T0189053

Lecture Notes in Computer Science 9908

Commenced Publication in 1973
Founding and Former Series Editors:
Gerhard Goos, Juris Hartmanis, and Jan van Leeuwen

More information about this series at http://www.springer.com/series/7412

Bastian Leibe · Jiri Matas
Nicu Sebe · Max Welling (Eds.)

Computer Vision – ECCV 2016

14th European Conference
Amsterdam, The Netherlands, October 11–14, 2016
Proceedings, Part IV

 Springer

Editors

Bastian Leibe
RWTH Aachen
Aachen
Germany

Nicu Sebe
University of Trento
Povo - Trento
Italy

Jiri Matas
Czech Technical University
Prague 2
Czech Republic

Max Welling
University of Amsterdam
Amsterdam
The Netherlands

ISSN 0302-9743   ISSN 1611-3349 (electronic)
Lecture Notes in Computer Science
ISBN 978-3-319-46492-3   ISBN 978-3-319-46493-0 (eBook)
DOI 10.1007/978-3-319-46493-0

Library of Congress Control Number: 2016951693

LNCS Sublibrary: SL6 – Image Processing, Computer Vision, Pattern Recognition, and Graphics

Printed on acid-free paper

This Springer imprint is published by Springer Nature
The registered company is Springer International Publishing AG
The registered company address is: Gewerbestrasse 11, 6330 Cham, Switzerland

Foreword

Welcome to the proceedings of the 2016 edition of the European Conference on Computer Vision held in Amsterdam! It is safe to say that the European Conference on Computer Vision is one of the top conferences in computer vision. It is good to reiterate the history of the conference to see the broad base the conference has built in its 13 editions. First held in 1990 in Antibes (France), it was followed by subsequent conferences in Santa Margherita Ligure (Italy) in 1992, Stockholm (Sweden) in 1994, Cambridge (UK) in 1996, Freiburg (Germany) in 1998, Dublin (Ireland) in 2000, Copenhagen (Denmark) in 2002, Prague (Czech Republic) in 2004, Graz (Austria) in 2006, Marseille (France) in 2008, Heraklion (Greece) in 2010, Florence (Italy) in 2012, and Zürich (Switzerland) in 2014.

For the 14th edition, many people worked hard to provide attendees with a most warm welcome while enjoying the best science. The Program Committee, Bastian Leibe, Jiri Matas, Nicu Sebe, and Max Welling, did an excellent job. Apart from the scientific program, the workshops were selected and handled by Hervé Jégou and Gang Hua, and the tutorials by Jacob Verbeek and Rita Cucchiara. Thanks for the great job. The coordination with the subsequent ACM Multimedia offered an opportunity to expand the tutorials with an additional invited session, offered by the University of Amsterdam and organized together with the help of ACM Multimedia.

Of the many people who worked hard as local organizers, we would like to single out Martine de Wit of the UvA Conference Office, who delicately and efficiently organized the main body. Also the local organizers Hamdi Dibeklioglu, Efstratios Gavves, Jan van Gemert, Thomas Mensink, and Mihir Jain had their hands full. As a venue, we chose the Royal Theatre Carré located on the canals of the Amstel River in downtown Amsterdam. Space in Amsterdam is sparse, so it was a little tighter than usual. The university lent us their downtown campuses for the tutorials and the workshops. A relatively new thing was the industry and the sponsors for which Ronald Poppe and Peter de With did a great job, while Andy Bagdanov and John Schavemaker arranged the demos. Michael Wilkinson took care to make Yom Kippur as comfortable as possible for those for whom it is an important day. We thank Marc Pollefeys, Alberto del Bimbo, and Virginie Mes for their advice and help behind the scenes. We thank all the anonymous volunteers for their hard and precise work. We also thank our generous sponsors. Their support is an essential part of the program. It is good to see such a level of industrial interest in what our community is doing!

Amsterdam does not need any introduction. Please emerge yourself but do not drown in it, have a nice time.

October 2016

Theo Gevers
Arnold Smeulders

Preface

Welcome to the proceedings of the 2016 European Conference on Computer Vision (ECCV 2016) held in Amsterdam, The Netherlands. We are delighted to present this volume reflecting a strong and exciting program, the result of an extensive review process. In total, we received 1,561 paper submissions. Of these, 81 violated the ECCV submission guidelines or did not pass the plagiarism test and were rejected without review. We employed the iThenticate software (www.ithenticate.com) for plagiarism detection. Of the remaining papers, 415 were accepted (26.6 %): 342 as posters (22.6 %), 45 as spotlights (2.9 %), and 28 as oral presentations (1.8 %). The spotlights – short, five-minute podium presentations – are novel to ECCV and were introduced after their success at the CVPR 2016 conference. All orals and spotlights are presented as posters as well. The selection process was a combined effort of four program co-chairs (PCs), 74 area chairs (ACs), 1,086 Program Committee members, and 77 additional reviewers.

As PCs, we were primarily responsible for the design and execution of the review process. Beyond administrative rejections, we were involved in acceptance decisions only in the very few cases where the ACs were not able to agree on a decision. PCs, as is customary in the field, were not allowed to co-author a submission. General co-chairs and other co-organizers played no role in the review process, were permitted to submit papers, and were treated as any other author.

Acceptance decisions were made by two independent ACs. There were 74 ACs, selected by the PCs according to their technical expertise, experience, and geographical diversity (41 from European, five from Asian, two from Australian, and 26 from North American institutions). The ACs were aided by 1,086 Program Committee members to whom papers were assigned for reviewing. There were 77 additional reviewers, each supervised by a Program Committee member. The Program Committee was selected from committees of previous ECCV, ICCV, and CVPR conferences and was extended on the basis of suggestions from the ACs and the PCs. Having a large pool of Program Committee members for reviewing allowed us to match expertise while bounding reviewer loads. Typically five papers, but never more than eight, were assigned to a Program Committee member. Graduate students had a maximum of four papers to review.

The ECCV 2016 review process was in principle double-blind. Authors did not know reviewer identities, nor the ACs handling their paper(s). However, anonymity becomes difficult to maintain as more and more submissions appear concurrently on arXiv.org. This was not against the ECCV 2016 double submission rules, which followed the practice of other major computer vision conferences in the recent past. The existence of arXiv publications, mostly not peer-reviewed, raises difficult problems with the assessment of unpublished, concurrent, and prior art, content overlap, plagiarism, and self-plagiarism. Moreover, it undermines the anonymity of submissions. We found that not all cases can be covered by a simple set of rules. Almost all controversies during the review process were related to the arXiv issue. Most of the reviewer inquiries were resolved by giving the benefit of the doubt to ECCV authors. However, the problem will have to be discussed by the community so that consensus is found on how to handle the issues brought by publishing on arXiv.

Particular attention was paid to handling conflicts of interest. Conflicts of interest between ACs, Program Committee members, and papers were identified based on the authorship of ECCV 2016 submissions, on the home institutions, and on previous collaborations of all researchers involved. To find institutional conflicts, all authors, Program Committee members, and ACs were asked to list the Internet domains of their current institutions. To find collaborators, the Researcher.cc database (http://researcher.cc/), funded by the Computer Vision Foundation, was used to find any co-authored papers in the period 2012–2016. We pre-assigned approximately 100 papers to each AC, based on affinity scores from the Toronto Paper Matching System. ACs then bid on these, indicating their level of expertise. Based on these bids, and conflicts of interest, approximately 40 papers were assigned to each AC. The ACs then suggested seven reviewers from the pool of Program Committee members for each paper, in ranked order, from which three were chosen automatically by CMT (Microsofts Academic Conference Management Service), taking load balancing and conflicts of interest into account.

The initial reviewing period was five weeks long, after which reviewers provided reviews with preliminary recommendations. With the generous help of several last-minute reviewers, each paper received three reviews. Submissions with all three reviews suggesting rejection were independently checked by two ACs and if they agreed, the manuscript was rejected at this stage ("early rejects"). In total, 334 manuscripts (22.5 %) were early-rejected, reducing the average AC load to about 30.

Authors of the remaining submissions were then given the opportunity to rebut the reviews, primarily to identify factual errors. Following this, reviewers and ACs discussed papers at length, after which reviewers finalized their reviews and gave a final recommendation to the ACs. Each manuscript was evaluated independently by two ACs who were not aware of each others, identities. In most of the cases, after extensive discussions, the two ACs arrived at a common decision, which was always adhered to by the PCs. In the very few borderline cases where an agreement was not reached, the PCs acted as tie-breakers. Owing to the rapid expansion of the field, which led to an unexpectedly large increase in the number of submissions, the size of the venue became a limiting factor and a hard upper bound on the number of accepted papers had to be imposed. We were able to increase the limit by replacing one oral session by a poster session. Nevertheless, this forced the PCs to reject some borderline papers that could otherwise have been accepted.

We want to thank everyone involved in making the ECCV 2016 possible. First and foremost, the success of ECCV 2016 depended on the quality of papers submitted by the authors, and on the very hard work of the ACs, the Program Committee members, and the additional reviewers. We are particularly grateful to Rene Vidal for his continuous support and sharing experience from organizing ICCV 2015, to Laurent Charlin for the use of the Toronto Paper Matching System, to Ari Kobren for the use of the Researcher.cc tools, to the Computer Vision Foundation (CVF) for facilitating the use of the iThenticate plagiarism detection software, and to Gloria Zen and Radu-Laurentiu Vieriu for setting up CMT and managing the various tools involved. We also owe a debt of gratitude for the support of the Amsterdam local organizers, especially Hamdi Dibeklioglu for keeping the website always up to date. Finally, the preparation of these proceedings would not have been possible without the diligent effort of the publication chairs, Albert Ali Salah and Robby Tan, and of Anna Kramer from Springer.

October 2016

Bastian Leibe
Jiri Matas
Nicu Sebe
Max Welling

Organization

General Chairs

Theo Gevers   University of Amsterdam, The Netherlands
Arnold Smeulders   University of Amsterdam, The Netherlands

Program Committee Co-chairs

Bastian Leibe   RWTH Aachen, Germany
Jiri Matas   Czech Technical University, Czech Republic
Nicu Sebe   University of Trento, Italy
Max Welling   University of Amsterdam, The Netherlands

Honorary Chair

Jan Koenderink   Delft University of Technology, The Netherlands
     and KU Leuven, Belgium

Advisory Program Chair

Luc van Gool   ETH Zurich, Switzerland

Advisory Workshop Chair

Josef Kittler   University of Surrey, UK

Advisory Conference Chair

Alberto del Bimbo   University of Florence, Italy

Local Arrangements Chairs

Hamdi Dibeklioglu   Delft University of Technology, The Netherlands
Efstratios Gavves   University of Amsterdam, The Netherlands
Jan van Gemert   Delft University of Technology, The Netherlands
Thomas Mensink   University of Amsterdam, The Netherlands
Michael Wilkinson   University of Groningen, The Netherlands

Workshop Chairs

Hervé Jégou   Facebook AI Research, USA
Gang Hua   Microsoft Research Asia, China

Tutorial Chairs

Jacob Verbeek   Inria Grenoble, France
Rita Cucchiara   University of Modena and Reggio Emilia, Italy

Poster Chairs

Jasper Uijlings   University of Edinburgh, UK
Roberto Valenti   Sightcorp, The Netherlands

Publication Chairs

Albert Ali Salah   Boğaziçi University, Turkey
Robby T. Tan   Yale-NUS College and National University
                               of Singapore, Singapore

Video Chair

Mihir Jain   University of Amsterdam, The Netherlands

Demo Chairs

John Schavemaker   Twnkls, The Netherlands
Andy Bagdanov   University of Florence, Italy

Social Media Chair

Efstratios Gavves   University of Amsterdam, The Netherlands

Industrial Liaison Chairs

Ronald Poppe   Utrecht University, The Netherlands
Peter de With   Eindhoven University of Technology, The Netherlands

Conference Coordinator, Accommodation, and Finance

Conference Office
Martine de Wit   University of Amsterdam, The Netherlands
Melanie Venverloo   University of Amsterdam, The Netherlands
Niels Klein   University of Amsterdam, The Netherlands

Area Chairs

Radhakrishna Achanta	Ecole Polytechnique Fédérale de Lausanne, Switzerland
Antonis Argyros	FORTH and University of Crete, Greece
Michael Bronstein	Universitá della Svizzera Italiana, Switzerland
Gabriel Brostow	University College London, UK
Thomas Brox	University of Freiburg, Germany
Barbara Caputo	Sapienza University of Rome, Italy
Miguel Carreira-Perpinan	University of California, Merced, USA
Ondra Chum	Czech Technical University, Czech Republic
Daniel Cremers	Technical University of Munich, Germany
Rita Cucchiara	University of Modena and Reggio Emilia, Italy
Trevor Darrell	University of California, Berkeley, USA
Andrew Davison	Imperial College London, UK
Fernando de la Torre	Carnegie Mellon University, USA
Piotr Dollar	Facebook AI Research, USA
Vittorio Ferrari	University of Edinburgh, UK
Charless Fowlkes	University of California, Irvine, USA
Jan-Michael Frahm	University of North Carolina at Chapel Hill, USA
Mario Fritz	Max Planck Institute, Germany
Pascal Fua	Ecole Polytechnique Fédérale de Lausanne, Switzerland
Juergen Gall	University of Bonn, Germany
Peter Gehler	University of Tübingen — Max Planck Institute, Germany
Andreas Geiger	Max Planck Institute, Germany
Ross Girshick	Facebook AI Research, USA
Kristen Grauman	University of Texas at Austin, USA
Abhinav Gupta	Carnegie Mellon University, USA
Hervé Jégou	Facebook AI Research, USA
Fredrik Kahl	Lund University, Sweden
Iasonas Kokkinos	Ecole Centrale Paris, France
Philipp Krähenbühl	University of California, Berkeley, USA
Pawan Kumar	University of Oxford, UK
Christoph Lampert	Institute of Science and Technology Austria, Austria
Hugo Larochelle	Université de Sherbrooke, Canada
Neil Lawrence	University of Sheffield, UK
Svetlana Lazebnik	University of Illinois at Urbana-Champaign, USA
Honglak Lee	Stanford University, USA
Kyoung Mu Lee	Seoul National University, Republic of Korea
Vincent Lepetit	Graz University of Technology, Austria
Hongdong Li	Australian National University, Australia
Julien Mairal	Inria, France
Yasuyuki Matsushita	Osaka University, Japan
Nassir Navab	Technical University of Munich, Germany

Sebastian Nowozin	Microsoft Research, Cambridge, UK
Tomas Pajdla	Czech Technical University, Czech Republic
Maja Pantic	Imperial College London, UK
Devi Parikh	Virginia Tech, USA
Thomas Pock	Graz University of Technology, Austria
Elisa Ricci	FBK Technologies of Vision, Italy
Bodo Rosenhahn	Leibniz-University of Hannover, Germany
Stefan Roth	Technical University of Darmstadt, Germany
Carsten Rother	Technical University of Dresden, Germany
Silvio Savarese	Stanford University, USA
Bernt Schiele	Max Planck Institute, Germany
Konrad Schindler	ETH Zürich, Switzerland
Cordelia Schmid	Inria, France
Cristian Sminchisescu	Lund University, Sweden
Noah Snavely	Cornell University, USA
Sabine Süsstrunk	Ecole Polytechnique Fédérale de Lausanne, Switzerland
Qi Tian	University of Texas at San Antonio, USA
Antonio Torralba	Massachusetts Institute of Technology, USA
Zhuowen Tu	University of California, San Diego, USA
Raquel Urtasun	University of Toronto, Canada
Joost van de Weijer	Universitat Autònoma de Barcelona, Spain
Laurens van der Maaten	Facebook AI Research, USA
Nuno Vasconcelos	University of California, San Diego, USA
Andrea Vedaldi	University of Oxford, UK
Xiaogang Wang	Chinese University of Hong Kong, Hong Kong, SAR China
Jingdong Wang	Microsoft Research Asia, China
Lior Wolf	Tel Aviv University, Israel
Ying Wu	Northwestern University, USA
Dong Xu	University of Sydney, Australia
Shuicheng Yan	National University of Singapore, Singapore
MingHsuan Yang	University of California, Merced, USA
Ramin Zabih	Cornell NYC Tech, USA
Larry Zitnick	Facebook AI Research, USA

Technical Program Committee

Austin Abrams	Pulkit Agrawal	Andrea Albarelli
Supreeth Achar	Jorgen Ahlberg	Alexandra Albu
Tameem Adel	Haizhou Ai	Saad Ali
Khurrum Aftab	Zeynep Akata	Daniel Aliaga
Lourdes Agapito	Ijaz Akhter	Marina Alterman
Sameer Agarwal	Karteek Alahari	Hani Altwaijry
Aishwarya Agrawal	Xavier Alameda-Pineda	Jose M. Alvarez

Mitsuru Ambai
Mohamed Amer
Senjian An
Cosmin Ancuti
Juan Andrade-Cetto
Marco Andreetto
Elli Angelopoulou
Relja Arandjelovic
Helder Araujo
Pablo Arbelaez
Chetan Arora
Carlos Arteta
Kalle Astroem
Nikolay Atanasov
Vassilis Athitsos
Mathieu Aubry
Yannis Avrithis
Hossein Azizpour
Artem Babenko
Andrew Bagdanov
Yuval Bahat
Xiang Bai
Lamberto Ballan
Arunava Banerjee
Adrian Barbu
Nick Barnes
Peter Barnum
Jonathan Barron
Adrien Bartoli
Dhruv Batra
Eduardo
    Bayro-Corrochano
Jean-Charles Bazin
Paul Beardsley
Vasileios Belagiannis
Ismail Ben Ayed
Boulbaba Benamor
Abhijit Bendale
Rodrigo Benenson
Fabian Benitez-Quiroz
Ohad Ben-Shahar
Dana Berman
Lucas Beyer
Subhabrata Bhattacharya
Binod Bhattarai
Arnav Bhavsar

Simone Bianco
Hakan Bilen
Horst Bischof
Tom Bishop
Arijit Biswas
Soma Biswas
Marten Bjoerkman
Volker Blanz
Federica Bogo
Xavier Boix
Piotr Bojanowski
Terrance Boult
Katie Bouman
Thierry Bouwmans
Edmond Boyer
Yuri Boykov
Hakan Boyraz
Steven Branson
Mathieu Bredif
Francois Bremond
Stefan Breuers
Michael Brown
Marcus Brubaker
Luc Brun
Andrei Bursuc
Zoya Bylinskii
Daniel Cabrini Hauagge
Deng Cai
Jianfei Cai
Simone Calderara
Neill Campbell
Octavia Camps
Liangliang Cao
Xiaochun Cao
Xun Cao
Gustavo Carneiro
Dan Casas
Tom Cashman
Umberto Castellani
Carlos Castillo
Andrea Cavallaro
Jan Cech
Ayan Chakrabarti
Rudrasis Chakraborty
Krzysztof Chalupka
Tat-Jen Cham

Antoni Chan
Manmohan Chandraker
Sharat Chandran
Hong Chang
Hyun Sung Chang
Jason Chang
Ju Yong Chang
Xiaojun Chang
Yu-Wei Chao
Visesh Chari
Rizwan Chaudhry
Rama Chellappa
Bo Chen
Chao Chen
Chao-Yeh Chen
Chu-Song Chen
Hwann-Tzong Chen
Lin Chen
Mei Chen
Terrence Chen
Xilin Chen
Yunjin Chen
Guang Chen
Qifeng Chen
Xinlei Chen
Jian Cheng
Ming-Ming Cheng
Anoop Cherian
Guilhem Cheron
Dmitry Chetverikov
Liang-Tien Chia
Naoki Chiba
Tat-Jun Chin
Margarita Chli
Minsu Cho
Sunghyun Cho
TaeEun Choe
Jongmoo Choi
Seungjin Choi
Wongun Choi
Wen-Sheng Chu
Yung-Yu Chuang
Albert Chung
Gokberk Cinbis
Arridhana Ciptadi
Javier Civera

James Clark
Brian Clipp
Michael Cogswell
Taco Cohen
Toby Collins
John Collomosse
Camille Couprie
David Crandall
Marco Cristani
James Crowley
Jinshi Cui
Yin Cui
Jifeng Dai
Qieyun Dai
Shengyang Dai
Yuchao Dai
Zhenwen Dai
Dima Damen
Kristin Dana
Kostas Danilidiis
Mohamed Daoudi
Larry Davis
Teofilo de Campos
Marleen de Bruijne
Koichiro Deguchi
Alessio Del Bue
Luca del Pero
Antoine Deleforge
Hervé Delingette
David Demirdjian
Jia Deng
Joachim Denzler
Konstantinos Derpanis
Frederic Devernay
Hamdi Dibeklioglu
Santosh Kumar Divvala
Carl Doersch
Weisheng Dong
Jian Dong
Gianfranco Doretto
Alexey Dosovitskiy
Matthijs Douze
Bruce Draper
Tom Drummond
Shichuan Du
Jean-Luc Dugelay

Enrique Dunn
Zoran Duric
Pinar Duygulu
Alexei Efros
Carl Henrik Ek
Jan-Olof Eklundh
Jayan Eledath
Ehsan Elhamifar
Ian Endres
Aykut Erdem
Anders Eriksson
Sergio Escalera
Victor Escorcia
Francisco Estrada
Bin Fan
Quanfu Fan
Chen Fang
Tian Fang
Masoud Faraki
Ali Farhadi
Giovanni Farinella
Ryan Farrell
Raanan Fattal
Michael Felsberg
Jiashi Feng
Michele Fenzi
Andras Ferencz
Basura Fernando
Sanja Fidler
Mario Figueiredo
Michael Firman
Robert Fisher
John Fisher III
Alexander Fix
Boris Flach
Matt Flagg
Francois Fleuret
Wolfgang Foerstner
David Fofi
Gianluca Foresti
Per-Erik Forssen
David Fouhey
Jean-Sebastien Franco
Friedrich Fraundorfer
Oren Freifeld
Simone Frintrop

Huazhu Fu
Yun Fu
Jan Funke
Brian Funt
Ryo Furukawa
Yasutaka Furukawa
Andrea Fusiello
David Gallup
Chuang Gan
Junbin Gao
Jochen Gast
Stratis Gavves
Xin Geng
Bogdan Georgescu
David Geronimo
Bernard Ghanem
Riccardo Gherardi
Golnaz Ghiasi
Soumya Ghosh
Andrew Gilbert
Ioannis Gkioulekas
Georgia Gkioxari
Guy Godin
Roland Goecke
Boqing Gong
Shaogang Gong
Yunchao Gong
German Gonzalez
Jordi Gonzalez
Paulo Gotardo
Stephen Gould
Venu M. Govindu
Helmut Grabner
Etienne Grossmann
Chunhui Gu
David Gu
Sergio Guadarrama
Li Guan
Matthieu Guillaumin
Jean-Yves Guillemaut
Guodong Guo
Ruiqi Guo
Yanwen Guo
Saurabh Gupta
Pierre Gurdjos
Diego Gutierrez

Abner Guzman Rivera
Christian Haene
Niels Haering
Ralf Haeusler
David Hall
Peter Hall
Onur Hamsici
Dongfeng Han
Mei Han
Xufeng Han
Yahong Han
Ankur Handa
Kenji Hara
Tatsuya Harada
Mehrtash Harandi
Bharath Hariharan
Tal Hassner
Soren Hauberg
Michal Havlena
Tamir Hazan
Junfeng He
Kaiming He
Lei He
Ran He
Xuming He
Zhihai He
Felix Heide
Janne Heikkila
Jared Heinly
Mattias Heinrich
Pierre Hellier
Stephane Herbin
Isabelle Herlin
Alexander Hermans
Anders Heyden
Adrian Hilton
Vaclav Hlavac
Minh Hoai
Judy Hoffman
Steven Hoi
Derek Hoiem
Seunghoon Hong
Byung-Woo Hong
Anthony Hoogs
Yedid Hoshen
Winston Hsu

Changbo Hu
Wenze Hu
Zhe Hu
Gang Hua
Dong Huang
Gary Huang
Heng Huang
Jia-Bin Huang
Kaiqi Huang
Qingming Huang
Rui Huang
Xinyu Huang
Weilin Huang
Zhiwu Huang
Ahmad Humayun
Mohamed Hussein
Wonjun Hwang
Juan Iglesias
Nazli Ikizler-Cinbis
Evren Imre
Eldar Insafutdinov
Catalin Ionescu
Go Irie
Hossam Isack
Phillip Isola
Hamid Izadinia
Nathan Jacobs
Varadarajan Jagannadan
Aastha Jain
Suyog Jain
Varun Jampani
Jeremy Jancsary
C.V. Jawahar
Dinesh Jayaraman
Ian Jermyn
Hueihan Jhuang
Hui Ji
Qiang Ji
Jiaya Jia
Kui Jia
Yangqing Jia
Hao Jiang
Tingting Jiang
Yu-Gang Jiang
Zhuolin Jiang
Alexis Joly

Shantanu Joshi
Frederic Jurie
Achuta Kadambi
Samuel Kadoury
Yannis Kalantidis
Amit Kale
Sebastian Kaltwang
Joni-Kristian Kamarainen
George Kamberov
Chandra Kambhamettu
Martin Kampel
Kenichi Kanatani
Atul Kanaujia
Melih Kandemir
Zhuoliang Kang
Mohan Kankanhalli
Abhishek Kar
Leonid Karlinsky
Andrej Karpathy
Zoltan Kato
Rei Kawakami
Kristian Kersting
Margret Keuper
Nima Khademi Kalantari
Sameh Khamis
Fahad Khan
Aditya Khosla
Hadi Kiapour
Edward Kim
Gunhee Kim
Hansung Kim
Jae-Hak Kim
Kihwan Kim
Seon Joo Kim
Tae Hyun Kim
Tae-Kyun Kim
Vladimir Kim
Benjamin Kimia
Akisato Kimura
Durk Kingma
Thomas Kipf
Kris Kitani
Martin Kleinsteuber
Laurent Kneip
Kevin Koeser
Effrosyni Kokiopoulou

Piotr Koniusz
Theodora Kontogianni
Sanjeev Koppal
Dimitrios Kosmopoulos
Adriana Kovashka
Adarsh Kowdle
Michael Kramp
Josip Krapac
Jonathan Krause
Pavel Krsek
Hilde Kuehne
Shiro Kumano
Avinash Kumar
Sebastian Kurtek
Kyros Kutulakos
Suha Kwak
In So Kweon
Roland Kwitt
Junghyun Kwon
Junseok Kwon
Jan Kybic
Jorma Laaksonen
Alexander Ladikos
Florent Lafarge
Pierre-Yves Laffont
Wei-Sheng Lai
Jean-Francois Lalonde
Michael Langer
Oswald Lanz
Agata Lapedriza
Ivan Laptev
Diane Larlus
Christoph Lassner
Olivier Le Meur
Laura Leal-Taixé
Joon-Young Lee
Seungkyu Lee
Chen-Yu Lee
Andreas Lehrmann
Ido Leichter
Frank Lenzen
Matt Leotta
Stefan Leutenegger
Baoxin Li
Chunming Li
Dingzeyu Li

Fuxin Li
Hao Li
Houqiang Li
Qi Li
Stan Li
Wu-Jun Li
Xirong Li
Xuelong Li
Yi Li
Yongjie Li
Wei Li
Wen Li
Yeqing Li
Yujia Li
Wang Liang
Shengcai Liao
Jongwoo Lim
Joseph Lim
Di Lin
Weiyao Lin
Yen-Yu Lin
Min Lin
Liang Lin
Haibin Ling
Jim Little
Buyu Liu
Miaomiao Liu
Risheng Liu
Si Liu
Wanquan Liu
Yebin Liu
Ziwei Liu
Zhen Liu
Sifei Liu
Marcus Liwicki
Roberto Lopez-Sastre
Javier Lorenzo
Christos Louizos
Manolis Lourakis
Brian Lovell
Chen-Change Loy
Cewu Lu
Huchuan Lu
Jiwen Lu
Le Lu
Yijuan Lu

Canyi Lu
Jiebo Luo
Ping Luo
Siwei Lyu
Zhigang Ma
Chao Ma
Oisin Mac Aodha
John MacCormick
Vijay Mahadevan
Dhruv Mahajan
Aravindh Mahendran
Mohammed Mahoor
Michael Maire
Subhransu Maji
Aditi Majumder
Atsuto Maki
Yasushi Makihara
Alexandros Makris
Mateusz Malinowski
Clement Mallet
Arun Mallya
Dixit Mandar
Junhua Mao
Dmitrii Marin
Elisabeta Marinoiu
Renaud Marlet
Ricardo Martin
Aleix Martinez
Jonathan Masci
David Masip
Diana Mateus
Markus Mathias
Iain Matthews
Kevin Matzen
Bruce Maxwell
Stephen Maybank
Scott McCloskey
Ted Meeds
Christopher Mei
Tao Mei
Xue Mei
Jason Meltzer
Heydi Mendez
Thomas Mensink
Michele Merler
Domingo Mery

Gregory Rogez
Marcus Rohrbach
Javier Romero
Matteo Ronchi
German Ros
Charles Rosenberg
Guy Rosman
Arun Ross
Paolo Rota
Samuel Rota Bulò
Peter Roth
Volker Roth
Brandon Rothrock
Anastasios Roussos
Amit Roy-Chowdhury
Ognjen Rudovic
Daniel Rueckert
Christian Rupprecht
Olga Russakovsky
Bryan Russell
Emmanuel Sabu
Fereshteh Sadeghi
Hideo Saito
Babak Saleh
Mathieu Salzmann
Dimitris Samaras
Conrad Sanderson
Enver Sangineto
Aswin Sankaranarayanan
Imari Sato
Yoichi Sato
Shin'ichi Satoh
Torsten Sattler
Bogdan Savchynskyy
Yann Savoye
Arman Savran
Harpreet Sawhney
Davide Scaramuzza
Walter Scheirer
Frank Schmidt
Uwe Schmidt
Dirk Schnieders
Johannes Schönberger
Florian Schroff
Samuel Schulter
William Schwartz

Alexander Schwing
Stan Sclaroff
Nicu Sebe
Ari Seff
Anita Sellent
Giuseppe Serra
Laura Sevilla-Lara
Shishir Shah
Greg Shakhnarovich
Qi Shan
Shiguang Shan
Jing Shao
Ling Shao
Xiaowei Shao
Roman Shapovalov
Nataliya Shapovalova
Ali Sharif Razavian
Gaurav Sharma
Pramod Sharma
Viktoriia Sharmanska
Eli Shechtman
Alexander Shekhovtsov
Evan Shelhamer
Chunhua Shen
Jianbing Shen
Li Shen
Xiaoyong Shen
Wei Shen
Yu Sheng
Jianping Shi
Qinfeng Shi
Yonggang Shi
Baoguang Shi
Kevin Shih
Nobutaka Shimada
Ilan Shimshoni
Koichi Shinoda
Takaaki Shiratori
Jamie Shotton
Matthew Shreve
Abhinav Shrivastava
Nitesh Shroff
Leonid Sigal
Nathan Silberman
Tomas Simon
Edgar Simo-Serra

Dheeraj Singaraju
Gautam Singh
Maneesh Singh
Richa Singh
Saurabh Singh
Vikas Singh
Sudipta Sinha
Josef Sivic
Greg Slabaugh
William Smith
Patrick Snape
Jan Sochman
Kihyuk Sohn
Hyun Oh Song
Jingkuan Song
Qi Song
Shuran Song
Xuan Song
Yale Song
Yi-Zhe Song
Alexander
    Sorkine Hornung
Humberto Sossa
Aristeidis Sotiras
Richard Souvenir
Anuj Srivastava
Nitish Srivastava
Michael Stark
Bjorn Stenger
Rainer Stiefelhagen
Martin Storath
Joerg Stueckler
Hang Su
Hao Su
Jingyong Su
Shuochen Su
Yu Su
Ramanathan Subramanian
Yusuke Sugano
Akihiro Sugimoto
Libin Sun
Min Sun
Qing Sun
Yi Sun
Chen Sun
Deqing Sun

Ganesh Sundaramoorthi

Jinli Suo

Supasorn Suwajanakorn

Tomas Svoboda

Chris Sweeney

Paul Swoboda

Raza Syed Hussain

Christian Szegedy

Yuichi Taguchi

Yu-Wing Tai

Hugues Talbot

Toru Tamaki

Mingkui Tan

Robby Tan

Xiaoyang Tan

Masayuki Tanaka

Meng Tang

Siyu Tang

Ran Tao

Dacheng Tao

Makarand Tapaswi

Jean-Philippe Tarel

Camillo Taylor

Christian Theobalt

Diego Thomas

Rajat Thomas

Xinmei Tian

Yonglong Tian

YingLi Tian

Yonghong Tian

Kinh Tieu

Joseph Tighe

Radu Timofte

Massimo Tistarelli

Sinisa Todorovic

Giorgos Tolias

Federico Tombari

Akihiko Torii

Andrea Torsello

Du Tran

Quoc-Huy Tran

Rudolph Triebel

Roberto Tron

Leonardo Trujillo

Eduard Trulls

Tomasz Trzcinski

Yi-Hsuan Tsai

Gavriil Tsechpenakis

Chourmouzios Tsiotsios

Stavros Tsogkas

Kewei Tu

Shubham Tulsiani

Tony Tung

Pavan Turaga

Matthew Turk

Tinne Tuytelaars

Oncel Tuzel

Georgios Tzimiropoulos

Norimichi Ukita

Osman Ulusoy

Martin Urschler

Arash Vahdat

Michel Valstar

Ernest Valveny

Jan van Gemert

Kiran Varanasi

Mayank Vatsa

Javier Vazquez-Corral

Ramakrishna Vedantam

Ashok Veeraraghavan

Olga Veksler

Jakob Verbeek

Francisco Vicente

Rene Vidal

Jordi Vitria

Max Vladymyrov

Christoph Vogel

Carl Vondrick

Sven Wachsmuth

Toshikazu Wada

Catherine Wah

Jacob Walker

Xiaolong Wang

Wei Wang

Limin Wang

Liang Wang

Hua Wang

Lijun Wang

Naiyan Wang

Xinggang Wang

Yining Wang

Baoyuan Wang

Chaohui Wang

Gang Wang

Heng Wang

Lei Wang

Linwei Wang

Liwei Wang

Ping Wang

Qi Wang

Qian Wang

Shenlong Wang

Song Wang

Tao Wang

Yang Wang

Yu-Chiang Frank Wang

Zhaowen Wang

Simon Warfield

Yichen Wei

Philippe Weinzaepfel

Longyin Wen

Tomas Werner

Aaron Wetzler

Yonatan Wexler

Michael Wilber

Kyle Wilson

Thomas Windheuser

David Wipf

Paul Wohlhart

Christian Wolf

Kwan-Yee Kenneth Wong

John Wright

Jiajun Wu

Jianxin Wu

Tianfu Wu

Yang Wu

Yi Wu

Zheng Wu

Stefanie Wuhrer

Jonas Wulff

Rolf Wurtz

Lu Xia

Tao Xiang

Yu Xiang

Lei Xiao

Yang Xiao

Tong Xiao

Wenxuan Xie

Lingxi Xie
Pengtao Xie
Saining Xie
Yuchen Xie
Junliang Xing
Bo Xiong
Fei Xiong
Jia Xu
Yong Xu
Tianfan Xue
Toshihiko Yamasaki
Takayoshi Yamashita
Junjie Yan
Rong Yan
Yan Yan
Keiji Yanai
Jian Yang
Jianchao Yang
Jiaolong Yang
Jie Yang
Jimei Yang
Michael Ying Yang
Ming Yang
Ruiduo Yang
Yi Yang
Angela Yao
Cong Yao
Jian Yao
Jianhua Yao
Jinwei Ye
Shuai Yi
Alper Yilmaz
Lijun Yin
Zhaozheng Yin

Xianghua Ying
Kuk-Jin Yoon
Chong You
Aron Yu
Felix Yu
Fisher Yu
Lap-Fai Yu
Stella Yu
Jing Yuan
Junsong Yuan
Lu Yuan
Xiao-Tong Yuan
Alan Yuille
Xenophon Zabulis
Stefanos Zafeiriou
Sergey Zagoruyko
Amir Zamir
Andrei Zanfir
Mihai Zanfir
Lihi Zelnik-Manor
Xingyu Zeng
Josiane Zerubia
Changshui Zhang
Cheng Zhang
Guofeng Zhang
Jianguo Zhang
Junping Zhang
Ning Zhang
Quanshi Zhang
Shaoting Zhang
Tianzhu Zhang
Xiaoqun Zhang
Yinda Zhang
Yu Zhang

Shiliang Zhang
Lei Zhang
Xiaoqin Zhang
Shanshan Zhang
Ting Zhang
Bin Zhao
Rui Zhao
Yibiao Zhao
Enliang Zheng
Wenming Zheng
Yinqiang Zheng
Yuanjie Zheng
Yin Zheng
Wei-Shi Zheng
Liang Zheng
Dingfu Zhou
Wengang Zhou
Tinghui Zhou
Bolei Zhou
Feng Zhou
Huiyu Zhou
Jun Zhou
Kevin Zhou
Kun Zhou
Xiaowei Zhou
Zihan Zhou
Jun Zhu
Jun-Yan Zhu
Zhenyao Zhu
Zeeshan Zia
Henning Zimmer
Karel Zimmermann
Wangmeng Zuo

Additional Reviewers

Felix Achilles
Sarah Adel Bargal
Hessam Bagherinezhad
Qinxun Bai
Gedas Bertasius
Michal Busta
Erik Bylow
Marinella Cadoni

Dan Andrei Calian
Lilian Calvet
Federico Camposeco
Olivier Canevet
Anirban Chakraborty
Yu-Wei Chao
Sotirios Chatzis
Tatjana Chavdarova

Jimmy Chen
Melissa Cote
Berkan Demirel
Zhiwei Deng
Guy Gilboa
Albert Gordo
Daniel Gordon
Ankur Gupta

Kun He
Yang He
Daniel Holtmann-Rice
Xun Huang
Liang Hui
Drew Jaegle
Cijo Jose
Marco Karrer
Mehran Khodabandeh
Anna Khoreva
Hyo-Jin Kim
Theodora Kontogianni
Pengpeng Liang
Shugao Ma
Ludovic Magerand
Francesco Malapelle
Julio Marco
Vlad Morariu

Rajitha Navarathna
Junhyuk Oh
Federico Perazzi
Marcel Piotraschke
Srivignesh Rajendran
Joe Redmon
Helge Rhodin
Anna Rohrbach
Beatrice Rossi
Wolfgang Roth
Pietro Salvagnini
Hosnieh Sattar
Ana Serrano
Zhixin Shu
Sven Sickert
Jakub Simanek
Ramprakash Srinivasan
Oren Tadmor

Xin Tao
Lucas Teixeira
Mårten Wädenback
Qing Wang
Yaser Yacoob
Takayoshi Yamashita
Huiyuan Yang
Ryo Yonetani
Sejong Yoon
Shaodi You
Xu Zhan
Jianming Zhang
Richard Zhang
Xiaoqun Zhang
Xu Zhang
Zheng Zhang

Contents – Part IV

Learning

Poster Session 5

Poster Session 4 (Continued)

Generating Visual Explanations

Lisa Anne Hendricks[1]([✉]), Zeynep Akata[2], Marcus Rohrbach[1,3], Jeff Donahue[1],
Bernt Schiele[2], and Trevor Darrell[1]

[1] UC Berkeley EECS, Berkeley, CA, USA
{lisa_anne,rohrbach,jdonahue,trevor}@eecs.berkeley.edu
[2] Max Planck Institute for Informatics, Saarbrücken, Germany
{akata,schiele}@mpi-inf.mpg.de
[3] ICSI, Berkeley, CA, USA

Abstract. Clearly explaining a rationale for a classification decision to an end user can be as important as the decision itself. Existing approaches for deep visual recognition are generally opaque and do not output any justification text; contemporary vision-language models can describe image content but fail to take into account class-discriminative image aspects which justify visual predictions. We propose a new model that focuses on the discriminating properties of the visible object, jointly predicts a class label, and explains why the predicted label is appropriate for the image. Through a novel loss function based on sampling and reinforcement learning, our model learns to generate sentences that realize a global sentence property, such as class specificity. Our results on the CUB dataset show that our model is able to generate explanations which are not only consistent with an image but also more discriminative than descriptions produced by existing captioning methods.

Keywords: Visual explanation · Image description · Language and vision

1 Introduction

Explaining why the output of a visual system is compatible with visual evidence is a key component for understanding and interacting with AI systems [4]. Deep classification methods have had tremendous success in visual recognition [8,10,20], but their outputs can be unsatisfactory if the model cannot provide a consistent justification of why it made a certain prediction. In contrast, systems which can justify why a prediction is consistent with visual elements to a user are more likely to be trusted [34]. Explanations of visual systems could also aid in understanding network mistakes and provide feedback to improve classifers.

We consider explanations as determining *why* a decision is consistent with visual evidence, and differentiate between *introspection* explanation systems

Electronic supplementary material The online version of this chapter (doi:10. 1007/978-3-319-46493-0_1) contains supplementary material, which is available to authorized users.

© Springer International Publishing AG 2016
B. Leibe et al. (Eds.): ECCV 2016, Part IV, LNCS 9908, pp. 3–19, 2016.
DOI: 10.1007/978-3-319-46493-0_1

Fig. 1. Our proposed model generates *explanations* that are both image relevant and class relevant. In contrast, *descriptions* are image relevant, but not necessarily class relevant, and *definitions* are class relevant but not necessarily image relevant. (Color figure online)

which explain how a model determines its final output (e.g., "This is a Western Grebe because filter 2 has a high activation...") and *justification* explanation systems which produce sentences detailing how visual evidence is compatible with a system output (e.g., "This is a Western Grebe because it has red eyes..."). We concentrate on justification explanation systems because they may be more useful to non-experts who do not have knowledge of modern computer vision systems [4].

We argue that visual explanations must satisfy two criteria: they must be *class discriminative* and *accurately describe* a specific image instance. As shown in Fig. 1, explanations are distinct from *descriptions*, which provide a sentence based only on visual information, and *definitions*, which provide a sentence based only on class information. Unlike descriptions and definitions, visual explanations detail why a certain category is appropriate for a given image while only mentioning image relevant features. For example, consider a classification system that predicts a certain image belongs to the class "western grebe" (Fig. 1, top). A standard captioning system might provide a description such as "This is a large bird with a white neck and black back in the water." However, as this description does not mention *discriminative* features, it could also be applied to a "laysan albatross" (Fig. 1, bottom). In contrast, we propose to provide *explanations*, such as "This is a western grebe because this bird has a long white neck, pointy yellow beak, and a red eye." The explanation includes the "red eye" property, which is important for distinguishing between "western grebe" and "laysan albatross". As such, our system explains *why* the predicted category is the most appropriate for the image.

We outline our approach in Fig. 2. In contrast to description models, we condition generation on an image and the predicted class label. We also use features extracted from a fine-grained recognition pipeline [10]. Like many contemporary description models [7,18,19,37,40], we use an LSTM [13] to generate word sequences. However, we design a novel loss function which encourages generated sentences to include class discriminative information; i.e., to be class specific. One challenge is that class specificity is a global sentence property: e.g., while

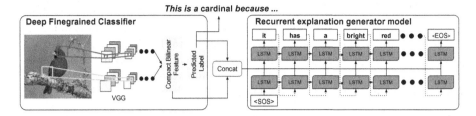

Fig. 2. Our joint classification and explanation model. We extract visual features using a fine-grained classifier before sentence generation and, unlike other sentence generation models, condition sentence generation on the predicted class label. A novel discriminative loss encourages generated sentences to include class specific attributes. (Color figure online)

a sentence "This is an all black bird with a bright red eye" is class specific to a "Bronzed Cowbird", words and phrases in this sentence, such as "black" or "red eye" are less class specific on their own. Our final output is a sampled sentence, so we backpropagate the discriminative loss through the sentence sampling mechanism via a technique from the reinforcement learning literature [39].

To the best of our knowledge, ours is the first framework to produce deep visual explanations using natural language justifications. We describe below that our novel joint vision and language explanation model combines classification and sentence generation by incorporating a loss function that operates over sampled sentences. We show that this formulation is able to focus generated text to be more discriminative and that our model produces better explanations than a description baseline. Our results also confirm that generated sentence quality improves with respect to traditional sentence generation metrics by including a discriminative class label loss during training. This result holds even when class conditioning is ablated at test time.

2   Related Work

Explanation. Automatic reasoning and explanation has a long and rich history within the artificial intelligence community [4,5,17,22,24,25,33,35]. Explanation systems span a variety of applications including explaining medical diagnosis [33], simulator actions [5,17,24,35], and robot movements [25]. Many of these systems are rule-based [33] or solely reliant on filling in a predetermined template [35]. Methods such as [33] require expert-level explanations and decision processes. As expert explanations or decision processes are not available during training, our model learns purely from visual features and fine-grained visual descriptions to fulfill our two proposed visual explanation criteria. In contrast to systems like [5,22,24,25,33,35] which aim to explain the underlying mechanism behind a decision, Biran et al. [4] concentrate on why a prediction is justifiable to a user. Such systems are advantageous because they do not rely on user familiarity with the design of an intelligent system in order to provide useful information.

Many vision methods focus on discovering visual features which can help "explain" an image classification decision [3, 6, 16]. Importantly, these models do not link discovered discriminative features to natural language expressions. We believe that the methods discovering discriminative visual features are complementary to our proposed system. In fact, discriminative visual features could be used as additional inputs to our model to produce better explanations.

Visual Description. Early image description methods rely on detecting visual concepts (e.g., subject, verb, and object) before generating a sentence with either a simple language model or sentence template [11, 21]. Recent deep models [7, 9, 18, 19, 28, 37, 40] outperform such systems and produce fluent, accurate descriptions. Though most description models condition sentence generation only on image features, [14] condition generation on auxiliary information, such as words used to describe a similar image in the train set. However, [14] does not condition sentence generation on category labels.

LSTM sentence generation models are generally trained with a cross-entropy loss between the probability distribution of predicted and ground truth words [7, 18, 28, 37, 40]. Frequently, however, the cross-entropy loss does not directly optimize for properties desirable at test time. [26] proposes a training scheme for generating unambiguous region descriptions which maximizes the probability of a region description while minimizing the probability of other region descriptions. In this work, we propose a novel loss function for sentence generation which allows us to specify a global constraint on generated sentences.

Fine-Grained Classification. Object classification, particularly fine-grained classification, is an attractive setting for explanation systems because describing image content does not suffice as an explanation. Explanation models must focus on aspects that are both class-specific and depicted in the image.

Most fine-grained zero-shot and few-shot image classification systems use attributes [23] as auxiliary information. Attributes discretize a high dimensional feature space into simple and readily interpretable decision statements that can act as an explanation. However, attributes have several disadvantages. They require experts for annotation which is costly and results in attributes which are hard for non-experts to interpret (e.g., "spatulate bill shape"). Attributes are not scalable as the list of attributes needs to be revised to ensure discriminativeness for new classes. Finally, attributes do not provide a natural language explanation like the user expects. We therefore use natural language descriptions [31] which achieved superior performance on zero-shot learning compared to attributes and also shown to be useful for text to image generation [32].

Reinforcement Learning in Computer Vision. Vision models which incorporate algorithms from reinforcement learning, specifically how to backpropagate through a sampling mechanism, have recently been applied to visual question answering [1] and activity detection [41]. Additionally, [40] use a sampling mechanism to attend to specific image regions for caption generation, but use the standard cross-entropy loss during training.

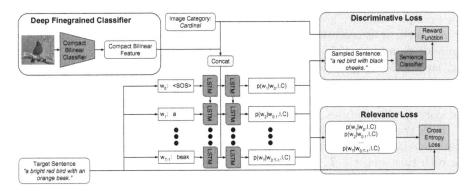

Fig. 3. Training our explanation model. Our explanation model differs from other caption models because it (1) includes the object category as an additional input and (2) incorporates a reinforcement learning based discriminative loss

3   Visual Explanation Model

Our visual explanation model (Fig. 3) aims to produce an explanation which describes visual content present in a specific image instance while containing appropriate information to explain why the image belongs to a specific category. We ensure generated descriptions meet these two requirements for explanation by including both a *relevance loss* (Fig. 3, bottom right) and *discriminative loss* (Fig. 3, top right). We propose a novel discriminative loss which acts on sampled word sequences during training. Our loss enables us to enforce global sentence constraints on sentences. By applying our loss to sampled sentences, we ensure that the final output of our system fulfills our explanation criteria. We consider a sentence to be either a complete sentence or a sentence fragment.

3.1   Relevance Loss

Image relevance can be accomplished by training a visual description model. Our model is based on LRCN [7], which consists of a convolutional network, which extracts high level visual features, and two stacked recurrent networks (specifically LSTMs), which generate descriptions conditioned on visual features. During inference, the first LSTM receives the previously generated word w_{t-1} as input and produces an output l_t. The second LSTM, receives the output of the first LSTM l_t and an image feature f and produces a probability distribution $p(w_t)$ over the next word. The word w_t is generated by sampling from the distribution $p(w_t)$. Generation continues until an "end-of-sentence" token is generated.

We propose two modifications to the LRCN framework to increase the image relevance of generated sequences (Fig. 3, top left). First, category predictions are used as an additional input to the second LSTM in the sentence generation model. Intuitively, category information can help inform the caption generation model which words and attributes are more likely to occur in a description.

For example, category level information can help the model decide if a red eye or red eyebrow is more likely for a given class. We experimented with a few methods to represent class labels, and found that training a language model, e.g., an LSTM, to generate word sequences conditioned on images, then using the average hidden state of the LSTM across all sequences for all classes in the train set as a vectorial representation of a class works best. Second, we use rich category specific features [10] to generate relevant explanations.

Each training instance consists of an image, category label, and a ground truth sentence. During training, the model receives the ground truth word w_t for each time step $t \in T$. We define the relevance loss for a specific image (I) and caption (C) as:

$$L_R(I,C) = \frac{1}{N} \sum_{n=0}^{N-1} \sum_{t=0}^{T-1} \log p(w_{t+1}|w_{0:t}, I, C) \qquad (1)$$

where w_t is a ground truth word and N is the batch size. By training the model to predict each word in a ground truth sentence, the model produces sentences which reflect the image content. However, this loss does not explicitly encourage generated sentences to discuss discerning visual properties. In order to generate sentences which are both image relevant and category specific, we include a discriminative loss to focus sentence generation on discriminative visual properties of the object.

3.2 Discriminative Loss

Our discriminative loss is based on a reinforcement learning paradigm for learning with layers which require sampling intermediate activations of a network. In our formulation, we first sample a sentence and then use the sampled sentence to compute a discriminative loss. By sampling the sentence before computing the loss, we ensure that sentences sampled from our model are more likely to be class specific. Our reinforcement based loss enables us to backpropagate through the sentence sampling mechanism.

We minimize the following overall loss function with respect to the explanation network weights W:

$$L_R(I,C) - \lambda \mathbb{E}_{\tilde{w} \sim p(w|I,C)} [R_D(\tilde{w})] \qquad (2)$$

which is a linear combination of the relevance loss L_R and the expectation of the negative discriminator reward $-R_D(\tilde{w})$ over descriptions $\tilde{w} \sim p(w|I,C)$, where $p(w|I,C)$ is the model's estimated conditional distribution over descriptions w given the image I and category C. Since $\mathbb{E}_{\tilde{w} \sim p(w|I,C)} [R_D(\tilde{w})]$ is intractable, we estimate it at training time using Monte Carlo sampling of descriptions from the categorical distribution given by the model's softmax output at each timestep. The sampling operation for the categorical distribution is non-smooth in the distribution's parameters $\{p_i\}$ as it is a discrete distribution. Therefore, $\nabla_W R_D(\tilde{w})$ for a given sample $\tilde{w}$ with respect to the weights W is undefined.

Following the REINFORCE [39] algorithm, we make use of the following equivalence property of the expected reward gradient:

$$\nabla_W \mathbb{E}_{\tilde{w} \sim p(w|I,C)} [R_D(\tilde{w})] = \mathbb{E}_{\tilde{w} \sim p(w|I,C)} [R_D(\tilde{w}) \nabla_W \log p(\tilde{w})] \qquad (3)$$

In this reformulation, the gradient $\nabla_W \log p(\tilde{w})$ is well-defined: $\log p(\tilde{w})$ is the log-likelihood of the sampled description $\tilde{w}$, just as L_R is the log-likelihood of the ground truth description. However, the sampled gradient term is weighted by the reward $R_D(\tilde{w})$, pushing the weights to increase the likelihood assigned to the most highly rewarded (and hence most discriminative) descriptions. Therefore, the final gradient we compute to update the weights W, given a description $\tilde{w}$ sampled from the model's softmax distribution, is:

$$\nabla_W L_R - \lambda R_D(\tilde{w}) \nabla_W \log p(\tilde{w}). \qquad (4)$$

$R_D(\tilde{w})$ should be high when sampled sentences are discriminative. We define our reward simply as $R_D(\tilde{w}) = p(C|\tilde{w})$, or the probability of the ground truth category C given only the generated sentence $\tilde{w}$. By placing the discriminative loss after the sampled sentence, the sentence acts as an information bottleneck. For the model to produce an output with a large reward, the generated sentence must include enough information to classify the original image properly.

For the sentence classifier, we train a single layer LSTM-based classification network to classify ground truth sentences. Our sentence classifier correctly predicts the class of unseen validation set sentences 22 % of the time. This number is possibly low because descriptions in the dataset do not necessarily contain discriminative properties (e.g., "This is a white bird with grey wings." is a valid description but can apply to multiple bird species). Nonetheless, we find that this classifier provides enough information to train our explanation model. Outside text sources (e.g., field guides) could be useful when training a sentence classifier. However, incorporating outside text can be challenging as this requires aligning our image annotation vocabulary to field-guide vocabulary. When training the explanation model, we do not update weights in the sentences classifier.

4   Experimental Setup

Dataset. We employ the Caltech UCSD Birds 200–2011 (CUB) dataset [38] which contains 200 classes of bird species and 11,788 images in total. Recently, [31] collected 5 sentences for each of the images which do not only describe the content of the image, e.g., "This is a bird", but also give a detailed description of the bird, e.g., "red feathers and has a black face patch". Unlike other image-sentence datasets, every image in the CUB dataset belongs to a class, and therefore sentences as well as images are associated with a single label. This property makes this dataset unique for the visual explanation task, where our aim is to generate sentences that are both discriminative and class-specific.

Though sentences collected in [31] were not originally collected for the visual explanation task, we observe that sentences include detailed and fine-grained category specific information. When ranking human annotations by output scores of our sentence classifier, we find that high-ranking sentences (and thus more discriminative sentences) include rich discriminative details. For example, the sentence "...mostly black all over its body with a small red and yellow portion in its wing" has a score of 0.99 for "Red winged blackbird" and includes details specific to this bird variety, such as "red and yellow portion in its wing". As ground truth annotations are descriptions as opposed to explanations, not all annotations are guaranteed to include discriminative information. For example, though the "bronzed-cowbird" has striking red eyes, not all humans mention this discrimitave feature. To generate satisfactory explanations, our model must learn which features are discriminative from descriptions and incorporate discriminative properties into generated explanations. Example ground truth images and annotations may be found in our supplemental.

Implementation. For image features, we extract 8,192 dimensional features from the penultimate layer of the compact bilinear fine-grained classification model [10] which has been pre-trained on the CUB dataset and achieves an accuracy of 84 %. We use one-hot vectors to represent input words at each time step and learn a 1000 dimensional embedding before inputting each word into an LSTM with 1000 hidden units. We train our models using *Caffe* [15], and determine model hyperparameters using the standard CUB validation set before evaluating on the test set. All reported results are on the standard CUB test set.

Baseline and Ablation Models. We propose two baseline models: a *description* model and a *definition* model. Our description baseline generates sentences conditioned only on images and is equivalent to LRCN [7] except we use image features from a fine-grained classifier [10]. Our definition baseline generates sentences using only an image label as input. Consequently, this model outputs the same sentence for every image of the same class. Our proposed model is both more image and class relevant than either of these baselines and thus superior for the explanation task.

Our explanation model differs from description models in two key ways. First, in addition to an image, generated sentences are conditioned on class predictions. Second, explanations are trained with a discriminative loss which enforces that generated sentences contain class specific information (see Eq. 2). To demonstrate that both class information and the discriminative loss are important, we compare our explanation model to an *explanation-label* model which is not trained with the discriminative loss, and to an *explanation-discriminative* model which is not conditioned on the predicted class.

Metrics. To evaluate our explanation model, we use automatic metrics and two human evaluations. Our automatic metrics rely on the common sentence evaluation metrics (METEOR [2] and CIDEr [36]) and are used to evaluate the quality of our explanatory text. METEOR is computed by matching words in generated and reference sentences, but unlike other common metrics such as BLEU [30], it uses WordNet [29] to also match synonyms. CIDEr measures the similarity of a generated sentence to reference sentence by counting common n-grams which are TF-IDF weighted. Consequently, CIDEr rewards sentences for correctly including n-grams which are uncommon in the dataset.

A generated sentence is *image relevant* if it mentions concepts which are mentioned in ground truth reference sentences for the image. Thus, to measure image relevance we simply report METEOR and CIDEr scores, with more relevant sentences producing higher METEOR and CIDEr scores.

Measuring *class relevance* is considerably more difficult. We could use the LSTM sentence classifier used to train our discriminative loss, but this is an unfair metric because some models were trained to directly increase the accuracy as measured by the LSTM classifier. Instead, we measure class relevance by considering how similar generated sentences for a class are to ground truth sentences for that class. Sentences which describe a certain bird class, e.g., "cardinal", should contain similar words and phrases to ground truth "cardinal" sentences, but not ground truth "black bird" sentences. We compute CIDEr scores for images from each bird class, but instead of using ground truth image descriptions as reference sentences, we pool all reference sentences which correspond to a particular class. We call this metric the *class similarity* metric.

Though class relevant sentences should have high class similarity scores, a model could achieve a better class similarity score by producing better overall sentences (e.g., better grammar) without producing more class relevant descriptions. To further demonstrate that our sentences are class relevant, we compute a *class rank* metric. Intuitively, class similarity scores computed for generated sentences about *cardinals* should be higher when compared to *cardinal* reference sentences than when compared to reference sentences from other classes. Consequently, more class relevant models should yield higher rank for ground truth classes. To compute class rank, we compute the class similarity for each generated sentence with respect to each bird category and rank bird categories by class similarity. We report the mean rank of the ground truth class. We emphasize the CIDEr metric because of the TF-IDF weighting over n-grams. If a bird has a unique feature, such as "red eyes", generated sentences which mention this attribute should be rewarded more than sentences which just mention attributes common across all bird classes. We apply our metrics to instances in which the compact bilinear classifier predicts the correct label as is unclear if the best explanatory text should be more similar to correct or predicted classes. However, the same trends hold if we apply our metrics to all generated sentences.

5   Results

We demonstrate that our model generates superior visual explanations and produces image and class relevant text. Additionally, generating visual explanations results in higher quality sentences based on common sentence generation metrics.

5.1   Quantitative Results

Image Relevance. Table 1, columns 2 & 3, record METEOR and CIDEr scores for our generated sentences. Importantly, our explanation model has higher

Table 1. Comparing our explanation model to our definition and description baseline, as well as the explanation-label and explanation-discriminative (explanation-dis.) ablation models. Our explanations are image relevant, as measured by METEOR and CIDEr scores (higher is better). They are also class relevant, as measured by class similarity metric (higher is better) and class rank metric (lower is better) (see Sect. 4 for details). Finally, our explanations are ranked better by experienced bird watchers.

	Image relevance		Class relevance		Best explanation
	METEOR	CIDEr	Similarity	Rank (1–200)	Bird expert rank (1–5)
Definition	27.9	43.8	42.60	15.82	2.92
Description	27.7	42.0	35.30	24.43	3.11
Explanation-label	28.1	44.7	40.86	17.69	2.97
Explanation-dis	28.8	51.9	43.61	19.80	3.22
Explanation	**29.2**	**56.7**	**52.25**	**13.12**	**2.78**

METEOR and CIDEr scores than our baselines. The explanation model also outperforms the explanation-label and explanation-discriminative model suggesting that both label conditioning and the discriminative loss are key to producing better sentences. Furthermore, METEOR and CIDEr are substantially higher when including a discriminative loss during training (compare rows 2 and 4 and rows 3 and 5) demonstrating that including this additional loss leads to better generated sentences. Moreover, the definition model produces more image relevant sentences than the description model suggesting that category information is important for fine-grained description. On the other hand, our explanation-label results are better than both the definition and description results showing that the image and label contain complementary information.

Class Relevance. Table 1, columns 4 & 5, report class similarity and class rank metrics (see Sect. 4 for details). Our explanation model produces a higher class similarity score than other models by a substantial margin. The class rank for our explanation model is also lower than for any other model suggesting that sentences generated by our explanation model more closely resemble the correct class than other classes in the dataset. Our ranking metric is quite difficult; sentences must include enough information to differentiate between very similar bird classes without looking at an image, and our results clearly show that our explanation model performs best at this difficult task. The accuracy of our LSTM sentence classifier follow the same general trend, with our explanation model achieves 59.13 % whereas the description model obtains 22.32 % accuracy.

Based on the success of our discriminator, we train a definition model with the discriminative loss and find that our loss does boost performance of the definition model (METEOR: 28.6, CIDEr: 51.7, Similarity: 48.8, Rank: 15.5). Importantly, the explanation still performs best on our evaluation metrics.

User Studies. The ultimate goal of our explanation system is to provide useful information about an unknown object to a user. We therefore also consulted experienced bird watchers to rate our explanations against our baseline and

 This is a pine grosbeak because this bird has a red head and breast with a gray wing and white wing.

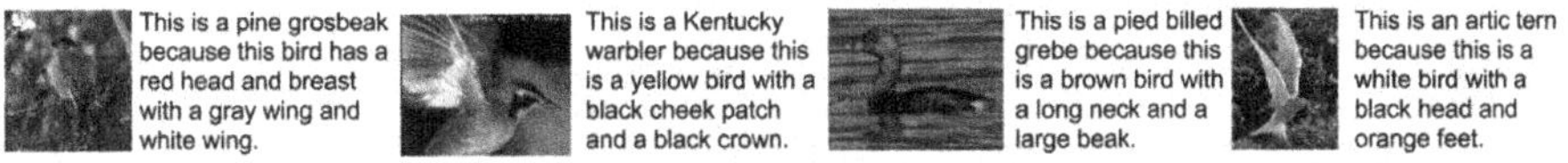

 This is a Kentucky warbler because this is a yellow bird with a black cheek patch and a black crown.

 This is a pied billed grebe because this is a brown bird with a long neck and a large beak.

 This is an artic tern because this is a white bird with a black head and orange feet.

Fig. 4. Visual explanations generated by our system. Our explanation model produces image relevant sentences that also discuss class discriminative attributes.

ablation models. Consulting experienced bird watchers is important because some sentences may provide correct, but non-discriminative properties, which an average person may not be able to properly identify. For example, *This is a Bronzed Cowbird because this bird is nearly all black with a short pointy bill.* is correct, but is a poor explanation as it does not mention unique attributes of a *Bronzed Cowbird* such as *red eye*. Two experienced bird watchers evaluated 91 randomly selected images and answered which sentence provided the best explanation for the bird class (Table 1, column 6). Our explanation model has the best mean rank (lower is better), followed by the definition model. This trend resembles the trend seen when evaluating class relevance.

We also demonstrate that explanations are more effective than descriptions at helping humans identify different bird species. We ask five Amazon Turk workers to choose between two images given a generated description and explanation. We evaluate 200 images (one for each bird category) and find that our explanations are more helpful to humans. When provided with an explanation, the correct image is chosen (with an image considered to be chosen correctly if 4 out of 5 workers select the correct image) 56 % of the time, whereas when provided with a description, the correct image is chosen less frequently (52 % of the time).

5.2 Qualitative Results

Figure 4 shows sample explanations which first declare a predicted class label ("This is a *Kentucky Warbler* because") followed by the explanatory text produced by the model described in Sect. 3. Qualitatively, our explanation model performs quite well. Note that our model accurately describes fine detail such as *black cheek patch* for *Kentucky Warbler* and *long neck* for *Pied Billed Grebe*.

Comparing Explanations, Baselines, and Ablations. Figure 5 compares sentences generated by our explanation, baseline, and ablation models. Each model produces reasonable sentences, however, we expect our explanation model to produce sentences which discuss class relevant properties. For many images, the explanation model uniquely mentions some relevant properties. In Fig. 5, row 1, the explanation model specifies that the *Bronzed Cowbird* has *red eyes* which is rarer than properties mentioned correctly by the definition and description models (*black, pointy bill*). For *White Necked Raven* (Fig. 5 row 3), the explanation model identifies the *white nape*, which is a unique attribute of that bird. Explanations are also more image relevant. For example, in Fig. 5 row 7 the explanation model correctly mentions visible properties of the *Hooded Merganser*, but other models fail in at least one property.

This is a **Bronzed Cowbird** *because ...*
Definition: this bird is **black** with blue on its wings and has a long **pointy beak**.
Description: this bird is **nearly all black** with a short **pointy bill**.
Explanation-Label: this bird is **nearly all black** with **bright orange eyes**.
Explanation-Dis.:   this is a **black bird** with a red eye and a white beak.
Explanation: this is a **black bird** with a red eye and a **pointy black beak**.

This is a **Black Billed Cuckoo** *because ...*
Definition: this bird has a **yellow belly** and a **grey head**.
Description: this bird has a **yellow belly** and **breast** with a **gray crown** and **green wing**.
Explanation-Label: this bird has a **yellow belly** and a **grey head** with a **grey throat**.
Explanation-Dis.:   this is a **yellow bird** with a **grey head** and a small beak.
Explanation: this is a **yellow bird** with a **grey head** and a pointy beak.

This is a **White Necked Raven** *because ...*
Definition: this bird is **black in color** with a **black beak** and **black eye rings**.
Description: this bird is **black** with a **white spot** and has a **long pointy beak**.
Explanation-Label: this bird is **black in color** with a **black beak** and **black eye rings**.
Explanation-Dis.:   this is a **black** bird with a **white nape** and a **black beak**.
Explanation: this is a **black** bird with a **white nape** and a **large black beak**.

This is a **Northern Flicker** *because ...*
Definition: this bird has a **speckled belly and breast** with a **long pointy bill**.
Description: this bird has a **long pointed bill** grey throat and spotted **black and white mottled crown**.
Explanation-Label: this bird has a **speckled belly and breast** with a **long pointy bill**.
Explanation-Dis.:   this is a **grey bird** with **black spots** and a red spotted crown.
Explanation: this is a **black and white spotted bird** with a red nape and a **long pointed black beak**.

This is a **American Goldfinch** *because ...*
Definition: this bird has a **yellow crown** a **short and sharp bill** and a **black wing** with a white breast.
Description: this bird has a **black crown** a **yellow bill** and a **yellow belly**.
Explanation-Label: this bird has a **black crown** a **short orange bill** and a **bright yellow breast and belly**.
Explanation-Dis.:   this is a **yellow bird** with a **black wing** and a black crown.
Explanation: this is a **yellow bird** with a **black and white wing** and an **orange beak**.

This is a **Yellow Breasted Chat** *because ...*
Definition: this bird has a **yellow belly and breast** with a **white eyebrow** and **gray crown**.
Description: this bird has a **yellow breast and throat** with a **white belly and abdomen**.
Explanation-Label: this bird has a **yellow belly and breast** with a **white eyebrow** and **gray crown**.
Explanation-Dis.:   this is a bird with a **yellow belly** and a **grey back and head**.
Explanation: this is a bird with a **yellow breast** and a **grey head and back**.

This is a **Hooded Merganser** *because ...*
Definition: this bird has a **black crown** a **white eye** and a **large black bill**.
Description: this bird has a **brown crown** a **white breast** and a large wingspan.
Explanation-Label: this bird has a **black and white head** with a large **long yellow bill** and **brown tarsus and feet**.
Explanation-Dis.:   this is a **brown bird** with a **white breast** and a white head.
Explanation: this bird has a **black and white head** with a **large black beak**.

Fig. 5. Example sentences generated by our baseline models, ablation models, and our proposed explanation model. Correct properties are highlighted in green, mostly correct ones are highlighted in yellow, and incorrect ones are highlighted in red. The explanation model correctly mentions image relevant and class relevant properties. (Color figure online)

Comparing Definitions and Explanations. Figure 6 directly compares explanations to definitions for three bird categories. Images on the left include a visual property of the bird species which is not present in the image on the right. Because the definition is the same for all image instances of a bird class, it can produce sentences which are not image relevant. For example, in the second row, the definition model says the bird has a *red spot on its head* which is true for the image on the left but not for the image on the right. In contrast, the explanation model mentions *red spot* only when it is present in the image.

Discriminative Loss. To determine how the discriminative loss impacts sentence generation, we compare the description and explanation- discriminative models in Fig. 7. Neither model receives class information at test time, though the explanation-discriminative model is explicitly trained to produced class

This is a **Red Bellied Woodpecker** because...

Definition: this bird has a bright red crown and nape **white breast and belly** and black and white spotted wings and secondaries.
Explanation: this bird has a red crown a black and white spotted wing and a **white belly**.

This is a **Downy Woodpecker** because...

Definition: this bird has a white breast black wings and a **red spot** on its head.
Explanation: this is a black and white bird with a **red spot** on its crown.

This is a **Shiny Cowbird** because...

Definition: this bird is black with a **long tail** and has a very short beak.
Explanation: this is a black bird with a **long tail feather** and a pointy black beak.

This is a **Red Bellied Woodpecker** because...

Definition: this bird has a bright red crown and nape **white breast and belly** and black and white spotted wings and secondaries.
Explanation: this bird has a bright red crown and nape with with black and white striped wings.

This is a **Downy Woodpecker** because...

Definition: this bird has a white breast black wings and a **red spot** on its head.
Explanation: this is a white bird with a black wing and a black and white striped head.

This is a **Shiny Cowbird** because...

Definition: this bird is black with a **long tail** and has a very short beak.
Explanation: this is a black bird with a small black beak.

Fig. 6. We compare generated explanations and definitions. All explanations on the left include an attribute which is not present on the image on the right. In contrast to definitions, our explanation model can adjust its output based on visual evidence. (Color figure online)

This is a **Black-Capped Vireo** because...

Description: this bird has a white belly and breast black and white wings with a white wingbar.
Explanation-Dis.: this is a bird with a white belly yellow wing and a **black head**.

This is a **Crested Auklet** because...

Description: this bird is black and white in color with a orange beak and black eye rings.
Explanation-Dis.: this is a black bird with a **white eye** and an orange beak.

This is a **Green Jay** because...

Description: this bird has a bright blue crown and a bright yellow throat and breast.
Explanation-Dis.: this is a yellow bird with a **blue head** and a **black throat**.

This is a **White Pelican** because...

Description: this bird is white and black in color with a long curved beak and white eye rings.
Explanation-Dis.: this is a large white bird with a **long neck** and a **large orange beak**.

This is a **Geococcyx** because...

Description: this bird has a long black bill a white throat and a brown crown.
Explanation-Dis.: this is a black and white spotted bird with a **long tail feather** and a pointed beak.

This is a **Cape Glossy Starling** because...

Description: this bird is blue and black in color with a stubby beak and black eye rings.
Explanation-Dis.: this is a blue bird with a **red eye** and a blue crown.

Fig. 7. Comparing sentences generated by description and explanation-discriminative models. Though both are capable of accurately describing visual attributes, the explanation-discriminative model captures more "class-specific" attributes. (Color figure online)

specific sentences. Both models generate visually relevant sentences. However, the model trained with our discriminative loss contains properties specific to a class more often than the ones generated using the description model. For instance, for the class *Black-Capped Vireo*, the explanation-discriminative model mentions *black head* which is one of the most prominent distinguishing properties of this vireo type. For the *White Pelican* image, the explanation-discriminative model mentions highly discriminative features like *long neck* and *orange beak*.

Incorrect Prediction. We qualitatively examine explanations for instances where the incorrect label is predicted (Fig. 8). In these scenarios, explanations are frequently image relevant and mention features common in both the image instance and the predicted class. For example, in the first row of Fig. 8 the model mistakes the "Laysan Albatross" for the "Cactus Wren". The explanation text

Correct: Laysan Albatross, **Predicted:** Cactus Wren

Explanation: this is a brown and white spotted bird with a long pointed beak.
Cactus Wren Definition: this bird has a long thin beak with a brown body and black spotted feathers.
Laysan Albatross Definition: this bird has a white head and breast a grey back and wing feathers and an orange beak.

Correct: Laysan Albatross, **Predicted:** Laysan Albatross

Explanation: this bird has a white head and breast with a long hooked bill.
Laysan Albatross Definition: this bird has a white head and breast a grey back and wing feathers and an orange beak.

Correct: Acadian Flycatcher, **Predicted:** Orange Crowned Warbler

Explanation: this is a small yellow bird with a grey head and small beak.
Acadian Flycatcher Definition: this bird is brown with white on its chest and has a very short beak.
Orange Crowned Warbler Definition: this bird is yellow with black on its wings and has a very short beak.

Correct: Acadian Flycatcher, **Predicted:** Acadian Flycatcher

Explanation: this is a small grey bird with a white belly and a small pointy beak.
Acadian Flycatcher Definition: this bird is brown with white on its chest and has a very short beak.

Correct: Great Crested Flycatcher, **Predicted:** Gray Kingbird

Explanation: this is a grey bird with a white throat and a long beak.
Great Crested Flycatcher Definition: this bird has a yellow belly and breast with a gray crown and brown back
Gray Kingbird Definition: this bird has a white belly and breast with a grey crown and wing.

Correct: Great Crested Flycatcher, **Predicted:** Great Crested Flycatcher

Explanation: this bird has a yellow belly and breast with a gray wing and head.
Great Crested Flycatcher Definition: this bird has a yellow belly and breast with a gray crown and brown back.

Fig. 8. When the model predicts the wrong class, the explanation is image relevant and frequently discusses attributes common between the image and the predicted class.

includes many features also mentioned in the "Cactus Wren" definition (for example color and the spotted feathers) and is relevant to the image.

6   Conclusion

Our work is an important step towards explaining deep visual models, a crucial capability required from intelligent systems. Visual explanation is a rich research direction, especially as the field of computer vision continues to employ and improve deep models which are not easily interpretable. We anticipate that future models will look "deeper" into networks to produce explanations and perhaps begin to explain the internal mechanism of deep models.

We propose a novel reinforcement learning based loss which allows us to influence the kinds of sentences generated with a sentence level loss function. Though we focus on a discriminative loss in this work, we believe the general principle of a loss which operates on a sampled sentence and optimizes for a global sentence property is potentially beneficial in other applications. For example, [12,27] propose introducing new vocabulary words into description systems. Though both models aim to optimize a global sentence property (whether or not a caption mentions a certain concept), neither optimizes for this property directly.

In summary, we have presented a novel image explanation framework which justifies the class prediction of a visual classifier. Our quantitative and qualitative evaluations demonstrate the potential of our proposed model and effectiveness of our novel loss function. Our explanation model goes beyond the capabilities of current captioning systems and effectively incorporates classification information to produce convincing explanations, a potentially key advance for adoption of many sophisticated AI systems.

Acknowledgements. This work was supported by DARPA, AFRL, DoD MURI award N000141110688, NSF awards IIS-1427425 and IIS-1212798, and the Berkeley

Artificial Intelligence Research (BAIR) Lab. Marcus Rohrbach was supported by a fellowship within the FITweltweit-Program of the German Academic Exchange Service (DAAD). Lisa Anne Hendricks is supported by an NDSEG fellowship. We thank our experienced bird watchers, Celeste Riepe and Samantha Masaki, for helping us evaluate our model.

References

1. Andreas, J., Rohrbach, M., Darrell, T., Klein, D.: Learning to compose neural networks for question answering. In: NAACL (2016)
2. Banerjee, S., Lavie, A.: Meteor: an automatic metric for MT evaluation with improved correlation with human judgments. In: Proceedings of the ACL Workshop on Intrinsic and Extrinsic Evaluation Measures for Machine Translation and/or Summarization, vol. 29 (2005)
3. Berg, T., Belhumeur, P.: How do you tell a blackbird from a crow? In: ICCV (2013)
4. Biran, O., McKeown, K.: Justification narratives for individual classifications. In: Proceedings of the AutoML Workshop at ICML 2014 (2014)
5. Core, M.G., Lane, H.C., Van Lent, M., Gomboc, D., Solomon, S., Rosenberg, M.: Building explainable artificial intelligence systems. In: Proceedings of the National Conference on Artificial Intelligence, vol. 21. AAAI Press, Menlo Park (1999). MIT Press, Cambridge (2006)
6. Doersch, C., Singh, S., Gupta, A., Sivic, J., Efros, A.: What makes Paris look like Paris? ACM Trans. Graph. **31**(4), 101:1–101:9 (2012). doi:10.1145/2185520. 2185597
7. Donahue, J., Hendricks, L.A., Guadarrama, S., Rohrbach, M., Venugopalan, S., Saenko, K., Darrell, T.: Long-term recurrent convolutional networks for visual recognition and description. In: CVPR (2015)
8. Donahue, J., Jia, Y., Vinyals, O., Hoffman, J., Zhang, N., Tzeng, E., Darrell, T.: DeCAF: a deep convolutional activation feature for generic visual recognition. In: ICML (2013)
9. Fang, H., Gupta, S., Iandola, F., Srivastava, R.K., Deng, L., Dollár, P., Gao, J., He, X., Mitchell, M., Platt, J.C., et al.: From captions to visual concepts and back. In: CVPR (2015)
10. Gao, Y., Beijbom, O., Zhang, N., Darrell, T.: Compact bilinear pooling. In: CVPR (2016)
11. Guadarrama, S., Krishnamoorthy, N., Malkarnenkar, G., Venugopalan, S., Mooney, R., Darrell, T., Saenko, K.: YouTube2Text: recognizing and describing arbitrary activities using semantic hierarchies and zero-shot recognition. In: ICCV (2013)
12. Hendricks, L.A., Venugopalan, S., Rohrbach, M., Mooney, R., Saenko, K., Darrell, T.: Deep compositional captioning: Describing novel object categories without paired training data. In: CVPR (2016)
13. Hochreiter, S., Schmidhuber, J.: Long short-term memory. Neural Comput. **9**(8), 1735–1780 (1997)
14. Jia, X., Gavves, E., Fernando, B., Tuytelaars, T.: Guiding long-short term memory for image caption generation. In: ICCV (2015)
15. Jia, Y., Shelhamer, E., Donahue, J., Karayev, S., Long, J., Girshick, R., Guadarrama, S., Darrell, T.: Caffe: Convolutional architecture for fast feature embedding. In: Proceedings of the ACM International Conference on Multimedia. ACM (2014)

16. Jiang, Z., Wang, Y., Davis, L., Andrews, W., Rozgic, V.: Learning discriminative features via label consistent neural network (2016). arXiv preprint arXiv:1602.01168

17. Johnson, W.L.: Agents that learn to explain themselves. In: AAAI (1994)

18. Karpathy, A., Li, F.: Deep visual-semantic alignments for generating image descriptions. In: CVPR (2015)

19. Kiros, R., Salakhutdinov, R., Zemel, R.: Multimodal neural language models. In: ICML (2014)

20. Krizhevsky, A., Sutskever, I., Hinton, G.E.: Imagenet classification with deep convolutional neural networks. In: NIPS (2012)

21. Kulkarni, G., Premraj, V., Dhar, S., Li, S., Choi, Y., Berg, A., Berg, T.: Baby talk: understanding and generating simple image descriptions. In: CVPR (2011)

22. Lacave, C., Díez, F.J.: A review of explanation methods for Bayesian networks. Knowl. Eng. Rev. **17**(02), 107–127 (2002)

23. Lampert, C., Nickisch, H., Harmeling, S.: Attribute-based classification for zero-shot visual object categorization. In: TPAMI (2013)

24. Lane, H.C., Core, M.G., Van Lent, M., Solomon, S., Gomboc, D.: Explainable artificial intelligence for training and tutoring. Technical report, DTIC Document (2005)

25. Lomas, M., Chevalier, R., Cross II., E.V., Garrett, R.C., Hoare, J., Kopack, M.: Explaining robot actions. In: Proceedings of the Seventh Annual ACM/IEEE International Conference on Human-Robot Interaction. ACM (2012)

26. Mao, J., Huang, J., Toshev, A., Camburu, O., Yuille, A., Murphy, K.: Generation and comprehension of unambiguous object descriptions. In: CVPR (2016)

27. Mao, J., Wei, X., Yang, Y., Wang, J., Huang, Z., Yuille, A.L.: Learning like a child: fast novel visual concept learning from sentence descriptions of images. In: ICCV (2015)

28. Mao, J., Xu, W., Yang, Y., Wang, J., Yuille, A.L.: Explain images with multimodal recurrent neural networks. In: NIPS Deep Learning Workshop (2014)

29. Miller, G.A., Beckwith, R., Fellbaum, C., Gross, D., Miller, K.J.: Introduction to wordnet: an on-line lexical database*. Int. J. Lexicogr. **3**(4), 235–244 (1990)

30. Papineni, K., Roukos, S., Ward, T., Zhu, W.J.: BLEU: a method for automatic evaluation of machine translation. In: ACL (2002)

31. Reed, S., Akata, Z., Lee, H., Schiele, B.: Learning deep representations of fine-grained visual descriptions. In: CVPR (2016)

32. Reed, S., Akata, Z., Yan, X., Logeswaran, L., Schiele, B., Lee, H.: Generative adversarial text to image synthesis. In: ICML (2016)

33. Shortliffe, E.H., Buchanan, B.G.: A model of inexact reasoning in medicine. Math. Biosci. **23**(3), 351–379 (1975)

34. Teach, R.L., Shortliffe, E.H.: An analysis of physician attitudes regarding computer-based clinical consultation systems. Use and Impact of Computers in Clinical Medicine. Springer, New York (1981)

35. Van Lent, M., Fisher, W., Mancuso, M.: An explainable artificial intelligence system for small-unit tactical behavior. In: Proceedings of the National Conference on Artificial Intelligence. AAAI Press, Menlo Park (1999). MIT Press, Cambridge (2006)

36. Vedantam, R., Lawrence Zitnick, C., Parikh, D.: CIDEr: consensus-based image description evaluation. In: CVPR (2015)

37. Vinyals, O., Toshev, A., Bengio, S., Erhan, D.: Show and tell: a neural image caption generator. In: CVPR (2015)

38. Wah, C., Branson, S., Welinder, P., Perona, P., Belongie, S.: The Caltech-UCSD Birds-200-2011 Dataset. Technical report CNS-TR-2011-001, California Institute of Technology (2011)
39. Williams, R.J.: Simple statistical gradient-following algorithms for connectionist reinforcement learning. Mach. Learn. **8**, 229–256 (1992)
40. Xu, K., Ba, J., Kiros, R., Courville, A., Salakhutdinov, R., Zemel, R., Bengio, Y.: Show, attend and tell: neural image caption generation with visual attention. In: ICML (2015)
41. Yeung, S., Russakovsky, O., Jin, N., Andriluka, M., Mori, G., Fei-Fei, L.: Every moment counts: dense detailed labeling of actions in complex videos. In: CVPR (2016)

Marker-Less 3D Human Motion Capture with Monocular Image Sequence and Height-Maps

Yu Du[1], Yongkang Wong[2], Yonghao Liu[1], Feilin Han[1], Yilin Gui[1],
Zhen Wang[1], Mohan Kankanhalli[2,3], and Weidong Geng[1(✉)]

[1] College of Computer Science, Zhejiang University, Hangzhou, China
{answeror,yonghaoliu,hanfeilin,ylgui,wangzh_cs,gengwd}@zju.edu.cn
[2] Interactive and Digital Media Institute,
National University of Singapore, Singapore, Singapore
yongkang.wong@nus.edu.sg
[3] School of Computing, National University of Singapore, Singapore, Singapore
mohan@comp.nus.edu.sg

Abstract. The recovery of 3D human pose with monocular camera is
an inherently ill-posed problem due to the large number of possible projections from the same 2D image to 3D space. Aimed at improving the
accuracy of 3D motion reconstruction, we introduce the additional built-
in knowledge, namely height-map, into the algorithmic scheme of reconstructing the 3D pose/motion under a single-view calibrated camera. Our
novel proposed framework consists of two major contributions. Firstly,
the RGB image and its calculated height-map are combined to detect
the landmarks of 2D joints with a dual-stream deep convolution network. Secondly, we formulate a new objective function to estimate 3D
motion from the detected 2D joints in the monocular image sequence,
which reinforces the temporal coherence constraints on both the camera
and 3D poses. Experiments with HumanEva, Human3.6M, and MCAD
dataset validate that our method outperforms the state-of-the-art algorithms on both 2D joints localization and 3D motion recovery. Moreover,
the evaluation results on HumanEva indicates that the performance of
our proposed single-view approach is comparable to that of the multi-
view deep learning counterpart.

Keywords: Human pose estimation · Height-map

1 Introduction

Marker-less motion capture is an active field of research in computer vision and
graphics with applications in computer animation, video surveillance, biomedical
research, and sports science. According to the recent study on world population
aging [1], the life expectancy at age 60 and above is expected to grow in the next

Electronic supplementary material The online version of this chapter (doi:10.
1007/978-3-319-46493-0_2) contains supplementary material, which is available to
authorized users.

B. Leibe et al. (Eds.): ECCV 2016, Part IV, LNCS 9908, pp. 20–36, 2016.
DOI: 10.1007/978-3-319-46493-0_2

few decades. This anticipates an emerging need in video-based analysis systems to monitor the elderly in nursing home as an event alert system.

Existing motion capture approaches can be broadly divided into two categories: (1) methods based on monocular camera [2–5], and (2) methods that rely on synchronous multi-view streams [6–8]. Nowadays, single view approaches are getting more attention in the industry. Although multi-view visual data presents richer information for marker-less motion capture, such data are not always available in reality, especially in the applications of video surveillance.

The recovery of 3D human poses with monocular image sequences is an inherently ill-posed problem, since the observed projection on a 2D image can be explained by multiple 3D poses and camera positions, when we try to infer poses from single-view images or motions from monocular video [9]. The problem becomes even more challenging if we consider realistic situations in which image features, such as the body silhouette, limbs or 2D joints, cannot be accurately detected due to environment factors or occlusions [10]. Nevertheless, human observers are able to accurately estimate the pose of a human body with a single eye. In most cases, they are also able to effortlessly organize the anatomical landmarks in three-dimensional space and predict the relative position of the camera, where the ambiguity is resolved by leveraging on vast memory of likely 3D configurations of humans [9]. A reasonable proxy for such capabilities can be available by learning from motion capture libraries, ensuring anthropometric plausibility while discarding impossible configurations. Motivated by this, we aim to achieve accurate 3D reconstruction of human motion from monocular image sequence recorded by a calibrated camera.

We propose a novel framework for marker-less 3D human motion capture with a single-view calibrated camera, where the 3D human pose is articulated as 3D pose or a skeleton model parameterized by joint locations. It consists of three key components, namely height-map generation, 2D joint localization, and 3D motion generation. Inspired by the recent success of deep learning approach on RGB-D camera [11,12], we propose a dual-stream Deep Convolution Network (ConvNet) to effectively detect 2D landmarks of human joints. The RGB images and the additional built-in knowledge (i.e., height-map) are independently modeled with one stream of ConvNet, which are then jointly fined-tuned for improved 2D joints detection. In addition, the nature of the dual-stream ConvNet architecture also allows the proposed method to be coupled with any improved RGB-based 2D joint detection algorithm in the future. Furthermore, in the 3D motion estimation stage, we propose to reinforce both the pose-conditioned joint velocity and the temporal coherence constraints of continuity of the camera and 3D poses in the optimization scheme. To the best of our knowledge, this is the first algorithm that utilizes the height-map to capture 3D articulated skeleton motion from a calibrated monocular camera.

The remaining of the paper is organized as follows. Section 2 reviews the related literature. Section 3 elaborates on the details of the proposed framework. Section 4 evaluates the proposed framework with both synthetic and real-world video dataset. Section 5 concludes the paper.

2 Literature Review

Human 3D pose estimation has received a lot of attention from the communities, and has been investigated using monocular camera [2–5], multi-view image sequences [6–8], and RGB-D sensor [11]. In the early research, Fischler and Elschlager [13] introduced the Pictorial Structures Model (PSM) to represent an object by a collection of parts in a deformable configuration. This is further adopted to represent human body as an articulated structure for tracking [4], recognition [14,15], and pose estimation [4,15–18] problems. Various approaches were proposed to learn PSM directly via RGB images [19,20] or depth images [17,21].

3D pose estimation from a single image is an inherently ill-posed problem due to the possibility of multiple plausible projections from the same 2D image to a variety of 3D poses. A common approach is to project the estimated 2D landmarks from single image to the 3D space by imposing certain constraints [5,9,10,22,23]. Simo-Serra et al. [10] imposed kinematic constraints to guarantee that the resulting pose resembles a human shape. In [5,9], 3D pose is represented as a sparse linear combination of an overcomplete dictionary. In [9], the sparse model is computed while enforcing anthropometric regularity on pose structure, whereas [5] enforced eight limb length constraints to eliminate errors generated from inaccurate 2D landmarks estimation. Simultaneous estimation of both 3D pose and camera parameters further improved the performance [5,9,23]. Recently, [24] considered the estimation of 3D pose as a Spatio-Temporal Matching problem that explore the correspondence between video and 3D motion capture data. The aforementioned approaches considered the 2D landmarks and 3D pose as separate problems, where [22] jointly models both problems using a Bayesian framework.

Recently, ConvNets has been applied to estimate human pose from a monocular camera. Specifically, it aims to label anatomical landmarks (or joints) on image. DeepPose [25] is the first work that holistically cast pose modeling as a joint regression problem. Chen and Yuille [2] further improved the estimation by modeling human pose as a graphical model where each local joint is considered as a node. They consider the part detection as a local image measurement and predict the spatial relationships between joints as an image dependent pairwise relations. Similarly, Tompson et al. [26] proposed a hybrid architecture that consists of ConvNet part detector and Markov Random Field inspired spatial-model to exploit the structural domain constraints. This approach is further improved by a cascaded architecture that combines fine and coarse scale ConvNet to accommodate the variance of human annotation errors [27]. Focusing on structured-output learning, Li et al. [28] embed image and pose into a high-dimensional space, whereas the image-pose embedding and score function are jointly trained using a maximum-margin cost function with a 2-stage optimization procedure. In contrast to the aforementioned approaches, [29–31] directly predicted the 3D pose from images.

While the single shot approach can be applied to model a human action from an image sequence, such approaches often result in unstable 3D motion

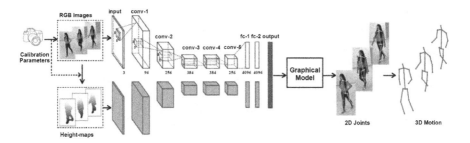

Fig. 1. Conceptual illustration of the proposed 3D human motion capture framework with a calibrated monocular camera. (Colour figure online)

reconstructions [3]. To address this, Wandt *et al.* [3] modeled 3D pose as a linear combination of base poses and proposed a periodic model for the mixing coefficients to improve the efficiency and accuracy for periodic motion (e.g., walking, running, *etc.*). The reconstruction on non-periodic motion is achieved with a regularization term on temporal bone length constancy. In [32], 3D pose estimation is considered as a sparsity-driven reconstruction problem with temporal smoothness prior. Furthermore, it regards 2D joints as a latent variable which the uncertainty maps can be jointly learned with deep learning based joint detector. Hasler *et al.* [7] proposed to perform automatic camera registration and audio synchronization for multiple cameras, followed by recovering 3D human pose by computing the correspondence between the extracted silhouettes. Hofmann and Gavrilla [6] proposed a multi-stage verification process for the shape hypotheses generated from each camera, and removed the temporal ambiguity by maximizing the best trajectories across cameras. Elhayek *et al.* [8] combined a ConvNet based part detection model [26] with a generative model-based tracking algorithm based on Sums of Gaussians framework, which captures temporally stable full articulated joints from multiple cameras.

To the best of our knowledge, there exist no work that employs height-map as built-in knowledge together with color image for 2D joints detection.

3 Proposed Method

3.1 Overview

In this work, the main objective is to accurately recover the 3D human poses with a calibrated monocular camera, where the 3D human motion is represented by a skeleton model parameterized by joint positions. Our proposed framework consists of three key components, namely, height-map generation, 2D joints localization, and 3D motion estimation. A conceptual diagram of the proposed framework is shown in Fig. 1.

The height-map is generated by existing height estimation algorithm [33] using calibrated camera parameters and the body silhouettes. Inspired by the

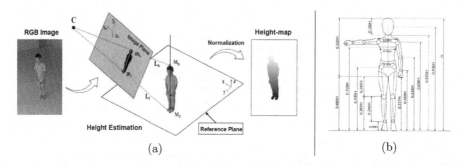

Fig. 2. (a) Illustration of height-map generation with pre-calibrated monocular camera, (b) Anatomical decomposition of Skeleton based on height [35].

recent success of skeleton pose recognition using RGB-D (color + depth) sensors [11,12], we propose a dual-stream deep ConvNet for 2D joints localization with RGB images and the computed height-maps (RGB-H). The dual-stream ConvNet is first trained with "Leeds Sports Poses" (LSP) dataset [34] (for the RGB stream), which is then used as an initial stream for the height-maps and trained with a synthetic dataset (for the H stream). The resulting model is then jointly fined-tuned on the target dataset with the computed RGB-H images. For the 3D human pose estimation, we consider both the reinforced temporal constraints of the camera and the pose-conditioned joint velocity.

3.2 Height-Map Generation

Height-map is a grayscale image designed to be an intermediate new representation of body parts, where pixels in a height-map indicate its height with respect to the reference plane rather than a measure of color, depth or intensity. For each pixel of the human body, we apply the height estimation method proposed by Park *et al.* [33] to calculate height from monocular RGB camera by back-projecting 2D features of an object into the 3D scene space (see Fig. 2). To accommodate variation in height across human subjects, we normalize the estimated height, $\boldsymbol{H}$, on each pixel to relative height, $\hat{\boldsymbol{H}}$, via:

$$\hat{\boldsymbol{H}}(x,y) = k \cdot \frac{\boldsymbol{H}(x,y)}{h_i} \qquad (1)$$

where x and y is the pixel coordinate, and h_i indicates the body height of ith person. k is a scale constant to map the relative height-map to a desired range, which is empirically set to 255 to mimic an intensity channel (see Fig. 2a). Given a height-map, we implicitly encode the spatial relationships among joints of a skeleton structure [35] (see Fig. 2b).

3.3 2D Joints Localization

Given an image sequence with m frames $\{\boldsymbol{I}_1, \ldots, \boldsymbol{I}_m | \boldsymbol{I}_t \in \mathbb{R}^{w \times h \times d}\}$, where w and h are the width and height of an image, and d is the number of channels. The goal is to localize the anatomical landmarks of human (i.e., 2D joints), $\{p_1, \ldots, p_m | p_t \in \mathbb{R}^{2n}\}$, in each image using both the RGB images and the estimated height-maps, where n is the pre-defined number of 2D joints. In this work, we assume that one pose is observed at each frame to simplify the mathematical formulation.

We adapt a ConvNet-based 2D joints localization method [2], which achieved state-of-the-art results on several public benchmark datasets[1]. This method depicts human pose as a graphical model and predicts the spatial relationship between joints as an image dependent pairwise relation. Inspired by the hybrid approach that use RGB-D sensor data [11,12], we design a dual-stream deep learning architecture, which operates on both RGB image and height-map, and a fully connected layer is deployed to fuse these two streams (conceptual diagram is shown in Fig. 1). This architecture is similar to other recent multi-stream approaches for recognition and segmentation tasks [36–39].

The localization of 2D joints in each stream is formulated as the optimization of a score function over a part based graphical model [16]:

$$F(l, t | I) = \sum_{i \in \mathcal{V}} U(l_i | I) + \sum_{(i,j) \in \mathcal{E}} R(l_i, l_j, t_{ij}, t_{ji} | I) + w_0 \qquad (2)$$

where $l = \{l_i | i \in \mathcal{V}\}$ is a set of joint positions, $t = \{t_{ij} | (i, j) \in \mathcal{E}\}$ is the pairwise relation type, and w_0 is a bias term. $\mathcal{V}$ and $\mathcal{E}$ are the sets of vertices and edges of the graphical model, respectively. U and R contain mixtures of part types and pairwise relation types, which are specified as the marginalization of a joint distribution modeled by ConvNet. The input of the ConvNet is an image patch while the output is the evidence for a part to lie in this patch with a certain relationship to its neighbours. We refer the reader to [2] for more details. Given the learned models, we discard the output layers of both streams and employ a new output layer to fuse the output of the last fully connected layers.

The dual-steam ConvNet employs a stage-wise training strategy. The RGB stream is pre-trained on LSP dataset [34], and the resultant network is further applied on our synthetic height-maps dataset to obtain the initial weights of the height stream. Note that in order to reuse the pre-trained network on color images to initialize the height stream, we recreate a RGB image by replicating height-map three times as that in [40]. The entire network is then jointly fine-tuned on a target training set.

Validation of Height-Map for 2D Joints Localization. To evaluate the feasibility of using height-map for effective localization of 2D joints, we conducted a preliminary experiment on the 8-persons test set of a real-world surveillance dataset, namely Multi-Camera Action Dataset (MCAD) [41]. The height-map based single-stream ConvNet is trained on our synthetic dataset using the pre-trained ConvNet provided by [2]. The preliminary result (see in Fig. 3) shows that the pure height-map based approach is comparable and a complement to that based on the pre-trained model with RGB images in [2]. Therefore, we

---

[1] http://human-pose.mpi-inf.mpg.de/#related_benchmarks.

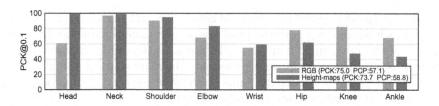

Fig. 3. Preliminary study of 2D joints localization with single-stream ConvNet on MCAD [41]. The values in the parenthesis are the mean value of PCK@0.1 and PCP [2].

argue that it is feasible to incorporate height-maps into the algorithmic pipeline of localizing landmark of joints from images. Please refer to Sect. 4 for details about databases and evaluation metrics.

3.4   3D Motion Estimation

Given a sequence of 2D joints $\{p_1, \cdots, p_m | p_t \in \mathbb{R}^{2n}\}$, the corresponding 3D poses $\{P_1, \cdots, P_m | P_t \in \mathbb{R}^{3n}\}$ can be estimated by optimizing the following objective function

$$\min_{\theta} \mathcal{L}(\theta; \mathbf{p}) + \mathcal{R}_t(\theta) + \mathcal{R}_a(\theta) \tag{3}$$

where $\theta = \{\mathbf{P}, \mathbf{V}, \mathbf{R}, \mathbf{T}\}$ is the union of all the 3D motion parameters, in which $\mathbf{p} = [p_1^T \cdots p_m^T]^T \in \mathbb{R}^{2mn}$, $\mathbf{P} = [P_1^T \cdots P_m^T]^T \in \mathbb{R}^{3mn}$, and $\mathbf{V} = [V_1^T \cdots V_m^T]^T \in \mathbb{R}^{3mn}$ denote the 2D position, the 3D position, and the 3D velocity of each joint, respectively; p_t is the concatenation of l at time t; $\mathbf{R} = \oplus_{t=1}^{m} (I_n \otimes R_t) \in \mathbb{R}^{3mn \times 3mn}$ and $\mathbf{T} = [\mathbf{1}_{n \times 1} \otimes T_1^T \cdots \mathbf{1}_{n \times 1} \otimes T_m^T]^T \in \mathbb{R}^{3mn}$ denote the orientation and position of the person in the camera frame; $\otimes$ and $\oplus$ are the Kronecker product and direct sum respectively; I is the identity matrix.

The first term is the reprojection error which is formulated as:

$$\mathcal{L}(\theta; \mathbf{p}) = \|\mathbf{p} - h(\mathbf{R}\mathbf{P} + \mathbf{T})\|^2 \tag{4}$$

where $h : \mathbb{R}^{3mn} \to \mathbb{R}^{2mn}$ performs perspective projection of the 3D joints to the 2D image plane.

The second term enforces the temporal constraints on each joint's movement speed, the orientation of the person with respect to the camera, and the corresponding position

$$\mathcal{R}_t(\theta) = \alpha \|\nabla_t (\mathbf{P} - \mathbf{V})\|^2 + \beta_r \|\nabla_t \mathbf{R}\|^2 + \beta_t \|\nabla_t \mathbf{T}\|^2 \tag{5}$$

where ∇_t is the discrete temporal derivative operator. The first sub-term penalizes the inconsistency between position and velocity. The second and third terms impose first-order smoothness on the orientation and position of the target person.

The last term imposes the anthropometric constraints on limb lengths

$$\mathcal{R}_a(\theta) = \gamma \|g(\mathbf{P})\|^2 \tag{6}$$

where g computes the length difference of arms and legs between the estimated poses and the training data.

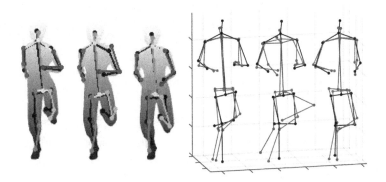

Fig. 4. Qualitative illustration of the robustness of the temporal coherence constraints to inaccurate localization of 2D joints. The ground-truth 2D and 3D skeletons are colored in black. On the left are three consecutive synthetic height-maps of running motion, where the localization of the left ankle in the second frame is incorrect. On the right are the estimated 3D poses by [9] (in blue) and by our method (in red). (Color figure online)

Pose-Conditioned Joint Velocity. We represent a 3D human pose P_t and the joint velocity of this pose V_t at time t by a linear combination of a set of bases $\mathbf{B} = \{b_1, \cdots, b_k\}$ and a mean vector μ

$$X_t = [P_t^T, V_t^T]^T = \mu + \mathbf{B}_t^* \omega_t \tag{7}$$

$$\{b_i\}_{i \in \mathcal{I}_{\mathbf{B}_t^*}} \in \mathbf{B}_t^* \subset \mathbf{B} \tag{8}$$

where ω_t are the basis coefficients, $\mathbf{B}_t^*$ is an optimal subset of an dictionary $\mathbf{B}$ where each column of matrix $\mathbf{B}_t^*$ is a basis b_i selected with index vector $\mathcal{I}_{\mathbf{B}_t^*}$ from $\mathbf{B}$. $\mathbf{B}$ is created by concatenating the bases computed from various types of motions using Principal Component Analysis (PCA).

When training the bases $\mathbf{B}$, each sample is formed by the concatenation of the 3D pose and the joint velocity of this pose. The joint velocity is approximated by the difference of joint positions in current and the k-th previous frames, where $k = \lfloor s_3/s_2 + 0.5 \rfloor$, in which s_2 and s_3 are the sampling rates of the input sequence and motion database respectively.

Based on this representation, the parameter P_t and V_t at time t are defined as $[I_n\ \mathbf{0}_n](\mu + \mathbf{B}_t^* \omega_t)$ and $[\mathbf{0}_n\ I_n](\mu + \mathbf{B}_t^* \omega_t)$, respectively. The parameter set can be re-written as $\theta = \{\mathbf{I}, \mathbf{\Omega}, \mathbf{R}, \mathbf{T}\}$, where $\mathbf{I} = \{\mathcal{I}_{\mathbf{B}_1^*}, \cdots, \mathcal{I}_{\mathbf{B}_m^*}\}$ is the index vectors, and $\mathbf{\Omega} = [\omega_1^T \cdots \omega_m^T]^T \in \mathbb{R}^{3mn}$ represents the coefficient vectors.

The sparse representation of human pose by an overcomplete dictionary has been adopted in recent work [9,23]. The key difference here is that our dictionary encodes not only the anthropomorphically plausible 3D poses, but also the pose-conditioned joint velocity. Figure 4 shows that the implausible 3D poses estimated from the inaccurate localization of 2D joints can be corrected by our temporal coherence constraints.

Synthetic height-maps   MCAD [41]   HumanEva [46]   Human3.6M [45]

Fig. 5. Samples from four datasets for evaluation.

Optimization. The objective function in (3) is solved by Projected Matching Pursuit [9]. In each iteration, we first compute the loss function in (3) for each frame with the available basis, followed by a frame level optimal basis selection with basis that contribute to minimum loss. The selected optimal basis is excluded for the next iteration. Then we estimate $\{\Omega, \mathbf{R}, \mathbf{T}\}$ in (3) by Levenberg-Marquardt algorithm [42]. The optimization terminates if the reprojection error is less than a threshold δ or the number of the basis selected for each frame reaches ϕ. $\mathbf{R}$ and $\mathbf{T}$ are initialized by EPnP algorithm [43] using the known intrinsic parameters of the calibrated camera.

4   Experiments

In this section, we evaluate the performance of the proposed method from three perspectives. First, we evaluate the efficacy of the proposed dual-stream ConvNet for 2D joints localization, which include various single-stream and dual-stream configurations, as well as comparison against [24]. Second, the evaluation of 3D motion recovery is made with the ground-truth 2D joint locations, and compared against [9,23]. Third, we compare the entire pipeline of the proposed framework against [5,10,28,44]. To keep the consistency with the literature, we use a skeleton of 14 joints [24] where a virtual root joint is added merely for visualization. Before computing the 3D error in Sects. 4.3 and 4.4, the estimated 3D pose is rigidly aligned with the ground-truth as that in existing works [10,22,23]. For the 3D evaluation on Human3.6M, we do not perform the rigid alignment on the resulting motion.

Based on the preliminary experiment, we fix the parameters of the proposed 3D motion estimation method in all experiments, where $\alpha = 0.1$, $\beta_r = 10$, $\beta_t = 1$, $\gamma = 1$, $\delta = 500$ and $\phi = 15$.

4.1   Datasets

We evaluate our approach on four datasets: (1) the synthetic height-maps dataset, (2) HumanEva dataset [45], (3) Human3.6M dataset [44], and (4) Multi-Camera Action Dataset (MCAD) [41]. The samples are shown in Fig. 5. We generate a large scale synthetic height-maps dataset, which consists of 184,872 synthetic height-maps along with the corresponding 2D and 3D joint locations, which are generated from 9 characters with 36 surrounding viewpoints. For each character there are around 570 poses extracted from five-hour motion capture data about dancing, walking, fighting, etc. HumanEva [45] is a benchmark dataset for 3D pose estimation. It contains synchronized multi-view videos captured by calibrated cameras and 3D ground-truth motion of 4 subjects performing 6 predefined actions with 3 repetitions. We use the walking and jogging motions of three subjects in the HumanEva, as that in [5,10], to evaluate the localization of 2D joints and the overall performance of our method. The third dataset we used is Human3.6M [44], which is currently the largest video pose dataset. It contains over 3.6 million frames of different human poses, viewed from 4 different angles, using an accurate human motion capture system. The motions were performed by 11 human subjects under 15 activity scenarios. Following [28], we split the dataset to have 5 subjects (S1, S5, S6, S7, S8) for training and 2 subjects (S9, S11) for testing. As far as the dataset is redundant, we select 1 out of 50 frames from all 4 cameras for training and every 5-th frame from camera 2 for testing, using the standard 17 joint skeleton from Human3.6M. The MCAD [41] consists of 20 persons and 18 actions recorded under 5 non-overlapping surveillance cameras, 14,298 action sequences in total. We manually labeled the 2D joints of all individuals in one of the cameras. 10 of the human subjects are used for training and the remaining ones are reserved for testing. All the data is converted into observer centric view during the pre-processing stage, as in [2].

4.2 Evaluation of 2D Joints Localization

We consider two metrics as indicators to evaluate the performance of 2D joint localization. The performance analyzed in terms of the Probability of Correct Keypoints (PCK) metric proposed in [16], which measures the accuracy using a curve of the percentage of correctly localized joints by varying localization precision threshold. In this work, we also adopt the strict Probability of Correct Pose (PCP) proposed by Chen *et al.* [2], where a body part is considered as correct if both of its joints lie within 50 % of the length of the ground-truth annotated endpoints. Based on the project site of [46][2], we select [2] as the baseline for 2D joint localization as it achieved the best performance for the time being.

Evaluation on MCAD. We first compare the proposed 2D joints localization method (RGB-H) with the one solely relying on color images (RGB) [2] or height-maps on the test set of MCAD. The ConvNets of these three methods are fine-tuned on the training set of MCAD with 30,000 iterations and a learning rate of 0.001. Then the part based graphical models are also re-trained based on the fine-tuned ConvNets. As shown in Fig. 6(a), although the model solely based on height-maps achieves lower accuracy than [2], combining color images and height-maps indeed improves the precision.

Next, we compare our dual-stream ConvNet against another single-stream ConvNet on the test set of MCAD. The single-stream ConvNet has exactly the same structure as the one in [2] except that the input dimension of the first layer is 4 (denoted as "4-channels RGB-H"). This model is trained from scratch on the

---

[2] https://cse.sc.edu/%7Efan23/projects/cvpr15/cvpr15.html.

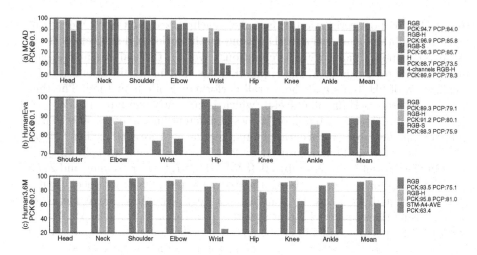

Fig. 6. Evaluation of 2D joints localization with RGB [2], RGB-H, RGB-S (RGB-Silhouette), H (height-maps), 4-channels RGB-H and STM-A4-AVE [24] respectively on the MCAD, HumanEva and Human3.6M.

Table 1. Evaluation of 2D joints localization on Human3.6M. The numbers are PCK accuracy at threshold 0.2.

	Directions	Discussion	Eating	Greeting	Phoning	Photo	Posing	Purchases
STM-A4-AVE [24]	67.6	62.3	55.1	68.9	56.5	54.9	57.6	47.7
Chen et al. [2]	98.8	95.5	98.1	97.6	93.9	89.5	98.6	85.6
Ours	99.0	96.9	98.9	98.4	96.5	94.0	99.2	93.8
	Sitting	SittingDown	Smoking	Waiting	WalkDog	Walking	WalkTogether	Mean
STM-A4-AVE [24]	42.4	26.2	58.7	65.9	61.2	81.5	79.4	59.1
Chen et al. [2]	94.1	70.5	94.4	96.3	88.6	98.0	97.7	93.5
Ours	95.0	77.2	96.1	98.2	94.3	98.7	98.9	95.8

training set of MCAD. As shown in Fig. 6(a), the performance of dual-stream ConvNet is much better than that of single-stream ConvNet, especially for wrist joints which registers an improvement of 32.6 % points.

To investigate whether the body silhouette could achieve similar performance as height-map, we train and test a RGB-Silhouette (RGB-S) based model using the exactly same settings in the RGB-H case. Fig. 6(a) shows that RGB-H outperforms RGB-S.

Evaluation on HumanEva. We compare three models (RGB, RGB-H and RGB-S) on the test set of HumanEva, where these models are trained on MCAD and not re-trained on this dataset. Because our definition of head and neck are different from HumanEva, we discard these two joints and evaluate with the remaining joints. As Fig. 6(b) shows, the precision of the estimated locations of the endsites are obviously improved by using RGB-H images, and the model based on the body silhouette does not generalize well on HumanEva.

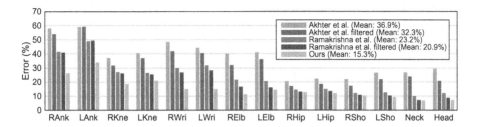

Fig. 7. Evaluation of 3D motion recovery with known 2D joints. The respective average error is shown in the legend. The estimated poses of [9, 23] are further filtered by zero-phase Butterworth filter (3rd order, 0.2 Hz for [23]; 2nd order, 1.7 Hz for [9]).

Evaluation on Human3.6M. We compare the proposed method with [2] and STM-A4-AVE [24] on the test set (S9 and S11) of Human3.6M. Our model and [2] are fine-tuned on the training set of Human3.6M using the same settings in the experiment on MCAD. As shown in Fig. 6(c) and Table 1, our method significantly outperforms others, especially in terms of PCP metric.

4.3   Evaluation of 3D Motion Recovery with Ground-Truth 2D Joints

We compare the proposed 3D motion recovery method with others on a sequence of 154 consecutive frames of synthetic motion of running around a circle, where the 2D joints locations are known. The character is driven by the retargeted motion capture data of CMU motion capture database [47]. We use the source codes provided by [9, 23]. We train the bases of our model and [9] on "running", "walking", "jumping" and "boxing" motions of CMU motion capture database by fixing the position and orientation of the root joint and concatenating PCA components which retrained 99 % of the variance from each motion category. For [23], we directly test the provided model without re-training. We also report the result of [9, 23] with simple smoothing filter. We use zero-phase Butterworth filter whose parameters are optimized with grid search. We report the relative reconstruction error proposed by [23], which is a distance measure relative to the length of the backbone of the ground-truth skeleton. Fig. 7 shows that our method achieves a lower reconstruction error.

4.4   Evaluation of 3D Motion Recovery with Predicted 2D Joints

In this section, we quantify the performance of 3D motion estimation as a distance measurement relative to the length of the backbone of the ground-truth skeleton [23]. Specifically, we report *Root Mean Square* (RMS) error on HumanEva and *mean per joint position error* on Human3.6M. Note that the difference in the evaluation scheme on HumanEva is to ensure consistency with [5]. Different from Sect. 4.3, we compare our entire pipeline which estimates 3D pose from raw RGB images and the corresponding height-maps.

Table 2. Evaluation of 3D motion estimation on 3 subjects of the HumanEva dataset. The value in each cell are the RMS error and standard deviation in millimeter.

	Walking				Jogging			
	S1	S2	S3	Mean	S1	S2	S3	Mean
[10]	99.6 (42.6)	108.3 (42.3)	127.4 (24.0)	111.8	109.2 (41.5)	93.1 (41.1)	115.8 (40.6)	106.0
[5]	71.9 (19.0)	75.7 (15.9)	85.3 (10.3)	77.6	62.6 (10.2)	77.7 (12.1)	**54.4** (9.0)	64.9
Ours	**62.2** (18.6)	**61.9** (13.2)	**69.2** (22.4)	**64.4**	**56.3** (15.4)	**59.3** (14.4)	59.3 (15.5)	**58.3**

Table 3. Evaluation of 3D motion estimation on Human3.6M dataset. The error are reported in mean per joint position error (MPJPE) [44].

	Directions	Discussion	Eating	Greeting	Phoning	Photo	Posing	Purchases	Sitting
LinKDE [44]	132.71	183.55	132.37	164.39	162.12	205.94	150.61	171.31	151.57
Li et al. [28]	–	136.88	96.94	124.74	–	168.68	–	–	–
Ours	**85.07**	**112.68**	104.90	**122.05**	**139.08**	135.91	**105.93**	166.16	**117.49**
	SittingDown	Smoking	Waiting	WalkDog	Walking	WalkTogether	Mean (6 actions)	Mean (15 actions)	
LinKDE [44]	243.03	162.14	170.69	177.13	96.60	127.88	160.00	162.14	
Li et al. [41]	–	–	–	132.17	69.97	–	121.56	–	
Ours	226.94	**120.02**	**117.65**	137.36	99.26	**106.54**	**118.69**	**126.47**	

We first evaluate our proposed framework against state-of-the-art [5,10] on the HumanEva. To ensure consistency with [5], the reconstruction error is computed on 12 joints[3]. As shown in Table 2, our method significantly outperforms others in 5 out of 6 tests and achieved the mean reconstruction error of 64.4 mm and 58.3 mm on walking and jogging motion respectively, which is around 17.0 % and 10.2 % reduction from [5]. In addition, our results is comparable to the state-of-the-art performance (66.5 mm) [8]. However, we would like to highlight

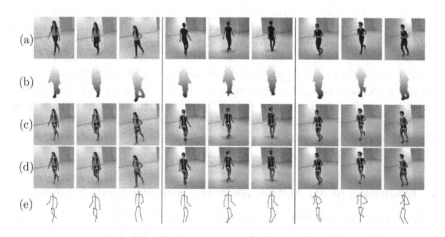

Fig. 8. Qualitative result of the proposed framework of 3 persons (left, middel and right) from the MCAD [41]. (a) Image sequence, (b) Computed height-maps, (c) Ground-truth of 2D joints, (d) Localized 2D joints, and (e) Recovered 3D motion.

---

[3] The left and right shoulders, elbows, wrists, hips, knees and ankles.

that [8] is a multi-view deep-learning based approach, which has the advantage of richer information from multiple views. It should also be noted that we didn't fine-tune our model on the HumanEva.

The second evaluation is conducted on the Human3.6 with results shown in Table 3. Our proposed approach outperforms [44] on almost all actions with an overall improvement of around 22 %. Comparing with [28], we achieved better results on 3 out of 6 actions and the mean error favors our framework. Note that [28] is significantly better on the *Walking* action, while our approach stands out on the *Discussion* and *Photo* action.

And finally, we show the qualitative results of our proposed method on three persons from the MCAD [41]. As shown in Fig. 8, the localized 2D joints resemble that from the ground-truth label and the resultant 3D pose from the recovered 3D motion is good.

5 Conclusion

Monocular 3D human pose estimation is a highly ambiguous problem that requires introducing additional knowledge [11]. In this work, we studied the efficacy of height-map as a type of built-in prior knowledge to detect the anatomical landmarks of a human body, as well as enforce the temporal constraints on the camera and 3D poses for improved skeleton-based human pose estimation. Together with both components, we achieved state-of-the-art performance for both 2D joints localization and 3D motion estimation over two benchmark datasets (HumanEva & Human3.6M) and a real-world surveillance dataset (MCAD). The codes and the annotations of MCAD are available at http://zju-capg.org/heightmap.

Moreover, we evaluate our single view RGB-H approach with a state-of-the-art multi-view approach [8] on the walking motion from HumanEva dataset. On average, the spatial precision difference in detected joints is very close to each other on the mean reconstruction error. This suggests that our single view RGB-H method is very competitive for some real-world applications, such as human behavior analysis for event alert system, which usually require highly accurate 3D motion recovery from monocular video clips. This also enables us to utilize the millions of monocular cameras from the existing surveillance networks where camera can be calibrated with a reasonable amount of effort.

For future work, we aim to extend our framework to accommodate complex human motion (e.g., break dance, yoga exercise, *etc.*), where the height-map may fail to indicate the anatomical structure. We are also interested in scenarios to recover 3D human motion with sporadic partial human body occlusion.

Acknowledgements. This work was supported by a grant from the National High Technology Research and Development Program of China (Program 863, 2013AA013705), and the National Natural Science Foundation of China (No. 61379067). This research was partly supported by the National Research Foundation, Prime Ministers Office, Singapore under its International Research Centre in Singapore Funding Initiative.

References

1. United Nations, Department of Economic, Social Affairs, Population Division: World population ageing 2013 (2013). ST/SEA/SER.A/348
2. Chen, X., Yuille, A.L.: Articulated pose estimation by a graphical model with image dependent pairwise relations. In: NIPS, pp. 1736–1744 (2014)
3. Wandt, B., Ackermann, H., Rosenhahn, B.: 3D human motion capture from monocular image sequences. In: CVPR Workshops, pp. 1–8 (2015)
4. Andriluka, M., Roth, S., Schiele, B.: Monocular 3D pose estimation and tracking by detection. In: CVPR, pp. 623–630 (2010)
5. Wang, C., Wang, Y., Lin, Z., Yuille, A.L., Gao, W.: Robust estimation of 3D human poses from a single image. In: CVPR, pp. 2369–2376 (2014)
6. Hofmann, M., Gavrila, D.M.: Multi-view 3D human pose estimation in complex environment. Int. J. Comput. Vis. **96**(1), 103–124 (2012)
7. Hasler, N., Rosenhahn, B., Thormählen, T., Wand, M., Gall, J., Seidel, H.: Markerless motion capture with unsynchronized moving cameras. In: CVPR, pp. 224–231 (2009)
8. Elhayek, A., de Aguiar, E., Jain, A., Tompson, J., Pishchulin, L., Andriluka, M., Bregler, C., Schiele, B., Theobalt, C.: Efficient ConvNet-based marker-less motion capture in general scenes with a low number of cameras. In: CVPR, pp. 3810–3818 (2015)
9. Ramakrishna, V., Kanade, T., Sheikh, Y.: Reconstructing 3D human pose from 2D image landmarks. In: Fitzgibbon, A., Lazebnik, S., Perona, P., Sato, Y., Schmid, C. (eds.) ECCV 2012. LNCS, vol. 7575, pp. 573–586. Springer, Heidelberg (2012). doi:10.1007/978-3-642-33765-9_41
10. Simo-Serra, E., Ramisa, A., Alenyà, G., Torras, C., Moreno-Noguer, F.: Single image 3D human pose estimation from noisy observations. In: CVPR, pp. 2673–2680 (2012)
11. Sridhar, S., Oulasvirta, A., Theobalt, C.: Interactive markerless articulated hand motion tracking using RGB and depth data. In: ICCV, pp. 2456–2463 (2013)
12. Gupta, S., Arbelaez, P., Girshick, R., Malik, J.: Aligning 3D models to RGB-D images of cluttered scenes. In: CVPR, pp. 4731–4740 (2015)
13. Fischler, M.A., Elschlager, R.A.: The representation and matching of pictorial structures. IEEE Trans. Comput. **22**(1), 67–92 (1973)
14. Felzenszwalb, P.F., Huttenlocher, D.P.: Pictorial structures for object recognition. Int. J. Comput. Vis. **61**(1), 55–79 (2005)
15. Andriluka, M., Roth, S., Schiele, B.: Pictorial structures revisited: people detection and articulated pose estimation. In: CVPR, pp. 1014–1021 (2009)
16. Yang, Y., Ramanan, D.: Articulated human detection with flexible mixtures of parts. IEEE Trans. Pattern Anal. Mach. Intell. **35**(12), 2878–2890 (2013)
17. Shotton, J., Sharp, T., Kipman, A., Fitzgibbon, A., Finocchio, M., Blake, A., Cook, M., Moore, R.: Real-time human pose recognition in parts from single depth images. Commun. ACM **56**(1), 116–124 (2013)
18. Zhang, D., Shah, M.: Human pose estimation in videos. In: ICCV, pp. 2012–2020 (2015)
19. Yasin, H., Iqbal, U., Krüger, B., Weber, A., Gall, J.: A dual-source approach for 3D pose estimation from a single image. In: CVPR, pp. 4948–4956 (2016)
20. Ionescu, C., Carreira, J., Sminchisescu, C.: Iterated second-order label sensitive pooling for 3D human pose estimation. In: CVPR, pp. 1661–1668 (2014)

21. Li, S., Chan, A.B.: 3D human pose estimation from monocular images with deep convolutional neural network. In: Cremers, D., Reid, I., Saito, H., Yang, M.-H. (eds.) ACCV 2014. LNCS, vol. 9004, pp. 332–347. Springer, Heidelberg (2015). doi:10.1007/978-3-319-16808-1_23

22. Simo-Serra, E., Quattoni, A., Torras, C., Moreno-Noguer, F.: A joint model for 2D and 3D pose estimation from a single image. In: CVPR, pp. 3634–3641 (2013)

23. Akhter, I., Black, M.J.: Pose-conditioned joint angle limits for 3D human pose reconstruction. In: CVPR, pp. 1446–1455 (2015)

24. Zhou, F., la Torre, F.D.: Spatio-temporal matching for human pose estimation in video. IEEE Trans. Pattern Anal. Mach. Intell. **38**(8), 1492–1504 (2016)

25. Toshev, A., Szegedy, C.: DeepPose: human pose estimation via deep neural networks. In: CVPR, pp. 1653–1660 (2014)

26. Tompson, J., Jain, A., LeCun, Y., Bregler, C.: Joint training of a convolutional network and a graphical model for human pose estimation. In: NIPS, pp. 1799–1807 (2014)

27. Tompson, J., Goroshin, R., Jain, A., LeCun, Y., Bregler, C.: Efficient object localization using convolutional networks. In: CVPR, pp. 648–656 (2015)

28. Li, S., Zhang, W., Chan, A.B.: Maximum-margin structured learning with deep networks for 3D human pose estimation. In: ICCV, pp. 2848–2856 (2015)

29. Tekin, B., Rozantsev, A., Lepetit, V., Fua, P.: Direct prediction of 3D body poses from motion compensated sequences. In: CVPR, pp. 991–1000 (2016)

30. Kostrikov, I.: Depth sweep regression forests for estimating 3D human pose from images. In: BMVC, pp. 1–13 (2014)

31. Hong, C., Yu, J., Wan, J., Tao, D., Wang, M.: Multimodal deep autoencoder for human pose recovery. IEEE Trans. Image Process. **24**(12), 5659–5670 (2015)

32. Zhou, X., Zhu, M., Leonardos, S., Derpanis, K., Daniilidis, K.: Sparseness meets deepness: 3D human pose estimation from monocular video. In: CVPR, pp. 4966–4975 (2016)

33. Park, S.-W., Kim, T.-E., Choi, J.-S.: Robust estimation of heights of moving people using a single camera. In: Kim, K.J., Ahn, S.J. (eds.) Proceedings of the International Conference on IT Convergence and Security 2011. LNEE, vol. 120, pp. 389–405. Springer, Heidelberg (2012). doi:10.1007/978-94-007-2911-7_36

34. Johnson, S., Everingham, M.: Clustered pose and nonlinear appearance models for human pose estimation. In: BMVC, pp. 1–11 (2010)

35. Benbakreti, S., Benyettou, M.: Gait recognition based on leg motion and contour of silhouette. In: ICITeS, pp. 1–5 (2012)

36. Srivastava, N., Salakhutdinov, R.R.: Multimodal learning with deep boltzmann machines. In: NIPS, pp. 2222–2230 (2012)

37. Hariharan, B., Arbeláez, P., Girshick, R., Malik, J.: Simultaneous detection and segmentation. In: Fleet, D., Pajdla, T., Schiele, B., Tuytelaars, T. (eds.) ECCV 2014. LNCS, vol. 8695, pp. 297–312. Springer, Heidelberg (2014). doi:10.1007/978-3-319-10584-0_20

38. Simonyan, K., Zisserman, A.: Two-stream convolutional networks for action recognition in videos. In: NIPS, pp. 568–576 (2014)

39. Eitel, A., Springenberg, J.T., Spinello, L., Riedmiller, M.A., Burgard, W.: Multimodal deep learning for robust RGB-D object recognition. In: IEEE/RSJ International Conference on Intelligent Robots and Systems, September 2015, pp. 681–687 (2015)

40. Gupta, S., Girshick, R., Arbeláez, P., Malik, J.: Learning rich features from RGB-D images for object detection and segmentation. In: Fleet, D., Pajdla, T., Schiele, B., Tuytelaars, T. (eds.) ECCV 2014. LNCS, vol. 8695, pp. 345–360. Springer, Heidelberg (2014). doi:10.1007/978-3-319-10584-0_23

41. Li, W., Wong, Y., Liu, A.A., Li, Y., Su, Y.T., Kankanhalli, M.: Multi-camera action dataset (MCAD): a dataset for studying non-overlapped cross-camera action recognition. CoRR abs/1607.06408 (2016)

42. Moré, J.J.: The levenberg-marquardt algorithm: implementation and theory. In: Watson, G.A. (ed.) Numerical Analysis, pp. 105–116. Springer, Heidelberg (1978)

43. Lepetit, V., Moreno-Noguer, F., Fua, P.: EPnP: an accurate $O(n)$ solution to the PnP problem. Int. J. Comput. Vis. **81**(2), 155–166 (2009)

44. Ionescu, C., Papava, D., Olaru, V., Sminchisescu, C.: Human3.6M: large scale datasets and predictive methods for 3D human sensing in natural environments. IEEE Trans. Pattern Anal. Mach. Intell. **36**(7), 1325–1339 (2014)

45. Sigal, L., Balan, A., Black, M.: HumanEva: synchronized video and motion capture dataset and baseline algorithm for evaluation of articulated human motion. Int. J. Comput. Vis. **87**(1–2), 4–27 (2010)

46. Fan, X., Zheng, K., Lin, Y., Wang, S.: Combining local appearance and holistic view: dual-source deep neural networks for human pose estimation. In: CVPR, pp. 1347–1355 (2015)

47. Carnegie Mellon University Motion Capture Database, http://mocap.cs.cmu.edu

Tensor Representations via Kernel Linearization for Action Recognition from 3D Skeletons

Piotr Koniusz[1,3]([✉]), Anoop Cherian[2,3], and Fatih Porikli[1,2,3]

[1] NICTA/Data61/CSIRO, Canberra, Australia
{piotr.koniusz,fatih.porikli}@data61.csiro.au
[2] Australian Centre for Robotic Vision, Canberra, Australia
anoop.cherian@data61.csiro.au
[3] Australian National University, Canberra, Australia
{piotr.koniusz,anoop.cherian,fatih.porikli}@anu.edu.au

Abstract. In this paper, we explore tensor representations that can compactly capture higher-order relationships between skeleton joints for 3D action recognition. We first define RBF kernels on 3D joint sequences, which are then linearized to form kernel descriptors. The higher-order outer-products of these kernel descriptors form our tensor representations. We present two different kernels for action recognition, namely (i) a *sequence compatibility kernel* that captures the spatio-temporal compatibility of joints in one sequence against those in the other, and (ii) a *dynamics compatibility kernel* that explicitly models the action dynamics of a sequence. Tensors formed from these kernels are then used to train an SVM. We present experiments on several benchmark datasets and demonstrate state of the art results, substantiating the effectiveness of our representations.

Keywords: Kernel descriptors · Skeleton action recognition · Higher-order tensors

1 Introduction

Human action recognition is a central problem in computer vision with potential impact in surveillance, human-robot interaction, elderly assistance systems, and gaming, to name a few. While there have been significant advancements in this area over the past few years, action recognition in unconstrained settings still remains a challenge. There have been research to simplify the problem from using RGB cameras to more sophisticated sensors such as Microsoft Kinect that can localize human body-parts and produce moving 3D skeletons [1]; these skeletons are then used for recognition. Unfortunately, these skeletons are often noisy due to the difficulty in localizing body-parts, self-occlusions, and sensor range

Electronic supplementary material The online version of this chapter (doi:10.1007/978-3-319-46493-0_3) contains supplementary material, which is available to authorized users.

B. Leibe et al. (Eds.): ECCV 2016, Part IV, LNCS 9908, pp. 37–53, 2016.
DOI: 10.1007/978-3-319-46493-0_3

errors; thus necessitating higher-order reasoning on these 3D skeletons for action recognition.

There have been several approaches suggested in the recent past to improve recognition performance of actions from such noisy skeletons. These approaches can be mainly divided into two perspectives, namely (i) generative models that assume the skeleton points are produced by a latent dynamic model [2] corrupted by noise and (ii) discriminative approaches that generate compact representations of sequences on which classifiers are trained [3]. Due to the huge configuration space of 3D actions and the unavailability of sufficient training data, discriminative approaches have been the trend in the recent years for this problem. In this line of research, the main idea has been to compactly represent the spatio-temporal evolution of 3D skeletons, and later train classifiers on these representations to recognize the actions. Fortunately, there is a definitive structure to motions of 3D joints relative to each other due to the connectivity and length constraints of body-parts. Such constraints have been used to model actions; examples include Lie Algebra [4], positive definite matrices [5,6], using a torus manifold [7], Hanklet representations [8], among several others. While modeling actions with explicit manifold assumptions can be useful, it is computationally expensive.

In this paper, we present a novel methodology for action representation from 3D skeleton points that avoids any manifold assumptions on the data representation, instead captures the higher-order statistics of how the body-joints relate to each other in a given action sequence. To this end, our scheme combines positive definite kernels and higher-order tensors, with the goal to obtain rich and compact representations. Our scheme benefits from using non-linear kernels such as radial basis functions (RBF) and it can also capture higher-order data statistics and the complexity of action dynamics.

We present two such kernel-tensor representations for the task. Our first representation *sequence compatibility kernel* (SCK), captures the spatio-temporal compatibility of body-joints between two sequences. To this end, we present an RBF kernel formulation that jointly captures the spatial and temporal similarity of each body-pose (normalized with respect to the hip position) in a sequence against those in another. We show that tensors generated from third-order outer-products of the linearizations of these kernels can be a simple yet powerful representation capturing higher-order co-occurrence statistics of body-parts and yield high classification confidences.

Our second representation, termed *dynamics compatibility kernel* (DCK) aims at representing spatio-temporal dynamics of each sequence explicitly. We present a novel RBF kernel formulation that captures the similarity between a pair of body-poses in a given sequence explicitly, and then compare it against such body-pose pairs in other sequences. As it might appear, such spatio-temporal modeling could be expensive due to the volumetric nature of space and time. However, we show that using an appropriate kernel model can shrink the time-related variable in a small constant size representation after kernel linearization. With this approach, we can model both spatial and temporal variations in the form of co-occurrences which could otherwise have been prohibitive.

We further show through experiments that the above two representations in fact capture complementary statistics regarding the actions, and combining them leads to significant benefits. We present experiments on three standard datasets for the task, namely (i) UTKinect-Actions [9], (ii) Florence3D-Actions [10], and (iii) MSR-Action3D [11] datasets and demonstrate state-of-the-art accuracy.

To summarize, the main contributions of this paper are (i) introduction of sequence and the dynamics compatibility kernels for capturing spatio-temporal evolution of body-joints for 3D skeleton based action sequences, (ii) derivations of linearization of these kernels, and (iii) their tensor reformulations. We review the related literature next.

2 Related Work

The problem of skeleton based action recognition has received significant attention over the past decades. Interested readers may refer to useful surveys [3] on the topic. In the sequel, we will review some of the more recent related approaches to the problem.

In this paper, we focus on action recognition datasets that represent a human body as an articulated set of connected body-joints that evolve in time [12]. A temporal evolution of the human skeleton is very informative for action recognition as shown by Johansson in his seminal experiment involving the moving lights display [13]. At the simplest level, the human body can be represented as a set of 3D points corresponding to body-joints such as elbow, wrist, knee, ankle, *etc.* Action dynamics has been modeled using the motion of such 3D points in [14,15], using joint orientations with respect to a reference axis [16] and even relative body-joint positions [17,18]. In contrast, we focus on representing these 3D body-joints by kernels whose linearization results in higher-order tensors capturing complex statistics. Noteworthy are also parts-based approaches that additionally consider the connected body segments [4,19–21].

Our work also differs from previous works in the way it handles the temporal domain. 3D joint locations are modeled as temporal hierarchy of coefficients in [14]. Pairwise relative positions of joints were modeled in [17] and combined with a hierarchy of Fourier coefficients to capture temporal evolution of actions. Moreover, this approach uses multiple kernel learning to select discriminative joint combinations. In [18], the relative joint positions and their temporal displacements are modeled with respect to the initial frame. In [4], the displacements and angles between the body parts are represented as a collection of matrices belonging to the special Euclidean group SE(3). Temporal domain is handled by the discrete time warping and Fourier temporal pyramid matching on a sequence of such matrices. In contrast, we model temporal domain with a single RBF kernel providing invariance to local temporal shifts and avoid expensive techniques such as time warping and multiple-kernel learning.

Our scheme also differs from prior works such as kernel descriptors [22] that aggregate orientations of gradients for recognition. Their approach exploits sums over the product of at most two RBF kernels handling two cues *e.g.*, gradient orientations and spatial locations, which are later linearized by Kernel PCA and Nyström techniques. Similarly, convolutional kernel networks [23] consider stacked layers of a variant of kernel descriptors [22]. Kernel trick was utilized for action recognition in kernelized covariances [24] which are obtained in Nyström-like process. A time series kernel [25] between auto-correlation matrices is proposed to capture spatio-temporal auto-correlations. In contrast, our scheme allows sums over several multiplicative and additive RBF kernels, thus, it allows handling multiple input cues to build a complex representation. We show how to capture higher-order statistics by linearizing a polynomial kernel and avoid evaluating costly kernels directly in contrast to kernel trick.

Third-order tensors have been found to be useful for several other vision tasks. For example, in [26], spatio-temporal third-order tensors on videos is proposed for action analysis, non-negative tensor factorization is used for image denoising in [27], tensor textures are proposed for texture rendering in [28], and higher order tensors are used for face recognition in [29]. A survey of multilinear algebraic methods for tensor subspace learning and applications is available in [30]. These applications use a single tensor, while our goal is to use the tensors as data descriptors similar to [31–34] for image recognition tasks. However, in contrast to these similar methods, we explore the possibility of using third-order representations for 3D action recognition, which poses a different set of challenges.

3   Preliminaries

In this section, we review our notations and the necessary background on shift-invariant kernels and their linearizations, which will be useful for deriving kernels on 3D skeletons for action recognition.

3.1   Tensor Notations

Let $\mathcal{V} \in \mathbb{R}^{d_1 \times d_2 \times d_3}$ denote a third-order tensor. Using Matlab style notation, we refer to the p-th slice of this tensor as $\mathcal{V}_{:,:,p}$, which is a $d_1 \times d_2$ matrix. For a matrix $V \in \mathbb{R}^{d_1 \times d_2}$ and a vector $\mathbf{v} \in \mathbb{R}^{d_3}$, the notation $\mathcal{V} = V \uparrow \otimes \mathbf{v}$ produces a tensor $\mathcal{V} \in \mathbb{R}^{d_1 \times d_2 \times d_3}$ where the p-th slice of $\mathcal{V}$ is given by $V v_p$, v_p being the p-th dimension of $\mathbf{v}$. Symmetric third-order tensors of rank one are formed by the outer product of a vector $\mathbf{v} \in \mathbb{R}^d$ in modes two and three. That is, a rank-one $\mathcal{V} \in \mathbb{R}^{d \times d \times d}$ is obtained from $\mathbf{v}$ as $\mathcal{V} = (\uparrow \otimes_3 \mathbf{v} \triangleq (\mathbf{v}\mathbf{v}^T) \uparrow \otimes \mathbf{v})$. Concatenation of n tensors in mode k is denoted as $[\mathcal{V}_i]_{i \in \mathcal{I}_n}^{\oplus_k}$, where $\mathcal{I}_n$ is an index sequence $1, 2, ..., n$. The Frobenius norm of tensor is given by $\|\mathcal{V}\|_F = \sqrt{\sum_{i,j,k} \mathcal{V}_{ijk}^2}$, where $\mathcal{V}_{ijk}$ represents the ijk-th element of $\mathcal{V}$. Similarly, the inner-product between two tensors $\mathcal{X}$ and $\mathcal{Y}$ is given by $\langle \mathcal{X}, \mathcal{Y} \rangle = \sum_{ijk} \mathcal{X}_{ijk} \mathcal{Y}_{ijk}$.

3.2   Kernel Linearization

Let $G_\sigma(\mathbf{u} - \bar{\mathbf{u}}) = \exp(-\|\mathbf{u} - \bar{\mathbf{u}}\|_2^2 / 2\sigma^2)$ denote a standard Gaussian RBF kernel centered at $\bar{\mathbf{u}}$ and having a bandwidth σ. Kernel linearization refers to rewriting this G_σ as an inner-product of two infinite-dimensional feature maps. To obtain these maps, we use a fast approximation method based on probability product kernels [35]. Specifically, we employ the inner product of d'-dimensional isotropic Gaussians given $u, u' \in \mathbb{R}^{d'}$. The resulting approximation can be written as:

$$G_\sigma(\mathbf{u} - \bar{\mathbf{u}}) = \left(\frac{2}{\pi\sigma^2}\right)^{\frac{d'}{2}} \int\limits_{\zeta \in \mathbb{R}^{d'}} G_{\sigma/\sqrt{2}}(\mathbf{u} - \zeta)\, G_{\sigma/\sqrt{2}}(\bar{\mathbf{u}} - \zeta)\, \mathrm{d}\zeta. \tag{1}$$

Equation (1) is then approximated by replacing the integral with the sum over Z pivots $\zeta_1, ..., \zeta_Z$, thus writing a feature map ϕ as:

$$\phi(\mathbf{u}) = \left[G_{\sigma/\sqrt{2}}(\mathbf{u} - \zeta_1), ..., G_{\sigma/\sqrt{2}}(\mathbf{u} - \zeta_Z)\right]^T, \tag{2}$$

$$\text{and } G_\sigma(\mathbf{u} - \bar{\mathbf{u}}) \approx \left\langle \sqrt{c}\phi(\mathbf{u}), \sqrt{c}\phi(\bar{\mathbf{u}}) \right\rangle, \tag{3}$$

where c represents a constant. We refer to (3) as the linearization of the RBF kernel.

4 Proposed Approach

In this section, we first formulate the problem of action recognition from 3D skeleton sequences, which precedes an exposition of our two kernel formulations for describing the actions, followed by their tensor reformulations through kernel linearization.

4.1 Problem Formulation

Suppose we are given a set of 3D human pose skeleton sequences, each pose consisting of J body-keypoints. Further, to simplify our notations, we assume each sequence consists of N skeletons, one per frame[1]. Mathematically, we can define such a pose sequence Π as:

$$\Pi = \left\{ \mathbf{x}_{is} \in \mathbb{R}^3, i \in \mathcal{I}_J, s \in \mathcal{I}_N \right\}. \tag{4}$$

Further, let each such sequence Π be associated with one of K action class labels $\ell \in \mathcal{I}_K$. Our goal is to use the skeleton sequence Π and generate an action descriptor for this sequence that can be used in a classifier for recognizing the action class. In the following, we will present two such action descriptors, namely (i) sequence compatibility kernel and (ii) dynamics compatibility kernel, which are formulated using the ideas of kernel linearization and tensor algebra. We present both these kernel formulations next.

---

[1] We assume that all sequences have N frames for simplification of presentation. Our formulations are equally applicable to sequences of arbitrary lengths e.g., M and N. Therefore, we apply in practice $G_{\sigma_3}(\frac{s}{M} - \frac{t}{N})$ in Eq. (5).

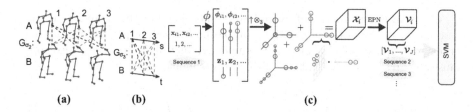

Fig. 1. Figures **(a)** and **(b)** show how SCK works – kernel G_{σ_2} compares exhaustively *e.g.* hand-related joint i for every frame in sequence A with every frame in sequence B. Kernel G_{σ_3} compares exhaustively the frame indexes. Figure **(c)** shows this burden is avoided by linearization – third-order statistics on feature maps $\phi(\mathbf{x}_{is})$ and $\mathbf{z}(s)$ for joint i are captured in tensor $\boldsymbol{\mathcal{X}}_i$ and whitened by EPN to obtain $\boldsymbol{\mathcal{V}}_i$ which are concatenated over $i = 1, ..., J$ to represent a sequence.

4.2   Sequence Compatibility Kernel

As alluded to earlier, the main idea of this kernel is to measure the compatibility between two action sequences in terms of the similarity between their skeletons and their temporal order. To this end, we assume each skeleton is centralized with respect to one of the body-joints (say, hip). Suppose we are given two such sequences Π_A and Π_B, each with J joints, and N frames. Further, let $\mathbf{x}_{is} \in \mathbb{R}^3$ and $\mathbf{y}_{jt} \in \mathbb{R}^3$ correspond to the body-joint coordinates of Π_A and Π_B, respectively. We define our *sequence compatibility kernel* (SCK) between Π_A and Π_B as (See footnote 1):

$$K_S(\Pi_A, \Pi_B) = \frac{1}{\Lambda} \sum_{(i,s) \in \mathcal{J}} \sum_{(j,t) \in \mathcal{J}} G_{\sigma_1}(i-j)\Big(\beta_1 G_{\sigma_2}(\mathbf{x}_{is} - \mathbf{y}_{jt}) + \beta_2\, G_{\sigma_3}\big(\frac{s-t}{N}\big)\Big)^r, \quad (5)$$

where Λ is a normalization constant and $\mathcal{J} = \mathcal{I}_J \times \mathcal{I}_N$. As is clear, this kernel involves three different compatibility subkernels, namely (i) G_{σ_1}, that captures the compatibility between joint-types i and j, (ii) G_{σ_2}, capturing the compatibility between joint locations $\mathbf{x}$ and $\mathbf{y}$, and (iii) G_{σ_3}, measuring the temporal alignment of two poses in the sequences. We also introduce weighting factors $\beta_1, \beta_2 \geq 0$ that adjusts the importance of the body-joint compatibility against the temporal alignment, where $\beta_1 + \beta_2 = 1$. Figures 1a and b illustrate how this kernel works. It might come as a surprise, why we need the kernel G_{σ_1}. Note that our skeletons may be noisy and there is a possibility that some of the keypoints are detected incorrectly (for example, elbows and wrists). Thus, this kernel allows incorporating some degree of uncertainty to the alignment of such joints. To simplify our formulations, in this paper, we will assume that such errors are absent from our skeletons, and thus $G_{\sigma_1}(i-j) = \delta(i-j)$. Further, the standard deviations σ_2 and σ_3 control the joint-coordinate selectivity and temporal shift-invariance respectively. That is, for $\sigma_3 \to 0$, two sequences will have to match perfectly in the temporal sense. For $\sigma_3 \to \infty$, the algorithm is invariant to any permutations of the frames. As will be clear in the sequel, the parameter r determines the order statistics of the kernel (we use $r = 3$).

Next, we present linearization of our kernel using the method proposed in Sect. 3.2 and Eq. (3) so that kernel $G_{\sigma_2}(\mathbf{x}-\mathbf{y}) \approx \phi(\mathbf{x})^T \phi(\mathbf{y})$ (see footnote[2]) while $G_{\sigma_3}(\frac{s-t}{N}) \approx \mathbf{z}(s/N)^T \mathbf{z}(t/N)$. With these approximations and simplification to G_{σ_1} we described above, we can rewrite our sequence compatibility kernel as:

$$K_S(\Pi_A, \Pi_B) = \frac{1}{\Lambda} \sum_{i \in \mathcal{I}_J} \sum_{s \in \mathcal{I}_N} \sum_{t \in \mathcal{I}_N} \left(\begin{bmatrix} \sqrt{\beta_1}\, \phi(\mathbf{x}_{is}), \text{ (see footnote 2)} \\ \sqrt{\beta_2}\, \mathbf{z}(s/N) \end{bmatrix}^T \cdot \begin{bmatrix} \sqrt{\beta_1}\phi(\mathbf{y}_{it}) \\ \sqrt{\beta_2}\mathbf{z}(t/N) \end{bmatrix} \right)^r \tag{6}$$

$$= \frac{1}{\Lambda} \sum_{i \in \mathcal{I}_J} \sum_{s \in \mathcal{I}_N} \sum_{t \in \mathcal{I}_N} \left\langle \uparrow \otimes_r \begin{bmatrix} \sqrt{\beta_1}\phi(\mathbf{x}_{is}) \\ \sqrt{\beta_2}\, \mathbf{z}(s/N) \end{bmatrix}, \uparrow \otimes_r \begin{bmatrix} \sqrt{\beta_1}\phi(\mathbf{y}_{it}) \\ \sqrt{\beta_2}\mathbf{z}(t/N) \end{bmatrix} \right\rangle \tag{7}$$

$$= \sum_{i \in \mathcal{I}_J} \left\langle \frac{1}{\sqrt{\Lambda}} \sum_{s \in \mathcal{I}_N} \uparrow \otimes_r \begin{bmatrix} \sqrt{\beta_1}\phi(\mathbf{x}_{is}) \\ \sqrt{\beta_2}\mathbf{z}(s/N) \end{bmatrix}, \frac{1}{\sqrt{\Lambda}} \sum_{t \in \mathcal{I}_N} \uparrow \otimes_r \begin{bmatrix} \sqrt{\beta_1}\phi(\mathbf{y}_{it}) \\ \sqrt{\beta_2}\mathbf{z}(t/N) \end{bmatrix} \right\rangle. \tag{8}$$

As is clear, (8) expresses $K_S(\Pi_A, \Pi_B)$ as a sum of inner-products on third-order tensors $(r = 3)$. This is illustrated by Fig. 1c. While, using the dot-product as the inner-product is a possibility, there are much richer alternatives for tensors of order $r >= 2$ that can exploit their structure or manipulate higher-order statistics in them, thus leading to better representations. An example of such a commonly encountered property is the so-called *burstiness* [36], which is the property that a given feature appears more often in a sequence than a statistically independent model would predict. A robust sequence representation should be invariant to the length of actions *e.g.*, a prolonged *hand waving* represents the same action as a short *hand wave*. The same is true for short versus repeated *head nodding*. Eigenvalue Power Normalization (EPN) [32] is known to suppress burstiness. It acts on higher-order statistics illustrated in Fig. 1c. Incorporating EPN, we generalize (8) as:

$$K_S^*(\Pi_A, \Pi_B) = \sum_{i \in \mathcal{I}_J} \left\langle \mathcal{G} \left(\frac{1}{\sqrt{\Lambda}} \sum_{s \in \mathcal{I}_N} \uparrow \otimes_r \begin{bmatrix} \sqrt{\beta_1}\phi(\mathbf{x}_{is}) \\ \sqrt{\beta_2}\mathbf{z}(s/N) \end{bmatrix} \right), \mathcal{G} \left(\frac{1}{\sqrt{\Lambda}} \sum_{t \in \mathcal{I}_N} \uparrow \otimes_r \begin{bmatrix} \sqrt{\beta_1}\phi(\mathbf{y}_{it}) \\ \sqrt{\beta_2}\mathbf{z}(t/N) \end{bmatrix} \right) \right\rangle, \tag{9}$$

where the operator $\mathcal{G}$ performs EPN by applying power normalization to the spectrum of the third-order tensor (by taking the higher-order SVD). Note that in general $K_S^*(\Pi_A, \Pi_B) \not\approx K_S(\Pi_A, \Pi_B)$ as $\mathcal{G}$ is intended to manipulate the spectrum of $\mathcal{X}$. The final representation, for instance for a sequence Π_A, takes the following form:

$$\mathcal{V}_i = \mathcal{G}(\mathcal{X}_i), \text{ where } \mathcal{X}_i = \frac{1}{\sqrt{\Lambda}} \sum_{s \in \mathcal{I}_N} \uparrow \otimes_r \begin{bmatrix} \sqrt{\beta_1}\, \phi(\mathbf{x}_{is}) \\ \sqrt{\beta_2}\mathbf{z}(s/N) \end{bmatrix}. \tag{10}$$

---

[2] In practice, we use $G'_{\sigma_2}(\mathbf{x}-\mathbf{y}) = G_{\sigma_2}(x^{(x)} - y^{(x)}) + G_{\sigma_2}(x^{(y)} - y^{(y)}) + G_{\sigma_2}(x^{(z)} - y^{(z)})$ so the kernel $G'_{\sigma_2}(\mathbf{x} - \mathbf{y}) \approx [\phi(x^{(x)}); \phi(x^{(y)}); \phi(x^{(z)})]^T [\phi(y^{(x)}); \phi(y^{(y)}); \phi(y^{(z)})]$ but for simplicity we write $G_{\sigma_2}(\mathbf{x} - \mathbf{y}) \approx \phi(\mathbf{x})^T \phi(\mathbf{y})$. Note that (x), (y), (z) are the spatial xyz-components of joints.

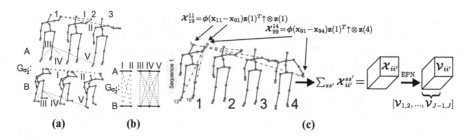

Fig. 2. Figure **(a)** shows that kernel $G_{\sigma_2'}$ in DCK captures spatio-temporal dynamics by measuring displacement vectors from any given body-joint to remaining joints spatially- and temporally-wise (*i.e.* see dashed lines). Figure **(b)** shows that comparisons performed by $G_{\sigma_2'}$ for any selected two joints are performed all-against-all temporally-wise which is computationally expensive. Figure **(c)** shows the encoding steps in the proposed linearization which overcome this burden.

We can further replace the summation over the body-joint indexes in (9) by concatenating $\mathcal{V}_i$ in (10) along the fourth tensor mode, thus defining $\mathcal{V} = [\mathcal{V}_i]_{i \in \mathcal{I}_J}^{\oplus_4}$. Suppose $\mathcal{V}_A$ and $\mathcal{V}_B$ are the corresponding fourth order tensors for Π_A and Π_B respectively. Then, we obtain:

$$K_S^*(\Pi_A, \Pi_B) = \langle \mathcal{V}_A, \mathcal{V}_B \rangle. \tag{11}$$

Note that the tensors $\mathcal{X}$ have the following properties: (i) super-symmetry $\mathcal{X}_{i,j,k} = \mathcal{X}_{\pi(i,j,k)}$ for indexes i, j, k and their permutation given by π, $\forall \pi$, and (ii) positive semi-definiteness of every slice, that is, $\mathcal{X}_{:,:,s} \in \mathcal{S}_+^d$, for $s \in \mathcal{I}_d$. Therefore, we need to use only the upper-simplex of the tensor which consists of $\binom{d+r-1}{r}$ coefficients (which is the total size of our final representation) rather than d^r, where d is the side-dimension of $\mathcal{X}$ *i.e.*, $d = 3Z_2 + Z_3$ (see footnote 2), and Z_2 and Z_3 are the numbers of pivots used in the approximation of G_{σ_2} (see footnote 2) and G_{σ_3} respectively. As we want to preserve the above listed properties in tensors $\mathcal{V}$, we employ slice-wise EPN which is induced by the Power-Euclidean distance and involves rising matrices to a power γ. Finally, we re-stack these slices along the third mode as:

$$\mathcal{G}(\mathcal{X}) = [\mathcal{X}_{:,:,s}^\gamma]_{s \in \mathcal{I}_d}^{\oplus_3}, \text{ for } 0 < \gamma \leq 1. \tag{12}$$

This $\mathcal{G}(\mathcal{X})$ forms our tensor representation for the action sequence.

4.3   Dynamics Compatibility Kernel

The SCK kernel that we described above captures the inter-sequence alignment, while the intra-sequence spatio-temporal dynamics is lost. In order to capture these temporal dynamics, we propose a novel dynamics compatibility kernel (DCK). To this end, we use the absolute coordinates of the joints in our kernel.

Using the notations from the earlier section, for two action sequences Π_A and Π_B, we define this kernel as:

$$K_D(\Pi_A, \Pi_B) = \frac{1}{\Lambda} \sum_{\substack{(i,s)\in\mathcal{J},\ (j,t)\in\mathcal{J}, \\ (i',s')\in\mathcal{J},\ (j',t')\in\mathcal{J}, \\ i\neq i, s\neq s \quad j\neq j, t\neq t}} \sum G'_{\sigma_1'}(i-j, i'-j')\, G_{\sigma_2'}\left((\mathbf{x}_{is} - \mathbf{x}_{i's'}) - (\mathbf{y}_{jt} - \mathbf{y}_{j't'})\right)$$

$$\cdot G'_{\sigma_3'}\left(\frac{s-t}{N}, \frac{s'-t'}{N}\right) G'_{\sigma_4'}(s-s', t-t'), \tag{13}$$

where $G'_\sigma(\boldsymbol{\alpha}, \boldsymbol{\beta}) = G_\sigma(\boldsymbol{\alpha}) G_\sigma(\boldsymbol{\beta})$. In comparison to the SCK kernel in (5), the DCK kernel uses the intra-sequence joint differences, thus capturing the dynamics. This dynamics is then compared to those in the other sequences. Figures 2a–c, depict schematically how this kernel captures co-occurrences. As in SCK, the first kernel $G'_{\sigma_1'}$ is used to capture sensor uncertainty in body-keypoint detection, and is assumed to be a delta function in this paper. The second kernel $G_{\sigma_2'}$ models the spatio-temporal co-occurrences of the body-joints. Temporal alignment kernels expressed as $G_{\sigma_3'}$ encode the temporal start and end-points from (s, s') and (t, t'). Finally, $G_{\sigma_4'}$ limits contributions of dynamics between temporal points if they are distant from each other, i.e. if $s' \gg s$ or $t' \gg t$ and σ_4' is small. Furthermore, similar to SCK, the standard deviations σ_2' and σ_3' control the selectivity over spatio-temporal dynamics of body-joints and their temporal shift-invariance for the start and end points, respectively. As discussed for SCK, the practical extensions described by the footnotes 1 and 2 apply to DCK as well.

As in the previous section, we employ linearization to this kernel. Following the derivations described above, it can be shown that the linearized kernel has the following form (see [37] or supplementary material for details):

$$K_D(\Pi_A, \Pi_B) = \sum_{\substack{i\in\mathcal{I}_J, \\ i'\in\mathcal{I}_J: \\ i'\neq i}} \left\langle \frac{1}{\sqrt{\Lambda}} \sum_{\substack{s\in\mathcal{I}_N, \\ s\in\mathcal{I}_N: \\ s\neq s}} G_{\sigma_4'}(s-s') \left(\phi(\mathbf{x}_{is} - \mathbf{x}_{i's'}) \cdot \mathbf{z}\left(\frac{s}{N}\right)^T \right) \uparrow \otimes \mathbf{z}\left(\frac{s'}{N}\right), \right.$$

$$\left. \frac{1}{\sqrt{\Lambda}} \sum_{\substack{t\in\mathcal{I}_N, \\ t\in\mathcal{I}_N: \\ t\neq t}} G_{\sigma_4'}(t-t') \left(\phi(\mathbf{y}_{it} - \mathbf{y}_{i't'}) \cdot \mathbf{z}\left(\frac{t}{N}\right)^T \right) \uparrow \otimes \mathbf{z}\left(\frac{t'}{N}\right) \right\rangle. \tag{14}$$

Equation (14) expresses $K_D(\Pi_A, \Pi_B)$ as a sum over inner-products on third-order non-symmetric tensors of third-order (c.f. Sect. 4.2 where the proposed kernel results in an inner-product between super-symmetric tensors). However, we can decompose each of these tensors with a variant of EPN which involves Higher Order Singular Value Decomposition (HOSVD) into factors stored in the so-called core tensor and equalize the contributions of these factors. Intuitively, this would prevent bursts in the statistically captured spatio-temporal co-occurrence dynamics of actions. For example, consider that a long *hand wave* versus a short one yield different temporal statistics, that is, the prolonged action results in bursts. However, the representation for action recognition should be invariant to such cases. As in the previous section, we introduce a non-linear operator $\mathcal{G}$ into Eq. (14) which will handle this. Our final representation, for example, for sequence Π_A can be expressed as:

$$\mathcal{V}_{ii'} = \mathcal{G}(\mathcal{X}_{ii'}), \text{ and } \mathcal{X}_{ii'} = \frac{1}{\sqrt{\Lambda}} \sum_{\substack{s \in \mathcal{I}_N, \\ s \in \mathcal{I}_N: \\ s \neq s}} G_{\sigma_4'}(s - s') \left(\phi(\mathbf{x}_{is} - \mathbf{x}_{i's'}) \cdot \mathbf{z}\left(\frac{s}{N}\right)^T \right) \uparrow \otimes \mathbf{z}\left(\frac{s'}{N}\right),$$

(15)

where the summation over the pairs of body-joint indexes in (14) becomes equivalent to the concatenation of $\mathcal{V}_{ii'}$ from (15) along the fourth mode such that we obtain tensor representations $[\mathcal{V}_{ii'}]^{\oplus 4}_{i > i': i, i' \in \mathcal{I}_J}$ for sequence Π_A and $[\bar{\mathcal{V}}_{ii'}]^{\oplus 4}_{i > i': i, i' \in \mathcal{I}_J}$ for sequence Π_B. The dot-product can be now applied between these representations for comparing them. For the operator $\mathcal{G}$, we choose HOSVD-based tensor whitening as proposed in [32]. However, they work with the super-symmetric tensors, such as the one we proposed in Sect. 4.2. We work with a general non-symmetric case in (15) and use the following operator $\mathcal{G}$:

$$(\mathcal{E}; \mathbf{A}_1, ..., \mathbf{A}_r) = HOSVD(\mathcal{X}) \tag{16}$$

$$\hat{\mathcal{E}} = Sgn(\mathcal{E}) |\mathcal{E}|^{\gamma} \tag{17}$$

$$\hat{\mathcal{V}} = ((\hat{\mathcal{E}} \otimes_1 \mathbf{A}_1) ...) \otimes_r \mathbf{A}_r \tag{18}$$

$$\mathcal{G}(\mathcal{X}) = Sgn(\hat{\mathcal{V}}) |\hat{\mathcal{V}}|^{\gamma^*} \tag{19}$$

In the above equations, we distinguish the core tensor $\mathcal{E}$ and its power normalized variants $\hat{\mathcal{E}}$ with factors that are being evened out by rising to the power $0 < \gamma \leq 1$, eigenvalue matrices $\mathbf{A}_1, ..., \mathbf{A}_r$ and operation $\otimes_r$ which represents a so-called tensor-product in mode r. We refer the reader to paper [32] for the detailed description of the above steps.

5   Computational Complexity

Non-linearized SCK with kernel SVM has complexity $\mathcal{O}(JN^2T^\rho)$ given J body joints, N frames per sequence, T sequences, and $2 < \rho < 3$ which concerns complexity of kernel SVM. Linearized SCK with linear SVM takes $\mathcal{O}(JNTZ_*^r)$ for a total of Z_* pivots and tensor order $r = 3$. Note that $N^2T^\rho \gg NTZ_*^r$. For $N = 50$ and $Z_* = 20$, this is $3.5\times$ (or $32\times$) faster than the exact kernel for $T = 557$ (or $T = 5000$) used in our experiments. Non-linearized DCK with kernel SVM has complexity $\mathcal{O}(J^2N^4T^\rho)$ while linearized DCK takes $\mathcal{O}(J^2N^2TZ^3)$ for Z pivots per kernel, e.g. $Z = Z_2 = Z_3$ given $G_{\sigma_2'}$ and $G_{\sigma_3'}$. As $N^4T^\rho \gg N^2TZ^3$, the linearization is $11000\times$ faster than the exact kernel, for say $Z = 5$. Note that EPN incurs negligible cost (see [37] for details).

6 Experiments

In this section, we present experiments using our models on three benchmark 3D skeleton based action recognition datasets, namely (i) the UTKinect-Action [9], (ii) Florence3D-Action [10], and (iii) MSR-Action3D [11]. We also present experiments evaluating the influence of the choice of various hyper-parameters, such as the number of pivots Z used for linearizing the body-joint and temporal kernels, the impact of Eigenvalue Power Normalization, and factor equalization.

6.1 Datasets

UTKinect-Action [9] dataset consists of 10 actions performed twice by 10 different subjects, and has 199 action sequences. The dataset provides 3D coordinate annotations of 20 body-joints for every frame. The dataset was captured with a stationary Kinect sensor and contains significant viewpoint and intra-class variations.

Florence3D-Action [10] dataset consists of 9 actions performed two to three times by 10 different subjects. It comprises 215 action sequences. 3D coordinate annotations of 15 body-joints are provided for every frame. This dataset was also captured with a Kinect sensor and contains significant intra-class variations *i.e.*, the same action may be articulated with the left or right hand. Moreover, some actions such as *drinking, performing a phone call*, etc., can be visually ambiguous.

MSR-Action3D [11] dataset is comprised from 20 actions performed two to three times by 10 different subjects. Overall, it consists of 557 action sequences. 3D coordinates of 20 body-joints are provided. This dataset was captured using a Kinect-like depth sensor. It exhibits strong inter-class similarity.

In all experiments we follow the standard protocols for these datasets. We use the cross-subject test setting, in which half of the subjects are used for training and the remaining half for testing. Similarly, we divide the training set into two halves for purpose of training-validation. Additionally, we use two protocols for MSR-Action3D according to approaches [11,17], where the latter protocol uses three subsets grouping related actions together.

6.2 Experimental Setup

For the sequence compatibility kernel, we first normalized all body-keypoints with respect to the hip joints across frames, as indicated in Sect. 4.2. Moreover, lengths of all body-parts are normalized with respect to a reference skeleton. This setup follows the pre-processing suggested in [4]. For our dynamics compatibility kernel, we use unnormalized body-joints and assume that the displacements of body-joint coordinates across frames capture their temporal evolution implicitly.

Sequence Compatibility Kernel. In this section, we first present experiments evaluating the influence of parameters σ_2 and σ_3 of kernels G_{σ_2} and G_{σ_3} which

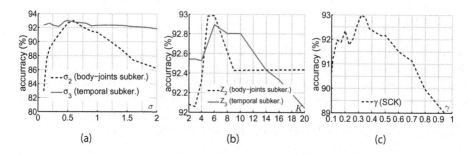

Fig. 3. Figure (**a**) illustrates the classification accuracy on Florence3d-Action for the sequence compatibility kernel when varying radii σ_2 (body-joints subkernel) and σ_3 (temporal subkernel). Figure (**b**) evaluates behavior of SCK w.r.t. the number of pivots Z_2 and Z_3. Figure (**c**) demonstrates effectiveness of our slice-wise Eigenvalue Power Normalization in tackling burstiness by varying parameter γ.

control the degree of selectivity for the 3D body-joints and temporal shift invariance, respectively. See Sect. 4.2 for a full definition of these parameters.

Furthermore, recall that the kernels G_{σ_2} and G_{σ_3} are approximated via linearizations according to Eqs. (1) and (3). The quality of these approximations and the size of our final tensor representations depend on the number of pivots Z_2 and Z_3 chosen. In our experiments, the pivots ζ are spaced uniformly within interval $[-1; 1]$ and $[0; 1]$ for kernels G_{σ_2} and G_{σ_3} respectively.

Figures 3a and b present the results of this experiment on the Florence3D-Action dataset – these are the results presented on the test set as we have also observed exactly the same trends on the validation set.

Figure 3a shows that the body-joint compatibility subkernel G_{σ_2} requires a choice of σ_2 which is not too strict as the specific body-joints (*e.g.*, elbow) would be expected to repeat across sequences in the exactly same position. On the one hand, very small σ_2 leads to poor generalization. On the other hand, very large σ_2 allows big displacements of the corresponding body-joints between sequences which results in poor discriminative power of this kernel. Furthermore, Fig. 3a demonstrates that the range of σ_3 for the temporal subkernel for which we obtain very good performance is large, however, as σ_3 becomes very small or very large, extreme temporal selectivity or full temporal invariance, respectively, result in a loss of performance. For instance, $\sigma_3 = 4$ results in 91 % accuracy only.

In Fig. 3b, we show the performance of our SCK kernel with respect to the number of pivots used for linearization. For the body-joint compatibility subkernel G_{σ_2}, we see that $Z_2 = 5$ pivots are sufficient to obtain good performance of 92.98 % accuracy. We have observed that this is consistent with the results on the validation set. Using more pivots, say $Z_2 = 20$, deteriorates the results slightly, suggesting overfitting. We make similar observations for the temporal subkernel G_{σ_3} which demonstrates good performance for as few as $Z_3 = 2$ pivots. Such a small number of pivots suggests that linearizing 1D variables and generating higher-order co-occurrences, as described in Sect. 4.2, is a simple, robust, and effective linearization strategy.

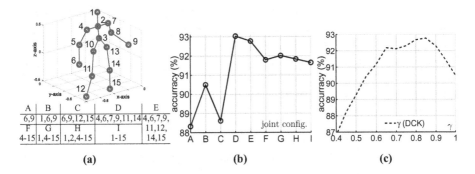

A	B	C	D	E
6,9	1,6,9	6,9,12,15	4,6,7,9,11,14	4,6,7,9,
F	G	H	I	11,12,
4-15	1,4-15	1,2,4-15	1-15	14,15

(a)   **(b)**   **(c)**

Fig. 4. Figure **(a)** enumerates the body-joints in the Florence3D-Action dataset. The table below lists subsets A-I of the body-joints used to build representations evaluated in Fig. **(b)**, which demonstrates the performance of our dynamics compatibility kernel w.r.t. these subsets. Figure **(c)** demonstrates effectiveness of equalizing the factors in non-symmetric tensor representation by HOSVD Eigenvalue Power Normalization by varying γ.

Further, Fig. 3c demonstrates the effectiveness of our slice-wise Eigenvalue Power Normalization (EPN) described in Eq. (12). When $\gamma = 1$, the EPN functionality is absent. This results in a drop of performance from 92.98 % to 88.7 % accuracy. This demonstrates that statistically unpredictable bursts of actions described by the body-joints, such as long versus short *hand waving*, are indeed undesirable. It is clear that in such cases, EPN is very effective, as in practice it considers correlated bursts, *e.g.* co-occurring *hand wave* and associated with it elbow and neck motion. For more details behind this concept, see [32]. For our further experiments, we choose $\sigma_2 = 0.6$, $\sigma_3 = 0.5$, $Z_2 = 5$, $Z_3 = 6$, and $\gamma = 0.36$, as dictated by cross-validation.

Dynamics Compatibility Kernel. In this section, we evaluate the influence of choosing parameters for the DCK kernel. Our experiments are based on the Florence3D-Action dataset. We present the scores on the test set as the results on the validation set match these closely. As this kernel considers all spatio-temporal co-occurrences of body-joints, we first evaluate the impact of the joint subsets we select for generating this representation as not all body-joints need to be used for describing actions.

Figure 4a enumerates the body-joints that describe every 3D human skeleton on the Florence3D-Action dataset whilst the table underneath lists the proposed body-joint subsets A-I which we use for computations of DCK. In Fig. 4b, we plot the performance of our DCK kernel for each subset. The plot shows that using two body-joints associated with the hands from Configuration-A in the DCK kernel construction, we attain 88.32 % accuracy which highlights the informativeness of temporal dynamics. For Configuration-D, which includes six body-joints such as the knees, elbows and hands, our performance reaches 93.03 %. This suggests that some not-selected for this configuration body-joints may be noisy and therefore detrimental to classification.

As configuration Configuration-E includes eight body-joints such as the feet, knees, elbows and hands, we choose it for our further experiments as it represents a reasonable trade-off between performance and size of representations. This configuration scores 92.77 % accuracy. We see that if we utilize all the body-joints according to Configuration-I, performance of 91.65 % accuracy is still somewhat lower compared to 93.03 % accuracy for Configuration-D highlighting again the issue of noisy body-joints.

In Fig. 4c, we show the performance of our DCK kernel when HOSVD factors underlying our non-symmetric tensors are equalized by varying the EPN parameter γ. For $\gamma = 1$, HOSVD EPN is absent which leads to 90.49 % accuracy only. For the optimal value of $\gamma = 0.85$, the accuracy rises to 92.77 %. This again demonstrates the presence of the burstiness effect in temporal representations.

Comparison to the State of the Art. In this section, we compare the performance of our representations against the best performing methods on the three datasets. Along with comparing SCK and DCK, we will also explore the complementarity of these representations in capturing the action dynamics by combining them.

On the Florence3D-Action dataset, we present our best results in Table 1a. Note that the model parameters for the evaluation was selected by cross-validation. Linearizing a sequence compatibility kernel using these parameters resulted in a tensor representation of size 26, 565 dimensions[3], and producing an accuracy of 92.98 % accuracy. As for the dynamics compatibility kernel (DCK), our model selected Configuration-E (described in Fig. 4a) resulting in a representation of dimensionality 16, 920 and achieved a performance of 92 %. However, somewhat better results were attained by Configuration-D, namely 92.27 % accuracy for size of 9, 450. Combining both SCK representation with DCK in Configuration-E results in an accuracy of 95.23 %. This constitutes a 4.5 % improvement over the state of the art on this dataset as listed in Table 1a and demonstrates the complementary nature of SCK and DCK. To the best of our knowledge, this is the highest performance attained on this dataset.

Action recognition results on the UTKinect-Action dataset are presented in Table 1b. For our experiments on this dataset, we kept all the parameters the same as those we used on the Florence3D dataset (described above). On this

Table 1. Evaluations of SCK and DCK and comparisons to the state-of-the-art results on **(a)** the Florence3D-Action and **(b)** UTKinect-Action dataset.

	SCK	DCK		SCK+DCK		SCK	DCK	SCK+DCK
accuracy	92.98 %	93.03 %	92.77 %	**95.23 %**	accuracy	96.08 %	97.5 %	**98.2 %**
size	26,565	9,450	16,920	43,485	size	40,480	16,920	57,400
Bag-of-Poses 82.00 % [10]			$SE(3)$ 90.88 % [4]		3D joints. hist. 90.92 % [9]			$SE(3)$ 97.08 % [4]
(a)					(b)			

---

[3] Note that this is the length of a vector per sequence after unfolding our tensor representation and removing duplicate coefficients from the symmetries in the tensor.

Table 2. Results on SCK and DCK and comparisons to the state of the art on MSR-Action3D.

	SCK	DCK	SCK+DCK	accuracy, protocol [17]	accuracy, protocol [11]
acc., prot. [17]	90.72 %	86.30 %	**91.45** %	Actionlets 88.20 % [17]	R. Forests 90.90 % [38]
acc., prot. [11]	93.52 %	91.71 %	**93.96** %	$SE(3)$ 89.48 % [4]	$SE(3)$ 92.46 % [4]
size	40,480	16,920	57,400	Kin. desc. 91.07 % [39]	

dataset, both SCK and DCK representations yield 96.08 % and 97.5 % accuracy, respectively. Combining SCK and DCK yields 98.2 % accuracy outperforming marginally a more complex approach described in [4] which uses Lie group algebra on $SE(3)$ matrix descriptors and requires practical extensions such as discrete time warping and Fourier temporal pyramids for attaining this performance, which we avoid completely.

In Table 2, we present our results on the MSR-Action3D dataset. Again, we kept all the model parameters the same as those used on the Florence3D dataset. Conforming to prior literature, we use two evaluation protocols on this dataset, namely (i) the protocol described in actionlets [17], for which the authors utilize the entire dataset with its 20 classes during the training and evaluation, and (ii) approach of [11], for which the authors divide the data into three subsets and report the average in classification accuracy over these subsets. The SCK representation results in the state-of-the-art accuracy of 90.72 % and 93.52 % for the two evaluation protocols, respectively. Combining SCK with DCK outperforms other approaches listed in the table and yields 91.45 % and 93.96 % accuracy for the two protocols, respectively.

Processing Time. For SCK and DCK, processing a single sequence with unoptimized MATLAB code on a single core i5 takes 0.2 s and 1.2 s, respectively. Training on full MSR Action3D with the SCK and DCK takes about 13 min. In comparison, extracting $SE(3)$ features [4] takes 5.3 s per sequence, processing on the full MSR Action3D dataset takes ~ 50 min. and with post-processing (time warping, Fourier pyramids, etc.) it goes to about 72 min. Therefore, SCK and DCK is about 5.4× faster.

7   Conclusions

We have presented two kernel-based tensor representations for action recognition from 3D skeletons, namely the sequence compatibility kernel (SCK) and dynamics compatibility kernel (DCK). SCK captures the higher-order correlations between 3D coordinates of the body-joints and their temporal variations, and factors out the need for expensive operations such as Fourier temporal pyramid matching or dynamic time warping, commonly used for generating sequence-level action representations. Further, our DCK kernel captures the action dynamics by modeling the spatio-temporal co-occurrences of the body-joints. This tensor representation also factors out the temporal variable, whose length depends on each sequence. Our experiments substantiate the effectiveness of our representations, demonstrating state-of-the-art performance on three challenging action recognition datasets.

Acknowledgements. AC is funded by the Australian Research Council Centre of Excellence for Robotic Vision (project number CE140100016).

References

1. Shotton, J., Sharp, T., Kipman, A., Fitzgibbon, A., Finocchio, M., Blake, A., Cook, M., Moore, R.: Real-time human pose recognition in parts from single depth images. Commun. ACM **56**, 116–124 (2013)
2. Turaga, P., Chellappa, R.: Locally time-invariant models of human activities using trajectories on the grassmannian. In: CVPR (2009)
3. Presti, L.L., La Cascia, M.: 3D skeleton-based human action classification: a survey. Pattern Recogn. **53**, 130–147 (2015)
4. Vemulapalli, R., Arrate, F., Chellappa, R.: Human action recognition by representing 3D skeletons as points in a Lie Group. In: CVPR, pp. 588–595 (2014)
5. Harandi, M., Salzmann, M., Porikli, F.: Bregman divergences for infinite dimensional covariance matrices. In: CVPR (2014)
6. Hussein, M.E., Torki, M., Gowayyed, M.A., El-Saban, M.: Human action recognition using a temporal hierarchy of covariance descriptors on 3D joint locations. In: IJCAI (2013)
7. Elgammal, A., Lee, C.S.: Tracking people on a torus. PAMI **31**, 520–538 (2009)
8. Li, B., Camps, O.I., Sznaier, M.: Cross-view activity recognition using hankelets. In: CVPR (2012)
9. Xia, L., Chen, C.C., Aggarwal, J.K.: View invariant human action recognition using histograms of 3D joints. In: CVPR Workshops, pp. 20–27(2012)
10. Seidenari, L., Varano, V., Berretti, S., Bimbo, A.D., Pala, P.: Recognizing actions from depth cameras as weakly aligned multi-part bag-of-poses. In: CVPR Workshop, June 2013
11. Li, W., Zhang, Z., Liu, Z.: Action recognition based on a bag of 3D points. In: CVPR Workshop, pp. 9–14 (2010)
12. Zatsiorsky, V.M.: Kinematic of Human Motion. Human Kinetics Publishers, Champaign (1997)
13. Johansson, G.: Visual perception of biological motion and a model for its analysis. Percept. Psychophysics **14**(2), 201–211 (1973)
14. Hussein, M.E., Torki, M., Gowayyed, M., El-Saban, M.: Human action recognition using a temporal hierarchy of covariance descriptors on 3D joint locations. In: IJCAI 2466–2472 (2013)
15. Lv, F., Nevatia, R.: Recognition and segmentation of 3-D human action using HMM and multi-class AdaBoost. In: Leonardis, A., Bischof, H., Pinz, A. (eds.) ECCV 2006. LNCS, vol. 3954, pp. 359–372. Springer, Heidelberg (2006). doi:10.1007/11744085_28
16. Parameswaran, V., Chellappa, R.: View invariance for human action recognition. IJCV **66**(1), 83–101 (2006)
17. Wu, Y., Liu, Z., Wu, Y., Yuan, J.: Mining actionlet ensemble for action recognition with depth cameras. In: CVPR, pp. 1290–1297 (2012)

18. Yang, X., Tian, Y.: Effective 3D action recognition using eigenjoints. J. Vis. Comun. Image Represent. **25**(1), 2–11 (2014)
19. Yacoob, Y., Black, M.J.: Parameterized modeling and recognition of activities. In: ICCV, pp. 120–128 (1998)
20. Ohn-Bar, E., Trivedi, M.M.: Joint angles similarities and HOG^2 for action recognition. In: CVPR Workshop (2013)
21. Ofli, F., Chaudhry, R., Kurillo, G., Vidal, R., Bajcsy, R.: Sequence of the most informative joints (SMIJ). J. Vis. Comun. Image Represent. **25**(1), 24–38 (2014)
22. Bo, L., Lai, K., Ren, X., Fox, D.: Object recognition with hierarchical kernel descriptors. In: CVPR (2011)
23. Mairal, J., Koniusz, P., Harchaoui, Z., Schmid, C.: Convolutional kernel networks. In: NIPS (2014)
24. Cavazza, J., Zunino, A., Biagio, M.S., Vittorio, M.: Kernelized covariance for action recognition. CoRR abs/1604.06582 (2016)
25. Gaidon, A., Harchoui, Z., Schmid, C.: A time series kernel for action recognition. BMVC **63**(1-63), 11 (2011)
26. Kim, T.K., Wong, K.Y.K., Cipolla, R.: Tensor canonical correlation analysis for action classification. In: CVPR (2007)
27. Shashua, A., Hazan, T.: Non-negative tensor factorization with applications to statistics and computer vision. In: ICML (2005)
28. Vasilescu, M.A., Terzopoulos, D.: Tensortextures: multilinear image-based rendering. ACM Trans. Graph. **23**(3), 336–342 (2004)
29. Vasilescu, M.A.O., Terzopoulos, D.: Multilinear analysis of image ensembles: tensorfaces. In: Heyden, A., Sparr, G., Nielsen, M., Johansen, P. (eds.) ECCV 2002. LNCS, vol. 2350, pp. 447–460. Springer, Heidelberg (2002). doi:10.1007/3-540-47969-4_30
30. Lu, H., Plataniotis, K.N., Venetsanopoulos, A.N.: A survey of multilinear subspace learning for tensor data. Pattern Recogn. **44**(7), 1540–1551 (2011)
31. Koniusz, P., Yan, F., Gosselin, P., Mikolajczyk, K.: Higher-order occurrence pooling on mid- and low-level features: visual concept detection. Technical report (2013)
32. Koniusz, P., Yan, F., Gosselin, P., Mikolajczyk, K.: Higher-order occurrence pooling for bags-of-words: visual concept detection. PAMI (2016)
33. Koniusz, P., Cherian, A.: Sparse coding for third-order super-symmetric tensor descriptors with application to texture recognition. In: CVPR (2016)
34. Zhao, X., Wang, S., Li, S., Li, J.: A comprehensive study on third order statistical features for image splicing detection. In: Digital Forensics and Watermarking, pp. 243–256 (2012)
35. Jebara, T., Kondor, R., Howard, A.: Probability product kernels. JMLR **5**, 819–844 (2004)
36. Jégou, H., Douze, M., Schmid, C.: On the burstiness of visual elements. In: CVPR, pp. 1169–1176(2009)
37. Koniusz, P., Cherian, A., Porikli, F.: Tensor representations via kernel linearization for action recognition from 3D skeletons (extended version). CoRR abs/1604.00239 (2016)
38. Zhu, Y., Chen, W., Guo, G.: Fusing spatiotemporal features and joints for 3D action recognition. In: CVPR Workshop, pp. 486–491(2013)
39. Zanfir, M., Leordeanu, M., Sminchisescu, C.: The moving pose: An efficient 3D kinematics descriptor for low-latency action recognition and detection. In: ICCV, pp. 2752–2759 (2013)

Manhattan-World Urban Reconstruction from Point Clouds

Minglei Li[1,2], Peter Wonka[1], and Liangliang Nan[1(✉)]

[1] Visual Computing Center, KAUST, Thuwal, Saudi Arabia
mingleili87@gmail.com, pwonka@gmail.com, liangliang.nan@gmail.com
[2] College of Electronic and Information Engineering, NUAA, Nanjing, China

Abstract. Manhattan-world urban scenes are common in the real world. We propose a fully automatic approach for reconstructing such scenes from 3D point samples. Our key idea is to represent the geometry of the buildings in the scene using a set of well-aligned boxes. We first extract plane hypothesis from the points followed by an iterative refinement step. Then, candidate boxes are obtained by partitioning the space of the point cloud into a non-uniform grid. After that, we choose an optimal subset of the candidate boxes to approximate the geometry of the buildings. The contribution of our work is that we transform scene reconstruction into a labeling problem that is solved based on a novel Markov Random Field formulation. Unlike previous methods designed for particular types of input point clouds, our method can obtain faithful reconstructions from a variety of data sources. Experiments demonstrate that our method is superior to state-of-the-art methods.

Keywords: Urban reconstruction · Manhattan-world scenes · Reconstruction · Box fitting

1 Introduction

Obtaining faithful reconstructions of urban scenes is an important problem in computer vision. Many methods have been proposed for reconstructing accurate and dense 3D point clouds from images [4,5,26,31]. Besides these point clouds computed from images, there exist an increasing amount of other types of point clouds, e.g., airborne LiDAR data and laser scans. Although these point clouds can be rendered in an impressive manner, many applications (e.g., navigation, simulation, virtual reality) still require polygonal models as a basis. However, few works have addressed the problem of converting these point clouds into surface models. In fact, reconstructing polygonal models from these point clouds still remains an open problem [17,23].

The main difficulty for urban reconstruction from point clouds is the low quality of the data. For example, the obtained point clouds of urban scenes

Electronic supplementary material The online version of this chapter (doi:10. 1007/978-3-319-46493-0_4) contains supplementary material, which is available to authorized users.

B. Leibe et al. (Eds.): ECCV 2016, Part IV, LNCS 9908, pp. 54–69, 2016.
DOI: 10.1007/978-3-319-46493-0_4

typically exhibit significant missing regions, as well as uneven point density. This is because the data acquisition process unavoidably suffers from occlusions. Therefore, incorporation of prior knowledge about the structure of the urban scenes into the reconstruction process becomes necessary. In this work, we aim to tackle the problem of reconstructing Manhattan-world urban scenes from the above mentioned point clouds. Such scenes are common in the real world [4].

Existing methods on urban reconstruction from point clouds are designed to handle particular types of input, i.e., either MVS point clouds [14, 29], airborne LiDAR data [12, 22, 30, 33], or laser scans [15, 19], and it may not be easy to extend these methods to handle data from other sources. Moreover, most of existing methods require segmentation of a scene into individual buildings [15, 28, 29], and some of them require to further extract individual facades [19], which often result in long processing times. The semantic segmentation of a scene into meaningful buildings or facades is still an unsolved problem that an automatic approach often generate unsatisfied segmentation [7]. Thus, we seek a fully automatic urban reconstruction solution that does not require this segmentation step.

The key observation in this work is that fitting a set of boxes to point clouds is much more robust than directly fitting a polygonal surface model. Thus, our strategy relies on choosing an optimal subset of boxes from a large number of box hypothesis through optimization. First, the input point cloud is aligned with a global coordinate system, and a large amount of planar segments are detected from the point cloud. Then, these planes are iteratively refined to best fit the input point cloud. The refined planes partition the space of the input data into a grid consisting of a compact set of boxes. We formulate the box selection as an energy minimization problem using a Markov Random Field formulation. After optimization, the chosen subset of boxes serve as lightweight polygonal models that faithfully represent the geometry of the buildings in the scene. Experiments show that our method can handle point clouds from a variety of data sources and obtains faithful reconstruction of the geometry of the scenes. Figure 1 shows an example of our reconstruction.

The main contributions of our work include:

- a framework for the automatic reconstruction of Manhattan-world scenes by directly fitting boxes into point clouds from various sources.
- a Markov Random Field formulation for selecting an optimal subset of candidate boxes to represent the geometry of the buildings in the scene.
- an urban reconstruction approach that does not require segmentation of the scene into individual buildings or facades, and it can handle point clouds from various data sources.

2   Related Work

Many approaches have been proposed for reconstructing physical objects represented by point clouds. A typical data-driven approach (e.g., Poisson reconstruction [11]) can generate very dense surface models from point clouds. These methods have strong requirements that data is complete and free of outliers. However, such requirements are unlikely to be guaranteed during data acquisition. To obtain complete reconstructions, model-driven approaches [4, 10, 13, 19, 28] take advantage of prior knowledge (e.g., facades are planar, facade elements are repeating) about the structure of the buildings, which seems to be more promising in reconstructing real world scenes. Some works [2, 21, 32] focus on recovering topologically correct assembly of hypothesized planes. However, since the initial planes are independent, these approaches may not produce accurate and simple polygonal models. In the following, we mainly review the model-driven approaches that are most related to our method.

Contour-based methods. These methods [12, 14, 22, 30, 33] were initially proposed to reconstruct urban scenes from airborne LiDAR data where the roofs of buildings are usually well captured. The typically work flow of these methods is as follows. First, contours or footprints of the buildings are extracted (usually followed by a refinement step) from the roofs of the buildings. Then, the extracted contours or footprints are extruded toward the ground plane, yielding 2.5D reconstructions that approximate the geometry of the buildings in the scene. Since only the data of the roofs of the buildings are considered, significant amount of critical information of the walls of the buildings are intentionally ignored. Thus, some important facade structures may be missing from the results.

Template-based methods. Urban scenes usually exhibit repeating structures, such as windows, doors, etc. A few template-based reconstruction methods have been proposed to reconstruct scenes containing these repeating structures. These methods first segment the point samples of a facade into meaningful segments and then obtain a detailed 3D model by replacing the segments with predefined templates. Starting from an initial coarse model consisting of few boxes constructed with user assistance, Nan et al. [18] perform 2D template matching to choose an appropriate set of detailed 3D templates and determine their locations in the 2D image domain. After that, the detailed 3D templates are positioned by projecting their 2D locations onto the faces of the 3D coarse model using the camera parameters recovered in the previous structure from motion step. Using supervised learning techniques, Lin et al. [15] first classify the input point cloud into different categories, and then decompose and fit the points of each individual building using predefined symmetric and convex blocks. Few works [20, 25] also exploit the idea of template matching to reconstruct indoor scenes. Rather than recovering detailed structures of buildings, our goal is to obtain an approximate reconstruction of the buildings in Manhattan-world scenes by fitting boxes directly into point clouds.

Graph-based methods. Many approaches represent the relationships between building elements using graphs and obtain polygonal models by partitioning or optimizing the graph presentation. Garcia et al. [6] propose a surface graph cuts approach for architectural modeling based on a volumetric representation. Hiep et al. [8] reconstruct mesh models of different scales by extracting a visibility consistent mesh from the dense point clouds using a minimum s-t cut-based

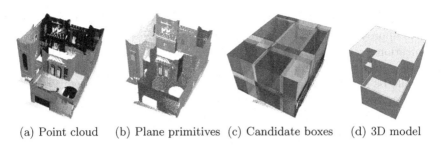

(a) Point cloud   (b) Plane primitives (c) Candidate boxes   (d) 3D model

Fig. 1. An overview of the proposed approach.

global optimization algorithm, followed by a refinement step using image information. Similarly, Verdie et al. [29] extract a surface model from a dense mesh representation using a min-cut algorithm. Following these methods, we represent the relationship between box hypothesis, and extract an optimal set of boxes to approximate the geometry of the buildings in the scene.

Manhattan-world scene reconstruction. Another large group of papers address the problem of Manhattan-world scene reconstruction. Matei et al. [16] and Venegas et al. [28] first extract regular grammars from LiDAR point clouds. Then, a volume description of the building is established from the classified points. By assuming repetitive structures, Nan et al. [19] interactively create and snap box-like detailed structures for facade reconstruction. To reconstruct indoor scenes complying with the Manhattan world assumption, Furukawa et al. [4] and Ikehata et al. [10] approximate the geometry of indoor scenes by placing axis-aligned planes to fit the MVS point clouds. Since high-level structure information of the scenes are exploited, the reconstruction results from these methods usually outperform those from data-driven approaches that are purely based on geometric fitting, in terms of controllability over both geometric and semantic complexity of the final models. Inspired by these methods, we tackle the problem of Manhattan-world scene reconstruction by fitting a set of boxes directly into the point clouds.

3   Overview

Given a point cloud of a Manhattan-world scene, our method establishes a box approximation of the scene in two major steps: candidate boxes generation and box selection. Figure 1 shows an overview of our method.

Candidate boxes generation. We first extract a large number of planar segments from the input point cloud using a RANSAC algorithm [24]. Considering that the detected planar segments unavoidably contain undesired elements due to noise, outliers, and missing data, we refine these planar segments by iteratively merging pairs of planes that are close to each other. After that, the refined planes partition the space of the input point cloud into a set of axis-aligned boxes with non-uniform sizes (see Sect. 4).

Box selection. In this step, we choose an optimal subset of the candidate boxes to approximate the scene. We formulate the boxes selection as an energy minimization problem, where the objective function is designed to encourage the final model to be confident with respect to the input point samples and meanwhile be simple and compact. Specifically, we design two energy terms, a data fitting term to ensure the fidelity of the final model with respect to the input point cloud, and a smoothness term to encourage geometric consistency of neighboring faces in the final model. The optimal set of boxes are then chosen by minimizing the above energy function using graph cut (see Sect. 5).

4   Candidate Box Generation

4.1   Plane Extraction

Using the Manhattan-world assumption, the major components of a building (i.e., walls and roofs) consist of axis-aligned planes. Thus, we first identify the three dominant directions of the scene, as well as a set of plane hypothesis on which most of the points lie. Then we iteratively refine these planar segments and generate candidate boxes from the refined planar segments.

To determine the three dominant directions of a scene, we identify the top three strong peaks from the histogram of the normal distribution of the point cloud [4]. Then the corresponding normal directions of the three peaks are regarded as the dominant directions. With these dominant directions, we transform the point cloud such that its dominant directions align with the axes of a given coordinate frame. We directly use the normal information if it is given. Otherwise, we estimate the normal at each point using Principal Component Analysis using K-nearest neighbors. Typically, a wide range [16, 30] of K can guarantee good normal estimation.

To extract planar segments from the noisy point clouds, we exploit the RANSAC-based primitive detection method proposed by Schnabel et al. [24]. Considering the noise and outliers in the point clouds, we run the RANSAC algorithm multiple times to generate a large number of initial plane hypothesis. By doing so, appropriate planar segments describing the structure of the scene are more likely to be present in the initial plane hypothesis. We discard planar segments if either their orientations are far away (i.e., more than 20°) from the three dominant directions, or they have a small number (i.e., 20) of supporting points.

Given the large number of plane hypothesis, we propose an algorithm that iteratively refines these initial planar segments. Specifically, we score each planar segment according to the number of its supporting points. Then, starting from the pair of planar segments with lowest average score, we merge them if the following two conditions are satisfied: (1) the angle between the two planes is less than a threshold θ_t, and (2) the distance from the center of mass of the points associated with one planar segment to that of the other one is less than a threshold d_t. After that, a new planar primitive is suggested by performing a least-squares fitting of the merged points. We repeat this process until no

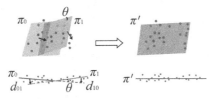

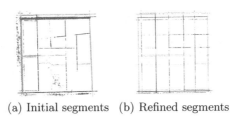

Fig. 2. The merging of two planar segments. Two planes π_0 and π_1 are merged if the angle between them is smaller than a threshold (i.e., $\theta < \theta_t$), and the distance from their mass centers is less than another threshold (i.e., $d_{01} < d_t$ and $d_{10} < d_t$). Then a new plane π' is proposed using a least-squares fitting of the union of the points.

(a) Initial segments   (b) Refined segments

Fig. 3. The refinement of the initially extracted planar segments (top-view).

more pairs of planar segments can be merged. As a result, the planar segments are refined such that they are supported by more points and meanwhile the number of planar segments is significantly reduced. Figure 2 shows the merging of two planar segments. Empirically, we set θ_t to 10° and d_t to 0.2 m. A visual comparison of the planar primitives before and after refinement is shown in Fig. 3. As can be seen from (b), the arrangement of the planar segments has been significantly regularized. Meanwhile, the number of planar segments is reduced from 66 to 45.

Missing walls. The above described plane extraction method can detect most of the major planes from the point cloud. However, some critical planes could still be omitted due to the large area of missing data. This is especially true when the data is obtained by airborne equipments. For example, in the point clouds computed from aerial images or obtained by an airborne LiDAR, the walls of the buildings are extremely sparse and incomplete (see Fig. 4(a)). To ensure sufficient information for the reconstruction, we propose to determine the missing walls from their neighboring planar segments. Specifically, we first generate a height map by projecting the points onto the ground plane and rasterizing the height values of the projected points. Then, we smooth the height map by using a bilateral filter [27]. After that, line segments are detected on the height map using the Hough Transform method [3]. Note that since the height map is generated using an orthographic projection, the detected line elements are in fact the intersections of walls and roofs of the building. Thus, these wall planes can be determined by fitting vertical planes to the detected line segments. An illustration of a missing wall detection is shown in Fig. 4. We add the wall planes to the initially detected planar segment set and run the refinement algorithm illustrated in Fig. 2.

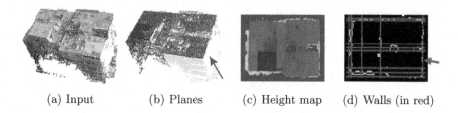

(a) Input   (b) Planes   (c) Height map   (d) Walls (in red)

Fig. 4. Detection of missing walls. The arrow indicates a missing wall. (Colour figure online)

4.2 Candidate Boxes

In this step, we generate box hypothesis from the planar segments extracted in the previous step. According to the orientations, the refined planar segments can be categorized into three groups, i.e. $\mathbf{G}_x$, $\mathbf{G}_y$, and $\mathbf{G}_z$, which are aligned with the three dominant directions, respectively. Intuitively, the supporting planes of these planar segments partition the space of the input point cloud into a set of axis-aligned boxes. Assuming N_x, N_y, and N_z are the numbers of the planes along the three dominant directions (i.e., $|\mathbf{G}_x| = N_x$, $|\mathbf{G}_y| = N_y$, and $|\mathbf{G}_z| = N_z$), the total number of candidate boxes can be computed by

$$N = (N_x - 1) \cdot (N_y - 1) \cdot (N_z - 1). \tag{1}$$

In the next step, we will propose an optimization-based box selection algorithm to choose appropriate candidate boxes to approximate the geometry of the buildings in the scene.

5   Box Selection

Given N candidate boxes $\mathbf{B} = \{b_i\}(1 \leq i \leq N)$ generated in the previous step, our goal is to choose a subset of the these boxes to approximate the 3D geometry of the buildings represented by the point samples $\mathbf{P}$. We formulate the box selection as a labeling problem so as to approximate the geometry of the buildings in the scene by a subset of the candidate boxes that favor high fidelity in data fitting and compactness in the structure of the final model. In the following, we first introduce our objectives. Then, we detail our energy function and a Markov Random Field formulation to minimize the energy function.

5.1   Objectives

To obtain a faithful reconstruction from the sampled points, we consider the following two main factors. First, the faces of the reconstructed model should be as close as possible to the input point cloud. Second, since we are seeking a set of boxes to approximate the 3D geometry of the Manhattan-world scene, the assembly of the chosen boxes should be compact and respect the structural

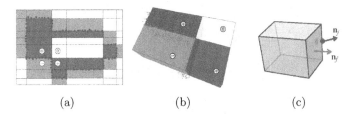

(a)   (b)   (c)

Fig. 5. Candidate boxes and supporting points. (a) A 2D illustration of the three types of candidate boxes: positive (blue), negative (green), and blank (white). (b) A zoom-in of the marked region in (a). (c) A supporting point of a face. (Color figure online)

property of the buildings, i.e., the planar facades containing the least number of holes and protrusions. We formulate these two factors as the following two objectives: data fitting and compactness.

Data fitting. We define the data fitting score $S(b_i)$ to measure how well a candidate box b_i is supported by the point cloud. Specifically, the score function $S(b_i)$ is defined as

$$S(b_i) = \sum_f^6 \sum_j^M \mathbf{n}_f \cdot \mathbf{n}_j \cdot dist(p_j)$$
$$dist(p_j) = \begin{cases} 1/(t + d_j), \ d_j < d_t \\ 0, \qquad\qquad \text{otherwise} \end{cases} \qquad (2)$$

where $\mathbf{n}_f$ denotes the normal of a face f in box b_i, and $\mathbf{n}_j$ the normal of a supporting point. To measure the fitting quality of f with respect to its supporting points $\{p_j\}(1 \le j \le M)$, we only consider points that are projected inside f and have distances smaller than a threshold d_t to this face (see Fig. 5(a)). Here, t is a constant to make sure that very small distances do not receive a huge weight. In our work, we set t to 1.0.

It is obvious that the data fitting score defined by Eq. 2 may have a negative value. We intended to design it in this way so as to distinguish three types of candidate boxes.

– *Positive boxes:* the boxes that have positive data fitting scores, and thus we prefer to choose them to represent the geometry of the building. Examples of this type of boxes are shown in blue in Fig. 5(a).
– *Negative boxes:* the boxes that have negative data fitting scores. The negative boxes are actually outside the volume of the building. This type of boxes are marked in green in Fig. 5(a).
– *Blank boxes:* the boxes supported either by no points, or by very few points, and thus their data fitting scores are close to zero. This type of boxes do not contribute to representing the geometry of the buildings and should be removed. Examples of blank boxes are shown in white in Fig. 5(a).

Boxes with few supporting points have very low data fitting score, thus they may be incorrectly identified as blank boxes resulting in holes in the final model.

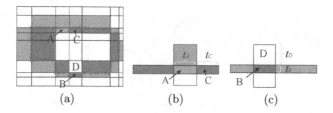

Fig. 6. A 2D illustration of holes and protrusions. Box A is misclassified as *negative* resulting in a hole; box B is misclassified as *positive* resulting in a protrusion. The thickness values t_A and t_C are used to computed the compactness for box pair A-C, and t_B and t_D for box pair B-D. Colors indicate different boxes bypes, i.e., blue for positive boxes, green for negative boxes, and white for blank boxes. (Color figure online)

To tackle this problem, we perform a smoothing procedure on the data fitting score of all blank candidate boxes. Specifically, we re-compute the data fitting score of a blank box as the area and distance weighted average of its neighbors.

$$\hat{S}(b_i) = \sum_{j \in Nb_i} w_j \cdot S(b_j)$$

$$w_j = \frac{A(f_{ij})/d_{ij}}{\sum_{j \in Nb_i} A(f_{ij})/d_{ij}}$$

(3)

where Nb_i are the direct neighboring boxes contacting b_i by a face; $S(b_j)$ is the data fitting score of box b_j originally computed by Eq. 2; w_j is a weight defined based on the area $A(f_{ij})$ of the contacting face of the two boxes and the distance d_{ij} between their centers.

Compactness. Since we are seeking a set of boxes as the approximate reconstruction of a building, any failure in assigning the label for a candidate box located on the surface of a building will result in a hole or a protrusion. Figure 6 shows two such examples.

To avoid holes and protrusions, we introduce the *compactness* for each pair of adjacent boxes. In our work, we say that a facade is not compact if holes or protrusion exist in this facade. Thus, to favor compactness (i.e., to avoid holes and protrusions), we prefer to assign the same label to two neighboring boxes. If the hole (or the protrusion) is caused by assigning a wrong label to a single box, the decrease in the compactness of the facade can be assessed by some value that is proportional to the thickness of the box. Specifically, we define a pairwise compactness between two neighboring boxes as

$$C_{i,j} = \frac{1}{min(t_i, t_j)}$$

(4)

where t_i and t_j are the thickness values of two adjacent boxes b_i and b_j. Intuitively, if one of two adjacent boxes is thin, the decrease in the compactness of assigning different labels to the boxes will be small.

5.2 Optimization

Now we describe how we select appropriate candidate boxes by using a Markov Random Field (MRF) formulation. We first construct an associated graph where the nodes represent all candidate boxes and each edge connects two adjacent boxes. This graph has a 3D grid structure where each node has a maximum number of 6 neighbors (for interior boxes) and a minimum number of 3 neighbors (for boxes at the corners of the 3D grid). We formulate the box selection as probability functions and compute the probabilities of each candidate box belonging to *positive* or *non-positive*. These box types are the labels that will be assigned to the nodes in the graph after the optimization. We employ a graph cut algorithm to partition this highly connected graph structure into optimal and consistent groups of boxes, where the boxes labeled as *positive* will then be assembled as the final approximate reconstruction of the buildings in the scene.

Our objective function consists of a data term and a smoothness term.

- *Data term.* The data term encourages to choose boxes that have higher data fitting scores.

$$D(b_i) = \begin{cases} -S(b_i), \text{ for positive boxes} \\ S(b_i), \text{ otherwise} \end{cases} \tag{5}$$

- *Smoothness term.* As has been discussed in Sect. 5.1, holes and protrusions should be avoided to ensure that the final reconstruction is compact. Thus, our smoothness term is defined to favor assigning the same label to neighboring boxes.

$$V(b_i, b_j) = \begin{cases} C_{i,j}, \text{ if } min(t_i, t_j) \leq 1 \\ 1, \phantom{C_{i,j}} \text{ otherwise} \end{cases} \tag{6}$$

Note that we set the smoothness weight to be a constant value of 1 if two adjacent boxes are both very thick. This is intended to handle very large boxes (i.e., boxes with a thickness larger than $1\,\text{m}$).

Now, our objective function can be defined as a linear combination of the sum of the above two terms.

$$E(\mathbf{X}) = \sum_{b_i} D(b_i) + \lambda \cdot \sum_{\{b_i, b_j\} \in \mathbb{E}} V(b_i, b_j), \tag{7}$$

where $\{x_i\} \in \mathbf{X}$ denote the binary label (i.e., *positive* or *non-positive*) assigned to each box; λ is a weight that balances between the data term and the smoothness term. Empirically, the value of λ can be approximately computed as the average of the number of neighboring points within d_t for all data samples, where d_t is the minimum distance between two parallel planes (see Sect. 4).

The above energy function can be efficiently minimized using an existing graph cut method [1]. After the energy being minimized, the assembly of candidate boxes labeled as *positive* approximate the geometry of the buildings represented by the input point cloud.

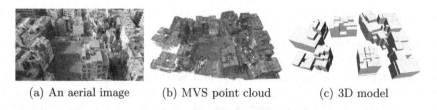

(a) An aerial image   (b) MVS point cloud   (c) 3D model

Fig. 7. Reconstruction of a scene consisting of a few complex buildings from MVS point cloud.

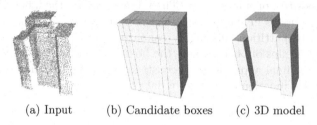

(a) Input   (b) Candidate boxes   (c) 3D model

Fig. 8. Reconstruction of a single building from airborne LiDAR data.

6   Results and Discussion

We have applied our approach on a variety of datasets (including MVS data, airborne LiDAR data, laser scans, and synthetic data) and conducted both qualitative and quantitative evaluations of the proposed method.

In Fig. 7, we show a scene consisting of a few buildings reconstructed from an MVS point cloud taken from Li et al. [14]. This point cloud was computed from aerial images using SfM and MVS [31]. As can be seen from (b), even though large portions of several walls are missing from the input, our method can recover the main structure of each building and obtain a compact 3D polygonal model for the entire scene without segmenting of the scene into individual buildings.

Figure 8 shows the reconstruction result of an individual building from aerial LiDAR data. Similar to the MVS data extracted from aerial images, aerial LiDAR data is even sparser and quite a few walls of the building are missing. As can be seen from this figure, our method successfully reconstructed a polygonal model consisting of a set of boxes approximating the geometry of this building.

We also tested our method on point clouds captured by a laser scanner. Figure 1 shows the reconstruction of a two-floor residential building. The point cloud is obtained using a Leica ScanStation C10 scanner. This data has higher accuracy, but it still contains large missing regions due to occlusions. We can observe that our method generates very faithful reconstruction.

Accuracy. Since the ground truth models are not available, we evaluate the accuracy of our reconstructed models by measuring the average distance of point samples to their nearest faces in the reconstructed models. Figure 9 visualizes our reconstruction error of two examples. For all the examples shown in the paper, our average reconstruction error is less than 8 cm.

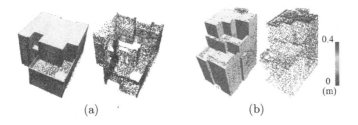

(a)   (b)

Fig. 9. The accuracy of two reconstructed models shown in Figs. 1 and 12.

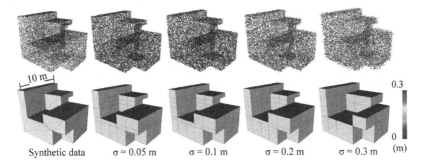

Synthetic data   σ = 0.05 m   σ = 0.1 m   σ = 0.2 m   σ = 0.3 m   (m)

Fig. 10. Reconstruction results from a synthetic data with increasing noise levels.

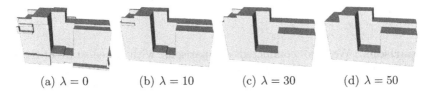

(a) $\lambda = 0$ (b) $\lambda = 10$ (c) $\lambda = 30$ (d) $\lambda = 50$

Fig. 11. The effect of the parameter λ on the final model. The suggested value of λ is 29.2, which is the average number of neighboring points within 0.2 m.

Robustness. In Fig. 10, we demonstrate the robustness of our approach with respect to different levels of noise using synthetic data. In this example, we can obtain good reconstruction results when the noise level σ is less than 30 cm. However, as the noise goes larger than the minimum distance between two actual planes in the building, the RANSAC failed in extracting appropriate planar segments, yielding an incorrect 3D model.

In the box selection step, the data fitting term and the compactness term work together resulting in faithful reconstruction. To understand how much each term contributes to the final reconstruction, we tested the effect of the weight parameter λ on the final results (Fig. 11). As can be seen from this figure, smaller values of λ (i.e., more data fitting) result in gaps and bumps (a) in the final model due to noise and outliers. Increasing the value of λ favors smooth surfaces (i.e., less holes and protrusions), and thus improves the compactness of the final models. However, a too large value leads to an overly smoothed 3D model (d).

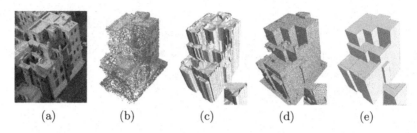

 (a)   (b)   (c)   (d)   (e)

Fig. 12. Comparisons with two state-of-the-art methods. (a) An aerial photograph of the building. (b) MVS point cloud. (c) Reconstruction result using the 2.5D dual contouring method [33]. (d) The result from L_1-based polycube method [9]. (e) Ours.

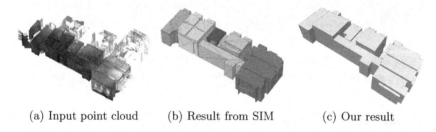

 (a) Input point cloud   (b) Result from SIM   (c) Our result

Fig. 13. A comparison with the structured indoor modeling method (SIM) on their data [10]. The SIM method requires segmenting the scene into individual rooms (color coded).

Comparisons. We also conducted comparisons with three state-of-the-art methods, namely the 2.5D Dual Contouring [33], L_1-based polycube generation [9], and a structured indoor modeling method [10] (see Figs. 12 and 13). As can be seen from Fig. 12, the result of the 2.5D Dual Contouring method (c) contains large areas of small bumps. This is because this method was initially designed to deal with data that has higher density and accuracy, and it mainly relies on roof information. Thus, it is sensitive to noise and the uneven point distribution in the roofs. The L_1-based polycube method can generate an isotropic dense surface model with more details (d). However, it usually produces undesirable surfaces (i.e., bumps and holes) passing through the outliers and the missing regions. Moreover, this method requires an initial dense 3D model as input (e.g., reconstructed using the Poisson reconstruction method [11]) and a remeshing step as preprocessing. In contrast, our method can generate more compact and visually pleasing reconstruction results (i.e., simple and clean polyhedra) as shown in (e).

In Fig. 13, we show a comparison with the structured indoor modeling approach [10]. Without segmenting the scenes into individual rooms, our method can generate comparable results.

Limitations. Our method is robust to high-levels of noise as shown in Fig. 10. To handle noise and outliers, we need to run the RANSAC algorithm multiple times during the candidate box generation step. Our experiments suggested that 10 iterations of RANSAC is usually enough to ensure that appropriate candidate boxes are proposed, but in extreme cases, it may require more iterations.

7   Conclusions

We presented a method for reconstruction of Manhattan-world scenes from point clouds. Our idea is to approximate the geometry of the buildings in the scene using a set of axis-aligned boxes. Our method is based on a *generate and select* strategy, i.e., we chose an optimal subset of boxes from a large number of candidates to assemble a compact polygonal mesh model. We formulated the box selection as a labeling problem and solved it based on a Markov Random Field formulation. Our reconstruction favors to represent the scene with a compact assembly of boxes and meanwhile respects the fitting to the input point cloud. Experiments demonstrated that our method can obtain good reconstruction for a variety of the data sources. The results of our method are polygonal models with simplified geometric structures, which can be directly used in various applications. Unlike previous methods that were designed to handle specific types of input data, our method does not have any particular requirements on the data source. Further, our method does not require semantically segmenting the input point clouds into individually buildings. Using a simple divide-and-conquer strategy (i.e., partition of the point clouds into small parts), our method can be directly applied for reconstructing large scale urban scenes.

Our method is dedicated to Manhattan-world scene reconstruction. However, it is still possible to reconstruct more general buildings by simply skipping the plane refinement step. As future work, we plan to extend our idea of box selection to polygon selection to handle more general scenes.

Acknowledgements. We thank the reviewers for their valuable comments. We also thank Dr. Neil Smith for providing us the data used in Fig. 7. This work was supported by the Office of Sponsored Research (OSR) under Award No. OCRF-2014-CGR3-62140401, and the Visual Computing Center at KAUST. Minglei Li was partially supported by NSFC (61272327). We also gratefully acknowledge the support of NVIDIA Corporation with the donation of the Quadro K5200 GPU used for this research.

References

1. Boykov, Y., Kolmogorov, V.: Computing geodesics and minimal surfaces via graph cuts. In: The 9th IEEE International Conference on Computer Vision, ICCV, vol. 2, pp. 26–33 (2003)
2. Chauve, A.L., Labatut, P., Pons, J.P.: Robust piecewise-planar 3d reconstruction and completion from large-scale unstructured point data. In: 2010 IEEE Conference on Computer Vision and Pattern Recognition (CVPR), pp. 1261–1268. IEEE (2010)

3. Fernandes, L.A.F., Oliveira, M.M.: Real-time line detection through an improved hough transform voting scheme. Pattern Recogn. **41**(1), 299–314 (2008)
4. Furukawa, Y., Curless, B., Seitz, S.M., Szeliski, R.: Manhattan-world stereo. In: CVPR, pp. 1422–1429 (2009)
5. Furukawa, Y., Ponce, J.: Accurate, dense, and robust multiview stereopsis. IEEE Trans. Pattern Anal. Mach. Intell. **32**(8), 1362–1376 (2010)
6. Garcia-Dorado, I., Demir, I., Aliaga, D.G.: Automatic urban modeling using volumetric reconstruction with surface graph cuts. Comput. Graph. **37**(7), 896–910 (2013)
7. Golovinskiy, A., Kim, V.G., Funkhouser, T.: Shape-based recognition of 3d point clouds in urban environments. In: ICCV, pp. 2154–2161 (2009)
8. Hiep, V., Keriven, R., Labatut, P., Pons, J.: Towards high resolution large-scale multi-view stereo. In: CVPR, pp. 1430–1437 (2009)
9. Huang, J., Jiang, T., Shi, Z., Tong, Y., Bao, H., Desbrun, M.: L1 based construction of polycube maps from complex shapes. ACM Trans. Graph. **33**(3), 25:1–25:11 (2014)
10. Ikehata, S., Yang, H., Furukawa, Y.: Structured indoor modeling. In: ICCV (2015)
11. Kazhdan, M., Hoppe, H.: Screened poisson surface reconstruction. ACM Trans. Graph. **32**(3), 29:1–29:13 (2013)
12. Lafarge, F., Descombes, X., Zerubia, J., Pierrot-Deseilligny, M.: Structural approach for building reconstruction from a single dsm. IEEE Trans. Pattern Anal. Mach. Intell. **32**(1), 135–147 (2010)
13. Li, M., Nan, L., Liu, S.: Fitting boxes to manhattan scenes using linear integer programming. Int. J. Digital Earth, 1–12 (2016)
14. Li, M., Nan, L., Smith, N., Wonka, P.: Reconstructing building mass models from uav images. Comput. Graph. **54**, 84–93 (2016)
15. Lin, H., Gao, J., Zhou, Y., Lu, G., Ye, M., Zhang, C., Liu, L., Yang, R.: Semantic decomposition and reconstruction of residential scenes from lidar data. SIGGRAPH **32**(4), 66:1–66:10 (2013)
16. Matei, B., Sawhney, H., Samarasekera, S., Kim, J., Kumar, R.: Building segmentation for densely built urban regions using aerial lidar data. In: CVPR, pp. 1–8 (2008)
17. Musialski, P., Wonka, P., Aliaga, D.G., Wimmer, M., van Gool, L., Purgathofer, W.: A survey of urban reconstruction. Comput. Graph. Forum **32**(6), 146–177 (2013)
18. Nan, L., Jiang, C., Ghanem, B., Wonka, P.: Template assembly for detailed urban reconstruction. Comput. Graph. Forum **35**, 217–228 (2015)
19. Nan, L., Sharf, A., Zhang, H., Cohen-Or, D., Chen, B.: Smartboxes for unteractive urban reconstruction. SIGGRAPH **29**(4), 93 (2010)
20. Nan, L., Xie, K., Sharf, A.: A search-classify approach for cluttered indoor scene understanding. ACM Trans. Graph. **31**(6), 1–10 (2012)
21. Oesau, S., Lafarge, F., Alliez, P.: Indoor scene reconstruction using feature sensitive primitive extraction and graph-cut. ISPRS J. Photogram. Remote Sens. **90**, 68–82 (2014)
22. Poullis, C., You, S.: Automatic reconstruction of cities from remote sensor data. In: CVPR, pp. 2775–2782 (2009)
23. Rottensteinera, F., Sohnb, G., Gerkec, M., Wegnerd, J., Breitkopfa, U., Jungb, J.: Results of the isprs benchmark on urban object detection and 3d building reconstruction. ISPRS J. Photogram. Remote Sens. **93**, 256–271 (2014)
24. Schnabel, R., Wahl, R., Klein, R.: Efficient ransac for point-cloud shape detection. Comput. Graph. Forum **26**(2), 214–226 (2007)

25. Shao, T., Xu, W., Zhou, K., Wang, J., Li, D., Guo, B.: An interactive approach to semantic modeling of indoor scenes with an rgbd camera. ACM Trans. Graph. **31**(6), 136:1–136:11 (2012). http://doi.acm.org/10.1145/2366145.2366155

26. Snavely, N., Seitz, S.M., Szeliski, R.: Photo tourism: exploring photo collections in 3d. In: SIGGRAPH, pp. 835–846 (2006)

27. Tomasi, C., Manduchi, R.: Bilateral filtering for gray and color images. In: ICCV, pp. 839–846 (1998)

28. Vanegas, C.A., Aliaga, D.G., Benes, B.: Building reconstruction using manhattan-world grammars. In: CVPR, pp. 358–365 (2010)

29. Verdie, Y., Lafarge, F., Alliez, P.: Lod generation for urban scenes. ACM Trans. Graph. **34**(3), 15 (2015)

30. Verma, V., Kumar, R., Hsu, S.: 3d building detection and modeling from aerial lidar data. In: CVPR, pp. 2213–2220 (2006)

31. Wu, C.: Visualsfm: A visual structure from motion system, 9 (2011). http://homes. cs.washington.edu/~ccwu/vsfm

32. Zebedin, L., Bauer, J., Karner, K., Bischof, H.: Fusion of feature- and area-based information for urban buildings modeling from aerial imagery. In: Forsyth, D., Torr, P., Zisserman, A. (eds.) ECCV 2008. LNCS, vol. 5305, pp. 873–886. Springer, Heidelberg (2008)

33. Zhou, Q.-Y., Neumann, U.: 2.5d dual contouring: a robust approach to creating building models from aerial LiDAR point clouds. In: Daniilidis, K., Maragos, P., Paragios, N. (eds.) ECCV 2010. LNCS, vol. 6313, pp. 115–128. Springer, Heidelberg (2010)

From Multiview Image Curves to 3D Drawings

Anil Usumezbas[1], Ricardo Fabbri[2(✉)], and Benjamin B. Kimia[3]

[1] SRI International, Providence, USA
anil.usumezbas@sri.com
[2] Polytechnic Institute, State University of Rio de Janeiro, Rio de Janeiro, Brazil
rfabbri@iprj.uerj.br
[3] Shool of Engineering, Brown University, Providence, USA
benjamin_kimia@brown.edu

Abstract. Reconstructing 3D scenes from multiple views has made impressive strides in recent years, chiefly by correlating isolated feature points, intensity patterns, or curvilinear structures. In the general setting – without controlled acquisition, abundant texture, curves and surfaces following specific models or limiting scene complexity – most methods produce unorganized point clouds, meshes, or voxel representations, with some exceptions producing unorganized clouds of 3D curve fragments. Ideally, many applications require structured representations of curves, surfaces and their spatial relationships. This paper presents a step in this direction by formulating an approach that combines 2D image curves into a collection of 3D curves, with topological connectivity between them represented as a 3D graph. This results in a **3D drawing**, which is complementary to surface representations in the same sense as a 3D scaffold complements a tent taut over it. We evaluate our results against truth on synthetic and real datasets.

Keywords: Multiview stereo · 3D reconstruction · 3D curve networks · Junctions

1 Introduction

The automated 3D reconstruction of *general* scenes from multiple views obtained using conventional cameras, under uncontrolled acquisition, is a paramount goal of computer vision, ambitious even by modern standards. While a fully complete working system addressing all the underlying challenges is beyond current technology, significant progress has been made in the past few years using approaches that fall into three broad classes, depending on whether one focuses on correlating isolated points, surface patches, or curvilinear structures across views, as described below.

A vast majority of multiview reconstruction methods rely on correlating isolated interest points across views to produce an unorganized 3D cloud of points.

Electronic supplementary material The online version of this chapter (doi:10.1007/978-3-319-46493-0_5) contains supplementary material, which is available to authorized users.

B. Leibe et al. (Eds.): ECCV 2016, Part IV, LNCS 9908, pp. 70–87, 2016.
DOI: 10.1007/978-3-319-46493-0_5

Fig. 1. Our approach transforms calibrated views of a scene into a "3D drawing" – a graph of 3D curves meeting at junctions. Each curve is shown in a different color. *(Please zoom in to examine closely. The 3D model is available as supplementary data.)* (Color figure online)

The **interest-point-based approach** has been highly successful in reconstructing large-scale scenes with *texture-rich images*, in systems such as in Photo-tourism and recent large-scale 3D reconstruction work [6,15,34,47]. Despite their manifest usefulness, these methods generally cannot represent smooth, texture-less regions (due to the sparsity of interest points in image regions with homogeneous appearance), or regions that change appearance drastically across views. This limits their applicability, especially in man-made environments [28] and objects such as cars [27], non-Lambertian surfaces such as that of the sea, appearance variation due to changing weather [2], and wide baseline [46].

Another approach matches intensity patterns across views using multiview stereo, producing denser point clouds or mesh reconstructions. **Dense multiview stereo** produces detailed 3D reconstructions of objects imaged under controlled conditions by a large number of precisely calibrated cameras [3,25,40–43,48]. For general, complex scenes with various kinds of objects and surface properties, this approach has shown most promise towards obtaining an accurate and dense 3D model of a given scene. Homogeneous areas, such as walls of a corridor, repeated texture, and areas with view-dependent intensities create challenges for these methods.

A smaller number of techniques correlate and reconstruct image **curvilinear structure** across views, resulting in 3D curvilinear structure. Pipelines based on straight lines (see [11,20,31] for recent reviews), algebraic and general curve features [8–10,21,23,29,36] have been proposed, but some lack generality, *e.g.*, requiring specific curve models [26]. The 3D Curve Sketch system [7,8,10] operates on multiple views by pairing curves from two arbitrary "hypothesis views" at a time via epipolar-geometric consistency. A curve pair reconstructs to a 3D curve fragment hypothesis, whose reprojection onto several other "confirmation views" gathers support from subpixel 2D edges. The curve pair hypotheses with enough support result in an unorganized set of 3D curve fragments, the "3D

Fig. 2. 3D drawings for urban planning and industrial design. A process from professional practice for communicating solution concepts with a blend of computer and handcrafted renderings [44,50]. New designs are often based off real object references, mockups or massing models for selecting viewpoints and rough shapes. These can be modeled *manually* in, *e.g.*, Google Sketchup (top-left), in some cases from reference imagery. The desired 2D views are rendered and *manually* traced into a reference curve sketch (center-left, bottom-left) easily modifiable to the designer's vision. The stylized drawings to be presented to a client are often produced by *manually* tracing and painting over the reference sketch (right). Our system can be used to generate reference *3D curve drawings* from video footage of the real site for urban planning, saving manual interaction, providing initial information such as rough dimensions, and aiding the selection of pose, editing and tracing. The condensed 3D curve drawings make room for the artist to overlay his concept and harness imagery as a clean reference, clear from details to be redesigned.

Curve Sketch". While the resulting 3D curve segments are visually appealing, they are fragmented, redundant, and lack explicit inter-curve organization.

The plethora of multiview representations, as documented above, arise because 3D structures are geometrically and semantically rich [12,32]. A building, for example, has walls, windows, doorways, roof, chimneys, etc. The structure can be represented by sample points (*i.e.*, unorganized cloud of points) or a surface mesh where connectivity among points is captured. This representation, especially when rendered with surface albedo or texture, is visually appealing. However, the representation also leaves out a great deal of semantic information: which points or mesh areas represent a window or a wall? Which two walls are adjacent? The representation of such components, or parts, requires an explicit representation of part boundaries such as ridges, as well as where these boundaries come together, such as junctions.

The same point can equally arise if objects in the scene were solely defined by their curve structures. A representation of a building by its ridges may usually give an appealing impression of its structure, but it fails to identify the walls, *i.e.*, which collection of 3D curves bound a wall and what its geometry is. Both surfaces and curves are important and needed across the board, *e.g.*, in applications such as robotics [4], urban planning and industrial design [44,50], Fig. 2.

In general, image curve fragments are attractive because they have good localization, they have greater invariance than interest points to changes in illumination, are stable over a greater range of baselines, and are typically denser than interest points. Furthermore, the reflectance or ridge curves provide boundary condition for surface reconstruction, while occluding contour variations across views lead to surfaces [37,39,45]. Recent studies strongly support the notion that image curves contain much of the image information [17,19,33,38]. Moreover, curves are structurally rich as reflected by their differential geometry, a fact which is exploited both in recent computer systems [1,8,10,33] and perception studies [13,33].

This paper develops the technology to process a series of (intrinsic and extrinsically) calibrated multiview images to generate a *3D curve drawing* as a graph of 3D curve segments meeting at junctions. The ultimate goal of this approach is to integrate the 3D curve drawing with the traditional recovery of surfaces so that 3D curves bound the 3D curve segments, towards a more semantic representation of 3D structures. The 3D curve drawing can also be of independent value in applications such as fast recognition of general 3D scenery [23], efficient transmission of general 3D scenes, scene understanding and modeling by reasoning at junctions [22], consistent non-photorealistic rendering from video [5], modeling of branching structures, among others [18,24,30].

The paper is organized as follows. In Sect. 2 we review the 3D curve sketch, identify three shortcomings and suggest solutions to each, resulting in the *Enhanced Curve Sketch*. Since the original 3D curve sketch was built around a few views at a time, it did not address fundamental issues surrounding integration of information from numerous views. Section 3 presents as our main contribution the multiview integration of information both at edge- and curve-level, which naturally leads to junctions. Section 4 validates the approach using real and synthetic datasets.

2   Enhanced 3D Curve Sketch

Image curve fragments formed from grouped edges are central to our framework. Each image V^v at view $v = 1, \ldots, N$ contains a number of curves γ_i^v, $i = 1, \ldots, M^v$. Reconstructed 3D curve fragments are referred as Γ_k, $k = 1, \ldots, K$, whose reprojection onto view v is $\gamma^{k,v}$. Indices may be omitted where clear from context.

The initial stage of our framework is built as an extension of the hypothesize-and-verify 3D Curve Sketch approach [10]. We use the same hypothesis generation mechanism with a novel verification step performing a finer-level analysis of image evidence and significantly reducing the fragmentation and redundancy in the 3D models.

Two image curves $\gamma_{l_1}^{v_1}$ and $\gamma_{l_2}^{v_2}$ are paired from two distinct views v_1 and v_2 at a time, the *hypothesis views*, provided they have sufficient epipolar overlap [10]. The verification of these K curve pair hypotheses, represented as ω_k,

$k = 1, \ldots, K$ with the corresponding 3D reconstruction denoted as $\boldsymbol{\Gamma}_k$, gauges the extent of edge support for the reprojection $\boldsymbol{\gamma}^{k,v}$ of $\boldsymbol{\Gamma}_k$ onto another set of *confirmation views*, $v = v_{i_3}, \ldots, v_{i_n}$. An image edge in view v suports $\boldsymbol{\gamma}^{k,v}$ if it is sufficiently close in distance *and* orientation. The total support a hypothesis ω receives from view v is

$$S_{\omega_k}^v \doteq \int_0^{L^{k,v}} \phi(\boldsymbol{\gamma}^{k,v}(s)) ds, \tag{1}$$

where $L^{k,v}$ is the length of $\boldsymbol{\gamma}^{k,v}$, and $\phi(\boldsymbol{\gamma}(s))$ is the extent of edge support at $\boldsymbol{\gamma}(s)$. A view is considered a *supporting view* for ω_k if $S_{\omega_k}^v > \tau_v$. Evidence from confirmation views is aggregated in the form

$$\mathcal{S}_{\omega_k} \doteq \sum_{v=i_3}^{i_n} \left[S_{\omega_k}^v > \tau_v \right] S_{\omega_k}^v. \tag{2}$$

The set of hypotheses ω_k whose support $\mathcal{S}_{\omega_k}$ exceeds a threshold are kept and the resulting $\boldsymbol{\Gamma}_k$ form the unorganized 3D curves.

Despite these advances, three major shortcomings remain: (i) some 3D curve fragments are correct for certain portions of the underlying curve and erroneous in other parts, due to multiview grouping inconsistencies; (ii) gaps in the 3D model, typically due to unreliable reconstructions near epipolar tangencies, where epipolar lines are nearly tangent to the curves; and (iii) multiple, redundant 3D structures. We now document each issue and describe our solutions.

Problem 1. **Erroneous grouping:** inconsistent multiview grouping of edges can lead to reconstructed curves which are veridical only along some portion, which are nevertheless wholly admitted, Fig. 3(a). Also, fully-incorrect hypotheses can accrue support coincidentally, as with repeated patterns or linear structures, Fig. 3(b). Both issues can be addressed by allowing for selective local reconstructions: only those portions of the curve receiving adequate edge support from sufficient views are reconstructed. This ensures that inconsistent 2D groupings do not produce spurious 3D reconstructions. The shift from cumulative global to multi-view local support results in greater selectivity and deals with coincidental alignment of edges with the reconstruction hypotheses.

Problem 2. **Gaps:** The geometric inaccuracy of curve segment reconstructions nearly parallel to epipolar lines led [10] to break off curves at epipolar tangencies, creating 2D gaps leading to gaps in 3D. We observe, however, that while reconstructions near epipolar tangency are *geometrically unreliable*, they are *topologically correct* in that they connect the reliable portions correctly but with highly inaccurate geometry. What is needed is to flag curve segments near epipolar tangency reconstructions as geometrically unreliable. We do this by the integration of support in Eq. 1, giving significantly lower weight to these unreliable portions instead of fully discarding them, which greatly reduces the presence of gaps in the resulting reconstruction.

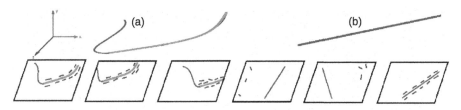

Fig. 3. (a) Due to a lack of consistency in grouping of edges at the image level, a correct 3D curve reconstruction, shown here in blue, can be erroneously grouped with an erroneous reconstruction, shown here in red, leading to partially correct reconstructions. When such a 3D curve is projected in its entirety to a number of image views, we only expect the correct portion to gather sustained image evidence, which argues for a hypothesis verification method that can distinguish between supported segments and outlier segments; (b) An incorrect hypothesis can at times coincidentally gather an extremely high degree of support from a limited set of views. The red 3D line shown here might be an erroneous hypothesis, but because parallel linear structures are common in man-made environments, such an incorrect hypothesis often gathers coincidental strong support from a particular view or two. Our hypothesis verification approach is able to handle such cases by requiring explicit support from a minimum number of viewpoints simultaneously. (Color figure online)

Problem 3. **Redundancy:** A 2D curve can pair up with dozens of curves from other views, all pointing to the same reconstruction, leading to redundant pairwise reconstructions as partially overlapping 3D curve segments, each localized slightly differently. Our solution is to detect and reconcile redundant reconstructions. Since redundancy changes as one traverses a 3D curve, we reconcile redundancy at the local level: each 3D edge is in one-to-one correspondence with a 2D edge of its primary hypothesis view (*i.e.*, the first view from which it was reconstructed), hence 3D edges can be grouped in a one-to-one manner,

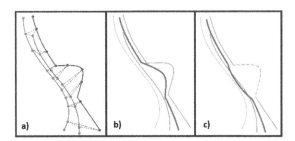

Fig. 4. (a) Redundant 3D curve reconstructions (orange, green and blue) can arise from a single 2D image curve in the primary hypothesis view. If the redundant curves are put in one-to-one correspondence and averaged, the resulting curve is shown in (b) in purple. Our robust averaging approach, on the other hand, is able to get rid of that bump by eliminating outlier segments, producing the purple curve shown in (c). (Color figure online)

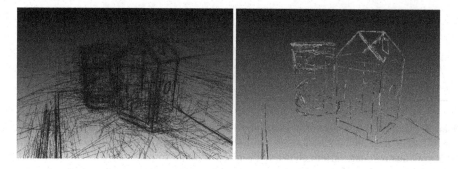

Fig. 5. A visual comparison of: (left) the curve sketch results [10], with (right) the results of our enhanced curve sketch algorithm presented in Sect. 2. Notice the significant reduction in both outliers and duplicate reconstructions, without sacrificing coverage.

all corresponding to a common 3D source. These are robustly averaged by data-driven outlier removal, where a Gaussian distribution is fit on all pairwise distances between corresponding samples, discarding samples farther than 2σ from the average, Fig. 4. Robust averaging improves localization accuracy, removes redundancy, and elongates shorter curve subsegments into longer 3D curves.

3   From 3D Curve Sketch to 3D Drawing

Despite the visible improvements of the Enhanced 3D Curve Sketch of Sect. 2, Fig. 5, curves are broken in many places, and there remains redundant overlap. The sketch representation as unorganized clouds of 3D curves are not able to capture the fine-level geometry or spatial organization of 3D curves, *e.g.* by using junction points to characterize proximity and neighborhood relations. The underlying cause of these issues is lack of integration across multiple views. The robust averaging approach of Sect. 2 is one step, anchored on one primary hypothesis view, but integrates evidence within that view only; a scene curve can be visible from multiple hypothesis view pairs, and some redundancy remains.

This lack of multiview integration is responsible for three problems observed in the enhanced curve sketch, Fig. 10: (*i*) localization inaccuracies, Fig. 10b, due to use of partial information; (*ii*) reconstruction redundancy, which lends to multiple curves with partial overlap, all arising from the same 3D structure, but remaining distinct, see Fig. 10c; (*iii*) excessive breaking because each curve segment arises from one curve in one initial view independently.

Multiview Local Consistency Network: The key idea underlying integration of reconstructions across views is the detection of a common image structure supporting two reconstruction hypotheses. Two 3D local curve segments depict the same single underlying 3D object feature if they are supported by the same 2D image edge structures. Since the identification of common image structure

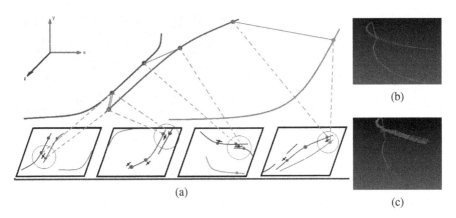

Fig. 6. The four bottlenecks of Fig. 10 are resolved by integration of information/cues from all views. (a) The shared edge supporting edges, which are marked with circles, create the purple links between the corresponding samples of the 3D curves. These purple bonds will then be used to pull the redundant segments together and reorganize the 3D model into a clean 3D graph. Observe how the determination of common image support can identify portions of the green and blue curves as identical while differentiating the red one as distinct. A real example for a bundle of related curves is shown in (b) and the links among their edges in (c). (Color figure online)

can vary along the curve, it must necessarily be a local process, operating at the level of a 3D local edge and not a 3D curve. Two 3D edge elements (edgels) depict the same 3D structure if they receive support from the same 2D edgels in a sufficient number of views, so 3D-2D links between a 2D edgel to the 3D edgel it supports must be kept. Typically, they share supporting image edges in many views; and the number of shared supporting edgels is the measure of strength for a 3D-3D link between them.

Formally, we define the Multiview Local geometric consistency Network (MLN) as pointwise alignments ϕ_{ij} between two 3D curves $\boldsymbol{\Gamma}_i$ and $\boldsymbol{\Gamma}_j$: let $\boldsymbol{\Gamma}_i(s_i)$ and $\boldsymbol{\Gamma}_j(s_j)$ be two points in two 3D curves, and define

$$S_{ij} \doteq \{v : \boldsymbol{\gamma}^{i,v}(s_i) \text{ and } \boldsymbol{\gamma}^{j,v}(s_j) \text{ share local support}\}. \tag{3}$$

Then the a kernel function ϕ defines a consistency link between these two points, weighted by the extent of multiview image support $\phi_{ij}(s_i, s_j) \doteq |S_{ij}|$. When the curves are sampled, ϕ becomes an adjacency matrix of a graph representing links between individual curve samples. The implementation goes through each image edgel which votes for a 3D curve point that has received support from it (see the supplementary material for details) (Fig. 6).

Multiview Curve-Level Consistency Network: The identification of 3D edges sharing 2D edges leads to high recall operating point with many false links due to accidental alignment of edge support. False positives can be reduced without affecting high recall by employing a notion of curve context for each 3D

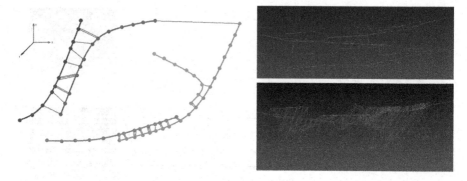

Fig. 7. The correspondence between 3D edge samples is skewed along a curve, which is a direct indication that these links cannot be used as-is when averaging and fusing redundant curve reconstructions. Instead, each point is assumed to be in correspondence with the point closest to it on another overlapping curve, during the iterative averaging step. Observe that corrections can be partial along related curves.

edgel: a link between two 3D edgels based on a supporting 2D edgel is more effective if the respective neighbors of the underlying 3D edge on the underlying 3D curve are also linked.

The curve context idea requires establishing new pairwise links between 3D curves using MLN, when there are a sufficient number of links with $\phi_{ij} > \tau_\epsilon$ between their constituent 3D edges (in our implementation, $\tau_\epsilon = 3$ and we require 5 such edges or more). The linking of 3D curves is represented by the Multiview Curve-level Consistency network (MCCN), a graph whose nodes are the 3D curves Γ_j and the edges represent the presence of high-weight 3D edge links between these 3D curves. The MCCN graph allows for a clustering of 3D curves by finding connected components; and once a link is established between two curves, there is a high likelihood of their edges corresponding in a regularized fashion, thus fewer common supporting 2D edges are required to establish a link between all their constituent 3D edges. This fact is used to perform gap filling, since even no edge support is acceptable to fill in small gaps and create a continuous and regularized correspondence if both neighbors of the gap are connected (see pseudocode in Supplementary Materials for details). The two stages in tandem, *i.e.*, high recall linking of 3D edges and use of curve context to reduce false positives leads to high recall and high precision, *i.e.*, all the 3D edges which need to be related are related and very few outlier connections remain.

Integrating Information Across Related Edges: The identification of a bundle of curves as arising from the same 3D source implies that we can improve the geometric accuracy of this bundle by allowing them to converge to a common solution. While this might appear straightforward, 3D edges are not consistently distributed along related curves, yielding a skew in the correspondence of related samples, Fig. 7, sometimes not a one-to-one correspondence, Fig. 8a. This argues for averaging 3D curves and not 3D edge samples, which in turn requires finding

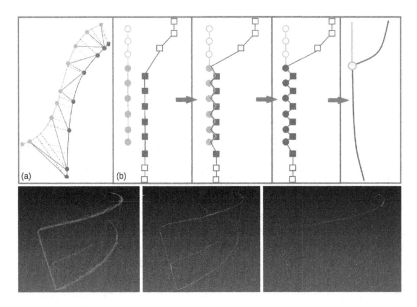

Fig. 8. (a) A schematic of sample correspondence along two related 3D curves, showing skewed correspondences that may not be one-to-one. (b) A sketch of how two curves are integrated. Bottom row: a real case.

a more regularized alignment between the 3D curves, without gaps; we find each curve samples's closest point on the other curve.

When post averaging a sample with its closest points on related curves, the order of resulting averaged samples is not clear. The order should be inferred from the underlying curves, but this information can be conflicting, unless the distance between two curves is substantially smaller than the sampling distance along the curves. This requires first updating each curve's geometry separately and iteratively, without merging curves until after convergence, Fig. 8d. This also improves the correspondence of samples at each iteration, as the closest points are continuously updated.

At each stage, the iterative averaging process simply replaces each 3D edge sample with the average of all closest points on curves related to it, Fig. 8b–d. This can be formulated as evolving all 3D curves by averaging along the MCCN using closest points. Formally, each $\boldsymbol{\Gamma}_i$ is evolved according to

$$\frac{\partial \boldsymbol{\Gamma}_i}{\partial t}(s) = \alpha \underset{\substack{(i,j)\in L \\ (\boldsymbol{\Gamma}_i,\boldsymbol{\Gamma}_j)\in \text{MCCN}}}{\text{avg}} \{\boldsymbol{\Gamma}_j(r) : \boldsymbol{\Gamma}_j(r) = \text{cp}_j(\boldsymbol{\Gamma}_i(s))\}, \tag{4}$$

where $\text{cp}_i(\mathbf{p})$ is the closest point in $\boldsymbol{\Gamma}_i$ to $\mathbf{p}$ and L is the link set defined as follows: Let the set S_{ij} of so-called strong local links between curves $\boldsymbol{\Gamma}_i$ and $\boldsymbol{\Gamma}_j$ be

$$S_{ij} \doteq \{(s,t) : \phi_{ij}(s,t) \geq \tau_\epsilon, \phi_{ij} \in \text{MLN}(\boldsymbol{\Gamma}_1,\ldots,\boldsymbol{\Gamma}_K)\}. \tag{5}$$

Then the set L of the MCCN is defined as

$$L \doteq \{(i,j) : |S_{ij}| \geq \tau_{sl}\}. \qquad (6)$$

In practice, the averaging is robust and α is chosen such that in one step we move to the average.

3D Curve Drawing Graph: Once all related curves have converged, they can be merged into single curves, separated by junctions where 3 or more curves meet. The order along the resulting curve is also dictated by closest points: The immediate neighbors of any averaged 3D edge are the two closest 3D edges to it among all converged 3D edges in a given MCCN cluster.

This where junctions naturally arise: as two distinct curves may merge along one portion they may diverge at one point, leaving two remaining, non-related subsegments behind, Fig. 8e. This is a *junction node* relating three or more curve segments, and its detection is done using the *merging primitives*, whose complete set are shown in Fig. 9. The intuition is this: a complex merging problem along the full length of two 3D curves actually consists of smaller, simpler and independent merging operations between different segments of each curve. A full merging problem between two complete curves can be expressed as a permutation of any number of simpler merging primitives. These primitives were worked out systematically to serve as the basic building blocks capable of constructing *all possible configurations* of our merging problem.

After iterative averaging, all resulting curves in any given cluster are processed in a pairwise fashion using these primitives: initialize the 3D graph with the longest curve in the cluster, and merge every curve in the cluster one by one into this graph. At each step, any number of these merging primitives arise and are handled appropriately. This process outputs the Multiview Curve Drawing Graph (MDG), which consists of multiple disconnected 3D graphs, one

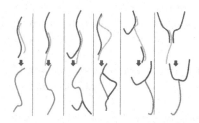

Fig. 9. The complete set of merging primitives, which were systematically worked out to cover all possible merging topologies between a pair of curves whose overlap regions are calculated beforehand. We claim that any configuration of overlap between two curves can be broken down into a series of these primitives along the length of one of the curves. The 5th primitive is representative of a bridge situation, where the connection at either end of the yellow curve can be any one of the first four cases shown, and 6th primitive is representative of a situation where only one end of the yellow curve connects to multiple existing curves, but not necessarily just two. (Color figure online)

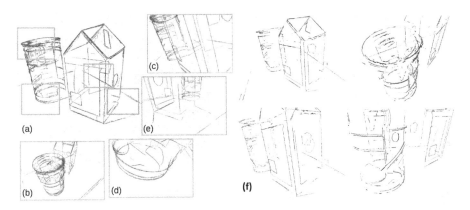

Fig. 10. (a) The four main issues with the enhanced curve sketch: (b) localization errors along the camera principal axis, which cause loss in accuracy if not corrected, (c) redundant reconstructions due to a lack of integration across different views, (d) the reconstruction of a single long curve as multiple, disconnected (but perhaps overlapping) short curve segments, and (e) the lack of connectivity among distinct 3D curves which naturally form junctions. (f) shows the 3D drawing reconstructed from this enhanced curve sketch, as described in Sect. 3. Observe how each of the four bottlenecks have been resolved. Additional results are evaluated visually and quantitatively, and are reported in Sect. 4 as well as Supplementary Materials.

for each 3D curve cluster in the MCCN. The nodes of each graph are the junctions (with curve endpoints) and the links are curve fragment geometries. This structure is the final 3D curve drawing.

4   Experiments and Evaluation

We have devised a number of large real and synthetic multiview datasets, available at multiview-3d-drawing.sourceforge.net.

The Barcelona Pavilion Dataset: a realistic synthetic dataset we created for validating the present approach with control over illumination, geometry and cameras. It consists of: 3D models composing a large, mostly man-made, scene professionally composed by eMirage studios using the 3D modeling software Blender; ground-truth cameras fly-by's around chairs with varied reflectance models and cluttered background; (*iii*) ground-truth videos realistically rendered with high quality ray tracing under 3 extreme illumination conditions (morning, afternoon, and night); (*iv*) ground-truth 3D *curve* geometry obtained by manually tracing over the meshes. This is the first synthetic 3D ground truth for evaluating multiview reconstruction algorithms that is realistically complex – most existing ground truth is obtained using either laser or structured light methods, both of which suffer from reconstruction inaccuracies and calibration errors. Starting from an existing 3D model ensures that our ground truth is not

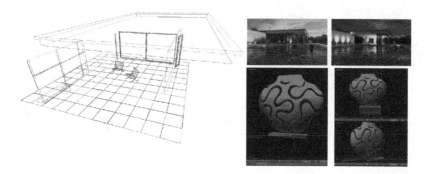

Fig. 11. Our publicly-available synthetic (left and top-right) and real (bottom-right) 3D ground truths modeled and rendered using Blender for the present work.

polluted by any such errors, since both 3D model and the calibration parameters are obtained from the 3D modeling software, Fig. 11. The result is the first publicly available, high-precision 3D curve ground truth dataset to be used in the evaluation of curve-based multiview stereo algorithms. For the experiments reported in the main manuscript we use 25 views out of 100 from this dataset, evenly distributed around the primary objects of interest, namely the two chairs, see Fig. 11.

The Vase Dataset: constructed for this research from the DTU Point Feature Dataset with calibration and 3D ground truth from structured light [16,35]. The images were taken using an automated robot arm from pre-calibrated positions and our test sequence was constructed using views from different illumination conditions to simulate varying illumination. To the best of our knowledge, these are the most exhaustive public multiview ground truth datasets. To generate ground-truth for curves, we have constructed a GUI based on Blender to manually remove all points of the ground-truth 3D point-cloud that correspond to homogeneous scene structures as observed when projected on all views, Fig. 11(bottom). What remains is a dense 3D point cloud ground truth where the points are restricted to be near abrupt intensity changes on the object, *i.e.* edges and curves. Our results on this real dataset showcase our algorithm's robustness under varying illumination.

The Amsterdam House Dataset: 50 calibrated multiview images, also developed for this research, comprising a wide variety of object properties, including but not limited to smooth surfaces, shiny surfaces, specific close-curve geometries, text, texture, clutter and cast shadows, Fig. 1. The camera reprojection error obtained by Bundler [34] is on average subpixel. There is no ground truth 3D geometry for this dataset; the intent here is: to qualitatively test on a scene that is challenging to approaches that rely on, *e.g.*, point features; and to be able to closely inspect expected geometries and junction arising from simple, known shapes of scene objects.

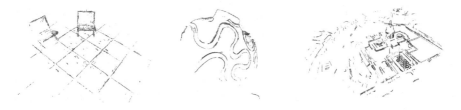

Fig. 12. The 3D drawing results on the Barcelona Pavilion, DTU Vase and Capitol Datasets. See Supplementary Materials for more extensive results and comparisons

The Capitol High Building: 256HD frames from a high 270° helicopter fly-by of the Rhode Island State Capitol [10]. Camera parameters are from the Matlab Calibration toolbox and tracking 30 points.

Qualitative Evaluation: The enhancements of Sect. 2 lead to significant improvements to the 3D curve sketch of [10] in increasing recall while maintaining precision. See Fig. 5 for a qualitative comparison. When the clean clouds of curves are organized into a set of connected 3D graphs, the results are more accurate, more visually pleasing and not redundant, Figs. 10(f) and 12. Each of the issues in Fig. 10(a–e) have been resolved and spatial organization of 3D curves have been captured as junctions, represented by small white spheres.

Quantitative Evaluation: Accuracy and coverage of 3D curve reconstructions is evaluated against ground truth. We compare 3 different results to quantify our improvements: (*i*) Original Curve Sketch [10] run exhaustively on all views, (*ii*) Enhanced Curve Sketch, Sect. 2, and (*iii*) Curve Drawing, Sect. 3. Edge maps are obtained using Third-Order Color Edge Detector [49], and are linked using

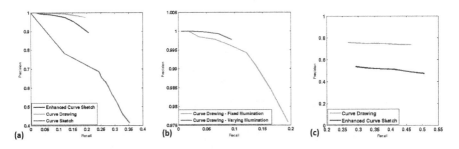

Fig. 13. Precision-recall curves for quantitative evaluation of 3D curve drawing algorithm: (a) Curve sketch, enhanced curve sketch and curve drawing results are compared on Barcelona Pavilion dataset with afternoon rendering, showing significant improvements in reconstruction quality; (b) A comparison of 3D curve drawing results on fixed and varying illumination version of Barcelona Pavilion dataset proves that 3D drawing quality does not get adversely affected by varying illumination; (c) 3D drawing improves reconstruction quality by a large margin in Vase dataset, which consists of images of a real object under slight illumination variation.

Symbolic Linker [14] to extract curve fragments for each view. Edge support thresholds are varied during reconstruction for each method, to obtain precision-recall curves. Here, **precision** is the percentage of accurately reconstructed curve samples: a ground truth curve sample is a true positive if its closer than a proximity threshold to the reconstructed 3D model. A reconstructed 3D sample is deemed a false positive if its not closer than τ_{prox} to any ground truth curve. This method ensures that redundant reconstructions aren't rewarded multiple times. All remaining curve samples in the reconstruction are false positives. **Recall** is the fraction of ground truth curve samples covered by the reconstruction. A ground truth sample is marked as a false negative if its farther than τ_{prox} to the test reconstruction. The precision-recall curves shown in Fig. 13 *quantitatively* measure the improvements of our algorithm and showcase its robustness under varying illumination.

5   Conclusion

We have presented a method to extract a 3D drawing as a graph of 3D curve fragments to represent a scene from a large number of multiview imagery. The 3D drawing is able to pick up contours of objects with homogeneous surfaces where feature and intensity based correlation methods fail. The 3D drawing can act as a scaffold to complement and assist existing feature and intensity based methods. Since image curves are generally invariant to image transformations such as illumination changes, the 3D drawing is stable under such changes. The approach does not require controlled acquisition, does not restrict the number of objects or object properties.

Acknowledgements. This research received support from FAPERJ/Brazil E25/ 2014/204167, UERJ/Brazil Prociencia 2014-2017, and NSF awards 1116140 and 1319914.

References

1. Abuhashim, T., Sukkarieh, S.: Incorporating geometric information into gaussian process terrain models from monocular images. In: IEEE/RSJ IROS 2012, pp. 4162–4168 (2012)
2. Baatz, G., Saurer, O., Köser, K., Pollefeys, M.: Large scale visual geo-localization of images in mountainous terrain. In: Fitzgibbon, A., Lazebnik, S., Perona, P., Sato, Y., Schmid, C. (eds.) ECCV 2012. LNCS, vol. 7573, pp. 517–530. Springer, Heidelberg (2012). doi:10.1007/978-3-642-33709-3_37
3. Calakli, F., Ulusoy, A.O., Restrepo, M.I., Taubin, G., Mundy, J.L.: High resolution surface reconstruction from multi-view aerial imagery. In: 3DIMPVT 2012, pp. 25–32 (2012)
4. Carlson, F.B., Vuong, N.D., Johansson, R.: Polynomial reconstruction of 3D sampled curves using auxiliary surface data. In: IEEE ICRA 2014, pp. 4411–4416 (2014)

5. Chen, T.-Y., Klette, R.: Animated non-photorealistic rendering in multiple styles. In: Huang, F., Sugimoto, A. (eds.) PSIVT 2013. LNCS, vol. 8334, pp. 12–23. Springer, Heidelberg (2014). doi:10.1007/978-3-642-53926-8_2

6. Diskin, Y., Asari, V.: Dense point-cloud representation of a scene using monocular vision. J. Electron. Imaging **24**(2), 023003 (2015)

7. Fabbri, R.: Multiview differential geometry in application to computer vision. Ph.D. dissertation. Division of Engineering, Brown University (2010)

8. Fabbri, R., Kimia, B.B., Giblin, P.J.: Camera pose estimation using first-order curve differential geometry. In: Fitzgibbon, A., Lazebnik, S., Perona, P., Sato, Y., Schmid, C. (eds.) ECCV 2012. LNCS, vol. 7575, pp. 231–244. Springer, Heidelberg (2012). doi:10.1007/978-3-642-33765-9_17

9. Fabbri, R., Kimia, B.B.: High-order differential geometry of curves for multiview reconstruction and matching. In: Rangarajan, A., Vemuri, B., Yuille, A.L. (eds.) EMMCVPR 2005. LNCS, vol. 3757, pp. 645–660. Springer, Heidelberg (2005). doi:10.1007/11585978_42

10. Fabbri, R., Kimia, B.B.: 3D curve sketch: flexible curve-based stereo reconstruction and calibration. In: CVPR (2010)

11. Fathi, H., Dai, F., Lourakis, M.: Automated as-built 3D reconstruction of civil infrastructure using computer vision. Adv. Eng. Inform. **29**, 149–161 (2015)

12. Feng, A., Shapiro, A., Ruizhe, W., Bolas, M., Medioni, G., Suma, E.: Rapid avatar capture and simulation using commodity depth sensors. In: SIGGRAPH 2014 (2014)

13. Fleming, R.W., Holtmann-Rice, D., Bülthoff, H.H.: Estimation of 3D shape from image orientations. PNAS **108**(51), 20438–20443 (2011)

14. Guo, Y., Kumar, N., Narayanan, M., Kimia, B.: A multi-stage approach to curve extraction. In: CVPR 2014 (2014)

15. Heinly, J., Schönberger, J.L., Dunn, E., Frahm, J.-M.: Reconstructing the world in six days. In: CVPR 2015 (2015)

16. Jensen, R., Dahl, A., Vogiatzis, G., Tola, E., Aanaes, H.: Large scale multi-view stereopsis evaluation. In: CVPR 2014 (2014)

17. Koenderink, J., van Doorn, A., Wagemans, J.: SFS? not likely.... i-Perception **4**(5), 299 (2013)

18. Kowdle, A., Batra, D., Chen, W.-C., Chen, T.: iModel: interactive co-segmentation for object of interest 3D modeling. In: Kutulakos, K.N. (ed.) ECCV 2010. LNCS, vol. 6554, pp. 211–224. Springer, Heidelberg (2012). doi:10.1007/978-3-642-35740-4_17

19. Kunsberg, B., Zucker, S.W.: Why shading matters along contours. In: Citti, G., Sarti, A. (eds.) Neuromathematics of Vision, pp. 107–129. Springer, Heidelberg (2014)

20. Lebeda, K., Hadfield, S., Bowden, R.: 2D or not 2D: bridging the gap between tracking and structure from motion. In: Cremers, D., Reid, I., Saito, H., Yang, M.-H. (eds.) ACCV 2014. LNCS, vol. 9006, pp. 642–658. Springer, Heidelberg (2014). doi:10.1007/978-3-319-16817-3_42

21. Litvinov, V., Yu, S., Lhuillier, M.: 2-manifold reconstruction from sparse visual features. In: IEEE IC3D 2012, pp. 1–8 (2012)

22. Mattingly, W.A., Chariker, J.H., Paris, R., Chang, D., Pani, J.R.: 3D modeling of branching structures for anatomical instruction. J. Vis. Lang. Comput. **29**, 54–62 (2015)

23. Pötsch, K., Pinz, A.: 3D geometric shape modeling by '3D contour cloud' reconstruction from stereo videos. In: Computer Vision Winter Workshop, p. 99 (2011)

24. Rao, D., Chung, S.-J., Hutchinson, S.: CurveSLAM: an approach for vision-based navigation without point features. In: IEEE/RSJ IROS, pp. 4198–4204 (2012)
25. Restrepo, M., Ulusoy, A., Mundy, J.: Evaluation of feature-based 3-D registration of probabilistic volumetric scenes. J. Photogrammetry Remote Sens. **98**, 1–18 (2014)
26. Rico Espino, J.G., Gonzalez-Barbosa, J.-J., Gómez Loenzo, R.A., Córdova Esparza, D.M., Gonzalez-Barbosa, R.: Vision system for 3D reconstruction with telecentric lens. In: Carrasco-Ochoa, J.A., Martínez-Trinidad, J.F., Olvera López, J.A., Boyer, K.L. (eds.) MCPR 2012. LNCS, vol. 7329, pp. 127–136. Springer, Heidelberg (2012). doi:10.1007/978-3-642-31149-9_13
27. Shinozuka, Y., Saito, H.: Sharing 3D object with multiple clients via networks using vision-based 3D object tracking. In: VRIC 2014, pp. 34:1–34:4 (2014)
28. Simoes, F., Almeida, M., Pinheiro, M., dos Anjos, R.: Challenges in 3D reconstruction from images for difficult large-scale objects. In: SVAR 2014, pp. 74–83 (2014)
29. Teney, D., Piater, J.: Sampling-based multiview reconstruction without correspondences for 3D edges. In: 3DIMPVT 2012, pp. 160–167 (2012)
30. Wang, R., Choi, J., Medioni, G.: 3D modeling from wide baseline range scans using contour coherence. In: CVPR 2014 (2014)
31. Zhang, L.: Line primitives and their applications in geometric computer vision. Ph.D. thesis (2013)
32. Zia, M., Stark, M., Schindler, K.: Towards scene understanding with detailed 3D object representations. IJCV **112**(2), 188–203 (2015)
33. Zucker, S.: Stereo, shading, and surfaces: curvature constraints couple neural computations. Proc. IEEE **102**(5), 812–829 (2014)
34. Agarwal, S., Snavely, N., Simon, I., Seitz, S.M., Szeliski, R.: Building Rome in a day. In: ICCV 2009 (2009)
35. Aanæs, H., Dahl, A.L., Pedersen, K.: Interesting interest points. IJCV **97**, 18–35 (2012)
36. Berthilsson, R., Åström, K., Heyden, A.: Reconstruction of general curves, using factorization and bundle adjustment. IJCV **41**(3), 171–182 (2001)
37. Cipolla, R., Giblin, P.: Visual Motion of Curves and Surfaces. Cambridge University Press, Cambridge (1999)
38. Cole, F., Sanik, K., DeCarlo, D., Finkelstein, A., Funkhouser, T., Rusinkiewicz, S., Singh, M.: How well do line drawings depict shape? In: SIGGRAPH 2009 (2009)
39. Taubin, G., Crispell, D., Lanman, D., Sibley, P., Zhao, Y.: Shape from depth discontinuities. In: Nielsen, F. (ed.) ETVC 2008. LNCS, vol. 5416, pp. 216–237. Springer, Heidelberg (2009). doi:10.1007/978-3-642-00826-9_9
40. Furukawa, Y., Ponce, J.: Accurate, dense, and robust multi-view stereopsis. In: CVPR 2007 (2007)
41. Goesele, M., Snavely, N., Curless, B., Hoppe, H., Seitz, S.: Multi-view stereo for community photo collections. In: ICCV 2007 (2007)
42. Habbecke, M., Kobbelt, L.: A surface-growing approach to multi-view stereo reconstruction. In: CVPR 2007 (2007)
43. Esteban, C.H., Schmitt, F.: Silhouette and stereo fusion for 3D object modeling. CVIU **96**(3), 367–392 (2004)
44. Leggitt, J.: Drawing Shortcuts: Developing Quick Drawing Skills Using Today's Technology. Wiley, New York (2015)
45. Liu, S., Kang, K., Tarel, J.-P., Cooper, D.B.: Freeform object reconstruction from silhouettes, occluding edges and texture edges. PAMI **30**, 131–146 (2007)
46. Moreels, P., Perona, P.: Evaluation of features detectors and descriptors based on 3D objects. IJCV **73**(3), 263–284 (2007)

47. Pollefeys, M., Gool, L.V., Vergauwen, M., Verbiest, F., Cornelis, K., Tops, J., Koch, R.: Visual modeling with a hand-held camera. IJCV **59**(3), 207–232 (2004)
48. Seitz, S., Curless, B., Diebel, J., Scharstein, D., Szeliski, R.: A comparison and evaluation of multi-view stereo reconstruction algorithms. In: CVPR 2006 (2006)
49. Tamrakar, A., Kimia, B.B.: No grouping left behind: from edges to curve fragments. In: ICCV 2007 (2007)
50. Yee, R.: Architectural Drawing: A Visual Compendium of Types and Methods. Wiley, New York (2012)

Shape from Selfies: Human Body Shape Estimation Using CCA Regression Forests

Endri Dibra[1]([⊠]), Cengiz Öztireli[1], Remo Ziegler[2], and Markus Gross[1]

[1] Department of Computer Science, ETH Zürich, Zürich, Switzerland
{edibra,cengizo,grossm}@inf.ethz.ch
[2] Vizrt, Zürich, Switzerland
rziegler@vizrt.com

Abstract. In this work, we revise the problem of human body shape estimation from monocular imagery. Starting from a statistical human shape model that describes a body shape with shape parameters, we describe a novel approach to automatically estimate these parameters from a single input shape silhouette using semi-supervised learning. By utilizing silhouette features that encode local and global properties robust to noise, pose and view changes, and projecting them to lower dimensional spaces obtained through multi-view learning with canonical correlation analysis, we show how regression forests can be used to compute an accurate mapping from the silhouette to the shape parameter space. This results in a very fast, robust and automatic system under mild self-occlusion assumptions. We extensively evaluate our method on thousands of synthetic and real data and compare it to the state-of-art approaches that operate under more restrictive assumptions.

1 Introduction

Estimating human body shape from imagery is an important problem in computer vision with diverse applications. The estimated body shape provides an accurate proxy geometry for further tasks such as rendering free viewpoint videos [10,48,49,53], surveillance [11], tracking [16], biometric authentication, medical and personal measurements, virtual cloth fitting [17,36,40,51], and artistic image reshaping [56]. Pose estimation is also tightly coupled with shape estimation. Knowing the body shape significantly reduces the complexity and improves the robustness of pose estimation algorithms and thus expands the space of poses that can be reliably estimated [2,55].

However, in contrast to pose estimation, body shape estimation has received substantially less attention from the community. Most existing algorithms rely on either manual input [25,40,56], restrictive assumptions on the acquired images [6],

Electronic supplementary material The online version of this chapter (doi:10.1007/978-3-319-46493-0_6) contains supplementary material, which is available to authorized users.

B. Leibe et al. (Eds.): ECCV 2016, Part IV, LNCS 9908, pp. 88–104, 2016.
DOI: 10.1007/978-3-319-46493-0_6

or require information other than just 2D images (e.g. depth) [23,37,50]. Furthermore, some of the methods have prohibitive complexity for real-time applications [6,25,50]. For practical applications, it is essential to have an automatic and fast algorithm that can work with images acquired under less restrictive conditions and body poses.

In this paper, we propose a fast and automatic method for estimating the 3D body shape of a person from images, utilizing *multi-view* semi-supervised learning. Our method relies on extracting novel features from a given silhouette of a single person under minimal self-occlusion like in a selfie, and a parametric human body shape model [3]. The latter is utilized to generate meshes spanning a spectrum of human body shapes, from which silhouettes are computed over multiple views, in poses compliant with the target applications for training. We firstly estimate viewing direction with high accuracy, by solving a classification task. Utilizing the information simultaneously captured in multiple synthetic views of the same body mesh, we apply Canonical Correlation Analysis (CCA) [24] to learn informative bases where the extracted features can be projected. A random forest regressor is then adopted to learn a mapping from projected feature space to parameter space. This results in lower feature dimensionality, reducing the training and test time drastically, and improves prediction as compared to plain regression forests. We demonstrate our results on real people and in a free-view-point video (supplementary [1]), and comprehensively evaluate our method by validating it on thousands of body shapes.

Contributions. In summary, the contributions of the paper are: (1) a fast and automatic system for shape estimation from monocular silhouette/s under no fixed pose and known camera assumptions, thanks to novel features that capture robust global and local information simultaneously, (2) demonstration of how CCA multi-view learning with regression forests can be applied to the task of shape estimation, leveraging synthetic data and improving prediction over random forests with raw data, (3) extensive validation on thousands of body shapes via thorough comparisons to state-of-the-art on a new bigger dataset.

2   Related Work

General methods for shape estimation. Estimating 3D geometry of body shapes from limited imagery is an inherently ill-posed problem. Early methods used simplifying assumptions such as the visual hull [30] or simple body models with geometric primitives [15,27,34]. Although these work well for coarse pose and shape approximations, an accurate shape estimation cannot be obtained.

Human body shape statistical priors. Instead of assuming general geometry, human body shape model based methods rely on the limited degrees of freedom for the possible body shapes. These parametric models are typically constructed from collected 3D scans of people [3,22,39]. Utilizing such a prior allows us to always stay within the space of realistic body shapes, and reduces the problem to estimating the parameters of the model. Such models can also be combined with articulation models to simultaneously represent pose as joint angles or transformations, and shape with parameters [3,22,35]. In this paper, we combine state-of-the-art 3D body shape databases [38,54] containing thousands of meshes, and utilize a deformation model based on SCAPE [3].

Fitting body shapes by silhouette matching. Once a statistical model of 3D shapes is defined, an error metric between the input silhouettes and those of the projections of the parameterized 3D body shape can be minimized [4,9,11,18,21,25,56]. Although this leads to accurate matching, despite promising results on deformable 2D shape matching [42,43], establishing correspondences between the input and output silhouettes is a very challenging problem especially when the body pose is not known or self occlusions are present. The simultaneous estimation of pose and shape is currently addressed by manual interaction to establish and refine matching or pose estimation [11,25,56], and under certain assumptions on the error metric, camera calibration, and views [9,18,25]. A recent work [29] aims at automatically finding a correspondence between 2D and 3D deformable objects by casting it as an energy minimization problem, demonstrating good results however for a shape retrieval task. Instead of fitting silhouettes directly and locally, we consider a global mapping from silhouettes to shape parameters that is invariant to various poses under mild self-occlusion assumptions. This allows us to sidestep pose estimation, avoid any manual interaction, and estimate the shape parameters for imperfect silhouettes interactively, all of which are essential components for a practical shape estimation system.

Fitting body shapes by statistical models. A recent body of works rely on global mappings between silhouettes and 3D body shapes [6,12–14,46,52]. These methods rely on a statistical model for body shapes as well as silhouettes. In this case, the problem reduces to estimating this mapping by various linear [52], or more complex techniques such as the shared Gaussian process latent variable model [12]. In order to generate robust and accurate shapes, these techniques typically require pre-defined and accurate poses [6,12,52], and have been validated with limited measurements except for the recent work of Boisvert et al. [6]. The running times can also be prohibitive for real-time applications [6,13]. We also define a mapping from the silhouette to a statistical shape space. However, we aim at robustness to pose changes and silhouette noise via computing specialized features, projecting them at correlated spaces and training a regressor with random forests. This allows close to real-time performance, unlocking further applications. We further present an extensive evaluation of our shape estimation with thousands of test cases and tens of body measurements.

Multi-view learning. Canonical Correlation Analysis (CCA) [24] and Kernel-CCA [20] are statistical learning techniques that find maximally correlated linear and non-linear projections of two random vectors. The projected spaces learn representations of two data views such that each view's predictive ability is mutually maximized. Hence, information present in either view that is uncorrelated with the other view is automatically removed in the projected space. That is a helpful property in predictive tasks. The aforementioned methods have been used for unsupervised data analysis with multiple views [19], fusing learned features for better prediction [41], reducing sample complexity using unlabeled data [26], or when multiple views are hallucinated from one single view [33]. A generalized version of CCA [45] has also been proposed but for a classification and retrieval task. Despite its power, CCA in combination with regression has found little usage since its proposal [26]. It has only been empirically evaluated for linear regression [33], and utilized for an action recognition classification task [28]. To the best of our knowledge, we are the first to apply CCA in a non-linear regression task for shape estimation, illustrating its power for such non-linear problems.

3   Shape Estimation Algorithm

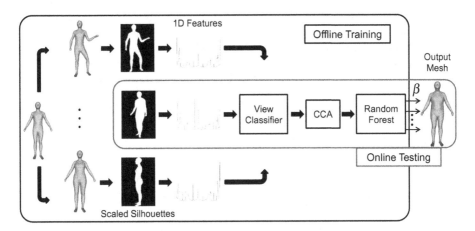

Fig. 1. Overview of our system. **Training:** Silhouettes from 36 views are extracted from meshes generated in various shapes and poses (Sect. 3.2). A View Classifier is learned (Sect. 3.4) from extracted silhouette features (Sect. 3.3). View specific Regression Forests are then trained to estimate shape parameters by first projecting features in CCA correlated spaces (Sect. 3.5). **Testing:** The extracted features from an input silhouette are used to first infer the camera view, and then the shape parameters by projecting them into CCA spaces and feeding them into the corresponding Regression Forest.

3.1   Method Overview

The goal of our system is to infer the 3D body shape of a person from a single or multiple monocular images fast and automatically. Specifically, we would like to estimate the parameters of a 3D body shape model (Sect. 3.2) such that the corresponding body shape best approximates the 3D body of the subject depicted in the input images. Despite the ambiguity that the 2D silhouette withholds, the projection of the transformed mesh in the image should at least best explain it.

An overview of our system is depicted in Fig. 1. The input to the shape estimation algorithm is a 2D silhouette of the desired individual under minimal self-occlusion (e.g. a selfie), which can be computed accurately for our target scenarios, by learning a background model through Gaussian mixture models and using Graphcuts [7]. The word "selfie" here is used interchangingly to describe the activity of taking a selfie in front of a mirror, and also as a label for poses representing mild self-occlusion (Fig. 2). We then compute features extracted from the silhouettes (Sect. 3.3). These are first used to train a classifier on the camera viewing direction (Sect. 3.4). The features from silhouettes of a particular view are then projected into bases obtained by CCA, such that the view itself and the most orthogonal one to it (e.g. front and side) are used to capture complementary information into the CCA correlated space, and fed to a Random Forest Regressor (Sect. 3.5) trained for each camera view. At test time, the extracted features from an input silhouette are used to first infer the camera view, and then the shape parameters by projecting them into CCA spaces and feeding them into the corresponding Regression Forest. The parameters are used to generate a mesh by solving a least-squares system on the vertex positions (Sect. 3.2). The generated mesh can then be utilized for various post-processing tasks such as human semantic parameter estimation, free view-point video with projective texturing, further shape refinement [6,56], or pose refinement [25].

3.2   Shape as a Geometric Model

We utilize the SCAPE model [3], which is a low-dimensional parametric model learned from 3D range scans of different people in different poses that captures correlated deformations due to shape and pose changes simultaneously. Specifically, SCAPE is defined as a set of triangle deformations applied to a reference template 3D mesh. Estimating a new shape requires estimating parameters α and β, which determine the deformations due to pose and intrinsic body shape, respectively. Given these parameters, each of the two edges $\mathbf{e}_{i1}$ and $\mathbf{e}_{i2}$ of the ith triangle of the template mesh (defined as the difference vectors between the vertices of the triangle), is deformed according to the following expression

$$\mathbf{e}'_{ij} = \mathbf{R}_i(\alpha)\mathbf{S}_i(\beta)\mathbf{Q}_i(\mathbf{R}_i(\alpha))\mathbf{e}_{ij}, \qquad (1)$$

with $j \in \{1, 2\}$. The matrices $\mathbf{R}_i(\alpha)$ correspond to joint rotations, and $\mathbf{Q}_i(\mathbf{R}_i(\alpha))$ to the pose induced non-rigid deformations, e.g. muscle bulging. $\mathbf{S}_i(\beta)$ are matrices modeling shape variation as a function of the shape parameters β. The body shape deformation space is learned by applying PCA to a set of meshes of different people in full correspondence and same pose, with transformations written as $\mathbf{s}(\beta) = \mathbf{U}\beta + \mu$, where $\mathbf{s}(\beta)$ is obtained by stacking all transformations $\mathbf{S}_i(\beta)$ for all triangles, $\mathbf{U}$ is a matrix with orthonormal columns, and μ is the mean of the triangle transformations over all meshes (please refer to Anguelov et al. [3] for further details). We therefore obtain the model by computing per-triangle deformations for each mesh of the dataset from a template mesh, which is the mean of all the meshes in the dataset (Fig. 2 left), and then applying PCA in

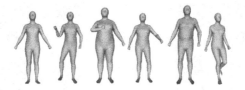

Fig. 2. 6 meshes from our database. The leftmost one is the mean mesh in the rest pose. The others are from different people in various poses.

order to extract the components capturing largest deformation variations. We chose to use 20 components ($\beta \in R^{20}$).

We would like to estimate the shape parameters β regardless of the pose. We take the common assumption that the body shape does not significantly change due to the range of poses we consider. Hence, we ignore pose dependent shape changes given by $\mathbf{Q}_i(\mathbf{R}(\alpha))$. Decoupling pose and shape changes allows us to adopt a fast and efficient method from the graphics community known as Linear Blend Skinning (LBS) [31] for pose changes, similar to previous works [25,38]. Starting from a rest pose shape with vertices $\mathbf{v}_1, ..., \mathbf{v}_n \in \mathbf{R}^4$ in homogenous coordinates, LBS computes the new position of each vertex by a weighted combination of the bone transformation matrices $\mathbf{T}_1, ..., \mathbf{T}_m$ in a skeleton controlling the mesh, and skinning weights $w_{i,1}, ..., w_{i,m} \in \mathbf{R}$ for each vertex $\mathbf{v}_i$, as given by the following formula:

$$\mathbf{v}_i^{'} = \sum_{j=1}^{m} w_{i,j} \mathbf{T}_j \mathbf{v}_i = \left(\sum_{j=1}^{m} w_{i,j} \mathbf{T}_j \right) \mathbf{v}_i \qquad (2)$$

In our model, the skinning weights are computed for a skeleton of 17 body parts (1 for the head, 2 for the torso, 2 for the hips and 3 for each of the lower and upper limbs) for the mean shape mesh using the heat diffusion method [5]. It has to be noted that $w_{i,j} \geq 0$ and $w_{i,1} + \cdots + w_{i,m} = 1$.

3.3 Feature Extraction

We extract novel features from the scaled silhouettes as the input to our learning method. These features are designed to capture local and global information on the silhouette shape, and be robust to pose and slight view changes. For each point in the silhouette, two feature values are calculated, namely the *(weighted) normal depth* and the *curvature*. In order to extract these, we first compute the 2D point normal for every point in the silhouette, and then smooth all normals with a circle filter of radius of 7 pixels. As different people have different silhouette lengths, we sample 1704 equidistant points from each silhouette starting from the topmost pixel of the silhouette. The sample size is set according to the smallest silhouette length over all our training data. Our feature vector per silhouette then consists of 3408 real valued numbers.

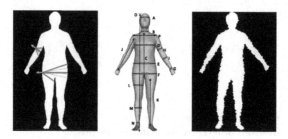

Fig. 3. (left) Normal depth computation in 2 different points. The arrows are the silhouette normals. The normal depth is computed as the weighted mean of the lengths of the red lines. (middle) 3D measurements on the meshes used for validation. (right) Noisy silhouette. (Colour figure online)

The normal depth is computed as follows. For any point from the sampled set, we send several rays starting from the point itself and oriented along the opposite direction of its normal, until they intersect the inner silhouette boundary. The lengths of the ray segments are defined as the normal depths as illustrated in Fig. 3 (left). The normals are represented in green and the ray segments in red for two different points in the silhouette. We allow an angle deviation of 50° from the silhouette normal axis. The feature for a point is defined as the weighted average of all normal depths falling within one std. dev. from the median of all the depths, with weights defined as the inverse of the angle between the rays and the normal axis.

The *normal depth* is a feature inspired by 3D geodesic shape descriptors [44,47], and different from the *Inner-Distance* 2D descriptor [32] used for classification of different object types while being noise sensitive, and the spectral features utilized in [29] for a shape retrieval task. The main ideas behind our feature are (a) for the same individual in different poses, under mild self-occlusions, the features look very similar with small local shifts, (b) each point feature serves as a robust body measurement, correlated with the breadth of the person in various parts of the body, which is analogous to estimating body circumference at each vertex of the real body mesh, and (c) the feature is robust to silhouette noise due to the median and averaging steps. The measure might differ though in some parts of the silhouette (e.g. elbow) for the same person in different poses. In order to alleviate this limitation, we apply smoothing on small neighborhoods of the silhouette. The *curvature* on the other hand is estimated as the local variance of the normals. Despite being a local feature, it provides a measure of roundness, especially around the hips, waist, belly and chest, which helps in discriminating between various shapes.

We illustrate that the combination of normal depth that captures global information on the silhouette and curvature encoding local details leads to estimators robust to limited self-occlusions, and discriminative enough to describe the silhouette and reconstruct the corresponding shape in Sect. 4.

3.4   View Direction Classification

To increase robustness with respect to view changes, we decided to train view-specific Regression Forests for 36 viewing directions around the body. In order to discriminate between the views, we train a Random Forest Classifier utilizing the 3408 features extracted (Sect. 3.3) from 100,000 silhouettes of people in multiple poses, shapes and views, having as labels the views numbered 1 to 36. We achieve a high accuracy of 99 % if we train and test on neutral and selfie-like poses. The accuracy decreases to 85.7 % if more involved poses (e.g. walking, running etc.) are added. However, by investigating class prediction probabilities, we observed that false positives are assigned only to the views that are contiguous to the view with the correct label. As it will be shown in Sect. 4, Table 2, a 10° view difference has a low reconstruction error when the features are projected into CCA bases.

3.5   Learning Shape Parameters

We pose shape parameter estimation as a regression task. Given the silhouette features, using supervised learning, we would like to estimate the shape parameters such that the reconstructed shape best explains the silhouette. To make the features more discriminative, we propose to correlate features extracted from silhouettes viewed from different directions. More specifically, we apply Canonical Correlation Analysis (CCA) [24] over features extracted from a pair of silhouettes from two camera views.

At training time, the views are selected such that they capture complementary information. While the first one is the desired view from which we want to estimate the shape (one of 36 views), the second one is chosen to be as orthogonal as possible to the first, e.g. (front and side view). Because the human body is symmetric, a complementary view to a desired one is always searched in the zero to 90° angle range to that view. In practice, we round the complementary view to the closest extreme (i.e. front or side view) to ease the offline computations.

We first apply PCA to reduce the dimensionality of the extracted features from 3408 to 300 in each view. Then, we stack the PCA projected features for all mesh silhouettes from the first and second views into the columns of the matrices $\mathbf{X}_1$ and $\mathbf{X}_2$, respectively. Then, CCA attempts to find basis vector pairs $\mathbf{b}_1$ and $\mathbf{b}_2$, such that the correlations between the projections of the variables onto these vectors are mutually maximized by solving:

$$\underset{\mathbf{b}_1,\mathbf{b}_2 \in R^N}{\arg \max}\; corr(\mathbf{b}_1^T \mathbf{X}_1, \mathbf{b}_2^T \mathbf{X}_2), \tag{3}$$

where $N = 300$. This results in a coordinate free mutual basis unaffected by rotation, translation or global scaling of the features. The features projected onto this basis thus capture mutual information coming from both views. The subsequent basis vector pairs are computed similarly, with the assumption that the new projected features are orthogonal to the existing projected ones. We use 200 basis pairs with CCA projections covering 99 % of the energy.

The final training is done on the 200 projected features extracted from one view, which is one of the 36 views we consider. These projected features are input to a Random Forest Regressor [8] of 4 trees and a maximum depth of 20. The labels for this regressor are the 20-dimensional shape parameter vectors β. Each component of β is weighted with weights set to the eigenvalues of the covariance matrix defined in Sect. 3.2 in the computation of the shape deformation space, and normalized to 1, to emphasize the large scale changes in 3D body shapes. At test time, the raw features extracted from a single given silhouette are first classified into a view. These are then projected with the obtained PCA and CCA matrices for that view to obtain a 200 dimensional vector. The projected features are finally fed into the corresponding Random Forest Regressor, in order to obtain the desired shape parameters β.

4   Validation and Results

Previous shape-from-silhouette methods lack extensive evaluation. Xi et al. [52] demonstrate results on two real images of people and 24 subjects in synthetic settings, Sigal et al. [46] validate on two measurements and two subjects in monocular settings, and Balan et al. [4] report silhouette errors for a few individuals in a sequence and height measurement for a single individual. To the best of our knowledge, only Boisvert et al. [6] perform a more extensive validation, for 220 synthetic humans consisting of scans from the CAESAR database [39], and four real individuals' front and side images. We present the largest validation experiment with 1500 synthetic body meshes as well as real individuals.

Data Generation. In order to learn a general model, we merge two large datasets [38,54] consisting of 3D models extracted from the commercially available CAESAR dataset[1]. We select 2900 meshes from the combined dataset for learning the shape model, leaving out around 1500 meshes for testing and experiments. In order to synthesize more training meshes, we sample from the 20 dimensional multivariate normal distribution spanned by the PCA space (Sect. 3.2), such that for a random sample $\beta = [\beta_1, \beta_2, ..., \beta_{20}]$, it holds that $\beta \sim \mathcal{N}(\mu, \Sigma)$ with μ being the 20-dimensional mean vector and Σ the 20×20 covariance matrix of the parameters. To synthesize meshes in different poses, we gather a set of animations comprising of various poses (e.g. selfie, walking, running, etc.). After transferring a generated pose to the template mesh using LBS, we compute the resulting per-triangle deformations $\mathbf{R}_i$. For a given mesh with parameters β, the final pose is then given by $\mathbf{e}'_{ij} = \mathbf{R}_i \mathbf{S}_i(\beta) \mathbf{e}_{ij}$, where $\mathbf{e}_{ij}$ are the edges of the template mesh (Sect. 3.2).

As the training set, we randomly generate 100000 samples from the multivariate distribution over the β parameters, and restrict them to fall into the $\pm 3 \times Std.Dev$ range for each dimension of the PCA projected parameters to avoid getting unrealistic human shapes. We project the generated meshes in each of the 36 camera viewpoints around the mesh (Sect. 3.4). The silhouette is

---

[1] http://store.sae.org/caesar/.

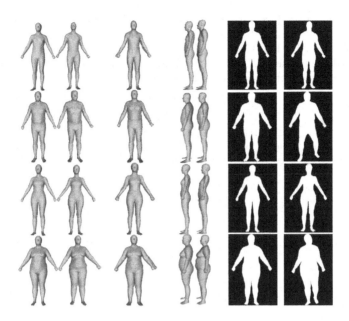

Fig. 4. Visual results for predictions on 4 test meshes. From left to right: predicted mesh, ground truth mesh, the two meshes frontally overlapping, the two meshes from the side view, silhouette from the predicted mesh, input silhouette.

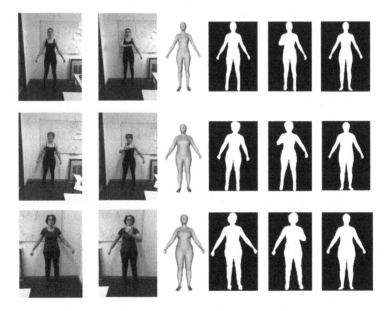

Fig. 5. Visual results for predictions on 3 females. From left to right: the two input images in a rest and selfie pose, the estimated mesh - same estimation is obtained for both poses, the two silhouettes from which features are extracted for each pose, the silhouette of the estimated mesh.

Table 1. Comparisons to state-of-the-art methods, variations of our method (*RF*, *CCA-RF-1*, *CCA-RF-2*) and ground truth, via various measurements. The measurements are illustrated in Fig. 3 (middle). Errors are represented as Mean ± Std. Dev and are expressed in millimeters. Note that we operate under a significantly more general setting than the state-of-the-art methods, please refer to the text.

Measurement	[6]	[13]	[52]	RF	CCA-RF-1	CCA-RF-2	GT
A. Head circumference	10 ± 12	23 ± 27	50 ± 60	16 ± 13	13 ± 10	**8 ± 8**	13 ± 9
B. Neck circumference	11 ± 13	27 ± 34	59 ± 72	13 ± 10	10 ± 8	**7 ± 7**	6 ± 6
C. Shoulder-blade/crotch length	4 ± 5	52 ± 65	119 ± 150	22 ± 18	18 ± 9	**18 ± 17**	14 ± 11
D. Chest circumference	10 ± 12	18 ± 22	36 ± 45	38 ± 31	30 ± 24	**25 ± 24**	24 ± 24
E. Waist circumference	22 ± 23	37 ± 39	55 ± 62	35 ± 28	29 ± 25	**24 ± 24**	16 ± 14
F. Pelvis circumference	11 ± 12	15 ± 19	23 ± 28	33 ± 26	30 ± 25	**26 ± 25**	14 ± 12
G. Wrist circumference	9 ± 12	24 ± 30	56 ± 70	10 ± 8	6 ± 5	**5 ± 5**	5 ± 5
H. Bicep circumference	17 ± 22	59 ± 76	146 ± 177	16 ± 13	13 ± 11	**11 ± 11**	9 ± 10
I. Forearm circumference	16 ± 20	76 ± 100	182 ± 230	14 ± 11	11 ± 9	**9 ± 8**	8 ± 8
J. Arm length	15 ± 21	53 ± 73	109 ± 141	19 ± 14	15 ± 12	**13 ± 12**	8 ± 8
K. Inside leg length	6 ± 7	9 ± 12	19 ± 24	26 ± 19	23 ± 18	**20 ± 19**	9 ± 9
L. Thigh circumference	9 ± 12	19 ± 25	35 ± 44	22 ± 18	19 ± 16	**18 ± 17**	11 ± 11
M. Calf circumference	6 ± 7	16 ± 21	33 ± 42	18 ± 13	14 ± 12	**12 ± 12**	7 ± 8
N. Ankle circumference	14 ± 16	28 ± 35	61 ± 78	10 ± 7	18 ± 6	**6 ± 6**	5 ± 5
O. Overall height	9 ± 12	21 ± 27	49 ± 62	60 ± 45	50 ± 42	**43 ± 41**	14 ± 11
P. Shoulder breadth	6 ± 7	12 ± 15	24 ± 31	15 ± 14	13 ± 6	**6 ± 6**	12 ± 11

computed by projecting all the mesh edges for which two coinciding triangles have normals pointing in opposite directions. The silhouettes are then uniformly scaled such that the height of the bounding box is equal to 528 pixels, and the width to 384 pixels. For testing, we evaluate our method with the meshes left out from the training dataset, as well as on real images.

Quantitative Experiments. We distinguish two test datasets, D1 and D2. D1 consists of 1500 meshes neither used to learn the parametric shape model nor to train the regression forests (RF) and D2 of 1000 meshes used to learn the parametric model but not to train the RF. These meshes consist of 50 % males and 50 % females, and are in roughly the same rest pose. In order to properly quantify our method, similar to Boisvert et al. [6], we perform 16 three-dimensional measurements on the meshes, which are commonly used in garment fitting as illustrated in Fig. 3 (middle). For the measurements represented with straight lines, we compute the Euclidean distance between the two extreme vertices. The ellipses represent circumferences and are measured on the body surface. For each of the 16 measurements, we compute the difference between the one from the ground truth mesh and the estimated mesh. We report the mean error and the standard deviation for each of the measurements in Table 1. We name our main method *CCA-RF*, with CCA applied to the features before passing them to the random forest, specifically *CCA-RF-1* and *CCA-RF-2* respectively tested on D1 and D2. Similarly, *RF*, for the method trained on raw features and tested on D1. The last table column provides the ground truth (GT) mean errors for D1, computed between the original test meshes and their reconstructions obtained by projecting them into the learned PCA space. This provides a lower limit for the obtainable errors with our 20 parameters shape model.

Before analyzing the results, it is crucial to highlight the differences between the settings and goals of the methods we compare to. Boisvert et al. [6] employ a setting where the pose is fixed to a rest pose and the distance from the camera is also fixed. The shape estimation method is based on utilizing silhouettes from two different views (front and side), with the application of garment fitting in mind. The same setting is considered for the other two methods mentioned above [13,52]. In contrast, we train and test for a more general setting, where we have a single silhouette as the input at test time, the pose can change, and no assumptions on the distance from the camera are made. Furthermore, our tests involve a significantly larger dataset with high variations.

Even though our method operates under a significantly more general setting than the previous works [6,13,52], with a single silhouette input and no distance information, it outperforms the non-linear and linear mapping methods. The mean absolute error for all the models is 19.4 mm for *CCA-RF-1* and 16.18 mm for *CCA-RF-2*. The errors are very close to those of GT, illustrating the accuracy of our technique. Note that some errors for *CCA-RF-2* are smaller than those of the GT, due to the different training as explained above. The higher error for D1 is due to the body shapes that cannot be represented with the parametric model learned from the rest of the shapes. The error is higher for the overall height, due to the fixed scale in the training and testing silhouettes that we use. It is important to note the differences in errors between the *RF* and *CCA-RF-1*. There is an overall decrease of error when CCA is utilized, which shows that the projection with the CCA bases significantly improves prediction. Additionally, we evaluate the performance of our method when the input comes from a less favorable view, the side view, achieving an error of 22.45 mm which is very close to the one from only the frontal view. For completeness, we compare also to Helten et al. [23], who utilize an RGB-D camera for capturing the body shapes, and a full RMSE map per vertex to measure the differences. Using two depth maps, fitting to the pose and testing only on 6 individuals they report a mean error of 10.1 mm while we have a mean error of 19.19 mm on 1500 meshes.

Poses, Views and Noise. We investigated accuracy in the presence of silhouette noise, various poses, and different or multiple views. We run the experiments with the data setup D1, explained above. For each experiment, we show the mean and standard deviation either of the accuracy gain or of the errors over all the body measurements in Table 2.

The first three columns show the *accuracy gain* of applying *CCA-RF* to the front view (F), side view (S) or when concatenating both views together (FS), as compared to *RF*. A larger gain is obtained in the side view as compared to the front view, due to additional information that is injected from the frontal view (the most representative one) in the projected space. An even bigger gain is obtained if both views are utilized for training and testing. This is very important, as it shows that having potentially more views improves the predictor. In fact, we have observed that utilizing the same amount (100000) of training

Table 2. Columns 1–3 show accuracy gain of applying CCA for the Frontal, Side and Frontal Side view altogether, over raw features. (VE) shows the error due to 10° view change and (VG), the gain of applying CCA. (N) is the error due to silhouette noise. (P12) shows the error of testing on 12 poses different from the training one, and the rest (Columns 8–11) demonstrate the errors while gradually adding more difficult poses from the training ones. Mean and Std. Deviation is computed over all the body measurements.

Measurement	(F)	(S)	(FS)	(VE)	(VG)	(N)	(P12)	(P1)	(W)	(R)	(PWR)
Mean (mm)	4.9	5.2	6.6	2.2	1.8	2.3	9.3	1.7	1.6	3.9	8.5
Std. Deviation (mm)	2.4	2.6	4.0	1.9	1.5	1.8	5.6	1.0	1.0	2.3	5.2

data, and training and testing on two views with the raw features, degrades the result as compared to just one view. This is alleviated with the CCA projection, improving the results as singular view noise in the data is removed.

The fourth column (VE), displays the *errors* obtained by testing on features extracted from a view 10° rotated from the frontal view, for a *CCA-RF* trained on the frontal view. The column for (VG) displays the *gain* of *CCA-RF* over *RF* for the same scenario. The CCA-RF is again more accurate, however the error for both is generally low, implying that a classification error of the camera view of 10° can be allowed in our system. (N) demonstrates the *error* due to random noise added to the silhouettes, as in Fig. 3 (right), showing robustness to noise to a certain extent. (P12) shows the *error* induced by training only on a rest pose, and testing on 12 different poses as in Fig. 2, as compared to testing on the same meshes in a rest pose, and (P1) describes the same measurement, however by training on 12 poses and testing on a different unseen one, demonstrating robustness to pose changes under minimal self occlusions. The last three columns demonstrate similar measurements, however, by increasing the articulations in the poses, with (W) consisting of poses from a walking sequence, (R) from a running sequence (supplementary [1]), and (PWR) combining all poses we have. The error increases in the latter case especially due to the introduction of poses with more self occlusions. However, when trained on individual sequences, the errors are lower, implying that for an application where a certain activity is known, one could adapt specialized regressors, especially due to the very fast training in the low dimensional spaces.

Algorithm Speed. The method is significantly faster than previous works, allowing for interactive applications. The method of Boisvert et al. [6] needs 6 s for body shape regression, 30 s for the MAP estimation, and 3 min for the silhouette based similarity optimization, with 6 s for their implementation of sGPLVM [13] (on an Intel Core i7 CPU 3 GHz and single-threaded implementation). We, on the other hand, reach 0.3 s using a single threaded implementation on an Intel Core i7 CPU 3.4 GHz (0.045 s for feature computation, 0.25 s for mesh computation, and 0.005 s for random forest regression), with even more speed-up opportunities as the feature computation and mesh vertices computation can be highly parallelized.

Qualitative Results. In Fig. 4, we show example samples from our tests. In each row, first the predicted mesh is shown along with the ground truth test mesh. Then, their overlap is illustrated. This is followed by the side views, and the silhouette of the estimated mesh and the input silhouette. Note that the input silhouettes are in different poses, but we show the estimated meshes in rest poses for easy comparisons. Our results are visually very close to the ground truth shapes even under such pose changes.

Finally, we show an experiment where real pictures of three females are taken in a rest and a selfie-like pose along with the estimated meshes in Fig. 5. It is important to note that despite the pose change, the retrieved mesh for each person is the same. Another important observation is that even though the input is scaled to the same size, the estimated parameters yield statistically plausible heights, which turned out to be sufficient in obtaining an ordering based on relative height between the estimated meshes. We believe that this is due to the statistical shape model, where semantic parameters like height and weight are correlated in the PCA parameter space. To the best of our knowledge, no previous work can resolve this task. For example, in the work by Sigal et al. [46], the mesh needs to be scaled if no camera calibration is provided.

5   Discussion and Conclusions

In this paper, we presented a novel technique that estimates 3D human body shape from a single silhouette. It allows different views, poses with mild occlusions, and various body shapes to be estimated. We extensively evaluated our technique on thousands of human bodies, by utilizing one of the biggest databases available to the community.

In the scope of this paper, we focused on shape extraction from a single silhouette because of its various applications such as selfies or utilizing limited video footage. However, this is an inherently ill-posed problem. Further views can be incorporated to obtain more accurate reconstructions, similar to methods we compare to. This would lead to a better estimation especially in the areas around the belly and chest, hence decrease the elliptical body measurement errors.

The accuracy of our method is tied to silhouette extraction. For the difficult cases of dynamic backgrounds or very loose clothes, the large scale silhouette deformations would skew our results. This could be tackled by fusing results over multiple frames. Unlike [13] though, our results always remain in the space of plausible human bodies. For small scale deformations (Fig. 3 right), we show in Table 2 (N) that our results stay robust.

We assume that the silhouettes come in poses with limited partial occlusion. Under this assumption, we showed robustness, the same mesh estimation is achieved from different poses (e.g. Fig. 5). However, under more pronounced occlusions, our results start degrading (Table 2 (PWR)), which could be alleviated by increasing the number of training poses and utilizing deeper learning.

Although we aimed at precise measurements for the evaluation, errors due to discretization are inevitable, hence a standardized procedure on a standard mesh dataset is needed as a benchmark. We believe that this work along with that of Boisvert et al. [6] has set an important step towards this direction.

Since our system is designed for a general setting, we apply a fixed scale to the silhouette, losing height information. We showed a fairly good performance on estimating the relative height and demonstrate better absolute height estimation, if camera calibration is incorporated (supplementary [1]).

Our fast system, running in minutes for training and milliseconds for execution in single core CPU's, while being memory lightweight due to the low feature dimensionality, could be integrated into smart phones, allowing body shapes to be reconstructed with one click of a button. Simultaneously, it can be used for 3D sport analysis, where estimation of a 3D shape of a player seen from a sparse set of cameras can improve projections of novel-views.

Finally, we showed how CCA, which captures relations in an unsupervised linear way, can be used to correlate different views in the data to improve the prediction power and speed of the algorithm. We believe that capturing non-linear relations with Kernel CCA's or deep architectures should lead to even better results. Our method illustrates the utility of CCA for other vision applications where two or more views describing the same object or event exists, such as multi-view pose estimation, video-to-text matching, or shape from various sources of information.

Acknowledgement. This work was funded by the KTI-grant 15599.1.

References

1. https://cgl.ethz.ch/publications/papers/paperDib16a.php
2. de Aguiar, E., Stoll, C., Theobalt, C., Ahmed, N., Seidel, H.P., Thrun, S.: Performance capture from sparse multi-view video. In: SIGGRAPH (2008)
3. Anguelov, D., Srinivasan, P., Koller, D., Thrun, S., Rodgers, J., Davis, J.: Scape: Shape completion and animation of people. In: SIGGRAPH (2005)
4. Balan, A.O., Sigal, L., Black, M.J., Davis, J.E., Haussecker, H.W.: Detailed human shape and pose from images. In: CVPR (2007)
5. Baran, I., Popovic, J.: Automatic rigging and animation of 3d characters. ACM Trans. Graph. **26**, 1–8 (2007)
6. Boisvert, J., Shu, C., Wuhrer, S., Xi, P.: Three-dimensional human shape inference from silhouettes: reconstruction and validation. Mach. Vis. Appl. **24**, 145–157 (2013)
7. Boykov, Y., Jolly, M.: Interactive graph cuts for optimal boundary and region segmentation of objects in N-D images. In: ICCV (2001)
8. Breiman, L.: Random forests. Mach. Learn. **26**, 123–140 (2001)
9. Bălan, A.O., Black, M.J.: The naked truth: estimating body shape under clothing. In: Forsyth, D., Torr, P., Zisserman, A. (eds.) ECCV 2008. LNCS, vol. 5303, pp. 15–29. Springer, Heidelberg (2008). doi:10.1007/978-3-540-88688-4_2
10. Casas, D., Volino, M., Collomosse, J., Hilton, A.: 4d video textures for interactive character appearance. Comp. Graph. Forum(Proc. Eurographics) **33**, 371–380 (2014)
11. Chen, X., Guo, Y., Zhou, B., Zhao, Q.: Deformable model for estimating clothed and naked human shapes from a single image. Vis. Comput. **29**, 1187–1196 (2013)

12. Chen, Y., Cipolla, R.: Learning shape priors for single view reconstruction. In: ICCV Workshops (2009)
13. Chen, Y., Kim, T.-K., Cipolla, R.: Inferring 3D shapes and deformations from single views. In: Daniilidis, K., Maragos, P., Paragios, N. (eds.) ECCV 2010. LNCS, vol. 6313, pp. 300–313. Springer, Heidelberg (2010). doi:10.1007/978-3-642-15558-1_22
14. Chen, Y., Kim, T., Cipolla, R.: Silhouette-based object phenotype recognition using 3d shape priors. In: ICCV (2011)
15. Delamarre, Q., Faugeras, O.: 3d articulated models and multi-view tracking with silhouettes. In: ICCV (1999)
16. Guan, L., Franco, J., Pollefeys, M.: Multi-object shape estimation and tracking from silhouette cues. In: CVPR (2008)
17. Guan, P., Reiss, L., Hirshberg, D.A., Weiss, A., Black, M.J.: Drape: dressing any person. ACM Trans. Graph **31**, 1–10 (2012)
18. Guan, P., Weiss, A., Balan, A.O., Black, M.J.: Estimating human shape and pose from a single image. In: ICCV (2009)
19. Hardoon, D.R., Mourão Miranda, J., Brammer, M., Shawe-Taylor, J.: Unsupervised analysis of fmri data using kernel canonical correlation. NeuroImage **37**, 1250–1259 (2007)
20. Hardoon, D.R., Szedmak, S.R., Shawe-taylor, J.R.: Canonical correlation analysis: an overview with application to learning methods. Neural Comput. **16**, 2639–2664 (2004)
21. Hasler, N., Ackermann, H., Rosenhahn, B., Thormählen, T., Seidel, H.: Multilinear pose and body shape estimation of dressed subjects from image sets. In: CVPR (2010)
22. Hasler, N., Stoll, C., Sunkel, M., Rosenhahn, B., Seidel, H.: A statistical model of human pose and body shape. Comput. Graph. Forum **28**, 337–246 (2009)
23. Helten, T., Baak, A., Bharaj, G., Müller, M., Seidel, H., Theobalt, C.: Personalization and evaluation of a real-time depth-based full body tracker. In: 3DV (2013)
24. Hotelling, H.: Relations between two sets of variates. Biometrika **28**, 321–377 (1936)
25. Jain, A., Thormählen, T., Seidel, H.-P., Theobalt, C.: MovieReshape: tracking and reshaping of humans in videos. ACM Trans. Graph. **29**(6), 148:1–148:10 (2010). doi:10.1145/1882261.1866174
26. Kakade, S.M., Foster, D.P.: Multi-view regression via canonical correlation analysis. In: Bshouty, N.H., Gentile, C. (eds.) COLT 2007. Lecture Notes in Artificial Intelligence (LNAI), vol. 4539, pp. 82–96. Springer, Heidelberg (2007). doi:10.1007/978-3-540-72927-3_8
27. Kakadiaris, I.A., Metaxas, D.: Three-dimensional human body model acquisition from multiple views. IJCV **30**, 191–218 (1998)
28. Kim, T.K., Wong, S.F., Cipolla, R.: Tensor canonical correlation analysis for action classification. In: CVPR (2007)
29. Lahner, Z., Rodola, E., Schmidt, F.R., Bronstein, M.M., Cremers, D.: Efficient globally optimal 2d-to-3d deformable shape matching. In: CVPR (2016)
30. Laurentini, A.: The visual hull concept for silhouette-based image understanding. PAMI **16**, 150–162 (1994)
31. Lewis, J.P., Cordner, M., Fong, N.: Pose space deformation: a unified approach to shape interpolation and skeleton-driven deformation. In: SIGGRAPH (2000)
32. Ling, H., Jacobs, D.W.: Shape classification using the inner-distance. PAMI **29**, 286–299 (2007)

33. McWilliams, B., Balduzzi, D., Buhmann, J.M.: Correlated random features for fast semi-supervised learning. In: NIPS (2013)
34. Mikic, I., Trivedi, M., Hunter, E., Cosman, P.: Human body model acquisition and tracking using voxel data. IJCV **53**, 199–223 (2003)
35. Neophytou, A., Hilton, A.: Shape and pose space deformation for subject specific animation. In: 3DV (2013)
36. Neophytou, A., Hilton, A.: A layered model of human body and garment deformation. In: 3DV (2014)
37. Perbet, F., Johnson, S., Pham, M.T., Stenger, B.: Human body shape estimation using a multi-resolution manifold forest. In: CVPR (2014)
38. Pishchulin, L., Wuhrer, S., Helten, T., Theobalt, C., Schiele, B.: Building statistical shape spaces for 3d human modeling. CoRR (2015)
39. Robinette, K.M., Daanen, H.A.M.: The caesar project: a 3-d surface anthropometry survey. In: 3DIM (1999)
40. Rogge, L., Klose, F., Stengel, M., Eisemann, M., Magnor, M.: Garment replacement in monocular video sequences. ACM Trans. Graph. **34**, 1–10 (2014)
41. Sargin, M.E., Yemez, Y., Erzin, E., Tekalp, A.M.: Audiovisual synchronization and fusion using canonical correlation analysis. Trans. Multimedia **9**, 1396–1403 (2007)
42. Schmidt, F.R., Farin, D., Cremers, D.: Fast matching of planar shapes in sub-cubic runtime. In: ICCV (2007)
43. Schmidt, F.R., Töppe, E., Cremers, D.: Efficient planar graph cuts with applications in computer vision. In: CVPR (2009)
44. Shapira, L., Shamir, A., Cohen-Or, D.: Consistent mesh partitioning and skeleton-isation using the shape diameter function. Visual Comput. **24**, 249–259 (2008)
45. Sharma, A., Kumar, A., Daume III, H., Jacobs, D.W.: Generalized multiview analysis: a discriminative latent space. In: CVPR (2012)
46. Sigal, L., Balan, A.O., Black, M.J.: Combined discriminative and generative articulated pose and non-rigid shape estimation. In: NIPS (2007)
47. Slama, R., Wannous, H., Daoudi, M.: Extremal human curves: a new human body shape and pose descriptor. In: FG (2013)
48. Starck, J., Miller, G., Hilton, A.: Video-based character animation. In: ACM SIGGRAPH Eurographics SCA (2005)
49. Stoll, C., Gall, J., de Aguiar, E., Thrun, S., Theobalt, C.: Video-based reconstruction of animatable human characters. In: SIGGRAPH Asia (2010)
50. Weiss, A., Hirshberg, D.A., Black, M.J.: Home 3d body scans from noisy image and range data. In: ICCV (2011)
51. Wuhrer, S., Pishchulin, L., Brunton, A., Shu, C., Lang, J.: Estimation of human body shape and posture under clothing. CVIU **127**, 31–42 (2014)
52. Xi, P., Lee, W., Shu, C.: A data-driven approach to human-body cloning using a segmented body database. In: Pacific Graphics (2007)
53. Xu, F., Liu, Y., Stoll, C., Tompkin, J., Bharaj, G., Dai, Q., Seidel, H.P., Kautz, J., Theobalt, C.: Video-based characters: Creating new human performances from a multi-view video database. In: SIGGRAPH (2011)
54. Yang, Y., Yu, Y., Zhou, Y., Du, S., Davis, J., Yang, R.: Semantic parametric reshaping of human body models. In: 3DV (2014)
55. Ye, M., Yang, R.: Real-time simultaneous pose and shape estimation for articulated objects using a single depth camera. In: CVPR (2014)
56. Zhou, S., Fu, H., Liu, L., Cohen-Or, D., Han, X.: Parametric reshaping of human bodies in images. ACM Trans. Graph. **29**(4), 126:1–126:10 (2010). doi:10.1145/1778765.1778863

Can We Jointly Register and Reconstruct Creased Surfaces by Shape-from-Template Accurately?

Mathias Gallardo$^{(\boxtimes)}$, Toby Collins, and Adrien Bartoli

ISIT, UMR 6284 CNRS/Université d'Auvergne, Clermont-Ferrand, France
mathiasgallardo@gmail.com

Abstract. Shape-from-Template (SfT) aims to reconstruct a deformable object from a single image using a texture-mapped 3D model of the object in a reference position. Most existing SfT methods require well-textured surfaces that deform smoothly, which is a significant limitation. Due to the sparsity of correspondence constraint and strong regularizations, they usually fail to reconstruct strong changes of surface curvature such as surface creases. We investigate new ways to solve SfT for creased surfaces. Our main idea is to implicitly model creases with a dense mesh-based surface representation with an associated robust bending energy term, which deactivates curvature smoothing automatically where needed. Crucially, the crease locations are not required *a priori* since they emerge as the lowest-energy state during optimization. We show with real data that by combining this model with correspondence and surface boundary constraints we can successfully reconstruct creases while also preserving smooth regions.

Keywords: 3D reconstruction · Shape-from-Template · Isometry · Boundaries · Bending energy · M-estimator · Creases · Sharpness

1 Introduction

The 3D reconstruction of deformable objects from images or videos is one of the biggest open challenges in computer vision. The main difficulty arises from the variability and complexity of deformations. Two main paradigms have emerged: Non-Rigid Structure-from-Motion (NRSfM), which uses multiple images, and Shape-from-Template (SfT), which uses a single image and a *template*. The template is composed of a texture map and a model of the object's 3D shape in a reference pose. Recent works in SfT made interesting theoretical and applicative contributions in the entertainment industry with augmented reality [2–4] and real-time animation deformation transfer [5,6]. Perspectives on using SfT in medical applications were also given [7,8]. The main advantage of SfT is that it

Electronic supplementary material The online version of this chapter (doi:10.1007/978-3-319-46493-0_7) contains supplementary material, which is available to authorized users.

© Springer International Publishing AG 2016
B. Leibe et al. (Eds.): ECCV 2016, Part IV, LNCS 9908, pp. 105–120, 2016.
DOI: 10.1007/978-3-319-46493-0_7

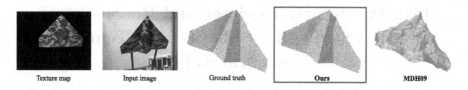

Texture map   Input image   Ground truth   **Ours**   MDH09

Fig. 1. An example of creased surface reconstruction by our method compared to a state-of-the-art method [1]. Unlike our method, [1] fails to reconstruct the creases.

needs only one image in order to achieve 3D reconstruction, which may be computed analytically [9]. SfT also registers the input image to the template, and so is well adapted to augmented reality. SfT is constrained by image data and deformation priors. The former includes feature correspondences [9–12] or (less commonly) direct pixel-wise matches [13–15]. Currently feature correspondences are the most common because they allow the problem to be solved globally. The latter includes conformity (angle preserving) [9], linear elasticity [7,8,16] and isometry (distance preserving) [9–11,17].

Most existing SfT methods break down when the surface creases, and this is for two reasons. Firstly, feature correspondences are not usually dense enough to tell us where creases occur. Secondly, most existing SfT methods use smoothed parameterizations for the surface and/or deformation to regularize the problem, which prefer smooth rather than creased solutions. The closest work to ours is [1], however this does not strictly model creases because the reconstructed creases are a by-product of the way it relaxes the isometry prior. We find that in practice it does not accurately reconstruct creases in many cases, as Fig. 1 shows. A fundamental problem with reconstructing deformable creased 3D surfaces from 2D image data is that we do not know *a priori* the crease locations. This makes it very difficult to employ existing parametric crease models used in other applications, such as b-splines, since we do not know *a priori* where to modify the spline to permit high changes in curvature. Instead our solution is to *implicitly model creases through an adaptive bending energy prior acting on a high-resolution non-parametric surface mesh.* Crucially, this does not require knowing anything *a priori* about the crease locations, since they emerge as the lowest-energy state during optimization.

While studying this problem we have found that correspondence constraints are often not sufficient data constraints. To remedy this, we complement them with a boundary constraint, which encourages the boundary of the surface to project to strong intensity edges in the image. This is a powerful constraint and should be used wherever possible. One main challenge is that we must ensure the boundary is attracted to correct image edges, which is not trivial. To deal with this we use statistical color models to help disambiguate non-boundary edges (*e.g.* from background clutter or texture). In the broader context of SfT, this is the first time that statistical color models has been exploited to solve the problem.

The paper is organized as follows. In Sect. 2, we give further background details and discuss state-of-the-art methods. In Sect. 3, we present our implicit crease energy model and its associated cost function. In Sect. 4, we present the full optimization framework. In Sect. 5, we validate our method with real data using ground truth generated by a high-precision structured-light scanner.

2   Background

We divide the background section into three parts. In the first part we discuss existing deformation models and priors in SfT. In the second part we discuss common data constraints used in SfT. In the third part we discuss how creases and surface discontinuities are modeled in other 3D reconstruction problems, then discuss a previous attempt to handle creases in [1].

2.1   Deformation Models and Priors in SfT

There are two main ways that deformations have been modeled in SfT. The first uses thin-shell models [9,11,12,17,18], where only the object's surface is modeled. The second way is volumetric models [19], where the object's surface and interior volume are modeled. Thin-shell models are the most common and give good approximations for thin or hollow surfaces made of e.g. paper, cloth and plastic. Most existing thin-shell models used in SfT use an approximate physical model of the object's material. The models have varied in complexity, from simple algebraic models such as smooth b-splines [18] or thin-plate splines [9,10]. Most recent methods use triangulated mesh models, which are conceptually simple and can handle general topologies [1,6,12,14,15].

Most of these methods use some forms of dimensionality reduction to reduce the problem's search space. This regularizes the problem and reduces the cost of optimization, and is based on the fundamental assumption that the surface can only deform smoothly. A significant problem with this is that when we want to reconstruct a creased surface, the deformations are non-smooth, so such dimensionality reduction will prevent the surface from being accurately reconstructed. Spline models such as b-splines and thin-plate splines reduce dimension by definition, because they model deformation with a finite set of control points. Thin-plate splines enforce global smooth deformations, and are not suitable to model surface creases. It is possible to model high-frequency and/or discontinuous deformations with b-splines by changing the spline's order and introducing repeated control points [20,21]. However, to correctly distribute the control points, one needs to know where the surface crease is, which in SfT is not known *a priori*. Other ways to reduce dimensionality have included using the eigen bases formed from the smooth modes of variation of the surface's stiffness matrix [12]. However a large number of bases are needed to model high frequency deformation such as creases, which dramatically increases the cost of optimization.

We propose to not enforce globally smooth deformations and to not apply such dimensionality reduction. Instead we use a so-called non-parametric approach where the surface is modelled by a dense triangulated mesh. We have found that creased surfaces such as folded paper can be recovered using mesh resolutions of $\mathcal{O}(10^4)$ vertices. We are able to work with such high resolution meshes because the constraints we apply on the mesh are very sparse (each constraint only applies to a small number of vertices), and this allows us to solve the resulting system iteratively with sparse linear solvers.

2.2   Data Constraints in SfT

To constrain the object's deformation data constraints must be extracted from the input image. There are three broad classes. The first and most common are *correspondence constraints* [9,11,18,22]. These match keypoints from the template's texture map and the input image using *e.g.* SURF [23], and tell us where points on the object's surface project to in the input image. The main advantages are that they do not require an initial estimate of the deformation and are reasonably fast to evaluate. However they only provide sparse constraints, and have only been used for smoothly deforming objects in the past. The second class of constraints are called *direct constraints*, and are computed directly from pixel values. They work by measuring the photometric agreement between the image and the deformed template and provide denser motion constraints than features. However direct constraints are highly non-convex and require a good initial estimate. They can also have difficulty handling strong photometric changes and when the object self-occludes or is occluded by other objects. The third type of constraints are contour constraints which are used to make the object's occluding contours align to edges in the image [24,25]. Similarly to direct constraints, these are highly non-convex constraints and require a good initial estimate. The main challenge with using contour constraints is they are difficult to apply robustly, particularly with strong background clutter.

2.3   Modelling Creases in Other Problem Domains and Previous Attempts in SfT

The problem of fitting unsmooth surfaces, including creases, has been extensively addressed in the curve [26] and surface [27–29] fitting literature. These generally address the problem of fitting 2D curves or 3D surfaces to 2D or 3D point sets respectively. Two approaches exist: one can densify the mesh [26–28] or adjust directly a model to the data [29,30]. [27] proposes the idea of tagging control points of a mesh and using subdivision surfaces to model discontinuities like creases and corners. This 3D concept is adapted to the 2D case by [26]. Another use of adaptive mesh is proposed by [28]. It starts by fitting a model to a downsampled set of points that excludes outliers. Then, to provide a better fitting, it selects new data points which have the smallest prediction residuals. The second category reconstructs 3D surfaces from 3D point cloud by having the user to select a set of global forms [30] or local shape examples [29].

The problem of reconstructing discontinuous 3D surfaces from 3D data is strongly data-driven, which is different to the SfT problem. In the SfT problem we do not have such 3D data. Instead we only have 2D projection data present in the input image, which is much weaker information. Indeed the whole reason why we require a 3D template is to form a well-posed problem by using the template's physical deformation constraints. To do this we must simultaneously register the template and reconstruct its deformed 3D shape (including creases). It would therefore particularly difficult to apply parametric models such as b-splines, because one would have to simultaneously register, reconstruct and restructure the b-spline's control points.

Practically all existing SfT methods use an ℓ_2 norm to regularize surface bending, but such norm cannot model creases because it incorrectly penalizes non-smooth solutions. The problem of creases or "sharp folds" has been looked at before in [1], via a convex formulation which maximizes the depth of each vertex and relaxes the inextensibility constraint. The inextensibility constraint preserves the geodesic distance between two vertices, but this distance may decrease when folds appear. [1] proposed to relax this constraint: the geodesic distance is replaced by the euclidean distance. Vertices may thus come closer to each other without making the surface shrink or extend. Two reasons make for this method difficult the reconstruction of 3D creases: correspondences are not sufficiently informative and it does not use smoother.

2.4 Contributions

Our main contribution is to use a high-density surface mesh model that implicitly model creases through the use of a robust smoothing regularizer known as an M-estimator. This deactivates excessive smoothing automatically during the optimization process. Crucially, crease location is not required *a priori* since it emerge as the lowest-energy state during optimization. Other problems such as optical flow [31, 32] use M-estimators for handling non-smooth solutions, and this gave much inspiration. However it was unclear whether M-estimators offered a good solution to handle the SfT problem, where 3D shape has to be reconstructed from 2D data. The second main contribution is to introduce robust boundary constraint that aligns the surface boundaries to the edges in the image. Importantly, we use color information to help determine where the true surface edges are.

3   Problem Formulation

3.1   Template Definition

The template consists of a *texture map* and a non-parametric *embedding* function φ that maps the texture map to 3D camera coordinates. The texture map, denoted by $\Im_{\mathcal{T}} : \mathbb{R}^2 \to \{1, ..., 255\}^3$ models the color at each point on the template's surface. This can be constructed by texture-mapping the template from one or more photographs. In the simple case when the template's surface can be seen entirely in a single calibrated image, texture-mapping is particularly simple, and can be done by inverting the image projection function, as shown in Fig. 2 (bottom left). We refer to the calibrated image as the *reference image*, and we assume the template is registered to the reference image. Here π_T denotes the projection function of the reference image's camera. We define the texture map's domain with $\Omega_T \subset \mathbb{R}^2$. We define $\Omega_{B_T} \triangleq \Omega_T$ as the boundary points of the texture map.

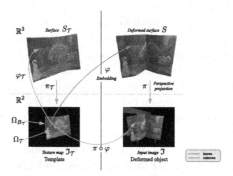

Fig. 2. Geometric setup of SfT with embedding functions.

We model the embedding function φ with a discrete dense triangular surface mesh of N vertices $\mathbf{x} = \{\mathbf{x}_1, ..., \mathbf{x}_N\} \in \mathbb{R}^{3 \times N}$ and F faces $\mathscr{F} = \{f_1, ..., f_F\} \in [1, N]^{3 \times F}$. We denote $E \in [1, N]^{2 \times N_E}$ as the set of mesh edges where N_E is the number of edges. We embed a point $\mathbf{u} \in \mathcal{I}_T$ using piecewise linear interpolation of the triangle vertices. Using its barycentric coordinates:

$$\varphi(\mathbf{u}; \mathbf{x}) = b_1 \mathbf{x}_{f_i(1)} + b_2 \mathbf{x}_{f_i(2)} + b_3 \mathbf{x}_{f_i(3)} \in \mathbb{R}^3, \tag{1}$$

where b_1, b_2 and $b_3 = 1 - b_1 - b_2$ are the barycentric coordinates of the point $\mathbf{x}$ on f_i. The embedding function φ_T gives the surface 3D reference 3D shape. The texture map and the reference image are known, then its corresponding embedding function φ_T is known. The embedding function φ is unknown, and the SfT problem is to determine its respective vertex positions $\mathbf{x} \subset \mathbb{R}^{3 \times N}$ in camera coordinates.

3.2 Global Cost Function

We solve the problem by combining *data constraints* (correspondence and boundary constraints) and *deformation priors* (isometry and bending constraints). The cost function is as follows:

$$C(\mathbf{x}) = C_{crsp}(\mathbf{x}) + \lambda_{iso} C_{iso}(\mathbf{x}) + \lambda_{bound} C_{bound}(\mathbf{x}) + \lambda_{bend} C_{bend}(\mathbf{x}). \tag{2}$$

Correspondence Constraint. We compute initial correspondences between the texture map image and the input image with an existing method. In all presented experiments we use SURF features that are matched with the graph-based method from [33][1]. Let M be the number of point correspondences in Ω_T, denoted $\mathbf{u}_j$, $j \in \{1, ..., M\}$. Let $\mathbf{q}_j \in \mathbb{R}^2$ be the pixel normalized coordinates of the jth correspondence in the input image $\mathfrak{I}$. Note that feature-matching method such as [33] are never guaranteed to be outlier free. We deal with this using a robust cost function as defined as follows:

$$C_{crsp}(\mathbf{x}) = \sum_{j=1}^{M} \rho\left((\pi \circ \varphi)(\mathbf{u}_j; \mathbf{x}) - \mathbf{q}_j\right), \tag{3}$$

where ρ is an M-estimator. This encourages the embedding function φ to project each point $\mathbf{u}_j$ onto the image at the correspondence position $\mathbf{q}_j$, but in a way that can tolerate outliers through an M-estimator ρ. We have investigated various M-estimators and found that $(\ell_1 - \ell_2)$ works well, with $\rho(\mathbf{y}) = 2(\sqrt{1 + \|\mathbf{y}\|_2^2/2} - 1)$.

Isometry Constraint. The isometry constraint is used to penalize surface extension and compression, and is required in general to make the SfT problem well posed. Following [1,34], we define the isometry constraint as:

$$C_{iso}(\mathbf{x}) = \sum_{(i,j) \in E} \left(l_{ij}^2 - \|\mathbf{x}_i - \mathbf{x}_j\|_2^2\right)^2, \tag{4}$$

where l_{ij} is the Euclidean distance between neighboring vertices (i, j) on the template's reference position.

Boundary Constraint. The aim of this constraint is to align Ω_{B_T} to wherever it is visible to the input image. We do this by defining a *boundariness* map I_B where likely surface boundaries locations behave like potential wells. I_B is computed using image edge information and is used to define the boundary constraint as follows:

$$C_{bound}(\mathbf{x}) = \int_{\Omega_{B_T}} \rho\left(I^B\left((\pi \circ \varphi)(\mathbf{u}_j; \mathbf{x})\right)\right) d\Omega, \tag{5}$$

where ρ is an M-estimator that we use to reduce the influence of false boundaries points on the energy function.

We base I^B on the fact that the surface's boundaries tend to coincide with strong image edges. We define I^G a blurred grayscale version of the input image $\mathfrak{I}$, which is computed using a Gaussian filter (h, σ). A naive way to compute the boundariness map would then be as follows:

$$I^B = \exp\left(-\frac{|\nabla I^G|}{\sigma^B}\right), \tag{6}$$

---

[1] The code is available at http://isit.u-clermont1.fr/~ab/Research/index.html.

where ∇I^G is the gradient of I^G, σ^B is a bandwidth term which governs the potential well's width. We illustrate this in Fig. 3, where an input image is shown in Fig. 3(a) and its corresponding boundariness map according to Eq. (6) is shown in Fig. 3(b). The true boundaries are represented with low potentials, but so are many false boundaries corresponding to background clutter and texture edges. This is a serious problem because they may attract the solution to a wrong local minimum.

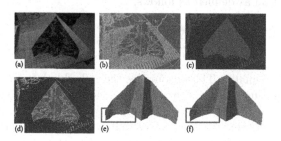

Fig. 3. (a) Input image, (b) naive boundariness map, (c) color model segmentation, (d) the enhanced boundariness map, (e) our 3D reconstruction *without* the enhanced boundariness map, (f) our 3D reconstruction *with* boundariness map using foreground color segmentation. (Color figure online)

We propose to exploit color information to significantly reduce false boundary edges. This works by applying a color-based foreground detector, trained on the target surface to each input image pixel, and setting $I^B = 1$ for any pixel which has a detection score below a threshold T_d. We train the detector using the foreground of input image (in our experiments we use an RGB Gaussian Mixture Model of 4 components) and use a default threshold of $T_d = 50$. In Fig. 3(b) and (d) we show the difference between the naive boundariness map and the boundariness map using the color-based statistical filter. Here we see that many false boundary edges in the background have been removed. Similarly to the correspondence constraint, we currently use the $(\ell_1 - \ell_2)$ M-estimator.

Bending Constraint. Our bending energy term robustly penalizes non-smooth embeddings, and is defined as follows:

$$C_{bend}(\mathbf{x}) = \int_{\Omega_T} \rho \left(\frac{\partial^2 \varphi(\mathbf{u}; \mathbf{x})}{\partial \mathbf{u}^2} \right) d\Omega, \tag{7}$$

where ρ is an M-estimator used to reduce the energy at creases.

4   Optimization

4.1   Overview

Equation (2) is a large-scale, sparse nonlinear optimization problem. The system is sparse because each constraint only depends on a small number of unknowns.

Regarding size, there are typically $\mathcal{O}(10^4)$ unknowns (the example in Fig. 1 has 11,557 unknowns and approximately 300,000 constraints). We propose to solve it with numerical gradient-based minimization, starting from an initial estimate $\mathbf{x}_0$. We determine $\mathbf{x}_0$ using an existing SfT method (specifically we use [10]), which does not use boundary constraints and assumes the surface is smooth. Given $\mathbf{x}_0$ our general strategy is to iteratively solve with Gauss-Newton iterations, by re-linearizing the constraints about the current estimate, then solving the corresponding linear system. For our problem sizes this can be done efficiently using sparse Cholesky decomposition, and we ensure convergence using backtracking line-search.

4.2 Improving Convergence

One caveat is that the boundary constraints are highly non-convex and can cause convergence on the wrong local minimum. The color-based filtering described in Sect. 3.2 partially deals with this, however we also introduce two more strategies. The first is to cascade the constraints, by first optimizing the solution without using boundary constraint until convergence. Once done, the detector detailed in Sect. 3.2 is trained using the region of the input image where the current estimate surface projects. Then, boundary constraints are introduced and the solution is refined. The second strategy is to use an image pyramid, which gives coarse-to-fine versions of the boundariness map and increases the convergence basin. This is a standard practice used in related problems such as optic flow. We currently use a two-level pyramid: the kernel sizes and standard-deviations are respectively $h_1 = (10, 10)$ and $\sigma_1 = 5$ and $h_2 = (5, 5)$ and $\sigma_2 = 2.5$ for a default image size of 1288×964 pixels. At the finest level, we do not apply the color-based filtering to the boundariness map. This is because assuming correct convergence, at the start of the finest level the boundaries should align reasonably closely to their true locations, and we therefore have less risk of false boundary edges steering the solution away to a wrong local minimum. The benefit is to use all edge information at the finest level, including edges where there is little color separation between the surface and its background.

5 Experimental Results

We compare the accuracy of our method with four others [1,9,10,12], which we denote respectively **ReD12**, **ReJ14**, **MDH09** and **LM16**. **MDH09** refers to the convex formulation of [1].

5.1 Ground Truth Acquisition

Some previous datasets with ground truth 3D exist [35], however these are low resolution, noisy and do not contain creased surfaces. To accurately evaluate our method new datasets with ground truth were required. We constructed three new data sets of three different objects with a highly-accurate commercial structured light system [36]. This consists of a HD data projector and an industrial machine vision camera [37], and captures depth maps to sub-millimeter accuracy. The advantage of this setup is that the depth maps are constructed in the camera's coordinate frame, so there is no need to register them to the camera's image. RGB images were captured from the camera at a resolution of 1288×964 pixels. It takes approximately 10 s to capture an image and its associated depth map. Our dataset consists of three creased objects scanned at approximately 20 cm from the camera: a *creased paper* (6 input images), a *folded aeroplane* (9 input images) and a *cardboard box* (8 input images). The 3D reference surfaces were obtained by flattening the objects. We also evaluated the accuracy of our method on an existing smooth dataset [35], to assess how our approach coped when creased reconstruction was not required.

5.2 Implementation Details and Evaluation Metrics

For all experiments we constructed the embedding meshes by laying a triangulated 100×100 vertex grid on the reference image which was then cropped to Ω_T. We found that this resolution was sufficient to accurately reconstruct creases. Correspondences were computed using the public code from [33], which gave approximately 300 correspondences per image. We discretized Ω_{B_T} to 1000 uniformly spaced points. For the state-of-the-art methods, there is no way to automatically optimize their free parameters. Therefore we tried our best to do this by hand, to obtain the best average error on all datasets. This was done by a search starting from the default values, and modifying each free parameter in turn to improve the average error. The values we used are found in the supplementary material. For our method, all experiments were ran using the same parameters, which were manually set.

On our new data sets we used two evaluation metrics. The first was the 3D position error (%), which was given by the average relative depth error over the region in the input image belonging to the surface. To do this, the template was fitted to the ground truth depth map, then distances between this deformed template and the estimated one were computed. The second metric was the normal error (in degrees), which was given by the average error in surface normal. To investigate the improvement at creased regions, we averaged results with two schemes. The first was to use the whole image region that corresponded to the surface. The second was using local neighborhoods around each crease, with a neighborhood distance of approximately 0.5 cm on the surface.

5.3 Results

The first part covers our investigation to see whether the choice of bending energy M-estimator had a significant impact on results (using our new data sets). The second part compares our results with the state-of-the-art methods using our new datasets. The third part compares our results with state-of-the-art methods using the dataset from [35].

Comparing Different Bending Energy M-estimators. Various M-estimators have been proposed in the literature (a good review can be found in [38]). Each have slightly different qualities and it is very hard to know *a priori* which work best for a given problem. M-estimators can either be parameterless, such as ℓ_1 or $(\ell_1 - \ell_2)$ or have at least one free parameter (usually it is only one), such as Huber and Cauchy. They may also be redescending or non-redescending. In this section we compared the performance of $(\ell_1 - \ell_2)$ and Huber, which are two non-redescending M-estimators. The purpose was two-fold. Firstly, to see if Huber's free parameter was sensitive and required careful tuning and secondly to see whether there was a significant performance difference between the two.

We run our method with 17 different bending energy M-estimator settings. The first 16 were with Huber using 16 different parameter values in the range $k = 10^2...10^{-6}$. The 17th was with $(\ell_1 - \ell_2)$. We evaluated performance using all input images in all three datasets. For each M-estimator setting, we run our method with 9 different bending energy weights from λ_{bend}, from 10^{-6} to 10^{-2} (which was a sufficient range), and then took the weight which produced the lowest average error. The corresponding results for all 17 M-estimator settings are shown in Fig. 4. We observe that with $(\ell_1 - \ell_2)$ we obtain very similar results to the best result obtained with Huber. The best k changes according to the error metric, but we can say reasonably that the best k varies between $k_7 = 0.05$ and $k_9 = 0.005$. This suggests that for our problem, given the optimal bending energy weight there is no clear difference between using $(\ell_1 - \ell_2)$ or Huber, and the choice for Huber's free parameter is important but not extremely sensitive in the range $k_7 = 0.05$ to $k_9 = 0.005$.

As a final experiment, we investigated the range of optimal bending energy weights for a given M-estimator. The purpose was to see how easy it is in practice to tune the bending energy weight for a given M-estimator. This was done by measuring the best bending energy weight for each test image independently, then measuring the corresponding spread. The results are shown in Fig. 4. Figure 4 shows that in general the spread of the best bending energy weight is similar for $(\ell_1 - \ell_2)$ and Huber with its parameter in the range k_7 to k_9. This implies that the difficulty of choosing a good weight for the bending energy is the same for the two M-estimators. From these experiments, we can conclude that there is very little difference in practice between using $(\ell_1 - \ell_2)$ or Huber with its parameter in the range $0.005 \leq k \leq 0.05$.

Results on Creased Datasets. For our method we used the $(\ell_1 - \ell_2)$ M-estimator for the bending energy with a corresponding weight of $\lambda_{bend} = 10^{-5}$. In Fig. 6 we show the result of the compared methods using a representative input image from each of the three datasets. In Fig. 5 we give summary statistics for each method across all images. These visual observations support the statistical results in Fig. 5. We notice that our method provides the best accuracy at the neighbors of the creases and a best global reconstruction. We remark that the large smooth regions of the surfaces are also reconstructed well in general. In Fig. 6, 5th row, 3rd column we show an example of a failure mode, where the

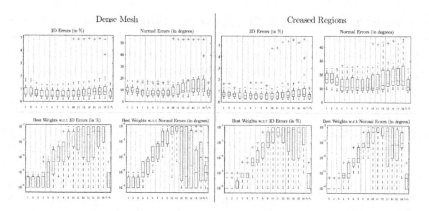

Fig. 4. Results of bending energy M-estimator analysis. We consider all input images of all the objects of our test datasets Sect. 5.3. **First row**: Errors obtained by running our method with 17 different M-estimators settings. In the first 16 settings we use Huber with 16 different hyper-parameter values. In the last setting, we use $(\ell_1 - \ell_2)$. **Second row**: the distribution of optimal weights λ_{bend} for each M-estimator setting.

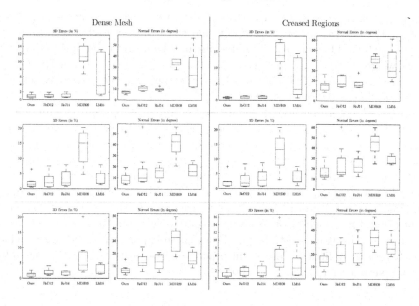

Fig. 5. Quantitative results comparison on the three new datasets. **First row**: *creased paper* dataset. **Second row**: *folded aeroplane* dataset. **Third row**: *cardboard box* dataset.

reconstruction at the bar code does not appear correct. The reason for this is because the boundary points were incorrectly fitted to the bottom of the bar code, which was compensated by the surface bending away from the camera in order to respect the isometric constraint.

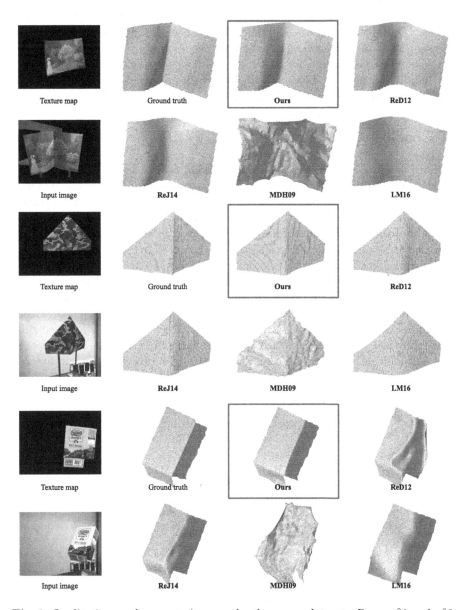

Fig. 6. Qualitative results comparison on the three new datasets. Rows $n°1$ and $n°2$: input image $n°1$ of the *creased paper* dataset. Rows $n°3$ and $n°4$: input image $n°1$ of the *folded aeroplane* dataset. Rows $n°5$ and $n°6$: input image $n°6$ of the *cardboard box* dataset.

Results on an Existing Smooth Dataset. We also tested whether our method also works well for simpler problems with smooth surfaces where ℓ_2 regularization is sufficient. We have found this to be the case with existing benchmark datasets. On the commonly-used public EPFL kinect paper dataset (193 frames) and using the same parameters, we evaluated accuracy using 40 images uniformly sampled, which produced a mean 3D error of 5.63 mm. This puts it among the best performing method, presented in [10], which uses an ℓ_2 regularization and which gives a mean 3D error of 5.74 mm.

6   Conclusion

We have developed a modeling and optimization framework for reconstructing smooth and creased 3D surfaces from a single image and a deformable 3D template. We implicitly model creases using a dense mesh-based surface representation with an associated robust bending energy term whose influence is governed by an M-estimator. We have shown that there is little difference in practice between two common M-estimators $((\ell_1 - \ell_2)$ and Huber with a correctly set hyper-parameter), and our results indicate significantly better performance compared to previous state-of-the-art methods. An important aspect of our approach is to combine motion constraints with boundary constraints, which can significantly improve results at the surface's boundaries. One difficulty with using them is potential confusion with non-boundary image edges. We have addressed this using statistical color models, which are particularly effective when the surface's color is significantly different to the background. In future work we will extend the approach to templates with arbitrary topologies and study dynamic crease modeling.

Acknowledgments. This research has received funding from Almerys Corporation and the EUs FP7 through the ERC research grant 307483 FLEXABLE.

References

1. Salzmann, M., Fua, P.: Reconstructing sharply folding surfaces: a convex formulation. In: International Conference on Computer Vision and Pattern Recognition, pp. 1054–1061 (2009)
2. Pilet, J., Lepetit, V., Fua, P.: Fast non-rigid surface detection, registration and realistic augmentation. Int. J. Comput. Vis. **76**(2), 109–122 (2007)
3. Herling, J., Broll, W.: High-quality real-time video inpainting with PixMix. IEEE Trans. Vis. Comput. Graph. **20**(6), 866–879 (2014)
4. Magnenat, S., Ngo, D.T., Zund, F., Ryffel, M., Noris, G., Rothlin, G., Marra, A., Nitti, M., Fua, P., Gross, M., Sumner, R.: Live texturing of augmented reality characters from colored drawings. IEEE Trans. Vis. Comput. Graph. **21**(11), 1201–1210 (2015)
5. Sumner, R.W., Popović, J.: Deformation transfer for triangle meshes. ACM Trans. Graph. **23**(3), 399–405 (2004)

6. Collins, T., Bartoli, A.: Realtime Shape-from-Template: system and applications. In: International Symposium on Mixed and Augmented Reality (2015)

7. Malti, A., Hartley, R., Bartoli, A., Kim, J.: Monocular template-based 3D reconstruction of extensible surfaces with local linear elasticity. In: International Conference on Computer Vision and Pattern Recognition (2013)

8. Haouchine, N., Dequidt, J., Berger, M.O., Cotin, S.: Single view augmentation of 3D elastic objects. In: International Symposium on Mixed and Augmented Reality, pp. 229–236 (2014)

9. Bartoli, A., Gérard, Y., Chadebecq, F., Collins, T., Pizarro, D.: Shape-from-Template. IEEE Trans. Pattern Anal. Mach. Intell. **37**(10), 2099–2118 (2015)

10. Chhatkuli, A., Pizarro, D., Bartoli, A.: Stable template-based isometric 3D reconstruction in all imaging conditions by linear least-squares. In: International Conference on Computer Vision and Pattern Recognition (2014)

11. Salzmann, M., Fua, P.: Linear local models for monocular reconstruction of deformable surfaces. IEEE Trans. Pattern Anal. Mach. Intell. **33**(5), 931–944 (2011)

12. Ngo, D.T., Östlund, J., Fua, P.: Template-based monocular 3D shape recovery using Laplacian meshes. IEEE Trans. Pattern Anal. Mach. Intell. **38**(1), 172–187 (2016)

13. Malti, A., Bartoli, A., Collins, T.: A pixel-based approach to template-based monocular 3D reconstruction of deformable surfaces. In: Proceedings of the IEEE International Workshop on Dynamic Shape Capture and Analysis at ICCV, pp. 1650–1657, November 2011

14. Ngo, T.D., Park, S., Jorstad, A.A., Crivellaro, A., Yoo, C., Fua, P.: Dense image registration and deformable surface reconstruction in presence of occlusions and minimal texture. In: International Conference on Computer Vision (2015)

15. Yu, R., Russell, C., Campbell, N.D.F., Agapito, L.: Direct, dense, and deformable: template-based non-rigid 3D reconstruction from RGB video. In: ICCV (2015)

16. Malti, A., Bartoli, A., Hartley, R.I.: A linear least-squares solution to elastic Shape-from-Template. In: International Conference on Computer Vision and Pattern Recognition (2015)

17. Collins, T., Bartoli, A.: Using isometry to classify correct/incorrect 3D-2D correspondences. In: Fleet, D., Pajdla, T., Schiele, B., Tuytelaars, T. (eds.) ECCV 2014. LNCS, vol. 8692, pp. 325–340. Springer, Heidelberg (2014). doi:10.1007/978-3-319-10593-2_22

18. Brunet, F., Hartley, R., Bartoli, A.: Monocular Template-Based 3D surface reconstruction: convex inextensible and nonconvex isometric methods. Computer Vis. Image Underst. **125**, 138–154 (2014)

19. Parashar, S., Pizarro, D., Bartoli, A., Collins, T.: As-rigid-as-possible volumetric Shape-from-Template. In: IEEE International Conference on Computer Vision (2015)

20. Gregorski, B.F., Hamann, B., Joy, K.I.: Reconstruction of B-spline surfaces from scattered data points. In: Computer Graphics International, 2000. Proceedings, pp. 163–170 (2000)

21. He, Y., Qin, H.: Surface reconstruction with triangular B-splines. In: Geometric Modeling and Processing, 2004. Proceedings, pp. 279–287 (2004)

22. Ostlund, J., Varol, A., Ngo, T., Fua., P.: Laplacian meshes for monocular 3D shape recovery. In: European Conference on Computer Vision (2012)

23. Bay, H., Ess, A., Tuytelaars, T., Van Gool, L.: Speeded-Up Robust Features (SURF). Comput. Vis. Image Underst. **110**(3), 346–359 (2008)

24. Ilić, S., Salzmann, M., Fua, P.: Implicit meshes for effective Silhouette handling. Int. J. Comput. Vis. **72**(2), 159–178 (2006)

25. Vicente, S., Agapito, L.: Balloon shapes: reconstructing and deforming objects with volume from images. In: 2013 International Conference on 3D Vision - 3DV 2013, June 2013

26. Kaess, M., Dellaert, F.: Reconstruction of objects with jagged edges through Rao-Blackwellized fitting of piecewise smooth subdivision curves. In: Proceedings of the First IEEE International Workshop on Higher-Level Knowledge in 3D Modeling and Motion Analysis, pp. 39–47 (2003)

27. Hoppe, H., DeRose, T., Duchamp, T., Halstead, M., Jin, H., McDonald, J., Schweitzer, J., Stuetzle, W.: Piecewise smooth surface reconstruction. In: Proceedings of the 21st Annual Conference on Computer Graphics and Interactive Techniques, pp. 295–302 (1994)

28. Fleishman, S., Cohen-Or, D., Silva, C.T.: Robust moving least-squares fitting with sharp features. ACM Trans. Graph. **24**(3), 544–552 (2005)

29. Gal, R., Shamir, A., Hassner, T., Pauly, M., Cohen-Or, D.: Surface reconstruction using local shape priors. In: Proceedings of the Fifth Eurographics Symposium on Geometry Processing. Eurographics Association, pp. 253–262 (2007)

30. Pauly, M., Mitra, N.J., Giesen, J., Gross, M., Guibas, L.J.: Example-based 3D scan completion. In: Proceedings of the Third Eurographics Symposium on Geometry Processing (2005)

31. Black, M.J., Anandan, P.: A Framework for the robust estimation of optical flow. In: Proceedings of Fourth International Conference on Computer Vision, pp. 231–236, May 1993

32. Zach, C., Pock, T., Bischof, H.: A duality based approach for realtime TV-L1 optical flow. In: Hamprecht, F.A., Schnörr, C., Jähne, B. (eds.) DAGM 2007. LNCS, vol. 4713, pp. 214–223. Springer, Heidelberg (2007). doi:10.1007/978-3-540-74936-3_22

33. Collins, T., Mesejo, P., Bartoli, A.: An analysis of errors in graph-based keypoint matching and proposed solutions. In: European Conference on Computer Vision (2014)

34. Perriollat, M., Hartley, R., Bartoli, A.: Monocular template-based reconstruction of inextensible surfaces. Int. J. Comput. Vis. **95**(2), 124–137 (2011)

35. Salzmann, M., Hartley, R., Fua, P.: Convex optimization for deformable surface 3D Tracking. In: International Conference on Computer Vision (2007)

36. David 3D Scanner (2014). http://www.david-3d.com/en/products/david4

37. Grey, P.: Flea2G 1.3 MP Color Firewire 1394b (Sony ICX445). https://www.ptgrey.com/

38. Zhang, Z.: Parameter estimation techniques: a tutorial with application to conic fitting. Image Vis. Comput, **15**(1), 59–76 (1997)

Distractor-Supported Single Target Tracking in Extremely Cluttered Scenes

Jingjing Xiao[1]([✉]), Linbo Qiao[2], Rustam Stolkin[1], and Aleš Leonardis[1]

[1] University of Birmingham, Birmingham B15 2TT, UK
shine636363@sina.com, {r.stolkin,a.leonardis}@cs.bham.ac.uk
[2] College of Computer, National University of Defense Technology,
Changsha 410073, China
qiao.linbo@nudt.edu.cn

Abstract. This paper presents a novel method for single target tracking in RGB images under conditions of extreme clutter and camouflage, including frequent occlusions by objects with similar appearance as the target. In contrast to conventional single target trackers, which only maintain the estimated target status, we propose a multi-level clustering-based robust estimation for online detection and learning of multiple target-like regions, called *distractors*, when they appear near to the true target. To distinguish the target from these distractors, we exploit a global dynamic constraint (derived from the target and the distractors) in a feedback loop to improve single target tracking performance in situations where the target is camouflaged in highly cluttered scenes. Our proposed method successfully prevents the estimated target location from erroneously jumping to a distractor during occlusion or extreme camouflage interactions. To gain an insightful understanding of the evaluated trackers, we have augmented publicly available benchmark videos, by proposing a new set of clutter and camouflage sub-attributes, and annotating these sub-attributes for all frames in all sequences. Using this dataset, we first evaluate the effect of each key component of the tracker on the overall performance. Then, the proposed tracker is compared to other highly ranked single target tracking algorithms in the literature. The experimental results show that applying the proposed global dynamic constraint in a feedback loop can improve single target tracker performance, and demonstrate that the overall algorithm significantly outperforms other state-of-the-art single target trackers in highly cluttered scenes.

1 Introduction

Visual object tracking remains an open and active research area, despite publication of numerous tracking algorithms over the last three to four decades [1,2]. A particularly difficult problem is how to track a target which moves through scenes featuring several other very similar objects, or which moves past extremely cluttered or camouflaged image regions, Fig. 1A. In these situations, it is difficult to distinguish the target using only its appearance information [3]. Additional information, such as dynamic models of the target and nearby distracting image

© Springer International Publishing AG 2016
B. Leibe et al. (Eds.): ECCV 2016, Part IV, LNCS 9908, pp. 121–136, 2016.
DOI: 10.1007/978-3-319-46493-0_8

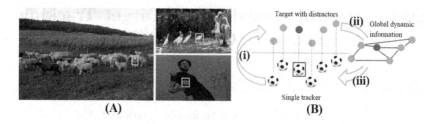

Fig. 1. (A) Sequences with many distractor objects used in our experiments. The cyan bounding boxes depict the single targets we want to track. (B) The proposed tracking framework. The yellow arrows show the feedback loop between the single target information and global dynamic information extracted from the tracker and the distractors. The red bounding box/dot represents the single target we want to track while the green dots denote the distractors. The proposed algorithm: (i) simultaneously tracks the target and the distractors using the proposed robust estimation method; (ii) extracts a global dynamic model from the relative target and distractor trajectories; (iii) feeds the global dynamic information back to the single target tracker to help identify the true target and infer occlusion situations. (Color figure online)

regions, may be useful to support robust tracking [4,5]. Therefore, in this paper, we show how a single target tracker can be used to detect and exploit contextual information. This contextual information is then fed back to the tracker to improve its robustness in problems of tracking a single target which is camouflaged against scenes containing a large number of similar non-target entities, which we call *distractors*.

Our proposed tracker is a *single*-target tracker, in the sense that it is initialised only with a bounding box of a single target in the first frame. However, unlike most single target trackers, it encodes information about other objects or image regions (distractors) with similar appearance to the target, and exploits a global dynamics constraint in a feedback loop to help disambiguate the target from these distractors, as illustrated in Fig. 1B. In scenes with clutter and camouflage, the proposed method detects multiple target-like regions and explicitly models this global information to improve the performance of the single target tracker, using methods which are somewhat analogous to the data association approaches used in multi-target tracking. However, in contrast to multi-target trackers, our proposed method (i) aims at using global information to improve a single target tracker at each frame; (ii) does not assign individual IDs to multiple other objects. The relationship of our tracker to single-target and multi-target trackers is illustrated in Fig. 2.

The main contributions of this paper are: (i) a novel coarse-to-fine multi-level clustering based robust estimation method for online detection and localisation of candidate image regions containing the true target and/or distractors; (ii) a novel global dynamics constraint applied in a feedback loop, which enables the motion of the target and an arbitrary number of distractors to be robustly disambiguated, while also making inferences about occlusion situations; (iii) for

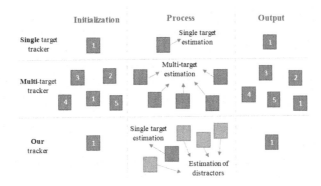

Fig. 2. Relationships between single target trackers, multi-target trackers and our proposed tracker during tracking. Single target trackers do not explicitly model information about distractor objects. Multi-target trackers model and identify *multiple* target regions, exploiting additional initialised prior knowledge. In contrast, our tracker is initialised in the same way as single-target trackers, but automatically detects and learns models for multiple distractor entities on the fly, to help improve the performance of the *single* target tracker.

performance evaluation, we propose a new set of sub-attributes to describe different kinds of cluttered scenes, and we augment publicly available benchmark data by per-frame annotations of all sequences with all sub-attributes. We perform two sets of experiments using publicly available ground-truthed datasets. First, on highly cluttered scenes, we (i) compare our tracker against other state-of-the-art single target trackers, demonstrating superior performance of the proposed algorithm, and (ii) study our tracker by evaluating the effectiveness of each designed component. Secondly, for an overall assessment of the tracker, we also evaluate its tracking performance on non-cluttered scenes from OTB100 [1] dataset, again with favourable results. The remainder of this paper is organised as follows. We review related work in Sect. 2. Section 3 explains technical details of our proposed tracker. Section 4 presents and discusses experimental results. Section 5 provides concluding remarks.

2 Related Work

We first review works on *single*-target tracking in highly cluttered scenes. Then, we review some related data association methods used in *multi*-target tracking literature to make a distinction between that work and our own (a single-target tracker which additionally models the global dynamics of multiple distractors).

To track a single target robustly in the presence of clutter, the tracker should learn and exploit contextual information. In [6,7] it was observed that non-target objects, known as *supporters*, may sometimes be associated with a target and can be used to help infer its position. However, in highly cluttered scenes, e.g. Fig. 1A, it may not be possible to find supporters that persistently move around the target with strong motion correlation. In contrast, we notice that identifying *distractors* in contextual clutter can also help robustify target identification. Other work [8–10] detected distractor regions with similar appearance to the target. However, tracking accuracy of such methods heavily depends on the pre-defined spatial density of samples, where sparse sampling cannot adequately distinguish adjacent objects, and dense sampling is computationally expensive. Even with dense sampling, such methods can still fail to distinguish adjacent or overlapping objects. In contrast, we propose a robust estimation method which uses a multi-level clustering scheme to efficiently search for objects at progressively finer granularities, and distinguishes inter-occluding objects using a novel method based on the disparity between mean and mode samples. Note that methods such as [8–10] maintain multiple image regions as target candidates, but do not specifically decide which region is the target at each frame. In contrast, our proposed method detects and learns distractors on-the-fly, and then exploits global target-distractor dynamics constraints to enable deterministic identification of the target at each frame. Appearance matching scores were used to distinguish the target from distractors in [11]. However, such algorithms are prone to failures when the target is camouflaged, occluded or undergoing deformation, when appearance matching methods can cause the tracker to erroneously fixate on clutter. A unified model to select the best matching metric (attribution selection) and most stable sub-region of the target (spatial selection) for tracking was proposed in [12]. Hong et al. [13] learned a discriminative (matching) metric that adaptively computed the importance of different features, and online adaptive attribute weighting was also proposed in [14–16]. Posseger et al. [17] recently proposed a distractor-aware target model to select salient colours in single target tracking. However, none of the methods [12–17] actively searches and memorises the trajectories of the distractors in scenes, or exploits a global dynamic constraint to improve single target tracking. In addition, our paper addresses video sequences that are so extreme that both target and distractors may have *identical* appearance, and cannot be disambiguated by any appearance features.

We now discuss the conceptual differences between our proposed global dynamic constraint and data association methods used in multi-target trackers, as illustrated in Fig. 2. Berclaz et al. [18] reformulated the data association problem as a constrained flow optimization convex problem, solved using a k-shortest paths algorithm. However, the computational cost of generating k paths is quite high, especially for our problem of finding a single target at each frame. Moreover, this method first obtains detections for every frame throughout an entire video sequence, and then mutually optimises the target IDs over all frames. Such post-processing methods cannot be used for online target tracking. Shitrit et al. [19] also relaxed the data association problem as a convex optimization problem which explicitly exploited image appearance cues to prevent erroneous identity switch. However, appearance cues are not sufficiently discriminating to distinguish between the target and the distractors in extremely challenging videos which we tackle in this paper, as shown in Fig. 1. Dicle et al. [3] utilized motion dynamics to distinguish targets with similar appearance, in order to reduce instances of target mislabelling and recover missing (occluded) data. However, their algorithm requires the number of targets to be known a-priori. In contrast, our method handles situations where the number of distractors is unknown and has to be learned on the fly during tracking. Chen et al. [20] proposed a constrained sequential labelling to solve the multi-target data association problem, which utilized learned cost functions and constraint propagation from captured complex dependencies. However, their approach is only designed to handle the case of piece-wise linear motion. The single target tracker of [21] was extended to online multi-target tracking [22] by using global data association. However, candidate target regions must be densely sampled which can be extremely computationally expensive. Moreover, the global identity-aware network flow graph of [22] depends heavily on target appearance models, which have difficulty in handling highly cluttered scenes, especially when both target and distractors share identical appearance. In [23], we learned and exploited the global movement of sports players to inform strong motion priors for key individual players. Information from the global team-level context dynamics enabled the tracker to overcome severe situations such as inter-player occlusions. However, the proposed context-conditioned latent behavior models do not readily generalise to non-sports tracking situations.

In contrast to the above-mentioned works, our proposed tracker explicitly exploits contextual information to detect and learn nearby distractors on-the-fly. It then simultaneously builds a tracking memory of both the target and the distractors, which is used to compute an online-learned global dynamic constraint which is finally fed back to help robustify the single-target tracker.

3   Proposed Distractor-Supported Single-Target Tracking Method

The proposed method consists of two steps. The first step uses the proposed robust estimation with coarse-to-fine multi-level clustering to find candidate image regions for the target and any distractors. The second step distinguishes the target from the distractors, and infers occlusion situations, by feeding back the extracted global dynamic constraint (based on the motion history of both the tracker and the distractors) to the single target tracker.

3.1   Robust Estimation with Coarse-to-fine Multi-level Clustering

Our proposed tracking algorithm first propagates a set of samples drawn from the region around the target position estimated at the preceding frame. We then propose a multi-level clustering-based robust estimation method to find regions that are similar to the target in the new frame. Multiple feature modalities and spatial information are used, level by level, in a coarse-to-fine sampling manner to incrementally achieve better results, shown in Fig. 3. This approach resolves the tradeoff between robustness and tracking speed, by first performing sparse

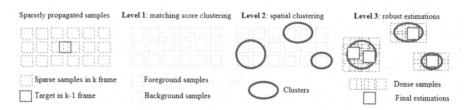

Fig. 3. Coarse-to-fine multi-level clustering-based robust estimation is used to find image regions containing the target or distractors. The algorithm: (i) sparsely propagates samples around the target position from the previous frame; (ii) clusters the propagated samples into two groups (foreground/background samples) according to their associated matching scores; (iii) clusters the foreground samples according to their spatial distribution; (iv) densely samples each clustered foreground region to perform robust estimations.

sampling to find initial candidates, and later applying dense sampling to a small subset of image regions where needed.

The algorithm begins by propagating only a sparse set of samples, with colour features initially used to compute matching scores for each sample. First, clustering is carried out according to colour matching scores to classify samples into *foreground* and *background* sets (level 1 clustering), defined as those with high and low matching scores respectively. Next, the spatial distribution of level 1 foreground samples is used to sub-cluster neighbouring samples (level 2 subclustering). For each level 2 cluster, we then apply a dense sampling, using an additional feature (HOG) for robust estimation (level 3 cluster subdividing). Note that we use the term *foreground* in a special sense, to denote *both the target and the distractors*. Everything else is called *background*.

A. Level 1 Clustering. The algorithm samples a sparse set of N_p locations surrounding the target location in a uniform way. The positions of the samples at the kth frame are denoted by $\{\mathbf{p}_k^i\}_{i=1,...,N_p}$. As colour histograms are acknowledged for their simplicity, computational efficiency, invariance to scale and resolution change [24], we first extract a colour histogram from each sample and compare it to the target appearance model to get matching scores $\{w_{C,k}^i\}_{i=1,...,N_p}$, where C indicates the colour feature. Within the information of the sample distributions and their associated matching scores, we use $\mathbf{x}_k^i = \{\mathbf{p}_k^i, w_{C,k}^i\}$ as the feature vector for a Gaussian Mixture Model in order to cluster the samples into two groups: foreground samples and background samples, according to Eq. 1:

$$p(\mathbf{x}_k^i; \theta) = \sum_{\mathbb{C}=1}^{2} \alpha_{\mathbb{C}} \mathcal{N}(\mathbf{x}_k^i; \mu_{\mathbb{C}}, \sum_{\mathbb{C}}) \qquad (1)$$

where $\alpha_{\mathbb{C}}$ is the weight of the cluster $\mathbb{C}$, $0 < \alpha_{\mathbb{C}} < 1$ for all components, and $\sum_{\mathbb{C}=1}^{2} \alpha_{\mathbb{C}} = 1$, where μ and $\sum$ are the mean and variance of the corresponding cluster. The parameter list:

$$\theta = \{\alpha_1, \mu_1, \sum_1, \alpha_2, \mu_2, \sum_2\} \qquad (2)$$

defines a Gaussian mixture model, which is estimated by maximising the likelihood [25]. The mean matching score of samples in each cluster is denoted by $\bar{w}_{C,k}^{C}$. Then, all samples in the cluster with the highest mean score are regarded as foreground samples, Eq. 3:

$$\mathbb{R}_f(\hat{i}) = 1, \quad \text{if } \hat{i} = \arg\max \bar{w}_{C,k}^{C(i)} \tag{3}$$

where $\mathbb{R}_f$ denotes whether sample $\hat{j}$ is regarded as foreground. The selected foreground samples $\mathbf{p}_k^i$ will next be used for level 2 sub-clustering using additional features, while all samples in the cluster with lower mean score are regarded as background and are discarded.

B. Level 2 Sub-clustering. In a highly cluttered environment, there may be many false positives among those samples labeled as foreground, caused by distractors (non-target image regions with target-like appearance). To distinguish individual objects in the scene (the target and the distractors) we therefore sub-cluster the samples within all level 1 clusters according to their spatial distribution:

$$\mathbb{C}_{sub}(i,j) = 1, \quad \text{if } \mathbb{N}(i,j) = 1, \ i,j \in \mathbb{R}_f \tag{4}$$

where $\mathbb{N}(i,j)$ denotes whether samples i and j are neighbours. $\mathbb{C}_{sub}(i,j) = 1$ labels samples i and j as belonging to the same sub-cluster. $\mathbb{R}_f$ represents the foreground sample cluster (level 1 cluster). Noticeably, the performance of this spatial distribution-based clustering method depends on the spatial density of propagated samples. If the samples are sparsely distributed, it is likely that a level 2 sub-cluster may contain more than one object (a similar problem was identified in [9,10]).

Figure 4 illustrates the results after level 1 and level 2 clustering, using a frame from the *Juggling* sequence. Even if there is a gap between two adjacent objects (Fig. 4A), it can be difficult to distinguish them using a sparse sampling density, Fig. 4B. Therefore, we next proceed to another level (level 3 cluster

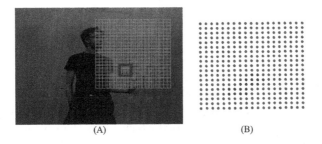

(A)   (B)

Fig. 4. Failure mode of levels 1 and 2 clustering, due to sparse sampling. (A) red grid denotes the sparsely distributed samples. Blue rectangle is the estimated object; (B) red dots denote background samples while blue dots denote foreground samples which have been erroneously merged into a single foreground cluster. Clearly levels 1 and 2 clustering can fail to disambiguate two adjacent objects. (Color figure online)

subdividing), where the foreground regions identified by levels 1 and 2 are more densely sampled and an additional appearance feature is added to achieve finer scale disambiguation.

C. Level 3 Robust Estimation with Cluster Subdividing. After we obtain the set of foreground samples from levels 1 and 2 clustering, we densely sample the region inside each level 2 sub-cluster to further improve the localisation of target and distractor regions. Each level 2 sub-cluster was obtained using colour features for matching, and all level 2 foreground samples therefore already have a high colour matching score. Therefore an additional feature modality is needed to achieve further disambiguation of target and distractor regions. At level 3 the algorithm therefore applies HOG features to compute the matching scores of the new samples, using a kernelised correlation filter [26].

Within each densely re-sampled level 2 sub-cluster, the most straightforward way to identify the object region is to search for the sample with the highest HOG feature matching score. However, as shown in Fig. 4, sometimes a coarse level 2 cluster may contain more than one object. If the target undergoes deformation, then a distractor within the same cluster often triggers a high matching score. In [24,27] they tried to detect the target by applying the expectation operator over the distributed samples with associated weights (i.e. taking the likelihood-weighted mean of all samples). However, the expectation estimation might be highly erroneous when multiple similar objects are present in the scene [28]. For example, taking the mean location of two similar objects will give an estimated location which lies on a background region, midway between both samples. To overcome this problem, we observe that the spatial ambiguity between the sample with the highest matching score (the *mode*) and the location of the *mean* sample (derived from the expectation operator) can indicate potential distractions within a cluster, and enable robust estimation.

Within the dense level 3 samples, the initial estimate of the object inside each cluster is taken to be the sample with the highest HOG matching score (i.e., the mode sample), denoted by $\mathbf{p}_k^{\mathbb{C}_{sub}(i_h)}$. We also use the expectation operator over all samples in the cluster to compute the mean sample:

$$\bar{\mathbf{p}}_k^{\mathbb{C}_{sub}} = \sum_{i=1}^{N_{\mathbb{C}}} w_{H,k}^{\mathbb{C}_{sub}(i)} \mathbf{p}_k^{\mathbb{C}_{sub}(i)} \tag{5}$$

where $w_{H,k}^{\mathbb{C}_{sub}(i)}$ is the associated HOG feature matching score of the dense sample i inside level 2 sub-cluster $\mathbb{C}_{sub}$ and $N_{\mathbb{C}}$ is the number of samples inside each cluster. If the overlap between $\mathbf{p}_k^{\mathbb{C}_{sub}(i_h)}$ and $\bar{\mathbf{p}}_k^{\mathbb{C}_{sub}}$ is small, it suggests there is another distractor inside the cluster, which is on the opposite side of $\mathbf{p}_k^{i_h}$ compared to $\bar{\mathbf{p}}_k$, see Fig. 5.

If we denote foreground samples in the other half of the cluster as $\mathbb{R}_{f,\mathbb{C}_{sub}/2}$, then a second object's location is estimated by:

$$\hat{i} = \arg\max w_{H,k}^{\mathbb{C}_{sub}(i)}$$
$$\textbf{s.t.}\quad i \in \mathbb{R}_{f,\mathbb{C}_{sub}/2}, \quad \mathbf{p}_k^{i_h} \cap \bar{\mathbf{p}}_k^{\mathbb{C}_{sub}} < \zeta \tag{6}$$

Fig. 5. Sub-image of Fig. 4B with level 3 clustering. Green dot denotes mode sample $\mathbf{p}_k^{\mathcal{C}_{sub}(i_h)}$. Black dot is the mean sample $\bar{\mathbf{p}}_k^{\mathcal{C}_{sub}}$. Yellow dots denote foreground samples in the other half of the same cluster. (Color figure online)

where ζ is the overlap threshold. This method will iteratively estimate the potential distractors inside each cluster until $\mathbf{p}_k^{i_h}$ and $\bar{\mathbf{p}}_k$ have significant overlap. Note that the difference between mode sample and mean sample is utilised in a novel way to indicate the search direction, which helps find the objects quickly, even when partly occluded, as illustrated in Fig. 7.

The final estimations from all clusters indicate "foreground" regions that might contain either the target or distractors, denoted by $\{\mathbf{p}_{o,k}^i\}_{i=1...N_{o,k}}$ where $N_{o,k}$ is the number of observed foreground regions (note we use foreground to refer to both the target and target-like distractors).

So far, we have presented a multi-level clustering-based robust estimation method with coarse-to-fine sampling to detect target-like regions. The method reduces the computational cost compared to dense sampling over the entire image, while improving tracking accuracy compared to methods using a fixed spatial sampling density. The algorithm will next combine the motion history information of both the target and the distractors to build a global dynamic constraint, described in Sect. 3.2. This global information will be fed back to the single-target tracker, deterministically associating a single foreground region to the target and also detecting occlusion situations.

3.2 Global Dynamic Constraint in a Feedback Loop

In highly cluttered scenes, motion cues are important for overcoming the ambiguity caused by appearance similarities between the target and the distractors [3]. Therefore, we use motion history of the target and the distractors to build a global dynamics constraint and feed it back to the individual tracker, which deterministically associates a single foreground region to the true target and prevents the estimated target location from erroneously jumping to a distractor during occlusion or extreme camouflage interactions.

A. Global Motion Regression Model of the Target and the Distractors. During rapid camera motion, the image coordinates of the objects (i.e., of the target and/or distractors) can jump abruptly. However, the *relative* positions between the objects remain relatively stable. Therefore, our global motion model is generated from the relative positions between the tracked target and the surrounding distractors. The multi-level clustering-based robust estimation (described in the previous section) outputs multiple detected foreground objects $\{\mathbf{p}_{o,k}^i\}_{i=1...N_{o,k}}$ at the kth frame. We now re-write the coordinates of these objects as:

$$\mathbf{p}_{o,k}^i = \bar{\mathbf{p}}_{o,k} + \Delta\mathbf{p}_{o,k}^i \tag{7}$$

where $\Delta\mathbf{p}_{o,k}^i$ represents the relative displacement between the ith object location and the spatial distribution centre $\bar{\mathbf{p}}_{o,k} = \frac{1}{N_{o,k}}\sum_{i=1}^{N_{o,k}}\mathbf{p}_{o,k}^i$ of all object position estimates.

Over a short time interval, the underlying dynamics of the target can reasonably be approximated as a linear regression model [3]. The global (relative) motion of the target in frame κ is then predicted by a linear regression model: $\Delta\mathbf{p}_{t,\kappa} = \beta_0 + \beta_1\kappa + \varepsilon_\kappa$, where β_0, β_1 are the coefficients and ε_k is a noise term. To estimate the parameters, the algorithm minimises the sum of squared residuals $\sum_{i=1}^{k-1}\varepsilon_\kappa^2$, where $\hat{\beta}_0, \hat{\beta}_1$ is obtained from the historic information of the relative position of the target, by least squares estimates. The predicted relative position of the target at frame k is:

$$\Delta\hat{\mathbf{p}}_{t,k} = \hat{\beta}_0 + \hat{\beta}_1 k \tag{8}$$

Note that the relative positions of the target and the distractors implicitly encode global information about the scene dynamics. The relative position of foreground object i at the kth frame can be denoted by $\Delta\mathbf{p}_{o,k}^i$, which is computed from Eq. 7. Note that our tracking algorithm is only concerned with solving the *single* target tracking problem, and does not assign or maintain individual IDs for all foreground objects in the scene. Using the relative target position predicted by the global motion model, we can calculate likelihood of a foreground object being the true target as:

$$w_{D,k}^i = e^{-|\Delta\mathbf{p}_{o,k}^i - \Delta\hat{\mathbf{p}}_{t,k}|} \tag{9}$$

where $w_{D,k}^i$ denotes the dynamic similarity score between the predicted target relative position $\Delta\hat{\mathbf{p}}_{t,k}$ and the relative position $\Delta\mathbf{p}_{o,k}^i$ of the ith foreground object.

Intuitively, the robustness of this dynamic similarity score, in Eq. 9, corresponds to the complexity and stability of the spatial distribution of the the detected foreground objects. If the number of detected foreground objects changes dramatically, this indicates either potential occlusion or newly emerged distractors.

B. Handling Dynamic Numbers of Distractors. While modelling the global dynamics, it is crucial to be able to handle situations where the number of detected foreground objects is changing. In such situations, the relative positions can be highly noisy or even invalid because of newly emerged/disappeared objects.

Newly emerged or disappeared foreground objects might either be the target or the distractors. Therefore, we use the image coordinates to associate each detected object i with a target-like dynamic matching score $w_{t,k}^i$ and distractor-like dynamic matching scores $w_{d,k}^{i,m}$, computed by:

$$\begin{cases} w_{t,k}^i = e^{-|\mathbf{p}_{o,k}^i - \mathbf{p}_{t,k-1}|} \\ w_{d,k}^{i,m} = e^{-|\mathbf{p}_{o,k}^i - \mathbf{p}_{d,k-1}^m|} \end{cases} \tag{10}$$

where $\mathbf{p}_{t,k-1}, \mathbf{p}_{d,k-1}^{m}$ are the positions of the target and the m-th distractor in the $k-1$th frame. $\mathbf{p}_{o,k}^{i}$ is the ith detected object at frame k. Here, the exponential function is applied to normalise the likelihood value to occupy the range $(0,1)$. The detected object corresponding to the target should have a high target-like dynamic matching score and also a low distractor-like dynamic matching score, giving a *global* dynamic score $w_{D,k}^{i}$ for the ith object as:

$$w_{D,k}^{i} = \begin{cases} N_{d,k-1} w_{t,k}^{i} / \sum_{m=1}^{N_{d,k-1}} w_{d,k}^{i,m} \ , & N_{d,k-1} \neq 0 \\ w_{t,k}^{i} \ , & others \end{cases} \tag{11}$$

where $N_{d,k-1}$ is the number of distractors in the $k-1$th frame.

C. Global Dynamic Constraint Fed Back to the Single-target Tracker. Our proposed algorithm feeds the generated global dynamic information back to the single-target tracker to constrain the estimated target trajectory and detect occlusion situations. Next, the newly estimated target state is used to update the global dynamic information for successive frames, as shown in Fig. 1B. With modelled global information, the final target region is optimally assigned to the candidate region with the highest dynamic similarity score $w_{D,k}^{i}$ by Eq. 12:

$$\hat{i} = \arg\max \ w_{D,k}^{i}$$
$$\textbf{s.t.} \ \ w_{t,k}^{i} \geq \lambda_{d} max \ \{w_{d,k}^{i,m}\}_{m=1,\ldots,N_{d,k-1}} \tag{12}$$

where $w_{D,k}^{i}$ is computed from Eq. 9 when the number of detected foreground objects is stable, and from Eq. 11 when the number of detected objects is changing. $N_{d,k-1}$ represents the number of the distractors in the $k-1$th frame while λ_{d} is a scaling factor in the range between 0 and 1. After confirming the target, the appearance model is updated using a linear combination of the reference model and the observation [24,29]. The global dynamic constraint is updated accordingly (Eqs. 9, 11).

4   Experimental Results

We first evaluate our proposed tracker by analysing the contributions of each of the key components (robust estimation with cluster subdividing, and the global dynamic constraint) on overall performance. Next we compare our tracker against the other state-of-the-art trackers which were ranked highest in recent benchmark studies [1,2,30]. Section 4.1 analyses performance specifically on highly cluttered scenes. Section 4.2 tests on all other scenes from OTB100 [1], confirming that our method also performs competitively on uncluttered scenes.

Evaluation Metrics. In this paper, we compare trackers in terms of the area under the curve (AUC) of the overlap rate curve [1]. **Implementation**. The proposed algorithm was implemented in Matlab2014a (linked to some C components) using an Intel Core i5-3570 CPU, giving average speed of 20.23 fps on non-cluttered scenes, and 4.01 fps on highly cluttered scenes with overhead computation cost from global dynamic model. All sequences and the code are publicly available.

4.1   Experiment on Highly Cluttered Dataset

Datasets. We have selected 28 highly cluttered sequences from publicly available data-sets [1–3,22]. Note that we do not use the full datasets in these first tests because: (i) these large datasets only contain a few sequences featuring extreme clutter and camouflage, which this paper specifically addresses; (ii) testing on all sequences introduces confounding factors (non-clutter conditions) making it hard to disambiguate the true capabilities of each algorithm to tackle clutter and camouflage. To gain a deeper understanding of the tracker performance on cluttered scenes, we propose a new set of *sub-attributes* for clutter and camou-flage: shape clutter, colour clutter, camera motion-caused camouflage motion, self-moving camouflage. We have *per-frame* annotated all sequences with all these sub-attributes.

A. Evaluation of the Tracker Sub-components. In this section, we decom-pose the method and evaluate the contribution of each of the key components to the overall performance. In the experiment, the baseline algorithm applies the colour feature used in Sect. 3.1A to estimate the target position from the sam-ple with the highest matching score. Next, we add HOG feature as described in Sect. 3.1C to identify the target region. Since the data association method SMOT [3] is explicitly designed for simultaneously tracking multiple targets which share similar appearance, we use this multi-target tracker to evaluate the effectiveness of the global dynamic constraint. Note that the original SMOT [3] is initialised with ground-truth positions for all objects (potential regions that con-tain the target or distractors). To conduct a meaningful comparison, we input the same detections from our proposed robust estimation to SMOT for data association and output the optimized path for the target. We provide the AUC results [1] of the decomposed algorithm for single target tracking, tested (i) over the entire dataset and (ii) for the frames corresponding to particular sub-attributes, Table 1.

Table 1 shows that our proposed multi-level clustering-based robust esti-mation improves tracking performance. The performance of our method ver-sus SMOT [3] demonstrates the effectiveness of our proposed global dynamic

Table 1. AUC for the decomposed single target tracking algorithm tested in extremely cluttered scenes. **B**: baseline algorithm (only colour feature); **H**: HOG feature used in Sect. 3.1C; **GDC**: global dynamic constraint in Sect. 3.2. (red: best performance; blue: second best performance).

Tracker	Overall	Clutter type		Camouflage motion	
		Colour	Shape	Camera-caused motion	Self-motion
B	6.204	5.6072	6.0677	5.7518	6.1285
B+H	7.8030	7.2776	7.6666	6.4885	7.6789
B+H+SMOT [3]	7.3545	6.7536	7.2065	6.5659	7.2558
B+H+GDC	8.7108	8.4086	8.5921	7.0662	8.6388

Fig. 6. Performance of our proposed single target tracker in extremely cluttered and camouflaged scenes. First row: *bolt 1*; second row: *marching*. Red bounding box: the target; yellow bounding box: adjacent distractors. (Color figure online)

Table 2. AUC for single target tracking performance in extremely cluttered scenes. Our proposed method significantly outperforms all compared methods on all sub-attributes. (red: best performance; blue: second best performance)

Tracker	Overall	Clutter type		Camouflage motion	
		Colour	Shape	Camera-caused motion	Self-motion
CT [11]	2.7215	2.5956	2.7984	1.9619	2.7641
CPF [24]	5.0872	4.1938	4.9113	4.9852	4.9120
Struck [21]	5.8647	5.2944	6.0627	3.6934	6.0705
SCM [31]	6.4292	5.6997	6.6102	4.1297	6.5985
KCF [29]	7.5602	6.9372	7.5118	5.5188	7.5591
HCF [32]	7.6767	7.0615	7.9109	6.5943	7.9219
Ours	8.7108	8.4086	8.5921	7.0662	8.6388

constraint. Since SMOT algorithm has difficulty handling scenes with highly dynamic number of distractors, it associates the wrong object to the target, impeding tracking performance. Of note, our proposed tracking method runs at 4.01 fps, while SMOT has a speed of 1.86 fps.

Figure 6 illustrates the strong performance of our proposed tracker in extreme clutter and camouflage. Distractors, detected and learned online by our tracker, are indicated by yellow bounding boxes, while the true target is shown with a red bounding box. In frame 139 of sequence *marching*, one distractor shares a major overlap with the target, however our proposed multi-level clustering process can still very accurately disambiguate and localise these two objects.

B. Overall Performance Comparison. To evaluate tracking performance under highly cluttered conditions, our proposed algorithm is compared against several state-of-the-art single target trackers including KCF [29], Struck [21], SCM [31], CPF [24] and the latest CNN-based tracker HCF [32], which were highly ranked in recent benchmark studies [1,2,30]. The CT algorithm [11] is considered as the most closely related work to ours, thus it also takes part in the comparison. We provide the AUC results [1] of each tracker in Table 2. The trade-off overlap rate curve is shown in Fig. 7.

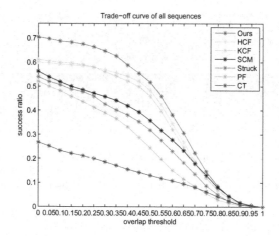

Fig. 7. The trade-off overlap rate curve of single target trackers, tested on 28 videos featuring highly cluttered scenes.

Our proposed tracker outperforms all compared trackers, both overall and also in all sub-attribute categories. KCF [29] and HCF [32] are both based on correlation filters but using different features. Since HCF applies the latest CNN features, it slightly outperforms KCF (using HOG). Note that our proposed method, even without our proposed global dynamic constraint (shown in Table 1), outperforms HCF (Table 2). This is because HCF densely samples the regions around the target, while our coarse-to-fine searching mechanism searches over an initially larger area to progressively finer granularities. CT [11] does exploit contextual information, but the algorithm is still based primarily on appearance matching. Since CT exploits more distracting information which is not properly eliminated, it performs the worst out of the compared methods.

4.2   Experiment on Non-cluttered Dataset

To check how the proposed algorithm performs on non-cluttered scenes, we also tested our algorithm on non-cluttered sequences (94 seq) from OTB100 [1], excluding the already used highly cluttered sequences. The ranks on the non-cluttered scenes are: HCF (11.04, AUC score), *ours* (9.78), KCF (9.44), Struck (9.34), SCM (9.00), CPF (6.82). HCF with CNN-based rich features achieves the best results on the non-cluttered sequences when handling other confounding factors, followed by our tracker with comparably good results.

5   Conclusions

In this paper we presented a novel method for tracking a single target in scenes of extreme clutter and camouflage. In contrast to conventional tracking algorithms which only maintain information about the target, the proposed algorithm incorporates a novel multi-level clustering method for online detection and learning of target-like contextual image regions, called distractors. To disambiguate the target's path among the distractors, a global dynamic constraint is proposed in a feedback loop to improve the single target tracker, and occlusion situations are also detected when no likely target path is found. The proposed method successfully prevents the estimated target location from erroneously jumping to distractors during occlusions or camouflage interactions. To evaluate our tracker, we have introduced a new set of sub-attributes, and have per-frame annotated a number of public benchmark test sequences with these sub-attributes. Using this dataset featuring extreme clutter and camouflage, we have first demonstrated the contribution of each key component of the tracker to the overall tracking performance, and then compared our tracker against highly ranked target tracking algorithms from the literature, demonstrating that our proposed method significantly outperforms other state-of-the-art trackers. In addition, we tested the tracker on non-cluttered scenes, where it also achieves competitive performance.

Acknowledgement. We acknowledge MoD/Dstl and EPSRC for providing the grant to support the UK academics (Ales Leonardis) involvement in a Department of Defense funded MURI project. This work was also supported by EU H2020 RoMaNS 645582 and EPSRC EP/M026477/1.

References

1. Wu, Y., Lim, J., Yang, M.H.: Online object tracking: A benchmark. In: CVPR, pp. 2411–2418. IEEE (2013)
2. Kristan, M., Matas, J., Leonardis, A., Vojir, T., Pflugfelder, R., Fernandez, G., Nebehay, G., Porikli, F., Cehovin, L.: A novel performance evaluation methodology for single-target trackers. PAMI (2015). http://ieeexplore.ieee.org/document/7379002/
3. Dicle, C., Camps, O.I., Sznaier, M.: The way they move: Tracking multiple targets with similar appearance. In: ICCV, pp. 2304–2311. IEEE (2013)
4. Kristan, M., Kovacic, S., Leonardis, A., Pers, J.: A two-stage dynamic model for visual tracking. IEEE Trans. Syst. Man Cybern. **40**(6), 1505–1520 (2010)
5. Xiao, J., Stolkin, R., Leonardis, A.: Single target tracking using adaptive clustered decision trees and dynamic multi-level appearance models. In: CVPR (2015)
6. Grabner, H., Matas, J., Van Gool, L., Cattin, P.: Tracking the invisible: Learning where the object might be. In: CVPR, pp. 1285–1292, June 2010
7. Yang, M., Wu, Y., Hua, G.: Context-aware visual tracking. PAMI **31**(7), 1195–1209 (2009)
8. Vermaak, J., Doucet, A., Pérez, P.: Maintaining multimodality through mixture tracking. In: ICCV, pp. 1110–1116. IEEE (2003)
9. Okuma, K., Taleghani, A., Freitas, N., Little, J.J., Lowe, D.G.: A boosted particle filter: multitarget detection and tracking. In: Pajdla, T., Matas, J. (eds.) ECCV 2004. LNCS, vol. 3021, pp. 28–39. Springer, Heidelberg (2004). doi:10.1007/978-3-540-24670-1_3
10. Yang, C., Duraiswami, R., Davis, L.: Fast multiple object tracking via a hierarchical particle filter. In: ICCV, vol. 1, pp. 212–219. IEEE (2005)
11. Dinh, T.B., Vo, N., Medioni, G.: Context tracker: Exploring supporters and distracters in unconstrained environments. In: CVPR, pp. 1177–1184. IEEE (2011)

12. Jiang, N., Wu, Y.: Unifying spatial and attribute selection for distracter-resilient tracking. In: CVPR, pp. 3502–3509 (2014)
13. Hong, Z., Mei, X., Tao, D.: Dual-force metric learning for robust distracter-resistant tracker. In: Fitzgibbon, A., Lazebnik, S., Perona, P., Sato, Y., Schmid, C. (eds.) ECCV 2012. LNCS, vol. 7572, pp. 513–527. Springer, Heidelberg (2012). doi:10.1007/978-3-642-33718-5_37
14. Talha, M., Stolkin, R.: Particle filter tracking of camouflaged targets by adaptive fusion of thermal and visible spectra camera data. IEEE Sens. J. **14**(1), 159–166 (2014)
15. Stolkin, R., Rees, D., Talha, M., Florescu, I.: Bayesian fusion of thermal and visible spectra camera data for region based tracking with rapid background adaptation. In: 2012 IEEE Conference on Multisensor Fusion and Integration for Intelligent Systems (MFI), pp. 192–199. IEEE (2012)
16. Xiao, J., Stolkin, R., Oussalah, M., Leonardis, A.: Continuously adaptive data fusion and model relearning for particle filter tracking with multiple features. IEEE Sens. J. **16**(8), 2639–2649 (2016)
17. Possegger, H., Mauthner, T., Bischof, H.: In defense of color-based model-free tracking. In: CVPR, pp. 2113–2120 (2015)
18. Berclaz, J., Fleuret, F., Turetken, E., Fua, P.: Multiple object tracking using k-shortest paths optimization. PAMI **33**(9), 1806–1819 (2011)
19. Ben Shitrit, H., Berclaz, J., Fleuret, F., Fua, P.: Tracking multiple people under global appearance constraints. In: ICCV, pp. 137–144. IEEE (2011)
20. Chen, S., Fern, A., Todorovic, S.: Multi-object tracking via constrained sequential labeling. In: CVPR, pp. 1130–1137. IEEE (2014)
21. Hare, S., Saffari, A., Torr, P.H.: Struck: Structured output tracking with kernels. In: ICCV, pp. 263–270. IEEE (2011)
22. Dehghan, A., Tian, Y., Torr, P.H., Shah, M.: Target identity-aware network flow for online multiple target tracking. In: CVPR, pp. 1146–1154 (2015)
23. Xiao, J., Stolkin, R., Leonardis, A.: Multi-target tracking in team-sports videos via multi-level context-conditioned latent behaviour models. In: BMVC (2014)
24. Nummiaro, K., Koller-Meier, E., Van Gool, L.: An adaptive color-based particle filter. Image Vis. Comput. **21**(1), 99–110 (2003)
25. Myung, I.J.: Tutorial on maximum likelihood estimation. J. Math. Psychol. **47**(1), 90–100 (2003)
26. Henriques, J.F., Caseiro, R., Martins, P., Batista, J.: Exploiting the circulant structure of tracking-by-detection with kernels. In: Fitzgibbon, A., Lazebnik, S., Perona, P., Sato, Y., Schmid, C. (eds.) ECCV 2012. LNCS, vol. 7575, pp. 702–715. Springer, Heidelberg (2012). doi:10.1007/978-3-642-33765-9_50
27. Mei, X., Ling, H.: Robust visual tracking using L1 minimization. In: ICCV, pp. 1436–1443. IEEE (2009)
28. Xiao, J., Oussalah, M.: Collaborative tracking for multiple objects in the presence of inter-occlusions. TCSVT **26**(2), 304–318 (2015)
29. Henriques, J.F., Caseiro, R., Martins, P., Batista, J.: High-speed tracking with kernelized correlation filters. PAMI **37**(3), 583–596 (2015)
30. Li, A., Lin, M., Wu, Y., Yang, M.H., Yan, S.: NUS-PRO: A new visual tracking challenge. PAMI **38**(2), 335–349 (2015)
31. Zhong, W., Lu, H., Yang, M.H.: Robust object tracking via sparsity-based collaborative model. In: CVPR, pp. 1838–1845. IEEE (2012)
32. Ma, C., Huang, J.B., Yang, X., Yang, M.H.: Hierarchical convolutional features for visual tracking. In: ICCV, pp. 3074–3082(2015)

Connectionist Temporal Modeling for Weakly Supervised Action Labeling

De-An Huang[(✉)], Li Fei-Fei, and Juan Carlos Niebles

Computer Science Department, Stanford University, Stanford, USA
{dahuang,feifeili,jniebles}@cs.stanford.edu

Abstract. We propose a weakly-supervised framework for action labeling in video, where only the order of occurring actions is required during training time. The key challenge is that the per-frame alignments
between the input (video) and label (action) sequences are unknown
during training. We address this by introducing the Extended Connectionist Temporal Classification (ECTC) framework to efficiently evaluate
all possible alignments via dynamic programming and explicitly enforce
their consistency with frame-to-frame visual similarities. This protects
the model from distractions of visually inconsistent or degenerated alignments without the need of temporal supervision. We further extend our
framework to the semi-supervised case when a few frames are sparsely
annotated in a video. With less than 1 % of labeled frames per video, our
method is able to outperform existing semi-supervised approaches and
achieve comparable performance to that of fully supervised approaches.

1 Introduction

With the rising popularity of video sharing sites like YouTube, there is a large
amount of visual data uploaded to the Internet. This has stimulated recent
developments of large-scale action understanding in videos [12,16,18]. Supervised
learning methods can be effective in this case, but fully annotating actions in
videos at large scale is costly in practice. An alternative is to develop methods
that require weak supervision, which may be automatically extracted from movie
scripts [3,5,9] or instructional videos [2,4,50] at a lower cost.

In this work, we address the problem of weakly-supervised action labeling in
videos. In this setting, only incomplete temporal localization of actions is available during training, and the goal is to train models that can be applied in new
videos to annotate each frame with an action label. This is challenging as the
algorithm must reason not only about whether an action occurs in a video, but
also about its exact temporal location. Our setting contrasts with most existing
works [19,26,32,48] for action labeling that require fully annotated videos with
accurate per frame action labels for training. Here, we aim at achieving comparable temporal action localization *without* temporal supervision in training.

The setting of our work is illustrated in Fig. 1. During training, only the
order of the occurring actions is given, and the goal is to apply the learned
model to unseen test videos. As no temporal localization is provided during

© Springer International Publishing AG 2016
B. Leibe et al. (Eds.): ECCV 2016, Part IV, LNCS 9908, pp. 137–153, 2016.
DOI: 10.1007/978-3-319-46493-0_9

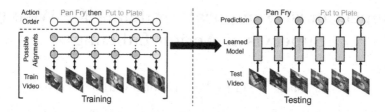

Fig. 1. We tackle the problem of weakly supervised action labeling where only the order of the occurring actions is given during training (left). We train a temporal model by maximizing the probability of all possible frame-to-label alignments. At testing time (right), no annotation is given. As our learned model already encodes the temporal structure of videos, it predicts the correct actions without further information.

training, the first challenge of our task is that there is a large number of possible alignments (or correspondences) between action labels and video frames, and it is infeasible to naively search through all of these alignments. We address this challenge by first introducing Connectionist Temporal Classification (CTC) [13], originally designed for speech recognition, to our video understanding task. CTC efficiently evaluates all of the possible alignments using dynamic programming.

Directly applying the original CTC framework to our weakly-supervised action labeling could not fully address the challenge of a large space of possible frame to action label alignments. Note that the duration of an action could be hundreds of frames, which is much longer than the duration of phonetic states in speech recognition. As a result, we are required to align videos of thousands of frames to only dozens of actions. This poses a unique challenge in comparison to speech, as our space of possible alignments is much larger and contains degenerated alignments that can deteriorate performance. We address this challenge by proposing the Extended Connectionist Temporal Classification (ECTC) framework, which explicitly enforces the alignments to be consistent with frame-to-frame visual similarities. The incorporation of similarity allows us to (1) explicitly encourage the model to output visually consistent alignments instead of fitting to the giant space of all possible alignments (2) down-weight degenerated paths that are visually inconsistent. In addition, we extend the forward-backward algorithm of [13] to incorporate visual similarity, which allows us to efficiently evaluate all of the possible alignments while explicitly enforcing their consistency with frame-to-frame similarities at the same time.

While our main focus is the weakly supervised setting, we also show how to extend our approach to incorporate supervision beyond action ordering. To this end, we introduce the *frame-level* semi-supervised setting, where action labels are temporally localized in a few annotated video frames. This supervision could be extracted from movie scripts [9,23] or by asking annotators to label actions for a small number of frames in the video, which is less costly than precisely annotating temporal boundaries of all actions. We model such supervision as a frame to label alignment constraints and naturally incorporate it in our ECTC framework to efficiently prune out inconsistent alignments. This significantly reduces the alignment space and boosts the performance of our approach.

The main contributions of our work can be summarized as: (1) We first introduce CTC to our video understanding task, as a way to efficiently evaluate all frame to action alignments. (2) We propose ECTC to explicitly enforce the consistency of alignments with visual similarities, which protects the model from distractions of visually inconsistent alignments without the need of temporal supervision. (3) We extend ECTC to incorporate *frame-level* semi-supervision in a unified framework to significantly reduce the space of possible alignments. (4) We test our model on long and complex activity videos from the Breakfast Actions Dataset [19] and a subset of the Hollywood2 dataset [5], and show that our method achieves state-of-the-art performance with less than 1 % of supervision.

2   Related Work

As significant progress has been made on categorizing temporally trimmed video clips, recent research of human activity analysis is shifting towards a higher level understanding in real-world settings [11,22,29,35,43,49]. Two tasks of action labeling have been explored extensively. The first is video classification, where the goal is to categorize each video to a discrete action class. Challenging datasets including UCF101 [38], HMDB51 [21], Sports1M [18], and ActivityNet [16] exemplify this. Deep neural networks trained directly from videos [8,36] have shown promising results on this task [46]. The second is dense action labeling, where the goal is to label each frame with the occurring actions [19,24,26,32,48], and the fully annotated temporal boundaries of actions are given during training.

In this paper, we aim to achieve action labeling with a weaker level of supervision that is easier to obtain than accurately time-stamped action labels. A similar goal has been explored in video to action alignment [4,5]. The closest to our work is the ordering constrained discriminative clustering (OCDC) approach [5], where the goal is to align video frames to an ordered list of actions. Using the ordering constraint, OCDC extends previous work [9] to deal with multiple actions in a video. As their focus is on video to action alignment, their method can assume that the ordering of actions is available both at training and testing. Our approach aims at a more general scenario, where the learned model is applied to unseen test videos that come without information about the actions appearing in the video. When applied to this more general scenario, OCDC is equivalent to a frame-by-frame action classifier that was implicitly learned during the training alignment. Therefore, OCDC does not fully exploit temporal information at test time, since it does not encapsulate the temporal relationships provided by the ordering supervision. This may limit its applicability to temporally structured complex activities. On the other hand, our temporal modeling exploits the temporal structure of actions in videos, such as the transitions between actions, by capturing them during training and leveraging at test time.

Our work is also related to recent progress on using instructional videos or movie scripts [2,4,9,25,30,35,51] as supervision for video parsing. These approaches also tackle the case when some text is available for alignment at testing time, and focus more on the natural language processing side of understanding the text in the instructions or the scripts. In this paper, we focus on training a temporal model that is applicable to unseen test videos that come without associated text. Our supervision could potentially be obtained with some of these text processing approaches, but this is not the focus of our work.

Our goal of understanding the temporal structure of video is related to [10, 31,34,37,39,40]. In contrast to their goal of classifying the whole video to a single action, our goal is to utilize the temporal structure of videos to guide the training of an action labeling model that can predict the occurring action at every frame in the unseen test video. Our use of visual similarities in the training is related to unsupervised video parsing [28,29,45], where frames are grouped into segments based on visual or semantic cues. We integrate visual similarity with weak supervision as a soft guidance of the model and go beyond just grouping video frames.

The core of our model builds upon Recurrent Neural Networks (RNN), which have been proved effective for capturing the temporal dependencies in data, and have been applied to challenging computer vision tasks including image captioning [7,8,17], video description [8,42,47], activity recognition [8,27], dense video labeling [48]. However, in the above tasks, accurate temporal localization of actions is either ignored or requires pre-segmented training data. Our ECTC framework enables learning recurrent temporal models with weak supervision, and we show empirically its effectiveness on the video action labeling task.

3   Ordering Constrained Video Action Labeling

Our goal is to train a temporal model to assign action labels to every frame of unseen test videos. We use a Recurrent Neural Network (RNN) at the core of our approach, as it has been successfully applied to label actions in videos [8,48]. While RNNs have been generally trained with full supervision in previous work, we aim to train them with weak supervision in the form of an ordered list of occurring actions. We address this challenge by proposing the Extended Connectionist Temporal Classification (ECTC) framework that efficiently evaluates all possible frame to action alignments and weights them by their consistency with the visual similarity of consecutive frames. The use of visual similarities sets our approach apart from the direct application of CTC [13] and alleviates the problem caused by visually inconsistent alignments. ECTC incorporates a frame dependent binary term on top of the original unary based model, and we show that this can be efficiently handled by our forward-backward algorithm.

3.1   Extended Connectionist Temporal Classification

The biggest challenge of our task is that only the order of the actions is given during training. Formally, given a training set consisting of video examples $X = [x_1, \cdots , x_T] \in \mathbb{R}^{d \times T}$ represented by d-dimensional features x_t extracted from each of their T frames, our goal is to infer the associated action labels $a = [a_1, \cdots , a_T] \in \mathcal{A}^{1 \times T}$, where $\mathcal{A}$ is a fixed set of possible actions. Note that a is not available for our training examples. Instead, the supervision we have for

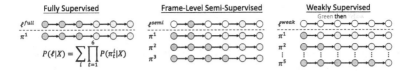

Fig. 2. Comparison of different levels of supervision (first row). Blank circles indicate frames without annotated action. The probability of ℓ is given by the sum of the probabilities of all the paths π^i that are consistent with it.

each video is the order of actions $\ell = \mathcal{B}(a)$, where $\mathcal{B}$ is the operator that removes the repeated labels. For example, $\mathcal{B}([b, b, c, c, c]) = [b, c]$. Our goal is to learn a temporal model using this supervision, and apply it to unseen test videos for which neither ℓ nor a are available. We build our temporal models with an RNN at the core. Let $Y = [y_1, \cdots, y_T] \in \mathbb{R}^{A \times T}$ be the RNN output at each frame, where $A = |\mathcal{A}|$ is the number of possible actions. We normalize the output vectors y_t using a softmax to get $z_t^k = P(k, t|X) = e^{y_t^k} / \sum_{k'} e^{y_t^{k'}}$, which can be interpreted as the probability of emitting action k at time t.

In the original CTC formulation [13], the conditional independence assumption states that the probability of a label sequence $\pi = [\pi_1, \cdots, \pi_T]$ is:

$$P(\pi|X) = \prod_{t=1}^{T} z_t^{\pi_t}, \tag{1}$$

which corresponds to the stepwise product of $z_t^{\pi_t}$ at each frame. Note that we distinguish a *path* π that indicates per-frame label information from the *label sequence* $\ell = \mathcal{B}(\pi)$ which only contains the ordering of actions and no precise temporal localization of labels. Label sequence ℓ is computed from path π by $\mathcal{B}(\pi)$, which removes all the consecutive label repetitions. We can compute the probability of emitting a label sequence ℓ, by summing the probability of all paths π that can be reduced to ℓ using the operator $\mathcal{B}$:

$$P(\ell|X) = \sum_{\{\pi|\mathcal{B}(\pi)=\ell\}} P(\pi|X). \tag{2}$$

Given the label sequence ℓ for each training video X, model learning is formulated as minimizing $\mathcal{L}(\ell, X) = -\log P(\ell|X)$, the negative log likelihood of emitting ℓ. The intuition is that, because we do not have the exact temporal location of a label, we sum over all the frame to label alignments that are consistent with ℓ [14]. One drawback of this original CTC formulation in Eq. (1) is that it does not take into account the fact that consecutive frames in the video are highly correlated, especially visually similar ones. This is important as the sum in Eq. (2) might thus include label paths π that are visually inconsistent with the video contents and thus deteriorate the performance. In the following, we discuss how our ECTC uses visual similarity to reweight the possible paths.

We introduce the Extended CTC framework to address such limitations. To illustrate our framework, assume that $z_t^a = z_t^b$ for all t in a short clip of visually

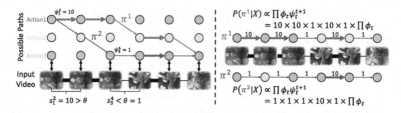

Fig. 3. Our ECTC framework uses the binary term ψ_t^{t+1} to re-weight paths. In this example, an input video has 6 frames and 3 annotated actions. Thicker connections between frames indicate higher similarity. In ECTC, π^1 has higher weight than π^2 since it stays in the same action for similar frames. In the example, π^1 actually matches the ground truth actions. In contrast, both paths are weighted equally in CTC.

similar frames. In this example, the probability of the path $[a, b, a, b]$ will be the same as $[a, a, b, b]$ using Eq. (1). Clearly the latter path should be more probable, as action labels are usually smooth and stay the same for visually similar frames. Such intuition, however, is not compatible with Eq. (1). While our RNN could implicitly encode such pattern from training observations, we reformulate Eq. (1) to explicitly enforce the incorporation of visual similarity between consecutive frames by rewarding visually consistent paths:

$$P(\pi|X) \propto \prod_{t=1}^{T} \phi_t \psi_t^{t+1}, \quad \phi_t = z_t^{\pi_t}, \quad \psi_t^{t+1} = \begin{cases} \max(\theta, s_t^{t+1}) & \pi_t = \pi_{t+1} \\ \theta & \pi_t \neq \pi_{t+1}. \end{cases} \quad (3)$$

The path probability now includes both a unary term ϕ_t and a binary term ψ_t^{t+1}. The unary term is defined as $z_t^{\pi_t}$ and represents the original formulation. We introduce the binary term ψ_t^{t+1} to explicitly capture the correlation between consecutive frames, where θ is a predefined minimum similarity, and $s_t^{t+1} = \mathrm{sim}(x_t, x_{t+1})$ is the similarity between frames. When $\pi_t = \pi_{t+1}$ and $s_t^{t+1} > \theta$ (the two frames are similar), $\psi_t^{t+1} = s_t^{t+1}$ can be seen as a reward for staying at the same action. Effectively, our binary term explicitly rewards the paths that have the same action for visually similar frames, which further encourages the model to generate visually consistent action labels. On the other hand, frames with low similarity are not penalized for having the same action. When $\pi_t = \pi_{t+1}$ and $s_t^{t+1} < \theta$ (low similarity), $\psi_t^{t+1} = \theta$ is simply the same for all and has no effect on the path probability after normalization. Consider an extreme case when $s_t^{t+1} = \infty$. This effectively imposes the constraint that $\pi_t = \pi_{t+1}$, as the probability of paths with $\pi_t \neq \pi_{t+1}$ will be zero after normalization. As we will show in the experiment, our explicit modeling of the frame-to-frame correlation with the binary term plays an important role to the success of our model, as it allows us to avoid visually inconsistent and trivial paths in our task. Figure 3 shows an example of how our ECTC reweights the paths using visual consistency.

3.2 ECTC Forward-Backward Algorithm

At first sight, the summation in Eq. (2) seems problematic, as the number of paths grows exponentially with the length of the input sequence. This is further complicated by the fact that our formulation in Eq. (3) involves a binary term ψ_t^{t+1} that depends on both frame t and $t+1$. We address this by proposing the ECTC forward-backward algorithm that extends the approach in [13] and naturally incorporates the visual similarity function in a unified framework. We will show how the proposed algorithm is still able to efficiently evaluate all of the possible paths using dynamic programming despite the introduction of the binary term in Eq. (3) to explicitly capture the correlation between consecutive frames. We define our *forward variable* as

$$\alpha(s,t) = \sum_{\{\pi_{1:t}|\mathcal{B}(\pi_{1:t})=\ell_{1:s}\}} P(\pi_{1:t}|X) \tag{4}$$

$$\propto \sum_{\{\pi_{1:t}|\mathcal{B}(\pi_{1:t})=\ell_{1:s}\}} \prod_{t'=1}^{t} \Psi_{t'}^{\pi_{t'}} z_{t'}^{\pi_{t'}}, \quad \Psi_t^k = \begin{cases} \max(\theta, s_{t-1}^t) & k = \pi_{t-1} \\ \theta & k \neq \pi_{t-1}, \end{cases} \tag{5}$$

which corresponds to the sum of probabilities of paths with length t $\pi_{1:t} = [\pi_1, \cdots, \pi_t]$ that satisfy $\mathcal{B}(\pi_{1:t}) = \ell_{1:s}$, where $\ell_{1:s}$ is the first s elements of the label sequence ℓ. We also introduce a new variable Ψ_t^k for explicitly modeling the dependence between consecutive frames and encourage the model to output visually consistent path. This makes the original CTC forward-backward algorithm not directly applicable to our formulation. By deriving all $\pi_{1:t}$ that satisfy $\mathcal{B}(\pi_{1:t}) = \ell_{1:s}$ from $\pi_{1:t-1}$, the forward recursion is formulated as:

$$\alpha(s,t) = \hat{z}_t^{\pi_t}\alpha(s, t-1) + \tilde{z}_t^{\pi_t}\alpha(s-1, t-1), \tag{6}$$

where

$$\hat{z}_t^{\pi_t} = \frac{\Psi_t^{\pi_t} z_t^{\pi_t}}{\sum_{k=1}^{A} \Psi_t^k z_t^k} = \frac{\max(\theta, s_{t-1}^t) z_t^{\pi_t}}{\max(\theta, s_{t-1}^t) z_t^{\pi_t} + \theta(1 - z_t^{\pi_t})} \tag{7}$$

$$\tilde{z}_t^{\pi_t} = \frac{\Psi_t^{\pi_t} z_t^{\pi_t}}{\sum_{k=1}^{A} \Psi_t^k z_t^k} = \frac{\theta z_t^{\pi_t}}{\max(\theta, s_{t-1}^t) z_t^{\pi_{t-1}} + \theta(1 - z_t^{\pi_{t-1}})}. \tag{8}$$

The key difference between our algorithm and that of [13] is the renormalization of z_t^k using frame similarity Ψ_t^k, which in turn gives the renormalized $\hat{z}_t^{\pi_t}$ and $\tilde{z}_t^{\pi_t}$. This efficiently incorporates visual similarity in the dynamic programming framework and encourages the model towards visually consistent paths. The first term in Eq. (6) corresponds to the case when $\pi_t = \pi_{t-1}$. Based on the definition, we have $\Psi_t^{\pi_t} = \Psi_t^{\pi_{t-1}} = \max(\theta, s_{t-1}^t)$. Intuitively, this reweighting using Ψ_t^k will reward and raise $z_t^{\pi_t}$ to $\hat{z}_t^{\pi_t}$ for having the same action label for similar consecutive frames. On the other hand, the second term in Eq. (6) is for the case when $\pi_t \neq \pi_{t-1}$, and thus $\Psi_t^{\pi_t} = \theta$. In this case, the probability is taken from $\tilde{z}_t^{\pi_t}$ to reward $\tilde{z}_t^{\pi_{t-1}}$, and thus $\tilde{z}_t^{\pi_t}$ will be smaller than $z_t^{\pi_t}$.

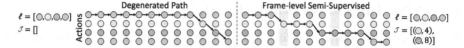

Fig. 4. Example of a degenerated path and a semi-supervised path. On the right, gray blocks constrain the path to be consistent with the two supervised frames. This significantly reduces the space of possible paths and prevents degenerated paths.

The *backward variable* is similarly defined as:

$$\beta(s,t) = \sum_{\{\pi_{t:T}|\mathcal{B}(\pi_{t:T})=\ell_{s:S}\}} P(\pi_{t:T}|X) \propto \sum_{\{\pi_{t:T}|\mathcal{B}(\pi_{t:T})=\ell_{s:S}\}} \prod_{t'=t}^{T} \tilde{\Psi}_{t'}^{\pi_{t'}} z_{t'}^{\pi_{t'}}, \quad (9)$$

the sum of the probability of all paths starting at t that will complete ℓ when appending from $t+1$ to any path of $\alpha(s,t)$. We also introduce $\tilde{\Psi}_t^k$ in the same way as Ψ_t^k, but by decomposing Eq. (3) backward rather than forward. The backward recursion to compute $\beta(s,t)$ can be derived similarly to the forward recursion in Eq. (6), but by deriving $\pi_{t:T}$ from $\pi_{t+1:T}$. Based on the definition of forward and backward variables, we have $P(\ell|X) = \sum_{s=1}^{S} \frac{\alpha(s,t)\beta(s,t)}{z_t^{\ell_s}}$.

Optimization. With this forward-backward algorithm, we are able to compute the gradient of the loss function $\mathcal{L}(\ell, X)$ w.r.t. the recurrent neural network output y_t^k, the response of label k at time t. The gradient is given by:

$$\frac{\partial \mathcal{L}(\ell, X)}{\partial y_t^k} = z_t^k - \frac{1}{P(\ell|X)} \sum_{s:\ell_s=k} \frac{\alpha(s,t)\beta(s,t)}{z_t^{\ell_s}}, \quad (10)$$

where the first term is the softmax output. The second term can be seen as the softmax target. The second term can be intuitively interpreted as $P(\pi_t = k|\mathcal{B}(\pi) = \ell, X)$, which is the probability of choosing action k at time t for paths that are consistent with the sequence label ℓ (reweighted by ψ_t^{t+1}). The recurrent neural network can then be optimized through back propagation [33].

4   Extension to Frame-Level Semi-supervised Learning

When only the ordering supervision is available, all of the paths π that are consistent with ℓ are considered in Eq. (2). A quick observation, however, shows that some undesirable or degenerate paths shown in Fig. 4 are also considered in the summation. This challenge is unique to our task as the length of the label sequence ℓ is usually much shorter than the number of frames, which is not the case in speech recognition. We have shown how our ECTC can be used in this case as soft constraints to down-weight such visually inconsistent paths and reward the ones that have consistent labels for visually similar frames. Nevertheless, when supervision beyond ordering is available, we can derive harder constraints for the paths and effectively remove undesirable paths from the summation.

In this section, we show that sparse temporal supervision can also be naturally incorporated in our framework and efficiently prune out the degenerated paths. We introduce the *frame-level* semi-supervised setting, where only a few frames in the video are annotated with the ground truth action. Such supervision could be automatically extracted from movie scripts [9,23] or by annotating a few frames of the video, which is much easier than finding the exact temporal boundaries of all the actions. Formally, the supervision we consider is a list of frames with the corresponding action labels: $\mathcal{J} = [(a_1, t_1), \cdots, (a_m, t_m), \cdots (a_M, t_M)]$, where each element of the list is a pair of frame index t_m and the corresponding action label a_m. This can significantly reduce the number of possible paths when combined with the order of the actions. For example, assuming that we have $\mathcal{J} = [(a, 2), (b, 4)]$ and $\ell = [a, b]$ for a video of length 6, then there are only two possible paths ($[a, a, b, b, b, b]$ and $[a, a, a, b, b, b]$) that are consistent with the supervision. This not only significantly reduces the space of consistent paths, but also avoids undesirable paths like $[a, a, a, a, a, b]$. Figure 4 also shows an example of the effect of the frame-level semi-supervision. This supervision can be naturally incorporated by extending the recursion in Eq. (6) as:

$$\alpha(s, t) = \begin{cases} 0, & \exists (a_m, t_m) \in \mathcal{J}, \text{ s.t. } t = t_m \text{ but } s \neq a_m \\ \hat{z}_t^{\pi_t} \alpha(s, t-1) + \tilde{z}_t^{\pi_t} \alpha(s-1, t-1), & \text{otherwise,} \end{cases} \quad (11)$$

where an extra checking step is applied to ensure that the path is consistent with the given semi-supervision. We will show that, with less than 1 % of frames being labeled, our approach can perform comparably to fully supervised model.

5 Experiments

We evaluate our model on two challenging tasks and datasets. The first is segmentation of cooking activity video in the Breakfast Actions Dataset [19]. The output action labeling divides the video into temporal segments of cooking steps. Because of the dependencies between temporally adjacent actions in cooking activities, the capacity of the model to handle temporal dynamics is especially important. The second task is action detection on videos in a subset of the Hollywood2 dataset [23], with a setting introduced by [5]. Our action labeling framework can be applied to action detection by considering an additional background label $\emptyset$ to indicate frames without actions of interest.

5.1 Implementation Details

Network Architecture. We use 1-layer Bidirectional LSTM (BLSTM) [15] with 256 hidden units for our approach. We cross-validate the learning rate and the weight decay. For the optimization, we use SGD with batch size 1. We clip gradients elementwise at 5 and scale gradients using RMSProp [41].

Visual Similarity. For our ECTC, we combine two types of visual similarity functions. The first is clustering of visually similar and temporally adjacent frames. We apply k-means clustering to frames in a way similar to SLIC [1] to over-segment the video. We initialize $\frac{T}{M}$ centers uniformly for a video, where T is the video length, and M is the average number of frames in a cluster. We empirically pick $M = 20$, which is much shorter than the average length of an action ($\sim$400 frames in the Breakfast Dataset) to conservatively over segment the video and avoid grouping frames that belong to different actions. The resulting grouping is in the form of constraints such as $\pi_t = \pi_{t+1}$, which can be easily incorporated in our ECTC by setting s_t^{t+1} to ∞. We thus set $s_t^{t+1} = \infty$ if the video frames x_t and x_{t+1} are in the same cluster and $s_t^{t+1} = 0$ otherwise. The second visual similarity function we consider is $s_t^{t+1} \propto \frac{x_t \cdot x_{t+1}}{|x_t||x_{t+1}|}$, the cosine similarity of the frames. This formulation will reward paths that assign visually similar frames to the same action and guide the search of alignment during the forward-backward algorithm. We combine the two similarity functions by setting s_t^{t+1} to the cosine similarity at the boundary between clusters instead of 0.

5.2 Evaluating Complex Activity Segmentation

In this task, the goal is to segment long activity videos into actions composing the activity. We follow [19] and define the *action units* as the shorter atomic actions that compose the longer and more complex activity. For example, "Take Cup" and "Pour Coffee" are action units that compose the activity "Make Coffee".

Dataset. We evaluate activity segmentation of our model on the Breakfast dataset [19]. The videos of the dataset were recorded from 52 participants in 18 different kitchens conducting 10 distinct cooking activities. This results in $\sim$77 h of videos of preparing dishes such as fruit salad and scrambled eggs.

Metrics. We follow the metrics used in previous work [19] to evaluate the parsing and segmentation of action units. The first is *frame accuracy*, the percentage of frames that are correctly labeled. The second is *unit accuracy*. The output action units sequence is first aligned to the ground truth sequence by dynamic time warping (DTW) before the error rate is computed. For weakly supervised approaches, high frame accuracy is harder to achieve than high unit accuracy because it directly measures the quality of the temporal localization of actions.

Features. We follow the feature extraction steps of [20] and use them for all competing methods. First, the improved dense trajectory descriptor [44] is extracted and encoded by Fisher Vector with GMMs = 64. L2 and power normalization, and PCA dimension reduction ($d = 64$) are then applied.

Baselines. We compare our method to three baselines. The first is per-frame Support Vector Machine (**SVM**) [6] with RBF kernels. We are interested in how well discriminative classification can do on the video segmentation task without exploiting the temporal information in the videos. The second is Hidden Markov Model Toolkit (**HTK**) used in previous work for this task [19,20]. The third is Order Constrained Discriminative Clustering (**OCDC**) of Bojanowski et al. [5], which has been applied to align video frames with actions.

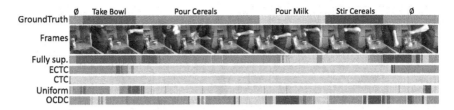

Fig. 5. Qualitative comparison of weakly supervised approaches in a testing video. Fully supervised results using BLSTM are also shown as reference (upper bound of our approach). Colors indicate different actions, and the horizontal axis is time. Per frame classification of OCDC is noisy and contains unrelated actions. The Uniform baseline produces the proper actions, but without alignment and ordering. CTC outputs a degenerated path in this case: while the order is correct, the sequence is dominated by a single action. Our ECTC has better localization and ordering of the actions since we incorporate visual similarity to prune out inconsistent and degenerated paths. (Color figure online)

Ablation Studies. First we analyze the effect of different components of our approach and compare to the baselines. The results are shown in Table 1. The first variation of our model is "**Uniform**". Instead of using our framework to evaluate all possible paths, the target of Uniform is a single path π given by uniformly distributing the occurring actions among frames. We also show the performance of direct application of **CTC** to our task. Without explicitly imposing the alignments to be consistent with the visual similarity, CTC only has the effect of trading-off frame accuracy for unit accuracy when compared to the Uniform baseline. The reason is that the original CTC objective is actually directly optimizing the unit accuracy, but ignoring the frame accuracy as long as the output action order is correct. The performance of our ECTC with only the clustering similarity is shown as "**ECTC (kmeans)**". This efficiently rules out the paths that are inconsistent with the visual grouping and improve the alignment of actions to frames. Using only the cosine similarity with ECTC ("**ECTC (cosine)**"), we are able to further improve the unit accuracy. Combining both similarities, the last column of Table 1 is our final ECTC model, which further improves the accuracy and outperforms fully supervised baselines. This verifies

Table 1. Ablation studies of our approach on the Breakfast dataset. Each component introduced in our approach gives an accuracy improvement. Our final ECTC model is able to outperform fully supervised baselines.

Supervision	Fully sup.		Weakly sup.					
Model	SVM [6]	HTK [19]	OCDC [5]	Uniform	CTC	ECTC (kmeans)	ECTC (cosine)	ECTC (Our full model)
Frame acc.	15.8	19.7	8.9	22.6	21.8	24.5	22.5	**27.7**
Unit acc.	15.7	20.4	10.4	33.1	36.3	35.0	**36.7**	35.6

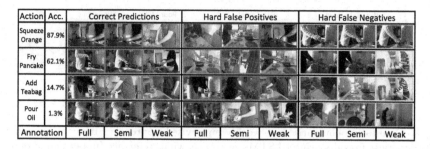

Action	Acc.	Correct Predictions			Hard False Positives			Hard False Negatives		
Squeeze Orange	87.9%									
Fry Pancake	62.1%									
Add Teabag	14.7%									
Pour Oil	1.3%									
Annotation		Full	Semi	Weak	Full	Semi	Weak	Full	Semi	Weak

Fig. 6. Example results for the two hardest and easiest actions. Correct Predictions illustrate the most confident correct frame predictions. Hard False Positives show incorrect predictions with high confidence. Our models can be confused by the appearance of objects in the scene (e.g., seeing the teabag box), or by similar motions (e.g., pouring milk instead of oil). Hard false negative show missing detections. We see challenges of viewpoint, illumination, and ambiguities near the annotated boundary between actions.

the advantage of using visual similarity in our ECTC to reward paths that are consistent with it. All variations of our temporal models outperform the linear classifier in OCDC on unseen test videos. Figure 5 shows the qualitative results.

Frame-Level Semi-supervision. Next we study the effect of having more supervision with our model. The results are shown in Fig. 7. The x-axis shows the fraction of labeled frames for our frame-level semi-supervision in each video. The minimum supervision we use is when only a single frame is labeled for each occurring action in the video (fraction 0.0025). Fraction 1 indicates our fully supervised performance. The annotation for the Uniform baseline in this case is equally distributed between two sparsely annotated frames. With our approach, the frame accuracy is dropping much slower than that of the Uniform baseline, since our approach is able to automatically and iteratively refine the alignment between action and frame during training. Our semi-supervised approach significantly outperforms OCDC with all fractions of labeled frames. The results of HTK, SVM, and our full ECTC are also plotted for reference. As noted earlier, our weakly supervised approach has the highest unit accuracy, as the CTC

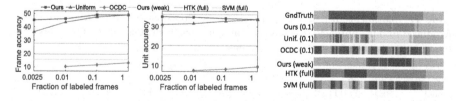

Fig. 7. Frame and unit accuracy in the Breakfast dataset plotted against fraction of labeled data in the frame-level semi-supervised setting. Horizontal lines are either fully-supervised or weakly supervised methods. On the right, qualitative results for one video follow the convention of Fig. 5.

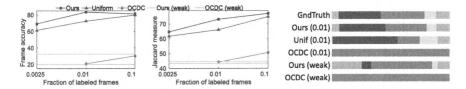

Fig. 8. Frame accuracy, Jaccard measure, and qualitative alignment results on the training set of the Breakfast dataset. Our models also produce good alignments for the training set in addition to the ability to segment unseen test videos.

objective is directly optimizing it. This is consistent with the fact that lower fraction of labeled frames of our approach actually has higher unit accuracy. Another interesting observation is the gap between our weakly supervised model and semi-supervised model. While our weakly supervised model already outperforms several baselines with full supervision, it can be seen that giving only a single frame annotation as an anchor for each segment significantly reduces the space of possible alignments and provides a strong cue to train our temporal model. Figure 6 shows results for different levels of supervision.

Training Set Alignment. While our framework aims at labeling unseen test videos when trained only with the ordering supervision, we also verify whether our action-frame alignment during training also outperforms the baselines. The frame accuracy and Jaccard measure are shown in Fig. 8. Jaccard measure is used to evaluate the alignment quality in [5]. OCDC that is directly designed for the alignment problem indeed performs closer to our method in this scenario.

5.3   Evaluating Action Detection

In this task, the goal is to localize actions in the video. This can be formulated as action labeling by introducing the background label $\emptyset$ to indicate frames without actions of interest. One practical challenge of this task is that the videos tend to

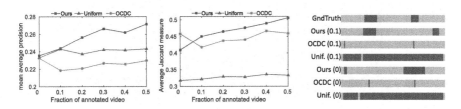

Fig. 9. Left plots mAP for action detection in unseen test videos. Middle plots the average Jaccard measure on the alignment evaluation set. Note that zero fraction of annotated video corresponds to the weakly-supervised setting, where all the videos in training set only have ordering supervision. Our approach consistently outperforms both baselines because of our temporal modeling and efficient evaluation of all possible alignments. On the right, we illustrate qualitative alignment results for all methods.

be dominated by $\emptyset$. This requires the model to deal with unbalanced data and poses a different challenge than the temporal segmentation task.

Dataset and Metrics. We evaluate action detection of our model on the dataset of Bojanowski et al. [5], which consists of clips taken from the 69 movies Hollywood2 [23] dataset were extracted. The full time-stamped annotation of 16 actions (e.g. "Open Door" and "Stand Up") are manually added. For metrics, we follow [5] and use mean average precision for evaluating action detection and average Jaccard measure for evaluating the action alignment.

Experimental Setup. We use the extracted features from Bojanowski et al. [5] for all the methods. All methods use the same random splitting of the dataset. As we follow the exact setup of [5] for evaluation, we would like to clarify that the semi-supervised here means *video-level* semi-supervised setting, where a fraction of the videos in the *supervised* set has full supervision, while the rest only has ordering as supervision. In this sense, the 0 fraction corresponds exactly to our weakly supervised setting, where all the videos only have ordering supervision. This is different from the *frame-level* semi-supervised setting we have discussed. All experiments are conducted over five random splits of the data.

Detection Results. The action detection results on the held-out testing set are shown in Fig. 9 (left). While the occurring actions do not have a strong correlation, the results still demonstrate the importance of temporal modeling for better performance on held-out data. Both of our approaches outperform the OCDC baseline of Bojanowski et al. [5] in this scenario. Figure 10 shows the qualitative results of our weakly-supervised action detection model.

Alignment Results. The action alignment result on the evaluation set is shown in Fig. 9 (middle). The uniform baseline performs the worst in this scenario, as there is no refinement of the alignment. On the other hand, our ECTC incorporates visual similarity and efficiently evaluates all possible alignments. This allows it to perform the best even for the alignment problem.

Fig. 10. Our weakly-supervised action detection results. Color means the output probability of the target action. Our model accurately localizes actions of varied lengths. (Color figure online)

6   Conclusions

We have presented ECTC, a novel approach for learning temporal models of actions in a weakly supervised setting. The key technical novelty lies in the incorporation of visual similarity to explicitly capture dependencies between consecutive frames. We propose a dynamic programming based algorithm to efficiently evaluate all of the possible alignments and weight their importance by the consistency with the visual similarity. We further extend ECTC to incorporate frame-level semi-supervision in a unified framework, which significantly reduce the space of possible alignments. We verify the effectiveness of this framework with two applications: activity segmentation and action detection. We demonstrate that our model is able to outperform fully supervised baselines with only weak supervision, and our model achieves comparable results to state-of-the-art fully supervised models with less than 1 % of supervision.

Acknowledgement. This work was supported by a grant from the Stanford AI Lab-Toyota Center for Artificial Intelligence Research.

References

1. Achanta, R., Shaji, A., Smith, K., Lucchi, A., Fua, P., Susstrunk, S.: Slic superpixels compared to state-of-the-art superpixel methods. IEEE Trans. Pattern Anal. Mach. Intell. **34**(11), 2274–2282 (2012)
2. Alayrac, J.B., Bojanowski, P., Agrawal, N., Sivic, J., Laptev, I., Lacoste-Julien, S.: Learning from narrated instruction videos (2015). arXiv preprint arXiv:1506.09215
3. Bojanowski, P., Bach, F., Laptev, I., Ponce, J., Schmid, C., Sivic, J.: Finding actors and actions in movies. In: Proceedings of the IEEE International Conference on Computer Vision, pp. 2280–2287 (2013)
4. Bojanowski, P., Lagugie, R., Grave, E., Bach, F., Laptev, I., Ponce, J., Schmid, C.: Weakly-supervised alignment of video with text. In: ICCV (2015)
5. Bojanowski, P., Lajugie, R., Bach, F., Laptev, I., Ponce, J., Schmid, C., Sivic, J.: Weakly supervised action labeling in videos under ordering constraints. In: Fleet, D., Pajdla, T., Schiele, B., Tuytelaars, T. (eds.) ECCV 2014. LNCS, vol. 8693, pp. 628–643. Springer, Heidelberg (2014). doi:10.1007/978-3-319-10602-1_41
6. Chang, C.C., Lin, C.J.: LIBSVM: a library for support vector machines. ACM Trans. Intell. Syst. Technol. **2**, 27:1–27:27 (2011). http://www.csie.ntu.edu.tw/~cjlin/libsvm
7. Chen, X., Zitnick, C.L.: Minds eye: a recurrent visual representation for image caption generation. In: CVPR (2015)
8. Donahue, J., Hendricks, L.A., Guadarrama, S., Rohrbach, M., Venugopalan, S., Saenko, K., Darrell, T.: Long-term recurrent convolutional networks for visual recognition and description (2014). arXiv preprint arXiv:1411.4389
9. Duchenne, O., Laptev, I., Sivic, J., Bach, F., Ponce, J.: Automatic annotation of human actions in video. In: ICCV (2009)
10. Fernando, B., Gavves, E., Oramas, J.M., Ghodrati, A., Tuytelaars, T.: Modeling video evolution for action recognition. In: CVPR (2015)
11. Gkioxari, G., Malik, J.: Finding action tubes. In: CVPR (2015)

12. Gorban, A., Idrees, H., Jiang, Y.G., Roshan Zamir, A., Laptev, I., Shah, M., Suk-thankar, R.: THUMOS challenge: action recognition with a large number of classes (2015). http://www.thumos.info/
13. Graves, A., Fernández, S., Gomez, F., Schmidhuber, J.: Connectionist temporal classification: labelling unsegmented sequence data with recurrent neural networks. In: ICML (2006)
14. Graves, A., Jaitly, N.: Towards end-to-end speech recognition with recurrent neural networks. In: ICML (2014)
15. Graves, A., Schmidhuber, J.: Framewise phoneme classification with bidirectional LSTM and other neural network architectures. Neural Netw. **18**(5), 602–610 (2005)
16. Heilbron, F.C., Escorcia, V., Ghanem, B., Niebles, J.C.: Activitynet: a large-scale video benchmark for human activity understanding. In: CVPR (2015)
17. Karpathy, A., Fei-Fei, L.: Deep visual-semantic alignments for generating image descriptions. In: CVPR (2015)
18. Karpathy, A., Toderici, G., Shetty, S., Leung, T., Sukthankar, R., Fei-Fei, L.: Large-scale video classification with convolutional neural networks. In: CVPR (2014)
19. Kuehne, H., Arslan, A., Serre, T.: The language of actions: recovering the syntax and semantics of goal-directed human activities. In: CVPR (2014)
20. Kuehne, H., Gall, J., Serre, T.: An end-to-end generative framework for video segmentation and recognition. In: WACV (2016)
21. Kuehne, H., Jhuang, H., Garrote, E., Poggio, T., Serre, T.: HMDB: a large video database for human motion recognition. In: ICCV (2011)
22. Lan, T., Zhu, Y., Zamir, A.R., Savarese, S.: Action recognition by hierarchical mid-level action elements. In: ICCV (2015)
23. Laptev, I., Marszałek, M., Schmid, C., Rozenfeld, B.: Learning realistic human actions from movies. In: CVPR (2008)
24. Lillo, I., Soto, A., Niebles, J.C.: Discriminative hierarchical modeling of spatio-temporally composable human activities. In: CVPR (2014)
25. Malmaud, J., Huang, J., Rathod, V., Johnston, N., Rabinovich, A., Murphy, K.: What's cookin'? Interpreting Cooking Videos Using Text, Speech and Vision. In: NAACL (2015)
26. Messing, R., Pal, C., Kautz, H.: Activity recognition using the velocity histories of tracked keypoints. In: CVPR (2009)
27. Ng, J.Y.H., Hausknecht, M., Vijayanarasimhan, S., Vinyals, O., Monga, R., Toderici, G.: Beyond short snippets: deep networks for video classification (2015). arXiv preprint arXiv:1503.08909
28. Niebles, J.C., Wang, H., Fei-Fei, L.: Unsupervised learning of human action categories using spatial-temporal words. Int. J. Comput. Vis. **79**(3), 299–318 (2008)
29. Pirsiavash, H., Ramanan, D.: Parsing videos of actions with segmental grammars. In: CVPR (2014)
30. Ramanathan, V., Joulin, A., Liang, P., Fei-Fei, L.: Linking peoplein videos with their names using conference resolution. In: ECCV (2014)
31. Ramanathan, V., Tang, K., Mori, G., Fei-Fei, L.: Learning temporal embeddings for complex video analysis. In: ICCV (2015)
32. Rohrbach, M., Amin, S., Andriluka, M., Schiele, B.: A database for fine grained activity detection of cooking activities. In: CVPR (2012)
33. Rumelhart, D.E., Hinton, G.E., Williams, R.J.: Learning representations by back-propagating errors. Cogn. Model. **5**, 3 (1988)
34. Ryoo, M.S., Aggarwal, J.K.: Spatio-temporal relationship match: video structure comparison for recognition of complex human activities. In: ICCV (2009)

35. Sener, O., Zamir, A., Savarese, S., Saxena, A.: Unsupervised semantic parsing of video collections. In: ICCV (2015)
36. Simonyan, K., Zisserman, A.: Two-stream convolutional networks for action recognition in videos. In: NIPS (2014)
37. Song, Y., Morency, L.P., Davis, R.: Action recognition by hierarchical sequence summarization. In: CVPR (2013)
38. Soomro, K., Roshan Zamir, A., Shah, M.: UCF101: A dataset of 101 human actions classes from videos in the wild. In: CRCV-TR-12-01 (2012)
39. Tang, K., Fei-Fei, L., Koller, D.: Learning latent temporal structure for complex event detection. In: CVPR (2012)
40. Taylor, G.W., Fergus, R., LeCun, Y., Bregler, C.: Convolutional learning of spatio-temporal features. In: Daniilidis, K., Maragos, P., Paragios, N. (eds.) ECCV 2010. LNCS, vol. 6316, pp. 140–153. Springer, Heidelberg (2010). doi:10.1007/978-3-642-15567-3_11
41. Tieleman, T., Hinton, G.: Lecture 6.5-rmsprop: divide the gradient by a running average of its recent magnitude. COURSERA: Neural Netw. Mach. Learn. (2012)
42. Venugopalan, S., Rohrbach, M., Donahue, J., Mooney, R., Darrell, T., Saenko, K.: Sequence to sequence-video to text. In: ICCV (2015)
43. Vo, N.N., Bobick, A.F.: From stochastic grammar to bayes network: probabilistic parsing of complex activity. In: CVPR (2014)
44. Wang, H., Schmid, C.: Action recognition with improved trajectories. In: ICCV (2013)
45. Wu, C., Zhang, J., Savarese, S., Saxena, A.: Watch-n-patch: unsupervised understanding of actions and relations. In: CVPR (2015)
46. Xu, Z., Zhu, L., Yang, Y., Hauptmann, A.G.: Uts-cmu at THUMOS. CVPR THUMOS Challenge (2015)
47. Yao, L., Torabi, A., Cho, K., Ballas, N., Pal, C., Larochelle, H., Courville, A.: Video description generation incorporating spatio-temporal features and a soft-attention mechanism. In: ICCV (2015)
48. Yeung, S., Russakovsky, O., Jin, N., Andriluka, M., Mori, G., Fei-Fei, L.: Every moment counts: dense detailed labeling of actions in complex videos (2015). arXiv preprint arXiv:1507.05738
49. Yeung, S., Russakovsky, O., Mori, G., Fei-Fei, L.: End-to-end learning of action detection from frame glimpses in videos. In: CVPR (2016)
50. Yu, S.I., Jiang, L., Hauptmann, A.: Instructional videos for unsupervised harvesting and learning of action examples. In: ACM Multimedia (2014)
51. Zhu, Y., Kiros, R., Zemel, R., Salakhutdinov, R., Urtasun, R., Torralba, A., Fidler, S.: Aligning books and movies: towards story-like visual explanations by watching movies and reading books. In: ICCV (2015)

Deep Joint Image Filtering

Yijun Li[1], Jia-Bin Huang[2], Narendra Ahuja[2], and Ming-Hsuan Yang[1(✉)]

[1] University of California, Merced, Merced, USA
{yli62,mhyang}@ucmerced.edu
[2] University of Illinois, Urbana-Champaign, Champaign, USA
{jbhuang1,n-ahuja}@illinois.edu
https://sites.google.com/site/yijunlimaverick/deepjointfilter

Abstract. Joint image filters can leverage the guidance image as a prior and transfer the structural details from the guidance image to the target image for suppressing noise or enhancing spatial resolution. Existing methods rely on various kinds of explicit filter construction or hand-designed objective functions. It is thus difficult to understand, improve, and accelerate them in a coherent framework. In this paper, we propose a learning-based approach to construct a joint filter based on Convolutional Neural Networks. In contrast to existing methods that consider only the guidance image, our method can selectively transfer salient structures that are consistent in both guidance and target images. We show that the model trained on a certain type of data, e.g., RGB and depth images, generalizes well for other modalities, e.g., Flash/Non-Flash and RGB/NIR images. We validate the effectiveness of the proposed joint filter through extensive comparisons with state-of-the-art methods.

Keywords: Joint filtering · Deep convolutional neural networks

1 Introduction

Image filtering with a guidance signal, known as *joint* or *guided filtering*, has been successfully applied to a variety of computer vision and computer graphics tasks, such as depth map enhancement [1–3], joint upsampling [1,4], cross-modality noise reduction [5–7], and structure-texture separation [8,9]. The wide applicability of joint filters can be attributed to their adaptability in handling visual signals in various visual domains and modalities, as shown in Fig. 1. For a target image, the guidance image can either be the target image itself [6,10], high-resolution RGB images [2,3,6], images from different sensing modalities [5,11,12], or filtering outputs from previous iterations [9]. The basic idea behind joint image filtering is that the guidance image often contains important structural details that can be transferred to the target image. The main goal of joint filtering is to enhance the degraded target image due to noise or low spatial resolution while

Electronic supplementary material The online version of this chapter (doi:10.1007/978-3-319-46493-0_10) contains supplementary material, which is available to authorized users.

© Springer International Publishing AG 2016
B. Leibe et al. (Eds.): ECCV 2016, Part IV, LNCS 9908, pp. 154–169, 2016.
DOI: 10.1007/978-3-319-46493-0_10

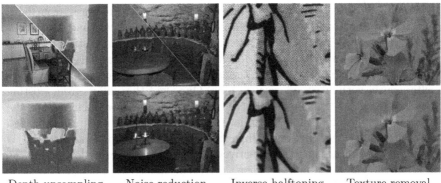

| Depth upsampling | Noise reduction | Inverse halftoning | Texture removal |

Fig. 1. Sample applications of joint image filtering: depth map upsampling, cross-modal noise reduction (flash/non-flash), inverse halftoning, and edge-preserving smoothing for texture removal. The *Target/Guidance* pair (top) can be various types of cross-modality visual data. With the help of the guidance image, important structures can be transferred to the degraded target image to help restore the blurred boundary or suppress noise (bottom).

avoiding transferring erroneous structures that are not originally presented in the target image, i.e., the texture-copying artifacts.

Several techniques have been proposed to transfer structures in the guidance image to the target image. One approach is based on explicit filter construction. For example, the bilateral filter [10] constructs spatially-varying filters that reflect local image structures (e.g., smooth regions, edges, textures) in the guidance image. These filters can then be applied to the target image to perform edge-aware smoothing [10] or joint upsampling [4]. Guided image filters [6] provide another type of filter construction by assuming a locally linear model over the guidance image. However, these filters share one common drawback. That is, the filter construction considers only the information in the guidance image and remains fixed (i.e., static guidance). When the local structures in the guidance and target images are not consistent, these techniques may transfer incorrect contents to the target image.

To address this issue, recent efforts focus on considering the contents of *both* the target and guidance images for exploiting common structures [7,9,13]. These frameworks typically build on iterative methods for minimizing a global objective function. The guidance signals are updated at each iteration (i.e., dynamic guidance) towards preserving the mutually consistent structures while suppressing structures that are not commonly shared in both images. However, these global optimization based techniques often use hand-crafted objective functions that may not reflect natural image priors well and are typically slow.

In this paper, we propose a *learning-based* joint filter based on Convolutional Neural Networks (CNNs). We propose a network architecture that consists of three sub-networks, as shown in Fig. 2. The first two sub-networks CNN_T and

CNN$_G$ act as feature extractors to determine informative features from both target and guidance images. These feature responses are then concatenated as inputs for the network CNN$_F$ to selectively transfer common structures and reconstruct the filtered output. We train the network using large quantities of real data (RGB and depth images) and learn all the network parameters simultaneously without stage-wise training. Our algorithm differs from existing methods in that our joint image filter is *completely data-driven*. This allows the network to handle complicated scenarios that may be difficult to capture through hand-crafted objective functions. While the network is trained using the RGB/D data, the network learns how to selectively transfer structures by leveraging the prior from the guidance image, rather than predicting specific depth values. As a result, the learned network generalizes well for handling images in various domains and modalities.

We make the following contributions in this paper:

- We propose a learning-based framework for constructing joint image filters. Our network takes both target and guidance images into consideration and naturally handles the inconsistent structure problem.
- With the learned joint filter, we demonstrate the state-of-the-art performance on four joint depth upsampling datasets.
- We show that the model trained on the RGB/D dataset generalizes well to handle image data in a variety of domains.

2   Related Work

Joint Image Filters. Joint image filters can be categorized into two main classes: (1) explicit filter based and (2) global optimization based. First, explicit joint filters compute the filtered output as a weighted average of neighboring pixels in the target image. The bilateral filters [1,4,9,10,14,15] and guided filters [6] are representative algorithms in this class. The filter weights, however, depend solely on the local structure of the guidance image. Therefore, erroneous structures may be transferred to the target image due to the lack of consistency check. In contrast, our model considers the contents of both images through extracting feature maps and handles this consistency issue implicitly through learning from examples.

Second, numerous approaches formulate joint filtering using a global optimization framework. The objective function typically consists of two terms: data fidelity and regularization terms. The data fidelity term ensures that the filtering output is close to the input target image. These techniques differ from each other mainly in the regularization term, which encourages the output to have a similar structure with the guidance. The regularization term can be defined according to texture derivatives [16], mid-level representations [2] such as segmentation and saliency, filtering outputs [13], or mutual structures shared by the target and guidance image [7]. However, global optimization based methods rely on hand-designed objective functions that may not reflect the complexities in natural images. Furthermore, these approaches are often time-consuming.

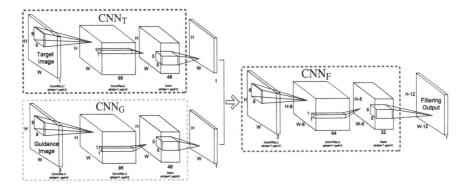

Fig. 2. The network architecture of our learning-based joint filters. The proposed model consists of three major components. Each component is a three-layer network. The sub-networks CNN$_T$ and CNN$_G$ aim to extract informative feature responses from the target and guidance images, respectively. These responses are then concatenated together as input for the network CNN$_F$. Finally, the CNN$_F$ model reconstructs the desired output by selectively transferring main structures while suppressing inconsistent structures.

In contrast, our method learns how to selectively transfer details directly from real RGB-depth datasets. Even though the training is time-consuming, the learned model is efficient during run time.

Deep Models for Low-Level Vision. While CNNs have achieved great success in high-level vision tasks [17], considerably less attention has been paid to apply these models to low-level vision problems. Recently, several methods apply CNNs for low-level vision and computational photography tasks. Examples include image denoising [18], rain drop removal [19], image super-resolution [20] and optical flow estimation [21]. Existing deep learning models for low-level vision take either one input image [18–20,22] or two images in the same domain [21]. In contrast, our network can take two streams of inputs in *heterogeneous* domains, e.g., RGB/NIR, Flash/Non-Flash, RGD/Depth, Intensity/Color. Our network architecture bears some resemblance to that in [21]. The main difference is that the merging layer in [21] uses a correlation operator while our model merges the inputs through stacking the feature responses. The closest work to ours is Xu et al. [22], which learns a CNN to approximate existing edge-aware filters from example images. Our method differs from [22] in two aspects. First, the goal of [22] is to use CNN for approximating *existing* edge-aware filters. In contrast, our goal is to learn a *new* joint image filter. Second, unlike the network in [22] that takes only one single RGB image, the proposed joint filter handles two images from different domains and modalities.

3   Learning Deep Joint Image Filters

Our CNN model consists of three sub-networks: CNN_T, CNN_G, and CNN_F, as shown in Fig. 2. First, the sub-network CNN_T takes the target image as input and extracts its feature map. Second, similar to CNN_T, the sub-network CNN_G extracts a feature map from the guidance image. Third, the sub-network CNN_F takes the concatenated feature responses from the sub-networks CNN_T and CNN_G as input and generates the final joint filtering result. Here, the major roles of the sub-network CNN_T and CNN_G are to serve as *non-linear* feature extractors that capture the local structural details in the respective target and guidance images. The sub-network CNN_F can be viewed as a non-linear regression function that maps the feature responses from both target and guidance images to the final filtered results. Note that the information from target and guidance images is simultaneously considered when predicting the final filtered result. Such a design allows us to selectively transfer structures and avoid texture-copying artifacts.

3.1   Network Architecture Design

To design a joint filter using CNNs, a straightforward implementation is to concatenate the target and guidance images together and directly train a generic CNN as in CNN_F. While in theory we can train a generic CNN to approximate the desired function for joint filtering, our empirical results show that such a network yields poor performance. Figure 3(c) shows one typical example of joint upsampling using only the network CNN_F. The main structures (e.g., the

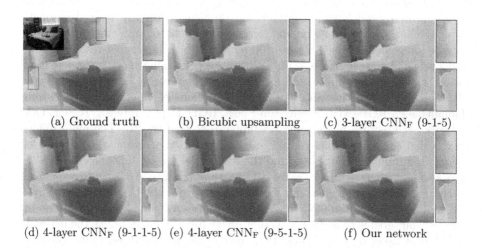

(a) Ground truth   (b) Bicubic upsampling   (c) 3-layer CNN_F (9-1-5)

(d) 4-layer CNN_F (9-1-1-5)   (e) 4-layer CNN_F (9-5-1-5)   (f) Our network

Fig. 3. Joint depth upsampling ($8\times$) results of using different network architectures f_1-f_2-... where f_i is the filter size of the i-th layer. (a) GT depth map (inset: Guidance). (b) Bicubic upsampling. (c)–(e) Results from the straightforward implementation using CNN_F. (f) Results from the proposed model.

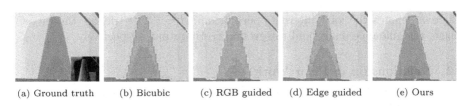

(a) Ground truth   (b) Bicubic   (c) RGB guided   (d) Edge guided   (e) Ours

Fig. 4. Joint depth upsampling ($8\times$) results under different types of guidance images. (a) Ground truth depth map (inset: guidance). (b) Bicubic upsampling. (c) RGB guided result. (d) Edge [24] guided result. Both (c) and (d) are trained using the CNN_F network. (e) Result of our final network design. Note the boundary of the sculpture (left) and the cone (middle).

boundary of the bed) presented in the guidance image are *not* well transferred to the target depth image, thereby resulting in blurry boundaries. Also, inconsistent texture structures in the guidance image (e.g., the stripe pattern of the curtain on the wall) are also incorrectly copied to the target image. A possible way that may improve the result is to adjust the architecture of CNN_F, such as increasing the network depth or using different filter sizes. However, as shown in Fig. 3(d) and (e), these variants do not show notable improvement. Blurry boundaries and the texture-copying problem still exist. Furthermore, we empirically find that there is no significant improvement using deeper models. We note that similar observations have also been reported in [23], which indicate that the effectiveness of deeper structures for low-level tasks is not as apparent as that shown in high-level tasks (e.g., image classification).

We attribute the limitation of using a generic network for joint filtering to the fact that the original RGB guidance image fails to provide direct and effective guidance as it mixes a variety of information (e.g., texture, intensity, edges). Figure 4 shows one example where we replace the original RGB guidance image with its edge map (extracted using [24]). Compared to the results guided by the RGB image (Fig. 4(c)), the result using edge map guidance (Fig. 4(d)) shows substantial improvement. Based on the above observation, we introduce two sub-networks CNN_T and CNN_G to create two separate processing streams for the two images first before concatenation. With the proposed architecture, we constrain the network to extract effective features from both images separately first and then combine them at a later stage to generate the final filtering output. This differs from conventional joint filters where the guidance information is mainly computed from the pixel-level intensity/color differences in the local neighborhood. As our models are jointly trained in an end-to-end fashion, our result (Fig. 4(e)) shows further improvements over that of using the edge guided filtering (Fig. 4(d)).

We adopt a three-layer structure for each sub-network as shown in Fig. 2. Given M training image samples $\{I_i^T, I_i^G, I_i^{gt}\}_{i=1}^M$, we learn the network parameters by minimizing the summed squared loss:

$$\|I^{gt} - \Phi(I^T, I^G)\|_2^2, \tag{1}$$

where Φ denotes the joint filtering operator, and I^T, I^G, I^{gt} denote the target image, the guidance image and the ground truth output, respectively.

3.2 Relationship to Prior Work

The proposed framework is closely related to weighted-average, optimization-based, and CNN-based models. In each layer of the network, the convolutional filters also perform a weighted-average process. In this context, our filter is similar to weighted-average filters. The key difference is that our weights are learned from data by considering both the contents of the target and guidance images while weighted-average filters (e.g., bilateral filters) depend only on the guidance image. Compared with optimization-based filters, our network plays a similar role of the fidelity and regularization terms in optimization methods by minimizing the error in (1). Through learning, our model implicitly ensures that the output does not deviate too much from the target image while sharing salient structures with the guidance image. For CNN-based models, our network architecture can be viewed as a unified model for different tasks. For example, if we remove CNN_G and use only CNN_T and CNN_F, the resulting network architecture resembles an image restoration model, e.g., SRCNN [20]. On the other hand, in cases of removing the network CNN_T, the remaining networks CNN_G and CNN_F can be viewed as using CNNs for depth prediction [25].

4   Experimental Results

In this section, we demonstrate the effectiveness of our approach through a broad range of joint image filtering tasks, including depth upsampling, colorization, texture-structure separation, and cross-modality image restoration.

Network Training. To train our network, we randomly collect 160,000 training patch pairs of size 32×32 from 1,000 RGB and depth maps in the NYU v2 dataset [26]. Images in the NYU dataset are real data taken in complicated indoor scenarios. We train two kinds of models for two different tasks: (1) joint image upsampling and (2) noise reduction. For the upsampling task, we obtain each low-quality target image from a ground-truth image ($4\times$, $8\times$, $16\times$) using nearest-neighbor downsampling. For noise reduction, we generate the low-quality target image by adding Gaussian noise to each ground-truth depth map with zero mean and variance of 1e-3. We use the MatConvNet toolbox [27] for constructing and learning our joint filters. We set the learning rate of the first two layers and the third layer as 1e-3 and 1e-4, respectively.

Testing. Using the RGB/D data for training, our model takes a 1-channel target image and a 3-channel guidance image. However, the trained model is not limited in the handling RGB/D data. We can apply our model to other modalities with a few modifications. For the multi-channel target image, we apply the model independently for each channel. For the single-channel guidance image, we replicate it three times to create the 3-channel image.

4.1 Depth Map Upsampling

Datasets. We present quantitative performance on depth upsampling in four benchmark datasets where the corresponding high-resolution RGB images are available.

- Middlebury dataset [30,31]: We collect 30 images from 2001–2006 datasets with the missing depth values provided by Lu [28].
- Lu [28]: This dataset contains six real depth maps captured with the ASUS Xtion Pro camera.
- NYU v2 dataset [26]: Since we use 1,000 images in this dataset for training, the rest of images (449) are used for testing.
- SUN RGB/D [29]: We use a random subset of 2,000 high-quality RGB/D image pairs from the 3,784 pairs obtained by the Kinect V2 sensor. These images contain a variety of complicated indoor scenes.

Evaluated Methods. We compare our model against several state-of-the-art joint image filters for depth map upsampling. Among them, JBU [4], GF [6] and Ham [13] are generic methods for joint image upsampling while MRF [16],

Table 1. Quantitative comparisons. Comparisons with the state-of-the-art methods in terms of RMSE. The depth values are scaled to the range [0, 255] for the Middlebury, Lu [28] and SUN RGB/D [29] datasets. For the NYU v2 dataset [26], the depth values are measured in centimeter. Note that the depth maps in the SUN RGB/D dataset may contain missing regions due to the limitation of depth sensors. We ignore these pixels in calculating the RMSE. Numbers in bold indicate the best performance and underscored numbers indicate the second best.

Methods	Middlebury [30,31]			Lu [28]			NYU v2 [26]			SUN RGB/D [29]		
	4×	8×	16×	4×	8×	16×	4×	8×	16×	4×	8×	16×
Bicubic	4.44	7.58	11.87	5.07	9.22	14.27	8.16	14.22	22.32	2.09	3.45	5.48
MRF [16]	4.26	7.43	11.80	4.90	9.03	14.19	7.84	13.98	22.20	1.99	3.38	5.45
GF [6]	4.01	7.22	11.70	4.87	8.85	14.09	7.32	13.62	22.03	1.91	3.31	5.41
JBU [4]	2.44	3.81	6.13	2.99	5.06	**7.51**	4.07	8.29	13.35	1.37	2.01	3.15
TGV [3]	3.39	5.41	12.03	4.48	7.58	17.46	6.98	11.23	28.13	1.94	3.01	5.87
Park [2]	2.82	4.08	7.26	4.09	6.19	10.14	5.21	9.56	18.10	1.78	2.76	4.77
Ham [13]	3.14	5.03	8.83	4.65	7.53	11.52	5.27	12.31	19.24	1.67	2.60	4.36
Ours	**2.14**	**3.77**	**6.12**	**2.54**	**4.71**	7.66	**3.54**	**6.20**	**10.21**	**1.28**	**1.81**	**2.78**

Table 2. Average run-time of depth map upsampling algorithms on images of 640×480 pixels from the NYU v2 dataset.

Methods	MRF [16]	GF [6]	JBU [4]	TGV [3]	Park [2]	Ham [13]	**Ours**
Time(s)	0.76	0.08	5.6	68	45	8.6	1.3

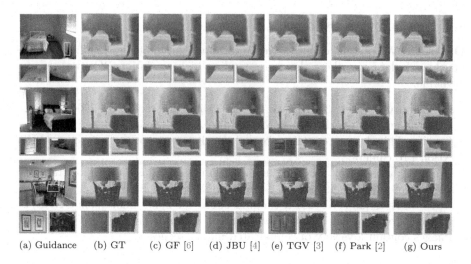

(a) Guidance   (b) GT   (c) GF [6]   (d) JBU [4]   (e) TGV [3]   (f) Park [2]   (g) Ours

Fig. 5. Qualitative comparisons of joint depth upsampling algorithms for a scaling factor of 8×.

Table 3. Quantitative comparisons of different upsampling methods for colorization.

Methods	Bicubic	GF [6]	Ham [13]	Ours
RMSE	6.01	5.74	6.31	5.48

TGV [3] and Park [2] are algorithms specifically designed for image guided depth upsampling. The low-quality target image is obtained from the ground-truth via nearest-neighbor downsampling [2,3,13].

Table 1 shows the quantitative results in terms of the root mean squared errors (RMSE). For other methods, we use default parameters suggested in their papers. The proposed model performs well against state-of-the-art methods on both synthetic and real datasets. The extensive evaluations on real depth maps demonstrate the effectiveness of our algorithm in handling complicated indoor scenes in the real world. We also compare the average run-time of different methods on the NYU v2 dataset in Table 2. We carry out the experiments on the same machine with an Intel i7 3.6 GHz CPU and 16GB RAM. Compared with other methods, the proposed algorithm performs efficiently with high-quality results.

We show in Fig. 5 three indoor scene examples (real data) for qualitative comparisons. The main advantage of the proposed joint filter is to selectively transfer salient structures in the guidance image while avoiding artifacts (see the green boxes). The GF [6] method does not recover the degraded boundary well under a large upsampling factor (e.g., 8×). The JBU [4], TGV [3] and Park [2] approaches are agnostic to structural consistency between the target and the guidance images, and thus transfer erroneous details. In contrast, our results are smoother, sharper and more accurate with respect to the ground truth.

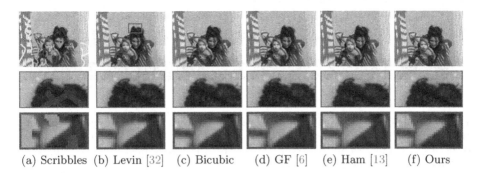

(a) Scribbles (b) Levin [32] (c) Bicubic (d) GF [6] (e) Ham [13] (f) Ours

Fig. 6. Joint image upsampling applied to colorization. The computational cost: (b) 8.2 s (c) 1.3 s (d) 1.5 s (e) 28.8 s (f) 2.8 s. The close-up areas clearly show that our joint upsampling results have fewer color bleeding artifacts and are comparable with the results computed using the full resolution image.

4.2 Joint Image Upsampling

Numerous computational photography applications require computing a solution (e.g., chromaticity, disparity, labels) over the pixel grid. However, it is often time-consuming to directly obtain the high-resolution solution maps. We demonstrate the use of joint image upsampling with colorization [32] as an example. We first compute the solution map (chromaticity) on the downsampled image using the user-specified color scribbles [32], and then use the original high-resolution intensity image as guidance to upsample the low-resolution chromaticity map. Figure 6 shows that our model is able to achieve visually pleasing results with much less color bleeding artifacts while being more efficient. Our results are visually similar to the direct solutions on the high-resolution intensity images (Fig. 6(b)). We also show quantitative comparisons in Table 3. We use the direct solution of [32] on the high-resolution image as GT and compute the RMSE over seven test images in [32]. Table 3 shows that our results approximate the direction solution best.

4.3 Structure-Texture Separation

We apply our model for texture removal and structure extraction. We use the target image itself as the guidance and adopt a similar strategy as in the rolling guidance filter (RGF) [9] to remove small-scale textures. We use inverse half-toning task as an example. A halftoned image is generated by the reprographic technique that simulates continuous tone imagery using various dot patterns [33], as shown in Fig. 7(a). The goal of inverse half-toning is to remove these dots and preserve main structures. We compare our results with those from RGF [9], L0 [34], Xu [8] and Kopf [33] for halftoned images reconstruction. Figure 7 shows that our filter can well preserve edges and achieve comparable performance against Kopf [33].

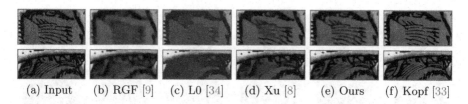

(a) Input (b) RGF [9] (c) L0 [34] (d) Xu [8] (e) Ours (f) Kopf [33]

Fig. 7. Comparisons of inverse halftoning results. For each method, we carefully select the parameter for the optimal results. (b) $\sigma_s = 3, \sigma_r = 0.1$. (c) $\lambda = 0.06$. (d) $\lambda = 0.005, \sigma = 3$. (e) Our result. (f) Result of [33]. Note that [33] is an algorithm specifically designed for reconstructing halftoned images.

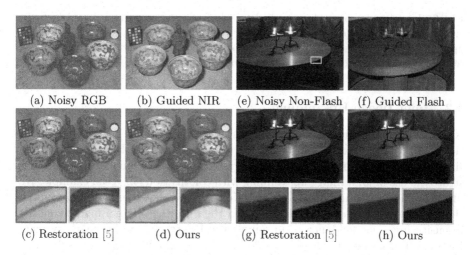

(a) Noisy RGB (b) Guided NIR (e) Noisy Non-Flash (f) Guided Flash

(c) Restoration [5] (d) Ours (g) Restoration [5] (h) Ours

Fig. 8. Sample results of noise reduction using RGB/NIR image pairs (a)–(d) and Flash/Non-Flash image pairs (e)–(h).

4.4 Cross-Modality Filtering for Noise Reduction

Finally, we demonstrate that our model can handle various visual domains through two noise reduction applications using RGB/NIR and Flash/Non-Flash image pairs. Figure 8(a)–(d) show sample results on joint image denoising with the NIR guidance image. The filtering results by our method are comparable to those of the state-of-the-art technique [5]. For Flash/Non-Flash image pairs, we aim to merge the ambient qualities of the no-flash image with the high-frequency details of the flash image. Guided by a flash image, the filtering result of our method is comparable to that of [5], as shown in Fig. 8(e)–(h).

5 Discussions

What Has the Network Learned? In Fig. 9(c), we visualize the learned guidance from $\mathrm{CNN_G}$ using two examples from the NYU v2 dataset [26].

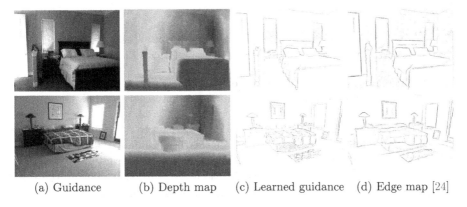

(a) Guidance   (b) Depth map   (c) Learned guidance   (d) Edge map [24]

Fig. 9. Comparison between the learned guidance feature maps from CNN_G and edge maps from [24]. It suggests that the network extracts informative, salient structures from the guidance image for content transfer.

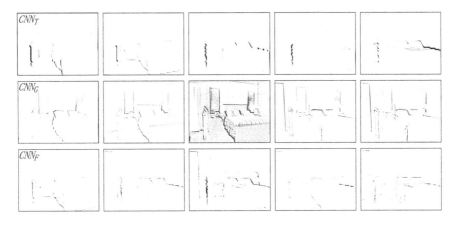

Fig. 10. Sample feature responses of the input in Fig. 9(a) at the first layer of CNN_T (top), and CNN_G (middle), and the second layer of CNN_F (bottom). Pixels with darker intensities indicate stronger responses. Note that with the help of CNN_F, inconsistent structures (e.g., the window on the wall) are successfully suppressed.

In general, the learned guidance appears like an edge map highlighting the salient structures in the guidance image. We show edge detection results from [24] in Fig. 9(d). Both results show strong responses to the main structures, but the guidance map generated by CNN_G appears to detect sharper boundaries while suppressing responses to small-scale textures, e.g., the wall in the first example. This is why using only CNN_F (Fig. 3(c)) does not perform well as it lacks the salient feature extraction step from the sub-network CNN_G. Similar observations are also found in [35] where a reference edge map is learned first from intermediate CNN features for the semantic segmentation.

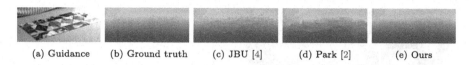

(a) Guidance	(b) Ground truth	(c) JBU [4]	(d) Park [2]	(e) Ours

Fig. 11. Comparisons of different joint upsampling methods on the texture-copying issue (the area carpet on the floor contains unwanted texture structures).

Selective Structure Transfer. Using the learned guidance alone to transfer details may sometimes be erroneous. In particular, the structures extracted from the guidance image may not exist in the target image. In Fig. 10, the top and middle rows show typical responses at the first layer of CNN_T and CNN_G. These two sub-networks show strong responses to edges from the target and guidance image respectively. Note that there are inconsistent structures (e.g., the window on the wall). The bottom row of Fig. 10 shows sample responses at the second layer of CNN_F. We observe that the sub-network CNN_F re-organizes the extracted structural features and suppresses inconsistent details.

We present another example in Fig. 11. We note that the ground truth depth map of the selected region is smooth. However, due to the high-contrast patterns on the mat in the guidance image, several methods, e.g., [2,4], incorrectly transfer the mat structure to the upsampled depth map. The reason is that these methods [2,4] rely only on structures in the guidance image. The problem, commonly known as texture-copying artifacts, often occurs when the texture in the guidance image has strong color contrast. With the help of the CNN_F, our filter successfully blocks the texture structure in the guidance image. Figure 11(e) shows our joint upsampling result.

Network Architecture. Based on our network configurations in Fig. 2, we analyze the effects of the performance under different hyper-parameter settings. As suggested in [23] that the number of layers does not play a significant role for low-level tasks (e.g., super-resolution), we vary the filter number n_i and size f_i $(i = 1, 2)$ of the first two layers in each sub-network. The training process is the same as described in Sect. 3.1 and the evaluation is conducted on the NYU v2 dataset [26] (449 test images). Table 4 shows that larger number and larger size of the filter may not always yield performance improvements. Therefore, the parameter selection of our method (shown in Fig. 2) strikes a good balance between performance and efficiency.

We set the output feature maps extracted from the target and guidance images as one single channel. That is, the input of CNN_F is of size $H \times W \times 2$. Intuitively, using multi-dimensional features may further improve the model capacity and performance. However, our experimental results (see the supplementary material) indicate that using multi-dimensional feature maps only slows down the training process without clear performance improvements.

Table 4. Depth upsampling results (RMSE in centimeters) of using different filter numbers and sizes in each sub-network. We apply the same parameters to all three sub-networks.

Size fixed	$n_1 = 128, n_2 = 64$	$n_1 = 96, n_2 = 48$	$n_1 = 64, n_2 = 32$
$Upscale = 8$	6.44	6.32	6.35
Number fixed	$f_1 = 11, f_2 = 1, f_3 = 7$	$f_1 = 9, f_2 = 1, f_3 = 7$	$f_1 = 9, f_2 = 1, f_3 = 5$
$Upscale = 8$	6.28	6.40	6.20

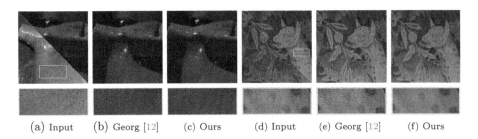

(a) Input   (b) Georg [12]   (c) Ours   (d) Input   (e) Georg [12]   (f) Ours

Fig. 12. Failure cases. Detailed small-scale textures (yellow rectangle) in the guidance image are over-smoothed by our filter. (Color figure online)

Failure Cases. We note that in some images, our model fails to transfer small-scale details from the guidance map. That is, our model incorrectly treats some small-scale details as noise. This can be explained by the fact that our training data is based on depth images. The depth map usually tends to be smooth and does not contain many details.

Figure 12 shows two examples of a Flash/Non-Flash pair for noise reduction. There are several spotty textures on the porcelain in the guided flash image that should be preserved when filtering the noisy non-flash image, and likewise the small-scale strip textures on the carpet. Compared with Georg [12] (Fig. 12(b) and (d)) that deals with Flash/Non-flash images, our filter treats these small-scale details as noise and tends to over-smooth the contents. We will use non-depth data to address the over-smoothing problem in our future work.

6   Conclusions

We present a learning-based approach for joint filtering based on convolutional neural networks. Instead of relying only on the guidance image, we design two sub-networks CNN_T and CNN_G to consider the contents of both the target and guidance images by extracting informative features respectively. These feature maps are then concatenated as inputs for the network CNN_F to selectively transfer salient structures from the guidance image to the target image while suppressing structures that are not consistent in both images. While we train our network on one type of data (RGB/D images), our model generalizes well on handling images in various modalities, e.g., RGB/NIR and Flash/Non-Flash image pairs. We show that the proposed model is efficient and achieves competitive performance against state-of-the-art techniques on various computer vision and computational photography applications.

Acknowledgment. This work is supported in part by the NSF CAREER Grant #1149783, gifts from Adobe and Nvidia, and Office of Naval Research under grant N00014-16-1-2314.

References

1. Yang, Q., Yang, R., Davis, J., Nistér, D.: Spatial-depth super resolution for range images. In: CVPR (2007)
2. Park, J., Kim, H., Tai, Y.W., Brown, M.S., Kweon, I.: High quality depth map upsampling for 3D-TOF cameras. In: ICCV (2011)
3. Ferstl, D., Reinbacher, C., Ranftl, R., Rüther, M., Bischof, H.: Image guided depth upsampling using anisotropic total generalized variation. In: ICCV (2013)
4. Kopf, J., Cohen, M.F., Lischinski, D., Uyttendaele, M.: Joint bilateral upsampling. In: SIGGRAPH (2007)
5. Yan, Q., Shen, X., Xu, L., Zhuo, S., Zhang, X., Shen, L., Jia, J.: Cross-field joint image restoration via scale map. In: ICCV (2013)
6. He, K., Sun, J., Tang, X.: Guided image filtering. PAMI **35**(6), 1397–1409 (2013)
7. Shen, X., Zhou, C., Xu, L., Jia, J.: Mutual-structure for joint filtering. In: ICCV (2015)
8. Xu, L., Yan, Q., Xia, Y., Jia, J.: Structure extraction from texture via relative total variation. ACM Trans. Graph. **31**(6), 139 (2012)
9. Zhang, Q., Shen, X., Xu, L., Jia, J.: Rolling guidance filter. In: Fleet, D., Pajdla, T., Schiele, B., Tuytelaars, T. (eds.) ECCV 2014. LNCS, vol. 8691, pp. 815–830. Springer, Heidelberg (2014). doi:10.1007/978-3-319-10578-9_53
10. Tomasi, C., Manduchi, R.: Bilateral filtering for gray and color images. In: ICCV (1998)
11. Eisemann, E., Durand, F.: Flash photography enhancement via intrinsic relighting. In: SIGGRAPH (2004)
12. Georg, P., Maneesh, A., Hugues, H., Richard, S., Michael, C., Kentaro, T.: Digital photography with flash and no-flash image pairs. In: SIGGRAPH (2004)
13. Ham, B., Cho, M., Ponce, J.: Robust image filtering using joint static and dynamic guidance. In: CVPR (2015)
14. Liu, M.Y., Tuzel, O., Taguchi, Y.: Joint geodesic upsampling of depth images. In: CVPR (2013)
15. Jampani, V., Kiefel, M., Gehler, P.V.: Learning sparse high dimensional filters: image filtering, dense crfs and bilateral neural networks. In: CVPR (2016)
16. Diebel, J., Thrun, S.: An application of Markov random fields to range sensing. In: NIPS (2005)
17. Krizhevsky, A., Sutskever, I., Hinton, G.E.: ImageNet classification with deep convolutional neural networks. In: NIPS (2012)
18. Burger, H.C., Schuler, C.J., Harmeling, S.: Image denoising: can plain neural networks compete with BM3D? In: CVPR (2012)
19. Eigen, D., Krishnan, D., Fergus, R.: Restoring an image taken through a window covered with dirt or rain. In: ICCV (2013)

20. Dong, C., Loy, C.C., He, K., Tang, X.: Learning a deep convolutional network for image super-resolution. In: Fleet, D., Pajdla, T., Schiele, B., Tuytelaars, T. (eds.) ECCV 2014. LNCS, vol. 8692, pp. 184–199. Springer, Heidelberg (2014). doi:10. 1007/978-3-319-10593-2_13

21. Philipp, F., Alexey, D., Eddy, I., Philip, H., Caner, H., Vladimir, G., van der Patrick, S., Daniel, C., Thomas, B.: FlowNet: learning optical flow with convolutional networks. In: ICCV (2015)

22. Xu, L., Ren, J., Yan, Q., Liao, R., Jia, J.: Deep edge-aware filters. In: ICML (2015)

23. Dong, C., Loy, C.C., He, K., Tang, X.: Image super-resolution using deep convolutional networks. PAMI **38**(2), 295–307 (2015)

24. Dollár, P., Zitnick, C.L.: Structured forests for fast edge detection. In: ICCV (2013)

25. David, E., Christian, P., Rob, F.: Depth map prediction from a single image using a multi-scale deep network. In: NIPS (2014)

26. Silberman, N., Hoiem, D., Kohli, P., Fergus, R.: Indoor segmentation and support inference from RGBD images. In: Fitzgibbon, A., Lazebnik, S., Perona, P., Sato, Y., Schmid, C. (eds.) ECCV 2012. LNCS, vol. 7576, pp. 746–760. Springer, Heidelberg (2012). doi:10.1007/978-3-642-33715-4_54

27. Andrea, V., Karel, L.: MatConvNet – convolutional neural networks for matlab. In: ACM MM (2015)

28. Lu, S., Ren, X., Liu, F.: Depth enhancement via low-rank matrix completion. In: CVPR (2014)

29. Song, S., Lichtenberg, S.P., Xiao, J.: Sun RGB-D: a RGB-D scene understanding benchmark suite. In: CVPR (2015)

30. Scharstein, D., Pal, C.: Learning conditional random fields for stereo. In: CVPR (2007)

31. Hirschmüller, H., Scharstein, D.: Evaluation of cost functions for stereo matching. In: CVPR (2007)

32. Levin, A., Lischinski, D., Weiss, Y.: Colorization using optimization. In: SIGGRAPH (2004)

33. Kopf, J., Lischinski, D.: Digital reconstruction of halftoned color comics. In: SIGGRAPH (2012)

34. Xu, L., Lu, C., Xu, Y., Jia, J.: Image smoothing via ℓ_0 gradient minimization. In: ACM SIGGRAPH ASIA (2011)

35. Chen, L.C., Barron, J.T., Papandreou, G., Murphy, K., Yuille, A.L.: Semantic image segmentation with task-specific edge detection using cnns and a discriminatively trained domain transform. In: CVPR (2016)

Efficient Multi-frequency Phase Unwrapping Using Kernel Density Estimation

Felix Järemo Lawin$^{(\boxtimes)}$, Per-Erik Forssén, and Hannes Ovrén

Computer Vision Laboratory, Linköping University, Linköping, Sweden
{felix.jaremo-lawin,per-erik.forssen,hannes.ovren}@liu.se

Abstract. In this paper we introduce an efficient method to unwrap multi-frequency phase estimates for time-of-flight ranging. The algorithm generates multiple depth hypotheses and uses a spatial kernel density estimate (KDE) to rank them. The confidence produced by the KDE is also an effective means to detect outliers. We also introduce a new closed-form expression for phase noise prediction, that better fits real data. The method is applied to depth decoding for the Kinect v2 sensor, and compared to the *Microsoft Kinect SDK* and to the open source driver *libfreenect2*. The intended Kinect v2 use case is scenes with less than 8 m range, and for such cases we observe consistent improvements, while maintaining real-time performance. When extending the depth range to the maximal value of 18.75 m, we get about 52 % more valid measurements than *libfreenect2*. The effect is that the sensor can now be used in large depth scenes, where it was previously not a good choice.

Keywords: Time-of-flight · Kinect v2 · Kernel-density-estimation

1 Introduction

Multi-frequency time-of-flight is a way to accurately estimate distance, that was originally invented for Doppler RADAR [1]. More recently it has also found an application in RGB-D sensors[1] that use time-of-flight ranging, such as the *Microsoft Kinect v2* [2].

Depth from time-of-flight requires very accurate time-of-arrival estimation. Amplitude modulation improves accuracy, by measuring phase shifts between the received and emitted signals, instead of time-of-arrival. However, a disadvantage with amplitude modulation is that it introduces a periodic depth ambiguity. By using multiple modulation frequencies in parallel, the ambiguity can be resolved in most cases, and the useful range can thus be extended.

---

[1] RGB-D sensors output both colour (RGB) and depth (D) images.

Electronic supplementary material The online version of this chapter (doi:10.1007/978-3-319-46493-0_11) contains supplementary material, which is available to authorized users.

B. Leibe et al. (Eds.): ECCV 2016, Part IV, LNCS 9908, pp. 170–185, 2016.
DOI: 10.1007/978-3-319-46493-0_11

Fig. 1. Single frame output on scene with greater than 18.75 m depth range. Left: *libfreenect2*, Center: proposed method. Right: corresponding RGB image. Pixels suppressed by outlier rejection are shown in green. The proposed method has more valid depth points than *libfreenect2* resulting in a denser and more well defined depth scene. While the suppressed areas are clean from outliers for the proposed method, the *libfreenect2* image is covered in salt and pepper noise. (Color figure online)

We introduce an efficient method to unwrap multi-frequency phase estimates for time-of-flight ranging. The algorithm uses *kernel density estimation* (KDE) in a spatial neighbourhood to rank different depth hypotheses. The KDE also doubles as a confidence measure which can be used to detect and suppress bad pixels. We apply our method to depth decoding for the Kinect v2 sensor. For large depth scenes we see a significant increase in coverage of about 52 % more valid pixels compared to *libfreenect2*. See Fig. 1 for a qualitative comparison. For 3D modelling with Kinect fusion [3], this results in fewer outlier points and more complete scene details. While the method is designed with the Kinect v2 in mind, it is also applicable to multi-frequency ranging techniques in general.

1.1 Related Work

The classic solution to the multi-frequency phase unwrapping problem, is to use the Chinese reminder theorem (CRT). This method is fast, but implicitly assumes noise free data, and in [1] it is demonstrated that by instead generating multiple unwrappings for each frequency, and then performing clustering along the range axis, better robustness to noise is achieved. However, due to its simplicity, CRT is still advocated, e.g. in [4,5], and is also used in the Kinect v2 drivers.

Simultaneous unwrapping of multiple phases with different frequencies is a problem that also occurs in fringe pattern projection techniques [5,6]. The algorithms are not fully equivalent though, as the phase is estimated by different means, and the relationship between phase and depth is different.

Another way to unwrap the time-of-flight phase shift is to use surface reflectivity constraints. As the amplitude associated with each phase measurement is a function of object distance and surface reflectivity, a popular approach in the literature is to assume locally constant reflectivity. Under this assumption, the depth can be unwrapped using e.g. a Markov Random Field (MRF) formulation with a data term and a reflectivity smoothness term. In [7], many different such unwrapping methods are discussed. A recent extension of this is [8], where distance, surface albedo and also the local surface normal are used to predict the reflectance.

The multi-frequency and reflectivity approaches are combined in [9] where a MRF with both reflectivity, and dual frequency data terms are used.

Detection of *multipath interference* (i.e. measurement problems due to light reflected from several different world locations reaching the same pixel) is studied in [10]. If four or more frequencies are used, pixels with multipath effects can be detected and suppressed. Recently in [11], a multipath detection algorithm based on blind source separation was applied to the Kinect v2. This required the firmware of the Kinect v2 to be modified to emit and receive at 5 frequencies instead of the default 3. As firmware modification currently requires reverse engineering of the transmission protocol we have not pursued this line of research.

In [12] a simulator for ToF measurements is developed and used to evaluate performance of a MRF that does simultaneous unwrapping and denoising using a wavelet basis. The performance on real data is however not shown.

Noise on the phase measurements is analyzed in [13] and it is suggested that the variance of phase is predicted by sensor variance divided by the phase amplitude squared. In this paper we derive a new model for phase noise that fits better with real data and utilize it as a measure of confidence for the measurements. In [12] a Gaussian mixture model for sensor noise is also derived, but its efficacy is never validated on real sensor data.

1.2 Structure

The paper is organized as follows: In Sect. 2 we describe how multi-frequency time-of-flight measurements are used to sense depth. In Sect. 3 we describe how we extend this by generating multiple hypotheses and selecting one based on kernel density estimation. We give additional implementation details and compare our method to other approaches in Sect. 4. The paper concludes with a discussion and outlook in Sect. 5.

2 Depth Decoding

In time-of-flight sensors, an amplitude modulated light signal is emitted to be reflected on objects in the environment. The reflected signal is then captured in the pixel array of the sensor, where it is correlated with the reference signal driving the light emitter. On the Kinect v2 this is achieved on the camera chip by using quantum efficiency modulation and integration [14,15] resulting in a voltage value v_k. In the general case N different reference signals are used, each phase shifted $\frac{2\pi}{N}$ radians from the others [13]. Often $N = 4$ is used [12], but in the Kinect v2 we have $N = 3$. The voltage values are used to calculate the phase shift between the emitted and the received signals using the complex phase

$$\mathbf{z} = \frac{2}{N} \sum_{k=0}^{N-1} v_k e^{-i(p_o + 2\pi k/N)}, \tag{1}$$

where p_o is a common phase offset. This expression is derived using least squares [13], and the actual phase shift and its corresponding amplitude are obtained as

$$\phi = \arg \mathbf{z} \quad \text{and} \quad a = |\mathbf{z}|. \tag{2}$$

The amplitude is proportional to the reflected signal strength, and increases when the voltage values make consistent contributions to $\mathbf{z}$. It is thus useful as a measure of confidence in the decoded phase.

From the phase shift ϕ in (2) the time-of-flight distance can be calculated as

$$d = \frac{c\phi}{4\pi f_m}, \tag{3}$$

where c is the speed of light, and f_m is the used modulation frequency (see e.g. [2]). This relationship holds both in multi-frequency RADAR [1] and RGB-D time-of-flight. In fringe projection profilometry [6], phase and amplitude values are also obtained for each frequency of the fringe pattern, resulting in a very similar problem. However, the relationship between phase and depth is different in this case.

The phase shift obtained from (2) is the true phase shift $\tilde{\phi}$ modulo 2π. Thus ϕ is ambiguous in an environment where d can be larger than $c/(2f_m)$. Finding the correct period, i.e. n in the expression

$$\tilde{\phi} = \phi_{\text{wrapped}} + 2\pi n, \quad n \in \mathbb{N}, \tag{4}$$

is called *phase unwrapping*. To reduce measurement noise, and increase the range in which ϕ is unambiguous, one can combine the phase measurements from multiple modulated signals with different frequencies.

Figure 2 shows the phase to distance relation for the three amplitude-modulated signals, with frequencies 16, 80 and 120 MHz, which is the setup used in the Kinect v2 [2]. For each of the three frequencies, three phase shifts are used to calculate a phase according to (2), and thus a total of nine measurements are used in each depth calculation. In the figure, we see that if the phase shifts are combined, a common wrap-around occurs at 18.75 m. This is thus the maximum range in which the Kinect v2 can operate without depth ambiguity.

As a final step, the phase shifts from the different modulation frequencies are combined using a phase unwrapping procedure and a weighted average.

It is of critical importance that the phase is correctly unwrapped, as choosing the wrong period will result in large depth errors. This is the topic of the following sub-sections.

2.1 Phase Unwrapping

Consider phase measurements of M amplitude modulated signals with different modulation frequencies. From (3) we get the following relations:

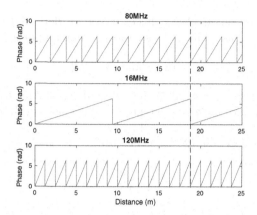

Fig. 2. Wrapped phases for Kinect v2, in the range 0 to 25 m. Top to bottom: ϕ_0, ϕ_1, ϕ_2. The dashed line at 18.75 m indicates the common wrap-around point for all three phases. Just before this line we have $n_0 = 9$, $n_1 = 1$, and $n_2 = 14$.

$$d = \frac{c\,(\phi_0 + 2\pi n_0)}{4\pi f_0} = \frac{c\,(\phi_1 + 2\pi n_1)}{4\pi f_1} = \cdots = \frac{c\,(\phi_{M-1} + 2\pi n_{M-1})}{4\pi f_{M-1}} \iff \quad (5)$$

$$\frac{k_0}{2\pi}\phi_0 + k_0 n_0 = \frac{k_1}{2\pi}\phi_1 + k_1 n_1 = \ldots = \frac{k_{M-1}}{2\pi}\phi_{M-1} + k_{M-1}n_{M-1} \quad (6)$$

where $\{k_m\}_{m=0}^{M-1}$ are the least common multiples for $\{f_m\}_{m=0}^{M-1}$ divided by the respective frequency and $\{n_m\}_{m=0}^{M-1}$ are the set of sought unwrapping coefficients. Now (6) can be simplified to a set of constraints on pairs of unwrapping coefficients (n_i, n_j):

$$k_i n_i - k_j n_j = \frac{k_j}{2\pi}\phi_j - \frac{k_i}{2\pi}\phi_i, \forall i, j \in [0, M-1] \text{ and } i > j. \quad (7)$$

In total there are $M(M-1)/2$ such equations. As the system is redundant, the correct unwrapping cannot be obtained by e.g. Gaussian elimination and in practice the equations are unlikely to hold due to measurement noise. The constraints can however be used to define a likelihood for a specific unwrapping.

2.2 CRT Based Unwrapping

The ambiguity of the phase measurements can be resolved by applying a variant of the Chinese reminder theorem (CRT) [4,5] to one equation at a time in (7):

$$n_i = k_i \cdot \text{round}\left(\frac{k_j\phi_j - k_i\phi_i}{k_i 2\pi}\right) \quad (8)$$

$$\tilde{\phi}_i = \phi_i + 2\pi n_i \quad (9)$$

In the case of more than two frequencies the unwrapped phase $\tilde{\phi}_i$ could be used in (8) for the next equation in (7) to unwrap the next phase. This is suggested and described in [5] and is also used in *libfreenect2*. In the end when all equations have been used, the full unambiguous range of the combined phase measurements has been unwrapped. The CRT method is fast but sensitive to noise as it unwraps each of the phase measurements in sequence. The consequence of this is that an error made early on will be propagated.

2.3 Phase Fusion

The unwrapped phase measurements are combined by using a weighted average:

$$t^* = \sum_{m=0}^{M-1} \frac{k_m \tilde{\phi}_m}{(k_m \sigma_{\phi_m})^2} \Big/ \left(\sum_{m=0}^{M-1} \frac{1}{(k_m \sigma_{\phi_m})^2} \right), \tag{10}$$

where σ_{ϕ_m} is the standard deviation of the noise in ϕ_m. The *pseudo distance* estimate t^* is later converted to a depth (i.e. distance in the forward direction), using the intrinsic camera parameters.

3 Kernel Density Based Unwrapping

In this paper, we propose a new method for multi-frequency phase unwrapping. The method considers several fused pseudo distances t^* (see (10)) for each pixel location $\mathbf{x}$, and select the one with the highest kernel density value [16]. Each such hypothesis $t^i(\mathbf{x})$ is a function of the unwrapping coefficients $\mathbf{n} = (n_0, \ldots, n_{M-1})$. The kernel density for a particular hypothesis $t^i(\mathbf{x})$ is a weighted sum of all considered hypotheses in the spatial neighbourhood:

$$p(t^i(\mathbf{x})) = \frac{\sum_{j \in \mathcal{I}, k \in \mathcal{N}(\mathbf{x})} w_{jk} K(t^i(\mathbf{x}) - t^j(\mathbf{x}_k))}{\sum_{j \in \mathcal{I}, k \in \mathcal{N}(\mathbf{x})} w_{jk}}. \tag{11}$$

Here $K(\cdot)$ is the kernel, and w_{jk} is a sample weight. The sets of samples to consider are defined by the hypothesis indices $\mathcal{I}$ (e.g. $\mathcal{I} = \{1, 2\}$ if we have two hypotheses in each pixel), and by the set of all spatial neighbours $\mathcal{N}(\mathbf{x}) = \{k : \|\mathbf{x}_k - \mathbf{x}\|_1 < r\}$ where r is a square truncation radius. The hypothesis weight w_{ik} is defined as

$$w_{ik} = g(\mathbf{x} - \mathbf{x}_k, \sigma) p(t^i(\mathbf{x}_k)|\mathbf{n}_i(\mathbf{x}_k)) p(t^i(\mathbf{x}_k)|\mathbf{a}_i(\mathbf{x}_k)). \tag{12}$$

The three factors in w_{ik} are:

- the *spatial weight* $g(\mathbf{x} - \mathbf{x}_k, \sigma)$, which is a Gaussian that downweights neighbours far from the considered pixel location $\mathbf{x}$.
- the *unwrapping likelihood* $p(t^i(\mathbf{x})|\mathbf{n}_i(\mathbf{x}))$, that depends on the consistency of the pseudo-distance estimate (10) given the unwrapping vector $\mathbf{n} = (n_0, \ldots, n_{M-1})$.

- the *phase likelihood* $p(t^i(\mathbf{x})|\mathbf{a}_i(\mathbf{x}))$, where $\mathbf{a}_i = (a_0, \ldots, a_{M-1})$, are the ampli-
tudes from (2). It defines the accuracy of the phase before unwrapping.

The kernel in (11) is defined as:

$$K(x) = e^{-x^2/2h^2}, \tag{13}$$

where h is the kernel scale.

In the following sub-sections we will describe the three weight terms in more
detail. For simplicity of notation, we will drop the pixel coordinate argument $\mathbf{x}$,
and e.g. write $p(t^*)$ instead of $p(t^*(\mathbf{x}))$.

3.1 Unwrapping Likelihood

Due to measurement noise, the constraints in (7) are never perfectly satisfied.
We thus subtract the left-hand side from the right-hand side of these equations
to form residuals ϵ_k, one for each of the $M(M-1)/2$ constraints. These are then
used to define a cost for a given unwrapping vector $\mathbf{n} = (n_0, \ldots, n_{M-1})$:

$$J(\mathbf{n}) = \sum_{k=1}^{M(M-1)/2} \epsilon_k^2 / \sigma_{\epsilon_k}^2. \tag{14}$$

This cost function corresponds to the following *unwrapping likelihood*:

$$p(t^*|\mathbf{n}) \propto e^{-J(\mathbf{n})/(2s_1^2)}, \tag{15}$$

where t^* is the fusion of the three unwrapped pseudo-distances, see (10), and s_1
is a scaling factor to be determined. For normally distributed residuals, and the
Kinect v2 case of $M = 3$, the constraints in (7) imply:

$$\sigma_{\epsilon_1}^2 = \left(\frac{k_1 \sigma_{\phi_1}}{2\pi}\right)^2 + \left(\frac{k_0 \sigma_{\phi_0}}{2\pi}\right)^2 \tag{16}$$

$$\sigma_{\epsilon_2}^2 = \left(\frac{k_2 \sigma_{\phi_2}}{2\pi}\right)^2 + \left(\frac{k_0 \sigma_{\phi_0}}{2\pi}\right)^2 \tag{17}$$

$$\sigma_{\epsilon_3}^2 = \left(\frac{k_2 \sigma_{\phi_2}}{2\pi}\right)^2 + \left(\frac{k_1 \sigma_{\phi_1}}{2\pi}\right)^2. \tag{18}$$

This gives us the weights in (14). The values of σ_{ϕ_m} could be predicted from the
phase amplitude a_m (more on this later), but they tend to deviate around a fixed
ratio, and we have observed better robustness of (15) if the ratio is always fixed.
We assume that the phase variances is equal for all modulation frequencies. This
assumption gives us their relative magnitudes, but not their absolute values,
which motivates the introduction of the parameter s_1 in (15).

3.2   Multiple Hypotheses

In contrast to the CRT approach to unwrapping, see Sect. 2.2, we will consider all meaningful unwrapping vectors $\mathbf{n} = (n_0, \ldots, n_{M-1})$ within the unambiguous range. A particular depth value corresponds to a unique unwrapping vector, but with the introduction of noise, neigbouring unwrappings need to be considered at wrap around points. For example, looking at the Kinect v2 case shown in Fig. 2, if $n_0 = n_1 = 0$, n_2 should either be 0 or 1. In total 30 different hypotheses for (n_0, n_1, n_2) are constructed in this way. These can then be ranked by (15).

Compared with the CRT approach, that only considers one hypothesis, the above approach is more expensive. On the other hand, the true maximum of (15) is guaranteed to be checked.

In the low noise case, we can expect the hypothesis with the largest likelihood according to (15) to be the correct one. This is however not necessarily the case in general. Therefore a subset $\mathcal{I}$ of hypotheses with high likelihoods are saved for further consideration, by evaluating the full kernel density (11).

3.3   Phase Likelihood

The amplitude, a, produced by (2) can be used to accurately propagate a noise estimate on the voltage values to noise in the phase estimate. In [13] this relationship is analysed and an expression is derived that can only be computed numerically. For practical use, [13] instead propose $\sigma_\phi^2 = 0.5(\sigma_v/a)^2$ as approximate propagation formula (for $N = 4$). For constant but unknown noise variance on the voltage values σ_v^2, the phase noise can be predicted from the amplitude, as:

$$\sigma_\phi = \gamma/a, \tag{19}$$

where γ is a parameter to be determined. While propagation of noise from voltage values to the complex phase vector $\mathbf{z}$ is linear, the final phase extraction is not, and we will now derive a more accurate approximation using sigma-point propagation [17]. Geometrically, phase extraction from the phase vector (2) is a projection onto a circle, and thus the noise propagation is also a projection of the noise distribution $p(\mathbf{z})$ onto the circle, see Fig. 4 (a). $p(\mathbf{z})$ is centered around the true amplitude a, and sigma-point candidates are located on a circle with radius σ_z. By finding the points where the circle tangents pass through the origin, we get an accurate projection of the noise distribution.

The points of tangency can be found using the pole-polar relationship [18]. For points (x, y) and $(x, -y)$ we get the expressions:

$$x = (a^2 - \sigma_z^2)/a \quad \text{and} \quad y = \frac{\sigma_z}{a}\sqrt{a^2 - \sigma_z^2}. \tag{20}$$

From these expressions, the phase noise can be predicted as:

$$\hat{\sigma}_\phi = \tan^{-1}(y/x) = \tan^{-1}(\sqrt{1/((a/\sigma_z)^2 - 1)}), \tag{21}$$

where σ_z is a model parameter to be determined. Values of $a < \sigma_z$ invalidate the geometric model in Fig. 4(a), and for these we use (19) with $\gamma = \sigma_z \pi/2$.

In *libfreenect2*, a bilateral filter is applied to the $\mathbf{z}$ vectors. The noise attenuation this results in is amplitude dependent, but it can be accurately modelled as a quadratic polynomial on a.

$$\hat{\sigma}_{\phi,\text{bilateral}} = \tan^{-1}(y/x) = \tan^{-1}(\sqrt{1/((\gamma_0 + a\gamma_1 + a^2\gamma_2)^2 - 1)}), \qquad (22)$$

We use the predicted phase noise to define a *phase likelihood*:

$$p(t^*|\mathbf{a}) = \prod_{m=0}^{M-1} p(t^*|a_m), \text{ where } p(t^*|a_m) \propto e^{-0.5\hat{\sigma}_{\phi m}^2/s_2^2}. \qquad (23)$$

where s_2 is a parameter to be tuned. The phase likelihood encodes the accuracy of the phases *before* unwrapping.

3.4   Hypothesis Selection

In each spatial position $\mathbf{x}$, we rank the considered hypotheses t^i, using the KDE (kernel density estimate) defined in (11). The final hypothesis selection is then made as:

$$i^* = \arg\max_{i\in\mathcal{I}} p(t^i). \qquad (24)$$

For the selected hypothesis, $p(t^{i^*})$ is also useful as a confidence measure that can be thresholded to suppress the output in problematic pixels. However, if the spatial support is small, e.g. 3×3, the weighted KDE occasionally encounters sample depletion problems (only very bad samples in a neighbourhood). This can be corrected by regularizing the confidence computation according to:

$$\text{conf}(t^i) = \frac{\sum_k w_k K(t^i - t^k)}{\max(p_{\min}, \sum_k w_k)} \approx p(t^i), \qquad (25)$$

where $p_{\min}$ is a small value, e.g. 0.5.

3.5   Spatial Selection Versus Smoothing

The proposed KDE approach, see (11), selects the best phase unwrapping by considering the distribution of hypotheses in the spatial neighbourhood of a pixel. Note that the spatial neighbourhood is only used to *select* among different hypotheses. This is different from a spatial smoothing, as is commonly used in e.g. depth from disparity [19]. A connection to kernel based smoothing approaches, such as channel smoothing [20,21] can be made by considering the limit where the number of hypotheses is the continuous set of t-values in the depth range of the sensor. The discrete selection in (24) will then correspond to decoding of the highest peak of the PDF, and thus to channel smoothing. In the experiments we will however use just $|\mathcal{I}| = 2$, or 3 hypotheses per pixel, which is far from this limit. After selection, the noise on each pixel is still uncorrelated from the noise of its neighbours, and each pixel can thus still be considered an independent measurement. This is beneficial when fusing data in a later step, using e.g. Kinect Fusion [3].

library(tuning)   **kitchen**(test)   **lecture**(test)

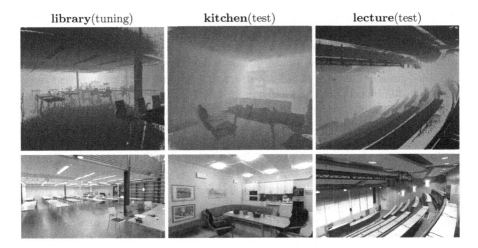

Fig. 3. Unwrapping ground truth for the three datasets. Top row: ground truth depth maps. Green pixels are suppressed, and not used in the evaluation. Bottom row: corresponding images from the RGB camera. (Color figure online)

4   Experiments

We apply the method to depth decoding for the Kinect v2 sensor, and compare it to the *Microsoft Kinect SDK*[2] in the following denoted *Microsoft* and to the open source driver *libfreenect2*. A first visual result is shown in Fig. 1. As can be seen in the figure, the proposed method has a better coverage in the depth images than *libfreenect2*. Another clear distinction between the methods is that *libfreenect2* produces salt and pepper noise all over the image. See also [22] for more examples, and corresponding RGB frames.

4.1   Implementation

The algorithm was implemented by modifying the *libfreenect2*[3] code for depth calculations using *OpenCL* [23] for GPU acceleration. When running the proposed pipeline with $|\mathcal{I}| = 2$ on a *Nvidia GeForce GTX 760* GPU, the frame rate for the depth calculations is above 30 fps for spatial supports up to 17×17. For e.g. a 3×3 support our method operates at 200 fps, which is marginally slower than *libfreenect2* (which also operates in a 3×3 neighbourhood) at 245 fps. The current implementation is however designed for ease of testing, and further speed optimization is be possible.

---

[2] Version 2.0.1409.

[3] As in *opencl_depth_packet_processor.cl* Feb 18 2016 commit: 1d06d2db04a9.

4.2   Ground Truth for Unwrapping

We construct our own ground truth data, which is used for quantitatively evaluating the correctness of the phase unwrappings. The accuracy of the ground truth must be good enough to tell a correct unwrapping from an incorrect one. As we have 30 unwrapping candidates in an 18.75 m range, the distance between the candidates is on average 60 cm. To ensure that no incorrect unwrappings are accidentally counted as inliers, we require an accuracy of at least half the candidate distance, i.e. better than 30 cm.

The required accuracy can easily be met using the Kinect sensor itself. By fusing many frames from the same camera pose, we can reduce the amount of unwrapping errors, and also increase the accuracy in correctly unwrapped measurements. For a given scene we place the camera at different locations corresponding to a spatial 3×3 grid. By fusing data from these poses we can detect and suppress multipath responses, which vary with camera position. Further details on the dataset generation can be found in the supplemental materials [22].

4.3   Datasets

We have used the procedure in Sect. 4.2 to collect three datasets with ground truth depth, shown in Fig. 3. The **kitchen** dataset has a maximal depth of 6.7 m, and is used to test the Kinect v2 under the intended usage with an 8 m depth limit. The **lecture** dataset has a maximal depth of 14.6 m and is used to evaluate methods without imposing the 8 m limit. The **library** dataset is used for parameter tuning, and has a maximal range of 17.0 m. For each dataset, we have additionally logged 25 raw-data frames from the central camera pose, using a data logger in Linux, and another 25 output frames using the *Microsoft SDK v2* API in Windows.

4.4   Comparison of Noise Propagation Models

The tuning dataset **library** was used to estimate the standard deviations σ_ϕ of the individual phase measurements over 40 frames. The model parameters in (19), (21) and (22)¯ were found by minimizing the residuals of the corresponding inverted expressions using non-linear least squares over all amplitude measurements a. The inversion of the expressions reduced bias effects due to large residuals for small amplitudes.

This procedure was performed for **z** with and without bilateral filtering (as implemented in *libfreenect2*). Figure 4((b) and (c)) shows the resulting predictions overlaid on the empirical distributions of the relation between the amplitude and the phase standard deviation. We see that the models proposed in (21) and (22) have a slightly better fit to the empirical distribution than [13] on raw phase measurements. However, for bilateral filtered **z**, the quadratic model suggested in expression (22) has the best fit. As bilateral filtering improves the final performance this is the model used in our method.

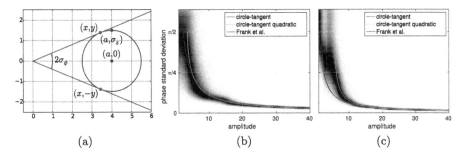

Fig. 4. (a): Geometrical illustration of the circle-tangents. (b): Predictions from raw phase overlaid on empirical distribution. (c): Predictions from bilateral-filtered phase.

4.5   Outlier Rejection

libfreenect2: outlier rejection is performed at several steps, each with one or several tuned thresholds:

– Pixels where any of the amplitudes is below a threshold are suppressed.
– Pixels where the pseudo-distances differ in magnitude are suppressed. The purpose of this is similar to (15), but an expression based on the cross-product of the pseudo phases with a reference relation is used.
– Pixels with a large depth, or amplitude variance in their 3×3 neighbourhood are suppressed.
– Pixels that deviate from their neighbours are suppressed.
– Pixels on edges in the voltage images are suppressed.

Proposed method: a single threshold is applied on the KDE-based confidence measure in (25).

4.6   Parameter Settings

The proposed method introduces the following parameters that needs to be set:

– the scaling s_1 in (15)
– the scaling s_2 in (23).
– the kernel scale h in (13).
– the spatial support r. (the Gaussian in (12) has a spatial support of $(2r+1) \times (2r+1)$ and $\sigma = r/2$.)
– the number of hypotheses $|\mathcal{I}|$.

The method is not sensitive to the selection of s_1, s_2 and h, and thus the same setting is used for all experiments. Unless otherwise stated, the parameters $r = 5$ and $|\mathcal{I}| = 2$ are used. The effects of these parameters are discussed further in the supplemental material [22].

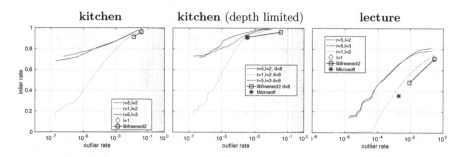

Fig. 5. Inlier and outlier rate plots. Each point or curve is the average over 25 frames.

4.7   Coverage Experiments

We have used the unwrapping datasets described in Sect. 4.3 to compare the methods in terms of inliers (correctly unwrapped points), and outliers (incorrectly unwrapped points). A point is counted as an inlier when a method outputs a depth estimate which is closer than 30 cm to the ground truth, and an outlier otherwise. These counts are then divided by the number of valid points in the ground truth to obtain inlier and outlier rates.

Figure 5 shows plots of inlier rate against outlier rate for our method, for the full range of thresholds on the output confidence in (25). As a reference, we also plot the output from *Microsoft* and *libfreenect2*, as well as *libfreenect2* without the outlier threshold, and *libfreenect2* where the hypothesis selection is done by minimising (14), instead of using the CRT approach in Sect. 2.2 (labelled $I = 1$ in the legend). As can be seen in Fig. 5 middle, the performance of *libfreenect2* and *Microsoft* are similar on short range scenes with a depth limit (this is expected, as the *libfreenect2* source mentions it being based on disassembly of the Microsoft SDK).

As can be seen, the proposed method consistently has a higher inlier rate at the same outlier rate, when compared to *libfreenect2* with the same spatial support, i.e. $r = 1$. When the spatial support size is increased, the improvement is more pronounced.

Performance for scenes with larger depth is exemplified with the **lecture** dataset. With the depth limit removed, we get significantly more valid measurements at the same outlier rate. The *Microsoft* method has a hard limit of 8 m and cannot really compete on this dataset; it only reaches about 35 % inlier rate. The *libfreenect2* method without the depth limit reaches 48 % inliers, at a 1 % outlier rate. At the 1 % outlier rate, the proposed method has a 73 % inlier rate, which is an relative improvement of 52 % over *libfreenect2*.

The performance is improved slightly for $|\mathcal{I}| = 3$ compared with $|\mathcal{I}| = 2$. While still having frame rates over 30 fps for a spatial support of $r = 5$, we consider the costs to outweigh the small improvement, and thus favour the setting of $|\mathcal{I}| = 2$.

Fig. 6. Meshes of **lecture** scene from KinFu. Left: unwrapped with *libfreenect2*. Right: unwrapped with the proposed method.

4.8   Kinect Fusion

We have implemented a data-logger that saves all output from the Kinect v2 to a file for later playback. This allows us to feed the Kinect Fusion implementation KinFu in the *Point Cloud Library* [24] with Kinect v2 output unwrapped with both *libfreenect2* and the proposed method. Figure 6 shows two meshes obtained in this way. As can be seen Kinect Fusion benefits from the proposed approach by generating models with fewer outlier points, and consistently more complete scene details. See [22] for more examples.

5   Concluding Remarks

This paper introduces a new multi-frequency phase unwrapping method based on kernel density estimation of phase hypotheses in a spatial neighbourhood. We also derive a new closed-form expression for prediction of phase noise and show how to utilize it as a measure of confidence for the measurements.

Our method was implemented and tested extensively on the Kinect v2 time-of-flight depth sensor. Compared to the previous methods in *libfreenect2* and *Microsoft Kinect SDK v2* it consistently produces more valid measurements when using the default depth limit of 8 m, while maintaining real-time performance. In large-depth environments, without the depth limit, the gains are however much larger, and the number of valid measurements increases by 52 % at the same outlier rate.

As we have shown, the proposed method allows better 3D scanning of large scenes, as the full 18.75 m depth range can be used. This is of interest for mapping and robotic navigation, where seeing further allows better planning. As the method is generic, future work includes applying it to other multi-frequency problems such as Doppler radar [1] and fringing [5,6].

Acknowledgements. This work has been supported by the Swedish Research Council in projects 2014-6227 (EMC2) and 2014-5928 (LCMM) and the EU's Horizon 2020 Programme grant No 644839 (CENTAURO).

References

1. Trunk, G., Brockett, S.: Range and velocity ambiguity resolution. In: IEEE National Radar Conference, pp. 146–149 (1993)
2. Sell, J., O'Connor, P.: The Xbox one system on a chip and kinect sensor. IEEE Micro **34**(2), 44–53 (2014)
3. Newcombe, R.A., et al.: KinectFusion: real-time dense surface mapping and tracking. In: IEEE ISMAR 2011, Basel, Switzerland, October 2011
4. Jongenelen, A.P.P., Bailey, D.G., Payne, A.D., Dorrington, A.A., Carnegie, D.A.: Analysis of errors in tof range imaging with dual-frequency modulation. IEEE Trans. Instrum. Measur. **60**(5), 1861–1868 (2011)
5. Wang, Z., Du, H., Park, S., Xie, H.: Three-dimensional shape measurement with a fast and accurate approach. Appl. Opt. **48**(6), 1052–1061 (2009)
6. Gorthi, S.S., Pastogi, P.: Fringe projection techniques: wither we are? Opt. Lasers Eng. **48**(2), 133–140 (2010)
7. Hansard, M.: Disambiguation of time-of-flight data. In: Time-of-Flight Cameras, Chap. 2. Springer Briefs in Computer Science, pp. 29–43. Springer, London (2013)
8. Crabb, R., Manduchi, R.: Fast single-frequenct time-of-flight range imaging. In: IEEE International Conference on Computer Vision and Pattern Recognition (CVPR 2015) (2015)
9. Droeschel, D., Holz, D., Behnke, S.: Multi-frequency phase unwrapping for time-of-flight cameras. In: IEEE International Conference on Intelligent Robots and Systems (2010)
10. Kirmani, A., Benedetti, A., Chou, P.A.: SPUMIC: simultaneous phase unwrapping and multipath interference cancellation in time-of-flight cameras using spectral methods. In: IEEE International Conference on Multimedia & Expo (ICME 2013) (2013)
11. Feigin, M., Bhandari, A., Izadi, S., Rhemann, C., Schmidt, M., Raskar, R.: Resolving multipath interference in Kinect: an inverse problem approach. IEEE Sens. J. **16**, 3419–3427 (2015)
12. Mei, J., Kirmani, A., Colaco, A., Goyal, V.K.: Phase unwrapping and denoising for time-of-flight imaging using generalized approximate message passing. In: IEEE International Conference on Image Processing (ICIP 2013) (2013)
13. Frank, M., Plaue, M., Rapp, H., Köthe, U., Jähne, B.: Theoretical and experimental error analysis of continuous-wave time-of-flight range cameras. Opt. Eng. **48**(1), 013602 (2009)
14. Bamji, C., Charbon, E.: US 6,515,740 B2: methods for CMOS-compatible three-dimensional image sensing using quantum efficiency modulation (2004)
15. Bamji, C.S., et al.: A 0.13 μm CMOS system-on-chip for a 512×424 time-of-flight image sensor with multi-frequency photo-demodulation up to 130 MHz and 2 GS/s ADC. IEEE J. Solid-State Circuits **50**(1), 303–319 (2015)
16. Murphy, K.P.: Machine Learning: A Probabilistic Perspective. MIT Press, Cambridge (2012)
17. Uhlmann, J.: Dynamic map building and localization: new theoretical foundations. Ph.D. thesis, University of Oxford (1995)
18. Hartley, R., Zisserman, A.: Multiple View Geometry in Computer Vision, 2nd edn. Cambridge University Press, Cambridge (2003)
19. Szeliski, R.: Computer Vision: Algorithms and Applications. Springer-Verlag New York Inc., New York (2010)

20. Forssén, P.E.: Low and medium level vision using channel representations. Ph.D. thesis, Linköping University, Sweden, SE-581 83 Linköping, Sweden, March 2004. Dissertation No. 858, ISBN 91-7373-876-X
21. Felsberg, M., Forssén, P.E., Scharr, H.: Channel smoothing: efficient robust smoothing of low-level signal features. IEEE TPAMI **28**(2), 209–222 (2006)
22. Järemo Lawin, F., Forssén, P.E., Ovrén, H.: Efficient multi-frequency phase unwrapping using kernel density estimation, supplemental material. Technical report, Linköing University (2016)
23. Khronos Group: OpenCL language specification (2015). https://www.khronos.org/opencl/
24. Rusu, R.B., Cousins, S.: 3D is here: point cloud library (PCL). In: IEEE ICRA, 9–13 May 2011

A Multi-scale CNN for Affordance Segmentation in RGB Images

Anirban Roy[✉] and Sinisa Todorovic

School of Electrical Engineering and Computer Science,
Oregon State University, Corvallis, USA
royani@oregonstate.edu, sinisa@eecs.oregonstate.edu

Abstract. Given a single RGB image our goal is to label every pixel with an affordance type. By affordance, we mean an object's capability to readily support a certain human action, without requiring precursor actions. We focus on segmenting the following five affordance types in indoor scenes: 'walkable', 'sittable', 'lyable', 'reachable', and 'movable'. Our approach uses a deep architecture, consisting of a number of multi-scale convolutional neural networks, for extracting mid-level visual cues and combining them toward affordance segmentation. The mid-level cues include depth map, surface normals, and segmentation of four types of surfaces – namely, floor, structure, furniture and props. For evaluation, we augmented the NYUv2 dataset with new ground-truth annotations of the five affordance types. We are not aware of prior work which starts from pixels, infers mid-level cues, and combines them in a feed-forward fashion for predicting dense affordance maps of a single RGB image.

Keywords: Object affordance · Mid-level cues · Deep learning

1   Introduction

This paper addresses the problem of affordance segmentation in an image, where the goal is to label every pixel with an affordance type. By affordance, we mean an object's capability to support a certain human action [1,2]. For example, when a surface in the scene affords the opportunity for a person to walk, sit or lie down on it, we say that the surface is characterized by affordance types 'walkable', 'sittable', or 'lyable'. Also, an object may be 'reachable' when someone standing on the floor can readily grasp the object. A surface or an object may be characterized by a number of affordance types. Importantly, affordance of an object exhibits only the possibility of some action, subject to the object's relationships with the environment, and thus is not an inherent (permanent) object's attribute. Thus, sometimes chairs are not 'sittable' and floors are not 'walkable' if other objects in the environment prevent performing the corresponding actions.

Electronic supplementary material The online version of this chapter (doi:10. 1007/978-3-319-46493-0_12) contains supplementary material, which is available to authorized users.

B. Leibe et al. (Eds.): ECCV 2016, Part IV, LNCS 9908, pp. 186–201, 2016.
DOI: 10.1007/978-3-319-46493-0_12

Affordance segmentation is an important, long-standing problem with a range of applications, including robot navigation, path planning, and autonomous driving [3–14]. Reasoning about affordances has been shown to facilitate object and action recognition [4,10,13]. Existing work typically leverages mid-level visual cues [3] for reasoning about spatial (and temporal) relationships among objects in the scene, which is then used for detection (and in some cases segmentation) of affordances in the image (or video). For example, Hoiem et al. [15,16] show that inferring mid-level cues – including: depth map, semantic cues, and occlusion maps – facilitates reasoning about the 3D geometry of a scene, which in turn helps affordance segmentation. This and other related work typically use a holistic framework aimed at "closing the loop" that iteratively improves affordance segmentation and estimation of mid-level cues, e.g., via energy minimization.

Motivated by prior work, our approach to affordance segmentation is grounded on estimation of mid-level cues, including depth map, surface normals and coarse-level semantic segmentation (e.g., general categories of surfaces such as walls, floors, furniture, props), as illustrated in Fig. 1. Our key difference from prior work is that, instead of "closing the loop", we use a *feed-forward* multi-scale convolutional neural network (CNN) in order to predict and integrate the mid-level cues for labeling pixels with affordance types. CNNs have been successfully used for low-level segmentation tasks [17–23]. Multi-scale CNNs have been demonstrated as suitable for computing hierarchical features, and successful in a range of pixel-level prediction tasks [17–19,23,24].

Given an RGB image, we independently infer its depth map, surface normals, and coarse-level semantic segmentation using the multi-scale CNN of Eigen et al. [24]. The three multi-scale CNNs produce corresponding mid-level cues at the output, which are then jointly feed as inputs to another multi-scale CNN for predicting N affordance maps for each of N affordance types. Our estimate of depth map, surface normals, and semantic segmentation can be explicitly analyzed for reasoning about important geometric properties of the scene – such as, e.g., identifying major surfaces, surface orientations, spatial extents of objects, object heights above the ground, etc. We treat the three mid-level cues as *latent* scene representations which are fused by the CNN for affordance segmentation. Therefore, in this paper, we do not evaluate inference of the mid-level cues.

In this paper, we focus on indoor scenes and typical affordances characterizing objects and surfaces in such scenes. Indoor scenes represent a challenging domain, because of relatively large variations in spatial layouts of objects affecting the feasibility of human-object interactions, and thus affordances. We consider the following five affordance types typical of indoor scenes:

1. **Walkable:** is any horizontal surface at a similar height as the ground that has free space vertically above (i.e., not occupied by any objects), since such a surface would afford a person to comfortably walk on it (even if soft);
2. **Sittable:** is any horizontal surface below a certain height from the ground (estimated relative to the human height) that has free space around and vertically above, as it would afford a person to comfortably sit on it;

3. **Lyable:** is any 'sittable' surface that is also sufficiently long and wide for a person to lie on it;
4. **Reachable:** can be any part of the scene that is within a reachable height for a person standing on the ground, and has free space around so that a person can stand next to it and readily grasp it;
5. **Movable:** is any 'reachable' small object (e.g., book) that can be easily moved by hand, and has free space around so as to afford the moving action.

In our specification, we consider that any 'walkable' surface is also 'standable'; therefore, 'standable' is not included in the above list. Also, we consider that the sitting action can be performed without a back support, which might be different from previous definitions in the literature. Note that almost everything under a certain height can be reachable if a person is allowed to bend, crawl, climb or perform other complex actions. In this paper, we only consider reachability by hand while a person is standing on the floor. Regarding 'movable', our definition may be too restrictive for a case when a relatively large object can be moved (e.g., chair); but, in such cases, the moving action cannot be easily performed.

It is also worth noting that we focus on "immediate" affordances, i.e., an object's capability to *immediately* support a human action, which can be readily executed without any precursor actions. For example, a chair is not immediately 'sittable' if it has to be moved before sitting on it. Therefore, we *cannot* resort to a deterministic mapping between object classes and their usual affordance types (chairs are in general sittable), since affordance types of particular object instances depend on the spatial context.

An obstacle that we have encountered in our work is the lack of datasets with ground truth pixel-wise annotations of affordances. Our literature review finds that most prior work focuses on affordance prediction at the image level, where the goal is to assign an affordance label to the entire image [4,5,9,11,25–27]. A few exceptions [28,29] seek to discover similar affordance types as ours in RGB images. They estimate ground truth by hallucinating human skeletons in various postures amidst the inferred 3D layout of the scene.

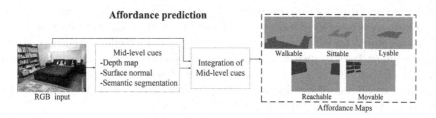

Fig. 1. An overview of our approach: given an RGB image, we use a multi-scale convolutional neural network (CNN) to compute mid-level cues – including: depth map, surface normals and segmentation of general surface categories (e.g., walls, floors, furniture, props). The CNN also fuses these mid-level cues in a feed-forward manner for predicting five affordance maps for each of the five affordance types considered: 'walkable', 'sittable', 'lyable', 'reachable', and 'movable'.

As human skeletons may provide a limited model for reasoning about certain human-object interactions in the scene, and may not be informative for some of our affordance types (e.g., 'movable'), we have developed a new semi-automated method for generating pixel-wise ground truth annotations of affordances. This is used to extend the NYU v2 dataset [30] with ground-truth dense affordance annotations, and our quantitative evaluation.

Contributions:

- We extend the NYUv2 dataset [30] with pixel-wise affordance ground truth.
- A new multi-scale deep architecture for extracting and fusing mid-level cues toward predicting dense affordance maps from an RGB image. Note that, unlike previous approaches [9,31–34], we do not rely on any additional cues based on human-object interaction (e.g., action, pose).

In the following, Sect. 2 reviews prior work, Sect. 3 explains our method for generating affordance ground truth, Sect. 4 specifies our deep architecture for affordance segmentation, Sect. 5 describes how to train our deep architecture, and Sect. 6 presents our experimental results.

2   Prior Work

Predicting affordances has a long history in computer vision [1,2]. Early work has typically considered a rule-based inference for affordance segmentation [35–37]. However, their hand-designed rules are too brittle for real-world indoor scenes abounding with clutter and occlusions.

Some recent approaches reason about affordance via interpreting human actions and human-objects interactions [9,31–34]. For example, recognizing human actions can provide informative cues for predicting affordance [31,32]. Other approaches leverage a fine-grained human pose estimation [33]. These visual cues are also used for predicting affordance of novel objects [9]. One of our key differences from these approaches is that they are aimed at predicting affordance of foreground objects, whereas we aim for a dense pixel-wise labeling.

A related line of work predicts affordance by hypothesizing possible human-object interactions in the scene [28,38,39]. For example, [28,39] use human-skeleton models in various postures. Our approach does not use human skeletons.

Another group of approaches [25–27,40,41] focus on affordances of small objects, such as spoon, knife, cup, etc., which are operated by hands. Thus, they address different affordance types from ours, including graspable, cuttable, liftable, fillable, scoopable, etc. In contrast, we consider affordance for human actions that involve the complete human body.

RGB and RGBD videos provide additional temporal cues for interpreting human-object interactions, and thus allow for robust affordance prediction [4,7,42,43]. Also, detecting objects and reconstructing a detailed 3D scene geometry can lead to robust affordance segmentation [25,28,42,44].

We are not aware of prior work which infers and combines mid-level cues in a feed-forward fashion using a deep architecture for predicting dense affordance maps of a single RGB image (Fig. 2).

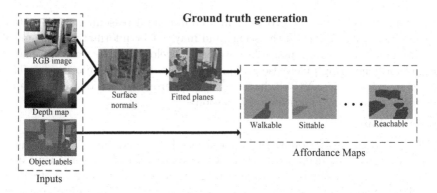

Fig. 2. For generating ground truth, we assume access to RGBD images. First, we compute surface normals from the RGB and depth information. Then, we use the RANSAC algorithm to fit 3D scene surfaces to a piece-wise planar approximation of the scene. The identified surface planes and their plane normals are combined with ground-truth object labels to decide affordance types present at every pixel.

3   Generation of Affordance Ground Truth

This section explains our semi-automated method for generating dense ground truth affordance maps in the NYUv2 dataset [30]. Importantly, for estimating such ground truth, we assume access to RGBD images and their pixel-wise annotations of object class labels. This is in contrast to our setting, where we have no access to depth information and object class labels, i.e., our approach takes only RGB images as input.

The NYUv2 dataset consists of 1449 indoor images with pixel-wise depth maps and object class labels for each image. There are 40 indoor object classes [45], including floor, wall, chair, sofa, table, bed, desk, books, bottle etc. Most of the scenes exhibit complex layouts of objects, clutter, and prominent occlusion. This makes affordance segmentation challenging.

Object Class Labels vs. Aaffordance Labels: Assigning affordance labels to pixels cannot be done using a direct mapping from available object class labels. This is because of two reasons. Different object parts may not support the same affordance (e.g., back-rest of a chair may not be sittable). Also, affordance of a particular object instance depends on the spatial context (e.g., a chair is placed under a table is not immediately sittable by our definition).

It follows that, in addition to object class labels, we also need to consider the spatial layout of objects in the scene for generating a reliable ground truth affordance maps. Thus, we develop an approach to systematically extract some essential geometrical cues from the scene, as explained below.

Understanding 3D Scene Geometry: We first align the RGB color and depth data, such that the floor represents the X-Y plane and Z axis represents height. From the RGB and depth map, we compute surface normals at every pixel. Then, we use the RANSAC algorithm to fit 3D scene surfaces to a piecewise planar approximation of the scene. This allows us to identify vertical and horizontal surface planes relative to the ground plane, as in [30]. For robustness, we allow some margin, such that we also account for near-horizontal and near-vertical surfaces (±10 degrees of the surface normal). Finally, for each horizontal and vertical surface plane, we compute its height and maximum height from the ground plane, respectively. Also, for every surface plane, we estimate its size, and if there is a free space around and vertically above. Surrounding clearance is considered at a distance of 1 foot from the surface plane, where distances in the 3D scene are estimated using the camera parameters and the depth data.

Combining Scene Geometry and Ground-Truth Object Labels: Given the aforementioned estimates of horizontal and vertical surface planes in the scene, we identify their ground-truth object class labels. This has two purposes: (a) to constrain the set of candidate affordance types that could be associated with each plane, and (b) to enforce smoothness in our generation of affordance ground truth. To this end, for each affordance type, we specify a list of object classes appearing in the NYUv2 dataset that could be characterized by that type. For example, objects that could be 'sittable' are {chair, bed, sofa, desk, table, ... }; objects that could be 'walkable' are {floor, floor-mat}; objects that could be 'lyable' are {bed, sofa, table, ... }. The detailed list of NYUv2 objects and affordances they could support is provided in the supplemental material.

After determining the object class labels of the surface planes, the above-mentioned manually specified affordance-object pairs are used for hypothesizing candidate affordances of each plane. The candidates are further constrained per affordance definitions, stated in Sect. 1 and specified in Table 1, taking into account the plane's size, height, and surrounding and vertical clearances. Thus, when the plane's size, height or clearance does not satisfy the definition of a particular candidate affordance, this candidate is removed from the solution. For example, a horizontal plane, estimated at 3 ft from the ground and with vertical clearance, whose majority ground-truth class is 'bed', could be 'sittable' and 'lyable'. But if the plane's size has been estimated as too small to comfortably accommodate a full human body, the plane is labeled only as 'sittable'.

Note that our approach to generating ground truth differs from that presented in [28,29]. Their approach hallucinates a human skeleton model in the scene to determine the ground-truth affordance labels. Specifically, they convolve a human skeleton corresponding to a particular human action with the 3D voxelized representation of the scene. Such an approach would not generate ground truth which respects our affordance definitions. For example, a skeleton representing a standing person can fit on top of a desk or a table, and as a result these surfaces would be labeled as 'walkable' or 'standable' [28]. However, our definition of 'walkable' is based on the expectation that walking on horizontal surfaces with non-zero heights from the ground cannot be readily performed (one needs to climb first). Also, a skeleton representing a sitting person can easily fit on a chair even if there are small objects on the chair preventing a comfort-

Table 1. Definitions of affordance types for surfaces identified in the scene. The heights are given in feet/meters, and sizes are given in feet^2/meters^2. We consider the maximum convex area of a surface to estimate its size. For all measurements, we allow $\pm 10\%$ tolerance to ensure robustness.

Affordance type	Definition				
	Surface type	Height (h)	Size (s)	Clearance above	Clearance side
Walkable	Horizontal	$h \leq 1/0.3$	$s \geq 2.5/0.23$	Yes	No
Sittable	Horizontal	$1.5/0.45 \leq h \leq 3.5/1$	$s \geq 1/0.1$	Yes	Yes
Lyable	Horizontal	$1.5/0.45 \leq h \leq 3.5/1$	$s \geq 10/0.9$	Yes	Yes
Reachable	Horizontal/Vertical	$1.5/0.45 \leq h \leq 7/2.1$	N/A	No	Yes
Movable	Horizontal/Vertical	$1.5/0.45 \leq h \leq 7/2.1$	$s \leq 2.5/0.23$	Either of two	

able sitting action. Unlike [28,29], we explicitly consider all requirements of the affordance definitions in order to generate affordance ground truth.

Manual Correction: The aforementioned automated generation of ground truth is prone to error. This is due to: (a) the stochastic nature of the RANSAC algorithm, (b) challenging elongated and thin surfaces that we fail to separate from the background, and (c) prominent occlusions and clutter that make our estimation of surface normals unreliable. Therefore, we have resorted to visual inspection of our results for corrections. We have used the Amazon mechanical turk to acquire multiple human corrections, and then applied majority voting to determine the final ground truth. Each user has been allowed to either add new regions to an affordance type, or remove wrongly labeled regions. The human corrections have been in relatively small disagreement, considering that our five affordance types are relatively complex cognitive concepts. Hence, the majority vote has helped resolve most disagreements.

Dataset Statistics: About 72% of the automatically generated affordance labelings have been corrected by human experts. Each manual correction takes about 30–40 s per affordance class. We compute the intersection over union (IoU) measure between the automatically generated and manually corrected ground truth to compute their similarity. The IoU value is 67%, which indicates that the manual correction is necessary. Affordance types 'walkable', 'sittable', 'lyable', 'reachable', and 'movable' appear in 83%, 60%, 22%, 100%, and 93% of the NYUv2 images, respectively. A similar pixel-level statistic estimates that 12%, 5%, 11%, 65% and 11% of pixels are occupied by the corresponding affordance, if that affordance is present in the image. 18% of pixels have multiple distinct affordance labels. We notice that pixels occupied by a particular object instance are not all labeled with the same affordance, as desired. Thus, for example, only 79% of pixels occupied by floors are labeled as 'walkable'.

Some example ground truths are shown in Fig. 3. Additional examples are presented in the supplemental material.

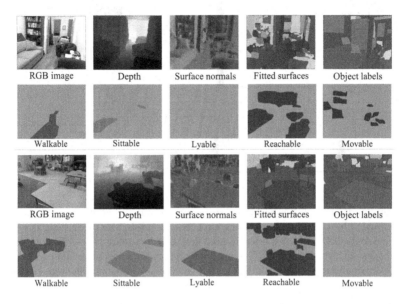

Fig. 3. Examples of our ground truth affordance maps: Top row represents the mid-level cues, i.e., depth map, surface normals and semantic segmentation. The bottom row represents the ground truth affordance maps.

4   Affordance Segmentation with a Multi-scale CNN

We use four multi-scale CNNs for affordance segmentation, as illustrated in Fig. 4. Each of these CNNs has the same architecture (e.g., number of convolutional layers, number and size of convolutional kernels) as the deep network presented in [24]. The three CNNs are aimed at extracting hierarchical features from the RGB image, via the coarse- and fine-scale networks, for estimating depth map, surface normals, and semantic segmentation, respectively. The coarse-scale CNN is designed to generate feature maps representing global visual cues in the image (e.g., large surfaces, context). The fine-scale CNN is designed to capture detailed visual cues, such as such as small objects, edges and object boundaries. As in [24], the outputs of the coarse-scale network is considered as inputs to the fine-scale network. The fourth CNN also consists of the coarse- and fine-scale networks, which serve for a multi-scale integration of the estimated mid-level cues and pixels of the input image for predicting the five affordance maps.

For semantic segmentation, we consider four high-level categories, including: 'floor', 'structure' (e.g., walls), 'furniture', and 'props' (small objects), defined in [30]. Note that this is in contrast to our method for generating ground truth,

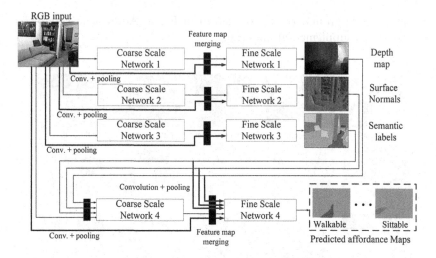

Fig. 4. Our multi-scale CNN architecture for predicting the affordance labels in the indoor scenes. The coarse scale network captures the global features such as context and the fine scale CNN captures finer details such as object boundaries. We combine the mid-level cues with the low-level RGB image to predict the affordance labels. Thin lines represent direct input and bold lines represent a convolution+pooling step, performed on the input before merging with the feature maps [24].

where we use as input ground-truth annotations of all fine-grained object classes (40 classes [45]). The four high-level categories allow for robust deep learning, since they provide significantly more training examples than there are instances for each fine-grained object class. Alternatively, we could have tried to conduct semantic segmentation of fine-grained object classes, and used the resulting segmentation for predicting affordance maps. However, such semantic scene labeling would limit the generalizability of our approach to scenes with novel objects.

Coarse-Scale Network: It takes pixels of the entire image as input, and generates feature maps as output. In this network, we use larger convolutional kernels with higher stride length than those used in the fine-scale network. As the deep architecture of [46], our coarse-scale network replaces the top fully connected layers by 1 × 1 convolution layers. The output is then upsampled in order to generate the final feature map. After every convolution+pooling step, the size of the output is reduced, such that the size of final output is 1/16 of the input. This final output is then upsampled to size 1/4 of the input.

Fine-Scale Network: The final output feature maps of the coarse-scale network and pixels of the image are jointly input to the fine-scale network for making the final prediction of the corresponding mid-level cue. In order to match the size of the RGB image with the size of the feature maps produced by the coarse-scale network, we perform a single step of convolution+pooling of the RGB image, as in [24]. For preserving fine details at the output, the convolution+pooling steps in this network do not reduce the output size. The final output of this network is upsampled to the size of the input RGB image, resulting either one of the mid-level cues or the affordance maps.

Details about both the coarse-scale and fine-scale network such as number of layers, kernel sizes, etc. are provided in the supplemental material. Note that, instead of using the three distinct scales as in [24], we consider only first two scales in our approach for efficiency.

5 Training

Our training of the deep architecture presented in Sect. 4 consists of four tasks aimed at training the four multi-scale CNNs. In each training task, the four coarse-scale networks are initialized with the VGG Net [47]. The fine-scale networks are initialized randomly. After initialization, the coarse-scale and fine-scale networks of each multi-scale CNN are trained jointly so as to minimize a suitable loss function, using the standard sub-gradient method with momentum. The momentum value is set to 0.9. Learning iterations are 2 M, 1.5 M, 1.5 M and 2 M for depth prediction, surface normal estimation, semantic segmentation and affordance segmentation respectively. Training takes 6–8 h/per task and inference takes $\approx$0.15 sec/per image, on a Nvidia Tesla K80 GPU. In the following, we specify the loss functions used for training.

Multi-scale CNN-1 is trained for depth map prediction. We use a scale-invariant and structure-aware loss function for depth prediction as in [48]. Let d denote a difference between a predicted depth and ground truth in the log scale. Then, this loss function is defined as

$$L_{depth} = \frac{1}{I}\sum_i d_i^2 - \frac{1}{2I^2}\left(\sum_i d_i\right)^2 + \frac{1}{I}\sum_i [(\nabla_x d_i)^2 + (\nabla_y d_i)^2] \qquad (1)$$

where i is the index of pixels, I is the total number of pixels, and $\nabla_x d_i$ and $\nabla_y d_i$ denote the gradients of the depth difference d along the x and y axes.

Multi-scale CNN-2 is trained for predicting surface normals. The loss function for normals prediction is specified as $L_{norm} = -\frac{1}{I}\sum_i \boldsymbol{n}_i \cdot \hat{\boldsymbol{n}}_i$, where $\boldsymbol{n}_i$ and $\hat{\boldsymbol{n}}_i$ denote the ground truth and predicted surface normals at pixel i, and the symbol '·' denotes the scalar product.

Multi-scale CNN-3 and multi-scale CNN-4 are trained for four-class semantic segmentation and predicting five binary affordance maps, respectively. For training both networks, we use the standard cross-entropy loss given the ground-truths of the four semantic categories, and our ground-truth affordance maps.

Data Augmentation: The NYUv2 dataset provides only 795 training images. The size of this training set is not sufficient to robustly train the multi-scale deep architecture. Therefore, we augment the training data by applying random translations, mirror flips, small rotations and contrast modifications. We also apply the same transformations to the corresponding ground truth maps. This results in a three times larger training set. Such data manipulation methods for increasing the training set are common [46,48].

6   Results

We first explain our experimental setup and then report our results.

Dataset. For evaluation, we use the NYUv2 dataset [30] which consists of 1449 RGBD images of indoor scenes with densely labeled object classes. Though the depth information is available for each image, we predict affordance only using RGB input. Following the standard split, we use 795 images for training and 654 images for testing. We augment the dataset with the additional five, ground-truth, binary, dense affordance maps of: 'sittable', 'walkable', 'lyable', 'reachable' and 'movable'.

Benchmark datasets for evaluating scene geometry and scene layout, such as the UIUC indoor dataset [49] and geometric context [15], are not suitable for our evaluation, because they do not provide dense ground-truth annotations of object classes and surface normals. This, in turn, prevents us to generate ground truth affordance maps for these datasets. The RGBD video datasets [4, 43] are also not suitable for our evaluation, since our goal is to segment affordance in a single RGB image. Moreover, we focus on five affordance types that are different from those annotated in the RGBD videos of [4, 43] – specifically, our affordances are defined in relation to the entire human body, whereas the RGBD videos show affordances of small objects manipulated by hands. Also, note that a direct comparison with the related approaches that densely predict similar (but not the same) affordance types in indoor scenes [28, 29] would not be possible. Their affordance labels are heuristically estimated, and their ground truth is not yet publicly available. Although we are not in a position to conduct direct comparison with the state of the art, in the following, we present multiple baselines and compare with them.

Evaluation Metric. For quantitative evaluation, we compare the binary ground-truth affordance map with our predicted binary map. Specifically, we compute the ratio of intersection over union (IOU) between pixel areas with value 1, i.e., where affordance is present in the binary map. This is a common metric used in semantic segmentation [24, 46]. Note that this metric is stricter than the pixel wise precision measure or classification accuracy as used in [7, 16, 29].

Baselines. The following baselines are used for our ablation studies, and thus systematically evaluate each component of our approach.

Without Predicting Depth Map (w/o Depth): In this baseline, we do not estimate depth maps, and do not use them for affordance segmentation. As shown in Table 2, ignoring depth cues significantly affects performance. This indicates that depth prediction is crucial for affordance segmentation as it helps reason about the 3D geometry of a scene.

Without Predicting Surface Normals (w/o Surf Norm): In this baseline, we ignore surface normals while predicting affordance. Surface normals help estimate a surface's orientation (i.e., horizontal or vertical), and in turn inform affordance segmentation (e.g., a 'walkable' surface must be horizontal). As shown in Table 2, ignoring surface normals in this baseline leads to poor performance.

Without Predicting Semantic Labels (w/o Sem): In this baseline, we ignore semantic labels for affordance segmentation. Table 2 shows that this baseline gives relatively poor performance, as semantic cues could help constrain ambiguities in affordance reasoning (e.g., floor is likely to be 'walkable').

Without Predicting Mid-Level Cues (w/o Mid-level): In this baseline, we ignore all three mid-level cues, i.e., affordance is predicted directly from pixels of the RGB image. Table 2 shows that the performance of this baseline is poor. This suggests that affordance maps cannot be reliably estimated directly from pixels, and that inference of our mid-level cues is critical.

With Ground Truth Cues (w GT): In this baseline, we directly use the ground truth depth maps, surface normals [30] and the semantic labels instead of predicting them from the image. This baseline amounts to an oracle prediction with correct mid-level cues for predicting affordance labels. Results of this baseline are shown in Table 2.

Table 2. Every baseline lacks one or more components of our approach and compered in terms of pixel wise IOU accuracy measure on the NYUv2 affordance dataset.

	Walkable	Sittable	Lyable	Reachable	Movable	Avg.
w/o Depth	63.23	31.44	36.10	57.24	43.84	46.37
w/o Surf Norm	64.36	32.32	37.77	57.70	44.64	47.36
w/o Sem	62.24	32.42	37.84	58.28	41.70	46.50
w/o Mid-level	58.45	24.63	31.20	50.54	34.20	39.80
w GT	70.43	37.61	43.33	63.41	51.37	53.23
Our approach	66.74	34.44	40.18	60.01	46.42	49.56

Evaluation of the Network Architecture. In this section, we empirically demonstrate the importance of multi-scale CNN architecture for affordance segmentation. Table 3 presents our results when using only coarse- or fine-scale network at a time, which amounts to considering features from a single scale – namely, either global visual cues or fine visual details. Table 3 shows that we get better performance when using only a coarse-scale network.

Table 3. Comparisons of the approaches with varying the network architechture in terms of pixel wise IOU accuracy measure on the NYUv2 affordance dataset.

	Walkable	Sittable	Lyable	Reachable	Movable	Avg.
Coarse scale only	62.41	29.01	35.43	55.54	40.25	44.53
Fine scale only	64.67	31.58	37.74	57.86	43.67	47.10
Our approach (both)	66.74	34.44	40.18	60.01	46.42	49.56

Qualitative Results. Figure 5 illustrates some of our results. As can be seen, some affordance classes may not be present in an image, and a pixel might be assigned multiple affordance labels. Pixels which are not assigned any affordance labels are considered as background.

| RGB Input | Walkable | Sittable | Lyable | Reachable | Movable |

Fig. 5. Qualitative results of affordance segmentation for each type of affrodacne class. For each RGB image, the top row represents the predicted affordance maps and the bottom row represents the ground truth maps.

Failure Case. Figure 6 shows a failure case, where some parts of the floor – under the table – are predicted as 'walkable'. Here, we fail to identify that the table is vertically above the floor, preventing the walking action. In this case, the presence of object clutter and partial occlusion cause our incorrect estimation of the 3D geometry, and consequently the wrong affordance map estimation.

Fig. 6. A failure case where we fail to identify that the table is vertically above the floor, preventing the walking action.

7   Conclusion

We have developed and evaluated a multiscale deep architecture for affordance segmentation in a single RGB image. Three multi-scale CNNs are applied independently to the image for extracting three mid-level cues – namely, depth map, surface normals and semantic segmentation of coarse-level surfaces in the scene. An additional multi-scale CNN is used to fuse these mid-level cues for pixel-wise affordance prediction. For evaluation, we have developed a semi-automated method for generating dense ground-truth affordance maps in images, using RGB and depth information along with ground-truth semantic segmentations as input. This method has been used to augment the NYUv2 dataset of indoor scenes with dense annotations of five affordance types: walkable, sittable, lyable, reachable and movable. Our experiments on the NYUv2 dataset demonstrate that each of the mid-level cues is crucial for the final affordance segmentation, as ignoring any of them significantly downgrades performance. Also, our multi-scale CNN architecture gives a significantly better performance than extracting visual cues at either a coarse or fine scale.

Acknowledgements. This work was supported in part by grant NSF RI 1302700.

References

1. Gibson, J.J.: The theory of affordances. In: Perceiving, Acting, and Knowing: Toward and Ecological Psychology, pp. 62–82. Erlbaum (1977)
2. Gibson, J.J.: The Ecological Approach to Visual Perception, Classic edn. Psychology Press, UK (2014)
3. Barrow, H., Tenenbaum, J.: Recovering intrinsic scene characteristics. Comput. Vis. Syst. 3–26 (1978)
4. Koppula, H.S., Saxena, A.: Anticipating human activities using object affordances for reactive robotic response. Pattern Anal. Mach. Intell. **38**(1), 14–29 (2016)
5. Koppula, H.S., Gupta, R., Saxena, A.: Learning human activities and object affordances from RGB-D videos. Int. J. Robot. Res. **32**(8), 951–970 (2013)
6. Gupta, A., Kembhavi, A., Davis, L.S.: Observing human-object interactions: using spatial and functional compatibility for recognition. Pattern Anal. Mach. Intell. **31**(10), 1775–1789 (2009)
7. Fouhey, D.F., Delaitre, V., Gupta, A., Efros, A.A., Laptev, I., Sivic, J.: People watching: human actions as a cue for single view geometry. Int. J. Comput. Vis. **110**(3), 259–274 (2014)

8. Delaitre, V., Fouhey, D.F., Laptev, I., Sivic, J., Gupta, A., Efros, A.A.: Scene semantics from long-term observation of people. In: Fitzgibbon, A., Lazebnik, S., Perona, P., Sato, Y., Schmid, C. (eds.) ECCV 2012. LNCS, vol. 7577, pp. 284–298. Springer, Heidelberg (2012)

9. Zhu, Y., Fathi, A., Fei-Fei, L.: Reasoning about object affordances in a knowledge base representation. In: Fleet, D., Pajdla, T., Schiele, B., Tuytelaars, T. (eds.) ECCV 2014. LNCS, vol. 8690, pp. 408–424. Springer, Heidelberg (2014). doi:10. 1007/978-3-319-10605-2_27

10. Kjellström, H., Romero, J., Kragić, D.: Visual object-action recognition: inferring object affordances from human demonstration. Comput. Vis. Image Underst. 115(1), 81–90 (2011)

11. Yao, B., Ma, J., Fei-Fei, L.: Discovering object functionality. In: ICCV (2013)

12. Farhadi, A., Endres, I., Hoiem, D., Forsyth, D.: Describing objects by their attributes. In: CVPR (2009)

13. Hoiem, D., Efros, A.A., Hebert, M.: Geometric context from a single image. In: ICCV (2005)

14. Chen, C., Seff, A., Kornhauser, A., Xiao, J.: Deepdriving: learning affordance for direct perception in autonomous driving. In: ICCV (2015)

15. Hoiem, D., Efros, A.A., Hebert, M.: Recovering surface layout from an image. Int. J. Comput. Vis. 75(1), 151–172 (2007)

16. Hoiem, D., Efros, A.A., Hebert, M.: Closing the loop in scene interpretation. In: CVPR (2008)

17. Farabet, C., Couprie, C., Najman, L., LeCun, Y.: Learning hierarchical features for scene labeling. Pattern Anal. Mach. Intell. 35(8), 1915–1929 (2013)

18. Pinheiro, P.H., Collobert, R.: Recurrent convolutional neural networks for scene parsing. In: ICML (2014)

19. Socher, R., Lin, C.C., Manning, C., Ng, A.Y.: Parsing natural scenes and natural language with recursive neural networks. In: ICML (2011)

20. Couprie, C., Farabet, C., Najman, L., LeCun, Y.: Indoor semantic segmentation using depth information. In: ICLR (2013)

21. Ning, F., Delhomme, D., LeCun, Y., Piano, F., Bottou, L., Barbano, P.E.: Toward automatic phenotyping of developing embryos from videos. Image Process. 14(9), 1360–1371 (2005)

22. Hariharan, B., Arbeláez, P., Girshick, R., Malik, J.: Simultaneous detection and segmentation. In: Fleet, D., Pajdla, T., Schiele, B., Tuytelaars, T. (eds.) ECCV 2014. LNCS, vol. 8695, pp. 297–312. Springer, Heidelberg (2014). doi:10.1007/ 978-3-319-10584-0_20

23. Ganin, Y., Lempitsky, V.: N^4-fields: neural network nearest neighbor fields for image transforms. In: ACCV (2014)

24. Eigen, D., Fergus, R.: Predicting depth, surface normals and semantic labels with a common multi-scale convolutional architecture. In: ICCV (2015)

25. Zhu, Y., Zhao, Y., Chun Zhu, S.: Understanding tools: task-oriented object modeling, learning and recognition. In: CVPR (2015)

26. Myers, A., Kanazawa, A., Fermuller, C., Aloimonos, Y.: Affordance of object parts from geometric features. In: Workshop on Vision meets Cognition, CVPR (2014)

27. Hermans, T., Rehg, J.M., Bobick, A.: Affordance prediction via learned object attributes. In: ICRA: Workshop on Semantic Perception, Mapping, and Exploration (2011)

28. Gupta, A., Satkin, S., Efros, A.A., Hebert, M.: From 3D scene geometry to human workspace. In: CVPR (2011)

29. Fouhey, D.F., Wang, X., Gupta, A.: In defense of the direct perception of affordances (2015). arXiv preprint arXiv:1505.01085

30. Silberman, N., Hoiem, D., Kohli, P., Fergus, R.: Indoor segmentation and support inference from RGBD images. In: Fitzgibbon, A., Lazebnik, S., Perona, P., Sato, Y., Schmid, C. (eds.) ECCV 2012. LNCS, vol. 7576, pp. 746–760. Springer, Heidelberg (2012). doi:10.1007/978-3-642-33715-4_54

31. Gupta, A., Davis, L.S.: Objects in action: an approach for combining action understanding and object perception. In: CVPR (2007)

32. Kjellström, H., Romero, J., Martínez, D., Kragić, D.: Simultaneous visual recognition of manipulation actions and manipulated objects. In: Forsyth, D., Torr, P., Zisserman, A. (eds.) ECCV 2008. LNCS, vol. 5303, pp. 336–349. Springer, Heidelberg (2008). doi:10.1007/978-3-540-88688-4_25

33. Yao, B., Fei-Fei, L.: Modeling mutual context of object and human pose in human-object interaction activities. In: CVPR (2010)

34. Castellini, C., Tommasi, T., Noceti, N., Odone, F., Caputo, B.: Using object affordances to improve object recognition. Auton. Mental Dev. 3(3), 207–215 (2011)

35. Winston, P.H., Binford, T.O., Katz, B., Lowry, M.: Learning physical descriptions from functional definitions, examples, and precedents. Department of Computer Science, Stanford University (1983)

36. Stark, L., Bowyer, K.: Achieving generalized object recognition through reasoning about association of function to structure. Pattern Anal. Mach. Intell. 13(10), 1097–1104 (1991)

37. Rivlin, E., Dickinson, S.J., Rosenfeld, A.: Recognition by functional parts. Comput. Vis. Image Underst. 62(2), 164–176 (1995)

38. Grabner, H., Gall, J., Van Gool, L.: What makes a chair a chair? In: CVPR (2011)

39. Jiang, Y., Koppula, H., Saxena, A.: Hallucinated humans as the hidden context for labeling 3D scenes. In: CVPR (2013)

40. Saxena, A., Driemeyer, J., Ng, A.Y.: Robotic grasping of novel objects using vision. Int. J. Robot. Res. 27(2), 157–173 (2008)

41. Yu, L.F., Duncan, N., Yeung, S.K.: Fill and transfer: a simple physics-based approach for containability reasoning. In: ICCV (2015)

42. Xie, D., Todorovic, S., Zhu, S.C.: Inferring dark matter and dark energy from videos. In: ICCV (2013)

43. Koppula, H.S., Saxena, A.: Physically grounded spatio-temporal object affordances. In: Fleet, D., Pajdla, T., Schiele, B., Tuytelaars, T. (eds.) ECCV 2014. LNCS, vol. 8691, pp. 831–847. Springer, Heidelberg (2014). doi:10.1007/978-3-319-10578-9_54

44. Zhao, Y., Zhu, S.C.: Scene parsing by integrating function, geometry and appearance models. In: CVPR (2013)

45. Gupta, S., Arbelaez, P., Malik, J.: Perceptual organization and recognition of indoor scenes from RGB-D images. In: CVPR (2013)

46. Long, J., Shelhamer, E., Darrell, T.: Fully convolutional networks for semantic segmentation. In: CVPR (2015)

47. Simonyan, K., Zisserman, A.: Very deep convolutional networks for large-scale image recognition (2014). arXiv preprint arXiv:1409.1556

48. Eigen, D., Puhrsch, C., Fergus, R.: Depth map prediction from a single image using a multi-scale deep network. In: NIPS (2014)

49. Hedau, V., Hoiem, D., Forsyth, D.: Recovering the spatial layout of cluttered rooms. In: ICCV (2009)

Hierarchical Dynamic Parsing and Encoding for Action Recognition

Bing Su[1(✉)], Jiahuan Zhou[2], Xiaoqing Ding[3], Hao Wang[4], and Ying Wu[2]

[1] Science and Technology on Integrated Information System Laboratory,
Institute of Software, Chinese Academy of Sciences, Beijing 100190, China
subingats@gmail.com
[2] Department of Electrical Engineering and Computer Science,
Northwestern University, Evanston, IL 60208, USA
{jzt011,yingwu}@eecs.northwestern.edu
[3] State Key Laboratory of Intelligent Technology and Systems,
Tsinghua National Laboratory for Information Science and Technology,
Department of Electronic Engineering, Tsinghua University, Beijing 100084, China
dingxq@tsinghua.edu.cn
[4] State Key Laboratory of Computer Science, Institute of Software,
Chinese Academy of Sciences, Beijing 100190, China
wanghao@iscas.ac.cn

Abstract. A video action generally exhibits quite complex rhythms and non-stationary dynamics. To model such non-uniform dynamics, this paper describes a novel hierarchical dynamic encoding method to capture both the locally smooth dynamics and globally drastic dynamic changes. It provides a multi-layer joint representation for temporal modeling for action recognition. At the first layer, the action sequence is parsed in an unsupervised manner into several smooth-changing stages corresponding to different key poses or temporal structures. The dynamics within each stage are encoded by mean-pooling or learning to rank based encoding. At the second layer, the temporal information of the ordered dynamics extracted from the previous layer is encoded again to form the overall representation. Extensive experiments on a gesture action dataset (Chalearn) and several generic action datasets (Olympic Sports and Hollywood2) have demonstrated the effectiveness of the proposed method.

Keywords: Action recognition · Hierarchical modeling · Dynamic encoding

1 Introduction

The performance of action recognition methods depends heavily on the representation of video data. For this reason, many recent efforts focus on developing various action representations in different levels. The state-of-the-art action representation is based on the Bag-of-Visual-Words (BoW) [1] framework, which includes three steps: local descriptors extraction, codebook learning, and descriptors encoding. The raw local descriptors themselves are noisy and the discriminative power of the distributed BoW representation comes from the efficient

© Springer International Publishing AG 2016
B. Leibe et al. (Eds.): ECCV 2016, Part IV, LNCS 9908, pp. 202–217, 2016.
DOI: 10.1007/978-3-319-46493-0_13

Fig. 1. The action "jump" can be roughly parsed into three divisions: running approach, body stay flew in the air and touch down. Each division can also be parsed into different sub-divisions

coding of these local descriptors. As a result, the temporal dependencies and dynamics of the video are seriously neglected.

Dynamics characterize the inherent global temporal dependencies of actions. Existing dynamic-based approaches generally view the video as a sequence of observations and model it with temporal models. The models can either be state-space-based such as HMM [2] and CRF [3] or exemplar-based such as DTW [4]. Such models generally not only require a large amount of training data to exactly estimate parameters, statistics and temporal alignments, but also cannot directly lead to vector representations with a fixed dimension. Recently, Fernando et al. [5] propose to pool frame-wide features via learning to rank within the BoW framework, which encodes the temporal evolution of appearances in a principled manner and results in a representation with the same dimension of the frame-wide features. The dynamics are considered as the ordering relations of frame-wide features and the changes of all successive frames are treated equally.

The dynamic behind an action is time-varying and not easy to be figuratively expressed. However, for a specific given action video, the dynamic does have some intuitive rhythms or regularities. One cue is that humans can recognize an action from some ordered key frames. Typically each frame captures a key pose, and the number of key poses is much smaller than the number of frames in the whole video. Taking an example of Fig. 1, a video recording an action "jump" may contain up to hundreds of frames, but only three key poses can represent the drastic changes in the dynamics: running approach, body stay flew in the air and touch down. There may be many similar frames corresponding to each key pose. These key poses segment the whole action into different divisions or stages, and each stage consists of the frames related to a key pose. Therefore, the dynamics of an action can also be viewed as a hierarchy. The dynamics within each stage are relatively stable, and the dynamics of the sequence of the stages or key poses represent the essential evolution of the action.

In this paper, we incorporate the dynamics in the hierarchy of two layers into a joint representation for action recognition. In the first layer, we parse the sequence of frame-wide features into different stages and encode the dynamics and appearances into a feature vector within each stage. In the second layer, we extract a high-level dynamic encoding representation by pooling the features produced in the first layer. The contributions of this work include: (1) The proposed hierarchical parsing and encoding is a new unsupervised representation learning method. It hierarchically abstracts the prominent dynamic and generates a representation that is robust to speed and local variations, meanwhile, it also captures the high-level semantic information for a video. (2) We propose an unsupervised method for temporal clustering to achieve efficient dynamic parsing. (3) The extracted representations from multi-scale parsings provide complementary discriminative information and hence can be readily combined.

2   Related Work

Appearance-Based Action Representation Approaches. BoW representation is widely used in appearance-based action representation approaches. Different methods differ in the local visual descriptors and the coding scheme. HOG, HOF and MBH are typical low-level descriptors used in video-based action recognition [6]. These descriptors can be computed either sparsely at local space-time cuboids [7] or by dense sampling scheme [6]. Various coding variants have also been proposed to encode these local descriptors, such as Fisher vector [8] and vector of locally aggregated descriptors [9,10]. Efforts have also been made to construct hierarchical feature representations based on BoW to capture context information and high-level concepts [11,12]. Besides these hand-crafted features, deep neural networks have also been applied to learn representations directly from videos, such as the trajectory-pooled deep-convolutional descriptors [13] and the pose-based convolutional neural network features [14].

Dynamic-Based Action Modeling Approaches. Both generative models and deterministic models have been studied to model and represent dynamics and motions in action recognition. Generative models are typically based on temporal (hidden) state-space, such as HMM [2,15,16], CRF [3,17], temporal AND-OR graph [18], and linear dynamic systems [19]. The dynamics in generative models refer to the internal hidden states and transitions, e.g., Multilevel motions of the bodies and parts are governed by such internal dynamics in [15]. A large amount of samples and complex computations are required to train such models. We use dynamics as a milder term to indicate the evolution of frame appearances. Our method directly captures such evolution from the single sequence in an unsupervised fashion.

For deterministic models, the temporal structures or alignments are explicitly modeled. Dynamic time warping (DTW) is used to align action sequences for recognition in [4]. Maximum margin temporal warping is proposed in [20] to learn temporal action alignments and phantom action templates. Actom sequence model [21] and graphs [22] are also used to model temporal structures and relationships among local features. Recently deep neural architectures are employed for modeling actions. In [23], spatial and temporal nets are incorporated into a two-stream ConvNet. In [24], salient dynamics of actions are modeled by the differential recurrent neural networks.

Temporal Clustering. Aligned Cluster Analysis [25] divides a sequence by minimizing the similarities among the segments, where the similarity between two segments is measured by a dynamic time alignment kernel. As the dynamics of each segment may not be stable, the segments do not correspond to stable action stages. In contrast, our method divides a sequence into segments by minimizing the within-segment variances so that the frames within each segment are similar. As each segment shows a stable dynamic, it can be viewed as a stage of an action. In MMTC [26], features in sequences are clustered into several common clusters, and a multi-class SVM is trained to assign clusters using all training sequences. Our method acts on each individual sequence independently and no training is needed, and the segments from different sequences are different and only account for the evolution of the specific sequence.

3   Hierarchical Dynamic Parsing and Encoding

Video-wide temporal evolution modeling method proposed in [5] aggregates the frame-wise features into a functional representation via a ranking machine. This representation captures the evolution of appearances over frames and hence provides the video-wide temporal information. However, the ranking function within the learning to rank machine attempts to rank all the frames in the video and these frames are equally treated, which ignores the non-stationary evolution of dynamic within different stages and cannot directly exploit the complex hierarchical temporal structures. Hierarchical architecture has the ability to learn a higher-level semantic representation by pooling local features in the lower layer and refining the features from the lower layer to the higher layer. In this section we propose a hierarchical temporal evolution modeling method, namely *Hierarchical Dynamic Parsing and Encoding or HDPE*, to take the rhythmic of stage-varying dynamic into account. The pipeline of HDPE is shown in Fig. 2. We construct the hierarchy with two layers in this paper, and note that it can be easily generalized to more layers.

3.1   Unsupervised Temporal Clustering

In order to capture the temporal structures corresponding to relatively-uniform local dynamics, we first propose an unsupervised temporal clustering method that learns the parse of an action sequence only from the sequence itself.

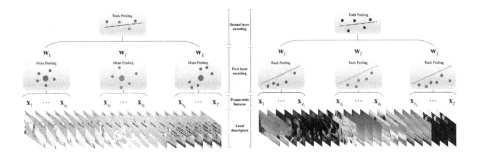

Fig. 2. The pipeline of the proposed method. The first layer can either adopt mean pooling (left) or rank pooling (right)

For each action video, we extract a feature vector from each frame. Thus the action video can be represented as a sequence of such features. We denote the video by $\mathbf{X} = [\mathbf{x}_1, \mathbf{x}_2, \cdots, \mathbf{x}_T]$, where $\mathbf{x}_t$ the feature vector extract from the t-th frame, and T is the number of frames in the whole video. We denote the partition of $\mathbf{X}$ by a segmentation path $\mathbf{P} = [\mathbf{p}_1, \mathbf{p}_2, \cdots, \mathbf{p}_L]$, where L is the number of divisions, typically $L < T$. $\mathbf{p}_t = [s_t, e_t]^T$ provides the range $\{s_t, s_t + 1, \cdots, e_t\}$ of the t-th division, s_t and e_t are the start and end indexes of the frames in this division. The number of frames divided into the t-th division is $l_t = e_t - s_t + 1$. We hope that each division contains a set of steady evolving frames corresponding to the same key pose or temporal structure. We require $\mathbf{P}$ being a non-overlapping and completing partition that covers the whole video. Non-overlap means no frame can be simultaneously divided into two divisions, complete means that every frame in the sequence must be divided into one and only one division, hence the elements of $\mathbf{P}$ satisfy the following constraints: $s_1 = 1, e_L = T, s_{t+1} = e_t + 1, \forall t = 1, \cdots, L-1$, $e_t \geq s_t, \forall t = 1, \cdots, L$. There may be noisy or outlier frame in the sequence, which is significantly different with its successive neighbor frames. To avoid assigning such outlier frame into a separate division and prevent extremely unbalance divisions, we make the restriction on the number of elements in each division. Specifically, we limit the maximum number of elements within one division by $f \cdot l_{ave}$, where f is the band factor, and $l_{ave} = \frac{T}{L}$ is the average number of elements in each division by uniform segmentation.

To parse the sequence $\mathbf{X}$ into different divisions, where each stage is related to a key pose, we define an essential sequence $\mathbf{U}$ of $\mathbf{X}$ as the sequence of key poses in $\mathbf{X}$: $\mathbf{U} = [\boldsymbol{\mu}_1, \boldsymbol{\mu}_2, \cdots, \boldsymbol{\mu}_L]$, where $\boldsymbol{\mu}_j$ is the mean of frame-wise features of the frames in the j-th division. Once $\mathbf{U}$ is given, the partition $\mathbf{P}$ can be obtained by computing the optimal alignment path along which the sum of distances between the aligned elements in $\mathbf{X}$ and the warped $\mathbf{U}$ is minimal among all possible paths:

$$\min_{\mathbf{P}} \sum_{j=1}^{L} \sum_{i=s_j}^{e_j} \|\mathbf{x}_i - \boldsymbol{\mu}_j\|_2^2 \qquad (1)$$

Consider a partial path that assigning the first i-th elements in $\mathbf{X}$ to the first j-th elements in $\mathbf{U}$, and the last l elements of the first i-th elements in $\mathbf{X}$ are assigned to the j-th element of $\mathbf{U}$. We denote the sum of element-wise distances along this partial path by the partial distance $d(i, j, l)$. The minimal partial distance can be determined recurrently:

$$d(i, j, l) = \begin{cases} \|\mathbf{x}_i - \boldsymbol{\mu}_j\|_2^2, l = 1, i = j = 1 \\ \|\mathbf{x}_i - \boldsymbol{\mu}_j\|_2^2 + \min_{k=1}^{f \cdot l_{ave}} d(i-1, j-1, k), l = 1 \\ \|\mathbf{x}_i - \boldsymbol{\mu}_j\|_2^2 + d(i-1, j, l-1), l \leq f \cdot l_{ave} \\ Inf, \; otherwise \end{cases} \qquad (2)$$

Equation (2) does not have aftereffect, hence Eq. (2) can be effectively solved by dynamic programming. When both partial sequences reach the end,

---

Algorithm 1. Unsupervised action parsing by temporal clustering

---

Input: a sequence $\mathbf{X}$, the number of divisions L, the maximal number of iterations Ite, the band factor f;
Output: the partition $\mathbf{P}$ of $\mathbf{X}$;
Initialize the partition path $\mathbf{P}$ to be a uniform partition;
while $\mathbf{P}$ has not converged and the number of iterations is less than Ite **do**
    Compute the essential sequence $\mathbf{U}$ using (3);
    Update the partition path $\mathbf{P}$ by solving ref using the dynamic programming algorithm (2) with the band factor f;
end while

---

the minimal distance along the optimal path is determined by $\min\limits_{l=1}^{f \cdot l_{ave}} d(T, L, l)$ and the optimal partition path $\mathbf{P}$ can be obtained by back tracking.

Given the partition $\mathbf{P}$ of the sequence $\mathbf{X}$, the essential sequence $\mathbf{U}$ can be obtained by computing the mean of each division. The essential sequence in turn can be used to parse the sequence $\mathbf{X}$ into different divisions. Determining the essential sequence $\mathbf{U}$ and computing the partition $\mathbf{P}$ rely on each other. We develop an unsupervised temporal clustering method to jointly mine temporal structures in the sequence $\mathbf{X}$ and learn the partition $\mathbf{P}$ that parses $\mathbf{X}$ into stages with respect to these temporal structures.

We first initialize the partition $\mathbf{P}$ to be a uniform partition that divides the sequence $\mathbf{X}$ into L equal segments. For example, if $L = 3, T = 9$, i.e. we divide a sequence $\mathbf{X}$ with 9 elements into 3 segments, the initial partition $\mathbf{P} = [[1,3]^T, [4,6]^T, [7,9]^T]$. Then we compute the essential sequence $\mathbf{U} = [\mu_1, \mu_2, \cdots, \mu_L]$, whose elements are the means of elements in the corresponding divisions:

$$\mu_j = \frac{1}{l_j} \sum_{k=s_j}^{e_j} \mathbf{x}_k, j = 1, \cdots, L \tag{3}$$

After that, we update the partition $\mathbf{P}$ by aligning the elements in $\mathbf{X}$ to those in $\mathbf{U}$ to parse $\mathbf{X}$ using the dynamic programming algorithm. The essential sequence $\mathbf{U}$ is recomputed in turn with the updated $\mathbf{P}$. The two procedures are continued until the partition is unchanged with the previous iteration or a prefixed number of iterations is reached. We summarize the joint partition learning and temporal clustering algorithm in Algorithm 1.

Convergency. Given $\mathbf{P}$, computing the essential sequence $\mathbf{U}$ by using Eq. (3) is equivalent to the solution of minimum mean square error problem: $\min\limits_{\mu} \sum\limits_{i=s_j}^{e_j} \|\mathbf{x}_i - \mu\|_2^2, j = 1, \cdots, L$. Given $\mathbf{U}$, computing $\mathbf{P}$ directly minimizes Eq. (1). Both procedures reduce the objective of Eq. (1). Equation (1) has a trivial lower bound $\sum\limits_{j=1}^{L} \sum\limits_{i=s_j}^{e_j} \|\mathbf{x}_i - \mu_j\|_2^2 \geq 0, \forall \mathbf{P}, \mathbf{U}$. Thus the partition learning algorithm will at least converge to a local minimum.

Computational Complexity. The complexities of dynamic programming Eq. (2) and calculating Eq. (3) are $O(LNd)$ and $O(Ld)$, L, N and d are the number of segments, the length of the input sequence and the dimension of the frame-wide features. Hence the complexity of the temporal clustering Algorithm 1 is $O(iLNd)$, i is the number of iterations. As the method processes each sequence separately, parallel speedup can be easily performed.

3.2 The First Layer Modeling

For an action sequence sample $\mathbf{X} = [\mathbf{x}_1, \mathbf{x}_2, \cdots, \mathbf{x}_T]$, we first parse it into L divisions using Algorithm 1. We denote the parsing result of $\mathbf{X}$ by $\mathbf{P} = [\mathbf{p}_1, \mathbf{p}_2, \cdots, \mathbf{p}_L]$. The evolution within each division is relatively steady and hence the frames in each division can be equally treated. An abstract feature vector can be extracted from each division via mean pooling or rank pooling [5].

Mean pooling simply uses the mean of the frame-wide features as the output of the division. For the l-th division, we denote the segmentation fragment as $\mathbf{X}^{[l]} = [\mathbf{x}_{s_l}, \mathbf{x}_{s_l+1}, \cdots, \mathbf{x}_{e_l}]$. The mean pooling result of the division can be calculated as:

$$\mathbf{w}_l = \frac{1}{e_l - s_l + 1} \sum_{\tau=0}^{e_l - s_l} \mathbf{x}_{s_l+\tau}$$

Rank pooling learns a linear ranking function to order the frame-wise features in each division via learning to rank and uses the parameters of the function as the representation of the temporal structure associated with the division. A vector valued function that transforms each element $\mathbf{x}_{s_l+t}$ to the corresponding time varying mean vector $\mathbf{v}_{s_l+t} = \frac{\mathbf{u}_{s_l+t}}{\|\mathbf{u}_{s_l+t}\|}$, where $\mathbf{u}_{s_l+t} = \frac{1}{t+1} \sum_{\tau=0}^{t} \mathbf{x}_{s_l+\tau}$, is first applied to $\mathbf{X}^{[l]}$, resulting in $\mathbf{V}^{[l]} = [\mathbf{v}_{s_l}, \mathbf{v}_{s_l+1}, \cdots, \mathbf{v}_{e_l}]$. A linear function $f(\mathbf{w}_l; \mathbf{v}) = \mathbf{w}_l^T \cdot \mathbf{v}$ is used to predict the ranking score for each $\mathbf{v}_{s_l+t}$. The parameters $\mathbf{w}_l$ of the linear function is learned to rank the orders of the elements in the division, such that $f(\mathbf{w}_l; \mathbf{v}_{s_l}) > f(\mathbf{w}_l; \mathbf{v}_{s_l+1}) > \cdots > f(\mathbf{w}_l; \mathbf{v}_{e_l})$.

$$\begin{aligned} \arg\min_{\mathbf{w}_l} \tfrac{1}{2}\|\mathbf{w}_l\|^2 + C \sum_{0 \le a < b \le e_l - s_l} \varepsilon_{ab} \\ s.t.\ \mathbf{w}_l^T \cdot (\mathbf{v}_{s_l+a} - \mathbf{v}_{s_l+b}) \ge 1 - \varepsilon_{ab}, \\ \varepsilon_{ab} \ge 0, \forall 0 \le a < b \le e_l - s_l \end{aligned} \tag{4}$$

$\mathbf{w}_l$ is used as the representation of the l-th temporal structure. After the first layer modeling, the original sequence $\mathbf{X}$ is mapped to the sequence of key temporal structures $\mathbf{W} = [\mathbf{w}_1, \mathbf{w}_2, \cdots, \mathbf{w}_L]$, which contains high-level abstract information based on the original representation.

For simple actions and fine-grained actions, compared with the dynamic of divisions, the dynamic within each division is quite uniform and contributes little to the discrimination of the whole actions. Changing the orders of frames in a division does not influence the understanding of the action. Mean pooling is suitable for such cases, which is equivalent to extract key frames. The key frames are more robust to individual frames and local distortions since each key frame is the mean of a division. For complex activities, the dynamics in divisions may be complex so that the orders of frames in each division cannot be changed, and hence it is better to apply rank pooling.

3.3 The Second Layer Modeling

The output sequence $\mathbf{W} = [\mathbf{w}_1, \mathbf{w}_2, \cdots, \mathbf{w}_L]$ from the first layer reflects the essential temporal evolution of the sequence, which can be thought as the sequence of key poses, each pose is a pooling of the frames in the corresponding stage and captures the stage-wide temporal evolution. The second layer extracts the video-wide temporal evolution from these ordered stage-wide temporal evolutions. The learning-to-rank modeling used in each division of the first layer is applied to $\mathbf{W}$. A ranking function $f(\mathbf{y}; \mathbf{w}') = \mathbf{y}^T \cdot \mathbf{w}'$ that aims at providing the orders of the time varying mean vectors $\mathbf{w}_1', \mathbf{w}_2', \cdots, \mathbf{w}_L'$ by applying vector valued function to elements of $\mathbf{W}$ such that $f(\mathbf{y}; \mathbf{w}_l') > f(\mathbf{y}; \mathbf{w}_k'), \forall 1 \leq k < l \leq L$. The parameter vector $\mathbf{y}$ of $f(\mathbf{y}; \mathbf{w}')$ serves as the final representation of the video sequence $\mathbf{X}$.

Several advantages of the proposed HDPE method are as follows. First, the method is totally unsupervised, simple and easy to perform. Both the parsing and the hierarchical encoding are built on a single action sequence. No annotations are needed to perform parsing or encoding, and no labels or negative data are needed for training. Second, the method is robust to local distortions and individual outliers or noisy frames. The abstract feature produced by the first layer for each division is a pooling of all the frame-wide features in the division, and few outliers or distortions have little effect on the pooling result. Third, the learned representation implicitly combines local appearances and global dynamic in a principled hierarchical manner. The orders within the parsed divisions are not so important, hence the pooling of the first layer focuses on capturing the local averaged appearances. The temporal orders among the divisions are crucial and reflect the inherent dynamic of the video. The encoding of the second layer focuses on capturing such global high-level dynamic.

4   Experiments

In this section we evaluate the performance of the proposed method on one gesture recognition dataset, i.e. the Chalearn dataset, and two challenging generic action recognition datasets, including the Olympic Sports dataset and the Hollywood2 dataset.

4.1   Datasets

ChaLearn Gesture Recognition Dataset [27]. This dataset consists of Kinect video data from 20 Italian gestures performed by 27 persons. There are

955 videos in total, and each video contains 8 to 20 non-continuous gestures with a length of 1 to 2 min. The dataset is split into training, validation and test sets. We report the multi-class (the mean over all classes) precision, recall and F-score measures on the validation set, as in [5, 27].

Olympic Sports Dataset [28]. This dataset contains 783 video sequences from 16 sports actions. The dataset is split into training and test sets. The training set includes 649 video sequences and the test set includes the remaining 134 video sequences. We report the mean average precision (mAP) as in [6] and the accuracy as in [20].

Hollywood2 Dataset [29]. This dataset contains RGB-video data from 12 generic action classes. There are in total 1,707 video clips in the dataset, which are collected from 69 different Hollywood movies. The dataset is split into training and test sets. The training set includes 823 videos and the test set includes the remaining 884 videos. The videos in the two sets are selected from different movies. We report mAP as in [6, 29].

4.2   Experimental Setup

Frame-Wide Features. For each action video, we extract a high-dimensional feature vector from each frame and represent the video by a sequence of frame-wide features. For the Olympic Sports dataset and the Hollywood2 dataset, we use the improved dense trajectories descriptors [6], which have achieved state-of-the-art results. We extract trajectory, HOG, HOF and MBH descriptors from the trajectories corresponding to a dense regular grid for all frames. The square-root trick is applied on these descriptors except trajectory descriptors. We learn a codebook with a size of 4,000 for each type of descriptors by k-means clustering as in [6] and quantize the descriptors to their nearest visual words in the codebook. The histogram of the quantized descriptors in one frame is used as the frame-wide feature of the frame. Hence the dimensionality of the frame-wide features is 4,000.

For the Chalearn Gesture recognition dataset, we employ the skeleton features provided by the authors of [5]. The normalized relative locations of body joints w.r.t the torso joints are calculated and clustered into a codebook with a size of 100. The histogram of the quantized relative locations in one frame is employed as the frame-wide feature with a dimensionality of 100.

Implementation Details. On the ChaLearn dataset and the Hollywood2 dataset, we apply chi-squared kernel map on each time varying mean vector when using rank pooling. On the Olympic Sports dataset, we apply chi-squared kernel map on the output representation of the second layer rather than in the second layer pooling, while the square-root trick is applied in the second layer pooling. The order in Eq. 4 can also be inverse, i.e., the rank value computed from the linear function of the previous frame is forced to be smaller than that of the current frame. If the first layer adopts rank pooling, the second layer encodes the results of the first layer with the same order and combines them together.

If the first layer adopts mean-pooling, the second layer encodes the results of the first layer in both forward and inverse orders and combines them together. Following [5], we also use the SVR solver of liblinear [30] to solve Eq. 4 and fix the value of C to 1. When improved dense trajectory features are used, the features of different descriptors are concatenated. We apply L_2-normalization to the final representation and train linear SVMs for classification.

4.3   Influence of Parameters

There are mainly two parameters of the proposed HDPE: the number of divisions L for parsing the action sequence by temporal clustering and the band factor f for aligning the sequence to the essential sequence by dynamic programming. We evaluate the influences of the two parameters on the final performance on the Chalearn Gesture recognition dataset. The average number of frames of the dataset is 39.7. We first fix f to be 2, and vary L from 2 to 10. The performances (the precision, recall and F-score) are shown in Fig. 3(a). We find that at first all performance measures improve with the increase of the number of divisions, because more temporal structures information can be captured. When L is larger than 7, the performances stop increasing. This may be because redundant divisions exist, which break the intrinsic temporal structures and slightly interfere the rank pooling of the second layer. However, the decline of the performances is not significant with redundant divisions. Thus we will set a relatively larger value for L in the subsequent experiments.

HDPE also supports to set different L for different sequences. For example, we can set L as N/r, r is a factor measuring averagely how many frames a state should contain and can be estimated according to prior knowledge on the data. We set L to be the same for all sequences, because as long as L is large enough, the evolution of L key stages should contain the information for discriminating different classes. Although the states of a more dynamic action are more complex, the local dynamics within these states are captured by the 1st layer modeling.

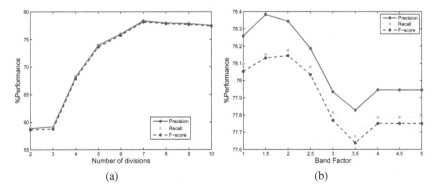

(a)   (b)

Fig. 3. The performances with the increase of (a) the number of divisions and (b) the value of band factor on the Chalearn Gusture dataset

We then fix the number of divisions to be 7, and vary the band factor f from 1 to 5 with a interval of 0.5. When $f = 1$, it means that the alignment is strictly restricted to the uniform alignment. When $f > 4$, the allowed maximal capacity of a division is larger than the length of the sequence, and it is equivalent to perform unconstrained dynamic time warping, which may mistake outliers as individual divisions and lead to extremely unbalanced alignment. We find that applying appropriate constraints on the capacity of each division benefits the performances. We set f in the range of 1.5 to 2 in the subsequent experiments. $f = 2$ means that the maximal number of elements within one division should not be larger than twice the average number of elements by uniform alignment.

4.4   Comparison of Pooling in the First Layer

In the first layer modeling, the encoding of each division could either be mean pooling or rank pooling as mentioned in Sect. 3.2. We compare the two pooling methods on the Chalearn Gesture dataset, the Olympic Sports dataset and the Hollywood2 dataset in Tables 1 and 2, respectively. M-HDPE and R-HDPE denote that the mean pooling and the rank pooling are used in the first layer modeling in HDPE, respectively. The mean pooling outperforms the rank pooling on the ChaLearn gesture dataset, while the rank pooling achieves better results on the Olympic sports and Hollywood2 datasets. This verifies the explanation in Sect. 3.2. That is, for fine-grained actions such as gestures, since the evolution within each division is quite uniform, the within-division dynamic can be ignored, and the local appearance information is enhanced by mean-pooling. For generic and complex actions, the complex dynamics within divisions contain important discriminative information of the action and hence cannot be eliminated.

Table 1. Comparison of performances using the two pooling methods on the ChaLearn dataset

Pooling method	Precision	Recall	F-score
M-HDPE	**78.34**	**78.18**	**78.15**
R-HDPE	75.95	75.83	75.79

Table 2. Comparison of MAPs using the two pooling methods on the Olympic Sports and Hollywood2 datasets

Pooling method	Olympic	Hollywood2
M-HDPE	84.58	62.90
R-HDPE	87.66	63.51

4.5   Comparison with State-of-the-Art

We compare the proposed HDPE with the improved dense trajectory features encoded by Bag-of-Words or Fisher Vector encoding [6] and learning to rank based temporal encoding (rank pooling) [5] of the whole video as well as the several other state-of-the-art results on the three datasets, as shown in Tables 3, 4 and 5. For HDPE, the number of divisions for each video is set to be 7, 10 and 10 for the ChaLearn Gesture dataset, the Olympic Sports dataset and the Hollywood2 dataset, respectively. The band factor is set to be 2 for all these datasets. Note that these parameters for the Olympic Sports dataset and the Hollywood2 dataset are set by intuitively judging the dynamic complexity from the average length of videos. Carefully tuning these parameters may further improve the performances. Mean pooling is adopted for the ChaLearn dataset and Rank pooling is adopted for the Olympic Sports dataset and the Hollywood2 dataset in the first layer modeling.

From Table 3, it can be observed that the proposed method outperforms the state-of-the-art method [5] on the ChaLearn gesture dataset. In [5], the results are achieved by combining the rank pooling representation with local method, and the results by rank pooling along are also reported, as denoted by

Table 3. Comparison of the proposed HDPE with state-of-the-art results on the ChaLearn gesture dataset

Method	Precision	Recall	F-score
Wu et al. [31]	59.9	59.3	59.6
Yao et al. [32]	-	-	56.0
Pfister et al. [33]	61.2	62.3	61.7
Fernando et al. [5]	75.3	75.1	75.2
Rank pooling [5]	74.0	73.8	73.9
HDPE	**78.34**	**78.18**	**78.15**

Table 4. Comparison of the proposed HDPE with state-of-the-art results on the Olympic Sports dataset. mAP is used as the performance measure

Method	Olympic Sports
Brendel et al. [22]	77.3
Gaidon et al. [34]	82.7
Jain et al. [10]	83.2
Wang et al. [6]	**91.1**
Local+BoW [6]	83.3
HDPE	87.66
HDPE+Rank pooling	**89.09**

Table 5. Comparison of the proposed HDPE with state-of-the-art results on the Hollywood2 dataset. mAP is used as the performance measure.

Method	Hollywood2
Jain et al. [10]	62.5
Wang et al. [6]	64.3
Hoai et al. [35]	73.6
Fernando et al. [5]	**73.7**
Local+BoW [6]	62.2
Rank pooling+BoW [5][a]	62.19
HDPE	**63.51**

[a]denotes that the result is reported by our reproduction with the BoW representation

"Rank pooling". Since we use the same frame-wide features provided by [5], the superior performance comes from the hierarchical parsing and modeling.

Table 4 shows that our result is slightly worse than the best result reported in [6], which is achieved by using the advanced Fisher Vector encoding. We use the Bag-of-Words encoding because the dimensionality of the frame-wide features encoded by Fisher Vector per descriptor is about 25,600, which is much higher than the Bag-of-Words encoding (4,000), and this will greatly increase the computation time of the temporal clustering Algorithm 1. [6] also reports their results with the Bag-of-words encoding, as denoted by "Local+BoW" in Table 4. Our method outperforms this method that encoding descriptors in all frames into a single representation without considering the temporal information by a margin of 4%. Since Fisher Vector encoding improves the mAP from 83.3% by BoW to 91.1% on this dataset [6], applying our method to frame-wide features with Fisher Vector encoding can also be expected to achieve much better result, with a cost of much more computation time. Carefully tuning the parameters L and f may also lead to performance improvement.

As shown in Table 5, on the Hollywood2 dataset, Fernando et al. [5] and Hoai et al. [35] achieve much higher mAPs. Besides the Fisher Vector encoding, both the two work also adopt the data augmentation technique proposed in [35], which double the training data by flipping each video and average the classification scores of each test video and its mirrored version. The performance of our method may also be improved by applying such data augmentation and Fisher Vector encoding to our method with the cost of time. We did not use this technique because both the time and space complexities are doubled, and we only focus on the evaluation of the proposed modeling method over other modeling method rather than the absolute performance. On the basis of the same BoW feature encoding method, our method outperforms the "Local+BoW" method reported in [6].

A potential advantage of the proposed method is the representations produced from different numbers of partitions in the first layer encode the temporal

Table 6. Comparison of the proposed HDPE with state-of-the-art results on the Olympic sports dataset. Accuracy is used as the performance measure

Method	Accuracy
Laptev et al. [29]	62.0
Niebles et al. [28]	72.1
Tang et al. [36]	66.8
Wang et al. [20]	73.8
HDPE	**81.34**
HDPE+Rank Pooling+Local	**83.58**

structures in different scales. If the number of divisions is set to 1, the temporal information is totally discarded and the proposed HDPE method boils down to the "Local+BoW" method [6]. If the number of divisions is set to be the length of the sequence, no local appearances are smoothed and the proposed HDPE method boils down to the "rank pooling" method [5]. The more divisions are parsed from the action, the finer the scale of the captured temporal information is. The representations generated in different scales provide complementary information to each other. Combining them together incorporates multi-scale temporal information together. We perform preliminary experiments on the Olympic Sports dataset to verify this. As shown in Table 4, concatenating the representations of the proposed method and the rank pooling method leads to a improvement of about 2 % in mAP. We also evaluate the multi-class accuracy in Table 6, the proposed HDPE representation itself significantly outperforms the reported results by a margin of 7.5 %, and the combination of the "local", rank pooling and the proposed HDPE representations further extends the margin to about 10 %.

5   Conclusions

In this paper we have presented a hierarchical dynamic parsing and encoding method for action recognition, which unsupervised learns higher-level representation from a single action sequence by exploring the temporal structures and building the hierarchical architecture. The hierarchy disentangles the local appearances and the global dynamic into different layers. In the lower layer, the sequence is parsed into different divisions, and local appearance information within each uniformly-evolved division is captured via local mean or rank pooling. In the higher layer, the global dynamic of the appearances among the divisions is encoded. The learned representation is robust, because outliers or noisy frames cannot directly impact on the global dynamic since they must be assigned to a corresponding division, while their influence within a division is greatly diminished by pooling. Experimental results on several action datasets have demonstrated the potential of the proposed method. Our future work involves exploring the fusion of multi-scale partitions to incorporate multi-scale temporal information.

Acknowledgements. This work was supported by National Basic Research Program of China (2013CB329305, 2013CB329403), Natural Science Foundation of China (61303164, 61402447, 61471214, 61502466) and Development Plan of Outstanding Young Talent from Institute of Software, Chinese Academy of Sciences (ISCAS2014-JQ02). This work was also supported by National Science Foundation grant IIS-0916607, IIS-1217302.

References

1. Sivic, J., Zisserman, A.: Video google: a text retrieval approach to object matching in videos. In: ICCV (2003)
2. Li, K., Hu, J., Fu, Y.: Modeling complex temporal composition of actionlets for activity prediction. In: Fitzgibbon, A., Lazebnik, S., Perona, P., Sato, Y., Schmid, C. (eds.) ECCV 2012. LNCS, vol. 7572, pp. 286–299. Springer, Heidelberg (2012). doi:10.1007/978-3-642-33718-5_21
3. Sminchisescu, C., Kanaujia, A., Li, Z., Metaxas, D.: Conditional models for contextual human motion recognition. In: ICCV (2005)
4. Yao, B., Zhu, S.C.: Learning deformable action templates from cluttered videos. In: ICCV (2009)
5. Fernando, B., Gavves, E., Oramas, J.M., Ghodrati, A., Tuytelaars, T.: Modeling video evolution for action recognition. In: CVPR (2015)
6. Wang, H., Schmid, C.: Action recognition with improved trajectories. In: ICCV (2013)
7. Laptev, I.: On space-time interest points. IJCV **64**(2), 107–123 (2005)
8. Perronnin, F., Sánchez, J., Mensink, T.: Improving the fisher kernel for large-scale image classification. In: Daniilidis, K., Maragos, P., Paragios, N. (eds.) ECCV 2010. LNCS, vol. 6314, pp. 143–156. Springer, Heidelberg (2010). doi:10.1007/978-3-642-15561-1_11
9. Jgou, H., Douze, M., Schmid, C., Prez, P.: Aggregating local descriptors into a compact image representation. In: CVPR (2010)
10. Jain, M., Jegou, H., Bouthemy, P.: Better exploiting motion for better action recognition. In: CVPR (2013)
11. Kovashka, A., Grauman, K.: Learning a hierarchy of discriminative space-time neighborhood features for human action recognition. In: CVPR (2010)
12. Peng, X., Zou, C., Qiao, Y., Peng, Q.: Action recognition with stacked fisher vectors. In: Fleet, D., Pajdla, T., Schiele, B., Tuytelaars, T. (eds.) ECCV 2014. LNCS, vol. 8693, pp. 581–595. Springer, Heidelberg (2014). doi:10.1007/978-3-319-10602-1_38
13. Wang, L., Qiao, Y., Tang, X.: Action recognition with trajectory-pooled deep-convolutional descriptors. In: CVPR (2015)
14. Chéron, G., Laptev, I., Schmid, C.: P-CNN: Pose-based CNN features for action recognition. In: ICCV (2015)
15. Bregler, C.: Learning and recognizing human dynamics in video sequences. In: CVPR (1997)
16. Su, B., Ding, X.: Linear sequence discriminant analysis: a model-based dimensionality reduction method for vector sequences. In: ICCV (2013)

17. Song, Y., Morency, L.P., Davis, R.: Action recognition by hierarchical sequence summarization. In: CVPR (2013)
18. Pei, M., Jia, Y., Zhu, S.C.: Parsing video events with goal inference and intent prediction. In: ICCV (2011)
19. Chaudhry, R., Ravichandran, A., Hager, G., Vidal, R.: Histograms of oriented optical flow and binet-cauchy kernels on nonlinear dynamical systems for the recognition of human actions. In: CVPR (2009)
20. Wang, J., Wu, Y.: Learning maximum margin temporal warping for action recognition. In: ICCV (2013)
21. Gaidon, A., Harchaoui, Z., Schmid, C.: Actom sequence models for efficient action detection. In: CVPR (2011)
22. Brendel, W., Todorovic, S.: Learning spatiotemporal graphs of human activities. In: ICCV (2011)
23. Simonyan, K., Zisserman, A.: Two-stream convolutional networks for action recognition in videos. In: NIPS (2014)
24. Veeriah, V., Zhuang, N., Qi, G.J.: Differential recurrent neural networks for action recognition. In: ICCV (2015)
25. Zhou, F., De la Torre, F., Cohn, J.F.: Unsupervised discovery of facial events. In: CVPR (2010)
26. Hoai, M., De la Torre, F.: Maximum margin temporal clustering. In: International Conference on Artificial Intelligence and Statistics (2012)
27. Shotton, J., Fitzgibbon, A., Cook, M., Sharp, T., Finocchio, M., Moore, R., Kipman, A., Blake, A.: Real-time human pose recognition in parts from a single depth image. In: CVPR (2011)
28. Niebles, J.C., Chen, C.-W., Fei-Fei, L.: Modeling temporal structure of decomposable motion segments for activity classification. In: Daniilidis, K., Maragos, P., Paragios, N. (eds.) ECCV 2010. LNCS, vol. 6312, pp. 392–405. Springer, Heidelberg (2010). doi:10.1007/978-3-642-15552-9_29
29. Laptev, I., Marszaek, M., Schmid, C., Rozenfeld, B.: Learning realistic human actions from movies. In: CVPR (2008)
30. Fan, R.E., Chang, K.W., Hsieh, C.J., Wang, X.R., Lin, C.J.: Liblinear: a library for large linear classification. JMLR 9, 1871–1874 (2008)
31. Wu, J., Cheng, J., Zhao, C., Lu, H.: Fusing multi-modal features for gesture recognition. In: ICMI (2013)
32. Yao, A., Gool, L.V., Kohli, P.: Gesture recognition portfolios for personalization. In: CVPR (2014)
33. Pfister, T., Charles, J., Zisserman, A.: Domain-adaptive discriminative one-shot learning of gestures. In: Fleet, D., Pajdla, T., Schiele, B., Tuytelaars, T. (eds.) ECCV 2014. LNCS, vol. 8694, pp. 814–829. Springer, Heidelberg (2014). doi:10.1007/978-3-319-10599-4_52
34. Gaidon, A., Harchaoui, Z., Schmid, C.: Recognizing activities with cluster-trees of tracklets. In: BMVC (2012)
35. Hoai, M., Zisserman, A.: Improving human action recognition using score distribution and ranking. In: Cremers, D., Reid, I., Saito, H., Yang, M.-H. (eds.) ACCV 2014. LNCS, vol. 9007, pp. 3–20. Springer, Heidelberg (2015). doi:10.1007/978-3-319-16814-2_1
36. Tang, K., Fei-Fei, L., Koller, D.: Learning latent temporal structure for complex event detection. In: CVPR (2012)

Distinct Class-Specific Saliency Maps for Weakly Supervised Semantic Segmentation

Wataru Shimoda and Keiji Yanai[✉]

Department of Informatics, The University of Electro-Communications,
1-5-1 Chofugaoka, Chofu-shi, Tokyo 182-8585, Japan
{shimoda-k,yanai}@mm.inf.uec.ac.jp

Abstract. In this paper, we deal with a weakly supervised semantic segmentation problem where only training images with image-level
labels are available. We propose a weakly supervised semantic segmentation method which is based on CNN-based class-specific saliency maps
and fully-connected CRF. To obtain distinct class-specific saliency maps
which can be used as unary potentials of CRF, we propose a novel method
to estimate class saliency maps which improves the method proposed by
Simonyan et al. (2014) significantly by the following improvements: (1)
using CNN derivatives with respect to feature maps of the intermediate
convolutional layers with up-sampling instead of an input image; (2) subtracting the saliency maps of the other classes from the saliency maps
of the target class to differentiate target objects from other objects; (3)
aggregating multiple-scale class saliency maps to compensate lower resolution of the feature maps. After obtaining distinct class saliency maps,
we apply fully-connected CRF by using the class maps as unary potentials. By the experiments, we show that the proposed method has outperformed state-of-the-art results with the PASCAL VOC 2012 dataset
under the weakly-supervised setting.

Keywords: Semantic segmentation · Weakly supervised segmentation ·
Fully convolutional neural network · Fully connected CRF

1   Introduction

Due to the recent advent of deep learning methods, convolutional neural network
(CNN) based methods have outperformed most of the previous state-of-the-art
in various kinds of image recognition tasks. In the task of semantic segmentation,
CNN achieved about 50 % improvement [3,4]. Semantic image segmentation is
a task to add object class labels to each of all the pixels in a given image,
which is more challenging task than object classification and object detection.
Semantic segmentation is expected to contribute detailed analysis of images in

Electronic supplementary material The online version of this chapter (doi:10.
1007/978-3-319-46493-0_14) contains supplementary material, which is available to
authorized users.

© Springer International Publishing AG 2016
B. Leibe et al. (Eds.): ECCV 2016, Part IV, LNCS 9908, pp. 218–234, 2016.
DOI: 10.1007/978-3-319-46493-0_14

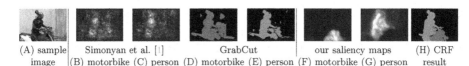

(A) sample | Simonyan et al. [1] | GrabCut | our saliency maps | (H) CRF
image | (B) motorbike (C) person | (D) motorbike (E) person | (F) motorbike (G) person | result

Fig. 1. (From the left) (A) sample image, (B), (C) its class saliency maps with respect to "motorbike" and "person" by [1], (D), (E) estimated regions of them by GrabCut, (F), (G) class saliency maps by the proposed method, and (H) estimated regions by Dense CRF.

various practical tasks such as food calorie estimation [5,6]. However, most of the CNN based semantic segmentation methods assume that pixel-wise annotation is available, which is costly to obtain in general.

On the other hand, collecting images with image-level annotation is easier than those with pixel-level annotation, since many images attached with tags are available on hand-crafted open image datasets such as ImageNet as well as on the Web. In this work, we focus on weakly-supervised semantic segmentation which requires not pixel-wise annotation as well as bounding box annotation but only image-level annotation.

In this paper, we propose a weakly supervised semantic segmentation method which is based on CNN-based class saliency maps and fully-connected CRF [2]. To obtain class saliency maps which are so distinct that we can use them as unary potentials terms of CRF, we propose a novel method to estimate class saliency maps which improves the method proposed by Simonyan et al. [1] significantly. Simonyan et al. [1] proposed class saliency maps based on the gradient of the class score with respect to the input image, which showed weakly-supervised object localization could be done by back-propagation-based visualization. However, their class saliency maps are vague and not distinct (Fig. 1(B), (C)). In addition, when different kinds of target objects are included in the image, the maps tend to respond to all the object regions. Although they adopted GrabCut for weakly-supervised segmentation based class saliency maps in their paper, their method is unable to distinguish multiple object regions (Fig. 1(D), (E)). To resolve the weaknesses of their method, we propose a new method to generate CNN-derivatives-based saliency maps. The proposed method can generate more distinct class saliency maps which discriminate the regions of a target class from the regions of the other classes (Fig. 1(F), (G)). The generated maps are so distinct that they can be used as unary potentials of CRF as they are (Fig. 1(H)). We call our new method for generating class saliency maps as "Distinct Class Saliency Maps (DCSM)".

To obtain DCSM, we propose three improvements over Simonyan et al. [1]: (1) using CNN derivatives with respect to feature maps of the intermediate convolutional layers with up-sampling instead of an input image; (2) subtracting the saliency maps of the other classes from the saliency maps of the target class to differentiate target objects from other objects; (3) aggregating multiple-scale class saliency maps to compensate lower resolution of the feature maps.

After obtaining distinct class saliency maps, we apply fully-connected CRF [2] by using the class maps as unary potentials. As a CNN, we use the VGG-16 pre-trained with 1000-class ILSVRC datasets and fine-tune it with multi-class training using only image-level labeled dataset. By the experiments, we show that the proposed method has outperformed state-of-the-arts on the PASCAL VOC 2012 dataset in the task of weakly supervised semantic segmentation under the standard condition.

To summarize our contributions in this paper, they are as follows:

- We propose a new weakly supervised segmentation method which combines distinct class saliency maps (DCSM) and fully connected CRF.
- We propose a novel method to estimate distinct class saliency maps:
  - based on CNN derivatives with respect to feature maps of the intermediate convolutional layers.
  - subtracting class saliency maps from each other.
  - aggregating multiple-scale class saliency maps.
- The obtained result outperforms those by the current state-of-the-arts on the Pascal VOC 2012 segmentation dataset under the weakly supervised setting.

2   Related Work

Recently, CNN-based semantic segmentation are being explored very actively, and the accuracy has been significantly improved compared to the non-CNN-based conventional methods. In this section, first we describe fully-supervised semantic segmentation, and next we explain weakly-supervised segmentation problem which is addressed in this work. Finally we describe some works based on gradient-based class saliency detection.

2.1   CNN-Based Fully-Supervised Semantic Segmentation

As early works on CNN-based semantic segmentation, Girshick et al. [7] and Hariharan et al. [8] proposed an object segmentation method using region proposal and CNN-based image classification. Firstly, they generated 2000 region candidates at most by Selective Search [9], and secondly apply CNN image classification by feed-forwarding of the CNN to each of the proposals. Finally they integrated all the classification results by non-maximum suppression and generated the final object regions. Although these methods outperformed the conventional methods greatly, they had a drawback that they required long processing time for CNN-based image classification of many region proposals.

While Girshick et al. [7] and Hariharan et al. [8] took advantage of excellent ability of a CNN on image classification task for semantic image segmentation in a relatively straightforward way, Long et al. [10] and Mostajabi et al. [11] proposed CNN-based semantic segmentation in a hierarchical way which achieved more robust and accurate segmentation. A CNN is much different from conventional bag-of-features framework regarding multi-layered structure consisting of multiple convolutional and pooling layers. Because CNN has several pooling layers, location information is gradually losing as the signal is transmitting from the lower layers to the upper layers. In general, the lower layers hold location information in their activations, while the upper layers holds weak local information. Therefore, it is difficult to estimate object regions by using only information in the last output layer. Long et al. [10] and Mostajabi et al. [11] pointed out that it can complement spatial information in the upper activations by up-sampling of the information in the middle layers and integrating them with the information in the upper layers. Upsampling in a CNN is generally called as "Deconvolution".

Long et al. [10] proposed a CNN-based segmentation method which integrates deconvolution from the intermediate layers and object heat map obtained by replacing all the full connection layers with 1×1 convolutional layers and providing a larger-size image than a usual 256×256 image. This replaces class score vectors with class score maps as outputs of the CNN, which express rough location of objects [12]. This idea was originally proposed by Sermanet et al. [13] and called as "fully convolutional network" or "sliding CNN", which plays important roles to raise performance on CNN-based segmentation. By using larger-size images as input images, more detailed location information can be obtained in the intermediate layers as well as in the class score maps from the last layer. This can be used as unary potentials of CRF [3,4,14].

On the other hand, Mostajabi et al. [11] proposed a method which associates up-sampled activation features of several intermediate layers with super-pixels and treat them as local features, which are called "zoom-out features".

In our work, we also aggregate location information in multiple intermediate layers for image segmentation. However, we adopt a back-propagation-based method, while they adopted feed-forward image segmentation.

2.2 CNN-Based Weakly-Supervised Segmentation

Most of the conventional non-CNN-based weakly supervised segmentation method employed Conditional Random Field (CRF) with unary potentials estimated by multiple instance learning [15], extremely randomized hashing forest [16], and GMM [17].

As a CNN-based method, Pedro et al. [18] addressed weakly-supervised segmentation by using multi-scale CNN proposed in [13]. They integrated the outputs which contain location information with log sum exponential, and limited object regions to the regions overlapped with object proposals [19].

Pathak et al. [20,21] and Papandreou et al. [22] proposed weakly-supervised semantic segmentation by adapting CNN models for fully-supervised segmentation to weakly-supervised segmentation. In MIL-FCN [20], they trained the CNN for fully-supervised segmentation proposed in Long et al. [10] with a global max-pooling loss which enables training of the CNN model using only training data with image-level labels which is the same idea as Multiple Instance Learning. Constrained Convolutional Neural Network (CCNN) [21] improved MIL-FCN by adding some constraints and using fully-connected CRF [2]. Papandreou et al. [22] trained the DeepLab model [3] proposed as a fully-supervised model with EM algorithm, which is called as "EM-adopt". Both CCNN and EM-adopt generated pseudo-pixel-level labels from image-level labels using constraints and EM algorithms to train FCN and DeepLab which were originally proposed for fully supervised segmentation, respectively. Both showed Dense CRF [2] were helpful to boost segmentation performance even in the weakly supervised setting.

While all the above-mentioned methods on weakly supervised segmentation employed only feed-forward computation, we adopted a method based on back-propagation (BP) computation. In this paper, our BP-based method outperforms all the methods based on feed-forward computation.

2.3   Gradient-Based Region Estimation with Back-Propagation

Simonyan et al. [1] showed that object segmentation without pixel-wise training data can be done by using back-propagation processing which is a method to train a CNN. To train a CNN, in general, we optimize CNN parameters so as to minimize the loss between groundtruth values and output values. In the back-propagation process, derivatives of the loss function are propagated from the top layers to the lower layers. Springenberg et al. [23] also proposed a method for object localization by back-propagating the derivatives of a maximum loss value of the object detected in the feed-forward computation. They achieved more accurate localization by limiting back-propagating values to positive values. Recently, Pan et al. [24] extended BP-based saliency maps by adding superpixel-based region refinements. BP-based methods was extended to temporal localization of events in a video by Gan et al. [25].

Although these methods can localize single objects in given images, it is difficult to localize multiple different kinds of objects in the same image as shown in Fig. 1(B), (C). This is because Pan et al. [24] proposed their method for generic salient object detection. BP-based methods have never been introduced into weakly-supervised semantic segmentation for multiple object images such as those of the PASCAL VOC dataset so far. To apply BP-based localization methods to the PASCAL VOC segmentation task, we need to modify them so that they can estimate class-specific saliency. In this paper, we have achieved that, and we show that our class-specific saliency maps (DCSM) are suitable for unary potentials of Dense CRF as shown in Fig. 1(F)–(H).

Moreover, all the existing BP-based methods used only the derivatives of the loss function with respect to an input image for object localization, and did not use derivatives or feed-forward activations in the intermediate layers. In our work, we obtained more distinctive class-specific saliency maps by using the derivatives of multiple intermediate layers.

3   Methods

In this section, we overview the proposed method, and explain the detail of the method which consists of three elements: multi-label training of CNN, multi-class object saliency map estimation which was inspired by [1], and fully connected CRF [2].

3.1   Overview

To achieve semantic segmentation for a given image, we (1) perform multi-label classification on a given image by feed-forward computation of the CNN, (2) calculate CNN derivatives with respect to feature maps of the intermediate convolutional layers with back-propagation by using each of the detected class labels as supervised signals in the loss function, (3) aggregate CNN derivatives of several intermediate layers with up-sampling to generate raw class saliency maps, (4) subtract raw saliency maps of the other candidate classes from the saliency maps of the target class, and (5) apply fully-connected CRF (Dense CRF) with subtracted class saliency maps as unary potential. Finally we obtain a segmentation result. The processing flow is shown in Fig. 2.

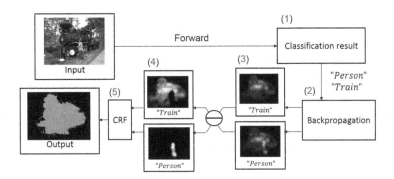

Fig. 2. Processing flow of the proposed method: (1) multi-label classification (2) computation of back-propagation with respect to each of the detected class labels (3) generating raw class saliency maps (4) subtracting raw saliency maps of the other candidate classes from the saliency maps of the target class (5) applying Dense CRF with subtracted class saliency maps as unary potential

3.2   Training CNN

For preparation, we train a CNN with a multi-label loss function. As an off-the-shelf basic CNN architecture, we use the VGG-16 [26] pre-trained with 1000-class ILSVRC datasets. In our framework, we fine-tune a CNN with training images with only image-level multi-label annotation.

Recently, fully convolutional networks (FCN) which accept arbitrary-sized inputs are used commonly in works on CNN-based detection and segmentation such as [10,12], in which fully connected layers with n units were replaced with the equivalent convolutional layers having n 1×1 filters. Following them, we introduce FCN to enable multi-scale generation of class saliency maps. When training, we insert global max pooling before the final loss function layer to deal with larger input images than the images used for pre-training of the VGG-16. We use images which are normalized to 500×500 by rescaling to have the largest size of the 500 pixels and zero-padding for training and testing in the same way as [12]. For multi-scale training, we resize training images randomly between the ratio 0.7 and 1.4 within a mini-batch.

To carry out multi-label training of the CNN, we use a Sigmoid cross entropy loss which is a standard loss function for multi-label annotation instead of a soft-max loss used in the original VGG-16 in the same way as [12,20]. The Sigmoid cross entropy loss function is represented in the following equation:

$$\text{loss} = \sum_{n=1}^{K} [-p_n \log \hat{p_n} - (1 - p_n)\log(1 - \hat{p_n})] \tag{1}$$

where K is the number of classes, $p_n = \{0, 1\}$ which represents the existence of the corresponding class label, and $\hat{p_n}$ means the output of Sigmoid function of the class score $f_n(x)$ represented in the following equation:

$$\hat{p_n} = \frac{1}{1 + e^{-f_n(x)}} \tag{2}$$

3.3   Class Saliency Maps

We propose a new method to estimate class-specific saliency maps by enhancing the method proposed by Simonyan et al. [1] greatly. It consists of (1) extracting CNN derivatives with respect to feature maps of the intermediate convolutional layers, (2) subtracting class saliency maps between the target class and the other classes, and (3) aggregation of multi-scale saliency maps.

Extracting CNN Derivatives. In [1], they regarded the derivatives of the class score with respect to the input image as class saliency maps. However, the position of an input image is the furthermost from the class score output on the deep CNN, which sometime causes weakening or vanishing of gradients. Instead of the derivatives of the class score with respect to the input image, we use the derivatives with respect to feature maps of the relatively upper intermediate layers which are expected to retain more high-level semantic information. We select the maximum absolute values of the derivatives with respect to the feature maps at each location of feature maps across all the kernels, and up-sample them with bilinear interpolation so that their size becomes the same as an input image (Fig. 3(C)–(G)). Finally we average them to obtain one saliency map (Fig. 3(B)). The idea on aggregating of information extracted from multiple feature layers was inspired by the work of [10], although they extracted not CNN derivatives but feature maps calculated by feed-forwarding.

The class score derivative v_i^c of a feature map in the i-th layer is the derivative of class score Sc with respect to the layer L_i at the point (activation signal) L_i^0:

$$v_i^c = \left. \frac{\partial S_c}{\partial L_i} \right|_{L_i^0} \tag{3}$$

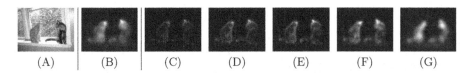

(A)   (B)   (C)   (D)   (E)   (F)   (G)

Fig. 3. Class saliency maps obtained from the VGG16-net fine-tuned with the PASCAL VOC 2012 dataset. (A) an input image, (B) average of [(E)–(G)], (C) conv1_1, (D) conv2_1, (E) conv3_2, (F) conv4_2, (G) conv5_2

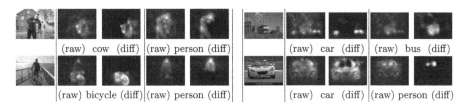

(raw) cow (diff)	(raw) person (diff)		(raw) car (diff)	(raw) bus (diff)
(raw) bicycle (diff)	(raw) person (diff)		(raw) car (diff)	(raw) person (diff)

Fig. 4. (raw) raw maps without subtraction (diff) maps with subtraction of other class maps.

v_i^c can be computed by back-propagation. After obtained v_i^c, we up-sample it to w_i^c with bilinear interpolation so that the size of an 2-D map of v_i^c becomes the same as an input image. Next, the class saliency map $M_i^c \in \mathcal{R}^{m \times n}$ is computed as $M_{i,x,y}^c = \max_{k_i} |w_{i,h_i(x,y,k)}^c|$, where $h_i(x,y,k)$ is the index of the element of w_i^c. Note that each value of the saliency map is normalized by $\tanh(\alpha M_{i,x,y} / \max_{x,y} M_{i,x,y})$ for visualization in Fig. 3 and all the other figures with $\alpha = 3$.

Subtracting Raw Class Saliency Maps. As shown in Fig. 1(B), (C), the saliency maps of two or more different classes tend to be similar to each other especially in the image-level. The saliency maps by [1] are likely to correspond to foreground regions rather than specific class regions. This problem is relaxed in the proposed methods, because we use saliency maps obtained from intermediate layers. However, the saliency regions of different classes are still overlapped with each other (Fig. 4(raw)).

To resolve that, we subtract saliency maps of the other candidate classes from the saliency maps of the target class to differentiate target objects from other objects. Here, we assume that we use the CNN trained with multi-label loss, and select several candidate classes the class score of which exceed a pre-defined threshold with a pre-defined minimum number. (In the experiments, we set 0.5 to the threshold and 3 to the minimum number.)

The improved class saliency maps with respect to class c, $\tilde{M}_i^c$, are represented as:

$$\tilde{M}_{i,x,y}^c = \sum_{c' \in candidates} \max\left(M_{i,x,y}^c - M_{i,x,y}^{c'}, 0\right) [c \neq c'], \tag{4}$$

where *candidates* is a set of the selected candidate classes. Figure 4 shows results without subtraction in the left (raw) and ones with subtraction in the right (diff). As we can see, subtraction of saliency maps resolved overlapped regions among the maps of the different classes.

Aggregating Multi-scale Class Saliency Maps. We use fully convolutional networks (FCN) which accept arbitrary-sized inputs for multi-scale generation of class saliency maps. If the larger input image than one for the original CNN is given to the fully-convolutionalized CNN, the output becomes class score maps represented as $h \times w \times C$ where C is the number of classes, and h and w are larger than 1. To obtain CNN derivatives with respect to enlarged feature maps, we simply back-propagate the target class score map which is define as $S_c(:,:,c) = 1$ (in the Matlab notation) with 0 for all the other elements, where c is the target class index.

The final class saliency map $\hat{M}^c$ averaged over the layers and the scales is obtained as follows:

$$\hat{M}^c_{x,y} = \frac{1}{|S||L|} \sum_{j \in S} \sum_{i \in L} \tanh(\alpha \tilde{M}^c_{j,i,x,y}), \tag{5}$$

where L is a set of the layers for which saliency maps are extracted, S is a set of the scale ratios, and α is a constant which we set to 3 in the experiments. Note that we assume the size of $\tilde{M}_{j,i}$ for all the layers are normalized to the same size as an input image before calculation of Eq. 5.

In the experiments, we adopted guided back-propagation (GBP) [23] as back-propagation method instead of normal back-propagation (BP) used in [1]. The difference between two methods is in the backward computation through ReLU. GBP can visualize saliency maps with less noise components than normal BP by back-propagating only positive values of CNN derivatives through ReLU [23].

3.4 Fully Connected CRF

Conditional Random Field (CRF) is a probabilistic graphical model which considers both node priors and consistency between nodes. Because class-specific saliency maps obtained in the previous subsection represent only probability of the target classes on each pixel and have no explicit information on object region boundaries, we apply CRF to estimate object boundaries. In this paper, we use fully connected CRF (noted as "FC-CRF" or "Dense CRF") [2] where every pixel is regarded as a node, and every node is connected to every other node. The energy function is defined as follows:

$$E(\mathbf{c}) = \sum_i \theta_i(c_i) + \sum_{i,j} \theta_{i,j}(c_i, c_j) \tag{6}$$

where c_i represents a class assignment on pixel i. The first unary term of the above equation is calculated from class saliency maps $\hat{M}^c_i$. We defined it as $\theta_i(c_i) = -\log(\hat{M}^c_{x,y})$.

Since the CNN we trained has no background class, we have no class maps on background class. To use CRF for image segmentation, a unary potential on the background class is needed as well as foreground potential. We estimate a unary potential on the background class from the maps of the candidate classes selected in the previous step by the following equation.

$$\hat{M}_{x,y}^{BG} = 1 - \max_{c \in target} \hat{M}_{x,y}^{c} \tag{7}$$

where $\hat{M}_{x,y}^{BG}$ is a saliency map of background class, and $target$ represents a set of the selected candidate classes.

The pairwise term of Eq. 6 is represented by $\theta_{i,j}(c_i, c_j) = u(c_i, c_j)k(f_i, f_j)$ where $u(x_i, x_j) = \begin{cases} 1 & (c_i \neq c_j) \\ 0 & others \end{cases}$ and $k(\mathbf{f}_i, \mathbf{f}_j)$ is a Gaussian kernel. Note that $\mathbf{f}_i, \mathbf{f}_j$ represents some kinds of image features extracted from pixel i and j. Following [2], we adopt bilateral position and color terms, and the kernels are

$$k(\mathbf{f}_i, \mathbf{f}_j) = w_1 \exp \left(-\frac{|p_i - p_j|^2}{2\gamma_\alpha^2} - \frac{|I_i - I_j|^2}{2\gamma_\beta^2} \right) + w_2 \exp \left(-\frac{|p_i - p_j|^2}{2\gamma_\gamma^2} \right) \tag{8}$$

where the first kernel depends on both pixel positions (denoted as p) and pixel color intensities (denoted as I), and the second kernel only depends on pixel positions. The hyper parameters γ_α, γ_β, and γ_γ control the scale of the Gaussian kernels. This model is amenable to efficient approximate probabilistic inference proposed by [2].

4   Experiments

We evaluated the proposed methods using the PASCAL VOC 2012 data. We compared the results with state-of-the-arts, and show significant improvements by the proposed methods.

4.1   Dataset

In the experiments, we used the PASCAL VOC 2012 segmentation data [27] to evaluate the proposed method. The PASCAL VOC 2012 segmentation dataset consists of 1464 training images, 1449 validation images, and 1456 test images including 20 class pixel-level labels as well as image-level labels. For training, we used the augmented PASCAL VOC training data including 10582 *train_aug* images provided by Hariharan et al. [28] in the same way as the other works on weakly-supervised segmentation such as MIL-FCN [20], EM-Adapt [22] and CCNN [21].

For evaluation, we used a standard intersection over union (IoU) metric which was the official evaluation metric in the PASCAL VOC segmentation task.

Table 1. Results of the mean IoU by Simonyan et al. and ours on Pascal VOC 2012 *val set*

Method \ α	2	2.5	3	4	5	6	7	8	9	10	15
Simonyan et al.	-	-	10.0	20.6	28.3	32.7	33.4	33.8	33.8	33.3	28.7
DCSM (ours)	40.0	44.0	44.1	40.6	36.4	-	-	-	-	-	

4.2   Experimental Setup

We used VGG-16 [26] as a basic CNN, modified it regarding Sigmoid entropy loss for multi-label training, random resizing of training images and global max pooling for multi-scale training following [12], and fine-tuned it with PASCAL VOC *train_aug* dataset. We used Caffe [29] to train the CNN with batchsize 2, learning rate 1e-5, momentum 0.9 and weight decay 0.0005. Note that we followed [21] regarding very small batchsize for fine-tuning of VGG-16. For the first 30000 iterations, we fine-tuned only the upper layers of the modified VGG-16 than Pool_5, and for the next 20000 iterations, we fine-tuned all the layers.

As hyperparameters of the fully-connected CRF, we used the following parameters which were chosen by grid search with validation data: $w_1 = w_2 = 1$, $\gamma_\alpha = 30$, $\gamma_\beta = 10$, and $\gamma_\gamma = 3$.

Using GPU, it takes about 0.3 s to perform segmentation for one image.

4.3   Evaluation on Class Saliency Maps

First, we compare the class saliency maps estimated by the proposed method (noted as DCSM (Distinct Class-specific Saliency Maps)) with ones by Simonyan et al. [1] qualitatively. Figure 5 shows both the results by Simonyan et al. and our method for three multiple object images and one single object images. From these results, it is shown that our method is much more effective for not only multiple object images but also single object images than the previous method. This figure shows our results are significantly better than [1], because we aggregate gradients in the multiple intermediate layers and carry out subtraction of raw class saliency maps. Our results clearly discriminated multiple regions of the different classes.

Figure 6 shows the results for images containing three or more objects. In even such cases, all the class saliency maps except for "chair" in the top-right sample were estimated successfully.

To compare both quantitatively, we carried out weakly supervised segmentation using estimated class saliency maps and Dense CRF. To obtain maps for unary potentials of CRF, we used Eq. 5 which contains a hyper-parameter, α. As shown in Table 1, we searched for the best values of α for both of Simonyan et al. and our method. As results, ours achieved 44.1 % as the best meanIoU with $\alpha = 3$, while Simonyan et al. achieved 33.8 % with $\alpha = 8$(or 9). From both the best results, our method is superior to Simonyan et al. significantly as a method to estimate CRF unary potentials under the weakly supervised setting.

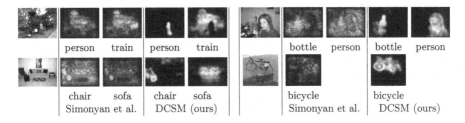

Fig. 5. Obtained class saliency maps (Left) by Simonyan et al. [1] (Right) by the proposed method (DCSM).

Fig. 6. Obtained class saliency maps for images containing three or more classes.

Table 2. Effects by layers from which CNN derivatives are extracted.

Layer	Mean IoU
Block1 (conv1_1, conv1_2)	5.5
Block2 (conv2_1, conv2_2)	21.5
Block3 (conv3_1, conv3_2, conv3_3)	32.5
Block4 (conv4_1, conv4_2, conv4_3)	**40.3**
Block5 (conv5_1, conv5_2, conv5_3)	26.3
Average block 1,2,3,4,5	41.3
Average block 2,3,4,5	42.2
Average block 3,4,5	**42.8**
Average block 4,5	42.5
Average block 3,4	37.97

Table 3. Effects by input image size and multi-scale aggregation.

Input image size	Mean IoU
(1) 300×300	34.5
(2) 400×400	41.0
(3) **500×500**	**42.4**
(4) 600×600	41.8
(5) 700×700	40.0
(6) 800×800	34.5
Average (1),(2),(3)	41.1
Average (2),(3)	42.9
Average (2),(3),(4)	**43.5**
Average (3),(4)	42.9
Average (3),(4),(5)	42.5
Average (3),(4),(5),(6)	42.8

4.4 Effects of Parameter Choices

Intermediate Layers. In the proposed method, we extract CNN derivatives from intermediate layers of the VGG-16, and averaged them to estimate class saliency maps. We examined the effects on which layers we use to extract

Table 4. Effects on the number of raw class maps for subtraction.

Class N	0	1	2	3	4	5	10	15
Mean IoU	38.2	42.2	43.5	44.1	44.2	44.0	43.7	43.3

Table 5. Effects on the way of back-propagation.

Method	BP	GBP
Mean IoU	41.2	44.1

Table 6. Results on PASCAL VOC 2012 *val set*.

Methods	bg	aero	bike	bird	boat	bottle	bus	car	cat	chair	cow	table	dog	horse	motor	person	plant	sheep	sofa	train	tv	mIoU
Weakly Supervised:																						
MIL-FCN [20]	-	-	-	-	-	-	-	-	-	-	-	-	-	-	-	-	-	-	-	-	-	25.7
EM-Adapt [22]	-	-	-	-	-	-	-	-	-	-	-	-	-	-	-	-	-	-	-	-	-	38.2
CCNN [21]	65.9	23.8	17.6	22.8	19.4	36.2	47.3	46.9	47.0	16.3	36.1	22.2	43.2	33.7	44.9	39.8	29.9	33.4	22.2	38.8	36.3	34.5
MIL-sppxl [18]	77.2	37.3	18.4	25.4	28.2	31.9	41.6	48.1	50.7	12.7	45.7	14.6	50.9	44.1	39.2	37.9	28.3	44.0	19.6	37.6	35.0	36.6
MIL-bb [18]	78.6	46.9	18.6	27.9	30.7	38.4	44.0	49.6	49.8	11.6	44.7	14.6	50.4	44.7	40.8	38.5	26.0	45.0	20.5	36.9	34.8	37.8
MIL-seg [18]	**79.6**	**50.2**	21.6	40.6	**34.9**	**40.5**	45.9	51.5	**60.6**	12.6	**51.2**	11.6	**56.8**	**52.9**	44.8	42.7	31.2	**55.4**	21.5	38.8	36.9	42.0
DCSM w/o CRF (ours)	72.5	35.0	23.7	33.6	20.9	32.8	57.6	49.2	51.4	14.7	42.9	32.8	51.9	43.1	53.2	47.6	35.2	47.7	28.6	40.3	36.7	40.5
DCSM w/ CRF (ours)	76.7	45.1	**24.6**	**40.8**	23.0	34.8	**61.0**	**51.9**	52.4	15.5	45.9	**32.7**	54.9	48.6	**57.4**	**51.8**	**38.2**	55.4	**32.2**	**42.6**	39.6	**44.1**

Table 7. Results on PASCAL VOC 2012 *test set*.

Methods	bg	aero	bike	bird	boat	bottle	bus	car	cat	chair	cow	table	dog	horse	motor	person	plant	sheep	sofa	train	tv	mIoU
Fully Supervised:																						
O2P [30]	85.4	69.7	22.3	45.2	44.4	49.6	66.7	57.8	56.2	13.5	46.1	32.3	41.2	59.1	55.3	51.0	36.2	50.4	27.8	46.9	44.6	47.6
SDS [8]	86.3	63.3	25.7	63.0	39.8	59.2	70.9	61.4	54.9	16.8	45.0	48.2	50.5	51.0	57.7	63.3	31.8	58.7	31.2	55.7	48.5	51.6
FCN-8s [10]	-	76.8	34.2	68.9	49.4	60.3	75.3	74.7	77.6	21.4	62.5	46.8	71.8	63.9	76.5	73.9	45.2	72.4	37.4	70.9	55.1	62.2
Zoom out [19]	89.8	81.9	35.1	78.2	57.4	56.5	80.5	74.0	79.8	22.4	69.6	53.7	74.0	76.0	76.6	68.8	44.3	70.2	40.2	68.9	55.3	64.4
DeepLab [4]	**93.1**	**84.4**	54.5	**81.5**	63.6	65.9	85.1	79.1	**83.4**	30.7	74.1	59.8	79.0	76.1	**83.2**	**80.8**	**59.7**	82.2	**50.4**	73.1	63.7	71.6
CRF as RNN [1]	87.5	39.0	**79.7**	64.2	**68.3**	**87.6**	80.8	**84.4**	30.4	**72.0**	**78.2**	60.4	80.5	77.8	83.1	80.6	59.5	**82.8**	47.8	**78.3**	67.1	**72.0**
Size tag Supervised:																						
CCNN w/size [21]	-	42.3	24.5	56.0	30.6	39.0	58.8	52.7	54.8	14.6	48.4	34.2	52.7	46.9	61.1	44.8	37.4	48.8	30.6	47.7	41.7	45.1
Weakly Supervised:																						
MIL-FCN [20]	-	-	-	-	-	-	-	-	-	-	-	-	-	-	-	-	-	-	-	-	-	24.9
EM-Adapt [22]	76.3	37.1	21.9	41.6	26.1	38.5	50.8	44.9	48.9	16.7	40.8	29.4	47.1	45.8	54.8	28.2	30.0	44.0	29.2	34.3	46.0	39.6
CCNN [21]	-	21.3	17.7	22.8	17.9	38.3	51.3	43.9	51.4	15.6	38.4	17.4	46.5	38.6	53.3	40.6	34.3	36.8	20.1	32.9	38.0	35.5
MIL-ILP-seg [18]	**78.7**	48.0	21.2	31.1	**28.4**	35.1	51.4	**55.5**	52.8	7.8	56.2	19.9	**53.8**	50.3	40.0	38.6	27.8	51.8	24.7	33.3	**46.3**	40.6
DCSM w/o CRF (ours)	73.9	34.1	24.4	39.6	18.0	37.6	57.8	49.0	51.5	13.3	42.3	33.5	47.8	44.2	63.7	44.3	34.5	48.3	31.2	35.7	37.1	41.0
DCSM w/ CRF (ours)	78.1	43.8	**26.3**	**49.8**	19.5	40.3	61.6	53.9	52.7	13.7	47.3	**34.8**	50.3	48.9	**69.0**	49.7	**38.4**	**57.1**	34.0	38.0	40.0	**45.1**

derivatives from. Table 2 shows the results evaluated with VOC *val set* varying the layer combinations. "Block1" in the table means the average of conv1_1 and conv1_2 in VGG-16, and "average Block 3,4,5" means the average of Block 3, Block 4, and Block 5. Among the single blocks, Block 4 achieved the best result, and among the block combinations, the combination of Block 3,4,5 achieved the best. Although Block 5 itself was less effective, adding Block 5 to combinations was effective to boost performance. This shows that aggregation of CNN derivatives extracted from multiple upper layers is the better choice.

Size of Input Images. Because we use fully convolutional CNN which can deal with arbitrary-sized input images, we examined the effects on input image size and multi-scale combination of input images. Note that we used bilinear up-scaling when the size of the original images were less than the indicated size. Table 3 shows the results, which indicates 500×500 was the best, and the combination of 400×400, 500×500 and 600×600 was the best. This is partly because we used training images with random resizing from 350 to 700 pixels. From these results, multi-scale aggregation helped boost performance.

Minimum Number of the Raw Class Maps for Subtraction. We use the raw class saliency maps of the top-N classes for raw class map subtraction which are estimated by feed-forward multi-class classification[1] of the input image in addition to the maps of the classes the output scores of which are more than the pre-defined threshold, 0.5. We examined effects on the top-N varying N. Note that exceptionally $N = 0$ means that subtraction was never carried out, that is, the results without subtraction. As shown in Table 4, using the top-4 ($N = 4$) raw class maps was the best[2]. Compared with $N = 0$, subtraction is always helpful to raise segmentation performance.

Guided BP vs. BP. We compared normal back propagation (BP) used in Simonyan et al. [1] with guided back propagation (GBP) proposed by Springenberg et al. [23]. GBP was better than BP as shown in Table 5.

4.5   Comparison with Other Methods

In the final subsection, we compare our results (DCSM) with other results by CNN-based methods quantitatively. Tables 6 and 7 show the results for PASCAL VOC 2012 *val set* and *test set*, respectively.

While MIL-FCN [20], EM-Adapt [22], CCNN [21] and our methods used PASCAL VOC training data and augmented training data provided by [28], MIL-{sppxl,bb,seg} by Pedro et al. [18] used their original additional training images which contains 700,000 images. Our method is different from other methods in terms of the way to use a CNN. While the existing methods employed only feed forward computation [18,20–22], we use backward computation as well as feed forward computation. Although the way to train CNN is the same as MIL-FCN [20] and MIL-{sppxl,bb,seg} [18], the method to localize objects is essentially different.

As shown in the tables, our results by DCSM with CRF outperformed all the *val* and *test* results by the weakly-supervised methods including MIL-{sppxl,bb,seg} which used about 70 times as many training images with the margin, 2.1 points and 4.5 points, respectively. Note that "CCNN w/size" used additional information on size of training images, the mean IoU of which was equivalent to ours.

---

[1] The classification accuracy of multi labels by the fine-tuned VGG-16 was 85.2 %.

[2] We used $N = 3$ in all the other experiments to save computation.

In Table 7, we also compared our results with the fully supervised methods. Our result is close to the result by one of the best non-CNN-based fully
supervised method, O2P [30]. Their difference is only 2.5 points.

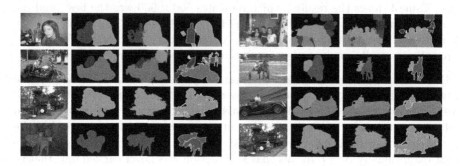

Fig. 7. Qualitative results on VOC 2012. Each row shows (left) input image, (middle
left) results estimated from class maps, (middle right) results after applying FC-CRF,
and (right) groundtruth. Please see the supplementary material for more results.

Finally, we show qualitative results by the proposed method without/with
Dense CRF in Fig. 7.

5   Conclusions

In this paper, we proposed a new weakly-supervised semantic segmentation
method consisting of a novel method of class saliency map estimation and Dense
CRF. The proposed distinct class saliency maps (DCSM) outperformed the maps
by Simonyan et al. [1] both qualitatively and quantitatively. The experimental
results proved the effectiveness of the proposed method, which achieved the
state-of-the-arts on the PASCAL VOC 2012 weakly supervised segmentation[3].

References

1. Simonyan, K., Vedaldi, A., Zisserman, A.: Deep inside convolutional networks:
   visualising image classification models and saliency maps. In: Proceedings of International Conference on Learning Representations (2014)
2. Krahenbuhl, P., Koltun, V.: Efficient inference in fully connected crfs with gaussian
   edge potentials. In: Advances in Neural Information Processing Systems (2011)
3. Chen, L., Papandreou, G., Kokkinos, I., Murphy, K., Yuille, A.L.: Semantic image
   segmentation with deep convolutional nets and fully connected CRFs. In: Proceedings of International Conference on Learning Representations (2015)

---

[3] At the time of publishing of this paper, the two works published as arXiv papers
[31,32] achieved the state-of-the-art results which were more than 50 % on the
PASCAL VOC 2012.

4. Zheng, S., Jayasumana, S., Paredes, B.R., Vineet, V., Su, Z.: Conditional random fields as recurrent neural networks. In: Proceedings of IEEE Computer Vision and Pattern Recognition (2015)

5. Myers, A., Johnston, N., Rathod, V., Korattikara, A., Gorban, A., Silberman, N., Guadarrama, S., Papandreou, G., Huang, J., Murphy, K.: Im2calories: towards an automated mobile vision food diary. In: Proceedings of IEEE International Conference on Computer Vision (2015)

6. Shimoda, W., Yanai, K.: CNN-based food image segmentation. In: Proceedings of International Workshop on Multimedia Assisted Dietary Management (MADIMA) (2015)

7. Girshick, R., Donahue, J., Darrell, T., Malik, J.: Rich feature hierarchies for accurate object detection and semantic segmentation. In: Proceedings of IEEE Computer Vision and Pattern Recognition (2014)

8. Hariharan, B., Arbeláez, P., Girshick, R., Malik, J.: Simultaneous detection and segmentation. In: Proceedings of European Conference on Computer Vision (2014)

9. Uijlings, J.R.R., van de Sande, K.E.A., Gevers, T., Smeulders, A.W.M.: Selective search for object recognition. Int. J. Comput. Vis. **104**, 154–171 (2013)

10. Long, J., Shelhamer, E., Darrell, T.: Fully convolutional networks for semantic segmentation. In: Proceedings of IEEE Computer Vision and Pattern Recognition (2015)

11. Mostajabi, M., Yadollahpour, P., Shakhnarovich, G.: Feedforward semantic segmentation with zoom-out features. In: Proceedings of IEEE Computer Vision and Pattern Recognition (2015)

12. Oquab, M., Bottou, L., Laptev, I., Sivic, J.: Is object localization for free? -weakly-supervised learning with convolutional neural networks. In: Proceedings of IEEE Computer Vision and Pattern Recognition (2015)

13. Sermanet, P., Eigen, D., Zhang, X., Mathieu, M., Fergus, R., LeCun, Y.: Overfeat: Integrated recognition, localization and detection using convolutional networks. In: Proceedings of International Conference on Learning Representations (2014)

14. Bell, S., Upchurch, P., Snavely, N., Bala, K.: Material recognition in the wild with the materials in context database. In: Proceedings of IEEE Computer Vision and Pattern Recognition (2015)

15. Vezhnevets, A., Buhmann, J.M.: Towards weakly supervised semantic segmentation by means of multiple instance and multitask learning. In: Proceedings of IEEE Computer Vision and Pattern Recognition (2010)

16. Vezhnevets, A., Buhmann, J.M.: Weakly supervised structured output learning for semantic segmentation. In: Proceedings of IEEE Computer Vision and Pattern Recognition (2012)

17. Zhang, L., Gao, Y., Xia, Y., Lu, K., Shen, J., Ji, R.: Representative discovery of structure cues for weakly-supervised image segmentation. IEEE Trans. Multimedia **16**(2), 470–479 (2014)

18. Pedro, P., Ronan, C.: From image-level to pixel-level labeling with convolutional networks. In: Proceedings of IEEE Computer Vision and Pattern Recognition (2015)

19. Pablo, A., Jordi, P.-T., Jon, B., Ferran, M., Jitendra, M.: Multiscale combinatorial grouping. In: Proceedings of IEEE Computer Vision and Pattern Recognition (2014)

20. Pathak, D., Shelhamer, E., Long, J., Darrell, T.: Fully convolutional multi-class multiple instance learning. In: Proceedings of International Conference on Learning Representations (2015)

21. Pathak, D., Krahenbuhl, P., Darrell, T.: Constrained convolutional neural networks for weakly supervised segmentation. In: Proceedings of IEEE International Conference on Computer Vision (2015)
22. Papandreou, G., Chen, L.C., Murphy, K., Yuille, A.L.: Weakly-and semi-supervised learning of a dcnn for semantic image segmentation. In: Proceedings of IEEE International Conference on Computer Vision (2015)
23. Springenberg, J.T., Dosovitskiy, A., Brox, T., Riedmiller, M.: Striving for simplicity: The all convolutional net. In: Proceedings of International Conference on Learning Representations (2015)
24. Pan, H., Hui, J.: A deep learning based fast image saliency detection algorithm. arXiv preprint arXiv:1602.00577 (2016)
25. Gan, C., Wang, N., Yang, Y., Yeung, D., Hauptmann, A.G.: Devnet: A deep event network for multimedia event detection and evidence recounting. In: Proceedings of IEEE Computer Vision and Pattern Recognition (2015)
26. Simonyan, K., Vedaldi, A., Zisserman, A.: Very deep convolutional networks for large-scale image recognition. In: Proceedings of International Conference on Learning Representations (2015)
27. Everingham, M., Eslami, S.M.A., Van Gool, L., Williams, C.K.I., Winn, J., Zisserman, A.: The pascal visual object classes challenge: a retrospective. Int. J. Comput. Vis. **111**(1), 98–136 (2015)
28. Hariharan, B., Arbelaez, P., Bourdev, L., Maji, S., Malik, J.: Semantic contours from inverse detectors. In: Proceedings of IEEE International Conference on Computer Vision (2011)
29. Jia, Y., Shelhamer, E., Donahue, J., Karayev, S., Long, J., Girshick, R., Guadarrama, S., Darrell, T.: Caffe: Convolutional architecture for fast feature embedding. arXiv preprint arXiv:1408.5093 (2014)
30. Carreira, J., Caseiro, R., Batista, J., Sminchisescu, C.: Semantic segmentation with second-order pooling. In: Proceedings of European Conference on Computer Vision (2012)
31. Wei, Y., Liang, X., Chen, Y., Shen, X., Cheng, M., Zhao, Y., Yan, S.: STC: A simple to complex framework for weakly-supervised semantic segmentation. arXiv:1509.03150 (2015)
32. Kolesnikov, A., Lampert, C.: Seed, expand and constrain: Three principles for weakly-supervised image segmentation. arXiv:1603.06098 (2016)

A Diagram is Worth a Dozen Images

Aniruddha Kembhavi[1]([✉]), Mike Salvato[1], Eric Kolve[1], Minjoon Seo[2],
Hannaneh Hajishirzi[2], and Ali Farhadi[1,2]

[1] Allen Institute for Artificial Intelligence, Seattle, USA
{anik,mikes,erick,alif}@allenai.org
[2] University of Washington, Seattle, USA
{minjoon,hannaneh}@washington.edu

Abstract. Diagrams are common tools for representing complex concepts, relationships and events, often when it would be difficult to portray the same information with natural images. Understanding natural images has been extensively studied in computer vision, while diagram understanding has received little attention. In this paper, we study the problem of diagram interpretation, the challenging task of identifying the structure of a diagram and the semantics of its constituents and their relationships. We introduce Diagram Parse Graphs (DPG) as our representation to model the structure of diagrams. We define syntactic parsing of diagrams as learning to infer DPGs for diagrams and study semantic interpretation and reasoning of diagrams in the context of diagram question answering. We devise an LSTM-based method for syntactic parsing of diagrams and introduce a DPG-based attention model for diagram question answering. We compile a new dataset of diagrams with exhaustive annotations of constituents and relationships for about 5,000 diagrams and 15,000 questions and answers. Our results show the significance of our models for syntactic parsing and question answering in diagrams using DPGs.

1 Introduction

For thousands of years visual illustrations have been used to depict the lives of people, animals, their environment, and major events. Archaeological discoveries have unearthed cave paintings showing lucid representations of hunting, religious rites, communal dancing, burial, etc. From ancient rock carvings and maps, to modern info-graphics and 3-D visualizations, to diagrams in science textbooks, the set of visual illustrations is very large, diverse and ever growing, constituting a considerable portion of visual data. These illustrations often represent complex concepts, such as events or systems, that are otherwise difficult to portray in a few sentences of text or a natural image (Fig. 1).

While understanding natural images has been a major area of research in computer vision, understanding rich visual illustrations has received scant attention. From a computer vision perspective, these illustrations are inherently different from natural images and offer a unique and interesting set of problems.

M. Salvato and E. Kolve—These authors contributed equally to this work.

© Springer International Publishing AG 2016
B. Leibe et al. (Eds.): ECCV 2016, Part IV, LNCS 9908, pp. 235–251, 2016.
DOI: 10.1007/978-3-319-46493-0_15

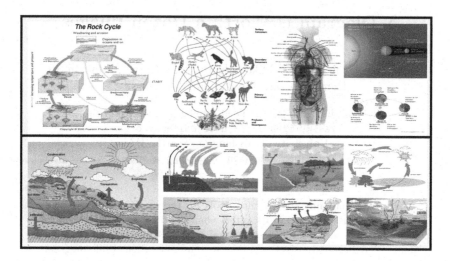

Fig. 1. The space of visual illustrations is very rich and diverse. The top palette shows the inter class variability for diagrams in our new diagram dataset, AI2D. The bottom palette shows the intra-class variation for the Water Cycles category.

Since they are purposefully designed to express information, they typically suppress irrelevant signals such as background clutter, intricate textures and shading nuances. This often makes the detection and recognition of individual elements inherently different than their counterparts, objects, in natural images. On the other hand, visual illustrations may depict complex phenomena and higher-order relations between objects (such as temporal transitions, phase transformations and inter object dependencies) that go well beyond what a single natural image can convey. For instance, one might struggle to find natural images that compactly represent the phenomena seen in some grade school science diagrams, as shown in Fig. 1. In this paper, we define the problem of understanding visual illustrations as identifying visual entities and their relations as well as establishing semantic correspondences to real-world concepts.

The characteristics of visual illustrations also afford opportunities for deeper reasoning than provided by natural images. Consider the food web in Fig. 1, which represents several relations such as foxes eating rabbits and rabbits eating plants. One can further reason about higher order relations between entities such as the effect on the population of foxes caused by a reduction in the population of plants. Similarly, consider the myriad of phenomena displayed in a single water cycle diagram in Fig. 1. Some of these phenomena are shown to occur on the surface of the earth while others occur either above or below the surface. The main components of the cycle (e.g. evaporation) are labeled and the flow of water is displayed using arrows. Reasoning about these objects and their interactions in such rich scenes provides many exciting research challenges.

In this paper, we address the problem of *diagram* interpretation and reasoning in the context of science diagrams, defined as the two tasks of *Syntactic parsing* and *Semantic interpretation*. *Syntactic parsing* involves detecting and recognizing constituents and their syntactic relationships in a diagram. This is most analogous to the problem of scene parsing in natural images. The wide variety of diagrams as well as large intra-class variation (Fig. 1 shows several varied images depicting a water cycle) make this step very challenging. *Semantic interpretation* is the task of mapping constituents and their relationships to semantic entities and events (real-world concepts). For example, an arrow in a food chain diagram typically corresponds to the concept of *consumption*, arrows in water cycles typically refer to *phase changes*, and arrows in a planetary diagram often refers to *rotatory motion*. This is a challenging task given the inherent ambiguities in the mapping functions. Hence we study it in the context of diagram question answering.

We introduce a representation to encode diagram constituents and their relationships in a graph, called diagram parse graphs (DPG) (example DPGs are shown in Fig. 6). The problem of syntactic parsing of diagrams is formulated as the task of learning to infer the DPG that best explains a diagram. We introduce a Deep Sequential Diagram Parser Network (DSDP-NET) that learns to sequentially add relationships and their constituents to form DPGs, using Long Short Term Memory (LSTM) networks. The problem of semantically interpreting a diagram and reasoning about the constituents and their relationships is studied in the context of diagram question answering. We present a neural network architecture (called DQA-NET) that learns to attend to useful relations in a DPG given a question about the diagram.

We compile a dataset named AI2 Diagrams (AI2D) of about 5000 grade school science diagrams with over 150000 rich annotations, their ground truth syntactic parses, and more than 15000 corresponding multiple choice questions. Our experimental results show that the proposed DSDP-NET for syntactic parsing outperforms several baseline methods. Moreover, we show that the proposed approach of incorporating diagram relations into question answering outperforms standard visual question answering methods.

Our contributions include: (a) We present two new tasks of diagram interpretation and reasoning, (b) we introduce the DPG representation to encode diagram parses and introduce a model that learns to map diagrams into DPGs, (c) we introduce a model for diagram question answering that learns the attention of questions into DPGs and (d) we present a new dataset to evaluate the above models with baselines[1].

2   Background

Understanding Diagrams. The problem of understanding diagrams received a fair amount of interest [13,29,41,49] in the 80's and 90's. However, many of these methods used hand written rules, assumed that the visual primitives were manually identified or worked on a specific set of diagrams. More recently, Futrelle et al. [14] proposed methods to analyze finite automata sketches but only worked with vector representations of diagrams. Recently, Seo et al. [36]

---

[1] Dataset and baselines available at http://allenai.org/plato/diagram_understanding.

proposed a method for understanding diagrams in geometry questions that identifies diagram elements by maximizing agreement between textual and visual data. In contrast to these approaches, we propose a unified approach to diagram understanding that builds upon the representational language of graphic representations proposed by Engelhardt [12] and works on a diverse set of diagrams.

The domain of abstract images has also received a considerable amount of interest over the past couple of years [5,48,54,58]. While abstract images significantly reduce the noise introduced by computer vision modules, thus bringing the semantics of the scene into focus, they still depict real world scenes, and hence differ significantly from diagrams which may depict more complex phenomena.

Parsing Natural Images. Several approaches to building bottom-up and top-down parsers have been proposed to syntactically parse natural images and videos. These include Bayesian approaches [45], And-Or graph structures [55], stochastic context free grammars [26], regular grammars [32], 3D Geometric Phrases [10] and a max margin structured prediction framework based on recursive neural networks [40]. Inspired by these methods, we adopt a graph based representation for diagrams.

Answering Questions. The task of question answering is an important area in the NLP community in several sub-domains including machine comprehension (MC) [16,35,50], science questions [7,20], geometry questions [37], algebra word problems [19,22] and open domain QA [52]. Our QA system is inspired from previous works, in particular from text based attention models [24,42] which we extend to diagrams. While MC systems attend on words or sentences from a reading passage, our system attends on the diagram via its parse graph. Analogously, the task of visual question answering (VQA) [4,15,25,34], which is to answer questions about an image has recently received considerable attention from the vision community. Attention models for VQA learn to attend on specific regions in the image, given the question [3,38,51,53,56]. Diagram images are vastly different from real images, and so are the corresponding questions. Hence, QA systems built for real images do not extend well, out of the box, for diagram QA tasks as we show in Sect. 7.4.

3   The Language of Diagrams

Much of the existing literature on graphic representations [9,18,46] covers only specific types of graphics or specific aspects of their syntactic structure. More recently, Engelhardt [12] proposed a coherent framework integrating various structural, semiotic and classification aspects that can be applied to the complete spectrum of graphic representations. We briefly describe some of his proposed principles below, as they apply to our space of diagrams, but refer the reader to [12] for a more thorough understanding.

A diagram is a composite graphic that consists of a graphic space, a set of constituents, and a set of relationships involving these constituents. A graphic space may be a metric space, distorted metric space (e.g. solar system diagram)

Table 1. Different types of relationships in our diagram parse graphs.

Intra-Object Label ($\mathbb{R}_1$): A text box naming the entire object
Intra-Object Region Label ($\mathbb{R}_2$): A text box referring to a region within an object
Intra-Object Linkage ($\mathbb{R}_3$): A text box referring to a region within an object via an arrow
Inter-Object Linkage ($\mathbb{R}_4$): Two objects related to one another via an arrow
Arrow Head Assignment ($\mathbb{R}_5$): An arrow head associated to an arrow tail
Arrow Descriptor ($\mathbb{R}_6$): A text box describing a process that an arrow refers to
Image Title ($\mathbb{R}_7$): The title of the entire image
Image Section Title ($\mathbb{R}_8$): Text box that serves as a title for a section of the image
Image Caption ($\mathbb{R}_9$): A text box that adds information about the entire image, but does not serve as the image title
Image Misc ($\mathbb{R}_{10}$): Decorative elements in the diagram

or a non-meaningful space (e.g. food web). Constituents in a diagram include illustrative elements (e.g. drawings of animals), textual elements, diagrammatic elements (e.g. arrows), informative elements (e.g. legends) and decorative elements. Relationships include spatial relations between constituents and the diagram space, and spatial and attribute-based relations between constituents (e.g. linkage, lineup, color variation, shape). An individual constituent may itself be a composite graphic, rendering this formulation recursive.

Our Representation: Diagram Parse Graph. We build upon Engelhardt's representation by introducing the concept of *Diagrammatic Objects* in our diagrams, defined as the primary entities being described in the diagram. Examples of objects include animals in the food web, the human body in an anatomy diagram, and the sun in water cycle (Fig. 1). The relationships within and between objects include intra-object, inter-object, and constituent-space relationships. We represent a diagram with a *Diagram Parse Graph* (DPG), in which nodes correspond to *constituents* and edges correspond to *relationships* between the constituents. We model four types of constituents: Blobs (Illustrations), Text Boxes, Arrows, and Arrow Heads.[2] We also model ten classes of relationships summarized in Table 1. Figure 6 shows some DPGs in our dataset.

---

[2] Separating arrow heads from arrow tails enables us to represent arrows with a single head, multiple heads or without heads in a uniform way.

4   Syntactic Diagram Parsing

Syntactic diagram parsing is the problem of learning to map diagrams into DPGs. Specifically, the goal is to detect and recognize constituents and their syntactic relationships in a diagram and find the DPG that best explains the diagram. We first generate proposals for nodes in the DPG using object detectors built for each constituent category (Sect. 7.1). We also generate proposals for edges in the DPG by combining proposal nodes using relationship classifiers (Sect. 7.2). Given sets of noisy node and edge proposals, our method then selects a subset of these to form a DPG by exploiting several local and global cues.

The constituent and relationship proposal generators result in several hundred constituent proposals and several thousand relationship proposals per diagram. These large sets of proposals, the relatively smaller number of true nodes and edges in the truth DPG and the rich nature of the structure of our DPGs, makes the search space for possible parse graphs incredibly large. We observe that forming a DPG amounts to choosing a subset of relationships among the proposals. Therefore, we propose a sequential formulation to this task that adds a relationship and its constituents at every step, exploiting local cues as well as long range global contextual cues using a memory-based model.

Model. We introduce a Deep Sequential Diagram Parser (DSDP-NET). Figure 2 depicts an unrolled illustration of DSDP-NET. Central to this is a stacked Long Short Term Memory (LSTM) recurrent neural network [17] with fully connected layers used prior to, and after the LSTM. Proposal relationships are then sequentially fed into the network, one at every time step, and the network predicts if this relationship (and its constituents) should be added to the DPG or not. Each relationship in our large candidate set is represented by a feature vector, capturing the spatial layout of its constituents in image space and their detection scores (more details in Sect. 7.3).

Training. LSTM networks typically require large amounts of training data. We provide training data to the DSDP-NET in the form of relationship sequences sampled from training diagrams. For each training diagram, we sample relationship sequences using sampling without replacement from thousands of relationship candidates, utilizing the relationship proposal scores as sampling weights. For each sampled sequence, we sequentially label the relationship at every time step by comparing the generated DPG to the ground truth DPG.[3]

The DSDP-NET is able to model dependencies between nodes and edges selected at different time steps in the sequence. It chooses relationships with large proposal scores but also learns to reject relationships that may lead to a high level of spatial redundancy or an incorrect structure in the layout. It also works well with a variable number of candidate relationships per diagram. Finally, it learns to stop adding relationships once the entire image space has been covered by the nodes and edges already present in the graph.

---

[3] A relationship labeled with a positive label in one sampled sequence may be labeled with a negative label in another sequence due to the presence of overlapping constituents and relationships in our candidate sets.

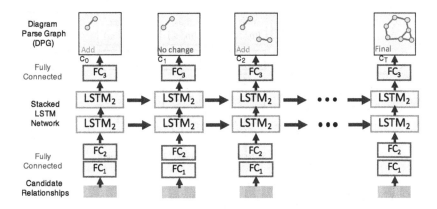

Fig. 2. An overview of the DSDP-NET solution to inferring DPGs from diagrams. The LSTM based network exploits global constrains such as overlap, coverage, and layout to select a subset of relations amongst thousands of candidates to construct a DPG.

Test. At test time, relationships in the candidate set are sorted by their proposal scores and presented to the network. Selected relationships are then sequentially added to form the final DPG.

5   Semantic Interpretation

DPGs represent the syntactic relationships between constituents of a diagram. They, however, do not encode the semantics of constituents and relationships. For example, the corresponding DPG in Fig. 4 indicates that `tree` and `mule deer` are related via in Inter-Object Linkage relationship, but it does not represent that the arrow corresponds to *consuming*. Constituents and relationships with a similar visual representation may have different semantic meanings in different diagrams. For example, the Inter-Object Linkage relationship can be interpreted as *consuming* in food webs and as *evaporation* in water cycles. Moreover, diagrams typically depict complex phenomena and reasoning about these phenomena goes beyond the tasks of matching and interpretation. For example, answering the question in Fig. 4 requires parsing the relationship between `trees` and `deer`, grounding the linkage to the act of *consuming* and reasoning about the effects of consumption on the populations of flora and fauna.

In order to evaluate the task of reasoning about the semantics of diagrams, we study semantic interpretation of diagrams in the context of diagram question answering. This is inspired by evaluation paradigms in school education systems and the recent progress in visual and textual question answering. Studying semantic interpretation of diagrams in the context of question answering also provides a well-defined problem definition, evaluation criteria, and metrics (Fig. 3).

Diagram Question Answering. A diagram question consists of a diagram d in raster graphics, a question sentence q, and multiple choices $\{c_1 \dots c_4\}$. The

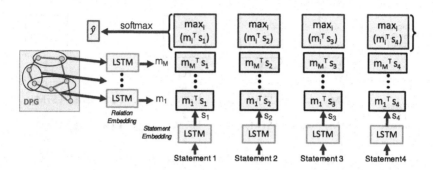

Fig. 3. An overview of the DQA-NET solution to diagram question answering. The network encodes the DPG into a set of facts, learns to attend on the most relevant fact, given a question and then answers the question.

goal of question answering is to select a single correct choice c_k given d and q (example questions in Fig. 7.)

We design a neural network architecture (called DQA-NET) to answer diagrammatic questions. The main intuition of the network is to encode the DPG into a set of facts and learn an attention model to find the closest fact to the question. For example, Fig. 7 shows facts that DQA-NET has selected to answer questions. More formally, DQA-NET consists of the following components: (a) a question embedding module that takes the question q and a choice $c_k, k \in \{1 \ldots 4\}$ to build a statement s_k and uses an LSTM to learn a d-dimensional embedding of the statement $s_k \in \mathbb{R}^d$; (b) a diagram embedding module that takes the DPG, extracts M relations $m_i, i \in \{1 \ldots M\}$ from DPG, and uses an LSTM to learn a d-dimensional embedding of diagram relations $m_i \in \mathbb{R}^d$; (c) an attention module that learns to attend to the relevant diagram relations by selecting the best statement choice that has a high similarity with the relevant diagram relations. For every statement s_k, our model computes a probability distribution over statement choices by feeding the best similarity scores between statements and diagram relations through a softmax layer.

$$\gamma_k = \max_i s_k^T \cdot m_i, \quad \hat{y} = \text{softmax}_k(\gamma_k) = \frac{\exp(\gamma_k)}{\sum_{k'} \exp(\gamma_{k'})}$$

We use cross entropy loss to train our model: $L(\theta) = H(y, \hat{y}) = -\sum_k y_k \log \hat{y}_k$. More details about the parameters can be found in Sect. 7.4.

6   Dataset

We build a new dataset (named AI2 Diagrams (AI2D)), to evaluate the task of diagram interpretation. AI2D is comprised of about 5000 diagrams representing topics from grade school science, each annotated with constituent segmentations and their relationships. In total, AI2D contains more than 118 K constituents and 53 K relationships. The dataset is also comprised of more than 15000 multiple

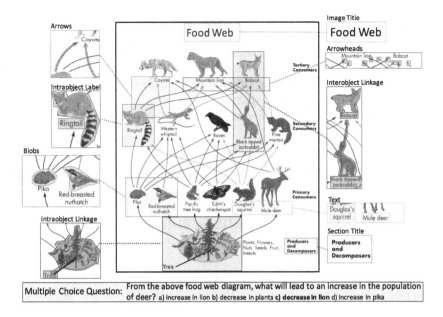

Fig. 4. An image from the AI2D dataset showing some of its rich annotations.

choice questions associated to the diagrams. We divide the AI2D dataset into a train set with about 4000 images and a blind test set with about 1000 images and report our numbers on this blind test set.

The images are collected by scraping Google Image Search with seed terms derived from the chapter titles in Grade 1–6 science textbooks. Each image is annotated using Amazon Mechanical Turk (AMT). Annotating each image with rich annotations such as ours, is a rather complicated task and must be broken down into several phases to maximize the level of agreement between turkers. Also, these phases need to be carried out sequentially to avoid conflicts in the annotations. The phases involve (1) annotating low-level constituents, (2) categorizing text boxes into one of four categories: relationship with the canvas, relationship with a diagrammatic element, intra-object and inter-object relationship, (3) categorizing arrows into one of three categories: intra-object, inter-object relationship or neither, (4) labelling intra-object linkage and inter-object linkage relationships. For this step, we display arrows to turkers and have them choose the origin and destination constituents in the diagram, (5) labelling intra-object label, intra-object region label and arrow descriptor relationships. For this purpose, we display text boxes to turkers and have them choose the constituents related to it, and finally (6) multiple choice questions with answers, representing grade school science questions are then obtained for each image. Figure 4 shows some of the rich annotations obtained for an image in the dataset.

7   Experiments

We describe methods used to generate constituent and relationship proposals with evaluations[4]. We also evaluate our introduced model DSDP-NET for syntactic parsing of diagrams that forms DPGs with comparisons to several baselines. Finally, we evaluate the proposed diagram question answering model DQA-NET and compare with standard visual question answering approaches.

7.1   Generating Constituent Proposals

Diagram Canvas: A diagram consists of multiple constituents overlaid onto a canvas, which may be uniformly colored, textured or have a blended image. We classify every pixel in the diagram into canvas vs constituent. We build nonparametric kernel density estimates (KDE) in RGB, texture and entropy spaces to generate features for a Random Forest (RF) classifier with 100 trees to obtain an Average Precision (AP) of 0.9142.

Detecting Blobs: Blobs exhibit a large degree of variability in their size, shape and appearance in diagrams, making them challenging to model. We combine segments at multiple levels of a segmentation hierarchy, obtained using Multiscale Combinatorial Grouping (MCG) [6] with segments produced using the canvas probability map to produce a set of candidates. Features capturing the location, size, central and Hu moments, etc. are provided to an RF classifier with 100 trees. *Baselines.* We evaluated several object proposal approaches including Edge Boxes [57], Objectness [2] and Selective Search [47]. Since these are designed to work on natural images, they do not provide good results on diagrams. We compare the RF approach to Edge Boxes, the most suitable of these methods, since it uses edge maps to propose objects and relies less on colors and gradients observed in natural images. **Results.** Our approach produces a significantly higher AP of 0.7829 compared to 0.02 (Fig. 5(a)).

Detecting Arrow Tails: Arrow tails are challenging to model since they are easily confused with other line segments present in the diagram and do not always have a corresponding arrow head to provide context. We generate proposal segments using a three pronged approach. We obtain candidates using the boundary detection method in [21], Hough transforms and by detecting parallel curved edge segments in a canny edge map; and recursively merge proximal segments that exhibit a low residual when fit to a 2nd degree polynomial. We then train a 2 class Convolutional Neural Network (CNN) resembling VGG-16 [39], with a fourth channel appended to the standard 3 channel RGB input. This fourth channel specifies the location of the arrow tail candidate smoothed with a Gaussian kernel of width 5. All filters except the ones for the fourth input channel at layer 1 are initialized from a publicly available VGG-16 model. The remaining filters are initialized with random values drawn from a Gaussian distribution. We use a batch size of 32 and a starting learning rate (LR) of 0.001.

---

[4] Constituent CNN models and DSDP-NET built using Keras [11], DQA-NET built using TensorFlow [1] and Random Forest models built using Scikit-learn [30].

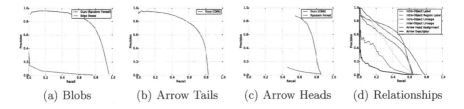

(a) Blobs	(b) Arrow Tails	(c) Arrow Heads	(d) Relationships

Fig. 5. Precision Recall curves for constituent and relationship proposal generators.

Results. Figure 5(b) shows the PR curve for our model with an AP of 0.6748. We tend to miss arrows that overlap significantly with more than three other arrows in the image as well as very thick arrows that are confused for blobs.

Detecting Arrow Heads: Arrow head proposals are obtained by a scanning window approach over 6 scales and 16 orientations. RGB pixels in each window undergo PCA followed by a 250 tree RF classifier. We then train a binary class CNN resembling the standard architecture of AlexNet [23] and initialize using a publicly available model. We use a batch size of 128 and a starting LR of 0.001. **Results.** Figure 5(c) shows the PR curves for our CNN model as well as the first pass RF model. We miss arrow heads which are extremely small and some which are present in poor quality images.

Detecting Text: We use Microsoft Project Oxford's Optical Character Recognition (OCR) service [27] to localize and recognize text. To improve the performance on single characters, we train a single character localizer using a CNN having the same architecture as AlexNet [23]. We use three training resources: (1) Chars74K (a character recognition dataset for natural images [8]), (2) a character dataset obtained from vector PDFs of scientific publications and (3) a set of synthetic renderings of single characters. The localized bounding boxes are then recognized using Tesseract [43]. **Results.** Using Tesseract end-to-end provides poor text localization results for diagrams with a 0.2 precision and a 0.46 recall. Our method improves the precision to 0.89 and recall to 0.75. Our false negatives comprise of vertically oriented and curved text, cursive fonts and unmerged multi-line blocks.

7.2 Generating Relationship Proposals

Relationship categories are presented in Table 1. Categories $\mathbb{R}_1$ through $\mathbb{R}_6$ relate two or more constituents with one another. We compute features capturing the spatial layout of the constituents with respect to one another as well as the diagram space and combine them with constituent detection probabilities. A 100 trees RF classifier is trained for each category. At test time, we generate proposal relationships from the large combinatorial set of candidate constituents using a proximity based pruning scheme. Categories $\mathbb{R}_7$ through $\mathbb{R}_{10}$ relate a single constituent with the entire image. We model each category using a non parametric Kernel Density Estimate (KDE) in X,Y space. **Results.** Figure 5(d)

Table 2. Results: (top) Syntactic parsing (bottom) QA (Q:question, I:image)

Method	Greedy Search	A* Search	Dsdp-Net
JIG Score	28.96	41.02	**51.45**

Method	Q + I (VQA)	Q	Q + I (VQA)	Q + OCR	Q + I + OCR	Dqa-Net
Train Set	VQA	AI2D	AI2D	AI2D	AI2D	AI2D
Accuracy	29.06	33.02	32.90	34.21	34.02	**38.47**

shows the PR curves for the relationships built using the RF classifier. The AP for several of relationships is low, owing to the inherent ambiguity in classifying relationships using local spatial decisions.

7.3   Syntactic Parsing: DPG Inference

Our Model DSDP-Net: The introduced DSDP-NET (depicted in Fig. 2) consists of a 2 layer stacked LSTM with each layer having a hidden state of dimensionality 512. The LSTM is preceded by two fully connected layers with an output dimensionality of 64 and a Rectified Linear Unit (ReLu) [28] activation function each. The LSTM is proceeded by a fully connected layer with a softmax activation function. This network is trained using RMSProp [44] to optimize the cross-entropy loss function. The initial learning rate is set to 0.0002.

Each candidate relationship is represented as a 92 dimensional feature vector that includes features for each constituent in the relationship (normalized x,y coordinates, detection score, overlap ratio with higher scoring candidates and the presence of this constituent in relationships presented to the network at prior time-steps) and features describing the relationship itself (relationship score and the presence of tuples of candidates in relationships presented to the network at previous time steps). We sample 100 relationship sequences per training image to generate roughly 400000 training samples. At test time, relationships are presented to the network in sorted order, based on their detection scores.

Baselines: GREEDY SEARCH: The first baseline is a greedy algorithm whereby nodes and edges are greedily added to the DPG using their proposal scores. It uses an *exit* model as a stopping condition. The exit model is trained to score DPGs based on their distance to the desired completed DPG. To train the exit model, we use features capturing the quality, coverage, redundancy and structure of the nodes and edges in the DPGs and use 100 tree RF models.
A* SEARCH: The second baseline is an A* search, which starts from an empty DPG and sequentially adds nodes and edges according to a cost. We improve upon the greedy algorithm by training a RF model that utilizes local and contextual cues to rank available constituents and relationships. The cost function for each step is a linear combination of the RF score and the distance of the resultant DPG to the desired complete DPG. We use the same exit model as before to approximate the distance from the goal.

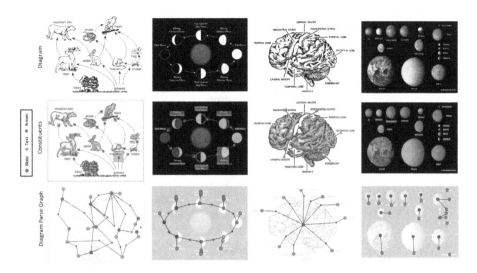

Fig. 6. Inferred DPGs using DSDP-NET. The first row shows the diagram, the second row shows the constituent segmentations and the third row shows the inferred DPGs.

DIRECT REGRESSION: We also trained a CNN to directly regress the DPG, akin to YOLO [33]. This generated no meaningful results on our dataset.

Evaluation. To evaluate these methods, we compute the Jaccard Index between the sets of nodes and edges in our proposed DPG and the ground truth DPG. We refer to this metric by the Jaccard Index for Graphs (JIG) score. The Jaccard Index, which measures similarity between finite sample sets, is defined as the size of the intersection divided by the size of the union of the sample sets.

Results. Table 2(*top*) shows the mean JIG scores, computed over the test set for each method. The DSDP-NET method outperforms both the GREEDY SEARCH and A* SEARCH by a considerable margin. This shows the importance of our sequential formulation to use LSTMs for adding relationships to form DPGs. Figure 6 shows qualitative examples of inferred DPGs using DSDP-NET.

7.4   Diagram Question Answering

Our Model DQA-Net: DQA-NET uses GloVe [31] model pre-trained on 6B tokens (Wikipedia 2014) to map each word to a 300D vector. The LSTM units have 1 layer, 50 hidden units, and forget bias of 2.5. We place a 50-by-300 FC layer between the word vectors and the LSTM units. The LSTM variables in all sentence embeddings (relation and statement) are shared. The loss function is optimized with stochastic gradient descent with batch size of 100. Learning rate starts at 0.01 and decays by 0.5 every 25 epochs, for 100 epochs in total.

Baselines. We use the best model (LSTM Q+I) from [4] as the baseline. Similar to the DQA-NET setup, a question-answer pair is translated to a statement and

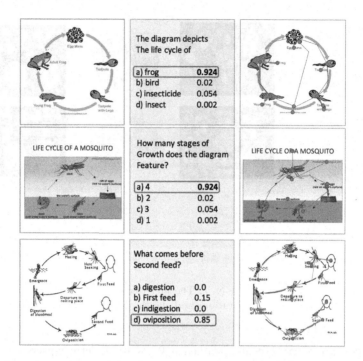

Fig. 7. Sample question answering results using DQA-NET. The second column shows the answer chosen and the third column shows the nodes and edges in the DPG that DQA-NET decided to attend to (indicated by red highlights). (Color figure online)

then passed through an LSTM into a 50D vector. The diagram is passed through a pre-trained VGG-16 model [39] followed by an FC layer into a 50D vector. We then compute the dot product between the statement and image vectors, followed by a softmax layer. We use cross entropy loss and the same optimization techniques as in DQA-NET. We also perform an ablation study using similar models but with just the question text (Q), question+image (Q+I) (VQA) and question + image + outputs of an OCR system (Q+I+OCR). **Results.** Table 2(*bottom*) reports the accuracy of different methods on the test set. DQA-NET outperforms VQA, both when it is trained on the VQA dataset as well as the AI2Ddataset. This shows that the DPG more effectively encodes high-level semantics of the diagrams, which are required to answer AI2D questions. Figure 7 shows examples of correctly answered questions by DQA-NET.

8   Conclusion

We introduced the task of diagram interpretation and reasoning. We proposed DSDP-NET to parse diagrams and create DPGs that encode the syntactical information depicted in the diagram. We introduced DQA-NET that learns to answer diagram questions by attending to diagram relations encoded with DPGs. Our experimental results show improvements of Dsdp-Net in parsing diagrams compared to strong baselines. We also show that Dqa-Net outperforms standard VQA techniques in diagram question answering. Diagram interpretation and reasoning raises new research questions that goes beyond natural image understanding. We release AI2D and our baselines to facilitate further research in diagram understanding and reasoning. Future work involves incorporating diagrammatic and commonsense knowledge in DQA.

Acknowledgements. This work is in part supported by ONR N00014-13-1-0720, NSF IIS-1338054, NSF IIS-1616112, Allen Distinguished Investigator Award and contracts from the Allen Institute for Artificial Intelligence.

References

1. Abadi, M., et al.: TensorFlow: large-scale machine learning on heterogeneous systems (2015)
2. Alexe, B., Deselaers, T., Ferrari, V.: Measuring the objectness of image windows. IEEE Trans. Pattern Anal. Mach. Intell. **34**, 2189–2202 (2012)
3. Andreas, J., Rohrbach, M., Darrell, T., Klein, D.: Learning to compose neural networks for question answering. In: NAACL (2016)
4. Antol, S., Agrawal, A., Lu, J., Mitchell, M., Batra, D., Lawrence Zitnick, C., Parikh, D.: Vqa: visual question answering. In: ICCV (2015)
5. Antol, S., Zitnick, C.L., Parikh, D.: Zero-shot learning via visual abstraction. In: Fleet, D., Pajdla, T., Schiele, B., Tuytelaars, T. (eds.) ECCV 2014. LNCS, vol. 8692, pp. 401–416. Springer, Heidelberg (2014). doi:10.1007/978-3-319-10593-2_27
6. Arbelaez, P.A., Pont-Tuset, J., Barron, J.T., Marques, F., Malik, J.: Multiscale combinatorial grouping. In: CVPR (2014)
7. Berant, J., Srikumar, V., Chen, P.C., Linden, A.V., Harding, B., Huang, B., Clark, P., Manning, C.D.: Modeling biological processes for reading comprehension. In: Proceedings of EMNLP (2014)
8. de Campos, T.E., Babu, B.R., Varma, M.: Character recognition in natural images. In: International Conference on Computer Vision Theory and Applications (2009)
9. Card, S.K., Mackinlay, J.D., Shneiderman, B.: Readings in Information Visualization: Using Vision to Think. Morgan Kaufmann, San Francisco (1999)
10. Choi, W., Chao, Y.W., Pantofaru, C., Savarese, S.: Understanding indoor scenes using 3d geometric phrases. In: CVPR (2013)
11. Chollet, F.: Keras (2015). https://github.com/fchollet/keras
12. von Engelhardt, J.: The Language of Graphics: A Framework for the Analysis of Syntax and Meaning in Maps, Charts and Diagrams. Yuri Engelhardt, Amsterdam (2002)
13. Ferguson, R.W., Forbus, K.D.: Telling juxtapositions: using repetition and alignable difference in diagram understanding. In: Holyoak, K., Gentner, D., Kokinov, B. (eds.) Advances in Analogy Research, pp. 109–117. New Bulgarian University, Sofia (1998)
14. Futrelle, R.P., Shao, M., Cieslik, C., Grimes, A.E.: Extraction, layout analysis and classification of diagrams in pdf documents. In: ICDAR (2003)
15. Gao, H., Mao, J., Zhou, J., Huang, Z., Wang, L., Xu, W.: Are you talking to a machine? dataset and methods for multilingual image question answering. In: NIPS (2015)

16. Hermann, K.M., Kocisky, T., Grefenstette, E., Espeholt, L., Kay, W., Suleyman, M., Blunsom, P.: Teaching machines to read and comprehend. In: NIPS (2015)
17. Hochreiter, S., Schmidhuber, J.: Long short-term memory. Neural Comput. **9**, 1735–1780 (1997)
18. Horn, R.: Visual Language: Global Communication for the 21st Century. MacroVU, Brainbridge Island (1998)
19. Hosseini, M.J., Hajishirzi, H., Etzioni, O., Kushman, N.: Learning to solve arithmetic word problems with verb categorization. In: EMNLP (2014)
20. Khashabi, D., Khot, T., Sabharwal, A., Clark, P., Etzioni, O., Roth, D.: Question answering via integer programming over semi-structured knowledge. In: IJCAI (2016)
21. Kokkinos, I.: Highly accurate boundary detection and grouping. In: CVPR (2010)
22. Koncel-Kedziorski, R., Hajishirzi, H., Sabharwal, A., Etzioni, O., Damon Ang, S.: Parsing algebraic word problems into equations. Trans. Assoc. Comput. Linguist. **3**, 585–597 (2015)
23. Krizhevsky, A., Sutskever, I., Hinton, G.E.: Imagenet classification with deep convolutional neural networks. In: NIPS (2012)
24. Kumar, A., Irsoy, O., Ondruska, P., Iyyer, M., Bradbury, J., Gulrajani, I., Zhong, V., Paulus, R., Socher, R.: Ask me anything: dynamic memory networks for natural language processing. In: ICML (2016)
25. Malinowski, M., Fritz, M.: A multi-world approach to question answering about real-world scenes based on uncertain input. In: NIPS (2014)
26. Martinovic, A., Gool, L.J.V.: Bayesian grammar learning for inverse procedural modeling. In: CVPR (2013)
27. Microsoft: Project oxford. https://www.projectoxford.ai/
28. Nair, V., Hinton, G.E.: Rectified linear units improve restricted boltzmann machines. In: ICML (2010)
29. O'Gorman, L., Kasturi, R.: Document Image Analysis. IEEE Computer Society Executive Briefings (1997)
30. Pedregosa, F., et al.: Scikit-learn: machine learning in Python. J. Mach. Learn. Res. **12**, 2825–2830 (2011)
31. Pennington, J., Socher, R., Manning, C.D.: Glove: global vectors for word representation. In: EMNLP (2014)
32. Pirsiavash, H., Ramanan, D.: Parsing videos of actions with segmental grammars. In: CVPR (2014)
33. Redmon, J., Divvala, S.K., Girshick, R.B., Farhadi, A.: You only look once: unified, real-time object detection. In: CVPR (2016)
34. Ren, M., Kiros, R., Zemel, R.: Exploring models and data for image question answering. In: NIPS (2015)
35. Richardson, M., Burges, C.J.C., Renshaw, E.: Mctest: a challenge dataset for the open-domain machine comprehension of text. In: EMNLP (2013)
36. Seo, M.J., Hajishirzi, H., Farhadi, A., Etzioni, O.: Diagram understanding in geometry questions. In: AAAI (2014)
37. Seo, M.J., Hajishirzi, H., Farhadi, A., Etzioni, O., Malcolm, C.: Solving geometry problems: combining text and diagram interpretation. In: EMNLP (2015)
38. Shih, K.J., Singh, S., Hoiem, D.: Where to look: focus regions for visual question answering. In: CVPR (2016)
39. Simonyan, K., Zisserman, A.: Very deep convolutional networks for large-scale image recognition. arXiv preprint arXiv:1409.1556 (2014)
40. Socher, R., Lin, C.C.Y., Ng, A.Y., Manning, C.D.: Parsing natural scenes and natural language with recursive neural networks. In: ICML (2011)

41. Srihari, R.K.: Computational models for integrating linguistic and visual information: a survey. Artif. Intell. Rev. **8**, 349–369 (1994)
42. Sukhbaatar, S., Szlam, A., Weston, J., Fergus, R.: End-to-end memory networks. In: NIPS (2015)
43. Tesseract: Open source ocr engine. https://github.com/tesseract-ocr/tesseract
44. Tieleman, T., Hinton, G.E.: Lecture 6.5-rmsprop: divide the gradient by a running average of its recent magnitude. In: COURSERA: Neural Networks for ML (2012)
45. Tu, Z., Chen, X., Yuille, A.L., Zhu, S.C.: Image parsing: unifying segmentation, detection, and recognition. In: CLOR (2003)
46. Twyman, M.: A schema for the study of graphic language (tutorial paper). In: Kolers, P.A., Wrolstad, M.E., Bouma, H. (eds.) Processing of Visible Language, pp. 117–150. Springer, New York (1979)
47. Uijlings, J.R.R., van de Sande, K.E.A., Gevers, T., Smeulders, A.W.M.: Selective search for object recognition. Int. J. Comput. Vis. **104**, 154–171 (2013)
48. Vedantam, R., Lin, X., Batra, T., Zitnick, C.L., Parikh, D.: Learning common sense through visual abstraction. In: ICCV (2015)
49. Watanabe, Y., Nagao, M.: Diagram understanding using integration of layout information and textual information. In: ACL (1998)
50. Weston, J., Bordes, A., Chopra, S., Mikolov, T.: Towards ai-complete question answering: a set of prerequisite toy tasks. In: ICLR (2016)
51. Xu, H., Saenko, K.: Ask, attend and answer: exploring question-guided spatial attention for visual question answering. arXiv preprint arXiv:1511.05234 (2015)
52. Yang, Y., Yih, W., Meek, C.: WikiQA: a challenge dataset for open-domain question answering. In: EMNLP (2015)
53. Yang, Z., He, X., Gao, J., Deng, L., Smola, A.: Stacked attention networks for image question answering. In: CVPR (2016)
54. Zhang, P., Goyal, Y., Summers-Stay, D., Batra, D., Parikh, D.: Yin and yang: balancing and answering binary visual questions. arXiv preprint arXiv:1511.05099 (2015)
55. Zhu, S.C., Mumford, D.: A stochastic grammar of images. Found. Trends Comput. Graph. Vis. **2**, 259–362 (2006)
56. Zhu, Y., Groth, O., Bernstein, M.S., Fei-Fei, L.: Visual7w: grounded question answering in images. In: CVPR (2016)
57. Zitnick, C.L., Dollár, P.: Edge boxes: locating object proposals from edges. In: Fleet, D., Pajdla, T., Schiele, B., Tuytelaars, T. (eds.) ECCV 2014. LNCS, vol. 8693, pp. 391–405. Springer, Heidelberg (2014). doi:10.1007/978-3-319-10602-1_26
58. Zitnick, C.L., Parikh, D.: Bringing semantics into focus using visual abstraction. In: CVPR (2013)

Automatic Attribute Discovery
with Neural Activations

Sirion Vittayakorn[1]([⊠]), Takayuki Umeda[2], Kazuhiko Murasaki[2], Kyoko Sudo[2], Takayuki Okatani[3], and Kota Yamaguchi[3]

[1] University of North Carolina at Chapel Hill, Chapel Hill, USA
sirionv@cs.unc.edu
[2] NTT Media Intelligence Laboratories, Yokosuka, Japan
[3] Tohoku University, Sendai, Japan

Abstract. How can a machine learn to recognize visual attributes emerging out of online community without a definitive supervised dataset? This paper proposes an automatic approach to discover and analyze visual attributes from a noisy collection of image-text data on the Web. Our approach is based on the relationship between attributes and neural activations in the deep network. We characterize the visual property of the attribute word as a divergence within weakly-annotated set of images. We show that the neural activations are useful for discovering and learning a classifier that well agrees with human perception from the noisy real-world Web data. The empirical study suggests the layered structure of the deep neural networks also gives us insights into the perceptual depth of the given word. Finally, we demonstrate that we can utilize highly-activating neurons for finding semantically relevant regions.

Keywords: Concept discovery · Attribute discovery · Saliency detection

1 Introduction

In a social photo sharing service such as Flickr, Pinterest or Instagram, a new word can emerge at any moment, and even the same word can change its semantics and transforms our vocabulary set at any time. For instance, the word *wicked* (literally means evil or morally wrong) is often used as a synonym of *really* among teenagers in these recent years - *"Wow, that game is wicked awesome!"*. In such a dynamic environment, how can we discover emerging visual concepts and build a visual classifier for each concept without a concrete dataset? It is unrealistic to manually build a high-quality dataset for learning every visual concepts for every application domains, even if some of the difficulty can be mitigated by the human-in-the-loop approach [2,3]. All we have are the observations but not definitions, provided in the form of co-occurring words and images.

In this paper, we consider an automatic approach to learn visual attributes from the open-world vocabulary on the Web. There have been numerous attempts of learning novel concepts from the Web in the past [1,5,6,9,37].

© Springer International Publishing AG 2016
B. Leibe et al. (Eds.): ECCV 2016, Part IV, LNCS 9908, pp. 252–268, 2016.
DOI: 10.1007/978-3-319-46493-0_16

What distinguishes our work from the previous efforts is in that we try to understand potentially-attribute words in terms of perception inside neural networks. Deep networks demonstrate outstanding performance in object recognition [11,15,27], and successfully apply to a wide range of tasks including learning from noisy data [30,31] or sentiment analysis [13,34]. In this paper, we focus on the analysis of neural activations to identify the degree of being visually perceptible, namely *visualness* of a given attribute, and take advantage of the layered structure of the deep model to determine the semantic depth of the attribute.

We collect two domain-specific datasets from online e-commerce and social networking websites. We study in domain-specific data rather than trying to learn general concept on the Web [5,6] to isolate contextual dependency of attributes to object categories. For example, the term *red eye* can refer to an overnight airline flight or an eye that appears red due to illness or injury. This contextual dependency can cause an ambiguity for the visual classifier (*red* classifier); i.e., sense disambiguation. In this paper, we use a single-domain dataset to reduce such a semantic shift to study consistent meaning of attributes under the fixed context [1,16].

We show that, using a trained neural network, we are able to characterize a visual attribute word by the divergence of neural activations in the weakly-annotated data. Figure 1 illustrates our framework. Our approach starts by cleaning the noisy Web data to find potentially visual attributes in the dataset, then splits the data into positive and negative sets. Using a pre-trained neural network, we identify highly activating neurons by KL divergence of activations. We show that we can use the identified neurons (prime units) for (1) learning a novel attribute classifier that is close to human perception, (2) understanding perceptual depth of the attribute, and (3) identifying attribute-specific saliency in the image. We summarize our contributions in the following.

1. We propose to utilize the divergence of neural activation as a descriptor to characterize visual concept in the noisy weakly annotated dataset. The neurons identified by the divergence can help learn a visual attribute classifier that has a close proximity to human perception.
2. We empirically study the relationship between human perception and the depth of activations to understand the visual semantics of attribute words.

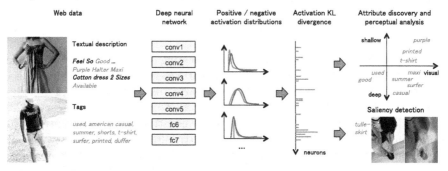

Fig. 1. Our attribute discovery framework. (Color figure online)

3. We show that the highly activating neurons according to the divergence are also useful for detecting attribute-specific saliency in the given image.
4. We collect two noisy datasets from the Web to evaluate our framework. The empirical study shows we are able to learn a domain-specific visual attributes without manual annotation.

2   Related Work

Attribute Discovery. Our work is related to the recent work on concept discovery from a collection of images from the Web [5,6,9,28,37]. Early work by Ferrari *et al.* [9] learns visual models of given attributes (e.g., red, spotted) from images collected from text search. NEIL [5] aims at discovering common sense knowledge from the Web starting from small exemplar images per concept. LEVAN [6] starts from mining bi-gram concepts from a large text corpus, and automatically retrieves training images from the Internet and learn a full-fledged detector for each concept. ConceptLearner [37] uses weakly labeled image collections from Flickr to train visual concept detectors. Shankar *et al.* [24] study the attribute discovery in weakly-supervised scenario, where the goal is to identify co-occurring but missing attributes in the dataset while learning a deep network. Recent work by Sun *et al.* [28] takes advantage of natural language to discover concepts for retrieval scenario. The automatic attribute discovery by Berg *et al.* [1] is close to our work in that the work tries to evaluate visualness of the discovered synsets of attributes in the e-commerce scenario. The major difference of our approach from the previous works is that we aim at discovering attribute words and also characterizing the attribute perception using neural activations.

Neural Representation. Thanks to the outstanding performance of deep neural networks in various tasks such as object recognition [11,15,27,29] or domain adaptation for visual recognition task [19], the deep analysis of the intermediate representation of the neural networks has been getting more attention [33,35,38]. Escorcia *et al.* [7] and Ozeki *et al.* [20] study the relationship between neural representation and attributes. In this paper, we aim at utilizing the intermediate representation for visually characterizing unknown words in the noisy dataset, and study how the representation relates to human perception of attributes.

Class-Specific Saliency Detection. Detecting class or attribute-specific saliency has been studied in the past in various forms, for example, as co-segmentation [4], parts [19,25] or latent parts discovery [14], and weakly-supervised [10,36] or fully-supervised labeling [21,22]. While Simonyan *et al.* [26] uses gradient as a class-specific saliency, we demonstrate that the receptive field of neurons [38] can effectively identify the attribute-specific regions with our activation divergence. Our neuron-level saliency detection performs comparable to gradient-based approach [26], and can also reveal us insight into how learning changes the neurons' response to visual stimuli.

3   Datasets and Pre-processing

3.1   Etsy Dataset

Etsy dataset is a collection of data from the online market of handcrafted products. Each product listing in Etsy contains an image, a title, a product description, and various metadata such as tags, category, or price. We initially crawl over 2.8 million product pages from etsy.com. Considering the trade-off between dataset size and domain specificity, we select the product images under the clothing category, which include 247 subcategories such as clothing/women/dress.

Near-Duplicate Removal. As common in any Web data, the raw data from Etsy contain a huge amount of near-duplicates. The major characteristics of Etsy data are the following: There are many shops, but the number of sold items per shop exhibits a long-tail. The same shop tends to sell similar items, e.g., the same black hoodie in the same background with a different logo patch, and in an extreme case, just a few words (proper nouns) are different in the product description. Our near-duplicate removal is primarily designed to prevent such proper nouns from building up a category. We observe that without the removal, we severely suffer from overfitting and end up with meaningless results.

Based on the above observation, we apply the following procedure to remove near-duplicates in Etsy: (1) Group product listings by shop. (2) Compute a bag-of-words from title and description except English stop words for each item within the group. (3) Compute the cosine distance between all pairs of products. (4) Apply agglomerative clustering by thresholding the pairwise cosine distance. (5) Randomly pick one product from each cluster. We apply the duplicate-removal for all shops in the dataset, and for each shop we merge any pairs of product having less than 0.1 cosine distance into the same cluster. After the near-duplicate removal, we observed that roughly 40 % of the products in Etsy were considered near-duplicates. We obtained 173,175 clothing products for our experiment.

Syntactic Analysis. Given the title and description of the product in Etsy dataset, we apply syntactic analysis [17] and extract part-of-speech (POS) tags for each word. In this paper, we consider 250 most frequent adjectives (JJ, JJR, and JJS tags) as potential attribute words. Unless noted, we use the (50 %, 25 %, 25 %) splits for train, test, and validation in the following experiments.

3.2   Wear Dataset

We crawled a large collection of images from the social fashion sharing website, wear.jp. The website contains an image, associated shots from different views, list of items, blog text, tags, and other metadata. The images in Wear dataset are extremely noisy; Many users take a photo with a mobile device under uncontrolled lighting conditions and inconsistent photo composition, making it very challenging to apply any existing fashion recognition approach [32]. From the crawled data, we use the random subset of 212,129 images for our experiments.

Merging Synonyms and Translations. From Wear dataset, we select user-annotated tags for candidate words. The majority of tags from Wear dataset are written in Japanese (some in English), but there are also multiple synonyms treated as different tags including typos. We observe such synonyms and translations creating many duplicates. To mitigate this problem, we remove synonyms by translating all words to English, using Google Translate, and merge words that maps to the same English word. After translation, we pick up the most frequent 250 tags as a set of attribute candidates and use for our experiment. Note that machine-translation is not perfect and we manually fix translation errors in the selected tags.

4   Attribute Discovery

Our attribute discovery framework starts by first splitting the weakly-annotated dataset into positive and negative sets, then computes Kullback-Leibler divergence (KL) for each activation unit in the deep neural network. We use the KL divergence to determine the important neurons for the given attributes. With these selected neurons, we can estimate the degree of *visualness* of attributes.

4.1   Divergence of Neural Activations

Although the image representation (neural activations) from the deep network captures numerous discriminative features in an image [35], each neuron in the network only sparsely responds to visual stimuli. We attempt to find neurons that highly respond to the visual pattern associated with a given attribute word. We propose to use the KL divergence of activations to identify these highly responding neurons or *prime units* for the given attribute.

Our framework starts by splitting the dataset D into positive and negative sets according to the weak annotation (adjectives or tags in Sect. 3). Positive or negative sets D_u^+, D_u^- are images with or without the candidate attribute-word u. Note the noisy annotation contains both false-positive and false-negative samples. Using a pre-trained neural network, we compute the empirical distribution of neural activations from all of the units in the network. Let us represent the empirical distribution of the positive/negative set by P_i^+ and P_i^- for each neuron i. For convolutional layers, we max-pool the spatial dimension in all channels and compute histograms P_i^+, P_i^-, since the maximum response is sufficient to identify unique units regardless of the location. Finally, we compute the symmetric KL divergence S_i for each activation unit i of the network:

$$
\begin{aligned}
S_i(u|D) &\equiv D_{\mathrm{KL}}(P_i^+||P_i^-) + D_{\mathrm{KL}}(P_i^-||P_i^+) \\
&= \sum_x P_i^+(x) \log \frac{P_i^+(x)}{P_i^-(x)} + \sum_x P_i^-(x) \log \frac{P_i^-(x)}{P_i^+(x)},
\end{aligned}
\tag{1}
$$

where x is the activation of the unit corresponding to histogram bins. The resulting KL divergence $S_i(u|D)$ serves as an indicator to find prime units for the word u.

The intuition is that if the word is associated to specific visual stimuli, the activation pattern of the positive set should be different from the negative set and that should result in a larger KL divergence for visual attributes (e.g., red, white, floral, stripped) than less visual attributes (e.g., expensive or handmade). In other word, we should be able to identify the visual pattern associated to the given word by finding neurons with higher KL divergence.

4.2 Visualness

We follow the previous work [1] and define the visualness in terms of the balanced classification accuracy given the positive and negative sets:

$$V(u|f) \equiv \text{accuracy}(f, D_u^+, D_u^-), \tag{2}$$

where f is a binary classification function. To eliminate the bias influence in the accuracy, we randomly subsample the positive and negative sets D_u^+, D_u^- to obtain balanced examples (50%-50%). We use neural activations as a feature representation to build a classifier, and use the KL divergence S_i as resampling and feature-selection criteria to identify important features for a given word u.

Selecting and Resampling by Activations. The noisy positive and negative sets D^+, D^- bring undesirable influence when evaluating the classification accuracy of the word (Eq. 2). Here, we propose to learn a visual classifier in two steps; we first learn an initial classifier based only on the activations from prime units, then we rank images based on the classification confidence. After that, we learn a stronger classifier from the confident samples using all of the activations in the network. More specifically, we first select 100 prime units according to the KL divergence (Eq. 1), and use the activations from these units as a feature (100 dimensions) to learn an initial classifier[1] using logistic regression [8] and identify the confident samples for the second classifier.

Learning Attribute Classifier. Once we learn the initial classifier, we rank images based on the confidence, resample the same number of images from both positive and negative sets according to the ranked order, and learn another attribute classifier using logistic regression from all of the activations (9,568 dimensions). Although more than 8,000 activations are from FC layers, the information gain is not necessarily proportional to the number of dimensions; FC layers tend to fire only a handful neurons, whereas convolutional layers after max-pooling give dense activations. Finally, the accuracy evaluation (Eq. 2) on the balanced test set gives the visualness of the given word.

---

[1] Gaussian Naive Bayes also works in our setting, but a stronger classifier such as SVM with RBF kernel tends to overfit.

4.3 Human Perception

To evaluate our approach, we collect human judgment of visualness using crowd-sourcing, and compute the correlation between our visualness and human perception. Following the observation in [23] that it is harder for humans to provide the absolute visualness score of attribute than the relative score. Thus, we design a task on Amazon Mechanical Turk as follows; given a word, we provide two images to the annotators where one is from the positive set and the other is from the negative set. We ask annotators to pick an image that is more relevant to the given attribute, or if there is none, answer none. We pick the 100 most frequent words in Etsy dataset for evaluation purpose. For each word, we randomly pick 50 pairs of positive and negative images, and asked 5 annotators to complete one task. We define the human visualness $H(u)$ of word u as the ratio of positive annotator agreements:

$$H(u) \equiv \frac{1}{N} \sum_{k}^{N} \mathbf{1} \left[h_k^+(u) > \theta \right], \tag{3}$$

where $\mathbf{1}$ is an indicator function, $h_k^+(u)$ is the number of positive votes for image pair k, N is the number of annotated images, and θ is a threshold. We set $\theta = 3$ for 5 annotators in our experiment. Equation 3 allows us to convert the relative comparison into agreement score, which is in absolute scale.

4.4 Experimental Results

We use the Etsy dataset to evaluate our visualness.[2] Since neurons activate differently depending on the training data, we compare the following models:

- **Pre-trained:** Reference CaffeNet model [15] implemented in [12], pre-trained on ImageNet 1000 categories.
- **Attribute-tuned:** A CNN fine-tuned to directly predict the weakly-annotated words in the dataset, ignoring the noise. We replaced the soft-max layer in CaffeNet with a sigmoid to predict 250 words (Sect. 3.1).
- **Category-tuned:** A CNN fine-tuned to predict the 247 sub-categories of clothing using metadata in Etsy dataset, such as t-shirt, dress, etc.

We choose the basic AlexNet to evaluate how fine-tuning affects in our attribute discovery task, but we can also apply a different CNN architecture such as VGG [27] to do the same. The category-tuned model is to see the effect of domain transfer without overfitting to the target labels. We compare the following different visualness definitions against human.

- **CNN+random:** Randomly subsample the same number of positive and negative images, learn a logistic regression from all of the neural activations (9,568 dimensions) in CNN, and use the testing accuracy to define the visualness. This is similar to the visualness prediction in the previous work [1] except that we use neural activations as a feature.

---

[2] Due to the translation issues, we were not able to get reliable human judgments in Wear dataset.

- **CNN+initial:** Testing accuracy of the initial classifier trained on the most activating neurons or prime units.
- **CNN+resample:** Testing accuracy of the attribute classifier trained on the resampled images according to the confidence of the initial classifier and learned from all of the neural activations, as described in Sect. 4.2.
- **Attribute-tuned:** Average precision of the direct prediction of the Attribute-tuned CNN in the balanced test set. We choose average precision instead of accuracy due to severe overfitting to our noisy training data.
- **Language prior:** The n-gram frequency of adjective-noun modification for the given attribute-word from the Google Books N-grams [18]. We show the language prior as a reference to understand the scenario when we do not have access to visual data at all. The assumption is that for each of the object category in Etsy, visual modifier should co-occur more than non-visual words. We compute the prior using the sum of n-gram probability on attribute-category modification to 20 nouns in the Etsy clothing categories.

Quantitative Evaluation. Table 1 summarizes the Pearson and Spearman correlation coefficients to human perception using different definitions of visualness together with the feature dimension. *Note that achieving the highest accuracy in classification does not mean the best proximity to human perception in the noisy dataset.* The results show that even though the initial classifiers learn from only 100 dimensional feature from prime units, they achieve the higher Spearman correlation to human perception than the random baselines with much larger feature. Moreover, resampling images by the initial classifier confidence improves the correlation to human perception over the random baseline in all models. These results confirm that feature-selection and resampling using the high-KL neurons help discovering visual attributes in the noisy dataset.

The result also suggests directly fine-tuning against the noisy annotation can harm the representational ability of neurons. We suspect that fine-tuning

Table 1. Visualness correlation to human perception.

Method	Feature dim.	Pearson	Spearman
Pre-trained+random (baseline)	9, 568	0.737	0.637
Pre-trained+initial	100	0.760	0.663
Pre-trained+resample	9, 568	**0.799**	0.717
Attribute-tuned	4, 096	0.662	0.549
Attribute-tuned+random	9, 568	0.716	0.565
Attribute-tuned+initial	100	0.716	0.603
Attribute-tuned+resample	9, 568	0.782	**0.721**
Category-tuned+random	9, 568	0.760	0.684
Category-tuned+initial	100	0.663	0.480
Category-tuned+resample	9, 568	0.783	0.704
Language prior	–	0.139	0.032

Table 2. Most and least visual attributes discovered in Etsy dataset.

Method	Most visual	Least visual
Human	Flip pink red floral blue	Url due last right additional
	Sleeve purple little black yellow	Sure free old possible cold
Pre-trained+resample	Flip pink red yellow green	Big great due much own
	Purple floral blue sexy elegant	Favorite new free different good
Attribute-tuned	Flip sexy green floral yellow	Right same own light happy
	Pink red purple lace loose	Best small different favorite free
Language prior	Top sleeve front matching waist	Organic lightweight classic gentle adjustable
	Bottom lace dry own right	Floral adorable url elastic super

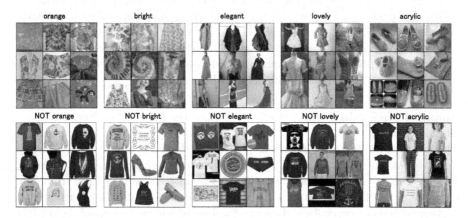

Fig. 2. Examples of most and least predicted images for some of the attributes. (Color figure online)

to a domain-specific data with possibly non-visual word leads to overfitting and suppresses neurons' activity even if they are important in recognition. The pre-trained network gives the slightly higher Pearson correlation perhaps because the neurons are trained on wider range of visual stimuli in the ImageNet than in a domain-specific data like Etsy, and that somehow helps reproducing human perception. The low correlation from language prior indicates the difficulty of detecting visual attributes only from textual knowledge.

Qualitative Evaluation. Table 2 lists the most and least visual attributes for selected methods. Note that the error in syntactic analysis incorrectly marked some nouns as adjective, such as *url* or *flip* (flip-flops) here. Generally, CNN-based methods result in a similar choice of the words. Language prior is picking very different vocabulary perhaps due to the lack of domain-specific knowledge in Google Books.

Figure 2 shows examples of the most or least confident images according to the pre-trained+resample model. From concrete concepts like *orange* to more abstract concepts *elegant*, we confirm that our automatic approach can learn various attributes only from the noisy dataset. Figure 3 shows examples of the

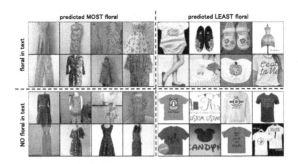

Fig. 3. Most and least *floral* images. With our automatically learned classifier, we can discover false-negatives and false-positives in the dataset. (Color figure online)

most and least *floral* images from both positive and negative sets. The noise in the dataset introduces a lot of false-negatives (not mentioned but actually floral product) and false-positives (mentioned floral in text but not relevant to the product). Our automatically learned attribute classifiers can function as a dataset purifier in a noisy dataset.

5   Understanding Perceptual Depth

In this section, we explore how each layer in the neural networks relates to attributes. It is well-known that neurons in a different layer activate to different types of visual pattern [7,35]. We further attempt to understand what type of semantic concepts directly relate to neurons using the KL divergence.

We consider the activation with respect to the layer depth. We compute the relative magnitude of max-pooled KL divergence for layer l:

$$S_l(u|D) \equiv \frac{1}{Z} \max_{i \in l} S_i(u|D), \text{ where } Z \equiv \sum_l \max_{i \in l} S_i(u|D). \tag{4}$$

We are able to identify the most *salient words* by ranking attribute vocabulary based on $S_l(u|D)$. In the following experiments, we use 7 layers in CaffeNet.

We use both Etsy and Wear dataset for finding salient words at each layer. Table 3 lists the most salient words for each layer of the pre-trained CNN in the two datasets. We can clearly see that more primitive visual concepts like color (e.g., *orange*, *green*) appear in the earlier stage of the CNN, and as we move down the network towards the output, we observe more complex visual concepts. We can observe the same trend from both Etsy and Wear datasets even though the two datasets are very different. Note that there are non-visual words in a general sense due to the dataset bias. For example, *genuine* in Etsy tends to appear in the context of *genuine leather*, and *many* appear in the context of *many designs available* for sweatshirt products. Such dataset bias results in higher divergence of neurons' activity. One approach to deal with such context-dependency is probably to consider a phrase instead of a word.

Table 3. Most salient words for each CNN layer.

(a) Etsy dataset

norm1	norm2	conv3	conv4	pool5	fc6	fc7
orange	green	bright	flattering	lovely	many	sleeve
colorful	red	pink	lovely	elegant	soft	sole
vibrant	yellow	red	vintage	natural	new	acrylic
bright	purple	purple	romantic	beautiful	upper	cold
blue	colorful	green	deep	delicate	sole	flip
welcome	blue	lace	waist	recycled	genuine	newborn
exact	vibrant	yellow	front	chic	friendly	large
yellow	ruffle	sweet	gentle	formal	sexy	floral
red	orange	french	formal	decorative	stretchy	waist
specific	only	black	delicate	romantic	great	american

(b) Wear dataset

norm1	norm2	conv3	conv4	pool5	fc6	fc7
blue	denim-jacket	border-	kids	shorts	white-skirt	long-skirt
green	pink	striped-tops	bucket-hat	half-length	flared-skirt	suit-style
red-black	red	border-	hat-n-glasses	pants	spring	midi-skirt
red	red-socks	stripes	black	denim	upper	gaucho-pants
denim-on-	red-black	dark-style	sleeveless	dotted	beret	handmade
denim	champion	stripes	american-	border-	shirt-dress	straw-hat
denim-shirt	blue	backpack	casual	stripes	overalls	white-n-
pink	white	red	long-	white-pants	hair-band	white
denim	shirt	dark-n-dark	cardigan	border-tops	loincloth-	white-
yellow	i-am-clumsy	denim-shirt	white-n-	gingham-	style	coordinate
leopard	yellow	navy	white	check	matched-	white-pants
		outdoor-	stole	sandals	pair	white
		style	mom-style	chester-coat		

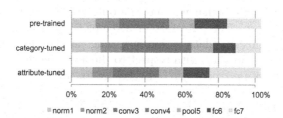

Fig. 4. Relative magnitude of average layer-wise maximum KL divergence. (Color figure online)

How Fine-Tuning Affects Perceptual Depth. Fine-tuning has an influence on the magnitude of the layer-wise max-pooled KL in that (1) the pre-trained model activates almost equally across layers and (2) the category-tuned model induced larger divergence in mid-layer (conv4), while (3) the attribute-tuned model activates more in the last layer (fc7). Figure 4 shows the relative magnitude of average layerwise max-pooled KL: $M_l \equiv \frac{1}{|U|} \sum_{u \in U} \sum_{i \in l} S_i(u|D)$. The attribute-tuning causes a direct change in the last layer as expected, whereas the category-tuning brings a representational change in the mid-layers. The result suggests the domain-specific knowledge is encoded inside the mid-to-higher level representation, but there are domain-agnostic features in the earliest layers perhaps useful for recognizing primitive attributes such as color. Moreover, we also

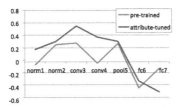

Fig. 5. Pearson correlation coefficients between human visualness and max KL divergence of each CNN layer. (Color figure online)

observe that the set of salient words per layer stay similar after fine-tuning in either cases; earlier layers activate more on primitive attributes, color or texture, and later layers activate more on abstract words.

How Each Layer Relates to Human Perception. Finally, we evaluate how each layer relates to human perception, using the annotation from Sect. 4.3. Figure 5 plots Pearson correlation of the layer-wise maximum KL divergence (Eq. 4) against human visualness. We show the correlation of pre-trained and attribute-tuned CNNs. The plot suggests the activation of mid-layers is closer to human visualness perception, but interestingly, the last fully-connected layers give negative correlation. We think that the last layers are more associated to abstract words that are not generally considered visual by humans, but they are contextually associated in a domain-specific data as in *genuine leather* case.

6 Saliency Detection

Cumulative Receptive Fields. We consider saliency detection with respect to the given attribute based on the receptive field [38]. The main idea is to accumulate neurons' response in the order of the largest KL divergence. Following [38], we first apply a sliding-window occluder to the given image, feed the occluded image to the CNN, and observe the difference in activation as a function of the occluder location $a_i(x, y)$ for unit i. We take the occluder patch at (x, y) from the mean image of the dataset, at different scales. In our experiment, we use 24×24, 48×48, and 96×96 occluder size with stride size 4 for the 256×256 image input to the CNN. After getting the response map $a_i(x, y)$, we apply a Gaussian filter with the scale proportional to the occluder size, and average out multiple scale responses to produce a single response map. The resulting response map $A_i(x, y)$ can have either positive or negative peaks to the input pattern, and we heuristically negate and invert the response map if the map has negative peaks. We normalize the response map within $[0, 1]$ scale. Let us denote this normalized response map of unit i by $R_i(x, y)$. We compute the final saliency map M by accumulating units ordered and weighted by the KL divergence:

$$M(x, y | u, I) \equiv \frac{1}{Z} \sum_i^K S_i(u|D) R_i(x, y|I), \tag{5}$$

where $Z = \sum_i^K S_i(u|D)$. We accumulate units by the largest unit divergence $S_i(u|D)$ up to K.

Human Annotation. We use Wear dataset for saliency evaluation, since the images in Etsy dataset are mostly a single object appearing in the center of the image frame and there is merely a localization need. Similarly to Sect. 4.3, we collect human annotation on the salient region for evaluation purpose. For the randomly selected set of 10 positive images for the most frequent 50 tags in Wear dataset, we ask 3 workers to draw bounding boxes around the relevant region to the specified tag-word. We consider pixels having 2 or more annotator votes to be the ground-truth salient regions. We discard images not having any worker agreement in the evaluation.

Experimental Results. Figure 6 plots the average performance from all the tags in terms of mean average precision (mAP) for predicting pixel-wise binary labels, and mean intersection-over-union (IoU) of the attribute-tuned model. We compute IoU for the binarized saliency map $M(x,y|u,I) \geq \theta$ at different threshold θ. The plots show the performance with respect to the number of accumulations K, as well as the baseline performance of the smoothed gradient magnitude [26] of the attribute-tuned model. The performance improves as more neurons accumulate in the saliency map according to the divergence, and gives on par or slightly better performance against the baseline. Note that even the pre-trained model can already reach the baseline by this simple accumulation based on KL divergence, without any optimization towards saliency. We observe improvement in both pre-trained and attribute-tuned models, but the pre-trained model tends to require more neurons. We believe that fine-tuning makes each neuron activate more to a specific pattern while reducing activations on irrelevant patterns, and that results in the diminishing accumulation effect.

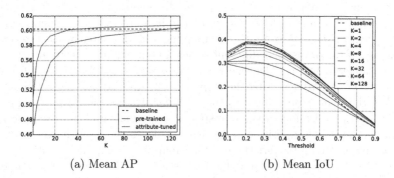

(a) Mean AP   (b) Mean IoU

Fig. 6. Saliency detection performance in terms of (a) mean average precision and (b) mean IoU of the attribute-tuned model over the heat-map threshold. (Color figure online)

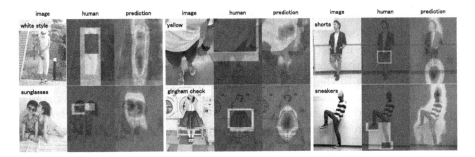

Fig. 7. Results of detected salient regions for the given attribute. The rightmost column shows failure cases due to distracting contexts or visibility issues. (Color figure online)

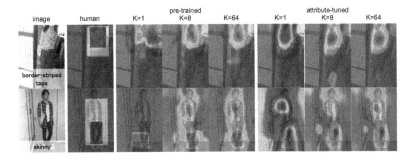

Fig. 8. Accumulating receptive fields by the largest KL divergence. As we add more neurons, the saliency heat-map becomes finer. (Color figure online)

The result also suggests that visual attributes are combinatorial visual stimuli rather than some visual pattern detectable only with a single neuron.

Figure 8 shows the detection results by human annotation and our cumulative receptive field using the pre-trained and fine-tuned CNNs, when the accumulation size K is 1, 8, and 64. Also, Fig. 7 shows the results of human annotation and the pre-trained CNN with accumulation size $K = 64$. Our saliency detection method works remarkably well *even without fine-tuning*. As we accumulate more neurons, the response map tends to produce finer localization. Accumulation helps most of the cases, but we observe failure cases when there is a distractor co-occuring with the given attribute. For example in Fig. 7, detecting shorts fails because legs always appear with shorts and we end up with legs detector instead of shorts (distractor issue). Moreover, our method tends to fail when the target attribute is associated to only small regions in the image (visibility issue).

7   Conclusion

We have shown that we are able to discover and analyze a new visual attribute from noisy Web data using neural activations. The key idea is the use of highly activating neurons in the network, identified by the divergence of activation distribution in the weakly annotated dataset. Empirical study using two real-world data gives us insights that our approach can automatically learn a visual attribute classifier that has a perceptual ability similar to humans, the depth in the network relates to the depth of attribute perception, and the neurons can detect salient regions in the given image. In the future, we wish to further study the relationship and similarity between discovered visual attributes and how the network architecture changes the neural perception in the hierarchical structure.

Acknowledgement. This work was partly supported by JSPS KAKENHI Grant Number 15H05919.

References

1. Berg, T.L., Berg, A.C., Shih, J.: Automatic attribute discovery and characterization from noisy web data. In: Daniilidis, K., Maragos, P., Paragios, N. (eds.) ECCV 2010. LNCS, vol. 6311, pp. 663–676. Springer, Heidelberg (2010). doi:10.1007/978-3-642-15549-9_48
2. Biswas, A., Parikh, D.: Simultaneous active learning of classifiers & attributes via relative feedback. In: CVPR, pp. 644–651 (2013)
3. Branson, S., Wah, C., Schroff, F., Babenko, B., Welinder, P., Perona, P., Belongie, S.: Visual recognition with humans in the loop. In: Daniilidis, K., Maragos, P., Paragios, N. (eds.) ECCV 2010. LNCS, vol. 6314, pp. 438–451. Springer, Heidelberg (2010). doi:10.1007/978-3-642-15561-1_32
4. Chai, Y., Rahtu, E., Lempitsky, V., Gool, L., Zisserman, A.: TriCoS: a tri-level class-discriminative co-segmentation method for image classification. In: Fitzgibbon, A., Lazebnik, S., Perona, P., Sato, Y., Schmid, C. (eds.) ECCV 2012. LNCS, vol. 7572, pp. 794–807. Springer, Heidelberg (2012). doi:10.1007/978-3-642-33718-5_57
5. Chen, X., Shrivastava, A., Gupta, A.: Neil: extracting visual knowledge from web data. In: ICCV, pp. 1409–1416, December 2013
6. Divvala, S., Farhadi, A., Guestrin, C.: Learning everything about anything: webly-supervised visual concept learning. In: CVPR (2014)
7. Escorcia, V., Niebles, J.C., Ghanem, B.: On the relationship between visual attributes and convolutional networks. In: CVPR, pp. 1256–1264 (2015)
8. Fan, R.E., Chang, K.W., Hsieh, C.J., Wang, X.R., Lin, C.J.: LIBLINEAR: A library for large linear classification. J. Mach. Learn. Res. **9**, 1871–1874 (2008)
9. Ferrari, V., Zisserman, A.: Learning visual attributes. In: Advances in Neural Information Processing Systems, pp. 433–440 (2007)
10. Guillaumin, M., Kuttel, D., Ferrari, V.: ImageNet auto-annotation with segmentation propagation. Int. J. Comput. Vis. **110**(3), 328–348 (2014)
11. He, K., Zhang, X., Ren, S., Sun, J.: Deep residual learning for image recognition. CVPR **7**(3), 171–180 (2015)
12. Jia, Y., Shelhamer, E., Donahue, J., Karayev, S., Long, J., Girshick, R., Guadarrama, S., Darrell, T.: Caffe: Convolutional architecture for fast feature embedding. arXiv preprint arXiv:1408.5093 (2014)
13. Jou, B., Chen, T., Pappas, N., Redi, M., Topkara, M., Chang, S.F.: Visual affect around the world: a large-scale multilingual visual sentiment ontology. ACM Multimed. (1), 159–168 (2015)

14. Kiapour, M.H., Yamaguchi, K., Berg, A.C., Berg, T.L.: Hipster wars: discovering elements of fashion styles. In: Fleet, D., Pajdla, T., Schiele, B., Tuytelaars, T. (eds.) ECCV 2014. LNCS, vol. 8689, pp. 472–488. Springer, Heidelberg (2014). doi:10.1007/978-3-319-10590-1_31

15. Krizhevsky, A., Sutskever, I., Hinton, G.E.: Imagenet classification with deep convolutional neural networks. In: NIPS (2012)

16. Lampert, C.H., Nickisch, H., Harmeling, S.: Learning to detect unseen object classes by between-class attribute transfer. In: CVPR, pp. 951–958 (2009)

17. de Marneffe, M.C., MacCartney, B., Manning, C.D.: Generating typed dependency parses from phrase structure parses. In: Proceedings of LREC, vol. 6, pp. 449–454 (2006)

18. Michel, J.B., Shen, Y.K., Aiden, A.P., Veres, A., Gray, M.K., Team, T.G.B., Pickett, J.P., Holberg, D., Clancy, D., Norvig, P., Orwant, J., Pinker, S., Nowak, M.A., Aiden, E.L.: Quantitative analysis of culture using millions of digitized books. Science **331**, 176–182 (2010)

19. Oquab, M., Bottou, L., Laptev, I., Sivic, J.: Learning and transferring mid-level image representations using convolutional neural networks. In: CVPR pp. 1717–1724 (2014)

20. Ozeki, M., Okatani, T.: Understanding convolutional neural networks in terms of category-level attributes. In: Cremers, D., Reid, I., Saito, H., Yang, M.-H. (eds.) ACCV 2014. LNCS, vol. 9004, pp. 362–375. Springer, Heidelberg (2015). doi:10.1007/978-3-319-16808-1_25

21. Pan, H., Jiang, H.: A deep learning based fast image saliency detection algorithm. arXiv preprint arXiv:1602.00577 (2016)

22. Pan, H., Wang, B., Jiang, H.: Deep learning for object saliency detection and image segmentation. arXiv preprint arXiv:1505.01173 (2015)

23. Parikh, D., Grauman, K.: Relative attributes. In: ICCV, pp. 503–510. IEEE (2011)

24. Shankar, S., Garg, V.K., Cipolla, R.: DEEP-CARVING: discovering visual attributes by carving deep neural nets. In: CVPR, pp. 3403–3412 (2015)

25. Simon, M., Rodner, E.: Neural Activation Constellations: Unsupervised Part Model Discovery with Convolutional Networks. CVPR **21**(1), 1–37 (2015)

26. Simonyan, K., Vedaldi, A., Zisserman, A.: Deep inside convolutional networks: visualising image classification models and saliency maps. In: ICLR, p. 1 (2014). https://arxiv.org/abs/1312.6034

27. Simonyan, K., Zisserman, A.: Very deep convolutional networks for large-scale image recognition. arXiv preprint arXiv:1409.1556, pp. 1–14 (2014)

28. Sun, C., Gan, C., Nevatia, R.: Automatic concept discovery from parallel text and visual corpora. In: ICCV, pp. 2596–2604 (2015)

29. Szegedy, C., Liu, W., Jia, Y., Sermanet, P., Reed, S., Anguelov, D., Erhan, D., Vanhoucke, V., Rabinovich, A.: Going deeper with convolutions. In: CVPR 2015 (2015)

30. Xiao, T., Xia, T., Yang, Y., Huang, C., Wang, X.: Learning from massive noisy labeled data for image classification. In: CVPR, pp. 2691–2699 (2015)

31. Vo, P.D., Ginsca, A., Borgne, H.L., Popescu, A.: On Deep Representation Learning from Noisy Web Images. arXiv preprint arXiv:1512.04785 (2015)

32. Yamaguchi, K., Kiapour, M.H., Ortiz, L.E., Berg, T.L.: Retrieving similar styles to parse clothing. TPAMI **37**(5), 1028–1040 (2015)

33. Yosinski, J., Clune, J., Nguyen, A., Fuchs, T., Lipson, H.: Understanding neural networks through deep visualization. In: Deep Learning Workshop, International Conference on Machine Learning (ICML) (2015)

34. You, Q., Luo, J., Jin, H., Yang, J.: Robust image sentiment analysis using progressively trained and domain transferred deep networks. In: AAAI, pp. 381–388 (2015)
35. Zeiler, M.D., Fergus, R.: Visualizing and understanding convolutional networks. In: Fleet, D., Pajdla, T., Schiele, B., Tuytelaars, T. (eds.) ECCV 2014. LNCS, vol. 8689, pp. 818–833. Springer, Heidelberg (2014). doi:10.1007/978-3-319-10590-1_53
36. Zhou, B., Khosla, A., Lapedriza, A., Oliva, A., Torralba, A.: Learning deep features for discriminative localization. In: CVPR (2016)
37. Zhou, B., Jagadeesh, V., Piramuthu, R.: Conceptlearner: discovering visual concepts from weakly labeled image collections. In: CVPR, June 2015
38. Zhou, B., Khosla, A., Lapedriza, A., Oliva, A., Torralba, A.: Object detectors emerge in deep scene CNNs. In: ICLR, p. 12 (2014)

"What Happens If..." Learning to Predict the Effect of Forces in Images

Roozbeh Mottaghi[1]([✉]), Mohammad Rastegari[1], Abhinav Gupta[1,2],
and Ali Farhadi[1,3]

[1] Allen Institute for AI, Seattle, USA
roozbehm@allenai.org
[2] Carnegie Mellon University, Pittsburgh, USA
[3] University of Washington, Seattle, USA

Abstract. *What happens if* one pushes a cup sitting on a table toward the edge of the table? How about pushing a desk against a wall? In this paper, we study the problem of understanding the movements of objects as a result of applying external forces to them. For a given force vector applied to a specific location in an image, our goal is to predict long-term sequential movements caused by that force. Doing so entails reasoning about scene geometry, objects, their attributes, and the physical rules that govern the movements of objects. We design a deep neural network model that learns long-term sequential dependencies of object movements while taking into account the geometry and appearance of the scene by combining Convolutional and Recurrent Neural Networks. Training our model requires a large-scale dataset of object movements caused by external forces. To build a dataset of forces in scenes, we reconstructed all images in SUN RGB-D dataset in a physics simulator to estimate the physical movements of objects caused by external forces applied to them. Our Forces in Scenes (ForScene) dataset contains 65,000 object movements in 3D which represent a variety of external forces applied to different types of objects. Our experimental evaluations show that the challenging task of predicting long-term movements of objects as their reaction to external forces is possible from a single image. The code and dataset are available at: http://allenai.org/plato/forces.

Keywords: Scene understanding · Forces · Motion estimation · Recurrent Neural Networks

1 Introduction

An important component in visual reasoning is the ability to understand the interaction between forces and objects; and the ability to predict the movements caused by those forces. We humans have an amazing understanding of how applied and action-reaction forces work. In fact, even with a static image [1,10], humans can perform a mental simulation of the future states and reliably predict the dynamics of the interactions. For example, a person can easily predict that the couch in Fig. 2(a) will not move if it is pushed against the wall and the mouse in Fig. 2(b) will eventually drop if it is pushed towards the edge of a desk.

© Springer International Publishing AG 2016
B. Leibe et al. (Eds.): ECCV 2016, Part IV, LNCS 9908, pp. 269–285, 2016.
DOI: 10.1007/978-3-319-46493-0_17

In this paper, we address the problem of predicting the effects of external forces applied to an object in an image. Figure 1 shows a long-term prediction of the sequence of movements of a cup when it is pushed toward the edge of the table. Solving this problem requires reliable estimates of the scene geometry, the underlying physics, and the semantic and geometric properties of objects. Additionally, it requires reasoning about interactions between forces and objects where subtle changes in how the force is applied might cause significant differences in how objects move. For example, depending on the magnitude of the force, the cup remains on the table or falls. What makes this problem more challenging is the sequential nature of the output where predictions about movements of objects depend on the estimates from the previous time steps. Finally, a data-driven approach to this problem requires a large-scale training dataset that includes movements of objects as their reaction to external forces. Active interaction with different types of scenes and objects to obtain such data is non-trivial.

Most visual scene understanding methods (e.g., [9, 25, 40]) are *passive* in that they are focused on predicting the scene structure, the objects, and their attributes and relations. These methods cannot estimate what happens if some parts of the scene are changed actively. For example, they can predict the

What happens if the cup is pushed towards the edge of the table?

Input

Output

Fig. 1. Our goal is to learn "What happens if Force X is applied to Point Y in the scene?". For example, from a single image, we can infer that the cup will drop if we push it towards the edge of the table. On the right we show the output of our method, i.e. a sequence of velocities in 3D.

(a)   (b)   (c)   (d)

Fig. 2. Subtle differences in forces cause significantly different movements. The force is shown in yellow and the direction of movement is shown in green. (a) No movement is caused by the force since there is a wall behind the sofa. (b) The force changes the height of the object. The mouse drops as the result of applying the force. (c) The object might move in the opposite direction of the force. The chair initially moves in the direction of the force, but it bounces back when it hits the desk. (d) The direction of the movement and the force is the same. (Color figure online)

location or 3D pose of a sofa, but they cannot predict how the sofa will move if it is pushed from behind. In this paper, we focus on an *active* setting, where the goal is to predict *"What happens if Force X is applied to Point Y in the scene?"*.

We design a deep neural network model that learns long-term sequential dependencies of object movements while taking into account the geometry and appearance of the scene by combining Convolutional and Recurrent Neural Networks. The RNN learns the underlying physical rules of movements while the CNN implicitly encodes the appearance and geometry of the object and the scene. To obtain a large number of observations of forces and objects to train this model, we collect a new dataset using physics engines; current datasets in the literature represent static scenes and are not suitable for active settings. Instead of training our model on synthetic images we do the inverse: we replicate the scenes in SUN RGB-D dataset [32] in a physics engine. The physics engine can then simulate forward the effect of applying forces to different objects in each image. We use the original RGB images, the forces, and their associated movements to form our dataset for training and evaluation.

Our experimental evaluations show that the challenging task of predicting long-term movements of objects as their reaction to external forces is possible from a single image. Our model obtains promising results in predicting the direction of the velocity of objects in 3D as the result of applying forces to them. We provide results for different variations of our method and show that our model outperforms baseline methods that perform regression and nearest neighbor search using CNN features. Furthermore, we show that our method generalizes to object categories that it has not seen during training.

2   Related Work

Passive scene understanding. There is a considerable body of work on scene understanding in the vision literature, e.g., [4,9,12,20,21,25,31,40,42]. However, most of these works propose *passive* approaches, where they infer the *current* configuration of the scenes (location of the objects, their 3D pose, support relationship, etc.) depicted in images or videos. In contrast, our method is an *active* approach, where we predict the result of interacting with objects using forces.

Physics-based prediction. [24] estimate the forces applied to the object and its trajectory for an action that is already happening in a scene. In this paper, we predict the future movements of the object for a *given force*. [8] predict the effect of forces in a billiard scene. Our method infers the movements based on a single image, while [8] uses a sequence of images. Also, [8] works on synthetic billiard scenes, while our method works on realistic images. [44] detect potentially falling objects given a point cloud representing the scene. In contrast, our method is based solely on visual cues and does not explicitly use physics equations.

Estimating physical properties. [2] estimate the physical parameters of rigid objects using video data. [3] estimates forces applied to a human using the dynamics of contacts with different surfaces. [39] learn a model for estimating physical properties of objects such as mass and friction based on a series of videos that show movement of objects on an inclined surface. These methods are not designed to predict the result of applying new forces to the scene and are limited to their controlled settings.

Stability inference. [43] reasons about the stability of objects in a given point cloud. [13] solves a joint optimization for segmentation, support relationships and stability. [14] propose a method to place a new object in a stable and semantically preferred location in a scene. Our method, in contrast, predicts the future movements of objects caused by applying forces to them.

Predicting sequences using neural networks. [28] propose a recurrent architecture to predict future frames of a video. [26] propose a recurrent neural net to predict the next frame in an Atari game given the current action and the previous frames. [33] propose Recurrent RBMs to model high dimensional sequences. [23] model temporal dependencies of a sequence and predict multiple steps in the future. These approaches either require a full sequence (past states and current actions) or work only on synthetic data and in limited environments. Also, [19] propose a deep-learning based method to perform a pre-defined set of tasks. They learn a distribution over actions given the current observation and configurations. In contrast, we predict how the scene changes as the result of an action (i.e. applying forces). In the language domain, [15,34] have used a combination of CNNs and RNNs to generate captions for images.

Data-driven prediction. [36] infers the future path of rigid objects according to learned models of appearance, context, and transition. [27,37] predict optical flow from a single image. [41] predict future events that might take place in a query image. [16] estimate future movements of humans in a given scene. [7] predicts relative movements of objects. Unlike these approaches, we explicitly represent forces and focus on the physics of the scene in order to infer future movements of objects in 3D.

Physics-based tracking. [30] recover 3D trajectories and the forces applied to objects in a tracking framework. [35] incorporates physical plausibility into a human tracking framework. Our problem is different from tracking since we perform inference using a single image.

3   Problem Statement

Given a query object in a single RGB image and a force vector, our goal is to predict the future movement of the object as the result of applying the force to the object. More specifically, for a force f and an impact point p on the object surface in the RGB image, our goal is to estimate a variable-length sequence of velocity directions $V = (v_0, v_1, \ldots, v_t)$ for the center of the mass of the object. These velocities specify how the location of the object changes over time.

For training we need to obtain the sequence V that is associated to force $f = (f_x, f_y, f_z)$ applied to point $p = (p_u, p_v)$ in the image. To this end, we automatically synthesize the scene in a physics engine (described in Sect. 4).

Fig. 3. Synthetic scenes. These example scenes are synthesized automatically from the images in the SUN RGB-D [32] dataset. Left: the original image, Middle: point cloud representation, Right: synthetic scene. The objects that belong to the same category are shown with the same color. For clarity, we do not visualize the walls.

The physics engine simulates forward the effect of applying the force to the point that corresponds to p in the 3D synthetic scene and generates the velocity profile and locations for the query object.

During testing, we do not have access to the synthesized scene or the physics engine, and our goal is to predict the sequence V given a query object in a single RGB image and a force[1].

We formulate the estimation of the movements as a sequential classification problem. Hence, each v_t takes a value from the set $\mathcal{L} = \{l_1, l_2, \ldots, l_N, s\}$, where each l_i denotes the index for a direction in the quantized space of 3D directions, and s represents 'stop' (no motion). The velocity at each time step v_t depends on the previous movements of the object. Therefore, a natural choice for modeling these temporal dependencies is a recurrent architecture. To couple the movement information with the appearance and geometry of the scene and also the force representation, our model integrates a Recurrent Neural Network (RNN) with a Convolutional Neural Network (CNN). Section 5 describes the details of the architecture.

4   Forces in Scenes (ForScene) Dataset

One of the key requirements of our approach is an *interactable* dataset. Most of the current datasets in the vision community are 'static' datasets in that we cannot apply forces to objects depicted in the scenes and modify the scenes. For example, we cannot move the constituent objects of the scenes shown in PASCAL [6] or COCO [22] images as we desire since inferring the depth map and the physics of the scene from a single RGB image is a challenging problem. An alternative would be to use RGB-D images, where the depth information is available. This solves the problem of depth estimation and moving the objects in perspective, but RGB-D images do not provide any information about the physics of the world either.

---

[1] We refer to the force and its impact point as *force* throughout the paper.

To make an *interactable* dataset, we transfer the objects and the scene layout shown in images to a physics engine. The physics engine takes a scene and a force as input and simulates the future states of the objects in the scene according to the applied forces. This enables us to collect the velocity sequences that we require for training our model.

Our dataset is based on the SUN RGB-D dataset [32], which includes 2D and 3D annotations in the form of 2D semantic segmentation and 3D bounding boxes for about 1,000 object categories. The 3D position and orientation of each bounding box is provided in the annotations, hence, we can transfer the 3D bounding boxes of the objects to the physics engine and reconstruct the same object arrangement in the physics engine. In addition, the SUN RGB-D dataset includes annotations for the scene layout (floors, walls, etc.). We replicate the scene layout in the physics engine as well. Figure 3 shows a few examples of the images and their corresponding scenes in the physics engine. More details about the dataset can be found in Sect. 6.1. Note that our training and evaluation is performed on real images. These synthetic scenes only supply the groundtruth velocity information.

5   Model

We now describe different components of our model, how we represent objects and forces in the model and how we formulate the problem to predict the movements.

5.1   Model Architecture

Our model has three main components: (1) A Convolutional Neural Network (CNN) to encode scene and object appearance and geometry. We refer to this part of the model as *image tower*. (2) Another CNN (parallel to the image tower) to capture force information. We refer to this part of the model as *force tower*. (3) A Recurrent Neural Network (RNN) that receives the output of the two CNNs and generates the object motion (or equivalently, a sequence of vectors that represent the velocity of the object at each time step). Note that the training is end-to-end and is performed jointly for all three components of the model. Figure 4 illustrates the architecture of the full network.

We use two different architectures for the image tower for the experiments: AlexNet [17] and ResNet-18 [11], where we remove their final classification layer. Similar to [24], the input to our image tower is a four-channel RGB-M image, where we add a mask channel (M) to the RGB image. The mask channel represents the location of the query object and it is obtained by applying a Gaussian kernel to a binary image that shows the bounding box of the query object. We propagate the output of the layer before the last layer of the CNN (e.g., FC7 when we use AlexNet) to the next stages of the network.

The force tower is structured as an AlexNet [17] and is parallel to the image tower. The input to the force tower is an RGB image that represents the impact

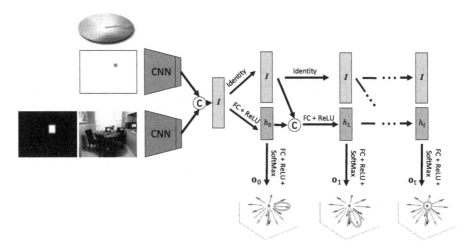

Fig. 4. Model. Our model consists of two CNNs for capturing the *force* and *image* information. We refer to these CNNs as force tower and image tower respectively. The input to the model is a force image and an RGB-M image (RGB image plus an M channel representing object bounding box). The color in the force image represents the direction and magnitude of the force (according to the color wheel). The symbol ©denotes concatenation. 'Identity' propagates the input to the output with no change. h_t represents the hidden layer of the RNN at time step t. Also, we use the abbreviation FC for a fully connected layer. The output of our model is a sequence of velocity *directions* at each time step. We consider 17 directions and an additional 'stop' class, which is shown by a red circle. The green ellipses show the chosen direction at each time step. The RNN stops when it generates the 'stop' class. (Color figure online)

point, direction and magnitude of the query force (we will explain in Sect. 6.2 how this image is created). The output of the FC7 layer of the force tower is propagated to the next stages of the network. Our experiments showed that using a separate force tower provides better results compared to adding the force as another input channel to the image tower. Probably, the reason is that there is too much variability in the real images, and the network is not able to capture the information in the force image when we have a single tower for both real images and force images. Therefore, we consider two separate towers and combine the output of these towers at a later stage. The outputs of the image tower and force tower are concatenated (referred to as I in Fig. 4) and provide a compact encoding of the visual cues and force representation for the recurrent part of the network.

The recurrent part of our network receives I as input and generates a sequence of velocity vectors. The advantage of using a Recurrent Neural Network (RNN) is two-fold. First, the velocities at different time steps are dependent on each other, and the RNN can capture these temporal dependencies. Second, RNNs enable us to predict a variable-length sequence of velocities (the objects move different distances depending on the magnitude of the force and the structure of the scene). We show the unfolded RNN in Fig. 4. The hidden layer of the RNN at time step t is a function of I and the previous hidden unit (h_{t-1}). More formally, $h_t = f(I, h_{t-1})$, where f is a linear function (fully connected layer) followed by a non-linear ReLU (Rectified Linear Unit). [18] show that RNNs composed of ReLUs and initialized with identity weight matrix are as powerful as standard LSTMs. The first hidden unit of the RNN (h_0) is only a function of I. The output at each time step $\mathbf{o}_t$ is a function of the hidden layer h_t. More concretely, $\mathbf{o}_t = \text{SoftMax}(g(h_t))$, where g is a linear function, which is augmented by a ReLU.

We use 1000 neurons for the hidden layer in the recurrent part of the network. The output $\mathbf{o}_t$ is of size $|\mathcal{L}|$. $\mathcal{L}$, as defined in Sect. 3, is a set of directions in 3D and a 'stop' class, which represents the end of the sequence.

5.2   Training

To train our model, in each iteration, we feed a random batch of RGB-M images from the training set into the image tower. The corresponding batch of force images is fed into the force tower. There is a sequence of velocity vectors associated to each pair of RGB-M and force images. These sequences have different lengths depending on the velocity profile of the query object in the groundtruth. If the object does not move as the result of applying the force, the sequence will be of length 1, where its value is 'stop'. The training is performed end-to-end, and each iteration involves a forward and a backward pass through the entire network.

The loss function is defined over the sequence of outputs $O = (\mathbf{o}_0, \mathbf{o}_1, \ldots, \mathbf{o}_{t'})$. Suppose the groundtruth velocity sequence is denoted by $V = (v_0, v_1, \ldots, v_t)$, the classification loss, $E(V, O)$, which is based on the cross entropy loss, is defined as follows:

$$E(V, O) = -\frac{1}{T} \sum_{t=0}^{T} q_t(v_t) \, \log(\mathbf{o}_t[v_t]), \qquad (1)$$

where $\mathbf{o}_t[v_t]$ represents the v_t-th element of $\mathbf{o}_t$, T is the maximum length of a sequence, and $q_t(v_t)$ is the inverse frequency of direction v_t in step t of the sequences in the training data. We pad the end of the sequences whose length is shorter than T (i.e. $|O| < T$ or $|V| < T$) with 'stop' so their length becomes equal to T. We could alternatively represent velocities as 3-dimensional vectors and use a regression loss instead. However, we achieved better performance using the classification formulation. A similar observation has been made by [37,38] that formulate a continuous variable estimation problem as classification.

5.3   Testing

The procedure for predicting a sequence of velocity vectors is as follows. We obtain I (the input to the RNN) by feeding the RGB-M and force images into the object and force towers, respectively. The hidden unit h_0 is computed according to the fully connected layer that is defined over I. The first velocity in the sequence, v_0, is computed by taking the argmax of the output of the SoftMax layer that is defined over h_0. We compute h_1 based on I and h_0 and similarly find the next velocity, v_1, in the sequence. More concretely, $v_t = \arg\max \mathbf{o}_t$ (recall that v_t is the index for a direction in the quantized set of directions or 'stop'). We continue this process until the RNN generates the 'stop' class (i.e. $v_t = \text{stop}$) or it reaches the maximum number of steps that we consider.

6 Experiments

In this section, we describe the evaluation of our method and compare our method with a set of baseline approaches. We provide the details of the dataset and explain how we interact with objects in the scenes. Additionally, we explain how we represent the force in the CNN and provide more implementation details about our network.

6.1 Dataset Details

Our dataset is based on the SUN RGB-D [32] dataset, which contains 10,335 images (we ignore 1,548 images that miss wall annotations or are not fully annotated). Each object is annotated with a 3D bounding box (position and orientation in 3D) and a segmentation mask (a 2D segmentation mask in the RGB image). There are more than 1,000 object categories in the dataset. Additionally, the room layout annotations (in the form of walls and floors) are provided for each image in the dataset. These annotations enable us to automatically reconstruct a similar scene in a physics engine. Therefore, for each image in [32], we have a synthetic scene, which will be used to simulate the effect of the forces.

We use Blender physics engine[2] to render the synthetic scenes. Some example scenes and their corresponding images are shown in Fig. 3[3]. To create our dataset, we use all ~1,000 categories and walls and floors to construct the synthetic scene, however, we apply the force to the 50 most frequent rigid categories in the dataset. These categories include: chair, keyboard, flower vase, etc. We represent each object as a cube in the synthetic scene.

For each object in the image, we randomly select a point on the surface of the object and apply the force to this point (note that during training for each point in the RGB image, we know the corresponding 3D point in the synthetic scene). The input force is also chosen at random. We simulate the scene after applying the force to the impact point. The simulation continues until the object to which the force is applied reaches a stable state, i.e. the linear and angular velocities of the object become zero. Over the entire dataset, it took a maximum of 32 simulation steps that the object converges to the stable position. We sample velocities every 6 steps, which results in a sequence of at most 6 velocity vectors (depending on the number of steps needed for reaching stability). We use

---

[2] http://www.blender.org.

[3] Some objects are missing in the synthetic scenes since they are not annotated in the SUN RGB-D dataset.

Fig. 5. Synthesizing the effect of the force. A force (shown by a yellow arrow) is applied to a point on the surface of the chair. The three pictures on the right show different time steps of the scene simulated in the physics engine. There is a red circle around the object that moves. (Color figure online)

this sequence as the groundtruth sequence for the query object and force. We represent these velocities in a quantized space of 3D directions (we ignore the magnitude of the velocities), where the directions are 45° apart from each other. Figure 4 shows these directions. We have 17 directions in total, hence, the size of the set $\mathcal{L}$ (defined in Sect. 3) will be 18 (17 directions + 1 'stop' class). We assign the velocity vector to the nearest direction class using angular distance. If the magnitude of the velocity vector is lower than a threshold we assign it to the 'stop' class. These directions cover a semi-sphere since the velocity directions in the other semi-sphere are rare in our dataset.

As the result of the simulations, we obtain 30,655 velocity sequences for training and validation and 34,777 sequences for test. Note that sometimes we apply the force in the same direction but with different magnitudes. In the real world, some of the objects such as toilets or kitchen cabinets are fixed to the floor. We consider those object categories as 'static' in the physics engine, which means we cannot move them by applying a force. Figure 5 shows a sequence of movement in a synthetic scene.

6.2 Force Representation

To feed the force to the CNN, we convert the force vector to an RGB image. Here we describe the procedure for creating the force image. For simplicity, we set the z component of our forces to zero (we refer to the axis that is perpendicular to the ground as the z axis). However, note that the z component of their corresponding velocities can be non-zero (e.g., a falling motion). The force image is the same size as the input RGB image. We represent the force as a Gaussian that is centered at the impact point of the force in the 2D image. We use a color from a color wheel (shown in Fig. 4) to represent the direction and the magnitude of the force. Each point on the color wheel specifies a unique direction and magnitude. The standard deviation of the Gaussian is 5 pixels in both directions.

6.3 Network and Optimization Parameters

We used Torch[4] to implement the proposed neural network. We run the experiments on a Tesla K40 GPU. We feed the training images to the network in

---

[4] http://torch.ch.

batches of size 128 when we use AlexNet for the image tower and of size 96 when we use ResNet-18 for the image tower. Our learning rate starts from 10^{-2} and gradually decreases to 10^{-4}. We initialize the image tower and the force tower by a publicly available AlexNet model[5] or ResNet model[6] that are pre-trained on ImageNet. We randomly initialize the 4th channel of the RGB-M image (the M channel) by a Gaussian distribution with mean 0 and standard deviation 0.01. The forward pass and the backward pass are performed for 15,000 iterations when we use AlexNet for the image tower (the loss value does not change after 15 K iterations). When we use ResNet-18 we use 35,000 iterations since it takes longer to converge.

6.4 Prediction of Velocity Sequences

We evaluate the performance of our method on predicting the 34,777 sequences of velocity vectors in the test portion of the dataset.

Evaluation criteria. To evaluate the performance of our method, we compare the estimated sequence of directions with the groundtruth sequence. If the predicted sequence has a different length compared to the groundtruth sequence, we consider it as incorrect. If both sequences have the same length, but they differ in at least one step, we consider that as an incorrect prediction as well. We report the percentage of sequences that we have predicted entirely correctly. We have about 1000 patterns of sequences in our test data so the chance performance is close to 0.001.

Results. We estimate 16.5 % of the sequences in the test data correctly using our method that uses AlexNet as image and force towers. We refer to this method as 'ours w/AlexNet' in Table 1. The criteria that we consider is a very strict criteria. Therefore, we also report our results using less strict criteria. We consider a direction as correct if it is among the closest k directions to the groundtruth direction. Figure 6(a) shows these results for $k = 0, \ldots, 4$ ($k = 0$ means we compare with the actual groundtruth class). We observe a significant improvement using this relaxed criteria. We also report the results using 'edit distance', which is a measure of dissimilarity between the groundtruth and the predicted sequences. Basically, it measures how many operations we need to convert a sequence to the other sequence. We report what percentage of predicted sequences are correct

Table 1. Ablative analysis of our method and comparison with baseline approaches. The evaluation metric is the percentage of sequences that we predict correctly.

ours w/ResNet + Depth	ours w/ResNet	ours w/AlexNet + Depth	ours w/AlexNet	Regression AlexNet	Nearest Neigh. AlexNet
19.8	16.9	17.5	16.5	10.4	8.5

---

[5] http://github.com/BVLC/caffe/tree/master/models/bvlc_alexnet.
[6] https://github.com/facebook/fb.resnet.torch/tree/master/pretrained.

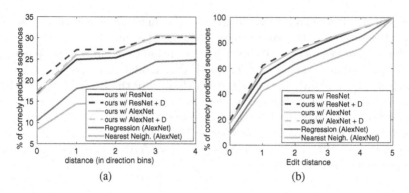

Fig. 6. Relaxation of the evaluation criteria. (a) We consider the prediction for each step as correct if it is among the k nearest directions to the groundtruth direction. The x-axis shows k. (b) We consider a predicted sequence as correct if it is within edit distance k of the groundtruth sequence. The x-axis shows k.

within edit distances 0 to 5. This result is shown in Fig. 6(b). The result of 'ours w/AlexNet' improves to 59.8 % from 16.5 % if we consider the predictions whose edit distance with the groundtruth is less than or equal to 1, as correct.

We also replaced the AlexNet in the image tower by the ResNet-18 [11] model. The performance for this case (referred to as 'ours w/ResNet') is reported in Table 1. The results using the relaxed criteria are shown in Figs. 6(a) and (b). To analyze the effect of depth on the predictions, we also incorporated depth into the image tower. We add the depth image as another channel in the input layer of the image tower. For obtaining the depth images, we use the method of [5], which estimates depth from a single image. We use their publicly available model, which is trained on a subset of the SUN RGB-D dataset. Using depth improves 'ours w/ResNet' and 'ours w/AlexNet' by 2.9 % and 1.0 %, respectively (Table 1). It seems ResNet better leverages this additional source of information. We initialize the additional depth channel randomly (random samples from a Gaussian distribution with mean 0 and standard deviation 0.01). The results for these ablative cases using the relaxed criteria are also shown in Fig. 6.

Some qualitative results are shown in Fig. 7. For example, Figs. 7(a) and (c) show two cases that the object moves in the same direction as the force. Figure 7(b) shows an example of falling, where the lamp moves straight for two steps and then it drops. Figure 7(e) shows an example that the object bounces back as the result of applying a large force. Figure 7(f) shows an example that object does not move no matter how large the force is. It probably learns that pushing objects against a wall cannot cause a movement. There are two other examples in Figs. 7(g) and (h), where the object does not move. We also show some failure cases in Fig. 8. In Fig. 8(a), the method ignores the wall behind the printer and infers a falling motion for the printer. In Fig. 8(b) the stove goes through the cabinet, which is not a correct prediction. Note that the synthetic

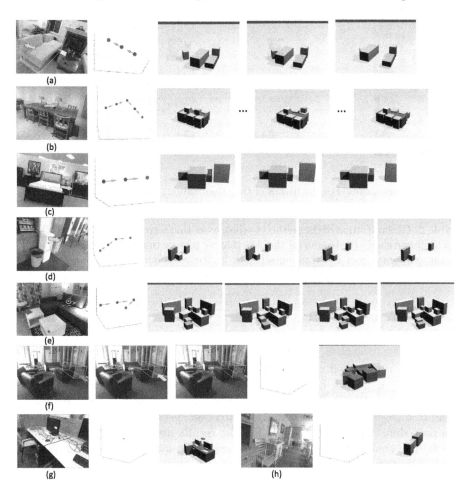

Fig. 7. Qualitative results. The left figure shows the force (color arrow) applied to the image. Different force magnitudes are shown with different colors, where blue, yellow, and red represent small, medium and large forces, respectively. The second image from the left shows the output of our method, which is a sequence of velocity vectors in 3D. The red point is the step that the velocity becomes zero. The resulted motion is visualized in the synthetic scenes. The object that moves is shown in yellow. Note that these synthetic scenes are for visualization purposes and they are not used during test. For clarity, we do not show walls. (Color figure online)

scenes are just for visualization of the movements and they are not used during testing and inference.

Baseline methods. The first baseline that we consider is a regression baseline, where we replace the RNN part of our network with a regressor that maps I (refer to Fig. 4) to 18 numbers (we have at most 6 steps and at each step we want to predict a 3-dimensional vector). If the length of the training sequence is

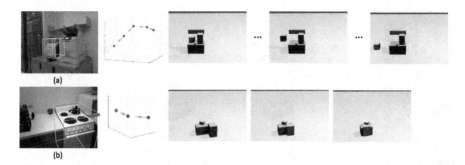

Fig. 8. Failure cases. For the details of the visualization, refer to the caption of Fig. 7.

Table 2. Generalization of the method to the classes that were not seen during training. Each column shows the results for the case that we remove the sequences corresponding to that category from the training set. The rightmost column ('All') shows the base case, where all training examples are seen.

Chair	Table	Desk	Pillow	Sofa chair	Sofa	Bed	Box	Garbage bin	Shelf	Avg.	All
17.7	17.0	15.4	15.5	15.9	17.2	15.9	14.6	16.1		15.9	16.12	16.53

less than 6, we set their corresponding elements in the 18-dimensional vector to zero. We use a smooth L1 loss function. As the result of regression, we obtain a vector of size 18, which corresponds to six 3-dimensional vectors. We assign them to different bins in the quantized direction space or the 'stop' class (using the procedure described in Sect. 6.1). The results are reported in Table 1 and Fig. 6. The result of the AlexNet-based regression method is 6.1 % lower than the result of 'ours w/AlexNet'.

Another baseline that we tried is a nearest neighbor baseline. For each query object and force in the test set, we forward the corresponding RGB-M and the force image to the our full network (which is already trained using our data). We obtain the features I. Then, we find the query object and force in our training data that produces the most similar I. We use the sequence that is associated to the most similar training data as the predicted sequence. The features are high dimensional. Hence, to find the nearest neighbor we use multiple index hashing method of [29]. The results of this AlexNet-based nearest neighbor is not competitive either (Table 1 and Fig. 6).

6.5   Unseen Categories

To evaluate how well our method generalizes to object categories that are not seen during training, we remove the training sequences that correspond to an object category and evaluate the method on the entire test set. For this experiment, we consider the ten most frequent object categories in our dataset.

We re-train the network each time we remove the sequences corresponding to an object category from our training set. The result of this experiment is shown in Table 2. We report the results using the strict evaluation criteria. We use the method that we refer to as 'ours w/AlexNet' for this experiment since its training time is faster than our other approaches. The results show that the average performance does not drop significantly compared to the case that we use the entire training set. This means that our method generalizes well to the categories that it has not seen during training.

7   Conclusion

Visual reasoning is a key component of any intelligent agent that is supposed to operate in the visual world. An important component in visual reasoning is the ability to predict the expected outcome of an action. This capability enables planing, reasoning about actions, and eventually successfully executing tasks. In this paper, we take one step toward this crucial component and study the problem of prediction the effect of an action (represented as a force vector) when applied to an object in an image. Our experimental evaluations show that our model can, in fact, predict sequential movements of objects when a force is applied to them.

Velocity magnitude and rotations: Our solution is mainly concerned with predicting translation vectors and velocity direction. Predicting velocity magnitude requires more complex reasoning about friction, materials, etc. Also our current model assumes uniform weights for all objects, resulting in a calibration issue for the magnitude of the force necessary to move an object. Our future work will involve addressing these issues.

Acknowledgements. This work is in part supported by ONR N00014-13-1-0720, ONR MURI N000141612007, NSF IIS- 1338054, Allen Distinguished Investigator Award, and the Allen Institute for Artificial Intelligence.

References

1. Battaglia, P., Hamrick, J., Tenenbaum, J.B.: Simulation as an engine of physical scene understanding. PNAS **110**, 18327–18332 (2013)
2. Bhat, K.S., Seitz, S.M., Popović, J., Khosla, P.K.: Computing the physical parameters of rigid-body motion from video. In: Heyden, A., Sparr, G., Nielsen, M., Johansen, P. (eds.) ECCV 2002. LNCS, vol. 2350, pp. 551–565. Springer, Heidelberg (2002). doi:10.1007/3-540-47969-4_37
3. Brubaker, M.A., Sigal, L., Fleet, D.J.: Estimating contact dynamics. In: ICCV (2009)
4. Choi, W., Chao, Y.W., Pantofaru, C., Savarese, S.: Understanding indoor scenes using 3d geometric phrases. In: CVPR (2013)
5. Eigen, D., Puhrsch, C., Fergus, R.: Depth map prediction from a single image using a multi-scale deep network. In: NIPS (2014)

6. Everingham, M., Gool, L., Williams, C.K., Winn, J., Zisserman, A.: The pascal visual object classes (voc) challenge. IJCV **88**, 303–338 (2010)
7. Fouhey, D.F., Zitnick, C.: Predicting object dynamics in scenes. In: CVPR (2014)
8. Fragkiadaki, K., Agrawal, P., Levine, S., Malik, J.: Learning predictive visual models of physics for playing billiards. In: ICLR (2016)
9. Gupta, A., Efros, A.A., Hebert, M.: Blocks world revisited: image understanding using qualitative geometry and mechanics. In: Daniilidis, K., Maragos, P., Paragios, N. (eds.) ECCV 2010. LNCS, vol. 6314, pp. 482–496. Springer, Heidelberg (2010). doi:10.1007/978-3-642-15561-1_35
10. Hamrick, J., Battaglia, P., Tenenbaum., J.B.: Internal physics models guide probabilistic judgments about object dynamics. In: Annual Meeting of the Cognitive Science Society (2011)
11. He, K., Zhang, X., Ren, S., Sun, J.: Deep residual learning for image recognition. In: CVPR (2016)
12. Heitz, G., Gould, S., Saxena, A., Koller, D.: Cascaded classification models: Combining models for holistic scene understanding. In: NIPS (2008)
13. Jia, Z., Gallagher, A., Saxena, A., Chen, T.: 3d-based reasoning with blocks, support, and stability. In: CVPR (2013)
14. Jiang, Y., Lim, M., Zheng, C., Saxena, A.: Learning to place new objects in a scene. IJRR **31**, 1021–1043 (2012)
15. Karpathy, A., Fei-Fei, L.: Deep visual-semantic alignments for generating image descriptions. In: CVPR (2015)
16. Kitani, K.M., Ziebart, B.D., Bagnell, J.A., Hebert, M.: Activity forecasting. In: Fitzgibbon, A., Lazebnik, S., Perona, P., Sato, Y., Schmid, C. (eds.) ECCV 2012. LNCS, vol. 7575, pp. 201–214. Springer, Heidelberg (2012). doi:10.1007/978-3-642-33765-9_15
17. Krizhevsky, A., Sutskever, I., Hinton, G.E.: Imagenet classification with deep convolutional neural networks. In: NIPS (2012)
18. Le, Q.V., Jaitly, N., Hinton, G.E.: A simple way to initialize recurrent networks of rectified linear units. In: ArXiv (2015)
19. Levine, S., Finn, C., Darrell, T., Abbeel, P.: End-to-end training of deep visuomotor policies. In: ArXiv (2015)
20. Li, L.J., Socher, R., Fei-Fei, L.: Towards total scene understanding: Classification, annotation and segmentation in an automatic framework. In: CVPR (2009)
21. Lin, D., Fidler, S., Urtasun, R.: Holistic scene understanding for 3d object detection with rgbd cameras. In: ICCV (2013)
22. Lin, T.-Y., Maire, M., Belongie, S., Hays, J., Perona, P., Ramanan, D., Dollár, P., Zitnick, C.L.: Microsoft COCO: common objects in context. In: Fleet, D., Pajdla, T., Schiele, B., Tuytelaars, T. (eds.) ECCV 2014. LNCS, vol. 8693, pp. 740–755. Springer, Heidelberg (2014). doi:10.1007/978-3-319-10602-1_48
23. Michalski, V., Memisevic, R., Konda, K.: Modeling deep temporal dependencies with recurrent grammar cells. In: NIPS (2014)
24. Mottaghi, R., Bagherinezhad, H., Rastegari, M., Farhadi, A.: Newtonian image understanding: Unfolding the dynamics of objects in static images. In: CVPR (2016)
25. Murphy, K., Torralba, A., Freeman, W.T.: Using the forest to see the trees: a graphical model relating features, objects, and scenes. In: NIPS (2003)
26. Oh, J., Guo, X., Lee, H., Lewis, R.L., Singh, S.P.: Action-conditional video prediction using deep networks in atari games. In: NIPS (2015)

27. Pintea, S.L., Gemert, J.C., Smeulders, A.W.M.: Déjà Vu: motion prediction in static. In: Fleet, D., Pajdla, T., Schiele, B., Tuytelaars, T. (eds.) ECCV 2014. LNCS, vol. 8691, pp. 172–187. Springer, Heidelberg (2014). doi:10.1007/978-3-319-10578-9_12

28. Ranzato, M., Szlam, A., Bruna, J., Mathieu, M., Collobert, R., Chopra, S.: Video (language) modeling: a baseline for generative models of natural videos. In: ArXiv (2014)

29. Rastegari, M., Keskin, C., Kohli, P., Izadi, S.: Computationally bounded retrieval. In: CVPR (2015)

30. Salzmann, M., Urtasun, R.: Physically-based motion models for 3d tracking: a convex formulation. In: ICCV (2011)

31. Silberman, N., Hoiem, D., Kohli, P., Fergus, R.: Indoor segmentation and support inference from RGBD images. In: Fitzgibbon, A., Lazebnik, S., Perona, P., Sato, Y., Schmid, C. (eds.) ECCV 2012. LNCS, vol. 7576, pp. 746–760. Springer, Heidelberg (2012). doi:10.1007/978-3-642-33715-4_54

32. Song, S., Lichtenberg, S.P., Xiao, J.: Sun rgb-d: A rgb-d scene understanding benchmark suite. In: CVPR (2015)

33. Sutskever, I., Hinton, G.E., Taylor, G.W.: The recurrent temporal restricted boltzmann machine. In: NIPS (2008)

34. Vinyals, O., Toshev, A., Bengio, S., Erhan, D.: Show and tell: A neural image caption generator. In: CVPR (2015)

35. Vondrak, M., Sigal, L., Jenkins, O.C.: Physical simulation for probabilistic motion tracking. In: CVPR (2008)

36. Walker, J., Gupta, A., Hebert, M.: Patch to the future: Unsupervised visual prediction. In: CVPR (2014)

37. Walker, J., Gupta, A., Hebert, M.: Dense optical flow prediction from a static image. In: ICCV (2015)

38. Wang, X., Fouhey, D.F., Gupta, A.: Designing deep networks for surface normal estimation. In: CVPR (2015)

39. Wu, J., Yildirim, I., Lim, J.J., Freeman, W.T., Tenenbaum, J.B.: Galileo: Perceiving physical object properties by integrating a physics engine with deep learning. In: NIPS (2015)

40. Yao, J., Fidler, S., Urtasun, R.: Describing the scene as a whole: Joint object detection, scene classification and semantic segmentation. In: CVPR (2012)

41. Yuen, J., Torralba, A.: A data-driven approach for event prediction. In: Daniilidis, K., Maragos, P., Paragios, N. (eds.) ECCV 2010. LNCS, vol. 6312, pp. 707–720. Springer, Heidelberg (2010). doi:10.1007/978-3-642-15552-9_51

42. Zhang, Y., Song, S., Tan, P., Xiao, J.: PanoContext: a whole-room 3D context model for panoramic scene understanding. In: Fleet, D., Pajdla, T., Schiele, B., Tuytelaars, T. (eds.) ECCV 2014. LNCS, vol. 8694, pp. 668–686. Springer, Heidelberg (2014). doi:10.1007/978-3-319-10599-4_43

43. Zheng, B., Zhao, Y., Yu, J.C., Ikeuchi, K., Zhu, S.C.: Beyond point clouds: Scene understanding by reasoning geometry and physics. In: CVPR (2013)

44. Zheng, B., Zhao, Y., Yu, J.C., Ikeuchi, K., Zhu, S.C.: Detecting potential falling objects by inferring human action and natural disturbance. In: ICRA (2014)

View Synthesis by Appearance Flow

Tinghui Zhou$^{(\boxtimes)}$, Shubham Tulsiani, Weilun Sun, Jitendra Malik,
and Alexei A. Efros

University of California, Berkeley, USA
tinghuiz@berkeley.edu

Abstract. We address the problem of *novel view synthesis*: given an input image, synthesizing new images of the same object or scene observed from arbitrary viewpoints. We approach this as a learning task but, critically, instead of learning to synthesize pixels from scratch, we learn to *copy* them from the input image. Our approach exploits the observation that the visual appearance of different views of the same instance is highly correlated, and such correlation could be explicitly learned by training a convolutional neural network (CNN) to predict *appearance flows* – 2-D coordinate vectors specifying which pixels in the input view could be used to reconstruct the target view. Furthermore, the proposed framework easily generalizes to multiple input views by learning how to optimally combine single-view predictions. We show that for both objects and scenes, our approach is able to synthesize novel views of higher perceptual quality than previous CNN-based techniques.

1 Introduction

Consider the car in Fig. 1(a). Actually, what you are *looking at* is a flat two-dimensional image that is but a projection of the three-dimensional physical car. Yet, numerous psychophysics experiments tell us that what you are *seeing* is not the 2D image but the 3D object that it represents. For example, one classic experiment demonstrates that people excel at "mental rotation" [2] – predicting what a given object would look like after a known 3D rotation is applied. In this paper, we study the computational equivalent of mental rotation called *novel view synthesis*. Given one or more input images of an object or a scene plus the desired viewpoint transformation, the goal is to synthesize a new image capturing this novel view, as shown in Fig. 1.

Besides purely academic interest (how well can this be done?), novel view synthesis has a plethora of practical applications, mostly in computer graphics and virtual reality. For example, it could enable photo editing programs like Photoshop to manipulate objects in 3D instead of 2D. Or it could help create full virtual reality environments based on historic images or video footage.

The ways that novel view synthesis has been approached in the past fall into two broad categories: geometry-based approaches and learning-based approaches. Geometric approaches try to first estimate (or fake) the approximate underlying 3D structure of the object, and then apply some transformation to

© Springer International Publishing AG 2016
B. Leibe et al. (Eds.): ECCV 2016, Part IV, LNCS 9908, pp. 286–301, 2016.
DOI: 10.1007/978-3-319-46493-0_18

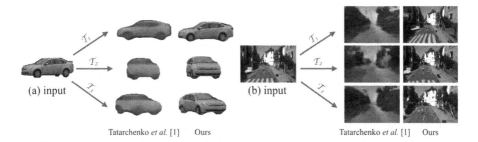

Tatarchenko *et al.* [1]   Ours   Tatarchenko *et al.* [1]   Ours

Fig. 1. Given an input image, our goal is to synthesize novel views of the same object (left) or scene (right) corresponding to various camera transformations (T_i). Our approach, based on learning appearance flows, is able to generate higher-quality results than the previous method that directly outputs pixels in the target view [1].

the pixels in the input image to produce the output [3–9]. Besides the requirement of somehow estimating the 3D structure, which is a difficult task by itself, the other major downside of these methods is that they produce holes in places where the source image does not have the appropriate visual content (e.g. the back side of an object). In such cases, various types of texture hole-filling are sometimes used but they are not always effective.

Learning-based approaches, on the other hand, argue that novel view synthesis is fundamentally a learning problem, because otherwise it is woefully underconstrained. Given a side of a car, there is no way to ever guess what the front of this car looks like, unless the system has observed other fronts of cars so it can make an educated guess. Such methods typically try, at training time, to build a parametric model of the object class, and then use it at test time, together with the input image, to generate a novel view. Unfortunately, parametric image generation is an open research topic, and currently the results of such methods are often too blurry (e.g. see [1] in Fig. 1).

In this paper, we propose to combine the benefits of both types of approaches, while also avoiding their pitfalls. Like geometric methods, we propose to use the pixels of the input image as much as possible, instead of trying to synthesize new ones from scratch. At the same time, we will use a learning-based approach to implicitly capture the approximate geometry of the object, avoiding the explicit estimation of the 3D structure. Our model also learns the appearance correlation between different parts of the object that enables synthesizing the backside of the object.

Conceptually, our approach is quite simple: we train a deep generative convolutional encoder-decoder model, similar to [1], but instead of generating RGB values for each pixel in the target view, we generate an *appearance flow* vector indicating the corresponding pixel in the input view to steal from. This way, the model does not need to learn how to generate pixels from scratch – just where to copy from the input view. In addition to making the learning problem more tractable, it also provides a natural way of preserving the identity and structure of the input instance – a task typically difficult for conventional learning approaches. We demonstrate the applicability of our approach by synthesizing views corresponding to rotation of objects and egomotion in scenes. We further extend our framework to leverage multiple input views and empirically show the quantitative as well as perceptual improvements obtained with our approach.

2   Related Work

Feature Learning by Disentangling Pose and Identity. Synthesizing novel views of objects can be thought of as decoupling pose and identity and has long been studied as part of feature learning and view-invariant recognition. Hinton et al. [10] learned a hierarchy of "capsules", computational units that locally transform their input, for generating small rotations to an input stereo pair, and argued for the use of similar units for recognition. More recently, Jaderberg et al. [11] demonstrated the use of computational layers that perform global spatial transformation over their input features as useful modules for recognition tasks. Jayaraman et al. [12] studied the task of synthesizing features transformed by ego-motion and demonstrated its utility as an auxiliary task for learning semantically useful feature space. Cheung et al. [13] proposed an auto-encoder with decoupled semantic units representing pose, identity etc. and latent units representing other factors of variation and showed that their approach was capable of generating novel views of faces. Kulkarni et al. [14] introduced a similarly motivated variational approach for decoupling and manipulating the factors of variation for images of faces. While the feature-learning approaches convincingly demonstrated the ability to disentangle factors of variation, the view manipulations demonstrated were typically restricted to small rotations or categories with limited shape variance like digits and faces.

CNNs for View Synthesis. A recent interest in learning to synthesize views for more challenging objects under diverse view variations has been driven by the ability of Convolutional Neural Networks (CNNs) [15,16] to function as image decoders. Dosovitiskiy et al. [17] learned a CNN capable of functioning as a renderer: given an input graphics code containing identity, pose, lighting etc. their model could render the corresponding image of a chair. Yang et al. [18] and Tatarchenko et al. [1] built on this work using the insight that the graphics code, instead of being presented explicitly, can be implicitly captured by an example source image along with the desired transformation. Yang et al. [18] learned a decoder to obtain implicit pose and identity units from the input source image, applied the desired transformation to the pose units, and used a decoder CNN to render the desired view. Concurrently, Tatarchenko et al. [1] followed a similar approach without the explicit decoupling of identity and pose to obtain similar results. A common module in these approaches is the use of a decoder CNN to generate the pixels corresponding to the transformed view from an implicit/explicit graphics code. Our work demonstrates that predicting appearance flows instead of pixels leads to significant improvements.

Geometric View Synthesis. An alternative paradigm for synthesizing novel views of an object is to explicitly model the underlying 3D geometry. In cases when more than one input view is available, modern multi-view stereo algorithms (see Furukawa and Hernandez [19] for an excellent tutorial) have demonstrated results of impressive visual quality. However, these methods fundamentally rely on finding visual correspondences – pixels that is in common across the views – so they break down when there are only a couple of views from very different viewpoints. In cases when only a single view is available, user interaction had typically been needed to help define a coarse geometry for the object or scene [3–5,7,8]. More recently, large Internet collections of stock 3D shape models have been leveraged to get 3D geometry for a wide range of common objects. For example, Kholgade *et al.* [9] obtained realistic renderings of novel views of an object by transferring texture from the corresponding 3D model, though they required manual annotation of the exact 3D model and its placement in the image. Rematas *et al.* [20] employed a similar technique after automatically inferring the closest 3D model from a shape collection as well as explicitly obtaining pose via a learnt system to situate the 3d model in the image. Their approach, however, is restricted to rendering the closest model in the shape collection instead of the original object. Su *et al.* [21] overcome this restriction by interpolating between several similar models from the shape collections, though they only demonstrate their technique for generating HOG [22] features for novel views. Unlike the CNN based learning approaches, these geometry-based methods require access to a shape collection during inference and are limited by the intermediate bottlenecks of inferring pose and retrieving similar models.

Image-Based Rendering. The idea of directly re-using the pixels from available images to generate new views has been popular in computer graphics. Debevec *et al.* [23] used the underlying geometry to composite multiple views for rendering novel views. Lightfield/lumigraph [24,25] rendering presented an alternate setup where a structured, dense set of views is available. Buehler *et al.* [26] presented a unifying framework for these image-based rendering techniques. The recent DeepStereo work by Flynn *et al.* [27] is a learning-based extension that performs compositing through learned geometric reasoning using a CNN, and can generate intermediate views of a scene by interpolating from a set of surrounding views. While these methods yield high-quality novel views, they do so by compositing the corresponding input image rays for each output pixel and can therefore only generate already seen content, (*e.g.* they cannot create the rear-view of a car from available frontal and side-view images).

Texture Synthesis and Epitomes. Reusing pixels of the input image to synthesize new visual context is also at the heart of non-parametric texture synthesis approaches. In texture synthesis [28,29], the synthesized image is pieced together by combining samples of the input texture image in a visually consistent way, whereas for texture transfer [30,31], an additional constraint aims to make the overall result also mimic a secondary "source" image. A related line of work uses *epitomes* [32] as a generative model for a set of images. The key idea is to use a condensed image as a palette for sampling patches to generate new images. In a similar spirit, our approach can be thought of as generating novel views of an object using the original image as an epitome.

3   Approach

Our approach to novel view synthesis is based on the observation that the appearance (texture, shape, color, etc.) of different views of the same object/scene is highly correlated, and in many cases even a single input view contains rich amount of information for inferring various novel views. For instance, given the side view of a car, one could extract appearance properties such as the 3D shape, body color, window layout and wheel types of the query instance that are sufficient for reconstructing many other views.

In this work, we *explicitly* infer the appearance correlation between different views of a given object/scene by training a convolutional neural network that takes (1) an input view and (2) a desired viewpoint transformation, and predicts a dense *appearance flow field* (AFF) that specifies how to reconstruct the target view using pixels from the input view. Specifically, for each pixel i in the target view, the appearance flow vector $f^{(i)} \in \mathbb{R}^2$ specifies the coordinate at the input view where the pixel value is sampled to reconstruct pixel i. The notion of appearance flow field is closely related to the nearest neighbor field (NNF) in PatchMatch [29], except that NNF is explicitly defined on a distance function between two patches, while our appearance flow field is the output of a CNN after end-to-end training for cross-view reconstruction.

The benefits of predicting the appearance flow field over raw pixels of the target view are three-fold: (1) It alleviates the perceptual blurriness in images generated by CNN trained with L_p loss. By constraining the CNN to only utilize pixels available in the input view, we are able to avoid the undesirable local minimum attained by predicting the mean (when $p = 2$) colors around texture/edge boundaries that lead to blurriness in the resulting image (e.g. see Sect. 4 for empirical comparison). (2) The color identity of the instance is preserved by construction since the synthesized view is reconstructed using only pixels from the same instance; (3) The appearance flow field enables intuitive interpretation of the network output since we can visualize exactly how the target view is constructed with the input pixels (e.g. see Fig. 6).

We first describe our training objective and the network architecture for the setting of a single input view in Sect. 3.1, and then present a simple extension in Sect. 3.2 that allows the network to learn how to combine individual predictions when multiple input views are available.

3.1   Learning View Synthesis via Appearance Flow

Recall that our goal is to train a CNN that, given an input view I_s and a relative viewpoint transformation T, synthesizes the target view I_t by sampling pixels from I_s according to the predicted appearance flow field. This can be formalized as minimizing the following objective:

$$\text{minimize} \sum_{<I_s,I_t,r>\in\mathcal{D}} \|I_t - g(I_s,T)\|_p, \quad \text{subject to} \quad g^{(i)}(I_s,T) \in \{I_s\}, \forall i, \quad (1)$$

where $\mathcal{D}$ is the set of training tuples, $g(\cdot)$ refers to the CNN whose weights we wish to optimize, $\| \cdot \|_p$ denotes the L_p norm[1], and i indexes over pixels of the synthesized view. Internally, the CNN computes a dense flow field f, where each element $f^{(i)} \triangleq (x^{(i)}, y^{(i)})$ specifies the pixel sampling location (in the coordinate frame of the input view) for constructing the output $g^{(i)}(I_s, T)$. To allow end-to-end training via stochastic gradient descent when $f^{(i)}$ falls into a sub-pixel coordinate, we rewrite the constraint of Eq. 1 in the form of bilinear interpolation:

$$g^{(i)}(I_s, T) = \sum_{q \in \{\text{neighbors of } (x^{(i)}, y^{(i)})\}} I_s^{(q)} (1 - |x^{(i)} - x^{(q)}|)(1 - |y^{(i)} - y^{(q)}|), \quad (2)$$

where q denotes the 4-pixel neighbors (top-left, top-right, bottom-left, bottom-right) of $(x^{(i)}, y^{(i)})$. This is also known as differentiable image sampling with a bilinear kernel, and its (sub)-gradient with respect to the CNN parameters could be efficiently computed [11].

Network Architecture. Our view synthesis network (Fig. 2) follows a similar high-level design as [1,18] with three major components:

1. Input view encoder – extracts relevant features (e.g. color, pose, texture, shape, etc.) of the query instance (6 conv + 2 fc layers).
2. Viewpoint transformation encoder – maps the specified relative viewpoint to a higher-dimensional hidden representation (2 fc layers).
3. Synthesis decoder – assembles features from the two feature encoders, and outputs the appearance flow field that reconstructs the target view with pixels from the input view (2 fc + 6 uconv layers).

All the convolution, fully-connected and fractionally-strided/up-sampling convolution (uconv) layers are followed by rectified linear units except for the last flow decoder layer.

Foreground Prediction. For synthesizing object views, we also train another network that predicts the foreground segmentation mask of the target view. The architecture is the same as the synthesis network in Fig. 2, except that in this case the last layer predicts a per-pixel binary classification mask (0 is background and 1 is foreground), and the network is trained with cross-entropy loss. At test time, we further apply the predicted foreground mask to the synthesized view.

3.2 Learning to Leverage Multiple Input Views

A single view of the object sometimes might not contain sufficient information for inferring an arbitrary target view. For instance, it would be very challenging to infer the texture details of the wheel spoke given only the frontal view of a car, and similarly, the side view of a car contains little to none information about the appearance of the head lights. Thus, it would be ideal to develop a

---

[1] We use $p = 1$ in all our experiments, but similar results can be obtained with L_2 norm as well.

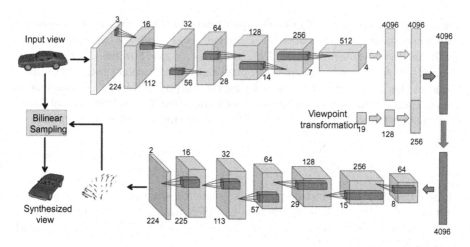

Fig. 2. Overview of our single-view network architecture. We follow an encoder-decoder framework where the input view and the desired viewpoint transformation are first encoded via several convolution and fully-connected layers, and then a decoder consisting of two fully-connected and six up-sampling convolution layers outputs an appearance flow field, which in conjunction with the input view yields the synthesized view through a bilinear sampling layer. All the layer weights are learned end-to-end through back-propagation.

mechanism that could leverage the individual strength of different input views to synthesize target views that might not be feasible with any input view alone.

To achieve this, we modify our view synthesis network to also output a *soft* confidence mask C_j that indicates per-pixel prediction quality using input view s_j, which could be implemented by adding an extra output channel to the last decoder layer. The confidence masks for all input views are further normalized to sum to one at each pixel location: $\bar{C}_j^{(i)} = C_j^{(i)} / \sum_{k=1}^{N} C_k^{(i)}$, where N denotes the number of input views. Intuitively, $\bar{C}_j^{(i)}$ is an estimator of *relative* prediction quality using input view j at pixel i, and by using $\bar{C}_j$ as a hypothesis selection mask, the final joint prediction is simply a weighted combination of hypotheses predicted by different input views: $\sum_{j=1}^{N} \bar{C}_j * g(I_{s_j}, r_j)$. Figure 3 illustrates the architecture of our multi-view network that is also end-to-end learnable.

Comparison with DeepStereo [27]. While the general idea of learning hypothesis selection for view synthesis has been recently explored in [27], there are a few key differences between our framework and [27]: (1) We do not require projecting the input image stack onto a planesweep volume that prohibits their method from synthesizing pixels that are invisible in the input views (i.e. view extrapolation); (2) Unlike [27], who have a fixed number of input views, our multi-view network is more flexible at both training and test time as it could take in an *arbitrary* number of input views for joint prediction, which is particularly beneficial when the number of input views varies at test time.

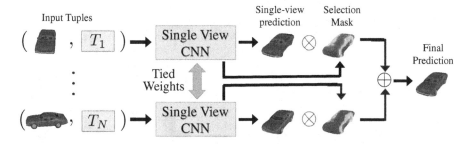

Fig. 3. Overview of our multi-view network architecture (⊗: per-pixel product, ⊕: per-pixel normalized sum). For each input view, we use a single-view CNN (same as Fig. 2 but with an extra output channel) with shared weights to independently predict the target view as well as a per-pixel selection/confidence mask. The final target view prediction is obtained by linearly combining the predictions from each view weighted by the selection masks.

4   Experiments

To evaluate the performance of our view synthesis approach, we conduct experiments on both objects (*car*, *chair* and *aeroplane*) and urban city scenes (KITTI [33]). Our main baseline is the recent work of Tatarchenko et al. [1] that synthesizes novel views by training a CNN to directly generate pixels. For fair comparison, we use the same number of network layers for their method and ours, and for experiments on multiple input views we extend their method to output hypothesis selection masks as described in Sect. 3.2.

Network Training Details. We train the networks using a modified version of Caffe [34] to support the bilinear sampling layer. We use the ADAM solver [35] with $\beta_1 = 0.9, \beta_2 = 0.999$, initial learning rate of 0.0001, step size of 50,000 and a step multiplier $\gamma = 0.5$.

4.1   Novel View Synthesis for Objects

Data Setup. We train and evaluate our view synthesis CNN for objects using the ShapeNet database [36]. In particular, we split the available shapes (7,497 cars and 700 chairs²) of each category into 80 % for training and 20 % for testing. For each shape, we render a total of 504 viewing angles (azimuth ranges from 0° to 355°, and elevation ranges from 0° to 30°, both at steps of 5°) with fixed camera distance. For simplicity, we limit the viewpoint transformation for CNN to a discrete set of 19 azimuth variations ranging from −180° to +180° at steps of 20°, and encode the transformation as a 19-D one-hot vector.

---

² The original ShapeNet core release contains a total of 6,778 chair models. However, a majority of the models are of low visual quality (e.g. texture-less), and we only keep a subset of 700 high-quality ones for our experiments.

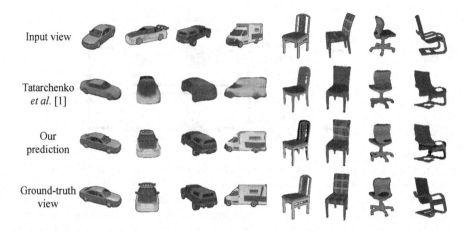

Input view

Tatarchenko
et al. [1]

Our
prediction

Ground-truth
view

Fig. 4. Comparison of our single-view synthesis results with the baseline method [1] on cars (left) and chairs (right). Our prediction tends to be consistently better at preserving high-frequency details (e.g. texture and edge boundaries) than the baseline.

At each training iteration, we randomly sample a batch of $< I_s, I_t, T >$ tuples from the training split for the single-view setting, and $< I_{s_1}, I_{s_2}, I_t, T_1, T_2 >$ tuples for the multi-view setting, where T_i denotes the relative viewpoint transformation between I_{s_i} and I_t, and T_i is randomly sampled from the set of valid transformations. For each category, we construct a test set of $20,000$ tuples by following the same sampling procedure above, except that the shapes are now sampled from the test split.

Appearance Flows Versus Direct Pixel Generation. Our first experiment compares the view synthesis performance of our appearance flow approach with the direct pixel generation method by [1] under the single input view setting.

Figure 4 compares the view synthesis results using different methods on examples from the test set of two categories (*car* and *chair*). Overall, our prediction tends to be much sharper and matches the ground-truth better than the baseline. In particular, our synthesized views using appearance flows are able to maintain detailed textures and edge boundaries that are lost in direct pixel generation despite both networks are trained with the same loss function.

For quantitative evaluation we measure the mean pixel L_1 error between the predicted views and the ground-truth on the foreground regions. As shown in Table 1, our method outperforms the baseline in both categories (*car* and *chair*). We further analyze the error statistics by computing the pairwise cross-view confusion matrix for both methods, which measures how predictive/informative a given view is for synthesizing another view (see the visualization in Fig. 5). The error statistics suggest that our method is especially strong in synthesizing views that share significant number of common pixels with the input view (within $\pm 45°$ azimuth variation from the input view – the diagonals in the plot) or along the corresponding symmetry planes (off-diagonals) that

Table 1. Mean pixel L_1 error between the ground-truth and predictions by different methods. Lower is better.

Input	Method	Car	Chair	KITTI
Single-view	Tatarchenko *et al.* [1]	0.404	0.345	0.492
	Ours	**0.368**	**0.323**	**0.471**
Multi-view	Tatarchenko *et al.* [1]	0.385	0.334	0.471
	Ours	**0.285**	**0.248**	**0.409**

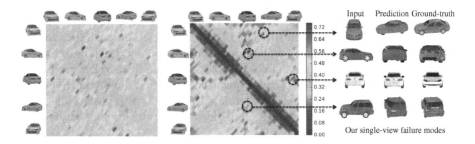

Fig. 5. Visualization of error statistics for generating novel views from a single input view on the *car* category. The heatmaps (blue–low, red–high) depict the mean pixel error for obtaining the target view (columns) from the input view (rows) for the baseline [1] (left) and our approach (middle). Some common failure modes of our method are visualized on the right. (Color figure online)

typically exhibit high appearance correlation with the input view (e.g. synthesizing the right view from the left view of a car), and slightly weaker than direct pixel generation in views that do not share much in common (e.g. from frontal to the side or rear views).

Interestingly though, when we conduct perceptual studies comparing the visual similarity between predicted views and the ground-truth, our method is far ahead of the baseline across the entire spectrum of the cross-view predictions. More specifically, we randomly sampled 1,000 test tuples, and asked users on Amazon Mechanical Turk to select the prediction that looks more similar to the ground-truth. We average the responses over 5 unique turkers for each test tuple, and find that 95 % of the time our prediction is chosen over the baseline for cars and 93 % for chairs, suggesting that the L_1 metric might not fully reflect the strength of our method.

One additional benefit of predicting appearance flows is that it allows intuitive visualization and understanding of exactly how the synthesized view is constructed. For instance, Fig. 6 shows sample appearance flow vectors predicted by our method. It is interesting to note that the appearance flows do not necessarily correspond to anatomically/symmetrically corresponding parts. For example, while the top-right pixels of the first car in Fig. 6 transfer appearance from their corresponding location in the source image, the pixels in the back wheel are generated using the front wheel of the source image.

Fig. 6. Sample appearance flow vectors predicted by our method. For randomly sampled points in the generated target image (left), the lines depict the corresponding appearance flow to the source image (right).

Multi-view Versus Single-view. In this experiment, we evaluate the synthesis performance of using multiple input views (two in this case). It turns out that having multiple input views is much more beneficial for our approach than for the baseline, as our synthesis error drops significantly compared to the single-view setting while less so for the baseline (see Table 1). This indicates that predicting appearance flows allows more effective utilization of different prediction hypotheses. Figure 7 shows sample visualization of how our multi-view synthesis network automatically combines high-quality predictions from individual input views to construct the final prediction.

Results on PASCAL VOC [37] Images. Although our synthesis network is trained on rendered synthetic images, it also exhibits potentials in generalizing to real images. In order to use our learnt models for synthesizing views for objects in PASCAL VOC, we require some pre-processing to ensure input statistics similar to the rendered training set. We therefore re-scale the input image to have similar number of foreground pixels as objects in the training set with the same aspect ratio. We visualize and compare a few example synthesis results on segmented PASCAL VOC images in Fig. 8.

4.2 Novel View Synthesis for Scenes

Data Setup. We evaluate our view synthesis CNN for scenes using the KITTI dataset [33], which provides odometry and image sequences taken during 11 short trips of a car travelling through urban city scenes. We split the 11 sequences into 9 for training and 2 for testing. The viewpoint transformation is computed using the odometry data by taking the difference between the 3×4 transformation matrices (Z-axis pointing forward) of the input and target frames, resulting in a 12-D vector of continuous values.

To sample a tuple for the single-view setting, we first randomly sample a sequence ID and then a input frame and a target frame within the sequence that are separated by at most ± 10 frames. For the multi-view setting, we sample an additional input view that is also at most ± 10 frames away from the target view. We randomly sample 10 tuples for training at each iteration and $20{,}000$ tuples for testing following the above procedure.

Comparison with Direct Pixel Generation. Similar to the evaluation on objects, we measure the mean pixel L_1 error between the predicted views and the ground-truth. As shown in Table 1, our method significantly outperforms the

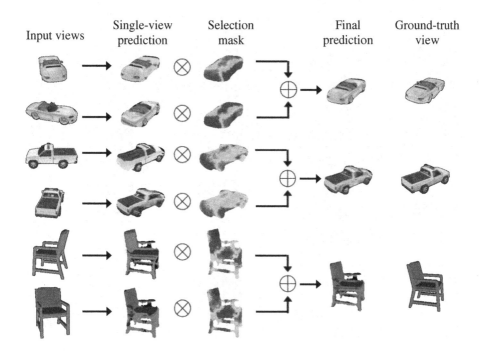

Fig. 7. View synthesis examples using our multi-view network. Each input view makes independent prediction of a candidate target view as well as a selection/confidence mask (blue–low, red–high). The final prediction is obtained by linearly combining the single-view predictions with weights normalized across the selection masks. Typically, the final prediction is more similar to the ground-truth than any independent prediction. (Color figure online)

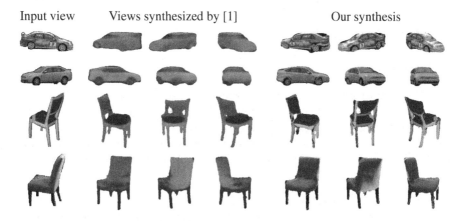

Fig. 8. View synthesis results for segmented objects in the PASCAL VOC dataset. Our method generalizes better and yields more realistic results than the baseline [1].

Input view	Prediction by [1]	Our prediction	Ground-truth view

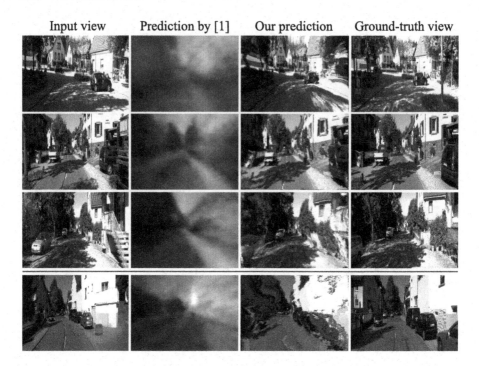

Fig. 9. View synthesis results on the KITTI dataset [33]. Our method typically preserves the scene structure and details of the objects in the synthesized view better than the baseline (a failure case is shown in the last row).

baseline [1] on both single-view and multi-view settings. The advantage is also visualized in Fig. 9, where we compare the predictions made by both methods on the single-view setting. Overall, our prediction tends to preserve the texture details and edge boundaries of objects depicted in the scene (Row 1–3), but sometimes might lead to severe distortions on failure cases (e.g. the last row).

5   Discussion

We have presented a framework that re-parametrizes image synthesis as predicting the appearance flow field between the input image(s) and the output, and demonstrated its successful application to novel view synthesis. But despite good performance on various benchmark evaluations, our method is by no means close to solving the problem in the general case. A number of major challenges are yet to be addressed:

– Our current method is incapable of hallucinating pixel values not present in the input view. While this is not as bad is it sounds (since the color palette of a typical image is quite rich), it would be beneficial to develop a mechanism that combines the hallucination capability of pixel generation CNN and the detail-preserving property of our flow-based synthesis.

- Empirically we observe that our network sometimes struggles in learning long-range appearance correlations, since the gradients derived from the flows are quite local. We conducted preliminary experiments with multi-scale reconstruction loss, and found it to alleviate the gradient locality to some extent.
- While the academic community around view synthesis is growing rapidly, we are still missing large-scale datasets of diverse real-world objects/scenes and a proper metric (L_1 pixel error is certainly not ideal) for measuring research progress.
- All the existing learning-based view synthesis approaches assume knowing the category of the object. An interesting direction is to develop a method that is category-agnostic, and once learned, can be applied to any real-world image.

Finally, we believe that our technique of leveraging appearance flows is also applicable to tasks beyond novel view synthesis, including image inpainting, video frame prediction, modeling effect of actions, super-resolution, *etc.*

Acknowledgements. We thank Philipp Krähenbühl and Abhishek Kar for helpful discussions. This work was supported in part by NSF award IIS-1212798, Intel/NSF Visual and Experiential Computing award IIS-1539099 and a Berkeley Fellowship. We gratefully acknowledge NVIDIA corporation for the donation of GPUs used for this research.

References

1. Tatarchenko, M., Dosovitskiy, A., Brox, T.: Single-view to multi-view: reconstructing unseen views with a convolutional network. arXiv preprint arXiv:1511.06702 (2015)
2. Shepard, R.N., Metzler, J.: Mental rotation of three-dimensional objects. Science **171**, 701–703 (1971)
3. Horry, Y., Anjyo, K.I., Arai, K.: Tour into the picture: using a spidery mesh interface to make animation from a single image. In: Proceedings of the 24th Annual Conference on Computer Graphics and Interactive Techniques (1997)
4. Oh, B.M., Chen, M., Dorsey, J., Durand, F.: Image-based modeling and photo editing. In: Proceedings of the 28th Annual Conference on Computer Graphics and Interactive Techniques (2001)
5. Zhang, L., Dugas-Phocion, G., Samson, J.S., Seitz, S.M.: Single-view modelling of free-form scenes. J. Vis. Comput. Anim. **13**, 225–235 (2002)
6. Hoiem, D., Efros, A.A., Hebert, M.: Automatic photo pop-up. ACM Trans. Graph. (TOG) **24**, 577–584 (2005)
7. Zheng, Y., Chen, X., Cheng, M.M., Zhou, K., Hu, S.M., Mitra, N.J.: Interactive images: cuboid proxies for smart image manipulation. ACM Trans. Graph. (TOG) (2012)
8. Chen, T., Zhu, Z., Shamir, A., Hu, S.M., Cohen-Or, D.: 3-sweep: Extracting editable objects from a single photo. ACM Trans. Graph. (TOG) **32**, 195 (2013)
9. Kholgade, N., Simon, T., Efros, A.A., Sheikh, Y.: 3d object manipulation in a single photograph using stock 3d models. ACM Trans. Graph. (TOG) (2014)
10. Hinton, G.E., Krizhevsky, A., Wang, S.D.: Transforming auto-encoders. In: Honkela, T., Duch, W., Girolami, M., Kaski, S. (eds.) ICANN 2011. LNCS, vol. 6791, pp. 44–51. Springer, Heidelberg (2011). doi:10.1007/978-3-642-21735-7_6

11. Jaderberg, M., Simonyan, K., Zisserman, A., et al.: Spatial transformer networks. In: Advances in Neural Information Processing Systems (2015)
12. Jayaraman, D., Grauman, K.: Learning image representations tied to egomotion. In: IEEE International Conference on Computer Vision (2015)
13. Cheung, B., Livezey, J.A., Bansal, A.K., Olshausen, B.A.: Discovering hidden factors of variation in deep networks. arXiv preprint arXiv:1412.6583 (2014)
14. Kulkarni, T.D., Whitney, W.F., Kohli, P., Tenenbaum, J.: Deep convolutional inverse graphics network. In: Advances in Neural Information Processing Systems (2015)
15. Fukushima, K.: Neocognitron: a self-organizing neural network model for a mechanism of pattern recognition unaffected by shift in position. Biol. Cybern. **36**, 193–202 (1980)
16. LeCun, Y., Boser, B., Denker, J., Henderson, D., Howard, R.E., Hubbard, W., Jackel, L.D.: Backpropagation applied to hand-written zip code recognition. In: Neural Computation (1989)
17. Dosovitskiy, A., Springenberg, J.T., Brox, T.: Learning to generate chairs with convolutional neural networks. In: IEEE International Conference on Computer Vision and Pattern Recognition (2015)
18. Yang, J., Reed, S.E., Yang, M.H., Lee, H.: Weakly-supervised disentangling with recurrent transformations for 3d view synthesis. In: Advances in Neural Information Processing Systems (2015)
19. Furukawa, Y., Hernández, C.: Multi-view stereo: a tutorial. Found. Trends Comput. Graph. Vis. **9**, 1–147 (2015)
20. Rematas, K., Nguyen, C., Ritschel, T., Fritz, M., Tuytelaars, T.: Novel views of objects from a single image. arXiv preprint arXiv:1602.00328 (2015)
21. Su, H., Wang, F., Yi, L., Guibas, L.: 3d-assisted image feature synthesis for novel views of an object. In: International Conference on Computer Vision (2015)
22. Dalal, N., Triggs, B.: Histograms of oriented gradients for human detection. In: IEEE Conference on Computer Vision and Pattern Recognition (2005)
23. Debevec, P.E., Taylor, C.J., Malik, J.: Modeling and rendering architecture from photographs: a hybrid geometry-and image-based approach. In: Proceedings of the 23rd Annual Conference on Computer Graphics and Interactive Techniques (1996)
24. Levoy, M., Hanrahan, P.: Light field rendering. In: Proceedings of the 23rd Annual Conference on Computer Graphics and Interactive Techniques, pp. 31–42. ACM (1996)
25. Gortler, S.J., Grzeszczuk, R., Szeliski, R., Cohen, M.F.: The lumigraph. In: Proceedings of the 23rd Annual Conference on Computer Graphics and Interactive Techniques, pp. 43–54. ACM (1996)
26. Buehler, C., Bosse, M., McMillan, L., Gortler, S., Cohen, M.: Unstructured lumigraph rendering. In: Proceedings of the 28th Annual Conference on Computer Graphics and Interactive Techniques, pp. 425–432. ACM (2001)
27. Flynn, J., Neulander, I., Philbin, J., Snavely, N.: Deepstereo: learning to predict new views from the world's imagery. In: IEEE Conference on Computer Vision and Pattern Recognition (2016)
28. Efros, A.A., Leung, T.K.: Texture synthesis by non-parametric sampling. In: The Proceedings of the Seventh IEEE International Conference on Computer Vision, 1999, vol. 2, pp. 1033–1038. IEEE (1999)
29. Barnes, C., Shechtman, E., Finkelstein, A., Goldman, D.: Patchmatch: a randomized correspondence algorithm for structural image editing. ACM Trans. Graph. (TOG) **28**, 24 (2009)

30. Hertzmann, A., Jacobs, C.E., Oliver, N., Curless, B., Salesin, D.H.: Image analogies. In: Proceedings of the 28th Annual Conference on Computer Graphics and Interactive Techniques, pp. 327–340. ACM (2001)

31. Efros, A.A., Freeman, W.T.: Image quilting for texture synthesis and transfer. In: Proceedings of the 28th Annual Conference on Computer Graphics and Interactive Techniques, pp. 341–346. ACM (2001)

32. Jojic, N., Frey, B.J., Kannan, A.: Epitomic analysis of appearance and shape. In: IEEE International Conference on Computer Vision (2003)

33. Geiger, A., Lenz, P., Urtasun, R.: Are we ready for autonomous driving? the kitti vision benchmark suite. In: IEEE Conference on Computer Vision and Pattern Recognition (2012)

34. Jia, Y., Shelhamer, E., Donahue, J., Karayev, S., Long, J., Girshick, R., Guadarrama, S., Darrell, T.: Caffe: Convolutional architecture for fast feature embedding. arXiv preprint arXiv:1408.5093 (2014)

35. Kingma, D., Ba, J.: Adam: A method for stochastic optimization. arXiv preprint arXiv:1412.6980 (2014)

36. Chang, A.X., Funkhouser, T., Guibas, L., Hanrahan, P., Huang, Q., Li, Z., Savarese, S., Savva, M., Song, S., Su, H., Xiao, J., Yi, L., Yu, F.: ShapeNet: an information-rich 3D model repository. Technical report arXiv:1512.03012 [cs.GR], Stanford University – Princeton University – Toyota Technological Institute at Chicago (2015)

37. Everingham, M., Van Gool, L., Williams, C.K.I., Winn, J., Zisserman, A.: The PASCAL Visual Object Classes Challenge (VOC2012) Results (2012). http://www.pascal-network.org/challenges/VOC/voc2012/workshop/index.html

Top-Down Learning for Structured Labeling with Convolutional Pseudoprior

Saining Xie[1(✉)], Xun Huang[2], and Zhuowen Tu[1]

[1] Department of CogSci and Department of CSE, UC San Diego, La Jolla, USA
s9xie@ucsd.edu, ztu@ucsd.edu
[2] Department of Computer Science, Cornell University, Ithaca, USA
xh258@cornell.edu

Abstract. Current practice in convolutional neural networks (CNN) remains largely bottom-up and the role of top-down process in CNN for pattern analysis and visual inference is not very clear. In this paper, we propose a new method for structured labeling by developing convolutional pseudoprior (ConvPP) on the ground-truth labels. Our method has several interesting properties: (1) compared with classic machine learning algorithms like CRFs and Structural SVM, ConvPP automatically learns rich convolutional kernels to capture both short- and long-range contexts; (2) compared with cascade classifiers like Auto-Context, ConvPP avoids the iterative steps of learning a series of discriminative classifiers and automatically learns contextual configurations; (3) compared with recent efforts combining CNN models with CRFs and RNNs, ConvPP learns convolution in the labeling space with improved modeling capability and less manual specification; (4) compared with Bayesian models like MRFs, ConvPP capitalizes on the rich representation power of convolution by automatically learning priors built on convolutional filters. We accomplish our task using pseudo-likelihood approximation to the prior under a novel fixed-point network structure that facilitates an end-to-end learning process. We show state-of-the-art results on sequential labeling and image labeling benchmarks.

Keywords: Structured prediction · Deep learning · Semantic segmentation · Top-down processing

1 Introduction

Structured labeling is a key machine learning problem: structured inputs and outputs are common in a wide range of machine learning and computer vision applications [1–3]. The goal of structured labeling is to simultaneously assign

---

S. Xie and X. Huang—Equally contributed.

Electronic supplementary material The online version of this chapter (doi:10.1007/978-3-319-46493-0_19) contains supplementary material, which is available to authorized users.

B. Leibe et al. (Eds.): ECCV 2016, Part IV, LNCS 9908, pp. 302–317, 2016.
DOI: 10.1007/978-3-319-46493-0_19

labels (from some fixed label set) to individual elements in a structured input. Markov random fields (MRFs) [4] and conditional random fields (CRFs) [2] have been widely used to model the correlations between the structured labels. However, due to the heavy computational burden in their training and testing/inference stages, MRFs and CRFs are often limited to capturing a few neighborhood interactions with consequent restrictions of their modeling capabilities. Structural SVM methods [5] and maximum margin Markov networks (M^3N) [6] capture correlations in a way similar to CRFs, but they try to specifically maximize the prediction margin; these approaches are likewise limited in the range of contexts, again due to associated high computational costs. When long range contexts are used, approximations are typically used to trade between accuracy and efficiency [7]. Other approaches to capture output variable dependencies have been proposed by introducing classifier cascades. For example, cascade models [8–10] in the spirit of stacking [11], are proposed to take the outputs of classifiers of the current layer as additional features for the next classifiers in the cascade. Since these approaches perform direct label prediction (in the form of functions) instead of inference as in MRFs or CRFs, the cascade models [8,9] are able to model complex and long-range contexts.

Despite the efforts in algorithmic development with very encouraging results produced in the past, the problem of structured labeling remains a challenge. To capture high-order configurations of the interacting labels, top-down information, or prior offers assistance in both training and testing/inference. The demonstrated role of top-down information in human perception [12–14] provides a suggestive indication of the form that top-down information could play in structured visual inference. Systems trying to explicitly incorporate top-down information under the Bayesian formulation point to a promising direction [15–18] but in the absence of a clear solution. Conditional random fields family models that learn the posterior directly [2,8,9,19] alleviates some burdens on learning the labeling configuration, but still with many limitations and constraints. The main difficulty is contributed by the level of complexity in building high-order statistics to capture a large number of interacting components within both short- and long- range contexts.

From a different angle, building convolutional neural networks for structured labeling [20] has resulted in systems that greatly outperform many previous algorithms. Recent efforts in combining CNN with CRF and RNN models [21,22] have also shed light onto the solution of extending CNN to structured prediction. However, these approaches still rely on CRF-like graph structure with limited neighborhood connections and heavy manual specification. More importantly, the explosive development in modeling data using layers of convolution has not been successfully echoed in modeling the prior in the label space.

In this paper, we propose a new structured labeling method by developing convolutional pseudoprior (ConvPP) on the ground-truth labels, which is infeasible by directly learning convolutional kernels using the existing CNN structure. We accomplish our task by developing a novel end-to-end fixed-point network structure using pseudo-likelihood approximation [23] to the prior that learns convolutional kernels and captures both the short- and the long- range contextual labeling information. We show state-of-the-art results on benchmark datasets in sequential labeling and popular image labeling.

2 Related Work

We first summarize the properties of our proposed convolutional pseudoprior (ConvPP) method: (1) compared with classical machine learning algorithms like CRFs [2], Structural SVM [5], and max-margin Markov networks [6], ConvPP automatically learns rich convolutional kernels to capture both the short- and the long- range contexts. (2) Compared with cascade classifiers [8,9], ConvPP avoids the time-consuming steps of iteratively learning a series of discriminative classifiers and it automatically learns the contextual configurations (we have tried to train a naive auto-context type of fully convolutional model instead of modeling prior directly from the ground-truth label space but without much success; the overall test error did not decrease after long-time training with many attempts of parameter tweaking; this is possibly due to the difficulty in capturing meaningful contexts on the predicted labels, which are noisy). (3) Compared with recent efforts combining CNN models with CRFs and RNNs [21,22], ConvPP learns convolution in the labeling space with improved modeling capability and less manual specification. (4) Compared with Bayesian models [16,24] ConvPP capitalizes on the rich representation power of CNN by automatically learning convolutional filters on the prior.

In addition, we will discuss some other related work. [25] addresses structured (image) labeling tasks by building a multi-scale CRF with handcrafted features and constrained context range, whereas in our work we learn the context automatically in an end-to-end network. [26] also combines RBM and CRF to incorporate shape prior for face segmentation. [19] is able to learn a large neighborhood graph but under a simplified model assumption; in [27] deep convolutional networks are learned on a graph but the focus there is not for structured labeling; deep belief nets (DBN) [28] and auto-encoders [29] are generative models that potentially can be adapted for learning the prior but it a clear path for structured labeling is lacking. Our work is also related to recurrent neural networks (RNNs) [1], but ConvPP has its particular advantage in: (1) modeling capability as explicit convolutional features are learned on the label space; (2) reduced training complexity as the time-consuming steps of computing recurrent responses are avoided by directly using the ground truth labels as a fixed-point model. In deep generative stochastic networks [30], pseudo-likelihood is used to train a deep generative model, but not for learning priors with CNN.

To summarize, ConvPP builds an end-to-end system by learning a novel hybrid model with convolutional pseudopriors on the labeling space and traditional bottom-up convolutional neural networks for the appearance.

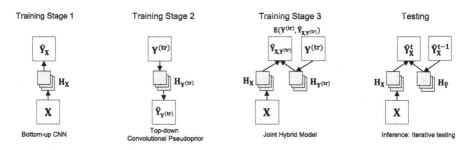

Fig. 1. The architecture of our ConvPP framework. At the first training stage, we train a bottom-up CNN model with image data as input; at the second training stage, we train a top-down convolutional pseudoprior model from ground-truth label maps. The hidden representations are then concatenated and the network is fine-tuned with the joint hybrid model. At inference, since we don't have the ground-truth label anymore, we iteratively feed predictions to the convolutional pseudoprior part.

3   Formulations

We first briefly discuss the structured labeling problem and understand it from the Bayesian point of view. Let $\mathcal{X}$ be the space of input observations and $\mathcal{Y}$ be the space of possible labels. Assume any data-label pairs $(\mathbf{X}, \mathbf{Y})$ follow a joint distribution $p(\mathbf{X}, \mathbf{Y})$. We seek to learn a mapping $F : \mathcal{X} \to \mathcal{Y}$ that minimizes the expected loss. For a new input sample $X \in \mathcal{X}$, we want to determine the optimal labeling $\mathbf{Y}^*$ that maximizes the posterior probability $p(\mathbf{Y}|\mathbf{X})$.

$$\mathbf{Y}^* = \arg\max_{\mathbf{Y}} p(\mathbf{Y}|\mathbf{X}) = \arg\max_{\mathbf{Y}} p(\mathbf{X}|\mathbf{Y})p(\mathbf{Y}) \tag{1}$$

In the scenario of structured labeling such as pixel-wise labeling, intuitively, the labeling decision should be made optimally by considering both the appearance and the prior, based on the Bayes rule in Eq. (1). However, learning both $p(\mathbf{X}|\mathbf{Y})$ and $p(\mathbf{Y})$ for complex structures is considered as very challenging. Our motivation here is to capitalize on the rich representational and compelling computational power of CNN for modeling both the appearance and prior. A large amount of work in the past using CNN has been primarily focused on training strong classifiers for predicting semantic labels (a discriminative way of modeling the appearance, [20]), but rarely on the prior part (top-down information).

To formulate our structured labeling problem, here we consider a graph, $\mathcal{G} = (\mathcal{V}, \mathcal{E})$. In a 1-D sequential labeling case, the graph is equivalent to a chain. The edge set $\mathcal{E}$ decides the graph topology, and hence the neighborhoods of every node. We denote $\mathcal{N}_i/i$ as the neighborhoods of node v_i. For each node v_i, we have its associated data $\mathbf{x}_i$, ground-truth label y_i, and ground-truth labels for all the neighborhoods of v_i as $\mathbf{y}_{\mathcal{N}_i/i}$. Inspired by pseudo-likelihood [23] and the hybrid model in [31], we make an approximation to the posterior in Eq. (1) as follows:

$$p(\mathbf{Y}|\mathbf{X}) \propto p(\mathbf{Y})p(\mathbf{X}|\mathbf{Y}) \dot{\propto} \prod_i p(y_i|\mathbf{Y}_{\mathcal{N}_i/i}) \cdot \prod_i p(y_i|\mathbf{X}) \tag{2}$$

where $\mathbf{Y}_{\mathcal{N}_i/i}$ encodes a neighborhood structure (contexts) of y_i for computing a pseudo-likelihood $p(y_i|\mathbf{Y}_{\mathcal{N}_i/i})$ [23] to approximate $p(\mathbf{Y})$, *but now as a prior*.

In addition, to see how the approximation to $p(\mathbf{X}|\mathbf{Y})$ by $\prod_i p(y_i|\mathbf{X})$ is obtained from Bayesian to conditional probability: (1) assume pseudo-likelihood on each pixel i to approximate the likelihood term $p(\mathbf{X}|\mathbf{Y})$, using $p(\mathbf{x}_i|x_{\mathcal{N}_i/i}, Y)$. Note that $\mathbf{x}_{\mathcal{N}_i/i}$ includes all the neighboring pixels of pixel i but excluding i; (2) assume independence, to approximate $p(\mathbf{x}_i|\mathbf{x}_{\mathcal{N}_i/i}, Y)$ by $p(\mathbf{x}_i|\mathbf{x}_{\mathcal{N}_i/i}, y_i)$; (3) $p(\mathbf{x}_i|\mathbf{x}_{\mathcal{N}_i/i}, y_i) = p(\mathbf{x}_i, y_i|\mathbf{x}_{\mathcal{N}_i/i})/P(y_i|\mathbf{x}_{\mathcal{N}_i/i}))$ and drop $p(y_i|\mathbf{x}_{\mathcal{N}_i/i})$ for another approximation. This leads to $p(\mathbf{x}_i, y_i|\mathbf{x}_{\mathcal{N}_i/i})$ which is $p(y_i|\mathbf{x}_{\mathcal{N}_i/i}, \mathbf{x}_i)p(\mathbf{x}_i|\mathbf{x}_{\mathcal{N}_i/i})$; (4) the above becomes $p(y_i|\mathbf{x}_{\mathcal{N}_i}) = p(y_i|\mathbf{X})$ when dropping $p(\mathbf{x}_i|\mathbf{x}_{\mathcal{N}_i/i})$.

This hybrid model is of special interest to us since: (1) our end-to-end deep learning framework allows a discriminative convolutional neural network (CNN) to be trained to compute $p(y_i|\mathbf{X})$ to model the appearance; (2) by directly working on the ground-truth labels $\mathbf{Y}$, we also learn a convolutional pseudoprior as $\prod_i p(y_i|\mathbf{Y}_{\mathcal{N}_i/i})$ using a pseudo-likelihood approximation.

Given a training data pair $p(\mathbf{X}, \mathbf{Y}^{(tr)})$, to solve an approximated MAP problem with convolutional pseudoprior,

$$\mathbf{Y}^{(tr)} = \arg\max_{\mathbf{Y}} \prod_i p(y_i|\mathbf{Y}_{\mathcal{N}_i/i}; \mathbf{w}_2) \cdot \prod_i p(y_i|\mathbf{X}; \mathbf{w}_1) \qquad (3)$$

From another perspective, the above learning/inference scheme can be motivated by the fixed-point model [32]. Denote $\mathbf{Q}$ as the one-hot encoding of labeling $\mathbf{Y}$, and therefore $\mathbf{Q}^{(tr)}$ as the one-hot encoding of ground-truth training labeling $\mathbf{Y}^{(tr)}$. The fixed-point model solve the problem with the formulation for a prediction function $\mathbf{f}$,

$$\mathbf{Q} = \mathbf{f}(\mathbf{x}_1, \mathbf{x}_2, \cdots, \mathbf{x}_n, \mathbf{Q}; \mathbf{w}) \qquad (4)$$

where $\mathbf{f}(\cdot) = [f(\mathbf{x}_1, \mathbf{Q}_{\mathcal{N}_1}; \mathbf{w}), \cdots, f(\mathbf{x}_n, \mathbf{Q}_{\mathcal{N}_n}; \mathbf{w})]^T$, $\mathbf{Q} = [\mathbf{q}_1, \mathbf{q}_2, \cdots, \mathbf{q}_n]^T$, and $\mathbf{q}_i = f(\mathbf{x}_i, \mathbf{Q}_{\mathcal{N}_i})$. $\mathbf{w} = (\mathbf{w}_1, \mathbf{w}_2)$. To get the labeling of a structured input graph $\mathcal{G}$, one can solve the non-linear system of equations $\mathbf{Q} = \mathbf{f}(\mathbf{x}_1, \mathbf{x}_2, \cdots, \mathbf{x}_n, \mathbf{Q}; \mathbf{w})$, which is generally a very difficult task. However, [32] shows that in many cases we can assume $\mathbf{f}$ represents so called contraction mappings, and so have an attractive fixed-point (a "stable state") for each structured input. When using the ground-truth labeling in the training process, that ground-truth labeling $\mathbf{Q}^{(tr)}$ is assumed to be the stable state: $\mathbf{Q}^{(tr)} = \mathbf{f}(\mathbf{x}_1, \mathbf{x}_2, \cdots, \mathbf{x}_n, \mathbf{Q}^{(tr)}; \mathbf{w})$.

Next, we discuss the specific network architecture design and our training procedure. The pipeline of our framework is shown in Fig. 1 consisting of three stages: (1) training $\mathbf{w}_1$ for $p(y_i|\mathbf{X}; \mathbf{w}_1)$; (2) training $\mathbf{w}_2$ for $p(y_i|\mathbf{Y}_{\mathcal{N}_i/i}; \mathbf{w}_2)$; and (3) fine-tuning for $\prod_i p(y_i|\mathbf{Y}_{\mathcal{N}_i/i}; \mathbf{w}_2) \cdot p(y_i|\mathbf{X}; \mathbf{w}_1)$ jointly.

At the first stage, we independently train a standard bottom-up CNN on the input data, in our work, we are especially interested in end-to-end architectures such as FCN [20]. Without loss of generality, we abstractly let the feature representations learned by FCN be $\mathbf{H_X}$, and network predictions be $\hat{\mathbf{Y}}_\mathbf{X}$, The error is computed with respect to the ground-truth label $\mathbf{Y}^{(tr)}$ and back-propagated during training. Similarly, at the second stage, we train a convolutional pseudo-prior network on the ground-truth label space. Conceptually the prior modeling is a top-down process. Implementation-wise, the ConvPP network is still a CNN. However, the most notable difference compared with a traditional CNN is that, the ground-truth labels are not only used as the supervision for back-propagation, but also used as the network input. We learn hidden representation $\mathbf{H}_{\mathbf{Y}^{(tr)}}$ and aim to combine this with the hierarchical representation $\mathbf{H}_{\mathbf{X}}$ learned in the bottom-up CNN model. Thus, combining pre-trained bottom-up CNN network and top-down ConvPP network, we build a joint hybrid model network in the third training stage. We concatenate $\mathbf{H}_{\mathbf{X}}$ and $\mathbf{H}_{\mathbf{Y}}$ (which can be fine-tuned) and learn a new classifier on top to produce the prediction $\hat{\mathbf{Y}}_{\mathbf{X},\mathbf{Y}^{(tr)}}$. The joint network is still trained with back-propagation in an end-to-end fashion.

At inference time, since we do not have the ground-truth label $\mathbf{Y}^{(tr)}$ available anymore, we follow the fixed-point motivation discussed above. We iteratively feed predictions $\hat{\mathbf{Y}}_{\mathbf{X}}^{t-1}$ made at previous iteration, to the ConvPP part of the hybrid model network. The starting point $\hat{\mathbf{Y}}_{\mathbf{X}}^{0} = \mathbf{0}$ can be a zero-initialized dummy prediction, or we can simply use $\hat{\mathbf{Y}}_{\mathbf{X}}^{0} = \hat{\mathbf{Y}}_{\mathbf{X}}$ given the pre-trained bottom-up CNN model.

This conceptually simple approach to approximate and model the prior naturally faces two challenges: (1) How do we avoid trivial solutions and make sure the ConvPP network can learn meaningful structures instead of converging to an identity function? (2) When the bottom-up CNN is deep and involves multiple pooling layers, how to match the spatial configurations and make sure that, $\mathbf{H}_{\mathbf{X}}$ and $\mathbf{H}_{\mathbf{Y}^{(tr)}}$ are compatible in terms of the appearances and structures they learn.

ConvPP Network Architectures. We will now explain the architecture design in ConvPP network to address the issues above. We have explored possible ways to avoid learning a trivial solution. Besides the ConvPP architecture design, one might think learning a convolutional auto-encoder on the ground-truth label space can achieve similar goal. However, we found that when training an auto-encoder on label space, the problem of trivial recovery is even more

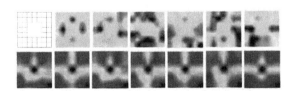

Fig. 2. The first row shows the donut filter we use for training the ConvPP network, and examples of learned real-valued filters after the ConvPP network training, originally initialized randomly. Note that a square hole (showing in light-green color) in the center is kept zero-valued during training, and it enforces the filter to learn non-trivial transformations. The second row shows trivial filters (close to identity transformation) are learned by a conventional auto-encoder.

severe compared to training auto-encoders on natural images. We tried different regularization and sparsification techniques presented in recent convolutional
auto-encoder works (e.g. [33]), but none of them work in our case. See Fig. 2 for a
visual comparison. We conjecture that the reasons could be (1) the ground-truth
labels are much simpler in their appearances, compared with natural images with
rich details. Thus the burden of being identically reconstructed is greatly eased;
(2) on the other hand, the structures like class inter-dependencies, shape context
and relative spatial configurations are highly complex and subtle, make it really
challenging to learn useful representations.

Donut Filter. Here we use a very simple yet effective approach to conquer the
issues: our ConvPP network contains only a single convolutional layer, where
we apply filters referred as "donut filters". The name comes from the way we
modify the traditional convolution kernels: we make a hole in the center of the
kernel. Figure 2 shows an example where a 3 by 3 hole is in the middle of a
7 by 7 convolution filter. Given that we only have one convolutional layer, we
impose a hard constraint on the ConvPP representation learning process: the
reconstruction of the central pixel label will never see its original value, instead
it can only be inferred from the neighboring labels. This is aligned with our
pseudoprior formulation in Eq. (3).

Donut filters are not supposed to be stacked to form a deep variant, since
the central pixel label information, even though cropped from one layer, can
be propagated from lower layers which enables the network to learn a trivial
solution. Empirically we found that one hidden convolution layer with multiple
filters is sufficient to approximate and model the useful prior in the label space.

Multi-scale ConvPP. A natural question then becomes, since there is only one
convolution layer in the ConvPP network, the receptive field size is effectively
the donut filter kernel size. Small kernel size will result in very limited range
of context that can be captured, while large kernel size will make the learning
process extremely hard and often lead to very poor local minimum.

To combat this issue, as illustrated in Fig. 3, we leverage the unique simplicity of ground-truth labeling maps, and directly downsample the input ground-
truth maps through multiple pooling layers to form a chain of multi-scale

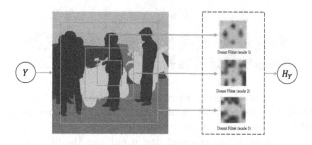

Fig. 3. Multiple donut filter layers with the same kernel size are integrated into different
depth of the joint network. Multi-scale context learning is naturally handled.

Table 1. An experimental comparison on the OCR dataset by varying the number of training data. It demonstrates that the generalization error monotonically decreases when adding more data.

Training data percentage (%)	10	20	30	40	50	60	70	80	90
Generalization error (%)		6.49	3.28	2.09	1.67	1.55	1.03	0.92	0.72	0.57

ground-truth maps. The in-network pooling layers also keep the network to be end-to-end trainable. This enables us to freely learn the ConvPP representations on different scales of the ground-truth label space. The flexibility of the useful context that ConvPP can capture, now comes from two aspects: (1) the convolution filter weights can be automatically learned during training. (2) the context range is also handled explicitly by multi-scale architecture design. One can imagine that ConvPP representations, learned on low-resolution ground-truth maps, are capable of modeling complex long range and high order semantic context, global object shape and spatial configuration, whereas representations learned on high-resolutions ground-truth maps are supposed to model local structures like local smoothness.

Given that we can learn $\mathbf{H_Y}$ from different scales, we are readily able to build the spatial correspondences between $\mathbf{H_X}$ and $\mathbf{H_Y^{(tr)}}$. One can concatenate the $\mathbf{H_Y}$ to any convolutional feature maps learned in the bottom-up CNN network, as long as they passed through the same number of downsampling layers.

Because our convolutional pseudoprior is learned directly from the ground-truth label space, and it does not condition on the input data at all, the choice of bottom-up CNN models are flexible. The complementary structural information provided by the ConvPP allows us to easily improve on state-of-the-art CNN architectures such as Fully Convolutional Neural Networks (FCN).

4   Experiments

In this section, we show experimental results on four benchmark datasets across different domains, namely FAQ (Natural language processing), OCR (Sequential image recognition), Pascal-Context (Semantic segmentation) and SIFT Flow (Scene labeling).

4.1   Sequential Labeling: 1-D Case

First, we explore the effectiveness of our proposed framework on two 1-D structured (sequential) labeling tasks: handwritten OCR [6] and FAQ sentence labeling [34]. In these two 1-D toy examples, the pseudoprior model is implemented as a fully connected layer whose inputs are one-hot-encoding of neighboring labels (excluding the to-be-predicted label itself). When we slide the model over the input sequences, this layer can be viewed as a 1D convolutional layer with kernel size m (m is the context window size) and hole size 1.

Handwritten OCR. This dataset contains 6,877 handwritten words, corresponding to various writings of 55 unique words. Each word is represented as a series of handwritten characters; there are 52,152 total characters. Each character is a binary 16 × 8 image, leading to 128-dimensional binary feature vectors. Each character is one of the 26 letters in the English alphabet. The task is to predict the identity of each character. We first resize all the OCR characters to the same size (28 × 28) and build a standard 5-layer LeNet [35]. The label context part has a single-hidden-layer MLP with 100 units. We normalize each image to zero-mean and unit-variance.

FAQ. The FAQ dataset consists of 48 files collecting questions and answers gathered from 7 multi-part UseNet FAQs. There are a total of 55,480 sentences across the 48 files. Each sentence is represented with 24-dimensional binary feature vector. [34] provides a description of the features). We extended the feature set with all pairwise products of the original 24 features, leading to a 600-dimensional feature representation. Each sentence in the FAQ dataset is given one of four labels: (1) head, (2) question, (3) answer, or (4) tail. The task is to predict the label for each sentence. We train a 3-hidden layer fully-connected network with [32, 64, 128] hidden units respectively. A single-hidden-layer MLP with 100 hidden units is trained on ground-truth labels.

For both of the dataset, two hyper-parameters are specified by cross-validation: we set the context window size to be 7 (for OCR) and 5 (for FAQ); the number of iterations during testing to be 10.

Results. The results in Tables 2 and 3 show that our proposed framework effectively models 1-D sequential structures and achieves better results for structured labeling as compared to previous methods. Several interesting observations: (1) on OCR dataset, compared to a kernel methods with hand-crafted features, our deep hybrid model performs worse on smaller dataset. But our deep learning approach performs better when the amount of training data increases (Table 1).

Table 2. Performance (error rate (%)) of structured labeling methods on the OCR dataset.

Methods	Small	Large
Linear-chain CRF [36]	21.62	14.20
M³N [36]	21.13	13.46
SEARN [10]	–	9.09
SVM + CRF [37]	–	5.76
Neural CRF [36]	10.8	4.44
Hidden-unit CRF [38]	18.36	1.99
Fixed-point [32]	**2.13**	0.89
NN without ConvPP	15.73	3.69
ConvPP (ours)	6.49	**0.57**

Table 3. Performance (error rate (%)) of structured labeling methods on the FAQ sentence labeling dataset.

Methods	Error
Linear SVM [36]	9.87
Linear CRF [38]	6.54
NeuroCRFs [36]	6.05
Hidden-unit CRF [38]	4.43
NN without ConvPP	5.25
ConvPP (ours)	**1.09**

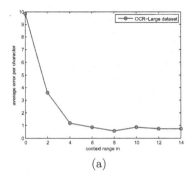
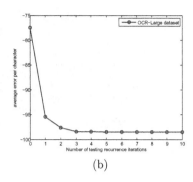

(a)   (b)

Fig. 4. (a) comparison of the generalization error on the OCR handwritten dataset by varying the context window length. (b) the generalization error on the OCR handwritten dataset as the number of testing iterations varies.

That is also the reason why ConvPP framework is important: handcrafted features and kernel methods are hard to be applied to many high-level vision tasks where big data is available. (2) ConvPP context window length reflects the range of context needed, we can see from Fig. 4(a) that the generalization error converges when the context window length is about 7, which is the typical length of a word in the dataset. (3) Fig. 4(b) shows that though we set the max number of testing iterations to be 10, with only 3 to 4 iterations at test time, the generalization error converges. That shows that the inference of our ConvPP model can be efficient. (4) The experiment in the simple sentence classification task shows that ConvPP has the potential to be applied on more NLP tasks such as sequence modeling. (5) To show the effectiveness of the proposed approach, especially the convolutional pseudoprior part, we also perform the ablation study where we train a bottom-up network with exactly the same parameter settings. From the results we can see that without the structural information learned from the output label space, the performance decreases a lot.

4.2   Image Semantic Labeling: 2-D Case

We then focus on two more challenging image labeling tasks: semantic segmentation and scene labeling. Most of deep structured labeling approaches evaluate their performance on the popular Pascal VOC object segmentation dataset [39], which contains only 20 object categories. Recently, CNN based methods, notably built on top of FCN [20], succeeded and dominated the Pascal-VOC leader-board where the performance (mean I/U) saturated to around 80 %. Here we instead evaluate our models on the much more challenging Pascal-Context dataset [40], which has 60 object/stuff categories and is considered as a fully labeled dataset (with much fewer pixels labeled as background). We believe the top-down contextual information should play a more crucial role in this case. We also evaluated our algorithm on SIFT Flow dataset [41] to evaluate our algorithm on the task

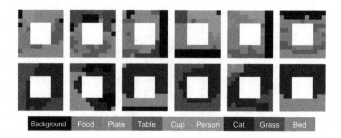

Fig. 5. Visualization of 2 filters. Each row displays top 6 label patches that produce highest activation for a filter.

of traditional scene labeling. In both experiments, the performance is measured by the standard mean intersection-over-union (mean I/U).

Multi-scale Integration with FCN. We build our hybrid model using FCN as the bottom-up CNN, and directly use the pre-trained models provided by the authors. FCN naturally handles multi-scale predictions by upgrading its 32-stride (32s) model to 16-stride (16s)/8-stride (8s) variants, where the final labeling decisions are made based on both high-level and low-lever representations of the network. For the 32s model and an input image size 384×512, the size of the final output of FCN, after 5 pooling layers, is 12×16. As discussed in our formulation, ConvPP can be integrated into FCN by downsampling the ground-truth maps accordingly.

Hyper-Parameter Settings. For all the 2-D labeling experiments, the number of channels in the donut filter convolution layer is 128. Adding more filters does not improve the performance. We keep all the hyper-parameters for the original bottom-up FCN network. The learning rates for the top-down ConvPP network are set to be 1e–7 for 32s, 1e–8 for 16s and 1e–9 for 8s variant. We choose the kernel size k of our donut filters by cross validation. The size of the hole in the middle is set to $\lfloor k/2 \rfloor \times \lfloor k/2 \rfloor$. In following two image labeling experiments we evaluate two configurations of donut filter, namely donut filter with small (7×7) kernel size, and large (11×11) kernel size. The comparison of results for those two configurations is shown in Table 4. The choice of donut filter size is crucial to the pseudoprior representation learning.

Sparse Donut Filter. We use 11×11 donut filters with 5×5 holes for Pascal-Context dataset since it achieves the best performance. The kernel covers a large portion of the 32-stride downsampled ground-truth map, and is therefore able to capture long range context. However, these large filters are typically very hard to learn. Inspired by [42],

Table 4. Comparison of the results by varying the donut filter kernel size.

Dataset	Kernel size	Mean IU
PASCAL-Context	7×7	40.3
	11×11	**41.0**
SIFT Flow	7×7	**40.7**
	11×11	32.4

we reduce the number of learnable parameters while keeping the context range. Starting from a randomly initialized 6×6 kernel, we dilate the convolution kernel by inserting zeros between every neighboring position. Zero-valued locations are fixed to zero throughout the training. The resulting kernel is of size 11×11 but only 6×6 parameters are learnable.

Training and Testing Process. We follow the procedure of FCN to train our multi-scale hybrid model by stages. We train the ConvPP-32s model first, then upgrade it to the ConvPP-16s model, and finally to the ConvPP-8s model. During testing, we found that 3 iterations are enough for our fixed-point approach to converge, thus we keep this parameter through out our experiments. One concern is if the iterative testing process could diverge. Interestingly, in all our experiments (1-D and 2-D), the results are improved monotonically and converged. This shows that the pseudoprior learning process is stable and the fixed-point solver is effective. The input of ConvPP part is initialized with original FCN prediction since it is readily available.

Computational Cost. Since we can utilize pretrained bottom-up network, training the single-layer top-down convolutional pseudoprior network is efficient. For Pascal-context dataset the training can be done in less than 1 hour on a single Tesla K40 GPU. The additional computational cost due to iterative inference procedure is also small. For 3 iterations of fixed-point inference, our ConvPP model only takes additional 150 ms. Note that all previous works using CRFs (either online or offline) also require testing-stage iterative process.

Pascal-Context. This dataset contains ground truth segmentations fully annotated with 60-category labels (including background), providing rich contextual information to be explored. We follow the standard training + validation split as in [20, 40], resulting in 4,998 training images and 5,105 validation images.

Table 5 shows the performance of our proposed structured labeling approach compared with FCN baselines and other state-of-the-art models.

We hope to evaluate our approach in a way that allows fair comparison with FCN, which does not explicitly handle structural information. Therefore we carefully control our experimental settings as follows: (1) We do not train the bottom-up CNN models for all the experiments in Training Stage 1, and use the pre-trained models provided by the

Table 5. Results on Pascal-Context dataset [40]. ConvPP outperforms FCN baselines and previous state-of-the-art models. † is trained with additional data from COCO.

	Mean IU
O$_2$P [43]	18.1
CFM (VGG+SS) [44]	31.5
CFM (VGG+MCG) [44]	34.4
CRF-RNN [21]	39.3
BoxSup† [45]	40.5
FCN-32s [20]	35.1
ConvPP-32s (ours)	37.1
FCN-16s [20]	37.6
ConvPP-16s (ours)	40.3
FCN-8s [20]	37.8
ConvPP-8s (ours)	**41.0**

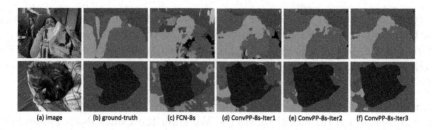

(a) image   (b) ground-truth   (c) FCN-8s   (d) ConvPP-8s-Iter1   (e) ConvPP-8s-Iter2   (f) ConvPP-8s-Iter3

Fig. 6. Iterative update of labeling results during testing. Segmentation results are gradually refined.

authors. **(2)** We train the top-down ConvPP network (Training stage 2) independently on each scale, namely 32s, 16s and 8s. **(3)** To train the hybrid models at a certain scale, we only use the pre-trained FCN models at the corresponding scale. (ConvPP-32s can only use the FCN-32s representations.) **(4)** For all the experiments, we fix the learning rate of the FCN part of the hybrid model, namely all the convolutional layers from Conv1_1 to fc7, to be zero. The reason we freeze the learning rate of FCN is to do an **ablation study**: we want to show the performance gain incorporating the ConvPP part. Intuitively context information should help more in high-level structural prediction rather than improving low-level appearance features. The experiment results support this claim: we get 40.89 when joint-tuning the parameters in the bottom-up FCN-8s network, the difference is negligible. Our methods consistently outperform the FCN baselines. We show the results for ConvPP 32s (structural information integrated in layer pool 5), ConvPP 16s (pool5 + pool4) and ConvPP 8s (pool5 + pool4 + pool3) to analyze the effect of multi-scale context learning. The results have been consistently improved by combining finer scales.

Our method also outperforms other state-of-the-art models built on FCN, notably CRF-RNN [21], which also explicitly handles structured labeling problem by integrating a fully-connected CRF model into the FCN framework; and BoxSup [45], which is trained with additional COCO data. This clearly shows the effectiveness of our ConvPP model in capturing complex inter-dependencies in structured output space. Example qualitative results of our ConvPP-8s compared to baseline FCN-8s model can be found in the supplementary material. Figure 6 shows how our labeling results are iteratively refined at inference time. With multi-scale architecture design, our method leverages both short- and long-range context to assist the labeling task. ConvPP is able to recover correct labels as well as suppress erroneous label predictions based on contextual information. In Fig. 5, we visualize 2 learned donut filters on 32-stride ground-truth maps by displaying label patches that produce top 6 activations (as done in [46]). It is shown that our filters are learned to detect complex label context patterns, such as "food-plate-table", "cat on the bed" and "cat on the grass".

SIFT Flow. We also evaluate our method on scene labeling task, where context is also important in accurate labeling. SIFT Flow dataset [41] contains 2,688 images with 33 semantic categories. A particular challenge for our ConvPP model for this dataset is the relatively small image/ground-truth map size (256×256), which means the 32-stride output is only 8×8. Downsampling the ground-truth map to this scale could potentially lead to loss in useful context information. In addition, the finest model provided by [20] is FCN-16s instead of FCN-8s.

To alleviate this problem, we train our own FCN-8s model (pre-trained with the provided FCN-16s model) as our baseline and build our ConvPP-8s on top of it. Also because of the size of the image in the dataset, as shown in Table 4, 11×11 donut filters perform poorly. Thus we choose the donut filters with kernel size 7×7 and hole size 3×3, and the sparsification operation is not needed. The testing procedure is the same as that of Pascal-Context dataset.

According to Table 6, our ConvPP models consistently outperform corresponding FCN baselines. The improvement of ConvPP-16s model is relatively small, which might result from the limited resolution of ground-truth maps (256×256). With higher ground-truth resolution, ConvPP-8s outperforms the stronger FCN-8s baseline by 1.2% in mean I/U. This substantiate that our proposed pseudoprior learning framework is effective in learning structural information from the ground-truth labeling space.

Table 6. Results on SIFT Flow dataset [41]. Our methods outperform the strong FCN baselines. Improvement of ConvPP-8s vs FCN-8s is more significant than that of ConvPP-16s vs FCN-16s, since higher resolution ground truth map carries more structured information.

	Mean IU
FCN-16s [20]	39.1
ConvPP-16s (ours)	39.7
FCN-8s [20]	39.5
ConvPP-8s (ours)	**40.7**

5   Conclusions

We propose a new method for structured labeling by developing convolutional pseudoprior (ConvPP) on the ground-truth labels. ConvPP learns convolution in the labeling space with improved modeling capability and less manual specification. The automatically learns rich convolutional kernels can capture both short- and long- range contexts combined with a multi-scale hybrid model architecture design. We use a novel fixed-point network structure that facilitates an end-to-end learning process. Results on structured labeling tasks across different domains shows the effectiveness of our method.

Acknowledgment. This work is supported by NSF IIS-1618477, NSF IIS-1360566, NSF IIS-1360568, and a Northrop Grumman Contextual Robotics grant. We thank Zachary C. Lipton, Jameson Merkow, Long Jin for helping improve this manuscript. We are grateful for the generous donation of the GPUs by NVIDIA.

References

1. Elman, J.L.: Finding structure in time. Cogn. Sci. **14**(2), 179–211 (1990)
2. Lafferty, J.D., McCallum, A., Pereira, F.C.N.: Conditional random fields. In: ICML (2001)
3. Shotton, J., Winn, J., Rother, C., Criminisi, A.: *TextonBoost*: joint appearance, shape and context modeling for multi-class object recognition and segmentation. In: Leonardis, A., Bischof, H., Pinz, A. (eds.) ECCV 2006. LNCS, vol. 3951, pp. 1–15. Springer, Heidelberg (2006). doi:10.1007/11744023_1
4. Geman, S., Geman, D.: Stochastic relaxation, Gibbs distributions, and the Bayesian restoration of images. IEEE PAMI **6**(6), 721–741 (1984)
5. Tsochantaridis, I., Joachims, T., Hofmann, T., Altun, Y.: Large margin methods for structured and interdependent output variables. JMLR **6**, 1453–1484 (2005)
6. Taskar, B., Guestrin, C., Koller, D.: Max-margin Markov networks. In: NIPS (2003)
7. Finley, T., Joachims, T.: Training structural SVMs when exact inference is intractable. In: ICML (2008)
8. Tu, Z.: Auto-context and its application to high-level vision tasks. In: CVPR (2008)
9. Heitz, G., Gould, S., Saxena, A., Koller, D.: Cascaded classification models. In: NIPS (2008)
10. Daumé, H.I., Langford, J., Marcu, D.: Search-based structured prediction. Mach. Learn. **75**, 297–325 (2009)
11. Wolpert, D.H.: Stacked generalization. Neural Netw. **5**(2), 241–259 (1992)
12. Ames Jr., A.: Visual perception and the rotating trapezoidal window. Psychol. Monogr. Gen. Appl. **65**(7), i (1951)
13. David, M.: Vision: A Computational Investigation into the Human Representation and Processing of Visual Information. Henry Holt and Co., Inc., New York (1982)
14. Gibson, J.J.: A theory of direct visual perception. In: Vision and Mind: Selected Readings in the Philosophy of Perception, pp. 77–90 (2002)
15. Kersten, D., Mamassian, P., Yuille, A.: Object perception as Bayesian inference. Ann. Rev. Psychol. **55**, 271–304 (2004)
16. Tu, Z., Chen, X., Yuille, A.L., Zhu, S.C.: Image parsing: unifying segmentation, detection, and recognition. IJCV **63**(2), 113–140 (2005)
17. Borenstein, E., Ullman, S.: Combined top-down/bottom-up segmentation. IEEE PAMI **30**(12), 2109–2125 (2008)
18. Wu, T., Zhu, S.C.: A numerical study of the bottom-up and top-down inference processes in and-or graphs. IJCV **93**(2), 226–252 (2011)
19. Krahenbuhl, P., Koltun, V.: Efficient inference in fully connected CRFs with Gaussian edge potentials. In: NIPS (2011)
20. Long, J., Shelhamer, E., Darrell, T.: Fully convolutional networks for semantic segmentation. In: CVPR (2015)
21. Zheng, S., Jayasumana, S., Romera-Paredes, B., Vineet, V., Su, Z., Du, D., Huang, C., Torr, P.: Conditional random fields as recurrent neural networks (2015). arXiv preprint arXiv:1502.03240
22. Lin, G., Shen, C., Reid, I., Hengel, A.v.d.: Deeply learning the messages in message passing inference. In: NIPS (2015)
23. Besag, J.: Efficiency of pseudolikelihood estimation for simple Gaussian fields. Biometrika **64**, 616–618 (1977)
24. Zhu, S.C., Mumford, D.: A stochastic grammar of images. Found. Trends Comput. Graph. Vis. **2**(4), 259–362 (2006)

25. He, X., Zemel, R.S., Carreira-Perpiñán, M.: Multiscale conditional random fields for image labeling. In: CVPR (2004)
26. Kae, A., Sohn, K., Lee, H., Learned-Miller, E.: Augmenting crfs with Boltzmann machine shape priors for image labeling. In: CVPR (2013)
27. Henaff, M., Bruna, J., LeCun, Y.: Deep convolutional networks on graph-structured data (2015). arXiv preprint arXiv:1506.05163
28. Hinton, G.E., Osindero, S., Teh, Y.-W.: A fast learning algorithm for deep belief nets. Neural Comput. 18(7), 1527–1554 (2006). MIT Press
29. Snoek, J., Adams, R.P., Larochelle, H.: Nonparametric guidance of autoencoder representations using label information. JMLR 13, 2567–2588 (2012)
30. Bengio, Y., Thibodeau-Laufer, E., Alain, G., Yosinski, J.: Deep generative stochastic networks trainable by backprop (2013). arXiv preprint arXiv:1306.1091
31. Tu, Z., Narr, K.L., Dollár, P., Dinov, I., Thompson, P.M., Toga, A.W.: Brain anatomical structure segmentation by hybrid discriminative/generative models. IEEE Trans. Med. Imaging 27(4), 495–508 (2008)
32. Li, Q., Wang, J., Wipf, D., Tu, Z.: Fixed-point model for structured labeling. ICML 28, 214–221 (2013)
33. Makhzani, A., Frey, B.: Winner-take-all autoencoders. In: NIPS (2015)
34. McCallum, A., Freitag, D., Pereira, F.C.: Maximum entropy Markov models for information extraction and segmentation. In: ICML (2000)
35. LeCun, Y., Bottou, L., Bengio, Y., Haffner, P.: Gradient-based learning applied to document recognition. In: Proceedings of the IEEE (1998)
36. Do, T., Arti, T.: Neural conditional random fields. In: AISTATS (2010)
37. Hoefel, G., Elkan, C.: Learning a two-stage SVM/CRF sequence classifier. In: CIKM, ACM (2008)
38. van der Maaten, L., Welling, M., Saul, L.K.: Hidden-unit conditional random fields. In: AISTATS (2011)
39. Everingham, M., Van Gool, L., Williams, C.K.I., Winn, J., Zisserman, A.: The PASCAL Visual Object Classes Challenge 2012 (VOC2012) results (2012). http://www.pascal-network.org/challenges/VOC/voc2012/workshop/index.html
40. Mottaghi, R., Chen, X., Liu, X., Cho, N.G., Lee, S.W., Fidler, S., Urtasun, R., et al.: The role of context for object detection and semantic segmentation in the wild. In: CVPR (2014)
41. Liu, C., Yuen, J., Torralba, A.: Nonparametric scene parsing: label transfer via dense scene alignment. In: CVPR (2009)
42. Chen, L.C., Papandreou, G., Kokkinos, I., Murphy, K., Yuille, A.L.: Semantic image segmentation with deep convolutional nets and fully connected CRFs. In: ICLR (2015)
43. Carreira, J., Caseiro, R., Batista, J., Sminchisescu, C.: Semantic segmentation with second-order pooling. In: Fitzgibbon, A., Lazebnik, S., Perona, P., Sato, Y., Schmid, C. (eds.) ECCV 2012. LNCS, vol. 7578, pp. 430–443. Springer, Heidelberg (2012). doi:10.1007/978-3-642-33786-4_32
44. Dai, J., He, K., Sun, J.: Convolutional feature masking for joint object and stuff segmentation. In: CVPR (2015)
45. Dai, J., He, K., Sun, J.: BoxSup: exploiting bounding boxes to supervise convolutional networks for semantic segmentation. In: ICCV (2015)
46. Zeiler, M.D., Fergus, R.: Visualizing and understanding convolutional networks. In: Fleet, D., Pajdla, T., Schiele, B., Tuytelaars, T. (eds.) ECCV 2014. LNCS, vol. 8689, pp. 818–833. Springer, Heidelberg (2014). doi:10.1007/978-3-319-10590-1_53

Generative Image Modeling Using Style and Structure Adversarial Networks

Xiaolong Wang[✉] and Abhinav Gupta

Robotics Institute, Carnegie Mellon University, Pittsburgh, USA
xiaolonw@cs.cmu.edu

Abstract. Current generative frameworks use end-to-end learning and generate images by sampling from uniform noise distribution. However, these approaches ignore the most basic principle of image formation: images are product of: (a) Structure: the underlying 3D model; (b) Style: the texture mapped onto structure. In this paper, we factorize the image generation process and propose Style and Structure Generative Adversarial Network (S^2-GAN). Our S^2-GAN has two components: the Structure-GAN generates a surface normal map; the Style-GAN takes the surface normal map as input and generates the 2D image. Apart from a real vs. generated loss function, we use an additional loss with computed surface normals from generated images. The two GANs are first trained independently, and then merged together via joint learning. We show our S^2-GAN model is interpretable, generates more realistic images and can be used to learn unsupervised RGBD representations.

1 Introduction

Unsupervised learning of visual representations is one of the most fundamental problems in computer vision. There are two common approaches for unsupervised learning: (a) using a discriminative framework with auxiliary tasks where supervision comes for free, such as context prediction [1,2] or temporal embedding [3–8]; (b) using a generative framework where the underlying model is compositional and attempts to generate realistic images [9–12]. The underlying hypothesis of the generative framework is that if the model is good enough to generate novel and realistic images, it should be a good representation for vision tasks as well. Most of these generative frameworks use end-to-end learning to generate RGB images from control parameters (z also called noise since it is sampled from a uniform distribution). Recently, some impressive results [13] have been shown on restrictive domains such as faces and bedrooms.

However, these approaches ignore one of the most basic underlying principles of image formation. Images are a product of two separate phenomena: **Structure:** this encodes the underlying geometry of the scene. It refers to the underlying mesh, voxel representation etc. **Style:** this encodes the texture on the objects and the illumination. In this paper, we build upon this IM101 principle of image formation and factor the generative adversarial network (GAN) into two generative processes as Fig. 1. The first, a structure generative model (namely

© Springer International Publishing AG 2016
B. Leibe et al. (Eds.): ECCV 2016, Part IV, LNCS 9908, pp. 318–335, 2016.
DOI: 10.1007/978-3-319-46493-0_20

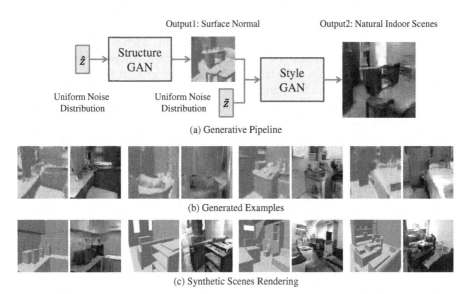

(a) Generative Pipeline

(b) Generated Examples

(c) Synthetic Scenes Rendering

Fig. 1. (a) Generative Pipeline: Given $\hat{z}$ sampled from uniform distribution, our Structure-GAN generates a surface normal map as output. This surface normal map is then given as input with $\tilde{z}$ to a second generator network (Style-GAN) and outputs an image. (b) We show examples of generated surface normal maps and images. (c) Our Style-GAN can be used as a rendering engine: given a synthetic scene, we can use it to render a realistic image. To visualize the normals, we represent facing right with blue, horizontal surface with green, facing left with red (blue → X; green → Y; red → Z). (Color figure online)

Structure-GAN), takes $\hat{z}$ and generates the underlying 3D structure (y_{3D}) for the scene. The second, a conditional generative network (namely Style-GAN), takes y_{3D} as input and noise $\tilde{z}$ to generate the image y_I. We call this factored generative network Style and Structure Generative Adversarial Network (S^2-GAN).

Why S^2-GAN? We believe there are fourfold advantages of factoring the style and structure in the image generation process. Firstly, factoring style and structure simplifies the overall generative process and leads to more realistic high-resolution images. It also leads to a highly stable and robust learning procedure. Secondly, due to the factoring process, S^2-GAN is more interpretable as compared to its counterparts. One can even factor the errors and understand where the surface normal generation failed as compared to texture generation. Thirdly, as our results indicate, S^2-GAN allows us to learn RGBD representation in an unsupervised manner. This can be crucial for many robotics and graphics applications. Finally, our Style-GAN can also be thought of as a learned rendering engine which, given any 3D input, allows us to render a corresponding image. It also allows us to build applications where one can modify the underlying 3D structure of an input image and render a completely new image.

However, learning S^2-GAN is still not an easy task. To tackle this challenge, we first learn the Style-GAN and Structure-GAN in an independent manner. We use the NYUv2 RGBD dataset [14] with more than 200 K frames for learning the initial networks. We train a Structure-GAN using the ground truth surface normals from Kinect. Because the perspective distortion of texture is more directly related to normals than to depth, we use surface normal to represent image structure in this paper. We learn in parallel our Style-GAN which is conditional on the ground truth surface normals. While training the Style-GAN, we have two loss functions: the first loss function takes in an image and the surface normals and tries to predict if they correspond to a real scene or not. However, this loss function alone does not enforce explicit pixel based constraints for aligning generated images with input surface normals. To enforce the pixel-wise constraints, we make the following assumption: if the generated image is realistic enough, we should be able to reconstruct or predict the 3D structure based on it. We achieve this by adding another discriminator network. More specifically, the generated image is not only forwarded to the discriminator network in GAN but also a input for the trained surface normal predictor network. Once we have trained an initial Style-GAN and Structure-GAN, we combine them together and perform end-to-end learning jointly where images are generated from $\hat{z}, \tilde{z}$ and fed to discriminators for real/fake task.

2   Related Work

Unsupervised learning of visual representation is one of the most challenging problems in computer vision. There are two primary approaches to unsupervised learning. The first is the discriminative approach where we use auxiliary tasks such that ground truth can be generated without labeling. Some examples of these auxiliary tasks include predicting: the relative location of two patches [2], ego-motion in videos [15,16], physical signals [17–19].

A more common approach to unsupervised learning is to use a generative framework. Two types of generative frameworks have been used in the past. Non-parametric approaches perform matching of an image or patch with the database for tasks such as texture synthesis [20] or super-resolution [21]. In this paper, we are interested in developing a parametric model of images. One common approach is to learn a low-dimensional representation which can be used to reconstruct an image. Some examples include the deep auto-encoder [22,23] or Restricted Boltzmann machines (RBMs) [24–28]. However, in most of the above scenarios it is hard to generate new images since sampling in latent space is not an easy task. The recently proposed Variational auto-encoders (VAE) [10,11] tackles this problem by generating images with variational sampling approach. However, these approaches are restricted to simple datasets such as MNIST. To generate interpretable images with richer information, the VAE is extended to be conditioned on captions [29] and graphics code [30]. Besides RBMs and auto-encoders, there are also many novel generative models in recent literature [31–34]. For example, Dosovitskiy et al. [31] proposed to use CNNs to generate chairs.

In this work, we build our model based on the Generative Adversarial Networks (GANs) framework proposed by Goodfellow et al. [9]. This framework was extended by Denton et al. [35] to generate images. Specifically, they proposed to use a Laplacian pyramid of adversarial networks to generate images in a coarse to fine scheme. However, training these networks is still tricky and unstable. Therefore, an extension DCGAN [13] proposed good practices for training adversarial networks and demonstrated promising results in generating images. There are more extensions include using conditional variables [36–38]. For instance, Mathieu et al. [37] introduced to predict future video frames conditioned on the previous frames. In this paper, we further simplify the image generation process by factoring out the generation of 3D structure and style.

In order to train our S^2-GAN we combine adversarial loss with 3D surface normal prediction loss [39–42] to provide extra constraints during learning. This is also related to the idea of combining multiple losses for better generative modeling [43–45]. For example, Makhzani et al. [43] proposed an adversarial auto-encoder which takes the adversarial loss as an extra constraint for the latent code during training the auto-encoder. Finally, the idea of factorizing image into two separate phenomena has been well studied in [46–49], which motivates us to decompose the generative process to structure and style. We use the RGBD data from NYUv2 to factorize and learn a S^2-GAN model.

3   Background for Generative Adversarial Networks

The Generative Adversarial Networks (GAN) [9] contains two models: generator G and discriminator D. The generator G takes the input which is a latent random vector z sampled from uniform noise distribution and tries to generate a realistic image. The discriminator D performs binary classification to distinguish whether an image is generated from G or it is a real image. Thus the two models are competing against each other (hence, adversarial): network G will try to generate images which will be hard for D to differentiate from real image, meanwhile network D will learn to avoid getting fooled by G.

Formally, we optimize the networks using gradient descent with batch size M. We are given samples as $\mathbf{X} = (X_1, ..., X_M)$ and a set of z sampled from uniform distribution as $\mathbf{Z} = (z_1, ..., z_M)$. The training of GAN is an iterative procedure with 2 steps: (i) fix the parameters of network G and optimize network D; (ii) fix network D and optimize network G. The loss for training network D is,

$$L^D(\mathbf{X}, \mathbf{Z}) = \sum_{i=1}^{M/2} L(D(X_i), 1) + \sum_{i=M/2+1}^{M} L(D(G(z_i)), 0). \qquad (1)$$

Inside a batch, half of images are real and the rest $G(z_i)$ are images generated by G given z_i. $D(X_i) \in [0, 1]$ represents the binary classification score given input image X_i. $L(y^*, y) = -[y \log(y^*) + (1 - y) log(1 - y^*)]$ is the binary entropy loss. Thus the loss Eq. 1 for network D is optimized to classify the real image as label

Table 1. Network architectures. Top: generator of Structure-GAN; bottom: discriminator of Structure-GAN (left) and discriminator of Style-GAN (right). "conv" means convolutional layer, "uconv" means fractionally-strided convolutional (deconvolutional) layer, where 2(*up*) stride indicates 2x resolution. "fc" means fully connected layer.

Structure-GAN(G)	fc	uconv	conv	conv	conv	conv	uconv	conv	uconv	conv
Input Size	–	9	18	18	18	18	18	36	36	72
Kernel Number	$9 \times 9 \times 64$	128	128	256	512	512	256	128	64	3
Kernel Size	–	4	3	3	3	3	4	3	4	5
Stride	–	2(*up*)	1	1	1	1	2(*up*)	1	2(*up*)	1

Structure-GAN(D)	conv	conv	conv	conv	conv	fc
Input Size	72	36	36	18	9	–
Kernel Number	64	128	256	512	128	1
Kernel Size	5	5	3	3	3	–
Stride	2	1	2	2	1	–

Style-GAN(D)	conv	conv	conv	conv	conv	fc
Input Size	128	64	32	16	8	–
Kernel Number	64	128	256	512	128	1
Kernel Size	5	5	3	3	3	–
Stride	2	2	2	2	1	–

1 and the generated image as 0. On the other hand, the generator G is trying to fool D to classify the generated image as a real image via minimizing the loss:

$$L^G(\mathbf{Z}) = \sum_{i=M/2+1}^{M} L(D(G(z_i)), 1). \tag{2}$$

4   Style and Structure GAN

GAN and DCGAN approaches directly generate images from the sampled z. Instead, we use the fact that image generation has two components: (a) generating the underlying structure based on the objects in the scene; (b) generating the texture/style on top of this 3D structure. We use this simple observation to decompose the generative process into two procedures: (i) Structure-GAN - this process generates surface normals from sampled $\hat{z}$ and (ii) Style-GAN - this model generates the images taking as input the surface normals and another latent variable $\tilde{z}$ sampled from uniform distribution. We train both models with RGBD data, and the ground truth surface normals are obtained from the depth.

4.1   Structure-GAN

We can directly apply GAN framework to learn how to generate surface normal maps. The input to the network G will be $\hat{z}$ sampled from uniform distribution and the output is a surface normal map. We use a 100-d vector to represent the $\hat{z}$ and the output is in size of $72 \times 72 \times 3$ (Fig. 2). The discriminator D will learn to classify the generated surface normal maps from the real maps obtained from depth. We introduce our network architecture as following.

Generator Network. As Table 1 (top row) illustrates, we apply a 10-layer model for the generator. Given a 100-d $\hat{z}$ as input, it is first fully connected to a 3D block ($9 \times 9 \times 64$). Then we further perform convolutional operations on top of

Fig. 2. Left: 4 Generated Surface Normal maps. Right: 2 Pairs of rendering results on ground truth surface normal maps using the Style-GAN without pixel-wise constraints.

it and generate the surface normal map in the end. Note that "uconv" represents fractionally-strided convolution [13], which is also called as deconvolution. We follow the settings in [13] and use Batch Normalization [50] and ReLU activations after each layer except for the last layer, where a TanH activation is applied.

Discriminator Network. We show the 6-layer network architecture in Table 1 (bottom left). Taking an image as input, the network outputs a single number which predicts the input surface normal is real or generated. We use LeakyReLU [51,52] for activation functions as in [13]. However, we do not apply Batch Normalization here. In our case, we find that the discriminator network easily finds trivial solutions with Batch Normalization.

4.2 Style-GAN

Given the RGB images and surface normal maps from Kinect, we train another GAN in parallel to generate images conditioned on surface normals. We call this network Style-GAN. First, we modify our generator network to a conditional GAN as proposed in [35,36]. The conditional information, i.e., surface normal maps, are given as additional inputs for both the generator G and the discriminator D. Augmenting surface normals as an additional input to D not only forces the generated image to look real, but also implicitly enforces the generated image to match the surface normal map. While training this discriminator, we only consider real RGB images and their corresponding surface normals as the positive examples. Given more cues from surface normals, we generate higher resolution of $128 \times 128 \times 3$ images with the Style-GAN.

Formally, we have a batch of RGB images $\mathbf{X} = (X_1, ..., X_M)$ and their corresponding surface normal maps $\mathbf{C} = (C_1, ..., C_M)$, as well as samples from noise distribution $\tilde{\mathbf{Z}} = (\tilde{z}_1, ..., \tilde{z}_M)$. We reformulate the generative function from $G(\tilde{z}_i)$ to $G(C_i, \tilde{z}_i)$ and discriminative function is changed from $D(X_i)$ to $D(C_i, X_i)$. Then the loss of discriminator network in Eq. 1 can be reformulated as,

$$L_{cond}^D(\mathbf{X}, \mathbf{C}, \tilde{\mathbf{Z}}) = \sum_{i=1}^{M/2} L(D(C_i, X_i), 1) + \sum_{i=M/2+1}^{M} L(D(C_i, G(C_i, \tilde{z}_i)), 0), \quad (3)$$

and the loss of generator network in Eq. 2 can be reformulated as,

$$L_{cond}^G(\mathbf{C}, \tilde{\mathbf{Z}}) = \sum_{i=M/2+1}^{M} L(D(C_i, G(C_i, \tilde{z}_i)), 1). \quad (4)$$

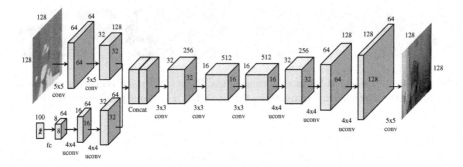

Fig. 3. The architecture of the generator in Style-GAN.

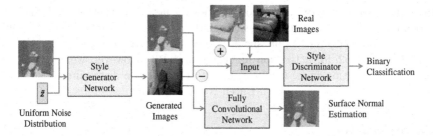

Fig. 4. Our Style-GAN. Given the ground truth surface normals and $\tilde{z}$ as inputs, the generator G learns to generate RGB images. The supervision comes from two networks: The discriminator network takes the generated images, real images and their corresponding normal maps as inputs to perform classification; The FCN takes the generated images as inputs and predict the surface normal maps.

We apply the same scheme of iterative training. By doing this, we can generate the images with network G as visualized in Fig. 2 (right).

Network Architecture. We show our generator as Fig. 3. Given a $128 \times 128 \times 3$ surface normal map and a 100-d $\tilde{z}$ as input, they are firstly forwarded to convolutional and deconvolutional layers respectively and then concatenated to form $32 \times 32 \times 192$ feature maps. On top of these feature maps, 7 layers of convolutions and deconvolutions are further performed. The output of the network is a $128 \times 128 \times 3$ RGB image. For the discriminator, we apply the similar architecture of the one in Structure-GAN (bottom right in Table 1). The input for the network is the concatenation of surface normals and images ($128 \times 128 \times 6$).

4.3   Multi-task Learning with Pixel-Wise Constraints

The Style-GAN can make the generated image look real and also enforce it to match the provided surface normal maps implicitly. However, as shown Fig. 2, the images are noisy and the edges are not well aligned with the edges in the surface normal maps. Thus, we propose to add a pixel-wise constraint to explicitly guide the generator to align the outputs with the input surface normal maps.

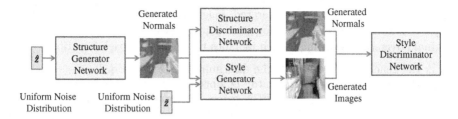

Fig. 5. Full model of our S²-GAN. It can directly generate RGB images given $\hat{z}, \tilde{z}$ as inputs. For simplicity, we do not visualize the positive samples in training. During joint learning, the loss from Style-GAN is also passed down to the Structure-GAN.

We make the following assumption: If the generated image is real enough, it can be used for reconstructing the surface normal maps. To encode this constraint, we train another network for surface normal estimation. We modify the Fully Convolutional Network (FCN) [53] with the classification loss as mentioned in [39] for this task. More specifically, we quantize the surface normals to 40 classes with k-means clustering as in [39,54] and the loss is defined as

$$L^{FCN}(\mathbf{X}, \mathbf{C}) = \frac{1}{K \times K} \sum_{i=1}^{M} \sum_{k=1}^{K \times K} L_s(F_k(X_i), C_{i,k}), \tag{5}$$

where L_s means the softmax loss and the output surface normal map is in $K \times K$ dimension, and $K = 128$ is in the same size of input image. $F_k(X_i)$ is the output of kth pixel in the ith sample. $C_{i,k}(1 \leqslant C_{i,k} \leqslant 40)$ is the label for the kth pixel in sample i. Thus the loss is designed to enforce each pixel in the image to generate accurate surface normal. Note that when training the FCN, we use the RGBD data which provides indoor scene images and ground truth surface normals. The model is trained from scratch without ImageNet pre-training.

FCN Architecture. We apply the AlexNet [55] following the same training scheme as [53], with modifications on the last 3 layers. Given a generated 128×128 image, it is first upsampled to 512×512 before feeding into the FCN. For the two layers before the last layer, we use smaller kernel numbers of 1024 and 512. The last layer is a deconvolutional layer with stride 2. In the end, upsampling (4x resolution) is further applied to generate the high quality results.

Given the trained FCN model, we can use it as an additional supervision (constraint) in the adversarial learning. Our final model is illustrated in Fig. 4. During training, not only the gradients from the classification loss of D will be passed down to G, but also the surface normal estimation loss from the FCN is passed through the generated image to G. This way, the adversarial loss from D will make the generated images look real, and the FCN will give pixel-wise constraints to make the generated images aligned with surface normal maps.

Formally, we combine the two losses in Eqs. 4 and 5 for the generator G,

$$L^G_{multi}(\mathbf{C}, \tilde{\mathbf{Z}}) = L^G_{cond}(\mathbf{C}, \tilde{\mathbf{Z}}) + L^{FCN}(G(\mathbf{C}, \tilde{\mathbf{Z}}), \mathbf{C}), \tag{6}$$

where $G(\mathbf{C}, \tilde{\mathbf{Z}})$ represents the generated images given a batch of surface normal maps $\mathbf{C}$ and noise $\tilde{\mathbf{Z}}$. The training procedure for this model is similar to the original adversarial learning, which includes three steps in each iteration:

- Fix the generator G, optimize the discriminator D with Eq. 3.
- Fix the FCN and the discriminator D, optimize the generator G with Eq. 6.
- Fix the generator G, fine-tune FCN using generated and real images.

Note that the parameters of FCN model are fixed in the beginning of multi-task learning, i.e., we do not fine-tune FCN in the beginning. The reason is the generated images are not good in the beginning, so feeding bad examples to FCN seems to make the surface normal prediction worse.

4.4   Joint Learning for $\mathbf{S}^2$-GAN

After training the Structure-GAN and Style-GAN independently, we merge all networks and train them jointly. As Fig. 5 shows, our full model includes surface normal generation from Structure-GAN, and based on it the Style-GAN generates the image. Note that the generated normal maps are first passed through an upsampling layer with bilinear interpolation before they are forwarded to the Style-GAN. Since we do not use ground truth surface normal maps to generate the images, we remove the FCN constraint from the Style-GAN. The discriminator in Style-GAN takes generated normals and images as negative samples, and ground truth normals and real images as positive samples.

For the Structure-GAN, the generator network receives not only the gradients from the discriminator of Structure-GAN, but also the gradients passed through the generator of Style-GAN. In this way, the network is forced to generate surface normals which not only are realistic but also help generate better RGB images. Formally, the loss for the generator network of Structure-GAN can be represented as combining Eqs. 2 and 4,

$$L_{joint}^G(\hat{\mathbf{Z}}, \tilde{\mathbf{Z}}) = L^G(\hat{\mathbf{Z}}) + \lambda \cdot L_{cond}^G(G(\hat{\mathbf{Z}}), \tilde{\mathbf{Z}}) \qquad (7)$$

where $\hat{\mathbf{Z}} = (\hat{z}_1, ..., \hat{z}_M)$ and $\tilde{\mathbf{Z}} = (\tilde{z}_1, ..., \tilde{z}_M)$ represent two sets of samples drawn from uniform distribution for Structure-GAN and Style-GAN respectively. The first term in Eq. 7 represents the adversarial loss from the discriminator of Structure-GAN and the second term represents that the loss of the Style-GAN is also passed down. We set the coefficient $\lambda = 0.1$ and smaller learning rate for Structure-GAN than Style-GAN in the experiments, so that we can prevent the generated normals from over fitting to the task of generating RGB images via Style-GAN. In our experiments, we find that without constraining λ and learning rates, the loss $L^G(\hat{\mathbf{Z}})$ easily diverges to high values and the Structure-GAN can no longer generate reasonable surface normal maps.

5   Experiments

We perform two types of experiments: (a) We qualitatively and quantitatively evaluate the quality of images generates using our model; (b) We evaluate the quality of unsupervised representation learning by applying the network for different tasks such as image classification and object detection.

Dataset. We use the NYUv2 dataset [14] in our experiment. We use the raw video data during training and extract 200 K frames from the 249 training video scenes. We compute the surface normals from the depth as [39,42].

Parameter Settings. We follow the parameters in [13] for training. We trained the models using Adam optimizer [56] with momentum term $\beta_1 = 0.5, \beta_2 = 0.999$ and batch size $M = 128$. The inputs and outputs for all networks are scaled to $[-1, 1]$ (including surface normals and RGB images). During training the Style and Structure GANs separately, we set the learning rate to 0.0002. We train the Structure-GAN for 25 epochs. For Style-GAN, we first fix the FCN model and train it for 25 epochs, then the FCN model are fine-tuned together with 5 more epochs. For joint learning, we set learning rate as 10^{-6} for Style-GAN and 10^{-7} for Structure-GAN and train them for 5 epochs.

Baselines. We have 4 baseline models trained on NYUv2 training set: (a) DCGAN [13]: it takes uniform noise as input and generate 64×64 images; (b) DCGAN + LAPGAN: we train a LAPGAN [35] on top of DCGAN, which takes lower resolution images as inputs and generates 128×128 images. We apply the same architecture as our Style-GAN for LAPGAN (Fig. 3 and Table 1). (c) DCGANv2: we train a DCGAN with the same architecture as our Structure-GAN (Table 1). (d) DCGANv2+LAPGAN: we train another LAPGAN on top of DCGANv2 as (b) with the same architecture. Note that baseline (d) has the same model complexity as our model.

5.1 Qualitative Results for Image Generation

Style-GAN Visualization. Before showing the image generation results of the full S^2-GAN model, we first visualize the results of our Style-GAN given the ground truth surface normals on the NYUv2 test set. As illustrated in the first 3 rows of Fig. 6, we can generate nice rendering results which are well aligned with the surface normal inputs. By comparing with the original RGB images, we show that our method can generate a different style (illumination, color, texture) of image with the same structure. We also make comparisons on the results of Style-GAN with/without pixel-wise constraints as visualized in Fig. 7. We show that if we train the model without the pixel-wise constraint, the output is less smooth and noisier than our approach.

Rendering on Synthetic Scenes. One application of our Style-GAN is rendering synthetic scenes. We use the 3D models annotated in [57] to generate the synthetic scenes. We use the scenes corresponding to the NYUv2 test set and make some modifications by rotation, zooming in/out. As the last two rows of Fig. 6 show, we can obtain very realistic rendering results on 3D models.

S^2-GAN Visualization. We now show the results of our full generative model. Given the noise $\hat{z}, \tilde{z}$, our model generate both surface normal maps (72×72) and

Input   Output   Original   Input   Output   Original   Input   Output   Original

Input   Output   Input   Output   Input   Output   Input   Output

Fig. 6. Results of Style-GAN conditioned on ground truth surface normals (first 3 rows) and synthetic scenes (last 2 rows). For ground truth normals, we show the input normals, our generated images and the original corresponding images.

W/O   With   W/O   With   W/O   With
Constraint Constraint   Constraint Constraint   Constraint Constraint

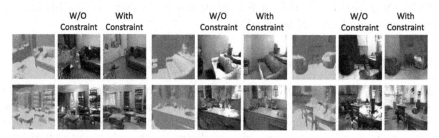

Fig. 7. Comparison between models with and without pixel-wise constraints.

RGB images (128 × 128) after that, as shown in Fig. 8(a). We compare with the baselines including DCGAN (Fig. 8(b)) and DCGAN + LAPGAN (Fig. 8(c)). We can see that our method can generate more structured indoor scenes, i.e., it is easier to figure out the structure and objects in our image. We also find that using LAPGAN does not help much improving the qualitative results.

Walking the Latent Space. One big advantage of our model is that it is interpretable. Recall that we have two random uniform vectors $\hat{z}, \tilde{z}$ as inputs for Structure and Style networks. We conduct two experiments here: (i) Fix $\tilde{z}$ (style) and manipulate the structure of images by changing $\hat{z}$; (ii) Fix $\hat{z}$ (structure) and manipulate the style of images by changing $\tilde{z}$. Specifically, given an initial set of

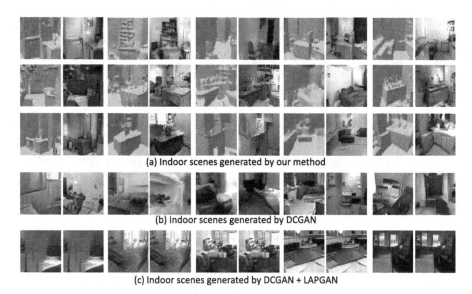

(a) Indoor scenes generated by our method

(b) Indoor scenes generated by DCGAN

(c) Indoor scenes generated by DCGAN + LAPGAN

Fig. 8. (a) Pairs of surface normals and images generated by S^2-GAN. (b) Results of DCGAN. (c) Results of DCGAN + LAPGAN. For each pair, result on the left is from DCGAN and on the right is applying LAPGAN after it.

$\hat{z}$ and $\tilde{z}$, we pick up a series of 10 random points in $\hat{z}$ or $\tilde{z}$ and gradually add 0.1 to these points for 6–7 times. We show that we can obtain smooth transitions in the outputs by interpolating the inputs as Fig. 9. For the example in the first two rows of Fig. 9, we show that by interpolating $\hat{z}$, we can gradually "grow" a 3D cube in the room and the style of the RGB images are consistent since we fix the $\tilde{z}$. For the last rows in Fig. 9, we fix the structure of the image and interpolate the $\tilde{z}$ so that the window of the room is gradually shut down.

User Study. We collect 1000 pairs of images randomly generated by our method and DCGAN. We let the AMT workers to judge which one is more realistic in each pair and 71 % of the time they think our approach generates better images.

5.2 Quantitative Results for Image Generation

To evaluate the generated images quantitatively, we apply the AlexNet pre-trained (supervised) on Places [58] and ImageNet dataset [59] to perform classification and detection on them. The motivation is: If the generated images are realistic enough, state of the art classifiers and detectors should fire on them with high scores. We compare our method with the three baselines mentioned in the beginning of experiment: DCGAN, DCGANv2 and DCGANv2 + LAPGAN. We generate 10 K images for each model and perform evaluation on them.

Classification on Generated Images. We apply the Places-AlexNet [58] to perform classification on the generated images. If the image is real enough, the

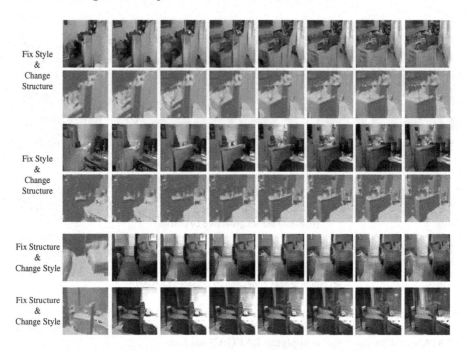

Fix Style
&
Change
Structure

Fix Style
&
Change
Structure

Fix Structure
&
Change Style

Fix Structure
&
Change Style

Fig. 9. Walking the latent space: Our latent space is more interpretable and we obtain smooth transitions of generated results by interpolating the inputs.

Places-AlexNet will give high response in one class during classification. Thus, we can use the maximum norm $|| \cdot ||_\infty$ of the softmax output (i.e., the maximum probability) of Places-AlexNet to represent the image quality. We compute the results for this metric on all generated images and show the mean for different models as Fig. 10(a). S^2-GAN is around 2 % better than the baselines.

Object Detection on Generated Images. We used Fast-RCNN detector [60] fine-tuned on the NYUv2 dataset with ImageNet pre-trained AlexNet. We then apply the detector on generated images. If the image is realistic enough, the detector should find objects (door, bed, sofa, table, counter etc.). Thus, we want to investigate on which images the detector can find more foreground objects. We plot the curves shown in Fig. 10(b) (the x-axis represents the detection threshold, and the y-axis represents average number of detections). We show that the detector can find more foreground objects in the images generated by S^2-GAN. At 0.3 threshold, there are on average 2.2 detections per image and 1.72 detections on images generated by DCGAN.

5.3   Representation Learning for Recognition Tasks

We now explore whether the representation learned by the discriminator network in our Style-GAN can be transferred to tasks such as scene classification and object detection. Since the input for the network is RGB image and surface

	S²-GAN	DCGAN	DCGANv2	DCGANv2 + LAPGAN
Maximum Norm	**29.0**	25.6	27.1	27.2

(a) Classification on generated images.

	S²-GAN	DCGAN	GIST	Places-AlexNet
RGB Accuracy	-	21.3	19.7	38.1
D Accuracy	-	19.1	20.1	27.7
RGBD Accuracy	35.3	27.1	23.0	39.0

(c) Classification on SUN RGB-D dataset.

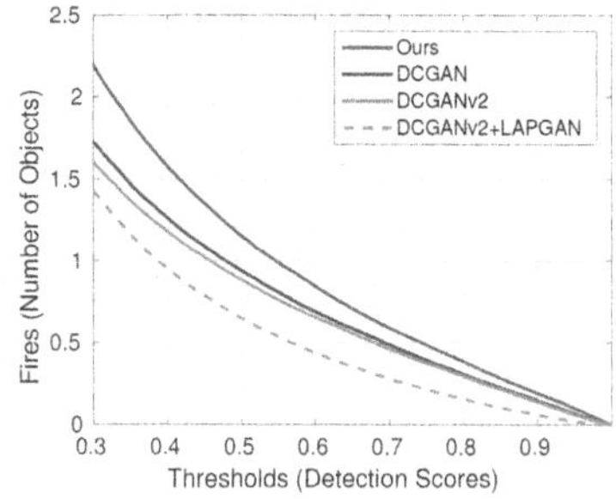

(b) Object detection on generated images.

Fig. 10. (a) The maximum norm of classification results on generated images. (b) Number of fires over different thresholds for object detection on generated images. (c) Scene classification on SUN RGB-D with our model and other methods (no fine-tuning).

normal map, our model can be applied to recognition tasks in RGBD data. We perform the experiments on scene classification on SUN RGB-D dataset [14,61–63] as well as object detection on NYUv2 dataset.

Scene Classification. We use the standard train/test split for scene classification in SUN RGB-D dataset, which includes 19 classes with 4852 training and 4660 testing images. We use our model, taking RGB images and normals as inputs, to extract the feature of the second-to-last layer and train SVM on top of it. We compare our method with the discriminator network in DCGAN and the baselines reported in [61]: GIST [64] feature as well as Places-AlexNet [58]. For the networks trained with only RGB data, we follow [61,65], which directly use them to extract feature on the depth representation. Then the features extracted from both RGB and depth are concatenated together as inputs for SVM classifier. Note that all models are not fine-tuned on the dataset. As Fig. 10(c) shows, our model is 8.2 % better than DCGAN and 3.7 % away from the Places-AlexNet.

Object Detection. In this task, we perform RGBD object detection on the NYUv2 dataset. We follow the Fast-RCNN pipeline [60] and use the code and parameter settings provided in [66]. In our case, we use surface normal to represent the depth. To apply our model for the detection task, we stacked two fully connected layer (4096-d) on top of the last convolutional layer and fine-tune the network end-to-end. We compare against four baselines: network with the same architecture trained from scratch, network pre-trained with DCGAN, DCGANv2, and ImageNet pre-trained AlexNet. For networks pre-trained on only RGB data, we fine-tune them on both the RGB and surface normal inputs separately and average the detection results during testing as [66]. We apply Batch Normalization [50] except for ImageNet pre-trained AlexNet. We show the results in Table 2. Our approach has 1.5 % improvement compared to the model trained from scratch.

Table 2. Detection results on NYU test set.

	mean	bath tub	bed	book shelf	box	chair	counter	desk	door	dresser	garbage bin	lamp	monitor	night stand	pillow	sink	sofa	table	tele vision	toilet
Ours	32.4	**44.0**	67.7	28.4	1.6	34.2	43.9	10.0	17.3	33.9	22.6	28.1	24.8	41.7	31.3	33.1	50.2	21.9	25.1	54.9
Scratch	30.9	35.6	67.7	23.1	2.1	33.1	40.5	10.1	15.2	31.2	19.4	26.8	29.1	39.9	30.5	36.6	43.8	20.4	29.5	52.8
DCGAN	30.4	38.9	67.6	26.3	**2.9**	32.5	39.1	10.6	16.9	23.6	23.0	26.5	25.1	44.5	29.6	**37.0**	45.2	21.0	28.5	38.4
DCGANv2	31.1	35.3	69.0	21.5	2.0	32.6	36.4	9.8	14.4	30.8	25.4	29.2	27.3	39.6	32.2	34.6	47.9	21.1	27.2	54.4
Imagenet	**37.6**	33.1	**69.9**	**39.6**	2.3	**38.1**	47.9	**16.1**	**24.6**	40.7	**26.5**	**37.8**	45.6	**49.5**	36.1	34.5	**53.2**	**25.0**	35.3	**58.4**

6 Conclusion

We present a novel Style and Structure GAN which factorizes the image generation process. We show our model is more interpretable and generates more realistic images compared to the baselines. We also show that our method can learn RGBD representations in an unsupervised manner.

Acknowledgement. This work was supported by ONR MURI N000141010934, ONR MURI N000141612007 and gift from Google. The authors would also like to thank David Fouhey and Kenneth Marino for many helpful discussions.

References

1. Doersch, C., Gupta, A., Efros, A.A.: Context as supervisory signal: discovering objects with predictable context. In: Fleet, D., Pajdla, T., Schiele, B., Tuytelaars, T. (eds.) ECCV 2014. LNCS, vol. 8691, pp. 362–377. Springer, Heidelberg (2014). doi:10.1007/978-3-319-10578-9_24
2. Doersch, C., Gupta, A., Efros, A.A.: Unsupervised visual representation learning by context prediction. In: ICCV (2015)
3. Wang, X., Gupta, A.: Unsupervised learning of visual representations using videos. In: ICCV (2015)
4. Goroshin, R., Bruna, J., Tompson, J., Eigen, D., LeCun, Y.: Unsupervised learning of spatiotemporally coherent metrics. In: ICCV (2015)
5. Zou, W.Y., Zhu, S., Ng, A.Y., Yu, K.: Deep learning of invariant features via simulated fixations in video. In: NIPS (2012)
6. Li, Y., Paluri, M., Rehg, J.M., Dollar, P.: Unsupervised learning of edges. In: CVPR (2016)
7. Walker, J., Gupta, A., Hebert, M.: Dense optical flow prediction from a static image. In: ICCV (2015)
8. Misra, I., Zitnick, C.L., Hebert, M.: Shuffle and learn: unsupervised learning using temporal order verification. In: ECCV (2016)
9. Goodfellow, I., Pouget-Abadie, J., Mirza, M., Xu, B., Warde-Farley, D., Ozair, S., Courville, A., Bengio, Y.: Generative adversarial nets. In: NIPS (2014)
10. Kingma, D., Welling, M.: Auto-encoding variational bayes. In: ICLR (2014)
11. Gregor, K., Danihelka, I., Graves, A., Rezende, D.J., Wierstra, D.: Draw: a recurrent neural network for image generation. CoRR abs/1502.04623 (2015)
12. Li, Y., Swersky, K., Zemel, R.: Generative moment matching networks. In: ICML (2014)
13. Radford, A., Metz, L., Chintala, S.: Unsupervised representation learning with deep convolutional generative adversarial networks. CoRR abs/1511.06434 (2015)

14. Silberman, N., Hoiem, D., Kohli, P., Fergus, R.: Indoor segmentation and support inference from RGBD images. In: Fitzgibbon, A., Lazebnik, S., Perona, P., Sato, Y., Schmid, C. (eds.) ECCV 2012. LNCS, vol. 7576, pp. 746–760. Springer, Heidelberg (2012). doi:10.1007/978-3-642-33715-4_54

15. Agrawal, P., Carreira, J., Malik, J.: Learning to see by moving. In: ICCV (2015)

16. Jayaraman, D., Grauman, K.: Learning image representations tied to ego-motion. In: ICCV (2015)

17. Owens, A., Isola, P., McDermott, J., Torralba, A., Adelson, E., Freeman, W.: Visually indicated sounds. In: CVPR (2016)

18. Pinto, L., Gupta, A.: Supersizing self-supervision: learning to grasp from 50 k tries and 700 robot hours. In: ICRA (2016)

19. Pinto, L., Gandhi, D., Han, Y., Park, Y.L., Gupta, A.: The curious robot: learning visual representations via physical interactions. In: ECCV (2016)

20. Efros, A.A., Leung, T.K.: Texture synthesis by non-parametric sampling. In: ICCV (1999)

21. Freeman, W.T., Jones, T.R., Pasztor, E.C.: Example-based super-resolution. In: Computer Graphics and Applications (2002)

22. Bengio, Y., Lamblin, P., Popovici, D., Larochelle, H.: Greedy layer-wise training of deep networks. In: NIPS (2007)

23. Le, Q.V., Ranzato, M.A., Monga, R., Devin, M., Chen, K., Corrado, G.S., Dean, J., Ng, A.Y.: Building high-level features using large scale unsupervised learning. In: ICML (2012)

24. Ranzato, M.A., Krizhevsky, A., Hinton, G.E.: Factored 3-way restricted Boltzmann machines for modeling natural images. In: AISTATS (2010)

25. Osindero, S., Hinton, G.E.: Modeling image patches with a directed hierarchy of Markov random fields. In: NIPS (2008)

26. Hinton, G.E., Salakhutdinov, R.R.: Reducing the dimensionality of data with neural networks. Science **313**, 504–507 (2006)

27. Lee, H., Grosse, R., Ranganath, R., Ng, A.Y.: Convolutional deep belief networks for scalable unsupervised learning of hierarchical representations. In: ICML (2009)

28. Taylor, G.W., Hinton, G.E., Roweis, S.: Modeling human motion using binary latent variables. In: NIPS (2006)

29. Mansimov, E., Parisotto, E., Ba, J.L., Salakhutdinov, R.: Generating images from captions with attention. CoRR abs/1511.02793 (2015)

30. Kulkarni, T.D., Whitney, W.F., Kohli, P., Tenenbaum, J.B.: Deep convolutional inverse graphics network. In: NIPS (2015)

31. Dosovitskiy, A., Springenberg, J.T., Brox, T.: Learning to generate chairs with convolutional neural networks. In: CVPR (2015)

32. Tatarchenko, M., Dosovitskiy, A., Brox, T.: Single-view to multi-view: reconstructing unseen views with a convolutional network. CoRR abs/1511.06702 (2015)

33. Theis, L., Bethge, M.: Generative image modeling using spatial LSTMs. CoRR abs/1506.03478 (2015)

34. Oord, A.V.D., Kalchbrenner, N., Kavukcuoglu, K.: Pixel recurrent neural networks. CoRR abs/1601.06759 (2016)

35. Denton, E., Chintala, S., Szlam, A., Fergus, R.: Deep generative image models using a laplacian pyramid of adversarial networks. In: NIPS (2015)

36. Mirza, M., Osindero, S.: Conditional generative adversarial nets. CoRR abs/1411.1784 (2014)

37. Mathieu, M., Couprie, C., LeCun, Y.: Deep multi-scale video prediction beyond mean square error. CoRR abs/1511.05440 (2015)

38. Im, D.J., Kim, C.D., Jiang, H., Memisevic, R.: Generating images with recurrent adversarial networks. CoRR abs/1602.05110 (2016)
39. Wang, X., Fouhey, D.F., Gupta, A.: Designing deep networks for surface normal estimation. In: CVPR (2015)
40. Eigen, D., Fergus, R.: Predicting depth, surface normals and semantic labels with a common multi-scale convolutional architecture. In: ICCV (2015)
41. Fouhey, D.F., Gupta, A., Hebert, M.: Data-driven 3D primitives for single image understanding. In: ICCV (2013)
42. Ladický, L., Zeisl, B., Pollefeys, M.: Discriminatively trained dense surface normal estimation. In: Fleet, D., Pajdla, T., Schiele, B., Tuytelaars, T. (eds.) ECCV 2014. LNCS, vol. 8693, pp. 468–484. Springer, Heidelberg (2014). doi:10.1007/978-3-319-10602-1_31
43. Makhzani, A., Shlens, J., Jaitly, N., Goodfellow, I.J.: Adversarial autoencoders. CoRR abs/1511.05644 (2015)
44. Larsen, A.B.L., Sønderby, S.K., Winther, O.: Autoencoding beyond pixels using a learned similarity metric. CoRR abs/1512.09300 (2015)
45. Dosovitskiy, A., Brox, T.: Generating images with perceptual similarity metrics based on deep networks. CoRR abs/1602.02644 (2016)
46. Barrow, H.G., Tenenbaum, J.M.: Recovering intrinsic scene characteristics from images. In: Computer Vision Systems (1978)
47. Tenenbaum, J.B., Freeman, W.T.: Separating style and content with bilinear models. In: Neural Computation (2000)
48. Fouhey, D.F., Hussain, W., Gupta, A., Hebert, M.: Single image 3D without a single 3D image. In: ICCV (2015)
49. Zhu, S.C., Wu, Y.N., Mumford, D.: Filters, random fields and maximum entropy (frame): towards a unified theory for texture modeling. In: IJCV (1998)
50. Ioffe, S., Szegedy, C.: Batch normalization: accelerating deep network training by reducing internal covariate shift. CoRR abs/1502.03167 (2015)
51. Maas, A.L., Hannun, A.Y., Ng, A.Y.: Rectifier nonlinearities improve neural network acoustic models. In: ICML (2013)
52. Xu, B., Wang, N., Chen, T., Li, M.: Empirical evaluation of rectified activations in convolutional network. CoRR abs/1505.00853 (2015)
53. Long, J., Shelhamer, E., Darrell, T.: Fully convolutional networks for semantic segmentation. In: CVPR (2015)
54. Ladický, L., Shi, J., Pollefeys, M.: Pulling things out of perspective. In: CVPR (2014)
55. Krizhevsky, A., Sutskever, I., Hinton, G.E.: Imagenet classification with deep convolutional neural networks. In: NIPS (2012)
56. Kingma, D., Ba, J.: Adam: a method for stochastic optimization. CoRR abs/1412.6980 (2014)
57. Guo, R., Hoiem, D.: Support surface prediction in indoor scenes. In: ICCV (2013)
58. Zhou, B., Lapedriza, A., Xiao, J., Torralba, A., Oliva, A.: Learning deep features for scene recognition using places database. In: NIPS (2014)
59. Russakovsky, O., Deng, J., Su, H., Krause, J., Satheesh, S., Ma, S., Huang, Z., Karpathy, A., Khosla, A., Bernstein, M., Berg, A.C., Fei-Fei, L.: ImageNet large scale visual recognition challenge. IJCV **115**(3), 211–252 (2015)
60. Girshick, R.: Fast r-cnn. In: ICCV (2015)
61. Song, S., Lichtenberg, S., Xiao, J.: Sun RGB-D: a RGB-D scene understanding benchmark suite. In: CVPR (2015)

62. Janoch, A., Karayev, S., Jia, Y., Barron, J., Fritz, M., Saenko, K., Darrell, T.: A category-level 3-D object dataset: Putting the kinect to work. In: Workshop on Consumer Depth Cameras in Computer Vision (with ICCV) (2011)
63. Xiao, J., Owens, A., Torralba, A.: SUN3D: a database of big spaces reconstructed using SfM and object labels. In: ICCV (2013)
64. Oliva, A., Torralba, A.: Modeling the shape of the scene: a holistic representation of the spatial envelope. IJCV **42**, 145–175 (2011)
65. Gupta, S., Girshick, R., Arbeláez, P., Malik, J.: Learning rich features from RGB-D images for object detection and segmentation. In: Fleet, D., Pajdla, T., Schiele, B., Tuytelaars, T. (eds.) ECCV 2014. LNCS, vol. 8695, pp. 345–360. Springer, Heidelberg (2014). doi:10.1007/978-3-319-10584-0_23
66. Gupta, S., Hoffman, J., Malik, J.: Cross modal distillation for supervision transfer. In: CVPR (2016)

Joint Learning of Semantic and Latent Attributes

Peixi Peng[1,4], Yonghong Tian[1,4(✉)], Tao Xiang[2], Yaowei Wang[3(✉)], and Tiejun Huang[1]

[1] National Engineering Laboratory for Video Technology,
Peking University, Beijing, China
{pxpeng,yhtian,tjhuang}@pku.edu.cn

[2] School of Electronic Engineering and Computer Science,
Queen Mary University of London, London, UK
t.xiang@qmul.ac.uk

[3] Department of Electronic Engineering,
Beijing Institute of Technology, Beijing, China
yaoweiwang@bit.edu.cn

[4] Cooperative Medianet Innovation Center, Beijing, China

Abstract. As mid-level semantic properties shared across object categories, attributes have been studied extensively. Recent approaches have attempted joint modelling of multiple attributes together with class labels so as to exploit their correlations for better attribute prediction and object recognition. However, they often ignore the fact that there exist some shared properties other than nameable/semantic attributes, which we call latent attributes. Basically, they can be further divided into discriminative and non-discriminative parts depending on whether they can contribute to an object recognition task. We argue that learning the latent attributes jointly with user-defined semantic attributes not only leads to better representation for object recognition but also helps with semantic attribute prediction. A novel dictionary learning model is proposed which decomposes the dictionary space into three parts corresponding to semantic, latent discriminative and latent background attributes respectively. An efficient algorithm is then formulated to solve the resultant optimization problem. Extensive experiments show that the proposed attribute learning method produces state-of-the-art results on both attribute prediction and attribute-based person re-identification.

Keywords: Attribute learning · Latent attributes · Person re-identification · Zero-shot learning · Dictionary learning

1 Introduction

Attributes are a type of mid-level semantic properties of visual objects that can be shared across different object categories. Typically, semantic attributes are

© Springer International Publishing AG 2016
B. Leibe et al. (Eds.): ECCV 2016, Part IV, LNCS 9908, pp. 336–353, 2016.
DOI: 10.1007/978-3-319-46493-0_21

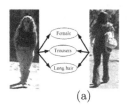 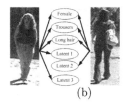

(a)   (b)

Fig. 1. (a) Given only three user-defined attributes as representation, the two people are mis-matched. (b) When complemented by latent attributes, the representation is more discriminative and solving the person re-identification problem becomes easier.

nameable and often annotated based on a user-defined ontology. Attribute learning has been studied extensively recently [1–9]. Existing approaches vary drastically depending on the objectives of learning attributes. Specifically, attributes learning methods have been developed for three objectives: (1) attribute prediction for image search [10], where each image is indexed by a list of predicted attributes and can thus be searched by text queries; (2) learning mid-level representation from low-level features for object recognition, typically at the fine-grained [6] or instance-level [11]; (3) zero-shot learning where given an attribute 'prototype' [12], unseen classes can be recognised by comparing the prototypes with the predicted attributes.

Earlier attribute learning works often tried to learn a set of binary attribute classifiers for each attribute separately and independently, whilst ignoring the existence of correlations among them, e.g., 'female' and 'long-hair' are correlated. This has been rectified by recent approaches [4–9] which jointly learn multiple attributes together with the object class labels so as to exploit their correlations. However, all these joint modelling approaches focus on the semantic user-defined attributes only, whilst ignoring the factors that (1) semantic attributes are often not exhaustively defined; and (2) there are also other shareable but not nameable/semantic properties. We call these shareable but undefined properties *latent attributes* and argue that they should also be jointly modelled with the user-defined semantic attributes and object class labels.

Jointly learning semantic and latent attributes is important for both attribute prediction and object recognition. This is due to two reasons: First, these latent attributes can also be discriminative and thus useful for object recognition. For example, Fig. 1 shows that a limited list of user-defined semantic attributes are often inadequate for instance-level object recognition such as person re-identification [13]. However, when a set of complementary and discriminative latent attributes are learned to augment the user-defined semantic attributes, recognition can be made easier. Second, even if predicting the user-defined attributes is the only goal, discovering and learning these latent attributes is still useful – it is certain that shareable properties that do not belong to the user-defined attributes are accounted for the model rather than act as a distractor to corrupt the learned semantic attribute predictor. Furthermore, by modelling latent attributes together with class labels, we can identify two types of latent attributes: those that are related to class labels and thus are potentially useful

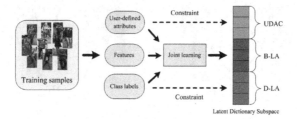

Fig. 2. Our framework for joint learning of user-defined-attribute-correlated (UDAC), discriminative latent attribute (D-LA), and background latent attribute (B-LA) dictionary subspaces.

for object recognition, and those that are not. The former is called discriminative latent attributes (D-LA), while the latter background latent attributes (B-LA) which could literally be object background that might appear in any object class.

To jointly learn both types of latent attributes as well as semantic attributes together with their correlations with the class labels, we propose a novel dictionary learning model with dictionary decomposition. Dictionary learning is naturally suited for learning a low-dimensional subspace corresponding to the latent attribute space. This is because by sharing the same dictionary with all object classes, it automatically discovers shareable properties. More importantly, we can easily decompose the learned dictionary into multiple parts and different parts are subject to different correlations with the available object annotations. Specifically, the learned dictionary subspace are decomposed into three parts: (1) The D-LA dictionary subspace part that is subject to the label correlation constraint so as to make sure that it is discriminative, (2) The B-LA dictionary subspace part that only helps data reconstruction and is subject to no constraint, and (3) The user-defined-attribute-correlated (UDAC) dictionary subspace part which is correlated to the user-defined attribute annotations. Note that in our framework, the user-defined attributes are learned through the latent attribute space. This is because a dictionary learning model aims to reconstruct the original signal using all dictionary atoms together, enforcing the learned three different types of attributes to be complementary to each other. Figure 2 illustrates the proposed dictionary learning framework.

2   Related Work

Learning Semantic Attributes. Earlier works on semantic attribution learning [1–3,14] consider predicting each attribute as a binary classification problem and solve them independently. Later works [4,5,7–9] realised that there exist correlations between different attributes, as well as between attributes and class labels, and proposed to learn different attributes jointly together with the class labels. For example, a unified multiplicative framework is proposed in [7] which projects images and category/class information into a shared feature space and the latent factors were disentangled and multiplied for attribute prediction. In [9,15], they learn the semantic attributes by incorporating class label information. Our model also learns user-defined semantic attributes and class labels jointly. Different from existing jointly attribute modelling works, we additionally model discriminative latent attributes and background latent attributes to improve the learn of user-defined semantic attributes as well as making the learned attribute-based representation more discriminative for the object classification task.

Learning Latent Attributes. The method for learning discriminative latent attributes has been exploited before [6,16–21]. However, in theses works, the latent attributes are not learned jointly and thus are not necessarily complementary to the user-defined attributes. Comparing to the few exceptions which learn them jointly [22,23], there is a significant difference: by using an additive dictionary, we aim to reconstruct the original feature representation; we thus devise the third type of attributes: background latent attributes (B-LA) to explicitly account for non-discriminant part of the representation (e.g. scene background, or what a person looks like in general) that is useless for the targeted task but has to be learned to avoid corrupting the other two types of useful attributes. Experimental results demonstrate clearly the importance of learning all three jointly. This novel concept can also be applied to existing joint attribute learning models.

Attribute-Based Person Re-identification. Semantic attributes have been exploited as a mid-level representation for matching people across non-overlapping camera views, or the person re-identification (Re-ID) problem [13,24–26]. However, these attribute-based Re-ID representations are not competitive on the benchmark datasets. This is because (1) the user-defined attribute representations have very low dimensions (dozens vs. tens of thousands for the typical low-level feature based representations used by the state-of-the-art Re-ID methods [27]); and (2) no latent attributes are exploited. Recently, user-defined attributes and low-level feature are modelled jointly in [28] in a multi-task learning framework to learn a discriminative representation for Re-ID. However, the user-defined attributes are predicted independently and no latent attributes are used. In contrast, our model is flexible in that discriminative latent attributes can still be learned when no annotation on user-defined attributes is available. Another relevant work is [11] which deploys a generative model to transfer attribute annotations from auxiliary data (fashion clothing) to the target data (surveillance video). Again, as a generative model, it is weak in learning discriminative representation.

Dictionary Learning. Beyond attribute learning, dictionary learning [29,30] has been studied widely as a method for learning a low-dimensional subspace. Originally designed for unsupervised learning, it has been extended for supervised learning for tasks such as face verification/recognition [31] and person Re-ID [32–34]. Our model is related to these dictionary-learning-based Re-ID models in that all models learn discriminative latent attributes through the learned dictionary subspace. However, only our model is able to additionally learn user-defined attributes and background latent attributes for better representation learning.

Contributions. Our contributions are as follows: (1) A unified framework for learning both user-defined semantic attributes and discriminative latent attributes is proposed. (2) We further develop a novel dictionary learning model which decomposes the learned dictionary subspace into three parts corresponding to the semantic, discriminative latent as well as background latent attributes respectively. An efficient optimisation algorithm is also formulated. Extensive experiments are carried out on benchmark attribute prediction and person Re-ID datasets. The results show that the proposed unified framework generates state-of-the-art results on both tasks.

3   Methodology

3.1   Formulation

Assume that a set of training data are given which are labelled with some user-defined (semantic) attributes[1] and object classes. In this paper, we focus on the problem of learning user-defined semantic and latent attributes jointly by dictionary learning. Specifically, the learned dictionary are decomposed into following three parts (see Fig. 2): (1) D^u corresponding to the user-defined-attribute-correlated (UDAC) dictionary subspace part which is correlated to the user-defined attribute annotations, (2) D^d corresponding to the discriminative latent attributes (D-LA) dictionary subspace part which is correlated to the class labels and thus useful for the given classification/recognition task, and (3) D^b corresponding to the background latent attributes (B-LA) dictionary subspace part which captures all the residual information in the training data which is uncorrelated to either user-defined attributes or class labels and thus is learned without any supervision.

Formally, we assume $Y \in \mathbb{R}^{m \times n}$ is a data matrix where each column y_i corresponds to an m-dimensional feature vector representing the ith object's appearance. n denotes the numbers of training samples. A is a $p \times n$ matrix where each column $a_i \in \{0,1\}^p$ indicates the absence or presence of all p binary user-defined attributes. The proposed method can be formulated as:

$$\left[D^u, D^d, D^b, W \right] = \arg\min \left\| Y - D^u X^u - D^d X^d \right\|_F^2 + \left\| Y - D^u X^u - D^d X^d - D^b X^b \right\|_F^2$$

$$+ \alpha \sum_{i,j=1}^{n} m_{i,j} \left\| x_i^d - x_j^d \right\|^2 + \beta^2 \left\| X^u - WA \right\|_F^2. \tag{1}$$

$$s.t. \ \left\| d_i^u \right\|_2^2 \le 1, \ \left\| d_i^d \right\|_2^2 \le 1, \ \left\| d_i^b \right\|_2^2 \le 1, \ \left\| w_i \right\|_2^2 \le 1 \ \forall i,$$

where matrices X^u, X^d and X^b are codes/coefficients corresponding to dictionaries D^u, D^d and D^b respectively; W is used to build correspondence between the codes obtained using D^u and the user-defined attribute annotation matrix A; d_i^u, d_i^d, d_i^b and w_i are the ith columns of D^u, D^d, D^b and W respectively; x_i^d is the ith column of X^d; α and β are free parameters controlling the strengths of

---

[1] We will show later that the requirement on the availability of user-defined attributes can be removed.

two regularisation terms to be explained later; M is an affinity matrix indicating the class-relationships (same/different class) among different training samples. Specifically, $m_{i,j} = 1$ if x_i^d and x_j^d are of same class, and $m_{i,j} = 0$ otherwise. The third term can be rewritten using the Laplacian matrix as:

$$\sum_{i,j=1}^{n} m_{i,j}\left\|x_i^d - x_j^d\right\|^2 = \text{Tr}(X^d L X^{d'}),\tag{2}$$

where $L = Q - M$ and Q is a diagonal matrix whose diagonal elements are the sums of the row elements of M. There are four terms of three categories in the cost function which are now explained in detail:

1. The first two terms are reconstruction errors that make sure the learned dictionaries can encode the data matrix Y well. Note that the two reconstruction error terms are stepwise ordered. Specifically, the minimisation of the first reconstruction error term enables D^u and D^d to encode Y as much as possible, while the minimisation of the second reconstruction error term enables D^b to encode and align the residual part of Y that cannot be coded by D^u and D^d. This stepwise two reconstruction error term formulation is important to prevent the B-LA D^b from dominating the reconstruction error leading to trivial solutions for D^u and D^d.
2. The third term is a graph Laplacian regularisation term which dictates that the projections of columns of Y in the D-LA subspace, i.e., X^d are close to each other if the corresponding data points belong to the same class. The goal of this term is thus to make the D-LA subspace parametrised by D^d to be more discriminative (class-dependent).
3. The last term is the constraint for learning the UDAC subspace part D^u. Note that we attempt to establish a linear constraint W between the projection in that subspace, X^u and user-defined attribute annotations A, rather than simply setting them to be equal ($X^u = A$), because user-defined attributes are always not additive. As explained earlier, modelling user-defined attributes via the same dictionary subspace makes the learned other two types of latent attributes to be complementary to the user-defined attributes.

3.2 Optimisation

Here we detail how the optimisation problem in (1) is solved. The problem is divided into the following subproblems:

1. *Computing codes X^u.* Given fixed D^u, D^d, D^d, W, X^d and X^b, the coding problem of estimating X^u becomes:

$$\min \left\|\tilde{Y} - \tilde{D} X^u\right\|_F^2,\tag{3}$$

where

$$\tilde{Y} = \begin{bmatrix} Y - D^d X^d \\ Y - D^d X^d - D^b X^b \\ \beta W A \end{bmatrix}, \tilde{D} = \begin{bmatrix} D^u \\ D^u \\ \beta I \end{bmatrix},$$

and I is the identity matrix. Let the derivative of (3) equal to 0 and the analytical solution of X^u can be obtained with:

$$X^u = \left(\tilde{D}'\tilde{D}\right)^{-1}\tilde{D}'\tilde{Y}. \tag{4}$$

2. *Computing codes X^d.* Given the other variables fixed, the coding problem of X^d becomes:

$$\min \left\|\tilde{Y} - \tilde{D}X^d\right\|_F^2 + \alpha \mathrm{Tr}(X^d L X^{d'}), \tag{5}$$

where

$$\tilde{Y} = \begin{bmatrix} Y - D^u X^u \\ Y - D^u X^u - D^b X^b \end{bmatrix}, \tilde{D} = \begin{bmatrix} D^d \\ D^d \end{bmatrix}.$$

and the analytical solution of x_i^d (the ith column of X^d) is:

$$x_i^d = \left(\tilde{D}'\tilde{D} + 2\alpha l_{t,i,i}I\right)^{-1}\left(\tilde{D}'\tilde{y}_i - 2\alpha \sum_{k \neq i} \tilde{y}_k l_{k,i}\right), \tag{6}$$

where $l_{k,i}$ is the (k,i) element of L and $\tilde{y}_i$ is the ith column of $\tilde{Y}$.

3. *Computing code X^b.* Fix other terms and X^b can be solved by:

$$\min \left\|Y - D^u X^u - D^d X^d - D^b X^b\right\|_F^2. \tag{7}$$

Let the derivative of (7) equal to 0 and the analytical solution of X^b is:

$$X^b = \left(D^{b'}D^b\right)^{-1}D^{b'}\left(Y - D^u X^u - D^d X^d\right). \tag{8}$$

4. *Updating dictionaries.* First, when D^b, X^u, X^d and X^b are given, D^u and D^d are estimated by the following optimisation problem:

$$\min \|\mathcal{Y} - \mathcal{D}\mathcal{X}\|_F^2, \ \text{s.t.} \ \|d_i^u\|_2^2 \leq 1, \ \left\|d_i^d\right\|_2^2 \leq 1, \tag{9}$$

where

$$\mathcal{D} = [D^u, D^d], \ \mathcal{Y} = [Y, Y - D^b X^b], \ \mathcal{X} = \begin{bmatrix} X^u & X^u \\ X^d & X^d \end{bmatrix}. \tag{10}$$

(9) can be optimised with the Lagrange dual. Thus, the analytical solution of $\mathcal{D}$ is: $\mathcal{D} = (\mathcal{Y}\mathcal{X}')(\mathcal{X}\mathcal{X}' + \Lambda)^{-1}$, where Λ is a diagonal matrix constructed from all the dual variables. Second, we fix other variables and solve D^b with the following objective function:

$$\min \left\|Y - D^u X^u - D^d X^d - D^b X^b\right\|_F^2, \ \text{s.t.} \ \left\|d_i^b\right\|_2^2 \leq 1(\forall i), \tag{11}$$

(11) can be solved similar to (9).

Algorithm 1. The proposed algorithm

Input: X_t; initialise D^u, D^d, D^b and W randomly; $X^d \rightarrow \mathbf{0}$,$X^b \rightarrow \mathbf{0}$;
Output: D^u, D^d, D^b, X^u, X^d, X^b and W.
while *Non-convergence* **do**
$\quad$ Coding problem:
$\qquad$ compute code X^u using (3),
$\qquad$ compute code X^d using (5),
$\qquad$ compute code X^b using (7).
$\quad$ Updating dictionaries:
$\qquad$ update D^u and D^d using (9),
$\qquad$ update D^b using (11).
$\quad$ Updating W:
$\qquad$ update W using (12),

---

5. *Updating W.* Similar to the dictionary updating procedure in Step 4, we fix other variables and solve W by:

$$\min \|X^u - WA\|_F^2, \quad s.t. \ \|w_i\|_2^2 \le 1(\forall i). \tag{12}$$

(12) can be optimised using the Lagrange dual. The analytical solution of W is: $D^u = (X^u A') (AA' + \Lambda)^{-1}$, where Λ is a diagonal matrix constructed from all the dual variables.

Algorithm 1 summaries the whole algorithm. In practice, we found that it always converges after a few (<50) iterations in our experiments.

3.3 Application to Person Re-ID

In the Person Re-ID problem, we assume that the training images are represented by some feature representation denoted as Y, and labelled with identities encoded in the matrix M, and a set of user-defined attributes A. Once the three dictionaries are learned using the training set as described above, each test image y can be encoded as $[x^u, x^d, x^b]$ via D^u, D^d and D^b respectively. The encoding problem can be formulated as:

$$[x^u, x^d, x^b] = \arg\min \left\| y - D^u x^u - D^d x^d - D^b x^b \right\|_2^2 + \gamma \|x^u\|_2^2 + \gamma \left\| x^d \right\|_2^2 + \gamma \left\| x^b \right\|_2^2, \tag{13}$$

where x^u, x^d and x^b are the projections of y in the UDAC, D-LA and B-LA part of the learned dictionary subspaces respectively, and γ is a weight for the regularisation terms. (13) can be solved easily with a linear system. After we obtain x^u, the user-defined attribute vector a can be predicted via the linear constraint W:

$$a = \arg\min \|x^u - Wa\|_2^2 + \gamma \|a\|_2^2. \tag{14}$$

Now, the test sample y can be represented as the predicted user-defined attributes a and D-LA x^d. Simply treating the predicted attributes as features, Re-ID could be performed by score-level fusion of computing the cosine distance of a and x^d between the attribute vectors of a probe sample and a gallery one.

Note that the proposed method can still work without the user-defined attribute annotations A in the training data. In this case, D^u, W and X^u will be dropped and (1) becomes:

$$\left[D^u, D^b\right] = \arg\min \left\|Y - D^d X^d\right\|_F^2 + \left\|Y - D^d X^d - D^b X^b\right\|_F^2 + \alpha \sum_{i,j=1}^{n} m_{i,j} \left\|x_i^d - x_j^d\right\|^2,$$

$$s.t. \left\|d_i^d\right\|_2^2 \le 1 \left\|d_i^b\right\|_2^2 \le 1, \forall i,$$

(15)

(15) can be solved as a special case of (1). Consequently, the test sample y is represented only by its D-LA x^d, which can be obtained by solving an optimisation problem similar to (13).

3.4   Application to User-Defined Attribute Prediction

In this task, our only goal is to predict the user-defined attributes, hence having a separate D-LA D^d is unnecessary and D^b alone can be used to explain any information that cannot be explained by D^u. Consequently, D^d, X^d and the graph Laplacian regularisation from (1) can be removed, and the optimisation problem for dictionary learning becomes:

$$\left[D^u, D^b, W\right] = \arg\min \left\|Y - D^u X^u\right\|_F^2 + \left\|Y - D^u X^u - D^b X^b\right\|_F^2 + \beta^2 \left\|X^u - WA\right\|_F^2$$

$$s.t. \left\|d_i^u\right\|_2^2 \le 1, \left\|d_i^b\right\|_2^2 \le 1, \|w_i\|_2^2 \le 1 \forall i.$$

(16)

It can also be solved as a special case of (1) with a similar solver as described in Sect. 3.2. Once the model is learned using a training set, a test sample y can be encoded with D^u and D^b by solving an optimisation problem similar to (13). Finally, the user-defined attribute vector a is predicted via (14).

4   Experiments

The proposed attribute learning model is evaluated on three tasks: attribute-based person re-identification (Re-ID), user-defined attribute prediction and zero-shot learning[2].

4.1   Person Re-ID

For this task, our attribute learning model is used to learn a discriminative mid-level representation for matching people across camera views.

Datasets. Four widely used benchmark datasets are chosen for person Re-ID. **VIPeR** [35] contains 1,264 images of 632 individuals from two distinct camera

---

[2] The code can be downloaded at http://pkuml.com/resources/code.html.

views (two images per individual) featured with large viewpoint changes and varying illumination conditions. All individuals are randomly divided into two equal-sized subsets for training and testing respectively with no overlapping in identity between the two subsets. This random partition process is repeated 10 times, and the averaged performance is reported. For fair comparison, we use the same data splits as in [36]. **PRID** [37] consists of images extracted from multiple person trajectories recorded from two surveillance static cameras. Camera view A contains 385 individuals, camera view B contains 749 individuals, and 200 of them appearing in both the two views. The single shot version of the dataset is used in our experiments as in [36], and we use the same data splits as in [36]. In each data split, 100 people with one image from each view are randomly chosen from the 200 present in both camera views for the training set, while the remaining 100 of View A are used as the probe set, and the remaining 649 of View B are used as gallery. Experiments are repeated over the 10 splits. **iLIDS** [38] has 476 images of 119 individuals captured in an airport terminal from three cameras of distinct viewpoints. It contains heavy occlusions caused by a large number of people and luggages. As in [39], 119 identities are randomly divided into two equal halves, one for training and the other for testing. The reported results are obtained by averaging over 10 trials. **Market-1501** [40] is the biggest re-id benchmark dataset to date, containing 32,668 detected person images of 1,501 identities. Each identity is captured by six cameras at most, and two cameras at least. We use the provided fixed training and test sets in [40], under both the single-query and multi-query evaluation settings.

Attribute Annotation. The training sets of all three datasets have labels indicating the identities of the people. In addition, a total of 105 user-defined attributes have been annotated on each training images in VIPeR, PRID and iLIDs as in [14]. We remove the user-defined attributes which appear in each dataset rarely, and the numbers of the remaining attributes are 85, 56 and 73 for VIPeR, PRID and iLIDs respectively. Note that the attribution annotation is unavailable on Market-1501. As mentioned in Sect. 3.3, our model works with and without the user-defined attributes. For fair comparisons with existing methods which do not use additional attribute annotations, we report results of our model both with and without user-defined attributes.

Features and Evaluation Metric. The low-level feature representation in [36] is employed in our experiments. These include colour histogram, HOG and LBP features which are concatenated resulting in 5,138 dimensions. For evaluation metric, we compute Cumulated Matching Characteristics (CMC) curves. Due to space constraint as well as for easier comparison with published results, we only report the cumulated matching accuracy at selected ranks in tables rather than reporting the actual CMC curves. The only exception is the Market-1501 dataset. Since there are on average 14.8 cross-camera ground truth matches for each query, we additionally use mean average precision (mAP) as in [40].

Parameter Settings. On the VIPeR, PRID and iLIDs datasets, the sizes of D^u, D^d and D^b are set to 100. We found that the performance of our model is insensitive to the dictionary size when it is between 100 to 200. The size of D^d is increased to 400 for Market-1501 due to the fact that the Market-1501 dataset is much bigger than the other three. The other free parameters in our model, α and β in (1) and γ in (13), are obtained using four-fold cross-validation.

Competitors. Twelve state-of-the-art Re-ID methods are selected for comparison. They fall into five categories: (1) Unsupervised: BoW features [40] based on Colour Names (CN) alone or in combination with Hue-Saturation Histograms (HS) are used to compute l_2 distance. (2) Distance metric leaning based methods: RPLM [41], Mid-level Filter [42], LADF [43], and Similarity Learning [44]. (3) Kernel-based Discriminative subspace learning methods: MFA [39], kLFDA [39], kCCA [36], XQDA [27], and MLAPG [45]; (4) Deep learning based: Improved Deep [46]; (5) Feature fusion based: Metric Ensembles [47]. Note that this method fuses more than one kind of features, which is known to be beneficial to all methods. (6) Attribute-based method: aMTL [28]. This is the most relevant to ours as it also utilises the user-defined attributes. Note that aMTL requires multiple images of each person for training, hence they apply data augmentation to generate more training samples on VIPeR and utilises the multi-shot setting of PRID rather than the single-shot one adopted by most other methods including ours. Furthermore, different from our model, aMTL cannot work without user-defined attributes. For fair comparison, we use the same features and the same training-test splits for the compared methods whenever possible (i.e. when the code is available we use the same features as ours). Three versions of our models are evaluated: "Ours_L" means only latent attributes are learned as representation, that is, the user-defined attribute annotation is not used as do most other compared methods. "Ours_U" means that only user-defined attributes are used to represent a person. "Ours_All" means both the user-defined and latent attributes are used.

Comparative Results. From the results shown in Table 1, we have the following key findings: (1) Even without using the additional attribute annotation, our method Ours_L outperforms all compared method particularly at low ranks. (2) If user-defined attributes are available, the results of Ours_U is very poor, showing that the user-defined attributes cannot represent a person discriminatively without latent attributes, because the user-defined attribute representations have very low dimensions as explained. Ours_All outperforms Ours_L and Ours_U on all datasets. That shows the learned user-defined attributes and discriminative latent attribute are indeed complementary to each other. (3) Compared to the alternative attribute-based Re-ID model aMTL, our model (Ours_All) is clearly better. In particular, the proposed method outperforms aMTL by a large margin even when they used more training data on PRID. In addition, aMTL can only be applied when there are user-defined attribute annotations, whilst our model is not restricted by that.

Table 1. Comparative results on four benchmark Re-ID datasets. '*' means we compare these methods with the same features using the author-provided code. '-' means no reported result is available.

(a) VIPeR

Rank	1	5	10	20
RPLM [41]	27.00	55.30	69.00	83.00
Mid-level [42]	29.11	52.34	65.95	79.87
Similarity[44]	36.80	70.40	83.70	91.70
LADF [43]	30.22	64.70	78.92	90.44
kCCA [36]	37.00	-	**85.00**	**93.00**
MFA* [39]	39.56	69.89	80.38	88.61
kLFDA* [39]	39.87	72.78	81.86	90.19
XQDA [27]	40.00	-	80.51	91.08
Deep [46]	34.81	63.61	75.63	84.49
MLAPG [45]	40.73	-	82.34	92.37
Ours_L	**41.25**	**73.60**	81.77	90.12
Metric Ensembles [47]	45.90	82.09	90.51	95.92
Ours_U	28.39	55.32	65.89	76.01
aMTL [28]	42.30	72.20	81.60	89.60
Ours_All	**45.03**	**74.11**	**83.13**	**90.51**

(b) PRID

Rank	1	5	10	20
RPLM [41]	15.00	32.00	42.00	54.00
kCCA [36]	15.00	-	47.00	60.00
MFA* [39]	20.90	50.30	57.90	68.10
kLFDA* [39]	21.60	51.50	60.00	68.10
Ours_L	**23.60**	**52.60**	**61.70**	**69.70**
Metric Ensembles [47]	17.90	39.00	50.00	62.00
Ours_U	16.30	27.60	34.80	43.20
aMTL [28]	18.00	37.40	50.10	66.60
Ours_All	**26.80**	**55.30**	**62.50**	**71.00**

(c) Market-1501

Query	singleQ		multiQ	
Evaluation metrics	Rank-1	mAP	Rank-1	mAP
BoW (CN) [40]	34.38	14.10	42.64	19.47
BoW(CN+HS) [40]	-	-	47.25	21.88
MFA* [39]	37.56	16.94	48.83	22.41
kLFDA* [39]	38.40	18.36	47.23	21.34
Ours_L	**47.39**	**21.06**	**56.17**	**26.85**

(d) iLIDs

Rank	1	5	10	20
MFA* [39]	49.20	80.41	87.90	94.28
kLFDA* [39]	48.41	78.40	87.73	**96.13**
Ours_L	**52.35**	**81.60**	**88.77**	94.91
Metric Ensembles [47]	50.34	72.50	81.50	91.00
Ours_U	39.19	65.38	75.49	83.52
Ours_All	**56.80**	**82.21**	**90.25**	**95.85**

4.2   User-Defined Attribute Prediction

Datasets and Settings. Three widely used benchmark datasets are chosen in this experiment. **AwA** is composed of 30,475 images from 50 animal categories and each category is annotated with 85 attributes. Following [2,3,9], we divide the dataset into two parts: 40 classes (24,295 images) for training and 10 classes (6,180 images) for testing. For fair comparison with the state-of-the-art methods, we adopt the same 4096-dimensional deep learning features DeCAF [48] provided by [3]. **CUB** contains 11,788 images of 200 bird classes. Each category is annotated with 312 attributes. We split the dataset following [8,9] to facilitate direct comparison with the state-of-the-art methods (150 classes for training and the rest 50 classes for testing). We also extract the same 4096-D DeCAF features as in [9]. **PETA** comprises 10 publicly available small-scale person image datasets totalling 19,000 images. Each image is labelled with 105 attributes. For fair comparison with [14], we follow the same setting and randomly select 9,500 images for training, 1,900 for validation and 7,600 for testing. We repeat 10 times and the average result is reported. As in [14], the same low-level color and texture features are extracted and the prediction results of the same selected 35 attributes are evaluated.

Competitors and Evaluation Metrics. Six state-of-the-art attribute learning approaches are compared. These include Direct Attribute Prediction (DAP)

Table 2. Comparative results on (a) predicting user-defined attributes and (b) zero-shot learning. "*" means same feature are used and "-" means no reported results.

(a) Attributes prediction

Approaches	AwA	CUB	PETA
DAP* [3]	72.80	61.80	69.50
IAP* [3]	72.10	-	-
ALE [8]	65.70	60.30	-
CSHAP* [9]	**74.30**	68.70	-
TbOs* [15]	67.55	68.37	70.20
MRF [14]	-	-	71.10
Ours	73.61	**74.85**	**73.12**

(b) Zero-shot learning

Approaches	AwA	CUB
DAP* [3]	57.23	-
UMF-IS [7]	48.60	18.20
CSHAP [9]	45.60	17.50
SSE-ReLU* [49]	76.33	30.41
Akata et al.* [50]	61.90	40.30
JLSE* [51]	80.46	42.11
Ours	**82.81**	**49.87**

[2,3], Indirect Attribute Prediction (IAP)[2,3], Attribute Label Embedding (ALE) [8], Class-Specific Hypergraph based Attribute Predictor (CSHAP) [9],"Two birds, One stone" (TbOs) [15] and Markov Random Field graph (MRF) [14]. For direct comparison with the reported results in the literature, the attribute prediction performance is measured by mean area under ROC curve (mAUC) on AwA and CUB, while the mean classification accuracy (mACC) is used on PETA.

Comparative Results. We report the user-defined attribute prediction performance in Table 2(a). The results show that the proposed method achieves state-of-the-art performance on CUB and PETA. In particular, on CUB, its mAUC is 6 % higher than the nearest competitor CSHAP. However, it is slightly inferior to CSHAP on AwA.

4.3   Zero-Shot Learning

Since images from different classes may share common attributes, we can recognize images from unseen classes based on transferred attribute concepts, which is referred as zero-shot learning [3]. Specifically, the user-defined attributes learned from seen classes are used to classify the images from unseen classes.

Datasets and Settings. Two benchmark datasets, **AwA** and **CUB**, are used in this experiment. For AWA, 40 classes are chosen as seen classes for training and the remanning 10 classes are chosen as unseen classes for testing. Also, we split CUB as 150 classes for training and 50 classes for testing. For both datasets, we utilize MatConvNet [52] with the "imagenet-vgg-verydeep-19" pretrained model [53] to extract a 4096-dim CNN feature vector for each image (or bounding box). The train-test split and features are as same as [49–51].

Comparative Results. In this experiments, we compare our methods with several state-of-the-art methods and the image classification accuracy is reported. As shown in Table 2(b), the performance of our method is significantly better than the state-of-the-art approaches on both datasets.

Table 3. Evaluation on the contributions of different model components for (a) user-defined attributes (att) prediction on AwA, (b) person Re-ID on VIPeR and (c) zero-shot learning (zsl) results on AWA. Note that D^d is not used for user-defined attributes prediction and zero-shot learning; there is thus no result under 'Without D^d' for AwA.

Dataset	AwA (att)	VIPeR (Re-ID)	AwA (zsl)
Evaluation metrics	mAUC	Rank 1	ACC
Without D^d	-	28.39	-
Without D^b	71.74	41.51	80.26
Without W	68.72	42.36	74.39
Ours_full	**73.61**	**45.03**	**82.81**

4.4 Further Evaluations

Contributions of Model Components. There are several key components in the proposed model (see (1)): (a) two types of latent attributes: D-LA (D^d) and B-LA (D^b) are learned together with the user-defined attributes; and (b) instead of learning it directly as part of the dictionary subspace, we model a linear transformation (W) from the user-defined attributes A to the UDAC dictionary subspace (D^u). In order to evaluate the effectiveness of these two components, we compare our full model (Ours_full) with various striped-down versions of our model. The results in Table 3 show clearly that all these components contribute positively to the final performance of the model.

Running Cost. All algorithms are implemented in Matlab and run on a server with 2.0 GHz CPU cores and 128 GB memory. For person Re-ID on the VIPeR dataset, our model takes 28.29 seconds to train and 0.35 seconds to match 312 images against 312 images. For predicting user-defined attributes on AwA, it takes 2,377 seconds to train and 0.33 seconds to predict 85 user-defined attributes on 6,180 images. It is thus extremely efficient during testing as a linear model.

5   Conclusions

We have proposed a novel attribute learning model which learns user-defined semantic attributes jointly with latent discriminative and background attributes. The model is based on dictionary learning with dictionary decomposition. An efficient algorithm is then formulated to solve the resultant optimization problem. Extensive experiments show that the proposed attribute learning method produces state-of-the-art results on attribute prediction, attribute-based person re-identification and zero-shot learning.

Acknowledgements. This work is partially supported by grants from the National Basic Research Program of China under grant 2015CB351806, the National Natural Science Foundation of China under contract No. 61390515, No. 61425025 and No. 61471042, Beijing Municipal Commission of Science and Technology under contract

No. Z151100000915070 and the National Key Technology and Development Program of China under contract No. 2014BAK10B02. These authors are also supported by Microsoft Research Asia Collaborative Research Program 2016, project ID FY16-RES-THEME-034.

References

1. Farhadi, A., Endres, I., Hoiem, D., Forsyth, D.: Describing objects by their attributes. In: IEEE Conference on Computer Vision and Pattern Recognition, CVPR 2009, pp. 1778–1785 (2009)
2. Lampert, C.H., Nickisch, H., Harmeling, S.: Learning to detect unseen object classes by between-class attribute transfer. In: IEEE Conference on Computer Vision and Pattern Recognition, CVPR 2009, pp. 951–958, June 2009
3. Lampert, C.H., Nickisch, H., Harmeling, S.: Attribute-based classification for zero-shot visual object categorization. IEEE Trans. Pattern Anal. Machine Intell. 36(3), 453–465 (2014)
4. Mahajan, D., Sellamanickam, S., Nair, V.: A joint learning framework for attribute models and object descriptions. In: IEEE International Conference on Computer Vision, pp. 1227–1234 (2011)
5. Jayaraman, D., Sha, F., Grauman, K.: Decorrelating semantic visual attributes by resisting the urge to share. In: 2014 IEEE Conference on Computer Vision and Pattern Recognition (CVPR), pp. 1629–1636 (2014)
6. Wang, Y., Mori, G.: A discriminative latent model of object classes and attributes. In: Daniilidis, K., Maragos, P., Paragios, N. (eds.) ECCV 2010. LNCS, vol. 6315, pp. 155–168. Springer, Heidelberg (2010). doi:10.1007/978-3-642-15555-0_12
7. Liang, K., Chang, H., Shan, S., Chen, X.: A unified multiplicative framework for attribute learning. In: 2015 IEEE International Conference on Computer Vision (ICCV), pp. 2506–2514, December 2015
8. Akata, Z., Perronnin, F., Harchaoui, Z., Schmid, C.: Label-embedding for attribute-based classification. In: 2013 IEEE Conference on Computer Vision and Pattern Recognition, pp. 819–826 (2013)
9. Huang, S., Elhoseiny, M., Elgammal, A., Yang, D.: Learning hypergraph-regularized attribute predictors. In: 2015 IEEE Conference on Computer Vision and Pattern Recognition (CVPR), pp. 409–417 (2015)
10. Kovashka, A., Parikh, D., Grauman, K.: Whittlesearch: Interactive image search with relative attribute feedback. Int. J. Comput. Vis. 115(2), 185–210 (2015)
11. Shi, Z., Hospedales, T.M., Xiang, T.: Transferring a semantic representation for person re-identification and search. In: Computer Vision and Pattern Recognition (CVPR) (2015)
12. Fu, Y., Hospedales, T.M., Xiang, T., Gong, S.: Transductive multi-view zero-shot learning. IEEE Trans. Pattern Anal. Mach. Intell. 37(11), 2332–2345 (2015)
13. Layne, R., Hospedales, T.M., Gong, S.: Attributes-Based Re-identification. Springer, London (2014)
14. Deng, Y., Luo, P., Loy, C.C., Tang, X.: Pedestrian attribute recognition at far distance. In: Proceedings of the ACM International Conference on Multimedia, pp. 789–792 (2014)
15. Li, Y., Wang, R., Liu, H., Jiang, H., Shan, S., Chen, X.: Two birds, one stone: jointly learning binary code for large-scale face image retrieval and attributes prediction. In: IEEE International Conference on Computer Vision, pp. 3819–3827 (2015)

16. Yu, F.X., Cao, L., Feris, R.S., Smith, J.R., Chang, S.F.: Designing category-level attributes for discriminative visual recognition. In: IEEE Conference on Computer Vision and Pattern Recognition, pp. 771–778 (2013)
17. Singh, S., Gupta, A., Efros, A.A.: Unsupervised discovery of mid-level discriminative patches. In: Fitzgibbon, A., Lazebnik, S., Perona, P., Sato, Y., Schmid, C. (eds.) ECCV 2012. LNCS, vol. 7573, pp. 73–86. Springer, Heidelberg (2012)
18. Rifai, S., Bengio, Y., Courville, A., Vincent, P., Mirza, M.: Disentangling factors of variation for facial expression recognition. In: Fitzgibbon, A., Lazebnik, S., Perona, P., Sato, Y., Schmid, C. (eds.) ECCV 2012. LNCS, vol. 7577, pp. 808–822. Springer, Heidelberg (2012). doi:10.1007/978-3-642-33783-3_58
19. Berg, T.L., Berg, A.C., Shih, J.: Automatic attribute discovery and characterization from noisy web data. In: Daniilidis, K., Maragos, P., Paragios, N. (eds.) ECCV 2010. LNCS, vol. 6311, pp. 663–676. Springer, Heidelberg (2010). doi:10.1007/978-3-642-15549-9_48
20. Rastegari, M., Farhadi, A., Forsyth, D.: Attribute discovery via predictable discriminative binary codes. In: Fitzgibbon, A., Lazebnik, S., Perona, P., Sato, Y., Schmid, C. (eds.) ECCV 2012. LNCS, vol. 7577, pp. 876–889. Springer, Heidelberg (2012). doi:10.1007/978-3-642-33783-3_63
21. Feng, J., Jegelka, S., Yan, S., Darrell, T.: Learning scalable discriminative dictionary with sample relatedness. In: IEEE Conference on Computer Vision and Pattern Recognition, pp. 1645–1652 (2014)
22. Fu, Y., Hospedales, T.M., Tao, X., Gong, S.: Learning multimodal latent attributes. IEEE Trans. Pattern Anal. Mach. Intell. 36(2), 303–316 (2014)
23. Sharmanska, V., Quadrianto, N., Lampert, C.H.: Augmented attribute representations. In: Fitzgibbon, A., Lazebnik, S., Perona, P., Sato, Y., Schmid, C. (eds.) ECCV 2012. LNCS, vol. 7576, pp. 242–255. Springer, Heidelberg (2012). doi:10.1007/978-3-642-33715-4_18
24. Layne, R., Hospedales, T.M., Gong, S.: Towards Person Identification and Re-identification with Attributes. In: Fusiello, A., Murino, V., Cucchiara, R. (eds.) ECCV 2012. LNCS, vol. 7583, pp. 402–412. Springer, Heidelberg (2012). doi:10.1007/978-3-642-33863-2_40
25. N Hospedales, T., Layne, R., Gong, S.: Re-id: hunting attributes in the wild. In: British Machine Vision Conference (BMVC) (2014)
26. Layne, R., Hospedales, T.M., Gong, S.: Person re-identification by attributes. In: British Machine Vision Conference (2012)
27. Liao, S., Hu, Y., Zhu, X., Li, S.Z.: Person re-identification by local maximal occurrence representation and metric learning. In: CVPR, pp. 2197–2206 (2015)
28. Su, C., Yang, F., Zhang, S., Tian, Q., Davis, L.S., Gao, W.: Multi-task learning with low rank attribute embedding for person re-identification. In: 2015 IEEE International Conference on Computer Vision (ICCV), pp. 3739–3747, December 2015
29. Kenneth, K., Joseph, M., Bhaskar, R., Kjersti, E., Te-Won, L., Terrence, S.: Dictionary learning algorithms for sparse representation. Neural Comput. 15(2), 349–396 (2003)
30. Aharon, M., Elad, M., Bruckstein, A.: K-svd: An algorithm for designing overcomplete dictionaries for sparse representation. IEEE Trans. Sig. Proces. 54, 4311–4322 (2006)
31. Guo, H., Jiang, Z., Davis, L.S.: Discriminative dictionary learning with pairwise constraints. In: Proceedings of the 11th Asian conference on Computer Vision (2014)

32. Zheng, J., Jiang, Z.: Learning view-invariant sparse representations for cross-view action recognition. In: 2013 IEEE International Conference on Computer Vision (ICCV), pp. 3176–3183. IEEE (2013)

33. Liu, X., Song, M., Tao, D., Zhou, X., Chen, C., Bu, J.: Semi-supervised coupled dictionary learning for person re-identification. In: 2014 IEEE Conference on Computer Vision and Pattern Recognition (CVPR) (2014)

34. Karanam, S., Li, Y., Radke, R.J.: Person re-identification with discriminatively trained viewpoint invariant dictionaries. In: 2015 IEEE International Conference on Computer Vision (ICCV) (2015)

35. Gray, D., Brennan, S., Tao, H.: Evaluating appearance models for recognition, reacquisition, and tracking. In: Proceedings of IEEE International Workshop on Performance Evaluation for Tracking and Surveillance (PETS), vol. 3. Citeseer (2007)

36. Lisanti, G., Masi, I., Del Bilmbo, A.: Matching people across camera views using kernel canonical correlation analysis. In: Proceedings of ICDSC (2014)

37. Hirzer, M., Beleznai, C., Roth, P.M., Bischof, H.: Person re-identification by descriptive and discriminative classification. In: Heyden, A., Kahl, F. (eds.) SCIA 2011. LNCS, vol. 6688, pp. 91–102. Springer, Heidelberg (2011). doi:10.1007/978-3-642-21227-7_9

38. Zheng, W., Gong, S., Xiang, T.: Associating groups of people. In: BMVC (2009)

39. Xiong, F., Gou, M., Camps, O., Sznaier, M.: Person re-identification using kernel-based metric learning methods. In: Fleet, D., Pajdla, T., Schiele, B., Tuytelaars, T. (eds.) ECCV 2014. LNCS, vol. 8695, pp. 1–16. Springer, Heidelberg (2014). doi:10.1007/978-3-319-10584-0_1

40. Zheng, L., Shen, L., Tian, L., Wang, S., Wang, J., Tian, Q.: Scalable person re-identification: a benchmark. In: 2015 IEEE International Conference on Computer Vision (ICCV), pp. 1116–1124, December 2015

41. Hirzer, M., Roth, P.M., Köstinger, M., Bischof, H.: Relaxed pairwise learned metric for person re-identification. In: Fitzgibbon, A., Lazebnik, S., Perona, P., Sato, Y., Schmid, C. (eds.) ECCV 2012. LNCS, vol. 7577, pp. 780–793. Springer, Heidelberg (2012). doi:10.1007/978-3-642-33783-3_56

42. Zhao, R., Ouyang, W., Wang, X.: Learning mid-level filters for person re-identification. In: Proceedings of CVPR (2014)

43. Li, Z., Chang, S., Liang, F., Huang, T.S., Cao, L., Smith, J.: Learning locally-adaptive decision functions for person verification. In: CVPR (2013)

44. Chen, D., Yuan, Z., Hua, G., Zheng, N., Wang, J.: Similarity learning on an explicit polynomial kernel feature map for person re-identification. In: Proceedings of the IEEE Conference on Computer Vision and Pattern Recognition, pp. 1565–1573 (2015)

45. Liao, S., Li, S.Z.: Efficient PSD constrained asymmetric metric learning for person re-identification. In: The IEEE International Conference on Computer Vision (ICCV), December 2015

46. Ahmed, E., Jones, M., Marks, T.K.: An improved deep learning architecture for person re-identification. In: CVPR (2015)

47. Paisitkriangkrai, S., Shen, C., van den Hengel, A.: Learning to rank in person re-identification with metric ensembles. arXiv preprint (2015). arXiv:1503.01543

48. Donahue, J., Jia, Y., Vinyals, O., Hoffman, J., Zhang, N., Tzeng, E., Darrell, T.: Decaf: A deep convolutional activation feature for generic visual recognition. University of California Berkeley, Brigham Young University, pp. 647–655 (2013)

49. Zhang, Z., Saligrama, V.: Zero-shot learning via semantic similarity embedding. In: 2015 IEEE International Conference on Computer Vision (ICCV), pp. 4166–4174, December 2015
50. Akata, Z., Reed, S., Walter, D., Lee, H., Schiele, B.: Evaluation of output embeddings for fine-grained image classification. In: 2015 IEEE Conference on Computer Vision and Pattern Recognition (CVPR), pp. 2927–2936, June 2015
51. Zhang, Z., Saligrama, V.: Zero-shot learning via joint latent similarity embedding. In: IEEE Conference on Computer Vision and Pattern Recognition (2016)
52. Vedaldi, A., Lenc, K.: Matconvnet - convolutional neural networks for matlab. Eprint Arxiv (2016)
53. Simonyan, K., Zisserman, A.: Very deep convolutional networks for large-scale image recognition. In: Computer Science (2014)

A Unified Multi-scale Deep Convolutional Neural Network for Fast Object Detection

Zhaowei Cai[1(✉)], Quanfu Fan[2], Rogerio S. Feris[2], and Nuno Vasconcelos[1]

[1] SVCL, UC San Diego, San Diego, USA
{zwcai,nuno}@ucsd.edu
[2] IBM T. J. Watson Research, Yorktown Heights, USA
{qfan,rsferi}@us.ibm.com

Abstract. A unified deep neural network, denoted the *multi-scale CNN* (MS-CNN), is proposed for fast multi-scale object detection. The MS-CNN consists of a proposal sub-network and a detection sub-network. In the proposal sub-network, detection is performed at multiple output layers, so that receptive fields match objects of different scales. These complementary scale-specific detectors are combined to produce a strong multi-scale object detector. The unified network is learned end-to-end, by optimizing a multi-task loss. Feature upsampling by deconvolution is also explored, as an alternative to input upsampling, to reduce the memory and computation costs. State-of-the-art object detection performance, at up to 15 fps, is reported on datasets, such as KITTI and Caltech, containing a substantial number of small objects.

Keywords: Object detection · Multi-scale · Unified neural network

1 Introduction

Classical object detectors, based on the sliding window paradigm, search for objects at multiple scales and aspect ratios. While real-time detectors are available for certain classes of objects, e.g. faces or pedestrians [1,2], it has proven difficult to build detectors of multiple object classes under this paradigm. Recently, there has been interest in detectors derived from deep convolutional neural networks (CNNs) [3–7]. While these have shown much greater ability to address the multiclass problem, less progress has been made towards the detection of objects at multiple scales. The R-CNN [3] samples object proposals at multiple scales, using a preliminary attention stage [8], and then warps these proposals to the size (e.g. 224×224) supported by the CNN. This is, however, very inefficient from a computational standpoint. The development of an effective and computationally efficient region proposal mechanism is still an open problem. The more recent Faster-RCNN [9] addresses the issue with a region proposal network (RPN), which enables end-to-end training. However, the RPN generates proposals of multiple scales by sliding a fixed set of filters over a fixed set of convolutional feature maps. This creates an inconsistency between the sizes of

© Springer International Publishing AG 2016
B. Leibe et al. (Eds.): ECCV 2016, Part IV, LNCS 9908, pp. 354–370, 2016.
DOI: 10.1007/978-3-319-46493-0_22

Fig. 1. In natural images, objects can appear at very different scales, as illustrated by the yellow bounding boxes. A single receptive field, such as that of the RPN [9] (shown in the shaded area), cannot match this variability.

objects, which are variable, and filter receptive fields, which are fixed. As shown in Fig. 1, a fixed receptive field cannot cover the multiple scales at which objects appear in natural scenes. This compromises detection performance, which tends to be particularly poor for small objects, like that in the center of Fig. 1. In fact, [4,5,9] handle such objects by upsampling the input image both at training and testing time. This increases the memory and computation costs of the detector.

This work proposes a unified multi-scale deep CNN, denoted the *multi-scale CNN* (MS-CNN), for fast object detection. Similar to [9], this network consists of two sub-networks: an object proposal network and an accurate detection network. Both of them are learned end-to-end and share computations. However, to ease the inconsistency between the sizes of objects and receptive fields, object detection is performed with multiple output layers, each focusing on objects within certain scale ranges (see Fig. 3). The intuition is that lower network layers, such as "conv-3," have smaller receptive fields, better matched to detect small objects. Conversely, higher layers, such as "conv-5," are best suited for the detection of large objects. The complimentary detectors at different output layers are combined to form a strong multi-scale detector. This is shown to produce accurate object proposals on detection benchmarks with large variation of scale, such as KITTI [10], achieving a recall of over 95 % for only 100 proposals.

A second contribution of this work is the use of feature upsampling as an alternative to input upsampling. This is achieved by introducing a deconvolutional layer that increases the resolution of feature maps (see Fig. 4), enabling small objects to produce larger regions of strong response. This is shown to reduce memory and computation costs. While deconvolution has been explored for segmentation [11] and edge detection [12], it is, as far as we know, for the first time used to speed up and improve detection. When combined with efficient context encoding and hard negative mining, it results in a detector that advances the state-of-the-art detection on the KITTI [10] and Caltech [13] benchmarks. Without image upsampling, the MS-CNN achieves speeds of 10 fps on KITTI (1250×375) and 15 fps on Caltech (640×480) images.

2   Related Work

One of the earliest methods to achieve real-time detection with high accuracy was the cascaded detector of [1]. This architecture has been widely used to implement sliding window detectors for faces [1,14], pedestrians [2,15] and cars [16]. Two main streams of research have been pursued to improve its speed: fast feature extraction [1,2] and cascade learning [14,15,17]. In [1], a set of efficient Haar features was proposed with recourse to integral images. The aggregate feature channels (ACF) of [2] made it possible to compute HOG features at about 100 fps. On the learning front, [14] proposed the soft-cascade, a method to transform a classifier learned with boosting into a cascade with certain guarantees in terms of false positive and detection rate. [17] introduced a Lagrangian formulation to learn cascades that achieve the optimal trade-off between accuracy and computational complexity. [15] extended this formulation for cascades of highly heterogeneous features, ranging from ACF set to deep CNNs, with widely different complexity. The main current limitation of detector cascades is the difficulty of implementing multiclass detectors under this architecture.

In an attempt to leverage the success of deep neural networks for object classification, [3] proposed the R-CNN detector. This combines an object proposal mechanism [8] and a CNN classifier [18]. While the R-CNN surpassed previous detectors [19,20] by a large margin, its speed is limited by the need for object proposal generation and repeated CNN evaluation. [6] has shown that this could be ameliorated with recourse to spatial pyramid pooling (SPP), which allows the computation of CNN features once per image, increasing the detection speed by an order of magnitude. Building on SPP, the Fast-RCNN [4] introduced the ideas of back-propagation through the ROI pooling layer and multi-task learning of a classifier and a bounding box regressor. However, it still depends on bottom-up proposal generation. More recently, the Faster-RCNN [9] has addressed the generation of object proposals and classifier within a single neural network, leading to a significant speedup for proposal detection. Another interesting work is YOLO [21], which outputs object detections within a 7×7 grid. This network runs at ~40 fps, but with some compromise of detection accuracy.

For object recognition, it has been shown beneficial to combine multiple losses, defined on intermediate layers of a single network [11,12,22,23]. GoogLeNet [22] proposed the use of three weighted classification losses, applied at layers of intermediate heights, showing that this type of regularization is useful for very deep models. The deeply supervised network architecture of [23] extended this idea to a larger number of layers. The fact that higher layers convey more semantic information motivated [11] to combine features from intermediate layers, leading to more accurate semantic segmentation. A similar idea was shown useful for edge detection in [12]. Similar to [11,12,22,23], the proposed MS-CNN is learned with losses that account for intermediate layer outputs. However, the aim is not to simply regularize the learning, as in [22,23], or provide detailed information for higher outputs, as in [11,12]. Instead, the goal is to produce a strong individual object detector at each intermediate output layer.

3   Multi-scale Object Proposal Network

In this section, we introduce the proposed network for the generation of object proposals.

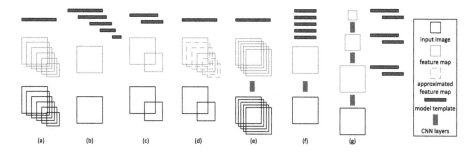

Fig. 2. Different strategies for multi-scale detection. The length of model template represents the template size.

3.1 Multi-scale Detection

The coverage of many object scales is a critical problem for object detection. Since a detector is basically a dot-product between a learned template and an image region, the template has to be matched to the spatial support of the object to recognize. There are two main strategies to achieve this goal. The first is to learn a single classifier and rescale the image multiple times, so that the classifier can match all possible object sizes. As illustrated in Fig. 2(a), this strategy requires feature computation at multiple image scales. While it usually produces the most accurate detection, it tends to be very costly. An alternative approach is to apply multiple classifiers to a single input image. This strategy, illustrated in Fig. 2(b), avoids the repeated computation of feature maps and tends to be efficient. However, it requires an individual classifier for each object scale and usually fails to produce good detectors. Several approaches have been proposed to achieve a good trade-off between accuracy and complexity. For example, the strategy of Fig. 2(c) is to rescale the input a few times and learn a small number of model templates [24]. Another possibility is the feature approximation of [2]. As shown in Fig. 2(d), this consists of rescaling the input a small number of times and interpolating the missing feature maps. This has been shown to achieve considerable speed-ups for a very modest loss of classification accuracy [2].

The implementation of multi-scale strategies on CNN-based detectors is slightly different from those discussed above, due to the complexity of CNN features. As shown in Fig. 2(e), the R-CNN of [3] simply warps object proposal patches to the natural scale of the CNN. This is somewhat similar to Fig. 2(a), but features are computed for patches rather than the entire image. The multi-scale mechanism of the RPN [9], shown in Fig. 2(f), is similar to that of Fig. 2(b). However, multiple sets of templates of the same size are applied to all feature maps. This can lead to a severe scale inconsistency for template matching. As shown in Fig. 1, the single scale of the feature maps, dictated by the (228×228) receptive field of the CNN, can be severely mismatched to small (e.g. 32×32) or large (e.g. 640×640) objects. This compromises object detection performance.

Inspired by previous evidence on the benefits of the strategy of Fig. 2(c) over that of Fig. 2(b), we propose a new multi-scale strategy, shown in Fig. 2(g).

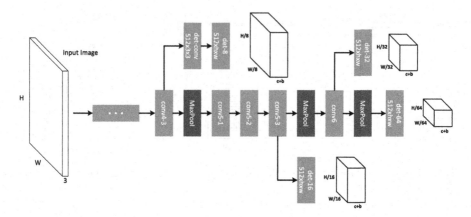

Fig. 3. Proposal sub-network of the MS-CNN. The bold cubes are the output tensors of the network. $h \times w$ is the filter size, c the number of classes, and b the number of bounding box coordinates.

This can be seen as the deep CNN extension of Fig. 2(c), but only uses a single scale of input. It differs from both Fig. 2(e) and (f) in that it exploits feature maps of several resolutions to detect objects at different scales. This is accomplished by the application of a set of templates at intermediate network layers. This results in a set of variable receptive field sizes, which can cover a large range of object sizes.

3.2 Architecture

The detailed architecture of the MS-CNN proposal network is shown in Fig. 3. The network detects objects through several detection branches. The results by all detection branches are simply declared as the final proposal detections. The network has a standard CNN trunk, depicted in the center of the figure, and a set of output branches, which emanate from different layers of the trunk. These branches consist of a single detection layer. Note that a buffer convolutional layer is introduced on the branch that emanates after layer "conv4-3". Since this branch is close to the lower layers of the trunk network, it affects their gradients more than the other detection branches. This can lead to some instability during learning. The buffer convolution prevents the gradients of the detection branch from being back-propagated directly to the trunk layers.

During training, the parameters $\mathbf{W}$ of the multi-scale proposal network are learned from a set of training samples $S = \{(X_i, Y_i)\}_{i=1}^{N}$, where X_i is a training image patch, and $Y_i = (y_i, b_i)$ the combination of its class label $y_i \in \{0, 1, 2, \cdots, K\}$ and bounding box coordinates $b_i = (b_i^x, b_i^y, b_i^w, b_i^h)$. This is achieved with a multi-task loss

$$\mathcal{L}(\mathbf{W}) = \sum_{m=1}^{M} \sum_{i \in S^m} \alpha_m l^m (X_i, Y_i | \mathbf{W}), \qquad (1)$$

where M is the number of detection branches, α_m the weight of loss l^m, and $S = \{S^1, S^2, \cdots, S^M\}$, where S^m contains the examples of scale m. Note that only a subset S^m of the training samples, selected by scale, contributes to the loss of detection layer m. Inspired by the success of joint learning of classification and bounding box regression [4,9], the loss of each detection layer combines these two objectives

$$l(X, Y|\mathbf{W}) = L_{cls}(p(X), y) + \lambda[y \geq 1] L_{loc}(b, \hat{b}), \tag{2}$$

where $p(X) = (p_0(X), \cdots, p_K(X))$ is the probability distribution over classes, λ a trade-off coefficient, $L_{cls}(p(X), y) = -\log p_y(X)$ the cross-entropy loss, $\hat{b} = (\hat{b}_x, \hat{b}_y, \hat{b}_w, \hat{b}_h)$ the regressed bounding box, and

$$L_{loc}(b, \hat{b}) = \frac{1}{4} \sum_{j \in \{x, y, w, h\}} smooth_{L_1}(b_j, \hat{b}_j), \tag{3}$$

the smoothed bounding box regression loss of [4]. The bounding box loss is only used for positive samples and the optimal parameters $\mathbf{W}^* = \arg\min_{\mathbf{W}} \mathcal{L}(\mathbf{W})$ are learned by stochastic gradient descent.

3.3 Sampling

This section describes the assembly of training samples $S^m = \{S_+^m, S_-^m\}$ for each detection layer m. In what follows, the superscript m is dropped for notional simplicity. An anchor is centered at the sliding window on layer m associated with width and height corresponding to filter size. More details can be found in Table 1. A sample X of anchor bounding box b is labeled as positive if $o^* \geq 0.5$, where

$$o^* = \max_{i \in S_{gt}} IoU(b, b_i). \tag{4}$$

S_{gt} is the ground truth and IoU the intersection over union between two bounding boxes. In this case, $Y = (y_{i^*}, b_{i^*})$, where $i^* = \arg\max_{i \in S_{gt}} IoU(b, b_i)$ and (X, Y) are added to the positive set S_+. All the positive samples in $S_+ = \{(X_i, Y_i)|y_i \geq 1\}$ contribute to the loss. Samples such that $o^* < 0.2$ are assigned to a preliminary negative training pool, and the remaining samples discarded. For a natural image, the distribution of objects and non-objects is heavily asymmetric. Sampling is used to compensate for this imbalance. To collect a final set of negative samples $S_- = \{(X_i, Y_i)|y_i = 0\}$, such that $|S_-| = \gamma|S_+|$, we considered three sampling strategies: random, bootstrapping, and mixture.

Random sampling consists of randomly selecting negative samples according to a uniform distribution. Since the distribution of hard and easy negatives is heavily asymmetric too, most randomly collected samples are easy negatives. It is well known that hard negatives mining helps boost performance, since hard negatives have the largest influence on the detection accuracy. Bootstrapping accounts for this, by ranking the negative samples according to their objectness scores, and then collecting top $|S_-|$ negatives. Mixture sampling combines the two, randomly sampling half of S_- and sampling the other half by bootstrapping. In our experiments, mixture sampling has very similar performance to bootstrapping.

To guarantee that each detection layer only detects objects in a certain range of scales, the training set for the layer consists of the subset of S that covers the corresponding scale range. For example, the samples of smallest scale are used to train the detector of "det-8" in Fig. 3. It is possible that no positive training samples are available for a detection layer, resulting in $|S_-|/|S_+| \gg \gamma$. This can make learning unstable. To address this problem, the cross-entropy terms of positives and negatives are weighted as follows

$$L_{cls} = \frac{1}{1+\gamma} \frac{1}{|S_+|} \sum_{i \in S_+} -\log p_{y_i}(X_i) + \frac{\gamma}{1+\gamma} \frac{1}{|S_-|} \sum_{i \in S_-} -\log p_0(X_i). \quad (5)$$

3.4   Implementation Details

Data Augmentation. In [4,6], it is argued that multi-scale training is not needed, since deep neural networks are adept at learning scale invariance. This, however, is not true for datasets such as Caltech [13] and KITTI [10], where object scales can span multiple octaves. In KITTI, many objects are quite small. Without rescaling, the cardinalities of the sets $S_+ = \{S_+^1, S_+^2, \cdots, S_+^M\}$ are wildly varying. In general, the set of training examples of largest object size is very small. To ease this imbalance, the original images are randomly resized to multiple scales.

Fine-Tuning. Training the Fast-RCNN [4] and RPN [9] networks requires large amounts of memory and a small mini-batch, due to the large size of the input (i.e. 1000×600). This leads to a very heavy training procedure. In fact, many background regions that are useless for training take substantially amounts of memory. Thus, we randomly crop a small patch (e.g. 448×448) around objects from the whole image. This drastically reduces the memory requirements, enabling four images to fit into the typical GPU memory of 12G.

Learning is initialized with the popular VGG-Net [25]. Since bootstrapping and the multi-task loss can make training unstable in the early iterations, a two-stage procedure is adopted. The first stage uses random sampling and a small trade-off coefficient λ (e.g. 0.05). 10,000 iterations are run with a learning rate of 0.00005. The resulting model is used to initialize the second stage, where random sampling is switched to bootstrapping and $\lambda = 1$. We set $\alpha_i = 0.9$ for "det-8" and $\alpha_i = 1$ for the other layers. Another 25,000 iterations are run with an initial learning rate of 0.00005, which decays 10 times after every 10,000 iterations. This two-stage learning procedure enables stable multi-task training.

4   Object Detection Network

Although the proposal network could work as a detector itself, it is not strong, since its sliding windows do not cover objects well. To increase detection

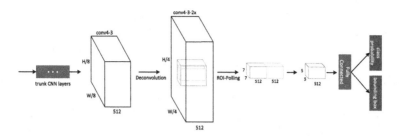

Fig. 4. Object detection sub-network of the MS-CNN. "trunk CNN layers" are shared with proposal sub-network. W and H are the width and height of the input image. The green (blue) cubes represent object (context) region pooling. "class probability" and "bounding box" are the outputs of the detection sub-network. (Color figure online)

accuracy, a detection network is added. Following [4], a ROI pooling layer is first used to extract features of a fixed dimension (e.g. $7 \times 7 \times 512$). The features are then fed to a fully connected layer and output layers, as shown in Fig. 4. A deconvolution layer, described in Sect. 4.1, is added to double the resolution of the feature maps. The multi-task loss of (1) is extended to

$$\mathcal{L}(\mathbf{W}, \mathbf{W}_d) = \sum_{m=1}^{M} \sum_{i \in S^m} \alpha_m l^m (X_i, Y_i | \mathbf{W}) + \sum_{i \in S^{M+1}} \alpha_{M+1} l^{M+1} (X_i, Y_i | \mathbf{W}, \mathbf{W}_d), \quad (6)$$

where l^{M+1} and S^{M+1} are the loss and training samples for the detection sub-network. S^{M+1} is collected as in [4]. As in (2), l^{M+1} combines a cross-entropy loss for classification and a smoothed L_1 loss for bounding box regression. The detection sub-network shares some of the proposal sub-network parameters $\mathbf{W}$ and adds some parameters $\mathbf{W}_d$. The parameters are optimized jointly, i.e. $(\mathbf{W}^*, \mathbf{W}_d^*) = \arg \min \mathcal{L}(\mathbf{W}, \mathbf{W}_d)$. In the proposed implementation, ROI pooling is applied to the top of the "conv4-3" layer, instead of the "conv5-3" layer of [4], since "conv4-3" feature maps performed better in our experiments. One possible explanation is that "conv4-3" corresponds to higher resolution and is better suited for location-aware bounding box regression.

4.1   CNN Feature Map Approximation

Input size has a critical role in CNN-based object detection accuracy. Simply forwarding object patches, at the original scale, through the CNN impairs performance (especially for small ones), since the pre-trained CNN models have a natural scale (e.g. 224×224). While the R-CNN naturally solves this problem through warping [3], it is not explicitly addressed by the Fast-RCNN [4] or Faster-RCNN [9]. To bridge the scale gap, these methods simply upsample input images (by ~ 2 times). For datasets, such as KITTI [10], containing large amounts of small objects, this has limited effectiveness. Input upsampling also has three side effects: large memory requirements, slow training and slow testing. It should be noted that input upsampling does not enrich the image details.

Instead, it is needed because the higher convolutional layers respond very weakly to small objects. For example, a 32×32 object is mapped into a 4×4 patch of the "conv4-3" layer and a 2×2 patch of the "conv5-3" layer. This provides limited information for 7×7 ROI pooling.

To address this problem, we consider an efficient way to increase the resolution of feature maps. This consists of upsampling feature maps (instead of the input) using a deconvolution layer, as shown in Fig. 4. This strategy is similar to that of [2], shown in Fig. 2(d), where input rescaling is replaced by feature rescaling. In [2], a feature approximator is learned by least squares. In the CNN world, a better solution is to use a deconvolution layer, similar to that of [11]. Unlike input upsampling, feature upsampling does not incur in extra costs for memory and computation. Our experiments show that the addition of a deconvolution layer significantly boosts detection performance, especially for small objects. To the best of our knowledge, this is the first application of deconvolution to jointly improve the speed and accuracy of an object detector.

4.2   Context Embedding

Context has been shown useful for object detection [5,7,26] and segmentation [27]. Context information has been modeled by a recurrent neural network in [26] and acquired from multiple regions around the object location in [5,7,27]. In this work, we focus on context from multiple regions. As shown in Fig. 4, features from an object (green cube) and a context (blue cube) region are stacked together immediately after ROI pooling. The context region is 1.5 times larger than the object region. An extra convolutional layer without padding is used to reduce the number of model parameters. It helps compress redundant context and object information, without loss of accuracy, and guarantees that the number of model parameters is approximately the same.

4.3   Implementation Details

Learning is initialized with the model generated by the first learning stage of the proposal network, described in Sect. 3.4. The learning rate is set to 0.0005, and reduced by a factor of 10 times after every 10,000 iterations. Learning stops after 25,000 iterations. The joint optimization of (6) is solved by back-propagation throughout the unified network. Bootstrapping is used and $\lambda = 1$. Following [4], the parameters of layers "conv1-1" to "conv2-2" are fixed during learning, for faster training.

5   Experimental Evaluation

The performance of the MS-CNN detector was evaluated on the KITTI [10] and Caltech Pedestrian [13] benchmarks. These were chosen because, unlike VOC [28] and ImageNet [29], they contain many small objects. Typical image sizes are 1250×375 on KITTI and 640×480 on Caltech. KITTI contains three

Table 1. Parameter configurations of the different models.

		det-8		det-16		det-32		det-64	ROI	FC
car	filter	5 × 5	7 × 7	5 × 5	7 × 7	5 × 5	7 × 7	5 × 5	7 × 7	4096
	anchor	40 × 40	56 × 56	80 × 80	112 × 112	160 × 160	224 × 224	320 × 320		
ped/cyc	filter	5 × 3	7 × 5	5 × 3	7 × 5	5 × 3	7 × 5	5 × 3	7 × 5	2048
	anchor	40 × 28	56 × 36	80 × 56	112 × 72	160 × 112	224 × 144	320 × 224		
caltech	filter	5 × 3	7 × 5	5 × 3	7 × 5	5 × 3	7 × 5	5 × 3	8 × 4	2048
	anchor	40 × 20	56 × 28	80 × 40	112 × 56	160 × 80	224 × 112	320 × 160		

Table 2. Detection recall of the various detection layers on KITTI validation set (car), as a function of object hight in pixels.

	det-8	det-16	det-32	det-64	combined
25≤height<50	0.9180	0.3071	0.0003	0	0.9360
50≤height<100	0.5934	0.9660	0.4252	0	0.9814
100≤height<200	0.0007	0.5997	0.9929	0.4582	0.9964
height≥200	0	0	0.9583	0.9792	0.9583
all scales	0.6486	0.5654	0.3149	0.0863	0.9611

object classes: car, pedestrian and cyclist, and three levels of evaluation: easy, moderate and hard. The "moderate" level is the most commonly used. In total, 7,481 images are available for training/validation, and 7,518 for testing. Since no ground truth is available for the test set, we followed [5], splitting the trainval set into training and validation sets. In all ablation experiments, the training set was used for learning and the validation set for evaluation. Following [5], a model was trained for car detection and another for pedestrian/cyclist detection. One pedestrian model was learned on Caltech. The model configurations for original input size are shown in Table 1. The detector was implemented in C++ within the Caffe toolbox [30], and source code is available at https://github. com/zhaoweicai/mscnn. All times are reported for implementation on a single CPU core (2.40 GHz) of an Intel Xeon E5-2630 server with 64 GB of RAM. An NVIDIA Titan GPU was used for CNN computations.

5.1 Proposal Evaluation

We start with an evaluation of the proposal network. Following [31], oracle recall is used as performance metric. For consistency with the KITTI setup, a ground truth is recalled if its best matched proposal has IoU higher than 70 % for cars, and 50 % for pedestrians and cyclists.

The Roles of Individual Detection Layers. Table 2 shows the detection accuracy of the various detection layers as a function of object height in pixels. As expected, each layer has highest accuracy for the objects that match its scale. While the individual recall across scales is low, the combination of all detectors achieves high recall for all object scales.

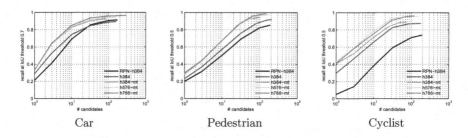

Car   Pedestrian   Cyclist

Fig. 5. Proposal recall on the KITTI validation set (moderate). "hXXX" refers to input images of height "XXX". "mt" indicates multi-task learning of proposal and detection sub-networks.

The Effect of Input Size. Fig. 5 shows that the proposal network is fairly robust to the size of input images for cars and pedestrians. For cyclist, performance increases between heights 384 and 576, but there are no gains beyond this. These results show that the network can achieve good proposal generation performance without substantial input upsampling.

Detection Sub-network Improves Proposal Sub-network. [4] has shown that multi-task learning can benefit both bounding box regression and classification. On the other hand [9] showed that, even when features are shared between the two tasks, object detection does not improve object proposals too much. Figure 5 shows that, for the MS-CNN, detection can substantially benefit proposal generation, especially for pedestrians.

Comparison with the State-of-the-art. Figure 6 compares the proposal generation network to BING [32], Selective Search [8], EdgeBoxes [33], MCG [34], 3DOP [5] and RPN [9]. The top row of the figure shows that the MS-CNN achieves a recall about 98 % with only 100 proposals. This should be compared to the ~2,000 proposals required by 3DOP and the ~10,000 proposals required by EdgeBoxbes. While it is not surprising that the proposed network outperforms unsupervised proposal methods, such as [8,33,34], its large gains over supervised methods [5,32], that can even use 3D information, are significant. The closest performance is achieved by RPN (input upsampled twice), which has substantially weaker performance for pedestrians and cyclists. When the input is not upsampled, RPN misses even more objects, as shown in Fig. 5. It is worth mentioning that the MS-CNN generates high quality proposals (high overlap with the ground truth) without any edge detection or segmentation. This is evidence for the effectiveness of bounding box regression networks.

5.2   Object Detection Evaluation

In this section we evaluate object detection performance. Since the performance of the cyclist detector has large variance on the validation set, due to the low number of cyclist occurrences, only car and pedestrian detection are considered in the ablation experiments.

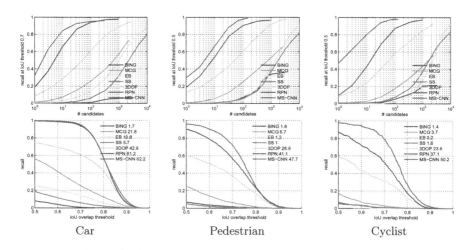

Car   Pedestrian   Cyclist

Fig. 6. Proposal performance comparison on KITTI validation set (moderate). The first row is proposal recall curves and the second row is recall v.s. *IoU* for 100 proposals.

Table 3. Results on the KITTI validation set. "hXXX" indicates an input of height "XXX", "2x" deconvolution, "ctx" context encoding, and "c" dimensionality reduction convolution. In columns "Time" and "# params", entries before the "/" are for car model and after for pedestrian/cyclist model.

Model	Time	# params	Cars			Pedestrians		
			Easy	Mod	Hard	Easy	Mod	Hard
h384	0.11 s/0.09 s	471M/217M	90.90	80.63	68.94	73.70	68.37	60.72
h576	0.22 s/0.19 s	471M/217M	90.42	88.14	73.44	75.35	70.77	63.07
h768	0.41 s/0.36 s	471M/217M	89.84	88.88	75.78	76.38	72.26	64.08
h576-random	0.22 s/0.19 s	471M/217M	90.94	87.50	71.27	70.69	65.91	58.28
h576-mixture	0.22 s/0.19 s	471M/217M	90.33	88.12	72.90	75.09	70.49	62.43
h384-2x	0.12 s/0.10 s	471M/217M	90.55	87.93	71.90	76.01	69.53	61.57
h576-2x	0.23 s/0.20 s	471M/217M	94.08	89.12	75.54	77.74	72.49	64.43
h768-2x	0.43 s/0.38 s	471M/217M	90.96	88.83	75.19	76.33	72.71	64.31
h576-ctx	0.24 s/0.20 s	863M/357M	92.89	88.88	74.34	76.89	71.45	63.50
h576-ctx-c	0.22 s/0.19 s	297M/155M	90.49	89.13	74.85	76.82	72.13	64.14
proposal network (h576)	0.19 s/0.18 s	80M/78M	82.73	73.49	63.22	64.03	60.54	55.07

The Effect of Input Upsampling. Table 3 shows that input upsampling can be a crucial factor for detection. A significant improvement is obtained by upsampling the inputs by 1.5~2 times, but we saw little gains beyond a factor of 2. This is smaller than the factor of 3.5 required by [5]. Larger factors lead to (exponentially) slower detectors and larger memory requirements.

Sampling Strategy. Table 3 compares sampling strategies: random ("h576-random"), bootstrapping ("h576") and mixture ("h576-mixture"). For car, these three strategies are close to each other. For pedestrian, bootstrapping and mixture are close, but random is much worse. Note that random sampling has many more false positives than the other two.

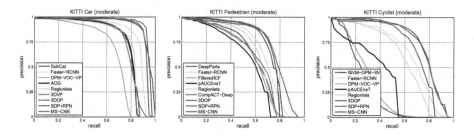

Fig. 7. Comparison to the state-of-the-art on KITTI benchmark test set (moderate).

Table 4. Results on the KITTI benchmark test set (only published works shown).

Method	Time	Cars			Pedestrians			Cyclists		
		Easy	Mod	Hard	Easy	Mod	Hard	Easy	Mod	Hard
LSVM-MDPM-sv [35]	10 s	68.02	56.48	44.18	47.74	39.36	35.95	35.04	27.50	26.21
DPM-VOC-VP [36]	8 s	74.95	64.71	48.76	59.48	44.86	40.37	42.43	31.08	28.23
SubCat [16]	0.7 s	84.14	75.46	59.71	54.67	42.34	37.95	-	-	-
3DVP [37]	40 s	87.46	75.77	65.38	-	-	-	-	-	-
AOG [38]	3 s	84.80	75.94	60.70	-	-	-	-	-	-
Faster-RCNN [9]	2 s	86.71	81.84	71.12	78.86	65.90	61.18	72.26	63.35	55.90
CompACT-Deep [15]	1 s	-	-	-	70.69	58.74	52.71	-	-	-
DeepParts [39]	1 s	-	-	-	70.49	58.67	52.78	-	-	-
FilteredICF [40]	2 s	-	-	-	67.65	56.75	51.12	-	-	-
pAUCEnsT [41]	60 s	-	-	-	65.26	54.49	48.60	51.62	38.03	33.38
Regionlets [20]	1 s	84.75	76.45	59.70	73.14	61.15	55.21	70.41	58.72	51.83
3DOP [5]	3 s	**93.04**	88.64	**79.10**	81.78	67.47	64.70	78.39	68.94	61.37
SDP+RPN [42]	0.4 s	90.14	88.85	78.38	80.09	70.16	64.82	81.37	73.74	65.31
MS-CNN	0.4 s	90.03	**89.02**	76.11	**83.92**	**73.70**	**68.31**	**84.06**	**75.46**	**66.07**

CNN Feature Approximation. Three methods were attempted for learning the deconvolution layer for feature map approximation: (1) bilinearly interpolated weights; (2) weights initialized by bilinear interpolation and learned with back-propagation; (3) weights initialized with Gaussian noise and learned by back-propagation. We found the first method to work best, confirming the findings of [11,12]. As shown in Table 3, the deconvolution layer helps in most cases. The gains are larger for smaller input images, which tend to have smaller objects. Note that the feature map approximation adds trivial computation and no parameters.

Context Embedding. Table 3 shows that there is a gain in encoding context. However, the number of model parameters almost doubles. The dimensionality reduction convolution layer significantly reduces this problem, without impairment of accuracy or speed.

Object Detection by the Proposal Network. The proposal network can work as a detector, by switching the class-agnostic classification to class-specific. Table 3 shows that, although not as strong as the unified network, it achieves

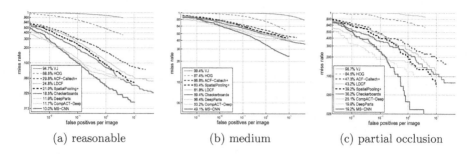

| (a) reasonable | (b) medium | (c) partial occlusion |

Fig. 8. Comparison to the state-of-the-art on Caltech.

fairly good results, which are better than those of some detectors on the KITTI leaderboard[1].

Comparison to the State-of-the-art. The results of model "h768-ctx-c" were submitted to the KITTI leaderboard. A comparison to previous approaches is given in Table 4 and Fig. 7. The MS-CNN set a new record for the detection of pedestrians and cyclists. The columns "Pedestrians-Mod" and "Cyclists-Mod" show substantial gains (6 and 7 points respectively) over 3DOP [5], and much better performance than the Faster-RCNN [9], Regionlets [20], etc. We also led a nontrivial margin over the very recent SDP+RPN [42], which used scale dependent pooling. In terms of speed, the network is fairly fast. For the largest input size, the MS-CNN detector is about 8 times faster than 3DOP. On the original images (1250 × 375) detection speed reaches 10 fps.

Pedestrian Detection on Caltech. The MS-CNN detector was also evaluated on the Caltech pedestrian benchmark. The model "h720-ctx" was compared to methods such as DeepParts [39], CompACT-Deep [15], CheckerBoard [40], LDCF [43], ACF [2], and SpatialPooling [41] on three tasks: reasonable, medium and partial occlusion. As shown in Fig. 8, the MS-CNN has state-of-the-art performance. Figure 8(b) and (c) show that it performs very well for small and occluded objects, outperforming DeepParts [39], which explicitly addresses occlusion. Moreover, it misses a very small number of pedestrians, due to the accuracy of the proposal network. The speed is approximately 8 fps (15 fps) on upsampled 960 × 720 (original 640 × 480) Caltech images.

6   Conclusions

We have proposed a unified deep convolutional neural network, denoted the MS-CNN, for fast multi-scale object detection. The detection is preformed at various intermediate network layers, whose receptive fields match various object scales. This enables the detection of all object scales by feedforwarding a single input image through the network, which results in a very fast detector. CNN feature

---

[1] http://www.cvlibs.net/datasets/kitti/.

approximation was also explored, as an alternative to input upsampling. It was shown to result in significant savings in memory and computation. Overall, the MS-CNN detector achieves high detection rates at speeds of up to 15 fps.

Acknowledgements. This work was partially funded by NSF grant IIS1208522 and a gift from KETI. We also thank NVIDIA for GPU donations through their academic program.

References

1. Viola, P.A., Jones, M.J.: Robust real-time face detection. Int. J. Comput. Vis. **57**(2), 137–154 (2004)
2. Dollár, P., Appel, R., Belongie, S.J., Perona, P.: Fast feature pyramids for object detection. IEEE Trans. Pattern Anal. Mach. Intell. **36**(8), 1532–1545 (2014)
3. Girshick, R.B., Donahue, J., Darrell, T., Malik, J.: Rich feature hierarchies for accurate object detection and semantic segmentation. In: CVPR, pp. 580–587(2014)
4. Girshick, R.B.: Fast R-CNN. In: ICCV, pp. 1440–1448(2015)
5. Chen, X., Kundu, K., Zhu, Y., Berneshawi, A., Ma, H., Fidler, S., Urtasun, R.: 3D object proposals for accurate object class detection. In: NIPS (2015)
6. He, K., Zhang, X., Ren, S., Sun, J.: Spatial pyramid pooling in deep convolutional networks for visual recognition. In: Fleet, D., Pajdla, T., Schiele, B., Tuytelaars, T. (eds.) ECCV 2014. LNCS, vol. 8691, pp. 346–361. Springer, Heidelberg (2014). doi:10.1007/978-3-319-10578-9_23
7. Gidaris, S., Komodakis, N.: Object detection via a multi-region and semantic segmentation-aware CNN model. In: ICCV, pp. 1134–1142(2015)
8. van de Sande, K.E.A., Uijlings, J.R.R., Gevers, T., Smeulders, A.W.M.: Segmentation as selective search for object recognition. In: ICCV, pp. 1879–1886(2011)
9. Ren, S., He, K., Girshick, R., Sun, J.: Faster R-CNN: Towards real-time object detection with region proposal networks. In: NIPS (2015)
10. Geiger, A., Lenz, P., Urtasun, R.: Are we ready for autonomous driving? the KITTI vision benchmark suite. In: CVPR, pp. 3354–3361(2012)
11. Long, J., Shelhamer, E., Darrell, T.: Fully convolutional networks for semantic segmentation. In: CVPR, pp. 3431–3440 (2015)
12. Xie, S., Tu, Z.: Holistically-nested edge detection. In: ICCV, pp. 1395–1403 (2015)
13. Dollár, P., Wojek, C., Schiele, B., Perona, P.: Pedestrian detection: An evaluation of the state of the art. IEEE Trans. Pattern Anal. Mach. Intell. **34**(4), 743–761 (2012)
14. Bourdev, L.D., Brandt, J.: Robust object detection via soft cascade. In: CVPR, pp. 236–243 (2005)
15. Cai, Z., Saberian, M.J., Vasconcelos, N.: Learning complexity-aware cascades for deep pedestrian detection. In: ICCV, pp. 3361–3369 (2015)
16. Ohn-Bar, E., Trivedi, M.M.: Learning to detect vehicles by clustering appearance patterns. IEEE Trans. Intell. Transp. Syst. **16**(5), 2511–2521 (2015)
17. Saberian, M.J., Vasconcelos, N.: Boosting algorithms for detector cascade learning. J. Mach. Learn. Res. **15**(1), 2569–2605 (2014)
18. Krizhevsky, A., Sutskever, I., Hinton, G.E.: Imagenet classification with deep convolutional neural networks. In: NIPS, pp. 1106–1114(2012)
19. Felzenszwalb, P.F., Girshick, R.B., McAllester, D.A., Ramanan, D.: Object detection with discriminatively trained part-based models. IEEE Trans. Pattern Anal. Mach. Intell. **32**(9), 1627–1645 (2010)

20. Wang, X., Yang, M., Zhu, S., Lin, Y.: Regionlets for generic object detection. In: ICCV, pp. 17–24 (2013)
21. Redmon, J., Divvala, S.K., Girshick, R.B., Farhadi, A.: You only look once: Unified, real-time object detection. In: CVPR (2016)
22. Szegedy, C., Liu, W., Jia, Y., Sermanet, P., Reed, S., Anguelov, D., Erhan, D., Vanhoucke, V., Rabinovich, A.: Going deeper with convolutions. In: CVPR, pp. 1–9 (2015)
23. Lee, C., Xie, S., Gallagher, P.W., Zhang, Z., Tu, Z.: Deeply-supervised nets. In: AISTATS (2015)
24. Benenson, R., Mathias, M., Timofte, R., Gool, L.J.V.: Pedestrian detection at 100 frames per second. In: CVPR, pp. 2903–2910 (2012)
25. Simonyan, K., Zisserman, A.: Very deep convolutional networks for large-scale image recognition. CoRR abs/1409.1556 (2014)
26. Bell, S., Zitnick, C.L., Bala, K., Girshick, R.B.: Inside-outside net: Detecting objects in context with skip pooling and recurrent neural networks. In: CVPR (2016)
27. Zhu, Y., Urtasun, R., Salakhutdinov, R., Fidler, S.: segDeepM: Exploiting segmentation and context in deep neural networks for object detection. In: CVPR, pp. 4703–4711 (2015)
28. Everingham, M., Gool, L.J.V., Williams, C.K.I., Winn, J.M., Zisserman, A.: The pascal visual object classes (VOC) challenge. Int. J. Comput. Vis. **88**(2), 303–338 (2010)
29. Russakovsky, O., Deng, J., Su, H., Krause, J., Satheesh, S., Ma, S., Huang, Z., Karpathy, A., Khosla, A., Bernstein, M.S., Berg, A.C., Li, F.: Imagenet large scale visual recognition challenge. Int. J. Comput. Vis. **115**(3), 211–252 (2015)
30. Jia, Y., Shelhamer, E., Donahue, J., Karayev, S., Long, J., Girshick, R.B., Guadarrama, S., Darrell, T.: Caffe: Convolutional architecture for fast feature embedding. In: MM, pp. 675–678 (2014)
31. Hosang, J., Benenson, R., Dollár, P., Schiele, B.: What makes for effective detection proposals? PAMI **38**(4), 814–830 (2015)
32. Cheng, M., Zhang, Z., Lin, W., Torr, P.H.S.: BING: binarized normed gradients for objectness estimation at 300fps. In: CVPR, pp. 3286–3293 (2014)
33. Zitnick, C.L., Dollár, P.: Edge boxes: locating object proposals from edges. In: Fleet, D., Pajdla, T., Schiele, B., Tuytelaars, T. (eds.) ECCV 2014. LNCS, vol. 8693, pp. 391–405. Springer, Heidelberg (2014). doi:10.1007/978-3-319-10602-1_26
34. Arbeláez, P.A., Pont-Tuset, J., Barron, J.T., Marqués, F., Malik, J.: Multiscale combinatorial grouping. In: CVPR, pp. 328–335 (2014)
35. Geiger, A., Wojek, C., Urtasun, R.: Joint 3D estimation of objects and scene layout. In: NIPS, pp. 1467–1475 (2011)
36. Pepik, B., Stark, M., Gehler, P.V., Schiele, B.: Multi-view and 3D deformable part models. IEEE Trans. Pattern Anal. Mach. Intell. **37**(11), 2232–2245 (2015)
37. Xiang, Y., Choi, W., Lin, Y., Savarese, S.: Data-driven 3D voxel patterns for object category recognition. In: CVPR, pp. 1903–1911 (2015)
38. Li, B., Wu, T., Zhu, S.-C.: Integrating context and occlusion for car detection by hierarchical and-or model. In: Fleet, D., Pajdla, T., Schiele, B., Tuytelaars, T. (eds.) ECCV 2014. LNCS, vol. 8694, pp. 652–667. Springer, Heidelberg (2014). doi:10.1007/978-3-319-10599-4_42
39. Tian, Y., Luo, P., Wang, X., Tang, X.: Deep learning strong parts for pedestrian detection. In: ICCV, pp. 1904–1912 (2015)
40. Zhang, S., Benenson, R., Schiele, B.: Filtered channel features for pedestrian detection. In: CVPR, pp. 1751–1760 (2015)

41. Paisitkriangkrai, S., Shen, C., van den Hengel, A.: Pedestrian detection with spatially pooled features and structured ensemble learning. CoRR abs/1409.5209 (2014)
42. Yang, F., Choi, W., Lin, Y.: Exploit all the layers: Fast and accurate CNN object detector with scale dependent pooling and cascaded rejection classifiers. In: CVPR. (2016)
43. Nam, W., Dollár, P., Han, J.H.: Local decorrelation for improved pedestrian detection. In: NIPS, pp. 424–432 (2014)

Deep Specialized Network
for Illuminant Estimation

Wu Shi[1], Chen Change Loy[1,2(✉)], and Xiaoou Tang[1,2]

[1] Department of Information Engineering,
The Chinese University of Hong Kong, Hong Kong, China
{sw015,ccloy,xtang}@ie.cuhk.edu.hk
[2] Shenzhen Institutes of Advanced Technology, CAS, Shenzhen, China

Abstract. Illuminant estimation to achieve color constancy is an ill-posed problem. Searching the large hypothesis space for an accurate illuminant estimation is hard due to the ambiguities of unknown reflections and local patch appearances. In this work, we propose a novel Deep Specialized Network (DS-Net) that is adaptive to diverse local regions for estimating robust local illuminants. This is achieved through a new convolutional network architecture with two interacting sub-networks, *i.e.* an *hypotheses network* (HypNet) and a *selection network* (SelNet). In particular, HypNet generates multiple illuminant hypotheses that inherently capture different modes of illuminants with its unique two-branch structure. SelNet then adaptively picks for confident estimations from these plausible hypotheses. Extensive experiments on the two largest color constancy benchmark datasets show that the proposed 'hypothesis selection' approach is effective to overcome erroneous estimation. Through the synergy of HypNet and SelNet, our approach outperforms state-of-the-art methods such as [1–3].

1 Introduction

The aim of color constancy is to recover the surface color under canonical (usually white) illumination from the observed color. Common computational approaches require estimating the spectral illumination of a scene to correct the extrinsic bias it induces. Illumination estimation can be understood as a process of searching through a hypothesis space to identify the best illuminant. It is often difficult to find a good one since the problem is underdetermined – both the illuminant and surface colors in an observed image are unknown. Finding a good hypothesis of illuminant becomes harder when there are ambiguities caused by complex interactions of extrinsic factors such as surface reflections and different texture appearances of objects.

Recent methods [2,4,5] attempt to exploit the exceptional modelling capacity of convolutional network for this problem. We argue that it is still non-trivial to

Electronic supplementary material The online version of this chapter (doi:10.1007/978-3-319-46493-0_23) contains supplementary material, which is available to authorized users.

B. Leibe et al. (Eds.): ECCV 2016, Part IV, LNCS 9908, pp. 371–387, 2016.
DOI: 10.1007/978-3-319-46493-0_23

(a) Input image (b) The restored image using CNN [2] (c) The restored image using DS-Net and the pixel-wise angular error
and the corresponding pixel-wise maps for branch-1 and -2 for HypNet. The last image is the angular error
angular error. map after the selection of SelNet.

Fig. 1. The proposed DS-Net shows superior performance over existing methods in handling regions with different intrinsic properties, thanks to the unique synergy between the hypotheses network (HypNet) and selection network (SelNet). In this example, the different branches of HypNet provide complementary illuminant estimations based on their specialization. SelNet automatically picks for the optimal estimations and yields a considerably lower angular error compared to that obtained from each respective branch in HypNet, as well as that obtained from CNN [2]. The angular error is the error in the illuminant estimate.

learn a model that can encompass the large and diverse hypothesis space given limited samples provided during the training stage. We believe that a model with higher flexibility could better handle ambiguous cases. The key principle advocated in [2,4,5] is to arrange multiple layers of neurons to extract increasingly abstract features for reconstructing a restored image. We start from a similar principle but introduce new considerations in our network design for addressing the problem of illuminant estimation. The proposed network, named as *Deep Specialized Network* (DS-Net) consists of two closely coupled sub-networks.

(1) *Hypotheses Network (HypNet)* – The sub-network learns to map an image patch to multiple hypotheses of illuminant of that patch. This is in contrast to existing network designs that usually provide just a single prediction. In our design, HypNet generates two competing hypotheses for an illuminant estimation of a patch through two branches that fork from a main CNN body. Each branch of HypNet is trained using a 'winner-take-all' learning strategy to automatically specialize to handle regions of certain appearance. For instance, as can be seen from Fig. 1, the first branch produces more accurate illuminant estimations for non-shadowed and bright regions like (*e.g.* sky), whilst the second branch is more effective on shadowed and textured areas (*e.g.* building and trees).

(2) *Selection Network (SelNet)* – This sub-network makes an unweighted vote on the hypotheses produced by HypNet. Specifically, it takes an image patch and generates a score vector to pick the final illuminant hypothesis generated from one of the branches in HypNet. In other words, the SelNet acts like a 'filter', whose job is to decide which particular illuminant is more likely given the local patch statistics. We show that SelNet yields much robust final predictions than simply averaging the hypotheses. The entire structure of the two networks is shown in Fig. 2.

The main contribution of this study is a new deep specialized network effective for illuminant estimation. Specifically, we design a single network (*i.e.* a HypNet) to output multiple hypotheses, which resembles multiple expert networks in an ensemble. A diversity-encouraging 'winner-take-all' learning scheme is proposed to train the specialized network. We further present a viable way to design a separate network (*i.e.* a SelNet) for hypothesis selection. Extensive experiments on standard benchmarks show the superiority of DS-Net over existing methods in both global-illuminant of multi-illuminants estimation.

2   Related Work

Color constancy is a well-studied topic in both vision science and computer vision. There is a rich body of literature on illuminant estimation. These methods can be broadly divided into two categories: (1) statistic-based methods that estimate the illuminant based on image statistics or physical properties. These methods consider the relationship between color statistics and achromatic colors [6,7], statistics inspired from the human visual system [8–12], spatial derivatives and frequency information from the image and scene illuminations [13–15], and specularity and shadows [16–18]; (2) learning-based approaches that estimate the illuminant using a model that is learned from training images. We refer readers to [19,20] for excellent surveys. In this section, we highlight learning-based approaches that are related to our work.

In general, learning-based methods are shown to be more accurate than statistics-based approaches. Features considered in these studies are mostly handcrafted, including chromaticity histograms [21–24], full three-dimensional RGB histogram [9,25], derivative and frequency features. Recent approaches have shown that relatively simple features, such as color and edge moments [26], or statistics of color chromaticity [1], could provide excellent performance.

While deep representation learned with CNN has achieved remarkable success in various high-level tasks [27–29] and a few low-level vision problems [30–35], it remains unclear if deep CNN can perform as well on the color constancy task. Barron [3] shows that his method can learn convolutional filters for accurate illuminant estimation. But he does not delve deeper into the use of deep CNNs. It is worth pointing out that Barron assumes that illuminant induces a global 2D translation in log-chrominance space. Such an assumption of uniform spectral distribution of light in an image may not work well in some common cases with multiple illuminants or scenes with in-shadow plus non-shadow regions. In contrast to [3], our approach does not assume single illuminant. We will show the effectiveness of the proposed approach over [3] on handling multi-illuminants.

Bianco *et al.* [2] make the first attempt to adopt a standard convolutional network for illuminant estimation. We show in the experiments that our network could provide more accurate estimates, thanks to the new network design with network-induced hypothesis selection. Under the global illuminant setting, while their method needs to specifically learn a separate support vector regressor to map local estimates to a global estimate, our approach can produce better results by just performing a simple median pooling on the already well-estimated illuminants from DS-Net.

A notable approach is proposed by Joze and Drew [36]. They adopt an exemplar-based approach - it finds similar surfaces in the training dataset, and estimating the illumination for each target surface through comparing the statistics of pixels belonging to similar surfaces with the target surface. This study shows the importance of capturing multiple modes through a non-parametric model. Our work is inspired by [36] but the proposed network does not require explicit nearest surface comparison. The multiple modes are inherently captured in the branch-level ensemble of HypNet.

There are other interesting approaches that exploit automatically detected objects such as faces [37] to guide the illuminant estimation. Approaches in [38, 39] require user guidance to deal with multiple illuminants.

3   Illuminant Estimation by Convolutional Network

Consider an image $\mathbf{I}_{rgb} = \{I_r, I_g, I_b\}$ taken from a linear RGB color camera with black level corrected and saturated pixels removed. The value of I_c for a Lambertian surface at pixel x is equal to the integral of the product of the illuminant spectral power distribution $E(x, \lambda)$, the surface reflectance $R(x, \lambda)$ and the sensor response function $S_c(\lambda)$:

$$I_c(x) = \int_{\Omega} E(x, \lambda)R(x, \lambda)S_c(\lambda)d\lambda, \qquad c \in \{r, g, b\}, \tag{1}$$

where λ is the wavelength, and Ω is the visible spectrum. From the Von Kries coefficient law [40], a simplified diagonal model is given by

$$I_c = E_c \times R_c, \qquad c \in \{r, g, b\}, \tag{2}$$

where E is the RGB illumination and R is the RGB value of reflectance under canonical (often white) illumination. Following this widely accepted model, the goal of color constancy is to estimate E from I, and then compute $R_c = I_c/E_c$.

Following existing studies [3,41], we process images in the space of UV chrominance[1]. Specifically, we first convert the RGB channels of I to the log-homogeneous chrominance (I_u, I_v) defined as follows:

$$I_u = \log(I_r/I_g) \qquad I_v = \log(I_b/I_g), \tag{3}$$

and estimate the illumination in that space:

$$E_u = \log(E_r/E_g) \qquad E_v = \log(E_b/E_g). \tag{4}$$

---

[1] As suggested by [3,41], the log-chrominance formulation is advantageous over the RGB formulation in that we have 2 unknown instead of 3, and R and I are related by simple linear constraint instead of a multiplicative constraint.

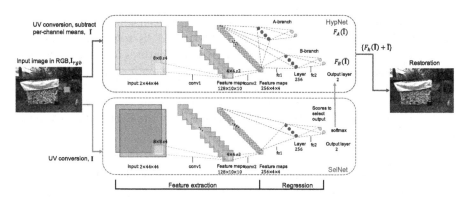

Fig. 2. The network architecture of Deep Specialized Network (DS-Net). It is trained to estimate illuminant of a given patch. It consists of two interacting networks, namely Hypotheses Network (HypNet) and Selection Network (SelNet). The former generates two hypotheses of illuminants from its two branches. The latter selects one of the hypotheses as the final estimation. It is possible to include more branches in HypNet.

One can easily recover (up to a scalar) the illumination E from UV to RGB [3] by following

$$E_r = \frac{\exp(-E_u)}{z} \quad E_g = \frac{1}{z} \quad E_b = \frac{\exp(-E_v)}{z} \tag{5}$$
$$z = \sqrt{\exp(-E_u)^2 + \exp(-E_v)^2 + 1}.$$

In this study we present a deep convolutional network named as DS-Net for illuminant estimation. An illustration of the proposed DS-Net structure is given in Fig. 2. As introduced in Sect. 1, the proposed network is unique in that its two sub-networks, namely HypNet and SelNet, can interact to collectively provide accurate illuminant estimation. We will detail each sub-networks and their interaction as follows.

3.1 Hypothesis Network - a Branch-Level Ensemble Network

Hypothesis Network (HypNet) is trained, given a patch of image, to estimate multiple hypotheses of illuminant for that patch. The network consists of two stages:

1. **Feature extraction:** extracts spectral and spatial features from a UV patch of image.
2. **Regression:** estimates the illuminants from the features extracted by the previous stage.

We will show in the following that these two stages can be modelled by a convolutional neural network. The structure of the network is illustrated in Fig. 2.

Feature extraction. Previous color constancy methods considered both spectral and spatial information, such as the average of RGB, the color of edges, and the double-opponent response [9]. Barron [3] achieved state-of-art results by using extended spatial features. Chen *et al.* [42] applied discrete cosine transform (DCT) in log-space to extract illumination invariant features in face recognition. Following the literature, our model takes into account both spectral and spatial features. These features can be captured by convolving an image with a bank of filters. The filters are learned during the training process of the network. Specifically, we use two convolutional layers and apply the Rectified Linear Unit ($\max(0, x)$) [43] on their outputs (see Fig. 2).

Regression. A straightforward method for regression is to use a stack of fully connected layers over the features from convolutional layers. However, we observe there are always some kinds of patches that the model cannot estimate well. We tried varying the number of layers, but the performance did not get any better. We conjecture that the difficulty may be due to the large complexity of the hypothesis space of this problem.

A plausible way to improve the performance of deep learning is to train an ensemble of neural networks and combine them during prediction. The benefits of ensemble methods are discussed in [44]. While the reasons combining models works so well are not fully comprehended, there is ample evidence that improvements over single models are the norm rather than the exception. The same observation has been frequently validated in many deep learning studies. For instance, Szegedy *et al.* [28] achieve top performance in ImageNet classification task through combining three residual and one inception network; DeepID2+ network [27] ensembles 25 networks for face verification. It is generally acknowledged that an ensemble is often much more accurate than the individual classifiers that make them up.

We wish to design a network that can covers a large and rich hypothesis space for improved performance. An ensemble network is a viable way to meet our objectives. To this end, we introduce a *branch-level ensemble* approach. Contrary to the convention of training multiple networks to form an ensemble, the proposed approach is implemented by forking after the last convolutional layer into two branches of fully connected layers, namely A-branch and B-branch[2]. Their mapping functions are represented as $F_A(\cdot)$ and $F_B(\cdot)$, respectively. The different branches constitute an ensemble. Such a design is computationally more attractive than a conventional network ensemble since they share common feature extraction layers. These two branches share only the input from the lower convolutional layer, but have individual parameters themselves and have no interactive connection. When the branches are trained with the 'winner-take-all' learning (discussed next), the two branches are able to cover different hypothesis spaces. As a result, the network will provide two intermediate hypotheses for any single patch.

To make a final decision for regression, two scores denoted as $\mathbf{s} = (s_A, s_B)$, are given for the respective A and B branches and the branch with a higher score

---

[2] We have tried more branches, but for this problem using more branches does not bring significant improvement. For efficiency and clarity, we present the two-branch version here.

is selected to provide the output, *i.e.*, the scores serve as a filter to determine which signal could pass.

Data preprocessing. We subtract per-channel means of a patch from each channel, and finally add those means to the output. Specifically, the 2-channel input is denoted as $\bar{\mathbf{I}} = (I_u - \bar{I}_u, I_v - \bar{I}_v)$, where $(\bar{I}_u, \bar{I}_v)$ are per-channel means. The output are $F_A(\bar{\mathbf{I}}) = (\tilde{E}_u - \bar{I}_u, \tilde{E}_v - \bar{I}_v)_A$ for the A-branch and $F_B(\bar{\mathbf{I}}) = (\tilde{E}_u - \bar{I}_u, \tilde{E}_v - \bar{I}_v)_B$ for the B-branch, where $\tilde{\mathbf{E}} = (\tilde{E}_u, \tilde{E}_v) = F(\bar{\mathbf{I}}) + (\bar{I}_u, \bar{I}_v)$ is the final estimated illumination. This operation makes the performance of our model stable to a variety of illuminants. Please refer to the supplementary material for a detailed explanation.

Winner-take-all learning of HypNet. In the training phase[3], a patch is extracted from an image and fed to the HypNet to obtain two hypotheses. The associated ground truth illuminant is provided. Then the score (s_A, s_B) for the branch whose hypothesis is closer to the ground truth is set to 1 and the other one to 0. We call these obtained scores as the *ground truth scores*, which will be used in SelNet training. Given a set of patches represented as $\{\bar{\mathbf{I}}\}$ and their corresponding ground truth illuminant $\{\mathbf{E}^*\}$, we use Euclidean loss[4] as the loss function to optimize HypNet. Specifically for each i-th patch, the loss is

$$L_i(\Theta) = \min_{k \in \{A,B\}} (||\tilde{\mathbf{E}}_i - \mathbf{E}^*_i||^2_2)_k, \tag{6}$$

where Θ represents the parameters of the convolutional layers and fully connected layers. The loss is minimized using stochastic gradient descent with the standard backpropagation. We adopt a batch-mode learning method with a batch size of 128.

Note that in our 'winner-take-all' learning scheme, only (the better) one of the branches is optimized and the other's forward signal and backward gradient are blocked[5]. In this way, at least one of the two branches is supposed to give a precise estimate and the two branches are able to complement each other to cover a larger hypothesis space. We attempted to back-propagate weighted sum errors to update the parameters of both branches but found that this scheme yielded much higher error in illuminant estimation.

In the test phase, the scores are obtained from another network, SelNet. We will introduce SelNet in the next section.

Discussion. We recommend using filters with a larger size in conv1 layer (see Fig. 2) to capture more spatial information. This follows several recent discoveries: (1) Barron [3] shows that using extended (spatial) features can improve their model by 10%–20%; (2) Gao *et al.* [9] demonstrates that using the structures analogous to the double-opponent cells in the human vision system will produce competitive results.

---

[3] Implemented using Caffe [45].

[4] Despite the loss we use does not directly optimize the angular error typically employed in color constancy evaluation, satisfactory results are still observed.

[5] This scheme is also related to the Multiple Choice Learning [54].

We note that there are different methods to create strong ensemble, *e.g.*, through enforcing interactions among the branches during training to increase diversity. We do not use deliberate method to create strong ensemble but just initialize the two branches differently with a similar spirit to random decision trees. Satisfactory performance is observed with this simple initialization approach, when it is used together with the proposed 'winner-take-all' learning.

3.2 Selection Network - A Hypothesis Selection Network

SelNet is trained to estimate the scores $\mathbf{s} = (s_A, s_B)$ that evaluate the quality of estimates, given the input patch and the hypotheses of that patch from HypNet. SelNet shares the same two-stage structure. However, the output of SelNet is not illuminant but a set of scores for the branches in HypNet. We apply a softmax operation on the output to get the scores normalized. Ideally, SelNet should give a higher score to the branch that is closer to the ground truth.

Input representation. We do not apply the data preprocessing of HypNet, since it may discard useful information such as local contrast. Consequently, we use the original patch in UV space. This representation only uses the information from the original data.

Learning for SelNet. In the training phase, an image patch and its ground truth illumination are extracted from an image. In addition, its two hypotheses and the ground truth scores are obtained from HypNet. We then arrange the input data in the corresponding form for SelNet and obtain an output from SelNet. The label is set to the ground truth scores. We optimize SelNet with multinomial logistic loss. In test phase, the output of SelNet is used to select one of the branches of HypNet.

3.3 Local to Global Estimation

Combining HypNet and SelNet, our DS-Net can predict patch-wise local illumination for an image. For the global-illuminant setting, a possible method is to learn a separate support vector regressor to aggregate local estimates to a global estimate [2]. Our approach can produce better results by simply performing a median pooling on all the local illuminant estimates of the image, without resorting to additional learning. Our unoptimized C++ code takes approximately 3 secs to process an image on a GPU.

4 Experiments

We evaluate the performance of our method in both global-illuminant and multi-illuminants settings in Sect. 4.1 and Sect. 4.2, respectively.

4.1 Global-Illuminant Setting

To evaluate the performance of our method in the global-illuminant setting, we use two standard datasets, *i.e.*, the Color Checker Dataset [25] reprocessed by Shi and Funt [46], and the NUS 8-camera dataset from Cheng *et al.* [47]. The Color Checker dataset contains 568 raw linear images with both indoor and outdoor scenes. The NUS 8-camera dataset from Cheng *et al.* consists of 1736 images from 8 different cameras, and about 210 individual scenes, where the same scene was photographed by each of the 8 cameras. For both of these datasets, the Macbeth Color Checker chart is placed in each image to estimate the ground truth illuminant. The color checker chart is masked out during the training and evaluation. Our model is learned and evaluated using a three-fold cross-validation. The angular error between the estimated illuminant $\tilde{E}_{rgb}$ and the ground truth illuminant E^*_{rgb} is computed for each image:

$$\epsilon = \arccos \left(\frac{\tilde{E}_{rgb} \cdot E^*_{rgb}}{\|\tilde{E}_{rgb}\| \cdot \|E^*_{rgb}\|} \right). \tag{7}$$

Table 1. Performance comparison of the proposed DS-Net against various other methods on the Color Checker dataset [25,46]. Some results were taken from past work therefore resulting in missing entries.

Methods	Mean	Median	Trimean	Best-25 %	Worst-25 %	95th percentile
White-Patch [40]	7.55	5.68	6.35	1.45	16.12	–
Edge-based Gamut [48]	6.52	5.04	5.43	1.90	13.58	–
Gray-World [6]	6.36	6.28	6.28	2.33	10.58	11.30
1st-order Gray-Edge [12]	5.33	4.52	4.73	1.86	10.03	11.00
2nd-order Gray-Edge [12]	5.13	4.44	4.62	2.11	9.26	–
Shades-of-Gray [49]	4.93	4.01	4.23	1.14	10.20	11.90
Bayesian [25]	4.82	3.46	3.88	1.26	10.49	–
General Gray-World [50]	4.66	3.48	3.81	1.00	10.09	–
Intersection-based Gamut [48]	4.20	2.39	2.93	0.51	10.70	–
Pixel-based Gamut [48]	4.20	2.33	2.91	0.50	10.72	14.10
Natural Image Statistics [10]	4.19	3.13	3.45	1.00	9.22	11.70
Bright Pixels [51]	3.98	2.61	–	–	–	–
Spatio-spectral (GenPrior) [52]	3.59	2.96	3.10	0.95	7.61	–
Cheng et al. [47]	3.52	2.14	2.47	0.50	8.74	–
Corrected-Moment (19 Color) [26]	3.50	2.60	–	–	–	8.60
Exemplar-based [36]	3.10	2.30	–	–	–	–
Corrected-Moment (19 Edge) [26]	2.80	2.00	–	–	–	6.90
CNN [2]	2.36	1.98	–	–	–	–
Regression Tree [1]	2.42	1.65	1.75	0.38	5.87	–
CCC (disc+ext) [3]	1.95	1.22	1.38	0.35	**4.76**	**5.85**
HypNet One Branch	2.18	1.35	1.54	0.38	5.42	6.69
HypNet (A-branch)	5.06	4.38	4.52	1.26	10.05	12.43
HypNet (B-branch)	4.55	2.35	3.10	0.50	12.21	15.50
DS-Net (Average)	3.74	2.99	3.18	0.86	7.83	9.27
DS-Net (HypNet+SelNet)	**1.90**	**1.12**	**1.33**	**0.31**	4.84	5.99
DS-Net (HypNet+Oracle)	1.15	0.76	0.86	0.22	2.72	3.35

Table 2. Performance comparison of the proposed DS-Net against various other methods on the Cheng et al. [47] dataset.

Methods	Mean	Median	Trimean	Best-25%	Worst-25%
White-Patch [40]	10.62	10.58	10.49	1.86	19.45
Edge-based Gamut [48]	8.43	7.05	7.37	2.41	16.08
Pixel-based Gamut [48]	7.70	6.71	6.90	2.51	14.05
Intersection-based Gamut [48]	7.20	5.96	6.28	2.20	13.61
Gray-World [6]	4.14	3.20	3.39	0.90	9.00
Bayesian [25]	3.67	2.73	2.91	0.82	8.21
Natural Image Statistics [10]	3.71	2.60	2.84	0.79	8.47
Shades-of-Gray [49]	3.40	2.57	2.73	0.77	7.41
Spatio-spectral (ML) [52]	3.11	2.49	2.60	0.82	6.59
General Gray-World [50]	3.21	2.38	2.53	0.71	7.10
2nd-order Gray-Edge [12]	3.20	2.26	2.44	0.75	7.27
Bright Pixels [51]	3.17	2.41	2.55	0.69	7.02
1st-order Gray-Edge [12]	3.20	2.22	2.43	0.72	7.36
Spatio-spectral (GenPrior) [52]	2.96	2.33	2.47	0.80	6.18
Cheng et al. [47]	2.92	2.04	2.24	0.62	6.61
CCC (disc+ext) [3]	2.38	1.48	1.69	**0.45**	5.85
Regression Tree [1]	2.36	1.59	1.74	0.49	5.54
HypNet One Branch	2.56	1.87	2.01	0.51	6.46
HypNet (A-branch)	3.49	2.94	3.03	0.90	7.00
HypNet (B-branch)	5.17	2.91	3.50	0.91	13.03
DS-Net (Average)	3.41	2.36	2.72	0.73	7.69
DS-Net (HypNet+SelNet)	**2.24**	**1.46**	**1.68**	0.48	**5.28**
DS-Net (HypNet+Oracle)	1.32	0.93	1.01	0.33	2.97

We report the following metrics following existing studies [1,3]: the mean, the median, the tri-mean, the means of the lowest-error 25% and the highest-error 25% of the data, and the 95 percentile for the Color Checker dataset. For the NUS 8-camera dataset, we run 8 different experiments on the subset for each camera, and report the geometric mean of each error metric for all the methods. A number of different color constancy algorithms are compared, and the reported baseline results were taken from past papers [3]. Experimental results of the Color Checker dataset and NUS 8-camera dataset are summarized in Tables 1 and 2, respectively.

Comparison with state-of-the-arts. On both the Color Checker and NUS 8-camera datasets, the proposed method 'DS-Net (HypNet+SelNet)' achieves the lowest mean and median errors in comparison to existing methods, including the CNN method presented in [2]. We show some examples of our performance against competitive methods in Fig. 3. In comparison to existing approaches, it is observed that our method performs better on complex and diverse regions, *e.g.* texture areas such as grass field, or smooth regions such as wall or sky. The results suggest the effectiveness of adopting a branch-level ensemble network with hypothesis selection.

Ablation analysis. We evaluated different variants of DS-Net:

- **HypNet One Branch** - it is a variant without the branch-level ensemble, i.e., it is a normal network with only one branch of fully connected layers, so SelNet is not needed for hypothesis selection.
- **HypNet (A-branch) or (B-branch)** - these variants refer to a model that generate estimations based on either A-branch or B-branch of HypNet.
- **DS-Net (Average)** - this variant generates an estimation by averaging the hypotheses from both A-branch and B-branch. It represents the typical way of generating predictions from an ensemble.
- **DS-Net (HypNet+SelNet)** - this is our full model with hypothesis selection using SelNet.
- **DS-Net (HypNet+Oracle)** - in this variant the hypothesis is selected by an oracle. The oracle selects the branch of which the estimation is closest to the ground truth.

From the results on the Color Checker dataset, it is observed that the mean and median errors are reduced by 13 % (from 2.18 to 1.90) and 17 % (from 1.35 to 1.12), respectively by using the branch-level ensemble in comparison to the variant 'HypNet One Branch'. It is interesting to point out that none of the two branches individually can achieve satisfactory performance. Averaging the hypotheses, *i.e.* HypNet (Average), does not improve the performance either. However, a significant improvement is obtained when SelNet is used for hypothesis selection. Note that if the best branch is selected by an oracle, the errors can be further reduced by a large margin (39 % and 32 % of the mean and median errors). The results suggest the large potential of hypothesis selection and there is still a room for further optimization. Our current SelNet achieves a selection accuracy of 75 %–77 % on the test folds. In Fig. 4, we show two examples of angular error maps obtained by using different variants of DS-Net. Figure 5 illustrates the evolution of illumination estimated by the two branches of Hyp-Net. It is observed that both branches are gradually converging to the ground truth and, at the same time, preserving their own specialities.

We also perform evaluation on SelNet by testing it with different input representations, *i.e.* with and without per-channel means subtraction. It is observed that with per-channel means subtraction the selection accuracy of SelNet drops to 67 %, leading to higher mean and median errors in the final illuminant estimation (3.81 and 2.80).

4.2   Multi-illuminant Setting

The proposed DS-Net by nature predicts patch-wise local illumination for an image. Thus it is capable of dealing with multi-illuminant settings although we do not introduce specific mechanisms, *e.g.* segmentation [53], to handle the different illuminants.

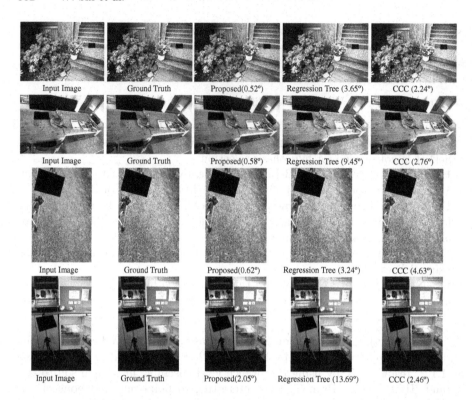

Fig. 3. *Global illuminant setting:* Restored images from the Color Checker dataset using the illuminants estimated from three different methods including the proposed DS-Net, Regression Tree [36] and CCC [3]. The angular error is provided at the bottom of each image. We follow [1] to apply gamma function on RAW images for better visualization. (Color figure online)

In this section, we evaluate the performance of our method on the popular outdoor multi-illuminant dataset proposed by Gijsenij *et al.* [53]. This dataset contains 9 challenging outdoor images with two illuminants for each image. Pixel-wise ground truth illuminants are provided for evaluation. The per-image error metric is the mean of pixel-wise angular error. Following [53], we report the mean and median errors of all images in the whole dataset. Considering the limited number of test images, global illuminant baselines and our method are first pre-trained on the Color Checker dataset, and then tested on the outdoor dataset. This also makes the task more challenging due to the cross-dataset evaluation.

We report the results of two state-of-art multi-illuminant methods, namely the Multiple Light Sources [53] (using White Patch and Gray World) and the Exemplar-Based [36] method using surface estimates, together with two state-of-art global-illuminant methods, Regression Tree [1] and CCC (dist+ext) [3]. The results of Multiple Light Sources and Exemplar-Based methods were obtained from the original paper [36,53]. We obtained the codes of Regression Tree [1] from its project page and retrained it on the Color Checker dataset.

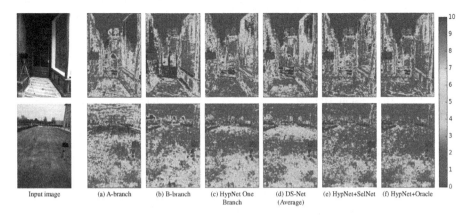

Fig. 4. *Global illuminant setting:* (a, b) The respective per-pixel angular error map of A-branch and B-branch of HypNet. (c) HypNet One Branch. (d) DS-Net (Average). (e) The full model DS-Net (HypNet+SelNet). (f) Upper bound DS-Net (HypNet+Oracle). (Color figure online)

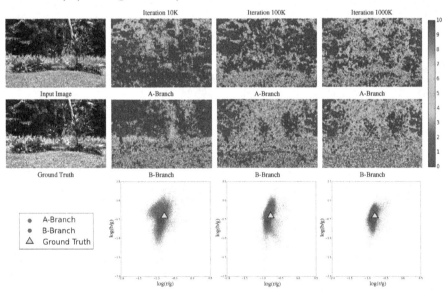

Fig. 5. *Global illuminant setting:* Column 1: the input image and the restored image using ground truth illumination. Column 2–4: the first two rows show the per-pixel angular error map of A-branch and B-branch of HypNet, using the models after 10K, 100K and 1000K training iterations. The last row depicts the UV chrominance of per-pixel illumination estimated by the two branches at the corresponding iterations. (Color figure online)

We reimplemented CCC (dist+ext) [3]. We ensure that both methods achieve comparable performance to their reported results under the global illuminant setting.

Table 3. Performance comparison of the proposed DS-Net against various other methods on the multi-illuminant outdoor dataset [53].

Methods	Mean	Median
Global state-of-the-arts		
Regression Tree [1]	9.3	7.8
CCC (disc+ext) [3]	8.4	9.0
Multi-illuminant state-of-the-arts		
Multiple Light Sources + White-Patch [53]	-	6.7
Multiple Light Sources + Gray-World [53]	-	6.4
Exemplar-Based Multi [36]	-	**4.3**
DS-Net (HypNet+SelNet)	4.8	4.6

Fig. 6. *Multi-illuminants setting:* Results from the outdoor multi-illuminant image dataset [53]. For each group, the images, from left to right, are respectively: the original image, the ground-truth pixel-wise illumination for that image, the estimated results using DS-Net (HypNet+SelNet), CCC [3], and Regression Tree [36]. Best viewed in color. (Color figure online)

The results are summarized in Table 3. It is observed that the proposed DS-Net outperforms existing global methods by a significant margin. Our approach also reports competitive performance in comparison to state-of-art multi-illuminant methods [36,53]. Note that unlike state-of-the-art exemplar-based method [36] that requires finding surfaces for both training and test images by mean-shift segmentation, and storing surfaces of all training images for nearest neighbor comparison, our approach only needs to perform pure feed-forward test given a new image. Qualitative results are shown in Fig. 6.

5   Conclusion

We have presented a new Deep Specialized Network (DS-Net) for illuminant estimation. The proposed network uniquely combines two networks: a multi-hypotheses network (HypNet) and a hypothesis selection network (SelNet), to work hand-in-hand for robust estimation. A novel notion of 'branch-level ensemble' is introduced. Through the proposed diversity-encouraging winner-take-all learning scheme, we observed that the two branches of HypNet automatically specialize on estimating illuminants for specific regions. When this capability is coupled with SelNet, state-of-the-art performances are achieved on the two largest color constancy dataset. Future work will investigate more effective selection scheme for a larger ensemble. In addition, it will be interesting to explore the applicability of specialized network for high-level vision task.

Acknowledgment. This work is partially supported by SenseTime Group Limited.

References

1. Cheng, D., Price, B., Cohen, S., Brown, M.S.: Effective learning-based illuminant estimation using simple features. In: IEEE Conference on Computer Vision and Pattern Recognition, pp. 1000–1008 (2015)
2. Bianco, S., Cusano, C., Schettini, R.: Single and multiple illuminant estimation using convolutional neural networks. arXiv preprint (2015). arXiv:1508.00998
3. Barron, J.T.: Convolutional color constancy. In: IEEE International Conference on Computer Vision, pp. 379–387 (2015)
4. Bianco, S., Cusano, C., Schettini, R.: Color constancy using CNNs. In: Proceedings of the IEEE Conference on Computer Vision and Pattern Recognition Workshops, pp. 81–89 (2015)
5. Lou, Z., Gevers, T., Hu, N., Lucassen, M.: Color constancy by deep learning. In: British Machine Vision Conference (2015)
6. Buchsbaum, G.: A spatial processor model for object colour perception. J. Franklin Inst. **310**(1), 1–26 (1980)
7. Land, E.H., McCann, J.J.: Lightness and retinex theory. J. Opt. Soc. Am. A **61**(1), 1–11 (1971)
8. Gao, S., Han, W., Yang, K., Li, C., Li, Y.: Efficient color constancy with local surface reflectance statistics. In: European Conference on Computer Vision, pp. 158–173 (2014)
9. Gao, S., Yang, K., Li, C., Li, Y.: A color constancy model with double-opponency mechanisms. In: IEEE International Conference on Computer Vision, pp. 929–936 (2013)
10. Gijsenij, A., Gevers, T.: Color constancy using natural image statistics and scene semantics. IEEE Trans. Pattern Anal. Mach. Intell. **33**(4), 687–698 (2011)
11. Gijsenij, A., Gevers, T., Van De Weijer, J.: Improving color constancy by photometric edge weighting. IEEE Trans. Pattern Anal. Mach. Intell. **34**(5), 918–929 (2012)
12. Van De Weijer, J., Gevers, T., Gijsenij, A.: Edge-based color constancy. IEEE Trans. Image Process. **16**(9), 2207–2214 (2007)
13. Bianco, S., Ciocca, G., Cusano, C., Schettini, R.: Improving color constancy using indoor-outdoor image classification. IEEE Trans. Image Process. **17**(12), 2381–2392 (2008)

14. Bianco, S., Ciocca, G., Cusano, C., Schettini, R.: Automatic color constancy algorithm selection and combination. Pattern Recogn. **43**(3), 695–705 (2010)
15. Drew, M.S., Funt, B.V.: Variational approach to interreflection in color images. J. Opt. Soc. Am. A **9**(8), 1255–1265 (1992)
16. Drew, M.S., Joze, H.R.V., Finlayson, G.D.: Specularity, the zeta-image, and information-theoretic illuminant estimation. In: European Conference on Computer Vision Workshop, pp. 411–420 (2012)
17. Lee, H.C.: Method for computing the scene-illuminant chromaticity from specular highlights. J. Opt. Soc. Am. A **3**(10), 1694–1699 (1986)
18. Tan, R.T., Nishino, K., Ikeuchi, K.: Color constancy through inverse-intensity chromaticity space. J. Opt. Soc. Am. A **21**(3), 321–334 (2004)
19. Hordley, S.D.: Scene illuminant estimation: past, present, and future. Color Res. Appl. **31**(4), 303–314 (2006)
20. Gijsenij, A., Gevers, T., Van De Weijer, J.: Computational color constancy: survey and experiments. IEEE Trans. Image Process. **20**(9), 2475–2489 (2011)
21. Cardei, V.C., Funt, B., Barnard, K.: Estimating the scene illumination chromaticity by using a neural network. J. Opt. Soc. Am. A **19**(12), 2374–2386 (2002)
22. Finlayson, G.D., Hordley, S.D., Hubel, P.M.: Color by correlation: a simple, unifying framework for color constancy. IEEE Trans. Pattern Anal. Mach. Intell. **23**(11), 1209–1221 (2001)
23. Funt, B., Xiong, W.: Estimating illumination chromaticity via support vector regression. In: Color and Imaging Conference, vol. 2004, pp. 47–52 (2004)
24. Rosenberg, C., Hebert, M., Thrun, S.: Color constancy using KL-divergence. In: IEEE International Conference on Computer Vision, vol. 1, pp. 239–246 (2001)
25. Gehler, P.V., Rother, C., Blake, A., Minka, T., Sharp, T.: Bayesian color constancy revisited. In: IEEE Conference on Computer Vision and Pattern Recognition, pp. 1–8 (2008)
26. Finlayson, G.: Corrected-moment illuminant estimation. In: IEEE International Conference on Computer Vision, pp. 1904–1911 (2013)
27. Sun, Y., Wang, X., Tang, X.: Deeply learned face representations are sparse, selective, and robust. In: IEEE Conference on Computer Vision and Pattern Recognition. pp. 2892–2900 (2015)
28. Szegedy, C., Ioffe, S., Vanhoucke, V.: Inception-v4, inception-resnet and the impact of residual connections on learning. arXiv preprint (2016). arXiv:1602.07261
29. Zhu, S., Liu, S., Loy, C.C., Tang, X.: Deep cascaded bi-network for face hallucination. In: European Conference on Computer Vision (2016)
30. Dong, C., Loy, C.C., He, K., Tang, X.: Image super-resolution using deep convolutional networks. IEEE Trans. Pattern Anal. Mach. Intell. **38**(2), 295–307 (2015)
31. Cui, Z., Chang, H., Shan, S., Zhong, B., Chen, X.: Deep network cascade for image super-resolution. In: Fleet, D., Pajdla, T., Schiele, B., Tuytelaars, T. (eds.) ECCV 2014. LNCS, vol. 8693, pp. 49–64. Springer, Heidelberg (2014). doi:10.1007/978-3-319-10602-1_4
32. Xu, L., Ren, J.S., Liu, C., Jia, J.: Deep convolutional neural network for image deconvolution. In: Advances in Neural Information Processing Systems, pp. 1790–1798 (2014)
33. Dong, C., Loy, C.C., Tang, X.: Accelerating the super-resolution convolutional neural network. In: European Conference on Computer Vision (2016)
34. Hui, T.W., Loy, C.C., Tang, X.: Depth map super resolution by deep multi-scale guidance. In: European Conference on Computer Vision (2016)
35. Xie, J., Xu, L., Chen, E.: Image denoising and inpainting with deep neural networks. In: Advances in Neural Information Processing Systems, pp. 341–349 (2012)

36. Joze, H.R.V., Drew, M.S.: Exemplar-based color constancy and multiple illumination. IEEE Trans. Pattern Anal. Mach. Intell. **36**(5), 860–873 (2014)
37. Bianco, S., Schettini, R.: Adaptive color constancy using faces. IEEE Trans. Pattern Anal. Mach. Intell. **36**(8), 1505–1518 (2014)
38. Hsu, E., Mertens, T., Paris, S., Avidan, S., Durand, F.: Light mixture estimation for spatially varying white balance. ACM Trans. Graph. **27**, 70 (2008)
39. Boyadzhiev, I., Bala, K., Paris, S., Durand, F.: User-guided white balance for mixed lighting conditions. ACM Trans. Graph. **31**(6), 200 (2012)
40. Brainard, D.H., Wandell, B.A.: Analysis of the retinex theory of color vision. J. Opt. Soc. Am. A **3**(10), 1651–1661 (1986)
41. Finlayson, G.D., Drew, M.S., Lu, C.: Intrinsic images by entropy minimization. In: Pajdla, T., Matas, J. (eds.) ECCV 2004. LNCS, vol. 3023, pp. 582–595. Springer, Heidelberg (2004). doi:10.1007/978-3-540-24672-5_46
42. Chen, W., Er, M.J., Wu, S.: Illumination compensation and normalization for robust face recognition using discrete cosine transform in logarithm domain. IEEE Trans. Syst. Man Cybern. Part B: Cybern. **36**(2), 458–466 (2006)
43. Nair, V., Hinton, G.E.: Rectified linear units improve restricted boltzmann machines. In: International Conference on Machine Learning, pp. 807–814 (2010)
44. Dietterich, T.G.: Ensemble methods in machine learning. In: Kittler, J., Roli, F. (eds.) MCS 2000. LNCS, vol. 1857, pp. 1–15. Springer, Heidelberg (2000). doi:10.1007/3-540-45014-9_1
45. Jia, Y., Shelhamer, E., Donahue, J., Karayev, S., Long, J., Girshick, R., Guadarrama, S., Darrell, T.: Caffe: convolutional architecture for fast feature embedding. In: ACM Multimedia, pp. 675–678 (2014)
46. Shi, L., Funt, B.: Re-processed version of the gehler color constancy dataset of 568 images. http://www.cs.sfu.ca/~colour/data/
47. Cheng, D., Prasad, D.K., Brown, M.S.: Illuminant estimation for color constancy: why spatial-domain methods work and the role of the color distribution. J. Opt. Soc. Am. A **31**(5), 1049–1058 (2014)
48. Barnard, K.: Improvements to gamut mapping colour constancy algorithms. In: Vernon, D. (ed.) ECCV 2000. LNCS, vol. 1842, pp. 390–403. Springer, Heidelberg (2000). doi:10.1007/3-540-45054-8_26
49. Finlayson, G.D., Trezzi, E.: Shades of gray and colour constancy. In: Color and Imaging Conference, vol. 2004, pp. 37–41 (2004)
50. Barnard, K., Martin, L., Coath, A., Fun, B.: A comparison of computational color constancy algorithms. II. Experiments with image data. IEEE Trans. Image Process. **11**(9), 985–996 (2002)
51. Joze, H.R.V., Drew, M.S., Finlayson, G.D., Rey, P.A.T.: The role of bright pixels in illumination estimation. In: Color and Imaging Conference, vol. 2012, pp. 41–46 (2012)
52. Chakrabarti, A., Hirakawa, K., Zickler, T.: Color constancy with spatio-spectral statistics. IEEE Trans. Pattern Anal. Mach. Intell. **34**(8), 1509–1519 (2012)
53. Gijsenij, A., Lu, R., Gevers, T.: Color constancy for multiple light sources. IEEE Trans. Image Process. **21**(2), 697–707 (2012)
54. Guzman-Rivera, A., Batra, D., Kohli, P.: Multiple choice learning: learning to produce multiple structured outputs. In: NIPS, pp. 1799–1807 (2012). https://papers.nips.cc/paper/4549-multiple-choice-learning-learning-to-produce-multiple-structured-outputs.pdf

Weakly-Supervised Semantic Segmentation Using Motion Cues

Pavel Tokmakov, Karteek Alahari$^{(\boxtimes)}$, and Cordelia Schmid

Inria, Grenoble, France
http://thoth.inrialpes.fr

Abstract. Fully convolutional neural networks (FCNNs) trained on a large number of images with strong pixel-level annotations have become the new state of the art for the semantic segmentation task. While there have been recent attempts to learn FCNNs from image-level weak annotations, they need additional constraints, such as the size of an object, to obtain reasonable performance. To address this issue, we present motion-CNN (M-CNN), a novel FCNN framework which incorporates motion cues and is learned from video-level weak annotations. Our learning scheme to train the network uses motion segments as soft constraints, thereby handling noisy motion information. When trained on weakly-annotated videos, our method outperforms the state-of-the-art approach [1] on the PASCAL VOC 2012 image segmentation benchmark. We also demonstrate that the performance of M-CNN learned with 150 weak video annotations is on par with state-of-the-art weakly-supervised methods trained with thousands of images. Finally, M-CNN substantially outperforms recent approaches in a related task of video co-localization on the YouTube-Objects dataset.

1 Introduction

The need for weakly-supervised learning for semantic segmentation has been highlighted recently [2–4]. It is particularly important, as acquiring a training set by labeling images manually at the pixel level is significantly more expensive than assigning class labels at the image level. Recent segmentation approaches have used weak annotations in several forms: bounding boxes around objects [5,6], image labels denoting the presence of a category [2,3] or a combination of the two [1]. All these previous approaches only use annotation in images, i.e., bounding boxes, image tags, as a weak form of supervision. Naturally, additional cues would come in handy to address this challenging problem. As noted in [7], motion is one such cue for semantic segmentation, which helps us identify the extent of objects and their boundaries in the scene more accurately. To our knowledge, motion has not yet been leveraged for weakly-supervised semantic segmentation. In this work, we aim to fill this gap by learning an accurate segmentation model with the help of motion cues extracted from weakly-annotated videos.

Thoth team, Laboratoire Jean Kuntzmann

B. Leibe et al. (Eds.): ECCV 2016, Part IV, LNCS 9908, pp. 388–404, 2016.
DOI: 10.1007/978-3-319-46493-0_24

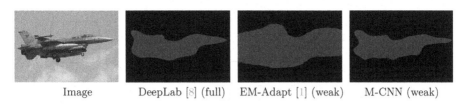

Image   DeepLab [8] (full)   EM-Adapt [1] (weak)   M-CNN (weak)

Fig. 1. Comparison of state-of-the-art fully [8] and weakly [1] supervised methods with our weakly-supervised M-CNN model.

Our proposed framework is based on fully convolutional neural networks (FCNNs) [8–11], which extend deep CNNs, and are able to classify every pixel in an input image in a single forward pass. While FCNNs show state-of-the-art results on segmentation benchmark datasets, they require thousands of pixel-level annotated images to train on—a requirement that limits their utility. Recently, there have been some attempts [1,3,12,13] to train FCNNs with weakly-annotated images, but they remain inferior in performance to their fully-supervised equivalents (see Fig. 1). In this paper, we develop a new CNN variant named M-CNN, which leverages motion cues in weakly-labeled videos, in the form of unsupervised motion segmentation, e.g., [14]. It builds on the architecture of FCNN by adding a motion segmentation based label inference step, as shown in Fig. 2. In other words, predictions from the FCNN layers and motion segmentation jointly determine the loss used to learn the network (see Sect. 3.2).

Our approach uses unsupervised motion segmentation from real-world videos, such as the YouTube-Objects [15] and the ImageNet-VID [16] datasets, to train the network. In this context, we are confronted with two main challenges. The first one is that even the best-performing algorithms cannot produce good motion segmentations consistently, and the second one is the ambiguity of video-level annotations, which cannot guarantee the presence of object in all the frames. We develop a novel scheme to address these challenges automatically without any manual annotations, apart from the labels assigned at the video level, denoting the presence of objects somewhere in the video. To this end, we use motion segmentations as soft constraints in the learning process, and also fine-tune our network with a small number of video shots to refine it.

We evaluated the proposed method on two related problems: semantic segmentation and video co-localization. When trained on weakly-annotated videos, M-CNN outperforms state-of-the-art EM-Adapt [1] on the PASCAL VOC 2012 image segmentation benchmark [17]. Furthermore, our trained model, despite using only 150 video labels, achieves performance similar to EM-Adapt trained on more than 10,000 VOC image labels. Augmenting our training set with 1,000 VOC images results in a further gain, achieving the best performance on VOC 2012 test set in the weakly-supervised setting (see Sect. 4.4). On the video co-localization task, where the goal is to localize common objects in a set of videos, M-CNN substantially outperforms a recent method [18] by over 16 % on the YouTube-Objects dataset.

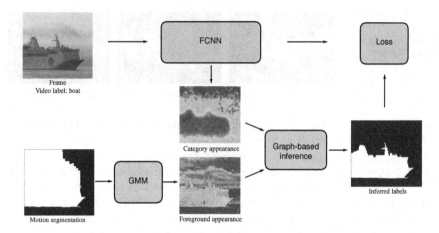

Fig. 2. Overview of our M-CNN framework, where we show only one frame from a video example for clarity. The soft potentials (foreground appearance) computed from motion segmentation and the FCNN predictions (category appearance) jointly determine the latent segmentation (inferred labels) to compute the loss, and thus the network update.

The contributions of this work are twofold: (i) We present a novel CNN framework for segmentation that integrates motion cues in video as soft constraints. (ii) Experimental results show that our segmentation model learned from weakly-annotated videos can indeed be applied to evaluate on challenging benchmarks and achieves top performance on semantic segmentation as well as video co-localization tasks.

2 Related Work

In addition to fully-supervised segmentation approaches, such as [19,20], several weakly-supervised methods have been proposed over the years: some of them use bounding boxes [5,6], while others rely on image labels [2]. Traditional approaches for this task, such as [2], used a variety of hand-crafted visual features, namely, SIFT histograms, color, texture, in combination with a graphical or a parametric structured model. Such early attempts have been recently outperformed by FCNN methods, e.g., [1].

FCNN architecture [1,3,8–13,21] adapts standard CNNs [22,23] to handle input images of any arbitrary size by treating the fully connected layers as convolutions with kernels of appropriate size. This allows them to output scores for every pixel in the image. Most of these methods [8–11,21] rely on strong pixel-level annotation to train the network.

Attempts [1,3,12,13] to learn FCNNs for the weakly-supervised case use either a multiple instance learning (MIL) scheme [3,12] or constraints on the distribution of pixel labels [1,13] to define the loss function. For example, Pathak *et al.* [12] extend the MIL framework used for object detection [24,25] to segmentation by treating the pixel with the highest prediction score for a category as its positive sample when computing the loss. Naturally, this approach is susceptible to standard issues suffered by MIL, like converging to the most discriminative parts of objects [24]. An alternative MIL strategy is used in [3], by introducing a soft aggregation function that translates pixel-level FCNN predictions into an image label distribution. The loss is then computed with respect to the image annotation label and backpropagated to update the network parameters. This strategy works better in practice than [12], but requires training images that contain only a single object, as well as explicit background images. Furthermore, it uses a complex post-processing step involving multi-scale segmentations when testing, which is critical to its performance.

Weakly-supervised FCNNs in [1,13] define constraints on the predicted pixel labels. Papandreou et al. [1] presented an expectation maximization (EM) approach, which alternates between predicting pixel labels (E-step) and estimating FCNN parameters (M-step). Here, the label prediction step is moderated with cardinality constraints, i.e., at least 20 % of the pixels in an image need to be assigned to each of the image-label categories, and at least 40 % to the background. This approach was extended in [13] to include generic linear constraints on the label space, by formulating label prediction as a convex optimization problem. Both these methods showed excellent results on the VOC 2012 dataset, but are sensitive to the linear/cardinality constraints. We address this drawback in our M-CNN framework, where motion cues act as more precise constraints. Fig. 1 shows the improvement due to these constraints. We demonstrate that FCNNs can be trained with videos, unlike all the previous methods restricted to images, and achieve the best performance using much less training data more effectively.

Weakly-supervised learning is also related to webly-supervised learning. Methods following this recent trend [26–29] are kick-started with either a small number of manually annotated examples, e.g., some fully-supervised training examples for the object detection task in [29], or automatically discovered "easy" samples [28], and then trained with a gradually increasing set of examples mined from web resources. However, none of them address the semantic segmentation problem. Other paradigms related to weakly-supervised learning, such as co-localization [15] and co-segmentation [30] require the video (or image) to contain a dominant object class. Co-localization methods aim to localize the common object with bounding boxes, whereas in co-segmentation, the goal is to estimate pixel-wise segment labels. Such approaches, e.g., [15,31,32], typically rely on a pre-computed candidate set of regions (or boxes) and choose the best one with an optimization scheme. Thus, they have no end-to-end learning mechanism and are inherently limited by the quality of the candidates.

3   Learning Semantic Segmentation from Video

We train our network by exploiting motion cues from video sequences. Specifically, we extract unsupervised motion segments from video, with algorithms such as [14], and use them in combination with the weak labels at the video level to learn the network. We sample frames from all the video sequences uniformly, and assign them the class label of the video. This collection forms our training dataset, along with their corresponding motion segments.

The parameters of M-CNN are updated with a standard mini-batch SGD, similar to other CNN approaches [1], with the gradient of a loss function. Here, the loss measures the discrepancy between the ground truth segmentation label and the label predicted at each pixel. Thus, in order to learn the network for the semantic segmentation task, we need pixel-level ground truth for all the training data. These pixel-level labels are naturally latent variables in the context of weakly-supervised learning. Now, the task is to estimate them for our weakly-labeled videos. An ideal scenario in this setting would be near-perfect motion segmentations, which can be directly used as object ground truth labels. However, in practice, not only are the segmentations far from perfect (see Fig. 3), but also fail to capture moving objects in many of the shots. This makes a direct usage of motion segmentation results suboptimal. To address this, we propose a novel scheme, where motion segments are only used as soft constraints to estimate the latent variables together with object appearance cues.

The other challenges when dealing with real-world video datasets, such as YouTube-Objects and ImageNet-VID, are related to the nature of video data itself. On one hand, not all parts of a video contain the object of interest. For instance, a video from a show reviewing boats may contain shots with the host talking about the boat, and showing it from the inside for a significant part—content that is unsuitable for learning a segmentation model for the VOC 'boat' category. On the other hand, a long video can contain many nearly identical object examples which leads to an imbalance in the training set. We address both problems by fine-tuning our M-CNN with an automatically selected, small subset of the training data.

3.1 Network Architecture

Our network is built on the DeepLab model for semantic image segmentation [8]. It is an FCNN, obtained by converting the fully-connected layers of the VGG-16 network [33] into convolutional layers. A few other changes are implemented to get a dense network output for an image at its full resolution efficiently. Our work builds on this network. We develop a more principled and effective label prediction scheme involving motion cues to estimate the latent variables, in contrast to the heuristic size constraints used in [1], which is based on DeepLab.

3.2 Estimating Latent Variables with Label Prediction

Given an image of N pixels, let $\mathbf{p}$ denote the output of the softmax layer of the convolutional network. Then, $p_i^l \in [0, 1]$ is the prediction score of the network at pixel i for label l. The parameters of the network are updated with the gradient of the loss function, given by:

$$\mathcal{L}(\mathbf{x}, \mathbf{p}) = \sum_{i=1}^{N} \sum_{l=0}^{L} \delta(x_i - l) \log(p_i^l), \tag{1}$$

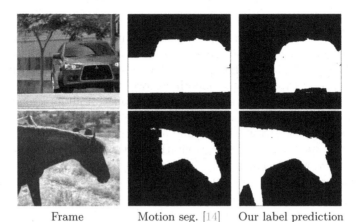

Frame   Motion seg. [14]   Our label prediction

Fig. 3. Examples highlighting the importance of label prediction for handling imprecise motion segmentations (second column). The soft potentials computed from motion segments along with network predictions produce better labels (third column) to learn the network.

where $\mathbf{x}$ denotes ground truth segmentation labels in the fully-supervised case, $\mathbf{p}$ is the current network prediction, and $\delta(x_i - l)$ is the Dirac delta function, i.e., $\delta(x_i - l) = 1$, if $x_i = l$, and 0 otherwise. The segmentation label x_i of pixel i takes values from the label set $\mathbf{L} = \{0, 1, \ldots, L\}$, containing the background class (0) and L object categories. Naturally, in the weakly-supervised case, ground truth segmentation labels are unavailable, and $\mathbf{x}$ represents latent segmentation variables, which need to be estimated. We perform this estimation with soft motion segmentation cues in this paper.

Given the motion segmentation $\mathbf{s} = \{s_i | i = 1, \ldots, N\}$, where $s_i \in \{0, 1\}$ denotes whether a pixel i belongs to foreground (1) or background (0).[1] The regions assigned to foreground can represent multiple objects when the video is tagged with more than one object label. A simple way of transforming motion segmentation labels s_i into latent semantic segmentation labels x_i is with a hard assignment, i.e., $x_i = s_i$. This hard assignment is limited to videos containing a single object label, and also makes the assumption that motion segments are accurate and can be used as they are. We will see in our experiments that this performs poorly when using real-world video datasets (cf. 'M-CNN* hard' in Table 1). We address this by using motion cues as soft constraints for estimating the label assignment $\mathbf{x}$ in the following.

Inference of the Segmentation $\mathbf{x}$. We compute the pixel-level segmentation $\mathbf{x}$ as the minimum of an energy function $E(\mathbf{x})$ defined by:

$$E(\mathbf{x}) = \sum_{i \in \mathcal{V}} \left(\psi_i^m(z_i) + \alpha \psi_i^{fc}(p_i^{x_i}) \right) + \sum_{(i,j) \in \mathcal{E}} \psi_{ij}(x_i, x_j), \qquad (2)$$

---

[1] We do not include an index denoting the frame number in the video for brevity.

where $\mathcal{V} = \{1, 2, \ldots, N\}$ is the set of all the pixels, z_i denotes the RGB color at pixel i and the set $\mathcal{E}$ denotes all pairs of neighboring pixels in the image. Unary terms ψ_i^m and ψ_i^{fc} are computed from motion cues and current predictions of the network respectively, with α being a scalar parameter balancing their impact. The pairwise term ψ_{ij} imposes a smoothness over the label space.

The first unary term ψ_i^m captures the appearance of all foreground objects obtained from motion segments. To this end, we learn two Gaussian mixture models (GMMs), one each for foreground and background, with RGB values of pixel colors, similar to standard segmentation methods [14, 34]. The foreground GMM is learned with RGB values of all the pixels assigned to foreground in the motion segmentation. The background GMM is learned in a similar fashion with the corresponding background pixels. Given the RGB values of a pixel i, $\psi_i^m(z_i)$ is the negative log-likelihood of the corresponding GMM (background one for $l = 0$ and foreground otherwise). Using motion cues to generate this soft potential ψ_i^m helps us alleviate the issue of imperfect motion segmentation. The second unary term ψ_i^{fc} represents the learned object appearance model determined by the current network prediction $p_i^{x_i}$ for pixel i, i.e., $\psi_i^{fc}(p_i^{x_i}) = -\log(p_i^{x_i})$.

The pairwise term is based on a contrast-sensitive Potts model [34, 35] as:

$$\psi_{ij}(x_i, x_j) = \lambda(1 - \Delta(i, j))(1 - \delta(x_i - x_j))\frac{\exp(-\gamma\|z_i - z_j\|^2)}{\mathrm{dist}(i, j)}, \qquad (3)$$

where z_i and z_j are colors of pixels i and j, λ is a scalar parameter to balance the order of magnitude of the pairwise term with respect to the unary term, and γ is a scalar parameter set to 0.5 as in [14]. The function $\mathrm{dist}(i, j)$ is the Euclidean distance between pixels. The Dirac delta function $\delta(x_i - x_j)$ ensures that the pairwise cost is only applicable when two neighboring pixels take different labels. In addition to this, we introduce the term $(1 - \Delta(i, j))$, where $\Delta(i, j) = 1$ if pixels i and j both fall in the boundary region around the motion segment, and 0 otherwise. This accounts for the fact that motion segments may not always respect color boundaries, and allows the minimization algorithm to assign different labels to neighboring pixels around motion edges.

We minimize the energy function (2) with an iterative GrabCut-like [34] approach, wherein we first apply the alpha expansion algorithm [36] to get a multi-label solution, use it to re-estimate the (background and foreground) GMMs, and then repeat the two steps a few times. We highlight the importance of our label prediction technique with soft motion-cue constraints in Fig. 3. Here, the original, binary motion predictions are imprecise (bottom) or incorrect (top), whereas using them as soft constraints in combination with the network prediction results in a more accurate estimation of the latent segmentation variables.

3.3   Fine-Tuning M-CNN

We learn an initial M-CNN model from all the videos in the dataset which have sufficient motion information (see Sect. 4.2 for implementation details). To refine this model we add a fine-tuning step, which updates the parameters of the network with a small set of unique and reliable video examples. This set is built automatically by selecting one shot from each video sequence, whose motion segment has the highest overlap (intersection over union) score with the current M-CNN prediction. The intuition behind this selection criterion is that our MCNN has already learned to discriminate categories of interest from the background, and thus, its predictions will have the highest overlap with precise motion segmentations. This model refinement leverages the most reliable exemplars and avoids near duplicates, often occurring within one video. In Sect. 4.3 we demonstrate the importance of this step for dealing with real-world non-curated video data.

4 Results and Evaluation

4.1 Experimental Protocol

We trained our M-CNN in two settings. The first one is on purely video data, and the second on a combination of image and video data. We performed experiments primarily with the weakly-annotated videos in the YouTube-Objects v2.2 dataset [37]. Additionally, to demonstrate that our approach adapts to other datasets automatically, we used the ImageNet video (ImageNet-VID) dataset [16]. The weakly-annotated images to train our network jointly on image and video data were taken from the training part of the PASCAL VOC 2012 segmentation dataset [17] with their image tags only. We then evaluated variants of our method on the VOC 2012 segmentation validation and test sets.

The YouTube-Objects dataset consists of 10 classes, with 155 videos in total. Each video is annotated with one class label and is split automatically into shots, resulting in 2511 shots overall. For evaluation, one frame per shot is annotated with a bounding box in some of the shots. We use this exclusively for evaluating our video co-localization performance in Sect. 4.5. For experiments with ImageNet-VID, we use 795 training videos corresponding to the 10 classes in common with YouTube-Objects. ImageNet-VID has bounding box annotations produced semi-automatically for every frame in a video shot (2120 shots in total). We accumulate the labels over a shot and assign them as class labels for the entire shot. As in the case of YouTube-Objects, we only use class labels at the video level, and none of the available additional annotations.

The VOC 2012 dataset has 20 foreground object classes and a background category. It is split into 1464 training, 1449 validation and 1456 test images. For experiments dealing with the subset of 10 classes in common with YouTube-Objects (see the list in Table 1), we treat the remaining 10 from VOC as irrelevant classes. In other words, we exclude all the training/validation images which contain only the irrelevant categories. This results in 914 training and 909 validation images. In images that contain an irrelevant class together with any of the 10 classes in YouTube-Objects, we treat their corresponding pixels as background for evaluation. Some of the state-of-art methods [1,13] use an augmented version of the VOC 2012 dataset, with over 10,000 additional training images [38]. Naturally the variants trained on this large dataset perform significantly better than those using the original VOC dataset. We do not use this augmented dataset in our work, but report state-of-the-art results due to our motion cues.

The segmentation performance of all the methods is measured as the intersection over union (IoU) score of the predicted segmentation and the ground truth. We compute IoU for each class as well as the average over all the classes, including background, following standard protocols [1,17]. We also evaluate our segmentation results in the co-localization setting with the CorLoc measure [14,15,31], which is defined as the percentage of images with IoU score, between ground truth and predicted bounding boxes, more than 0.5.

4.2 Implementation Details

Motion Segmentation. In all our experiments we used [14], a state-of-the-art method for motion segmentation. We perform two pruning steps before training the network. First, we discard all shots with less than 20 frames (2× the batch size of our SGD training). Second, we remove shots without relevant motion information: (i) when there are nearly no motion segments, or (ii) a significant part of the frame is assigned to foreground. We prune them out by a simple criterion based on the size of the foreground segments. We keep only the shots where the estimated foreground occupies between 2.5 % and 50 % of the frame area in each frame, for at least 20 contiguous frames in the shot. In cases where motion segmentation fails in the middle of a shot, but recovers later, producing several valid sequences, we keep the longest one. These two steps combined remove about a third of the shots, with 1675 and 1691 shots remaining in YouTube-Objects and ImageNet-VID respectively. We sample 10 frames uniformly from each of these remaining shots to train the network.

Training. We use a mini-batch of size 10 for SGD, where each mini-batch consists of the 10 frame samples of one shot. Our CNN learning parameters follow the setting in [1]. The initial learning rate is set to 0.001 and multiplied by 0.1 after a fixed number of iterations. We use a momentum of 0.9 and a weight decay of 0.0005. Also, the loss term $\delta(x_i - l)\log(p_i^l)$ computed for each object class l with num_l training samples, in (1), is weighted by $\min_{j=1...L}\text{num}_j/\text{num}_l$. This accounts for imbalanced number of training samples for each class in the dataset.

In the energy function (2), the parameter α, which controls the relative importance of the current network prediction and the soft motion cues, is set to 1 when training on the entire dataset. It is increased to 2 for fine-tuning, where the predictions are more reliable due to an improved network. We perform 4 iterations of the graph cut based inference algorithm, updating the GMMs at each step. The inference algorithm is either alpha expansion (for videos with multiple objects) or graph cut (when there is only one object label for the video). Following [14], we learn GMMs for a frame t with the motion segments from all the 10 frames in a batch, weighting each of them inversely according to their distance from t. The fine-tuning step is performed very selectively with the best shot for each video, where the average overlap is no less than 0.2. A systematic evaluation on the VOC 2012 validation set confirmed that the performance is not sensitive

Table 1. Performance of M-CNN and EM-Adapt variants, trained with YouTube-Objects, on the VOC 2012 validation set. '*' denotes the M-CNN models without fine-tuning. 'M-CNN* hard' is the variant without the label prediction step. 'M-CNN' is our complete method: with fine-tuning and label prediction.

Method	FOV	bkg	aero	bird	boat	car	cat	cow	dog	horse	mbike	train	Average
EM-Adapt	Small	65.7	25.1	20.5	9.3	21.6	23.7	12.4	17.7	14.9	19.5	25.4	23.2 ± 3.0
EM-Adapt	Large	69.1	12.9	14.7	9.0	12.9	15.4	5.6	9.9	7.8	15.9	23.0	17.9 ± 4.4
M-CNN*	Small	83.4	30.3	35.2	13.5	11.6	36.5	22.1	19.8	22.2	5.2	13.7	26.7 ± 1.0
M-CNN*	Large	84.6	35.3	44.8	24.7	21.7	44.4	26.3	26.5	27.9	10.0	22.9	33.6 ± 0.2
M-CNN* Hard	Large	83.6	35.3	38.6	24.0	21.2	39.6	20.2	21.3	19.2	7.9	17.9	29.9 ± 0.7
M-CNN	Large	86.3	46.5	43.5	27.6	34.0	47.5	28.7	31.0	30.8	32.4	43.4	41.2 ± 1.3

to the number of iterations and the α parameter. More details on this and our implementation in the Caffe framework [39] are available online [40].

4.3 Evaluation of M-CNN

We start by evaluating the different components of our M-CNN approach and compare to the state-of-the-art EM-Adapt method, see Table 1. We train EM-Adapt and M-CNN with the pruned shots from our YouTube-Objects training set in two network settings: large and small field of view (FOV). The large FOV is 224×224, while the small FOV is 128×128. We learn 5 models which vary in the order of the training samples and their variations (cropping, mirroring), and report the mean score and standard deviation.

The small FOV M-CNN without the fine-tuning step achieves an IoU of 26.7 %, whereas large FOV gives 33.6 % on the PASCAL VOC 2012 validation set. In contrast, EM-Adapt [1] trained[2] on the same dataset performs poorly with large FOV. Furthermore, both the variants of EM-Adapt are lower in performance than our M-CNN. This is because EM-Adapt uses a heuristic (where background and foreground are constrained to a fraction of the image area) to estimate the latent segmentation labels, and fails to leverage the weak supervision in our training dataset effectively. Our observation on this failure of EM-Adapt is further supported by the analysis in [1], which notes that a large FOV network performs poorer than its small FOV counterpart when only a "small amount of supervision is leveraged". The label prediction step (Sect. 3.2) proposed in our method leverages training data better than EM-Adapt, by optimizing an energy function involving soft motion constraints and network responses. We also evaluated the significance of using motion cues as soft constraints (M-CNN*) instead of introducing them as hard labels (M-CNN* hard), i.e., directly using motion segmentation result as latent labels **x**. 'M-CNN* hard' achieves 29.9 compared to 33.6 with soft constraints. We then take our best variant (M-CNN with large FOV) and fine-tune it, improving the performance further to 41.2 %. In all the remaining experiments, we use the best variants of EM-Adapt and M-CNN.

---

[2] We used the original implementation provided by the authors to train EM-Adapt.

Table 2. Performance of our M-CNN variants on the VOC 2012 validation set is shown as IoU scores. We also compare with the best variants of EM-Adapt [1] trained on YouTube-Objects (YTube), ImageNet-VID (ImNet), VOC, and augmented VOC (VOC aug.) datasets. † denotes the average result of 5 trained models.

Method	Dataset	bkg	aero	bird	boat	car	cat	cow	dog	horse	mbike	train	Average
EM-Adapt	YTube	65.7	25.1	20.5	9.3	21.6	23.7	12.4	17.7	14.9	19.5	25.4	23.2†
EM-Adapt	ImNet	66.1	22.8	18.7	16.9	26.7	35.7	22.4	23.6	21.4	28.4	24.3	27.9
EM-Adapt	VOC	75.5	30.5	27.4	24.1	41.8	36.8	25.5	33.3	29.3	40.0	29.7	35.8
EM-Adapt	VOC aug	77.4	32.1	30.8	26.4	42.6	40.7	32.8	37.8	35.1	45.2	41.1	40.2
M-CNN	YTube	86.3	46.5	43.5	27.6	34.0	47.5	28.7	31.0	30.8	32.4	43.4	41.2†
M-CNN	VOC+YTube	85.4	54.5	40.8	35.5	41.2	47.5	38.3	42.0	41.5	45.0	47.8	47.2†
M-CNN	VOC aug.+YTube	82.5	47.8	35.3	29.6	45.6	54.6	40.3	46.6	44.8	52.2	56.6	48.7
M-CNN	ImNet	85.6	41.4	45.3	23.2	38.6	42.3	36.0	35.1	21.1	15.3	44.8	39.0
M-CNN	VOC+ImNet	85.1	53.3	46.8	32.5	33.9	37.3	40.7	32.3	34.2	40.0	45.0	43.7
M-CNN	VOC aug.+ImNet	83.1	47.6	40.3	26.4	44.1	51.1	41.7	51.0	34.9	44.6	52.7	47.0

4.4   Training on Weakly-Annotated Videos and Images

We also trained our M-CNN with weakly-annotated videos and images. To this end, we used images from the VOC 2012 training set. We added the 914 images from the VOC 2012 training set containing the 10 classes, and used only their weak annotations, i.e., image-level labels. In this setting, we first trained the network with the pruned video shots from YouTube-Objects, fine-tuned it with a subset of shots (as described in Sect. 3.3), and then performed a second fine-tuning step with these selected video shots and VOC images. To estimate the latent segmentation labels we use our optimization framework (Sect. 3.2) when the training sample is from the video dataset and the EM-Adapt label prediction step when it is from the VOC set. We can alternatively use our framework with only the network prediction component for images, but this is not viable when training on classes without video data, i.e., the remaining 10 classes in VOC. As shown in Table 2, using image data, with additional object instances, improves the IoU score from 41.2 to 47.2. In comparison, EM-Adapt re-trained for 10 classes on the original VOC 2012 achieves only 35.8. Augmenting the dataset with several additional training images [38], improves it to 40.2, but this remains considerably lower than our result. M-CNN trained with ImageNet-VID achieves 39.0 (ImNet in the table), which is comparable to our result with YouTube-Objects. The performance is significantly lower for the motorbike class (15.3 vs 32.4) owing to the small number of video shots available for training. In this case, we only have 67 shots compared to 272 from YouTube-Objects. Augmenting this dataset with VOC images boosts the performance to 43.7 (VOC+ImNet). Augmenting the training set with additional images (VOC aug.) further increases the performance.

Qualitative Results. Figure 4 shows qualitative results of M-CNN (trained on VOC and YouTube-Objects) on a few sample images. These have much more accurate object boundaries than the best variant of EM-Adapt [1], which tends to localize the object well, but produces a 'blob-like' segmentation, see the last

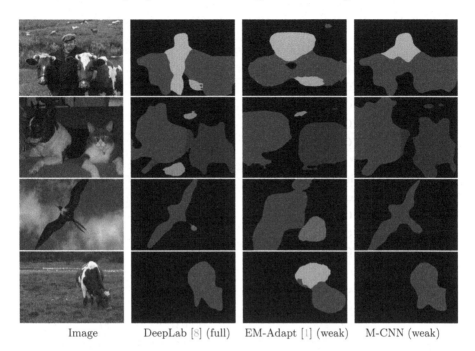

| Image | DeepLab [8] (full) | EM-Adapt [1] (weak) | M-CNN (weak) |

Fig. 4. Sample results on the VOC 2012 validation set. Results of fully-supervised DeepLab [8], weakly-supervised EM-Adapt [1] trained on augmented VOC, and our weakly-supervised M-CNN trained on VOC+YouTube-Objects are shown in 2nd, 3rd and 4th columns respectively. (*Best viewed in color.*)

three rows in the figure in particular. The first two rows show example images containing multiple object categories. M-CNN recognizes object classes more accurately, e.g., cow in row 4, than EM-Adapt, which confuses cow (shown in green) with horse (shown in magenta). Furthermore, our segmentation results compare favorably with the fully-supervised DeepLab [8] approach (see rows 3–4), highlighting the impact of motion to learn segmentation. There is scope for further improvement, e.g., overcoming the confusion between similar classes in close proximity to each other, as in the challenging case in row 2 for cat vs dog.

Comparison to the State of the Art. Table 3 shows evaluation on the VOC 2012 test set, with our M-CNN trained on 20 classes using image and video data for 10 classes and image data only for the other 10. We performed this by uploading our segmentation results to the evaluation server, as ground truth is not publicly available for the test set. We compare with several state-of-the-art methods with scores taken directly from the publications, except [1] without the post-processing CRF step. This result, shown as '[1]' in the table, is with a model we trained on the VOC augmented dataset. We train M-CNN on all the 20 VOC classes with the model trained (and fine-tuned) on YouTube-Objects and perform a second fine-tuning step together with videos from YouTube-Objects

Table 3. Evaluation on the VOC 2012 test set shown as IoU scores.

Method	Training data	# train. samples	Average	Average 10-class
Strong/Full supervision				
[3] + bb	VOC+ImNet	~762,500	37.0	43.8
[3] + seg	VOC+ImNet	~761,500	40.6	48.0
[1] + seg	VOC aug.	12,031	69.0	78.2
[41] (full)	VOC aug.	10,582	69.6	79.3
[11] (full)	VOC aug.+COCO	77,784	74.7	82.9
Weak supervision with additional info.				
[3] + sp	ImNet	~760,000	35.8	42.3
[13] + sz	VOC aug.	10,582	43.3	48.9
[13] + sz + CRF	VOC aug.	10,582	45.1	51.2
[1] + CRF	VOC aug.	12,031	39.6	45.2
Weak supervision				
[12]	VOC aug.	12,031	25.7	-
[13]	VOC aug.	10,582	35.6	39.5
[1]	VOC aug.	12,031	35.2	40.3
Ours	VOC+YTube	3,139	**39.8**	**49.6**
Ours	VOC+ImNet	3,155	36.9	48.0

and images from VOC. This achieves 39.8 mean IoU over all the 20 classes, and 49.6 on the 10 classes with video data. This result is significantly better than methods using only weak labels, which achieve 25.7 [12], 35.6 [13] and 35.2 [1]. The improvement shown by our M-CNN is more prominent when we consider the average over 10 classes where we use soft motion segmentation cues, and the background, with nearly 10 % and 9 % boost over [1,13] respectively. We also show the evaluation of the model trained on ImageNet-VID in the table.

A few methods have used additional information in the training process, such as the size of objects (+ sz in the table), superpixel segmentation (+ sp), or post-processing steps, e.g., introducing a CRF with pairwise terms learned from fully-annotated data (+ CRF), or even strong or full supervision, such as bounding box (+ bb) or pixel-level segmentation (+ seg) annotations. Even though our pure weakly-supervised method is not directly comparable to these approaches, we have included these results in the table for completeness. Nevertheless, M-CNN outperforms some of these methods [1,3], due to our effective learning scheme. Also from Table 3, the number of training samples used for M-CNN (number of videos shots + number of VOC training images) is significantly lower than those for all the other methods.

Table 4. Co-localization performance of M-CNN on the YouTube-Objects dataset. We report per class and average CorLoc scores, and compare with state-of-the-art unsupervised and weakly-supervised methods.

Method	aero	bird	boat	car	cat	cow	dog	horse	mbike	train	Average
Unsupervised											
[7]	53.9	19.6	38.2	37.8	32.2	21.8	27.0	34.7	45.4	37.5	34.8
[14]	65.4	67.3	38.9	65.2	46.3	40.2	65.3	48.4	39.0	25.0	50.1
[18]	55.2	58.7	53.6	72.3	33.1	58.3	52.5	50.8	45.0	19.8	49.9
Weakly-supervised											
[15]	51.7	17.5	34.4	34.7	22.3	17.9	13.5	26.7	41.2	25.0	28.5
[31]	25.1	31.2	27.8	38.5	41.2	28.4	33.9	35.6	23.1	25.0	31.0
[18]	56.5	66.4	58.0	76.8	39.9	69.3	50.4	56.3	53.0	31.0	55.7
M-CNN	76.1	57.7	77.7	68.8	71.6	75.6	87.9	71.9	80.0	52.6	**72.0**

4.5   Co-localization

We perform co-localization in the standard setting, where videos contain a common object. Here, we use our M-CNN trained on the YouTube-Objects dataset with 10 categories. We evaluate it on all the frames in YouTube-Objects to obtain prediction scores $\mathbf{p}_i$ for each pixel i. With these scores, we compute a foreground GMM by considering pixels with high predictions for the object category as foreground. A background GMM is also computed in a similar fashion. These form the unary term ψ_i^m in the energy function (2). We then minimize this function with graph cut based inference to compute the binary (object vs background) segmentation labels. Since we estimate segmentations for all the video frames, we do this at the superpixel level [42] to reduce computation cost. We then extract the bounding box enclosing the largest connected component in each frame, and evaluate them following [15]. Quantitative results with this are summarized as CorLoc scores in Table 4. We observe that our result outperforms previous state of the art [18] by over 16 %. Performing this experiment with ImageNet-VID data we obtain 42.1 on average, in comparison to 37.9 of [14]. ImageNet-VID being a more challenging dataset than YouTube-Objects results in a lower performance for both these methods.

5   Summary

This paper introduces a novel weakly-supervised learning approach for semantic segmentation, which uses only class labels assigned to videos. It integrates motion cues computed from video as soft constraints into a fully convolutional neural network. Experimental results show that our soft motion constraints can handle noisy motion information and improve significantly over the heuristic size constraints used by state-of-the-art approaches for weakly-supervised semantic

segmentation, i.e., EM-Adapt [1]. We show that our approach outperforms previous state of the art [1,13] on the PASCAL VOC 2012 image segmentation
dataset, thereby overcoming domain-shift issues typically seen when training
on video and testing on images. Furthermore, our weakly-supervised method
shows excellent results for video co-localization and improves over several methods [14,18,31].

Acknowledgements. This work was supported in part by the ERC advanced grant
ALLEGRO, the MSR-Inria joint project, a Google research award and a Facebook gift.
We gratefully acknowledge the support of NVIDIA with the donation of GPUs used
for this research.

References

1. Papandreou, G., Chen, L.C., Murphy, K., Yuille, A.L.: Weakly-and semi-supervised
   learning of a DCNN for semantic image segmentation. In: ICCV (2015)
2. Vezhnevets, A., Ferrari, V., Buhmann, J.: Weakly supervised structured output
   learning for semantic segmentation. In: CVPR (2012)
3. Pinheiro, P.O., Collobert, R.: From image-level to pixel-level labeling with convolutional networks. In: CVPR (2015)
4. Hartmann, G., Grundmann, M., Hoffman, J., Tsai, D., Kwatra, V., Madani, O.,
   Vijayanarasimhan, S., Essa, I., Rehg, J., Sukthankar, R.: Weakly supervised learning of object segmentations from web-scale video. In: ECCV (2012)
5. Monroy, A., Ommer, B.: Beyond bounding-boxes: learning object shape by model-
   driven grouping. In: Fitzgibbon, A., Lazebnik, S., Perona, P., Sato, Y., Schmid,
   C. (eds.) ECCV 2012. LNCS, vol. 7574, pp. 580–593. Springer, Heidelberg (2012).
   doi:10.1007/978-3-642-33712-3_42
6. Wu, J., Zhao, Y., Zhu, J., Luo, S., Tu, Z.: MILCut: a sweeping line multiple instance
   learning paradigm for interactive image segmentation. In: CVPR (2014)
7. Brox, T., Malik, J.: Object segmentation by long term analysis of point trajectories.
   In: Daniilidis, K., Maragos, P., Paragios, N. (eds.) ECCV 2010. LNCS, vol. 6315,
   pp. 282–295. Springer, Heidelberg (2010). doi:10.1007/978-3-642-15555-0_21
8. Chen, L.C., Papandreou, G., Kokkinos, I., Murphy, K., Yuille, A.L.: Semantic
   image segmentation with deep convolutional nets and fully connected CRFs. In:
   ICLR (2015)
9. Farabet, C., Couprie, C., Najman, L., LeCun, Y.: Learning hierarchical features
   for scene labeling. PAMI **35**(8), 1915–1929 (2013)
10. Long, J., Shelhamer, E., Darrell, T.: Fully convolutional networks for semantic
    segmentation. In: CVPR (2015)
11. Zheng, S., Jayasumana, S., Romera-Paredes, B., Vineet, V., Su, Z., Du, D., Huang,
    C., Torr, P.: Conditional random fields as recurrent neural networks. In: ICCV
    (2015)
12. Pathak, D., Shelhamer, E., Long, J., Darrell, T.: Fully convolutional multi-class
    multiple instance learning. In: ICLR (2015)
13. Pathak, D., Krähenbühl, P., Darrell, T.: Constrained convolutional neural networks
    for weakly supervised segmentation. In: ICCV (2015)
14. Papazoglou, A., Ferrari, V.: Fast object segmentation in unconstrained video. In:
    ICCV (2013)

15. Prest, A., Leistner, C., Civera, J., Schmid, C., Ferrari, V.: Learning object class detectors from weakly annotated video. In: CVPR (2012)
16. http://www.vision.cs.unc.edu/ilsvrc2015/download-videos-3j16.php#vid
17. Everingham, M., Van Gool, L., Williams, C.K.I., Winn, J., Zisserman, A.: The PASCAL Visual Object Classes Challenge 2012 (VOC2012) Results http://www.pascal-network.org/challenges/VOC/voc2012/workshop/index.html
18. Kwak, S., Cho, M., Laptev, I., Ponce, J., Schmid, C.: Unsupervised object discovery and tracking in video collections. In: ICCV (2015)
19. Carreira, J., Sminchisescu, C.: CPMC: automatic object segmentation using constrained parametric min-cuts. PAMI **34**(7), 1312–1328 (2012)
20. Carreira, J., Caseiro, R., Batista, J., Sminchisescu, C.: Semantic segmentation with second-order pooling. In: Fitzgibbon, A., Lazebnik, S., Perona, P., Sato, Y., Schmid, C. (eds.) ECCV 2012. LNCS, vol. 7578, pp. 430–443. Springer, Heidelberg (2012). doi:10.1007/978-3-642-33786-4_32
21. Lin, G., Shen, C., van dan Hengel, A., Reid, I.: Efficient piecewise training of deep structured models for semantic segmentation. In: CVPR (2016)
22. LeCun, Y., Boser, B., Denker, J.S., Henderson, D., Howard, R.E., Hubbard, W., Jackel, L.D.: Backpropagation applied to handwritten zip code recognition. Neural Comput. **1**(4), 541–551 (1989)
23. Krizhevsky, A., Sutskever, I., Hinton, G.E.: ImageNet classification with deep convolutional neural networks. In: NIPS (2012)
24. Cinbis, R.G., Verbeek, J., Schmid, C.: Multi-fold MIL training for weakly supervised object localization. In: CVPR (2014)
25. Russakovsky, O., Lin, Y., Yu, K., Fei-Fei, L.: Object-centric spatial pooling for image classification. In: Fitzgibbon, A., Lazebnik, S., Perona, P., Sato, Y., Schmid, C. (eds.) ECCV 2012. LNCS, vol. 7573, pp. 1–15. Springer, Heidelberg (2012)
26. Chen, X., Shrivastava, A., Gupta, A.: NEIL: Extracting visual knowledge from web data. In: CVPR (2013)
27. Divvala, S.K., Farhadi, A., Guestrin, C.: Learning everything about anything: Webly-supervised visual concept learning. In: CVPR (2014)
28. Chen, X., Gupta, A.: Webly supervised learning of convolutional networks. In: ICCV (2015)
29. Liang, X., Liu, S., Wei, Y., Liu, L., Lin, L., Yan, S.: Towards computational baby learning: A weakly-supervised approach for object detection. In: ICCV (2015)
30. Rother, C., Minka, T., Blake, A., Kolmogorov, V.: Cosegmentation of image pairs by histogram matching - incorporating a global constraint into MRFs. In: CVPR (2006)
31. Joulin, A., Tang, K., Fei-Fei, L.: Efficient image and video co-localization with Frank-wolfe algorithm. In: Fleet, D., Pajdla, T., Schiele, B., Tuytelaars, T. (eds.) ECCV 2014. LNCS, vol. 8694, pp. 253–268. Springer, Heidelberg (2014). doi:10.1007/978-3-319-10599-4_17
32. Tang, K.D., Sukthankar, R., Yagnik, J., Li, F.: Discriminative segment annotation in weakly labeled video. In: CVPR (2013)
33. Simonyan, K., Zisserman, A.: Very deep convolutional networks for large-scale image recognition. In: ICLR (2015)
34. Rother, C., Kolmogorov, V., Blake, A.: Grabcut: interactive foreground extraction using iterated graph cuts. ACM Trans. Graph. **23**(3), 309–314 (2004)
35. Boykov, Y., Jolly., M.P.: Interactive graph cuts for optimal boundary and region segmentation of objects in N-D images. In: ICCV (2001)
36. Boykov, Y., Veksler, O., Zabih, R.: Fast approximate energy minimization via graph cuts. PAMI **23**(11), 1222–1239 (2001)

37. http://www.calvin.inf.ed.ac.uk/datasets/youtube-objects-dataset
38. Hariharan, B., Arbelaez, P., Bourdev, L., Maji, S., Malik, J.: Semantic contours from inverse detectors. In: ICCV (2011)
39. Jia, Y., Shelhamer, E., Donahue, J., Karayev, S., Long, J., Girshick, R., Guadarrama, S., Darrell, T.: Caffe: convolutional architecture for fast feature embedding. In: ACM Multimedia (2014)
40. http://www.thoth.inrialpes.fr/research/weakseg
41. Mostajabi, M., Yadollahpour, P., Shakhnarovich, G.: Feedforward semantic segmentation with zoom-out features. In: CVPR (2015)
42. Achanta, R., Shaji, A., Smith, K., Lucchi, A., Fua, P., Süsstrunk, S.: Slic superpixels compared to state-of-the-art superpixel methods. PAMI **34**(11), 2274–2282 (2012)

Human-in-the-Loop Person Re-identification

Hanxiao Wang$^{(\boxtimes)}$, Shaogang Gong, Xiatian Zhu, and Tao Xiang

School of EECS, Queen Mary University of London, London, UK
{hanxiao.wang,s.gong,xiatian.zhu,t.xiang}@qmul.ac.uk

Abstract. Current person re-identification (re-id) methods assume that
(1) pre-labelled training data are available for every camera pair, (2) the
gallery size for re-identification is moderate. Both assumptions scale
poorly to real-world applications when camera network size increases
and gallery size becomes large. Human verification of automatic model
ranked re-id results becomes inevitable. In this work, a novel human-in-
the-loop re-id model based on Human Verification Incremental Learning
(HVIL) is formulated which does not require any pre-labelled training
data to learn a model, therefore readily scalable to new camera pairs.
This HVIL model learns cumulatively from human feedback to provide
instant improvement to re-id ranking of each probe on-the-fly enabling
the model scalable to large gallery sizes. We further formulate a Regularised Metric Ensemble Learning (RMEL) model to combine a series of
incrementally learned HVIL models into a single ensemble model to be
used when human feedback becomes unavailable.

Keywords: Person re-identification · Incremental learning · Human-in-
the-loop · Metric ensemble

1 Introduction

State-of-the-art person re-identification (re-id) models are dominated by supervised learning approaches [1–12], which employ a *train-once-and-deploy* scheme
(Fig. 1(a)). That is, a pre-labelled training data set with given cross-view true-
matching identities is first collected and used to learn a model. The learned model
is then deployed to new data without any modification. Based on this approach,
the re-id community has witnessed over the past two years ever-increased re-id
matching accuracy on increasingly larger sized benchmarks with more identities. For instance, the CUHK03 benchmark [9] contains 13,164 images of 1,360
identities which is significantly larger than the early VIPeR [13] and iLIDS [14]
benchmarks. The state-of-the-art Rank-1 matching accuracy on CUHK03 is now
in 50–60 % [12], doubling the best performance reported merely a year ago [9].

One inevitable question arises: Are we close to an automated re-id solution
capable of deployment in the real-world? The answer is no. This is because
existing supervised learning based re-id methods make two critical assumptions,
both of which are invalid in the real-world (unscalable): (1) A manually pre-
labelled pairwise training data set is assumed available for every camera pair.

© Springer International Publishing AG 2016
B. Leibe et al. (Eds.): ECCV 2016, Part IV, LNCS 9908, pp. 405–422, 2016.
DOI: 10.1007/978-3-319-46493-0_25

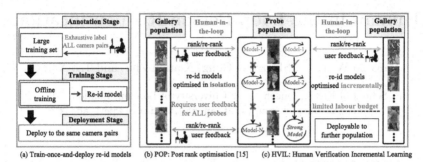

Fig. 1. (a) Conventional *train-once-and-deploy* re-id strategy requires pre-labelled training data collection. (b) POP [15]: A recent *human-in-the-loop re-id* approach which optimises probe-specific models in isolation. (c) HVIL: The proposed new incremental human-in-the-loop re-id model.

However, this is neither scalable (prohibitive to collect in the real-world as there are quadratic number of camera pairs), nor plausible (there may not exist sufficiently large number of training people reappearing in every pair of camera views). (2) The size of the training dataset is assumed either significantly greater or no less than that of test gallery population on which the learned model will be deployed. For instance, given the standard splits of the CUHK03 benchmark, the training set consists of paired images of 1,260 person identities from six different camera views (on average 4.8 image samples per person per camera view), whilst the test gallery set consists of only 100 identities each with a single image (one-shot setting). The test set's identity size is thus 10 times less than that of the training set, and has approximately 50 times less images. In a real-world, the size of any deployment gallery population is almost always much greater than any pre-labelled training data size even if such training data were made available. In a public space such as an underground station, there are easily over 1,000 people passing through a camera network every hour, resulting in a typical gallery population size of over 10,000 in a day. It was observed from our experiments that a 10-fold increase in gallery size leads to a 10-fold decrease in re-id Rank-1 performance, resulting in a single-digit Rank-1 score, even when the state-of-the-art re-id models were trained from sufficiently sized labelled data. Given such single-digit Rank-1 scores, human operators are required to verify any true match given a probe from a rather large rank list.

To overcome the inherent limitations of the two aforementioned assumptions from pre-labelling based supervised learning, an attractive alternative approach is to explore *human-in-the-loop* for person re-identification (Fig. 1(b)). Such an approach is inherently more scalable compared to conventional pre-trained re-id models because it does not assume the collection of pre-labelled training data. Human-in-the-loop verification can be considered as a form of "labelling effort". However, this on-the-fly verification approach has two significant advantages over the conventional approach that requires pre-labelling data for training: (1) It requires much less labelling-effort (the number of feedback from human verification is typically in tens rather than thousands required for pre-labelling training data); (2) It focuses on optimising the re-id ranking of each probe directly in the test gallery population, rather than learning a distance metric in a separate training set and blindly assuming its adaptability to the test gallery population.

In this work we develop a re-id model without the need for pre-labelled training. Crucially, it can be improved incrementally by human verification and benefits from more flexible human feedback (similar/dissimilar). As a result, it enables a human to re-id rapidly a given probe image after only a handful of feedback verifications even when the gallery size is large. More specifically, a Human Verification Incremental Learning (HVIL) model (Fig. 1(c)) is formulated to maximise the effectiveness of human-in-the-loop feedback by incorporating: (1) *Flexible feedback* - HVIL allows for weak human feedback (similar/dissimilar) without the need for exhaustive user search in the ranked list, instead of being restricted to only true/false verifications. (2) *Immediate benefit* - By introducing a new online incremental distance metric learning model, HVIL enables real-time response to human feedback by rapidly presenting a freshly optimised ranking list. (3) *The older the wiser* - HVIL is updated cumulatively on-the-fly utilising multiple user feedback per probe and optimised incrementally for each new probe given what been learned from all previous probes. (4) *A strong ensemble model* - An additional Regularised Metric Ensemble Learning (RMEL) model is introduced by taking all the incrementally optimised per-probe models as a set of "weak" models [16,17] and constructing a "strong" ensemble model for performing re-id tasks when human feedback becomes unavailable.

Related Work - Current best performing person re-id methods are fully supervised but they require a large number of pre-labelled training data from every camera pair for building camera-pair specific distance metric models [2–12,18–20]. Their usefulness and scalability are inherently limited in real-world applications especially with large camera networks. This problem becomes more acute for the more recent deep learning based methods [9,19,21–23] which need more labelled training data to function. To relax this need for labelling, existing attempts include semi-supervised [24,25], unsupervised [26–28], and transfer learning [29–32]. However, all of these strategies are weak in performance compared to fully supervised learning - without labelled data, they are unable to learn strong discriminative information for cross-view people re-identification. In contrast, the proposed HVIL model learns discriminatively from human feedback instead of pre-labelled image pairs, and is capable of yielding much superior person re-id matching accuracy than the state-of-the-art supervised re-id models, with added advantages of costing much less human feedback as "labelling effort" and being more scalable to large test gallery sizes.

Very few human-in-the-loop re-id methods were reported before, nor received much attention. Abir et al. [33] assumed a pre-labelled training set available per person *in addition* to human-in-the-loop verification. Hirzer et al. [34] considered a form of human feedback which is ill-posed: It only allows a user to verify whether a *true* match is within the top-N ranking list. This limits significantly the effectiveness of human feedback and can waste expensive human labour when a true match cannot be found in the top-N ranks. More recently, Liu et al. [15]

proposed the POP model (Fig. 1(b)), which allows a user to identify correct matches more rapidly and accurately by accommodating more flexible feedback information. However, both [15,34] are limited inherently due to the fact that they treat each probe as an independent retrieval task, i.e. the process of learning a model for each probe does not benefit learning models for other probes. This lack of improving model-learning cumulatively with increasing human feedback is both suboptimal and in danger of disengaging the human in the loop. In contrast, the proposed HVIL re-id framework (Fig. 1(c)) enables incremental model improvement from cumulative human feedback. Moreover, the proposed RMEL ensemble model further benefits from previous human verification effort even when human feedback is no long available.

Contributions - (1) We formulate a new approach to person re-id for a model to be optimised cumulatively by human feedback on-the-fly with each re-id task at hand without pre-labelled training and being effective for large gallery sizes. (2) A Human Verification Incremental Learning (HVIL) model is introduced for distance metric optimisation by flexible human feedback continuously in real-time and from cumulative feedback when more probe images are searched. (3) A Regularised Metric Ensemble Learning (RMEL) model is constructed for a strong ensemble model when human feedback becomes unavailable. The advantages of the proposed approach is validated by extensive comparisons against contemporary image retrieval methods and state-of-the-art supervised person re-id models on two largest re-id benchmarks CUHK03 [9] and Market-1501 [35].

2 Human-in-the-Loop Incremental Learning

2.1 Problem Formulation

Suppose an image is denoted by a feature vector $x \in \mathbb{R}^d$. The *human-in-the-loop re-id* problem is formulated as: (1) For each image x^p in a probe set $\mathcal{P} = \{x_i^p\}_{i=1}^{N_p}$, x^p is matched against a gallery set $\mathcal{G} = \{x_i^g\}_{i=1}^{N_g}$ and an initial ranking list is generated by a re-id ranking function $f(\cdot) : \mathbb{R}^d \to \mathbb{R}$, according to ranking scores $f_{x^p}(x_i^g)$. (2) A human operator (user) browses the gallery ranking list to verify the existence and the rank of any true match for x^p. Human feedback is generated when a ranked gallery image x^g is selected by the user with a label $y \in \{$true, dissimilar, similar$\}$. Once a feedback on probe x^p is received, parameters of $f(\cdot)$ are updated instantly to re-order the gallery ranking list and give the user immediate reward for the feedback. (3) When either a true match is found or a pre-determined maximum round of feedback is reached, the next probe is presented for re-id in the gallery set. In contrast to pre-labelling training data required by conventional *train-once-and-deploy* re-id schemes, *human-in-the-loop re-id* has two unique characteristics: (a) Due to human patience and limited labour budget [34], a user is only interested in the top ranked gallery images, and a user's feedback on each probe is limited. (b) Rather than verifying *only* true (positive) matches in the gallery for each probe, which are inherently very few if any among the top ranks[1], it is a much easier and more rewarding task for the user to give feedback on the many top ranked negative gallery instances: *strong-negative* (dissimilar) - *"definitely not the one I am looking for"*, and *weak-negative* (similar) - *"looks similar but not the same person"* [15].

2.2 Modelling Human Feedback as a Loss Function

Formally, we wish to construct an incrementally optimised ranking function, $f_{\boldsymbol{x}^p}(\boldsymbol{x}_i^g) : \mathbb{R}^d \to \mathbb{R}$, where $f(\cdot)$ can be estimated by three types of human feedback $y \in L = \{m, s, w\}$ as *true-match, strong-negative*, and *weak-negative* respectively. Inspired by [36–38], we define a ranking error ($\mathcal{L}$oss) function for a feedback y on a human selected gallery sample $\boldsymbol{x}^g$ given a probe $\boldsymbol{x}^p$ as:

$$err(f_{\boldsymbol{x}^p}(\boldsymbol{x}^g), y) = \mathcal{L}_y(rank(f_{\boldsymbol{x}^p}(\boldsymbol{x}^g))), \tag{1}$$

where $rank(f_{\boldsymbol{x}^p}(\boldsymbol{x}^g))$ denotes the rank of $\boldsymbol{x}^g$ given by $f_{\boldsymbol{x}^p}(\cdot)$, defined as:

$$rank(f_{\boldsymbol{x}^p}(\boldsymbol{x}^g)) = \sum_{\boldsymbol{x}_i^g \in G \setminus \boldsymbol{x}^g} \mathcal{I}(f_{\boldsymbol{x}^p}(\boldsymbol{x}_i^g) \geqslant f_{\boldsymbol{x}^p}(\boldsymbol{x}^g)), \tag{2}$$

where $\mathcal{I}(\cdot)$ is the indicator function. The loss function $\mathcal{L}_y(\cdot) : \mathbb{Z}^+ \to \mathbb{R}^+$ transforms a rank into a loss. We introduce a novel re-id ranking loss defined as:

$$\mathcal{L}_y(k) = \begin{cases} \sum_{i=1}^k \alpha_i, & \text{if } y \in \{m, w\} \\ \sum_{i=k+1}^{n_g} \alpha_i, & \text{if } y \in \{s\}, \end{cases} \quad \text{with} \quad \alpha_1 \geqslant \alpha_2 \geqslant \cdots \geqslant 0. \tag{3}$$

Note, different choices of α_i lead to specific model responses to human feedback. We set $\alpha_i = \frac{1}{i}$ (large penalty with steep slope) when y indicates a *true-match*, and $\alpha_i = \frac{1}{n_g - 1}$ with n_g the gallery size (small penalty with gentle slope) when y represents a *weak-negative* or *strong-negative*. Such a ranking loss is designed to favour a model update behaviour so that: (1) *true-matches* are quickly pushed up to the top ranks, whilst (2) *weak-/strong-negatives* are mildly moved towards the top/bottom rank direction. Our experiments (Sect. 4.1) show that such a ranking loss criterion boosts very effectively the Rank-1 matching rate and pushes quickly *true-matches* to the top ranks at each iteration of human feedback.

2.3 Real-Time Model Update for Instant Feedback Reward

Given the re-id ranking loss function defined in Eq. (3), we wish to have real-time model update to human feedback therefore providing instant reward to user labour effort. To that end, we consider the re-id ranking model $f(\cdot)$ as a negative Mahalanobis distance metric:

$$f_{\boldsymbol{x}^p}(\boldsymbol{x}^g) = -\left[(\boldsymbol{x}^p - \boldsymbol{x}^g)^\top M (\boldsymbol{x}^p - \boldsymbol{x}^g)\right], \quad M \in S_+^d. \tag{4}$$

---

[1] In a large size gallery set, true matches are often scarce (only one-shot) and overwhelmed (appear in low-ranks) by false matches of high-ranks in the rank list.

The positive semi-definite matrix M consists of model parameters to be learned.

Knowledge Cumulation by Online Learning - In previous works [15,34], $f(\cdot)$ is only optimised in isolation for each probe without benefiting from previous feedback on other probes. To overcome this limitation, we wish to optimise $f(\cdot)$ incrementally in an online manner [39] for maximising the value of limited human feedback labour budget. Moreover, to achieve real-time human-in-the-loop feedback and reward, $f(\cdot)$ needs be estimated on each human feedback.

Formally, given a new probe $\boldsymbol{x}_t^p$ at time step $t \in \{1, \cdots, \tau\}$ (τ the pre-defined budget), a user is presented with a gallery rank list computed by the previously estimated model M_{t-1} instead of re-initialising a new ranking function from scratch for this new probe. The user then verifies a gallery image $\boldsymbol{x}_t^g$ in the top ranks with a label y_t, generating a labelled triplet $(\boldsymbol{x}_t^p, \boldsymbol{x}_t^g, y_t)$. Given Eq. (3), this triplet has a corresponding loss as $\mathcal{L}^{(t)} = \mathcal{L}_{y_t}(rank(f_{\boldsymbol{x}_t^p}(\boldsymbol{x}_t^g)))$. We update the ranking model by minimising the following object function:

$$M_t = \underset{M \in S_+^d}{argmin}\, \Delta_F(M, M_{t-1}) + \eta\mathcal{L}^{(t)}, \tag{5}$$

where Δ_F is a Bregman divergence measure, defined by an arbitrary differentiable convex function F, for regularising the discrepancy between M and M_{t-1}. The set S_+^d defines a PSD cone, and the tradeoff parameter $\eta > 0$ balances the model update divergence and empirical loss. This optimisation updates incrementally the ranking model adopted from the previous probe by encoding user feedback on the current probe.

Loss Approximation for Real-Time Optimisation - In order to encourage and maintain user engagement in verification feedback, real-time online incremental metric learning is required. However, as $\mathcal{L}^{(t)}$ is discontinuous, the overall objective function cannot be optimised efficiently by gradient-based methods. We thus approximate the loss function by a continuous upper bound [36] so that it is differentiable w.r.t. M:

$$\widetilde{\mathcal{L}}^{(t)} = \frac{1}{\mathcal{N}_t^-} \sum_{\boldsymbol{x}_i^g \in G \backslash \boldsymbol{x}_t^g} \mathcal{L}_{y_t}\left(rank\left(f_{\boldsymbol{x}_t^p}(\boldsymbol{x}_t^g|M_{t-1})\right)\right) h_{y_t}\left(f_{\boldsymbol{x}_t^p}(\boldsymbol{x}_t^g|M_t) - f_{\boldsymbol{x}^p}(\boldsymbol{x}_i^g|M_t)\right)^2, \tag{6}$$

where $f_{\boldsymbol{x}_t^p}(\boldsymbol{x}_t^g|M_{t-1})$ denotes the function value of $f_{\boldsymbol{x}_t^p}(\boldsymbol{x}_t^g)$ parametrised by M_{t-1}, and $h_{y_t}(\cdot)$ represents a hinge loss function defined as:

$$h_{y_t}(f_{\boldsymbol{x}_t^p}(\boldsymbol{x}_t^g) - f_{\boldsymbol{x}_t^p}(\boldsymbol{x}_i^g)) = \begin{cases} max(0, 1 - f_{\boldsymbol{x}_t^p}(\boldsymbol{x}_t^g) + f_{\boldsymbol{x}_t^p}(\boldsymbol{x}_i^g)), & \text{if } y_t \in \{m, w\} \\ max(0, 1 - f_{\boldsymbol{x}_t^p}(\boldsymbol{x}_i^g) + f_{\boldsymbol{x}_t^p}(\boldsymbol{x}_t^g)), & \text{if } y_t \in \{s\}. \end{cases} \tag{7}$$

The normaliser $\mathcal{N}_t^-$ in Eq. (6) is the amount of violators, i.e. the gallery instances that generate non-zero hinge loss in Eq. (7) w.r.t. triplet $(\boldsymbol{x}_t^p, \boldsymbol{x}_t^g, y_t)$.

Learning Speed-Up by Most Violator Update - Given the approximation in Eq. (6), we can exploit the stochastic gradient descent (SGD) algorithm [40] for optimising Eq. (5) by iteratively updating on sub-sampled batches of all violators. However, the computational overhead of iterative updates can be large due to possibly many violators, and thus not meeting the real-time requirement. To address this problem, we explore a *most violator update* strategy, that is, to perform metric updates using *only* the violator x_v^g with the most violation (Eq. (7)). The final approximated empirical loss is then estimated as:

$$\widetilde{\mathcal{L}}_v^{(t)} = \mathcal{L}_{y_t}\left(rank\left(f_{x_t^p}(x_t^g|M_{t-1})\right)\right) h_{y_t}\left(f_{x_t^p}(x_v^g|M_t) - f_{x^p}(x_v^g|M_t)\right)^2. \quad (8)$$

By replacing $\mathcal{L}^{(t)}$ in Eq. (5) with $\widetilde{\mathcal{L}}_v^{(t)}$, and setting the gradient of Eq. (5) to zero, we yield the following ranking metric online update criterion:

$$M_t = g^{-1}\left(g(M_{t-1}) - \eta\nabla_M\widetilde{\mathcal{L}}_v^{(t)}\right), \quad (9)$$

where $g(\cdot)$ denotes the derivative of F (Eq. (5)) w.r.t. M [41]. For the form of F, we adopt Burg matrix divergence [42]:

$$\Delta_F(M, M_{t-1}) = tr\left(MM_{t-1}^{-1}\right) - logdet\left(MM_{t-1}^{-1}\right). \quad (10)$$

Equation (9) can be readily optimised by any gradient-based update schemes [41, 43]. We adopted the LogDet Exact Gradient Online (LEGO) algorithm [44]. This is desirable because Eq. (9) is solved with a computational complexity of $\mathcal{O}(d^2)$ where d is the feature vector dimension. This avoids eigenvector computation with a cost of $\mathcal{O}(d^3)$ required by most other schemes. Given all the components described above, our final model for Human Verification Incremental Learning (HVIL) enables real-time incremental person re-id model learning with human-in-the-loop feedback. Our extensive experiments (Sect. 4.1) show that this HVIL model provides the fastest human-in-the-loop feedback-reward cycle over other competitors. An overview of the HVIL model is given in Algorithm 1.

Algorithm 1. Human Verification Incremental Learning (HVIL)

Data: Unlabelled probe set $\mathcal{P}$ and gallery set $\mathcal{G}$;
Result: Per probe optimised ranking lists; re-id models $\{M_t\}_{t=1}^{\mathcal{T}}$;
Initialisation: $M_0 = I$ (identity matrix, equivalent to L_2 distance)
while $t < \tau$ **do**
    Present the next probe $x_t^p \in \mathcal{P}$;
    for $iter = 1 : maxIter$ **do**
        // maxIter: maximum interaction rounds per probe
        Rank $\mathcal{G}$ with M_{t-1} against x_t^p (Eq. (4));
        Collect human feedback (x_t^g, y_t);
        Locate the most violator x_v^g and calculate $\widetilde{\mathcal{L}}_v^{(t)}$ (Eqs. (7) and (8));
        $M_t = update(M_{t-1}, \widetilde{\mathcal{L}}_v^{(t)})$ (Eq. (9)), $t = t + 1$;
    end
end
Return $\{M_t\}_{t=1}^{\mathcal{T}}$.

---

3   Metric Ensemble Learning for Automated Re-id

Finally, we consider a situation when limited human labour budget is exhausted at time τ and an automated re-id strategy is required for any further probes. In this case, as the HVIL re-id model is optimised incrementally, the model M_τ optimised by the human verified probe at time τ can be directly deployed. However, it is desirable to construct an even "stronger" model based on metric ensemble learning. Specifically, a side-product of HVIL is a series of models incrementally optimised *locally* for a set of probes with human feedback. We consider them as a set of *globally* "weak" models $\{M_j\}_{j=1}^\tau$, and wish to construct a *single globally strong model* for re-id further probes without human feedback.

Regularised Metric Ensemble Learning - Given weak models $\{M_j\}_{j=1}^\tau$, we compute a distance vector $\boldsymbol{d}_{ij} \in \mathbb{R}^\tau$ for any probe-gallery pair $(\boldsymbol{x}_j^g, \boldsymbol{x}_i^p)$:

$$\boldsymbol{d}_{ij} = - \left[f_{\boldsymbol{x}_i^p}(\boldsymbol{x}_j^g | M_1), \cdots, f_{\boldsymbol{x}_i^p}(\boldsymbol{x}_j^g | M_t), \cdots, f_{\boldsymbol{x}_i^p}(\boldsymbol{x}_j^g | M_\tau) \right]^\top. \qquad (11)$$

The objective of metric ensemble learning is to obtain an optimal combination of these distances for producing a single globally optimal distance. Here we consider the ensemble ranking function $f_{\boldsymbol{x}_i^p}^{ens}(\boldsymbol{x}_j^g)$ in a bi-linear form (shortened as f_{ij}^{ens}):

$$f_{ij}^{ens} = f_{\boldsymbol{x}_i^p}^{ens}(\boldsymbol{x}_j^g) = -\boldsymbol{d}_{ij}^\top \boldsymbol{W} \boldsymbol{d}_{ij}, \quad \text{s.t. } \boldsymbol{W} \in S_+^\tau, \qquad (12)$$

with $\boldsymbol{W}$ being the model parameters capturing the correlations among all the weak model metrics. In this context, previous work such as [20] is a special case of our model when $\boldsymbol{W}$ is restricted to be diagonal only.

Objective Function - To estimate an optimal ensemble weights $\boldsymbol{W}$ with most identity-discriminative power, we re-use the true matching pairs verified during the human verification procedure (Sect. 2) as "training data": $\mathcal{X}_{tr} = \{(\boldsymbol{x}_i^p, \boldsymbol{x}_i^g)\}_{i=1}^{N_l}$, and their corresponding person identities are denoted by $\mathcal{C} = \{c_i\}_{i=1}^{N_l}$. Note, "training data" here are only for estimating ensemble weights, not for learning a distance metric. Since the ranking score f_{ij}^{ens} in Eq. (12) is either negative or zero, we consider that in the extreme case, an *ideal* ensemble function f^* should provide the following ranking scores : $f_{ij}^* = 0$ for $c_i = c_j$, and $f_{ij}^* = -1$ for $c_i \neq c_j$. Using $\boldsymbol{F}^*$ to denote such an ideal ranking score matrix and $\boldsymbol{F}^{ens}$ to denote an estimated score matrix by a given $\boldsymbol{W}$ with Eq. (12), our proposed objective function for metric ensemble learning is then defined as:

$$\min_{\boldsymbol{W}} \|\boldsymbol{F}^{ens} - \boldsymbol{F}^*\|_F^2 + \nu \mathcal{R}(\boldsymbol{W}), \quad \text{s.t. } \boldsymbol{W} \in S_+^\tau, \qquad (13)$$

where $\|\cdot\|_F$ denotes a Frobenius norm, and $\mathcal{R}(\boldsymbol{W})$ a regulariser on $\boldsymbol{W}$ with parameter ν controlling the regularisation strength. Whilst common choices of $\mathcal{R}(\boldsymbol{W})$ include L_1, Frobenius norm, or matrix trace, we introduce the following regularisation for a Regularised Metric Ensemble Learning (RMEL) re-id model:

$$\mathcal{R}(\boldsymbol{W}) = -\sum_{i,j} f_{ij}^{ens}, \quad for \ c_i = c_j. \qquad (14)$$

Our intuition is to impose severe penalties for true match pairs with low ranking scores since they deliver the most informative discriminative information for cross-view person re-id, whilst false match pairs are either less informative (strong-negative) or non-discriminative (weak-negative).

Optimisation - Equation (13) is strictly convex with a guaranteed global optimal so it can be optimised by any off-the-shelf toolboxes [45]. We adopt the standard first-order projected gradient descent algorithm [46]. Given the estimated optimal ensemble weight matrix W and the weak models $\{M_j\}_{j=1}^{\tau}$, a single strong ensemble model (Eq. (12)) is made available for performing automated re-id of any further probes on the gallery population. Our experiments (Sect. 4.2) show that the proposed RMEL algorithm achieves superior performance compared to state-of-the-arts supervised re-id models given the same amount of labelled data.

4 Experiments

Two experiments were conducted: (1) The proposed HVIL model was evaluated under a *human-in-the-loop re-id* setting and an *enlarged* test gallery population was used to reflect real-world use-cases. (2) In the event of limited human labour budget being exhausted and human feedback becoming unavailable, the proposed HVIL-RMEL model was evaluated under an *automated re-id* setting.

Datasets - Two largest person re-id benchmarks: CUHK03 [9] and Market-1501 [35] were chosen for evaluation due to the need for large test gallery size. CUHK03 contains 13,164 automatically detected bounding boxes of 1,360 people; Market-1501 consists of 32,668 detections of 1,501 people. Both datasets cover 6 outdoor surveillance cameras with severely divergent and unknown viewpoints, illumination conditions, (self)-occlusion and background clutter.

Data Partitions - For each dataset, we randomly selected 1,000 identities D_{p1} (p stands for population) as the partition to perform *human-in-the-loop re-id* experiments. The remaining partition of people D_{p2} (360 on CUHK03, and 501 on Market-1501) were separated for evaluating the proposed model against state-of-the-art supervised re-id methods for *automated re-id* (see details in Sects. 4.1 and 4.2). To obtain statistical reliability, we generated 6 different trials $\{D_{p1}^i, D_{p2}^i\}_{i=1}^6$ for experiments and reported their averaged results.

Visual Features - The descriptor of [47] was adopted for person image representation. The feature vector (5,138 dimensions) was a concatenation of colour, HOG [48] and LBP [49] histograms extracted from horizontal rectangular stripes.

4.1 Evaluation on Human-in-the-Loop Person Re-id

We evaluated the performance of our HVIL model in *human-in-the-loop re-id* setting, along with detailed human feedback statistics analysis.

Human Feedback Protocol - Human feedback were collected on all 6 trials of D_{p1}^i partitions in 6 independent sessions by 2 volunteers as users, i.e. each trial for one different session. The human labour budget in each session was limited to the maximum of 300 probes. For testing, the standard single-shot re-id scheme [1] is considered, i.e. from the partition D_{p1}^i we selected randomly a single image per identity to form a 300 people/image probe set $\mathcal{P}^i$ and crucially, a much larger 1,000 people/image gallery set $\mathcal{G}^i$ ($\mathcal{P}^i$ and $\mathcal{G}^i$ are from different camera views). During each session, a user was asked to perform *human-in-the-loop re-id* on probes in probe set $\mathcal{P}^i$ against gallery set $\mathcal{G}^i$. For each probe, a *maximum* of 3 rounds of user interaction are allowed. We limited the users to verify only the top-50 in the rank list (5 % of 1,000 gallery set). During each interaction: (1) A user selects one gallery image as either *strong-negative*, *weak-negative*, or *true-match*; and (2) the system takes the feedback, updates the ranking function and returns the re-ordered ranking list, all in real-time (Sect. 2). The HVIL model was evaluated against six existing models for *human-in-the-loop re-id* as follows.

Competitors A - Three existing human-in-the-loop models were compared: (1) POP [15]: The current state-of-the-art *human-in-the-loop re-id* method based on Laplacian SVMs and graph label propagation; (2) Rocchio [50]: A probe vector modification model updates iteratively the probe's feature vector based on human feedback, widely used for image retrieval tasks [51]; (3) EMR [52]: A graph-based ranking model that optimises the ranking function by least square regression. For a fair comparison of all four human-in-the-loop models, the users were asked to verify the same probe and gallery data ($\mathcal{P}^i, \mathcal{G}^i$) with three-types of feedback given the ranking-list generated by each model.

Competitors B - In addition, three state-of-the-art conventional supervised person re-id models were also compared: (4) kLFDA [10], (5) XQDA [11], and (6) MLAPG [12]. These supervised re-id methods were trained using fully pre-labelled data in the separate partition D_{p2}^i (CUHK03: averagely 3,483 images of 360 identities; Market-1501: averagely 7,737 images of 501 identities) before being deployed to $\mathcal{P}^i$ (300) and $\mathcal{G}^i$ (1,000) for testing. Note, the underlying human labour effort for pre-labelling the training data to learn these supervised models was significantly greater – exhaustively searching 3,483 and 7,737 *true* matched images respectively for CUHK03 and Market-1501, than that required by the human-in-the-loop methods – between 300 to 900 *indicative* verification (similar, dissimilar, or true) given a maximum of 300 probes on both CUHK03 and Market-1501, so only 1/10th of and weaker user input than supervised models.

Implementation Details - For implementing the HVIL model (Sect. 2), the only hyper-parameter η (Eq. (5)) was set to 0.5 on both datasets. We found that HVIL is insensitive to η with a wide satisfiable range from 10^{-1} to 10^1. For POP, EMR, and Rocchio, we adopted the authors' recommended parameter settings as in [15,50]. For all methods above, we applied L_2 distance as the initial ranking function $f_0(\cdot)$ without loss of generalisation[2]. Note that for HVIL, once $f_0(\cdot)$ was initialised for only the very first probe, it was then optimised incrementally across

---

[2] No limitation on considering any distance/similarity metrics, either learned or not.

Table 1. Evaluating human-in-the-loop person re-id with CMC performances.

Dataset	CUHK03 [9] ($N_g = 1000$)				Market-1501 [35] ($N_g = 1000$)			
Rank (%)	1	50	100	200	1	50	100	200
L2	2.9	31.1	43.2	58.2	16.1	66.6	76.6	85.0
kLFDA [10]	5.9	47.3	60.1	75.0	21.8	85.8	**91.5**	**96.3**
XQDA [11]	3.7	40.2	53.6	68.5	18.3	75.1	83.5	91.1
MLAPG [12]	4.2	39.5	52.4	66.7	24.1	84.5	91.2	95.7
EMR [52]	46.0	47.3	51.3	60.0	53.3	64.3	75.7	85.0
Rocchio [50]	43.1	49.9	57.3	65.1	52.7	69.6	77.6	87.3
POP [15]	46.3	55.7	64.0	74.3	56.0	72.7	80.6	86.3
HVIL (ours)	**56.1**	**64.7**	**75.7**	**87.4**	**78.0**	**86.0**	90.3	93.4

different probes. In contrast, for POP and EMR and Rocchio, each probe had its own $f_0(\cdot)$ initialised as L_2 since the models are not cumulative across different probes. For supervised methods kLFDA, XQDA and MLAPG, the parameters were determined by cross-validation on D_{p2} with the authors' published codes. All models adopted the same feature descriptor [47].

Evaluation Metrics - Cumulative Match Characteristic (CMC) curves were adopted for performance evaluation. Specifically, we calculated the cumulative recognition rate at each rank position. Expected Rank (ER) is also used for evaluation, defined as the average rank of all true matches. For all human-in-the-loop models, we used the ranking result after the final interaction on each probe for CMC evaluation. The averaged results over all 6 trials are reported.

Comparative Results - The person re-id performance of all methods on $\mathcal{P}^i$ and $\mathcal{G}^i$ is shown in Table 1. First, it is evident that when the testing gallery size was enlarged from their standard settings (100 identities for CUHK03 and 751 for Market-1501) to 1,000 identities, *all* conventional supervised re-id models suffered severely, e.g. a 10-fold drop at Rank-1 for XQDA on CUHK03. More importantly, even though the supervised models were trained on a large-sized pre-labelled data in D_{p2} with an average of 3,483 cross-view images of 360 identities on CUHK03, and 7,737 images of 501 identities on Market-1501, their re-id performance was still significantly outperformed by *human-in-the-loop* models with 10-fold less human verification effort. This suggests the necessity of *human-in-the-loop* in real-world person re-id applications when the gallery population size becomes inevitably large. Moreover, to learn functionable supervised models, substantially more exhaustive pre-labelled training data are required. Such results suggest that *human-in-the-loop re-id* is a much better strategy for more efficiently exploiting human labour in real-world applications.

Second, HVIL improves significantly over the state-of-the-art human-in-the-loop model POP on Rank-1 score: from 46.3 % to 56.1 % on CUHK03 (~10 % in absolute terms) and from 56.0 % to 78.0 % on Market-1501 (over 20 % in

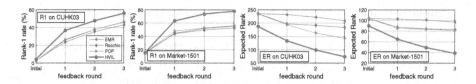

Fig. 2. Comparing Rank-1 score and Expected Rank (ER) on human feedback rounds.

absolute terms). HVIL's advantage continues over all ranks. This demonstrates compellingly the advantages of the HVIL model in cumulatively exploiting human verification feedback, whilst the existing human-in-the-loop models have no mechanisms for sharing human feedback knowledge among different probes.

Statistics Analysis on Human Verification - Figure 2 shows the comparisons of Rank-1 and Expected Rank (ER) on the 4 human-in-the-loop models over three verification feedback rounds. It is evident that the proposed HVIL model is more effective than the other three models in boosting Rank-1 scores and pushing up true matches' ranking orders. The reasons are: (1) Given a large gallery population with potentially complex manifold structure, it is difficult to perform accurately graph label propagation for graph-based methods like POP and EMR. (2) Unlike POP/EMR/Rocchio, the proposed HVIL model optimises on re-id ranking losses (Eq. (3)) specifically designed to maximise the three types of human verification feedback. (3) The HVIL model enables knowledge cumulation (Eq. (5)). This is evident in Fig. 2 where HVIL yields notably better (lower) Expected Ranks (ER), even for the initial ER before verification feedback takes place on a probe (due to benefiting cumulative effect from other probes). In contrast, other models do not improve initial ER on each probe due to the lack of a mechanism to cumulate experience.

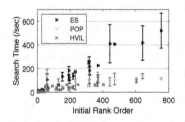

Fig. 3. Search time from different human-in-the-loop models on the same 25 randomly selected probes.

Table 2. Human verification effort vs. benefit. All measures are from averaging over all probes. ↓: lower better; ↑: higher better.

Dataset	CUHK03 [9]			Market-1501 [35]		
Method	HVIL	POP	ES	HVIL	POP	ES
Found-matches (%) ↑	56.1	46.3	100	78.0	56.0	100
Browsed-images ↓	32.9	42.1	234.1	19.5	38.3	108.7
Feedback ↓	2.1	2.3	-	1.6	1.9	-
Search-time (s) ↓	31.7	58.1	172.8	28.1	49.8	106.2

We further evaluated the human verification effort in relation to re-id performance benefit, collected from the human-in-the-loop re-id evaluation experiments reported above. We compared the HVIL model with the POP model and Exhaustive Search (ES) where a user performs exhaustive visual searching over

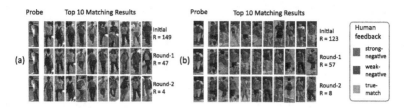

Fig. 4. HVIL re-id examples on CUHK03 (a) and Market-1501 (b). The ranks of true matches before user feedback are shown.

the whole gallery ranking list (1,000) until finding a true match. The averaged statistics over all 6 trials were compared in Table 2. It is evident that though ES is guaranteed to locate a true match for every probe if it existed, it is much more expensive than POP (3×) and HVIL (5×) in search time given a 1,000-sized gallery. This difference will increase further on larger galleries. Comparing HVIL and POP, it is evident that HVIL is both more cost-effective (less Search-time, Browsed-images and Feedback) and more accurate (more Found-matches).

To better understand model convergence given human feedback, we conducted a separate experiment to measure the search time by different human-in-the-loop models given the initial rank lists on 25 randomly selected probes verified by multiple users. This experiment was evaluated by 10 independent sessions with the same set of 25 probes provided. In each session, the users were required to find a true match for all 25 probes. Specifically, for HVIL and POP, if a true match was not identified after 3 (maximum) feedback, the users then performed an exhaustive searching until it was found. The search time statistics for all 25 probes are shown in Fig. 3, where a bar shows the variance between 10 different sessions. It is unsurprising that ES is the least efficient whilst HVIL is the quickest in finding a true match, i.e. the data points of HVIL are much lower in search time. Moreover, it is evident that HVIL yields much better initial ranks, i.e. the data points of HVIL are more centred towards the bottom-left corner. This further shows the benefit of cumulative learning in HVIL (Sect. 2.3). Figure 4 shows two visual examples of the HVIL model in action, where user feedback efficiently push true matches to top ranks within 2 rounds of interactions.

4.2 Evaluation on Automated Person Re-Id

The proposed RMEL model was evaluated for *automated person re-id* against both state-of-the-art supervised models and baseline ensemble models as follows.

Training/Testing Protocol - In each of the overall 6 trials, we employed the human verified true matches on D_{p1}^i (168 pairs on CUHK03 and 234 pairs on Market-1501 in average, as not all probe images found their true matches with a maximum of three feedback) to learn the weights for constructing a strong ensemble model using all the verified weak models $\{M_j\}_{j=1}^{\tau}$ collected from our previous experiments on *human-in-the-loop re-id*. The strong ensemble model was then deployed for testing on the separate partition D_{p2}^i with the gallery

Table 3. Evaluating automated person re-id with CMC performances.

Dataset	CUHK03 [9] ($N_g = 360$)				Market-1501 [35] ($N_g = 501$)				VIPeR ($N_g = 316$)			
Rank (%)	1	5	10	20	1	5	10	20	1	5	10	20
L2	4.6	14.0	21.1	28.7	23.0	44.0	55.1	65.7	14.7	28.0	40.6	52.1
kLFDA [10]	6.2	19.0	28.3	39.1	29.1	58.9	71.2	82.2	32.3	65.8	79.7	90.9
XQDA [11]	5.3	14.2	21.1	30.0	28.7	54.5	65.6	75.3	40.0	68.1	80.5	91.1
MLAPG [12]	5.3	15.2	23.5	33.9	25.2	51.4	65.3	77.4	40.7	69.9	82.3	**92.4**
HVIL - M_{avg}	5.8	17.6	26.3	36.3	27.3	56.7	68.2	80.1	21.8	51.0	66.3	82.4
HVIL - M_τ	6.5	19.0	27.4	37.6	31.6	60.1	72.7	**83.5**	34.7	63.2	78.0	90.3
HVIL - RMEL	**9.3**	**20.7**	**29.0**	**39.5**	**33.8**	**61.0**	**73.6**	**83.5**	**42.4**	**72.6**	**83.0**	90.4

size of 360 and 501 for CUHK03 and Market-1501 respectively. For performance evaluation, we adopted the standard single-shot test setting, i.e. randomly sampling 360 cross-camera person image pairs from CUHK03 and 501 pairs from Market-1501 on $\{D_{p2}^i\}_{i=1}^6$ to construct the test gallery and probe sets over six trials. The averaged CMC performance over all trials was reported.

Competitors A - Three state-of-the-art supervised re-id models are compared: kLFDA [10], XQDA [11], and MLAPG [12] were trained using 300 ground-truth labelled data from $\mathcal{P}^i$ (300) and $\mathcal{G}^i$ (1,000) of D_{p1}^i, for both CUHK03 and Market-1501. The trained models were tested on the separate partition D_{p2}^i with same testing protocol as above.

Competitors B - For fully evaluating the effect of the HVIL-RMEL model, two more ensemble baseline models are compared: (1) HVIL - M_τ: The incrementally optimised re-id model M_τ obtained by HVIL from the last probe image at time τ during the *human-in-the-loop* process. (2) HVIL - M_{avg}: An naive approach to ensemble weak models, that is, simply taking an average weighting of all weak models $\{M_j\}_{j=1}^\tau$ as the ensemble re-id model.

Results on CUHK03 and Market-1501 - Table 3 reports the result. For CUHK03, there is insufficient labelled data for all camera pairs during training, given only one pair of randomly selected single-shot images per identity. All models including HVIL-RMEL generated poor re-id performances (Rank-1 < 10 %), much less than state-of-the-art reported in the literature. For Market-1501, a similar problem exists although less pronounced. Note, the results in Table 3 are based on a single-shot test setting. This is a much harder problem than the multi-shot test setting [35] where on average 14.8 true matches exist in the gallery for each probe. When HVIL-RMEL was evaluated under the same multi-shot setting on Market-1501, it yields 53.5 %, 83.0 %, 89.0 %, 94.1 % for Rank-1/5/10/20 respectively, significantly outperforms [35]. Given the experimental results above, it is evident that: Due to (1) a much larger unlabelled test gallery population than the labelled training set, (2) a lack of sufficient multi-shot training/testing data in many camera pairs, *human-in-the-loop* approach to re-id is not only desirable, but essential for re-id in real world applications.

Nevertheless, for *automated person re-id*, the proposed HVIL-RMEL still achieves the best performance among all models with a Rank-1 of 9.3 % on CUHK03 and 33.8 % on Market-1501. More importantly, even though less true-match data (168 pairs for CUHK03 and 234 pairs for Market-1501) were used to learn the ensemble weighting for the RMEL model as compared to the ground-truth data (300 pairs for both benchmarks) used to train kLFDA, XQDA and MLAPG, it is evident that the human verification feedback process yields more discriminative information for optimising probe re-id directly in the gallery population, resulting in a more optimal ensemble model. It is also evident that naively taking an average ensemble model (HVIL - M_{avg}) gives even poorer performance than the cumulatively learned single model (HVIL - M_τ).

Results on VIPeR - To compare HVIL-RMEL in a more comparable context defined in the literature on *automated person re-id*, we tested the HVIL-RMEL model on the VIPeR [13] benchmark under the exact setting of the established protocol: splitting the 632 identities into $50-50$ % partitions for training and testing sets. For obtaining weak re-id models, we simulated HVIL feedback update by simply giving the ground-true matching pairs instead of weak/strong-negatives (Eq. (9)); therefore each weak model was obtained by a true-match, using the same information as training a conventional supervised model. The last/right panel of Table 3 compares the performance of such a HVIL-RMEL model against the published results of kLFDA, XQDA and MLAPG[3]. It is evident that the proposed model yields state-of-the-art performance under the same conventional re-id settings, with Rank-1 score of 42.4 %, slightly better, by 2.4 % and 1.7 % respectively, than the current state-of-the-art XQDA and MLAPG.

5   Conclusions

We formulated a novel approach to human-in-the-loop person re-id by introducing a Human Verification Incremental Learning (HVIL) model, designed to overcome two unrealistic assumptions adopted by existing re-id models that prevent them to be scalable to real world applications. In particular, the proposed HVIL model avoids the need for collecting off-line pre-labelled training data and is scalable to re-id tasks in large gallery sizes. The advantage of HVIL over other human-in-the-loop models is its ability to learn cumulatively from human feedback on more probe images when available. We further developed a regularised metric ensemble learning (RMEL) method to explore HVIL for automated re-id tasks when human feedback is unavailable. Extensive comparisons on the CUHK03 [9] and the Market-1501 [35] benchmarks show the potentials of the proposed HVIL-RMEL model for real-world re-id deployments.

---

[3] A different 26,960-dim LOMO feature [11] were used for the published XQDA and MLAPG results [11,12] shown in Table 3. They were worsened using the 5,138-dim feature [47] adopted in our experiments, not shown here due to space limitation.

References

1. Gong, S., Cristani, M., Yan, S., Loy, C.C.: Person Re-identification, vol. 1. Springer, London (2014)
2. Mignon, A., Jurie, F.: PCCA: a new approach for distance learning from sparse pairwise constraints. In: IEEE Conference on Computer Vision and Pattern Recognition, Providence, Rhode Island, United States, June 2012
3. Koestinger, M., Hirzer, M., Wohlhart, P., Roth, P.M., Bischof, H.: Large scale metric learning from equivalence constraints. In: IEEE Conference on Computer Vision and Pattern Recognition, Providence, Rhode Island, United States, June 2012
4. Zheng, W.S., Gong, S., Xiang, T.: Re-identification by relative distance comparison. IEEE Trans. Pattern Anal. Mach. Intell. **35**, 653–668 (2013)
5. Pedagadi, S., Orwell, J., Velastin, S.A., Boghossian, B.A.: Local fisher discriminant analysis for pedestrian re-identification. In: IEEE Conference on Computer Vision and Pattern Recognition, Portland, Oregon, United States, June 2013
6. Zhao, R., Ouyang, W., Wang, X.: Learning mid-level filters for person re-identification. In: IEEE Conference on Computer Vision and Pattern Recognition, Columbus, Ohio, United States, June 2014
7. Wang, T., Gong, S., Zhu, X., Wang, S.: Person re-identification by video ranking. In: European Conference on Computer Vision, Zurich, Switzerland, September 2014
8. Wang, T., Gong, S., Zhu, X., Wang, S.: Person re-identification by discriminative selection in video ranking. IEEE Trans. Pattern Anal. Mach, Intell (2016). doi:10.1109/TPAMI.2016.2522418. in press
9. Li, W., Zhao, R., Xiao, T., Wang, X.: DeepReID: deep filter pairing neural network for person re-identification. In: IEEE Conference on Computer Vision and Pattern Recognition, Columbus, Ohio, United States, June 2014
10. Xiong, F., Gou, M., Camps, O., Sznaier, M.: Person re-identification using kernel-based metric learning methods. In: European Conference on Computer Vision, Zurich, Switzerland, September 2014
11. Liao, S., Hu, Y., Zhu, X., Li, S.Z.: Person re-identification by local maximal occurrence representation and metric learning. In: IEEE Conference on Computer Vision and Pattern Recognition, Boston, Massachusetts, United States, June 2015, pp. 2197–2206 (2015)
12. Liao, S., Li, S.Z.: Efficient PSD constrained asymmetric metric learning for person re-identification. In: IEEE International Conference on Computer Vision, December 2015
13. Gray, D., Brennan, S., Tao, H.: Evaluating appearance models for recognition, reacquisition and tracking. In: IEEE International Workshop on Performance Evaluation for Tracking and Surveillance (2007)
14. Zheng, W.S., Gong, S., Xiang, T.: Associating groups of people. In: British Machine Vision Conference (2009)
15. Liu, C., Loy, C.C., Gong, S., Wang, G.: Pop: person re-identification post-rank optimisation. In: IEEE International Conference on Computer Vision, Sydney, Australia, December 2013
16. Schapire, R.E.: The strength of weak learnability. Mach. Learn. **5**(2), 197–227 (1990)
17. Amit, Y., Geman, D.: Shape quantization and recognition with randomized trees. Neural Comput. **9**(7), 1545–1588 (1997)

18. Gong, S., Cristani, M., Chen, C.L., Hospedales, T.M.: The re-identification challenge. In: Gong, S., Cristani, M., Yan, S., Loy, C.C. (eds.) Person Re-Identification. Springer, London (2014)
19. Ding, S., Lin, L., Wang, G., Chao, H.: Deep feature learning with relative distance comparison for person re-identification. Pattern Recogn. **48**, 2993–3003 (2015)
20. Paisitkriangkrai, S., Shen, C., van den Hengel, A.: Learning to rank in person re-identification with metric ensembles. In: IEEE Conference on Computer Vision and Pattern Recognition, pp. 1846–1855 (2015)
21. Ustinova, E., Ganin, Y., Lempitsky, V.: Multiregion bilinear convolutional neural networks for person re-identification. arXiv preprint arXiv:1512.05300 (2015)
22. Shi, H., Zhu, X., Liao, S., Lei, Z., Yang, Y., Li, S.Z.: Constrained deep metric learning for person re-identification. arXiv preprint arXiv:1511.07545 (2015)
23. Ahmed, E., Jones, M.J., Marks, T.K.: An improved deep learning architecture for person re-identification. In: CVPR, pp. 3908–3916. IEEE (2015)
24. Liu, X., Song, M., Tao, D., Zhou, X., Chen, C., Bu, J.: Semi-supervised coupled dictionary learning for person re-identification. In: IEEE Conference on Computer Vision and Pattern Recognition, Columbus, Ohio, United States, June 2014
25. Kodirov, E., Xiang, T., Gong, S.: Dictionary learning with iterative Laplacian regularisation for unsupervised person re-identification. In: British Machine Vision Conference, Swansea, United Kingdom, September 2015
26. Farenzena, M., Bazzani, L., Perina, A., Murino, V., Cristani, M.: Person re-identification by symmetry-driven accumulation of local features. In: IEEE Conference on Computer Vision and Pattern Recognition, San Francisco, California, United States, June 2010
27. Zhao, R., Ouyang, W., Wang, X.: Unsupervised salience learning for person re-identification. In: IEEE Conference on Computer Vision and Pattern Recognition, Portland, Oregon, United States, June 2013
28. Wang, H., Gong, S., Xiang, T.: Unsupervised learning of generative topic saliency for person re-identification. In: British Machine Vision Conference, Nottingham, United Kingdom, September 2014
29. Layne, R., Hospedales, T.M., Gong, S.: Domain transfer for person re-identification. In: Workshop of ACM International Conference on Multimedia, Barcelona, Catalunya, Spain, October 2013
30. Ma, A.J., Yuen, P.C., Li, J.: Domain transfer support vector ranking for person re-identification without target camera label information. In: IEEE International Conference on Computer Vision, Sydney, Australia, December 2013
31. Wang, X., Zheng, W.S., Li, X., Zhang, J.: Cross-scenario transfer person re-identification. IEEE Trans. Circ. Syst. Video Technol. **PP**(99), 1447–1460 (2015)
32. Ma, A.J., Li, J., Yuen, P.C., Li, P.: Cross-domain person reidentification using domain adaptation ranking svms. IEEE Trans. Image Process. **24**(5), 1599–1613 (2015)
33. Das, A., Panda, R., Roy-Chowdhury, A.: Active image pair selection for continuous person re-identification. In: IEEE International Conference on Image Processing, Quebec, Canada, September 2015
34. Hirzer, M., Beleznai, C., Roth, P.M., Bischof, H.: Person re-identification by descriptive and discriminative classification. In: Heyden, A., Kahl, F. (eds.) SCIA 2011. LNCS, vol. 6688, pp. 91–102. Springer, Heidelberg (2011). doi:10.1007/978-3-642-21227-7_9
35. Zheng, L., Shen, L., Tian, L., Wang, S., Wang, J., Tian, Q.: Scalable person re-identification: a benchmark. In: Proceedings of the IEEE International Conference on Computer Vision, pp. 1116–1124 (2015)

36. Lim, D., Lanckriet, G.: Efficient learning of mahalanobis metrics for ranking. In: Jebara, T., Xing, E.P. (eds.) International Conference on Machine Learning, pp. 1980–1988 (2014)
37. Weston, J., Bengio, S., Usunier, N.: Large scale image annotation: Learning to rank with joint word-image embeddings. In: European Conference of Machine Learning (2010)
38. Usunier, N., Buffoni, D., Gallinari, P.: Ranking with ordered weighted pairwise classification. In: Proceedings of the 26th Annual International Conference on Machine Learning, ICML 2009, pp. 1057–1064. ACM, New York (2009)
39. Chechik, G., Sharma, V., Shalit, U., Bengio, S.: Large scale online learning of image similarity through ranking. J. Mach. Learn. Res. **11**, 1109–1135 (2010)
40. Bottou, L.: Large-scale machine learning with stochastic gradient descent. In: Lechevallier, Y., Saporta, G. (eds.) Proceedings of COMPSTAT 2010, pp. 177–186. Springer, Heidelberg (2010)
41. Tsuda, K., Rätsch, G., Warmuth, M.K.: Matrix exponentiated gradient updates for on-line learning and bregman projection. J. Mach. Learn. Res. **6**, 995–1018 (2005)
42. Higham, N.J.: Matrix nearness problems and applications. Department of Mathematics, University of Manchester (1988)
43. Kivinen, J., Warmuth, M.K.: Exponentiated gradient versus gradient descent for linear predictors. Inf. Comput. **132**, 1–63 (1997)
44. Jain, P., Kulis, B., Dhillon, I.S., Grauman, K.: Online metric learning and fast similarity search. In: Advances in Neural Information Processing Systems, Vancouver, British Columbia, Canada, December 2009, pp. 761–768 (2009)
45. Grant, M., Boyd, S.: CVX: Matlab software for disciplined convex programming, version 2.1. http://cvxr.com/cvx
46. Boyd, S., Vandenberghe, L.: Convex Optimization. Cambridge University Press, New York, NY, USA (2004)
47. Lisanti, G., Masi, I., Del Bimbo, A.: Matching people across camera views using kernel canonical correlation analysis. In: ACM International Conference on Distributed Smart Cameras, Venice, Italy, November 2014
48. Wang, X., Han, T.X., Yan, S.: An HOG-LBP human detector with partial occlusion handling. In: IEEE International Conference on Computer Vision, Kyoto, Japan, September 2009
49. Ahonen, T., Hadid, A., Pietikainen, M.: Face description with local binary patterns: application to face recognition. IEEE Trans. Pattern Anal. Mach. Intell. **28**, 2037–2041 (2006)
50. Lin, W.C., Chen, Z.Y., Ke, S.W., Tsai, C.F., Lin, W.Y.: The effect of low-level image features on pseudo relevance feedback. Neurocomputing **166**, 26–37 (2015)
51. Datta, R., Joshi, D., Li, J., Wang, J.Z.: Image retrieval: Ideas, influences, and trends of the new age. ACM Comput. Surv. **40**, 5:1–5:60 (2008)
52. Xu, B., Bu, J., Chen, C., Cai, D., He, X., Liu, W., Luo, J.: Efficient manifold ranking for image retrieval. In: ACM SIGIR Conference on Research and Development in Information Retrieval, Beijing, China, July 2011, pp. 525–534 (2011)

Real-Time Monocular Segmentation and Pose Tracking of Multiple Objects

Henning Tjaden[1]([✉]), Ulrich Schwanecke[1], and Elmar Schömer[2]

[1] Computer Science Department,
RheinMain University of Applied Sciences, Wiesbaden, Germany
{henning.tjaden,ulrich.schwanecke}@hs-rm.de
[2] Institute of Computer Science,
Johannes Gutenberg University Mainz, Mainz, Germany
schoemer@uni-mainz.de

Abstract. We present a real-time system capable of segmenting multiple 3D objects and tracking their pose using a single RGB camera, based on prior shape knowledge. The proposed method uses twist-coordinates for pose parametrization and a pixel-wise second-order optimization approach which lead to major improvements in terms of tracking robustness, especially in cases of fast motion and scale changes, compared to previous region-based approaches. Our implementation runs at about 50–100 Hz on a commodity laptop when tracking a single object without relying on GPGPU computations. We compare our method to the current state of the art in various experiments involving challenging motion sequences and different complex objects.

Keywords: Tracking · Segmentation · Real-time · Monocular · Pose estimation · Model-based · Shape knowledge

1 Introduction

Tracking the 3D motion of a rigid object from its 2D projections into image sequences of a single camera is one of the main research areas in computer vision. This involves estimating the pose, i.e. the 3D translation and rotation, of the object relative to the camera in each image. The fields of application for visual 3D object tracking are numerous, such as visual servoing of robots, medical navigation and visualization, sports therapy, augmented reality systems and human computer interaction. Many different solutions to this problem have been developed over the years and are now part of a variety of practical applications. For a survey of monocular 3D tracking of rigid objects see e.g. [1].

Recently so-called region-based pose estimation methods have emerged, which are mainly based on statistical level-set segmentation approaches [2].

Electronic supplementary material The online version of this chapter (doi:10. 1007/978-3-319-46493-0_26) contains supplementary material, which is available to authorized users.

B. Leibe et al. (Eds.): ECCV 2016, Part IV, LNCS 9908, pp. 423–438, 2016.
DOI: 10.1007/978-3-319-46493-0_26

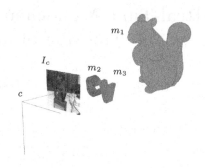

Fig. 1. Example of region-based 3D tracking of three different objects with partial occlusions. All poses are determined by the proposed method within about 30 ms. Left: Augmented reality view of the scene, where the rendered models yield a segmentation of the objects in the image. Right: 3D overview of the scene.

These do not require any kind of artificial marker or other augmentation of the object of interest. They only rely on a 3D model of the object. Therefore, they fall into the category of model-based pose estimation methods. These are very attractive for application scenarios where it is undesirable or even impossible to modify the objects. For example in case of sports therapy, where ergonomics might be affected or for tracking objects in public environments such as cars or planes that cannot be modified beforehand.

Some model-based approaches use edge or point features associated with the surface model of the 3D object for pose estimation [3–6]. The main disadvantages of these methods are that they struggle with motion blur and are prone to local minima especially with cluttered backgrounds. Using point-based features also requires the objects' surfaces to be sufficiently textured, which significantly limits the variety of suitable objects.

In contrast to feature-based approaches, region-based methods minimize the discrepancy between silhouettes. Thereby, the object's contour is estimated and its 3D pose is determined in an interleaved manner. Here the model is used to generate synthetic projections of the object's silhouette under a currently estimated pose. For pose estimation the similarity between this silhouette and the silhouette stemming from the currently segmented object region in the real image is maximized by varying the pose parameters. Vice versa, the synthetic silhouette which is rendered using an estimated pose is assumed to provide a ground truth segmentation for the current image that is used in order to update the foreground and background image segmentation model (Fig. 1).

1.1 Related Work

Due to the large amount of literature about optical pose estimation and tracking, in the following we focus on the pose optimization strategies and real-time capabilities of region-based methods. One class of object pose estimation approaches that couple image segmentation and pose estimation is based on explicit point correspondences between the segmented and the projected contour of the object [7–9]. These correspondences are used to set up a linear system describing the spatial distance between the projection rays of the points on the segmented contour and the corresponding 3D object points that belong to the projected contour with respect to the pose parameters. The linear system is then solved iteratively by recalculating the point correspondences after each iteration. Over the years, region-based methods involving this point-based pose optimization procedure, which can be seen as an ICP (iterative closest points) algorithm, have been improved [10,11] and shown to produce promising results in many challenging scenarios. Unfortunately, the overall computations take several seconds per frame. In [8] an optical flow approach matching the contours by minimizing the pixel-wise quadratic difference between their level-set functions was introduced which determines the object's pose with 13 frames per second for small images.

In [12] the authors present PWP3D, the first region-based approach that achieved real-time frame rates (20–25 Hz) using GPUs by solving the pose estimation problem in a pixel-wise minimization scheme. The presented approach is similar to the variational approach suggested in [13] but uses level-set functions instead of separately integrating over the foreground and background region to simplify computations and make it real-time capable. More recently, a further improved version of PWP3D was presented, that runs with more than 30 Hz on a mobile phone [14]. The performance increase was mainly due to an hierarchical approach, an approximation of the level set transform and its derivatives, as well as an estimation of the rotation using a gyroscope which is visually corrected for drift based on a single gradient descent step every tenth frame. The authors state that solving the problem in a fully analytical manner without any approximations is only possible with about 20–25 Hz, even when using GPUs.

Other approaches building upon PWP3D have been proposed in [15,16]. They mainly focus on improving the segmentation part but also suggest different strategies for replacing the simple gradient descent approach. In [15] the Levenberg-Marquardt algorithm is suggested but neither elaborately illustrated nor evaluated with regard to runtime. Gradient descent with two different step sizes, one for rotation and one for translation, is used in [16]. The two gradients are normalized to unit rotation and unit pixel size and a 2D search for the optimal step sizes is conducted. The authors' implementation is much slower than PWP3D but they predict that their algorithm could be further optimized in order to achieve similar runtimes to PWP3D. Both of these methods as well as [13,14] use a decoupled rotation and translation vector for pose parametrization.

1.2 Motivation

To our best knowledge PWP3D is still the state of the art monocular region-based pose estimation approach achieving fairly high frame rates. Therefore, we built upon PWP3D and improved it with regard to computation time and tracking robustness. We identified two main areas of potential improvement, image segmentation and pose optimization strategy. Issues resulting from the global foreground and background statistics used for image segmentation have recently been addressed by [15,16]. As the suggested improvements are not yet real-time capable, we are not using them in our current implementation. In fact, our work disregards the image segmentation part and focusses on improving the pose optimization part to improve the general performance and robustness.

The PWP3D implementation provided by the authors uses a simple gradient descent with predefined, decreasing step sizes in order to minimize the defined energy function. The number of iterations and the choice of three different step sizes (one each for rotation, translation along the optical axis and translation within the camera's image plane) depend on the model complexity and the size of the projected silhouette. Since these parameters have to be adapted at least once for each new object the algorithm is difficult to configure. In general this problem can not be solved by simply using smaller step sizes as real-time frame rates are only achieved with about eight iterations per frame and the number of necessary gradient descent iterations increases if the step sizes decrease. Although others have developed strategies for improving the simple gradient descent in their works where PWP3D was used, to our knowledge the problem has not yet been adequately investigated or improved regarding tracking robustness and runtime reduction for real-time scenarios.

1.3   Contributions

This paper includes three main contributions. First, we present a novel pixel-wise optimization strategy based on a Gauß-Newton-like algorithm using linearized twists for pose parametrization. Our approach has significantly improved convergence properties, especially for rotational motion, as we demonstrate in our experiments. The number of iterations and the common step size can thus be adjusted regardless of the model complexity and its distance to the camera. Second, we describe an implementation that uses the GPU only for rendering purposes, performing all other computations on the CPU and achieving frame rates of about 50–100 Hz when tracking a single object on a commodity laptop. Finally, we present real-time multiple object tracking using region-based pose estimation.

The rest of the paper is structured as follows: Sect. 2 gives an overview of the used mathematical concepts. Section 3 details our implementation and runtime analysis. A comparison of our approach and previous state of the art based on various experiments is given in Sect. 4, whereas Sect. 5 concludes with a brief summary and potential future work.

2   Method

In the following we give a condensed overview of the mathematical concepts and notations used throughout this paper. A camera color image is denoted by $I_c :$ $\Omega \to \mathbb{R}^3$ where $\Omega \subset \mathbb{R}^2$ is the image domain (see Fig. 1). The color of each pixel $\mathbf{x}_c := (x_c, y_c)^\top \in \Omega$ is given by $\mathbf{y} = I_c(\mathbf{x}_c)$. Each object is represented by a dense surface model (triangle mesh) consisting of 3D points $\mathbf{X}_m^i := (X_m^i, Y_m^i, Z_m^i)^\top \in \mathbb{R}^3$, with $i = 1, \ldots, N$ where N is the number of objects. The pose of a model m_i with respect to the camera coordinate frame c is given by

$$T_{cm}^i = \begin{bmatrix} R_{cm}^i & \mathbf{t}_{cm}^i \\ \mathbf{0}_{1\times3} & 1 \end{bmatrix} \in \mathbb{SE}(3), \tag{1}$$

describing the rigid transformation between surface points $\mathbf{X}_m^i$ in the model's reference frame and $\mathbf{X}_c^i$ in the camera's reference frame by $\tilde{\mathbf{X}}_c^i = T_{cm}^i \tilde{\mathbf{X}}_m^i$. The tilde denotes the corresponding homogenous representation of a vector $\tilde{\mathbf{X}} = (X, Y, Z, W)^\top$, with $W = 1$. $R_{cm}^i \in \mathbb{SO}(3)$ denotes the model's orientation and $\mathbf{t}_{cm}^i \in \mathbb{R}^3$ the model's origin relative to the camera's reference frame.

For pose optimization we represent the rigid body motion that occurred between two consecutive frames using twists

$$\theta\hat{\xi} = \theta \begin{bmatrix} \hat{\mathbf{w}} & \mathbf{v} \\ \mathbf{0}_{1\times3} & 0 \end{bmatrix} \in \mathfrak{se}(3), \text{ with } \hat{\mathbf{w}} = \begin{bmatrix} 0 & -\omega_3 & \omega_2 \\ \omega_3 & 0 & -\omega_1 \\ -\omega_2 & \omega_1 & 0 \end{bmatrix} \in \mathfrak{so}(3), \tag{2}$$

which are parametrized by the vector $\theta\xi = \theta \left(\omega_1, \omega_2, \omega_3, v_1, v_2, v_2\right)^\top \in \mathbb{R}^6$, with $\mathbf{w} = (w_1, w_2, w_3)^\top$, $\|\mathbf{w}\|_2 = 1$, where θ is a one-parametric coupling of the rotation and translation parameters describing the motion along a screw. This coupling qualifies twist coordinates as the natural choice for gradient-based pose optimization methods. For more information on the *Lie group* $\mathbb{SE}(3)$ and the corresponding *Lie algebra* $\mathfrak{se}(3)$ see [17]. Each twist can be transformed to its corresponding group element via the exponential map

$$exp(\theta\hat{\xi}) = \begin{bmatrix} exp(\theta\hat{\mathbf{w}}) \ (\mathbb{I}_{3\times3} - exp(\theta\hat{\mathbf{w}}))\hat{\mathbf{w}}\mathbf{v} + \mathbf{w}\mathbf{w}^\top \mathbf{v}\theta \\ \mathbf{0}_{1\times3} & 1 \end{bmatrix} \in \mathbb{SE}(3), \tag{3}$$

where $exp(\theta\hat{\mathbf{w}})$ can be computed according to Rodrigues's formula as

$$exp(\theta\hat{\mathbf{w}}) = \mathbb{I}_{3\times3} + sin(\theta)\hat{\mathbf{w}} + (1 - cos(\theta))\hat{\mathbf{w}}^2. \tag{4}$$

Our camera is pre-calibrated and its intrinsic matrix

$$K = \begin{bmatrix} f_x & 0 & c_x \\ 0 & f_y & c_y \\ 0 & 0 & 1 \end{bmatrix} \tag{5}$$

is assumed to be fixed. All images are undistorted removing non-linear distortion and allowing the perspective projection of a 3D surface point to a 2D image point to be described by $\mathbf{x}_c = \pi(K(T_{cm}\tilde{\mathbf{X}}_m)_{3\times1})$, with $\pi(\mathbf{X}) = (X/Z, Y/Z)^\top$.

Our method builds upon PWP3D where the pixel-wise posterior probability of a projected contour, given the current camera image is described by

$$P(\Phi^i|I) = \prod_{\mathbf{x}_c \in \Omega} \left(H_e(\Phi^i(\mathbf{x}_c))P_f^i(\mathbf{y}) + (1 - H_e(\Phi^i(\mathbf{x}_c)))P_b^i(\mathbf{y}) \right). \tag{6}$$

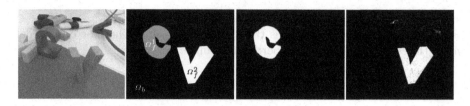

Fig. 2. Pixel-wise posterior image segmentation. From left to right: Camera image of two 3D objects to be segmented: A red C and a green V. Silhouettes of corresponding surface models drawn in a grey value corresponding to its index. Per pixel difference $P_f^1(\mathbf{y}) - P_b^1(\mathbf{y})$ and $P_f^2(\mathbf{y}) - P_b^2(\mathbf{y})$ respectively, visualizing the resulting segmentation (Color figure online)

$P_f^i(\mathbf{y})$ and $P_b^i(\mathbf{y})$ represent the per object foreground and background region membership probability of each pixel's color, as illustrated in Sect. 2.1. H_e is the smoothed Heaviside step function

$$H_e(x) = \frac{1}{\pi}\left(-\operatorname{atan}(b \cdot x) + \frac{\pi}{2}\right),\tag{7}$$

with b determining its reach. Φ^i is the level-set embedding of each object's contour defined by its pose as described in Sect. 2.2. Assuming pixel-wise independency and by taking the negative log of $P(\Phi|I)$, this results in the energy

$$E^i = -\sum_{\mathbf{x}_c \in \Omega} \log\left(H_e(\Phi^i(\mathbf{x}_c))P_f^i(\mathbf{y}) + (1 - H_e(\Phi^i(\mathbf{x}_c)))P_b^i(\mathbf{y})\right),\tag{8}$$

to be minimized with respect to the respective object's pose. Our approach to efficiently perform this minimization is described in Sect. 2.3.

2.1   Pixel-Wise Posterior Object Segmentation

We are basically using the same image segmentation method as PWP3D, based on the pixel-wise posteriors presented in [18] (see Fig. 2). Assuming that the pose of each object is known for the current image, their 3D models are used to render synthetic silhouettes splitting the image domain in multiple foreground regions Ω_f^i and a common background region Ω_b. Thus the individual background regions are given by $\Omega_b^i = \Omega \setminus \Omega_f^i$. These regions are used to determine foreground and background RGB color histograms with 32 bins per channel modelling the foreground and background posteriors $P_f^i(\mathbf{y})$ and $P_b^i(\mathbf{y})$ for each color. We are also using PWP3D's temporal consistency strategy for histogram updating.

2.2   Level-Set Pose Embedding

Each object projects to a silhouette region Ω_f^i, that depends on the object's pose and is bounded by its 2D contour $\mathbf{C}^i$ (see Fig. 3). A level-set function Φ

implicitly defines such a closed curve as its zero level. Here Euclidian signed distance transforms are used to define this level-set embedding as

$$\Phi^i(\mathbf{x}_c) = \begin{cases} -d(\mathbf{x}_c, \mathbf{C}^i) & \forall \mathbf{x}_c \in \Omega^i_f \\ d(\mathbf{x}_c, \mathbf{C}^i) & \forall \mathbf{x}_c \in \Omega^i_b \end{cases}, \quad \text{with} \quad d(\mathbf{x}_c, \mathbf{C}) = \min_{\mathbf{c} \in \mathbf{C}} |\mathbf{c} - \mathbf{x}_c|, \quad (9)$$

where each pixel is mapped to the shortest distance between its location and the contour (see Fig. 3). Such signed distance transforms can be efficiently computed with the method presented in [19]. By a simple extension, this algorithm can also be used to compute a mapping of each pixel to the corresponding location of its closest contour pixel, which is needed during pose optimization, as explained in the following section.

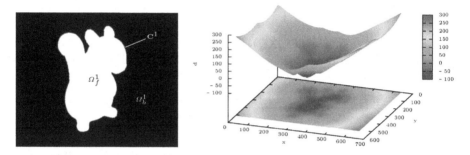

Fig. 3. An illustration of the level-set pose embedding $\Phi(\mathbf{x}_c)$ applied to a squirrel figurine. Left: The projected silhouette with indicated contour $\mathbf{C}^1$ as well as inner region Ω^1_f and outer region Ω^1_b. Right: A combined 2D/3D plot of the signed distance transform of $\mathbf{C}^1$

2.3 Iterative Pose Optimization

In contrast to the originally applied gradient descent approach, we optimize the energy functional (Eq. 8) with respect to the pose parameters based on an iterative Gauß-Newton-like method. For nonlinear optimization methods the number of required gradient calculations and function evaluations has the greatest impact on runtime. In our situation rendering a silhouette and computing its signed distance transform are quite costly operations making a function evaluation similarly computationally demanding as calculating its gradient. We therefore neglected optimization methods using any kind of line-search strategy to determine step sizes, such as conjugate gradients, DFP, BFGS or Levenberg-Marquardt [20]. Calculating the Hessian matrix in order to determine the step size can be done with an acceptable increase of runtime, but our experiments proved it to be numerically unstable, as commonly reported in literature.

We instead selected an iterative Gauß-Newton-like optimization strategy, where the Hessian is approximated from first order derivatives. Thereby, the gradient of the energy functional is given by

$$\frac{\partial E^i(\theta\xi)}{\partial\theta\xi} = -\sum_{\mathbf{x}_c\in\Omega}\frac{P_f(\mathbf{y})-P_b(\mathbf{y})}{H_e(\Phi^i(\mathbf{x}_c,\theta\xi))(P_f(\mathbf{y})-P_b(\mathbf{y}))+P_b(\mathbf{y})}\delta_e\frac{\partial\Phi^i(\mathbf{x}_c,\theta\xi)}{\partial\theta\xi} \quad (10)$$

where δ_e is the smoothed Dirac delta function corresponding to H_e and the derivatives of the signed distance function with respect to twist coordinates are

$$\frac{\partial\Phi^i(\mathbf{x}_c,\theta\xi)}{\partial\theta\xi} = \frac{\partial\Phi^i}{\partial\mathbf{x}_c}\frac{\partial\pi}{\partial K(exp(\theta\hat{\xi})T^i_{cm}\tilde{\mathbf{X}}^i_m)_{3\times1}}\frac{\partial K(exp(\theta\hat{\xi})T^i_{cm}\tilde{\mathbf{X}}^i_m)_{3\times1}}{\partial\theta\xi}. \quad (11)$$

Assuming small motion it holds $exp(\theta\hat{\xi})\approx\mathbb{I}_{4\times4}+\theta\hat{\xi}$ and therefore we get

$$\frac{\partial\Phi^i(\mathbf{x}_c,\theta\xi_0)}{\partial\theta\xi} = \left[\frac{\partial\Phi^i}{\partial x_c},\frac{\partial\Phi^i}{\partial y_c}\right]\begin{bmatrix}\frac{f_x}{Z^i_c} & 0 & -\frac{X^i_c f_x}{(Z^i_c)^2} \\ 0 & \frac{f_y}{Z^i_c} & -\frac{Y^i_c f_y}{(Z^i_c)^2}\end{bmatrix}\begin{bmatrix}0 & Z^i_c & -Y^i_c & 1 & 0 & 0 \\ -Z^i_c & 0 & X^i_c & 0 & 1 & 0 \\ Y^i_c & -X^i_c & 0 & 0 & 0 & 1\end{bmatrix}, \quad (12)$$

with $\mathbf{X}^i_c = (X^i_c, Y^i_c, Z^i_c)^\top = (T^i_{cm}\tilde{\mathbf{X}}^i_m)_{3\times1}$. For a pixel $\mathbf{x}_c\in\Omega^i_b$, $\mathbf{X}_c$ is the surface point in the camera's frame of reference that projects to its closest contour pixel. The first-order derivatives of Φ^i are simply calculated as central differences

$$\frac{\partial\Phi^i}{\partial x_c} = \frac{\Phi^i(x_c+1,y_c)-\Phi^i(x_c-1,y_c)}{2}, \quad \frac{\partial\Phi^i}{\partial y_c} = \frac{\Phi^i(x_c,y_c+1)-\Phi^i(x_c,y_c-1)}{2}. \quad (13)$$

This results in the 1×6 per pixel Jacobi vector $J^i(\mathbf{x}_c,\theta\xi_0) = \partial E^i(\mathbf{x}_c,\theta\xi_0)/\partial\theta\xi$, evaluated at $\theta\xi_0 = \mathbf{0}^\top$. At each iteration the twist parameter step is calculated as

$$\Delta\theta\xi^i = -\left(\sum_{\mathbf{x}_c\in\Omega}J^i(\mathbf{x}_c,\theta\xi_0)^\top J^i(\mathbf{x}_c,\theta\xi_0)\right)^{-1}\sum_{\mathbf{x}_c\in\Omega}J^i(\mathbf{x}_c,\theta\xi_0)^\top, \quad (14)$$

using Cholesky decomposition. The resulting step is mapped to its corresponding group element in $\mathbb{SE}(3)$ and applied to the initial transform estimate as

$$T^i_{cm} \leftarrow exp(\Delta\theta\xi^i)T^i_{cm}. \quad (15)$$

In order to increase tracking robustness in case of fast movement or motion blur and to decrease runtime, we compute the pose optimization in a coarse to fine manner as explained in detail in Sect. 3.2.

2.4   Initialization

The whole tracking process is currently initialized manually. We render each model as an overlay to the live camera feed using a pre-defined initial pose. The user is then required to roughly align this mask with the objects in the scene. On key press these silhouette masks along with the current camera image are used to calculate the initial color histograms that provide posterior segmentation for the subsequent first pose optimization. After initialization pose optimization and color histogram updates are performed in an interleaved fashion for each following camera image as described above.

3   Implementation

In the following we provide an overview of our C++ implementation with regard to runtime optimization. It is based on CPU parallelization and OpenGL for rendering purposes.

3.1   Rendering Engine

As PWP3D we use a mesh representation of the 3D surface models. In contrast to PWP3D we do not involve a reverse Z-buffer since it did not show any significant advantage in our experiments. Instead of a custom software renderer we use the standard pipeline of OpenGL in order to render the object's silhouettes along with the depth-buffer. Using hardware rendering, runtime scales well even for complex models composed of a large number of polygons.

To generate synthetic views that match the real images, the camera's intrinsic parameters need to be included (see Eq. 5). We model perspective projection to the canonical view volume v as $\mathbf{X}_v = P_{gl}T_{glc}T_{cm}^i\tilde{\mathbf{X}}_m^i$, with

$$
P_{gl} = \begin{bmatrix} \frac{2f_x}{w} & 0 & 1-\frac{2c_x}{w} & 0 \\ 0 & -\frac{2f_y}{h} & 1-\frac{2c_y}{h} & 0 \\ 0 & 0 & \frac{Z_f+Z_n}{Z_n-Z_f} & \frac{2Z_fZ_n}{Z_n-Z_f} \\ 0 & 0 & -1 & 0 \end{bmatrix} \quad \text{and} \quad T_{glc} = \begin{bmatrix} 1 & 0 & 0 & 0 \\ 0 & -1 & 0 & 0 \\ 0 & 0 & -1 & 0 \\ 0 & 0 & 0 & 1 \end{bmatrix}, \quad (16)
$$

where w, h are the camera image width and height, and Z_n, Z_f are the near- and far-plane of the OpenGL view frustum. The matrix T_{glc} describes the transform from the coordinate frame of the real camera to that of the OpenGL camera.

Hierarchical rendering is achieved by changing the width and height of the viewport according to the current pyramid level. As we perform the image processing on the CPU, offscreen rendering to a *FrameBufferObject* is used, which is then downloaded to host memory as the silhouette mask $I_s : \Omega \to \mathbb{R}$ and the corresponding depth-buffer $I_d : \Omega \to \mathbb{R}$. Based on the depth-buffer I_d the surface points $\mathbf{X}_c^i$ can be determined via backprojection as

$$
\mathbf{X}_c^i = D(\mathbf{x}_c)K^{-1}\tilde{\mathbf{x}}_c, \text{ with } D(\mathbf{x}_c) = \frac{2Z_nZ_f}{Z_f + Z_n - (2I_d(\mathbf{x}_c) - 1)(Z_f - Z_n)}, \quad (17)
$$

for all $\mathbf{x}_c \in \Omega_f^i$, where $\tilde{\mathbf{x}}_c = (x_c, y_c, 1)^\top$ denotes the homogeneous extension of the image point $\mathbf{x}_c = (x_c, y_c)^\top$.

3.2   Image Processing

For every image I_c and each object m_i we compute two maps $I_{Pf}^i, I_{Pb}^i : \Omega \to \mathbb{R}$ mapping each pixel to its foreground and its background posterior probability as

$$
I_{Pf}^i(\mathbf{x}_c) = P_f^i\left(I_c(\mathbf{x}_c)\right) \forall \mathbf{x}_c \in \Omega \quad \text{and} \quad I_{Pb}^i(\mathbf{x}_c) = P_b^i\left(I_c(\mathbf{x}_c)\right) \forall \mathbf{x}_c \in \Omega \quad (18)
$$

Fig. 4. Multiple object tracking with occlusion. Left: Input frame showing a red squirrel figurine occluding a green letter V. Middle: Silhouette mask I_s of corresponding surface models m_1 and m_2. Right: Φ^2 within ± 8 pixels around the occluded contour C^2 (grey values) and pixels influenced by occlusion (bright red inside, dark red outside of Ω_f^2). (Color figure online)

based on the current color histograms. Due to our hierarchical coarse to fine pose optimization strategy we build a three level image pyramid using a scale factor of 2, resulting in corresponding camera matrices $1/4K$, $1/2K$ and K. Overall, we perform six optimization iterations for each object per image. The first three iterations are conducted at the lowest pyramid level, followed by two iterations in the next level and a single iteration at full image resolution.

To distinguish multiple objects, we render each model silhouette region Ω_f^i using a unique intensity corresponding to the model index i. Analog to PWP3D we only evaluate the energy in a narrow band (± 8 pixels) around the contour of each object. Thereby, we use the same width for each pyramid level. All subsequent image processing steps are restricted to a 2D ROI (region of interest) containing this contour band. This ROI is given by the 2D bounding rectangle of the projected bounding box of a model expanded by 8 pixels in each direction.

The last three image processing steps are implemented using one thread per CPU core, each processing a bunch of image rows. First, the signed distance transform (Eq. 9) of each silhouette region Ω_f^i is computed. Thereby, we do not explicitly extract the contour using Scharr kernels as done in PWP3D, but use forward finite differences within the algorithm presented in [19]. Next, the derivatives of the signed distance transform are calculated (Eq. 13). Finally, the Hessian approximation and the gradient of the energy needed for the parameter step (Eq. 14) are calculated, where each thread calculates the sums over $(J^i)^\top J^i$ and $(J^i)^\top$ for its pixels, which are added up afterwards in the main thread. Note that only the upper triangular part of $(J^i)^\top J^i$ has to be calculated as it is symmetrical.

3.3   Occlusion Handling

Tracking multiple objects simultaneously mutual occlusions are very likely to emerge (Fig. 4), which must be handled appropriately. In our approach occlusions can be modeled using the silhouette mask I_s. Thereby, the natural approach as realized in PWP3D is to render each model's silhouette I_s^i separately

Fig. 5. Example scenes used for performance analysis. The scenes vary in the number of objects, their polygon count and distances to the camera

and determine its individual signed distance transform Φ^i. Then, the common silhouette mask I_s is also rendered, identifying whether a pixel belongs to the region of a different object and thus has to be discarded for the current object.

Although this approach is easy to compute it does not scale well with the number of objects as each I_s^i, I_d^i and I_s have to be rendered and transferred to host memory. Thereby, computing Φ^i directly from I_d^i avoids downloading I_s^i, but the number of renderings is still linear in the number of objects. In order to minimize rendering and memory transfer we instead render the entire scene once per iteration, download a common silhouette mask I_s and the according depth-buffer I_d, and compute each Φ^i directly from I_s as described in Sect. 3.2. Thereby, the respective contours C^i can contain segments resulting from occlusions that are considered in the respective signed distance transform. To handle this, for each object all pixels with a distance value that was influenced by occlusion have to be discarded for pose optimization (Fig. 4). By only using I_s and I_d this detection is split into two cases. For a pixel $\mathbf{x}_c \in \Omega_b^i$ outside of the silhouette region, we simply check whether $I_s(\mathbf{x}_c)$ equals another object index. In that case, $\mathbf{x}_c$ is discarded if the depth at $I_d(\mathbf{x}_c)$ of the other object is smaller than that of the closest contour pixel to $\mathbf{x}_c$, meaning that the other surface is actually in front of the current object (indicated with dark red in Fig. 4). For $\mathbf{x}_c \in \Omega_f^i$ inside of the silhouette region we perform the same checks for all neighboring pixels outside of Ω_f^i to the closest contour pixel to $\mathbf{x}_c$. If any of these pixels next to the contour passes the mask and depth checks, $\mathbf{x}_c$ is discarded (indicated with bright red in Fig. 4).

4 Evaluation

This section provides an in-depth performance analysis of our method. We give detailed runtime measurements and experimental evaluations comparing our approach to PWP3D in challenging motion sequences. For all experiments a commodity laptop with Intel Core i7 quad core CPU @ 2.6 GHz and NVIDIA GeForce GT 650M GPU as well as a 640×512 pixel resolution camera were used.

4.1 Performance Analysis

For model-based methods, the runtime not only depends on the number of objects but also on the models' complexity (polygon count and distance to camera), which hamper general performance measurements. We therefore demonstrate the performance of our implementation by providing chronometries (Table 1) of several different example scenes (Fig. 5). Note that the significant runtime difference in the third row of Table 1 is due to the fact that we do not need to download the silhouette mask I_s in case of a single object as in this case we can compute Φ^1 directly from I_d.

4.2 Experimental Comparison

We compare our method to PWP3D in three real image data experiments using image sequences pre-recorded at 50 Hz (featured in supplementary video material). Our approach was able to track the single object in the first two sequences in real-time while PWP3D needed about 60 – 80 ms per frame. In order to neglect the influence of the runtime on the frame rate and the resulting pose difference between consecutive frames, all sequences were post-processed at full frame rate by both algorithms. For PWP3D we used eight optimization iterations since this would enable at least 20 – 25 Hz when using more powerful hardware. While our method was used with the same settings (number of iterations per hierarchy, see Sect. 3.2) throughout, we had to adjust all step sizes individually for PWP3D for each experiment and each object in order to achieve the best results.

In the first experiment we moved the camera around a scene tracking a stationary squirrel figurine (Fig. 6). Thereby, we endeavored to generate fast rotational motion at different distances between camera and object. The results show the dependency of the step sizes in PWP3D on the distance to the camera. If the distance of the object in Z direction becomes too small, the step sizes are too large and the pose starts to oscillate (e.g. frames 150–230), but if the distance between the object and the camera increases the overall optimization quality degrades, resulting in the step sizes to be too small to reach the minimum (e.g. starting around frame 280). We tried to scale the step sizes with regard to

Table 1. Average runtimes (in ms) for the example scenes depicted in Fig. 5 for each main processing step combined for all objects and separated by the three pyramid levels. Also the overall runtime per frame is given

Processing step	Fig. 5(a)	Fig. 5(b)	Fig. 5(c)	Fig. 5(d)
Posterior pyramid	1.0	1.2	2.5	5.1
Scene rendering	0.2, 0.2, 0.3	0.5, 0.4, 0.4	0.2, 0.2, 0.3	0.3, 0.3, 0.3
Transfer I_d (and I_s)	0.6, 0.4, 0.4	0.6, 0.4, 0.4	1.1, 0.8, 0.7	1.1, 0.8, 0.7
Level-set transforms Φ^i	0.4, 0.2, 0.1	2.9, 0.9, 0.3	1.1, 0.4, 0.3	1.2, 0.7, 0.4
Derivatives $\partial\Phi^i/\partial\mathbf{x}_c$	0.1, 0.05, 0.04	0.2, 0.1, 0.1	0.2, 0.1, 0.1	0.3, 0.2, 0.1
$(J^i)^\top J^i$ and $(J^i)^\top$	0.4, 0.2, 0.1	1.0, 0.5, 0.3	0.9, 0.5, 0.3	1.3, 0.8, 0.6
Histogram update	2.7	3.2	6.4	9.0
Overall per frame	10.4	18.8	22.0	30.2

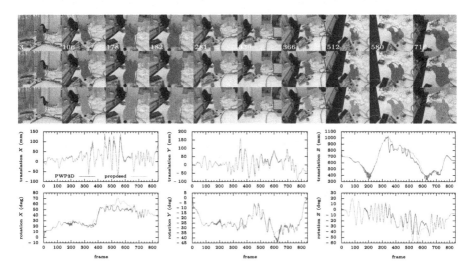

Fig. 6. Top: Visual result of the first pose tracking experiment for both methods (Top row: input images. Middle row: Result of PWP3D. Bottom row: Result of proposed method). Bottom: Determined pose parameters. The color of the plots corresponds to the mesh color drawn in the example frames with respect to the algorithm used

the translation in Z-direction which slightly reduced these effects but did not solve the problem. In contrast, our method performed equally well producing pleasing results throughout the whole sequence. If the step sizes of PWP3D suit the distance, both methods perform equally well, which shows that our approach does not degrade the tracking quality (e.g. frames 20–150). At initialization our method always converged within the first three frames (18 iterations) while PWP3D needed at least about 12 frames (96 iterations) until alignment.

In the second experiment we tracked a hand held screwdriver that was moved in front of the stationary camera (Fig. 7). The sequence contains a challenging full $360°$ turn around the X-axis of the screwdriver that shows the advantage of our parametrization compared to that used in PWP3D (frames 180–400). We set the rotation step size for PWP3D to a large value such that it was close to oscillating (e.g. frames 105–150) since this produced the best overall results. While our method is able to correctly track this motion, PWP3D fails to determine the rotation of the object despite the large step size for rotation. Starting at around frame 450, the screwdriver was moved closer towards the camera, leading to a tracking loss of PWP3D at frame 586, while the proposed method remained stable even though both methods suffer from poor segmentation caused by the occlusion by the hands and the heterogenous appearance of the screwdriver.

The third experiment compares our occlusion detection method to the straightforward approach of PWP3D (Fig. 8). Here, the green letter V and the camera were stationary while the red squirrel figurine was attached to a stick and moved around. The plots show that both methods struggle with heavy occlusions (e.g. example frames 318, 371, 450) but in general are robust. The unwanted motion of the letter (frames 762–827) was caused by ambient occlusion polluting

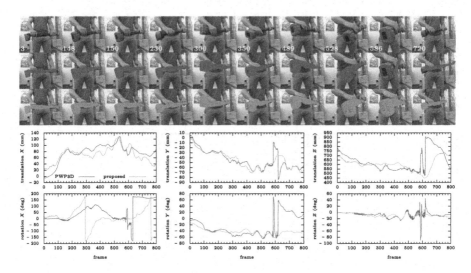

Fig. 7. Results of the second experiment, where a screwdriver was moved in front of the stationary camera. The visualization of the tracking results is analogous to Fig. 6

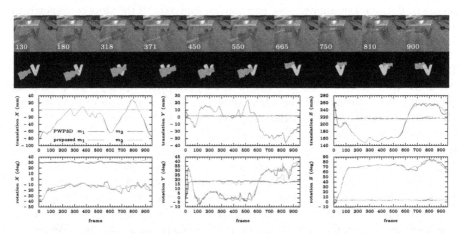

Fig. 8. Results of the third experiment, with two objects occluding one another. Top: Example frames with the proposed corresponding silhouette masks I_s below. Bottom: Plots of determined pose parameters for PWP3D and the proposed method (Color figure online)

the color histograms. Due to its overall faster convergence our method in general is more sensitive to these kinds of distortions.

5 Conclusions

We presented an improvement to the current state of the art region-based pose estimation methods. The proposed optimization strategy has fewer parameters to set and better convergence properties compared to previous approaches, which lead to a major increase of tracking robustness and reduction of runtime.

Pose ambiguities caused by object symmetries are inherent to pose estimation methods solely based on silhouette information. In future work we plan on extending the energy functional by a photometric term that incorporates the inner structure such as texture or edges of the objects for resolving these ambiguities. We will also investigate integrating recent approaches improving the image segmentation part (e.g. [16]). Finally detecting tracking losses and subsequent re-localization in real-time were not addressed and remain future work.

References

1. Lepetit, V., Fua, P.: Monocular model-based 3D tracking of rigid objects: A survey. Found. Trends. Comput. Graph. Vis. **1**(1), 1–89 (2005)
2. Cremers, D., Rousson, M., Deriche, R.: A review of statistical approaches to level set segmentation: Integrating color, texture, motion and shape. Int. J. Comput. Vis. **72**(2), 195–215 (2007)
3. Harris, C., Stennet, C.: RAPiD - A video-rate object tracker. In: British Machine Vision Conference, pp. 73–77, September 1990
4. Vacchetti, L., Lepetit, V., Fua, P.: Stable real-time 3D tracking using online and offline information. IEEE Trans. Pattern Anal. Mach. Intell. **26**(10), 1385–1391 (2004)
5. Park, Y., Lepetit, V., Woo, W.: Multiple 3D object tracking for augmented reality. In: 2008 7th IEEE/ACM International Symposium on Mixed and Augmented Reality, ISMAR 2008, pp. 117–120, September 2008
6. Kim, K., Lepetit, V., Woo, W.: Keyframe-based modeling and tracking of multiple 3D objects. In: 2010 9th IEEE International Symposium on Mixed and Augmented Reality, ISMAR 2010, pp. 193–198, October 2010
7. Rosenhahn, B., Brox, T., Weickert, J.: Three-dimensional shape knowledge for joint image segmentation and pose tracking. Int. J. Comput. Vis. **73**(3), 243–262 (2006)
8. Rosenhahn, B., Brox, T., Cremers, D., Seidel, H.-P.: A comparison of shape matching methods for contour based pose estimation. In: Reulke, R., Eckardt, U., Flach, B., Knauer, U., Polthier, K. (eds.) IWCIA 2006. LNCS, vol. 4040, pp. 263–276. Springer, Heidelberg (2006). doi:10.1007/11774938_21
9. Schmaltz, C., Rosenhahn, B., Brox, T., Cremers, D., Weickert, J., Wietzke, L., Sommer, G.: Region-based pose tracking. In: Martí, J., Benedí, J.M., Mendonça, A.M., Serrat, J. (eds.) IbPRIA 2007. LNCS, vol. 4478, pp. 56–63. Springer, Heidelberg (2007). doi:10.1007/978-3-540-72849-8_8
10. Brox, T., Rosenhahn, B., Gall, J., Cremers, D.: Combined region and motion-based 3D tracking of rigid and articulated objects. IEEE Trans. Pattern Anal. Mach. Intell. **32**(3), 402–415 (2010)
11. Schmaltz, C., Rosenhahn, B., Brox, T., Weickert, J.: Region-based pose tracking with occlusions using 3D models. Mach. Vis. Appl. **23**(3), 557–577 (2011)
12. Prisacariu, V.A., Reid, I.D.: PWP3D: Real-time segmentation and tracking of 3D objects. Int. J. Comput. Vis. **98**(3), 335–354 (2012)
13. Dambreville, S., Sandhu, R., Yezzi, A., Tannenbaum, A.: A geometric approach to joint 2D region-based segmentation and 3D pose estimation using a 3D shape prior. SIAM J. Img. Sci. **3**(1), 110–132 (2010)

14. Prisacariu, V., Kahler, O., Murray, D., Reid, I.: Real-time 3D tracking and reconstruction on mobile phones. IEEE Trans. Visual. Comput. Graph. **21**(5), 557–570 (2015)
15. Zhao, S., Wang, L., Sui, W., yu Wu, H., Pan, C.: 3D object tracking via boundary constrained region-based model. In: 2014 IEEE International Conference on Image Processing (ICIP), pp. 486–490, October 2014
16. Hexner, J., Hagege, R.R.: 2D–3D pose estimation of heterogeneous objects using a region based approach. Int. J. Comput. Vis. **118**, 95–112 (2016). ISSN: 1573-1405
17. Murray, R.M., Li, Z., Sastry, S.S.: A Mathematical Introduction to Robotic Manipulation, 3rd edn. CRC Press Inc., Boca Raton (1994)
18. Bibby, C., Reid, I.: Robust real-time visual tracking using pixel-wise posteriors. In: Forsyth, D., Torr, P., Zisserman, A. (eds.) ECCV 2008. LNCS, vol. 5303, pp. 831–844. Springer, Heidelberg (2008). doi:10.1007/978-3-540-88688-4_61
19. Felzenszwalb, P.F., Huttenlocher, D.P.: Distance transforms of sampled functions. Theory Comput. **8**(1), 415–428 (2012)
20. Press, W.H., Teukolsky, S.A., Vetterling, W.T., Flannery, B.P.: Numerical Recipes 3rd Edition: The Art of Scientific Computing, 3rd edn. Cambridge University Press, New York (2007)

Estimation of Human Body Shape in Motion with Wide Clothing

Jinlong Yang[1,2], Jean-Sébastien Franco[1,2], Franck Hétroy-Wheeler[1,2], and Stefanie Wuhrer[1,2(✉)]

[1] Inria Grenoble Rhône-Alpes, Grenoble, France
{jinlong.yang,jean-sebastien.franco,
franck.hetroy,stefanie.wuhrer}@inria.fr
[2] Laboratoire Jean Kuntzmann, Université Grenoble Alpes, Grenoble, France

Abstract. Estimating 3D human body shape in motion from a sequence of unstructured oriented 3D point clouds is important for many applications. We propose the first automatic method to solve this problem that works in the presence of loose clothing. The problem is formulated as an optimization problem that solves for identity and posture parameters in a shape space capturing likely body shape variations. The automation is achieved by leveraging a recent robust pose detection method [1]. To account for clothing, we take advantage of motion cues by encouraging the estimated body shape to be inside the observations. The method is evaluated on a new benchmark containing different subjects, motions, and clothing styles that allows to quantitatively measure the accuracy of body shape estimates. Furthermore, we compare our results to existing methods that require manual input and demonstrate that results of similar visual quality can be obtained.

Keywords: Human body modeling · Shape and motion estimation · Statistical shape space

1 Introduction

Estimating 3D human body shape in motion is important for applications ranging from virtual change rooms to security. While it is currently possible to effectively track the surface of the clothing of dressed humans in motion [2] or to accurately track body shape and posture of humans dressed in tight clothing [3], it remains impossible to automatically estimate the 3D body shape in motion for humans captured in loose clothing.

Given an input motion sequence of raw 3D meshes or oriented point clouds (with unknown correspondence information) showing a dressed person, the goal

Electronic supplementary material The online version of this chapter (doi:10.1007/978-3-319-46493-0_27) contains supplementary material, which is available to authorized users.

B. Leibe et al. (Eds.): ECCV 2016, Part IV, LNCS 9908, pp. 439–454, 2016.
DOI: 10.1007/978-3-319-46493-0_27

of this work is to estimate the body shape and motion of this person. Existing techniques to solve this problem are either not designed to work in the presence of loose clothing [4,5] or require manual initialization for the pose [6,7], which limits their use in general scenarios. The reason is that wide clothing leads to strong variations of the acquired surface that is challenging to handle automatically. We propose an *automatic* framework that allows to estimate the human body shape and motion that is robust to the presence of *loose clothing*.

Existing methods that estimate human body shape based on an input motion sequence of 3D meshes or oriented point clouds use a shape space that models human body shape variations caused by different identities and postures as prior. Such a prior allows to reduce the search space to likely body shapes and postures. Prior works fall into two lines of work. On the one hand, there are human body shape estimation methods specifically designed to work in the presence of loose clothing [6,7]. These techniques take advantage of the fact that observations of a dressed human in motion provides important cues about the underlying body shape as different parts of the clothing are close to the body shape in different frames. However, these methods require manually placed markers to initialize the posture. On the other hand, there are human body shape estimation methods designed to robustly and automatically compute the shape and posture estimate over time [4,5]. However, these methods use strong priors of the true human body shape to track the posture over time and to fit the shape to the input point cloud, and may therefore fail in the presence of loose clothing.

In this work, we combine the advantages of these two lines of work by proposing an automatic framework that is designed for body shape estimation under loose clothing. Like previous works, our method restricts the shape estimate to likely body shapes and postures, as defined by a shape space. We use a shape space that models variations caused by different identities and variations caused by different postures as linear factors [8]. This simple model allows for the development of an efficient fitting approach. To develop an automatic method, we employ a robust pose detection method that accounts for different identities [1] and use the detected pose to guide our model fitting. To account for clothing, we take advantage of motion cues by encouraging the estimated body shape to be located inside the acquired observation at each frame. This constraint, which is expressed as a simple energy that is optimized over all input frames jointly, allows to account for clothing without the need to explicitly detect skin regions on all frames as is the case for previous methods [7,9].

To the best of our knowledge, existing datasets in this research area do not provide 3D sequences of both body shape as ground truth and dressed scans for estimation. Therefore, visual quality is the only evaluation choice. To quantitatively evaluate our framework and allow for future comparisons, we propose the first dataset consisting of synchronized acquisitions of dense unstructured geometric motion data and sparse motion capture data of 6 subjects with 3 clothing styles (tight, layered, wide) under 3 representative motions, where the capture in tight clothing serves as ground truth body shape.

The main contributions of this work are the following.

- An automatic approach to estimate 3D human body shape in motion in the presence of loose clothing.
- A new benchmark consisting of 6 subjects captured in 3 motions and 3 clothing styles each that allows to quantitatively compare human body shape estimates.

2   Related Work

Many works estimate human posture without aiming to estimate body shape, or track a known body shape over time. As our goal is to simultaneously estimate body shape and motion automatically and in the presence of loose clothing, we will focus our discussion on this scenario.

Statistical Shape Spaces. To model human body shape variations caused by different identities, postures, and motions, statistical shape spaces are commonly used. These shape spaces represent a single frame of a motion sequence using a low-dimensional parameter space that typically models shape variations caused by different identities and caused by different postures using separate sets of parameters. Such shape spaces can be used as prior when the goal is to predict a likely body shape under loose clothing.

Anguelov et al. [10] proposed a statistical shape space called SCAPE that combines an identity model computed by performing principal component analysis (PCA) on a population of 3D models in standard posture with a posture model computed by analyzing near-rigid body parts corresponding to bones. This model performs statistics on triangle transformations, which allows to model non-rigid deformations caused by posture changes. Achieving this accuracy requires solving an optimization problem to reconstruct a 3D mesh from its representation in shape space. To improve the accuracy of the SCAPE space, Chen et al. [11] propose to combine the SCAPE model with localized multilinear models for each body part. To model the correlation of the shape changes caused by identity and posture changes, Hasler et al. [12] perform PCA on a rotation-invariant encoding of the model's triangles. These models may be used as priors when estimating human body shape in motion, but none of them allow to efficiently reconstruct a 3D human model from the shape space.

To speed up the reconstruction time from the SCAPE representation, Jain et al. [13] propose a simplified SCAPE model, denoted by S-SCAPE in the following, that computes the body shape by performing PCA on the vertex coordinates of a training set in standard posture and combines this with a linear blend skinning (LBS) to model posture changes. Any posture variations present in the training data cause posture variation to be modeled in identity space, which is known to cause counter-intuitive deformations [8]. To remedy this, recently proposed shape spaces start by normalizing the posture of the training data before performing statistics and model shape changes caused by different factors such as identity and posture as multilinear factors [8,14,15]. We use the normalized

S-SCAPE model [8] in this work; however, any of these shape spaces could be used within our framework.

Recently, Pons-Moll et al. [16] proposed a statistical model that captures fine-scale dynamic shape variation of the naked body shape. We do not model dynamic geometry in this work, as detailed shape changes are typically not observable under loose clothing.

Estimation of Static Body Shape Under Clothing. To estimate human body shape based on a static acquisition in loose clothing and in arbitrary posture, the following two approaches have been proposed. Balan et al. [9] use a SCAPE model to estimate the body shape under clothing based on a set of calibrated multi-view images. This work is evaluated on a static dataset of different subjects captured in different postures and clothing styles. Our evaluation on 3D motion sequences of different subjects captured in different motions and clothing styles is inspired by this work. Hasler et al. [17] use a rotation-invariant encoding to estimate the body shape under clothing based on a 3D input scan. While this method leads to accurate results, it cannot easily be extended to motion sequences, as identity and posture parameters are not separated in this encoding.

Both of these methods require manual input for posture initialization. In this work, we propose an automatic method to estimate body shape in motion.

Estimation of Body Shape in Motion. The static techniques have been extended to motion sequences with the help of shape spaces that separate shape changes caused by identity and posture. Several methods have been proposed to fit a SCAPE or S-SCAPE model to Kinect data by fixing the parameters controlling identity over the sequence [4,5]. These methods are not designed to work with clothing, and it is assumed that only tight clothing is present.

Two more recent methods are designed to account for the presence of clothing. The key idea of these methods is to take advantage of temporal motion cues to obtain a better identity estimate than would be possible based on a single frame. Our method also takes advantage of motion cues.

Wuhrer et al. [6] use a shape space that learns local information around each vertex to estimate human body shape for a 3D motion sequence. The final identity estimate is obtained by averaging the identity estimates over all frames. While this shape space leads to results of high quality, the fitting is computationally expensive, as the reconstruction of a 3D model from shape space requires solving an optimization problem. Our method uses a simpler shape space while preserving a similar level of accuracy by using an S-SCAPE model that prenormalizes the training shapes with the help of localized information.

Neophytou and Hilton [7] propose a faster method based on a shape space that models identity and posture as linear factors and learns shape variations on a posture-normalized training database. To constrain the estimate to reliable regions, the method detects areas that are close to the body surface. In contrast, our method constrains the estimate to be located inside the observed clothing at every input frame, which results in an optimization problem that does not require a detection.

Both of these methods require manual input for posture initialization on the first frame. Additionally, a temporal alignment is required by Neophytou and Hilton. Computing temporal alignments is a difficult problem, and manual annotation is tedious when considering larger sets of motion sequences. In contrast, our method is fully automatic and addresses both aspects.

3   S-SCAPE Model

In this work, we use the S-SCAPE model as prior for human body shape changes caused by different identities and postures. While we choose this shape space, any shape space that models identity and posture as multilinear factors could be used [14,15]. Although such a simple shape space does not accurately model correlated shape changes, such as muscle bulging, it allows to effectively separate the different variations and can be fitted efficiently to input scans.

This section briefly reviews the S-SCAPE model introduced by Jain et al. [13] that allows to separate the influence of parameters controlling identity and parameters controlling posture of a human body shape. In the following, we denote by β and Θ the parameter vectors that influence shape changes caused by identity and posture changes, respectively. In this work, we use the publicly available posture-normalized S-SCAPE model [8], where each training shape was normalized with the help of localized coordinates [18].

In the following, let N_v denote the number of vertices on the S-SCAPE model, let $s\left(\beta,\Theta\right) \in \mathbb{R}^{3N_v}$ denote the vector containing the vertex coordinates of identity β in posture Θ, and let $\widetilde{s}\left(\beta,\Theta\right) \in \mathbb{R}^{4N_v}$ denote the vector containing the corresponding homogeneous vertex coordinates. For the fixed posture Θ_0 that was used to train the identity space, S-SCAPE models the shape change caused by identity using a PCA model as

$$\widetilde{s}\left(\beta,\Theta_0\right) = \widetilde{A}\beta + \widetilde{\mu}, \tag{1}$$

where $\widetilde{\mu} \in \mathbb{R}^{4N_v}$ contains the homogeneous coordinates of the mean body shape, $\widetilde{A} \in \mathbb{R}^{4N_v \times d_{id}}$ is the matrix found by PCA, and d_{id} is the dimensionality of the identity shape space. For a fixed identity β_0, S-SCAPE models the shape change caused by posture using LBS as

$$s_i\left(\beta_0,\Theta\right) = \sum_{j=1}^{N_b} \omega_{ij}\,T_j\left(\Theta\right)\widetilde{s}_i\left(\beta_0,\Theta_0\right), \tag{2}$$

where s_i and $\widetilde{s}_i$ denote the standard and homogenous coordinate vector of the i-th vertex of s, N_b denotes the number of bones used for LBS, $T_j\left(\Theta\right) \in \mathbb{R}^{3\times 4}$ denotes the transformation matrix applied to the j-th bone, and ω_{ij} denotes the rigging weight binding the i-th vertex to the j-th bone.

Combining Eqs. 1 and 2 in matrix notation leads to

$$s\left(\beta,\Theta\right) = T\left(\Theta\right)\widetilde{A}\beta + T\left(\Theta\right)\widetilde{\mu}, \tag{3}$$

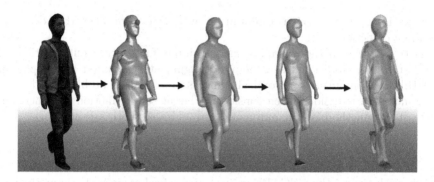

Fig. 1. Overview of the proposed pipeline. From left to right: input frame, result of Stitched Puppet [1] with annotated landmarks, result after estimation of initial identity and posture, final result, and overlay of input and final result.

where $T(\Theta) \in \mathbb{R}^{3N_v \times 4N_v}$ is a sparse matrix containing the per-vertex transformations. Using this notation, it is easy to see that S-SCAPE is linear in both β and $T(\Theta)$, which allows for a simple optimization w.r.t. β and Θ.

4   Estimating Model Parameters for a Motion Sequence

We start by providing an overview of the proposed method. Figure 1 shows the different parts of the algorithm visually. Given as input a trained S-SCAPE model and a motion sequence consisting of N_f frames F_i represented by triangle meshes with unknown correspondence, we aim to compute a single parameter vector β controlling the shape of the identity (as the identity of the person is fixed during motion) along with N_f parameter vectors Θ_i controlling the postures in each frame, such that $s_i(\beta, \Theta_i)$ is close to F_i.

To fit the S-SCAPE model to a single frame F, we aim to minimize

$$E(F,\beta,\Theta)=\omega_{lnd}E_{lnd}(F,\beta,\Theta)+\omega_{data}E_{data}(F,\beta,\Theta)+\omega_{cloth}E_{cloth}(F,\beta,\Theta) \qquad (4)$$

w.r.t. β and Θ subject to constraints that keep β in the learned probability distribution of parameter values. Here, ω_{lnd}, ω_{data}, and ω_{cloth} are weights that trade off the influence of the different energy terms. The energy E_{lnd} measures the distance between a sparse set of provided landmarks, which correspond to distinctive positions on the human body, to their corresponding locations on $s(\beta, \Theta)$. The provided landmarks are computed automatically in the following. The energy E_{data} measures the distance between $s(\beta, \Theta)$ and F using a nearest neighbor cost. The energy E_{cloth} is designed to account for loose clothing by encouraging $s(\beta, \Theta)$ to be located inside the observation F.

For a motion sequence of N_f frames, our goal is then to minimize

$$E\left(F_{1:N_f},\beta,\Theta_{1:N_f}\right)=\sum_{i=1}^{N_f} E(F_i,\beta,\Theta_i) \qquad (5)$$

w.r.t. $\boldsymbol{\beta}$ and $\Theta_{1:N_f}$ subject to constraints that keep $\boldsymbol{\beta}$ in the learned probability distribution of parameter values. Here, $\boldsymbol{F}_{1:N_f} = \{\boldsymbol{F}_1,\ldots,\boldsymbol{F}_{N_f}\}$ is the set of frames and $\Theta_{1:N_f} = \{\Theta_1,\ldots,\Theta_{N_f}\}$ is the set of posture parameters. The energy E_{cloth} allows to take advantage of motion cues in this formulation as it encourages the body shape to lie inside all observed frames.

In the following sections, we detail the prior that is used to constrain $\boldsymbol{\beta}$ as well as the different energy terms. Optimizing Eq. 5 w.r.t. all parameters jointly results in a high-dimensional optimization problem that is inefficient to solve and prone to get stuck in undesirable local minima. After introducing all energy terms, we discuss how this problem can be divided into smaller problems that can be solved in order, thereby allowing to find a good minimum in practice.

4.1   Prior Model for $\boldsymbol{\beta}$

A prior model is used to ensure that the body shape stays within the learned shape space that represents plausible human shapes. The identity shape space is learned using PCA, and has zero mean and standard deviation σ_i along the i-th principal component. Similarly to previous work [9], we do not penalize values of $\boldsymbol{\beta}$ that stay within $3\sigma_i$ of the mean to avoid introducing a bias towards the mean shape. However, rather than penalizing a larger distance from the mean, we constrain the solution to lie inside the hyperbox $\pm 3\sigma_i$ using a constrained optimization framework. This constraint can be handled by standard constrained optimizers since the hyperbox is axis-aligned, and using this hard constraint removes the need to appropriately weigh a prior energy w.r.t. other energy terms.

4.2   Landmark Energy

The landmark energy helps to guide the solution towards the desired local minimum with the help of distinctive anatomical landmarks. This energy is especially important during the early stages of the optimization as it allows to find a good initialization for the identity and posture parameters. In the following, we consider the use of N_{lnd} landmarks and assume without loss of generality that the vertices corresponding to landmarks are the first N_{lnd} vertices of $\boldsymbol{s}$. The landmark term is defined as

$$E_{lnd}\left(\boldsymbol{F},\boldsymbol{\beta},\Theta\right) = \sum_{i=1}^{N_{lnd}} \left\| \boldsymbol{s}_i\left(\boldsymbol{\beta},\Theta\right) - \boldsymbol{l}_i(\boldsymbol{F})\right\|^2, \qquad (6)$$

where $\boldsymbol{l}_i(\boldsymbol{F})$ denotes the i-th landmark of frame $\boldsymbol{F}$, $\boldsymbol{s}_i\left(\boldsymbol{\beta},\Theta\right)$ denotes the vertex corresponding to the i-th landmark of $\boldsymbol{s}\left(\boldsymbol{\beta},\Theta\right)$, and $\|\cdot\|$ denotes the ℓ^2 norm.

The landmarks $\boldsymbol{l}_i(\boldsymbol{F})$ are computed automatically with the help of the state of the art Stitched Puppet [1], which allows to robustly fit a human body model to a single scan using a particle-based optimization. Specifically, we once manually select a set of vertex indices to be used as landmarks on the Stitched Puppet model, which is then fixed for all experiments. To fit the Stitched Puppet to a single frame, randomly distributed particles are used to avoid getting stuck in

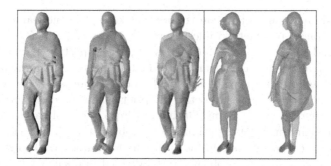

Fig. 2. Left: overfitting problem of Stitched Puppet in the presence of clothing. Input frame, Stitched Puppet result with 160 particles, and Stitched Puppet result with 30 particles are shown in order. Right: the failure case from our database caused by mismatching of Stitched Puppet.

undesirable local minima. We fit the Stitched Puppet model to frame F, and report the 3D positions of the pre-selected indices after fitting as landmarks $l_i(F)$. While the Stitched Puppet aims to fit the body shape and posture of F, only the coordinates $l_i(F)$ are used by our framework. Note that our method does not require accurate $l_i(F)$, since $l_i(F)$ are only used to initialize the optimization.

Using many particles on each frame of a motion sequence is inefficient. Furthermore, since the Stitched Puppet is trained on a database of minimally dressed subjects, using many particles to fit to a frame in wide clothing may lead to overfitting problems. This is illustrated in Fig. 2. To remedy this, we choose to use a relatively small number of particles which is set to 30. Starting at the second frame, we initialize the particle optimization to the result of the previous frame to guide the optimization towards the desired optimum.

4.3 Data Energy

The data energy pulls the S-SCAPE model towards the observation F using a nearest neighbor term. This energy, which unlike the landmark energy considers all vertices of s, is crucial to fit the identity and posture of s to the input F as

$$E_{data}(F,\beta,\Theta) = \sum_{i=1}^{N_v} \delta_{NN} \|s_i(\beta,\Theta) - NN(s_i(\beta,\Theta),F)\|^2, \qquad (7)$$

where N_v denotes the number of vertices of s and $NN(s_i(\beta,\Theta),F)$ denotes the nearest neighbour of vertex $s_i(\beta,\Theta)$ on F. To remove the influence of outliers and reduce the possibility of nearest neighbour mismatching, we use a binary weight δ_{NN} that is set to one if the distance between s_i and its nearest neighbor on F is below 200 mm and the angle between their outer normal vectors is below $60°$, and to zero otherwise.

4.4 Clothing Energy

The clothing energy is designed to encourage the predicted body shape s to be located entirely inside the observation F. This energy is particularly important when considering motion sequences acquired with loose clothing. In such cases, merely using E_{lnd} and E_{data} leads to results that overestimate the circumferences of the body shape because β is estimated to fit to F rather than to fit inside of F, see Fig. 3. To remedy this, we define the clothing energy as

$$E_{cloth}(F,\beta,\Theta)=\sum_{i=1}^{N_v} \delta_{out}\delta_{NN}\|s_i(\beta,\Theta)-NN(s_i(\beta,\Theta),F)\|^2+\omega_r\|\beta-\beta_0\|^2, \tag{8}$$

where δ_{out} is used to identify vertices of s located outside of F. This is achieved by setting δ_{out} to one if the angle between the outer normal of $NN(s_i(\beta,\Theta),F)$ and the vector $s_i(\beta,\Theta)-NN(s_i(\beta,\Theta),F)$ is below $90°$, and to zero otherwise. Furthermore, ω_r is a weight used for the regularization term, and β_0 is an initialization of the identity parameters used to constrain β.

When observing a human body dressed in loose clothing in motion, different frames can provide valuable cues about the true body shape. The energy E_{cloth} is designed to exploit motion cues when optimizing E_{cloth} w.r.t. all available observations F_i. This allows to account for clothing using a simple optimization without the need to find skin and non-skin regions as in previous work [7,9,19]. The regularization $\|\beta-\beta_0\|^2$ used in Eq. 8 is required to avoid excessive thinning of limbs due to small misalignments in posture.

Figure 3 shows the influence of E_{cloth} on the result of a walking sequence in layered clothing. The left side shows overlays of the input and the result for $\omega_{cloth}=0$ and $\omega_{cloth}=1$. Note that while circumferences are overestimated when $\omega_{cloth}=0$, a body shape located inside the input frame is found for $\omega_{cloth}=1$. The comparison to the ground truth body shape computed as discussed in Sect. 6 is visualized in the middle and the right of Fig. 3, and shows that E_{cloth} leads to a significant improvement of the accuracy of β.

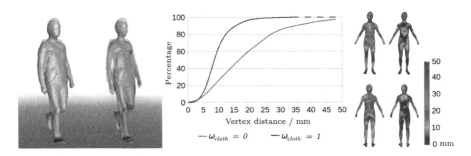

Fig. 3. Influence of E_{cloth} on walking sequence. Left: input data overlayed with result with $\omega_{cloth}=0$ (left) and $\omega_{cloth}=1$ (right). Middle: cumulative per-vertex error of estimated body shape with $\omega_{cloth}=0$ and $\omega_{cloth}=1$. Right: color-coded per-vertex error with $\omega_{cloth}=0$ (left) and $\omega_{cloth}=1$ (right).

4.5   Optimization Schedule

Minimizing $E\left(\boldsymbol{F}_{1:N_f}, \boldsymbol{\beta}, \Theta_{1:N_f}\right)$ defined in Eq. 5 over all N_f frames w.r.t. $\boldsymbol{\beta}$ and Θ_i jointly is not feasible when considering motion sequences containing hundreds of frames as this is a high-dimensional optimization problem. To solve this problem without getting stuck in undesirable local minima, we optimize three smaller problems in order.

Initial Identity Estimation. We start by computing an initial estimate β_0 based on the first N_k frames of the sequence by optimizing $E\left(\boldsymbol{F}_{1:N_k}, \boldsymbol{\beta}, \Theta_{1:N_k}\right)$ w.r.t. $\boldsymbol{\beta}$ and Θ_i. For increased efficiency, we start by computing optimal β_i and Θ_i for each frame using Eq. 4 by alternating the optimization of Θ_i for fixed β_i with the optimization of β_i for fixed Θ_i. This is repeated for N_{it} iterations. Temporal consistency is achieved by initializing Θ_{i+1} as Θ_i and β_{i+1} as β_i starting at the second frame. As it suffices for the identity parameters to roughly estimate the true body shape at this stage, we set $\omega_{cloth} = 0$. In the first iterations, E_{lnd} is essential to guide the fitting towards the correct local optimum, while in later iterations E_{data} gains in importance. We therefore set $\omega_{data} = 1 - \omega_{lnd}$ and initialize ω_{lnd} to one. We linearly reduce ω_{lnd} to zero in the last two iterations. We then initialize the posture parameters to the computed Θ_i, and the identity parameters to the mean of the computed β_i and iteratively minimize $E\left(\boldsymbol{F}_{1:N_k}, \boldsymbol{\beta}, \Theta_{1:N_k}\right)$ w.r.t. $\Theta_{1:N_k}$ and $\boldsymbol{\beta}$. This leads to stable estimates for $\Theta_{1:N_k}$ and an initial estimate of the identity parameter, which we denote by β_0 in the following.

Posture Estimation. During the next stage of our framework, we compute the posture parameters $\Theta_{N_k+1:N_f}$ for all remaining frames by sequentially minimizing Eq. 4 w.r.t. Θ_i. As before, Θ_{i+1} is initialized to the result of Θ_i. As the identity parameters are not accurate at this stage, we set $\omega_{cloth} = 0$. For each frame, the energy is optimized N_{it} times while reducing the influence of ω_{lnd} in each iteration, using the same weight schedule as before. This results in posture parameters Θ_i for each frame.

Identity Refinement. In a final step, we refine the identity parameters to be located inside all observed frames $\boldsymbol{F}_{1:N_f}$. To this end, we initialize the identity parameters to β_0, fix all posture parameters to the computed Θ_i, and minimize $E\left(\boldsymbol{F}_{1:N_f}, \boldsymbol{\beta}, \Theta_{1:N_f}\right)$ w.r.t. $\boldsymbol{\beta}$. As the landmarks and observations are already fitted adequately, we set $\omega_{lnd} = \omega_{data} = 0$ at this stage of the optimization.

5   Implementation Details

The S-SCAPE model used in this work consists of $N_v = 6449$ vertices, and uses $d_{id} = 100$ parameters to control identity and $d_{pose} = 30$ parameters to control posture by rotating the $N_b = 15$ bones. The bones, posture parameters, and rigging weights are set as in the published model [8].

For the Stitched Puppet, we use 60 particles for the first frame, and 30 particles for subsequent frames. We use a total of $N_{lnd} = 14$ landmarks that have been shown sufficient for the initialization of posture fitting [6], and are located at forehead, shoulders, elbows, wrists, knees, toes, heels, and abdomen. Figure 1 shows the chosen landmarks on the Stitched Puppet model. During the optimization, we set $N_{it} = 6$ and $N_k = 25$. The optimization w.r.t. β uses analytic gradients, and we use Matlab L-BFGS-B to optimize the energy. The setting of the regularization weight ω_r depends on the clothing style. The looser the clothing, the smaller ω_r, as this allows for more corrections of the identity parameters. In our experiments, we use $\omega_r = 1$ for all the sequences with layered and wide clothing in our dataset.

6   Evaluation

6.1   Dataset

This section introduces the new dataset we acquired to allow quantitative evaluation of human body shape estimation from dynamic data. The dataset consists of synchronized acquisitions of dense unstructured geometric motion data and sparse motion capture (MoCap) data of 6 subjects (3 female and 3 male) captured in 3 different motions and 3 clothing styles each. The geometric motion data are sequences of meshes obtained by applying a visual hull reconstruction to a 68-color-camera (4M pixels) system at 30FPS. The basic motions that were captured are walk, rotating the body, and pulling the knees up. The captured clothing styles are very tight, layered (long-sleeved layered clothing on upper body), and wide (wide pants for men and dress for women). The body shapes of 6 subjects vary significantly. Figure 4 shows some frames of the database.

To evaluate algorithms using this dataset, we can compare the body shapes estimated under loose clothing with the tight clothing baseline. The comparison is done per vertex on the two body shapes under the same normalized posture. Cumulative plots are used to show the results.

Fig. 4. Six representative examples of frames of our motion database. From left to right, a female and male subject is shown for tight, layered, and wide clothing each.

6.2   Evaluation of Posture and Shape Fitting

We applied our method to all sequences in the database. For one sequence of a female subject captured while rotating the body in wide clothing, Stitched Puppet fails to find the correct posture, which leads to a failure case of our method (see Fig. 2). We exclude this sequence from the following evaluation.

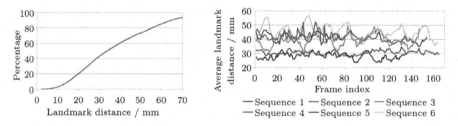

Fig. 5. Accuracy of posture estimation over the walking sequences in tight clothing. Left: cumulative landmark errors. Right: average landmark error for each sequence.

To evaluate the accuracy of the posture parameters Θ, we compare the 3D locations of a sparse set of landmarks captured using a MoCap system with the corresponding model vertices of our estimate. This evaluation is performed in very tight clothing, as no accurate MoCap markers are available for the remaining clothing styles. Figure 5 summarizes the per-marker errors over the walking sequences of all subjects. The results show that most of the estimated landmarks are within 35 mm of the ground truth and that our method does not suffer from drift for long sequences. As the markers on the Stitched Puppet and the MoCap markers were placed by non-experts, the landmark placement is not fully repeatable, and errors of up to 35 mm are considered fairly accurate.

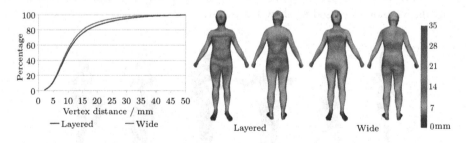

Fig. 6. Summary of shape accuracy computed over the frames of all motion sequences of all subjects captured in layered and wide clothing. Left: cumulative plots showing the per-vertex error. Right: mean per-vertex error color-coded from blue to red.

To evaluate the accuracy of the identity parameters β, we use for each subject the walking sequence captured in very tight clothing to establish a ground truth identity β_0 by applying our shape estimation method. Applying our method to sequences in looser clothing styles of the same subject leads identity parameters β, whose accuracy can be evaluated by comparing the 3D geometry of $s\,(\beta_0, \Theta_0)$ and $s\,(\beta, \Theta_0)$ for a standard posture Θ_0.

Figure 6 summarizes the per-vertex errors over all motion sequences captured in layered and wide clothing, respectively. The left side shows the cumulative errors, and the right side shows the color-coded mean per-vertex error. The color coding is visualized on the mean identity of the training data. The result shows that our method is robust to loose clothing with more than 50 % of all the vertices having less than 10 mm error for both layered and wide clothing. The right side shows that as expected, larger errors occur in areas where the shape variability across different identities is high.

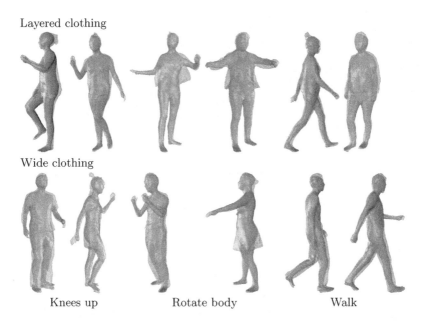

Fig. 7. Overlay of input data and our result.

Figure 7 shows some qualitative results for all three types of motions and two clothing styles. Note that accurate body shape estimates are obtained for all frames. Consider the frame that shows a female subject performing a rotating motion in layered clothing. Computing a posture or shape estimate based on this frame is extremely challenging as the geometry of the layered cloth locally resembles the geometry of an arm, and as large portions of the body shape are occluded. Our method successfully leverages temporal consistency and motion cues to find reliable posture and body shape estimates.

6.3   Comparative Evaluation

As we do not have results on motion sequences with ground truth for existing methods, this section presents visual comparisons, shown in Fig. 8. We compare to Wuhrer et al. [6] on the dancer sequence [20] presented in their work. Note that unlike the results of Wuhrer et al., our shape estimate does not suffer from unrealistic bending at the legs even in the presence of wide clothing. Furthermore, we compare to Neophytou and Hilton [7] on the swing sequence [21] presented in their work. Note that we obtain results of similar visual quality without the need for manual initializations and pre-aligned motion sequences. In summary, we present the first fully automatic method for body shape and motion estimation, and show that this method achieves state of the art results.

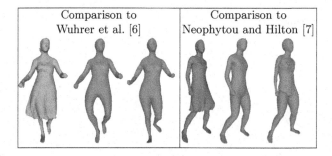

| Comparison to Wuhrer et al. [6] | Comparison to Neophytou and Hilton [7] |

Fig. 8. Per comparison from left to right: input, result of prior works, our result.

7   Conclusion

We presented an approach to automatically estimate the human body shape under motion based on a 3D input sequence showing a dressed person in possibly loose clothing. The accuracy of our method was evaluated on a newly developed benchmark[1] containing 6 different subjects performing 3 motions in 3 different styles each. We have shown that, although being fully automatic, our posture and shape estimation achieves state of the art performance. In the future, the body shape and motion estimated by our algorithm have the potential to aid in a variety of tasks including virtual change rooms and security applications.

Acknowledgements. Funded by France National Research grant ANR-14-CE24-0030 ACHMOV. We thank Yannick Marion for help with code to efficiently fit an S-SCAPE model to a single frame, Leonid Pishchulin for helpful discussions, Alexandros Neophytou and Adrian Hilton for providing comparison data, and Mickaël Heudre, Julien Pansiot and volunteer subjects for help acquiring the database.

---

[1] The benchmark can be downloaded at http://dressedhuman.gforge.inria.fr/.

References

1. Zuffi, S., Black, M.: The stitched puppet: a graphical model of 3D human shape and pose. In: Conference on Computer Vision and Pattern Recognition, pp. 3537–3546 (2015)
2. Newcombe, R.A., Fox, D., Seitz, S.M.: Dynamicfusion: reconstruction and tracking of non-rigid scenes in real-time. In: Conference on Computer Vision and Pattern Recognition, pp. 343–352 (2015)
3. Bogo, F., Black, M.J., Loper, M., Romero, J.: Detailed full-body reconstructions of moving people from monocular RGB-D sequences. In: ICCV (2015)
4. Weiss, A., Hirshberg, D., Black, M.: Home 3D body scans from noisy image and range data. In: International Conference on Computer Vision, pp. 1951–1958 (2011)
5. Helten, T., Baak, A., Bharai, G., Müller, M., Seidel, H.P., Theobalt, C.: Personalization and evaluation of a real-time depth-based full body scanner. In: International Conference on 3D Vision, pp. 279–286 (2013)
6. Wuhrer, S., Pishchulin, L., Brunton, A., Shu, C., Lang, J.: Estimation of human body shape and posture under clothing. Comput. Vis. Image Underst. **127**, 31–42 (2014)
7. Neophytou, A., Hilton, A.: A layered model of human body and garment deformation. In: International Conference on 3D Vision, pp. 171–178 (2014)
8. Pishchulin, L., Wuhrer, S., Helten, T., Theobalt, C., Schiele, B.: Building statistical shape spaces for 3D human modeling. Technical report 1503.05860, arXiv (2015)
9. Balan, A.O., Black, M.J.: The naked truth: estimating body shape under clothing. In: European Conference on Computer Vision, pp. 15–29 (2008)
10. Anguelov, D., Srinivasan, P., Koller, D., Thrun, S., Rodgers, J., Davis, J.: SCAPE: shape completion and animation of people. In: Proceedings of SIGGRAPH ACM Transactions on Graphics, vol. 24, no. 3, pp. 408–416 (2005)
11. Chen, Y., Liu, Z., Zhang, Z.: Tensor-based human body modeling. In: Conference on Computer Vision and Pattern Recognition, pp. 105–112 (2013)
12. Hasler, N., Stoll, C., Sunkel, M., Rosenhahn, B., Seidel, H.P.: A statistical model of human pose and body shape. In: Proceedings of Eurographics Computer Graphics Forum, vol. 28, no. 2, pp. 337–346 (2009)
13. Jain, A., Thormählen, T., Seidel, H.P., Theobalt, C.: MovieReshape: tracking and reshaping of humans in videos. In: Proceedings of SIGGRAPH Asia ACM Transactions on Graphics, vol. 29, no. 148, pp. 1–10 (2010)
14. Neophytou, A., Hilton, A.: Shape and pose space deformation for subject specific animation. In: International Conference on 3D Vision, pp. 334–341 (2013)
15. Loper, M., Mahmood, N., Romero, J., Pons-Moll, G., Black, M.: SMPL: A skinned multi-person linear model. In: Proceedings of SIGGRAPH Asia Transactions on Graphics, vol. 34, no. 6, pp. 248:1–248:16 (2015)
16. Pons-Moll, G., Romero, J., Mahmood, N., Black, M.: DYNA: a model of dynamic human shape in motion. In: Proceedings of SIGGRAPH Transactions on Graphics, vol. 34, no. 4, pp. 120:1–120:14 (2015)
17. Hasler, N., Stoll, C., Rosenhahn, B., Thormählen, T., Seidel, H.P.: Estimating body shape of dressed humans. In: Proceedings of Shape Modeling International Computers and Graphics, vol. 33, no. 3, pp. 211–216 (2009)
18. Wuhrer, S., Shu, C., Xi, P.: Posture-invariant statistical shape analysis using Laplace operator. In: Proceedings of Shape Modeling International Computers and Graphics, vol. 36, no. 5, pp. 410–416 (2012)

19. Stoll, C., Gall, J., de Aguiar, E., Thrun, S., Theobalt, C.: Video-based reconstruction of animatable human characters. In: Proceedings of SIGGRAPH Asia ACM Transactions on Graphics, vol. 29, no. 6, pp. 139:1–139:10 (2010)
20. de Aguiar, E., Stoll, C., Theobalt, C., Ahmed, N., Seidel, H.P., Thrun, S.: Performance capture from sparse multi-view video. In: Proceedings of SIGGRAPH ACM Transactions on Graphics, vol. 27, no. 3, pp. 98:1–98:10 (2008)
21. Vlasic, D., Baran, I., Matusik, W., Popović, J.: Articulated mesh animation from multi-view silhouettes. In: Proceedings of SIGGRAPH ACM Transactions on Graphics, vol. 27, no. 3, pp. 97:1–97:10 (2008)

A Shape-Based Approach for Salient Object Detection Using Deep Learning

Jongpil Kim[(✉)] and Vladimir Pavlovic

Department of Computer Science,
Rutgers, The State University of New Jersey, Piscataway, USA
{jpkim,vladimir}@cs.rutgers.edu

Abstract. Salient object detection is a key step in many image analysis tasks as it not only identifies relevant parts of a visual scene but may also reduce computational complexity by filtering out irrelevant segments of the scene. In this paper, we propose a novel salient object detection method that combines a shape prediction driven by a convolutional neural network with the mid and low-region preserving image information. Our model learns a shape of a salient object using a CNN model for a target region and estimates the full but coarse saliency map of the target image. The map is then refined using image specific low-to-mid level information. Experimental results show that the proposed method outperforms previous state-of-the-arts methods in salient object detection.

Keywords: Salient object detection · Deep learning · Convolutional neural networks

1 Introduction

Visual saliency is one of the fundamental problems in computer vision. It aims to automatically identify the most important and salient regions/objects in an image. The saliency detection slightly differs from general semantic image segmentation in that it seeks to elucidate salient foreground structures from otherwise "irrelevant" background whereas semantic segmentation algorithms partition an image into regions of coherent properties [4]. As it can also reduce computational complexity by focusing on the interest regions, saliency detection has recently received attention in the context of many computer vision problems including object detection, image segmentation and classification.

Many recent works have focused on the specific task of detecting salient objects [4,8,9,11,19,20,27,29,30,33,35,37]. The central task there is to estimate a saliency score of an image patch/superpixel using visual features extracted on the patch/superpixel. To this end, classifiers (or regressors) are trained on the extracted features to determine the saliency score [8,11,27,35].

For training the classifiers, a single binary label is traditionally assigned to the patch based on the normalized overlap rate between the patch and its ground truth salient map [27,35]. The overlap rate ranges from 0 to 1; 0 represents no salient

© Springer International Publishing AG 2016
B. Leibe et al. (Eds.): ECCV 2016, Part IV, LNCS 9908, pp. 455–470, 2016.
DOI: 10.1007/978-3-319-46493-0_28

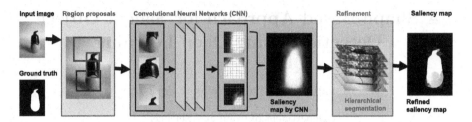

Fig. 1. The overview of the proposed saliency detection framework. First, we generate region proposals from an input image. The regions' saliency map is then assessed by a specifically structured and trained CNN. Finally, we refine the saliency map using a hierarchical segmentation.

region in the patch, and 1 means that the patch is fully contained in the salient region. Then the binary label is obtained by thresholding the overlap rate.

The binary classification-based approaches are limited in that they ignore the shape of the salient region in the patch by assigning a single (univariate) output value to an input (patch or superpixel). Moreover, the patches whose overlap rates are around 0.5 are often ignored to prevent the classifiers from being confused. This results in two critical drawbacks: (1) the valuable data is excluded from the training process and (2) the geometric precision of saliency, in particular for overlaps around 0.5, will be significantly degraded.

To overcome the aforementioned limitations of the binary classification approach, we propose a new method that takes explicit shape of the salient region into consideration. In the proposed method, we model the prediction of the shape of the salient region as a multi-label classification problem. An image patch is assigned to a binary $m \times n$ map so that the map closely resembles the ground truth salient map of the image patch. Therefore, the proposed method can be considered as a structured output prediction approach by considering correlations of saliency "pixels" in the output. This results in more accurate shape-preserving saliency prediction compared to the binary all-salient or all-non-salient traditional representation. Our goal is to learn the image representation to accurately predict the binary map.

An overview of our salient object detection approach is depicted in Fig. 1. Our specific computational model uses a convolutional neural network (CNN) as a multi-label classifier not only because of CNN's strong empirical performance in many vision problems but also because they leverage and directly encode spatial image content. The spatial information is one of the important properties for our task because we want to discover locations and shapes of the salient regions. Unlike the binary classification approaches, the proposed method does not ignore the patches whose overlap rates are around 0.5. Instead, it uses all the patches by extending the binary representation into the $m \times n$ binary map and learns rich representations of the salient regions. To achieve this goal, we propose a new CNN framework to capture not only the local context of a local region of an image but also address the global information of the image.

Despite this geometrically more accurate representation, the predicted saliency map using the CNN may be insufficient to accurately delineate salient shape boundaries as the CNN does not explicitly take the global image context, such as the object placement or image boundaries, into consideration. For instance, as illustrated in Fig. 1, the saliency map detected by the CNN model largely agree with the ground truth maps. However, the boundaries are excessively blurred. Therefore, we combine the output of the CNN with the target-driven hierarchical image segmentation. This combination eliminates over-smoothing and results in improved salient object boundaries.

In summary, this paper makes the following key contributions: (1) we propose a novel method that accurately estimates the shape of the salient region by treating the prediction problem as a structured multi-label classification task, (2) a new CNN architecture that addresses both global and local context of an image is proposed, (3) by effectively combining the deep learning method and the hierarchical segmentation, the proposed method assures accurate delineation of saliency boundaries through the use of image context. As a result it outperforms previous approaches and shows the state-of-the-art performance in saliency detection.

2   Related Work

Over the recent years, the convolutional neural network (CNN) model has demonstrated significant gains in performance for many tasks in computer vision, where sufficient training data is available. Aided by computational speedups resulting from highly-parallelized and efficient GPU implementations, tasks such as object detection, segmentation, and recognition [6,7,14,31,32,34] have seen significant gains in performance. In this paper, we use the CNN framework for the saliency detection as a multi-class classifier. Instead of training the CNN from scratch, we train our model in a similar manner of fine-tuning a pre-trained convolutional network for our purpose so that the proposed method can adapt the knowledge gained on a large dataset to the current task. The fine-tuning methods are known to successfully perform in a variety of problems in computer vision [18,22,34,36].

Salient object detection has attracted key interest in many computer vision applications. Comprehensive surveys of salient object detection and visual attention modeling can be found in [3,4]. A seminal work, Itti et al. proposed bottom-up visual saliency using biologically inspired center-surround differences across multi-scale image features [9]. An alternative approach to use local contrast using a fuzzy growth model is proposed in [19]. In [30], a bottom-up method to detect salient regions using graph-based manifold raking was proposed. Jiang et al. [11] proposed a method to integrate discriminative regional features to compute the saliency scores. Image boundary prior, which assumes that most image boundary regions are background, has been shown to be effective for object saliency detection [25,30,33].

Salient object detection methods using the deep learning methods have been recently proposed [8,27,35,37]. Wang *et al.* [27] proposed to use two convolutional neural networks. One of them is used to learn local patch features to estimate a saliency value of each pixel and the other to incorporate global features such as global contrast and geometric information. Hierarchy-associated features to represent the global context of the salient object were proposed in [37]. Zhao *et al.* [35] proposed a CNN architecture that considers both global-context and local context saliency. Our method is different from the previous approaches in that we estimate a shape of a salient object in a region instead of determining the binary saliency score on each pixel or region.

Several other approaches have been proposed to use shape dictionaries for segmentation [13,16,24] to address the shape of the object beyond the binary representation. In those methods, the shape dictionaries, whose words represented pre-defined shapes, constructed by clustering image patches or descriptors. During prediction, the word closest to the input image in the shape dictionaries is assigned as the prediction result. Unlike the traditional binary representation, these models can attempt to preserve the underlying object/boundary shape. The shape dictionary-based approaches, however, have limitations. First, they predict the shape of the object in the scope of the pre-defined dictionaries. Therefore, how to construct the shape dictionaries (*e.g.*, the number of the clusters) must be carefully examined to assure accurate generalized performance and boundary accuracy. Second, by treating the problem as a multi-class (basis shape) classification, they inadvertently impose the 0–1 loss among classes which does not reflect difference degrees of basis shape similarities. To address this problem, we use the CNN as a multi-label classifier, which will lead to the Hamming, shape-sensitive, loss required for fine boundary delineation.

3   Proposed Method

In this section, we first define the patch-based representation of saliency, which will be the key representation used in our predictive model. Then we describe our architecture of a convolutional neural network (CNN) for salient object detection and how to train it. Next we explain the proposed framework to predict a saliency map using the trained CNN model. Lastly, we describe the refinement of the saliency map using the mid and low-level information such as hierarchical segmentations.

3.1   Saliency Representation

In the previous binary-based or shape dictionary-based approaches for the salient object detection, an image patch associated with a binary value (*e.g.*, presence or absence of the object in the patch) or a label (representing the dictionary shape closest in appearance to the saliency map). Instead, we directly represent the saliency map in the patch using an $m \times n$ binary map, as illustrated in Fig. 2. Note that the resolution of this map need not to be the same as the resolution of

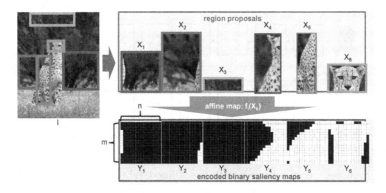

Fig. 2. Visualization of region proposals and their encoded binary saliency map representations. We generate region proposals, $\{X_1, \ldots, X_6\}$, on image I. Then we map them to encoded binary saliency maps of size $m \times n$, $\{Y_1, \ldots, Y_6\}$ by affine map $f_I(X_k)$.

the original saliency map, instead it typically represents a coarse approximation. Our goal is to predict this binary map by treating the prediction problem as a multi-label classification.

Image-based saliency could, in principle, be encoded based on saliency of a set of dense, overlapping, patches that fully span the image. However, this representation is typically highly (computationally) inefficient. Instead, we define image saliency based solely on the saliency of representative image regions. In particular, we use selective search [26] to extract category-independent region proposals as it is fast and showed successful performance in the object detection tasks [1,7].

Formally, for image I we generate K region proposals, $\{X_1, X_2, \ldots, X_K\}$ by a region proposal method (selective search), where X_k is the k-th representative region of size $h_k \times w_k$ centered at position (s_k, t_k). Each X_k is mapped to Y_k of size $m \times n$, the encoded binary saliency map of region X_k, $Y_k = f_I(X_k)$, where $f_I(\cdot)$ is the affine map from X_k to Y_k. We aim at predicting all entries of Y_k as the multi-label classification.

Figure 2 depicts sample region proposals and corresponding encoded binary saliency maps. We can observe that our saliency representation accurately preserves the shape information of the objects.

3.2 Convolutional Neural Networks for Shape Prediction

In this section, we explain our *shape-based* saliency detection framework (SSD) using convolutional neural networks (CNN) for salient object detection. We aim at training the CNN for the multi-label classification so that it will be able to predict the salient shape of the object accurately.

Figure 3 shows the architecture of the CNN designed for our purpose. The CNN contains two branches, one for fine representation (top) and the other

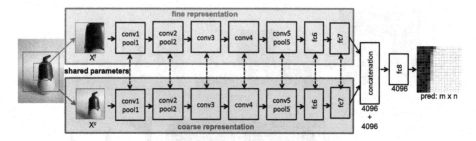

Fig. 3. The architecture of our shape-based saliency detection model. The CNN contains two branches: the top branch processes a fine-level image patch to handle local-context while the bottom addresses global-context contained in a coarse-level image patch. Two branches are combined to fully connected layer `fc8`. We adopt AlexNet [14] for two branches up to `fc7`. We tie weights between two branches, denoted by dashed arrows, so that the same `fc`-level feature embedding functions is used for two input patches. Then joint relationship is estimated at `fc8`.

for coarse representation (bottom). For the fine representation, we feed region proposal X^f of size $h \times w$ centered at position (s, t) to the CNN to predict the saliency. However, an isolated image patch may be insufficient to determine the saliency as it contains only the local information, excluding the important regional context. To include contextual information from the neighborhood of X^f to the CNN, we extract a larger image patch X^c so that X^c has the same center position (s, t) with size $\alpha h \times \alpha w$ where $\alpha > 1$ is a magnification factor. In this way, the CNN leverages the local content within X^f and combines it with the regional context in X^c.

For the implementation, we use a pair of AlexNet-like architectures [14] each of which has the same architecture as AlextNet up to `fc7` as illustrated in Fig. 3. The fine representation branch processes X^f to address the local information while the coarse representation branch exploits the global context contained in X^c. We tie weights between two branches up to `fc7` so that the same `fc`-level feature embedding function is used for both coarse and fine patches. Then two `fc7`s in both branches are concatenated and fully connected to `fc8` where joint relationship between X^f and X^c is estimated. We use the sigmoid layer for `pred` so that each entry in the output has a real value in the range of 0 and 1. We train the proposed architecture in an end-to-end manner.

Training. We can train AlexNet by minimizing a negative log-likelihood cost function as follows:

$$L = -\frac{1}{N} \sum_{i=1}^{N} \sum_{l=1}^{L} \delta(y_i = l) \cdot \log\left(\hat{p}_l(x_i)\right), \quad (1)$$

where N and L are the numbers of the training samples and the labels, respectively, x_i the i-th input, $y_i \in (1, 2, \ldots, L)$ the ground truth label for x_i, $\hat{p}_l(x_i)$ the prediction probability of x_i for the l-th label, and $\delta(\cdot)$ the indicator function.

Our goal is to predict entries of a $m \times n$ patch under the multi-label classification. To achieve this, we use the sigmoid cross entropy loss function to optimize the proposed CNN as follows:

$$L = -\frac{1}{N} \sum_{i=1}^{N} \sum_{l=1}^{mn} \left[Y_i(l) \log \left(\hat{p}_l(X_i^f, X_i^c) \right) + (1 - Y_i(i)) \log \left(1 - \hat{p}_l(X_i^f, X_i^c) \right) \right],$$

(2)

where N is the number of training samples, $Y_i(l)$ the l-th binary value of i-th encoded saliency map Y_i, and $\hat{p}_l(X_i^f, X_i^c)$ the prediction probability of our CNN taking X_i^f and X_i^c as inputs. We can train our convolutional neural network by minimizing the loss function in (2).

Prediction. To predict a saliency map for a given image, we first generate region proposals using selective search to obtain category-free object regions on the image. The region proposal method reduces the search space by allowing us to focus on the interest regions where objects are likely to appear. Therefore, we can reduce the number of the CNN evaluations instead of exhaustively running the CNN on the entire image.

For a given image $I^{h \times w}$, we generate region proposals $\{X_1^f, \ldots, X_K^f\}$ by selective search, and corresponding $\{X_1^c, \ldots, X_K^c\}$ as explained. We then run the CNN by feeding X_k^f and X_k^c as inputs and predict a salient object shape, p_k. Next, we perform the affine transformation to map $p_k^{m \times n}$ back to the position (s_k, y_k) with size (h_k, w_k), pad zeros outside the transformed area to obtain a saliency prediction map $P_k^{h \times w}$.

The final saliency map for the whole image is the average of the prediction results, $\{P_1, P_2, \ldots, P_K\}$. Let $C^{h \times w}$ be a matrix for normalization where $C(l)$ denotes the number of the region proposals containing the l-th entry (pixel). Then the saliency map S for input image I is computed as follows:

$$S(l) = \begin{cases} 0 & \text{if } C(l) = 0 \\ \frac{\sum_{k=1}^{K} P_k(l)}{C(l)} & \text{if } C(l) > 0 \end{cases},$$

(3)

where l denotes the l-th entry.

3.3 Refinement of Saliency Maps Using Hierarchical Segmentations

In this section, we explain our shape-based saliency detection using the hierarchical segmentation (SSD-HS) method for refinement. The CNN-based prediction proposed above may not consider spatial consistency or boundaries of objects in the image as it processes the region proposals independently. As a results, the predicted salient maps usually show fuzzy object boundaries as depicted in Fig. 4 (third column, SSD).

To overcome this limitation, we refine the predicted saliency map using the target image-specific segmentation proposals. The main role of the segmentation is to provide informative boundary cues so that we can find pixel-wise accurate candidates of the objects as well as maintain the global spatial consistency.

To achieve this, we generate a set of L-level hierarchical segmentation proposals $M = \{M_1, M_2, \ldots, M_L\}$ where M_1 is the finest segmentation with the largest number of segmented regions and M_L is the coarsest with the smallest number of regions for image I. Note that M_l is computed by merging the regions in M_{l-1}. In this way, we build a hierarchy in the set of L-level segmentations. We use an ultrametric contour map (UCM) generated by the gPb (globalized probability of boundary based contour detection) [2] to build the hierarchical segmentation for our purpose. The UCM contains a set of real valued contours to reflect the contrast between neighboring regions. We generate the hierarchical segmentation maps by thresholding the UCM with L different values.

Let $R_l(i)$ be the i-th region (superpixel) on the l-th level segmentation M_l. We define the saliency score in $R_l(i)$, $M_l(i)$, as the expected saliency prediction score computed by the CNN in that region as follows:

$$M_l(i) = \frac{1}{|R_l(i)|} \sum_{p \in R_l(i)} S(p), \tag{4}$$

where p is a pixel in region $R_l(i)$, $S(p)$ the predicted saliency value at pixel p, and $|R_l(i)|$ the number of the pixels in $R_l(i)$. Then we compute the refined saliency map for the l-th level, S_l, by assigning $M_l(i)$ to all pixels in $R_l(i)$:

$$S_l(p) = M_l(i), \qquad p \in R_l(i). \tag{5}$$

In this way, we have L refined saliency maps, $\{S_1, S_2, \ldots, S_L\}$ for image I.

Figure 4 shows the refined multi-level saliency maps generated by (5). In the finer level, boundaries of the objects are preserved while there are many artifacts in the background. As we move toward the coarser level, those artifacts become weaker. On the other hand, we lose the accurate object boundaries. Therefore, we need to combine the multi-level saliency maps to both preserve accurate delineation of saliency boundaries and reduce the artifacts.

A problem of fusing the multi-level saliency maps to generate a final output has been previously discussed including approaches to use the conditional random field (CRF) [17] or the regression method [11]. In this paper, we use a least-square estimator as it is fast to compute and results in strong performance. Formally, we formulate the following optimization problem to find weights $\mathbf{w} = \{w_1, \ldots, w_l\}$ to linearly combine the multi-level saliency maps:

$$\arg\min_{\mathbf{w}} \sum_{I \in \mathbf{V}} \left\| Y^I - \sum_{l=1}^{L} w_l S_l^I \right\|_F^2, \tag{6}$$

$$\text{s.t.} \sum_{l=1}^{L} w_l = 1, \qquad w_l \geq 0 \quad (l = 1, 2, \ldots, L)$$

where $\mathbf{V}$ denotes the validation set, and Y^I the ground truth saliency map for image I. The final saliency map is computed as the weighted linear sum of the multi-level saliency maps, $\sum_{l=1}^{L} w_l S_l$. As desired, the fused map shows accurate boundaries and little artifacts as depicted in Fig. 4 (last column, SSD-HS).

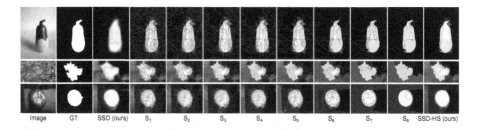

Fig. 4. Visualization of multi-level saliency maps using the hierarchical segmentations. SSD, detected by the CNN, initially shows fuzzy boundaries and artifacts. By aggregating saliency maps from S_1 (finest) to S_8 (coarsest), SSD-HS successfully delineates accurate object boundaries and smooths out the artifacts.

4   Experimental Results

In this section, we explain our experimental settings including the datasets we used in the paper and the CNN settings. We then examine the performance of our saliency representation and compare it to other baseline methods. Next, we show the saliency prediction results using the proposed method and compare to state-of-the-art methods in saliency detection. Lastly, we analyze the multi-context representation used in our CNN architecture.

4.1   Experimental Settings

Benchmark Datasets. To evaluate the performance of the proposed method, we use several datasets that are widely used for saliency detection including MSRA-5000 [17], SOD [21,28], ECSSD [29] and PASCAL-S [15]. Each dataset provides pixel-wise ground truth annotation for the salient objects. MSRA-5000 is the largest dataset, consisting of 5000 images that cover a large variety of image contents including natural scenes, animals, indoor, outdoor and so on. SOD is a collection of salient object boundaries based on Berkeley Segmentation Dataset. SOD is challenging as it has 300 images with multiple objects. ECSSD includes many semantically meaningful but structurally complex images in 1000 images. PASCAL-S dataset contains 850 natural images with complex objects and backgrounds.

Evaluation Criteria. We evaluate the performance of the proposed method using the precision-recall (PR) curve and the F-measure. For the PR curve, we increase the threshold from 0 to 255 and measure the precision and recall of a saliency map. We compute the maximal F-measure of the average precision-recall curve as in [4]. The F-measure is a harmonic mean of precision and recall defined as:

$$F_\beta = \frac{(1 + \beta^2) \cdot (P \times R)}{\beta^2 \cdot P + R}, \tag{7}$$

where P and R are precision and recall, respectively. We set β^2 to 0.3 because we want to emphasize the precision more than the recall [4,27].

Fig. 5. Visualization of selected shape classes.

Experimental Settings and Training CNN. We split the MSRA-5000 dataset into training, validation and test sets as suggested in [11]. We do not use other datasets during training because not only they do not have as many images as MSRA-5000 does but also we want to examine how well the proposed model can be adapted to different datasets without overfitting. We use selective search to generate patches on the training set and randomly select 100,000 patches to train our CNN model.

We use the open-source package Caffe [10] to implement our CNN model. In our implementation, we initialized the weights of our network by adopting those of AlexNet trained on ImageNet [5] where possible in a fine-tunning manner instead of training the CNN from scratch. As our CNN takes a pair of two images whose sizes are 227×227, we resize the input images by the bilinear interpolation before we feed them to the CNN.

We set $\alpha = 2$ such that $X^c \in \mathcal{R}^{2m \times 2n}$ includes the neighborhood information of $X^f \in \mathcal{R}^{m \times n}$. We use a square encoded binary saliency map, *i.e.*, $m = n$. For the hierarchical segmentation maps, we empirically set the number of the maps L to 16 by thresholding the UCM map from 0.2 to 0.95 quantiles with a step size 0.05.

4.2   Experimental Results

Evaluation on Various Schemes for Saliency Representation. To determine the optimal size of the encoded saliency map, we perform experiments with various sizes, $m \in \{8, 16, 24, 32\}$. The experimental results are shown in Table 1. If m is too small, it may be insufficient to represent accurate shapes because the affine map loses much information. On the other hand, as we increase m, the complexity of the encoded map increases. Consequently, SSD (16×16) shows the best performance so that we set $m = 16$ hereafter.

Experimental results with two additional $\alpha \in \{1.5, 3\}$ are also shown in Table 1. $\alpha = 3$ shows worse performance than $\alpha = 2$ (*i.e.*, SSD 16×16) because the coarse patch may be too large, losing the information of the object shape. On the other hand, if the coarse patch looks at a smaller region, *i.e.*, $\alpha = 1.5$, it may fail to consider the global context, resulting in worse performance than $\alpha = 2$.

To set baseline methods, we adopt binary representation-based and shape dictionary-based approaches, and fully convolutional networks as follows:

– Binary representation (BIN)
  We use the traditional binary representation as a baseline method. In this approach, a region proposal is mapped to a binary value by thresholding the

Table 1. F-measure scores for baseline and proposed methods on four benchmark datasets. Red and blue colors denote the best and the second best results, respectively.

Data Set	BIN	DIC	FCN	SSD (8x8)	SSD (16x16)	SSD (24x24)	SSD (32x32)	SSD ($\alpha = 1.5$)	SSD ($\alpha = 3$)
MSRA-5000	0.663	0.830	0.788	0.875	**0.888**	0.883	0.878	**0.885**	0.865
PASCAL-S	0.642	0.761	0.783	0.786	**0.802**	**0.794**	0.785	0.792	0.788
ECSSD	0.619	0.789	0.778	**0.844**	**0.853**	0.842	0.828	0.832	0.831
SOD	0.575	0.692	0.693	0.715	**0.733**	0.729	0.705	**0.738**	0.718

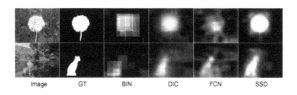

Image   GT   BIN   DIC   FCN   SSD

Fig. 6. Saliency maps generated by baseline and proposed methods. GT: ground truth. BIN: binary representation. DIC: dictionary-based representation. FCN: fully convolutional networks. SSD: our shape-based salient detection method.

normalized overlap rate between the region and its ground truth map. Note that BIN can be easily implemented by setting $m = n = 1$ in our framework.
- Dictionary-based representation (DIC)
  We encode the saliency map using pre-defined shape classes as in [13,16,24]. For this purpose, we cluster normalized region proposals to construct a dictionary with D shape classes, $\{V_1, V_2, \ldots, V_D\}$. Sample shape classes are depicted in Fig. 5. Then we train a CNN^{DIC} as a multi-class classifier to predict the shape class closest to the region proposal. For region proposal X_k, we compute its local saliency map as an expected shape over prediction of the CNN^{DIC}:

$$P_k^{\text{DIC}} = \sum_{d=1}^{D} V_d \cdot \text{CNN}_d^{\text{DIC}}(X_k), \qquad (8)$$

where $\text{CNN}_d^{\text{DIC}}(X_k)$ is the prediction probability of X_k for shape class d. Then we can compute the final saliency map by replacing P_k with P_k^{DIC} in (3). We set D to 64 as in [13].
- Fully convolutional network (FCN)
  FCN allows us to predict a full sized saliency map by introducing deconvolution layers [18]. FCN is similar to our approach in that it directly estimates the shape of the salient object. However, FCN takes the entire image into consideration while our method focuses on the salient object areas by employing the region proposal method. For the implementation, we fine-tune a pre-trained model provided by the authors of [18]. We set the number of classes to two (0 for a background pixel, 1 for a salient object pixel). We normalize the output of FCN using the softmax function for our purpose.

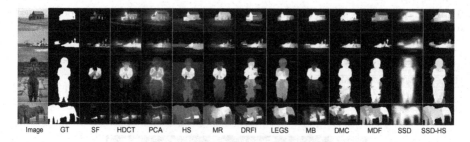

Image   GT   SF   HDCT   PCA   HS   MR   DRFI   LEGS   MB   DMC   MDF   SSD   SSD-HS

Fig. 7. Saliency maps generated by different methods for comparison including SF [23], HDCT [12], PCA [20] HS [29], MR [30], DRFI [11], LEGS [27], MB [33], DMC [35], and MDF [8]. GT denotes ground truth. SSD and SSD-HS are the proposed methods.

Experimental results in Table 1 confirm that the proposed shape-based approach outperforms the other baseline methods. For the qualitative analysis, we depict sample saliency maps in Fig. 6. BIN performs the worst because it ignores the shape information and therefore fails to delineate accurate object boundaries. FCN computes the saliency values on the entire image while the proposed SSD focuses on the object regions. Therefore, SSD can highlight the salient regions without being distracted by the background areas, resulting in better performance than FCN as shown in Fig. 6. DIC performs worse than the proposed method as it represents the object's shape as a combination of the pre-defined shape classes while the proposed method can estimate an arbitrary shape. As a result, DIC results in coarse saliency maps while our SSD detects accurate silhouettes of objects as illustrated in Fig. 6.

Comparison to Previous Methods. To evaluate the performance of the proposed method, we compare our method to 10 state-of-the-art methods in salient object detection including SF [23], HDCT [12], PCA [20] HS [29], MR [30], DRFI [11], LEGS [27], MB [33], DMC [35], and MDF [8]. Figure 8 shows the performance evaluation results in terms of the Precision-Recall curve (PR-curve). Our SSD-HS shows the best performance among the other methods over the four datasets as shown in Fig. 8. The performance of SSD is also comparable to the other methods in all the benchmark datasets. These results confirm the importance of the shape prediction-based approach for salient object detection. The F-measure scores over the four benchmark datasets also verify that the proposed method outperforms the others as shown in Table 2.

We also compare our saliency maps to those computed by the other method for the qualitative analysis in Fig. 7. It is interesting to observe that SSD accurately detects silhouettes of the salient objects even though it does not take the spatial consistency or boundaries of objects in the image into consideration. Combined with the hierarchical segmentation, SSD-HS can highlight the salient objects more accurately than the others.

Multi-context Representation. To analyze the effect of the multi-context representation, we construct a single-context framework (fiSSD-HD) by using

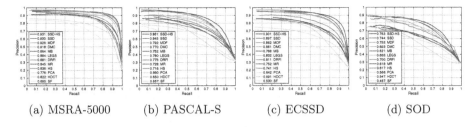

(a) MSRA-5000   (b) PASCAL-S   (c) ECSSD   (d) SOD

Fig. 8. Precision-Recall curves on four benchmark datasets. The number next to the method name denotes the AUC (area under curve) score.

Table 2. F-measure scores for different methods including ours on four benchmark datasets. Red and blue colors denote the best and the second best results, respectively.

Data Set	SF	HDCT	PCA	HS	MR	DRFI	LEGS	MB	DMC	MDF	SSD	SSD-HS
MSRA-5000	0.701	0.813	0.752	0.813	0.824	0.845	0.870	0.826	**0.894**	0.885	0.888	**0.902**
PASCAL-S	0.557	0.653	0.651	0.694	0.701	0.738	0.776	0.724	0.763	0.792	**0.802**	**0.820**
ECSSD	0.548	0.704	0.642	0.727	0.739	0.778	0.827	0.739	0.837	0.832	**0.853**	**0.865**
SOD	0.493	0.576	0.578	0.619	0.610	0.677	0.700	0.625	0.699	**0.738**	0.733	**0.756**

only the fine representation branch in Fig. 3 and compare it to SSD-HD. fiSSD-HD is trained and evaluated under the same experimental settings as SSD-HD.

Figure 9a shows the PR-curves on ECSSD for SSD-HD and fiSSD-HD. Because SSD-HS uses both contextual and local information together, it consequently outperforms fiSSD-HD that relies only on the local context.

We measure the classification performance of the CNNs used in fiSSD-HD and SSD-HD to understand their different behaviors. For this purpose, we test both CNNs on 10000 random region proposals from the test dataset and measure the mean absolute error (MAE) as the evaluation criteria. We found that the MAE values are 0.1734 for SSD-HS and 0.2240 for fiSSD-HS. This result verifies that the multi-context representation used in SSD-HS significantly reduces the classification error of the CNN, and consequently increases the performance of the saliency detection.

We also draw the MAE as a function of the normalized overlap rate (between the patch and its ground truth salient map) as shown in Fig. 9b. The figure depicts that multi-context representation significantly reduces the classification error when the overlap rate is around 0 (absence of salient object pixels) or 1 (full of object pixels). These results imply that if the region proposal is outside or inside the salient object, the single-context representation may be insufficient to predict the saliency. The multi-context representation, however, can overcome this limitation by looking at wide areas to determine the uniqueness of the local region.

Figure 9c visualizes prediction results for region proposals. The CNN in fiSSD-HS produces a completely wrong prediction if the region proposal is inside the object (broccoli). It also has difficulty to separate the salient object from

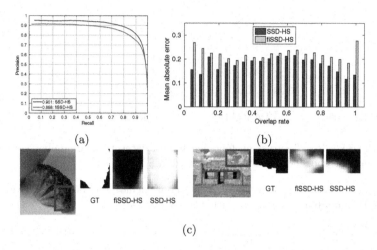

Fig. 9. (a) Precision-Recall curves on ECSSD. (b) The mean average error (MAE) as a function of the overlap rate. (c) The multi representation (SSD-HS) predicts accurately the shapes of the salient objects in the region proposals. However, the coarse representation (fiSSD-HS) results in a completely wrong prediction (left), or does not accurately detect the salient object when the background is complex (right).

complex backgrounds (cloudy sky). However, the multi-context representation is able to detect the salient objects accurately by exploiting the global context.

5   Conclusions

In this paper, we proposed a novel method to detect salient objects in an image using a specially designed convolutional neural network (CNN) model. For this purpose, we formulated the salient object detection problem as the multi-label classification. Our method directly estimates the shape of the salient object using the CNN trained to predict the shape of the object. We further refine the saliency map predicted by the CNN using the hierarchical segmentation maps to exploit the global information such as spatial consistency and object boundaries. The quantitative and the qualitative analyses on various benchmark datasets confirm that the proposed method outperforms the state-of-the-art methods in saliency detection.

References

1. Alexe, B., Deselaers, T., Ferrari, V.: Measuring the objectness of image windows. IEEE Trans. Pattern Anal. Mach. Intell. (TPAMI) **34**, 2189–2202 (2012)
2. Arbelaez, P., Maire, M., Fowlkes, C., Malik, J.: Contour detection and hierarchical image segmentation. IEEE Trans. Pattern Anal. Mach. Intell. (TPAMI) **33**(5), 898–916 (2011)

3. Borji, A., Itti, L.: State-of-the-art in visual attention modeling. IEEE Trans. Pattern Anal. Mach. Intell. (TPAMI) **35**(1), 185–207 (2013)
4. Borji, A., Sihite, D.N., Itti, L.: Salient object detection: a benchmark. In: European Conference on Computer Vision (ECCV) (2012)
5. Deng, J., Dong, W., Socher, R., Li, L.J., Li, K., Fei-Fei, L.: ImageNet: a large-scale hierarchical image database. In: IEEE Conference on Computer Vision and Pattern Recognition (CVPR) (2009)
6. Donahue, J., Jia, Y., Vinyals, O., Hoffman, J., Zhang, N., Tzeng, E., Darrell, T.: DeCAF: a deep convolutional activation feature for generic visual recognition. In: International Conference on Machine Learning (ICML) (2014)
7. Girshick, R., Donahue, J., Darrell, T., Malik, J.: Rich feature hierarchies for accurate object detection and semantic segmentation. In: IEEE Conference on Computer Vision and Pattern Recognition (CVPR) (2014)
8. Guanbin Li, Y.Y.: Visual saliency based on multiscale deep features. In: IEEE Conference on Computer Vision and Pattern Recognition (CVPR) (2015)
9. Itti, L., Koch, C., Niebur, E.: A model of saliency-based visual attention for rapid scene analysis. IEEE Trans. Pattern Anal. Mach. Intell. (TPAMI) **20**(11), 1254–1259 (1998)
10. Jia, Y., Shelhamer, E., Donahue, J., Karayev, S., Long, J., Girshick, R., Guadarrama, S., Darrell, T.: Caffe: convolutional architecture for fast feature embedding. arXiv preprint arXiv:1408.5093 (2014)
11. Jiang, H., Wang, J., Yuan, Z., Wu, Y., Zheng, N., Li, S.: Salient object detection: a discriminative regional feature integration approach. In: IEEE Conference on Computer Vision and Pattern Recognition (CVPR) (2013)
12. Kim, J., Han, D., Tai, Y.W., Kim, J.: Salient region detection via high-dimensional color transform. In: IEEE Conference on Computer Vision and Pattern Recognition (CVPR) (2014)
13. Kim, J., Pavlovic, V.: A shape preserving approach for salient object detection using convolutional neural networks. In: International Conference on Pattern Recognition (ICPR) (2016)
14. Krizhevsky, A., Sutskever, I., Hinton, G.E.: ImageNet classification with deep convolutional neural networks. In: Advances in Neural Information Processing Systems (NIPS), pp. 1–9 (2012)
15. Li, Y., Hou, X., Koch, C., Rehg, J.M., Yuille, A.L.: The secrets of salient object segmentation. In: IEEE Conference on Computer Vision and Pattern Recognition (CVPR) (2014)
16. Lim, J.J., Zitnick, C.L., Dollár, P.: Sketch tokens: a learned mid-level representation for contour and object detection. In: CVPR (2013)
17. Liu, T., Yuan, Z., Sun, J., Wang, J., Zheng, N., Tang, X., Shum, H.Y.: Learning to detect a salient object. IEEE Trans. Pattern Anal. Mach. Intell. (TPAMI) **33**(2), 353–367 (2011)
18. Long, J., Shelhamer, E., Darrell, T.: Fully convolutional networks for semantic segmentation. In: IEEE Conference on Computer Vision and Pattern Recognition (CVPR) (2015)
19. Ma, Y.F., Zhang, H.J.: Contrast-based image attention analysis by using Fuzzy growing. In: ACM International Conference on Multimedia (MM) (2003)
20. Margolin, R., Tal, A., Zelnik-Manor, L.: What makes a patch distinct? In: IEEE Conference on Computer Vision and Pattern Recognition (CVPR) (2013)
21. Movahedi, V., Elder, J.H.: Design and perceptual validation of performance measures for salient object segmentation. In: Perceptual Organization in Computer Vision (POCV) (2010)

22. Oquab, M., Bottou, L., Laptev, I., Sivic, J.: Learning and transferring mid-level image representations using convolutional neural networks. In: IEEE Conference on Computer Vision and Pattern Recognition (CVPR) (2014)

23. Perazzi, F., Krähenbühl, P., Pritch, Y., Hornung, A.: Saliency filters: contrast based filtering for salient region detection. In: IEEE Conference on Computer Vision and Pattern Recognition (CVPR), pp. 733–740 (2012)

24. Shen, W., Wang, X., Wang, Y., Bai, X., Zhang, Z.: DeepContour: a deep convolutional feature learned by positive-sharing loss for contour detection. In: IEEE Conference on Computer Vision and Pattern Recognition (CVPR) (2015)

25. Sun, J., Lu, H., Li, S.: Saliency detection based on integration of boundary and soft-segmentation. In: International Conference on Image Processing (ICIP) (2012)

26. Uijlings, J., van de Sande, K., Gevers, T., Smeulders, A.: Selective search for object recognition. Int. J. Comput. Vis. (IJCV) **104**, 154–171 (2013)

27. Wang, L., Lu, H., Ruan, X., Yang, M.H.: Deep networks for saliency detection via local estimation and global search. In: IEEE Conference on Computer Vision and Pattern Recognition (CVPR) (2015)

28. Wei, Y., Wen, F., Zhu, W., Sun, J.: Geodesic saliency using background priors. In: European Conference on Computer Vision (ECCV) (2012)

29. Yan, Q., Xu, L., Shi, J., Jia, J.: Hierarchical saliency detection. In: IEEE Conference on Computer Vision and Pattern Recognition (CVPR) (2013)

30. Yang, C., Zhang, L., Lu, H., Ruan, X., Yang, M.H.: Saliency detection via graph-based manifold ranking. In: IEEE Conference on Computer Vision and Pattern Recognition (CVPR) (2013)

31. LeCun, Y., Bottou, L., Bengio, Y., Haffner, P.: Gradient-based Learning applied to Document Recognition. In: Proceedings of the IEEE (1998)

32. Zeiler, M.D., Fergus, R.: Visualizing and understanding convolutional networks. In: European Conference on Computer Vision (ECCV) (2014)

33. Zhang, J., Sclaroff, S., Lin, Z., Shen, X., Price, B., Měch, R.: Minimum barrier salient object detection at 80 FPS. In: International Conference on Computer Vision (ICCV) (2015)

34. Zhang, N., Donahue, J., Girshick, R., Darrell, T.: Part-based R-CNNs for fine-grained category detection. In: European Conference on Computer Vision (ECCV) (2014)

35. Zhao, R., Ouyang, W., Li, H., Wang, X.: Saliency detection by multi-context deep learning. In: IEEE Conference on Computer Vision and Pattern Recognition (CVPR) (2015)

36. Zhou, B., Lapedriza, A., Xiao, J., Torralba, A., Oliva, A.: Learning deep features for scene recognition using places database. In: Neuarl Information Processing Systems (NIPS) (2014)

37. Zou, W., Komodakis, N.: HARF: Hierarchy-associated rich features for salient object detection. In: International Conference on Computer Vision (ICCV) (2015)

Fast Optical Flow Using Dense Inverse Search

Till Kroeger[1]([⊠]), Radu Timofte[1], Dengxin Dai[1], and Luc Van Gool[1,2]

[1] Computer Vision Laboratory, D-ITET, ETH Zurich, Zurich, Switzerland
{kroegert,timofter,dai,vangool}@vision.ee.ethz.ch
[2] VISICS/iMinds, ESAT, KU Leuven, Leuven, Belgium

Abstract. Most recent works in optical flow extraction focus on the accuracy and neglect the time complexity. However, in real-life visual applications, such as tracking, activity detection and recognition, the time complexity is critical. We propose a solution with very low time complexity and competitive accuracy for the computation of dense optical flow. It consists of three parts: (1) inverse search for patch correspondences; (2) dense displacement field creation through patch aggregation along multiple scales; (3) variational refinement. At the core of our *Dense Inverse Search*-based method (DIS) is the efficient search of correspondences inspired by the inverse compositional image alignment proposed by Baker and Matthews (2001, 2004). DIS is competitive on standard optical flow benchmarks. DIS runs at 300 Hz up to 600 Hz on a single CPU core (1024 × 436 resolution. 42 Hz/46 Hz when including preprocessing: disk access, image re-scaling, gradient computation. More details in Sect. 3.1.), reaching the temporal resolution of human's biological vision system. It is order(s) of magnitude faster than state-of-the-art methods in the same range of accuracy, making DIS ideal for real-time applications.

1 Introduction

Optical flow estimation is under constant pressure to increase both its quality and speed. Such progress allows for new applications. A higher speed enables its inclusion into larger systems with extensive subsequent processing (*e.g.* reliable features for motion segmentation, tracking or action/activity recognition) and its deployment in computationally constrained scenarios (*e.g.* embedded systems, autonomous robots, large-scale data processing).

A robust optical flow algorithm should cope with discontinuities (outliers, occlusions, motion discontinuities), appearance changes (illumination, chromaticity, blur, deformations), and large displacements. Decades after the pioneering research of Horn and Schunck [4] and Lucas and Kanade [5] we have solutions for the first two issues [6,7] and recent endeavors lead to significant progress in handling large displacements [8–21]. This came at the cost of high run-times usually not acceptable in computationally constrained scenarios such as real-time applications. Recently, only very few works aimed at balancing accuracy

Electronic supplementary material The online version of this chapter (doi:10.1007/978-3-319-46493-0_29) contains supplementary material, which is available to authorized users.

© Springer International Publishing AG 2016
B. Leibe et al. (Eds.): ECCV 2016, Part IV, LNCS 9908, pp. 471–488, 2016.
DOI: 10.1007/978-3-319-46493-0_29

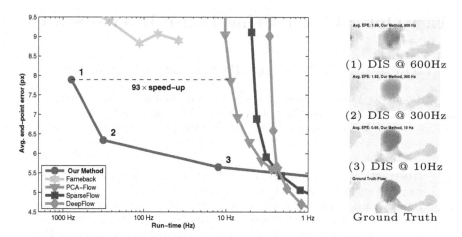

Fig. 1. Our DIS method runs at 10 Hz up to 600 Hz on a single core CPU for an average end-point pixel error smaller or similar to top optical flow methods at similar speed. This plot excludes preprocessing time for *all* methods. Details in Sects. 3.1 and 3.3.

and run-time in favor of efficiency [19, 22, 23], or employed massively parallelized dedicated hardware to achieve acceptable run-times [21, 24, 25]. In contrast to this, recently it has been noted for several computer vision tasks [3, 26–29], that it is often desirable to trade-off powerful but complex algorithms for simple and efficients methods, and rely on high frame-rates and smaller search spaces for good accuracy. In this paper we focus on improving the speed of optical flow in general, non-domain-specific scenarios, while remaining close to the state-of-the-art flow quality. We propose two novel components with low time complexity, one using inverse search for fast patch correspondences, and one based on multi-scale aggregation for fast dense flow estimation. Additionally, a fast variational refinement step further improves the accuracy of our *dense inverse search*-based method. Altogether, we obtain speed-ups of 1–2 orders of magnitude over state-of-the-art methods at similar flow quality operating points (Fig. 1). The run-times are in the range of 10–600 Hz on 1024 × 436 resolution images, depending on the selected trade-off between run-time and accuracy, by using a single CPU core on a common desktop PC. The method reaches the temporal resolution of human's biological vision system [3]. To the best of our knowledge, this is the first time that optical flow at several hundred frames-per-second has been reached with such high flow quality on any hardware.

1.1   Related Work

Providing an exhaustive overview [30] of optical flow estimation is beyond the scope of this paper. Most of the work on improving the time complexity (without trading-off quality) combines some of the following ideas:

While, initially, the **feature descriptors** of choice were extracted sparsely, invariant under scaling or affine transformations [31], the recent trend in optical flow estimation is to densely extract rigid (square) descriptors from local frames [9,32,33]. HOG [34], SIFT [35], and SURF [36] are among the most popular square patch support descriptors. In the context of scene correspondence, the SIFT-flow [33] and PatchMatch [37] algorithms use descriptors or small patches. The descriptors are invariant only to similarities which may be insufficient especially for large displacements and challenging deformations [9]. Godot *et al.* [38] learn descriptors appropriate for optical flow using siamese CNNs.

The **feature matching** usually employs a (reciprocal) nearest neighbor operation [9,35,37,38]. Important exceptions are the recent works of Weinzaepfel *et al.* [17] (non-rigid matching inspired by deep convolutional nets), of Leordeanu *et al.* [11] (enforcing affine constraints), and of Timofte *et al.* [12] (robust matching inspired by compressed sensing). They follow Brox and Malik [9] and guide a variational optical flow estimation through (sparse) correspondences from the descriptor matcher and can thus handle arbitrarily large displacements. Xu *et al.* [20] combine SIFT [35] and PatchMatch [37] matching for refined flow level initialization at the expense of computational costs.

An **optimization** problem is often at the core of the flow extraction methods. The flow is estimated by minimizing an energy that sums up matching errors and smoothness constraints. While Horn and Schunck [4] proposed a variational approach to globally optimize the flow, Lucas and Kanade [5] solve the correspondence problem locally and independently for image patches. Local [5,23,39] methods are usually faster but less accurate than the global ones. Given location and smoothness priors over the image, MRF formulations are used [40,41]. Recently full optimization over discrete grids has been successfully applied [14,42].

Parallel computation is a natural way of improving the run-time of the optical flow methods by (re)designing them for parallelization. The industry historically favored specialized hardware such as FPGAs [43], while the recent years brought the advance of GPUs [21,24,25,44]. Yet, multi-core design on the same machine is the most common parallelization. However, many complex flow methods are difficult to adapt for parallel processing.

Learning. Most of the optical flow methods exploit training images for parameter tuning. However, this is only a rough embedding of prior knowledge. Only recently methods were proposed that successfully learn specific models from such training material. Wulff *et al.* [19] assume that any flow field can be approximated by a decomposition over a learned basis of flow fields. Fischer *et al.* [21] construct Convolutional Neural Networks (CNNs) to solve the optical flow estimation. Gadot *et al.* [38] learn patch similarities using siamese CNNs.

Coarse-to-fine optimizations have been applied frequently to flow estimation [9,45,46] to avoid poor local minima, especially for large motions, and thus to improve the performance and to speed up the convergence.

Branch and bound and **priority queues** have been used to find smart strategies to first explore the flow in the most favorable image regions and gradually refine it for the more ambiguous regions. This often leads to a reduction in computational costs. The PatchMatch methods [37,38,46] follow a branch and bound strategy, gradually fixing the most promising correspondences. Bao *et al.* [24] propose an edge-preserving extension (EPPM) based on PatchMatch.

Dynamic Vision Sensors [47], asynchronously capturing illumination changes at microsecond latency, have been used to compute optical flow. Benosman [3] and Barranco [29] note that realistic motion estimation, even with large displacements, becomes simple when capturing image evidence in the kilohertz-range.

1.2   Contributions

We present a novel optical flow method based on dense inverse search (DIS), which we demonstrate to provide high quality flow estimation at 10–600 Hz on a single CPU core. This method is 1–2 orders of magnitude times faster than previous results [12,17,19] on the Sintel [48] and KITTI [49] datasets when considering all methods at similar flow quality operating points. At the same time it is significantly more accurate compared to existing methods running at *equal speed* [5,22]. This result is based on two main contributions:

Fast inverse search for correspondences. Inspired by the inverse compositional image alignment of [1,2] we devise our inverse search procedure (explained in Sect. 2.1) for fast mining of a grid of patch-based correspondences between two input images. While usually less robust than exhaustive feature matching, we can extract a uniform grid of correspondences in microseconds.

Fast optical flow with multi-scale reasoning. Many methods assume sparse and outlier-free correspondences, and rely heavily on variational refinement to extract pixel-wise flow [12,17]. This helps to smooth-out small errors, and cover regions with flat and ambigious textures, where exhaustive feature matching fails. Other methods rely directly on pixel-wise refinement [24,25]. We chose a middle ground and propose a very fast and robust patch-averaging-scheme, performed only once per scale, after grid-based correspondences have been extracted. This step gains robustness against outlier correspondences, and initializes a pixel-wise variational refinement, performed once per scale. We reach an optimal trade-off between accuracy and speed at 300 Hz on a single CPU core, and reach 600 Hz without variational refinement at the cost of accuracy. Both operating points are marked as **(2)** and **(1)** in Figs. 1, 4 and 5.

Related to our approach is [25]. Here, the inverse image warping idea [2] is used on *all* the pixels, while our method optimizes patches independently. In contrast to our densification, done once per scale, [25] relies on frequent flow interpolations, requiring a high-powered GPU, and still is significantly slower than our CPU-only method. The paper is structured as follows: In Sect. 2 we introduce our DIS method. In Sect. 3 we describe the experiments, separately evaluate the patch-based correspondence search, and analyse the complete DIS algorithm with and without the variational refinement. In Sect. 4 we conclude the paper.

2   Proposed Method

In the following, we introduce our dense inverse search-based method (DIS) by describing: how we extract single point correspondences between two images in Sect. 2.1, how we merge a set of noisy point correspondences on each level s of a scale-pyramid into a dense flow field $\mathbf{U}_s$ in Sect. 2.2, how we refine $\mathbf{U}_s$ using variational refinement in Sect. 2.3, and possible extensions of DIS in Sect. 2.4.

2.1   Fast Inverse Search for Correspondences

The core component in our method to achieve high performance is the efficient search for patch correspondences. In the following we will detail how we extract one single point correspondence between two frames.

For a given template patch T in the reference image I_t, with a size of $\theta_{ps} \times \theta_{ps}$ pixels, centered on location $\mathbf{x} = (x, y)^T$, we find the best-matching sub-window of $\theta_{ps} \times \theta_{ps}$ pixels in the query image I_{t+1} using gradient descent. We are interested in finding a warping vector $\mathbf{u} = (u, v)$ such that we minimize the sum of squared differences over the sub-window between template and query location:

$$\mathbf{u} = \mathrm{argmin}_{\mathbf{u}'} \sum_x \left[I_{t+1}(\mathbf{x} + \mathbf{u}') - T(\mathbf{x}) \right]^2 . \tag{1}$$

Minimizing this quantity is non-linear and is optimized iteratively using the inverse Lukas-Kanade algorithm as proposed in [2]. For this method two steps are alternated for a number of iterations or until the quantity (1) converges. For the first step, the quantity (2) is minimized around the current estimate $\mathbf{u}$ for an update vector $\Delta\mathbf{u}$ such that

$$\Delta\mathbf{u} = \mathrm{argmin}_{\Delta\mathbf{u}'} \sum_x \left[I_{t+1}(\mathbf{x} + \mathbf{u} + \Delta\mathbf{u}') - T(\mathbf{x}) \right]^2 . \tag{2}$$

The first step requires extraction and bilinear interpolation of a sub-window $I_{t+1}(\mathbf{x} + \mathbf{u})$ for sub-pixel accurate warp updates. The second step updates the warping $\mathbf{u} \leftarrow \mathbf{u} + \Delta\mathbf{u}$.

The original Lukas-Kanade algorithm [5] required expensive re-evaluation of the Hessian of the image warp at every iteration. As proposed in [2] the inverse objective function $\sum_x \left[T(\mathbf{x} - \Delta\mathbf{u}) - I_{t+1}(\mathbf{x} + \mathbf{u}) \right]^2$ can be optimized instead of (2), removing the need to extract the image gradients for $I_{t+1}(\mathbf{x} + \mathbf{u})$ and to re-compute the Jacobian and Hessian at every iteration. Due to the large speed-up this inversion has been used for point tracking in SLAM [50], camera pose estimation [51], and is covered in detail in [2] and our supplementary material.

In order to gain some robustness against absolute illumination changes, we mean-normalize each patch. One challenge of finding sparse correspondences with this approach is that the true displacements cannot be larger than the patch size θ_{ps}, since the gradient descent is dependent on similar image context in both patches. Often a coarse-to-fine approach with fixed window-size but changing image size is used [50,51], firstly, to incorporate larger smoothed contexts at coarser scales and thereby lessen the problem of falling into local optima, secondly, to find larger displacements, and, thirdly, to ensure fast convergence.

Algorithm 1.   Dense Inverse Search (DIS)

1: Set initial flow field $\mathbf{U}_{\theta_{ss}+1} \leftarrow \mathbf{0}$
2: **for** $s = \theta_{ss}$ to θ_{sf} **do**
3:       (**1.**) Create uniform grid of N_s patches
4:       (**2.**) Initialize displacements from $\mathbf{U}_{s+1}$
5:       **for** $i = 1$ to N_s **do**
6:             (**3.**) Inverse search for patch i
7:       (**4.**) Densification: Compute dense flow field $\mathbf{U}_s$
8:       (**5.**) Variational refinement of $\mathbf{U}_s$

2.2   Fast Optical Flow with Multi-scale Reasoning

We follow such a multi-scale approach, but, instead of optimizing patches independently, we compute an intermediate dense flow field and re-initialize patches at each level. We do this because of two reasons: (1) the intermediate dense flow field smooths displacements and provides robustness, effectively filtering outliers and (2) it reduces the number of patches on coarser scales, thereby providing a speed-up. We operate in a coarse-to-fine fashion from a first (coarsest) level θ_{ss} in a scale pyramid with a downscaling quotient of θ_{sd} to the last (finest) level θ_{sf}. On each level our method consists of five steps, summarized in Algorithm 1, yielding a dense flow field $\mathbf{U}_s$ in each iteration s.

(**1.**) **Creation of a grid:** We initialize patches in a uniform grid over the image domain. The grid density and number of patches N_s is implicitly determined by the parameter $\theta_{ov} \in [0,1)$ which specifies the overlap of adjacent patches and is always floored to an integer overlap in pixels. A value of $\theta_{ov} = 0$ denotes a patch adjacency with no overlap and $\theta_{ov} = 1 - \epsilon$ results in a dense grid with one patch centered on each pixel in the reference image.

(**2.**) **Initialization:** For the first iteration ($s = \theta_{ss}$) we initialize all patches with the trivial zero flow. On each subsequent scale s we initialize the displacement of each patch $i \in N_s$ at its location $\mathbf{x}$ with the flow from the previous (coarser) scale: $\mathbf{u}_{i,\text{init}} = \mathbf{U}_{s+1}(\mathbf{x}/\theta_{sd}) \cdot \theta_{sd}$.

(**3.**) **Inverse search:** Optimal displacements are computed independently for all patches, as detailed in Sect. 2.1. The search time required for each patch lies in the range of 1–2 μs, as detailed in the supplementary material.

(**4.**) **Densification:** After step three we have updated displacement vectors $\mathbf{u}_i$. For more robustness against outliers, we reset all patches to their initial flow $\mathbf{u}_{i,\text{init}}$ for which the displacement update $\|\mathbf{u}_{i,\text{init}} - \mathbf{u}_i\|_2$ exceeds the patch size θ_{ps}. We create a dense flow field $\mathbf{U}_s$ in each pixel $\mathbf{x}$ by applying weighted averaging to displacement estimates of all patches overlapping at $\mathbf{x}$ in the reference image:

$$\mathbf{U}_s(\mathbf{x}) = \frac{1}{Z} \sum_i^{N_s} \frac{\lambda_{i,\mathbf{x}}}{\max(1, \|d_i(\mathbf{x})\|_2)} \cdot \mathbf{u}_i, \tag{3}$$

where the indicator $\lambda_{i,\mathbf{x}} = 1$ iff patch i overlaps with location $\mathbf{x}$ in the reference image, $d_i(\mathbf{x}) = I_{t+1}(\mathbf{x} + \mathbf{u}_i) - T(\mathbf{x})$ denotes the intensity difference between template patch and warped image at this pixel, $\mathbf{u}_i$ denotes the estimated displacement of patch i, and normalization $Z = \sum_i \lambda_{i,\mathbf{x}} / \max(1, \|d_i(\mathbf{x})\|_2)$.

(5.) Variational energy minimization of flow $\mathbf{U_s}$, as detailed in Sect. 2.3.

2.3   Fast Variational Refinement

We use the variational refinement of [17] with three simplifications: (i) We use no feature matching term, (ii) intensity images only, and (iii) refine only on the current scale. The energy is a weighted sum of intensity and gradient data terms (E_I, E_G) and a smoothness term (E_S) over the image domain Ω:

$$E(\mathbf{U}) = \int_\Omega \sigma \Psi(E_I) + \gamma \Psi(E_G) + \alpha \Psi(E_S) \, d\mathbf{x} \qquad (4)$$

We use a robust penalizer $\Psi(a^2) = \sqrt{a^2 + \epsilon^2}$, with $\epsilon = 0.001$ for all terms as proposed in [52]. We use a separate penalization of intensity and gradient constancy assumption, with normalization as proposed in [53]: With the brightness constancy assumption $(\nabla_3^T I)\mathbf{u} = 0$, where $\nabla_3 = (\partial x, \partial y, \partial z)^T$ denotes the spatio-temporal gradient, we can model the intensity data term as $E_I = \mathbf{u}^T \bar{\mathbf{J}}_0 \mathbf{u}$. We use the normalized tensor $\bar{\mathbf{J}}_0 = \beta_0 (\nabla_3 I)(\nabla_3^T I)$ to enforce brightness constancy, with normalization $\beta_0 = (\|\nabla_2 I\|^2 + 0.01)^{-1}$ by the spatial derivatives and a term to avoid division by zero as in [53].

Similarly, E_G penalizes the gradient constancy: $E_G = \mathbf{u}^T \bar{\mathbf{J}}_{xy} \mathbf{u}$ with $\bar{\mathbf{J}}_{xy} = \beta_x (\nabla_3 I_{dx})(\nabla_3^T I_{dx}) + \beta_y (\nabla_3 I_{dy})(\nabla_3^T I_{dy})$, and normalizations $\beta_x = (\|\nabla_2 I_{dx}\|^2 + 0.01)^{-1}$ and $\beta_y = (\|\nabla_2 I_{dy}\|^2 + 0.01)^{-1}$. The smoothness term is a penalization over the norm of the gradient of displacements: $E_S = \|\nabla u\|^2 + \|\nabla v\|^2$. The non-convex energy $E(\mathbf{U})$ is minimized iteratively with θ_{vo} fixed point iterations and θ_{vi} iterations of Successive-Over-Relaxation for the linear system, as in [54].

2.4   Extensions

Our method lends itself to five extensions as follows:

i. Parallelization of all time-sensitive parts of our method (step 3, 5 in Sect. 2.2) is trivially achievable, since patch optimization operates independently. In the variational refinement the linear systems per pixel are solved independently in each inner iteration. With OpenMP we receive an almost linear speed-up with number of cores. Since the overhead of thread creation and management is significant for fast run-times, we use only one core in all experiments.

ii. Using RGB color images, instead of intensity only, boosts the score in most top-performing optical flow methods. In our experiments, we found that using color is not worth the observed increase of the run-time.

iii. Merging forward-backward flow estimations increases the accuracy. We found that the boost is not worth the observed doubling of the run-time.

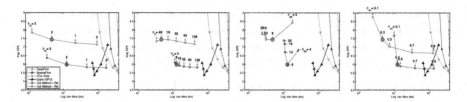

Fig. 2. Optical Flow result on Sintel with changing parameters. We set $\theta_{sf} = 2$, $\theta_{it} = 8$, $\theta_{ps} = 8$, $\theta_{ov} = 0.3$, marked with a black circle in all plots. From the left to right we vary the parameters θ_{sf}, θ_{it}, θ_{ps}, and θ_{ov} independently in each plot.

iv. Robust error norms, such as L1 and the Huber-norm [55], can be used instead of the L2-norm, implicit in the optimization of (1). Experimentally, we found that the gained robustness is not worth the slower convergence.

v. Using DIS for stereo depth, requires the estimation of the horizontal pixel displacement. Removing the vertical degree of freedom from DIS is trivial.

See the supplementary material for experiments on **i.-v.**

3   Experiments

In order to evaluate the performance of our method, we present three sets of experiments. Firstly, we conduct an analysis of our parameter selection in Sect. 3.1. Here, we also study the impact of variational refinement in our method. Secondly, we evaluate the inverse search (step 3 in Algorithm 1) in Sect. 3.2 without densification (step 4). The complete pipeline for optical flow is evaluated in Sects. 3.3 and 3.4. Thirdly, since the problem of recovering large displacements can also be handled by higher frame-rates combined with lower run-time per frame-pair, we conduct an experiment in Sect. 3.5 to analyse the benefit of higher frame-rates.

3.1   Implementation and Parameter Selection

We implemented[1] our method in C++ and run all experiments and baselines on a Core i7 CPU using a single core, and a GTX780 GPU for the EPPM [24] baseline. For *all* experiments on the Sintel and KITTI training datasets we report timings from which we exclude all operations which, in a typical robotics vision application, would be unnecessary, performed only once, or shared between multiple tasks: Disk access, creation of an image pyramid including image gradients with a downsampling quotient of 2, all initializations of the flow algorithms. We do this for our method and *all* baselines within their provided code. For EPPM, where only an executable was available, we subtracted the average overhead time of our method for fair comparison. Please see the supplementary material for variants of these experiments where preprocessing times are included for

---

[1] Source code available: http://www.vision.ee.ethz.ch/~kroegert/OFlow/.

Table 1. Parameters of our method. Parameters in **bold** have a significant impact on performance and are cross-validated in Sect. 3.1.

Parameter	Function
$\theta_{\mathbf{sf}}$	**Finest scale in multi-scale pyramid**
$\theta_{\mathbf{it}}$	**Number of gradient descent iterations per patch**
$\theta_{\mathbf{ps}}$	**Rectangular patch size in (pixel)**
$\theta_{\mathbf{ov}}$	**Patch overlap on each scale (percent)**
θ_{sd}	Downscaling quotient in scale pyramid
θ_{ss}	Coarsest scale in multi-scale pyramid
θ_{vo}, θ_{vi}	Number of outer and inner iterations for variational refinement
δ, γ, α	Intensity, gradient and smoothness weights for variational refinement

all methods. Our method requires 20 ms of preprocessing, spent on disk access (11 ms), image scaling and gradients (9 ms, unoptimized). For experiments on the Sintel and KITTI test datasets (Tables 3 and 4) we *include* this preprocessing time to be comparable with reported timings in the online benchmarks.

Parameter selection. Our method has four main parameters which affect speed and performance as explained in Sect. 2: θ_{ps} size of each rectangular patch, θ_{ov} patch overlap, θ_{it} number of iterations for the inverse search, θ_{sf} finest and final scale on which to compute the flow. We plot the change in the *average end-point error* (EPE) versus *run-time* on the Sintel (*training, final*) dataset [48] in Fig. 2. We draw three conclusions: Firstly, operating on finer scales (lower θ_{sf}), more patch iterations (higher θ_{it}), higher patch density (higher θ_{ov}) generally lowers the error, but, depending on the time budget, may not be worth it. Secondly, the patch size θ_{ps} has a clear optimum at 8 and 12 pixels. This also did not change when varying θ_{ps} at lower θ_{sf} or higher θ_{it}. Thirdly, using variational refinement always significantly reduced the error for a moderate increase in run-time.

In addition we have several parameters of lower importance, which are fixed for all experiments. We set $\theta_{sd} = 2$, *i.e.* we use an image pyramid, where the resolution is halved with each downscaling. We set the coarsest image scale $\theta_{ss} = 5$ for Sect. 3.3 and $\theta_{ss} = 6$ for Sect. 3.4 due to higher image resolutions. For different patch sizes and image pyramids the coarsest scale can be selected as $\theta_{ss} = \log_{\theta_{sd}}(2 \cdot width)/(f \cdot \theta_{ps})$ and raised to the nearest integer, to capture motions of at least $1/f$ of the image width. For the variational refinement we fix intensity, gradient and smoothness weights as $\delta = 5, \gamma = 10, \alpha = 10$ and keep iteration numbers fixed at $\theta_{vo} = 1 \cdot (s+1)$, where s denotes the current scale and $\theta_{vi} = 5$. In contrast to our comparison baselines [12,17,19], we do not fine-tune DIS for a specific dataset. We use a 20 percent subset of Sintel training to develop our method, and only the remaining training material is used for evaluation. All parameters are summarized in Table 1. If the flow is not computed up to finest scale ($\theta_{sf} = 0$), we scale-up the result (linearly interpolated) to full resolution for comparison for all methods. More details on implementation and timings of all parts of Algorithm 1 are provided in the supplementary material.

Table 2. Error of sparse correspondences (pixels). Columns left to right: (i) average end-point error over complete flow field, (ii) error in displacement range < 10 px., (iii) 10–40 px., (iv) > 40 px.

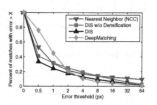

	EPE all	s0–10	s10–40	s40+
NN	32.06	13.64	53.77	101.00
DIS w/o Densification	7.76	2.16	8.65	37.94
DIS	4.16	**0.84**	4.98	23.09
DeepMatching [17]	**3.60**	1.27	**3.91**	**16.49**

Fig. 3. Percent of sparse correspondences above error threshold.

3.2   Evaluation of Inverse Search

In this section we evaluate the sparse point correspondences created by inverse search on the Sintel training dataset. For each frame pair we initialized a sparse grid (given by Deep Matching [17]) in the first image and computed point correspondences in the second image. The correspondences are computed by (i) exhaustive *Nearest Neighbor* search on normalized cross-correlation (*NCC*), (ii) our method where we skip the densification step between each scale change (*DIS w/o Densification*), (iii) our method including the densification step (*DIS*), and using (iv) *DeepMatching* [17]. The results are shown in Fig. 3 and Table 2.

We have four observations: (i) Nearest Neighbor search has a low number of incorrect matches, but precise correspondences and is very prone to outliers. (ii) DeepMatching has a high percentage of erroneous correspondences (with small errors), but is very good at large displacements. (iii) In contrast to this, our method (DIS w/o Densification) generally performs well in the range of small displacements, but is strongly affected by outliers. This is due to the fact that the implicit SSD (sum of squared differences) error minimization is not invariant to changes in orientation, contrast, and deformations. (iv) Averaging all patches in each scale (DIS), taking into account their photometric error as described in Eq. (3), introduces robustness towards these outliers. It also decreases the error for approximately correct matches. Furthermore, it enables reducing the number of patches at coarser scales, leading to lower run-time.

3.3   MPI Sintel Optical Flow Results

Following our parameter evaluation in Sect. 3.1, we selected four operating points:

(1) $\theta_{sf} = 3, \theta_{it} = 016, \theta_{ps} = 08, \theta_{ov} = 0.30$, **at 600/46² Hz,**
(2) $\theta_{sf} = 3, \theta_{it} = 012, \theta_{ps} = 08, \theta_{ov} = 0.40$, **at 300/42 Hz,**
(3) $\theta_{sf} = 1, \theta_{it} = 016, \theta_{ps} = 12, \theta_{ov} = 0.75$, **at 10/8.3 Hz,**
(4) $\theta_{sf} = 0, \theta_{it} = 256, \theta_{ps} = 12, \theta_{ov} = 0.75$, **at 0.5/0.5 Hz,**

---

[2] Without/with image preprocessing: disk access, image gradients and re-scaling.

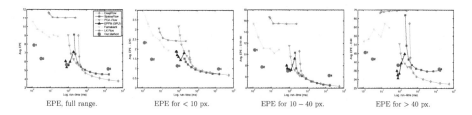

| EPE, full range. | EPE for < 10 px. | EPE for 10 − 40 px. | EPE for > 40 px. |

Fig. 4. Sintel-training results: average end-point error (EPE, in pixels) versus run-time (millisecond) on various displacement ranges.

Table 3. Sintel test errors in pixels (http://sintel.is.tue.mpg.de/results), retrieved on 25th of July 2016 for *final* subset. Run-times are measured by us, except: [†]self-reported, and [‡]on other datasets with same or smaller resolution.

	EPE all	s0–10	s10–40	s40+	Time (s)	CPU	GPU
FlowFields [16]	**5.81**	1.16	**3.74**	**33.89**	18 [†]	✓	
DeepFlow [17]	7.21	1.28	4.11	44.12	55	✓	
SparseFlow [12]	7.85	**1.07**	3.77	51.35	16	✓	
EPPM [24]	8.38	1.83	4.96	49.08	0.31		✓
PCA-Flow [19]	8.65	1.96	4.52	51.84	0.37	✓	
LDOF [9]	9.12	1.49	4.84	57.30	60 [†‡]	✓	
Classic+NL-fast [52]	10.09	1.09	4.67	67.81	120 [†‡]	✓	
DIS-Fast	10.13	2.17	5.93	59.70	**0.023**	✓	
SimpleFlow [23]	13.36	1.48	9.58	81.35	1.6 [†‡]		✓

We compare our method against a set of recently published baselines running on a single CPU core: DeepFlow [17], SparseFlow [12], PCA-Flow [19]; two older established methods: Pyramidal Lukas-Kanade Flow [5,56], Farneback's method [22]; and one recent GPU-based method: EPPM [24]. Since run-times for optical flow methods are strongly linked to image resolution, we incrementally speed-up all baselines by downscaling the input images by factor of 2^n, where n starting at $n = 0$ is increased in increments of 0.5. We chose this *non-intrusive* parameter of image resolution to analyse each method's trade-off between run-time and flow error. We bilinearly interpolate the resulting flow field to the original resolution for evaluation. We also experiment with temporal instead of spatial downsampling for the same purpose, as described in Sect. 3.5.

We run all baselines and DIS for all operating points on the Sintel [48] *final* training (Fig. 4) and testing (Table 3) benchmark. On the testing benchmark we report operating point **(2)** for DIS. As noted in Sect. 3.1, run-times for all methods are reported *without* preprocessing for the training dataset to facilitate comparison of algorithms running in the same environment at high speed, and *with* preprocessing for the online testing benchmark to allow comparison with self-reported times. From the experiments on the testing and training dataset,

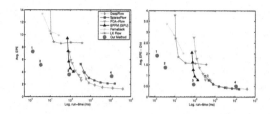

Fig. 5. KITTI (training) result. Average end-point error (px) versus run-time (ms) for all (left) and small displacements (right, s0–10). See supplementary material for large displacement errors.

Table 4. KITTI test results (http://www.cvlibs.net/datasets/kitti/eval_flow.php), retrieved on 25th of July 2016, for *all pixels, at 3px threshold*.

	Out-Noc	Out-All	Avg-Noc	Avg-All	Time (s)	CPU	GPU
PH-Flow [57]	**5.76 %**	**10.57 %**	**1.3 px**	**2.9 px**	800	✓	
DeepFlow [17]	7.22 %	17.79 %	1.5 px	5.8 px	17	✓	
SparseFlow [12]	9.09 %	19.32 %	2.6 px	7.6 px	10	✓	
EPPM [24]	12.75 %	23.55 %	2.5 px	9.2 px	0.25		✓
PCA-Flow [19]	15.67 %	24.59 %	2.7 px	6.2 px	0.19	✓	
eFolki [25]	19.31 %	28.79 %	5.2 px	10.9 px	0.026		✓
LDOF [9]	21.93 %	31.39 %	5.6 px	12.4 px	60	✓	
FlowNetS+ft [21]	37.05 %	44.49 %	5.0 px	9.1 px	0.08		✓
DIS-Fast	38.58 %	46.21 %	7.8 px	14.4 px	**0.024**	✓	
RLOF [39]	38.60 %	46.13 %	8.7 px	16.5 px	0.488		✓

we draw several conclusions: *Operating point* **(2)** points to the best trade-off between run-time and flow error. For the average EPE of around 6 pixels, DIS is approximately two orders of magnitude faster than the fastest CPU baseline (PCA-Flow [19]) and also more than one order of magnitude faster than the fastest GPU baseline (EPPM [24]). DIS can be further sped-up by removing the variational refinement as in *operating point* **(1)** while maintaining reasonable flow quality (see Fig. 6). We also tested using only the variational refinement without sparse initialization ($\theta_{it} = 0$), and found experimentally that the result is close to the trivial zero-flow solution. Finer resolution changes over scales and more iterations for the refinement will yield better results at significantly increased cost. *Operating point* **(3)** is comparable with the performance of EPPM, but slightly better for small displacements and worse for large displacements. If we use all available scales, and increase the number of iterations, we obtain *operating point* **(4)**. At the run-time of several seconds per frame pair, more complex methods, such as DeepFlow, perform better, in particular for large displacements. The supplementary material includes variants of Figs. 4 and 5, where preprocessing times are included, and flow error maps on Sintel, where typical failure cases of DIS at motion discontinuities and frame boundaries are observable.

3.4   KITTI Optical Flow Results

Complementary to the experiment on the synthetic Sintel dataset, we ran our method on the KITTI Optical Flow benchmark [49] for realistic driving scenarios. We use the same experimental setup and operating points as in Sect. 3.3. The result is presented in Figs. 5, 7 (training) and Table 4 (testing). Our conclusions from the Sintel dataset in Sect. 3.3 also apply for this dataset, suggesting a stable performance of our method, since we did not optimize any parameters for this dataset. On the online test benchmark, for which we *include* our preprocessing time, we are on par with RLOF [39] and the recently published FlowNet [21]. Even though both take advantage of a GPU, we are still significantly faster at comparable performance. In the supplementary material we include plots of more operating points on the training set of Sintel and KITTI, as well as the same plots as Figs. 4 and 5 where all preprocessing times are *included*.

3.5   High Frame-Rate Optical Flow

Often, a simpler and faster algorithm, combined with a higher temporal resolution in the data, can yield better accuracy than a more powerful algorithm, on lower temporal resolutions. This has been analysed in detail in [26] for the task of visual odometry. As noted in [3,29] this is also the case for optical flow, where large displacements, due to low-frame rate or strong motions are significantly more difficult to estimate than small displacements. In contrast to the recent focus on handling ever larger displacements [9,12,14,17,20,46], we want to analyse how *decreasing* the run-time while *increasing* the frame-rate affects our algorithm. For this experiment we selected a random subset of the Sintel training dataset, and synthesized new ground truth flow for lower frame-rates

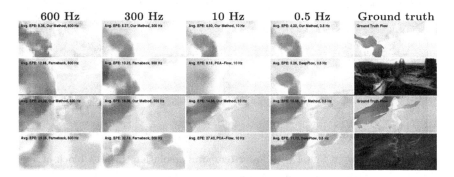

Fig. 6. Examplary results on Sintel (training). In each block of 2 × 6, top row, left to right: Our method for operating points (**1**)–(**4**), Ground Truth. Bottom row: Farneback 600 Hz, Farneback 300 Hz, PCA-Flow 10 Hz, DeepFlow 0.5 Hz, Original Image.

484   T. Kroeger et al.

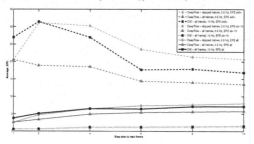

600 Hz	300 Hz	10 Hz	0.5 Hz	Ground truth

Fig. 7. Same as Fig. 6 but for KITTI (training) with Pyramidal LK as 300 Hz baseline.

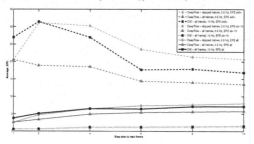

Fig. 8. Flow result on Sintel with low temporal resolution. Accuracy of DeepFlow on large displacements versus DIS on small displacements, tracked through *all intermediate* frames. As baseline we included the accuracy of DeepFlow for tracking small displacements. Note: While we use the same frame pairs to compute each vertical set of points, frame pairs differ over stepsizes.

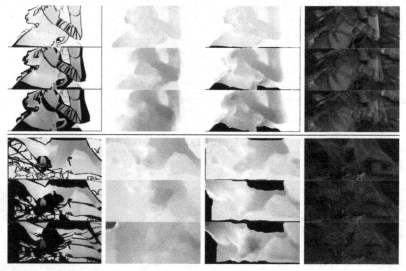

Fig. 9. Optical flow on Sintel with lower temporal resolution. In each block of 3 × 4: Rows, top to bottom, correspond to step sizes 1 (original frame-rate), 6, 10 frames. Columns, left to right, correspond to new ground truth, DeepFlow result, DIS result (through *all intermediate frames*), original images. Large displacements are significantly better preserved by DIS through higher frame-rates.

from the one provided in the dataset. We create new ground truth for $1/2$ to $1/10$ of the source frame-rate from the original ground truth and the additionally provided segmentation masks to invalidate occluded regions. We compare Deep-Flow at a speed of 0.5 Hz on this lower temporal resolution against DIS (*operating point* (**3**), 10 Hz), running through *all intermediate frames* at the original, higher frame-rate. Thus, while DeepFlow has to handle larger displacements in one frame pair, DIS has to handle smaller displacements, tracked through multiple frames and accumulates error drift. We observe (Fig. 8) that DIS starts to outperform DeepFlow when running at 2× the original frame-rate, notably for large displacements, while still being 10× faster. Figure 9 shows examples of the new ground truth, results of DeepFlow and DIS. We conclude, that it is advantageous to choose DIS over DeepFlow, aimed at recovering large displacements, when the combination of frame-rate and run-time per frame can be chosen freely.

4   Conclusions

In this paper we presented a novel and simple way of computing dense optical flow. The presented approach trades off a lower flow estimation error for large decreases in run-time: For the same level of error, the presented method is two orders of magnitude faster than current state-of-the-art approaches, as shown in experiments on synthetic (Sintel) and realistic (KITTI) optical flow benchmarks. In the future we will address open problems with our method: Due to the coarse-to-fine approach small and fast motions can sometimes get lost beyond recovery. A sampling-based approach to recover over-smoothed object motions at finer scales may alleviate this problem. The implicit minimization of the L2 matching error in our method is not invariant to many modes of change, such as in contrast, deformations, and occlusions. More robust error metrics may be helpful here. Furthermore, a GPU implementation may yield another significant speed-up.

Acknowledgments. This work was supported by ERC *VarCity (#273940)* and SNF *Tracking in the Wild (CRSII2_147693/1)*, and a NVIDIA GPU grant. We thank Richard Hartley for his pertinent input on this work.

References

1. Baker, S., Matthews, I.: Equivalence and efficiency of image alignment algorithms. In: CVPR (2001)
2. Baker, S., Matthews, I.: Lucas-Kanade 20 years on: a unifying framework. In: IJCV (2004)
3. Benosman, R., Clercq, C., Lagorce, X., Ieng, S.H., Bartolozzi, C.: Event-based visual flow. IEEE Trans. Neural Netw. Learn. Syst. **25**(2), 407–417 (2014)
4. Horn, B.K., Schunck, B.G.: Determining optical flow. In: Proceedings of SPIE 0281, Techniques and Applications of Image Understanding (1981)
5. Lucas, B.D., Kanade, T.: An iterative image registration technique with an application to stereo vision. IJCAI **81**, 674–679 (1981)

6. Black, M.J., Anandan, P.: The robust estimation of multiple motions: parametric and piecewise-smooth flow fields. In: CVIU (1996)
7. Papenberg, N., Bruhn, A., Brox, T., Didas, S., Weickert, J.: Highly accurate optic flow computation with theoretically justified warping. IJCV **67**(2), 141–158 (2006)
8. Steinbrucker, F., Pock, T., Cremers, D.: Large displacement optical flow computation without warping. In: ICCV (2009)
9. Brox, T., Malik, J.: Large displacement optical flow: descriptor matching in variational motion estimation. IEEE Trans. PAMI **33**(3), 500–513 (2011)
10. Braux-Zin, J., Dupont, R., Bartoli, A.: A general dense image matching framework combining direct and feature-based costs. In: ICCV (2013)
11. Leordeanu, M., Zanfir, A., Sminchisescu, C.: Locally affine sparse-to-dense matching for motion and occlusion estimation. In: ICCV (2013)
12. Timofte, R., Van Gool, L.: Sparseflow: Sparse matching for small to large displacement optical flow. In: WACV, pp. 1100–1106, January 2015
13. Kennedy, R., Taylor, C.J.: Optical flow with geometric occlusion estimation and fusion of multiple frames. In: Tai, X.-C., Bae, E., Chan, T.F., Lysaker, M. (eds.) EMMCVPR 2015. LNCS, vol. 8932, pp. 364–377. Springer, Heidelberg (2015). doi:10.1007/978-3-319-14612-6_27
14. Menze, M., Heipke, C., Geiger, A.: Discrete optimization for optical flow. In: Gall, J., Gehler, P., Leibe, B. (eds.) GCPR 2015. LNCS, vol. 9358, pp. 16–28. Springer, Heidelberg (2015). doi:10.1007/978-3-319-24947-6_2
15. Revaud, J., Weinzaepfel, P., Harchaoui, Z., Schmid, C.: EpicFlow: edge-preserving interpolation of correspondences for optical flow. In: CVPR (2015)
16. Bailer, C., Taetz, B., Stricker, D.: Flow fields: Dense correspondence fields for highly accurate large displacement optical flow estimation. In: ICCV (2015)
17. Weinzaepfel, P., Revaud, J., Harchaoui, Z., Schmid, C.: Deepflow: large displacement optical flow with deep matching. In: ICCV (2013)
18. Wills, J., Agarwal, S., Belongie, S.: A feature-based approach for dense segmentation and estimation of large disparity motion. IJCV **68**, 125–143 (2006)
19. Wulff, J., Black, M.J.: Efficient sparse-to-dense optical flow estimation using a learned basis and layers. In: CVPR, pp. 120–130 (2015)
20. Xu, L., Jia, J., Matsushita, Y.: Motion detail preserving optical flow estimation. IEEE Trans. PAMI **34**(9), 1744–1757 (2012)
21. Fischer, P., Dosovitskiy, A., Ilg, E., Häusser, P., Hazırbaş, C., Golkov, V., van der Smagt, P., Cremers, D., Brox, T.: Flownet: learning optical flow with convolutional networks. In: ICCV (2015)
22. Farnebäck, G.: Two-frame motion estimation based on polynomial expansion. In: Bigun, J., Gustavsson, T. (eds.) SCIA 2003. LNCS, vol. 2749, pp. 363–370. Springer, Heidelberg (2003). doi:10.1007/3-540-45103-X_50
23. Tao, M., Bai, J., Kohli, P., Paris, S.: Simpleflow: A non-iterative, sublinear optical flow algorithm. In: Computer Graphics Forum, vol. 31, pp. 345–353. Wiley Online Library (2012)
24. Bao, L., Yang, Q., Jin, H.: Fast edge-preserving patchmatch for large displacement optical flow. IEEE Trans. Image Process. **23**(12), 4996–5006 (2014)
25. Plyer, A., Le Besnerais, G., Champagnat, F.: Massively parallel lucas kanade optical flow for real-time video processing applications. J. Real-Time Image Proc. **11**(4), 1–18 (2014)
26. Handa, A., Newcombe, R.A., Angeli, A., Davison, A.J.: Real-Time camera tracking: when is high frame-rate best? In: Fitzgibbon, A., Lazebnik, S., Perona, P., Sato, Y., Schmid, C. (eds.) ECCV 2012. LNCS, vol. 7578, pp. 222–235. Springer, Heidelberg (2012). doi:10.1007/978-3-642-33786-4_17

27. Dai, D., Kroeger, T., Timofte, R., Van Gool, L.: Metric imitation by manifold transfer for efficient vision applications. In: IEEE Conference on Computer Vision and Pattern Recognition (CVPR) (2015)
28. Srinivasan, N., Roberts, R., Dellaert, F.: High frame rate egomotion estimation. In: Chen, M., Leibe, B., Neumann, B. (eds.) ICVS 2013. LNCS, vol. 7963, pp. 183–192. Springer, Heidelberg (2013). doi:10.1007/978-3-642-39402-7_19
29. Barranco, F., Fermuller, C., Aloimonos, Y.: Contour motion estimation for asynchronous event-driven cameras. Proc. IEEE 102(10), 1537–1556 (2014)
30. Fortun, D., Bouthemy, P., Kervrann, C.: Optical flow modeling and computation: a survey. Comput. Vis. Image Underst. 134, 1–21 (2015). Image Understanding for Real-world Distributed Video Networks
31. Mikolajczyk, K., Tuytelaars, T., Schmid, C., Zisserman, A., Matas, J., Schaffalitzky, F., Kadir, T., Van Gool, L.: A comparison of affine region detectors. IJCV 65, 43–72 (2005)
32. Tola, E., Lepetit, V., Fua, P.: A fast local descriptor for dense matching. In: CVPR (2008)
33. Liu, C., Yuen, J., Torralba, A.: SIFT flow: Dense correspondence across scenes and its applications. TPAMI 33(5), 978–994 (2011)
34. Dalal, N., Triggs, B.: Histograms of oriented gradients for human detection. In: CVPR (2005)
35. Lowe, D.G.: Distinctive image features from scale-invariant keypoints. IJCV 60(2), 91–110 (2004)
36. Baya, H., Essa, A., Tuytelaarsb, T., Van Gool, L.: Speeded-up robust features (surf). CVIU 110(3), 346–359 (2008)
37. Barnes, C., Shechtman, E., Goldman, D.B., Finkelstein, A.: The generalized patchmatch correspondence algorithm. In: Daniilidis, K., Maragos, P., Paragios, N. (eds.) ECCV 2010. LNCS, vol. 6313, pp. 29–43. Springer, Heidelberg (2010). doi:10.1007/978-3-642-15558-1_3
38. Gadot, D., Wolf, L.: Patchbatch: a batch augmented loss for optical flow. In: The IEEE Conference on Computer Vision and Pattern Recognition (CVPR), June 2016
39. Senst, T., Eiselein, V., Sikora, T.: Robust local optical flow for feature tracking. IEEE Trans. Circ. Syst. Video Technol. 22(9), 1377–1387 (2012)
40. Heitz, F., Bouthemy, P.: Multimodal estimation of discontinuous optical flow using markov random fields. TPAMI 15(12), 1217–1232 (1993)
41. Szeliski, R., Zabih, R., Scharstein, D., Veksler, O., Kolmogorov, V., Agarwala, A., Tappen, M., Rother, C.: A comparative study of energy minimization methods for markov random fields with smoothness-based priors. TPAMI 30(6), 1068–1080 (2008)
42. Chen, Q., Koltun, V.: Full flow: optical flow estimation by global optimization over regular grids. In: The IEEE Conference on Computer Vision and Pattern Recognition (CVPR), June 2016
43. Pauwels, K., Tomasi, M., Alonso, J.D., Ros, E., Van Hulle, M.: A comparison of FPGA and GPU for real-time phase-based optical flow, stereo, and local image features. IEEE Trans. Comput. 61(7), 999–1012 (2012)
44. Zach, C., Pock, T., Bischof, H.: A duality based approach for realtime TV-L1 optical flow. In: Annual Symposium on German Association Pattern Recognition (2007)
45. Enkelmann, W.: Investigations of multigrid algorithms for the estimation of optical flow fields in image sequences. Comput. Vis. Graph. Image Process. 43, 150–177 (1988)

46. Hu, Y., Song, R., Li, Y.: Efficient coarse-to-fine patchmatch for large displacement optical flow. In: The IEEE Conference on Computer Vision and Pattern Recognition (CVPR), June 2016
47. Lichtsteiner, P., Posch, C., Delbruck, T.: A 128×128 120 db 15 μs latency asynchronous temporal contrast vision sensor. IEEE J. Solid-State Circ. **43**(2), 566–576 (2008)
48. Butler, D.J., Wulff, J., Stanley, G.B., Black, M.J.: A naturalistic open source movie for optical flow evaluation. In: Fitzgibbon, A., Lazebnik, S., Perona, P., Sato, Y., Schmid, C. (eds.) ECCV 2012. LNCS, vol. 7577, pp. 611–625. Springer, Heidelberg (2012). doi:10.1007/978-3-642-33783-3_44
49. Geiger, A., Lenz, P., Stiller, C., Urtasun, R.: Vision meets robotics: the KITTI dataset. In: IJRR (2013)
50. Klein, G., Murray, D.: Parallel tracking and mapping for small AR workspaces. In: ISMAR (2007)
51. Forster, C., Pizzoli, M., Scaramuzza, D.: SVO: Fast semi-direct monocular visual odometry. In: ICRA, pp. 15–22, May 2014
52. Sun, D., Roth, S., Black, M.J.: Secrets of optical flow estimation and their principles. In: CVPR (2010)
53. Zimmer, H., Bruhn, A., Weickert, J.: Optic flow in harmony. IJCV **93**, 368–388 (2011)
54. Brox, T., Bruhn, A., Papenberg, N., Weickert, J.: High accuracy optical flow estimation based on a theory for warping. In: Pajdla, T., Matas, J. (eds.) ECCV 2004. LNCS, vol. 3024, pp. 25–36. Springer, Heidelberg (2004). doi:10.1007/978-3-540-24673-2_3
55. Werlberger, M., Trobin, W., Pock, T., Wedel, A., Cremers, D., Bischof, H.: Anisotropic huber-L1 optical flow. In: BMVC (2009)
56. Bouguet, J.Y.: Pyramidal implementation of the affine lucas kanade feature tracker description of the algorithm. Intel Corporation **5**, 1–10 (2001)
57. Yang, J., Li, H.: Dense, accurate optical flow estimation with piecewise parametric model. In: CVPR, pp. 1019–1027 (2015)

Global Registration of 3D Point Sets
via LRS Decomposition

Federica Arrigoni[1(✉)], Beatrice Rossi[2], and Andrea Fusiello[1]

[1] DPIA - Università di Udine, Via Delle Scienze, 208, Udine, Italy
arrigoni.federica@spes.uniud.it, andrea.fusiello@uniud.it
[2] AST Lab - STMicroelectronics, Via Olivetti, 2, Agrate Brianza, Italy
beatrice.rossi@st.com

Abstract. This paper casts the global registration of multiple 3D point-sets into a low-rank and sparse decomposition problem. This neat mathematical formulation caters for missing data, outliers and noise, and it benefits from a wealth of available decomposition algorithms that can be plugged-in. Experimental results show that this approach compares favourably to the state of the art in terms of precision and speed, and it outperforms all the analysed techniques as for robustness to outliers.

Keywords: Point-set registration · Motion synchronization · Matrix completion · Low-rank and sparse matrix decomposition

1 Introduction

The goal of multiple point-set registration is to find the rigid transformations that bring multiple ($n \geq 2$) 3D point sets into alignment, where each rigid transformation is represented by an element of the Special Euclidean Group SE(3), namely the semi-direct product of the Special Orthogonal Group SO(3) with $\mathbb{R}^3$. This is a fundamental problem in the reconstruction of 3D models of objects, covering a wide range of applications, including (but not limited to) cultural heritage, engineering modelling and virtual reality.

If $n = 2$ then we are dealing with a *pairwise* (two point-sets) registration problem. The gold standard in this context is the Iterative Closest Point (ICP) Algorithm [1,2], which computes correspondences between the point sets given an estimate for the rigid transformation, then updates the transformation based on the current correspondences, and iterates through these steps until convergence – to a local minimum – is reached. See [3] for an overview of several variants of the ICP Algorithm.

If $n > 2$ then we are dealing with a *multiple* point-set registration problem, which is more complex than the $n = 2$ case due to the high amount of parameters that have to be estimated. Among the initial attempts to address this problem are the *sequential* techniques introduced in [2,4], that repeatedly register a new point set into a growing model, until all the sets are considered. This approach however returns suboptimal solutions since it does not take into account all the

© Springer International Publishing AG 2016
B. Leibe et al. (Eds.): ECCV 2016, Part IV, LNCS 9908, pp. 489–504, 2016.
DOI: 10.1007/978-3-319-46493-0_30

available constraints, *e.g.* the constraint between the last and first point set is not used if the sets are obtained using a turntable. *Global* methods, on the other hand, consider simultaneously all the points sets. They are able to exploit the redundancy in the constraints between pairs of point sets, to compensate and distribute the error, thereby preventing drift in the solution. Global registration can be solved in *point space* or in *frame space*. In the former case, all the rigid transformations are computed by optimizing a cost function that depends on the distance between corresponding points. In the latter case, the optimization criterion is related to the internal consistency of the network of rigid transformations applied to the local coordinate frames. This instance is also known as *motion synchronization* [5] or *motion averaging* [6].

Early point-space solutions include the methods presented in [7–10]. More recently, [11] solves the problem on the manifold of rotations with Gauss-Newton iterations and then computes translations through least-squares. Such approach is improved in [12] by reducing computational time and it is embedded in a Bayesian framework in [13], in order to take into account reliability of correspondences. A similar formulation is adopted in [14] where the authors cast the registration problem to a semidefinite program, proving conditions for exact and stable recovery of rigid transformations. In [15] a robust solution is derived by minimizing a cost function based on the ℓ_1-norm. A generalization of the ICP Algorithm to $n > 2$ is described in [16], which builds on the Levenberg-Marquardt ICP formulation of [17], while in [18] multiple point-set registration is solved by combining ICP and Generalized Procrustes Analysis [19]. A related approach employs rank minimization for global registration of multiple depth images [20].

Frame-space methods originate from the pioneering works of [21], that distributes the error along all cycles in a cycle basis, and [22], that casts the problem as the optimization of an objective function in SE(3) where rotations are parameterized as unit quaternions. The authors of [23] represent rigid transformations as dual quaternions, and propose a graph diffusion algorithm where each transformation is updated in turn through linear or geodesic averaging. In [6,24] the Lie-group structure of SE(3) is exploited and an iterative scheme is proposed in which at each step the rigid transformations are updated by averaging two-view transformations in the tangent space. In [5,25] motion synchronization is formulated as a null-space problem.

At the border between frame-space and point-space methods is the formulation in [26], where 3D points are used to compute a second-order approximation of the cost function, but they are not involved in subsequent computations.

Among the aforementioned methods, [11–14,21] first recover the rotation component of the rigid transformations and then compute translations, while [6,15,16,18,20,22,23,25,26] and our approach compute rotations and translations simultaneously, as elements of SE(3).

In this paper we concentrate on frame-space methods, for they are faster and less memory-demanding than point-space ones. It goes without saying that any optimal formulation *must* include points in the cost function, in analogy to bundle adjustment in the context of structure from motion. Nevertheless, frame-space approaches yield a fairly accurate registration.

Many frame-space methods are deceived by gross errors (outliers), caused by failure of ICP to estimate the correct transformation between two point-sets. To overcome this drawback, we propose a global frame-space approach to multiple point-set registration which is *robust* to outliers.

We show that the registration problem can be cast to a *low-rank and sparse* (LRS) matrix decomposition. Our proposal is a general framework, not a specific method, since – in principle – any LRS decomposition algorithm can be plugged-in. However, in order to make our approach concrete, we analyse three LRS algorithms, namely R-GoDec [27], Grasta [28] and L1-Alm [29], showing that they can be profitably applied to address the registration problem. Experimental results show that our approach compares favourably to the state of the art as for precision and speed, and it outperforms all the analysed techniques in terms of robustness to outliers. Failure cases appear when the percentage of missing data is extremely high.

This paper builds on [27] and extends it in two respects. From the theoretical point of view, our approach generalizes to SE(3) the original formulation for SO(3). From the experimental point of view, we tackle the problem of multiple point-set registration, while [27] concentrates on structure from motion.

The next section provides the background on LRS decomposition, Sect. 3 defines the multiple point-set registration problem, whereas Sect. 4 describes how such a problem can be translated into a LRS decomposition of an incomplete matrix, corrupted by noise and outliers. Experiments on synthetic and real dataset are reported in Sect. 5, and conclusions are drawn in Sect. 6.

2 Low-Rank and Sparse Decomposition

Low-rank and sparse (LRS) matrix decompositions have become interesting to researchers due to their profitable application in different areas, such as image analysis, pattern recognition, and graph clustering. A survey of such decompositions and a wide overview of available algorithms can be found in [30]. LRS decompositions work by imposing constraints on the rank and sparsity of the addends and have the following general form

$$\mathcal{F}(\widehat{X}) = \mathcal{F}(L) + S + N \tag{1}$$

where $\widehat{X}$ is a known data matrix, L is an unknown low-rank matrix representing some meaningful structure contained into the data, S is an unknown sparse matrix representing outliers, N accounts for a diffuse noise and $\mathcal{F}$ is a linear operator. The goal is to recover L (and possibly S) under conditions on S, N and $\mathcal{F}$ to be further specified.

Examples of LRS decompositions are Robust Principal Component Analysis (RPCA) [31] and Matrix Completion (MC) [32,33]. RPCA looks for the lowest-rank matrix L and the sparsest matrix S such that a given data matrix $\widehat{X}$ can be decomposed as $\widehat{X} = L + S + N$. Note that this is an instance of Eq. (1) with $\mathcal{F}$ being the identity operator. MC is concerned with the problem of recovering missing entries of an *incomplete* low-rank data matrix $\widehat{X}$. Entries of $\widehat{X}$ are specified on a subset of indices Ω (a.k.a. *sampling set*), namely $\Omega_{ij} = 1$ if $\widehat{X}_{ij}$ is specified and $\Omega_{ij} = 0$ otherwise. MC can be cast as an instance of Eq. (1) if $S = 0$ and $\mathcal{F}$ is the projection onto the space of matrices that vanish out of Ω, namely $\mathcal{F}(X) = \mathcal{P}_\Omega(X) = X \circ \Omega$, where $\circ$ is the Hadamard (or entry-wise) product.

We briefly recall some of the available approaches to compute LRS decompositions in the general form (1) with $S, N \neq 0$, L of fixed rank r, and $\mathcal{F} = \mathcal{P}_\Omega$.

The R-GODEC algorithm [27] is a modified version of GODEC [34], which was originally conceived to solve RPCA or MC problems separately. R-GODEC expresses the sparse term S as the sum of two terms S_1 and S_2 having complementary supports: S_1 has support on Ω and represents outliers, while S_2 has support on $\mho$ (the complementary of Ω) and it is an approximation of $-\mathcal{P}_\mho(L)$, *i.e.* it represents completion of missing entries. The associated problem is

$$\min_{L, S_1, S_2} \frac{1}{2} \left\| \mathcal{P}_\Omega(\widehat{X}) - L - S_1 - S_2 \right\|_F^2 + \lambda \|S_1\|_1$$
$$\text{s.t. } \operatorname{rank}(L) \leq r, \operatorname{supp}(S_1) \subseteq \Omega, \operatorname{supp}(S_2) = \mho \tag{2}$$

which is solved using a block-coordinate minimization scheme that alternates the update of L (with S_1, S_2 fixed), and S_1, S_2 (with L fixed). L is computed as the the rank-r projection of $\mathcal{P}_\Omega(\widehat{X}) - S_1 - S_2$ using Bilateral Random Projections [34], S_1 is computed via soft-thresholding [35] of $\mathcal{P}_\Omega(\widehat{X} - L)$, and S_2 is updated as $-\mathcal{P}_\mho(L)$.

Another option is to express the LRS decomposition problem in terms of *subspace identification*, as done in [28,29]. The goal of subspace identification methods is to identify the column space of the unknown low-rank term L. Indeed, since any matrix L of fixed rank r admits a factorization of the form $L = UY^T$ where U and Y have r columns, the problem of recovering L can be translated into recovering U and Y. Specifically, the GRASTA algorithm [28] solves

$$\min_{S, U, Y} \|S\|_1$$
$$\text{s.t. } \mathcal{P}_\Omega(\widehat{X}) = \mathcal{P}_\Omega(UY^T) + S \tag{3}$$

with U belonging to the Grasmannian manifold, i.e. the set of all r-dimensional subspaces of a Euclidean space. GRASTA considers one data vector $\hat{x}$ at a time, representing one column of $\widehat{X}$, and alternates between estimating U and a triple of vectors (s, y, w) which represent respectively the sparse corruptions in $\hat{x}$, the weights for the fit to the subspace U, and the dual vector. For computing U, GRASTA uses gradient descent on the Grasmannian with (s, y, w) fixed, while for computing (s, y, w), it uses the Alternating Direction Method of Multipliers (ADMM) [36]. The L1-ALM algorithm presented in [29] exploits a similar approach and solves instead

$$\min_{U,Y} \left\| \mathcal{P}_\Omega(\hat{X} - UY^T) \right\|_1 + \lambda \left\| Y^T \right\|_*$$

$$\text{s.t. } U^T U = I_r \tag{4}$$

where $\|\cdot\|_*$ denotes the trace-norm of a matrix, *i.e.* the sum of its singular values. The trace-norm regularization term is introduced to improve convergence. The optimization problem is solved via the augmented Lagrange multiplier (ALM) method [37]. At each iteration, the augmented Lagrange function with orthogonal U is minimized via the Gauss-Seidel iteration, then the Lagrange multiplier and the dual parameter are updated.

3   Problem Definition

Let $P = \{\mathbf{p}_k\}_{k=1}^m$ be a set of 3D points representing a given object expressed in an absolute (world) coordinate system. Let $\{P^i\}_{i=1}^n$ denote multiple views of the object taken from different positions and viewing directions, where each 3D point set $P^i = \{\mathbf{p}_k^i\}_{k \in V_i}$ refers to a subset $V_i \subseteq \{1, \ldots, m\}$ of the original m points. Let $M_i \in SE(3)$ denote the 3D displacement between the local reference frame of view i and the world coordinate system

$$M_i = \begin{pmatrix} R_i & \mathbf{t}_i \\ \mathbf{0}^\mathsf{T} & 1 \end{pmatrix} \in SE(3) \tag{5}$$

where $R_i \in SO(3)$ represents the rotation component of the transformation, and $\mathbf{t}_i \in \mathbb{R}^3$ represents the translation component. In this paper $M_i \in SE(3)$ is referred to as the *absolute motion* of view i. Using this notation, the (homogeneous) coordinates of the k-th point can be expressed in the reference frame of view i as $\mathbf{p}_k^i = M_i \mathbf{p}_k$ and the relation between the coordinates of $\mathbf{p}_k$ in references i and j is given by

$$\mathbf{p}_k^i = M_i M_j^{-1} \mathbf{p}_k^j \tag{6}$$

assuming that $k \in V_i \cap V_j$, where the index set $V_i \cap V_j$ defines corresponding points between P_i and P_j.

The goal of multiple point-set registration is to estimate the absolute transformations $M_i \in SE(3)$ starting from the knowledge of the point sets $\{P^i\}_{i=1}^n$. Since P can be recovered from $\mathbf{p}_k^i = M_i \mathbf{p}_k$ by applying the inverse of absolute motions to each point, the absolute motions can be viewed as the transformations that bring multiple point sets into alignment. The index sets $\{V_i\}_{i=1}^n$ are in general unknown, and therefore they have to be computed beforehand or during the registration process.

The registration problem can be profitably formulated in frame space without involving 3D points [21–25]. Let $M_{ij} \in SE(3)$ denote the rigid transformation between the reference frame of view i and that of view j, which is referred to as the *relative motion* of the pair (i, j). It follows from Eq. (6) that the following condition holds

$$M_{ij} = M_i M_j^{-1} \tag{7}$$

which means that the registration problem can be reduced to finding the absolute motions $M_i \in SE(3)$ given measurements of their ratios. Such a problem is known in the literature as *motion synchronization* [5] or *motion averaging* [6].

Let $\mathcal{E} \subseteq \{1, \ldots, n\} \times \{1, \ldots, n\}$ denote the set of available pairs, which can be viewed as the set of edges of a finite simple graph $\mathcal{G} = (\mathcal{V}, \mathcal{E})$ with $\mathcal{V} = \{1, \ldots, n\}$, referred to as the *measurement graph*. Obviously, it is possible to recover the absolute motions – up to a global transformation – only if such a graph is connected. If $\mathcal{G}$ is a tree then there is no counteraction of the errors in the solution. However, as soon as redundant measures are considered (*i.e.* the graph has at least one cycle), they are exploited by the synchronization process to globally compensate the errors.

4   Proposed Approach

Let X denote the $4n \times 4n$ block-matrix containing the relative motions, let M denote the $4n \times 4$ block-matrix containing the absolute motions, and let M^{-b} denote the $4 \times 4n$ block-matrix containing the inverse of absolute motions, namely

$$
X = \begin{pmatrix} I_4 & M_{12} & \ldots & M_{1n} \\ M_{21} & I_4 & \ldots & M_{2n} \\ & \ldots & & \\ M_{n1} & M_{n2} & \ldots & I_4 \end{pmatrix}, \quad M = \begin{bmatrix} M_1 \\ M_2 \\ \ldots \\ M_n \end{bmatrix}, \quad M^{-b} = \begin{bmatrix} M_1^{-1} & M_2^{-1} & \ldots & M_n^{-1} \end{bmatrix}
$$
(8)

where I_4 denotes the 4×4 identity matrix. Using this notation, the compatibility constraint (7) can be expressed in a compact form as $X = M M^{-b}$, which implies that $\text{rank}(X) = 4$.

Let $\widehat{M}_{ij} \in SE(3)$ denote an estimate of the true relative motion $M_{ij} \in SE(3)$. In the presence of noise the measured relative motions will not satisfy Eq. (7), thus the goal is to average them so as to maximally satisfy $\widehat{M}_{ij} \approx M_i M_j^{-1}$. A possible approach consists in formulating the following optimization problem

$$
\min_{M_i \in SE(3)} \sum_{(i,j) \in \mathcal{E}} \left\| \widehat{M}_{ij} - M_i M_j^{-1} \right\|_F^2
$$
(9)

where the Frobenius norm $|| \cdot ||_F$ defines a left-invariant metric on $SE(3)$.

Let $\widehat{X}$ denote the $4n \times 4n$ block-matrix containing the measured relative motions $\widehat{M}_{ij} \in SE(3)$, and let A be the adjacency matrix of the measurement graph $\mathcal{G} = (\mathcal{V}, \mathcal{E})$, *i.e.* $A_{ij} = 1$ if $(i,j) \in \mathcal{E}$ and $A_{ij} = 0$ otherwise. In practical scenarios the measurement graph is not complete, since a point set do not overlap with all the others, thus $\widehat{X}$ has missing entries, which are represented as zero blocks. In other words, the available relative information is represented by $\mathcal{P}_\Omega(\widehat{X})$, where the sampling set has a 4×4 block-structure: $\Omega = A \otimes \mathbb{1}_{4\times 4}$ ($\mathbb{1}_{4\times 4}$ is a 4×4 matrix filled by ones, and $\otimes$ denotes the Kronecker product). Using this notation, the minimization problem (9) can be expressed as

$$\min_{X} \left\| \mathcal{P}_\Omega(\widehat{X} - X) \right\|_F^2 \tag{10}$$
$$\text{s.t. } X = MM^{-\flat}, \ M \in SE(3)^n.$$

This formulation can successfully average noisy relative motions, but it is not resistant to outliers. For this reason we consider the following problem

$$\min_{X,S} \left\| \mathcal{P}_\Omega(\widehat{X} - X) - S \right\|_F^2 \tag{11}$$
$$\text{s.t. } X = MM^{-\flat}, \ M \in SE(3)^n, \ S \text{ is sparse in } \Omega$$

where the additional variable S represents outliers, which are sparse over the measurement graph (by assumption).

If the *rank relaxation* is adopted, *i.e.* all the constraints except of the rank property are ignored, then the following relaxed optimization problem is obtained

$$\min_{L,S} \left\| \mathcal{P}_\Omega(\widehat{X} - L) - S \right\|_F^2 \tag{12}$$
$$\text{s.t. } \mathrm{rank}(L) \le 4, \ S \text{ is sparse in } \Omega$$

where L denotes a low-rank matrix which approximates the theoretical X defined in (8). Note that if the optimal solution to (12) satisfies $L = MM^{-\flat}$ with $M \in SE(3)^n$, then it is the global minimizer of (11). Otherwise, the optimal L only provides an estimate for the theoretical X, since it solves a relaxed version of Problem (11). In particular, the 4×4 blocks of L are not constrained to be Euclidean motions, thus they need to be projected onto $SE(3)$. Specifically, every fourth row is set equal to $[0\ 0\ 0\ 1]$ and 3×3 rotation blocks are projected onto $SO(3)$ through Singular Value Decomposition. Any block-column of the resulting matrix can be taken as an estimate of M, as we already know that the solution is up to a global rigid transformation.

Note that Problem (12) is indeed a LRS decomposition problem, since it is associated to the general formulation (1) with $\mathcal{F} = \mathcal{P}_\Omega$, namely $\mathcal{P}_\Omega(\widehat{X}) = \mathcal{P}_\Omega(L) + S + N$, thus the absolute motions can be recovered by means of any algorithm that computes such decomposition.

5 Experiments

We evaluated our approach on both simulated and real datasets analysing resilience to noise, robustness to outliers, sensitivity to missing data and computational cost. We considered three LRS decomposition algorithms, namely R-GoDec [27], Grasta [28] and L1-Alm [29], showing that they can be successfully applied to perform multiple point-set registration in a robust and efficient manner. We compared such algorithms to other registration techniques which work in frame space (*i.e.* not requiring point correspondences), namely the methods developed by Sharp *et al.* [21], Torsello *et al.* (Diffusion) [23], Bernard *et al.* (Null-space) [25] and Govindu [6]. The codes of Grasta, L1-Alm and

DIFFUSION are available online, the one by Govindu has been provided by the author, while in the other cases we used our implementation. All the simulations were performed in MATLAB on a dual-core computer with 1.3 GHz processor.

5.1 Simulated Data

We evaluated the aforementioned methods assuming that pairwise motions have been computed beforehand, thus 3D points are not involved in these simulations. Specifically, we generated a redundant set of relative motions (possibly corrupted by noise and/or outliers) – simulating the output of a pairwise registration algorithm such as ICP – which were given as input to all the techniques, and we evaluated the final estimates of absolute motions.

We considered n absolute motions in which rotations were sampled from random Euler angles and translation coordinates follow a standard Gaussian distribution. The measurement graph $\mathcal{G} = (\mathcal{V}, \mathcal{E})$ is a random graph drawn from the Erdős-Rényi model with parameters (n, p), i.e. given a vertex set $\mathcal{V} = \{1, 2, \ldots, n\}$ each edge (i, j) is in the set $\mathcal{E}$ with probability $p \in [0, 1]$, independently of all other edges. Thus $(1 - p)$ controls the degree of sparsity of the graph ($p = 1$ corresponds to the complete graph). The inlier pairwise motions were corrupted by a multiplicative noise $\widehat{M}_{ij} = M_{ij} E_{ij}$, with $E_{ij} \in SE(3)$ representing a small perturbation of the identity matrix. The rotation component of E_{ij} has axis uniformly distributed over the unit sphere and angle following a Gaussian distribution with zero mean and standard deviation $\sigma_R \in [1°, 10°]$, and the translation components were sampled from a Gaussian distribution with zero mean and standard deviation $\sigma_T \in [0.01, 0.1]$. All the results were averaged over 50 trials. In order to compare estimated and theoretical absolute motions we computed the transformation that aligns them by applying single averaging [38] for the rotation term and least-squares for the translation term. We used the angular distance and Euclidean norm to measure the accuracy of estimated rotations and translations respectively, where the angular (or geodesic) distance between two rotations $R, S \in SO(3)$ is the angle (in the angle-axis space) of the rotation SR^T which lies in the range $[0, 180°]$.

It is hard to evaluate the performances of a registration method as a whole, since several parameters are involved, thus in the following simulations we let one parameter vary at a time and keep the others fixed.

Noise. In this experiment we evaluate the effect of noise on relative motions in the absence of outliers. We considered $n = 100$ absolute motions and $p = 0.3$, which corresponds to about 70 % of missing pairs. Results with higher values of p correspond to better conditioned problems, with the same qualitative behaviour as $p = 0.3$, and hence they are not reported. Figure 1 shows the mean errors on absolute motions (rotation errors are measured in degrees while translation errors are commensurate with the simulated data) obtained by all the analysed techniques, as a function of the standard deviation of noise. The worst resilience to noise is achieved by Sharp et al. while LRS decomposition techniques and

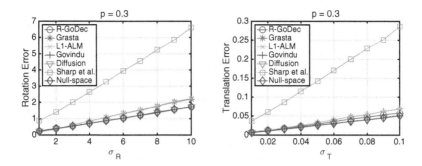

Fig. 1. Mean errors on absolute motions as a function of σ_R and σ_T.

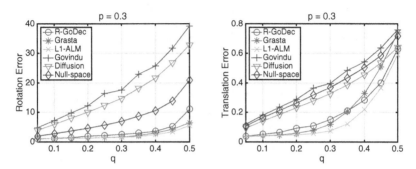

Fig. 2. Mean errors on absolute motions as a function of q.

the remaining algorithms return good estimates of absolute motions. A possible explanation of such behaviour is that in Sharp *et al.*'s method the error is distributed among the motions but it is not reduced. The best accuracy is achieved by non robust methods: DIFFUSION, NULL-SPACE and Govindu's. In general, robust techniques are not optimal with respect to noise, since they trade robustness for statistical efficiency.

Outliers. In this experiment we study the robustness to outliers of our approach. Each edge $(i, j) \in \mathcal{E}$ was designated as an outlier with uniform probability $q \in [0, 1]$, independently of all other edges. Outlier edges were assigned random elements of $SE(3)$. We considered $n = 100$ absolute motions sampled as before, we chose $p = 0.3$ to define the density of the measurement graph, and we introduced a fixed level of noise on relative motions ($\sigma_T = 0.05, \sigma_R = 5°$). The probability q that an edge is outlier ranges from 0.05 to 0.5, which correspond to about 5 % and 50 % of effective outliers. Figure 2 shows the mean errors on absolute motions as a function of q obtained by our approach, DIFFUSION, NULL-SPACE and Govindu's. The errors obtained by Sharp *et al.* are not reported in Fig. 2 so as to better visualize differences between the remaining algorithms (the method by Sharp *et al.* yields an average rotation error of 20° for $q = 0.05$ and 100°

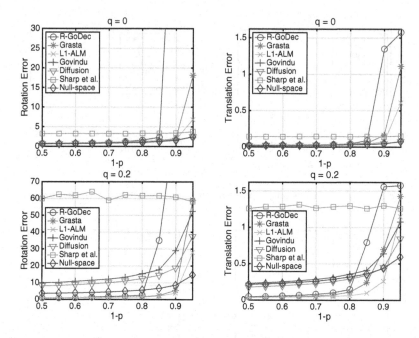

Fig. 3. Mean errors on absolute motions as a function of $(1-p)$, with $q = 0$ (top) and $q = 0.2$ (bottom). In the left sub-figures, the average rotation errors of R-GoDec are approximately $90°$ for $(1-p) = 0.9$ and $120°$ for $(1-p) = 0.95$.

for $q = 0.5$). Figure 2 confirms that DIFFUSION, NULL-SPACE and the method by Govindu are not robust, and it clearly shows the resilience to outliers gained by R-GoDec, GRASTA and L1-ALM. In particular, the errors obtained by LRS decomposition techniques remain almost unchanged until $q = 0.4$ for rotations and $q = 0.3$ for translations.

Missing Data. In this experiment we study how missing data influence the performances of our approach. We considered $n = 100$ absolute motions sampled as before and we introduced a fixed level of noise on relative motions ($\sigma_T = 0.05, \sigma_R = 5°$). The sparsity parameter $(1-p)$ ranges from 0.5 to 0.95, which correspond to about 50 % and 95 % of missing pairs. Results with lower values of $(1-p)$ yield the same behaviour as $(1-p) = 0.5$, and hence they are not reported. We considered both the ideal case where outliers are absent ($q = 0$) and a more realistic situation in which a fixed percentage of outliers is introduced ($q = 0.2$). Results are reported in Fig. 3, which shows the mean errors on absolute motions as a function of the sparsity parameter $(1-p)$. The errors obtained by Sharp *et al.* remain constant as $(1-p)$ increases, showing no sensitivity to missing data. The same holds for the method by Govindu, DIFFUSION and NULL-SPACE, if outliers are not present. As for our approach, GRASTA and L1-ALM can tolerate up to 90 % of missing pairs in the case $q = 0.2$, whereas R-GoDec

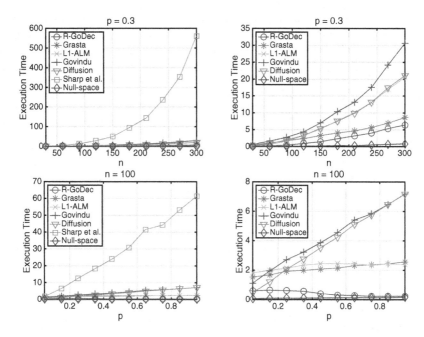

Fig. 4. Execution times (seconds) as a function of n (top) and p (bottom). The right figures are a magnification of the left ones.

breaks down with 80 % of missing pairs. If there are no outliers ($q = 0$), all the LRS methods can tolerate an extra 5 % of missing data.

Execution Time. In this experiment we assess the computational efficiency of all the methods in two scenarios. First, we kept the density level of the measurement graph fixed ($p = 0.3$) and let n vary between 30 and 300. Then, we kept the number of absolute motions fixed ($n = 100$) and let p vary between 0.05 (about 95 % of missing data) and 0.95 (about 5 % of missing data). In both cases we introduced a fixed level of noise and outliers on relative motions ($\sigma_T = 0.05, \sigma_R = 5°$, $q = 0.2$). DIFFUSION is implemented in C++ (by the authors), while the remaining algorithms are implemented in MATLAB. Results are reported in Fig. 4, showing that the method by Sharp *et al.* is remarkably slower than the other techniques. In particular, L1-ALM is comparable to DIFFUSION and faster than Govindu's, while both R-GODEC and GRASTA are slower than NULL-SPACE but faster than the other methods. The bottom row in Fig. 4 shows that the execution time of matrix decomposition techniques and NULL-SPACE do not change significantly when p varies, whereas the other techniques require more time as the measurement graph gets denser.

The rundown of these tests is that, collectively, motion synchronization methods based on LRS decomposition qualify among the fastest solutions and provide

Table 1. Mean errors (rotations in degrees, translations in millimetres) on absolute motions for the Stanford repository. The number of point sets and the percentage of missing pairs are also reported.

Dataset	n	% miss.	R-GoDec rot.	R-GoDec tra.	Grasta rot.	Grasta tra.	L1-ALM rot.	L1-ALM tra.	Govindu rot.	Govindu tra.	Diffusion rot.	Diffusion tra.	Sharp et al. rot.	Sharp et al. tra.	Null-space rot.	Null-space tra.
Bunny	10	0	0.82	2.9	0.84	1.9	0.78	1.6	1.07	3.7	1.07	3.7	1.07	4.5	1.07	3.7
Buddha	15	0	0.85	0.3	0.79	0.4	0.94	0.4	1.28	0.4	1.28	0.4	2.22	0.6	1.27	0.4
Dragon	15	0	0.79	0.3	0.91	0.4	0.77	0.4	1.52	0.4	1.52	0.4	1.45	0.6	1.51	0.4

Table 2. Execution times (seconds) of motion synchronization. The number of point sets and the percentage of missing pairs are also reported.

Dataset	n	% miss.	R-GoDec	Grasta	L1-ALM	Govindu	Diffusion	Sharp et al.	Null-space
Gargoyle	27	40	0.05	0.47	0.15	0.13	0.35	1.94	0.03
Capital	100	71	0.67	1.62	1.66	0.98	2.53	25.27	0.09

a good trade-off between statistical efficiency and resilience to outliers. However, they are more affected than the other methods by the sparsity of the graph.

5.2 Real Data

In this section we report the outcome of tests on real datasets of range images. Relative motion estimates were produced thanks to the MATLAB implementation of ICP (`pcregrigid`). The measurements graph was defined by discarding all the pairs with registration error higher than a threshold. This produced a redundant set of relative motions which were compensated by solving a motion synchronization problem, returning the transformations that align the original point sets. These estimates could have been improved by alternating motion synchronization and computing relative motions, as suggested in [23,24]; however, such a refinement was not applied in these experiments, i.e. we performed motion synchronization only once. Experimentally we observed that LRS decompositions perform better when translation components have values comparable to rotations, namely in the range $[-1, 1]$. For this reason, before performing motion synchronization, we divided all the relative translations by the maximum of the translations norm (and eventually multiplied the absolute translations by such a scale). This normalization also improves the results of the other algorithms.

From the Stanford 3D Scanning Repository [39] we used the Bunny, Happy Buddha (standing) and Dragon (standing) datasets, which contain 10, 15 and 15 point sets, respectively. As for the initialization of the ICP algorithm, we perturbed the available ground-truth motions by a rotation with random axis and angle uniformly distributed over $[0, 2°]$, similarly to the experiments carried out in [24]. Since ground-truth motions are available for these datasets, we evaluated quantitatively the results by reporting the mean errors in Table 1. Differences in execution time are meaningless for such relatively small datasets and are not

Table 3. Cross-sections of registered point-sets.

reported. The errors obtained by R-GoDec, Grasta and L1-Alm are always lower than the other techniques, highlighting the benefit of robustness.

In another experiment we considered two datasets, named `Gargoyle` and `Capital`, which contain 27 and 100 point sets respectively. Since there is no information about the scans, we simply initialized the ICP algorithm with identity matrices. Execution times are reported in Table 2. They are referred to the motion synchronization step, *i.e.* computing absolute motions from relative motions, and they do not include the time for computing relative motions, which is the same for all the techniques. R-GoDec is slower than Null-space but faster than the other solutions, the method by Sharp *et al.* is the slowest technique, while Grasta and L1-Alm are faster than Diffusion but slower than Null-space and Govindu's method.

The different registration techniques can be appraised qualitatively from the cross-sections of output 3D models reported Table 3, as it is customary in the registration literature. The cross-sections obtained by our approach are crisper than the others, proving the effectiveness of LRS decomposition in handling measurement errors in the context of multiple point-set registration. In particular, the best visual accuracy is achieved by L1-Alm and Grasta, while R-GoDec get slightly worse results, yet better than the remaining methods. There is no significant difference between the cross-sections obtained by Diffusion, Null-space and Govindu's, while the misalignment produced by Sharp *et al.* is evident, especially for the Gargoyle dataset. Figure 5 shows the 3D models produced by L1-Alm with different colours for each point cloud.

In summary, these experiments with real data confirms the conclusions drawn from the simulations.

(a) Bunny   (b) Buddha   (c) Dragon   (d) Gargoyle   (e) Capital

Fig. 5. 3D models obtained with L1-ALM. Different point sets are colour coded. (Color figure online)

6   Conclusions

For the first time in the literature we formulated frame-space registration as a low-rank and sparse decomposition problem that neatly caters for missing-data, outliers and noise, and it benefits from a wealth of available decomposition algorithms that can be seamlessly used as alternatives. Experimental results show that this approach is efficient and provides a good trade-off between statistical efficiency and resilience to outliers. However, it is more affected than the other methods by the sparsity of the measurement graph. It must be said, though, that the goal of synchronization is to exploit redundancy: if the measures are barely sufficient the problem looses significance.

Acknowledgements. Thanks to Massimiliano Corsini (ISTI-CNR) for providing the Gargoyle and Capital datasets, and to Avishek Chatterjee and Venu Madhav Govindu for providing the MATLAB implementation of [6].

References

1. Besl, P., McKay, N.: A method for registration of 3-D shapes. IEEE Trans. Pattern Anal. Mach. Intell. **14**(2), 239–256 (1992)
2. Chen, Y., Medioni, G.: Object modeling by registration of multiple range images. In: Proceedings of the IEEE International Conference on Robotics and Automation, pp. 2724–2729 (1991)
3. Rusinkiewicz, S., Levoy, M.: Efficient variants of the ICP algorithm. In: Proceedings of the International Conference on 3-D Digital Imaging and Modeling, pp. 145–152 (2001)
4. Pulli, K.: Multiview registration for large data sets. In: Proceedings of the International Conference on 3-D Digital Imaging and Modeling, pp. 160–168 (1999)
5. Arrigoni, F., Fusiello, A., Rossi, B.: Spectral motion synchronization in SE(3). ArXiv e-prints (1506.08765) (2015)
6. Govindu, V.M.: Lie-algebraic averaging for globally consistent motion estimation. In: Proceedings of the IEEE Conference on Computer Vision and Pattern Recognition, pp. 684–691 (2004)

7. Williams, J., Bennamoun, M.: Simultaneous registration of multiple corresponding point sets. Comput. Vis. Image Underst. **81**(1), 117–141 (2001)
8. Pennec, X.: Multiple registration and mean rigid shape: applications to the 3D case. In: 16th Leeds Annual Statistical Workshop, pp. 178–185 (1996)
9. Benjemaa, R., Schmitt, F.: A solution for the registration of multiple 3D point sets using unit quaternions. In: Burkhardt, H., Neumann, B. (eds.) ECCV 1998. LNCS, vol. 1407, pp. 34–50. Springer, Heidelberg (1998). doi:10.1007/BFb0054732
10. Bergevin, R., Soucy, M., Gagnon, H., Laurendeau, D.: Towards a general multiview registration technique. IEEE Trans. Pattern Anal. Mach. Intell. **18**(5), 540–547 (1996)
11. Krishnan, S., Lee, P.Y., Moore, J.B., Venkatasubramanian, S.: Optimisation-on-a-manifold for global registration of multiple 3D point sets. Int. J. Intell. Syst. Technol. Appl. **3**(3/4), 319–340 (2007)
12. Bonarrigo, F., Signoroni, A.: An enhanced 'optimization-on-a-manifold' framework for global registration of 3D range data. In: Proceedings of the Joint 3DIM/3DPVT Conference: 3D Imaging, Modeling, Processing, Visualization and Transmission, pp. 350–357 (2011)
13. Mateo, X., Orriols, X., Binefa, X.: Bayesian perspective for the registration of multiple 3D views. Comput. Vis. Image Underst. **118**, 84–96 (2014)
14. Chaudhury, K.N., Khoo, Y., Singer, A.: Global registration of multiple point clouds using semidefinite programming. SIAM J. Optim. **25**(1), 468–501 (2015)
15. Raghuramu, A.C.: Robust multiview registration of 3D surfaces via ℓ_1-norm minimization. In: British Machine Vision Conference (2015)
16. Fantoni, S., Castellani, U., Fusiello, A.: Accurate and automatic alignment of range surfaces. In: Second Joint 3DIM/3DPVT Conference: 3D Imaging, Modeling, Processing, Visualization and Transmission (3DIMPVT), pp. 73–80 (2012)
17. Fitzgibbon, A.: Robust registration of 2D and 3D point sets. Image Vis. Comput. **21**(13–14), 1145–1153 (2003)
18. Toldo, R., Beinat, A., Crosilla, F.: Global registration of multiple point clouds embedding the generalized procrustes analysis into an ICP framework. In: 3D Data Processing Visualization and Transmission Conference (2010)
19. Beinat, A., Crosilla, F.: Generalized procrustes analysis for size and shape 3D object reconstruction. In: Optical 3-D Measurement Techniques, pp. 345–353. Wichmann Verlag (2001)
20. Thomas, D., Matsushita, Y., Sugimoto, A.: Robust simultaneous 3D registration via rank minimization. In: Proceedings of the Joint 3DIM/3DPVT Conference: 3D Imaging, Modeling, Processing, Visualization and Transmission, pp. 33–40 (2012)
21. Sharp, G.C., Lee, S.W., Wehe, D.K.: Multiview registration of 3D scenes by minimizing error between coordinate frames. In: Heyden, A., Sparr, G., Nielsen, M., Johansen, P. (eds.) ECCV 2002. LNCS, vol. 2351, pp. 587–597. Springer, Heidelberg (2002). doi:10.1007/3-540-47967-8_39
22. Fusiello, A., Castellani, U., Ronchetti, L., Murino, V.: Model acquisition by registration of multiple acoustic range views. In: Heyden, A., Sparr, G., Nielsen, M., Johansen, P. (eds.) ECCV 2002. LNCS, vol. 2351, pp. 805–819. Springer, Heidelberg (2002). doi:10.1007/3-540-47967-8_54
23. Torsello, A., Rodola, E., Albarelli, A.: Multiview registration via graph diffusion of dual quaternions. In: Proceedings of the IEEE Conference on Computer Vision and Pattern Recognition, pp. 2441–2448 (2011)
24. Govindu, V.M., Pooja, A.: On averaging multiview relations for 3D scan registration. IEEE Trans. Image Process. **23**(3), 1289–1302 (2014)

25. Bernard, F., Thunberg, J., Gemmar, P., Hertel, F., Husch, A., Goncalves, J.: A solution for multi-alignment by transformation synchronisation. In: Proceedings of the IEEE Conference on Computer Vision and Pattern Recognition (2015)
26. Shih, S., Chuang, Y., Yu, T.: An efficient and accurate method for the relaxation of multiview registration error. IEEE Trans. Image Process. **17**(6), 968–981 (2008)
27. Arrigoni, F., Magri, L., Rossi, B., Fragneto, P., Fusiello, A.: Robust absolute rotation estimation via low-rank and sparse matrix decomposition. In: Proceedings of the International Conference on 3D Vision (3DV), pp. 491–498 (2014)
28. He, J., Balzano, L., Szlam, A.: Incremental gradient on the Grassmannian for online foreground and background separation in subsampled video. In: Proceedings of the IEEE Conference on Computer Vision and Pattern Recognition, pp. 1568–1575 (2012)
29. Zheng, Y., Liu, G., Sugimoto, S., Yan, S., Okutomi, M.: Practical low-rank matrix approximation under robust L_1-norm. In: Proceedings of the IEEE Conference on Computer Vision and Pattern Recognition, pp. 1410–1417 (2012)
30. Zhou, X., Yang, C., Zhao, H., Yu, W.: Low-rank modeling and its applications in image analysis. ACM Comput. Surv. **47**(2), 36:1–36:33 (2014)
31. Candès, E.J., Li, X., Ma, Y., Wright, J.: Robust principal component analysis? J. ACM **58**(3), 11:1–11:37 (2011)
32. Candès, E.J., Recht, B.: Exact matrix completion via convex optimization. Found. Comput. Math. **9**(6), 717–772 (2009)
33. Candès, E.J., Tao, T.: The power of convex relaxation: near-optimal matrix completion. IEEE Trans. Inf. Theory **56**(5), 2053–2080 (2010)
34. Zhou, T., Tao, D.: GoDec: randomized low-rank & sparse matrix decomposition in noisy case. In: Proceedings of the 28th International Conference on Machine Learning (ICML11), pp. 33–40. ACM, June 2011
35. Beck, A., Teboulle, M.: A fast iterative shrinkage-thresholding algorithm for linear inverse problems. SIAM J. Imaging Sci. **2**(1), 183–202 (2009)
36. Boyd, S., Parikh, N., Chu, E., Peleato, B., Eckstein, J.: Distributed optimization and statistical learning via the alternating direction method of multipliers. Found. Trends Mach. Learn. **3**(1), 1–122 (2011)
37. Bertsekas, D.P.: Constrained Optimization and Lagrange Multiplier Methods. Academic Press, New York (1982)
38. Hartley, R., Aftab, K., Trumpf, J.: L1 rotation averaging using the Weiszfeld algorithm. In: Proceedings of the IEEE Conference on Computer Vision and Pattern Recognition, pp. 3041–3048 (2011)
39. Stanford University: 3D scanning repository. http://graphics.stanford.edu/data/3Dscanrep/

Recognition from Hand Cameras:
A Revisit with Deep Learning

Cheng-Sheng Chan, Shou-Zhong Chen, Pei-Xuan Xie, Chiung-Chih Chang,
and Min Sun$^{(\boxtimes)}$

Departmant of Electrical Engineering, National Tsing Hua University,
Hsinchu, Taiwan
{s104061526,s104061545}@m104.nthu.edu.tw,
{s101061230,s101060006}@m101.nthu.edu.tw, sunmin@ee.nthu.edu.tw

Abstract. We revisit the study of a wrist-mounted camera system
(referred to as HandCam) for recognizing activities of hands. HandCam
has two unique properties as compared to egocentric systems (referred
to as HeadCam): (1) it avoids the need to detect hands; (2) it more consistently observes the activities of hands. By taking advantage of these
properties, we propose a deep-learning-based method to recognize hand
states (free vs. active hands, hand gestures, object categories), and discover object categories. Moreover, we propose a novel two-streams deep
network to further take advantage of both HandCam and HeadCam. We
have collected a new synchronized HandCam and HeadCam dataset with
20 videos captured in three scenes for hand states recognition. Experiments show that our HandCam system consistently outperforms a deep-
learning-based HeadCam method (with estimated manipulation regions)
and a dense-trajectory-based HeadCam method in all tasks. We also
show that HandCam videos captured by different users can be easily
aligned to improve free vs. active recognition accuracy (3.3 % improvement) in across-scenes use case. Moreover, we observe that finetuning
Convolutional Neural Network consistently improves accuracy. Finally,
our novel two-streams deep network combining HandCam and HeadCam
achieves the best performance in four out of five tasks. With more data,
we believe a joint HandCam and HeadCam system can robustly log hand
states in daily life.

Keywords: Activity recognition · Wearable camera

1 Introduction

Recently, the technological advance of wearable devices has led to significant
interests in recognizing human behaviors in daily life (i.e., uninstrumented environment). Among many devices, egocentric camera systems have drawn significant attention, since the camera is aligned with the wearer's field-of-view, it
naturally captures what a person sees. These systems have shown great potential in recognizing daily activities (e.g., making meals, watching TV, etc.) [1],
estimating hand poses [2,3], generating how-to videos [4], etc.

© Springer International Publishing AG 2016
B. Leibe et al. (Eds.): ECCV 2016, Part IV, LNCS 9908, pp. 505–521, 2016.
DOI: 10.1007/978-3-319-46493-0_31

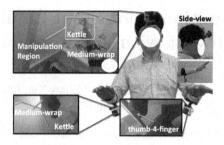

Fig. 1. Illustration of our wearable camera system: consisting of three wide-angle cameras, two mounted on the left and right wrists to capture hands (referred to as Hand-Cam) and one mounted on the head (referred to as HeadCam). We use our HandCam system to robustly recognize object categories (e.g., kettle) and hand gestures (see red arrows for illustration). (Color figure online)

Despite many advantages of egocentric camera systems, there exists two main issues which are much less discussed [2]. Firstly, hand localization is not solved especially for passive camera systems. Even for active camera systems like Kinect, hand localization is challenging when two hands are interacting or a hand is interacting with an object. Secondly, the limited field-of-view of an egocentric camera implies that hands will inevitably move outside the images sometimes. On the other hand, cameras have been mounted on other locations to avoid similar issues. In project Digit [5], a camera is mounted on a user's wrist to always observe the user's hand pose. This allows a user to issue gesture commands at any time. Similarly, a camera has been mounted on a robot arm for accurately picking up an object [6]. In fact, the seminal work [7] has conducted simulation on 3D model of the human body to analyze the effects of field of view and body motion, when cameras are mounted at different locations. Hence, we argue that egocentric camera system might not be the best wearable system for recognizing human behaviors.

We revisit the wrist-mounted camera system (similar to [8]) to capture activities of both hands (Fig. 1). We name our system "HandCam" which is very different from egocentric systems with cameras on head or chest (e.g., [2,4,9]). By wearing cameras on wrists, HandCam directly recognizes the states of hands (e.g., object: kettle; gesture: medium-wrap in Fig. 1). It avoids the needs to detect hands and infer manipulation regions as required in classical egocentric systems [9]. A few methods have been proposed to recognize activities using wrist-mounted camera [8,10]. They show that wrist-mounted sensor system can be small and user-friendly. They also primarily focus on fusing different sensing modalities. However, we focus on designing a deep-learning-based vision algorithm to improve recognition accuracy (see Sect. 2.3 for more comparison). Most importantly, we are one of the first to propose a novel two-streams deep network taking advantages of both HandCam and HeadCam. All our methods are design to classify hand states including free vs. active (i.e., hands holding objects or not), object categories, and hand gestures (Sect. 3.3). A similar method is also proposed to discover object categories in an unseen scene (Sect. 3.7).

To evaluate our system, we collected a new synchronized HandCam and HeadCam dataset for hand state recognition. The dataset consists of 20 sets of video sequences (i.e., each set includes two HandCams and one HeadCam synchronized videos) captured in three scenes: a small office, a mid-size lab, and a large home. In order to thoroughly analyze recognition tasks, we ask users to interact with multiple object categories and multiple object instances. We also ask multiple users to wear HandCam in a casual way to consider the variation introduced by multiple users. To overcome this variation, a fully automatic hand alignment method is proposed (Sect. 3.2).

Experiments show that our HandCam system consistently outperforms a deep-learning-based HeadCam method (with estimated manipulation regions [11]) and a dense-trajectory-based [12] HeadCam method in all tasks. Moreover, we show that HandCam videos captured by different users can be easily aligned to improve free vs. active recognition accuracy (3.3 % acc. improvement) in across-scenes use case. In all experiments, we use state-of-the-art Convolutional Neural Network (CNN) [13] features. We observe that finetuning CNN consistently improves accuracy (at most 4.9 % improvement). Finally, our method combining HandCam and HeadCam features achieves the best performance.

2   Related Work

A few non-vision-based methods have been proposed to recognize human daily activities based on recognizing hand states [14, 15]. Wu et al. [16] combine sparse RFID data with a third-person video to recognize human daily activities based on objects used. In the following, we focus on the vision-based methods and review related work in egocentric recognition, hand detection and pose estimation, and a few works inspired our HandCam system.

2.1   Egocentric Recognition

[9, 17, 18] are the early egocentric works learning to recognize objects, actions, and activities. These methods assume foreground objects and hands can be easily separated from background using appearance, geometric, and motion cues. Their methods are evaluated on an egocentric activity dataset where the users move mainly their hands in front of a static table. In contrast, we allow users to naturally move to different places in a scene, which creates addition challenge for egocentric system to localize hands. For instance, Pirsiavash and Ramanan [1] also propose to recognize activities through recognizing objects while users is moving in their homes. Since their approach is based on detecting hand-object manipulation in the egocentric field-of-view, it is confused mainly with activities observing similar objects in the field-of-view without manipulation. However,

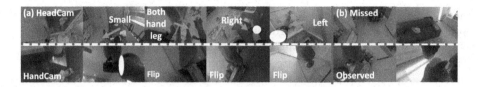

Fig. 2. HandCam (bottom-row) vs. HeadCam (top-row). Panel (a) compares the hand location variation. The variation in HandCam (bottom) is significantly less than variation in HeadCam (top). We also know exactly which video captures left or right hand. We flip left hand images to mimic right hand images and train a single deep network. Panel (b) shows typical examples of missed hands in HeadCam but observed hands in HandCam. For example, we do not require consistent hand-eye coordination for opening a water bottle while walking.

since our HandCam significantly reduces hand location variation (Fig. 2(a)), this scenario won't be a big issue for our HandCam system.

[11,19,20] further show the importance of gaze to help recognizing actions requiring "hand-eye coordination". We argue that not all daily activities consistently requires hand-eye coordinate. For instance, we do not require consistent hand-eye coordination for opening a water bottle while walking (Fig. 2-b-Right). In such case, head movement and gaze information might be misleading, and the user's hand and object of interest might move outside the field-of-view of the egocentric camera (Fig. 2(b)). On the other hand, our HandCam system more consistently captures hand-object interaction for a variety of daily activities. Finally, a few works [21–23] focus on summarizing egocentric videos by recognizing objects, people, and scenes.

Extra Sensors. Fernando et al. [24] utilize motion capture techniques, static cameras, wearable IMUs, and a head-mounted camera to study food preparation process in an instrumented kitchen. [4] proposes to combine egocentric camera with gaze tracker to robustly "discover" objects of interest given multiple sequences recorded in the same scene conducting the same tasks by different subjects. Moghimi et al. [25] propose to use a head-mounted RGBD camera to recognize both manipulation and non-manipulation activities. Damen et al. [26] also propose to use RGBD camera to model background and "discover" foreground objects. In this work, we show that with our HandCam system, objects can also be discovered without the need of gaze tracker or RGBD sensor (Sect. 3.7).

2.2 Hand Detection and Pose Estimation

[2,3] focus on estimating 3D hand poses using wearable RGBD camera. Despite many success in 3D hand pose recognition, Rogez et al. [2] show that egocentric 3D hand poses estimation is very challenging due to common interaction between hands and other objects or scene elements. [27–29] focus on detecting hand pixels in RGB images while users are moving around various environments. Betancourt et al. [30] study the weakness of [27] and proposes method for reducing false

positive detection of hands. Although these RGB methods are not as robust as RGBD methods, these methods have been applied to discover hand gestures [31].

2.3   Camera for Hands

A few work have proposed to wear cameras on wrists or other body parts to recognize gestures, poses, and activities of hands. In [5,32], cameras are mounted on a user's wrists to always observe user's hand pose. This allows a user to issue gesture commands at any time. However, the project assumes that a user is hand free of objects. In contrast, our HandCam system focuses on recognizing hand-object interactions. Similarly, a camera has been mounted on a robot arm for it to accurately pick up an object [6]. Although the robot has other sensors like a stereo camera and a lazer range finder which are not mounted on the robot arm, it has been shown that the HandCam is essential for picking up an object. Chan et al. [33] recently propose to wear a camera on hand webbings to recognize hand gestures and context-aware interactions such as events triggered by object recognition. However, they assume that objects are instrumented with QR codes. These works suggest that egocentric camera systems might not be the only wearable options for understanding human behaviors.

Maekawa et al. [8] is the most relevant prior work aiming for object-based activity recognition using sensors on wrist including a camera. We share the same idea to take advantage of wrist-mounted camera to recognize human-object interaction. However, it focuses on fusing the observation of heterogeneous sensors including a camera, a microphone, and an accelerometer. Compared to our deep learning approach, they utilize simple and efficient color histogram as the feature. Moreover, they train/test in the same environment and use same object instances, whereas we train/test different object instances across different environments (e.g., train: lab+office; test: home). Ohnishi et al. [34] present a recent paper that achieves an outstanding recognition accuracy using a wrist-mounted camera (only on right hand). They also focus on vision approach using deep features and dense-trajectory-based features [12]. Our HandCam method does not use motion feature [12], since it is time consuming to compute (on average a few seconds for each prediction). On the other hand, our deep feature can be computed in real-time on a GPU. Moreover, they use pre-trained CNN feature only, whereas we train a novel two-streams CNN to learn representation for wearable cameras. Finally, in their experiments, they assume that the temporal segment of each action is given. Hence, they evaluate per-segment classification accuracy, whereas we evaluate per-frame classification accuracy.

3   Our System

Our wearable camera system (Fig. 1) consists of three wide-angle cameras: two HandCams and one HeadCam. We first propose a method utilizing deep-learning techniques to classify hand states (free vs. active, object categories, and hand gestures) observed by either HandCam or HeadCam separately. Finally, we propose a novel two-streams CNN model to take advantage of all cameras in Sect. 3.8.

Fig. 3. Across-videos Hand Alignment. Panel (a)-left shows the across-videos hand variation. Panel (a)-right shows aligned images. Panel (b) shows example of median and diversity images on the top and bottom, respectively.

3.1 Wearable Cues

The strength of a wearable system essentially lies in the unique cues it can extract. For an egocentric system, these cues include gaze, hand, and foreground information. Some systems utilize active sensors to reliably localize hands (e.g., RGBD sensor in [3]) or predict user's attention (e.g., gaze tracker in [4]). However, they require extra hardware expenses and more power consumption. Many other egocentric systems require only a camera. However, sophisticated pre-processing steps [9,11,17,20] are required for removing background information.

Our HandCam system is designed with two focuses:

- Stable Hand Cue. Significantly reduced hand location variation (Fig. 2(a)-bottom) as compared to egocentric systems which have larger hand location variation (Fig. 2(a)-top). Our system also typically won't be confused between left and right hands, since they are recorded by different cameras. Moreover, we augment our dataset by flipping left hand images to mimic right hand images. We found that the data augmentation procedure [35] improves the accuracy of our deep network.
- Consistent Observation. Almost all hand related activities are observed as compared to egocentric systems which have limited field-of-view that missed some hand related activities (Fig. 2(b)).

Human Factors. As we design our system to be used by general users, we let each user to wear the HandCam under a general guideline. As a consequence, different users mount the HandCam with slightly different distances and orientation. Therefore, the hand location variation "across" video sequences (Fig. 3(a)-left) is noticeable. However, once the camera is mounted on a user's wrists, the spatial variation of hand regions are small within the video. By utilizing this fact, we propose a fully automatic across-videos hand alignment method.

3.2 Hand Alignment

In each video sequence, we model the pixel value (i.e., a value between $0 \sim 255$) distribution across time for each pixel and each color channel as a Laplace distribution parameterized by its center (μ) and its diversity (β). We estimate the

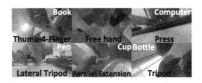

Fig. 4. Typical hand states in HandCam view: object category (top-white-font) and hand gesture (bottom-red-font). The statisitcs of states in our dataset in shown in Fig. 8. (Color figure online)

parameters of the distribution using maximum likelihood estimators, where the median image represents the common pattern (Fig. 3(b)-top) and the diversity image represents the variation of pixel values (black indicates small variation in Fig. 3(b)-bottom). We simply treat the pixels with diversity β smaller than β_{th} for all color channel as "stable" hand mask (within blue box in Fig. 3(b)-bottom). We find the video with the smallest "stable" hand mask across all videos as the reference video, and use the median image within the mask as alignment template (blue box in Fig. 3(b)-top). We apply multiscale normalized cross-correlation to align the template to the median images of other videos. Then, we apply cropping and replicate padding to generate hand aligned images (Fig. 3(a)-right).

3.3   Hand States Recognition

Given the aligned (Fig. 3(a)-right) and stable (Fig. 2(b)-bottom) observation of hand, we propose to recognize the hand states for multiple tasks (Fig. 4).

Free vs. Active. The most fundamental states of interests is to recognize whether the hand is manipulating an object (referred to as "active state"), or not (referred to as "free state"). In this work, we explicitly evaluate the performance of active hands recognition undergoing some unseen activities.

Hand Gesture Recognition. At a slightly finer level of granularity (12 gesture classes shown in technical report [36]), we propose to recognize hand gestures of active hands. Note that gesture is an important affordance cue for recognizing activities without the need to recognize a large number of object categories involving in the same activity.

Object Category Recognition. At the finest level of granularity (23 object categories), we propose to recognize object categories which have been manipulated by hands. Categorical recognition allows our system to recognize an unseen object instance within a know category.

We take a fully supervised approach and train a frame-based multiclass state classifier. The classifier generates a confidence $u(s_i)$ for state s_i in the ith frame. For example, $u(s_i = Active)$ specifies the confidence that the ith frame contains an active hand. $u(s_i = Notebook)$ specifies the confidence that the ith frame contains a hand manipulating a notebook. We take advantage of the recent breakthrough in deep learning and extract frame-based feature f_i from Convolutional

Neural Network (CNN) [13], where i denotes the frame index. The deep feature f_i is a high-level representation used as the input of the state classifier and the state change detector described next. We describe the setting of the CNN model that we use in our application in Sects. 3.6 and 3.8.

3.4 State Change Detection

Since frame-based state recognition inevitably will contain spurious error predictions, we propose to detect possible state changes.

Frame-Based Change. We train a frame-base binary state change classifier (i.e., change or no change) by treating frames within d frames distance away from a ground truth change frame as positive examples and remaining frames as negative examples. The large value of d will increase the number of positive examples, but decreasing the localization ability of the true change locations. In order to reduce the visual variation of changes, we propose the following feature,

$$cf_i = |f_{i-d} - f_{i+d}| = |f_{i+d} - f_{i-d}|, \tag{1}$$

where f is the same deep feature used for state classifier. Note that f is a high-level semantic feature. Hence, cf measures semantic changes, but not low-level motion or lighting condition changes. Moreover, cf implies that transition from active to free should have a similar feature representation as transition from free to active. Given cf, we apply a change classifier to obtain frame-based state change confidences for all frames (Fig. 5).

Change Candidates. Similar to classical edge detection [37], we need to remove redundant change candidates with high confidences. Hence, we apply non-maximum suppression to find local maximum with respect to state change confidences (Fig. 5). We define the local maximum locations as change candidates $\{i\}_{i \in C}$, where C contains a set of local maximum change locations. Note that we prefer high recall (i.e., $>95\,\%$) at this step.

3.5 Full Model

We now combine frame-based state classification with detected change candidates to improve the classification of states. Both information are captured into a pairwise scoring function below,

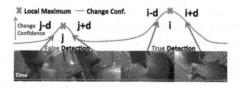

Fig. 5. Illustration of state change detection. Two change candidates are shown, where the first one corresponds to a false detection and the second one corresponds to a true detection. Our system ensures high recall of state changes at this step.

$$R(S) = \sum_{i=1}^{N} u(s_i) + \lambda \sum_{i=1}^{N-1} b(s_i, s_{i+1}), \qquad (2)$$

where $R(S)$ is the score as a function of a set of states $S = [s_1, s_2, ..., s_i, ...]$, i is the index of frame, s_i is the state of the ith frame, the space of s_i is $\{state1, state2, ...\}$, N is the total number of frames, λ balances the potentials, and $u(.), b(.)$ are the unary and binary scoring functions, respectively.

Scoring Functions. The unary scoring function is exactly the same as the scores in Sect. 3.3. The binary scoring function is defined below,

$$for \ i \notin C; \ if \ s_i \neq s_{i+1}, \ b(s_i, s_{i+1}) = -\inf; \ otherwise, \ b(s_i, s_{i+1}) = 0, \qquad (3)$$

which means no change is allowed when the ith frame is not a change candidate;

$$for \ i \in C; \ if \ s_i \neq s_{i+1}, \ b(s_i, s_{i+1}) = -S(\bar{f}_i, \bar{f}_{i+1}); \ otherwise, \ b(s_i, s_{i+1}) = S(\bar{f}_i, \bar{f}_{i+1}),$$

where $S(\bar{f}_i, \bar{f}_{i+1})$ is the cosine similarity between $\bar{f}_i, \bar{f}_{i+1}$, $\bar{f}_i$ is the average frame-based deep features between the change candidate immediately before the ith frame and the change candidate at the ith frame, and $\bar{f}_{i+1}$ is the average frame-based deep features between the change candidate at the ith frame and the change candidate immediately after the ith frame. We apply a dynamic programming inference procedure to predict the states maximizing $R(S)$.

3.6 Deep Feature

We extract our deep feature from the well-known AlexNet [13][1] CNN model. Instead of using the pre-trained $1K$ dimension final output as feature, we try

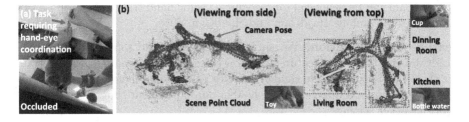

Fig. 6. Panel (a) shows an example where HandCam (bottom) is occluded but Head-Cam (top) observed the activity requiring hand-eye coordination. Panel (b) shows 3D Structure [38] of the Scene reconstructed from HeadCam images. A pair of blue and red dots indicates the recovered camera 3D pose and other color-coded dots show the color of the scene. This shows that HeadCam contains place information which potentially is useful for hand states recognition. (Color figure online)

---

[1] VGG [39] can be used to achieve $1 - 2\%$ improvement in general.

different design choices to address the following questions: (1) which layer should we extract feature? and (2) will finetuning improve recognition from the new HandCam observation? In our pilot experiment, we found that a compact six layers model achieves the best accuracy, while being more computationally efficient than the original AlexNet (see technical report [36]). Hence, we use the fc6 output of AlexNet by default in all experiments of this paper. In Sect. 6, we also show that finetuning consistently improves state prediction accuracy.

3.7   Object Discovery

Given many observation of how users interact with objects in a new scene, we propose a simple method to discover common object categories. Firstly, we predict the active hand segments which is typically over-segmented. Then, we calculate segment-base feature $\bar{f}$ as the average of the frame-based features and apply a hierarchical clustering method using cosine similarity to group similar segments into clusters. By assuming that the same object category is manipulated by hands multiple-times in a similar way, two similar segments likely corresponds to the same object categories. In Sect. 6.3, we show that our HandCam system can discover categories more accurately than a HeadCam system.

3.8   Combining HandCam with HeadCam

Since our goal is to achieve the best accuracy, we would like to combine HandCam with HeadCam to do even better. Intuitively, HeadCam should be complementary to HandCam in some ways. Firstly, sometimes HandCam is occluded by other objects, whereas HeadCam keeps a clear view of the hands (Fig. 6(a)) due to required hand-eye coordination. Second, HeadCam observed more scene/place information which might be useful. For instance, we have used the observation from HeadCam to reconstruct[2] the scene as well as localize the HeadCam in the scene as shown in Fig. 6(b). It is possible that certain place information observed by HeadCam can be beneficial for recognizing some hand states. We propose two approaches to combine HeadCam and HandCam.

Feature Concatenation. We simply concatenate the separately finetuned HeadCam and HandCam features. Then, we use the concatenate feature to train the state classifier and state change detector as described before. Although this is a straight forward approach, we show in our experiment that it already outperforms other settings.

Two-Streams CNN. Inspired by [40], we treat each camera as one unique stream and design a novel two-streams CNN. Each stream first feeds-forward through a CNN of six layers with the same first six layers in the AlexNet [13] architecture. Then, the fc6 (each with 4096 dimension) outputs of both streams are concatenated (total 8192 dimension) before forwarding to the next two fully connected layers. We use this two-streams CNN to predict Free/Active states,

---

[2] We use visualsfm [38] for reconstruction.

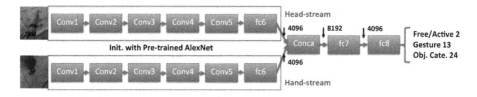

Fig. 7. Architecture of our two-streams CNN. The top and bottom streams take the HeadCam and the HandCam, respectively, as inputs. The two-streams CNN is used to predict Free/Active states, 13 hand gesture states, or 24 object category states. Conv, fc, and Conca denote convolution, fully-connected, and concatenate, respectively.

13 hand gesture states, or 24 object category states. Please see Fig. 7 for the detail architecture. The model weights of both streams are initialized with the ImageNet pre-trained AlexNet model. Then, we finetune the full two-streams CNN with parameters detailed in Sect. 5. After finetuning, we take the last hidden representation of our two-streams CNN as feature to train the state classifier and state change detector as described before. Our experiment shows that jointly finetuning two-streams achieves the best performance in four out of five tasks.

4 Dataset

We have collected a new synchronized "HandCam" and "HeadCam" video data for hand states recognition. Our dataset contains 20 round of data collection (60 video sequences), where each round consists of three synchronized video sequences (two from HandCam and one from HeadCam). In total, our dataset contains ~115.5 min of videos, which is at a similar scale of the egocentric video dataset [4]. For HandCam, we ask each user to mount the camera so that the palm is in the center of the camera. For HeadCam, we found it is much harder to be mounted correctly by each user. Hence, we help each user to mount the HeadCam so that the user's gaze is in the center of the camera while manipulating objects. Our dataset can be accessed at http://aliensunmin. github.io/project/handcam/.

	# Vid.	# Fra.	# Users	#TO	#Cat.	#Inst.	#Gest.	Categories Instances
Office	6	7213	6	1	6	30	10	lamp switch 1; whiteboard pen 6; thermos bottle 5; book 6; computer 6; magnet 6
Lab	8	9299	8	3	9	58	11	whiteboard eraser 1; computer 7; cellphone 8; coin 4; ruler 8; thermos bottle 7; whiteboard pen 7; pen 8; cup 8
Home	6	11390	4	3	12	35	11	TV remote 1; AC remote 1; switch 1; window 1; fridge 1; cupboard 1; water tap 1; toy 4; kettle 6; cup 6; bottle 6; snack 6
Total	20	27902	11	7	23	111	12	

Fig. 8. Statistics of our HandCam dataset. Vid., Fra., RO, Cars., Inst., and Gest. stand for videos, frames, task-order, categories, instances,and gestures, respectively.

In order to thoroughly analyze tasks involving recognizing object category, hand gesture, etc., we explicitly collect videos in multiple indoor scenes, interacting with multiple object categories, and multiple object instances within each category. A thorough statistics is shown in Fig. 8. We summarize the properties of our dataset below.

- Scene: We have collected videos in three scenes: a small office, a mid-size lab, and a large home (Fig. 6(b)), where office and lab involve many similar object interactions, but involve very different object interactions as in home.
- Task: We pre-define a number of tasks for users to follow. To increase variation, each user randomly selects a task-order to perform.
- Object category: We prepare many instances for most movable objects in Fig. 8. We ensure that these instances are separable in our train/test splits.
- User: We have 11 unique users involved in collecting the videos.

Annotating Interface. For annotating hand states, we ask annotators to watch the synchronized three videos (i.e., two HandCams and one HeadCam) to make label decision. A snapshot of our viewer is shown in technical report [36].

Training vs. Testing Set. We have two settings. Firstly, we train on office and lab. Then, we test on home. We refer this as "Home" setting. This is a challenging setting, since home is an unseen scene and there are many unseen object categories and activities. In the second setting, we evenly divide the video sequences into half for training and the remaining half for testing in all scenes. We refer this as "AllScenes" setting.

5   Implementation Details

Camera System. Our system consists of three synchronized GoPro 3+ cameras to record videos with 1920×1080 resolution at 60 fps and we process them at 6 fps. In the future, we will use small fisheye cameras to to mitigate the issues of unnatural behavior and self-occlusion due to the relatively big GoPro cameras.

Alignment. We achieve stable result by setting $\beta^{th} = 40$ and trying seven scales (i.e., $[0.9, 1, 1.1, 1.2, 1.3, 1.4, 1.5]$) in our multi-scales alignment method.

Training. We set SVM regularization parameters, parameter d of state change features, and λ automatically using 5-fold cross-validation for each setting. We finetune an imagenet pre-trained AlexNet on our dataset using the following parameters consistently for all tasks: maximum iterations = 40000, step-size = 10000, momentum = 0.9, every 10000 iteration weight decay =0.1, and learning rate = 0.001. To augment our dataset, we flip the left HandCam frames horizontally and jointly trained with the right HandCam frames.

Training Two-Streams CNN. For finetuning the two-streams CNN on our dataset, we set maximum iterations = 10000, step-size = 2500, momentum = 0.9, every 2500 iteration weight decay =0.1, and learning rate = 0.001. We also augment our dataset by horizontal flipping frames.

Table 1. Frame-based classification accuracy of hand states: free vs. active, gesture, and object category. Unary denotes the method relying on unary scoring function. Full denotes our full model. See method abbreviation for the naming of each column.

	NoAlign	Align	AlignFT	BL	BLCrop	BCropFT	BCropFTv2	IDT
Free vs. Active								
Home-Unary	70.1%	71.4%	74.1%	60.7%	61.1%	61.7%	57.0%	59.9%
Home-Full	71.4%	74.7%	75.5%	62.1%	63.0%	64.7%	57.8%	60.8%
AllScene-Unary	76.1%	75.5%	79.3%	65.7%	68.9%	69.5%	64.5%	70.5%
AllScene-Full	77.2%	76.9%	80.6%	67.1%	70.6%	73.1%	62.3%	70.9%
Gesture								
Home-Unary	53.9%	53.8%	54.1%	48.9%	47.4%	44.7%	52.1%	54.5%
Home-Full	55.2%	55.6%	56.6%	51.3%	48.9%	50.1%	55.4%	55.3%
AllScene-Unary	60.5%	60.2%	63.1%	55.7%	57.1%	53.7%	53.0%	59.9%
AllScene-Full	61.8%	62.4%	65.1%	56.8%	58.3%	59.1%	56.1%	60.1%
Object								
AllScene-Unary	60.0%	59.5%	62.8%	53.6%	55.2%	51.4%	51.6%	56.1%
AllScene-Full	61.8%	61.5%	66.5%	54.9%	56.6%	57.4%	54.9%	58.6%

6 Experiment Results

We evaluate recognition tasks of three hand state: free vs. active, gesture, and object category. Most tasks are conducted in two train/test settings: Home? and AllScenes? as described in Sect. 4. All the following experiments are conducted using fc6 features in Alexnet.

HeadCam Baseline. We apply two state-of-the-art hand segmentation methods [28,29] to predict manipulation region. Similar to [11], we predict at most two boxes, one for left and one for right hands. Typical ground truth and predicted boxes are shown in technical report [36]. Next, we crop the HeadCam images with respect to the predict manipulation region and apply the same methods introduced in this paper to recognize hand states (see technical report [36] for more details). We also use improved dense trajectory [12] of the whole frame to capture the motion cues as a strong but time-consuming baseline.

Method Abbreviation. To facilitate discussion, we introduce the following abbreviations for different methods.

- HeadCam: IDT, BL, BLCrop, BCropFT, and BCropFTv2. IDT is a HeadCam baseline using [12]. BL is a HeadCam baseline using pre-trained feature of the whole frame. BLCrop is a HeadCam baseline using pre-trained feature with regions cropped by [28]. BCropFT is using finetuned feature with regions cropped by [28]. BCropFTv2 is using finetuned feature with regions cropped by [29].
- HandCam: NoAlign, Align, and AlignFT. NoAlign is HandCam without hand alignment using pre-trained feature. Align is HandCam with alignment using pre-trained feature. AlignFT is Align using finetuned feature.

518   C.-S. Chan et al.

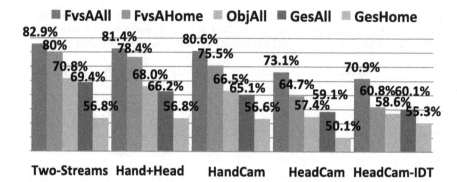

Fig. 9. Comparing two-streams CNN with HandCam+HeadCam, HandCam (AlignFT), HeadCam (BLCropFT), and HeadCam-IDT in five tasks: FvsA stands for free vs. active. Obj stands for object category. Ges stands for gesture.

6.1 Free Vs. Active Recognition

Free vs. active recognition accuracy is shown in the top part of Table 1.

Pre-trained CNN. Using pre-trained CNN feature, our full method already outperforms the non-cropped, cropped, and IDT HeadCam baselines. These results confirm that HandCam is a great alternative to HeadCam systems.

Unary vs. Full. Our full model also consistently outperforms the unary model in all settings and for both HandCam and HeadCam.

Hand Alignment. Although hand alignment shows no critical improvement in AllScenes, we confirm that hand alignment improves from 71.4 % to 74.7 % acc. in the challenging Home setting.

Finetune CNN. Finetuning CNN shows consistent improvement in all settings and for both HandCam and HeadCam. Our finetuned full method achieves 75.5 % acc. in Home and 80.6 % acc. in AllScenes.

6.2 Gesture Recognition

Gesture recognition (see the middle part of Table 1) shares the same trend in free vs. active recognition. Except that, in Home setting, hand alignment only shows 0.4 % acc. improvement using pre-trained feature. Nevertheless, our finetuned full method achieves 56.6 % acc. in Home and 65.1 % acc. in AllScenes. They are 6.6 % (Home) and 6 % (AllScenes) better than the finetuned cropped baseline, and 1.3 % (Home) and 5 % (AllScenes) better than IDT.

6.3 Object Category Recognition

Object category recognition accuracy in AllScenes setting is shown in the last part of Table 1. We found that it shares the same trend in Sect. 6.1. Most importantly, our finetuned full method achieves the best accuracy (66.5 %). In Home

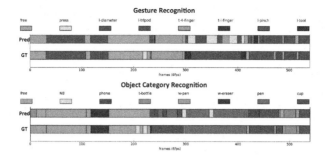

Fig. 10. Temporal visualization of predicted hand gesture (top-row) and object category (bottom-row) using two-streams CNN in AllScenes. Pred and GT stands for prediction and ground truth. The color-code of states are on top of each visualization.

setting, since many object categories are not observed in training, we evaluate object discovery task. We treat object category discovery as a clustering task, and compare the clustering results between our best HandCam configuration (i.e., AlignFT) and the best HeadCam configuration (i.e., BLCropFT). We report a modified purity (defined in technical report [36]) to focus on discovering object categories (not free-hand?). We calculate the purity with different number of clusters (see technical report [36]), and find that HandCam outperforms HeadCam by about 10 % from 30 to 100 clusters.

6.4 Combining HandCam with HeadCam

We show comparison among HeadCam (BLCropFT), HeadCam motion (HeadCam-IDT), HandCam (AlignFT), HandCam+HeadCam (feature concatenation), and our novel two-streams CNN in Fig. 9. HandCam+HeadCam with simple feature concatenation already outperforms the single camera settings in all five tasks. Most importantly, our novel two-streams CNN achieves the best performance in four our of five tasks (except gesture in Home setting). We show temporal visualization of predicted vs. ground truth hand gesture and object category of our two-streams CNN in Fig. 10 (see more in technical report [36]).

7 Conclusion

We revisit a wrist-mounted camera system (HandCam) for recognizing various hand states. To evaluate our system, we collect a new dataset with synchronized HandCam and HeadCam observing multiple object categories, instances, gestures in multiple scenes. HandCam with deep-learning-based method consistently outperforms HeadCam systems in all tasks by at most 10.8 % improvement in accuracy. Most importantly, we show that combining HandCam with HeadCam using a novel two-streams CNN gives the best performance in four out of five tasks. With more data and a more sophisticated network, we believe the recognition performance of our system can be greatly improved in the future.

Acknowledgements. We thank MOST 104-2221-E-007-089-MY2 in Taiwan for their support. We also thank Hou Ning Hu for collaboration.

References

1. Pirsiavash, H., Ramanan, D.: Detecting activities of daily living in first-person camera views. In: CVPR (2012)
2. Rogez, G., Supani, J.S., Khademi, M., Montiel, J.M.M., Ramanan, D.: 3d hand pose detection in egocentric RGB-D images. CoRR abs/1412.0065 (2014)
3. Rogez, G., Supani, J.S., Ramanan, D.: First-person pose recognition using egocentric workspaces. In: CVPR (2015)
4. Damen, D., Leelasawassuk, T., Haines, O., Calway, A., Mayol-Cuevas, W.: Youdo, i-learn: discovering task relevant objects and their modes of interaction from multi-user egocentric video. In: BMVC (2014)
5. Kim, D., Hilliges, O., Izadi, S., Butler, A.D., Chen, J., Oikonomidis, I., Olivier, P.: Digits: freehand 3d interactions anywhere using a wrist-worn gloveless sensor. In: UIST (2012)
6. Saxena, A., Driemeyer, J., Ng, A.: Robotic grasping of novel objects using vision. Int. J. Rob. Res. **27**(2), 157–173 (2008)
7. Mayol-Cuevas, W., Tordoff, B., Murray, D.: On the choice and placement of wearable vision sensors. IEEE Trans. Syst. Man Cybern. Part A: Syst. Hum. **39**(2), 414–425 (2009)
8. Maekawa, T., Yanagisawa, Y., Kishino, Y., Ishiguro, K., Kamei, K., Sakurai, Y., Okadome, T.: Object-based activity recognition with heterogeneous sensors on wrist. In: Floréen, P., Krüger, A., Spasojevic, M. (eds.) Pervasive 2010. LNCS, vol. 6030, pp. 246–264. Springer, Heidelberg (2010). doi:10.1007/978-3-642-12654-3_15
9. Fathi, A., Ren, X., Rehg, J.M.: Learning to recognize objects in egocentric activities. In: CVPR (2011)
10. Maekawa, T., Kishino, Y., Yanagisawa, Y., Sakurai, Y.: Wristsense: wrist-worn sensor device with camera for daily activity recognition. In: PERCOM Workshops. IEEE (2012)
11. Li, Y., Fathi, A., Rehg, J.M.: Learning to predict gaze in egocentric video. In: ICCV(2013)
12. Wang, H., Schmid, C.: Action recognition with improved trajectories. In: ICCV (2013)
13. Krizhevsky, A., Sutskever, I., Hinton, G.E.: Imagenet classification with deep convolutional neural networks. In: NIPS (2012)
14. Patterson, D.J., Fox, D., Kautz, H., Philipose, M.: Fine-grained activity recognition by aggregating abstract object usage. In: ISWC (2005)
15. Stikic, M., Huynh, T., Laerhoven, K.V., Schiele, B.: ADL recognition based on the combination of RFID, and accelerometer sensing. In: Pervasive Computing Technologies for Healthcare (2008)
16. Wu, J., Osuntogun, A., Choudhury, T., Philipose, M., Rehg, J.M.: A scalable approach to activity recognition based on object use. In: ICCV (2007)
17. Fathi, A., Farhadi, A., Rehg, J.M.: Understanding egocentric activities. In: ICCV (2011)
18. Fathi, A., Rehg, J.M.: Modeling actions through state changes. In: CVPR (2013)

19. Fathi, A., Li, Y., Rehg, J.M.: Learning to recognize daily actions using gaze. In: Fitzgibbon, A., Lazebnik, S., Perona, P., Sato, Y., Schmid, C. (eds.) ECCV 2012. LNCS, vol. 7572, pp. 314–327. Springer, Heidelberg (2012). doi:10.1007/978-3-642-33718-5_23

20. Li, Y., Ye, Z., Rehg, J.M.: Delving into egocentric actions. In: CVPR (2015)

21. Ghosh, J., Lee, Y.J., Grauman, K.: Discovering important people and objects for egocentric video summarization. In: CVPR (2012)

22. Lu, Z., Grauman, K.: Story-driven summarization for egocentric video. In: CVPR (2013)

23. Sun, M., Farhadi, A., Taskar, B., Seitz, S.: Salient montages from unconstrained videos. In: Fleet, D., Pajdla, T., Schiele, B., Tuytelaars, T. (eds.) ECCV 2014. LNCS, vol. 8695, pp. 472–488. Springer, Heidelberg (2014). doi:10.1007/978-3-319-10584-0_31

24. De la Torre, F., Hodgins, J.K., Montano, J., Valcarcel, S.: Detailed human data acquisition of kitchen activities: the CMU-multimodal activity database (CMU-MMAC). In: Workshop on Developing Shared Home Behavior Datasets to Advance HCI and Ubiquitous Computing Research, in conjuction with CHI 2009 (2009)

25. Moghimi, M., Azagra, P., Montesano, L., Murillo, A.C., Belongie, S.: Experiments on an rgb-d wearable vision system for egocentric activity recognition. In: CVPR Workshop on Egocentric (First-person) Vision (2014)

26. Damen, D., Gee, A., Mayol-Cuevas, W., Calway, A.: Egocentric real-time workspace monitoring using an rgb-d camera. In: IROS (2012)

27. Li, C., Kitani, K.M.: Pixel-level hand detection in egocentric videos. In: CVPR (2013)

28. Li, C., Kitani, K.M.: Model recommendation with virtual probes for egocentric hand detection. In: ICCV (2013)

29. Bambach, S., Lee, S., Crandall, D.J., Yu, C.: Lending a hand: Detecting hands and recognizing activities in complex egocentric interactions. In: ICCV (2015)

30. Betancourt, A., Lopez, M., Regazzoni, C., Rauterberg, M.: A sequential classifier for hand detection in the framework of egocentric vision. In: CVPRW (2014)

31. Huang, D.A., Ma, M., Ma, W.C., Kitani., K.M.: How do we use our hands? discovering a diverse set of common grasps. In: CVPR (2015)

32. Vardy, A., Robinson, J., Cheng, L.T.: The wristcam as input device. In: ISWC (1999)

33. Chan, L., Chen, Y.L., Hsieh, C.H., Liang, R.H., Chen, B.Y.: Cyclopsring: enabling whole-hand and context-aware interactions through a fisheye ring. In: UIST (2015)

34. Ohnishi, K., Kanehira, A., Kanezaki, A., Harada, T.: Recognizing activities of daily living with a wrist-mounted camera. In: CVPR (2016)

35. Wu, R., Yan, S., Shan, Y., Dang, Q., Sun, G.: Deep image: scaling up image recognition. CoRR abs/1501.02876 (2015)

36. Chan, C.S., Chen, S.Z., Xie, P.X., Chang, C.C., Sun, M.: Technical report of recognition from hand cameras. http://aliensunmin.github.io/project/handcam/

37. Canny, J.: A computational approach to edge detection. PAMI **PAMI-8**(6), 679–698 (1986)

38. Wu, C.: Towards linear-time incremental structure from motion. In: 3DV (2013)

39. Simonyan, K., Zisserman, A.: Very deep convolutional networks for large-scale image recognition. In: ICLR (2015)

40. Simonyan, K., Zisserman, A.: Two-stream convolutional networks for action recognition in videos. In: NIPS (2014)

Learning

XNOR-Net: ImageNet Classification Using Binary Convolutional Neural Networks

Mohammad Rastegari[1](✉), Vicente Ordonez[1], Joseph Redmon[2],
and Ali Farhadi[1,2]

[1] Allen Institute for AI, Seattle, USA
{mohammadr,vicenteor}@allenai.org
[2] University of Washington, Seattle, USA
{pjreddie,ali}@cs.washington.edu

Abstract. We propose two efficient approximations to standard convolutional neural networks: Binary-Weight-Networks and XNOR-Networks. In Binary-Weight-Networks, the filters are approximated with binary values resulting in 32× memory saving. In XNOR-Networks, both the filters and the input to convolutional layers are binary. XNOR-Networks approximate convolutions using primarily binary operations. This results in 58× faster convolutional operations (in terms of number of the high precision operations) and 32× memory savings. XNOR-Nets offer the possibility of running state-of-the-art networks on CPUs (rather than GPUs) in real-time. Our binary networks are simple, accurate, efficient, and work on challenging visual tasks. We evaluate our approach on the ImageNet classification task. The classification accuracy with a Binary-Weight-Network version of AlexNet is the same as the full-precision AlexNet. We compare our method with recent network binarization methods, BinaryConnect and BinaryNets, and outperform these methods by large margins on ImageNet, more than 16 % in top-1 accuracy. Our code is available at: http://allenai.org/plato/xnornet.

1 Introduction

Deep neural networks (DNN) have shown significant improvements in several application domains including computer vision and speech recognition. In computer vision, a particular type of DNN, known as Convolutional Neural Networks (CNN), have demonstrated state-of-the-art results in object recognition [1–4] and detection [5–7].

Convolutional neural networks show reliable results on object recognition and detection that are useful in real world applications. Concurrent to the recent progress in recognition, interesting advancements have been happening in virtual reality (VR by Oculus) [8], augmented reality (AR by HoloLens) [9], and smart wearable devices. Putting these two pieces together, we argue that it is the right time to equip smart portable devices with the power of state-of-the-art recognition systems. However, CNN-based recognition systems need large amounts of

© Springer International Publishing AG 2016
B. Leibe et al. (Eds.): ECCV 2016, Part IV, LNCS 9908, pp. 525–542, 2016.
DOI: 10.1007/978-3-319-46493-0_32

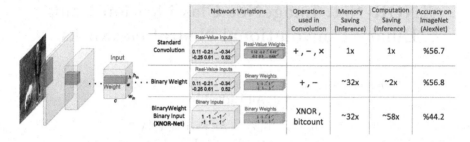

Fig. 1. We propose two efficient variations of convolutional neural networks. **Binary-Weight-Networks**, when the weight filters contains binary values. **XNOR-Networks**, when both weigh and input have binary values. These networks are very efficient in terms of memory and computation, while being very accurate in natural image classification. This offers the possibility of using accurate vision techniques in portable devices with limited resources. (Color figure online)

memory and computational power. While they perform well on expensive, GPU-based machines, they are often unsuitable for smaller devices like cell phones and embedded electronics.

For example, AlexNet [1] has 61 M parameters (249 MB of memory) and performs 1.5 B high precision operations to classify one image. These numbers are even higher for deeper CNNs *e.g.,* VGG [2] (see Sect. 4.1). These models quickly overtax the limited storage, battery power, and compute capabilities of smaller devices like cell phones.

In this paper, we introduce simple, efficient, and accurate approximations to CNNs by binarizing the weights and even the intermediate representations in convolutional neural networks. Our binarization method aims at finding the best approximations of the convolutions using binary operations. We demonstrate that our way of binarizing neural networks results in ImageNet classification accuracy numbers that are comparable to standard full precision networks while requiring a significantly less memory and fewer floating point operations.

We study two approximations: Neural networks with binary weights and XNOR-Networks. In **Binary-Weight-Networks** all the weight values are approximated with binary values. A convolutional neural network with binary weights is significantly smaller ($\sim$32$\times$) than an equivalent network with single-precision weight values. In addition, when weight values are binary, convolutions can be estimated by only addition and subtraction (without multiplication), resulting in $\sim$2$\times$ speed up. Binary-weight approximations of large CNNs can fit into the memory of even small, portable devices while maintaining the same level of accuracy (See Sects. 4.1 and 4.2).

To take this idea further, we introduce **XNOR-Networks** where both the weights and the inputs to the convolutional and fully connected layers are approximated with binary values[1]. Binary weights and binary inputs allow an efficient way of implementing convolutional operations. If all of the operands of the convolutions are binary, then the convolutions can be estimated by XNOR and bitcounting operations [11]. XNOR-Nets result in accurate approximation of CNNs while offering $\sim58\times$ speed up in CPUs (in terms of number of the high precision operations). This means that XNOR-Nets can enable real-time inference in devices with small memory and no GPUs (Inference in XNOR-Nets can be done very efficiently on CPUs).

To the best of our knowledge this paper is the first attempt to present an evaluation of binary neural networks on large-scale datasets like ImageNet. Our experimental results show that our proposed method for binarizing convolutional neural networks outperforms the state-of-the-art network binarization method of [11] by a large margin (16.3 %) on top-1 image classification in the ImageNet challenge ILSVRC2012. Our contribution is two-fold: First, we introduce a new way of binarizing the weight values in convolutional neural networks and show the advantage of our solution compared to state-of-the-art solutions. Second, we introduce XNOR-Nets, a deep neural network model with binary weights and binary inputs and show that XNOR-Nets can obtain similar classification accuracies compared to standard networks while being significantly more efficient. Our code is available at: http://allenai.org/plato/xnornet.

2   Related Work

Deep neural networks often suffer from over-parametrization and large amounts of redundancy in their models. This typically results in inefficient computation and memory usage [12]. Several methods have been proposed to address efficient training and inference in deep neural networks.

Shallow networks: Estimating a deep neural network with a shallower model reduces the size of a network. Early theoretical work by Cybenko shows that a network with a large enough single hidden layer of sigmoid units can approximate any decision boundary [13]. In several areas (*e.g.*, vision and speech), however, shallow networks cannot compete with deep models [14]. [15] trains a shallow network on SIFT features to classify the ImageNet dataset. They show it is difficult to train shallow networks with large number of parameters. [16] provides empirical evidence on small datasets (*e.g.*, CIFAR-10) that shallow nets are capable of learning the same functions as deep nets. In order to get the similar accuracy, the number of parameters in the shallow network must be close to the number of parameters in the deep network. They do this by first training a state-of-the-art deep model, and then training a shallow model to mimic the deep model. These methods are different from our approach because we use the standard deep architectures not the shallow estimations.

---

[1] Fully connected layers can be implemented by convolution, therefore, in the rest of the paper, we refer to them also as convolutional layers [10].

Compressing pre-trained deep networks: Pruning redundant, non-informative weights in a previously trained network reduces the size of the network at inference time. Weight decay [17] was an early method for pruning a network. Optimal Brain Damage [18] and Optimal Brain Surgeon [19] use the Hessian of the loss function to prune a network by reducing the number of connections. Recently [20] reduced the number of parameters by an order of magnitude in several state-of-the-art neural networks by pruning. [21] proposed to reduce the number of activations for compression and acceleration. Deep compression [22] reduces the storage and energy required to run inference on large networks so they can be deployed on mobile devices. They remove the redundant connections and quantize weights so that multiple connections share the same weight, and then they use Huffman coding to compress the weights. HashedNets [23] uses a hash function to reduce model size by randomly grouping the weights, such that connections in a hash bucket use a single parameter value. Matrix factorization has been used by [24,25]. We are different from these approaches because we do not use a pretrained network. We train binary networks from scratch.

Designing compact layers: Designing compact blocks at each layer of a deep network can help to save memory and computational costs. Replacing the fully connected layer with global average pooling was examined in the Network in Network architecture [26], GoogLenet [3] and Residual-Net [4], which achieved state-of-the-art results on several benchmarks. The bottleneck structure in Residual-Net [4] has been proposed to reduce the number of parameters and improve speed. Decomposing 3×3 convolutions with two 1×1 is used in [27] and resulted in state-of-the-art performance on object recognition. Replacing 3×3 convolutions with 1×1 convolutions is used in [28] to create a very compact neural network that can achieve $\sim 50\times$ reduction in the number of parameters while obtaining high accuracy. Our method is different from this line of work because we use the full network (not the compact version) but with binary parameters.

Quantizing parameters: High precision parameters are not very important in achieving high performance in deep networks. [29] proposed to quantize the weights of fully connected layers in a deep network by vector quantization techniques. They showed just thresholding the weight values at zero only decreases the top-1 accuracy on ILSVRC2012 by less than %10. [30] proposed a provably polynomial time algorithm for training a sparse networks with $+1/0/-1$ weights. A fixed-point implementation of 8-bit integer was compared with 32-bit floating point activations in [31]. Another fixed-point network with ternary weights and 3-bits activations was presented by [32]. Quantizing a network with L_2 error minimization achieved better accuracy on MNIST and CIFAR-10 datasets in [33]. [34] proposed a back-propagation process by quantizing the representations at each layer of the network. To convert some of the remaining multiplications into binary shifts the neurons get restricted values of power-of-two integers. In [34] they carry the full precision weights during the test phase, and only quantize the neurons during the back-propagation process, and not during the forward-propagation. Our work is similar to these methods since we are quantizing the parameters in the network. But our quantization is the extreme scenario $+1, -1$.

Network binarization: These works are the most related to our approach. Several methods attempt to binarize the weights and the activations in neural networks. The performance of highly quantized networks (*e.g.,* binarized) were believed to be very poor due to the destructive property of binary quantization [35]. Expectation BackPropagation (EBP) in [36] showed high performance can be achieved by a network with binary weights and binary activations. This is done by a variational Bayesian approach, that infers networks with binary weights and neurons. A fully binary network at run time presented in [37] using a similar approach to EBP, showing significant improvement in energy efficiency. In EBP the binarized parameters were only used during inference. BinaryConnect [38] extended the probabilistic idea behind EBP. Similar to our approach, BinaryConnect uses the real-valued version of the weights as a key reference for the binarization process. The real-valued weight updated using the back propagated error by simply ignoring the binarization in the update. BinaryConnect achieved state-of-the-art results on small datasets (*e.g.,* CIFAR-10, SVHN). Our experiments shows that this method is not very successful on large-scale datsets (*e.g.,* ImageNet). BinaryNet [11] propose an extention of BinaryConnect, where both weights and activations are binarized. Our method is different from them in the binarization method and the network structure. We also compare our method with BinaryNet on ImageNet, and our method outperforms BinaryNet by a large margin. [39] argued that the noise introduced by weight binarization provides a form of regularization, which could help to improve test accuracy. This method binarizes weights while maintaining full precision activation. [40] proposed fully binary training and testing in an array of committee machines with randomized input. [41] retraine a previously trained neural network with binary weights and binary inputs.

3   Binary Convolutional Neural Network

We represent an L-layer CNN architecture with a triplet $\langle \mathcal{I}, \mathcal{W}, * \rangle$. $\mathcal{I}$ is a set of tensors, where each element $\mathbf{I} = \mathcal{I}_{l(l=1,...,L)}$ is the input tensor for the lth layer of CNN (Green cubes in Fig. 1). $\mathcal{W}$ is a set of tensors, where each element in this set $\mathbf{W} = \mathcal{W}_{lk(k=1,...,K^l)}$ is the kth weight filter in the lth layer of the CNN. K^l is the number of weight filters in the lth layer of the CNN. $*$ represents a convolutional operation with $\mathbf{I}$ and $\mathbf{W}$ as its operands[2]. $\mathbf{I} \in \mathbb{R}^{c \times w_{in} \times h_{in}}$, where (c, w_{in}, h_{in}) represents *channels, width* and *height* respectively. $\mathbf{W} \in \mathbb{R}^{c \times w \times h}$, where $w \leq w_{in}$, $h \leq h_{in}$. We propose two variations of binary CNN: **Binary-weights**, where the elements of $\mathcal{W}$ are binary tensors and **XNOR-Networks**, where elements of both $\mathcal{I}$ and $\mathcal{W}$ are binary tensors.

3.1   Binary-Weight-Networks

In order to constrain a convolutional neural network $\langle \mathcal{I}, \mathcal{W}, * \rangle$ to have binary weights, we estimate the real-value weight filter $\mathbf{W} \in \mathcal{W}$ using a binary filter

---

[2] In this paper we assume convolutional filters do not have bias terms.

$\mathbf{B} \in \{+1, -1\}^{c \times w \times h}$ and a scaling factor $\alpha \in \mathbb{R}^+$ such that $\mathbf{W} \approx \alpha\mathbf{B}$. A convolutional operation can be approximated by:

$$\mathbf{I} * \mathbf{W} \approx (\mathbf{I} \oplus \mathbf{B})\,\alpha \qquad (1)$$

where, $\oplus$ indicates a convolution without any multiplication. Since the weight values are binary, we can implement the convolution with additions and subtractions. The binary weight filters reduce memory usage by a factor of $\sim 32\times$ compared to single-precision filters. We represent a CNN with binary weights by $\langle \mathcal{I}, \mathcal{B}, \mathcal{A}, \oplus \rangle$, where $\mathcal{B}$ is a set of binary tensors and $\mathcal{A}$ is a set of positive real scalars, such that $\mathbf{B} = \mathcal{B}_{lk}$ is a binary filter and $\alpha = \mathcal{A}_{lk}$ is an scaling factor and $\mathcal{W}_{lk} \approx \mathcal{A}_{lk}\mathcal{B}_{lk}$

Estimating Binary Weights: Without loss of generality we assume $\mathbf{W}, \mathbf{B}$ are vectors in $\mathbb{R}^n$, where $n = c \times w \times h$. To find an optimal estimation for $\mathbf{W} \approx \alpha\mathbf{B}$, we solve the following optimization:

$$\begin{aligned} J(\mathbf{B}, \alpha) &= \|\mathbf{W} - \alpha\mathbf{B}\|^2 \\ \alpha^*, \mathbf{B}^* &= \operatorname*{argmin}_{\alpha, \mathbf{B}} J(\mathbf{B}, \alpha) \end{aligned} \qquad (2)$$

by expanding Eq. 2, we have

$$J(\mathbf{B}, \alpha) = \alpha^2 \mathbf{B}^\mathsf{T}\mathbf{B} - 2\alpha\mathbf{W}^\mathsf{T}\mathbf{B} + \mathbf{W}^\mathsf{T}\mathbf{W} \qquad (3)$$

since $\mathbf{B} \in \{+1, -1\}^n$, $\mathbf{B}^\mathsf{T}\mathbf{B} = n$ is a constant. $\mathbf{W}^\mathsf{T}\mathbf{W}$ is also a constant because $\mathbf{W}$ is a known variable. Lets define $\mathbf{c} = \mathbf{W}^\mathsf{T}\mathbf{W}$. Now, we can rewrite the Eq. 3 as follow: $J(\mathbf{B}, \alpha) = \alpha^2 n - 2\alpha\mathbf{W}^\mathsf{T}\mathbf{B} + \mathbf{c}$. The optimal solution for $\mathbf{B}$ can be achieved by maximizing the following constrained optimization: (note that α is a positive value in Eq. 2, therefore it can be ignored in the maximization)

$$\mathbf{B}^* = \operatorname*{argmax}_{\mathbf{B}}\{\mathbf{W}^\mathsf{T}\mathbf{B}\} \quad s.t. \ \ \mathbf{B} \in \{+1, -1\}^n \qquad (4)$$

This optimization can be solved by assigning $\mathbf{B}_i = +1$ if $\mathbf{W}_i \geq 0$ and $\mathbf{B}_i = -1$ if $\mathbf{W}_i < 0$, therefore the optimal solution is $\mathbf{B}^* = \operatorname{sign}(\mathbf{W})$. In order to find the optimal value for the scaling factor α^*, we take the derivative of J with respect to α and set it to zero:

$$\alpha^* = \frac{\mathbf{W}^\mathsf{T}\mathbf{B}^*}{n} \qquad (5)$$

By replacing $\mathbf{B}^*$ with $\operatorname{sign}(\mathbf{W})$

$$\alpha^* = \frac{\mathbf{W}^\mathsf{T}\operatorname{sign}(\mathbf{W})}{n} = \frac{\sum |\mathbf{W}_i|}{n} = \frac{1}{n}\|\mathbf{W}\|_{\ell 1} \qquad (6)$$

therefore, the optimal estimation of a binary weight filter can be simply achieved by taking the sign of weight values. The optimal scaling factor is the average of absolute weight values.

Training Binary-Weights-Networks: Each iteration of training a CNN involves three steps; forward pass, backward pass and parameters update. To train a CNN with binary weights (in convolutional layers), we only binarize the weights during the forward pass and backward propagation. To compute the gradient for sign function sign(r), we follow the same approach as [11], where $\frac{\partial \text{sign}}{\partial r} = r1_{|r| \le 1}$. The gradient in backward after the scaled sign function is $\frac{\partial C}{\partial W_i} = \frac{\partial C}{\widetilde{W_i}}(\frac{1}{n} + \frac{\partial \text{sign}}{\partial W_i}\alpha)$. For updating the parameters, we use the high precision (real-value) weights. Because, in gradient descend the parameter changes are tiny, binarization after updating the parameters ignores these changes and the training objective can not be improved. [11,38] also employed this strategy to train a binary network.

Algorithm 1. Training an L-layers CNN with binary weights:

Input: A minibatch of inputs and targets $(\mathbf{I}, \mathbf{Y})$, cost function $C(\mathbf{Y}, \hat{\mathbf{Y}})$, current weight $\mathcal{W}^t$ and current learning rate η^t.
Output: updated weight $\mathcal{W}^{t+1}$ and updated learning rate η^{t+1}.
 1: Binarizing weight filters:
 2: **for** $l = 1$ to L **do**
 3:     **for** k^{th} filter in l^{th} layer **do**
 4:         $\mathcal{A}_{lk} = \frac{1}{n}\|\mathcal{W}_{lk}^t\|_{\ell 1}$
 5:         $\mathcal{B}_{lk} = \text{sign}(\mathcal{W}_{lk}^t)$
 6:         $\widetilde{\mathcal{W}}_{lk} = \mathcal{A}_{lk}\mathcal{B}_{lk}$
 7: $\hat{\mathbf{Y}} = $ **BinaryForward**$(\mathbf{I}, \mathcal{B}, \mathcal{A})$ // standard forward propagation except that convolutions are computed using Eq. 1 or 11
 8: $\frac{\partial C}{\partial \mathcal{W}} = $ **BinaryBackward**$(\frac{\partial C}{\partial \hat{\mathbf{Y}}}, \widetilde{\mathcal{W}})$ // standard backward propagation except that gradients are computed using $\widetilde{\mathcal{W}}$ instead of $\mathcal{W}^t$
 9: $\mathcal{W}^{t+1} = $ **UpdateParameters**$(\mathcal{W}^t, \frac{\partial C}{\partial \mathcal{W}}, \eta_t)$ // Any update rules (e.g., SGD or ADAM)
10: $\eta^{t+1} = $ **UpdateLearningrate**(η^t, t) // Any learning rate scheduling function

---

Algorithm 1 demonstrates our procedure for training a CNN with binary weights. First, we binarize the weight filters at each layer by computing $\mathcal{B}$ and $\mathcal{A}$. Then we call forward propagation using binary weights and its corresponding scaling factors, where all the convolutional operations are carried out by Eq. 1. Then, we call backward propagation, where the gradients are computed with respect to the estimated weight filters $\widetilde{\mathcal{W}}$. Lastly, the parameters and the learning rate gets updated by an update rule e.g., SGD update with momentum or ADAM [42].

Once the training finished, there is no need to keep the real-value weights. Because, at inference we only perform forward propagation with the binarized weights.

3.2   XNOR-Networks

So far, we managed to find binary weights and a scaling factor to estimate the real-value weights. The inputs to the convolutional layers are still real-value

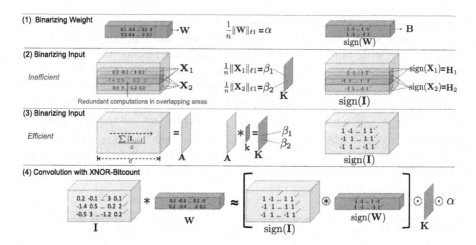

Fig. 2. This figure illustrates the procedure explained in Sect. 3.2 for approximating a convolution using binary operations.

tensors. Now, we explain how to binarize both weights and inputs, so convolutions can be implemented efficiently using XNOR and bitcounting operations. This is the key element of our XNOR-Networks. In order to constrain a convolutional neural network $\langle \mathcal{I}, \mathcal{W}, * \rangle$ to have binary weights and binary inputs, we need to enforce binary operands at each step of the convolutional operation. A convolution consist of repeating a shift operation and a dot product. Shift operation moves the weight filter over the input and the dot product performs elementwise multiplications between the values of the weight filter and the corresponding part of the input. If we express dot product in terms of binary operations, convolution can be approximated using binary operations. Dot product between two binary vectors can be implemented by XNOR-Bitcounting operations [11]. In this section, we explain how to approximate the dot product between two vectors in $\mathbb{R}^n$ by a dot product between two vectors in $\{+1, -1\}^n$. Next, we demonstrate how to use this approximation for estimating a convolutional operation between two tensors.

Binary Dot Product: To approximate the dot product between $\mathbf{X}, \mathbf{W} \in \mathbb{R}^n$ such that $\mathbf{X}^\mathsf{T}\mathbf{W} \approx \beta \mathbf{H}^\mathsf{T} \alpha \mathbf{B}$, where $\mathbf{H}, \mathbf{B} \in \{+1, -1\}^n$ and $\beta, \alpha \in \mathbb{R}^+$, we solve the following optimization:

$$\alpha^*, \mathbf{B}^*, \beta^*, \mathbf{H}* = \underset{\alpha, \mathbf{B}, \beta, \mathbf{H}}{\operatorname{argmin}} \|\mathbf{X} \odot \mathbf{W} - \beta\alpha\mathbf{H} \odot \mathbf{B}\| \qquad (7)$$

where $\odot$ indicates element-wise product. We define $\mathbf{Y} \in \mathbb{R}^n$ such that $\mathbf{Y}_i = \mathbf{X}_i\mathbf{W}_i$, $\mathbf{C} \in \{+1, -1\}^n$ such that $\mathbf{C}_i = \mathbf{H}_i\mathbf{B}_i$ and $\gamma \in \mathbb{R}^+$ such that $\gamma = \beta\alpha$. The Eq. 7 can be written as:

$$\gamma^*, \mathbf{C}^* = \underset{\gamma, \mathbf{C}}{\operatorname{argmin}} \|\mathbf{Y} - \gamma\mathbf{C}\| \qquad (8)$$

the optimal solutions can be achieved from Eq. 2 as follow

$$\mathbf{C}^* = \text{sign}(\mathbf{Y}) = \text{sign}(\mathbf{X}) \odot \text{sign}(\mathbf{W}) = \mathbf{H}^* \odot \mathbf{B}^* \qquad (9)$$

Since $|\mathbf{X}_i|, |\mathbf{W}_i|$ are independent, knowing that $\mathbf{Y}_i = \mathbf{X}_i \mathbf{W}_i$ then,
$\mathbf{E}\left[|\mathbf{Y}_i|\right] = \mathbf{E}\left[|\mathbf{X}_i||\mathbf{W}_i|\right] = \mathbf{E}\left[|\mathbf{X}_i|\right] \mathbf{E}\left[|\mathbf{W}_i|\right]$ therefore,

$$\gamma^* = \frac{\sum |\mathbf{Y}_i|}{n} = \frac{\sum |\mathbf{X}_i||\mathbf{W}_i|}{n} \approx \left(\frac{1}{n}\|\mathbf{X}\|_{\ell 1}\right)\left(\frac{1}{n}\|\mathbf{W}\|_{\ell 1}\right) = \beta^* \alpha^* \qquad (10)$$

Binary Convolution: Convolving weight filter $\mathbf{W} \in \mathbb{R}^{c \times w \times h}$ (where $w_{in} \gg w$, $h_{in} \gg h$) with the input tensor $\mathbf{I} \in \mathbb{R}^{c \times w_{in} \times h_{in}}$ requires computing the scaling factor β for all possible sub-tensors in $\mathbf{I}$ with same size as $\mathbf{W}$. Two of these sub-tensors are illustrated in Fig. 2 (second row) by $\mathbf{X}_1$ and $\mathbf{X}_2$. Due to overlaps between subtensors, computing β for all possible sub-tensors leads to a large number of redundant computations. To overcome this redundancy, first, we compute a matrix $\mathbf{A} = \frac{\sum |\mathbf{I}_{:,:,i}|}{c}$, which is the average over absolute values of the elements in the input $\mathbf{I}$ across the channel. Then we convolve $\mathbf{A}$ with a 2D filter $\mathbf{k} \in \mathbb{R}^{w \times h}$, $\mathbf{K} = \mathbf{A} * \mathbf{k}$, where $\forall ij \ \mathbf{k}_{ij} = \frac{1}{w \times h}$. $\mathbf{K}$ contains scaling factors β for all sub-tensors in the input $\mathbf{I}$. $\mathbf{K}_{ij}$ corresponds to β for a sub-tensor centered at the location ij (across width and height). This procedure is shown in the third row of Fig. 2. Once we obtained the scaling factor α for the weight and β for all sub-tensors in $\mathbf{I}$ (denoted by $\mathbf{K}$), we can approximate the convolution between input $\mathbf{I}$ and weight filter $\mathbf{W}$ mainly using binary operations:

$$\mathbf{I} * \mathbf{W} \approx (\text{sign}(\mathbf{I}) \circledast \text{sign}(\mathbf{W})) \odot \mathbf{K}\alpha \qquad (11)$$

where $\circledast$ indicates a convolutional operation using XNOR and bitcount operations. This is illustrated in the last row in Fig. 2. Note that the number of non-binary operations is very small compared to binary operations.

Training XNOR-Networks: A typical block in CNN contains several different layers. Figure 3(left) illustrates a typical block in a CNN. This block has four layers in the following order: 1-Convolutional, 2-Batch Normalization, 3-Activation and 4-Pooling. Batch Normalization layer [43] normalizes the input batch by its mean and variance. The activation is an element-wise non-linear

Fig. 3. This figure contrasts the block structure in our XNOR-Network (right) with a typical CNN (left).

function (*e.g.*, Sigmoid, ReLU). The pooling layer applies any type of pooling (*e.g.*, max,min or average) on the input batch. Applying pooling on binary input results in significant loss of information. For example, max-pooling on binary input returns a tensor that most of its elements are equal to +1. Therefore, we put the pooling layer after the convolution. To further decrease the information loss due to binarization, we normalize the input before binarization. This ensures the data to hold zero mean, therefore, thresholding at zero leads to less quantization error. The order of layers in a block of binary CNN is shown in Fig. 3(right).

The binary activation layer (BinActiv) computes $\mathbf{K}$ and sign($\mathbf{I}$) as explained in Sect. 3.2. In the next layer (BinConv), given $\mathbf{K}$ and sign($\mathbf{I}$), we compute binary convolution by Eq. 11. Then at the last layer (Pool), we apply the pooling operations. We can insert a non-binary activation (*e.g.*, ReLU) after binary convolution. This helps when we use state-of-the-art networks (*e.g.*, AlexNet or VGG).

Once we have the binary CNN structure, the training algorithm would be the same as Algorithm 1.

Binary Gradient: The computational bottleneck in the backward pass at each layer is computing a convolution between weight filters (w) and the gradients with respect of the inputs (g^{in}). Similar to binarization in the forward pass, we can binarize g^{in} in the backward pass. This leads to a very efficient training procedure using binary operations. Note that if we use Eq. 6 to compute the scaling factor for g^{in}, the direction of maximum change for SGD would be diminished. To preserve the maximum change in all dimensions, we use $\max_i(|g_i^{in}|)$ as the scaling factor.

k-**bit Quantization:** So far, we showed 1-bit quantization of weights and inputs using sign(x) function. One can easily extend the quantization level to k-bits by using $q_k(x) = 2(\frac{[(2^k-1)(\frac{x+1}{2})]}{2^k-1} - \frac{1}{2})$ instead of the sign function. Where [.] indicates rounding operation and $x \in [-1, 1]$.

4 Experiments

We evaluate our method by analyzing its efficiency and accuracy. We measure the efficiency by computing the computational speedup (in terms of number of high precision operation) achieved by our binary convolution vs. standard convolution. To measure accuracy, we perform image classification on the large-scale ImageNet dataset. This paper is the first work that evaluates binary neural networks on the ImageNet dataset. Our binarization technique is general, we can use any CNN architecture. We evaluate AlexNet [1] and two deeper architectures in our experiments. We compare our method with two recent works on binarizing neural networks; BinaryConnect [38] and BinaryNet [11]. The classification accuracy of our binary-weight-network version of AlexNet is as accurate as the full precision version of AlexNet. This classification accuracy outperforms competitors on binary neural networks by a large margin. We also present an

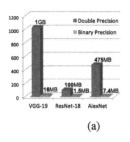
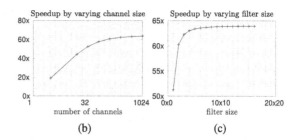

(a)   (b)   (c)

Fig. 4. This figure shows the efficiency of binary convolutions in terms of memory (a) and computation (b–c). (a) is contrasting the required memory for binary and double precision weights in three different architectures (AlexNet, ResNet-18 and VGG-19). (b, c) Show speedup gained by binary convolution under (b)-different number of channels and (c)-different filter size

ablation study, where we evaluate the key elements of our proposed method; computing scaling factors and our block structure for binary CNN. We shows that our method of computing the scaling factors is important to reach high accuracy.

4.1 Efficiency Analysis

In an standard convolution, the total number of operations is $cN_{\mathbf{W}}N_{\mathbf{I}}$, where c is the number of channels, $N_{\mathbf{W}} = wh$ and $N_{\mathbf{I}} = w_{in}h_{in}$. Note that some modern CPUs can fuse the multiplication and addition as a single cycle operation. On those CPUs, Binary-Weight-Networks does not deliver speed up. Our binary approximation of convolution (Eq. 11) has $cN_{\mathbf{W}}N_{\mathbf{I}}$ binary operations and $N_{\mathbf{I}}$ non-binary operations. With the current generation of CPUs, we can perform 64 binary operations in one clock of CPU, therefore the speedup can be computed by $S = \frac{cN_{\mathbf{W}}N_{\mathbf{I}}}{\frac{1}{64}cN_{\mathbf{W}}N_{\mathbf{I}}+N_{\mathbf{I}}} = \frac{64cN_{\mathbf{W}}}{cN_{\mathbf{W}}+64}$.

The speedup depends on the channel size and filter size but not the input size. In Fig. 4(b–c) we illustrate the speedup achieved by changing the number of channels and filter size. While changing one parameter, we fix other parameters as follows: $c = 256$, $n_{\mathbf{I}} = 14^2$ and $n_{\mathbf{W}} = 3^2$ (majority of convolutions in ResNet [4] architecture have this structure). Using our approximation of convolution we gain 62.27× theoretical speed up, but in our CPU implementation with all of the overheads, we achieve 58× speed up in one convolution (Excluding the process for memory allocation and memory access). With the small channel size ($c = 3$) and filter size ($N_{\mathbf{W}} = 1 \times 1$) the speedup is not considerably high. This motivates us to avoid binarization at the first and last layer of a CNN. In the first layer the channel size is 3 and in the last layer the filter size is 1×1. A similar strategy was used in [11]. Figure 4a shows the required memory for three different CNN architectures (AlexNet, VGG-19, ResNet-18) with binary and double precision weights. Binary-weight-networks are so small that can be easily fitted into portable devices. BinaryNet [11] is in the same order of memory and computation efficiency as our method. In Fig. 4, we show an analysis of computation and memory cost for a binary convolution. The same analysis is valid for BinaryNet and BinaryConnect. The key difference of our method is using a scaling-factor, which does not change the order of efficiency while providing a significant improvement in accuracy.

4.2   Image Classification

We evaluate the performance of our proposed approach on the task of natural image classification. So far, in the literature, binary neural network methods have presented their evaluations on either limited domain or simplified datasets *e.g.,* CIFAR-10, MNIST, SVHN. To compare with state-of-the-art vision, we evaluate our method on ImageNet (ILSVRC2012). ImageNet has ∼1.2 M train images from 1 K categories and 50 K validation images. The images in this dataset are natural images with reasonably high resolution compared to the CIFAR and MNIST dataset, which have relatively small images. We report our classification performance using Top-1 and Top-5 accuracies. We adopt three different CNN architectures as our base architectures for binarization: AlexNet [1], Residual Networks (known as ResNet) [4], and a variant of GoogLenet [3]. We compare our Binary-weight-network (**BWN**) with BinaryConnect (**BC**) [38] and our XNOR-Networks (**XNOR-Net**) with BinaryNeuralNet (**BNN**) [11]. BinaryConnect (BC) is a method for training a deep neural network with binary weights during forward and backward propagations. Similar to our approach, they keep the real-value weights during the updating parameters step. Our binarization is different from BC. The binarization in BC can be either deterministic or stochastic. We use the deterministic binarization for BC in our comparisons because the stochastic binarization is not efficient. The same evaluation settings have been used and discussed in [11]. BinaryNeuralNet (BNN) [11] is a neural network with binary weights and activations during inference and gradient computation in training. In concept, this is a similar approach to our XNOR-Network but the binarization method and the network structure in BNN is different from ours. Their training algorithm is similar to BC and they used deterministic binarization in their evaluations.

CIFAR-10: BC and BNN showed near state-of-the-art performance on CIFAR-10, MNIST, and SVHN dataset. BWN and XNOR-Net on CIFAR-10 using the same network architecture as BC and BNN achieve the error rate of 9.88 % and 10.17 % respectively. In this paper we explore the possibility of obtaining near state-of-the-art results on a much larger and more challenging dataset (ImageNet).

AlexNet: [1] is a CNN architecture with 5 convolutional layers and two fully-connected layers. This architecture was the first CNN architecture that showed to be successful on ImageNet classification task. This network has 61 M parameters. We use AlexNet coupled with batch normalization layers [43].

Train: In each iteration of training, images are resized to have 256 pixel at their smaller dimension and then a random crop of 224 × 224 is selected for

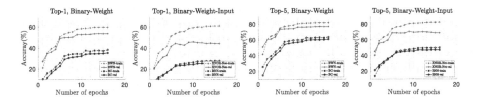

Fig. 5. This figure compares the imagenet classification accuracy on Top-1 and Top-5 across training epochs. Our approaches BWN and XNOR-Net outperform BinaryConnect (BC) and BinaryNet (BNN) in all the epochs by large margin ($\sim$17%).

Table 1. This table compares the final accuracies (Top1 - Top5) of the full precision network with our binary precision networks; Binary-Weight-Networks (BWN) and XNOR-Networks (XNOR-Net) and the competitor methods; BinaryConnect (BC) and BinaryNet (BNN).

Classification accuracy (%)									
Binary-weight				Binary-input-binary-weight				Full-precision	
BWN		BC [11]		XNOR-Net		BNN [11]		AlexNet [1]	
Top-1	Top-5	Top-1	Top-5	Top-1	Top-5	Top-1	Top-5	Top-1	Top-5
56.8	**79.4**	35.4	61.0	**44.2**	**69.2**	27.9	50.42	56.6	80.2

training. We run the training algorithm for 16 epochs with batch size equal to 512. We use negative-log-likelihood over the soft-max of the outputs as our classification loss function. In our implementation of AlexNet we do not use the Local-Response-Normalization (LRN) layer[3]. We use SGD with momentum = 0.9 for updating parameters in BWN and BC. For XNOR-Net and BNN we used ADAM [42]. ADAM converges faster and usually achieves better accuracy for binary inputs [11]. The learning rate starts at 0.1 and we apply a learning-rate-decay = 0.01 every 4 epochs.

Test: At inference time, we use the 224×224 center crop for forward propagation.

Figure 5 demonstrates the classification accuracy for training and inference along the training epochs for top-1 and top-5 scores. The dashed lines represent training accuracy and solid lines shows the validation accuracy. In all of the epochs our method outperforms BC and BNN by large margin ($\sim$17%). Table 1 compares our final accuracy with BC and BNN. We found that the scaling factors for the weights (α) is much more effective than the scaling factors for the inputs (β). Removing β reduces the accuracy by a small margin (less than 1% top-1 alexnet).

Binary Gradient: Using XNOR-Net with binary gradient the accuracy of top-1 will drop only by 1.4%.

---

[3] Our implementation is followed by https://gist.github.com/szagoruyko/dd032c 529048492630fc.

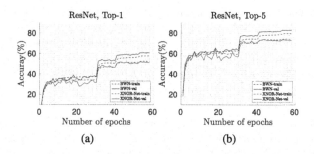

Fig. 6. This figure shows the classification accuracy; (a) Top-1 and (b) Top-5 measures across the training epochs on ImageNet dataset by Binary-Weight-Network and XNOR-Network using ResNet-18.

Table 2. This table compares the final classification accuracy achieved by our binary precision networks with the full precision network in ResNet-18 and GoogLenet architectures.

	ResNet-18		GoogLenet	
Network variations	Top-1	Top-5	Top-1	Top-5
Binary-weight-network	60.8	83.0	65.5	86.1
XNOR-network	51.2	73.2	N/A	N/A
Full-precision-network	69.3	89.2	71.3	90.0

Residual Net: We use the ResNet-18 proposed in [4] with short-cut type B.[4].

Train: In each training iteration, images are resized randomly between 256 and 480 pixel on the smaller dimension and then a random crop of 224×224 is selected for training. We run the training algorithm for 58 epochs with batch size equal to 256 images. The learning rate starts at 0.1 and we use the learning-rate-decay equal to 0.01 at epochs number 30 and 40.

Test: At inference time, we use the 224×224 center crop for forward propagation.

Figure 6 demonstrates the classification accuracy (Top-1 and Top-5) along the epochs for training and inference. The dashed lines represent training and the solid lines represent inference. Table 2 shows our final accuracy by BWN and XNOR-Net.

GoogLenet Variant: We experiment with a variant of GoogLenet [3] that uses a similar number of parameters and connections but only straightforward convolutions, no branching[5]. It has 21 convolutional layers with filter sizes alternating between 1 × 1 and 3 × 3.

---

[4] We used the Torch implementation in https://github.com/facebook/fb.resnet.torch.
[5] We used the Darknet [44] implementation: http://pjreddie.com/darknet/image net/#extraction.

Table 3. In this table, we evaluate two key elements of our approach; computing the optimal scaling factors and specifying the right order for layers in a block of CNN with binary input. (a) demonstrates the importance of the scaling factor in training binary-weight-networks and (b) shows that our way of ordering the layers in a block of CNN is crucial for training XNOR-Networks. C,B,A,P stands for Convolutional, BatchNormalization, Active function (here binary activation), and Pooling respectively.

Binary-Weight-Network			XNOR-Network		
Strategy for computing α	top-1	top-5	Block Structure	top-1	top-5
Using equation 6	56.8	79.4	C-B-A-P	30.3	57.5
Using a separate layer	46.2	69.5	B-A-C-P	44.2	69.2

| (a) | (b) |

Train: Images are resized randomly between 256 and 320 pixel on the smaller dimension and then a random crop of 224×224 is selected for training. We run the training algorithm for 80 epochs with batch size of 128. The learning rate starts at 0.1 and we use polynomial rate decay, $\beta = 4$.

Test: At inference time, we use a center crop of 224×224.

4.3 Ablation Studies

There are two key differences between our method and the previous network binarization methods; the binarization technique and the block structure in our binary CNN. For binarization, we find the optimal scaling factors at each iteration of training. For the block structure, we order the layers in a block in a way that decreases the quantization loss for training XNOR-Net. Here, we evaluate the effect of each of these elements in the performance of the binary networks. Instead of computing the scaling factor α using Eq. 6, one can consider α as a network parameter. In other words, a layer after binary convolution multiplies the output of convolution by an scalar parameter for each filter. This is similar to computing the affine parameters in batch normalization. Table 3a compares the performance of a binary network with two ways of computing the scaling factors. As we mentioned in Sect. 3.2 the typical block structure in CNN is not suitable for binarization. Table 3b compares the standard block structure C-B-A-P (Convolution, Batch Normalization, Activation, Pooling) with our structure B-A-C-P. (A, is binary activation).

5   Conclusion

We introduce simple, efficient, and accurate binary approximations for neural networks. We train a neural network that learns to find binary values for weights, which reduces the size of network by $\sim 32\times$ and provide the possibility of loading very deep neural networks into portable devices with limited memory. We also propose an architecture, XNOR-Net, that uses mostly bitwise operations to approximate convolutions. This provides ~58× speed up and enables the possibility of running the inference of state of the art deep neural network on CPU (rather than GPU) in real-time.

Acknowledgements. This work is in part supported by ONR N00014-13-1-0720, NSF IIS- 1338054, Allen Distinguished Investigator Award, and the Allen Institute for Artificial Intelligence.

References

1. Krizhevsky, A., Sutskever, I., Hinton, G.E.: Imagenet classification with deep convolutional neural networks. In: Advances in neural information processing systems, pp. 1097–1105 (2012)
2. Simonyan, K., Zisserman, A.: Very deep convolutional networks for large-scale image recognition. arXiv preprint arXiv:1409.1556 (2014)
3. Szegedy, C., Liu, W., Jia, Y., Sermanet, P., Reed, S., Anguelov, D., Erhan, D., Vanhoucke, V., Rabinovich, A.: Going deeper with convolutions. In: Proceedings of the IEEE Conference on Computer Vision and Pattern Recognition, pp. 1–9 (2015)
4. He, K., Zhang, X., Ren, S., Sun, J.: Deep residual learning for image recognition. CoRR (2015)
5. Girshick, R., Donahue, J., Darrell, T., Malik, J.: Rich feature hierarchies for accurate object detection and semantic segmentation. In: Proceedings of the IEEE Conference on Computer Vision and Pattern Recognition, pp. 580–587 (2014)
6. Girshick, R.: Fast r-cnn. In: Proceedings of the IEEE International Conference on Computer Vision, pp. 1440–1448 (2015)
7. Ren, S., He, K., Girshick, R., Sun, J.: Faster r-cnn: towards real-time object detection with region proposal networks. In: Advances in Neural Information Processing Systems, pp. 91–99 (2015)
8. Oculus, V.: Oculus rift-virtual reality headset for 3d gaming (2012). http://www.oculusvr.com
9. Gottmer, M.: Merging reality and virtuality with microsoft hololens (2015)
10. Long, J., Shelhamer, E., Darrell, T.: Fully convolutional networks for semantic segmentation. In: Proceedings of the IEEE Conference on Computer Vision and Pattern Recognition, pp. 3431–3440 (2015)
11. Courbariaux, M., Bengio, Y.: Binarynet: training deep neural networks with weights and activations constrained to +1 or −1. CoRR (2016)
12. Denil, M., Shakibi, B., Dinh, L., de Freitas, N., et al.: Predicting parameters in deep learning. In: Advances in Neural Information Processing Systems, pp. 2148–2156 (2013)
13. Cybenko, G.: Approximation by superpositions of a sigmoidal function. Math. Control Sig. Syst. **2**(4), 303–314 (1989)
14. Seide, F., Li, G., Yu, D.: Conversational speech transcription using context-dependent deep neural networks. In: Interspeech, pp. 437–440 (2011)
15. Dauphin, Y.N., Bengio, Y.: Big neural networks waste capacity. arXiv preprint arXiv:1301.3583 (2013)
16. Ba, J., Caruana, R.: Do deep nets really need to be deep?. In: Advances in Neural Information Processing Systems, pp. 2654–2662 (2014)

17. Hanson, S.J., Pratt, L.Y.: Comparing biases for minimal network construction with back-propagation. In: Advances in Neural Information Processing Systems, pp. 177–185 (1989)
18. LeCun, Y., Denker, J.S., Solla, S.A., Howard, R.E., Jackel, L.D.: Optimal brain damage. In: NIPs, vol. 89 (1989)
19. Hassibi, B., Stork, D.G.: Second Order Derivatives for Network Pruning: Optimal Brain Surgeon. Morgan Kaufmann, San Francisco (1993)
20. Han, S., Pool, J., Tran, J., Dally, W.: Learning both weights and connections for efficient neural network. In: Advances in Neural Information Processing Systems, pp. 1135–1143 (2015)
21. Van Nguyen, H., Zhou, K., Vemulapalli, R.: Cross-domain synthesis of medical images using efficient location-sensitive deep network. In: Navab, N., Hornegger, J., Wells, W.M., Frangi, A.F. (eds.) MICCAI 2015. LNCS, vol. 9349, pp. 677–684. Springer, Heidelberg (2015). doi:10.1007/978-3-319-24553-9_83
22. Han, S., Mao, H., Dally, W.J.: Deep compression: compressing deep neural networks with pruning, trained quantization and huffman coding. arXiv preprint arXiv:1510.00149 (2015)
23. Chen, W., Wilson, J.T., Tyree, S., Weinberger, K.Q., Chen, Y.: Compressing neural networks with the hashing trick. arXiv preprint arXiv:1504.04788 (2015)
24. Denton, E.L., Zaremba, W., Bruna, J., LeCun, Y., Fergus, R.: Exploiting linear structure within convolutional networks for efficient evaluation. In: Advances in Neural Information Processing Systems, pp. 1269–1277 (2014)
25. Jaderberg, M., Vedaldi, A., Zisserman, A.: Speeding up convolutional neural networks with low rank expansions. arXiv preprint arXiv:1405.3866 (2014)
26. Lin, M., Chen, Q., Yan, S.: Network in network. arXiv preprint arXiv:1312.4400 (2013)
27. Szegedy, C., Ioffe, S., Vanhoucke, V.: Inception-v4, inception-resnet and the impact of residual connections on learning. CoRR (2016)
28. Iandola, F.N., Moskewicz, M.W., Ashraf, K., Han, S., Dally, W.J., Keutzer, K.: Squeezenet: alexnet-level accuracy with 50x fewer parameters and <1mb model size. arXiv preprint arXiv:1602.07360 (2016)
29. Gong, Y., Liu, L., Yang, M., Bourdev, L.: Compressing deep convolutional networks using vector quantization. arXiv preprint arXiv:1412.6115 (2014)
30. Arora, S., Bhaskara, A., Ge, R., Ma, T.: Provable bounds for learning some deep representations. arXiv preprint arXiv:1310.6343 (2013)
31. Vanhoucke, V., Senior, A., Mao, M.Z.: Improving the speed of neural networks on cpus. In: Proceedings of Deep Learning and Unsupervised Feature Learning NIPS Workshop, vol. 1 (2011)
32. Hwang, K., Sung, W.: Fixed-point feedforward deep neural network design using weights +1, 0, and −1. In: 2014 IEEE Workshop on Signal Processing Systems (SiPS), pp. 1–6. IEEE (2014)
33. Anwar, S., Hwang, K., Sung, W.: Fixed point optimization of deep convolutional neural networks for object recognition. In: 2015 IEEE International Conference on Acoustics, Speech and Signal Processing (ICASSP), pp. 1131–1135. IEEE (2015)
34. Lin, Z., Courbariaux, M., Memisevic, R., Bengio, Y.: Neural networks with few multiplications. arXiv preprint arXiv:1510.03009 (2015)
35. Courbariaux, M., Bengio, Y., David, J.P.: Training deep neural networks with low precision multiplications. arXiv preprint arXiv:1412.7024 (2014)
36. Soudry, D., Hubara, I., Meir, R.: Expectation backpropagation: parameter-free training of multilayer neural networks with continuous or discrete weights. In: Advances in Neural Information Processing Systems, pp. 963–971 (2014)

37. Esser, S.K., Appuswamy, R., Merolla, P., Arthur, J.V., Modha, D.S.: Backpropagation for energy-efficient neuromorphic computing. In: Advances in Neural Information Processing Systems, pp. 1117–1125 (2015)

38. Courbariaux, M., Bengio, Y., David, J.P.: Binaryconnect: training deep neural networks with binary weights during propagations. In: Advances in Neural Information Processing Systems, pp. 3105–3113 (2015)

39. Wan, L., Zeiler, M., Zhang, S., Cun, Y.L., Fergus, R.: Regularization of neural networks using dropconnect. In: Proceedings of the 30th International Conference on Machine Learning (ICML-13), pp. 1058–1066 (2013)

40. Baldassi, C., Ingrosso, A., Lucibello, C., Saglietti, L., Zecchina, R.: Subdominant dense clusters allow for simple learning and high computational performance in neural networks with discrete synapses. Phys. Rev. Lett. **115**(12), 128101 (2015)

41. Kim, M., Smaragdis, P.: Bitwise neural networks. arXiv preprint arXiv:1601.06071 (2016)

42. Kingma, D., Ba, J.: Adam: a method for stochastic optimization. arXiv preprint arXiv:1412.6980 (2014)

43. Ioffe, S., Szegedy, C.: Batch normalization: accelerating deep network training by reducing internal covariate shift. arXiv preprint arXiv:1502.03167 (2015)

44. Redmon, J.: Darknet: open source neural networks in c (2013–2016). http://pjreddie.com/darknet/

Top-Down Neural Attention
by Excitation Backprop

Jianming Zhang[1(✉)], Zhe Lin[2], Jonathan Brandt[2], Xiaohui Shen[2],
and Stan Sclaroff[1]

[1] Boston University, Boston, USA
{jmzhang,sclaroff}@bu.edu
[2] Adobe Research, San Jose, USA
{zlin,jbrandt,xshen}@adobe.com

Abstract. We aim to model the top-down attention of a Convolutional
Neural Network (CNN) classifier for generating task-specific attention
maps. Inspired by a top-down human visual attention model, we propose a new backpropagation scheme, called Excitation Backprop, to pass
along top-down signals downwards in the network hierarchy via a probabilistic Winner-Take-All process. Furthermore, we introduce the concept
of contrastive attention to make the top-down attention maps more discriminative. In experiments, we demonstrate the accuracy and generalizability of our method in weakly supervised localization tasks on the MS
COCO, PASCAL VOC07 and ImageNet datasets. The usefulness of our
method is further validated in the text-to-region association task. On the
Flickr30k Entities dataset, we achieve promising performance in phrase
localization by leveraging the top-down attention of a CNN model that
has been trained on weakly labeled web images.

1 Introduction

Top-down task-driven attention is an important mechanism for efficient visual
search. Various top-down attention models have been proposed, *e.g.* [1–4].
Among them, the Selective Tuning attention model [3] provides a biologically
plausible formulation. Assuming a pyramidal neural network for visual processing, the Selective Tuning model is composed of a bottom-up sweep of the network
to process input stimuli, and a top-down Winner-Take-ALL (WTA) process to
localize the most relevant neurons in the network for a given top-down signal.

Inspired by the Selective Tuning model, we propose a top-down attention formulation for modern CNN classifiers. Instead of the deterministic WTA process
used in [3], which can only generate binary attention maps, we formulate the
top-down attention of a CNN classifier as a *probabilistic* WTA process.

The probabilistic WTA formulation is realized by a novel backpropagation scheme, called *Excitation Backprop*, which integrates both top-down and

---

Electronic supplementary material The online version of this chapter (doi:10.
1007/978-3-319-46493-0_33) contains supplementary material, which is available to
authorized users.

© Springer International Publishing AG 2016
B. Leibe et al. (Eds.): ECCV 2016, Part IV, LNCS 9908, pp. 543–559, 2016.
DOI: 10.1007/978-3-319-46493-0_33

Fig. 1. A CNN classifier's top-down attention maps generated by our Excitation Backprop can localize common object categories, *e.g.* chair and glass, as well as fine-grained categories like boy, man and woman in this example image, which is resized to 224×224 for our method. The classifier used in this example is trained to predict ~ 18 K tags using only weakly labeled web images. Visualizing the classifier's top-down attention can also help interpret what has been learned by the classifier. For couple, we can tell that our classifier uses the two adults in the image as the evidence, while for father, it mostly concentrates on the child. This indicates that the classifier's understanding of father may strongly relate to the presence of a child.

bottom-up information to compute the winning probability of each neuron efficiently. Interpretable attention maps can be generated by Excitation Backprop at intermediate convolutional layers, thus avoiding the need to perform a complete backward sweep. We further introduce the concept of contrastive top-down attention, which captures the differential effect between a pair of contrastive top-down signals. The contrastive top-down attention can significantly improve the discriminativeness of the generated attention maps.

In experiments, our method achieves superior weakly supervised localization performance *vs.* [5–9] on challenging datasets such as PASCAL VOC [10] and MS COCO [11]. We further explore the scalability of our method for localizing a large number of visual concepts. For this purpose, we train a CNN tag classifier to predict ~ 18 K tags using 6M weakly labeled web images. By leveraging our top-down attention model, our image tag classifier can be used to localize a variety of visual concepts. Moreover, our method can also help to understand what has been learned by our tag classifier. Some examples are shown in Fig. 1.

The performance of our large-scale tag localization method is evaluated on the challenging Flickr30k Entities dataset [12]. Without using a language model or any localization supervision, our top-down attention based approach achieves competitive phrase-to-region performance *vs.* a fully-supervised baseline [12].

To summarize, the **main contributions** of this paper are:

- a top-down attention model for CNN based on a probabilistic Winner-Take-All process using a novel Excitation Backprop scheme;
- a contrastive top-down attention formulation for enhancing the discriminativeness of attention maps; and
- a large-scale empirical exploration of weakly supervised text-to-region association by leveraging the top-down neural attention model.

2   Related Work

There is a rich literature about modeling the top-down influences on selective attention in the human visual system (see [13] for a review). It is hypothesized that top-down factors like knowledge, expectations and behavioral goals can affect the feature and location expectancy in visual processing [1,4,14,15], and bias the competition among the neurons [3,15–18]. Our attention model is related to the Selective Tuning model of [3], which proposes a biologically inspired attention model using a top-down WTA inference process.

Various methods have been proposed for grounding a CNN classifier's prediction [5–9,19]. In [5,6,20], error backpropagation based methods are used for visualizing relevant regions for a predicted class or the activation of a hidden neuron. Recently, a layer-wise relevance backpropagation method is proposed by [9] to provide a pixel-level explanation of CNNs' classification decisions. Cao *et al.* [7] propose a feedback CNN architecture for capturing the top-down attention mechanism that can successfully identify task relevant regions. In [19], it is shown that replacing fully-connected layers with an average pooling layer can help generate coarse class activation maps that highlight task relevant regions. Unlike these previous methods, our top-down attention model is based on the WTA principle, and has an interpretable probabilistic formulation. Our method is also conceptually simpler than [7,19] as we do not require modifying a network's architecture or additional training. The ultimate goal of our method goes beyond visualization and explanation of a classifier's decision [6,9,20], as we aim to maneuver CNNs' top-down attention to generate highly discriminative attention maps for the benefits of localization.

Training CNN models for weakly supervised localization has been studied by [21–25]. In [21,24,25], a CNN model is transformed into a fully convolutional net to perform efficient sliding window inference, and then Multiple Instance Learning (MIL) is integrated in the training process through various pooling methods over the confidence score map. Due to the large receptive field and stride of the output layer, the resultant score maps only provide very coarse location information. To overcome this issue, a variety of strategies, *e.g.* image re-scaling and shifting, have been proposed to increase the granularity of the score maps [21,24,26]. Image and object priors are also leveraged to improve the object localization accuracy in [22–24]. Compared with weakly supervised localization, the problem setting of our task is essentially different. We assume a pre-trained deep CNN model is given, which may not use any dedicated training process or model architecture for the purpose of localization. Our focus, instead, is to model the top-down attention mechanism of *generic* CNN models to produce interpretable and useful task-relevant attention maps.

3   Method

3.1   Top-Down Neural Attention Based on Probabilistic WTA

We consider a generic feedforward neural network model. The goal of a top-down attention model is to identify the task-relevant neurons in the network.

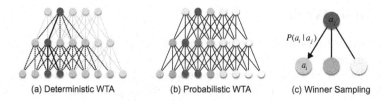

(a) Deterministic WTA   (b) Probabilistic WTA   (c) Winner Sampling

Fig. 2. Deterministic WTA [3] *vs.* our probabilistic WTA for modeling top-down attention. (a) Given a selected output unit, the red dots denote the winners identified by the top-down layer-wise deterministic WTA scheme in the processing cone, and the cyan ones are inhibited. (b) In our probabilistic WTA scheme, winner neurons are generated by a stochastic sampling process (shown in (c)). The top-down signal is specified by a probability distribution over the output units. The shading of a dot in (b) indicates the its relative likelihood of winning against the other ones in the same layer.

Given a selected output unit, a deterministic top-down WTA scheme is used in the biologically inspired Selective Tuning model [3] to localize the most relevant neurons in the processing cone (see Fig. 2 (a)) and generate a binary attention map. Inspired by the deterministic WTA, we propose a *probabilistic WTA* formulation to model a neural network's top-down attention (Fig. 2(b) and (c)), which leverages more information in the network and generates soft attention maps that can capture subtle differences between top-down signals. This is critical to our contrastive attention formulation in Sect. 3.3.

In our formulation, the top-down signal is specified by a prior distribution $P(A_0)$ over the output units, which can model the uncertainty in the top-down control process. Then the winner neurons are recursively sampled in a top-down fashion based on a conditional winning probability $P(A_t|A_{t-1})$, where $A_t, A_{t-1} \in \mathcal{N}$ denote the selected winner neuron at the current and the previous step respectively, and $\mathcal{N}$ is the overall neuron set. We formulate the top-down relevance of each neuron as its probability of being selected as a winner in this process. Formally, given a neuron $a_i \in \mathcal{N}$ (note that a_i denotes a specific neuron and A_t denotes a variable over the neurons), we would like to compute its *Marginal Winning Probability* (MWP) $P(a_i)$. The MWP $P(a_i)$ can be factorized as

$$P(a_i) = \sum_{a_j \in \mathcal{P}_i} P(a_i|a_j)P(a_j), \tag{1}$$

where $\mathcal{P}_i$ is the parent node set of a_i (in top-down order). As Eq. 1 indicates, given $P(a_i|a_j)$, $P(a_i)$ is a function of the marginal winning probability of the parent nodes in the preceding layers. It follows that $P(a_i)$ can be computed in a top-down layer-wise fashion.

Our formulation is equivalent to an absorbing Markov chain process [27] with $p_{ij} := P(a_i|a_j)$ as the transition probability and neurons at the network bottom as the absorbing nodes. $P(a_i)$ can then be interpreted as the expected number of visits when a walker randomly starts from a node in the output layer according to $P(A_0)$. This expected number of visits can be computed by a simple matrix

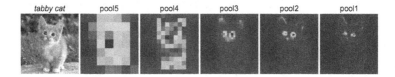

Fig. 3. Example Marginal Winning Probability (MWP) maps computed via Excitation Backprop from different layers of the public `VGG16` model [29] trained on ImageNet. The input image is shown on the right. The MWP maps are generated for the category `tabby cat`. Neurons at higher-level layers have larger receptive fields and strides. Thus, they can capture larger areas but with lower spatial accuracy. Neurons at lower layers tend to more precisely localize features at smaller scale.

multiplication using the fundamental matrix of the absorbing Markov chain [27]. (Detailed explanation can be found in the supplementary material.) In this light, the MWP $P(a_i)$ is a linear function of the the top-down signal $P(A_0)$, which will be shown to be convenient later (see Sect. 3.3).

3.2   Excitation Backprop

In this section, we propose the Excitation Backprop method to realize the probabilistic WTA formulation for modern CNN models.

A modern CNN model [28–30] is mostly composed of a basic type of neuron a_j, whose response is computed by $\widehat{a}_j = \varphi(\sum_i w_{ij}\widehat{a}_i + b_i)$. Here w_{ij} is the weight, $\widehat{a}_i$ is the input, b_i is the bias and φ is the nonlinear activation function. We call this type of neuron an *Activation Neuron*. We have the following assumptions about the activation neurons.

A1. The response of the activation neuron is non-negative.

A2. An activation neuron is tuned to detect certain visual features. Its response is positively correlated to its confidence of the detection.

A1 holds for a majority of the modern CNN models, as they adopt the Rectified Linear Unit (ReLU) as the activation function[1]. **A2** has been empirically verified by many recent works [6,19,31,32]. It is observed that neurons at lower layers detect simple features like edge and color, while neurons at higher layers can detect complex features like objects and body parts.

Between activation neurons, we define a connection to be *excitatory* if its weight is non-negative, and *inhibitory* otherwise. Our Excitation Backprop passes top-down signals through excitatory connections between activation neurons. Formally, let $\mathcal{C}_j$ denote the child node set of a_j (in the top-down order). For each $a_i \in \mathcal{C}_j$, the conditional winning probability $P(a_i|a_j)$ is defined as

$$P(a_i|a_j) = \begin{cases} Z_j \widehat{a}_i w_{ij} & \text{if } w_{ij} \geq 0, \\ 0 & \text{otherwise.} \end{cases} \qquad (2)$$

---

[1] We discuss some exceptions and the remedies in the supplementary material.

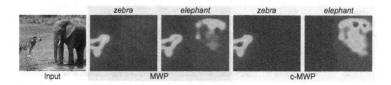

Fig. 4. Marginal Winning Probability (MWP) *vs.* contrastive MWP (c-MWP). The input image is resized to 224×224, and we use GoogleNet pretrained on ImageNet to generate the MWP maps and c-MWP maps for "zebra" and "elephant". The MWP map for "elephant" does not successfully suppress the zebra. In contrast, by cancelling out common winner neurons for "elephant" and "non-elephant", the c-MWP map more effectively highlights the elephant.

$Z_j = 1/\sum_{i:w_{ij}\geq 0} \widehat{a}_i w_{ij}$ is a normalization factor so that $\sum_{a_i \in C_j} P(a_i|a_j) = 1$. In the special case when $\sum_{i:w_{ij}\geq 0} \widehat{a}_i w_{ij} = 0$, we define Z_i to be 0. Note that the formulation of $P(a_i|a_j)$ is valid due to **A1**, since $\widehat{a}_i$ is always non-negative.

Equation 2 assumes that if a_j is a winner neuron, the next winner neuron will be sampled among its child node set C_j based on the connection weight w_{ij} and the input neuron's response $\widehat{a}_i$. The weight w_{ij} captures the top-down feature expectancy, while $\widehat{a}_i$ represents the bottom-up feature strength, as assumed in **A2**. Due to **A1**, child neurons of a_j with negative connection weights always have an inhibitory effect on a_j, and thus are excluded from the competition.

Equation 2 recursively propagates the top-down signal layer by layer, and we can compute attention maps from any intermediate convolutional layer. For our method, we simply take the sum across channels to generate a marginal winning probability (MWP) map as our attention map, which is a 2D probability histogram. Figure 3 shows some example MWP maps generated using the pretrained VGG16 model [29]. Neurons at higher-level layers have larger receptive fields and strides. Thus, they can capture larger areas but with lower spatial accuracy. Neurons at lower layers tend to more precisely localize features at smaller scales.

3.3 Contrastive Top-Down Attention

Since the MWP is a linear function of the top-down signal (see Sect. 3.1), we can compute any linear combination of MWP maps for an image by a single backward pass. All we need to do is linearly combine the top-down signal vectors at the top layer before performing the Excitation Backprop. In this section, we take advantage of this property to generate highly discriminative top-down attention maps by passing down pairs of contrastive signals.

For each output unit o_i, we virtually construct a dual unit $\bar{o}_i$, whose input weights are the negation of those of o_i. For example, if an output unit corresponds to an elephant classifier, then its dual unit will correspond to a non-elephant classifier. Subtracting the MWP map for non-elephant from the one for elephant will cancel out common winner neurons and amplify the discriminative neurons for `elephant`. We call the resulting map a *contrastive* MWP map, which can be computed by a single backward pass. More details can be found in our supplementary material. In practice we weight the target unit and its dual equally, and truncate the contrastive MWP map at zero so that only positive parts are kept. Our probabilistic formulation ensures that there are always some positive parts on the contrastive MWP map, unless the MWP map and its dual are identical. Figure 4 shows some examples.

4   Experiments

We implement Excitation Backprop in Caffe [33] (available at our project website[2]). Implementation details are included in our supplementary material.

4.1   The Pointing Game

The goal of this section is to evaluate the *discriminativeness* of different top-down attention maps for localizing target objects in crowded visual scenes.

Evaluation setting. Given a pre-trained CNN classifier, we test different methods in generating a top-down attention map for a target object category present in an image. Ground truth object labels are used to cue the method. We extract the maximum point on the top-down attention map. A hit is counted if the maximum point lies on one of the annotated instances of the cued object category, otherwise a miss is counted. We measure the localization accuracy by $Acc = \frac{\#Hits}{\#Hits + \#Misses}$ for each object category. The overall performance is measured by the mean accuracy across different categories.

We call this the *Pointing Game*, as it asks the CNN model to point at an object of designated category in the image. The pointing game does not require highlighting the full extent of an object, and it does not account for the CNN model's classification accuracy. Therefore, it purely compares the *spatial selectiveness* of the top-down attention maps. Moreover, the pointing game only involves minimum post-processing of the attention maps, so it can evaluate different types of attention maps more fairly.

Datasets. We use the test split of the PASCAL VOC07 dataset [10] (4952 images) and the validation split of the MS COCO dataset [11] (40137 images). In particular, COCO contains 80 object categories, and many of its images have multiple object categories, making even the simple Pointing Game rather challenging. To evaluate success in the Pointing Game, we use the groundtruth bounding boxes for VOC07 and the provided segmentation masks for COCO.

CNN classifiers. We consider three popular CNN architectures: `CNN-S` [34] (an improved version of AlexNet [28]), `VGG16` [29], and `GoogleNet` [30]. These models vary a lot in depth and structure. We download these models from the Caffe Model Zoo website [35]. These models are pre-trained on ImageNet [36].

---

[2] http://www.cs.bu.edu/groups/ivc/excitation-backprop.

For both VOC07 and COCO, we use the training split to fine-tune each model. We follow the basic training procedure for image classification, and thus no multi-scale training is used. Only the output layer is fine-tuned using the multi-label cross-entropy loss for simplicity, since the classification accuracy is not our focus. More details are included in our supplementary material.

Test methods. We compare Excitation Backprop (MWP and c-MWP) with the following methods: (Grad) the error backprogation method [5], (Deconv) the deconvolution method originally designed for internal neuron visualization [6], (LRP) layer-wise relevance propagation [9], and (CAM) the class activation map method [8]. We implement Grad, Deconv and CAM in Caffe. For Deconv, we use an improved version proposed in [20], which generates better maps than the original version [6]. For Grad and Deconv, we follow [5] to use the maximum absolute value across color channels to generate the final attention map. Taking the mean instead of maximum will degrade their performance. For LRP, we use the software provided by the authors, which only supports CPU computation. For VGG16, this software can take 30 s to generate an attention map on an Intel Xeon 2.90GHz×6 machine[3]. Due to limited computational resources, we only evaluate LRP for CNN-S and GoogleNet.

Note that CAM is only applicable to certain architectures like GoogleNet, which do not have fully connected layers. At test time, it acts like a fully convolutional model to perform dense sliding window evaluation [21,37]. Therefore, the comparison with CAM encompasses the comparison with the dense evaluation approach for weakly supervised localization [21].

To generate the full attention maps for images of arbitrary aspect ratios, we convert each testing CNN classifier to a fully convolutional architecture as in [21]. All the compared methods can be easily extended to fully convolutional models. In particular, for Excitation Backprop, Grad and Deconv, the output confidence map of the target category is used as the top-down signal to capture the spatial weighting. However, all input images are resized to 224 in the smaller dimension, and no multi-scale processing is used.

For different CNN classifiers, we empirically select different layers to compute our attention maps based on a held-out set. We use the conv5 layer for CNN-S, pool4 for VGG16 and pool2 for GoogleNet. We use bicubic interpolation to upsample the generated attention maps. The effect of the layer selection will be analysed below. For Grad, Deconv and LRP we blur their maps by a Gaussian kernel with $\sigma = 0.02 \cdot \max\{W, H\}$, which slightly improves their performance since their maps tend to be sparse and noisy at the pixel level. In the evaluation, we expand the groundtruth region by a tolerance margin of 15 pixels, so that the attention maps produced by CAM, which are only 7 pixels in the shortest dimension, can be more fairly compared.

Results. The results are reported in Table 1. As the pointing game is trivial for images with large dominant objects, we also report the performance on a difficult

---

[3] On COCO, we need to compute about 116 K attention maps, which leads to over 950 h of computation on a single machine for LRP using VGG16.

Table 1. Mean accuracy (%) in the pointing game. For each method, we report two scores for the overall test set and a difficult subset respectively. `Center` is the baseline that points at image center. The second best score of each column is underlined.

	VOC07 Test (All/Diff.)			COCO Val. (All/Diff.)		
	CNN-S	VGG16	GoogleNet	CNN-S	VGG16	GoogleNet
Center	69.5/42.6	69.5/42.6	69.5/42.6	27.7/19.4	27.7/19.4	27.7/19.4
Grad [5]	78.6/59.8	76.0/56.8	79.3/61.4	38.7/30.1	37.1/30.7	42.6/36.3
Deconv [6]	73.1/45.9	75.5/52.8	74.3/49.4	36.4/28.4	38.6/30.8	35.7/27.9
LRP [9]	68.1/41.3	-	72.8/50.2	32.5/24.0	-	40.2/32.7
CAM [8]	-	-	80.8/61.9	-	-	41.6/35.0
MWP	73.7/52.9	76.9/55.1	79.3/60.4	35.0/27.7	39.5/32.5	43.6/37.1
c-MWP	**78.7/61.7**	**80.0/66.8**	**85.1/72.3**	**43.0/37.0**	**49.6/44.2**	**53.8/48.3**

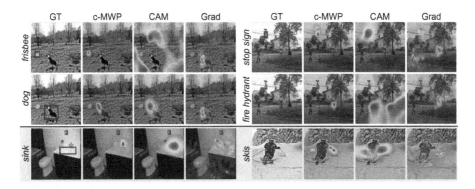

Fig. 5. Example attention maps using `GoogleNet`. For visualization, the maps are superimposed on the images after some postprocessing (slight blur for Grad and thresholding for CAM). (*Top two rows*) Our c-MWP is very discriminative and can often localize challengingly small objects like `frisbee`, `stop sign` and `fire hydrant`. (*Bottom row*) Two typical failure cases of top-down neural attention are shown. Since `faucet` often co-occurs with `sink`, the CNN's attention falsely focuses on the faucet in the image. It is the same case for `ski poles` and `skis`.

subset of images for each category. The difficult set includes images that meet two criteria: (1) the total area of bounding boxes (or segments in COCO) of the testing category is smaller than 1/4 the size of the image and (2) there is at least one other distracter category in the image.

Our c-MWP consistently outperforms the other methods on both VOC07 and COCO across different CNN models. c-MWP is also substantially better than MWP, which validates the idea of contrastive attention. `GoogleNet` provides the best localization performance for different methods, which is also observed by [7,8]. Using `GoogleNet`, our c-MWP outperforms the second best method by about 10 % points on the difficult sets of VOC07 and COCO. In particular, our c-

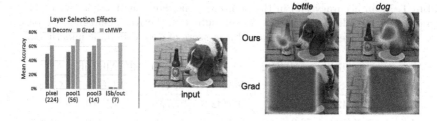

Fig. 6. Effects of layer selection on VOC07 *difficult* set. (*Left*) For Grad, Deconv and our c-MWP, we compare their attention maps from three different layers in the GoogleNet. At I5b/out, Grad and Deconv fail to generate meaningful attention maps, while our method can still achieve reasonable accuracy. (*Right*) We show example attention maps by our c-MWP and Grad from the I5b/out layer.

Table 2. Analysis of contrastive attention on VOC07 *difficult* set using GoogleNet. We evaluate two variants of Excitation Backprop for the contrastive attention map computation compared with our full model. We also test the contrastive attention idea for Grad, Deconv and CAM and their original scores are shown in brackets. See text for details.

	Excitation backprop			Other methods		
	full	post-norm	w/o norm	c-Grad	c-Deconv	c-CAM
Mean Acc. (%)	**70.6**	58.1	41.6	N.A	67.7 (49.4)	61.9 (61.9)

MWP gives the best performance in 69/80 object categories of COCO, especially for small objects like remote, tie and baseball bat (see our supplementary material).

Example attention maps are shown in Fig. 5. As we can see, our c-MWP maps can accurately localize the cued objects in rather challenging scenes. More examples are included in our supplementary material.

Layer selection effects. We use GoogleNet to analyze the effects of layer selection. For a comparison, we also report the performance of Grad and Deconv by taking the maximum gradient magnitude across feature map channels in the intermediate layers. Results are reported in Fig. 6. We choose three intermediate layers in GoogleNet: pool1, pool3 and Inception_5b/output (I5b/out), whose spatial resolutions are 56, 14 and 7 in the shortest dimension respectively. Performance does not vary much across all methods at the chosen layers except I5b/out. Our c-MWP only gets a slight decrease in accuracy (mainly due to the map's low spatial resolution), while Grad and Deconv do not generate meaningful attention maps (see Fig. 6). This is because the attention maps of Grad and Deconv at I5b/out are not conditioned on the activation values of I5b/out, and thus fail to leverage the spatial information captured by I5b/out.

Analysis of contrastive top-down attention. The proposed contrastive attention is conceptually simple, which basically subtracts one attention map

Table 3. Bounding box localization error on ImageNet Val. using `GoogleNet`. *The score of Feedback is from the original paper.

	Grad [5]	Deconv [6]	LRP [9]	CAM [8]	Feedback* [7]	c-MWP	MWP
Opt. α	5.0	4.5	1.0	1.0	-	0.0	1.5
Loc. Error (%)	41.6	41.6	57.8	48.1	<u>38.8</u>	57.0	**38.7**

from its dual using the virtual contrastive output unit. We test this idea for Grad, Deconv and CAM and the performance is reported in Table 2. For Grad, the gradient magnitude map is identical to its dual since the gradients of the dual map are just the negation of the reference map. As a result, the subtraction gives a zero map. For CAM, the performance remains the same because the dual map is again a negation of the reference attention map and the maximum point will not be changed by the subtraction. However, the proposed contrastive attention works for Deconv, when the attention map and its dual are L1-normalized before subtraction. Deconv shares a similar spirit of our method as it discards negative/inhibitory signals by thresholding at ReLU layers, but it also introduces non-linearity in the propagation process. Therefore, it requires two backward passes and proper normalization, while our method can directly propagate the contrastive signal via a single pass and achieves better performance.

Our probabilistic WTA formulation produces well-normalized attention maps that enable direct subtraction. We report the performance of two variants of our method in Table 2. We remove the normalization factor Z_i in Eq. 2 and pass down the contrastive signal. This leads to a significant degradation in performance (w/o norm). Then we compute the attention map and its dual separately and do the subtraction after L1-normalization (post-norm). The performance is improved but still substantially lower than our full method. This analysis further confirms the importance of our probabilistic formulation.

4.2   Localizing Dominant Objects

We now turn to a different evaluation setting [7]. The goal of this setting is bounding box (bbox) localization of dominant objects in the image.

Dataset and evaluation. We follow the protocol of Feedback Net [7] for a fair comparison. The test is performed on the ImageNet Val. set ($\sim$50 K images), where each image has a label representing the category of dominant objects in it. The label is given, so the evaluation is based on the localization error rate with an IOU threshold at 0.5. Images are resized to 224×224.

As in [7], simple thresholding is used to extract a bbox from an attention map. We set the threshold $\tau = \alpha\mu_I$, where μ_I is the mean value of the map. Then the tightest bbox covering the white pixels is extracted. The parameter α is optimized in the range $[0 : 0.5 : 10]$ for each method on a held out set.

Results. Table 3 reports the results based on the same `GoogleNet` model obtained from Caffe Model Zoo [35] as in [7]. We find that c-MWP performs poorly, but our MWP obtains competitive results against Feedback and other methods. Compared with Feedback, our method is conceptually much simpler. Feedback requires modification of a CNN's architecture and needs 10–50 iterations of forward-backward passes for computing an attention map.

Note that this task favors attention maps that fully cover the *dominant* object in an image. Thus, it is very different from the Pointing Game, which favors discriminativeness instead. Our c-MWP usually only highlights the most discriminative part of an object due to the competition between the contrastive pair of top-down signals. This experiment highlights the versatility of our method, and the value of the non-contrastive version (MWP) for dominant object localization.

4.3 Text-to-Region Association

Text-to-region association in unconstrained images [12] is very challenging compared to the object detection task, due to the lack of fully-annotated datasets and the large number of words/phrases used in the natural language. Moreover, an image region can be referred to by potentially many different words/phrases, which further increases the complexity of the fully-supervised approach.

By leveraging the top-down attention of a CNN image tag classifier, we propose a highly scalable approach to weakly supervised word-to-region association. We train an image tag classifier using ~6M weakly labeled thumbnail images collected from a commercial stock image website[4] (Stock6M). Each image is 200-pixels in the longest dimension and comes with about 30–50 user tags. These tags cover a wide range of concepts, including objects, scenes, body parts, attributes, activities, and abstract concepts, but are also very noisy. We picked ~18 K most frequent tags for our dictionary. We empirically found that the first few tags of each image are usually more relevant, and consequently use only the first 5 tags of an image in the training.

Tag classifier training. We use the pre-trained `GoogleNet` model from Caffe Model Zoo, and fine-tune the model using the multi-label cross-entropy objective function for the 18 K tags. Images are padded to square shape by mirror padding and upsampled to 256×256. Random flipping and cropping are used for data augmentation. We use SGD with a batch size of 64 and a starting learning rate of 0.01. The learning rate is lowered by a factor of 0.1 when the validation error plateaus. The training process passes through the data for three epochs and takes ~55 h on an NVIDIA K40c GPU.

Dataset and evaluation. To quantitatively evaluate our top-down attention method and the baselines in text-to-region association, we use the recently proposed Flickr30k Entities (Flickr30k) dataset [12]. Evaluation is performed on the test split of Flickr30k (1000 images), where every image has five sentential descriptions. Each Noun Phrase (NP) in a sentence is manually associated with the bounding box (bbox) regions it refers to in the image. NPs are grouped into

---

[4] https://stock.adobe.com.

Table 4. Performance comparison on the Flickr30k Entities dataset. We report performance for both the whole dataset and a subset of small instances. The R@N refers to the overall recall rate regardless of phrase types. mAP (Group) and mAP (Phrase) should be interpreted differently, because most phrases belong to the group `people`. CCA* refers to the precomputed results provided by [12], while CCA and SPE are the results reported in the original paper. MCG_base is the performance using MCG's original proposal scores. EB is EdgeBoxes [39].

	opt. γ	R@1	R@5	R@10	mAP (Group)	mAP (Phrase)
MCG_base	–	10.7/ 7.7	30.3/22.4	40.5/30.3	6.9/ 4.5	16.8/12.9
Grad (MCG)	0.50	24.3/ 7.6	49.6/32.9	59.7/45.8	10.2/ 3.8	28.8/15.6
Deconv (MCG)	0.50	21.5/11.3	48.4/34.5	58.5/46.0	10.0/ 4.0	26.5/16.7
LRP (MCG)	0.50	24.3/11.8	51.6/36.8	61.3/48.5	10.3/ 4.3	28.9/18.1
CAM (MCG)	0.75	21.7/ 6.5	47.1/27.9	56.1/39.1	7.5/ 2.0	26.0/11.9
MWP (MCG)	0.50	**28.5**/15.0	52.7/39.1	61.3/49.8	11.8/ 5.3	**31.1**/20.3
c-MWP (MCG)	0.50	26.2/**21.2**	**54.3/43.4**	**62.2/51.7**	**15.2**/10.8	30.8/**24.0**
CCA* [12] (EB)	–	25.2/**21.8**	50.3/**41.0**	58.1/**47.3**	12.8/**11.5**	28.8/**23.6**
CCA [12] (EB)	–	25.3/ –	–	**59.7**/ –	11.2/ –	–
c-MWP (EB)	0.25	**27.0**/18.4	49.9/35.2	57.7/43.9	**13.2**/ 8.1	**29.4**/20.0

Table 5. Per group recall@5 (%) on the Flickr30k Entities dataset. The mean scores are computed over different group types, which are different from the overall recall rates reported in Table 4.

	People	Clothing	Bodypart	Animal	Vehicle	Instrument	Scene	Other	Mean
MCG_base	36.1	30.1	9.9	50.8	37.8	26.5	31.5	19.1	30.3
Grad (MCG)	65.0	32.4	14.0	**70.1**	63.0	40.7	58.8	32.5	47.1
Deconv (MCG)	65.4	31.6	18.7	67.0	64.0	46.9	53.6	28.9	47.0
LRN (MCG)	64.6	37.7	16.4	62.9	63.5	45.7	59.4	37.9	48.5
CAM (MCG)	60.5	28.4	9.6	57.0	57.5	37.0	**64.4**	32.7	43.4
MWP (MCG)	**68.6**	37.7	16.1	68.7	66.3	53.7	54.5	36.8	50.3
c-MWP (MCG)	63.5	**47.6**	**24.5**	69.9	**72.0**	54.3	61.0	40.2	**54.1**
CCA* [12] (EB)	**63.6**	**43.7**	**22.9**	57.0	69.0	50.6	45.0	**36.2**	48.5
c-MWP (EB)	62.8	35.0	17.6	**65.1**	**73.5**	**58.6**	**53.2**	36.2	**50.3**

eight types (see [12]). Given an NP, the task is to provide a list of scored bboxes, which will be measured by the recall rate (similar to the object proposal metric) or per-group/per-phrase Average Precision (AP) (similar to the object detection metric). We use the evaluation code from [12].

To generate scored bboxes for an NP, we first compute the word attention map for each word in the NP using our tag classifier. Images are resized to 300 pixels in the shortest dimension to better localize small objects. Then we simply average the word attention maps to get an NP attention map. Advanced language models can be used for better fusing the word attention maps, but we adopt the simplest fusion scheme to demonstrate the effectiveness of our top-down attention model. We skip a small proportion of words that are not covered by our 18 K dictionary. MCG [38] is used to generate 500 segment proposals, which are re-scored based on the phrase attention map. The re-scored segments are then converted to bboxes, and redundant bboxes are removed via Non-maximum Suppression using the IOU threshold of 0.7.

The segment scoring function is defined as $f(R) = S_R/A_R^\gamma$ where S_R is the sum of the values inside the segment proposal R on the given attention map and A_R is the segment's area. The parameter γ is to control the penalty of the segment's area, which is optimized for each method in the range $[0 : 0.25 : 1]$.

Results. The recall rates and mAP scores are reported in Table 4. For our method and the baselines, we additionally report the performance on a subset of small instances whose bbox area is below 0.25 of the image size, as we find small regions are much more difficult to localize. Our c-MWP consistently outperforms all the attention map baselines across different metrics. In particular, the group-level mAP of our method is better than the second best by a large margin.

We also compare with a recent fully supervised method [12], which is trained directly on the Flickr30k Entities dataset using CNN features. For fair comparison, we use the same bbox proposals used in [12], which are generated by EdgeBoxes (EB) [39]. These proposals are pre-computed and provided by [12]. Our performance using EB is lower than using MCG, mainly due to the lower accuracy of the EB's bbox proposals. Compared with the segmentation proposals, the bbox proposals can also affect our ranking function for small and thin objects. However, our method still attains competitive performance against [12]. Note that our method is weakly supervised and does not use any training data from the Flickr30k Entities dataset.

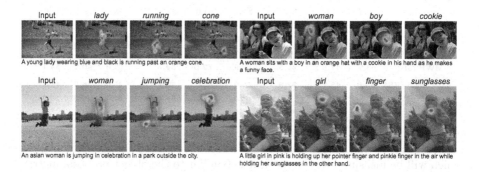

Fig. 7. Word attention maps obtained by c-MWP using our image tag classifier. For each test image, one of its caption annotations from Flickr30k Entities is displayed below. We show the attention maps for the words in red in each caption. By leveraging a large-scale weakly labeled dataset, our method can localize a large number of visual concepts, *e.g.* objects (cone, sunglasses and cookie), fine-grain categories of people (woman and boy), body parts (finger) and actions (jumping, running and celebration). More examples are included in our supplementary material.

We further report the per-group Recall@5 score in Table 5. Our method achieves promising results in many group types, *e.g.* `vehicle` and `instrument`. Note that the fully supervised CCA (EB) [12] gives significantly worse performance than c-MWP (EB) in `animal`, `vehicle` and `instrument`, which are the three rarest types in the Flickr30k Entities dataset. This again shows the limitation of fully-supervised approaches due to the lack of fully-annotated data.

Some example word attention maps are shown in Fig. 7 to demonstrate the localization ability of our method. As we can see, our method can localize not only noun phrases but also actions verbs in the text.

5   Conclusion

We propose a probabilistic Winner-Take-All formulation to model the top-down neural attention for CNN classifiers. Based on our formulation, a novel propagation method, Excitation Backprop, is presented to compute the Marginal Winning Probability of each neuron. Using Excitation Backprop, highly discriminative attention maps can be efficiently computed by propagating a pair of contrastive top-down signals via a single backward pass in the network. We demonstrate the accuracy and the generalizability of our method in a large-scale Pointing Game. We further show the usefulness of our method in localizing dominant objects. Moreover, without using any localization supervision or language model, our neural attention based method attains competitive localization performance *vs.* the state-of-the-art fully supervised methods on the challenging Flickr30k Entities dataset.

Acknowledgments. This research was supported in part by Adobe Research, US NSF grants 0910908 and 1029430, and gifts from NVIDIA.

References

1. Koch, C., Ullman, S.: Shifts in selective visual attention: towards the underlying neural circuitry. In: Vaina, L.M. (ed.) Matters of Intelligence. Conceptual Structures in Cognitive Neuroscience. Synthese Library, vol. 188, pp. 115–141. Springer, New York (1987)
2. Anderson, C.H., Van Essen, D.C.: Shifter circuits: a computational strategy for dynamic aspects of visual processing. Proc. Natl. Acad. Sci. **84**(17), 6297–6301 (1987)
3. Tsotsos, J.K., Culhane, S.M., Wai, W.Y.K., Lai, Y., Davis, N., Nuflo, F.: Modeling visual attention via selective tuning. Artif. Intell. **78**(1), 507–545 (1995)
4. Wolfe, J.M.: Guided search 2.0 a revised model of visual search. Psychon. Bull. Rev. **1**(2), 202–238 (1994)
5. Simonyan, K., Vedaldi, A., Zisserman, A.: Deep inside convolutional networks: visualising image classification models and saliency maps. In: ICLR Workshop (2014)
6. Zeiler, M.D., Fergus, R.: Visualizing and understanding convolutional networks. In: Fleet, D., Pajdla, T., Schiele, B., Tuytelaars, T. (eds.) ECCV 2014. LNCS, vol. 8689, pp. 818–833. Springer, Heidelberg (2014). doi:10.1007/978-3-319-10590-1_53

7. Cao, C., Liu, X., Yang, Y., Yu, Y., Wang, J., Wang, Z., Huang, Y., Wang, L., Huang, C., Xu, W., et al.: Look and think twice: capturing top-down visual attention with feedback convolutional neural networks. In: ICCV (2015)
8. Zhou, B., Khosla, A., Lapedriza, A., Oliva, A., Torralba, A.: Learning deep features for discriminative localization (2016)
9. Bach, S., Binder, A., Montavon, G., Klauschen, F., Müller, K.R., Samek, W.: On pixel-wise explanations for non-linear classifier decisions by layer-wise relevance propagation. PloS One **10**(7), e0130140 (2015)
10. Everingham, M., Van Gool, L., Williams, C.K.I., Winn, J., Zisserman, A.: The pascal visual object classes (VOC) challenge. Int. J. Comput. Vis. **88**(2), 303–338 (2010)
11. Lin, T.-Y., Maire, M., Belongie, S., Hays, J., Perona, P., Ramanan, D., Dollár, P., Zitnick, C.L.: Microsoft COCO: common objects in context. In: Fleet, D., Pajdla, T., Schiele, B., Tuytelaars, T. (eds.) ECCV 2014. LNCS, vol. 8693, pp. 740–755. Springer, Heidelberg (2014). doi:10.1007/978-3-319-10602-1_48
12. Plummer, B.A., Wang, L., Cervantes, C.M., Caicedo, J.C., Hockenmaier, J., Lazebnik, S.: Flickr30k entities: collecting region-to-phrase correspondences for richer image-to-sentence models. In: CVPR (2015)
13. Baluch, F., Itti, L.: Mechanisms of top-down attention. Trends Neurosci. **34**(4), 210–224 (2011)
14. Treisman, A.M., Gelade, G.: A feature-integration theory of attention. Cogn. Psychol. **12**(1), 97–136 (1980)
15. Desimone, R., Duncan, J.: Neural mechanisms of selective visual attention. Ann. Rev. Neurosci. **18**(1), 193–222 (1995)
16. Reynolds, J.H., Heeger, D.J.: The normalization model of attention. Neuron **61**(2), 168–185 (2009)
17. Abrial, J.-R.: On B. In: Bert, D. (ed.) B 1998. LNCS, vol. 1393, pp. 1–8. Springer, Heidelberg (1998). doi:10.1007/BFb0053350
18. Beck, D.M., Kastner, S.: Top-down and bottom-up mechanisms in biasing competition in the human brain. Vis. Res. **49**(10), 1154–1165 (2009)
19. Zhou, B., Khosla, A., Lapedriza, A., Oliva, A., Torralba, A.: Object detectors emerge in deep scene cnns. In: ICLR (2015)
20. Springenberg, J.T., Dosovitskiy, A., Brox, T., Riedmiller, M.: Striving for simplicity: the all convolutional net. arXiv preprint (2014). arXiv:1412.6806
21. Oquab, M., Bottou, L., Laptev, I., Sivic, J.: Is object localization for free?-weakly-supervised learning with convolutional neural networks. In: CVPR (2015)
22. Pathak, D., Krahenbuhl, P., Darrell, T.: Constrained convolutional neural networks for weakly supervised segmentation. In: ICCV (2015)
23. Papandreou, G., Chen, L.C., Murphy, K., Yuille, A.L.: Weakly-and semi-supervised learning of a dcnn for semantic image segmentation. In: ICCV (2015)
24. Pinheiro, P.O., Collobert, R.: From image-level to pixel-level labeling with convolutional networks. In: CVPR (2015)
25. Fang, H., Gupta, S., Iandola, F., Srivastava, R.K., Deng, L., Dollár, P., Gao, J., He, X., Mitchell, M., Platt, J.C., et al.: From captions to visual concepts and back. In: CVPR (2015)
26. Pinheiro, P.H., Collobert, R.: Recurrent convolutional neural networks for scene parsing. In: ICLR (2014)
27. Kemeny, J.G., Snell, J.L., et al.: Finite Markov Chains. Springer, New York, Berlin, Heidelberg, Tokyo (1960)
28. Krizhevsky, A., Sutskever, I., Hinton, G.E.: Imagenet classification with deep convolutional neural networks. In: NIPS (2012)

29. Simonyan, K., Zisserman, A.: Very deep convolutional networks for large-scale image recognition. In: ICLR (2015)
30. Szegedy, C., Liu, W., Jia, Y., Sermanet, P., Reed, S., Anguelov, D., Erhan, D., Vanhoucke, V., Rabinovich, A.: Going deeper with convolutions. In: CVPR (2015)
31. Zhou, B., Lapedriza, A., Xiao, J., Torralba, A., Oliva, A.: Learning deep features for scene recognition using places database. In: NIPS (2014)
32. Yosinski, J., Clune, J., Nguyen, A., Fuchs, T., Lipson, H.: Understanding neural networks through deep visualization. arXiv preprint (2015). arXiv:1506.06579
33. Caffe: convolutional architecture for fast feature embedding. In: ACM International Conference on Multimedia (2014)
34. Chatfield, K., Simonyan, K., Vedaldi, A., Zisserman, A.: Return of the devil in the details: delving deep into convolutional nets. In: BMVC (2014)
35. Caffe Model Zoo. https://github.com/BVLC/caffe/wiki/Model-Zoo
36. Russakovsky, O., Deng, J., Su, H., Krause, J., Satheesh, S., Ma, S., Huang, Z., Karpathy, A., Khosla, A., Bernstein, M., Berg, A.C., Fei-Fei, L.: Imagenet large scale visual recognition challenge. Int. J. Comput. Vis. (IJCV) 115(3), 211–252 (2015)
37. Sermanet, P., Eigen, D., Zhang, X., Mathieu, M., Fergus, R., LeCun, Y.: Overfeat: integrated recognition, localization and detection using convolutional networks. In: ICLR (2014)
38. Arbeláez, P., Pont-Tuset, J., Barron, J., Marques, F., Malik, J.: Multiscale combinatorial grouping. In: CVPR (2014)
39. Zitnick, C.L., Dollár, P.: Edge boxes: locating object proposals from edges. In: Fleet, D., Pajdla, T., Schiele, B., Tuytelaars, T. (eds.) ECCV 2014. LNCS, vol. 8693, pp. 391–405. Springer, Heidelberg (2014). doi:10.1007/978-3-319-10602-1_26

Learning Recursive Filters for Low-Level Vision via a Hybrid Neural Network

Sifei Liu[1], Jinshan Pan[1,2], and Ming-Hsuan Yang[1(✉)]

[1] UC Merced, Merced, USA
{sliu32,mhyang}@ucmerced.edu
[2] Dalian University of Technology, Dalian, China
sdluran@gmail.com

Abstract. In this paper, we consider numerous low-level vision problems (e.g., edge-preserving filtering and denoising) as recursive image filtering via a hybrid neural network. The network contains several spatially variant recurrent neural networks (RNN) as equivalents of a group of distinct recursive filters for each pixel, and a deep convolutional neural network (CNN) that learns the weights of RNNs. The deep CNN can learn regulations of recurrent propagation for various tasks and effectively guides recurrent propagation over an entire image. The proposed model does not need a large number of convolutional channels nor big kernels to learn features for low-level vision filters. It is significantly smaller and faster in comparison with a deep CNN based image filter. Experimental results show that many low-level vision tasks can be effectively learned and carried out in real-time by the proposed algorithm.

1 Introduction

Recursive filters, also called Infinite Impulse Response (IIR) filters, are efficient algorithms that account for signals with infinite duration. As such, recursive implementations are commonly exploited to accelerate image filtering methods, such as spatially invariant/variant Gaussian filters [1–3], bilateral filters [4] and domain transforms [5]. However, few methods are developed based on recursive formulations for low-level vision tasks mainly due to the difficulty in filter design.

Recently, several deep CNN based methods have been proposed for low-level vision tasks [6–10]. A convolutional filter can be considered as equivalent to a finite impulse response (FIR) filter. Unlike IIR filters, it is easier to design FIR filters at the expense of using more parameters to support non-local dependency. In deep CNNs, Xu et al. [7] approximate a number of edge-preserving filters by a data-driven approach which uses hundreds of convolutional channels to support spatially variant filtering or large (up to 16×16) kernels to support global convolution. In spite of using a large number of parameters, this model does not present local image structures well. Furthermore, it is difficult to extend the deep

Electronic supplementary material The online version of this chapter (doi:10. 1007/978-3-319-46493-0_34) contains supplementary material, which is available to authorized users.

B. Leibe et al. (Eds.): ECCV 2016, Part IV, LNCS 9908, pp. 560–576, 2016.
DOI: 10.1007/978-3-319-46493-0_34

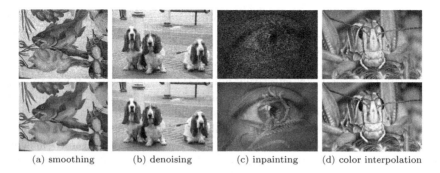

(a) smoothing   (b) denoising   (c) inpainting   (d) color interpolation

Fig. 1. Several applications of the proposed algorithm. (a) Approximation of relative total variation (RTV) [11] for edge-preserving smoothing. (b) Denoising. (c) Restoration of an image with random 50 % pixels occluded. (d) Restoration of an image with only 3 % color informations retained. Several applications of the proposed algorithm. (Color figure online)

CNN model to other low-level vision problems such as colorization and image completion.

Figure 1 shows a number of low-level vision tasks, e.g., denoising and inpainting, which can be efficiently carried out by the proposed algorithm. In this work, we incorporate a group of RNNs as an equivalent of a recursive filter. As an important class of neural networks, RNNs have been used for modeling contextual information in sequential data [12–14]. The linear formulation of a RNN is equivalent to a first order recursive filter, and the weight matrix corresponds to the coefficients. In addition, higher order recursive filters can be formulated with several RNNs integrated in cascade, or in parallel. To design a data-driven RNN filter, a straightforward approach is to take each pixel as a hidden recurrent node in a two-dimensional (2D) spatial sequence [15–17], and use the recurrent structure to learn the propagation weight matrix. However, a standard RNN uses an invariant weight matrix, which makes all pixels share one single recursive filter. Thus, this approach cannot be directly applied to filters that are conditioned on an input image with spatially variant structures, e.g. edge-preserving smoothing.

To address these issues, we propose a spatially variant RNN by introducing a weight map conditioned on the input image structure. The map has a set of distinct values for each node which control the node-wise recurrent propagation, or equivalently, each node has a distinct recursive filter. The weight map is associated with an image representation that reveals important structures e.g., salient edges (useful for edge-preserving smoothing and denoising). It can be jointly trained through a deep CNN that is combined with RNNs in an end-to-end fashion. The proposed hybrid network is shown in Fig. 3, which is significantly different from existing pure data-driven CNN models [6–10]. It is worth emphasizing that the CNN is not used to extract hierarchical image features, but to learn the coefficients of RNNs. We show that a variety of low-level vision tasks can be carried out as recursive image filtering by the proposed neural network.

The contributions of this work are summarized as: (a) A hybrid neural network is proposed to learn recursive filters for low-level vision tasks. The network contains several spatially variant RNNs as equivalents of a group of distinct recursive filters for each pixel, and a deep CNN that learns the weights of the RNNs. (b) The deep CNN effectively guides the propagation of RNNs through learned regulations in a data-driven fashion. Specifically, the weight map from the CNN is highly correlated to the corresponding image structures, which plays an important role in low-level vision problems. (c) The proposed model achieves promising results without any special design, regularization of the coefficients, pre-training or post-processing, and is suitable for real-time applications.

2   Related Work

Low-Level Vision. The recent years have witnessed significant advances in numerous low-level vision problems due to the use of designed priors and propagation methods under the guidance of image structures. In edge-preserving image smoothing, the key problem is to design structural priors to preserve sharp edges. Some explicit weight-averaging filters, e.g., bilateral filters [18] and guided image filters [19] exploit internal or guided image structures to preserve the edges of filtered images. Most energy-based edge-preserving methods explicitly or implicitly design adaptive weight maps through image structures (e.g., image gradients), such as edge-preserving decompositions [20], relative total variation [11], to achieve this goal. In PDE-based image processing, the edge-preserving effect is achieved by hand-craft anisotropic diffusion operators [21]. These adaptive weight maps control whether the image regions should be smoothed or not, and similar ideas have been used in image denoising and inpainting.

Numerous recent image processing methods, e.g., colorization [22,23] and image matting [23,24], involve propagation that is equivalent to implicitly filtering an image according to its structure. Although significant progress has been made, solving any of these problems is not a trivial task as specific operations are required. Furthermore, it is difficult to solve them in a unified framework.

Deep Learning Models. Several data-driven deep learning methods for low-level vision have been explored in recent years [6–10]. One significant advantage is that these data-driven models are good approximations to multiple conventional filters/enhancers via one learning paradigm. The uniform edge-preserving CNN filter [7] achieves 200 times acceleration against some conventional methods. In addition, CNNs have been applied to image denoising [25–27], super resolution [10], and deconvolution [6], among others. However, there are two factors that limit the performance of deep CNN based models. First, these models are generally large due to numerous convolutional operations. Second, it is difficult to generalize CNN based models to a variety of low-level vision problems. As another class of neural networks, RNNs have been recently exploited for high-level vision problems such as object recognition [14] and scene labeling [13], through applying recurrent propagations over spatial domain. In this work, we show that recurrent structures can be better exploited for effective and efficient image filtering for low-level vision.

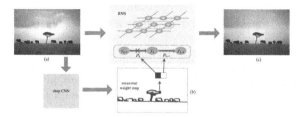

Fig. 2. An illustrative example of the proposed model for edge-preserving image smoothing with a single RNN. The deep CNN generates a weight map (b) that guides the propagation of the RNN. We consider an image as a group of sequences, and take the left-to-right recurrent propagation in 1D as an example, where k denotes a spatial location. For a single RNN, the weight map corresponds to the edges of an image and can be clearly visualized. When p_k is close to zero, it cuts off the propagations from $k - 1$ to k so that the edge is preserved (i.e., near boundary). On the other hand, p_{k+1} maintains the propagation from k to $k + 1$ so that the image is smoothed at any non-edge location. The CNN and RNN are jointly trained (see Fig. 1).

3   Recursive Filter via RNNs

The proposed model contains two parts, a deep CNN, and a set of RNNs that take the output of the CNN as their input. Different from existing CNN based methods [6–8], the filtered images are generated only through the set of RNNs. The deep CNN, on the other hand, does not contribute any features or outputs for the filtered result. Instead, it learns the internal regulations (see Fig. 2, an example of a single RNN for edge-preserving smoothing) to guide the propagation process for each hidden node. In terms of the network structure, the deep CNN does not need to have a large number of channels or large kernels, since it focuses on learning the guidance for recurrent propagation instead of kernels for low-level filters. In comparison to recent deep CNN models for [6,7,10], the proposed model is much more efficient and light-weighted.

In this section, we describe the algorithmic details of the low-level part in the proposed network. We show that a recursive filter can be equally expressed by a set of RNNs, with its coefficients corresponding to the weight matrices of RNNs. We present two schemes to combine a group of RNNs for constructing a recursive filter, and show how to ensure the stability of the system.

3.1   Preliminaries of Recursive Filters

We first review recursive IIR filters [28] before presenting the hybrid neural network. For illustration, we use a one-dimensional (1D) convolution FIR filter, in which the output $y[k]$ is composed of a weighed sum of the input signal $x[k - i]$, expressed in the causal, discrete-time formulation:

$$y[k] = \sum_{i=0}^{M} a_i x[k-i], \quad k = 0, \ldots, N, \tag{1}$$

where N is the range of the sequence to be filtered, k is one point in the signal which practically corresponds to a frame, character, or pixel in the sequential data. A 1D IIR filter is different in the sense that the output also contains the previously computed values:

$$y[k] = \sum_{i=0}^{P} a_i x[k-i] + \sum_{j=1}^{Q} b_j y[k-j], \quad k = 0, \ldots, N, \tag{2}$$

where $x[k-i]$ is the input and $y[k]$ is the output sequence, $\{a_i, b_i\} \in \mathbb{R}$ are filter coefficients, P and M are the order of convolutional filters, and Q is the order of the recursive filter. A 0-th order IIR filter is reduced to a FIR filter. An IIR filter (2) is equivalent to a FIR filter (1) by recursively expanding its second term. For an impulse input, the expended terms can be infinitely long with exponentially decaying coefficients. That is, an IIR filter bypasses a long convolution, with only a few coefficients involved. The causal IIR system from (2) is equivalently described in the z-domain by its transfer function $H(z)$ [28]:

$$H(z) = \frac{\sum_{i=0}^{P} a_i z^{-i}}{1 - \sum_{j=1}^{Q} b_j z^{-j}}. \tag{3}$$

It describes the frequency properties of IIRs independent of specific input signals. The output sequence $y[k]$ can be obtained from the z-transform of the input signal $X(z)$ and $H(z)$ by computing the inverse z-transform of $H(z)X(z)$. Note that for causal filters, we need to define the initial conditions of the input signal $x[-i]$ where $i = 1, \ldots, P$, and the output signal $y[-j]$ where $j = 1, \ldots, Q$. In this work, we set the initial conditions to zero in the training process since we only use up to the second order ($Q \le 2$). Similarly, we obtain the testing results by padding image borders.

3.2 Recursive Decomposition

The Q-th order IIR filter can be decomposited into a set of first order filters in two different forms.

Cascade Decomposition. A recursive filter can be described in the z-plane with poles and zeros [28]. Denoting the poles by $\{p_j\}_{j=1}^{Q}$ and the nonzero zeros by $\{q_i\}_{i=1}^{P}$, we have

$$H(z) = H_r(z) H_c(z),$$
$$H_r = \prod_{j=1}^{Q} \frac{g_j}{1 - p_j z^{-1}}, \quad H_c = \prod_{i=1}^{P} h_i(1 - q_i z^{-1}), \tag{4}$$

where H_r and H_c are recursive and convolutional parts, g_i and h_j are their coefficients respectively, $\{g, h, p, q\} \in \mathbb{C}$. While H_c is equivalent to an ordinary

0-th order FIR that can be constructed through a convolutional layer, H_r is a cascade of Q first order IIR units. The spatial domain formulation with respect to the j-th unit from sequences of input $x^r[k]$ and output $y^r[k]$ is:

$$y_j^r[k] = g_j x_j^r[k] + p_j y_j^r[k-1].$$ (5)

We denote this formulation as a cascade decomposition.

Parallel Decomposition. In [29], it is shown that $H(z)$ can be decomposed into a sum of Q first order recursive filters:

$$H(z) = H_r(z) + H_c(z),$$
$$H_r = \sum_{j=1}^{Q} \frac{g_j}{1-p_j z^{-1}}, \quad H_c = \sum_{i=0}^{P-Q} h_i z^{-i},$$ (6)

where $\{g, h, p\} \in \mathbb{C}$. Similar to the cascade formulation, the parallel decomposition also contains a FIR H_c with different kernel size $(P - Q + 1)$ of a convolutional layer, as well as Q summed first order IIR units. Each one shares the same formulation as in (5). We refer to this formulation as a parallel decomposition.

To simplify the framework, we do not apply H_c from (4) and (6) in this work. Therefore, the parallel way has $P = Q - 1$, which is greater than the cascade one with $P = 0$ when $Q > 1$. It is more amenable to be designed as a high-pass filter (e.g., for enhancement effect) compared to the cascade connection [28].

3.3   Constructing Recursive Filter via Linear RNNs

Single Linear RNN is 1st Order Filter. RNNs have been used to learn sequential data of varying length for various tasks. Let $x \in X$ be the input signal, $h \in H$ be the hidden state, and $\{W_x, W_h\}$ be the weight matrices, then the recurrent relation over spatial or time is modeled by

$$h[k] = f\{W_x x[k] + W_h(h[k-1] + b)\}.$$ (7)

The formulation (7) is slightly different from the first order recursive filter, as expressed in (5), where the sigmoid is often used for f to ensure the output is bounded and the recurrent system is stable in transition.

To model the recursive filter (5), we set f as an identity function $f(x) = x$, and $\{W_x, W_h\}$ as diagonal matrixes. We refer to this neural network as the Linear Recurrent Neural Network (LRNN) in this paper. With this method, we ignore the bias term in (7) and formulate LRNN using the dot product:

$$h[k] = g \cdot x[k] + p \cdot h[k-1],$$ (8)

where $x[k] \in \mathbb{R}^{n \times 1}$. The $\{g, p\} \in \mathbb{R}^{n \times 1}$ can be regarded as the diagonal values of W_x and W_h, where $\cdot$ is a dot product operator.

We further formulate (8) in a normalized filter which has unit gain at some specified frequency. For example, a low-pass filter commonly has unit gain at $z = 1$, which implies that its discrete impulse response should sum to one. Normalizing a filter is carried out by scaling its impulse response by an appropriate factor, where (8) is computed by setting $g = 1 - p$ such that the prediction of coefficients is reduced to estimating the parameter p only:

$$h[k] = (1 - p) \cdot x[k] + p \cdot h[k - 1]. \tag{9}$$

Its backward pass can be generalized by back propagation thorough time (BPTT) used in RNNs [30]. The derivations with respect to $h[k]$, denoted as $\theta[k]$ is,

$$\theta[k] = \delta[k] + p \cdot \theta[k + 1]. \tag{10}$$

The stability of LRNN (9) is different from the standard RNN (7) because the range of $h[k]$ is not controlled through some nonlinear functions (e.g., sigmoid). The output sequence is likely to go to infinity when p is greater than one. According to z-transform [28], the causal recursive system can be stabilized by regularizing p inside the unit circle $|p| < 1$, which we discuss in the next section. In addition, the propagation of (9) can reach to a long range when p is close to one, thereby enabling global propagation over an entire image.

Construction of High Order Filters. High order recursive filters [29] can be constructed by combining a group of LRNNs in cascade or parallel schemes as discussed in Sect. 3.2. In the cascade decomposition, LRNNs are stacked with the input signal passing through one to the next. In the parallel approach, each LRNN receives the input signal respectively, where the outputs are integrated with node-wise operations. The FIR terms (which we do not use in this work) can be implemented by convolutional layers that are integrated in the same way.

Two Dimensional Image. To filter an image we need to extend the 1D LRNN in (9) to 2D. We adopt a strategy similar to the 4-way directional propagation for two-dimensional data in [31]. First, the 1D LRNN is processed respectively along left-to-right, top-to-bottom and their reverse directions, as shown in Fig. 3. In any direction, we treat each row or column as 1D sequence. Taking the left-to-right case as an example, the LRNN scans each row from left to right. As a result, four hidden activation maps are generated. We integrate the four maps through selecting the optimal direction based on the maximum response at each location. This is carried out by a node-wise max pooling, which effectively selects the maximally responded direction as the desired information to be propagated and rejects noisy information from other directions. We note that the four directions can be executed in parallel for acceleration as they are independent.

4   Learning Spatially Variant Recursive Filters

One problem with the standard or linear RNN in (7) and (9) is that it takes a group of fixed weights for every point k. Filtering an image in such a way means that each pixel is processed with the same recursive filter, which is not effective for many low-level tasks, e.g., edge-preserving smoothing, where the edge and texture areas need to be processed differently.

4.1 Spatially Variant LRNN

Therefore, we propose a spatially variant recurrent network by extending the fixed parameter p to $p[k]$, so that each pixel has a distinct recursive filter. Taking edge-preserving smoothing as an example (see Fig. 2), and considering the first order recursive filter (a single LRNN), $\{p[k]\}$, namely the weight map, is supposed to be associate with an "edge map". Specifically, the weights that lie on the edge regions should be close to zero such that the input $x[k]$ is preserved, and one otherwise so that the other regions can be smoothed out via recurrent propagation (as in (9)). For higher order recursive filters and some other tasks, e.g., inpainting, the weight maps are more complex and do not correspond to some explicit image structures. However, they reveal the propagation regulations with respect to specific tasks, which are conditioned on the input image.

We have two types of input to a LRNN, i.e., an image X and a weight map P. Given a hidden node $h[k]$ and similar to (9), the spatially variant LRNN is:

$$h[k] = (1 - p[k]) \cdot x[k] + p[k] \cdot h[k-1].\qquad(11)$$

In the back propagation pass, the derivative $\sigma[k]$ with respect to $p[k]$ is:

$$\sigma[k] = \theta[k] \cdot (h[k-1] - x[k]),\qquad(12)$$

such that the weight map $p[k]$ of a spatially variant recursive filter can be learned.

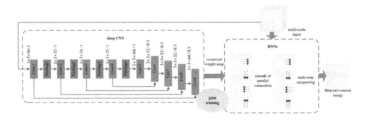

Fig. 3. Proposed hybrid network that contains a group of RNNs to filter/restore an image and a deep CNN to learn to propagate the RNNs. The process of filtering/restoration is carried out through RNNs with two inputs and one output result. Both parts are trained jointly in an end-to-end fashion. (Color figure online)

4.2 Learning LRNN Weight Maps via CNN

We propose to learn the weight maps through a deep CNN, which takes an image to be filtered as its input. The CNN can be small and deep since it learns the guidance of propagation instead of learning convolutional filters. The proposed network is equipped with 10 convolutional layers. The first five layers are followed by a max pooling, while the other five ones are followed by a bilinear upsampling. The RELUs are used between adjacent convolutional layers. In addition, 4 links between corresponding downsampling and upsampling units connect feature maps of the same size at different levels in order to learn better representations, where similar settings can be found in [32]. We use 3×3 kernels with the number of channels ranging from 16 to 64, as shown in Fig. 3.

To connect with the LRNNs of different directions (4 distinct hidden layers, see Fig. 3), the weight map can be equally split into 4 parts for the 4 directions. To simplify the network implementation, each axis is allowed to share the same part (e.g., the left-to-right and right-to-left directions share a common horizontal map). Thus, for each LRNN we have two parts of weight map for the x and y-axis, respectively. We find that better results can be obtained by linearly transferring the RGB input of LRNN into a feature space, e.g., through one convolutional layer, and then perform LRNN on the proposed transform space. We are then able to select a best direction at each point on the feature space using a node-wise integration strategy, which combines the four directions. The combined maps can be transferred back to a 3-channel image through another convolutional layer. We configure both of the transform convolutional layers using 3×3 kernels. We set the number of channels in each hidden layer of LRNNs to $m = 16$ in all experiments so that each $x[k]$ and $p[k]$ in (11) are vectors with dimension of 16. The number of output channels for CNN is $2 \times m \times R$, where R denotes the order of recursive filter (equivalently the number of LRNNs), e.g., it should be set to 64 with a network configured with a $2nd$ order recursive filter. Importantly, we equip a hyperbolic tangent function as the topmost layer of the CNN, so that the weight map is restricted to $(-1, 1)$ to stabilize the LRNN, as introduced in Sect. 3.3.

5   Experimental Results

We apply the proposed model to a variety of low-level vision problems including edge-preserving smoothing, enhancement, image denoising, inpainting and colorization. All the following applications share the same model size as well as the run-time. Specifically, our model reaches real-time performance on images of 320×240 pixels (QVGA) using a Nvidia Geforce GTX Ti GPU with 3 GB memory. Due to space limitation, we present some results in this section. More and large images are included in the supplemental materials. The trained models and source code will be made available at sifeiliu.net/project.

Experimental Settings. To obtain rich information from different scales of an image, we use multi-scale input through downsampling the color image with ratio of $\{1/2, 1/4, 1/8, 1/16\}$, resizing them to the original size, and concatenating them as a single input. Therefore, nodes in a LRNN can reach to a more global range via processing on coarse scales, without increasing the number of coefficient maps to be learned. We use 96×96 image patches as the original inputs that are randomly cropped from training images, which are then processed as multi-scale input through average pooling and upsampling. All patches are augmented through perturbation using the similarity transform, so as to adapt to the scale-variant property for some existing filters. We use about 400,000 image patches that are randomly cropped from the MS COCO dataset [33] in the training

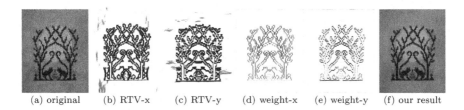

(a) original   (b) RTV-x   (c) RTV-y   (d) weight-x   (e) weight-y   (f) our result

Fig. 4. Visualization of weight maps for approximating the RTV filter using first order recursive filter. (a) original image; (b) and (c): manually designed edge prior maps in RTV for x and y axes; (d) and (e): weight maps generated from the CNN for x and y; (f) our filtered result.

process with data augmentations. For all the following applications, the order of filter is set to 2 with specific structures shown in Fig. 3. The only difference lies in the integration manner with respect to these 2 LRNNs, e.g., in cascade or parallel way, which is specified in each application.

5.1 Edge-Preserving Smoothing

Xu et al. in [7] propose a CNN model to approximate various filters such that many conventional implementations can be accelerated significantly. We show that the proposed algorithm is able to approximate various filters and performs favorably against [7] in terms of accuracy, run time, and model size. We selectively learn a group of local and global filters including bilateral filter (BLF) [18], weighted least square (WLS) [20], L0 smoothing [34], RTV texture smoothing [11], weighted median filter (WMF) [35], and rolling guidance filter (RGF) [36].

Visualization of Weight Maps. We first demonstrate through a first order recursive filter using a single scale RGB image without any linear transformation as the input to both CNN and LRNN, where the weight maps with respect to x and y axes accurately correspond to the edges of the image. This is carried out by setting the number of output channels of the CNN to 2, such that the maps for x and y axes, which are then shared by all channels of the hidden layers in the LRNN, can be obtained and visualized.

We note that some edge-preserving methods, e.g., RTV [11], focus on extracting the main structures of an image. The RTV weight maps (Fig. 4(b) and (c)), which reflects the main structures of an image, determine whether the image regions are smoothed or not in the propagation step [11]. Interestingly, the learned data-driven weight maps by our model (see Fig. 4(d) and (e)) have the similar effects to the hand-craft maps. They accurately locate the image edges with cleaner background, and effectively remove the grid-like texture in the input image, as shown in Fig. 4(f). As our method is data-driven, different weight maps are generated for different tasks. The data-driven approach allows the proposed algorithm to be generalized to a variety of applications without hand-designed priors.

Table 1. Quantitative evaluations for learning various image filters.

Methods	L_0 [34]	BLF [18]	RTV [11]	RGF [36]	WLS [20]	WMF [35]	Shock [37]
PSNRs of [7]	32.8	38.4	32.1	35.9	36.2	31.6	30.0
Our PSNRs	30.9	**38.6**	**37.1**	**42.2**	**39.4**	**34.0**	**31.8**

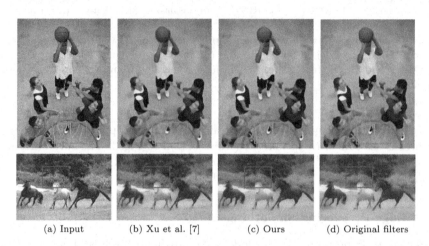

(a) Input   (b) Xu et al. [7]   (c) Ours   (d) Original filters

Fig. 5. Approximation of edge-preserving filters. (a) input images. (b) results by Xu et al. [7]. (c) results of our model. (d) results from the original filters. First row: Results by approximating RGF [36]. Second row: Results by approximating WLS smoothing [20].

Quantitative Comparisons. We show the applications that are based on a second order filter. Specifically for edge-smoothing tasks (e.g., L0, WLS and RTV, etc.), the two LRNNs are connected in cascade since it is more amicable to low-pass filtering. On the other hand, we use the parallel integration scheme for learning shock filters [37] with enhancement effects. We quantitatively evaluate the proposed algorithm against [7] on the dataset used in [7]. Table 1 shows that our method generates high quality filtered images with significant improvements over the state-of-art CNN based method. In addition, the proposed model is much smaller and faster due to the hybrid structure, which can be used to accelerate more conventional algorithms, e.g., region covariance filter (RegCov) [38] and local laplacian filter (LLF) [39].

Figure 5 shows approximations of RGF [36] and WLS smoothing [20]. The results by our model preserve more accurate structures without including details that are supposed to be removed. The filtered images are visually the same with those generated by the original implementations. We note that the CNN based filter [7] misses important local structures by approximating the RGF, and includes some details that should be removed by approximating the WLS, as shown in Fig. 5(b). More results are included in the supplemental material.

Run Time and Model Size. We evaluate all the following methods with the same computer introduced in the beginning of this section. The proposed method achieves favorable speed as shown in Table 2, and is significantly smaller than that of [7] (0.54 vs 5.60 MB). It can speed up a variety of conventional filters for denoising, inpainting and colorization, etc.

Table 2. Run-time (second) performance against [7] and some conventional methods at different resolutions of color images.

Method	BLF [18]	WLS [20]	RTV [11]	WMF [35]	EPLL [40]	Levin [22]	Xu et al. [7]	Ours
QVGA	0.46	0.71	0.81	0.67	33.82	2.10	0.23	**0.05**
VGA	1.41	3.40	3.51	1.70	466.79	9.24	0.83	**0.16**
720p	3.18	11.38	9.94	3.80	1395.61	31.09	2.10	**0.37**

5.2   Image Denoising

The proposed method can be used to learn filters for image denoising. Specifically, we train the model with thousands of patches in which white Gaussian noise with the standard deviation of 0.01 is added. At the output end, the model is supervised by the original image patches. We apply the parallel connection to the two LRNNs to preserve more details. The other settings are the same as those used in Sect. 5.1.

Figure 6 shows the results with two state-of-art algorithms including expected patch log likelihood (EPLL) [40] and a deep CNN based model [9]. The denoising method [40] is based on image patch prior, and the vectorization-based deep CNN [9] used for image denoising is based on a two-layer convolutional model. Although significant noise has been removed by both methods, some details are not preserved well and the restored results are over-smoothed. The learned filter by the proposed model generates clear images with well preserved fine details, as shown in Fig. 6(d). It retains important image contents such as brushstrokes of oil painting in the first row, or pattens of the feather in the second row.

The deep CNN method is likely to be slower in terms of run-time (was not specified in [9]) due to large model size, while the EPLL takes more than hundreds of seconds to process one image. In contrast, the proposed method achieves several order of magnitude accelerations (see Sect. 5.1).

5.3   Image Propagation Examples

In this section, we validate the effectiveness of propagation-study of the network by restoring images from degraded frames with masks. In this case, the deep CNN learns more complex rules than the edges that are used for smoothing. We apply the proposed model to two interesting applications for pixel and color interpolation (e.g., inpainting and colorizaiton). Specifically, we retain randomly 50 % pixels for the image interpolation and 3 % monochrome pixels for the color interpolation. The proposed model takes degraded images as well as masks as input channels, and learns the weight maps with the supervision of the original

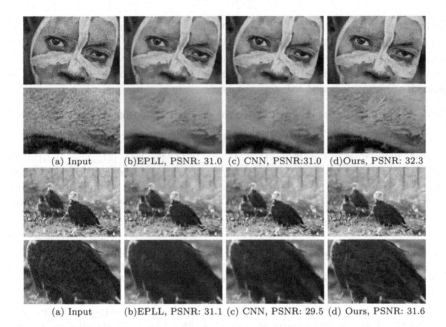

(a) Input   (b)EPLL, PSNR: 31.0 (c) CNN, PSNR:31.0 (d)Ours, PSNR: 32.3

(a) Input   (b)EPLL, PSNR: 31.1 (c) CNN, PSNR: 29.5 (d) Ours, PSNR: 31.6

Fig. 6. Image denoising. (b) denotes the results of image patch prior based method EPLL [40]. (c) denotes the results by end-to-end trainable CNN method [9].

images. It learns complex regulations including identifying the occluded pixels and restoring them by propagating information from the other pixels, and identifying the image structures such that the restored pixels can naturally adapt to them.

Pixel Interpolation. The goal of pixel interpolation is to restore the values in missing regions according to a mask of pixels that are to be restored. In this model, the random mask is concatenated with the degraded image as the input, such that it learns the propagation rules according to all the visual information. The LRNNs filter the degraded image according to the learned rules and output an interpolated result. It does not require explicit regulations to compute the missing data, nor expensive optimizations for each test image. Therefore, it is accurate and fast to execute through forward propagation.

We show that the proposed algorithm can restore fine details (e.g., pattens on a butterfly) in Fig. 7 with randomly half pixels are masked. We discover that the proposed model trained for image interpolation can be directly applied to image inpainting with texts, as shown in the first row of Fig. 8. Both results are visually very similar to the original images, as shown in Figs. 7(b) and 8(c).

Color Interpolation. The proposed algorithm can be applied to color image restoration and editing despite providing little color information, e.g., user inputs. Given the brightness channels (y channel in the YCbCr color space), we retain only 3 % color pixels, as shown in Fig. 8(e). Taking a degraded images

(a) occluded	(b) restored	(c) original

Fig. 7. Pixel interpolation. (a) input image. (b) restored image for masking half pixels in (a).

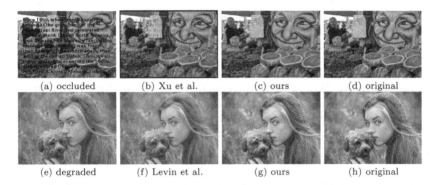

(a) occluded	(b) Xu et al.	(c) ours	(d) original
(e) degraded	(f) Levin et al.	(g) ours	(h) original

Fig. 8. First row: image inpainting on the regions of texts with comparison to Xu et al. [8]. We directly apply the pixel interpolation model to inpainting. The model does not require any network finetuning on texts masks. Second row: color interpolation with comparison to Levin et al. [22]. (Color figure online)

as well as the masks as input, the proposed model learns to propagate the known colors to other regions to be restored. Specifically, the proposed model generates favorable results (visually the same with the original image) compared to the state-of-the-art method [22], which takes more than 3 s on a QVGA image.

The proposed model can also be generalized to image re-colorization by applying the brightness channel of an input image, and directly taking 3 % color pixels from the monochrome channels in a reference image of the same size. The re-colored image has the contents of the original image, but with the color style of the reference image. Figure 9 shows one example of image re-colorization. More results are included in the supplemental material.

6 Conclusion

In this work, we propose a novel hybrid neural network for low-level vision tasks, based on the recursive filters whose coefficients can be learned by a deep CNN. We show that the proposed model is faster as well as significantly smaller than the deep CNN filters. It is also more generic, and can effectively and efficiently

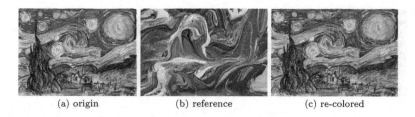

(a) origin   (b) reference   (c) re-colored

Fig. 9. Re-colorization by applying the brightness channel of (a) and directly taking 3 % color pixels from the monochrome channels in a reference image with the same size. (Color figure online)

handle a variety of applications including image smoothing, image denoising and pixel interpolation.

Acknowledgments. This work is supported in part by the NSF CAREER grant #1149783, NSF IIS grant #1152576, gifts from Adobe/Nvidia Preliminary work is carried out at Multimedia Laboratory in Chinese University of Hong Kong.

References

1. Deriche, R.: Recursively implementating the Gaussian and its derivatives. Ph.D. thesis, INRIA (1993)
2. Young, I.T., Vliet, L.J.V.: Recursive implementation of the gaussian filter. Sig. Process. **44**(2), 139–151 (1995)
3. Tan, S., Dale, J.L., Johnston, A.: Performance of three recursive algorithms for fast space-variant gaussian filtering. Real-Time Imaging **9**(3), 215–228 (2003)
4. Yang, Q.: Recursive bilateral filtering. In: ECCV
5. Gastal, E.S., Oliveira, M.M.: Domain transform for edge-aware image and video processing. ACM TOG **30**, 69 (2011)
6. Xu, L., Ren, J.S., Liu, C., Jia, J.: Deep convolutional neural network for image deconvolution. In: NIPS, pp. 1790–1798 (2014)
7. Xu, L., Ren, J.S., Yan, Q., Liao, R., Jia, J.: Deep edge-aware filters. In: ICML, pp. 1669–1678 (2015)
8. Sj, R.J., Li, X., Qiong, Y., Wenxiu, S.: Shepard convolutional neural networks. In: NIPS, pp. 901–909 (2015)
9. Ren, J.S.J., Xu, L.: On vectorization of deep convolutional neural networks for vision tasks. In: AAAI, pp. 1840–1846 (2015)
10. Dong, C., Loy, C.C., He, K., Tang, X.: Learning a deep convolutional network for image super-resolution. In: ECCV, pp. 184–199 (2014)
11. Xu, L., Yan, Q., Xia, Y., Jia, J.: Structure extraction from texture via relative total variation. ACM TOG **31**(6), 139 (2012)
12. Graves, A., Fernndez, S., Schmidhuber, J.: Multi-dimensional recurrent neural networks. In: ICANN (2007)
13. Byeon, W., Breuel, T.M., Raue, F., Liwicki, M.: Scene labeling with LSTM recurrent neural networks. In: CVPR, pp. 3547–3555 (2015)
14. Visin, F., Kastner, K., Cho, K., Matteucci, M., Courville, A., Bengio, Y.: Renet: a recurrent neural network based alternative to convolutional networks. arXiv preprint arXiv:1505.00393 (2015)

15. Oord, A.V.D., Kalchbrenner, N., Kavukcuoglu, K.: Pixel recurrent neural networks. arXiv preprint arXiv:1601.06759 (2016)
16. Stollenga, M.F., Byeon, W., Liwicki, M., Schmidhuber, J.: Parallel multi-dimensional LSTM, with application to fast biomedical volumetric image segmentation. arXiv preprint arXiv:1506.07452 (2015)
17. Kalchbrenner, N., Danihelka, I., Graves, A.: Grid long short-term memory. arXiv preprint arXiv:1507.01526 (2015)
18. Tomasi, C., Manduchi, R.: Bilateral filtering for gray and color images. In: ICCV, pp. 839–846 (1998)
19. He, K., Sun, J., Tang, X.: Guided image filtering. IEEE PAMI 35(6), 1397–1409 (2013)
20. Farbman, Z., Fattal, R., Lischinski, D., Szeliski, R.: Edge-preserving decompositions for multi-scale tone and detail manipulation. ACM TOG 27, 67 (2008)
21. Weickert, J.: Anisotropic Diffusion in Image Processing. B.G Teubner Stuttgart, Stuttgart (1998)
22. Levin, A., Lischinski, D., Weiss, Y.: Colorization using optimization. ACM TOG 23(3), 689–694 (2004)
23. Xu, L., Yan, Q., Jia, J.: A sparse control model for image and video editing. ACM TOG 32(6), 197:1–197:10 (2013)
24. Levin, A., Lischinski, D., Weiss, Y.: A closed-form solution to natural image matting. IEEE PAMI 30(2), 228–242 (2008)
25. Burger, H.C., Schuler, C.J., Harmeling, S.: Image denoising: can plain neural networks compete with bm3d? In: CVPR, pp. 2392–2399 (2012)
26. Xie, J., Xu, L., Chen, E.: Image denoising and inpainting with deep neural networks. In: NIPS, pp. 341–349 (2012)
27. Agostinelli, F., Anderson, M.R., Lee, H.: Adaptive multi-column deep neural networks with application to robust image denoising. In: NIPS, pp. 1493–1501 (2013)
28. John, G.P., Dimitris, G.M.: Digital Signal Processing, Principles, Algorithms, and Applications. Prentice Hall, Upper Saddle River (1996)
29. Gastal, E.S., Oliveira, M.M.: High-order recursive filtering of non-uniformly sampled signals for image and video processing. Comput. Graph. Forum 34, 81–93 (2015)
30. Graves, A., Schmidhuber, J.: Offline handwriting recognition with multidimensional recurrent neural networks. In: NIPS (2009)
31. Chen, L., Barron, J.T., Papandreou, G., Murphy, K., Yuille, A.L.: Semantic image segmentation with task-specific edge detection using CNNS and a discriminatively trained domain transform. arXiv preprint arXiv:1511.03328 (2015)
32. Long, J., Shelhamer, E., Darrell, T.: Fully convolutional networks for semantic segmentation. In: CVPR (2015)
33. Lin, T., Maire, M., Belongie, S., Bourdev, L.D., Girshick, R.B., Hays, J., Perona, P., Ramanan, D., Dollár, P., Zitnick, C.L.: Microsoft COCO: common objects in context (2014)
34. Xu, L., Lu, C., Xu, Y., Jia, J.: Image smoothing via l-0 gradient minimization. ACM TOG 30, 174 (2011)
35. Zhang, Q., Xu, L., Jia, J.: 100+ times faster weighted median filter (WMF). In: CVPR, pp. 2830–2837 (2014)
36. Zhang, Q., Shen, X., Xu, L., Jia, J.: Rolling guidance filter. In: ECCV, pp. 815–83 (2014)
37. Osher, S., Rudin, L.I.: Feature-oriented image enhancement using shock filters. SIAM J. Numer. Anal. 27(4), 919–940 (1990)

38. Karacan, L., Erdem, E., Erdem, A.: Structure-preserving image smoothing via region covariances. ACM TOG **32**, 176 (2013)
39. Paris, S., Hasinoff, S.W., Kautz, J.: Local laplacian filters: edge-aware image processing with a laplacian pyramid. ACM Trans. Graph. **30**(4), 68 (2011)
40. Zoran, D., Weiss, Y.: From learning models of natural image patches to whole image restoration. In: ICCV, pp. 479–486 (2011)

Learning Representations
for Automatic Colorization

Gustav Larsson[1]([⊠]), Michael Maire[2], and Gregory Shakhnarovich[2]

[1] University of Chicago, Chicago, USA
larsson@cs.uchicago.edu
[2] Toyota Technological Institute at Chicago, Chicago, USA
{mmaire,greg}@ttic.edu

Abstract. We develop a fully automatic image colorization system. Our approach leverages recent advances in deep networks, exploiting both low-level and semantic representations. As many scene elements naturally appear according to multimodal color distributions, we train our model to predict per-pixel color histograms. This intermediate output can be used to automatically generate a color image, or further manipulated prior to image formation. On both fully and partially automatic colorization tasks, we outperform existing methods. We also explore colorization as a vehicle for self-supervised visual representation learning.

1 Introduction

Colorization of grayscale images is a simple task for the human imagination. A human need only recall that sky is blue and grass is green; for many objects, the mind is free to hallucinate several plausible colors. The high-level comprehension required for this process is precisely why the development of fully automatic colorization algorithms remains a challenge. Colorization is thus intriguing beyond its immediate practical utility in graphics applications. Automatic colorization serves as a proxy measure for visual understanding. Our work makes this connection explicit; we unify a colorization pipeline with the type of deep neural architectures driving advances in image classification and object detection.

Both our technical approach and focus on fully automatic results depart from past work. Given colorization's importance across multiple applications (*e.g.* historical photographs and videos [40], artist assistance [31,37]), much research strives to make it cheaper and less time-consuming [3,5–7,13,19,21,26,41]. However, most methods still require some level of user input [3,6,13,19,21,33]. Our work joins the relatively few recent efforts on fully automatic colorization [5,7,26]. Some [5,7] show promising results on typical scenes (*e.g.* landscapes), but their success is limited on complex images with foreground objects.

At a technical level, existing automatic colorization methods often employ a strategy of finding suitable reference images and transferring their color onto a target grayscale image [7,26]. This works well if sufficiently similar reference

Electronic supplementary material The online version of this chapter (doi:10. 1007/978-3-319-46493-0_35) contains supplementary material, which is available to authorized users.

B. Leibe et al. (Eds.): ECCV 2016, Part IV, LNCS 9908, pp. 577–593, 2016.
DOI: 10.1007/978-3-319-46493-0_35

Fig. 1. Our automatic colorization of grayscale input; more examples in Figs. 3 and 4. (Color figure online)

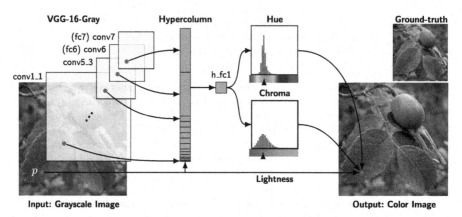

Fig. 2. System overview. We process a grayscale image through a deep convolutional architecture (VGG) [36] and take spatially localized multilayer slices (hypercolumns) [14,25,27], as per-pixel descriptors. We train our system end-to-end for the task of predicting hue and chroma distributions for each pixel p given its hypercolumn descriptor. These predicted distributions determine color assignment at test time. (Color figure online)

images can be found, but is difficult for unique grayscale input images. Such a strategy also requires processing a large repository of reference images at test time. In contrast, our approach is free of database search and fast at test time. Section 2 provides a complete view of prior methods, highlighting differences.

Our approach to automatic colorization converts two intuitive observations into design principles. First, semantic information matters. In order to colorize arbitrary images, a system must interpret the semantic composition of the scene (what is in the image: faces, cars, plants, ...) as well as localize objects (where things are). Deep convolutional neural networks (CNNs) can serve as tools to incorporate semantic parsing and localization into a colorization system.

Our second observation is that while some scene elements can be assigned a single color with high confidence, others (*e.g.* clothes or cars) may draw from many suitable colors. Thus, we design our system to predict a color histogram, instead of a single color, at every image location. Figure 2 sketches the CNN architecture we use to connect semantics with color distributions by exploiting features across multiple abstraction levels. Section 3 provides details.

Section 4 experimentally validates our algorithm against competing methods [7,41] in two settings: fully (grayscale input only) and partially (grayscale input with reference global color histogram) automatic colorization. Across every metric and dataset [30,32,42], our method achieves the best performance. Our system's fully automatic output is superior to that of prior methods relying on additional information such as reference images or ground-truth color histograms. To ease the comparison burden for future research, we propose a new colorization benchmark on ImageNet [32]. We also experiment with colorization itself as an objective for learning visual representations from scratch, thereby replacing use of ImageNet pretraining in a traditional semantic labeling task.

Section 5 summarizes our contributions: (1) a novel technical approach to colorization, bringing semantic knowledge to bear using CNNs, and modeling color distributions; (2) state-of-the-art performance across fully and partially automatic colorization tasks; (3) a new ImageNet colorization benchmark; (4) proof of concept on colorization for self-supervised representation learning.

2 Related Work

Previous colorization methods broadly fall into three categories: scribble-based [15,21,24,31,44], transfer [3,6,13,19,26,38,41], and automatic direct prediction [5,7].

Scribble-based methods, introduced by Levin *et al.* [21], require manually specifying desired colors of certain regions. These scribble colors are propagated under the assumption that adjacent pixels with similar luminance should have similar color, with the optimization relying on Normalized Cuts [35]. Users can interactively refine results via additional scribbles. Further advances extend similarity to texture [24,31], and exploit edges to reduce color bleeding [15].

Transfer-based methods rely on availability of related *reference* image(s), from which color is transferred to the target grayscale image. Mapping between source and target is established automatically, using correspondences between local descriptors [3,26,41], or in combination with manual intervention [6,19]. Excepting [26], reference image selection is at least partially manual.

In contrast to these method families, our goal is *fully automatic* colorization. We are aware of two recent efforts in this direction. Deshpande *et al.* [7] colorize an entire image by solving a linear system. This can be seen as an extension of patch-matching techniques [41], adding interaction terms for spatial consistency. Regression trees address the high-dimensionality of the system. Inference requires an iterative algorithm. Most of the experiments are focused on a dataset (SUN-6) limited to images of a few scene classes, and best results are obtained when the scene class is known at test time. They also examine another partially automatic task, in which a desired global color histogram is provided.

The work of Cheng *et al.* [5] is perhaps most related to ours. It combines three levels of features with increasing receptive field: the raw image patch, DAISY features [39], and semantic features [23]. These features are concatenated and fed into a three-layer fully connected neural network trained with an L_2 loss. Only this last component is optimized; the feature representations are fixed.

Unlike [5,7], our system does not rely on hand-crafted features, is trained end-to-end, and treats color prediction as a histogram estimation task rather than as regression. Experiments in Sect. 4 justify these principles by demonstrating performance superior to the best reported by [5,7] across all regimes.

Two concurrent efforts also present feed-forward networks trained end-to-end for colorization. Iizuka *et al.* [16] propose a network that concatenates two separate paths, specializing in global and local features, respectively. This concatenation can be seen as a two-tiered hypercolumn; in comparison, our 16-layer hypercolumn creates a continuum between low- and high-level features. Their network is trained jointly for classification (cross-entropy) and colorization (L_2 loss in Lab). We initialize, but do not anchor, our system to a classification-based network, allowing for fine-tuning of colorization on unlabeled datasets.

Zhang *et al.* [45] similarly propose predicting color histograms to handle multi-modality. Some key differences include their usage of up-convolutional layers, deep supervision, and dense training. In comparison, we use a fully convolutional approach, with deep supervision implicit in the hypercolumn design, and, as Sect. 3 describes, memory-efficient training via spatially sparse samples.

3   Method

We frame the colorization problem as learning a function $f : \mathcal{X} \rightarrow \mathcal{Y}$. Given a grayscale image patch $\mathbf{x} \in \mathcal{X} = [0,1]^{S \times S}$, f predicts the color $\mathbf{y} \in \mathcal{Y}$ of its center pixel. The patch size $S \times S$ is the receptive field of the colorizer. The output space $\mathcal{Y}$ depends on the choice of color parameterization. We implement f according to the neural network architecture diagrammed in Fig. 2.

Motivating this strategy is the success of similar architectures for semantic segmentation [4,10,14,23,27] and edge detection [1,11,25,34,43]. Together with colorization, these tasks can all be viewed as image-to-image prediction problems, in which a value is predicted for each input pixel. Leading methods commonly adapt deep convolutional neural networks pretrained for image classification [32, 36]. Such classification networks can be converted to *fully convolutional* networks that produce output of the same spatial size as the input, *e.g.* using the shift-and-stitch method [23] or the more efficient *à trous* algorithm [4]. Subsequent training with a task-specific loss fine-tunes the converted network.

Skip-layer connections, which directly link low- and mid-level features to prediction layers, are an architectural addition beneficial for many image-to-image problems. Some methods implement skip connections directly through concatenation layers [4,23], while others equivalently extract per-pixel descriptors by reading localized slices of multiple layers [14,25,27]. We use this latter strategy and adopt the recently coined *hypercolumn* terminology [14] for such slices.

Though we build upon these ideas, our technical approach innovates on two fronts. First, we integrate domain knowledge for colorization, experimenting with output spaces and loss functions. We design the network output to serve as an intermediate representation, appropriate for direct or biased sampling. We introduce an energy minimization procedure for optionally biasing sampling towards a reference image. Second, we develop a novel and efficient computational strategy for network training that is widely applicable to hypercolumn architectures.

3.1   Color Spaces

We generate training data by converting color images to grayscale according to $L = \frac{R+G+B}{3}$. This is only one of many desaturation options and chosen primarily to facilitate comparison with Deshpande *et al.* [7]. For the representation of color predictions, using RGB is overdetermined, as lightness L is already known. We instead consider output color spaces with L (or a closely related quantity) conveniently appearing as a separate pass-through channel:

- **Hue/chroma.** Hue-based spaces, such as HSL, can be thought of as a color cylinder, with angular coordinate H (hue), radial distance S (saturation), and height L (lightness). The values of S and H are unstable at the bottom (black) and top (white) of the cylinder. HSV describes a similar color cylinder which is only unstable at the bottom. However, L is no longer one of the channels. We wish to avoid both instabilities and still retain L as a channel. The solution is a color bicone, where chroma (C) takes the place of saturation. Conversion to HSV is given by $V = L + \frac{C}{2}$, $S = \frac{C}{V}$.
- **Lab and $\alpha\beta$.** Lab (or L*a*b) is designed to be perceptually linear. The color vector (a, b) defines a Euclidean space where the distance to the origin determines chroma. Deshpande *et al.* [7] use a color space somewhat similar to Lab, denoted "ab". To differentiate, we call their color space $\alpha\beta$.

3.2   Loss

For any output color representation, we require a loss function for measuring prediction errors. A first consideration, also used in [5], is L_2 regression in Lab:

$$L_{\text{reg}}(\mathbf{x}, \mathbf{y}) = \|f(\mathbf{x}) - \mathbf{y}\|^2 \tag{1}$$

where $\mathcal{Y} = \mathbb{R}^2$ describes the (a, b) vector space. However, regression targets do not handle multimodal color distributions well. To address this, we instead predict distributions over a set of color bins, a technique also used in [3]:

$$L_{\text{hist}}(\mathbf{x}, \mathbf{y}) = D_{\text{KL}}(\mathbf{y}\|f(\mathbf{x})) \tag{2}$$

where $\mathcal{Y} = [0, 1]^K$ describes a histogram over K bins, and D_{KL} is the KL-divergence. The ground-truth histogram $\mathbf{y}$ is set as the empirical distribution in a rectangular region of size R around the center pixel. Somewhat surprisingly, our experiments see no benefit to predicting smoothed histograms, so we simply set $R = 1$. This makes $\mathbf{y}$ a one-hot vector and Eq. (2) the log loss. For histogram predictions, the last layer of neural network f is always a softmax.

There are several choices of how to bin color space. We bin the Lab axes by evenly spaced Gaussian quantiles ($\mu = 0, \sigma = 25$). They can be encoded separately for a and b (as marginal distributions), in which case our loss becomes the sum of two separate terms defined by Eq. (2). They can also be encoded as a joint distribution over a and b, in which case we let the quantiles form a 2D grid of bins. In our experiments, we set $K = 32$ for marginal distributions and

$K = 16 \times 16$ for joint. We determined these numbers, along with σ, to offer a good compromise of output fidelity and output complexity.

For hue/chroma, we only consider marginal distributions and bin axes uniformly in $[0, 1]$. Since hue becomes unstable as chroma approaches zero, we add a sample weight to the hue based on the chroma:

$$L_{\text{hue/chroma}}(\mathbf{x}, \mathbf{y}) = D_{\text{KL}}(\mathbf{y}_C \| f_C(\mathbf{x})) + \lambda_H y_C D_{\text{KL}}(\mathbf{y}_H \| f_H(\mathbf{x})) \qquad (3)$$

where $\mathcal{Y} = [0, 1]^{2 \times K}$ and $y_C \in [0, 1]$ is the sample pixel's chroma. We set $\lambda_H = 5$, roughly the inverse expectation of y_C, thus equally weighting hue and chroma.

3.3 Inference

Given network f trained according to a loss function in the previous section, we evaluate it at every pixel n in a test image: $\hat{\mathbf{y}}_n = f(\mathbf{x}_n)$. For the L_2 loss, all that remains is to combine each $\hat{\mathbf{y}}_n$ with the respective lightness and convert to RGB. With histogram predictions, we consider options for inferring a final color:

- **Sample.** Draw a sample from the histogram. If done per pixel, this may create high-frequency color changes in areas of high-entropy histograms.
- **Mode.** Take the $\arg\max_k \hat{y}_{n,k}$ as the color. This can create jarring transitions between colors, and is prone to vote splitting for proximal centroids.
- **Median.** Compute cumulative sum of $\hat{\mathbf{y}}_n$ and use linear interpolation to find the value at the middle bin. Undefined for circular histograms, such as hue.
- **Expectation.** Sum over the color bin centroids weighted by the histogram.

For Lab output, we achieve the best qualitative and quantitative results using expectations. For hue/chroma, the best results are achieved by taking the median of the chroma. Many objects can appear both with and without chroma, which means $C = 0$ is a particularly common bin. This mode draws the expectation closer to zero, producing less saturated images. As for hue, since it is circular, we first compute the complex expectation:

$$z = \mathbb{E}_{H \sim f_h(\mathbf{x})}[H] \triangleq \frac{1}{K} \sum_k [f_h(x)]_k e^{i\theta_k}, \quad \theta_k = 2\pi \frac{k + 0.5}{K} \qquad (4)$$

We then set hue to the argument of z remapped to lie in $[0, 1)$.

In cases where the estimate of the chroma is high and z is close to zero, the instability of the hue can create artifacts. A simple, yet effective, fix is chromatic fading: downweight the chroma if the absolute value of z is too small. We thus redefine the predicted chroma by multiplying it by a factor of $\max(\eta^{-1}|z|, 1)$. In our experiments, we set $\eta = 0.03$ (obtained via cross-validation).

Original   Chromatic fading

3.4   Histogram Transfer from Ground-Truth

So far, we have only considered the fully automatic color inference task. Deshpande *et al.* [7], test a separate task where the ground-truth histogram in the two non-lightness color channels of the original color image is made available.[1] In order to compare, we propose two histogram transfer methods. We refer to the predicted image as the *source* and the ground-truth image as the *target*.

Lightness-normalized quantile matching. Divide the RGB representation of both source and target by their respective lightness. Compute marginal histograms over the resulting three color channels. Alter each source histogram to fit the corresponding target histogram by quantile matching, and multiply by lightness. Though it does not exploit our richer color distribution predictions, quantile matching beats the cluster correspondence method of [7] (see Table 3).

Energy minimization. We phrase histogram matching as minimizing energy:

$$E = \frac{1}{N} \sum_n D_{\text{KL}}(\hat{\mathbf{y}}_n^* \| \hat{\mathbf{y}}_n) + \lambda D_{\chi^2}(\langle \hat{\mathbf{y}^*} \rangle, \mathbf{t}) \tag{5}$$

where N is the number of pixels, $\hat{\mathbf{y}}, \hat{\mathbf{y}}^* \in [0,1]^{N \times K}$ are the predicted and posterior distributions, respectively. The target histogram is denoted by $\mathbf{t} \in [0,1]^K$. The first term contains unary potentials that anchor the posteriors to the predictions. The second term is a symmetric χ^2 distance to promote proximity between source and target histograms. Weight λ defines relative importance of histogram matching. We estimate the source histogram as $\langle \hat{\mathbf{y}}^* \rangle = \frac{1}{N} \sum_n \hat{\mathbf{y}}_n^*$. We parameterize the posterior for all pixels n as: $\hat{\mathbf{y}}_n^* = \text{softmax}(\log \hat{\mathbf{y}}_n + \mathbf{b})$, where the vector $\mathbf{b} \in \mathbb{R}^K$ can be seen as a global bias for each bin. It is also possible to solve for the posteriors directly; this does not perform better quantitatively and is more prone to introducing artifacts. We solve for $\mathbf{b}$ using gradient descent on E and use the resulting posteriors in place of the predictions. In the case of marginal histograms, the optimization is run twice, once for each color channel.

3.5   Neural Network Architecture and Training

Our base network is a fully convolutional version of VGG-16 [36] with two changes: (1) the classification layer (fc8) is discarded, and (2) the first filter layer (conv1_1) operates on a single intensity channel instead of mean-subtracted RGB. We extract a hypercolumn descriptor for a pixel by concatenating the features at its spatial location in all layers, from data to conv7 (fc7), resulting in a 12,417 channel descriptor. We feed this hypercolumn into a fully connected layer with 1024 channels (h_fc1 in Fig. 2), to which we connect output predictors.

Processing each pixel separately in such manner is quite costly. We instead run an entire image through a single forward pass of VGG-16 and approximate hypercolumns using bilinear interpolation. Even with such sharing, densely extracting hypercolumns requires significant memory (1.7 GB for 256 × 256 input).

---

[1] Note that if the histogram of the L channel were available, it would be possible to match lightness to lightness exactly and thus greatly narrow down color placement.

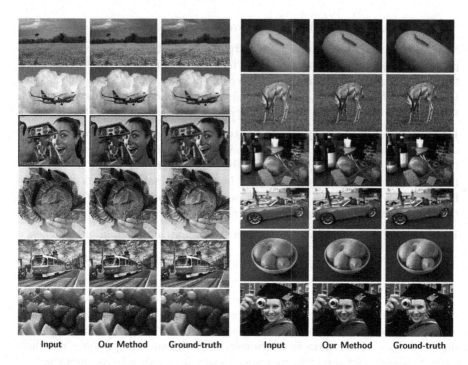

| Input | Our Method | Ground-truth | Input | Our Method | Ground-truth |

Fig. 3. Fully automatic colorization results on ImageNet/ctest10k. Our system reproduces known object color properties (*e.g.* faces, sky, grass, fruit, wood), and coherently picks colors for objects without such properties (*e.g.* clothing). (Color figure online)

To fit image batches in memory during training, we instead extract hypercolumns at only a sparse set of locations, implementing a custom Caffe [20] layer to directly compute them.[2] Extracting batches of only 128 hypercolumn descriptors per input image, sampled at random locations, provides sufficient training signal. In the backward pass of stochastic gradient descent, an interpolated hypercolumn propagates its gradients to the four closest spatial cells in each layer. Locks ensure atomicity of gradient updates, without incurring any performance penalty. This drops training memory for hypercolumns to only 13 MB per image.

We initialize with a version of VGG-16 pretrained on ImageNet, adapting it to grayscale by averaging over color channels in the first layer and rescaling appropriately. Prior to training for colorization, we further fine-tune the network for one epoch on the ImageNet classification task with grayscale input. As the original VGG-16 was trained without batch normalization [17], scale of responses in internal layers can vary dramatically, presenting a problem for learning atop their hypercolumn concatenation. Liu *et al.* [22] compensate for such variability

---

[2] https://github.com/gustavla/autocolorize.

Fig. 4. Additional results. *Top:* our automatic colorizations of these ImageNet examples are difficult to distinguish from real color images. *Bottom:* B & W photographs. (Color figure online)

by applying layer-wise L_2 normalization. We use the alternative of balancing hypercolumns so that each layer has roughly unit second moment ($\mathbb{E}[X^2] \approx 1$); the supplementary material provides additional details.

4   Experiments

Starting from pretrained VGG-16-Gray, described in the previous section, we attach h_fc1 and output prediction layers with Xavier initialization [12], and fine-tune the entire system for colorization. We consider multiple prediction layer variants: Lab output with L_2 loss, and both Lab and hue/chroma marginal or joint histogram output with losses according to Eqs. (2) and (3). We train each system variant end-to-end for one epoch on the 1.2 million images of the ImageNet training set, each resized to at most 256 pixels in smaller dimension.

| Grayscale only | GT Scene | GT Scene & Hist | Grayscale only | GT Histogram | Ground-truth |
| Welsh et al. [41] | Deshpande et al. [7] | | | Our Method | |

Fig. 5. SUN-6. GT Scene: test image scene class is available. GT Hist: test image color histogram is available. We obtain colorizations with visual quality better than those from prior work, even though we do not exploit reference images or known scene class. Our energy minimization method (Sect. 3.4) for GT Hist further improves results. In either mode, our method appears less dependent on spatial priors: note splitting of the sky in the first row and correlation of green with actual grass in the last row. (Color figure online)

Table 1. ImageNet/cval1k. Validation performance of system variants. Hue/chroma is best, but only with chromatic fading.

Model\Metric	RMSE	PSNR
No colorization	0.343	22.98
Lab, L_2	0.318	24.25
Lab, $K = 32$	0.321	24.33
Lab, $K = 16 \times 16$	0.328	24.30
Hue/chroma, $K = 32$	0.342	23.77
+ chromatic fading	**0.299**	**24.45**

Table 2. ImageNet/cval1k. Ablation study of hypercolumn components.

Model\Metric	RMSE	PSNR
data..fc7	**0.299**	**24.45**
data..conv5_3	0.306	24.13
conv4_1..fc7	0.302	**24.45**
conv5_1..fc7	0.307	24.38
fc6..fc7	0.323	24.22
fc7	0.324	24.19

A single epoch takes approximately 17 h on a GTX Titan X GPU. At test time, colorizing a single 512×512 pixel image takes 0.5 s.

We setup two disjoint subsets of the ImageNet validation data for our own use: 1000 validation images (**cval1k**) and 10000 test images (**ctest10k**). Each set has a balanced representation for ImageNet categories, and excludes any images encoded as grayscale, but may include images that are naturally grayscale (*e.g.* closeup of nuts and bolts), where an algorithm should know not to add color. Category labels are discarded; only images are available at test time. We propose **ctest10k** as a standard benchmark with the following metrics:

- **RMSE**: root mean square error in $\alpha\beta$ averaged over all pixels [7].
- **PSNR**: peak signal-to-noise ratio in RGB calculated per image [5]. We use the arithmetic mean of PSNR over images, instead of the geometric mean as in Cheng *et al.* [5]; geometric mean is overly sensitive to outliers.

By virtue of comparing to ground-truth color images, quantitative colorization metrics can penalize reasonable, but incorrect, color guesses for many objects (*e.g.* red car instead of blue car) more than jarring artifacts. This makes qualitative results for colorization as important as quantitative; we report both.

Figures 1, 3, and 4 show example test results of our best system variant, selected according to performance on the validation set and trained for a total of 10 epochs. This variant predicts hue and chroma and uses chromatic fading during image generation. Table 1 provides validation benchmarks for all system variants, including the trivial baseline of no colorization. On ImageNet test (**ctest10k**), our selected model obtains 0.293 (RMSE, $\alpha\beta$, avg/px) and 24.94 dB (PSNR, RGB, avg/im), compared to 0.333 and 23.27 dB for the baseline.

Table 2 examines the importance of different neural network layers to colorization; it reports validation performance of ablated systems that include only the specified subsets of layers in the hypercolumn used to predict hue and chroma. Some lower layers may be discarded without much performance loss, yet higher layers alone (`fc6..fc7`) are insufficient for good colorization.

Our ImageNet colorization benchmark is new to a field lacking an established evaluation protocol. We therefore focus on comparisons with two recent papers [5,7], using their self-defined evaluation criteria. To do so, we run our ImageNet-trained hue and chroma model on two additional datasets:

- **SUN-A** [30] is a subset of the SUN dataset [42] containing 47 object categories. Cheng *et al.* [5] train a colorization system on 2688 images and report results on 1344 test images. We were unable to obtain the list of test images, and therefore report results averaged over five random subsets of 1344 SUN-A images. We do not use any SUN-A images for training.
- **SUN-6**, another SUN subset, used by Deshpande *et al.* [7], includes images from 6 scene categories (beach, castle, outdoor, kitchen, living room, bedroom). We compare our results on 240 test images to those reported in [7] for their method as well as for Welsh *et al.* [41] with automatically matched reference images as in [26]. Following [7], we consider another evaluation regime in which ground-truth target color histograms are available.

Figure 5 shows a comparison of results on SUN-6. Forgoing usage of ground-truth global histograms, our fully automatic system produces output qualitatively superior to methods relying on such side information. Tables 3 and 4 report quantitative performance corroborating this view. The partially automatic systems in Table 4 adapt output to fit global histograms using either: (C) cluster correspondences [7], (Q) quantile matching, or (E) our energy minimization described in Sect. 3.4. Our quantile matching results are superior to those of [7] and our new energy minimization procedure offers further improvement.

Table 3. SUN-6. Comparison with competing methods.

Method	RMSE
Grayscale (no colorization)	0.285
Welsh *et al.* [41]	0.353
Deshpande *et al.* [7]	0.262
+ GT Scene	0.254
Our Method	**0.211**

Table 4. SUN-6 (GT Hist). Comparison using ground-truth histograms. Results for Deshpande *et al.* [7] use GT Scene.

Method	RMSE
Deshpande *et al.* (C) [7]	0.236
Deshpande *et al.* (Q)	0.211
Our Method (Q)	0.178
Our Method (E)	**0.165**

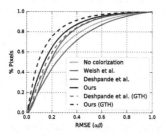

Fig. 6. SUN-6. Cumulative histogram of per pixel error (higher = more pixels with lower error). Results for Deshpande *et al.* [7] use GT Scene.

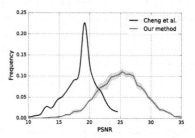

Fig. 7. SUN-A. Histogram of per-image PSNR for [5] and our method. The highest geometric mean PSNR reported for experiments in [5] is 24.2, vs. **32.7±2.0** for us.

Figures 6 and 7 compare error distributions on SUN-6 and SUN-A. As in Table 3, our fully automatic method dominates all competing approaches, even those which use auxiliary information. It is only outperformed by the version of itself augmented with ground-truth global histograms. On SUN-A, Fig. 7 shows clear separation between our method and [5] on per-image PSNR.

Our supplementary material provides anecdotal comparisons to one additional method, that of Charpiat *et al.* [2], which can be considered an automatic system if reference images are available. Unfortunately, source code of [2] is not available and reported time cost is prohibitive for large-scale evaluation (30 minutes per image). We were thus unable to benchmark [2] on large datasets.

With regard to concurrent work, Zhang *et al.* [45] include a comparison of our results to their own. The two systems are competitive in terms of quantitative measures of colorization accuracy. Their system, set to produce more vibrant colors, has an advantage in terms of human-measured preferences. In contrast, an off-the-shelf VGG-16 network for image classification, consuming our system's color output, more often produces correct labels, suggesting a realism advantage. We refer interested readers to [45] for the full details of this comparison.

Fig. 8. Failure modes. *Top row, left-to-right:* texture confusion, too homogeneous, color bleeding, unnatural color shifts (×2). *Bottom row:* inconsistent background, inconsistent chromaticity, not enough color, object not recognized (upside down face partly gray), context confusion (sky). (Color figure online)

Fig. 9. Sampling colorizations. *Left:* Image & 3 samples; *Right:* Uncertainty map. (Color figure online)

Though we achieve significant improvements over prior state-of-the-art, our results are not perfect. Figure 8 shows examples of significant failures. Minor imperfections are also present in some of the results in Figs. 3 and 4. We believe a common failure mode correlates with gaps in semantic interpretation: incorrectly identified or unfamiliar objects and incorrect segmentation. In addition, there are "mistakes" due to natural uncertainty of color – *e.g.* the graduation robe at the bottom right of Fig. 3 is red, but could as well be purple.

Since our method produces histograms, we can provide interactive means of biasing colorizations according to user preferences. Rather than output a single color per pixel, we can sample color for image regions and evaluate color uncertainty. Specifically, solving our energy minimization formulation (Eq. (5)) with global biases **b** that are not optimized based on a reference image, but simply "rotated" through color space, induces changed color preferences throughout the image. The uncertainty in the predicted histogram modulates this effect.

Figure 9 shows multiple sampled colorizations, together with a visualization of uncertainty. Here, uncertainty is the entropy of the predicted hue multiplied by the chroma. Our distributional output and energy minimization framework open the path for future investigation of human-in-the-loop colorization tools.

Table 5. ImageNet/cval1k. Compares methods of initialization before colorization training. Hue/chroma with chromatic fading is used in both cases (see in Table 1).

Initialization	RMSE	PSNR
Classifier	0.299	24.45
Random	0.311	24.25

Table 6. VOC 2012 segmentation validation set. Pretraining uses ImageNet images (X), labels (Y). VOC 2012 images are in color (C).

Initialization	Architecture	X	Y	C	mIU (%)
Classifier	VGG-16	✓	✓		64.0
Colorizer	VGG-16	✓			50.2
Random	VGG-16				32.5
Classifier [9,29]	AlexNet	✓	✓	✓	48.0
BiGAN [9]	AlexNet	✓		✓	34.9
Inpainter [29]	AlexNet	✓		✓	29.7
Random [29]	AlexNet			✓	19.8

4.1 Representation Learning

High-level visual understanding is essential for the colorization of grayscale images, motivating our use of an ImageNet pretrained network as a starting point. But with enough training data, perhaps we can turn this around and use colorization as means of learning networks for capturing high-level visual representations. Table 5 shows that a colorization network, trained from scratch using only unlabeled color images, is surprisingly competitive. It converges slower, but requires not more than twice the number of epochs.

Our preliminary work shows that the networks learned via training colorization from scratch generalize well to other visual tasks. This is significant because such training requires no human annotation effort. It follows a recent trend of learning representations through self-supervision (*e.g.* context prediction [8], solving jigsaw puzzles [28], inpainting [29], adversarial feature learning [9]).

We examine self-supervised colorization as a replacement for supervised ImageNet pretraining on the Pascal VOC 2012 semantic segmentation task, with results on grayscale validation set images. We train colorization from scratch on ImageNet (Table 5) and fine-tune for Pascal semantic segmentation. We make the one adjustment of employing cross-validated early stopping to avoid overfitting. Table 6 shows this strategy to be promising as a drop-in replacement for supervised ImageNet pretraining. Self-supervised colorization more than halfway bridges the gap between random initialization and supervised pretraining.

As VGG-16 is a more performant architecture, comparison with prior work is not straightforward. Yet, Table 6 still indicates that colorization is a front-runner among the self-supervision methods, leading to an 18-point improvement in mIU over the baseline. To our knowledge, 50.2 % is the highest reported result that does not supplement training with additional annotated data [18].

5 Conclusion

We present a system that demonstrates state-of-the-art ability to automatically colorize grayscale images. Two novel contributions enable this progress: a deep neural architecture that is trained end-to-end to incorporate semantically meaningful features of varying complexity into colorization, and a color histogram prediction framework that handles uncertainty and ambiguities inherent in colorization while preventing jarring artifacts. Our fully automatic colorizer produces strong results, improving upon previously leading methods by large margins on all datasets tested; we also propose a new large-scale benchmark for automatic image colorization, and establish a strong baseline with our method to facilitate future comparisons. Our colorization results are visually appealing even on complex scenes, and allow for effective post-processing with creative control via color histogram transfer and intelligent, uncertainty-driven color sampling. We further reveal colorization as a promising avenue for self-supervised visual learning.

Acknowledgements. We thank Ayan Chakrabarti for suggesting lightness-normalized quantile matching and for useful discussions, and Aditya Deshpande and Jason Rock for discussions on their work. We gratefully acknowledge the support of NVIDIA Corporation with the donation of GPUs for this research.

References

1. Bertasius, G., Shi, J., Torresani, L.: Deepedge: a multi-scale bifurcated deep network for top-down contour detection. In: CVPR (2015)
2. Charpiat, G., Bezrukov, I., Altun, Y., Hofmann, M., Schölkopf, B.: Machine learning methods for automatic image colorization. In: Computational Photography: Methods and Applications. CRC Press (2010)
3. Charpiat, G., Hofmann, M., Schölkopf, B.: Automatic image colorization via multimodal predictions. In: Forsyth, D., Torr, P., Zisserman, A. (eds.) ECCV 2008. LNCS, vol. 5304, pp. 126–139. Springer, Heidelberg (2008). doi:10.1007/978-3-540-88690-7_10
4. Chen, L.C., Papandreou, G., Kokkinos, I., Murphy, K., Yuille, A.L.: Semantic image segmentation with deep convolutional nets and fully connected CRFs. In: ICLR (2015)
5. Cheng, Z., Yang, Q., Sheng, B.: Deep colorization. In: ICCV (2015)
6. Chia, A.Y.S., Zhuo, S., Gupta, R.K., Tai, Y.W., Cho, S.Y., Tan, P., Lin, S.: Semantic colorization with internet images. ACM Trans. Graph. (TOG) 30(6) (2011)
7. Deshpande, A., Rock, J., Forsyth, D.: Learning large-scale automatic image colorization. In: ICCV (2015)
8. Doersch, C., Gupta, A., Efros, A.A.: Unsupervised visual representation learning by context prediction. In: Proceedings of the IEEE International Conference on Computer Vision, pp. 1422–1430 (2015)
9. Donahue, J., Krähenbühl, P., Darrell, T.: Adversarial feature learning (2016). arXiv preprint arXiv:1605.09782
10. Farabet, C., Couprie, C., Najman, L., LeCun, Y.: Learning hierarchical features for scene labeling. IEEE Trans. Pattern Anal. Mach. Intell. **35**(8), 1915–1929 (2013)
11. Ganin, Y., Lempitsky, V.S.: N^4-fields: neural network nearest neighbor fields for image transforms. In: ACCV (2014)
12. Glorot, X., Bengio, Y.: Understanding the difficulty of training deep feedforward neural networks. In: AISTATS (2010)

13. Gupta, R.K., Chia, A.Y.S., Rajan, D., Ng, E.S., Zhiyong, H.: Image colorization using similar images. In: ACM International Conference on Multimedia (2012)
14. Hariharan, B., an R. Girshick, P.A., Malik, J.: Hypercolumns for object segmentation and fine-grained localization. In: CVPR (2015)
15. Huang, Y.C., Tung, Y.S., Chen, J.C., Wang, S.W., Wu, J.L.: An adaptive edge detection based colorization algorithm and its applications. In: ACM International Conference on Multimedia (2005)
16. Iizuka, S., Simo-Serra, E., Ishikawa, H.: Let there be color!: joint end-to-end learning of global and local image priors for automatic image colorization with simultaneous classification. ACM Trans. Graph. (Proc. SIGGRAPH 2016) 35(4) (2016)
17. Ioffe, S., Szegedy, C.: Batch normalization: accelerating deep network training by reducing internal covariate shift. In: ICML (2015)
18. Ion, A., Carreira, J., Sminchisescu, C.: Probabilistic joint image segmentation and labeling by figure-ground composition. Int. J. Comput. Vision **107**(1), 40–57 (2014)
19. Irony, R., Cohen-Or, D., Lischinski, D.: Colorization by example. In: Eurographics Symposium on Rendering (2005)
20. Jia, Y., Shelhamer, E., Donahue, J., Karayev, S., Long, J., Girshick, R., Guadarrama, S., Darrell, T.: Caffe: convolutional architecture for fast feature embedding (2014). arXiv preprint arXiv:1408.5093
21. Levin, A., Lischinski, D., Weiss, Y.: Colorization using optimization. ACM Trans. Graph. (TOG) **23**(3), 689–694 (2004)
22. Liu, W., Rabinovich, A., Berg, A.C.: Parsenet: looking wider to see better (2015). arXiv preprint arXiv:1506.04579
23. Long, J., Shelhamer, E., Darrell, T.: Fully convolutional networks for semantic segmentation. In: CVPR (2015)
24. Luan, Q., Wen, F., Cohen-Or, D., Liang, L., Xu, Y.Q., Shum, H.Y.: Natural image colorization. In: Eurographics Conference on Rendering Techniques (2007)
25. Maire, M., Yu, S.X., Perona, P.: Reconstructive sparse code transfer for contour detection and semantic labeling. In: Cremers, D., Reid, I., Saito, H., Yang, M.-H. (eds.) ACCV 2014. LNCS, vol. 9006, pp. 273–287. Springer, Heidelberg (2015). doi:10.1007/978-3-319-16817-3_18
26. Morimoto, Y., Taguchi, Y., Naemura, T.: Automatic colorization of grayscale images using multiple images on the web. In: SIGGRAPH: Posters (2009)
27. Mostajabi, M., Yadollahpour, P., Shakhnarovich, G.: Feedforward semantic segmentation with zoom-out features. In: CVPR (2015)
28. Noroozi, M., Favaro, P.: Unsupervised learning of visual representations by solving jigsaw puzzles (2016). arXiv preprint arXiv:1603.09246
29. Pathak, D., Krahenbuhl, P., Donahue, J., Darrell, T., Efros, A.A.: Context encoders: feature learning by inpainting. In: CVPR (2016)
30. Patterson, G., Xu, C., Su, H., Hays, J.: The sun attribute database: beyond categories for deeper scene understanding. Int. J. Comput. Vision **108**(1–2), 59–81 (2014)
31. Qu, Y., Wong, T.T., Heng, P.A.: Manga colorization. ACM Trans. Graph. (TOG) **25**(3), 1214–1220 (2006)
32. Russakovsky, O., Deng, J., Su, H., Krause, J., Satheesh, S., Ma, S., Huang, Z., Karpathy, A., Khosla, A., Bernstein, M., Berg, A.C., Fei-Fei, L.: ImageNet large scale visual recognition challenge. Int. J. Comput. Vision (IJCV) **115**(3), 211–252 (2015)
33. Sapiro, G.: Inpainting the colors. In: ICIP (2005)

34. Shen, W., Wang, X., Wang, Y., Bai, X., Zhang, Z.: Deepcontour: a deep convolutional feature learned by positive-sharing loss for contour detection. In: CVPR (2015)
35. Shi, J., Malik, J.: Normalized cuts and image segmentation. IEEE Trans. Pattern Anal. Mach. Intell. **22**(8), 888–905 (2000)
36. Simonyan, K., Zisserman, A.: Very deep convolutional networks for large-scale image recognition. In: ICLR (2015)
37. Sỳkora, D., Buriánek, J., Žára, J.: Unsupervised colorization of black-and-white cartoons. In: International Symposium on Non-Photorealistic Animation and Rendering (2004)
38. Tai, Y.W., Jia, J., Tang, C.K.: Local color transfer via probabilistic segmentation by expectation-maximization. In: CVPR (2005)
39. Tola, E., Lepetit, V., Fua, P.: A fast local descriptor for dense matching. In: CVPR (2008)
40. Tsaftaris, S.A., Casadio, F., Andral, J.L., Katsaggelos, A.K.: A novel visualization tool for art history and conservation: automated colorization of black and white archival photographs of works of art. Stud. Conserv. **59**(3), 125–135 (2014)
41. Welsh, T., Ashikhmin, M., Mueller, K.: Transferring color to greyscale images. ACM Trans. Graph. (TOG) **21**(3), 277–280 (2002)
42. Xiao, J., Hays, J., Ehinger, K.A., Oliva, A., Torralba, A.: Sun database: large-scale scene recognition from abbey to zoo. In: CVPR (2010)
43. Xie, S., Tu, Z.: Holistically-nested edge detection. In: ICCV (2015)
44. Yatziv, L., Sapiro, G.: Fast image and video colorization using chrominance blending. IEEE Trans. Image Process. **15**(5), 1120–1129 (2006)
45. Zhang, R., Isola, P., Efros, A.A.: Colorful image colorization. In: ECCV (2016)

Poster Session 5

Deep Reconstruction-Classification Networks for Unsupervised Domain Adaptation

Muhammad Ghifary[1,3]($\boxtimes$), W. Bastiaan Kleijn[1], Mengjie Zhang[1],
David Balduzzi[1], and Wen Li[2]

[1] Victoria University of Wellington, Wellington, New Zealand
{bastiaan.kleijn,mengjie.zhang}@ecs.vuw.ac.nz, david.balduzzi@vuw.ac.nz
[2] ETH Zürich, Zürich, Switzerland
liwen@vision.ee.ethz.ch
[3] Weta Digital, Wellington, New Zealand
mghifary@gmail.com

Abstract. In this paper, we propose a novel unsupervised domain adaptation algorithm based on deep learning for visual object recognition. Specifically, we design a new model called Deep Reconstruction-Classification Network (DRCN), which jointly learns a shared encoding representation for two tasks: (i) supervised classification of labeled source data, and (ii) unsupervised reconstruction of unlabeled target data. In this way, the learnt representation not only preserves discriminability, but also encodes useful information from the target domain. Our new DRCN model can be optimized by using backpropagation similarly as the standard neural networks.

We evaluate the performance of DRCN on a series of cross-domain object recognition tasks, where DRCN provides a considerable improvement (up to ~8% in accuracy) over the prior state-of-the-art algorithms. Interestingly, we also observe that the reconstruction pipeline of DRCN transforms images from the source domain into images whose appearance resembles the target dataset. This suggests that DRCN's performance is due to constructing a single composite representation that encodes information about both the structure of target images and the classification of source images. Finally, we provide a formal analysis to justify the algorithm's objective in domain adaptation context.

Keywords: Domain adaptation · Object recognition · Deep learning · Convolutional networks · Transfer learning

1 Introduction

An important task in visual object recognition is to design algorithms that are robust to *dataset bias* [1]. Dataset bias arises when labeled training instances are available from a source domain and test instances are sampled from a related, but different, target domain. For example, consider a person identification

Electronic supplementary material The online version of this chapter (doi:10.1007/978-3-319-46493-0_36) contains supplementary material, which is available to authorized users.

B. Leibe et al. (Eds.): ECCV 2016, Part IV, LNCS 9908, pp. 597–613, 2016.
DOI: 10.1007/978-3-319-46493-0_36

application in *unmanned aerial vehicles* (UAV), which is essential for a variety of tasks, such as surveillance, people search, and remote monitoring [2]. One of the critical tasks is to identify people from a bird's-eye view; however collecting labeled data from that viewpoint can be very challenging. It is more desirable that a UAV can be trained on some already available *on-the-ground* labeled images (source), e.g., people photographs from social media, and then success-fully applied to the actual UAV view (target). Traditional supervised learning algorithms typically perform poorly in this setting, since they assume that the training and test data are drawn from the same domain.

Domain adaptation attempts to deal with dataset bias using unlabeled data from the target domain so that the task of manual labeling the target data can be reduced. Unlabeled target data provides auxiliary training information that should help algorithms generalize better on the target domain than using source data only. Successful domain adaptation algorithms have large practical value, since acquiring a huge amount of labels from the target domain is often expensive or impossible. Although domain adaptation has gained increasing attention in object recognition, see [3] for a recent overview, the problem remains essentially unsolved since model accuracy has yet to reach a level that is satisfactory for real-world applications. Another issue is that many existing algorithms require optimization procedures that do not scale well as the size of datasets increases [4–10]. Earlier algorithms were typically designed for relatively small datasets, e.g., the Office dataset [11].

We consider a solution based on learning representations or features from raw data. Ideally, the learned feature should model the label distribution as well as reduce the discrepancy between the source and target domains. We hypothesize that a possible way to approximate such a feature is by (supervised) learning the *source label* distribution and (unsupervised) learning of the *target data distribu-tion*. This is in the same spirit as *multi-task learning* in that learning auxiliary tasks can help the main task be learned better [12,13]. The goal of this paper is to develop an accurate, scalable multi-task feature learning algorithm in the context of domain adaptation.

Contribution: To achieve the goal stated above, we propose a new deep learn-ing model for unsupervised domain adaptation. Deep learning algorithms are highly scalable since they run in linear time, can handle streaming data, and can be parallelized on GPUs. Indeed, deep learning has come to dominate object recognition in recent years [14,15].

We propose *Deep Reconstruction-Classification Network* (DRCN), a convolu-tional network that jointly learns two tasks: (i) supervised source label prediction and (ii) unsupervised target data reconstruction. The encoding parameters of the DRCN are shared across both tasks, while the decoding parameters are sepa-rated. The aim is that the learned label prediction function can perform well on classifying images in the target domain – the data reconstruction can thus be viewed as an auxiliary task to support the adaptation of the label prediction. Learning in DRCN alternates between unsupervised and supervised training, which is different from the standard *pretraining-finetuning* strategy [16,17].

From experiments over a variety of cross-domain object recognition tasks, DRCN performs better than the state-of-the-art domain adaptation algorithm [18], with up to $\sim 8\%$ accuracy gap. The DRCN learning strategy also provides a considerable improvement over the pretraining-finetuning strategy, indicating that it is more suitable for the unsupervised domain adaptation setting. We furthermore perform a visual analysis by reconstructing source images through the learned reconstruction function. It is found that *the reconstructed outputs resemble the appearances of the target images* suggesting that the encoding representations are successfully adapted. Finally, we present a probabilistic analysis to show the relationship between the DRCN's learning objective and a semi-supervised learning framework [19], and also the soundness of considering only data from a target domain for the data reconstruction training.

2   Related Work

Domain adaptation is a large field of research, with related work under several names such as class imbalance [20], covariate shift [21], and sample selection bias [22]. In [23], it is considered as a special case of transfer learning. Earlier work on domain adaptation focused on text document analysis and NLP [24,25]. In recent years, it has gained a lot of attention in the computer vision community, mainly for object recognition application, see [3] and references therein. The domain adaptation problem is often referred to as *dataset bias* in computer vision [1].

This paper is concerned with *unsupervised domain adaptation* in which labeled data from the target domain is not available [26]. A range of approaches along this line of research in object recognition have been proposed [4,5,9,27–30], most were designed specifically for small datasets such as the Office dataset [11]. Furthermore, they usually operated on the SURF-based features [31] extracted from the raw pixels. In essence, the unsupervised domain adaptation problem remains open and needs more powerful solutions that are useful for practical situations.

Deep learning now plays a major role in the advancement of domain adaptation. An early attempt addressed large-scale sentiment classification [32], where the concatenated features from fully connected layers of stacked denoising autoencoders have been found to be domain-adaptive [33]. In visual recognition, a fully connected, shallow network pretrained by denoising autoencoders has shown a certain level of effectiveness [34]. It is widely known that deep convolutional networks (ConvNets) [35] are a more natural choice for visual recognition tasks and have achieved significant successes [14,15,36]. More recently, ConvNets pretrained on a large-scale dataset, ImageNet, have been shown to be reasonably effective for domain adaptation [14]. They provide significantly better performances than the SURF-based features on the Office dataset [37,38]. An earlier approach on using a convolutional architecture without pretraining on ImageNet, DLID, has also been explored [39] and performs better than the SURF-based features.

To further improve the domain adaptation performance, the pretrained ConvNets can be *fine-tuned* under a particular constraint related to minimizing a domain discrepancy measure [18,40–42]. Deep Domain Confusion (DDC) [41] utilizes the maximum mean discrepancy (MMD) measure [43] as an additional loss function for the fine-tuning to adapt the last fully connected layer. Deep Adaptation Network (DAN) [40] fine-tunes not only the last fully connected layer, but also some convolutional and fully connected layers underneath, and outperforms DDC. Recently, the deep model proposed in [42] extends the idea of DDC by adding a criterion to guarantee the class alignment between different domains. However, it is limited only to the *semi-supervised* adaptation setting, where a small number of target labels can be acquired.

The algorithm proposed in [18], which we refer to as ReverseGrad, handles the domain invariance as a binary classification problem. It thus optimizes two contradictory objectives: (i) minimizing label prediction loss and (ii) maximizing domain classification loss via a simple *gradient reversal* strategy. ReverseGrad can be effectively applied both in the pretrained and randomly initialized deep networks. The randomly initialized model is also shown to perform well on cross-domain recognition tasks other than the Office benchmark, i.e., large-scale handwritten digit recognition tasks. Our work in this paper is in a similar spirit to ReverseGrad in that it does not necessarily require pretrained deep networks to perform well on some tasks. However, our proposed method undertakes a fundamentally different learning algorithm: finding a good label classifier while simultaneously learning the structure of the target images.

3   Deep Reconstruction-Classification Networks

This section describes our proposed deep learning algorithm for unsupervised domain adaptation, which we refer to as *Deep Reconstruction-Classification Networks* (DRCN). We first briefly discuss the unsupervised domain adaptation problem. We then present the DRCN architecture, learning algorithm, and other useful aspects.

Let us define a *domain* as a probability distribution $\mathbb{D}_{XY}$ (or just $\mathbb{D}$) on $\mathcal{X} \times \mathcal{Y}$, where $\mathcal{X}$ is the input space and $\mathcal{Y}$ is the output space. Denote the source domain by $\mathbb{P}$ and the target domain by $\mathbb{Q}$, where $\mathbb{P} \neq \mathbb{Q}$. The aim in *unsupervised domain adaptation* is as follows: given a labeled i.i.d. sample from a source domain $S^s = \{(x_i^s, y_i^s)\}_{i=1}^{n_s} \sim \mathbb{P}$ and an unlabeled sample from a target domain $S_u^t = \{(x_i^t)\}_{i=1}^{n_t} \sim \mathbb{Q}_X$, find a good labeling function $f : \mathcal{X} \to \mathcal{Y}$ on S_u^t. We consider a feature learning approach: finding a function $g : \mathcal{X} \to \mathcal{F}$ such that the discrepancy between distribution $\mathbb{P}$ and $\mathbb{Q}$ is minimized in $\mathcal{F}$.

Ideally, a discriminative representation should model both the label and the structure of the data. Based on that intuition, we hypothesize that a domain-adaptive representation should satisfy two criteria: (i) classify well the source domain labeled data and (ii) reconstruct well the target domain unlabeled data, which can be viewed as an approximate of the ideal discriminative representation. Our model is based on a convolutional architecture that has two pipelines with a shared encoding representation. The first pipeline is a standard convolutional network for *source label prediction* [35], while the second one is a convolutional autoencoder for *target data reconstruction* [44,45]. Convolutional architectures are a natural choice for object recognition to capture spatial correlation of images. The model is optimized through multitask learning [12], that is, jointly learns the (supervised) source label prediction and the (unsupervised) target data reconstruction tasks.[1] The aim is that the encoding shared representation should learn the commonality between those tasks that provides useful information for cross-domain object recognition. Figure 1 illustrates the architecture of DRCN.

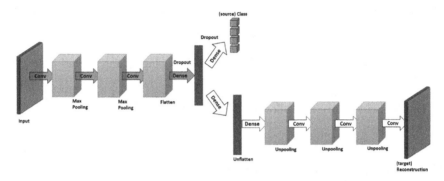

Fig. 1. Illustration of the DRCN's architecture. It consists of two pipelines: (i) label prediction and (ii) data reconstruction pipelines. The shared parameters between those two pipelines are indicated by the red color. (Color figure online)

We now describe DRCN more formally. Let $f_c : \mathcal{X} \to \mathcal{Y}$ be the (supervised) label prediction pipeline and $f_r : \mathcal{X} \to \mathcal{X}$ be the (unsupervised) data reconstruction pipeline of DRCN. Define three additional functions: (1) an encoder/feature mapping $g_{\text{enc}} : \mathcal{X} \to \mathcal{F}$, (2) a decoder $g_{\text{dec}} : \mathcal{F} \to \mathcal{X}$, and (3) a feature labeling $g_{\text{lab}} : \mathcal{F} \to \mathcal{Y}$. For m-class classification problems, the output of g_{lab} usually forms an m-dimensional vector of real values in the range $[0, 1]$ that add up to 1, i.e., *softmax* output. Given an input $x \in \mathcal{X}$, one can decompose f_c and f_r such that

$$f_c(x) = (g_{\text{lab}} \circ g_{\text{enc}})(x), \tag{1}$$
$$f_r(x) = (g_{\text{dec}} \circ g_{\text{enc}})(x). \tag{2}$$

Let $\Theta_c = \{\Theta_{\text{enc}}, \Theta_{\text{lab}}\}$ and $\Theta_r = \{\Theta_{\text{enc}}, \Theta_{\text{dec}}\}$ denote the parameters of the supervised and unsupervised model. Θ_{enc} are shared parameters for the feature mapping g_{enc}. Note that $\Theta_{\text{enc}}, \Theta_{\text{dec}}, \Theta_{\text{lab}}$ may encode parameters of multiple layers. The goal is to seek a single feature mapping g_{enc} model that supports both f_c and f_r.

Learning algorithm: The learning objective is as follows. Suppose the inputs lie in $\mathcal{X} \subseteq \mathbb{R}^d$ and their labels lie in $\mathcal{Y} \subseteq \mathbb{R}^m$. Let $\ell_c : \mathcal{Y} \times \mathcal{Y} \to \mathbb{R}$ and

---

[1] The unsupervised convolutional autoencoder is not trained via the greedy layer-wise fashion, but only with the standard back-propagation over the whole pipeline.

$\ell_r : \mathcal{X} \times \mathcal{X} \to \mathbb{R}$ be the classification and reconstruction loss respectively. Given labeled source sample $S^s = \{(\mathbf{x}_i^s, \mathbf{y}_i^s)\}_{i=1}^{n_s} \sim \mathbb{P}$, where $\mathbf{y}_i \in \{0,1\}^m$ is a *one-hot* vector, and unlabeled target sample $S_u^t = \{(\mathbf{x}_j^t)\}_{j=1}^{n_t} \sim \mathbb{Q}$, we define the empirical losses as:

$$\mathcal{L}_c^{n_s}(\{\Theta_{\text{enc}}, \Theta_{\text{lab}}\}) := \sum_{i=1}^{n_s} \ell_c \left(f_c(\mathbf{x}_i^s; \{\Theta_{\text{enc}}, \Theta_{\text{lab}}\}), \mathbf{y}_i^s \right), \tag{3}$$

$$\mathcal{L}_r^{n_t}(\{\Theta_{\text{enc}}, \Theta_{\text{dec}}\}) := \sum_{j=1}^{n_t} \ell_r \left(f_r(\mathbf{x}_j^t; \{\Theta_{\text{enc}}, \Theta_{\text{dec}}\}), \mathbf{x}_j^t \right). \tag{4}$$

Typically, ℓ_c is of the form *cross-entropy loss* $\sum_{k=1}^{m} y_k \log[f_c(\mathbf{x})]_k$ (recall that $f_c(\mathbf{x})$ is the softmax output) and ℓ_r is of the form *squared loss* $\|\mathbf{x} - f_r(\mathbf{x})\|_2^2$.

Our aim is to solve the following objective:

$$\min \lambda \mathcal{L}_c^{n_s}(\{\Theta_{\text{enc}}, \Theta_{\text{lab}}\}) + (1 - \lambda)\mathcal{L}_r^{n_t}(\{\Theta_{\text{enc}}, \Theta_{\text{dec}}\}), \tag{5}$$

where $0 \leq \lambda \leq 1$ is a hyper-parameter controlling the trade-off between classification and reconstruction. The objective is a convex combination of supervised and unsupervised loss functions. We justify the approach in Sect. 5.

Objective (5) can be achieved by alternately minimizing $\mathcal{L}_c^{n_s}$ and $\mathcal{L}_r^{n_t}$ using *stochastic gradient descent* (SGD). In the implementation, we used RMSprop [46], the variant of SGD with a gradient normalization – the current gradient is divided by a moving average over the previous root mean squared gradients. We utilize dropout regularization [47] during $\mathcal{L}_c^{n_s}$ minimization, which is effective to reduce overfitting. Note that dropout regularization is applied in the fully-connected/dense layers only, see Fig. 1.

The stopping criterion for the algorithm is determined by monitoring the average reconstruction loss of the unsupervised model during training – the process is stopped when the average reconstruction loss stabilizes. Once the training is completed, the optimal parameters $\hat{\Theta}_{\text{enc}}$ and $\hat{\Theta}_{\text{lab}}$ are used to form a classification model $f_c(\mathbf{x}^t; \{\hat{\Theta}_{\text{enc}}, \hat{\Theta}_{\text{lab}}\})$ that is expected to perform well on the target domain. The DRCN learning algorithm is summarized in Algorithm 1 and implemented using Theano [48].

Data augmentation and denoising: We use two well-known strategies to improve DRCN's performance: data augmentation and denoising. Data augmentation generates additional training data during the supervised training with respect to some plausible transformations over the original data, which improves generalization, see e.g. [49]. Denoising involves reconstructing *clean* inputs given their *noisy* counterparts. It is used to improve the feature invariance of denoising autoencoders (DAE) [33]. Generalization and feature invariance are two properties needed to improve domain adaptation. Since DRCN has both classification and reconstruction aspects, we can naturally apply these two tricks simultaneously in the training stage.

Algorithm 1. The Deep Reconstruction-Classification Network (DRCN) learning algorithm.

Input:
- Labeled source data: $S^s = \{(\mathbf{x}_i^s, y_i^s)\}_{i=1}^{n_s}$;
- Unlabeled target data: $S_u^t = \{\mathbf{x}_j^t\}_{i=j}^{n_t}$;
- Learning rates: α_c and α_r;

1: Initialize parameters $\Theta_{\mathrm{enc}}, \Theta_{\mathrm{dec}}, \Theta_{\mathrm{lab}}$
2: **while** not stop **do**
3:     **for each** source batch of size m_s **do**
4:         Do a forward pass according to (1);
5:         Let $\Theta_c = \{\Theta_{\mathrm{enc}}, \Theta_{\mathrm{lab}}\}$. Update Θ_c:

$$\Theta_c \leftarrow \Theta_c - \alpha_c \lambda \nabla_{\Theta_c} \mathcal{L}_c^{m_s}(\Theta_c);$$

6:     **end for**
7:     **for each** target batch of size m_t **do**
8:         Do a forward pass according to (2);
9:         Let $\Theta_r = \{\Theta_{\mathrm{enc}}, \Theta_{\mathrm{dec}}\}$. Update Θ_r:

$$\Theta_r \leftarrow \Theta_r - \alpha_r(1 - \lambda)\nabla_{\Theta_r} \mathcal{L}_r^{m_t}(\Theta_r).$$

10:   **end for**
11: **end while**

Output:
- DRCN learnt parameters: $\hat{\Theta} = \{\hat{\Theta}_{\mathrm{enc}}, \hat{\Theta}_{\mathrm{dec}}, \hat{\Theta}_{\mathrm{lab}}\}$;

Let $\mathbb{Q}_{\tilde{X}|X}$ denote the noise distribution given the original data from which the noisy data are sampled from. The classification pipeline of DRCN f_c thus actually observes additional pairs $\{(\tilde{\mathbf{x}}_i^s, y_i^s)\}_{i=1}^{n_s}$ and the reconstruction pipeline f_r observes $\{(\tilde{\mathbf{x}}_i^t, \mathbf{x}_i^t)\}_{i=1}^{n_t}$. The noise distribution $\mathbb{Q}_{\tilde{X}|X}$ are typically geometric transformations (translation, rotation, skewing, and scaling) in data augmentation, while either zero-masked noise or Gaussian noise is used in the denoising strategy. In this work, we combine all the fore-mentioned types of noise for denoising and use only the geometric transformations for data augmentation.

4   Experiments and Results

This section reports the evaluation results of DRCN. It is divided into two parts. The first part focuses on the evaluation on large-scale datasets popular with deep learning methods, while the second part summarizes the results on the Office dataset [11].

4.1   Experiment I: SVHN, MNIST, USPS, CIFAR, and STL

The first set of experiments investigates the empirical performance of DRCN on five widely used benchmarks: MNIST [35], USPS [50], Street View House Numbers (SVHN) [51], CIFAR [52], and STL [53], see the corresponding references for more detailed configurations. The task is to perform cross-domain recognition: *taking the training set from one dataset as the source domain and the test set from another dataset as the target domain.* We evaluate our algorithm's recognition accuracy over three cross-domain pairs: (1) MNIST vs USPS, (2) SVHN vs MNIST, and (3) CIFAR vs STL.

MNIST (MN) vs USPS (US) contains 2D grayscale handwritten digit images of 10 classes. We preprocessed them as follows. USPS images were rescaled into 28×28 and pixels were normalized to $[0, 1]$ values. From this pair, two cross-domain recognition tasks were performed: MN $\rightarrow$ US and US $\rightarrow$ MN.

In SVHN (SV) vs MNIST (MN) pair, MNIST images were rescaled to 32×32 and SVHN images were grayscaled. The $[0, 1]$ normalization was then applied to all images. Note that we did not preprocess SVHN images using local contrast normalization as in [54]. We evaluated our algorithm on SV $\rightarrow$ MN and MN $\rightarrow$ SV cross-domain recognition tasks.

STL (ST) vs CIFAR (CI) consists of RGB images that share eight object classes: *airplane, bird, cat, deer, dog, horse, ship*, and *truck*, which forms $4,000$ (train) and $6,400$ (test) images for STL, and $40,000$ (train) and $8,000$ (test) images for CIFAR. STL images were rescaled to 32×32 and pixels were standardized into zero-mean and unit-variance. Our algorithm was evaluated on two cross-domain tasks, that is, ST $\rightarrow$ CI and CI $\rightarrow$ ST.

The architecture and learning setup: The DRCN architecture used in the experiments is adopted from [44]. The label prediction pipeline has three convolutional layers: 100 5×5 filters (CONV1), 150 5×5 filters (CONV2), and 200 3×3 filters (CONV3) respectively, two max-pooling layers of size 2×2 after the first and the second convolutional layers (POOL1 and POOL2), and three fully-connected layers (FC4, FC5, and FC_out) – FC_out is the output layer. The number of neurons in FC4 or FC5 was treated as a tunable hyper-parameter in the range of $[300, 350, ..., 1000]$, chosen according to the best performance on the validation set. The shared encoder g_{enc} has thus a configuration of CONV1-POOL1-CONV2-POOL2-CONV3-FC4-FC5. Furthermore, the configuration of the decoder g_{dec} is the inverse of that of g_{enc}. Note that the unpooling operation in g_{dec} performs by upsampling-by-duplication: inserting the pooled values in the appropriate locations in the feature maps, with the remaining elements being the same as the pooled values.

We employ ReLU activations [55] in all hidden layers and linear activations in the output layer of the reconstruction pipeline. Updates in both classification and reconstruction tasks were computed via RMSprop with learning rate of 10^{-4} and moving average decay of 0.9. The control penalty λ was selected according to accuracy on the source validation data – typically, the optimal value was in the range $[0.4, 0.7]$.

Benchmark algorithms: We compare DRCN with the following methods. (1) ConvNet$_{src}$: a supervised convolutional network trained on the labeled source domain only, with the same network configuration as that of DRCN's label prediction pipeline, (2) SCAE: ConvNet preceded by the layer-wise pretraining of stacked convolutional autoencoders on all unlabeled data [44], (3) SCAE$_t$:

similar to SCAE, but only unlabeled data from the target domain are used during pretraining, (4) SDA$_{sh}$ [32]: the deep network with three fully connected layers, which is a successful domain adaptation model for sentiment classification, (5) Subspace Alignment (SA) [27],[2] and (6) ReverseGrad [18]: a recently published domain adaptation model based on deep convolutional networks that provides the state-of-the-art performance.

All deep learning based models above have the same architecture as DRCN for the label predictor. For ReverseGrad, we also evaluated the "original architecture" devised in [18] and chose whichever performed better of the original architecture or our architecture. Finally, we applied the data augmentation to all models similarly to DRCN. The ground-truth model is also evaluated, that is, a convolutional network trained from and tested on images from the target domain only (ConvNet$_{tgt}$), to measure the difference between the cross-domain performance and the ideal performance.

Classification accuracy: Table 1 summarizes the cross-domain recognition accuracy (*mean $\pm$ std*) of all algorithms over ten independent runs. DRCN performs best in all but one cross-domain tasks, better than the prior state-of-the-art ReverseGrad. Notably on the SV $\rightarrow$ MN task, DRCN outperforms ReverseGrad with $\sim 8\%$ accuracy gap. DRCN also provides a considerable improvement over ReverseGrad ($\sim 5\%$) on the reverse task, MN $\rightarrow$ SV, but the gap to the groundtruth is still large – this case was also mentioned in previous work as a failed case [18]. In the case of CI $\rightarrow$ ST, the performance of DRCN almost matches the performance of the target baseline.

DRCN also convincingly outperforms the greedy-layer pretraining-based algorithms (SDA$_{sh}$, SCAE, and SCAE$_t$). This indicates the effectiveness of the simultaneous reconstruction-classification training strategy over the standard pretraining-finetuning in the context of domain adaptation.

Comparison of different DRCN flavors: Recall that DRCN uses only the unlabeled target images for the unsupervised reconstruction training. To verify

Table 1. Accuracy (*mean $\pm$ std* %) on five cross-domain recognition tasks over ten independent runs. Bold and underline indicate the best and second best domain adaptation performance. ConvNet$_{tgt}$ denotes the ground-truth model: training and testing on the target domain only.

Methods	MN $\rightarrow$ US	US $\rightarrow$ MN	SV $\rightarrow$ MN	MN $\rightarrow$ SV	ST $\rightarrow$ CI	CI $\rightarrow$ ST
ConvNet$_{src}$	85.55 $\pm$ 0.12	65.77 $\pm$ 0.06	62.33 $\pm$ 0.09	25.95 $\pm$ 0.04	54.17 $\pm$ 0.21	63.61 $\pm$ 0.17
SDA$_{sh}$ [32]	43.14 $\pm$ 0.16	37.30 $\pm$ 0.12	55.15 $\pm$ 0.08	8.23 $\pm$ 0.11	35.82 $\pm$ 0.07	42.27 $\pm$ 0.12
SA [27]	85.89 $\pm$ 0.13	51.54 $\pm$ 0.06	63.17 $\pm$ 0.07	28.52 $\pm$ 0.10	54.04 $\pm$ 0.19	62.88 $\pm$ 0.15
SCAE [44]	85.78 $\pm$ 0.08	63.11 $\pm$ 0.04	60.02 $\pm$ 0.16	27.12 $\pm$ 0.08	54.25 $\pm$ 0.13	62.18 $\pm$ 0.04
SCAE$_t$ [44]	86.24 $\pm$ 0.11	65.37 $\pm$ 0.03	65.57 $\pm$ 0.09	27.57 $\pm$ 0.13	54.68 $\pm$ 0.08	61.94 $\pm$ 0.06
ReverseGrad [18]	91.11 $\pm$ 0.07	**74.01 $\pm$ 0.05**	73.91 $\pm$ 0.07	35.67 $\pm$ 0.04	56.91 $\pm$ 0.05	66.12 $\pm$ 0.08
DRCN	**91.80 $\pm$ 0.09**	73.67 $\pm$ 0.04	**81.97 $\pm$ 0.16**	**40.05 $\pm$ 0.07**	**58.86 $\pm$ 0.07**	**66.37 $\pm$ 0.10**
ConvNet$_{tgt}$	96.12 $\pm$ 0.07	98.67 $\pm$ 0.04	98.67 $\pm$ 0.04	91.52 $\pm$ 0.05	78.81 $\pm$ 0.11	66.50 $\pm$ 0.07

---

[2] The setup follows one in [18]: the inputs to SA are the last hidden layer activation values of ConvNet$_{src}$.

the importance of this strategy, we further compare different flavors of DRCN: DRCN_s and DRCN_{st}. Those algorithms are conceptually the same but different only in utilizing the unlabeled images during the unsupervised training. DRCN_s uses only unlabeled source images, whereas DRCN_{st} combines both unlabeled source and target images.

The experimental results in Table 2 confirm that DRCN always performs better than DRCN_s and DRCN_{st}. While DRCN_{st} occasionally outperforms ReverseGrad, its overall performance does not compete with that of DRCN. The only case where DRCN_s and DRCN_{st} flavors can closely match DRCN is on MN→ US. This suggests that the use of *unlabeled source data* during the reconstruction training do not contribute much to the cross-domain generalization, which verifies the DRCN strategy in using the unlabeled target data only.

Table 2. Accuracy (%) of DRCN_s and DRCN_{st}.

Methods	MN → US	US → MN	SV → MN	MN → SV	ST → CI	CI → ST
DRCN$_s$	89.92 ± 0.12	65.96 ± 0.07	73.66 ± 0.04	34.29 ± 0.09	55.12 ± 0.12	63.02 ± 0.06
DRCN$_{st}$	91.15 ± 0.05	68.64 ± 0.05	75.88 ± 0.09	37.77 ± 0.06	55.26 ± 0.06	64.55 ± 0.13
DRCN	91.80 ± 0.09	73.67 ± 0.04	81.97 ± 0.16	40.05 ± 0.07	58.86 ± 0.07	66.37 ± 0.10

Data reconstruction: A useful insight was found when reconstructing source images through the reconstruction pipeline of DRCN. Specifically, we observe the visual appearance of $f_r(x_1^s), \ldots, f_r(x_m^s)$, where $x_1^s, \ldots, x_m^s$ are some images from the source domain. Note that $x_1^s, \ldots, x_m^s$ are unseen during the unsupervised reconstruction training in DRCN. We visualize such a reconstruction in the case of SV →MN training in Fig. 2. Figure 2(a) and (b) display the original source (SVHN) and target (MNIST) images.

The main finding of this observation is depicted in Fig. 2(c): the reconstructed images produced by DRCN given some SVHN images as the source inputs. We found that *the reconstructed SVHN images resemble MNIST-like digit appearances, with white stroke and black background,* see Fig. 2(b). Remarkably, DRCN still can produce "correct" reconstructions of some noisy SVHN images. For example, all SVHN digits 3 displayed in Fig. 2(a) are clearly reconstructed by DRCN, see the fourth row of Fig. 2(c). DRCN tends to pick only the digit in the middle and ignore the remaining digits. This may explain the superior cross-domain recognition performance of DRCN on this task. However, such a cross-reconstruction appearance does not happen in the reverse task, MN → SV, which may be an indicator for the low accuracy relative to the groundtruth performance.

We also conduct such a diagnostic reconstruction on other algorithms that have the reconstruction pipeline. Figure 2(d) depicts the reconstructions of the SVHN images produced by ConvAE trained on the MNIST images only. They do not appear to be digits, suggesting that ConvAE recognizes the SVHN images as noise. Figure 2(e) shows the reconstructed SVHN images produced by DRCN_{st}. We can see that they look almost identical to the source images shown in Fig. 2(a), which is not surprising since the source images are included during the reconstruction training.

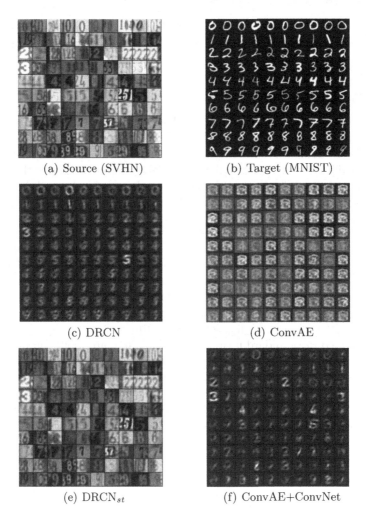

(a) Source (SVHN)

(b) Target (MNIST)

(c) DRCN

(d) ConvAE

(e) DRCN$_{st}$

(f) ConvAE+ConvNet

Fig. 2. Data reconstruction after training from SVHN → MNIST. Figure (a)–(b) show the original input pixels, and (c)–(f) depict the reconstructed source images (SVHN). The reconstruction of DRCN appears to be MNIST-like digits, see the main text for a detailed explanation.

Finally, we evaluated the reconstruction induced by ConvNet$_{src}$ to observe the difference with the reconstruction of DRCN. Specifically, we trained ConvAE on the MNIST images in which the encoding parameters were initialized from those of ConvNet$_{src}$ and not updated during training. We refer to the model as ConvAE+ConvNet$_{src}$. The reconstructed images are visualized in Fig. 2(f). Although they resemble the style of MNIST images as in the DRCN's case, only a few source images are correctly reconstructed.

To summarize, the results from this diagnostic data reconstruction correlate with the cross-domain recognition performance. More visualization on other cross-domain cases can be found in the Supplemental materials.

4.2 Experiments II: Office Dataset

In the second experiment, we evaluated DRCN on the standard domain adaptation benchmark for visual object recognition, OFFICE [11], which consists of three different domains: AMAZON (A), DSLR (D), and WEBCAM (W). OFFICE has 2817 labeled images in total distributed across 31 object categories. The number of images is thus relatively small compared to the previously used datasets.

We applied the DRCN algorithm to *finetune* AlexNet [14], as was done with different methods in previous work [18,40,41].[3] The fine-tuning was performed only on the fully connected layers of AlexNet, $fc6$ and $fc7$, and the last convolutional layer, $conv5$. Specifically, the label prediction pipeline of DRCN contains $conv4$-$conv5$-$fc6$-$fc7$-$label$ and the data reconstruction pipeline has $conv4$-$conv5$-$fc6$-$fc7$-$fc6'$-$conv5'$-$conv4'$ (the ' denotes the inverse layer) – it thus does not reconstruct the original input pixels. The learning rate was selected following the strategy devised in [40]: cross-validating the base learning rate between 10^{-5} and 10^{-2} with a multiplicative step-size $10^{1/2}$.

We followed the standard unsupervised domain adaptation training protocol used in previous work [7,39,40], that is, using *all* labeled source data and unlabeled target data. Table 3 summarizes the performance accuracy of DRCN based on that protocol in comparison to the state-of-the-art algorithms. We found that DRCN is competitive against DAN and ReverseGrad – the performance is either the best or the second best except for one case. In particular, DRCN performs best with a convincing gap in situations when the target domain has relatively many data, i.e., AMAZON as the target dataset.

Table 3. Accuracy (*mean ± std %*) on the Office dataset with the standard unsupervised domain adaptation protocol used in [7,39].

Method	A → W	W → A	A → D	D → A	W → D	D → W
DDC [41]	61.8 ± 0.4	52.2 ± 0.4	64.4 ± 0.3	52.1 ± 0.8	98.5 ± 0.4	95.0 ± 0.5
DAN [40]	68.5 ± 0.4	$\underline{53.1} \pm 0.3$	$\underline{67.0} \pm 0.4$	54.0 ± 0.4	$\underline{99.0} \pm 0.2$	$\underline{96.0} \pm 0.3$
ReverseGrad [18]	$\mathbf{72.6} \pm 0.3$	52.7 ± 0.2	$\mathbf{67.1} \pm 0.3$	$\underline{54.5} \pm 0.4$	$\mathbf{99.2} \pm 0.3$	$\mathbf{96.4} \pm 0.1$
DRCN	$\underline{68.7} \pm 0.3$	$\mathbf{54.9} \pm 0.5$	66.8 ± 0.5	$\mathbf{56.0} \pm 0.5$	$\underline{99.0} \pm 0.2$	$\mathbf{96.4} \pm 0.3$

5   Analysis

This section provides a first step towards a formal analysis of the DRCN algorithm. We demonstrate that optimizing (5) in DRCN relates to solving a semi-supervised learning problem on the target domain according to a framework

---

[3] Recall that AlexNet consists of five convolutional layers: $conv1, \ldots, conv5$ and three fully connected layers: $fc6, fc7$, and $fc8/output$.

proposed in [19]. The analysis suggests that unsupervised training using only unlabeled target data is sufficient. That is, adding unlabeled source data might not further improve domain adaptation.

Denote the labeled and unlabeled distributions as $\mathbb{D}_{XY} =: \mathbb{D}$ and $\mathbb{D}_X$ respectively. Let $P^\theta(\cdot)$ refer to a family of models, parameterized by $\theta \in \Theta$, that is used to learn a maximum likelihood estimator. The DRCN learning algorithm for domain adaptation tasks can be interpreted probabilistically by assuming that $P^\theta(x)$ is Gaussian and $P^\theta(y|x)$ is a multinomial distribution, fit by logistic regression.

The objective in Eq. (5) is equivalent to the following maximum likelihood estimate:

$$\hat{\theta} = \underset{\theta}{\operatorname{argmax}} \lambda \sum_{i=1}^{n_s} \log P^\theta_{Y|X}(y_i^s|x_i^s) + (1 - \lambda) \sum_{j=1}^{n_t} \log P^\theta_{X|\tilde{X}}(x_j^t|\tilde{x}_j^t), \quad (6)$$

where $\tilde{x}$ is the noisy input generated from $\mathbb{Q}_{\tilde{X}|X}$. The first term represents the model learned by the supervised convolutional network and the second term represents the model learned by the unsupervised convolutional autoencoder. Note that the discriminative model only observes labeled data from the source distribution $\mathbb{P}_X$ in objectives (5) and (6).

We now recall a semi-supervised learning problem formulated in [19]. Suppose that labeled and unlabeled samples are taken from the *target domain* $\mathbb{Q}$ with probabilities λ and $(1 - \lambda)$ respectively. By Theorem 5.1 in [19], the maximum likelihood estimate ζ is

$$\zeta = \underset{\zeta}{\operatorname{argmax}} \lambda \underset{\mathbb{Q}}{\mathbb{E}}[\log P^\zeta(x,y)] + (1 - \lambda) \underset{\mathbb{Q}_X}{\mathbb{E}}[\log P^\zeta_X(x)] \quad (7)$$

The theorem holds if it satisfies the following assumptions: *consistency*, the model contains true distribution, so the MLE is consistent; and *smoothness and measurability* [56]. Given target data $(x_1^t, y_1^t), \ldots, (x_{n_t}^t, y_{n_t}^t) \sim \mathbb{Q}$, the parameter ζ can be estimated as follows:

$$\hat{\zeta} = \underset{\zeta}{\operatorname{argmax}} \lambda \sum_{i=1}^{n_t} [\log P^\zeta(x_i^t, y_i^t)] + (1 - \lambda) \sum_{i=1}^{n_t} [\log P^\zeta_X(x_i^t)] \quad (8)$$

Unfortunately, $\hat{\zeta}$ cannot be computed in the unsupervised domain adaptation setting since we do not have access to target labels.

Next we inspect a certain condition where $\hat{\theta}$ and $\hat{\zeta}$ are closely related. Firstly, by the *covariate shift* assumption [21]: $\mathbb{P} \neq \mathbb{Q}$ and $\mathbb{P}_{Y|X} = \mathbb{Q}_{Y|X}$, the first term in (7) can be switched from an expectation over target samples to source samples:

$$\underset{\mathbb{Q}}{\mathbb{E}}\left[\log P^\zeta(x,y) \right] = \underset{\mathbb{P}}{\mathbb{E}}\left[\frac{\mathbb{Q}_X(x)}{\mathbb{P}_X(x)} \cdot \log P^\zeta(x,y) \right]. \quad (9)$$

Secondly, it was shown in [57] that $P^\theta_{X|\tilde{X}}(x|\tilde{x})$, see the second term in (6), defines an ergodic Markov chain whose asymptotic marginal distribution of X converges to the data-generating distribution $\mathbb{P}_X$. Hence, Eq. (8) can be rewritten as

$$\hat{\zeta} \approx \underset{\zeta}{\operatorname{argmax}} \, \lambda \sum_{i=1}^{n_s} \frac{\mathbb{Q}_X(x_i^s)}{\mathbb{P}_X(x_i^s)} \log P^\zeta(x_i^s, y_i^s) + (1-\lambda) \sum_{j=1}^{n_t} [\log P_{X|\tilde{X}}^\zeta(x_j^t | \tilde{x}_j^t)]. \quad (10)$$

The above objective differs from objective (6) only in the first term. Notice that $\hat{\zeta}$ would be approximately equal $\hat{\theta}$ if the ratio $\frac{\mathbb{Q}_X(x_i^s)}{\mathbb{P}_X(x_i^s)}$ is constant for all x^s. In fact, it becomes the objective of DRCN$_{st}$. Although the constant ratio assumption is too strong to hold in practice, comparing (6) and (10) suggests that $\hat{\zeta}$ can be a reasonable approximation to $\hat{\theta}$.

Finally, we argue that using unlabeled source samples during the unsupervised training may not further contribute to domain adaptation. To see this, we expand the first term of (10) as follows

$$\lambda \sum_{i=1}^{n_s} \frac{\mathbb{Q}_X(x_i^s)}{\mathbb{P}_X(x_i^s)} \log P_{Y|X}^\zeta(y_i^s | x_i^s) + \lambda \sum_{i=1}^{n_s} \frac{\mathbb{Q}_X(x_i^s)}{\mathbb{P}_X(x_i^s)} \log P_X^\zeta(x_i^s).$$

Observe the second term above. As $n_s \to \infty$, P_X^θ will converge to $\mathbb{P}_X$. Hence, since $\int_{x \sim \mathbb{P}_X} \frac{\mathbb{Q}_X(x)}{\mathbb{P}_X(x)} \log \mathbb{P}_X(x) \leq \int_{x \sim \mathbb{P}_X} \mathbb{P}_X^t(x)$, adding more unlabeled source data will only result in a constant. This implies an optimization procedure equivalent to (6), which may explain the *uselessness* of unlabeled source data in the context of domain adaptation.

Note that the latter analysis does not necessarily imply that incorporating unlabeled source data degrades the performance. The fact that DRCN$_{st}$ performs worse than DRCN could be due to, e.g., the model capacity, which depends on the choice of the architecture.

6   Conclusions

We have proposed Deep Reconstruction-Classification Network (DRCN), a novel model for unsupervised domain adaptation in object recognition. The model performs multitask learning, i.e., alternately learning (source) label prediction and (target) data reconstruction using a shared encoding representation. We have shown that DRCN provides a considerable improvement for some cross-domain recognition tasks over the state-of-the-art model. It also performs better than deep models trained using the standard *pretraining-finetuning* approach. A useful insight into the effectiveness of the learned DRCN can be obtained from its data reconstruction. The appearance of DRCN's reconstructed source images resemble that of the target images, which indicates that DRCN learns the domain correspondence. We also provided a theoretical analysis relating the DRCN algorithm to semi-supervised learning. The analysis was used to support the strategy in involving only the target unlabeled data during learning the reconstruction task.

References

1. Torralba, A., Efros, A.A.: Unbiased look at dataset bias. In: CVPR, pp. 1521–1528 (2011)
2. Hsu, H.J., Chen, K.T.: Face recognition on drones: issues and limitations. In: Proceedings of ACM DroNet 2015 (2015)
3. Patel, V.M., Gopalan, R., Li, R., Chellapa, R.: Visual domain adaptation: a survey of recent advances. IEEE Signal Process. Mag. **32**(3), 53–69 (2015)
4. Aljundi, R., Emonet, R., Muselet, D., Sebban, M.: Landmarks-based kernelized subspace alignment for unsupervised domain adaptation. In: CVPR (2015)
5. Baktashmotlagh, M., Harandi, M.T., Lovell, B.C., Salzmann, M.: Unsupervised domain adaptation by domain invariant projection. In: ICCV, pp. 769–776 (2013)
6. Bruzzone, L., Marconcini, M.: Domain adaptation problems: a DASVM classification technique and a circular validation strategy. IEEE TPAMI **32**(5), 770–787 (2010)
7. Gong, B., Grauman, K., Sha, F.: Connecting the dots with landmarks: discriminatively learning domain-invariant features for unsupervised domain adaptation. In: ICML (2013)
8. Long, M., Ding, G., Wang, J., Sun, J., Guo, Y., Yu, P.S.: Transfer sparse coding for robust image representation. In: CVPR, pp. 404–414 (2013)
9. Long, M., Wang, J., Ding, G., Sun, J., Yu, P.S.: Transfer joint matching for unsupervised domain adaptation. In: CVPR, pp. 1410–1417 (2014)
10. Pan, S.J., Tsang, I.W.H., Kwok, J.T., Yang, Q.: Domain adaptation via transfer component analysis. IEEE Trans. Neural Netw. **22**(2), 199–210 (2011)
11. Saenko, K., Kulis, B., Fritz, M., Darrell, T.: Adapting visual category models to new domains. In: Daniilidis, K., Maragos, P., Paragios, N. (eds.) ECCV 2010. LNCS, vol. 6314, pp. 213–226. Springer, Heidelberg (2010). doi:10.1007/978-3-642-15561-1_16
12. Caruana, R.: Multitask learning. Mach. Learn. **28**, 41–75 (1997)
13. Argyriou, A., Evgeniou, T., Pontil, M.: Multi-task feature learning. In: Schölkopf, B., Platt, J., Hoffman, T. (eds.) Advances in Neural Information Processing Systems, vol. 19, pp. 41–48. MIT Press, Cambridge (2006)
14. Krizhevsky, A., Sutskever, I., Hinton, G.E.: Classification with deep convolutional neural networks. In: NIPS, vol. 25, pp. 1106–1114 (2012)
15. Simonyan, K., Zisserman, A.: Very deep convolutional networks for large-scale image recognition. In: ICLR (2015)
16. Hinton, G.E., Osindero, S.: A fast learning algorithm for deep belief nets. Neural Comput. **18**(7), 1527–1554 (2006)
17. Bengio, Y., Lamblin, P., Popovici, D., Larochelle, H.: Greedy Layer-Wise training of deep networks. In: NIPS, vol. 19, pp. 153–160 (2007)
18. Ganin, Y., Lempitsky, V.S.: Unsupervised domain adaptation by backpropagation. In: ICML, pp. 1180–1189 (2015)
19. Cohen, I., Cozman, F.G.: Risks of semi-supervised learning: how unlabeled data can degrade performance of generative classifiers. In: Semi-Supervised Learning. MIT Press (2006)
20. Japkowicz, N., Stephen, S.: The class imbalance problem: a systematic study. Intell. Data Anal. **6**(5), 429–450 (2002)
21. Shimodaira, H.: Improving predictive inference under covariate shift by weighting the log-likelihood function. J. Stat. Plann. Infer. **90**(2), 227–244 (2000)

22. Zadrozny, B.: Learning and evaluating classifiers under sample selection bias. In: Proceedings of the 21th Annual International Conference on Machine Learning, pp. 114–121 (2004)
23. Pan, S.J., Yang, Q.: A survey on transfer learning. IEEE Trans. Knowl. Data Eng. **22**(10), 1345–1359 (2010)
24. Blitzer, J., McDonald, R., Pereira, F.: Domain adaptation with structural correspondence learning. In: Proceedings of the 2006 Conference on Empirical Methods in Natural Language Processing, pp. 120–128 (2006)
25. Daumé-III, H.: Frustratingly easy domain adaptation. In: Proceedings of ACL (2007)
26. Margolis, A.: A literature review of domain adaptation with unlabeled data. Technical report, University of Washington (2011)
27. Fernando, B., Habrard, A., Sebban, M., Tuytelaars, T.: Unsupervised visual domain adaptation using subspace alignment. In: ICCV, pp. 2960–2967 (2013)
28. Ghifary, M., Balduzzi, D., Kleijn, W.B., Zhang, M.: Scatter component analysis: a unified framework for domain adaptation and domain generalization. CoRR abs/1510.04373 (2015)
29. Gopalan, R., Li, R., Chellapa, R.: Domain adaptation for object recognition: an unsupervised approach. In: ICCV, pp. 999–1006 (2011)
30. Gong, B., Shi, Y., Sha, F., Grauman, K.: Geodesic flow Kernel for unsupervised domain adaptation. In: CVPR, pp. 2066–2073 (2012)
31. Bay, H., Tuytelaars, T., Gool, L.V.: SURF: speeded up robust features. CVIU **110**(3), 346–359 (2008)
32. Glorot, X., Bordes, A., Bengio, Y.: Domain adaptation for large-scale sentiment classification: a deep learning approach. In: ICML, pp. 513–520 (2011)
33. Vincent, P., Larochelle, H., Lajoie, I., Bengio, Y., Manzagol, P.A.: Stacked denoising autoencoders: learning useful representations in a deep network with a local denoising criterion. J. Mach. Learn. Res. **11**, 3371–3408 (2010)
34. Ghifary, M., Kleijn, W.B., Zhang, M.: Domain adaptive neural networks for object recognition. In: Pham, D.-N., Park, S.-B. (eds.) PRICAI 2014. LNCS (LNAI), vol. 8862, pp. 898–904. Springer, Heidelberg (2014). doi:10.1007/978-3-319-13560-1_76
35. LeCun, Y., Bottou, L., Bengio, Y., Haffner, P.: Gradient-based learning applied to document recognition. Proc. IEEE **86**, 2278–2324 (1998)
36. Girshick, R., Donahue, J., Darrell, T., Malik, J.: Rich feature hierarchies for accurate object detection and semantic segmentation. In: CVPR (2014)
37. Donahue, J., Jia, Y., Vinyals, O., Hoffman, J., Zhang, N., Tzeng, E., Darrell, T.: DeCAF: a deep convolutional activation feature for generic visual recognition. In: ICML (2014)
38. Hoffman, J., Tzeng, E., Donahue, J., Jia, Y., Saenko, K., Darrell, T.: One-Shot Adaptation of Supervised Deep Convolutional Models (2013). CoRR abs/1312.6204
39. Chopra, S., Balakrishnan, S., Gopalan, R.: DLID: deep learning for domain adaptation by interpolating between domains. In: ICML Workshop on Challenges in Representation Learning (2013)
40. Long, M., Cao, Y., Wang, J., Jordan, M.I.: Learning transferable features with deep adaptation networks. In: ICML (2015)
41. Tzeng, E., Hoffman, J., Zhang, N., Saenko, K., Darrell, T.: Deep domain confusion: maximizing for domain invariance (2014). CoRR abs/1412.3474
42. Tzeng, E., Hoffman, J., Darrell, T., Saenko, K.: Simultaneous deep transfer across domains and tasks. In: ICCV (2015)

43. Borgwardt, K.M., Gretton, A., Rasch, M.J., Kriegel, H.P., Schölkopf, B., Smola, A.J.: Integrating structured biological data by Kernel maximum mean discrepancy. Bioinformatics **22**(14), e49–e57 (2006)

44. Masci, J., Meier, U., Cireşan, D., Schmidhuber, J.: Stacked convolutional auto-encoders for hierarchical feature extraction. In: Honkela, T., Duch, W., Girolami, M., Kaski, S. (eds.) ICANN 2011. LNCS, vol. 6791, pp. 52–59. Springer, Heidelberg (2011). doi:10.1007/978-3-642-21735-7_7

45. Zeiler, M.D., Krishnan, D., Taylor, G.W., Fergus, R.: Deconvolutional networks. In: CVPR, pp. 2528–2535 (2010)

46. Tieleman, T., Hinton, G.: Lecture 6.5–RmsProp: divide the gradient by a running average of its recent magnitude. COURSERA: Neural Netw. Mach. Learn. (2012)

47. Srivastava, N., Hinton, G., Krizhevsky, A., Sutskever, I., Salakhutdinov, R.: Dropout: a simple way to prevent neural networks from overfitting. JMLR **15**, 1929–1958 (2014)

48. Bastien, F., Lamblin, P., Pascanu, R., Bergstra, J., Goodfellow, I.J., Bergeron, A., Bouchard, N., Bengio, Y.: Theano: new features and speed improvements. In: Deep Learning and Unsupervised Feature Learning NIPS 2012 Workshop (2012)

49. Simard, P.Y., Steinkraus, D., Platt, J.C.: Best practices for convolutional neural networks applied to visual document analysis. In: ICDAR, vol. 2, pp. 958–962 (2003)

50. Hull, J.J.: A database for handwritten text recognition research. IEEE TPAMI **16**(5), 550–554 (1994)

51. Netzer, Y., Wang, T., Coates, A., Bissacco, A., Wu, B., Ng, A.Y.: Reading digits in natural images with unsupervised feature learning. In: NIPS Workshop on Deep Learning and Unsupervised Feature Learning (2011)

52. Krizhevsky, A.: Learning multiple layers of features from tiny images. Master's thesis, Department of Computer Science, University of Toronto, April 2009

53. Coates, A., Lee, H., Ng, A.Y.: An analysis of single-layer networks in unsupervised feature learning. In: AISTATS, pp. 215–223 (2011)

54. Sermanet, P., Chintala, S., LeCun, Y.: Convolutional neural networks applied to house number digit classification. In: ICPR, pp. 3288–3291 (2012)

55. Nair, V., Hinton, G.E.: Rectified linear units improve restricted Boltzmann machines. In: ICML (2010)

56. White, H.: Maximum likelihood estimation of misspecified models. Econometrica **50**(1), 1–25 (1982)

57. Bengio, Y., Yao, L., Guillaume, A., Vincent, P.: Generalized denoising auto-encoders as generative models. In: NIPS, pp. 899–907 (2013)

Learning Without Forgetting

Zhizhong Li$^{(\boxtimes)}$ and Derek Hoiem

Department of Computer Science,
University of Illinois Urbana Champaign, Champaign, USA
{zli115,dhoiem}@illinois.edu

Abstract. When building a unified vision system or gradually adding new capabilities to a system, the usual assumption is that training data for all tasks is always available. However, as the number of tasks grows, storing and retraining on such data becomes infeasible. A new problem arises where we add new capabilities to a Convolutional Neural Network (CNN), but the training data for its existing capabilities are unavailable. We propose our Learning without Forgetting method, which uses only new task data to train the network while preserving the original capabilities. Our method performs favorably compared to commonly used feature extraction and fine-tuning adaption techniques and performs similarly to multitask learning that uses original task data we assume unavailable. A more surprising observation is that Learning without Forgetting may be able to replace fine-tuning as standard practice for improved new task performance.

Keywords: Convolutional neural networks · Transfer learning · Multi-task learning · Deep learning · Visual recognition

1 Introduction

Many practical vision applications require learning new visual capabilities while maintaining performance on existing ones. For example, a robot may be delivered to someone's house with a set of default object recognition capabilities, but new site-specific object models need to be added. Or for construction safety, a system can identify whether a worker is wearing a safety vest or hard hat, but a superintendent may wish to add the ability to detect improper footware. Ideally, the new tasks could be learned while sharing parameters from old ones, without degrading performance on old tasks or having access to the old training data. Legacy data may be unrecorded, proprietary, or simply too cumbersome to use in training a new task. Though similar in spirit to transfer, multitask, and lifelong learning, we are not aware of any work that provides a solution to the problem of continually adding new prediction tasks based on adapting shared parameters *without access to training data* for previously learned tasks.

In this paper, we demonstrate a simple but effective solution on a variety of image classification problems with Convolutional Neural Network (CNN) classifiers. In our setting, a CNN has a set of shared parameters θ_s (e.g., five convolutional layers and two fully connected layers for AlexNet [11] architecture),

© Springer International Publishing AG 2016
B. Leibe et al. (Eds.): ECCV 2016, Part IV, LNCS 9908, pp. 614–629, 2016.
DOI: 10.1007/978-3-319-46493-0_37

	Fine Tuning	Duplicating and Fine Tuning	Feature Extraction	Joint Training	Learning without Forgetting
new task performance	good	good	X medium	best	√ best
original task performance	X bad	good	good	good	√ good
training efficiency	fast	fast	fast	X slow	√ fast
testing efficiency	fast	X slow	fast	fast	√ fast
storage requirement	medium	X large	medium	X large	√ medium
requires previous task data	no	no	no	X yes	√ no

Fig. 1. We wish to add new prediction tasks to an existing CNN vision system without requiring access to the training data for existing tasks. This table shows relative advantages of our method compared to commonly used methods.

task-specific parameters for previously learned tasks θ_o (e.g., the output layer for ImageNet [19] classification and corresponding weights), and randomly initialized task-specific parameters for new tasks θ_n (e.g., scene classifiers). It is useful to think of θ_o and θ_n as classifiers that operate on features parameterized by θ_s. Currently, there are three common approaches (Figs. 1 and 2) to learning θ_n while benefiting from previously learned θ_s:

Feature extraction (e.g., [6]): θ_s and θ_o are unchanged, and the outputs of one or more layers are used as features for the new task in training θ_n.

Fine-tuning (e.g., [9]): θ_s and θ_n are optimized for the new task, while θ_o is fixed. A low learning rate is typically used to prevent large drift in θ_s. Potentially, the original network could be duplicated and fine-tuned for each new task to create a set of specialized networks.

Joint Training (e.g., [3]): All parameters θ_s, θ_o, θ_n are jointly optimized, for example by interleaving samples from each task.

Each of these strategies has a major drawback. Feature extraction typically underperforms on the new task because the shared parameters fail to represent some information that is discriminative for the new task. Fine-tuning degrades performance on previously learned tasks because the shared parameters change without new guidance for the original task-specific prediction parameters. Duplicating and fine-tuning for each task results in linearly increasing test time as new tasks are added, rather than sharing computation for shared parameters. Joint training becomes increasingly cumbersome in training as more tasks are learned and is not possible if the training data for previously learned tasks is unavailable.

We propose a new strategy that we call **Learning without Forgetting** (LwF). Using only examples for the new task, we optimize both for high accuracy for the new task and for preservation of responses on the existing tasks from the original network. Clearly, if the new network produces exactly the same outputs on all relevant images, its accuracy will be the same as the original network. In practice, the images for the new task may provide a poor sampling of the original task domain, but our experiments show that preserving outputs on these examples is still an effective strategy to preserve performance on the old task and also has an unexpected benefit of acting as a regularizer to improve

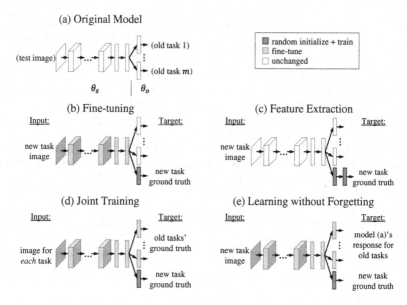

Fig. 2. Illustration for our method (e) and methods we compare to (b–d). Images and labels used in training are shown. Data for different tasks are used in alternation in joint training.

performance on the new task. Our Learning without Forgetting approach has several advantages:

(1) Classification performance: Learning without Forgetting outperforms feature extraction and, more surprisingly, fine-tuning on the new task while greatly outperforming using fine-tuned parameters θ_s on the old task.
(2) Computational efficiency: Training time is faster than joint training and only slightly slower than fine-tuning, and test time is faster than if one uses multiple fine-tuned networks for different tasks.
(3) Simplicity in deployment: Once a task is learned, the training data does not need to be retained or reapplied to preserve performance in the adapting network.

2   Related Work

Multi-task learning, transfer learning, and related methods have a long history. In brief, our Learning without Forgetting approach could be seen as a combination of Distillation Networks [10] and fine-tuning [9]. Fine-tuning initializes with parameters from an existing network trained on a related data-rich problem and finds a new local minimum by optimizing parameters for a new task with a low learning rate. The idea of Distillation Networks is to learn parameters in a simpler network that produce the same outputs as a more complex ensemble of networks either on the original training set or a large unlabeled set of data. Our approach differs in that we solve for a set of parameters that works well on both old and new tasks using the same data to supervise learning of the new tasks and to provide unsupervised output guidance on the old tasks.

We now summarize existing methods for transfer and multitask learning and compare them to our approach.

Feature Extraction [6,17] uses a pre-trained deep CNN to compute features for an image. The extracted features are the activations of one layer (usually the last hidden layer) or multiple layers given the image. Classifiers trained on these features can achieve competitive results, sometimes outperforming human-engineered features [6]. Further studies [2] show how hyper-parameters, e.g. original network structure, should be selected for better performance. Feature extraction does not modify the original network and allows new tasks to benefit from complex features learned from previous tasks. However, these features are not specialized for the new task and can often be improved by fine-tuning.

Fine-tuning [9] modifies the parameters of an existing CNN to train a new task. The output layer is extended with randomly intialized weights for the new task and a small learning rate is used to tune parameters from their original values to minimize the loss on the new task. Using appropriate hyper-parameters for training, the resulting model often outperforms feature extraction [2,9] or learning from a randomly initialized network [1,26]. Fine-tuning adapts the shared parameters θ_s to make them more discriminative for the new task, and the low learning rate is an indirect mechanism to preserve some of the representational structure learned in the original tasks. Our method provides a more direct way to preserve representations that are important for the original task, improving both original and new task performance relative to fine-tuning.

Adding new nodes to each network layer is a way to preserve the original network parameters while learning new discriminative features. For example, Terekhov et al. [21] proposes Deep Block-Modular Neural Networks for fully-connected neural networks. Parameters for the original network are untouched, and newly added nodes are fully connected to the layer beneath them. This method has the downside of substantially expanding the number of parameters in the network, and can underperform both fine-tuning and feature extraction if insufficient training data is available to learn the new parameters. We experiment with expanding the fully connected layers of original network but find that the expansion does not provide an improvement on our original approach.

Our work also relates to **methods that transfer knowledge** between networks. Hinton et al. [10] propose Knowledge Distillation, where knowledge is transferred from a large network or a network assembly to a smaller network for efficient deployment. The smaller network is trained using a modified cross-entropy loss (further described in Sect. 3) that encourages both large and small responses of the original and new network to be similar. Romero et al. [18] builds on this work to transfer to a deeper network by applying extra guidance on the middle layer. Chen et al. [5] proposes the Net2Net method that immediately generates a deeper, wider network that is functionally equivalent to an existing one. This technique can quickly initialize networks for faster hyper-parameter exploration. These methods aim to produce a differently structured network that approximates the original network, while we aim to find new parameters for the original network structure (θ_s, θ_o) that approximate the original outputs while tuning shared parameters θ_s for new tasks.

Feature extraction and fine-tuning are special cases of **Domain Adaptation** (when old and new tasks are the same) or **Transfer Learning** (different tasks). Transfer Learning uses knowledge from one task to help another, as surveyed by Pan et al. [15]. The Deep Adaption Network by Long et al. [13] matches the RKHS embedding of the deep representation of both source and target tasks to reduce domain bias. Another similar domain adaptation method is by Tzeng et al. [23], which encourages the shared deep representation to be indistinguishable across domains. This method also uses knowledge distillation, but to help train the *new* domain instead of preserving the old task. Domain adaptation and transfer learning require that at least unlabeled data is present for both task domains. In contrast, we are interested in the case when training data for the original tasks (i.e. source domains) are not available.

Multitask learning (e.g., [3]) differs from transfer learning in that it aims at improving all tasks simultaneously by combining the common knowledge from all tasks. Each task provides extra training data for the parameters that are shared or constrained, serving as a form of regularization for the other tasks [4]. For neural networks, Caruana [3] gives a detailed study of multi-task learning. Usually the bottom layers of the network are shared, while the top layers are task-specific. Multitask learning requires data from all tasks to be present, while our method requires only data for the new tasks.

Methods that **integrate knowledge over time**, e.g. Lifelong Learning [22] and Never Ending Learning [14], are also related. Lifelong learning focuses on flexibly adding new tasks while transferring knowledge between tasks. Never Ending Learning focuses on building diverse knowledge and experience (e.g. by reading the web every day). Though topically related to our work, these methods do not provide a way to preserve performance on existing tasks without the original training data. Ruvolo et al. [7] describe a method to efficiently add new tasks to a multitask system, co-training all tasks while using only new task data. However, the method assumes that weights for all classifiers and regression models can be linearly decomposed into a set of bases. In contrast with our method, the algorithm applies only to logistic or linear regression on engineered features, and these features cannot be made task-specific, e.g. by fine-tuning.

3   Learning Without Forgetting

Given a CNN with shared parameters θ_s and task-specific parameters θ_o (Fig. 2(a)), our goal is to add task-specific parameters θ_n for a new task and to learn parameters that work well on old and new tasks, using images and

LEARNINGWITHOUTFORGETTING:
Start with:
θ_s: shared parameters
θ_o: task specific parameters for each old task
X_n, Y_n: training data and ground truth on the new task
Initialize:
$Y_o \leftarrow$ CNN$(X_n, \theta_s, \theta_o)$ // compute output of old tasks for new data
$\theta_n \leftarrow$ RANDINIT$(|\theta_n|)$ // randomly initialize new parameters
Train:
Define $\hat{Y}_o \equiv$ CNN$(X_n, \hat{\theta}_s, \hat{\theta}_o)$ // old task output
Define $\hat{Y}_n \equiv$ CNN$(X_n, \hat{\theta}_s, \hat{\theta}_n)$ // new task output
$\theta_s^*, \theta_o^*, \theta_n^* \leftarrow \underset{\hat{\theta}_s, \hat{\theta}_o, \hat{\theta}_n}{\text{argmin}} \left(\mathcal{L}_{old}(Y_o, \hat{Y}_o) + \mathcal{L}_{new}(Y_n, \hat{Y}_n) + \mathcal{R}(\hat{\theta}_s, \hat{\theta}_o, \hat{\theta}_n) \right)$

Fig. 3. Procedure for learning without forgetting.

labels from only the new task (i.e., *without using data from existing tasks*). Our algorithm is outlined in Fig. 3, and the network structure illustrated in Fig. 2(e).

First, we record responses $\mathbf{y}_o$ on each new task image from the original network for outputs on the old tasks (defined by θ_s and θ_o). Our experiments involve classification, so the responses are the set of label probabilities for each training image. Nodes for each new class are added to the output layer, fully connected to the layer beneath, with randomly initialized weights θ_n. The number of new parameters is equal to the number of new classes times the number of nodes in the last shared layer, typically a very small percent of the total number of parameters. In our experiments (Sect. 4.2), we also compare alternate ways of modifying the network for the new task.

Next, we train the network to minimize loss for all tasks and regularization $\mathcal{R}$ using stochastic gradient descent. The regularization $\mathcal{R}$ corresponds to a simple weight decay of 0.0005. When training, we first freeze θ_s and θ_o and train θ_n to convergence. Then, we jointly train all weights until convergence.

For simplicity, we denote the loss functions, outputs, and ground truth for single examples. The total loss is averaged over all images in a batch in training. For new tasks, the loss encourages predictions $\hat{\mathbf{y}}_n$ to be consistent with the ground truth $\mathbf{y}_n$. The tasks in our experiments are multiclass classification, so we use the common [11,20] multinomial logistic loss:

$$\mathcal{L}_{new}(\mathbf{y}_n, \hat{\mathbf{y}}_n) = -\mathbf{y}_n \cdot \log \hat{\mathbf{y}}_n \tag{1}$$

where $\hat{\mathbf{y}}_n$ is the softmax output of the network and $\mathbf{y}_n$ is the one-hot ground truth label vector. If there are multiple new tasks, or if the task is multi-label classification where we make true/false predictions for each label, we take the sum of losses across the new tasks and the labels.

For each original task, we want the output probabilities for each image to be close to the recorded output from the original network. We use the Knowledge Distillation loss, which was found by Hinton et al. [10] to work well for encouraging the outputs of one network to approximate the outputs of another. This is a modified cross-entropy loss that increases the weight for smaller probabilities:

$$\mathcal{L}_{old}(\mathbf{y}_o, \hat{\mathbf{y}}_o) = -H(\mathbf{y}'_o, \hat{\mathbf{y}}'_o) = -\sum_{i=1}^{l} y_o'^{(i)} \log \hat{y}_o'^{(i)} \tag{2}$$

where l is the number of labels and $y_o'^{(i)}$, $\hat{y}_o'^{(i)}$ are the modified versions of recorded and current probabilities $y_o^{(i)}$, $\hat{y}_o^{(i)}$:

$$y_o'^{(i)} = \frac{(y_o^{(i)})^{1/T}}{\sum_j (y_o^{(j)})^{1/T}}, \quad \hat{y}_o'^{(i)} = \frac{(\hat{y}_o^{(i)})^{1/T}}{\sum_j (\hat{y}_o^{(j)})^{1/T}}. \tag{3}$$

If there are multiple old tasks, or if an old task is multi-label classification, we take the sum of the loss for each old task and label. Hinton et al. [10] suggest that setting $T > 1$, which increases the weight of smaller logit values and encourages the network to better encode similarities among classes. We use $T = 2$ according to a grid search on a held out set, which aligns with the author's recommendations. In experiments, use of knowledge distillation loss leads to similar performance to other reasonable losses. Therefore, it is important to constrain outputs for original tasks to be similar to the original network, but the similarity measure is not crucial.

Implementation Details. We use MatConvNet [24] to train our networks using stochastic gradient descent with momentum of 0.9 and dropout enabled in the fully connected layers. The data normalization of the original task is used for the new task. The resizing follows the implementation of the original network, which is 256×256 for AlexNet and 256 pixels in the shortest edge with aspect ratio preserved for VGG. We randomly jitter the training data by taking random fixed-size crops of the resized images and adding variance to the RGB values, as with AlexNet. This data augmentation is applied to feature extraction too.

When training networks, we follow the standard practices for fine-tuning existing networks. We use a learning rate much smaller than when training the original network ($0.1 \sim 0.02$ times the original rate), and lower it once by $10\times$ after the accuracy on a held out set plateaus. The learning rates are selected to maximize new task performance with a reasonable number of epochs. The compared methods converge at similar speeds, so we used the same number of epochs for each method (but not the same for different task pairs). For each scenario, the same learning rate are shared by all methods except feature extraction, which uses $5\times$ the learning rate due to its small number of parameters.

For the feature extraction baseline, we extract features as the last hidden layer of the original network and classify with a two-layer network with 4096 nodes in the hidden layer. For joint training, loss for one task's output nodes is only applied for its own training images. The same number of images are subsampled for every task in each epoch to balance their loss, and we interleave batches of different tasks for gradient descent.

Efficiency Comparison. The most computationally expensive part of using the neural network is evaluating or back-propagating through the shared parameters θ_s, especially the convolutional layers. For training, feature extraction is the fastest because only the new task parameters are tuned. LwF is slightly slower than fine-tuning because it needs to back-propagate through θ_o for old tasks but needs to evaluate and back-propagate through θ_s only once. Joint training is the slowest, because different images are used for different tasks, and each task requires separate back-propagation through the shared parameters.

All methods take approximately the same amount of time to evaluate a test image. However, duplicating the network and fine-tuning for each task takes m times as long to evaluate, where m is the total number of tasks.

4   Experiments

Our experiments are designed to evaluate whether Learning without Forgetting (LwF) is an effective method to learn a new task while preserving performance on old tasks. We compare to baselines of *feature extraction* and *fine-tuning*, which are common approaches to leverage an existing network for a new task without requiring training data for the original tasks. Feature extraction maintains the exact performance on the original task. We also compare to *joint training* (sometimes called multitask learning) as an upper-bound on possible performance, since joint training uses images and labels for original and new tasks, while LwF uses only images and labels for the new tasks.

We experiment on a variety of image classification problems with varying degrees of inter-task similarity. For the original ("old") task, we consider the ILSVRC 2012 subset of *ImageNet* [19] and the *Places2* [27] taster challenge in ILSVRC 2015 [19]. ImageNet has 1,000 object category classes and more than 1,000,000 training images. Places2 has 401 scene classes and more than 8,000,000 training images. We use these large datasets also because we assume we start from a well-trained network, which implies a large-scale dataset. For the new tasks, we consider PASCAL *VOC 2012 image classification* [8] ("VOC"), *Caltech-UCSD Birds-200-2011 fine-grained classification* [25] ("CUB"), and *MIT indoor scene classification* [16] ("Scenes"). These datasets have a moderate number of images for training: 5,717 for VOC; 5,994 for CUB; and 5,360 for Scenes. Among these, VOC is very similar to ImageNet, as subcategories of its labels can be found in ImageNet classes. MIT indoor scene dataset is in turn similar to Places2. CUB is dissimilar to both, since it includes only birds and requires capturing the fine details of the image to make a valid prediction. In one experiment, we use MNIST [12] as the new task expecting our method to underperform, since the hand-written characters are completely unrelated to ImageNet classes.

We mainly use the AlexNet [11] network structure because it is fast to train and well-studied by the community [2,9,26]. We also verify that similar results hold using 16-layer VGGnet [20] on a smaller set of experiments. The original networks pre-trained on ImageNet and Places2 are obtained from public online

Table 1. Performance for the single new task scenario. For all tables, the **difference** of methods' performance with LwF (our method) is reported to facilitate comparison. Mean Average Precision is reported for VOC and accuracy for all others. On the new task, LwF outperforms baselines, and performs comparably with joint training, which uses old task training data we consider unavailable for the other methods. On the old task, our method greatly outperforms fine-tuning and achieves similar performance to joint training. An exception is the MNIST task where LwF does not perform well.

(a) Using AlexNet structure (validation performance for ImageNet/Places2/VOC)

	ImageNet→VOC		ImageNet→CUB		ImageNet→Scenes		Places2→VOC		Places2→CUB		Places2→Scenes		ImageNet→MNIST	
	old	new	old	new	old	new	old	new	old	new	old	new	old	new
LwF (ours)	56.5	75.8	55.1	57.5	55.9	64.5	43.3	72.1	38.4	41.7	43.0	75.3	52.1	99.0
fine-tuning	-1.4	-0.3	-5.1	-1.5	-3.4	-1.0	-1.8	-0.1	-9.1	-0.8	-4.1	-0.8	-4.9	0.2
feat. extraction	0.5	-1.1	2.0	-5.3	1.2	-3.7	-0.2	-3.9	4.7	-19.4	0.2	-0.5	5.0	-0.8
joint training	0.2	0.0	0.5	-0.9	0.5	-0.6	-0.1	0.1	3.3	-0.2	0.2	0.1	4.7	0.2

(b) Test set performance   (c) Using VGGnet structure

	Places2→VOC	
	old	new
LwF (ours)	41.1	75.2
fine-tuning	-1.9	-0.1
feat. extraction	0.1	-3.5
joint training	0.0	0.0

	ImageNet→CUB		ImageNet→Scenes	
	old	new	old	new
LwF (ours)	65.6	72.3	68.1	74.7
fine-tuning	-11.0	-0.2	-5.6	-0.7
feat. extraction	3.1	-9.1	0.7	-5.1
joint training	2.5	2.3	2.0	0.8

sources. At suggestion of the authors of Places2, we fine-tuned the provided Places2 original network on the Places2 training set, due to its sensitivity to image rescaling methods, which slightly improved performance (44% top-1 validation accuracy with 10 jitters) compared to the reported 43%.

We report the center image crop mean average precision for VOC, and center image crop accuracy for all other tasks. We report the accuracy of the validation set of VOC, ImageNet and Places2, and on the test set of CUB and Scenes dataset. Since the test performance of the former three cannot be evaluated frequently, we only provide the performance on their test sets in one experiment.

Our experiments investigate adding a single new task to the network or adding multiple tasks one-by-one. We also examine effect of dataset size and network design. In ablation studies, we examine alternative response-preserving losses, the utility of expanding the network structure, and fine-tuning with a lower learning rate as a method to preserve original task performance.

4.1   Main Experiments

Single New Task Scenario. First, we compare the results of learning one new task among different task pairs and different methods. Table 1(a) and (b) shows the performance of our method, and the relative performance of other methods compared to it using AlexNet. We make the following observations:

On the new task, our method consistently outperforms fine-tuning and feature extraction except for ImageNet→MNIST. The gain over fine-tuning was unexpected and indicates that preserving outputs on the old task is an effective regularizer. (See Sect. 5 for a brief discussion). This finding motivates replacing fine-tuning with LwF as the standard approach for adapting a network to a new task.

On the old task, our method performs better than fine-tuning but often underperforms feature extraction. By changing shared parameters θ_s, fine-tuning significantly degrades performance on the task for which the original network was trained. By jointly adapting θ_s and θ_o to generate similar outputs to the original network on the old task, the performance loss is greatly reduced.

Our method performs similarly to joint training. Our method tends to slightly outperform joint training on the new task but underperform on the old task, which we attribute to a different balance of the losses in the two methods. Overall, the methods perform similarly, a positive result since our method does not require access to the old task training data and is faster to train.

Dissimilar new tasks degrade old task performance more. For example, CUB is very dissimilar task from Places2 [2], and adapting the network to CUB leads to a Places2 accuracy loss of 13.8 % (4.7 % + 9.1 %) for fine-tuning, 4.7 % for LwF, and 1.4 % (4.7 % − 3.3 %) for joint training. In these cases, learning the new task causes considerable drift in the shared parameters, which cannot fully be accounted for by LwF because the distribution of CUB and Places2 images is very different. Even joint training leads to more accuracy loss on Places2→CUB's old task because it cannot find a set of shared parameters that works well for both tasks. As expected, our method does not outperform fine-tuning for ImageNet-¿MNIST on the new task, since the hand-written characters provide poor indirect supervision for the old task, and the old task accuracy drops substantially with both methods, though more with fine-tuning.

Similar observations hold for both VGG and AlexNet structures, except that joint training outperforms consistently for VGG (Table 1(c)), indicating that these results are likely to hold for other network structures as well, though joint training may have a larger benefit on networks with more representational power.

Multiple New Task Scenario. Second, we compare different methods when we cumulatively add new tasks to the system, simulating a scenario in which new object or scene categories are gradually added to the prediction vocabulary. We experiment on gradually adding VOC task to AlexNet trained on Places2, and adding Scene task to AlexNet trained on ImageNet. These pairs have moderate difference between original task and new tasks. We split the new task classes into three parts according to their similarity – VOC into transport, animals and objects, and Scenes into large rooms, medium rooms and small rooms. The images in Scenes are split into these three subsets. Since VOC is a multilabel dataset, it is not possible to split the images into different categories, so the labels are split for each task and images are shared among all the tasks.

Each time a new task is added, the responses of all other tasks Y_o are recomputed, to emulate the situation where data for *all* original tasks are unavailable. Therefore, Y_o for older tasks changes each time. For feature extractor and

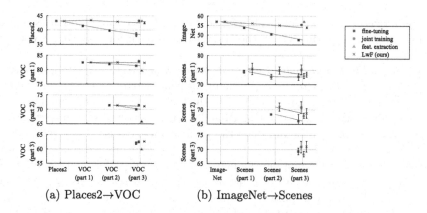

(a) Places2→VOC   (b) ImageNet→Scenes

Fig. 4. Performance of each task when gradually adding new tasks to a pre-trained network. Different tasks are shown in different sub-graphs. The x-axis labels indicate the new task added to the network each time. Error bars shows ± 2 standard deviations for 3 runs with different θ_n random initializations. Markers are jittered horizontally for visualization, but line plots are not jittered to facilitate comparison. For all tasks, our method degrades slower over time than fine-tuning and outperforms feature extraction. For Places2→VOC, our method performs comparably to joint training.

joint training, cumulative training does not apply, so we only report their performance on the final stage where all tasks are added. Figure 4 shows the results on both dataset pairs. Our findings are usually consistent with the single new task scenario: *LwF outperforms fine-tuning on all tasks, outperforms feature extraction for new tasks, and except on the old tasks in ImageNet→Scenes, performs similarly overall to joint training.*

Influence of Dataset Size. We inspect whether the size of the new task dataset affects our performance relative to other methods. We perform this experiment on adding VOC to Places2 AlexNet. We subsample the VOC dataset to 30 %, 10 % and 3 % when training the network, and report the result on the entire validation set. Note that for joint training, since each dataset has a different size, the same number of images are subsampled to train both tasks (resampled each epoch), which means a smaller number of Places2 images being used at one time. Our results are shown in Fig. 5. Results show that *the same observations hold, except that our method suffers more than joint training on the old task as the number of examples is decreased. Differences between LwF and fine-tuning on the old task and between LwF and feature extraction on the new task increase with less data.*

4.2   Design Choices and Alternatives

Choice of Task-Specific Layers. It is possible to regard more layers as task-specific θ_o, θ_n (see Fig. 6(a)) instead of regarding only the output nodes as task-specific. This may provide advantage for both tasks because later layers

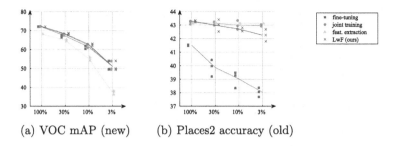

(a) VOC mAP (new)   (b) Places2 accuracy (old)

Fig. 5. Influence of subsampling new task training set on compared methods. The x-axis indicates diminishing training set size. Three runs of our experiments with different random θ_n initialization and dataset subsampling are shown. Scatter points are jittered horizontally for visualization, but line plots are not jittered to facilitate comparison. Differences between LwF and fine-tuning on the old task and between LwF and feature extraction on the new task increase with less data.

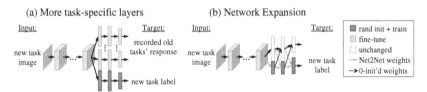

Fig. 6. Illustration for alternative network modification methods. In (a), more fully connected layers are task-specific, rather than shared. In (b), nodes for multiple old tasks (not shown) are connected in the same way. LwF can also be applied to Network Expansion by unfreezing all nodes and matching output responses on the old tasks

tend to be more task specific [2]. However, doing so requires more storage, as most parameters in AlexNet are in the first two fully connected layers. Table 2(a) shows the comparison on three task pairs. *Our results do not indicate any advantage to having additional task-specific layers.*

Network Expansion. We explore another way of modifying the network structure, which we refer to as "network expansion", which adds nodes to some layers. This allows for extra new-task-specific information in the earlier layers while still using the original network's information.

Figure 6(b) illustrates this method. We add 1024 nodes to each layer of the top 3 layers. The weights from all nodes at previous layer to the new nodes at current layer are initialized the same way Net2Net [5] would expand a layer by copying nodes. Weights from new nodes at previous layer to the original nodes at current layer are initialized to zero. The top layer weights of the new nodes are randomly re-initialized. Then we either freeze the existing weights and fine-tune the new weights on the new task ("network expansion"), or train using Learning without Forgetting as before ("network expansion + LwF").

Table 2(b) shows the comparison with our original method. *Network expansion by itself performs better than feature extraction, but neither variant performs*

Table 2. Performance of our method versus various alternative design choices. In most cases, these alternative choices do not provide consistent advantage or disadvantage compared to our method.

(a) Changing the number of task-specific layers

	Places2→VOC		ImageNet→Scenes		ImageNet→CUB	
starting from	old	new	old	new	old	new
output layer (ours)	43.3	72.1	55.9	64.5	55.1	57.5
last hidden layer	43.1	72.5	55.5	64.2	54.8	56.5
2nd last hidden (Fig. 6(a))	43.1	72.6	55.8	64.2	55.2	56.1

(b) Comparison of our method, network expansion, and L2 soft-constraint. Performance relative to Learning without Forgetting is reported. Fine-tuning and feature extraction are shown for comparison. Network expansion by itself underperforms on the new task. Using it with LwF yields worse to similar performance as LwF. L2 soft-constraint produces results between fine-tuning and feature extraction.

	ImageNet→VOC		ImageNet→CUB		ImageNet→Scenes		Places2→VOC		Places2→CUB		Places2→Scenes	
	old	new	old	new	old	new	old	new	old	new	old	new
LwF (ours)	56.5	75.8	55.1	57.5	55.9	64.5	43.3	72.1	38.4	41.7	43.0	75.3
fine-tuning	-1.4	-0.3	-5.1	-1.5	-3.4	-1.0	-1.8	-0.1	-9.1	-0.8	-4.1	-0.8
feat. extraction	0.5	-1.1	2.0	-5.3	1.2	-3.7	-0.2	-3.9	4.7	-19.4	0.2	-0.5
network expansion	0.5	-1.1	2.0	-3.6	1.2	-2.0	-0.2	-3.6	4.7	-6.9	0.2	0.0
network expansion + LwF	0.0	0.1	-0.3	-0.5	-0.2	-0.4	0.0	0.2	1.3	-0.1	-0.3	-0.2
L2 weight soft-constraint	-1.0	-0.4	-4.2	-2.0	-3.0	-1.0	-1.5	-0.5	-8.5	-3.3	-4.0	-0.4

(c) Changing the response-preserving loss. Only L_2 underperforms on the old task.

	Places2	VOC
LwF (L_1)	43.5	71.9
LwF (L_2)	42.2	72.3
LwF (cross-entropy)	43.6	71.8
LwF (know. distill.)	43.3	72.1

(d) Attempt to lower θ_s's learning rate when fine-tuning. The degradation of old task performance is not avoided, and the new task performance drops.

	ImageNet→VOC		Places2→VOC	
	old	new	old	new
fine-tuning	55.2	75.6	41.5	71.9
fine-tuning (10% θ_s learning rate)	55.9	75.5	41.5	71.4

as well as LwF on new tasks. We leave exploration of other possible versions of network expansion (e.g. number of top layers to expand, number of new nodes at each layer, parameter initialization method) as future work.

L2 Soft-Constrained Weights. Perhaps an obvious alternative to LwF is to keep the network parameters (instead of the response) close to the original. We compare with the baseline that adds $\frac{1}{2}\lambda_c\|w - w_0\|^2$ to the loss for fine-tuning, where w and w_0 are flattened vectors of all shared parameters θ_s and their original values. Coefficient λ is set to 0.5 for VOC and 0.05 for other new tasks.

As shown in Table 2(b), *our method outperforms this baseline, which produces a result between feature extraction (no parameter change) and fine-tuning (free parameter change).* We believe that by regularizing the output, our method maintains old task performance better than regularizing individual parameters, since many small parameter changes could cause big changes in the outputs.

Choice of Response Preserving Loss. We compare the use of L_1, L_2, cross-entropy loss, and knowledge distillation loss with $T = 2$ for keeping $\mathbf{y}'_o, \hat{\mathbf{y}}'_o$

similar. We test on adding VOC to Places2 AlexNet. Table 2(c) shows our results. *Results indicate no clear overall advantage or disadvantage for any loss, though L_2 underperforms on the original task.*

Effect of Lower Learning Rate of Shared Parameters. We investigate whether simply lowering the learning rate of the shared parameters θ_s would preserve the original task performance. The result is shown in Table 2(d). A reduced learning rate does not prevent fine-tuning from significantly reducing original task performance, and it reduces new task performance. This shows that *simply reducing the learning rate of shared layers is insufficient for original task preservation.*

5 Discussion

We address the problem of adapting a vision system to a new task while preserving performance on original tasks, without access to training data for the original tasks. We propose the Learning without Forgetting method for convolutional neural networks, which can be seen as a hybrid of knowledge distillation and fine-tuning, learning parameters that are discriminative for the new task while preserving outputs for the original tasks on the training data.

This work has implications for two uses. First, if we want to expand the set of possible predictions on an existing network, our method performs similarly to joint training but is faster to train and does not require access to the training data for previous tasks. Second, if we care only about the performance for the new task, our method consistently outperforms the current standard practice of fine-tuning. Fine-tuning approaches use a low learning rate in hopes that the parameters will settle in a "good" local minimum not too far from the original values. Preserving outputs on the old task is a more direct and interpretable way to retain the important shared structures learned for the previous tasks.

We see several directions for future work. We have demonstrated the effectiveness of LwF for image classification but would like to further experiment on semantic segmentation, detection, and problems outside of computer vision. Additionally, one could explore variants of the approach, such as maintaining a set of unlabeled images to serve as representative examples for previously learned tasks. Theoretically, it would be interesting to bound the old task performance based on preserving outputs for a sample drawn from a different distribution. More generally, there is a need for approaches that are suitable for online learning across different tasks, especially when classes have heavy tailed distributions.

Acknowledgement. This work is supported in part by NSF Awards 14-46765 and 10-53768 and ONR MURI N000014-16-1-2007.

References

1. Agrawal, P., Girshick, R., Malik, J.: Analyzing the performance of multilayer neural networks for object recognition. In: Fleet, D., Pajdla, T., Schiele, B., Tuytelaars, T. (eds.) ECCV 2014, Part VII. LNCS, vol. 8695, pp. 329–344. Springer, Heidelberg (2014)
2. Azizpour, H., Razavian, A., Sullivan, J., Maki, A., Carlsson, S.: Factors of transferability for a generic convnet representation. IEEE Trans. Pattern Anal. Mach. Intell. **38**, 1790–1802 (2014)
3. Caruana, R.: Multitask learning. Mach. Learn. **28**(1), 41–75 (1997)
4. Chapelle, O., Shivaswamy, P., Vadrevu, S., Weinberger, K., Zhang, Y., Tseng, B.: Boosted multi-task learning. Mach. Learn. **85**(1–2), 149–173 (2011)
5. Chen, T., Goodfellow, I., Shlens, J.: Net2net: accelerating learning via knowledge transfer. In: Proceedings of the International Conference on Learning Representations (ICLR) (2016, to appear)
6. Donahue, J., Jia, Y., Vinyals, O., Hoffman, J., Zhang, N., Tzeng, E., Darrell, T.: DeCAF: a deep convolutional activation feature for generic visual recognition. In: International Conference in Machine Learning (ICML) (2014)
7. Eaton, E., Ruvolo, P.L.: Ella: an efficient lifelong learning algorithm. In: Proceedings of the 30th International Conference on Machine Learning, pp. 507–515 (2013)
8. Everingham, M., Eslami, S.M.A., Van Gool, L., Williams, C.K.I., Winn, J., Zisserman, A.: The pascal visual object classes challenge: a retrospective. Int. J. Comput. Vis. **111**(1), 98–136 (2015)
9. Girshick, R., Donahue, J., Darrell, T., Malik, J.: Rich feature hierarchies for accurate object detection and semantic segmentation. In: The IEEE Conference on Computer Vision and Pattern Recognition (CVPR), June 2014
10. Hinton, G., Vinyals, O., Dean, J.: Distilling the knowledge in a neural network. In: NIPS Workshop (2014)
11. Krizhevsky, A., Sutskever, I., Hinton, G.E.: Imagenet classification with deep convolutional neural networks. In: Advances in Neural Information Processing Systems, pp. 1097–1105 (2012)
12. LeCun, Y., Bottou, L., Bengio, Y., Haffner, P.: Gradient-based learning applied to document recognition. Proc. IEEE **86**(11), 2278–2324 (1998)
13. Long, M., Wang, J.: Learning transferable features with deep adaptation networks. arXiv preprint (2015). arXiv:1502.02791
14. Mitchell, T., Cohen, W., Hruschka, E., Talukdar, P., Betteridge, J., Carlson, A., Dalvi, B., Gardner, M., Kisiel, B., Krishnamurthy, J., Lao, N., Mazaitis, K., Mohamed, T., Nakashole, N., Platanios, E., Ritter, A., Samadi, M., Settles, B., Wang, R., Wijaya, D., Gupta, A., Chen, X., Saparov, A., Greaves, M., Welling, J.: Never-ending learning. In: Proceedings of the Twenty-Ninth AAAI Conference on Artificial Intelligence (AAAI 2015) (2015)
15. Pan, S.J., Yang, Q.: A survey on transfer learning. IEEE Trans. Knowl. Data Eng. **22**(10), 1345–1359 (2010)
16. Quattoni, A., Torralba, A.: Recognizing indoor scenes. In: IEEE Conference on Computer Vision and Pattern Recognition, CVPR 2009, pp. 413–420 (2009)
17. Razavian, A., Azizpour, H., Sullivan, J., Carlsson, S.: CNN features off-the-shelf: an astounding baseline for recognition. In: Proceedings of the IEEE Conference on Computer Vision and Pattern Recognition Workshops, pp. 806–813 (2014)
18. Romero, A., Ballas, N., Kahou, S.E., Chassang, A., Gatta, C., Bengio, Y.: Fitnets: hints for thin deep nets. In: Proceedings of the International Conference on Learning Representations (ICLR) (2015)

19. Russakovsky, O., Deng, J., Su, H., Krause, J., Satheesh, S., Ma, S., Huang, Z., Karpathy, A., Khosla, A., Bernstein, M., Berg, A.C., Fei-Fei, L.: Imagenet large scale visual recognition challenge. Int. J. Comput. Vis. (IJCV) **115**(3), 211–252 (2015)
20. Simonyan, K., Zisserman, A.: Very deep convolutional networks for large-scale image recognition. CoRR abs/1409.1556 (2014)
21. Terekhov, A.V., Montone, G., ORegan, J.K.: Knowledge transfer in deep block-modular neural networks. In: Wilson, S.P., Verschure, P.F.M.J., Mura, A., Prescott, T.J. (eds.) Living Machines 2015. LNCS, vol. 9222, pp. 268–279. Springer, Heidelberg (2015)
22. Thrun, S.: Lifelong learning algorithms. In: Thrun, S., Pratt, L. (eds.) Learning to Learn, pp. 181–209. Springer, New York (1998)
23. Tzeng, E., Hoffman, J., Darrell, T., Saenko, K.: Simultaneous deep transfer across domains and tasks. In: Proceedings of the IEEE International Conference on Computer Vision, pp. 4068–4076 (2015)
24. Vedaldi, A., Lenc, K.: Matconvnet - convolutional neural networks for matlab. In: Proceeding of the ACM International Conference on Multimedia (2015)
25. Wah, C., Branson, S., Welinder, P., Perona, P., Belongie, S.: The Caltech-UCSD Birds-200-2011 Dataset. Technical report. CNS-TR-2011-001, California Institute of Technology (2011)
26. Yosinski, J., Clune, J., Bengio, Y., Lipson, H.: How transferable are features in deep neural networks? In: Advances in Neural Information Processing Systems, pp. 3320–3328 (2014)
27. Zhou, B., Khosla, A., Lapedriza, A., Torralba, A., Oliva, A.: Places2: a large-scale database for scene understanding. arXiv preprint (2015) (to appear)

Identity Mappings in Deep Residual Networks

Kaiming He[✉], Xiangyu Zhang, Shaoqing Ren, and Jian Sun

Microsoft Research, Beijing, China
kmh.kaiminghe@gmail.com

Abstract. Deep residual networks have emerged as a family of extremely deep architectures showing compelling accuracy and nice convergence behaviors. In this paper, we analyze the propagation formulations behind the residual building blocks, which suggest that the forward and backward signals can be directly propagated from one block to any other block, when using identity mappings as the skip connections and after-addition activation. A series of ablation experiments support the importance of these identity mappings. This motivates us to propose a new residual unit, which makes training easier and improves generalization. We report improved results using a 1001-layer ResNet on CIFAR-10 (4.62 % error) and CIFAR-100, and a 200-layer ResNet on ImageNet. Code is available at: https://github.com/KaimingHe/resnet-1k-layers.

1 Introduction

Deep residual networks (ResNets) [1] consist of many stacked "Residual Units". Each unit (Fig. 1(a)) can be expressed in a general form:

$$\mathbf{y}_l = h(\mathbf{x}_l) + \mathcal{F}(\mathbf{x}_l, \mathcal{W}_l),$$
$$\mathbf{x}_{l+1} = f(\mathbf{y}_l),$$

where $\mathbf{x}_l$ and $\mathbf{x}_{l+1}$ are input and output of the l-th unit, and $\mathcal{F}$ is a residual function. In [1], $h(\mathbf{x}_l) = \mathbf{x}_l$ is an identity mapping and f is a ReLU [2] function.

ResNets that are over 100-layer deep have shown state-of-the-art accuracy for several challenging recognition tasks on ImageNet [3] and MS COCO [4] competitions. The central idea of ResNets is to learn the additive residual function $\mathcal{F}$ with respect to $h(\mathbf{x}_l)$, with a key choice of using an identity mapping $h(\mathbf{x}_l) = \mathbf{x}_l$. This is realized by attaching an identity skip connection ("shortcut").

In this paper, we analyze deep residual networks by focusing on creating a "direct" path for propagating information—not only within a residual unit, but through the entire network. Our derivations reveal that *if both $h(\mathbf{x}_l)$ and $f(\mathbf{y}_l)$ are identity mappings*, the signal could be *directly* propagated from one unit to any other units, in both forward and backward passes. Our experiments empirically show that training in general becomes easier when the architecture is closer to the above two conditions.

To understand the role of skip connections, we analyze and compare various types of $h(\mathbf{x}_l)$. We find that the identity mapping $h(\mathbf{x}_l) = \mathbf{x}_l$ chosen in [1]

B. Leibe et al. (Eds.): ECCV 2016, Part IV, LNCS 9908, pp. 630–645, 2016.
DOI: 10.1007/978-3-319-46493-0_38

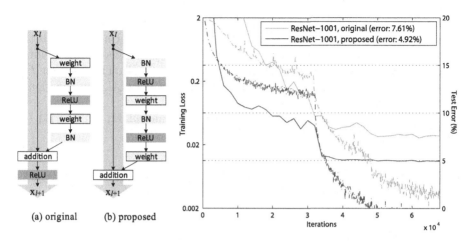

Fig. 1. Left: (a) original Residual Unit in [1]; (b) proposed Residual Unit. The grey arrows indicate the easiest paths for the information to propagate, corresponding to the additive term "$\mathbf{x}_l$" in Eq. (4) (forward propagation) and the additive term "1" in Eq. (5) (backward propagation). **Right**: training curves on CIFAR-10 of **1001-layer** ResNets. Solid lines denote test error (y-axis on the right), and dashed lines denote training loss (y-axis on the left). The proposed unit makes ResNet-1001 easier to train.

achieves the fastest error reduction and lowest training loss among all variants we investigated, whereas skip connections of scaling, gating [5–7], and 1×1 convolutions all lead to higher training loss and error. These experiments suggest that keeping a "clean" information path (indicated by the grey arrows in Figs. 1, 2 and 4) is helpful for easing optimization.

To construct an identity mapping $f(\mathbf{y}_l) = \mathbf{y}_l$, we view the activation functions (ReLU and BN [8]) as *"pre-activation"* of the weight layers, in contrast to conventional wisdom of "post-activation". This point of view leads to a new residual unit design, shown in (Fig. 1(b)). Based on this unit, we present competitive results on CIFAR-10/100 with a 1001-layer ResNet, which is much easier to train and generalizes better than the original ResNet in [1]. We further report improved results on ImageNet using a 200-layer ResNet, for which the counterpart of [1] starts to overfit. These results suggest that there is much room to exploit the dimension of *network depth*, a key to the success of modern deep learning.

2   Analysis of Deep Residual Networks

The ResNets developed in [1] are *modularized* architectures that stack building blocks of the same connecting shape. In this paper we call these blocks *"Residual Units"*. The original Residual Unit in [1] performs the following computation:

$$\mathbf{y}_l = h(\mathbf{x}_l) + \mathcal{F}(\mathbf{x}_l, \mathcal{W}_l), \tag{1}$$

$$\mathbf{x}_{l+1} = f(\mathbf{y}_l). \tag{2}$$

Here $\mathbf{x}_l$ is the input feature to the l-th Residual Unit. $\mathcal{W}_l = \{W_{l,k}|_{1 \le k \le K}\}$ is a set of weights (and biases) associated with the l-th Residual Unit, and K is the number of layers in a Residual Unit (K is 2 or 3 in [1]). $\mathcal{F}$ denotes the residual function, e.g., a stack of two 3×3 convolutional layers in [1]. The function f is the operation after element-wise addition, and in [1] f is ReLU. The function h is set as an identity mapping: $h(\mathbf{x}_l) = \mathbf{x}_l$.[1]

If f is also an identity mapping: $\mathbf{x}_{l+1} \equiv \mathbf{y}_l$, we can put Eq. (2) into Eq. (1) and obtain:

$$\mathbf{x}_{l+1} = \mathbf{x}_l + \mathcal{F}(\mathbf{x}_l, \mathcal{W}_l). \tag{3}$$

Recursively $\left(\mathbf{x}_{l+2} = \mathbf{x}_{l+1} + \mathcal{F}(\mathbf{x}_{l+1}, \mathcal{W}_{l+1}) = \mathbf{x}_l + \mathcal{F}(\mathbf{x}_l, \mathcal{W}_l) + \mathcal{F}(\mathbf{x}_{l+1}, \mathcal{W}_{l+1})\text{, etc.}\right)$ we will have:

$$\mathbf{x}_L = \mathbf{x}_l + \sum_{i=l}^{L-1} \mathcal{F}(\mathbf{x}_i, \mathcal{W}_i), \tag{4}$$

for *any deeper unit* L and *any shallower unit* l. Equation (4) exhibits some nice properties. **(i)** The feature $\mathbf{x}_L$ of any deeper unit L can be represented as the feature $\mathbf{x}_l$ of any shallower unit l plus a residual function in a form of $\sum_{i=l}^{L-1} \mathcal{F}$, indicating that the model is in a *residual* fashion between any units L and l. **(ii)** The feature $\mathbf{x}_L = \mathbf{x}_0 + \sum_{i=0}^{L-1} \mathcal{F}(\mathbf{x}_i, \mathcal{W}_i)$, of any deep unit L, is the *summation* of the outputs of all preceding residual functions (plus $\mathbf{x}_0$). This is in contrast to a "plain network" where a feature $\mathbf{x}_L$ is a series of matrix-vector *products*, say, $\prod_{i=0}^{L-1} W_i \mathbf{x}_0$ (ignoring BN and ReLU).

Equation (4) also leads to nice backward propagation properties. Denoting the loss function as $\mathcal{E}$, from the chain rule of backpropagation [9] we have:

$$\frac{\partial \mathcal{E}}{\partial \mathbf{x}_l} = \frac{\partial \mathcal{E}}{\partial \mathbf{x}_L} \frac{\partial \mathbf{x}_L}{\partial \mathbf{x}_l} = \frac{\partial \mathcal{E}}{\partial \mathbf{x}_L} \left(1 + \frac{\partial}{\partial \mathbf{x}_l} \sum_{i=l}^{L-1} \mathcal{F}(\mathbf{x}_i, \mathcal{W}_i)\right). \tag{5}$$

Equation (5) indicates that the gradient $\frac{\partial \mathcal{E}}{\partial \mathbf{x}_l}$ can be decomposed into two additive terms: a term of $\frac{\partial \mathcal{E}}{\partial \mathbf{x}_L}$ that propagates information directly without concerning any weight layers, and another term of $\frac{\partial \mathcal{E}}{\partial \mathbf{x}_L} \left(\frac{\partial}{\partial \mathbf{x}_l} \sum_{i=l}^{L-1} \mathcal{F}\right)$ that propagates through the weight layers. The additive term of $\frac{\partial \mathcal{E}}{\partial \mathbf{x}_L}$ ensures that information is directly propagated back to *any shallower unit* l. Equation (5) also suggests that it is unlikely for the gradient $\frac{\partial \mathcal{E}}{\partial \mathbf{x}_l}$ to be canceled out for a mini-batch, because in general the term $\frac{\partial}{\partial \mathbf{x}_l} \sum_{i=l}^{L-1} \mathcal{F}$ cannot be always -1 for all samples in a mini-batch. This implies that the gradient of a layer does not vanish even when the weights are arbitrarily small.

---

[1] It is noteworthy that there are Residual Units for increasing dimensions and reducing feature map sizes [1] in which h is not identity. In this case the following derivations do not hold strictly. But as there are only a very few such units (two on CIFAR and three on ImageNet, depending on image sizes [1]), we expect that they do not have the exponential impact as we present in Sect. 3. One may also think of our derivations as applied to all Residual Units within the same feature map size.

Discussions. Equations (4) and (5) suggest that the signal can be directly propagated from any unit to another, both forward and backward. The foundation of Eq. (4) is two identity mappings: (i) the identity skip connection $h(\mathbf{x}_l) = \mathbf{x}_l$, and (ii) the condition that f is an identity mapping.

These directly propagated information flows are represented by the grey arrows in Figs. 1, 2 and 4. And the above two conditions are true when these grey arrows cover no operations (expect addition) and thus are "clean". In the following two sections we separately investigate the impacts of the two conditions.

3 On the Importance of Identity Skip Connections

Let's consider a simple modification, $h(\mathbf{x}_l) = \lambda_l \mathbf{x}_l$, to break the identity shortcut:

$$\mathbf{x}_{l+1} = \lambda_l \mathbf{x}_l + \mathcal{F}(\mathbf{x}_l, \mathcal{W}_l), \tag{6}$$

where λ_l is a modulating scalar (for simplicity we still assume f is identity). Recursively applying this formulation we obtain an equation similar to Eq. (4): $\mathbf{x}_L = (\prod_{i=l}^{L-1} \lambda_i)\mathbf{x}_l + \sum_{i=l}^{L-1}(\prod_{j=i+1}^{L-1} \lambda_j)\mathcal{F}(\mathbf{x}_i, \mathcal{W}_i)$, or simply:

$$\mathbf{x}_L = (\prod_{i=l}^{L-1} \lambda_i)\mathbf{x}_l + \sum_{i=l}^{L-1} \hat{\mathcal{F}}(\mathbf{x}_i, \mathcal{W}_i), \tag{7}$$

where the notation $\hat{\mathcal{F}}$ absorbs the scalars into the residual functions. Similar to Eq. (5), we have backpropagation of the following form:

$$\frac{\partial \mathcal{E}}{\partial \mathbf{x}_l} = \frac{\partial \mathcal{E}}{\partial \mathbf{x}_L} \left((\prod_{i=l}^{L-1} \lambda_i) + \frac{\partial}{\partial \mathbf{x}_l} \sum_{i=l}^{L-1} \hat{\mathcal{F}}(\mathbf{x}_i, \mathcal{W}_i) \right). \tag{8}$$

Unlike Eq. (5), in Eq. (8) the first additive term is modulated by a factor $\prod_{i=l}^{L-1} \lambda_i$. For an extremely deep network (L is large), if $\lambda_i > 1$ for all i, this factor can be exponentially large; if $\lambda_i < 1$ for all i, this factor can be exponentially small and vanish, which blocks the backpropagated signal from the shortcut and forces it to flow through the weight layers. This results in optimization difficulties as we show by experiments.

In the above analysis, the original identity skip connection in Eq. (3) is replaced with a simple scaling $h(\mathbf{x}_l) = \lambda_l \mathbf{x}_l$. If the skip connection $h(\mathbf{x}_l)$ represents more complicated transforms (such as gating and 1×1 convolutions), in Eq. (8) the first term becomes $\prod_{i=l}^{L-1} h_i'$ where h' is the derivative of h. This product may also impede information propagation and hamper the training procedure as witnessed in the following experiments.

3.1 Experiments on Skip Connections

We experiment with the 110-layer ResNet as presented in [1] on CIFAR-10 [10]. This extremely deep ResNet-110 has 54 two-layer Residual Units (consisting of

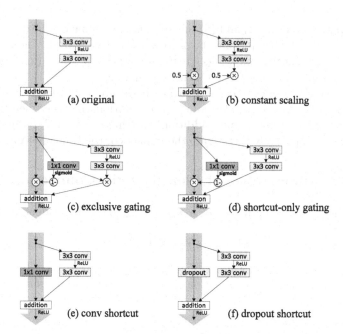

Fig. 2. Various types of shortcut connections used in Table 1. The grey arrows indicate the easiest paths for the information to propagate. The shortcut connections in (b–f) are impeded by different components. For simplifying illustrations we do not display the BN layers, which are adopted right after the weight layers for all units here.

3×3 convolutional layers) and is challenging for optimization. Our implementation details (see appendix) are the same as [1]. Throughout this paper we report the median accuracy of **5 runs** for each architecture on CIFAR, reducing the impacts of random variations.

Though our above analysis is driven by identity f, the experiments in this section are all based on $f =$ ReLU as in [1]; we address identity f in the next section. Our baseline ResNet-110 has 6.61 % error on the test set. The comparisons of other variants (Fig. 2 and Table 1) are summarized as follows:

Constant Scaling. We set $\lambda = 0.5$ for all shortcuts (Fig. 2(b)). We further study two cases of scaling $\mathcal{F}$: (i) $\mathcal{F}$ is not scaled; or (ii) $\mathcal{F}$ is scaled by a constant scalar of $1 - \lambda = 0.5$, which is similar to the highway gating [6,7] but with frozen gates. The former case does not converge well; the latter is able to converge, but the test error (Table 1, 12.35 %) is substantially higher than the original ResNet-110. Figure 3(a) shows that the training error is higher than that of the original ResNet-110, suggesting that the optimization has difficulties when the shortcut signal is scaled down.

Exclusive Gating. Following the Highway Networks [6,7] that adopt a gating mechanism [5], we consider a gating function $g(\mathbf{x}) = \sigma(W_g\mathbf{x} + b_g)$ where a transform is represented by weights W_g and biases b_g followed by the sigmoid

Table 1. Classification error on the CIFAR-10 test set using ResNet-110 [1], with different types of shortcut connections applied to all Residual Units. We report "fail" when the test error is higher than 20 %.

Case	Fig.	On shortcut	On $\mathcal{F}$	Error (%)	Remark
Original [1]	Fig. 2(a)	1	1	**6.61**	
Constant scaling	Fig. 2(b)	0	1	fail	This is a plain net
		0.5	1	fail	
		0.5	0.5	12.35	frozen gating
Exclusive gating	Fig. 2(c)	$1 - g(\mathbf{x})$	$g(\mathbf{x})$	fail	init b_g=0 to -5
		$1 - g(\mathbf{x})$	$g(\mathbf{x})$	8.70	init $b_g = -6$
		$1 - g(\mathbf{x})$	$g(\mathbf{x})$	9.81	init $b_g = -7$
Shortcut-only gating	Fig. 2(d)	$1 - g(\mathbf{x})$	1	12.86	init $b_g = 0$
		$1 - g(\mathbf{x})$	1	6.91	init $b_g = -6$
1×1 conv shortcut	Fig. 2(e)	1×1 conv	1	12.22	
Dropout shortcut	Fig. 2(f)	dropout 0.5	1	fail	

function $\sigma(x) = \frac{1}{1+e^{-x}}$. In a convolutional network $g(\mathbf{x})$ is realized by a 1×1 convolutional layer. The gating function modulates the signal by element-wise multiplication.

We investigate the "exclusive" gates as used in [6,7]—the $\mathcal{F}$ path is scaled by $g(\mathbf{x})$ and the shortcut path is scaled by $1 - g(\mathbf{x})$. See Fig. 2(c). We find that the initialization of the biases b_g is critical for training gated models, and following the guidelines[2] in [6,7], we conduct hyper-parameter search on the initial value of b_g in the range of 0 to -10 with a decrement step of -1 on the training set by cross-validation. The best value (-6 here) is then used for training on the training set, leading to a test result of 8.70 % (Table 1), which still lags far behind the ResNet-110 baseline. Figure 3(b) shows the training curves. Table 1 also reports the results of using other initialized values, noting that the exclusive gating network does not converge to a good solution when b_g is not appropriately initialized.

The impact of the exclusive gating mechanism is two-fold. When $1 - g(\mathbf{x})$ approaches 1, the gated shortcut connections are closer to identity which helps information propagation; but in this case $g(\mathbf{x})$ approaches 0 and suppresses the function $\mathcal{F}$. To isolate the effects of the gating functions on the shortcut path alone, we investigate a non-exclusive gating mechanism in the next.

Shortcut-Only Gating. In this case the function $\mathcal{F}$ is not scaled; only the shortcut path is gated by $1 - g(\mathbf{x})$. See Fig. 2(d). The initialized value of b_g is still essential in this case. When the initialized b_g is 0 (so initially the expectation of $1 - g(\mathbf{x})$ is 0.5), the network converges to a poor result of 12.86 % (Table 1). This is also caused by higher training error (Fig. 3(c)).

---

[2] See also: `people.idsia.ch/~rupesh/very_deep_learning/` by [6,7].

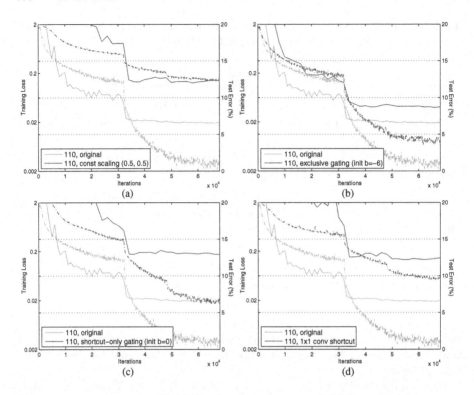

Fig. 3. Training curves on CIFAR-10 of various shortcuts. Solid lines denote test error (y-axis on the right), and dashed lines denote training loss (y-axis on the left).

When the initialized b_g is very negatively biased (*e.g.*, -6), the value of $1 - g(\mathbf{x})$ is closer to 1 and the shortcut connection is nearly an identity mapping. Therefore, the result (6.91 %, Table 1) is much closer to the ResNet-110 baseline.

1×1 Convolutional Shortcut. Next we experiment with 1×1 convolutional shortcut connections that replace the identity. This option has been investigated in [1] (known as option C) on a 34-layer ResNet (16 Residual Units) and shows good results, suggesting that 1×1 shortcut connections could be useful. But we find that this is not the case when there are many Residual Units. The 110-layer ResNet has a poorer result (12.22 %, Table 1) when using 1×1 convolutional shortcuts. Again, the training error becomes higher (Fig. 3(d)). When stacking so many Residual Units (54 for ResNet-110), even the shortest path may still impede signal propagation. We witnessed similar phenomena on ImageNet with ResNet-101 when using 1×1 convolutional shortcuts.

Dropout Shortcut. Last we experiment with dropout [11] (at a ratio of 0.5) which we adopt on the output of the identity shortcut (Fig. 2(f)). The network fails to converge to a good solution. Dropout statistically imposes a scale of λ with an expectation of 0.5 on the shortcut, and similar to constant scaling by 0.5, it impedes signal propagation.

Table 2. Classification error (%) on the CIFAR-10 test set using different activation functions.

Case	Fig.	ResNet-110	ResNet-164
Original Residual Unit [1]	Fig. 4(a)	6.61	5.93
BN after addition	Fig. 4(b)	8.17	6.50
ReLU before addition	Fig. 4(c)	7.84	6.14
ReLU-only pre-activation	Fig. 4(d)	6.71	5.91
Full pre-activation	Fig. 4(e)	**6.37**	**5.46**

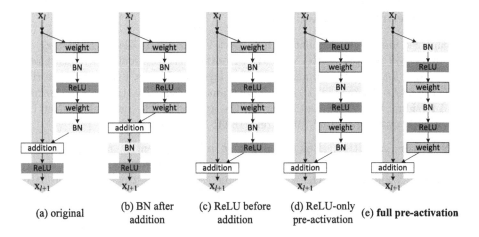

(a) original   (b) BN after addition   (c) ReLU before addition   (d) ReLU-only pre-activation   (e) **full pre-activation**

Fig. 4. Various usages of activation in Table 2. All these units consist of the same components—only the orders are different.

3.2   Discussions

As indicated by the grey arrows in Fig. 2, the shortcut connections are the most direct paths for the information to propagate. *Multiplicative* manipulations (scaling, gating, 1×1 convolutions, and dropout) on the shortcuts can hamper information propagation and lead to optimization problems.

It is noteworthy that the gating and 1×1 convolutional shortcuts introduce more parameters, and should have stronger *representational* abilities than identity shortcuts. In fact, the shortcut-only gating and 1×1 convolution cover the solution space of identity shortcuts (*i.e.*, they could be optimized as identity shortcuts). However, their training error is higher than that of identity shortcuts, indicating that the degradation of these models is caused by optimization issues, instead of representational abilities.

4   On the Usage of Activation Functions

Experiments in the above section support the analysis in Eqs. (5) and (8), both being derived under the assumption that the after-addition activation f is the identity mapping. But in the above experiments f is ReLU as designed in [1], so Eqs. (5) and (8) are approximate in the above experiments. Next we investigate the impact of f.

We want to make f an identity mapping, which is done by re-arranging the activation functions (ReLU and/or BN). The original Residual Unit in [1] has a shape in Fig. 4(a)—BN is used after each weight layer, and ReLU is adopted after BN except that the last ReLU in a Residual Unit is after element-wise addition (f = ReLU). Figure 4(b–e) show the alternatives we investigated, explained as following.

4.1 Experiments on Activation

In this section we experiment with ResNet-110 and a 164-layer *Bottleneck* [1] architecture (denoted as ResNet-164). A bottleneck Residual Unit consist of a 1×1 layer for reducing dimension, a 3×3 layer, and a 1×1 layer for restoring dimension. As designed in [1], its computational complexity is similar to the two-3×3 Residual Unit. More details are in the appendix. The baseline ResNet-164 has a competitive result of 5.93 % on CIFAR-10 (Table 2).

BN After Addition. Before turning f into an identity mapping, we go the opposite way by adopting BN after addition (Fig. 4(b)). In this case f involves BN and ReLU. The results become considerably worse than the baseline (Table 2). Unlike the original design, now the BN layer alters the signal that passes through the shortcut and impedes information propagation, as reflected by the difficulties on reducing training loss at the beginning of training (Fig. 6 left).

ReLU Before Addition. A naïve choice of making f into an identity mapping is to move the ReLU before addition (Fig. 4(c)). However, this leads to a *non-negative* output from the transform $\mathcal{F}$, while intuitively a "residual" function should take values in $(-\infty, +\infty)$. As a result, the forward propagated signal is monotonically increasing. This may impact the representational ability, and the result is worse (7.84 %, Table 2) than the baseline. We expect to have a residual function taking values in $(-\infty, +\infty)$. This condition is satisfied by other Residual Units including the following ones.

Post-activation or Pre-activation? In the original design (Eqs. (1) and (2)), the activation $\mathbf{x}_{l+1} = f(\mathbf{y}_l)$ affects *both paths* in the *next* Residual Unit: $\mathbf{y}_{l+1} = f(\mathbf{y}_l) + \mathcal{F}(f(\mathbf{y}_l), \mathcal{W}_{l+1})$. Next we develop an *asymmetric* form where an activation $\hat{f}$ only affects the $\mathcal{F}$ path: $\mathbf{y}_{l+1} = \mathbf{y}_l + \mathcal{F}(\hat{f}(\mathbf{y}_l), \mathcal{W}_{l+1})$, for any l (Fig. 5(a) to (b)). By renaming the notations, we have the following form:

$$\mathbf{x}_{l+1} = \mathbf{x}_l + \mathcal{F}(\hat{f}(\mathbf{x}_l), \mathcal{W}_l), \tag{9}$$

It is easy to see that Eq. (9) is similar to Eq. (4), and can enable a backward formulation similar to Eq. (5). For this new Residual Unit as in Eq. (9), the new after-addition activation becomes an identity mapping. This design means that

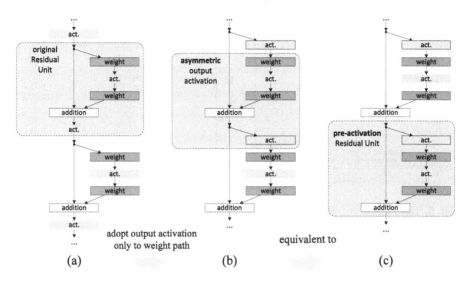

Fig. 5. Using asymmetric after-addition activation is equivalent to constructing a *pre-activation* Residual Unit.

Table 3. Classification error (%) on the CIFAR-10/100 test set using the original Residual Units and our pre-activation Residual Units.

Dataset	Network	Baseline unit	Pre-activation unit
CIFAR-10	ResNet-110 (1layer skip)	9.90	8.91
	ResNet-110	6.61	6.37
	ResNet-164	5.93	5.46
	ResNet-1001	7.61	4.92
CIFAR-100	ResNet-164	25.16	24.33
	ResNet-1001	27.82	22.71

if a new after-addition activation $\hat{f}$ is asymmetrically adopted, it is equivalent to recasting $\hat{f}$ as the *pre-activation* of the next Residual Unit. This is illustrated in Fig. 5.

The distinction between post-activation/pre-activation is caused by the presence of the element-wise *addition*. For a plain network that has N layers, there are $N - 1$ activations (BN/ReLU), and it does not matter whether we think of them as post- or pre-activations. But for branched layers merged by addition, the position of activation matters.

We experiment with two such designs: (i) ReLU-only pre-activation (Fig. 4(d)), and (ii) full pre-activation (Fig. 4(e)) where BN and ReLU are both adopted before weight layers. Table 2 shows that the ReLU-only pre-activation performs very similar to the baseline on ResNet-110/164. This ReLU layer is not used in conjunction with a BN layer, and may not enjoy the benefits of BN [8].

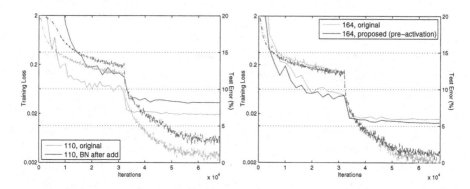

Fig. 6. Training curves on CIFAR-10. **Left**: BN after addition (Fig. 4(b)) using ResNet-110. **Right**: pre-activation unit (Fig. 4(e)) on ResNet-164. Solid lines denote test error, and dashed lines denote training loss.

Somehow surprisingly, when BN and ReLU are both used as pre-activation, the results are improved by healthy margins (Tables 2 and 3). In Table 3 we report results using various architectures: (i) ResNet-110, (ii) ResNet-164, (iii) a 110-layer ResNet architecture in which each shortcut skips only 1 layer (*i.e.*, a Residual Unit has only 1 layer), denoted as "ResNet-110(1layer)", and (iv) a 1001-layer bottleneck architecture that has 333 Residual Units (111 on each feature map size), denoted as "ResNet-1001". We also experiment on CIFAR-100. Table 3 shows that our "pre-activation" models are consistently better than the baseline counterparts. We analyze these results in the following.

4.2   Analysis

We find the impact of pre-activation is twofold. First, the optimization is further eased (comparing with the baseline ResNet) because f is an identity mapping. Second, using BN as pre-activation improves regularization of the models.

Ease of Optimization. This effect is particularly obvious when training the *1001-layer* ResNet. Figure 1 shows the curves. Using the original design in [1], the training error is reduced very slowly at the beginning of training. For $f =$ ReLU, the signal is impacted if it is negative, and when there are many Residual Units, this effect becomes prominent and Eq. (3) (so Eq. (5)) is not a good approximation. On the other hand, when f is an identity mapping, the signal can be propagated directly between any two units. Our 1001-layer network reduces the training loss very quickly (Fig. 1). It also achieves the lowest loss among all models we investigated, suggesting the success of optimization.

We also find that the impact of $f =$ ReLU is not severe when the ResNet has fewer layers (*e.g.*, 164 in Fig. 6(right)). The training curve seems to suffer a little bit at the beginning of training, but goes into a healthy status soon. By monitoring the responses we observe that this is because after some training, the weights are adjusted into a status such that $\mathbf{y}_l$ in Eq. (1) is more frequently above zero and f does not truncate it ($\mathbf{x}_l$ is always non-negative due to the previous ReLU, so $\mathbf{y}_l$ is below zero only when the magnitude of $\mathcal{F}$ is very negative). The truncation, however, is more frequent when there are 1000 layers.

Reducing Overfitting. Another impact of using the proposed pre-activation unit is on regularization, as shown in Fig. 6 (right). The pre-activation version reaches slightly higher training loss at convergence, but produces lower test error. This phenomenon is observed on ResNet-110, ResNet-110(1-layer), and ResNet-164 on both CIFAR-10 and 100. This is presumably caused by BN's regularization effect [8]. In the original Residual Unit (Fig. 4(a)), although the BN normalizes the signal, this is soon added to the shortcut and thus the merged signal is not normalized. This unnormalized signal is then used as the input of the next weight layer. On the contrary, in our pre-activation version, the inputs to all weight layers have been normalized.

5   Results

Comparisons on CIFAR-10/100. Table 4 compares the state-of-the-art methods on CIFAR-10/100, where we achieve competitive results. We note that we do not specially tailor the network width or filter sizes, nor use regularization techniques (such as dropout) which are very effective for these small datasets. We obtain these results via a simple but essential concept—going deeper. These results demonstrate the potential of *pushing the limits of depth*.

Comparisons on ImageNet. Next we report experimental results on the 1000-class ImageNet dataset [3]. We have done preliminary experiments using the skip connections studied in Figs. 2 and 3 on ImageNet with ResNet-101 [1], and observed similar optimization difficulties. The training error of these non-identity shortcut networks is obviously higher than the original ResNet at the first learning rate (similar to Fig. 3), and we decided to halt training due to limited resources. But we did finish a "BN after addition" version (Fig. 4(b)) of ResNet-101 on ImageNet and observed higher training loss and validation error. This model's single-crop (224×224) validation error is 24.6 %/7.5 %, *vs.* the original ResNet-101's 23.6 %/7.1 %. This is in line with the results on CIFAR in Fig. 6 (left).

Table 5 shows the results of ResNet-152 [1] and ResNet-200[3], all trained from scratch. We notice that the original ResNet paper [1] trained the models using scale jittering with shorter side $s \in [256, 480]$, and so the test of a 224×224 crop on $s = 256$ (as did in [1]) is negatively biased. Instead, we test a single 320×320 crop from $s = 320$, for all original and our ResNets. Even though the ResNets are trained on smaller crops, they can be easily tested on larger crops because the ResNets are fully convolutional by design. This size is also close to 299×299 used by Inception v3 [19], allowing a fairer comparison.

---

[3] The ResNet-200 has 16 more 3-layer bottleneck Residual Units than ResNet-152, which are added on the feature map of 28×28.

Table 4. Comparisons with state-of-the-art methods on CIFAR-10 and CIFAR-100 using *"moderate data augmentation"* (flip/translation), except for ELU [12] with no augmentation. Better results of [13,14] have been reported using stronger data augmentation and ensembling. For the ResNets we also report the number of parameters. Our results are the median of 5 runs with mean±std in the brackets. All ResNets results are obtained with a mini-batch size of 128 except [†] with a mini-batch size of 64 (code available at https://github.com/KaimingHe/resnet-1k-layers).

CIFAR-10	Error (%)	CIFAR-100	Error (%)
NIN [15]	8.81	NIN [15]	35.68
DSN [16]	8.22	DSN [16]	34.57
FitNet [17]	8.39	FitNet [17]	35.04
Highway [7]	7.72	Highway [7]	32.39
All-CNN [14]	7.25	All-CNN [14]	33.71
ELU [12]	6.55	ELU [12]	24.28
FitResNet, LSUV [18]	5.84	FitNet, LSUV [18]	27.66
ResNet-110 [1] (1.7 M)	6.61	ResNet-164 [1] (1.7 M)	25.16
ResNet-1202 [1] (19.4 M)	7.93	ResNet-1001 [1] (10.2 M)	27.82
ResNet-164 [ours] (1.7M)	5.46	ResNet-164 [ours] (1.7 M)	24.33
ResNet-1001 [ours] (10.2M)	4.92 (4.89±0.14)	ResNet-1001 [ours] (10.2M)	**22.71** (22.68±0.22)
ResNet-1001 [ours] (10.2M)[†]	**4.62** (4.69±0.20)		

The original ResNet-152 [1] has top-1 error of 21.3 % on a 320×320 crop, and our pre-activation counterpart has 21.1 %. The gain is not big on ResNet-152 because this model has not shown severe generalization difficulties. However, the original ResNet-200 has an error rate of 21.8 %, higher than the baseline ResNet-152. But we find that the original ResNet-200 has *lower* training error than ResNet-152, suggesting that it suffers from overfitting.

Our pre-activation ResNet-200 has an error rate of 20.7 %, which is **1.1 %** lower than the baseline ResNet-200 and also lower than the two versions of ResNet-152. When using the scale and aspect ratio augmentation of [19,20], our ResNet-200 has a result better than Inception v3 [19] (Table 5). Concurrent with our work, an Inception-ResNet-v2 model [21] achieves a single-crop result of 19.9 %/4.9 %. We expect our observations and the proposed Residual Unit will help this type and generally other types of ResNets.

Computational Cost. Our models' computational complexity is linear on depth (so a 1001-layer net is ~10× complex of a 100-layer net). On CIFAR, ResNet-1001 takes about 27 h to train on 2 GPUs; on ImageNet, ResNet-200 takes about 3 weeks to train on 8 GPUs (on par with VGG nets [22]).

Table 5. Comparisons of single-crop error on the ILSVRC 2012 validation set. All ResNets are trained using the same hyper-parameters and implementations as [1]). Our Residual Units are the full pre-activation version (Fig. 4(e)). †: code/model available at https://github.com/facebook/fb.resnet.torch/tree/master/pretrained, using scale and aspect ratio augmentation in [20].

Method	Augmentation	Train crop	Test crop	Top-1	top-5
ResNet-152, original Residual Unit [1]	scale	224×224	224×224	23.0	6.7
ResNet-152, original Residual Unit [1]	scale	224×224	320×320	21.3	5.5
ResNet-152, **pre-act** Residual Unit	scale	224×224	320×320	21.1	5.5
ResNet-200, original Residual Unit [1]	scale	224×224	320×320	21.8	6.0
ResNet-200, **pre-act** Residual Unit	scale	224×224	320×320	**20.7**	**5.3**
ResNet-200, **pre-act** Residual Unit	scale+asp ratio	224×224	320×320	**20.1**†	**4.8**†
Inception v3 [19]	scale+asp ratio	299×299	299×299	21.2	5.6

6   Conclusions

This paper investigates the propagation formulations behind the connection mechanisms of deep residual networks. Our derivations imply that identity shortcut connections and identity after-addition activation are essential for making information propagation smooth. Ablation experiments demonstrate phenomena that are consistent with our derivations. We also present 1000-layer deep networks that can be easily trained and achieve improved accuracy.

Appendix: Implementation Details

The implementation details and hyper-parameters are the same as those in [1]. On CIFAR we use only the translation and flipping augmentation in [1] for training. The learning rate starts from 0.1, and is divided by 10 at 32k and 48k iterations. Following [1], for all CIFAR experiments we warm up the training by using a smaller learning rate of 0.01 at the beginning 400 iterations and go back to 0.1 after that, although we remark that this is not necessary for our proposed Residual Unit. The mini-batch size is 128 on 2 GPUs (64 each), the weight decay is 0.0001, the momentum is 0.9, and the weights are initialized as in [23].

On ImageNet, we train the models using the same data augmentation as in [1]. The learning rate starts from 0.1 (no warming up), and is divided by 10 at 30 and 60 epochs. The mini-batch size is 256 on 8 GPUs (32 each). The weight decay, momentum, and weight initialization are the same as above.

When using the pre-activation Residual Units (Figs. 4(d), (e) and 5), we pay special attention to the first and the last Residual Units of the entire network. For the first Residual Unit (that follows a stand-alone convolutional layer, conv$_1$), we adopt the first activation right after conv$_1$ and before splitting into two paths; for the last Residual Unit (followed by average pooling and a fully-connected classifier), we adopt an extra activation right after its element-wise addition. These two special cases are the natural outcome when we obtain the pre-activation network via the modification procedure as shown in Fig. 5.

The bottleneck Residual Units (for ResNet-164/1001 on CIFAR) are constructed following [1]. For example, a $\begin{bmatrix} 3 \times 3, 16 \\ 3 \times 3, 16 \end{bmatrix}$ unit in ResNet-110 is replaced with a $\begin{bmatrix} 1 \times 1, 16 \\ 3 \times 3, 16 \\ 1 \times 1, 64 \end{bmatrix}$ unit in ResNet-164, both of which have roughly the same number of parameters. For the bottleneck ResNets, when reducing the feature map size we use projection shortcuts [1] for increasing dimensions, and when pre-activation is used, these projection shortcuts are also with pre-activation.

References

1. He, K., Zhang, X., Ren, S., Sun, J.: Deep residual learning for image recognition. In: CVPR (2016)
2. Nair, V., Hinton, G.E.: Rectified linear units improve restricted boltzmann machines. In: ICML (2010)
3. Russakovsky, O., Deng, J., Su, H., Krause, J., Satheesh, S., Ma, S., Huang, Z., Karpathy, A., Khosla, A., Bernstein, M., Berg, A.C., Fei-Fei, L.: Imagenet large scale visual recognition challenge. IJCV **115**, 211–252 (2015)
4. Lin, T.-Y., Maire, M., Belongie, S., Hays, J., Perona, P., Ramanan, D., Dollár, P., Zitnick, C.L.: Microsoft COCO: common objects in context. In: Fleet, D., Pajdla, T., Schiele, B., Tuytelaars, T. (eds.) ECCV 2014, Part V. LNCS, vol. 8693, pp. 740–755. Springer, Heidelberg (2014)
5. Hochreiter, S., Schmidhuber, J.: Long short-term memory. Neural Comput. **9**, 1735–1780 (1997)
6. Srivastava, R.K., Greff, K., Schmidhuber, J.: Highway networks. In: ICML Workshop (2015)
7. Srivastava, R.K., Greff, K., Schmidhuber, J.: Training very deep networks. In: NIPS (2015)
8. Ioffe, S., Szegedy, C.: Batch normalization: accelerating deep network training by reducing internal covariate shift. In: ICML (2015)
9. LeCun, Y., Boser, B., Denker, J.S., Henderson, D., Howard, R.E., Hubbard, W., Jackel, L.D.: Backpropagation applied to handwritten zip code recognition. Neural Comput. **1**, 541–551 (1989)
10. Krizhevsky, A.: Learning multiple layers of features from tiny images. Technical report (2009)
11. Hinton, G.E., Srivastava, N., Krizhevsky, A., Sutskever, I., Salakhutdinov, R.R.: Improving neural networks by preventing co-adaptation of feature detectors (2012). arXiv:1207.0580
12. Clevert, D.A., Unterthiner, T., Hochreiter, S.: Fast and accurate deep network learning by exponential linear units (ELUs). In: ICLR (2016)
13. Graham, B.: Fractional max-pooling (2014). arXiv:1412.6071
14. Springenberg, J.T., Dosovitskiy, A., Brox, T., Riedmiller, M.: Striving for simplicity: the all convolutional net (2014). arXiv:1412.6806
15. Lin, M., Chen, Q., Yan, S.: Network in network. In: ICLR (2014)
16. Lee, C.Y., Xie, S., Gallagher, P., Zhang, Z., Tu, Z.: Deeply-supervised nets. In: AISTATS (2015)
17. Romero, A., Ballas, N., Kahou, S.E., Chassang, A., Gatta, C., Bengio, Y.: Fitnets: hints for thin deep nets. In: ICLR (2015)

18. Mishkin, D., Matas, J.: All you need is a good init. In: ICLR (2016)
19. Szegedy, C., Vanhoucke, V., Ioffe, S., Shlens, J., Wojna, Z.: Rethinking the inception architecture for computer vision. In: CVPR (2016)
20. Szegedy, C., Liu, W., Jia, Y., Sermanet, P., Reed, S., Anguelov, D., Erhan, D., Vanhoucke, V., Rabinovich, A.: Going deeper with convolutions. In: CVPR (2015)
21. Szegedy, C., Ioffe, S., Vanhoucke, V.: Inception-v4, inception-resnet and the impact of residual connections on learning (2016). arXiv:1602.07261
22. Simonyan, K., Zisserman, A.: Very deep convolutional networks for large-scale image recognition. In: ICLR (2015)
23. He, K., Zhang, X., Ren, S., Sun, J.: Delving deep into rectifiers: surpassing human-level performance on imagenet classification. In: ICCV (2015)

Deep Networks with Stochastic Depth

Gao Huang[1]([✉]), Yu Sun[1], Zhuang Liu[2], Daniel Sedra[1],
and Kilian Q. Weinberger[1]

[1] Cornell University, Ithaca, USA
{gh349,ys646,dms422,kqw4}@cornell.edu
[2] Tsinghua University, Beijing, China
liuzhuang13@mails.tsinghua.edu.cn

Abstract. Very deep convolutional networks with hundreds of layers
have led to significant reductions in error on competitive benchmarks.
Although the unmatched expressiveness of the many layers can be highly
desirable at test time, training very deep networks comes with its own
set of challenges. The gradients can vanish, the forward flow often dimin-
ishes, and the training time can be painfully slow. To address these problems, we propose *stochastic depth*, a training procedure that enables the
seemingly contradictory setup to *train short* networks and *use deep* networks at test time. We start with very deep networks but during training, for each mini-batch, randomly drop a subset of layers and bypass
them with the identity function. This simple approach complements the
recent success of residual networks. It reduces training time substantially
and improves the test error significantly on almost all data sets that we
used for evaluation. With stochastic depth we can increase the depth
of residual networks even beyond 1200 layers and still yield meaningful
improvements in test error (4.91 % on CIFAR-10).

1   Introduction

Convolutional Neural Networks (CNNs) were arguably popularized within the
vision community in 2009 through AlexNet [1] and its celebrated victory at the
ImageNet competition [2]. Since then there has been a notable shift towards
CNNs in many areas of computer vision [3–8]. As this shift unfolds, a second
trend emerges; deeper and deeper CNN architectures are being developed and
trained. Whereas AlexNet had 5 convolutional layers [1], the VGG network and
GoogLeNet in 2014 had 19 and 22 layers respectively [5,7], and most recently
the ResNet architecture featured 152 layers [8].

Network depth is a major determinant of model expressiveness, both in theory [9,10] and in practice [5,7,8]. However, very deep models also introduce new
challenges: vanishing gradients in backward propagation, diminishing feature
reuse in forward propagation, and long training time.

G. Huang and Y. Sun are contributed equally.

© Springer International Publishing AG 2016
B. Leibe et al. (Eds.): ECCV 2016, Part IV, LNCS 9908, pp. 646–661, 2016.
DOI: 10.1007/978-3-319-46493-0_39

Vanishing Gradients is a well known nuisance in neural networks with many layers [11]. As the gradient information is back-propagated, repeated multiplication or convolution with small weights renders the gradient information ineffectively small in earlier layers. Several approaches exist to reduce this effect in practice, for example through careful initialization [12], hidden layer supervision [13], or, recently, Batch Normalization [14].

Diminishing feature reuse during forward propagation (also known as loss in information flow [15]) refers to the analogous problem to vanishing gradients in the forward direction. The features of the input instance, or those computed by earlier layers, are "washed out" through repeated multiplication or convolution with (randomly initialized) weight matrices, making it hard for later layers to identify and learn "meaningful" gradient directions. Recently, several new architectures attempt to circumvent this problem through direct identity mappings between layers, which allow the network to pass on features unimpededly from earlier layers to later layers [8,15].

Long training time is a serious concern as networks become very deep. The forward and backward passes scale linearly with the depth of the network. Even on modern computers with multiple state-of-the-art GPUs, architectures like the 152-layer ResNet require several weeks to converge on the ImageNet dataset [8].

The researcher is faced with an inherent dilemma: shorter networks have the advantage that information flows efficiently forward and backward, and can therefore be trained effectively and within a reasonable amount of time. However, they are not expressive enough to represent the complex concepts that are commonplace in computer vision applications. Very deep networks have much greather model complexity, but are very difficult to train in practice and require a lot of time and patience.

In this paper, we propose *deep networks with stochastic depth*, a novel training algorithm that is based on the seemingly contradictory insight that ideally we would like to have a *deep* network during *testing* but a *short* network during *training*. We resolve this conflict by creating deep Residual Network [8] architectures (with hundreds or even thousands of layers) with sufficient modeling capacity; however, during training we shorten the network significantly by randomly removing a substantial fraction of layers independently for each sample or mini-batch. The effect is a network with a small *expected* depth during training, but a large depth during testing. Although seemingly simple, this approach is surprisingly effective in practice.

In extensive experiments we observe that training with stochastic depth substantially reduces training time and test error (resulting in multiple new records to the best of our knowledge at the time of initial submission to ECCV). The reduction in training time can be attributed to the shorter forward and backward propagation, so the training time no longer scales with the full depth, but the shorter *expected depth* of the network. We attribute the reduction in test error to two factors: (1) shortening the (expected) depth during training reduces the chain of forward propagation steps and gradient computations, which strengthens the gradients especially in earlier layers during backward propagation;

(2) networks trained with stochastic depth can be interpreted as an implicit *ensemble* of networks of different depths, mimicking the record breaking ensemble of depth varying ResNets trained by He et al. [8].

We also observe that similar to Dropout [16], training with stochastic depth acts as a regularizer, even in the presence of Batch Normalization [14]. On experiments with CIFAR-10, we increase the depth of a ResNet beyond 1000 layers and still obtain significant improvements in test error.

2   Background

Many attempts have been made to improve the training of very deep networks. Earlier works adopted greedy layer-wise training or better initialization schemes to alleviate the vanishing gradients and diminishing feature reuse problems [12, 17,18]. A notable recent contribution towards training of very deep networks is Batch Normalization [14], which standardizes the mean and variance of hidden layers with respect to each mini-batch. This approach reduces the vanishing gradients problem and yields a strong regularizing effect.

Recently, several authors introduced extra skip connections to improve the information flow during forward and backward propagation. Highway Networks [15] allow earlier representations to flow unimpededly to later layers through parameterized skip connections known as "information highways", which can cross several layers at once. The skip connection parameters, learned during training, control the amount of information allowed on these "highways".

Residual networks (ResNets) [8] simplify Highway Networks by shortcutting (mostly) with identity functions. This simplification greatly improves training efficiency, and enables more direct feature reuse. ResNets are motivated by the observation that neural networks tend to obtain *higher training error* as the depth increases to very large values. This is counterintuitive, as the network gains more parameters and therefore better function approximation capabilities. The authors conjecture that the networks become *worse* at function approximation because the gradients and training signals vanish when they are propagated through many layers. As a fix, they propose to add *skip connections* to the network. Formally, if H_ℓ denotes the output of the ℓth layer (or sequence of layers) and $f_\ell(\cdot)$ represents a typical convolutional transformation from layer $\ell-1$ to ℓ, we obtain

$$H_\ell = \text{ReLU}(f_\ell(H_{\ell-1}) + \text{id}(H_{\ell-1})), \tag{1}$$

where $\text{id}(\cdot)$ denotes the identity transformation and we assume a ReLU transition function [19]. Figure 1 illustrates an example of a function f_ℓ, which consists of multiple convolutional and Batch Normalization layers. When the output dimensions of f_ℓ do not match those of $H_{\ell-1}$, the authors redefine $\text{id}(\cdot)$ as a linear projection to reduce the dimensions of $\text{id}(H_{\ell-1})$ to match those of $f_\ell(H_{\ell-1})$. The propagation rule in (1) allows the network to pass gradients and features (from the input or those learned in earlier layers) back and forth between the layers via the identity transformation $\text{id}(\cdot)$.

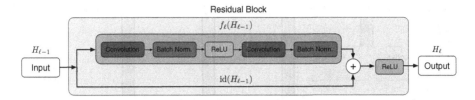

Fig. 1. A close look at the ℓth ResBlock in a ResNet.

Dropout. Stochastically dropping hidden nodes or connections has been a popular regularization method for neural networks. The most notable example is Dropout [16], which multiplies each hidden activation by an independent Bernoulli random variable. Intuitively, Dropout reduces the effect known as "co-adaptation" of hidden nodes collaborating in groups instead of independently producing useful features; it also makes an analogy with training an ensemble of exponentially many small networks. Many follow up works have been empirically successful, such as DropConnect [20], Maxout [21] and DropIn [22].

Similar to Dropout, stochastic depth can be interpreted as training an ensemble of networks, but with different depths, possibly achieving higher diversity among ensemble members than ensembling those with the same depth. Different from Dropout, we make the network shorter instead of thinner, and are motivated by a different problem. Anecdotally, Dropout loses effectiveness when used in combination with Batch Normalization [14,23]. Our own experiments with various Dropout rates (on CIFAR-10) show that Dropout gives practically no improvement when used on 110-layer ResNets with Batch Normalization.

We view all of these previous approaches to be extremely valuable and consider our proposed training with stochastic depth complimentary to these efforts. In fact, in our experiments we show that training with stochastic depth is indeed very effective on ResNets with Batch Normalization.

3   Deep Networks with Stochastic Depth

Learning with stochastic depth is based on a simple intuition. To reduce the *effective* length of a neural network during training, we randomly skip layers entirely. We achieve this by introducing skip connections in the same fashion as ResNets, however the connection pattern is randomly altered for each mini-batch. For each mini-batch we randomly select sets of layers and remove their corresponding transformation functions, only keeping the identity skip connection. Throughout, we use the architecture described by He et al. [8]. Because the architecture already contains skip connections, it is straightforward to modify, and isolates the benefits of stochastic depth from that of the ResNet identity connections. Next we describe this network architecture and then explain the stochastic depth training procedure in detail.

ResNet architecture. Following He et al. [8], we construct our network as the functional composition of L *residual blocks* (ResBlocks), each encoding the

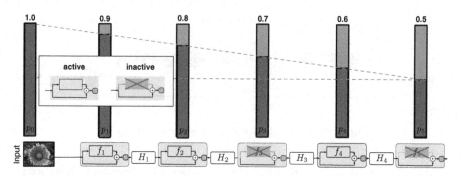

Fig. 2. The linear decay of p_ℓ illustrated on a ResNet with stochastic depth for $p_0 = 1$ and $p_L = 0.5$. Conceptually, we treat the input to the first ResBlock as H_0, which is always active.

update rule (1). Figure 1 shows a schematic illustration of the ℓth ResBlock. In this example, f_ℓ consists of a sequence of layers: `Conv-BN-ReLU-Conv-BN`, where `Conv` and `BN` stand for Convolution and Batch Normalization respectively. This construction scheme is adopted in all our experiments except ImageNet, for which we use the bottleneck block detailed in He et al. [8]. Typically, there are 64, 32, or 16 filters in the convolutional layers (see Sect. 4 for experimental details).

Stochastic depth aims to shrink the depth of a network during training, while keeping it unchanged during testing. We can achieve this goal by randomly dropping entire ResBlocks during training and bypassing their transformations through skip connections. Let $b_\ell \in \{0, 1\}$ denote a Bernoulli random variable, which indicates whether the ℓth ResBlock is active ($b_\ell = 1$) or inactive ($b_\ell = 0$). Further, let us denote the "survival" probability of ResBlock ℓ as $p_\ell = \Pr(b_\ell = 1)$.

With this definition we can bypass the ℓth ResBlock by multiplying its function f_ℓ with b_ℓ and we extend the update rule from (1) to

$$H_\ell = \texttt{ReLU}(b_\ell f_\ell(H_{\ell-1}) + \text{id}(H_{\ell-1})). \tag{2}$$

If $b_\ell = 1$, Eq. (2) reduces to the original ResNet update (1) and this ResBlock remains unchanged. If $b_\ell = 0$, the ResBlock reduces to the identity function,

$$H_\ell = \text{id}(H_{\ell-1}). \tag{3}$$

This reduction follows from the fact that the input $H_{\ell-1}$ is always non-negative, at least for the architectures we use. For $\ell \geq 2$, it is the output of the previous ResBlock, which is non-negative because of the final `ReLU` transition function (see Fig. 1). For $\ell = 1$, its input is the output of a `Conv-BN-ReLU` sequence that begins the architecture before the first ResBlock. For non-negative inputs the `ReLU` transition function acts as an identity.

The survival probabilities p_ℓ are new hyper-parameters of our training procedure. Intuitively, they should take on similar values for neighboring Res-Blocks. One option is to set $p_\ell = p_L$ uniformly for all ℓ to obtain a single hyper-parameter p_L. Another possibility is to set them according to a smooth function of ℓ. We propose a simple linear decay rule from $p_0 = 1$ for the input, to p_L for the last ResBlock:

$$p_\ell = 1 - \frac{\ell}{L}(1 - p_L). \tag{4}$$

See Fig. 2 for a schematic illustration. The linearly decaying survival probability originates from our intuition that the earlier layers extract low-level features that will be used by later layers and should therefore be more reliably present. In Sect. 4 we perform a more detailed empirical comparison between the uniform and decaying assignments for p_ℓ. We conclude that the linear decay rule (4) is preferred and, as training with stochastic depth is surprisingly stable with respect to p_L, we set $p_L = 0.5$ throughout (see Fig. 8).

Expected network depth. During the forward-backward pass the transformation f_ℓ is bypassed with probability $(1 - p_\ell)$, leading to a network with reduced depth. With stochastic depth, the number of effective ResBlocks during training, denoted as $\tilde{L}$, becomes a random variable. Its expectation is given by: $E(\tilde{L}) = \sum_{\ell=1}^{L} p_\ell$.

Under the linear decay rule with $p_L = 0.5$, the expected number of ResBlocks during training reduces to $E(\tilde{L}) = (3L - 1)/4$, or $E(\tilde{L}) \approx 3L/4$ when L is large. For the 110-layer network with $L = 54$ commonly used in our experiments, we have $E(\tilde{L}) \approx 40$. In other words, with stochastic depth, we train ResNets with an average number of 40 ResBlocks, but recover a ResNet with 54 blocks at test time. This reduction in depth significantly alleviates the vanishing gradients and the information loss problem in deep ResNets. Note that because the connectivity is random, there will be updates with significantly shorter networks and more direct paths to individual layers. We provide an empirical demonstration of this effect in Sect. 5.

Training time savings. When a ResBlock is bypassed for a specific iteration, there is no need to perform forward-backward computation or gradient updates. As the forward-backward computation dominates the training time, stochastic depth significantly speeds up the training process. Following the calculations above, approximately 25 % of training time could be saved under the linear decay rule with $p_L = 0.5$. The timings in practice using our implementation are consistent with this analysis (see the last paragraph of Sect. 4). More computational savings can be obtained by switching to a uniform probability for p_ℓ or lowering p_L accordingly. In fact, Fig. 8 shows that with $p_L = 0.2$, the ResNet with stochastic depth obtains the same test error as its constant depth counterpart on CIFAR-10 but gives a 40 % speedup.

Implicit model ensemble. In addition to the predicted speedups, we also observe significantly lower testing errors in our experiments, in comparison with ResNets of constant depth. One explanation for our performance improvements is that training with stochastic depth can be viewed as training an ensemble of ResNets _implicitly_. Each of the L layers is either active or inactive, resulting

Table 1. Test error (%) of ResNets trained with stochastic depth compared to other most competitive methods previously published (whenever available). A "+" in the name denotes standard data augmentation. ResNet with constant depth refers to our reproduction of the experiments by He et al.

	CIFAR10+	CIFAR100+	SVHN	ImageNet
Maxout [21]	9.38	-	2.47	-
DropConnect [20]	9.32	-	1.94	-
Net in Net [24]	8.81	-	2.35	-
Deeply Supervised [13]	7.97	-	1.92	33.70
Frac. Pool [25]	-	27.62	-	-
All-CNN [6]	7.25	-	-	41.20
Learning Activation [26]	7.51	30.83	-	-
R-CNN [27]	7.09	-	1.77	-
Scalable BO [28]	6.37	27.40	1.77	-
Highway Network [29]	7.60	32.24	-	-
Gen. Pool [30]	6.05	-	1.69	28.02
ResNet with constant depth	6.41	27.76	1.80	21.78
ResNet with stochastic depth	5.25	24.98	1.75	21.98

in 2^L possible network combinations. For each training mini-batch one of the 2^L networks (with shared weights) is sampled and updated. During testing all networks are averaged using the approach in the next paragraph.

Stochastic depth during testing requires small modifications to the network. We keep all functions f_ℓ active throughout testing in order to utilize the full-length network with all its model capacity. However, during training, functions f_ℓ are only active for a fraction p_ℓ of all updates, and the corresponding weights of the next layer are calibrated for this survival probability. We therefore need to re-calibrate the outputs of any given function f_ℓ by the expected number of times it participates in training, p_ℓ. The forward propagation update rule becomes:

$$H_\ell^{\text{Test}} = \text{ReLU}(p_\ell f_\ell(H_{\ell-1}^{\text{Test}}; W_\ell) + H_{\ell-1}^{\text{Test}}). \tag{5}$$

From the model ensemble perspective, the update rule (5) can be interpreted as combining all possible networks into a single test architecture, in which each layer is weighted by its survival probability.

4   Results

We empirically demonstrate the effectiveness of stochastic depth on a series of benchmark data sets: CIFAR-10, CIFAR-100 [1], SVHN [31], and ImageNet [2].

Implementation details. For all data sets we compare the results of ResNets with our proposed stochastic depth and the original constant depth, and other

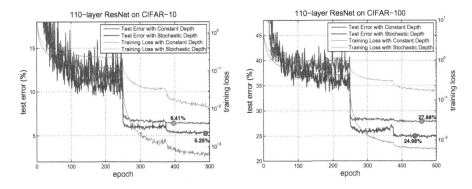

Fig. 3. Test error on CIFAR-10 (*left*) and CIFAR-100 (*right*) during training, with data augmentation, corresponding to results in the first two columns of Table 1.

most competitive benchmarks. We set p_ℓ with the linear decay rule of $p_0 = 1$ and $p_L = 0.5$ throughout. In all experiments we report the test error from the epoch with the lowest validation error. For best comparisons we use the same construction scheme (for constant and stochastic depth) as described by He et al. [8]. In the case of CIFAR-100 we use the same 110-layer ResNet used by He et al. [8] for CIFAR-10, except that the network has a 100-way softmax output. Each model contains three groups of residual blocks that differ in number of filters and feature map size, and each group is a stack of 18 residual blocks. The numbers of filters in the three groups are 16, 32 and 64, respectively. For the transitional residual blocks, i.e. the first residual block in the second and third group, the output dimension is larger than the input dimension. Following He et al. [8], we replace the identity connections in these blocks by an average pooling layer followed by zero paddings to match the dimensions. Our implementations are in Torch 7 [32]. The code to reproduce the results is publicly available on GitHub at https://github.com/yueatsprograms/Stochastic_Depth.

CIFAR-10. CIFAR-10 [1] is a dataset of 32-by-32 color images, representing 10 classes of natural scene objects. The training set and test set contain 50,000 and 10,000 images, respectively. We hold out 5,000 images as validation set, and use the remaining 45,000 as training samples. Horizontal flipping and translation by 4 pixels are the two standard data augmentation techniques adopted in our experiments, following the common practice [6,13,20,21,24,26,30].

The baseline ResNet is trained with SGD for 500 epochs, with a mini-batch size 128. The initial learning rate is 0.1, and is divided by a factor of 10 after epochs 250 and 375. We use a weight decay of 1e-4, momentum of 0.9, and Nesterov momentum [33] with 0 dampening, as suggested by [34]. For stochastic depth, the network structure and all optimization settings are exactly the same as the baseline. All settings were chosen to match the setup of He et al. [8].

The results are shown in Table 1. ResNets with constant depth result in a competitive 6.41 % error on the test set. ResNets trained with stochastic depth yield a further relative improvement of 18 % and result in 5.25 % test error. To

our knowledge this is significantly lower than the best existing single model performance (6.05 %) [30] on CIFAR-10 prior to our submission, without resorting
to massive data augmentation [6,25].[1] Figure 3 (*left*) shows the test error as a
function of epochs. The point selected by the lowest validation error is circled
for both approaches. We observe that ResNets with stochastic depth yield lower
test error but also slightly higher fluctuations (presumably due to the random
depth during training).

CIFAR-100. Similar to CIFAR-10, CIFAR-100 [1] contains 32-by-32 color
images with the same train-test split, but from 100 classes. For both the baseline and our method, the experimental settings are exactly the same as those
of CIFAR-10. The constant depth ResNet yields a test error of 27.22 %, which
is already the state-of-the-art in CIFAR-100 with standard data augmentation.
Adding stochastic depth drastically reduces the error to 24.98 %, and is again
the best published single model performance to our knowledge (see Table 1 and
Fig. 3 *right*).

We also experiment with CIFAR-10 and CIFAR-100 without data augmentation. ResNets with constant depth obtain 13.63 % and 44.74 % on CIFAR-10
and CIFAR-100 respectively. Adding stochastic depth yields consistent improvements of about 15 % on both datasets, resulting in test errors of 11.66 % and
37.8 % respectively.

SVHN. The format of the Street View House Number (SVHN) [31] dataset
that we use contains 32-by-32 colored images of cropped out house numbers
from Google Street View. The task is to classify the digit at the center. There
are 73,257 digits in the training set, 26,032 in the test set and 531,131 easier
samples for additional training. Following the common practice, we use all the
training samples but do not perform data augmentation. For each of the ten
classes, we randomly select 400 samples from the training set and 200 from the
additional set, forming a validation set with 6,000 samples in total. We preprocess
the data by subtracting the mean and dividing the standard deviation. Batch
size is set to 128, and validation error is calculated every 200 iterations.

Our baseline network has 152 layers. It is trained for 50 epochs with a beginning learning rate of 0.1, divided by 10 after epochs 30 and 35. The depth
and learning rate schedule are selected by optimizing for the validation error of
the baseline through many trials. This baseline obtains a competitive result of
1.80 %. However, as seen in Fig. 4, it starts to overfit at the beginning of the
second phase with learning rate 0.01, and continues to overfit until the end of
training. With stochastic depth, the error improves to 1.75 %, the second-best
published result on SVHN to our knowledge after [30].

Training time comparison. We compare the training efficiency of the constant
depth and stochastic depth ResNets used to produce the previous results. Table 2
shows the training (clock) time under both settings with the linear decay rule
$p_L = 0.5$. Stochastic depth consistently gives a 25 % speedup, which confirms our

---

[1] The only model that performs even better is the 1202-layer ResNet with stochastic
depth, discussed later in this section.

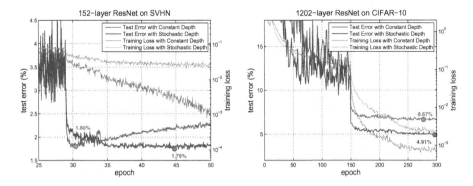

Fig. 4. Left: Test error on SVHN, corresponding to results on column three in Table 1. *right*: Test error on CIFAR-10 using 1202-layer ResNets. The points of lowest validation errors are highlighted in each case.

Table 2. Training time comparison on benchmark datasets.

	CIFAR10+	CIFAR100+	SVHN
Constant depth	20 h 42 m	20 h 51 m	33 h 43 m
Stochastic depth	15 h 7 m	15 h 20 m	25 h 33 m

analysis in Sect. 3. See Fig. 8 and the corresponding section on hyper-parameter sensitivity for more empirical analysis.

Training with a 1202-layer ResNet. He et al. [8] tried to learn CIFAR-10 using an aggressively deep ResNet with 1202 layers. As expected, this extremely deep network overfitted to the training set: it ended up with a test error of 7.93 %, worse than their 110-layer network. We repeat their experiment on the same 1202-layer network, with constant and stochastic depth. We train for 300 epochs, and set the learning rate to 0.01 for the first 10 epochs to "warm-up" the network and facilitate initial convergence, then restore it to 0.1, and divide it by 10 at epochs 150 and 225.

The results are summarized in Fig. 4 (*right*) and 5. Similar to He et al. [8], the ResNets with constant depth of 1202 layers yields a test error of 6.67 %, which is worse than the 110-layer constant depth ResNet. In contrast, if trained with stochastic depth, this extremely deep ResNet performs remarkably well. We want to highlight two trends: (1) Comparing the two 1202-layer nets shows that training with stochastic depth leads to a 27 % relative improvement; (2) Comparing the two networks trained with stochastic depth shows that increasing the architecture from 110 layers to 1202 yields a further improvement on the previous record-low 5.25 %, to a 4.91 % test error without sign of overfitting, as shown in Fig. 4 (*right*)[2].

---

[2] We do not include this result in Table 1 since this architecture was only trained on one of the datasets.

To the best of our knowledge, this is the lowest known test error on CIFAR-10 with moderate image augmentation and the first time that a network with more than 1000 layers has been shown to *further reduce* the test error[3]. We consider these findings highly encouraging and hope that training with stochastic depth will enable researchers to leverage extremely deep architectures in the future.

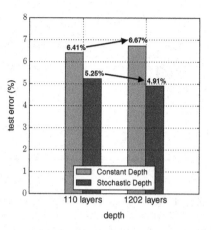

Fig. 5. With stochastic depth, the 1202-layer ResNet still significantly improves over the 110-layer one.

ImageNet. The ILSVRC 2012 classification dataset consists of 1000 classes of images, in total 1.2 million for training, 50,000 for validation, and 100,000 for testing. Following the common practice, we only report the validation errors. We follow He et al. [8] to build a 152-layer ResNet with 50 bottleneck residual blocks. When input and output dimensions do not match, the skip connection uses a learned linear projection for the mismatching dimensions, and an identity transformation for the other dimensions. Our implementation is based on the github repository `fb.resnet.torch`[4] [34], and the optimization settings are the same as theirs, except that we use a batch size of 128 instead of 256 because we can only spread a batch among 4 GPUs (instead of 8 as they did).

We train the constant depth baseline for 90 epochs (following He et al. and the default setting in the repository) and obtain a final error of 23.06 %. With stochastic depth, we obtain an error of 23.38 % at epoch 90, which is slightly higher. We observe from Fig. 6 that the downward trend of the validation error with stochastic depth is still strong, and from our previous experience, could benefit from further training. Due to the 25 % computational saving, we can add 30 epochs (giving 120 in total, after decreasing the learning rate to 1e-4 at epoch 90),

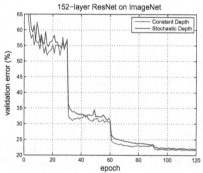

Fig. 6. Validation error on ILSVRC 2012 classification.

and still finish in almost the same total time as 90 epochs of the baseline. This reaches a final error of 21.98 %. We have also kept the baseline running for 30 more epochs. This reaches a final error of 21.78 %.

---

[3] This is, until early March, 2016, when this paper was submitted to ECCV. Many new developments have further decreased the error on CIFAR-10 since then (and some are based on this work).

[4] https://github.com/facebook/fb.resnet.torch.

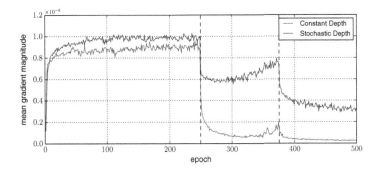

Fig. 7. The first convolutional layer's mean gradient magnitude for each epoch during training. The vertical dotted lines indicate scheduled reductions in learning rate by a factor of 10, which cause gradients to shrink.

Because ImageNet is a very complicated and large dataset, the model complexity required could potentially be much more than that of the 152-layer ResNet [35]. In the words of an anonymous reviewer, the current generation of models for ImageNet are still in a different regime from those of CIFAR. Although there seems to be no immediate benefit from applying stochastic depth on this particular architecture, it is possible that stochastic depth will lead to improvements on ImageNet with larger models, which the community might soon be able to train as GPU capacities increase.

5   Analytic Experiments

In this section, we provide more insights into stochastic depth by presenting a series of analytical results. We perform experiments to support the hypothesis that stochastic depth effectively addresses the problem of vanishing gradients in backward propagation. Moreover, we demonstrate the robustness of stochastic depth with respect to its hyper-parameter.

Improved gradient strength. Stochastically dropping layers during training reduces the effective depth on which gradient back-propagation is performed, while keeping the test-time model depth unmodified. As a result we expect training with stochastic depth to reduce the vanishing gradient problem in the backward step. To empirically support this, we compare the magnitude of gradients to the first convolutional layer of the first ResBlock ($\ell = 1$) with and without stochastic depth on the CIFAR-10 data set.

Figure 7 shows the mean absolute values of the gradients. The two large drops indicated by vertical dotted lines are due to scheduled learning rate division. It can be observed that the magnitude of gradients in the network trained with stochastic depth is always larger, especially after the learning rate drops. This seems to support out claim that stochastic depth indeed significantly reduces the vanishing gradient problem, and enables the network to be trained more

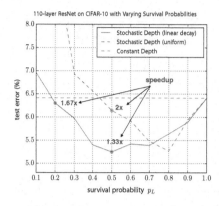
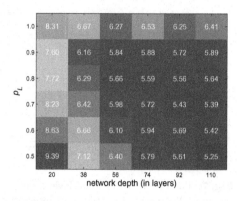

Fig. 8. Left: Test error (%) on CIFAR-10 with respect to the p_L with uniform and decaying assignments of p_ℓ. Right: Test error (%) heatmap on CIFAR-10 varyied over p_L and network depth.

effectively. Another indication of the effect is in the left panel of Fig. 3, where one can observe that the test error of the ResNets with constant depth approximately plateaus after the first drop of learning rate, while stochastic depth still improves the performance even after the learning rate drops for the second time. This further supports that stochastic depth combines the benefits of shortened network during training with those of deep models at test time.

Hyper-parameter sensitivity. The survival probability p_L is the only hyper-parameter of our method. Although we used $p_L = 0.5$ throughout all our experiments, it is still worth investigating the sensitivity of stochastic depth with respect to its hyper-parameter. To this end, we compare the test error of the 110-layer ResNet under varying values of p_L ($L = 54$) for both linear decay and uniform assignment rules on the CIFAR-10 data set in Fig. 8 (*left*). We make the following observations: (1) both assignment rules yield better results than the baseline when p_L is set properly; (2) the linear decay rule outperforms the uniform rule consistently; (3) the linear decay rule is relatively robust to fluctuations in p_L and obtains competitive results when p_L ranges from 0.4 to 0.8; (4) even with a rather small survival probability e.g. $p_L = 0.2$, stochastic depth with linear decay still performs well, while giving a 40 % reduction in training time. This shows that stochastic depth can save training time substantially without compromising accuracy.

The heatmap on the right shows the test error varied over both p_L and network depth. Not surprisingly, deeper networks (at least in the range of our experiments) do better with a $p_L = 0.5$. The "valley" of the heatmap is along the diagonal. A deep enough model is necessary for stochastic depth to significantly outperform the baseline (an observation we also make with the ImageNet data set), although shorter networks can still benefit from less aggressive skipping.

6   Conclusion

In this paper we introduced deep networks with *stochastic depth*, a procedure to train very deep neural networks effectively and efficiently. Stochastic depth reduces the network depth during training *in expectation* while maintaining the full depth at testing time. Training with stochastic depth allows one to increase the depth of a network well beyond 1000 layers, and still obtain a reduction in test error. Because of its simplicity and practicality we hope that training with stochastic depth may become a new tool in the deep learning "toolbox", and will help researchers scale their models to previously unattainable depths and capabilities.

Acknowledgements. We thank the anonymous reviewers for their kind suggestions. Kilian Weinberger is supported by NFS grants IIS-1550179, IIS-1525919 and EFRI-1137211. Gao Huang is supported by the International Postdoctoral Exchange Fellowship Program of China Postdoctoral Council (No. 20150015). Yu Sun is supported by the Cornell University Office of Undergraduate Research. We also thank our lab mates, Matthew Kusner and Shuang Li for useful and interesting discussions.

References

1. Krizhevsky, A., Hinton, G.: Learning multiple layers of features from tiny images (2009)
2. Deng, J., Dong, W., Socher, R., Li, L.J., Li, K., Fei-Fei, L.: Imagenet: a large-scale hierarchical image database. In: IEEE Conference on Computer Vision and Pattern Recognition, 2009, CVPR 2009. IEEE, pp. 248–255 (2009)
3. Krizhevsky, A., Sutskever, I., Hinton, G.E.: Imagenet classification with deep convolutional neural networks. In: Advances in Neural Information Processing Systems, pp. 1097–1105 (2012)
4. Sermanet, P., Eigen, D., Zhang, X., Mathieu, M., Fergus, R., LeCun, Y.: Overfeat: integrated recognition, localization and detection using convolutional networks. arXiv preprint arXiv:1312.6229 (2013)
5. Simonyan, K., Zisserman, A.: Very deep convolutional networks for large-scale image recognition. arXiv preprint arXiv:1409.1556 (2014)
6. Springenberg, J.T., Dosovitskiy, A., Brox, T., Riedmiller, M.: Striving for simplicity: the all convolutional net. arXiv preprint arXiv:1412.6806 (2014)
7. Szegedy, C., Liu, W., Jia, Y., Sermanet, P., Reed, S., Anguelov, D., Erhan, D., Vanhoucke, V., Rabinovich, A.: Going deeper with convolutions. In: Proceedings of the IEEE Conference on Computer Vision and Pattern Recognition, pp. 1–9 (2015)
8. He, K., Zhang, X., Ren, S., Sun, J.: Deep residual learning for image recognition. arXiv preprint arXiv:1512.03385 (2015)
9. Håstad, J., Goldmann, M.: On the power of small-depth threshold circuits. Comput. Complex. **1**(2), 113–129 (1991)
10. Håstad, J.: Computational Limitations of Small-Depth Circuits. MIT Press, Cambridge (1987)
11. Bengio, Y., Simard, P., Frasconi, P.: Learning long-term dependencies with gradient descent is difficult. IEEE Trans. Neural Networks **5**(2), 157–166 (1994)

12. Glorot, X., Bengio, Y.: Understanding the difficulty of training deep feedforward neural networks. In: International Conference on Artificial Intelligence and Statistics, pp. 249–256 (2010)

13. Lee, C.Y., Xie, S., Gallagher, P., Zhang, Z., Tu, Z.: Deeply-supervised nets. arXiv preprint arXiv:1409.5185 (2014)

14. Ioffe, S., Szegedy, C.: Batch normalization: accelerating deep network training by reducing internal covariate shift. arXiv preprint arXiv:1502.03167 (2015)

15. Srivastava, R.K., Greff, K., Schmidhuber, J.: Highway networks. arXiv preprint arXiv:1505.00387 (2015)

16. Srivastava, N., Hinton, G., Krizhevsky, A., Sutskever, I., Salakhutdinov, R.: Dropout: a simple way to prevent neural networks from overfitting. J. Mach. Learn. Res. **15**(1), 1929–1958 (2014)

17. Fahlman, S.E., Lebiere, C.: The Cascade-Correlation Learning Architecture. Morgan Kaufmann Publishers Inc., San Francisco (1989)

18. Erhan, D., Bengio, Y., Courville, A., Manzagol, P.A., Vincent, P., Bengio, S.: Why does unsupervised pre-training help deep learning? J. Mach. Learn. Res. **11**, 625–660 (2010)

19. Nair, V., Hinton, G.E.: Rectified linear units improve restricted Boltzmann machines. In: Proceedings of the 27th International Conference on Machine Learning (ICML-10), pp. 807–814 (2010)

20. Wan, L., Zeiler, M., Zhang, S., Cun, Y.L., Fergus, R.: Regularization of neural networks using dropconnect. In: Dasgupta, S., Mcallester, D. (eds.): Proceedings of the 30th International Conference on Machine Learning (ICML-13), JMLR Workshop and Conference Proceedings, vol. 28, pp. 1058–1066, May 2013

21. Goodfellow, I.J., Warde-Farley, D., Mirza, M., Courville, A., Bengio, Y.: Maxout networks. arXiv preprint arXiv:1302.4389 (2013)

22. Smith, L.N., Hand, E.M., Doster, T.: Gradual dropin of layers to train very deep neural networks. In: CVPR (2016)

23. Zagoruyko, S.: 92.45% on cifar-10 in torch (2015)

24. Lin, M., Chen, Q., Yan, S.: Network in network. arXiv preprint arXiv:1312.4400 (2013)

25. Graham, B.: Fractional max-pooling. arXiv preprint arXiv:1412.6071 (2014)

26. Agostinelli, F., Hoffman, M., Sadowski, P., Baldi, P.: Learning activation functions to improve deep neural networks. arXiv preprint arXiv:1412.6830 (2014)

27. Liang, M., Hu, X.: Recurrent convolutional neural network for object recognition. In: Proceedings of the IEEE Conference on Computer Vision and Pattern Recognition, pp. 3367–3375 (2015)

28. Snoek, J., Rippel, O., Swersky, K., Kiros, R., Satish, N., Sundaram, N., Patwary, M., Ali, M., Adams, R.P., et al.: Scalable bayesian optimization using deep neural networks. arXiv preprint arXiv:1502.05700 (2015)

29. Srivastava, R.K., Greff, K., Schmidhuber, J.: Training very deep networks. In: Advances in Neural Information Processing Systems, pp. 2368–2376 (2015)

30. Lee, C.Y., Gallagher, P.W., Tu, Z.: Generalizing pooling functions in convolutional neural networks: mixed, gated, and tree. arXiv preprint arXiv:1509.08985 (2015)

31. Netzer, Y., Wang, T., Coates, A., Bissacco, A., Wu, B., Ng, A.Y.: Reading digits in natural images with unsupervised feature learning. In: NIPS Workshop on Deep Learning and Unsupervised Feature Learning, Granada, Spain, vol. 2011, p. 4 (2011)

32. Collobert, R., Kavukcuoglu, K., Farabet, C.: Torch7: a matlab-like environment for machine learning. In: BigLearn, NIPS Workshop (2011)

33. Sutskever, I., Martens, J., Dahl, G., Hinton, G.: On the importance of initialization and momentum in deep learning. In: Proceedings of the 30th International Conference on Machine Learning (ICML-13), pp. 1139–1147 (2013)
34. Gross, S., Wilber, M.: Training and investigating residual nets (2016)
35. He, K., Zhang, X., Ren, S., Sun, J.: Identity mappings in deep residual networks. arXiv preprint arXiv:1603.05027 (2016)

Less Is More: Towards Compact CNNs

Hao Zhou[1]([✉]), Jose M. Alvarez[2], and Fatih Porikli[2,3]

[1] University of Maryland, College Park, College Park, USA
hzhou@cs.umd.edu
[2] Data61/CSIRO, Eveleigh, Australia
jose.alvarez@data61.csiro.au
[3] Australian National University, Canberra, Australia
fatih.porikli@anu.edu.au

Abstract. To attain a favorable performance on large-scale datasets, convolutional neural networks (CNNs) are usually designed to have very high capacity involving millions of parameters. In this work, we aim at optimizing the number of neurons in a network, thus the number of parameters. We show that, by incorporating sparse constraints into the objective function, it is possible to decimate the number of neurons during the training stage. As a result, the number of parameters and the memory footprint of the neural network are also reduced, which is also desirable at the test time. We evaluated our method on several well-known CNN structures including AlexNet, and VGG over different datasets including ImageNet. Extensive experimental results demonstrate that our method leads to compact networks. Taking first fully connected layer as an example, our compact CNN contains only 30 % of the original neurons without any degradation of the top-1 classification accuracy.

Keywords: Convolutional neural network · Neuron reduction · Sparsity

1 Introduction

Last few years have witnessed the success of deep convolutional neural networks (CNN) in many computer vision applications. One important reason is the emergence of large annotated datasets and the development of high-performance computing hardware facilitating the training of high capacity CNNs with an exceptionally large number of parameters.

When defining the structure of a network, large networks are often preferred, and strong regularizers [36] tend to be applied to give the network as much discriminative power as possible. As such, the state-of-the-art CNNs nowadays contain hundreds of millions of parameters [34]. Most of these parameters come from one or two layers that host a large number of neurons. Take AlexNet [23] as an example. The first and the second fully connected layers, which have 4096

Electronic supplementary material The online version of this chapter (doi:10.1007/978-3-319-46493-0_40) contains supplementary material, which is available to authorized users.

© Springer International Publishing AG 2016
B. Leibe et al. (Eds.): ECCV 2016, Part IV, LNCS 9908, pp. 662–677, 2016.
DOI: 10.1007/978-3-319-46493-0_40

Table 1. Neuron reduction in the first fully connected layer, the total parameter compression, reduced memory, the top-1 validation error rate (red: error rate without sparse constraints).

Network	Compression (%)		Memory reduced[a]	Top-1 error (%)
	Neurons[b]	Parameters[c]		
LeNet	97.80	92.00	1.52 (MB)	0.63 (0.72)
CIFAR-10 quick	73.44	33.42	0.19 (MB)	25.25 (24.75)
AlexNet	73.73	65.42	152.14 (MB)	46.10 (45.57)
VGG-13	76.21	61.29	311.06 (MB)	39.26 (37.50)

[a]Supposing a single type is used to store the weight
[b]Results on number of neurons in the first fully connected layer
[c]Results on the number of parameters of the whole network

neurons each, contain around 89 % of all the parameters. Having to use such a large number of parameters leads to high memory requirements when mapping and running the network on computational platforms. Consequently, using deep CNNs obligates significant hardware resources, which hinders their practicability for mobile computing devices that have limited memory specifications.

Several recent studies have focused on reducing the size of the network concluding that there is substantial redundancy in the number of parameters of a CNN. For instance, [10,20] represent the filters in a CNN using a linear combination of basis filters. However, these methods can only apply to an already trained network. Other works have investigated directly reducing the number of parameters in a CNN by using sparse filters instead of its original full-size filters. To the best of our knowledge, existing deep learning toolboxes [6,21,38] do not support sparse data structures yet. Therefore, special structures need to be implemented. Moreover, FFT is shown to be very efficient to compute convolutions on GPUs [29]. However, a sparse matrix is usually no longer sparse in the Fourier domain, which limits the applicability (i.e., reduction of memory footprint) of these methods.

To address the shortcomings of the aforementioned works, we propose an efficient method to decimate the number of neurons. Our approach has four key advantages: (1) Neurons are assessed and reduced during the training phase. Therefore, no pre-trained network is required. (2) The reduction of parameters do not rely on the sparsity of neurons; thus, our method can be directly included in popular deep learning toolboxes. (3) The number of filters in Fourier domain is proportional to the number of neurons in spatial domain. Therefore, our method can also reduce the number of parameters in the Fourier domain. (4) Reducing the number of neurons of a layer directly condenses the data dimensionality when the output of an internal layer is utilized as image features [3,12].

Our method consists of imposing sparse constraints on the neurons of a CNN in the objective function during the training process. Furthermore, to minimize the extra computational cost of adding these constraints, we solve the sparse constrained optimization problem using forward-backward splitting method [11,14].

The main advantage of forward-backward splitting is the bypass of the sparse constraint evaluations during the standard back-propagation step, making the implementation very practical. We also investigate the importance of rectified linear units in sparse constrained CNNs. Our experiments show that rectified linear units help to reduce the number of neurons leading to even more compact networks.

We conduct a comprehensive set of experiments to validate our method using four well-known models (i.e., LeNet, CIFAR-10 quick, AlexNet and VGG) on three public datasets including ImageNet. Table 1 summarizes a representative set of our results when constraints are applied to the first fully connected layer of each model, which has the largest number of neurons and parameters. As shown, even with a large portion of neurons removed and, therefore, a significant reduction in the memory footprint of the original model; the resulting networks still perform as good as the original ones. These results are also convenient for deployment in mobile platforms where computational resources are relevant. For instance, using single float type (4 bytes) to store the network, the amount of memory saved for AlexNet in Table 1 is 152 MB.

To reiterate, the contribution of this paper is threefold. First, we remove neurons of a CNN during the training stage. Second, we analyze the importance of rectified linear units for sparse constraints. Finally, our experimental results on four well-known CNN architectures demonstrate a significant reduction in the number of neurons and the memory footprint of the testing phase without affecting the classification accuracy.

2   Related Work

Deep CNNs demand large memory and excessive computational times. This motivated studies to simplify the structure of CNNs. However, so far only one pioneering work explored the redundancy in the number of neurons [36].

We organize the related work in three categories; network distillation, approximating parameters or neurons by memory efficient structures, and parameter pruning in large networks.

Network Distillation: The work in [2] is among the first papers that tried to mimic a complicated model with a simple one. The key idea is to train a powerful ensemble model and use it to label a large amount of unlabeled data. Then a neural network is trained on these data so as to perform similarly to the ensemble model. Following the idea of [1,2,19,32] presenting training of a simple neural network based on the soft output of a complicated one. Their results show that a much simpler network can imitate a complicated network. However, these methods require a two-step training process and the simple network must be trained after the complicated one.

Memory Efficient Structures: Most of the studies in this category are inspired by the work of Denil et al. [9] that demonstrated redundancy in the parameters of neural networks. It proposed to learn only 5 % of the parameters and predicted the rest by choosing an appropriate dictionary. Inspired by this, [10,20,27] proposed to represent the filters in convolutional layers by a linear combination of basis filters. As a result, convolving with the original filters is equivalent to convolving with the base filters followed by a linear combination of the output of these convolutions. These methods focus on speeding up the testing phase of CNNs. In [24], the use of the CP-decomposition to approximate the filter in each layer as a sequence of four convolutional layers with small kernels is investigated in order to speed up testing time on CPU mode of a network. In [15] several schemes to quantize the parameters in CNNs are presented. All these methods require a trained network and then fine tuning for the new structures. [31] applied Tensor Train (TT) format to approximate the fully connected layers and train the TT format CNN from scratch. They can achieve a high compression rate with little loss of accuracy. However, it is not clear whether TT format can be applied to convolutional layers.

Parameter Pruning: A straightforward way to reduce the size of CNNs is directly removing some of the unimportant parameters. Back to 1990, LeCun et al. [26] introduced computing the second derivatives of the objective function with respect to the parameters as the saliency, and removing the parameters with low saliency value. Later, Hassibi and Stork [18] followed their work and proposed an optimal brain surgeon, which achieved better results. These two methods, nevertheless, require computation of the second derivatives, which is computationally costly for large-scale neural networks [17]. In [5], directly adding sparse constraints on the parameters was discussed. This method, different from ours, cannot reduce the number of neurons.

Another approach [16] combines the memory efficient structures and parameter pruning. First, unimportant parameters are removed, and then, after a fine-tuning process, the remaining parameters are quantized for further compression. This work is complementary to ours and can be used to further compress the network trained using our method.

Directly related to our proposed method is [36]. Given a pretrained CNN, it proposes a theoretically sound approach to combine similar neurons together. Yet, their method is mainly for pruning a trained network whereas our method directly removes neurons during training. Although [36] is *data-free* when pruning, it requires a pretrained network, which is data dependent. Moreover, our results show that, without degrading the performance, we can remove more neurons than the suggested cut-off value reported in [36].

3   Sparse Constrained Convolutional Neural Networks

Notation: In the following discussion, if not otherwise specified, $|\cdot|$ is the ℓ_1 norm, $||\mathbf{x}|| = \sqrt{\sum_i x_i^2}$ is the ℓ_2 norm for a vector (Frobenius norm for a matrix). We use $\mathbf{W}$ and $\mathbf{b}$ to denote all the parameters in filters and bias terms in a CNN, respectively. $\mathbf{w}_l$ and $\mathbf{b}_l$ represent the filter and bias parameters in the l-th layer. $\mathbf{w}_l$ is a tensor whose size is $w \times h \times m \times n$, where w and h are the width and the height of a 2D filter, m represents the number of channels for the input feature and n is the number of channels for the output feature. $\mathbf{b}_l$ is a n dimensional vector, i.e. each output feature of this layer has one bias term. $\mathbf{w}_{lj}$ represents a $w \times h \times m$ filter that creates the j-th channel of the output feature for layer l, b_{lj} is its corresponding bias term. $\mathbf{w}_{lj}$ and b_{lj} together form a neuron. We use $\hat{\mathbf{W}}$, $\hat{\mathbf{w}}_l$ and $\hat{\mathbf{w}}_{lj}$ to represent the augmented filters (they contain the corresponding bias term).

3.1 Training a Sparse Constrained CNN

Let $\{\mathbf{X}, \mathbf{Y}^*\}$ be the training samples and corresponding ground-truth label. Then, a CNN can be represented as a function $\mathbf{Y} = f(\hat{\mathbf{W}}, \mathbf{X})$, where $\mathbf{Y}$ is the output of the network. $\hat{\mathbf{W}}$ is learned through minimizing an objective function:

$$\min_{\hat{\mathbf{W}}} \psi(f(\hat{\mathbf{W}}, \mathbf{X}), \mathbf{Y}^*). \tag{1}$$

We use $\psi(\hat{\mathbf{W}})$ to represent the objective function for simplicity. The objective function $\psi(\hat{\mathbf{W}})$ is usually defined as the average cross entropy of the ground truth labels with respect to the output of the network for each training image. Equation (1) is usually solved using a gradient descend based method such as back-propagation [25].

Our goal is adding sparse constraints on the neurons of a CNN. Therefore, the optimization problem of (1) can be written as:

$$\min_{\hat{\mathbf{W}}} \psi(\hat{\mathbf{W}}) + g(\hat{\mathbf{W}}), \tag{2}$$

where $g(\hat{\mathbf{W}})$ represents the set of constraints added to $\hat{\mathbf{W}}$. Given this new optimization problem, the k-th iteration of a standard back-propagation can be defined as:

$$\hat{\mathbf{W}}^k = \hat{\mathbf{W}}^{k-1} - \tau \frac{\partial \psi(\hat{\mathbf{W}})}{\partial \hat{\mathbf{W}}} \big|_{\hat{\mathbf{W}} = \hat{\mathbf{W}}^{k-1}} - \tau \frac{\partial g(\hat{\mathbf{W}})}{\partial \hat{\mathbf{W}}} \big|_{\hat{\mathbf{W}} = \hat{\mathbf{W}}^{k-1}}, \tag{3}$$

where $\hat{\mathbf{W}}^k$ represents the parameters learned at k-th iteration and τ is the learning rate. Based on (3), a new term $\frac{\partial g(\hat{\mathbf{W}})}{\partial \hat{\mathbf{W}}} \big|_{\hat{\mathbf{W}} = \hat{\mathbf{W}}^{k-1}}$ must be added to the gradient of each constrained layer during back-propagation. In those cases where $g(\hat{\mathbf{W}})$ is non-differentiable at some points, sub-gradient methods of $g(\hat{\mathbf{W}})$ are usually needed. However, these methods have three main problems. First, iterates of the sub-gradient at the points of non-differentiability hardly ever occur [11]. Second, sub-gradient methods usually cannot generate an accurate sparse solution [39]. Finally, sub-gradients of some sparse constraints are difficult to choose due to their complex form or they may not be unique [14]. To avoid these problems, and in particular with l_1 constrained optimization problems, [5,37] proposed to use proximal mapping. Following their idea, in the next section, we apply proximal operator to our problem.

3.2 Forward-Backward Splitting

Our proposal to solve the problem (2) and therefore, train a constrained CNN, consists of using forward-backward splitting algorithm [11,14]. Forward-backward splitting provides a way to solve non-differentiable and constrained large-scale optimization problem of the generic form:

$$\min_{\mathbf{z}} f(\mathbf{z}) + h(\mathbf{z}), \qquad (4)$$

where $\mathbf{z} \in \mathbb{R}^N$, $f(\mathbf{z})$ is differentiable and $h(\mathbf{z})$ is an arbitrary convex function [11,14]. The algorithm consists of two stages: First, a forward gradient descent on $f(\mathbf{z})$. Then, a backward gradient step evaluating the proximal operator of $h(\mathbf{z})$. Using this algorithm has two main advantages. First, it is usually easy to estimate the proximal operator of $h(\mathbf{z})$ or even having a closed form solution. Second, backward analysis has an important effect on the convergence of the method when $f(\mathbf{z})$ is convex [14].

Though there is no guarantee about convergence when $f(\mathbf{z})$ is non-convex, forward-backward splitting method usually works quite well for non-convex optimization problems [14]. By treating $\psi(\hat{\mathbf{W}})$ in Eq. (2) as $f(\mathbf{z})$, the forward gradient descent can be computed exactly as the standard back-propagation algorithm in training CNNs. As a result, using forward-backward splitting method to solve sparse constrained CNNs has two steps in one iteration. Algorithm 1 shows how to apply this method to optimize Eq. (2), where τ^k is the learning rate of forward step at k-th iteration.

Algorithm 1. Forward-backward splitting for sparse constrained CNNs

---

1: **while** Not reaching maximum number of iterations **do**
2:     One step back-propagation for $\psi(\hat{\mathbf{W}})$ to get $\hat{\mathbf{W}}^{k*}$
3:     $\hat{\mathbf{W}}^{k+1} = \arg\min_{\hat{\mathbf{W}}} g(\hat{\mathbf{W}}) + \frac{1}{2\tau^k}||\hat{\mathbf{W}} - \hat{\mathbf{W}}^{k*}||^2$
4: **end while**

In practice, we define one step in line 2 of Algorithm 1 as one epoch instead of one iteration of the stochastic gradient descent algorithm. There are two main reasons for this. First, to minimize the computational training overhead of the algorithm as we need to estimate fewer proximal operators of $g(\hat{\mathbf{W}})$. Second, the gradient of $\psi(\hat{\mathbf{W}})$ at each iteration is an approximation to the exact gradient which is noisy [37]. Computing the gradient after certain number of iterations would make the learned parameters more stable [39].

4   Sparse Constraints

Our goal is removing neurons $\hat{\mathbf{w}}_{lj}$, each of which is a tensor. To this end, we consider two sparse constraints for $g(\hat{\mathbf{W}})$ in Eq. (2): tensor low rank constraints [28] and group sparsity [8].

4.1   Tensor Low Rank Constraints

Although the low-rank constraints for 2D matrices and their approximations have been extensively studied, as far as we know, there are few works considering the low-rank constraints for higher dimensional tensors. In [28], the authors proposed to minimize the average rank of different unfolding of a tensor matrix. To relax the problem to convex, they proposed to approximate the average rank using the average of trace norms, which is called tensor trace norm, for different unfolding [28]. We use this formulation as our tensor low rank constraints.

The tensor trace norm of a neuron $\hat{\mathbf{w}}_{lj}$ is $||\hat{\mathbf{w}}_{lj}||_{tr} = \frac{1}{n} \sum_{i=1}^{n} ||\hat{\mathbf{w}}_{lj(i)}||_{tr}$, where n is the order of tensor $\hat{\mathbf{w}}_{lj}$, and $\hat{\mathbf{w}}_{lj(i)}$ is the result of unfolding the tensor $\hat{\mathbf{w}}_{lj}$ along the i-th mode. Under this definition, function $g(\hat{\mathbf{W}})$ can be defined as:

$$g(\hat{\mathbf{W}}) = \lambda \sum_{(j,l)\in\Omega} \frac{1}{n} \sum_{i=1}^{n} ||\hat{\mathbf{w}}_{lj(i)}||_{tr}, \tag{5}$$

where Ω is a set containing all the neurons to be constrained and λ is the weight for the sparse constraint.

As a result, the backward step in the forward-backward splitting is given by:

$$\hat{\mathbf{w}}_{lj}^{k} = \arg\min_{\hat{\mathbf{w}}_{lj}} \frac{1}{n} \sum_{i=1}^{n} ||\hat{\mathbf{w}}_{lj(i)}||_{tr} + \frac{1}{2\tau\lambda n} \sum_{i=1}^{n} ||\hat{\mathbf{w}}_{lj(i)}^{k} - \hat{\mathbf{w}}_{lj(i)}^{k*}||^2. \tag{6}$$

This problem can be solved using the Low Rank Tensor Completion (LRTC) algorithm proposed in [28].[1]

4.2   Group Sparse Constraints

These are defined as $l_{2,1}$ regularizer. Applying $l_{2,1}$ to our objective function, we have:

$$g(\hat{\mathbf{W}}) = \lambda \sum_{(j,l)\in\Omega} ||\hat{\mathbf{w}}_{lj}||, \tag{7}$$

where λ and Ω are the same as in Sect. 4.1. $||.||$ is defined in Sect. 3. According to [8], backward step in forward backward splitting method at k-th iteration now becomes:

$$\hat{\mathbf{w}}_{lj}^{k} = \max\{||\hat{\mathbf{w}}_{lj}^{k*}|| - \tau\lambda, 0\} \frac{\hat{\mathbf{w}}_{lj}^{k*}}{||\hat{\mathbf{w}}_{lj}^{k*}||}, \tag{8}$$

where τ is the learning rate and $\hat{\mathbf{w}}_{lj}^{k*}$ is the optimized neuron from the forward step in forward backward splitting.

---

[1] Please refer to the supplementary material for the specific details of the algorithm.

5   Importance of Rectified Linear Units in Sparse Constrained CNNs

Convolutional layers in a CNN are usually followed by a nonlinear activation function. Rectified Linear Units (ReLU) [23] has been heavily used in CNNs for computer vision tasks. Besides the advantages of ReLU discussed in [13,30,40], we show that $\hat{\mathbf{w}}_{lj} = \mathbf{0}$ is a local minimum in sparse constrained CNNs, of which the non-linear function is ReLU. This can explain our findings that ReLU can help removing more neurons and inspires us to set momentum to 0 for neurons which reach their sparse local minimum during training as discussed in Sect. 6.1.

ReLU function was defined as $ReLU(x) = max(0,x)$ which is non-differentiable at 0. This brings us difficulty to analyze the local minimum of sparse constrained CNNs. Based on the observation that, in practical implementations, the gradient of ReLU function at 0 is set to 0 [6,21,38]. We consider the following practical definition of ReLU:

$$ReLU(x) = \begin{cases} x & \text{if } x > \epsilon \\ 0 & \text{if } x \leq \epsilon. \end{cases} \qquad (9)$$

where ϵ is chosen such that for any real number x that a computer can represent, if $x > 0$, then $x > \epsilon$; if $x \leq 0$, then $x < \epsilon$. The non-differentiable point of ReLU function is now at ϵ which will never appear in practice. Under this definition, ReLU function is differentiable and continuous at point 0, the gradient of $ReLU(x)$ at 0 is now 0. As a result, this practical definition of ReLU is consistent with the implementations of ReLU function in practice [6,21,38].

By fixing all other neurons, it is not difficult to show that a particular neuron $\hat{\mathbf{w}}_{lj} = \mathbf{0}$ lies in a flat region of $\psi(\hat{\mathbf{w}}_{lj})$ under the above definition of ReLU. Moreover, $g(\hat{\mathbf{w}}_{lj})$ contains a sparse constrains, so $\hat{\mathbf{w}}_{lj} = \mathbf{0}$ is the local minimum of the objective function $\psi(\hat{\mathbf{w}}_{lj}) + g(\hat{\mathbf{w}}_{lj}).^2$

The fact that $\hat{\mathbf{w}}_{lj} = \mathbf{0}$ is a local minimum for sparse constrained CNNs using ReLU as nonlinear activation function can explain the improvement in the number of neurons removed as discussed in Sect. 6.1. Importantly, we find that using momentum during the optimization may push a zero neuron away from being $\mathbf{0}$ since momentum memorizes the gradient of this neuron in previous steps. As a consequence, using momentum would lead to more non-zero neurons without performance improvement. In practice, once a neuron reaches $\mathbf{0}$, we set its momentum to zero, forcing the neuron to maintain its value. As we will demonstrate in Sect. 6.1 this results in more zero neurons without affecting the performance.

6   Experiments

We test our method on four well-known convolutional neural networks on three well-known datasets: LeNet on MNIST [25], CIFAR10-quick [35] on CIFAR-10

---

^{2} Please find the detailed discussion in supplementary material.

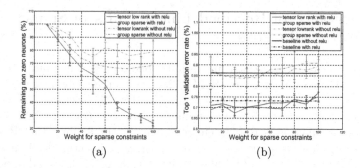

Fig. 1. (a) Percentage of nonzero neurons on the second convolutional layer for LeNet under different weights for sparse constraints with and without adding ReLU layer. (b) Corresponding top 1 validation error rate. Baseline in (b) shows the top 1 validation error rate without adding any sparse constraints. Error bars represent the standard deviation over the four experiments.

[22] and AlexNet [23] and VGG [34] on ILSVRC-2012 [33]. We use LeNet and CIFAR10-quick provided by Matconvnet [38] and AlexNet and VGG provided by [4] to carry out all our experiments.

All the structures of the networks are provided by Matconvnet [38] or [4], the only change we made is to add ReLU function after each convolutional layer in LeNet, which we will discuss in detail later. For all our experiments, data augmentation and pre-processing strategies are provided by [4,38].

6.1 LeNet on MNIST

MNIST is a well-known dataset for machine learning and computer vision. It contains $60,000$ handwritten digits for training and $10,000$ for testing. All these digits are images of 28×28 with a single channel. All the data will be subtracted by the mean as suggested in [38]. The average top 1 validation error rate of LeNet on MNIST adding ReLU layer is 0.73%. As training a LeNet on MNIST is fast, we use this experiment as a sanity check. Results are computed as the average over four runs of each experiment using different random seeds.

ReLU helps removing more neurons: The LeNet structure provided by Matconvnet has two convolutional layers and two fully connected layers. The two convolutional layers are followed by a max pooling layer respectively. Under this structure, the sparse solution may not be a local minimum. Based on the discussion in Sect. 5, we add a ReLU layer after each of these two convolutional layers so that $\hat{\mathbf{w}}_{lj} = \mathbf{0}$ is a local minimum. We compare these two structures by using different weights for sparse constraints added to the second convolutional layer and show the results in Fig. 1.

As shown in Fig. 1, adding ReLU improves the performance of LeNet no matter whether we add sparse constraints or not. Comparing these two structures, adding ReLU layer always leads to more zero neurons compared with the

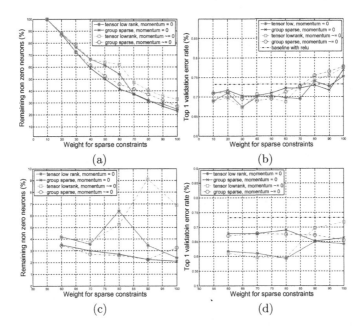

Fig. 2. Comparison of the proposed results with setting momentum to be zero. (a) and (c) show the percentage of non zero neurons for second convolutional layer and first fully connected layer under different weights for sparse constraints respectively. (b) and (d) show their corresponding top 1 validation error rate.

original structure. What is more interesting is that, with ReLU layer, the top 1 validation error rate of LeNet with sparse constraints is more close to, if not better than, the performance without sparse constraints. This may be explained by the fact the $\hat{\mathbf{w}}_{lj} = \mathbf{0}$ is a local minimum of the structure with ReLU and this local minimum is usually a good one. In the following discussion, when LeNet is mentioned, we mean LeNet with ReLU function after each of its convolutional layers.

Momentum for Sparse Local Minimum: Momentum plays a significant role in training CNNs. It can be treated as a memory of the gradient computed in previous iterations and has been proved to accelerate the convergence of SGD. However, this memory of gradient effect may push a neuron in its sparse local minimum away, leading to results with more non-zero neurons with no improvement in performance. To avoid this problem we can directly set the momentum of the neurons to be zero for those reached sparse local minimum.

In Fig. 2, we compare the number of non-zero neurons with and without setting the momentum to be zero for LeNet on MNIST dataset. We add the sparse constraints on the second convolutional layer and the first fully connected layer since they have most of the filters. As shown in Fig. 2, the performance does not drop when momentum is set to be zero for local sparse minimum. Additionally, we sporadically achieve better performance. Moreover, for first

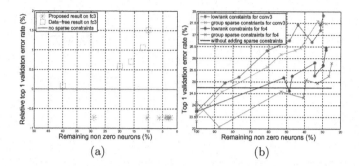

Fig. 3. (a) **MNIST** Comparison between of single layer results of the proposed method and the data-free method presented in [36] using LeNet on MNIST. (b) **CIFAR-10** Top 1 validation error rate versus percentage of remaining non zero neurons on conv3 and fc4 using CIFAR10-quick.

fully connected layer, setting momentum to be zero leads to results with more zero neurons under large sparse weights.[3]

From Figs. 1 and 2, we find that the top-1 error rates of using tensor low-rank constraints are a little better than using group sparse constraints. Group sparse constraints, however, can give more zero neurons which can result in more compact networks. These differences are very small, so we conclude that both of these methods can help removing neurons without hurting the performance of the network. In the following discussion, only results from group sparse constraints are shown when necessary.

Compression for LeNet: Figure 3 (a) shows the comparison of the proposed method with [36]. Since [36] only adds sparse constraints on first fully connected layer of LeNet (fc3), we only show our results using group sparse constraints on fc3. The compression rate and top 1 validation error are averaged over 4 results with different random seeds. Since the two networks may be trained differently, we show the relative top 1 validation error rate, which is defined as top 1 validation error rate of the proposed method minus that without sparse constraints. A smaller value means better performance. As shown in this figure, our method outperforms the one proposed in [36] in both compression and accuracy. Please, note that [36] predicts the cut-off number of neurons for fc3 to be 440 and a drop of performance of 1.07 %. The proposed method, on the contrary, can remove 489 neurons while maintaining the performance of the original one.

To improve the compression rate, we add group sparse constraints to the layers containing most of the parameters in LeNet: the second convolutional layer (conv2) and the first fully connected layer (fc3). We compare two strategies. First, adding sparse constraints in a layer by layer fashion and second, jointly constraining both layers. Empirically we found that the first strategy performs better. Thus, we first add sparse constraints on fc3 and, after the number of zero-

---
[3] For a clear comparison, we only show results under large weights for the first fully connected layer in the figure.

Table 2. Results of adding group sparse constraints on three layers.

τ			Non-zero Neurons			Number of Parameters	Top-1 error (%)
conv1	conv2	fc3	conv1	conv2	fc3		
100	80	90	7	23	20	11820	0.72
100	120	80	7	13	21	7079	0.76
120	120	90	6	14	20	6980	0.81

neurons in this layer is stable, we add sparse constraints on conv2. We report the results of using group sparse constraints. The weight used for fc3 is set to 100, and the weights for conv2 are set to 60, 80, 100. Table 3 summarizes the average results over the four runs of the experiment. As shown, our method not only reduces significantly the number of neurons, which leads to significant reduction in the number of parameters in these two layers but also compresses the total number of parameters of the network for more than 90 %, leading to a memory footprint reduction larger than 1 MB.

We further try to add group sparse constraints on all three layers of LeNet to check whether our method can work on more layers. To introduce more redundancy on conv1 and conv2, we initialize the number of non zero neurons for conv1 and conv2 to be 100. Similar to adding sparse constraints on two layers, we add sparse constraints layer by layer. We show some of our results in Table 2. To compare, the best compression result of adding sparse constraints on conv2 and fc3 leads to a model with 13062 parameters (third row of LeNet in Table 2). We find that by adding sparse constraints on three layers, a more compact network can be achieved though we initialize the network with more neurons.

6.2 CIFAR-10 Quick on CIFAR-10

CIFAR-10 [22] is a database consisting of 50,000 training and 10,000 testing RGB images with a resolution of 32 × 32 pixels split into 10 classes. As suggested in [38], data is standardized using zero-mean unit length normalization followed by a whitening process. Furthermore, we use random flips as data augmentation. For a fair comparison, we train the original network, CIFAR10-quick, without any sparse constraints using the same training set-up and achieve a top 1 validation error rate of 24.75 %.

Since the third convolutional layer (conv3) and the first fully connected layer (fc4) contain most of the parameters, we add sparse constraints on these two layers independently. Figure 3(b) shows the top 1 validation error rate versus the percentage of remaining non-zero neurons. As shown, 20 % and 70 % of neurons for conv3 and fc4 can be removed without a noticeable drop in performance.

To obtain the best compression results, we jointly constraint conv3 and fc4 as we did with LeNet. To this end, we first add the constraints on fc4, and then, we include the same ones on conv3. We run the experiment for more epochs compared to the default values in Matconvnet [38]. For a fair comparison, we

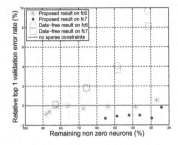

Fig. 4. ImageNet. Comparison between single layer results on fc6 and fc7 and the data-free method in [36] using AlexNet on ImageNet. Data-free results are from [36].

train the baseline (i.e., CIFAR-10 quick without sparse constraints) for the same number of epochs. As a result, we obtain a top 1 validation error of 22.33 %. We used this result to compute relative top 1 validation error rate. The weight of group sparse constraints for fc4 is fixed to 280 while the three different weights for conv3 are $220, 240, 280$. A summary of results is listed in the second part of Table 3. Through this experiment, it can be seen that even for this simple network, we can remove a large number of neurons which leads to a great compression in the number of parameters. Considering that there are only 64 neurons on each of these two layers, the compression results are significant.

6.3 AlexNet and VGG on ImageNet

ImageNet [7] is a dataset with over 15 million labeled images split into 22,000 categories. AlexNet [23] was proposed to be trained on ILSVRC-2012 [33] which is a subset of ImageNet with 1.2 million training images and 50,000 validation images. We use the implementation of AlexNet and VGG-13 provided by [4] in order to test ImageNet on our cluster. Random flipping is applied to augment the data. Quantitative results are reported using a single crop in the center of the image. For comparison, we consider the network trained without adding any sparse constraints. The top 1 validation error for this baseline is 45.57 % and 37.50 % for AlexNet and VGG-13 respectively. For the rest of experiments we only report results using group sparse constraints.

Figure 4 shows the top 1 validation error rate versus the percentage of nonzero neurons for AlexNet. Group sparse constraints are added on first and second fully connected layers (fc6 and fc7) independently. Results from [36] are copied from their paper and shown in this figure for comparison. Similar to Sect. 6.1, we show the relative top 1 validation error rates due to the training of two methods may be different. This figure clearly shows that compared with [36], the proposed method can remove a large number of neurons without decreasing the performance. For instance, the best compression results of the proposed method can eliminate 76.76 % of all the parameters of AlexNet with a negligible drop in performance (0.57 % in top 1 validation error). The best performance model in [36], on the other hand, can only remove 34.89 % of the parameters with top

Less Is More: Towards Compact CNNs   675

Table 3. Results of adding group sparse constraints on two layers. The best compression results within 1 % decrease in top 1 error rate is shown in bold.

	τ		Neurons pruned (%)		Top-1 error (%)		Parameter reduction (%)	Memory reduced (MB)
	conv2	fc3	conv2	fc3	Absolute	Relative		
LeNet	60	100	45.5	97.75	0.73	0.00	95.35	1.57
	80	100	56.5	97.75	0.77	0.04	96.31	1.58
	100	100	63.0	97.75	0.76	0.03	**96.79**	**1.59**
	τ		Neurons pruned (%)		Top-1 error (%)		Parameter reduction (%)	Memory reduced (MB)
	conv3	fc4	conv3	fc4	Absolute	Relative		
cifar-10 quick	220	280	31.25	70.31	22.21	−0.12	47.17	268.24
	240	280	46.88	71.86	22.73	0.4	**55.15**	**313.62**
	280	280	54.69	70.31	23.78	1.45	58.56	333.01
	τ		Neurons pruned (%)		Top-1 error (%)		Parameter reduction (%)	Memory reduced (MB)
	fc6	fc7	fc6	fc7	Absolute	Relative		
AlexNet	40	35	48.46	56.49	44.58	−0.98	55.15	128.26
	45	30	77.05	60.21	46.14	0.57	**76.76**	**178.52**
	45	35	73.39	65.80	45.88	0.31	74.88	174.14

1 validation error rate decreased by 2.24 %. A representative set of compression results obtained using sparse constraints on two layers is shown in the third part of Table 3.

We test the proposed method on VGG-13 on the first fully connected layer as it contains most of the parameters of the network. Table 4 summarizes the outcomes of the experiment for different group sparsity weights. As shown, for this state-of-the-art network structure, our method can reduce nearly half of the parameters and significantly reduce the memory footprint at the expenses of a slight drop in performance.

Table 4. Some compression results of proposed method on fc1 for vgg-B. Neuron: compression of neurons in the fc1. Parameter: compression of total parameters.

Layer	τ	Compression %		Memory	Top 1 error (%)	
		neurons	Parameters	Reduced (MB)	Absolute	Relative
fc1	5	39.04	35.08	178.02	38.30	0.80
fc1	10	49.27	44.28	224.67	38.54	1.04
fc1	20	76.21	61.30	311.06	39.26	1.76

7 Conclusion

We proposed an algorithm to significantly reduce of the number of neurons in a convolutional neural network by adding sparse constraints during the training step. The forward-backward splitting method is applied to solve the sparse constrained problem. We also analyze the benefits of using rectified linear units as non-linear activation function to remove a larger number of neurons.

Experiments using four popular CNNs including AlexNet and VGG-B demonstrate the capacity of the proposed method to reduce the number of neurons, therefore, the number of parameters and memory footprint, with a negligible loss in performance.

Acknowledgment. The authors thank NVIDIA for generous hardware donations.

References

1. Ba, J., Caruana, R.: Do deep nets really need to be deep?. In: NIPS (2014)
2. Bucila, C., Caruana, R., Niculescu-Mizil, A.: Model compression. In: ACM SIGKDD (2006)
3. Chen, L., Papandreou, G., Kokkinos, I., Murphy, K., Yuille, A.L.: Semantic image segmentation with deep convolutional nets and fully connected CRFS. In: ICLR (2014)
4. Chintala, S.: soumith/imagenet-multigpu.torch (2015). https://github.com/soumith/imagenet-multiGPU.torch
5. Collins, M.D., Kohli, P.: Memory bounded deep convolutional networks. CoRR abs/1412.1442 (2014)
6. Collobert, R., Kavukcuoglu, K., Farabet, C.: Torch7: a matlab-like environment for machine learning. In: BigLearn, NIPS Workshop (2011)
7. Deng, J., Dong, W., Socher, R., Li, L.J., Li, K., Fei-Fei, L.: Imagenet: a large-scale hierarchical image database. In: CVPR (2009)
8. Deng, W., Yin, W., Zhang, Y.: Group sparse optimization by alternating direction method. In: SPIE. vol. 8858 (2013)
9. Denil, M., Shakibi, B., Dinh, L., Ranzato, M., Freitasa, N.D.: Predicting parameters in deep learning. In: NIPS (2013)
10. Denton, E.L., Zaremba, W., Bruna, J., LeCun, Y., Fergus, R.: Exploiting linear structure within convolutional networks for efficient evaluation. In: NIPS (2014)
11. Duchi, J., Singer, Y.: Efficient online and batch learning using forward backward splitting. J. Mach. Learn. Res. **10**, 2899–2934 (2009)
12. Girshick, R., Donahue, J., Darrell, T., Malik, J.: Rich feature hierarchies for accurate object detection and semantic segmentation. In: CVPR (2014)
13. Glorot, X., Bordes, A., Bengio, Y.: Deep sparse rectifier neural networks. In: AISTATS (2011)
14. Goldstein, T., Studer, C., Baraniuk, R.G.: A field guide to forward-backward splitting with a FASTA implementation. arXiv eprint arXiv.abs/1411.3406 (2014)
15. Gong, Y., Liu, L., Yang, M., Bourdev, L.D.: Compressing deep convolutional networks using vector quantization. CoRR abs/1412.6115 (2014)
16. Han, S., Mao, H., Dally, W.J.: Deep compression: Compressing deep neural network with pruning, trained quantization and huffman coding. In: ICLR (2016)

17. Han, S., Pool, J., Tran, J., Dally, W.J.: Learning both weights and connections for efficient neural networks. In: NIPS (2015)
18. Hassibi, B., Stork, D.G.: Second order derivatives for network pruning: Optimal brain surgeon. In: NIPS (1993)
19. Hinton, G.E., Vinyals, O., Dean, J.: Distilling the knowledge in a neural network. In: NIPS 2014 Deep Learning Workshop (2014)
20. Jaderberg, M., Vedaldi, A., Zisserman, A.: Speeding up convolutional neural networks with low rank expansions. In: BMVC (2014)
21. Jia, Y., Shelhamer, E., Donahue, J., Karayev, S., Long, J., Girshick, R., Guadarrama, S., Darrell, T.: Caffe: Convolutional architecture for fast feature embedding. arXiv preprint (2014). arXiv:1408.5093
22. Krizhevsky, A.: Learning multiple layers of features from tiny images. Technical report, Department of Computer Science, University of Toronto (2009)
23. Krizhevsky, A., Sutskever, I., Hinton, G.E.: Imagenet classification with deep convolutional neural networks. In: NIPS (2012)
24. Lebedev, V., Ganin, Y., Rakhuba, M., Oseledets, I.V., Lempitsky, V.S.: Speeding-up convolutional neural networks using fine-tuned cp-decomposition. In: ICLR (2015)
25. LeCun, Y., Bottou, L., Bengio, Y., Haffner, P.: Gradient-based learning applied to document recognition. Proc. IEEE **86**(11), 2278–2324 (1998)
26. LeCun, Y., Denker, J.S., Solla, S.A.: Optimal brain damage. In: NIPS (1990)
27. Liu, B., Wang, M., Foroosh, H., Tappen, M., Penksy, M.: Sparse convolutional neural networks. In: CVPR (2015)
28. Liu, J., Musialski, P., Wonka, P., Ye, J.: Tensor completion for estimating missing values in visual data. IEEE Trans. PAMI **35**(1), 208–220 (2013)
29. Mathieu, M., Henaff, M., LeCun, Y.: Fast training of convolutional networks through FFTS. CoRR abs/1312.5851, http://arxiv.org/abs/1312.5851 (2013)
30. Nair, V., Hinton, G.E.: Rectified linear units improve restricted boltzmann machines. In: ICML (2010)
31. Novikov, A., Podoprikhin, D., Osokin, A., Vetrov, D.P.: Tensorizing neural networks. In: NIPS (2015)
32. Romero, A., Ballas, N., Kahou, S.E., Chassang, A., Gatta, C., Bengio, Y.: Fitnets: Hints for thin deep nets. In: ICLR (2015)
33. Russakovsky, O., Deng, J., Su, H., Krause, J., Satheesh, S., Ma, S., Huang, Z., Karpathy, A., Khosla, A., Bernstein, M., Berg, A.C., Fei-Fei, L.: Imagenet large scale visual recognition challenge. IJCV **115**(3), 211–252 (2015)
34. Simonyan, K., Zisserman, A.: Very deep convolutional networks for large-scale image recognition. CoRR abs/1409.1556 (2014)
35. Snoek, J., Larochelle, H., Adams, R.P.: Practical bayesian optimization of machine learning algorithms. In: NIPS (2012)
36. Srinivas, S., Babu, R.V.: Data-free parameter pruning for deep neural networks. In: BMVC (2015)
37. Tsuruoka, Y., Tsujii, J., Ananiadou, S.: Stochastic gradient descent training for l1-regularized log-linear models with cumulative penalty. In: ACL-IJCNLP (2009)
38. Vedaldi, A., Lenc, K.: Matconvnet - convolutional neural networks for matlab. In: ACM MM (2014)
39. Yu, D., Seide, F., Li, G., Deng, L.: Exploiting sparseness in deep neural networks for large vocabulary speech recognition. In: ICASSP (2012)
40. Zeiler, M.D., Ranzato, M., Monga, R., Mao, M., Yang, K., Le, Q., Nguyen, P., Senior, A., Vanhoucke, V., Dean, J., Hinton, G.: On rectified linear units for speech processing. In: ICASSP (2013)

Unsupervised Visual Representation Learning by Graph-Based Consistent Constraints

Dong Li[1], Wei-Chih Hung[2], Jia-Bin Huang[3], Shengjin Wang[1(✉)],
Narendra Ahuja[3], and Ming-Hsuan Yang[2]

[1] Tsinghua University, Beijing, China
wgsgj@tsinghua.edu.cn
[2] University of California, Merced, Merced, USA
[3] University of Illinois, Urbana-Champaign, Champaign, USA
https://sites.google.com/site/lidonggg930/feature-learning

Abstract. Learning rich visual representations often require training on datasets of millions of manually annotated examples. This substantially limits the scalability of learning effective representations as labeled data is expensive or scarce. In this paper, we address the problem of unsupervised visual representation learning from a large, unlabeled collection of images. By representing each image as a node and each nearest-neighbor matching pair as an edge, our key idea is to leverage graph-based analysis to discover positive and negative image pairs (i.e., pairs belonging to the same and different visual categories). Specifically, we propose to use a cycle consistency criterion for mining positive pairs and geodesic distance in the graph for hard negative mining. We show that the mined positive and negative image pairs can provide accurate supervisory signals for learning effective representations using Convolutional Neural Networks (CNNs). We demonstrate the effectiveness of the proposed unsupervised constraint mining method in two settings: (1) unsupervised feature learning and (2) semi-supervised learning. For unsupervised feature learning, we obtain competitive performance with several state-of-the-art approaches on the PASCAL VOC 2007 dataset. For semi-supervised learning, we show boosted performance by incorporating the mined constraints on three image classification datasets.

Keywords: Unsupervised feature learning · Semi-supervised learning · Image classification · Convolutional neural networks

1 Introduction

Convolutional neural networks have recently achieved impressive performance on a broad range of visual recognition tasks [1–3]. However, the success of CNNs

Electronic supplementary material The online version of this chapter (doi:10. 1007/978-3-319-46493-0_41) contains supplementary material, which is available to authorized users.

© Springer International Publishing AG 2016
B. Leibe et al. (Eds.): ECCV 2016, Part IV, LNCS 9908, pp. 678–694, 2016.
DOI: 10.1007/978-3-319-46493-0_41

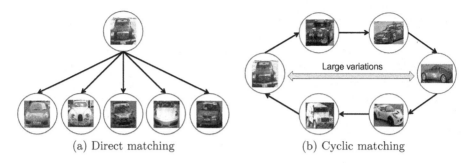

(a) Direct matching   (b) Cyclic matching

Fig. 1. Illustration of positive mining based on cycle consistency. (a) Direct image matching using similarity of the appearance features often results in matching pairs with very similar appearances (e.g., certain pose of cars). (b) By finding cycles in the graph, we observe that image pairs in the cycle are likely to belong to the same visual category but with large appearance variations (e.g., under different viewpoints).

is mainly attributed to supervised learning over massive amounts of human-labeled data. The need of large-scale manual annotations substantially limits the scalability of learning effective representations as labeled data is expensive or scarce. In this paper, we address the problem of *unsupervised* visual representation learning. Given only a large, unlabeled image collection, we aim to learn rich visual representations without using any manual supervision. This particular setting is important for many practical applications because large amounts of interconnected visual data is readily available on the Internet. However, it remains challenging to learn effective representations for visual recognition in an unsupervised fashion.

Numerous efforts have been made on unsupervised learning [4–8]. Existing approaches aim to use reconstruction as a pretext task for visual representation learning. The most commonly used architecture is an autoencoder which aims at reconstructing input images from noisy ones [6–8]. However, current reconstruction-based algorithms tend to learn filters detecting low-level patterns (e.g., edges, textures). Such algorithms may not generalize well to high-level visual recognition tasks. Recent work explores various types of supervisory signals freely available in images and videos for unsupervised visual representation learning. Examples include ego-motion [9,10], context prediction [11], and tracking [12]. However, ego-motion information does not correlate with semantic information well. Spatial context prediction [11] and tracking [12] consider only *instance-level* data as the training samples are taken *within* the same image and video.

In this paper, we propose a new way to generate *category-level* training samples for unsupervised visual representation learning. The general idea is that we can discover underlying *semantic* similarity among images by leveraging graph-based analysis over a large collection of images. We construct the k-nearest neighbor (k-NN) graph by representing each image as a node and each nearest-neighbor matching pair as an edge. Unlike other methods that use the nearest neighbor graphs to learn similarity functions [13,14], we use the graph to mine constraints for learning rich visual representations. Specifically, we propose to use a cycle consistency criterion for mining positive pairs. Compared to the direct image matching, cycle consistency allows us to mine image pairs from the same category yet with large appearance variations. The basic idea for positive mining is illustrated in Fig. 1. For negative image pair mining, we propose to use geodesic distance in the graph to discover hard negative samples. Image pairs with large geodesic distance are likely to belong to different categories but may have a small Euclidean distance in the original feature space. We observe that the mined positive and negative image pairs can provide accurate supervisory signals to train a CNN for learning effective representations. We validate the effectiveness of the proposed unsupervised constraint mining method in two settings: (1) unsupervised feature learning and (2) semi-supervised learning. For unsupervised feature learning, we obtain competitive performance with several state-of-the-art approaches on the PASCAL VOC 2007 dataset. For semi-supervised learning, we improve the classification results by incorporating the mined constraints on three datasets.

We make the following three contributions in this work:

1. We propose a simple but effective approach to mine semantically similar and dissimilar image pairs from a large, unlabeled collection of images.
2. We tackle the problem of learning rich visual representations in an unsupervised manner. Using the mined image pairs, we train a Siamese network to perform binary classification (i.e., same or different categories). Using the CNN model trained on the large-scale ImageNet dataset without any labels, we obtain competitive performance with the state-of-the-art unsupervised learning approaches on the PASCAL VOC 2007 dataset.
3. We show how the unsupervised constraint mining approach can also be used in a semi-supervised learning problem. We improve the classification accuracy by incorporating the mined constraints, particularly when the number of available training samples is limited.

2   Related Work

Visual Representation Learning. Convolutional neural networks have achieved great success on various recognition tasks [1–3]. Typical CNN-based visual representation learning approaches rely on full supervision, i.e., images with manually annotated class labels. Recent research on visual representation learning has been explored in a weakly supervised [15–18], semi-supervised [19, 20] and unsupervised [11,12] fashion. Various types of supervisory signals are exploited to train CNNs as the substitutes for class labels. For example, Agrawal et al. [9] and Jayaraman et al. [10] train CNNs by exploiting ego-motion information. Wang et al. [12] track image patches in a video to train the network with a ranking loss. Doersch et al. [11] extract pairs of patches from an image and train the network to predict their relative positions. Chen et al. [21] and Joulin et al. [22] utilize the available large-scale web resources for learning CNN representations. However, ego-motion information [9,10] does not correlate with semantic information well. Spatial context prediction [11] and tracking [12] consider only *instance-level* data as the training samples are taken *within* the same image and video. In contrast, we use graph-based analysis to generate *category-level* training samples *across* different images. These category-level samples contain positive image pairs that are semantically similar but may have large intra-class appearance variations. Such information is crucial for learning visual representations for factoring out nuisance appearance variations.

Unsupervised Object/Patch Mining. Another line of related work is unsupervised object/patch mining. Existing methods use various forms of clustering or matching algorithms for object discovery [23], ROI detection [24] and patch mining [25,26]. Examples include spectral clustering [27], discriminative clustering [25,26], and alternating optimization algorithms [23,24]. However, clustering methods are typically sensitive to the pre-defined number of clusters. In contrast, our unsupervised constraint mining method aims at finding semantically similar and dissimilar image pairs instead of multiple image clusters. Compared to iterative optimization methods, our mining algorithm is more efficient and can be easily applied to large-scale datasets. In addition, we rely on CNNs to learn effective visual representations while most unsupervised object/patch mining methods use only hand-crafted features.

Cycle Consistency. Cycle consistency in a graph has been applied to various computer vision and graphics problems, including co-segmentation [28,29], structure from motion [30,31] and image matching [32,33]. These approaches exploit cycles as constraints and solve constrained optimization problems for establishing correspondences among pixels/keypoints/patches across different images. In this work, we observe that cycle consistency can be used for finding semantically similar images. With detecting cycles in the k-NN graph, we can mine positive image pairs with large appearance variations from an unlabeled image collection. Our work is also related to symmetric nearest neighbor matching [34,35]. For example, Dekel et al. [35] match pairs of points where each point is the nearest neighbor of the other. This is a particular case (i.e., 2-cycle) of cycle consistency in our setup.

3   Overview

Our goal is to learn rich visual representations in an unsupervised manner. We propose an unsupervised constraint mining algorithm to generate category-level image pairs from an unlabeled image collection (Sect. 4). For positive pair mining, we detect cycles in the k-NN graph and take all the matching pairs in the cycles as positive samples. Compared to the direct image matching, image pairs mined by cycle consistency are likely to belong to the same visual category but with large appearance variations. For negative pair mining, we take image pairs with large geodesic distance in the graph as negative samples. Such mined negative pairs are likely to belong to different categories but may have a small Euclidean distance in the original feature space. We validate the effectiveness of the proposed unsupervised constraint mining algorithm in two settings: unsupervised feature learning (Sect. 5.1) and semi-supervised learning (Sect. 5.2). Figure 2 shows the overview of the two settings.

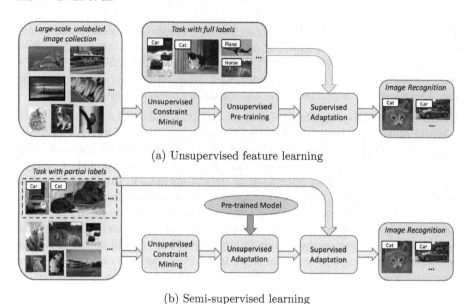

(a) Unsupervised feature learning

(b) Semi-supervised learning

Fig. 2. Overview of the two settings for visual representation learning. For unsupervised feature learning, our goal is learning visual representations from a large-scale unlabeled image collection and employing the learned representations for specific recognition tasks with full labels. For semi-supervised learning, our goal is adapting visual representations from the supervised pre-trained model to specific recognition tasks with partial annotations.

4   Unsupervised Constraint Mining

In this section, we introduce the unsupervised constraint mining algorithm. We start with computing the Euclidean distance between each image pair in the original feature space. We then construct a k-NN graph $G = (V, E)$. Each node $v \in V = \{I_1, I_2, \ldots, I_N\}$ denotes an image. Each directed edge e_{ij} denotes a matching pair "$I_i \rightarrow I_j$" if I_j belongs to the k-nearest neighbors of I_i. The edge weight w_{ij} is defined by the Euclidean distance between the matching pair.

4.1   Positive Constraint Mining

We define that I_j is an n-order k-nearest neighbor of the image I_i if there exists a directed path of length n from image I_i to image I_j. The set of n-order k-nearest neighbors for image I_i is denoted as $\mathcal{N}_k^{(n)}(I_i)$. For example, if I_b belongs to the 5-nearest neighbors of I_a and I_c belongs to the 5-nearest neighbors of I_b, we have $I_c \in \mathcal{N}_5^{(2)}(I_a)$. Naturally, if I_i belongs to its own n-order k-nearest neighbors, we then obtain a directed cycle.

$$I_i \in \mathcal{N}_k^{(n)}(I_i), \ n = 2, 3, 4, \ldots . \tag{1}$$

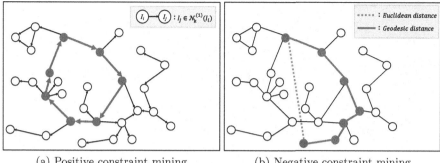

(a) Positive constraint mining   (b) Negative constraint mining

Fig. 3. Illustration of the graph-based unsupervised constraint mining algorithm. (a) For positive mining, we propose to use cycle consistency to mine image pairs from the same class but with large appearance variations. (b) For negative mining, we propose to use geodesic distance to mine image pairs from the different classes but with a relatively small Euclidean distance in the original feature space.

For each node in the k-NN graph, we search its n-order k-nearest neighbors and detect cycles according to (1). An n-cycle constraint can generate $n(n-1)/2$ different pairs of images. We take these pairs as positive samples for the subsequent CNN training. Figure 3(a) illustrates the process for positive constraint mining.

Cycle consistency offers two advantages for generating positive image pairs. (1) It helps mine indirect matching pairs from the same category yet with large appearance variations. For example, a 4-cycle constraint "$I_a \rightarrow I_b \rightarrow I_c \rightarrow I_d \rightarrow I_a$" will generate two indirect pairs as (I_a, I_c) and (I_b, I_d). Although the image I_a and I_c may have dramatically different appearances, the third image I_b (or I_d) provides indirect evidence supporting their match. (2) It filters the large candidate set of k-NN matching pairs and selects the most representative ones (e.g., the adjacent pair (I_a, I_b) in the 4-cycle constraint).

4.2   Negative Constraint Mining

Geodesic distance is widely used in manifold learning and has recently been applied to foreground/background segmentation as a low-level metric [36–38]. In our method, we use geodesic distance to mine hard negative image pairs in a k-NN graph. Specifically, we first use the Floyd-Warshall algorithm [39] for finding shortest paths between each node in the graph. The geodesic distance g_{ij} is the accumulated edge weights along the shortest path from I_i to I_j. We then perform random selection among those image pairs with large geodesic distance as negative samples. Figure 3(b) illustrates the process for negative constraint mining.

Geodesic distance brings two advantages for generating negative image pairs. (1) Image pairs with large Euclidean distance are often easy samples, which do not contain much information for learning a good CNN representation. This is

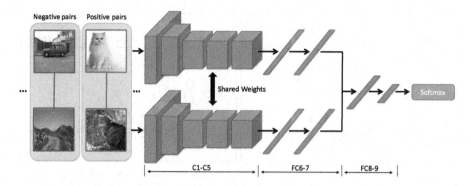

Fig. 4. The proposed Siamese network for binary classification. C1-FC7 layers follow the AlexNet architecture and share weights. FC8-9 layers have 64 and 2 neurons, respectively. A binary softmax classifier is used to predict whether the two images belong to the same category.

because the original Euclidean distance only expresses the appearance similarity between two images. In contrast, image pairs with large geodesic distance are likely to belong to different categories but may have small Euclidean distances in the original feature space. (2) Within a typical multi-class image dataset (e.g., the 1,000 classes in the ImageNet classification task), an overwhelming majority of random image pairs are negative samples. It is thus more efficient to select hard negative pairs based on geodesic distance for learning effective representations than collecting large amounts of easy samples.

5   Visual Representation Learning

To learn visual representations by the mined positive and negative pairs, we design a two-branch Siamese network for binary pair classification. Figure 4 shows the Siamese network architecture. In our experiments, we take two images with size 227×227 as input. The layers of C1-FC7 follow the AlexNet architecture and share weights. We concatenate the two FC7 outputs and stack two fully connected layers of FC8-9 with 64 and 2 neurons, respectively. A softmax loss function is used to train the entire network for predicting whether the two images belong to the same category.

5.1   Unsupervised Feature Learning

In the setting of unsupervised feature learning (Fig. 2(a)), the goal is learning visual representations from a large-scale unlabeled image collection and employing the learned representations for specific recognition tasks with full labels. To this end, we first use the proposed unsupervised constraint mining algorithm to discover positive and negative pairs from the ImageNet 2012 dataset [40] without any labels. We use Fisher Vectors based on dense SIFT [41] as feature descriptors.[1] Instead of directly applying our algorithm to the entire large-scale dataset with 1.2 million nodes, we randomly divide the training set into multiple subsets. Image pairs are mined in each subset and assembled eventually. In the unsupervised pre-training stage, we use the mined pairs to train the Siamese network (Fig. 4) for binary pair classification. Mini-batch Stochastic Gradient Descent (SGD) is used to train the network with random initialization. Section 6.1 describes more training details. In the supervised adaptation stage, we use the ground-truth data to fine-tune the network with a softmax loss for image classification.

5.2 Semi-supervised Learning

In the setting of semi-supervised learning (Fig. 2(b)), the goal is adapting visual representations from the supervised pre-trained model to specific recognition tasks with partial annotations. We first use the proposed unsupervised constraint mining algorithm to mine positive and negative image pairs on the entire dataset. In the unsupervised adaptation stage, we use the mined pairs to train the Siamese network (Fig. 4), which is initialized using the pre-trained parameters on ImageNet with class labels. In the supervised adaptation stage, we use the partial ground-truth data to fine-tune the base network with the softmax loss for image classification.

6 Experiments

6.1 Implementation Details

We use Caffe [42] to train our network with a Tesla K40 GPU. In all experiments, SGD is used for optimization with the batch size of 50. Each batch contains 25 positive pairs and 25 negative pairs.

For unsupervised feature learning, we randomly divide the entire ImageNet training set into 128 subsets where each subset contains $\sim$10 k images. In total, our method mines $\sim$1 million positive pairs and $\sim$13 million negative pairs. We train the network from random initialization with 400 k iterations. The learning rate is initially set to 0.01 and follows a polynomial decay with the power parameter of 0.5. It takes six hours to mine the pairs and five days to train the network.

For semi-supervised learning, we use the unsupervised mined pairs to train the Siamese network with the fixed learning rate of 0.001 for 50 k iterations. In the supervised adaption stage, all available image labels are used to fine-tune the base network with the fixed learning rate of 0.001 for 5k iterations.

The source code, as well as the pre-trained models, is available at the project webpage.

---

[1] For efficiency, PCA is used to project the high-dimensional FV descriptors to 512 dimensions.

6.2   Datasets and Evaluation Metrics

We evaluate the image classification performance of the unsupervised learned representations on the PASCAL VOC 2007 dateset [43]. The challenging PAS-CAL VOC dataset contains 20 objects categories with large intra-class variations in complex scenes. We use three datasets to evaluate the recognition performance of semi-supervised learning: (1) CIFAR-10 for object recognition [44], (2) CUB-200-2011 for fine-grained recognition [45] and (3) MIT indoor-67 for scene recognition [46]. We use average precision (AP) as the metric for image classification on VOC 2007 and top-1 classification accuracy for the other three datasets.

6.3   Controlled Experiments

Evaluation on Positive Mining. We compare the proposed positive mining method with random sampling and direct matching for image classification on CIFAR-10. For fair comparisons, we randomly sample the same set of 500 k true negative pairs for the three positive mining methods.[2]

- Random sampling: Randomly sampling 10 k pairs.
- Direct matching: The top 10 k pairs with the smallest Euclidean distance.
- Cycle consistency: The 10 k pairs mined by n-cycle constraints with $k = 4$.

We use the positive pairs mined by different methods (along with the same negative pairs) to train the Siamese network. We initialize the base network using the pre-trained parameters on ImageNet with class labels. For testing, we extract 4096-d FC7 features and train linear SVMs for classification. Table 1 shows the mining and classification results with different positive mining methods. In terms of true positive rate, cycle consistency significantly outperforms random sampling and direct matching. The results demonstrate that our method can handle large intra-class variations and discover accurate pairs from the same category. Regarding the classification accuracy, using 4-cycle constraints achieves significant improvement over direct similarity matching by around 3 points. The experimental results demonstrate that cycle consistency helps learn better CNN feature representations. We also observe that the recognition performance is insensitive to the cycle length, which shows the stability and robustness of the proposed method. Notably, although 2-cycle and 3-cycle constraints do not generate indirect matching pairs, they are crucial for selecting representative positive pairs for feature learning. Without cycle consistency, acyclic transitive matching easily generates false positive pairs, particularly when the cycle length n is large. We believe that cycle consistency provides an effective criterion to discover good positive pairs for learning effective representations.

Parameter Analysis. Figure 5 shows the statistics of mined cycles with different k (the number of nearest neighbors) and n (the length of cycle). The amount of mined cycles increases as k increases because larger k results in more

---

[2] True positives (TP) and true negatives (TN) are denoted as those pairs belonging to the same and different visual categories, respectively.

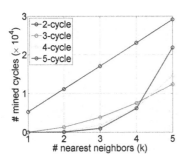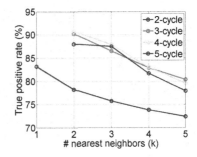

Fig. 5. The statistics of the mined cycle constraints on the CIFAR-10 *train* set. **Left:** Total amount of mined cycles. **Right:** True positive rate among all the mined pairs.

Table 1. Comparisons of different positive mining methods on CIFAR-10.

	Random sampling	Direct matching	2-cycle	3-cycle	4-cycle	5-cycle
TP rate	10.0	59.0	73.8	82.9	**83.0**	81.7
Accuracy	73.7	78.0	79.9	80.5	**80.9**	80.2

Table 2. Comparisons of different negative mining methods on CIFAR-10.

	Random sampling	Original distance	Geodesic distance
TN rate	90.0	**95.5**	91.0
Accuracy	83.8	68.3	**85.2**

linked nodes in the graph. On the other hand, as k increases, the true positives rate drops due to the noise introduced by nearest neighbor matching. However, using 4-cycle constraints, we obtain a much higher true positive rate with a 40 % relative improvement over direct matching (see Table 1). The results show that cycles do help get rid of the noise in the matching process.

Effect of Different Features. We evaluate different features for constructing the graph and obtain similar classification performance on CIFAR-10 (LBP: 76.7 %, HOG: 80.7 %, and SIFT+FV: 80.9 %). The results show that cycle consistency works well on different hand-crafted features. We also use the initial ImageNet-pretrained CNN features to construct the graph. It achieves 81.6 % accuracy on CIFAR-10, slightly higher than that of using SIFT+FV (80.9 %).

Evaluation on Negative Mining. We conduct controlled experiments to examine the effectiveness of the proposed negative mining method on CIFAR-10. The same 500 k true positive pairs are randomly sampled for the following three methods.

- Random sampling: Randomly sampling 500 k pairs.
- Original distance: The top 500 k pairs with the largest Euclidean distance.
- Geodesic distance: The 500 k pairs mined with geodesic distance.

Fig. 6. Examples of positive and negative image pairs mined from the ImageNet 2012 dataset using our unsupervised constraint mining method.

We use the negative pairs mined by different methods (along with the same positive pairs) to train the Siamese network. Table 2 shows the mining and classification results with the three negative mining methods on CIFAR-10. The graph-based geodesic distance achieves classification accuracy of 85.2%, significantly outperforming the method by the original Euclidean distance by 17 points. Although more accurate pairs are mined by the original distance, they are often easy negative samples and do not provide much information for learning effective representations. Negative mining by random sampling performs well because an overwhelming majority of image pairs are negative in a typical image dataset, e.g., 90% on CIFAR-10. In general, the experimental results demonstrate that the proposed graph-based geodesic distance can generate hard negative samples to learn better representations for visual recognition.

6.4 Unsupervised Learning Results

Qualitative Evaluation. We first show qualitative results obtained by our unsupervised feature learning method. Figure 6 shows some examples of image pairs mined from the ImageNet 2012 dataset using the proposed unsupervised constraint mining method. Cycle consistency can mine positive pairs with large appearance variations (e.g., different viewpoints and shape deformations). Geodesic distance can mine hard negative pairs which share appearance similarities to an extent (e.g., bird and aeroplane, monkey and human). Figure 7 shows examples of nearest neighbor search results using different feature representations. Our unsupervised method obtains similar retrieval results with the supervised pre-trained AlexNet for different types of visual categories.

Quantitative Evaluation. We compare the proposed unsupervised feature learning method with several state-of-the-art approaches for image classification on VOC 2007 in Table 3. All the results are obtained by fine-tuning using

Fig. 7. Examples of nearest neighbor search results. The query images are shown on the far left. For each query, the three rows show the top 8 nearest neighbors obtained by AlexNet with random parameters, AlexNet trained with full supervision, and AlexNet trained using our unsupervised method, respectively. FC7 features are used to compute Euclidean distance for all the three methods.

Table 3. Comparisons of classification performance on the VOC 2007 *test* set.

Methods	Supervision	Classification
Agrawal et al. [9]	Ego-motion	52.9
Doersch et al. [11]	Context	55.3
Wang et al. [12]	Tracking triplet	**58.4**
Ours	Matching pair	56.5
Krizhevsky et al. [1]	Class labels	**69.5**

the VOC 2007 training data.[3] We achieve competitive performance with the state-of-the-art unsupervised approaches. Compared to Agrawal et al. [9], we show a significant performance gain by 3.6 points. Ego-motion information does not correlate well with semantic similarity, and hence the trained model does not perform well for visual recognition. Our method outperforms Doersch et al. [11] which use context prediction as supervision. They consider only instance-level training samples within the same image while we mine category-level samples across different images. Wang et al. [12] achieve better performance by leveraging visual tracking of video data. However, our method aims at mining matching pairs from an unlabeled image collection. For fair comparisons, we use random initialization as in existing unsupervised feature learning work and do not include other initialization strategies.

We compare the classification performance using SIFT+FV and our learned features. Our learned features significantly outperform SIFT+FV by 10.5 points (56.5 % vs. 46.0 %). The results show that we do not train the network to replicate hand-crafted features. While we use hand-crafted features to construct the graph, the proposed graph-based analysis can discover underlying semantic similarity among unlabeled images for learning effective representations.

Effect of Network Architectures. We also evaluate the performance using GoogLeNet as the base network. We achieve 56.6 % mAP on VOC 2007, which is similar with that of using AlexNet (56.5 %).[4]

6.5   Semi-supervised Learning Results

We also evaluate the proposed unsupervised constraint mining algorithm in the semi-supervised setting. For the three datasets used, we randomly select several images per class on the training set as the partial annotated data. Figure 8(a) shows that we achieve significant performance gains compared with directly fine-tuning on CIFAR-10. In the extreme case that only one image label per class is known, our method largely improves the mean accuracy by 7.5 points (34.1 % vs. 26.6 %). Using 4,000 labels of CIFAR-10, our method outperforms Rasmus et al. [48] from 79.6 % to 84.3 %. The experimental results demonstrate

---

[3] The baseline numbers of [9,11,12] are from [47].

[4] The GoogLeNet-based Siamese network is trained with a batch size of 32 and 960 k iterations.

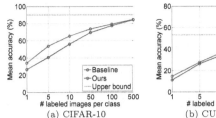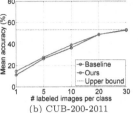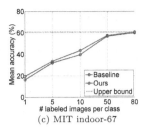

(a) CIFAR-10   (b) CUB-200-2011   (c) MIT indoor-67

Fig. 8. Mean classification accuracy in the semi-supervised leaning tasks on three datasets: (a) CIFAR-10, (b) CUB-200-2011, and (c) MIT indoor-67. The upper bound represents the mean classification accuracy when images in the training set are fully annotated.

that our unsupervised constraint mining method provides new useful constraints beyond annotations and helps better transfer the pre-trained network for visual recognition.

Figure 8(b) and (c) show another two semi-supervised learning results on CUB-200-2011 and MIT indoor-67, respectively. The results show boosted classification performance for both fine-grained objects and scene categories. We obtain the true positive rate of 55.8 % by 4-cycle constraints on CUB-200-2011 (only 0.5 % by random sampling) and 65.8 % on MIT indoor-67 (only 1.5 % by random sampling). The results demonstrate that our method can generate accurate image pairs despite small inter-class differences among visual categories.

7 Conclusions

In this paper, we propose to leverage graph-based analysis to mine constraints from an unlabeled image collection for visual representation learning. We use a cycle consistency criterion to mine positive image pairs and geodesic distance to mine hard negative samples. The proposed unsupervised constraint mining method is applied to both unsupervised feature learning and semi-supervised learning. In the unsupervised setting, we mine a collection of image pairs from the large-scale ImageNet dataset without any labels for learning CNN representations. The learned features achieve competitive recognition results on VOC 2007 compared with existing unsupervised approaches. In the semi-supervised setting, we show boosted performance on three image classification datasets. In summary, our method provides new insights into data mining, unsupervised feature learning, and semi-supervised learning, and has broad applications for large-scale recognition tasks.

Acknowledgments. This work is supported in part by the Initiative Scientific Research Program of Ministry of Education under Grant #20141081253. J.-B. Huang and N. Ahuja are supported in part by Office of Naval Research under Grant N00014-16-1-2314. W.-C. Hung and M.-H. Yang are supported in part by the NSF CAREER Grant #1149783 and gifts from Adobe and Nvidia.

References

1. Krizhevsky, A., Sutskever, I., Hinton, G.E.: ImageNet classification with deep convolutional neural networks. In: NIPS (2012)
2. Girshick, R., Donahue, J., Darrell, T., Malik, J.: Rich feature hierarchies for accurate object detection and semantic segmentation. In: CVPR (2014)
3. Long, J., Shelhamer, E., Darrell, T.: Fully convolutional networks for semantic segmentation. In: CVPR (2015)
4. Le, Q.V.: Building high-level features using large scale unsupervised learning. In: ICML (2012)
5. Srivastava, N., Salakhutdinov, R.R.: Multimodal learning with deep boltzmann machines. In: NIPS (2012)
6. Bengio, Y., Lamblin, P., Popovici, D., Larochelle, H.: Greedy layer-wise training of deep networks. In: NIPS (2007)
7. Vincent, P., Larochelle, H., Bengio, Y., Manzagol, P.A.: Extracting and composing robust features with denoising autoencoders. In: ICML (2008)
8. Ranzato, M.A., Huang, F.J., Boureau, Y.L., LeCun, Y.: Unsupervised learning of invariant feature hierarchies with applications to object recognition. In: CVPR (2007)
9. Agrawal, P., Carreira, J., Malik, J.: Learning to see by moving. In: ICCV (2015)
10. Jayaraman, D., Grauman, K.: Learning image representations tied to ego-motion. In: ICCV (2015)
11. Doersch, C., Gupta, A., Efros, A.A.: Unsupervised visual representation learning by context prediction. In: ICCV (2015)
12. Wang, X., Gupta, A.: Unsupervised learning of visual representations using videos. In: ICCV (2015)
13. Malisiewicz, T., Efros, A.: Beyond categories: the visual memex model for reasoning about object relationships. In: NIPS (2009)
14. Cao, S., Snavely, N.: Graph-based discriminative learning for location recognition. In: CVPR (2013)
15. Oquab, M., Bottou, L., Laptev, I., Sivic, J.: Is object localization for free?-weakly-supervised learning with convolutional neural networks. In: CVPR (2015)
16. Li, D., Huang, J.B., Li, Y., Wang, S., Yang, M.H.: Weakly supervised object localization with progressive domain adaptation. In: CVPR (2016)
17. Wu, J., Yu, Y., Huang, C., Yu, K.: Deep multiple instance learning for image classification and auto-annotation. In: CVPR (2015)
18. Liang, X., Liu, S., Wei, Y., Liu, L., Lin, L., Yan, S.: Towards computational baby learning: A weakly-supervised approach for object detection. In: ICCV (2015)
19. Chen, X., Shrivastava, A., Gupta, A.: NEIL: Extracting visual knowledge from web data. In: ICCV (2013)
20. Divvala, S., Farhadi, A., Guestrin, C.: Learning everything about anything: webly-supervised visual concept learning. In: CVPR (2014)
21. Chen, X., Gupta, A.: Webly supervised learning of convolutional networks. In: ICCV (2015)
22. Joulin, A., van der Maaten, L., Jabri, A., Vasilache, N.: Learning visual features from large weakly supervised data. In: ECCV (2016)
23. Cho, M., Kwak, S., Schmid, C., Ponce, J.: Unsupervised object discovery and localization in the wild: part-based matching with bottom-up region proposals. In: CVPR (2015)

24. Kim, G., Torralba, A.: Unsupervised detection of regions of interest using iterative link analysis. In: NIPS (2009)
25. Singh, S., Gupta, A., Efros, A.A.: Unsupervised discovery of mid-level discriminative patches. In: Fitzgibbon, A., Lazebnik, S., Perona, P., Sato, Y., Schmid, C. (eds.) ECCV 2012, Part II. LNCS, vol. 7573, pp. 73–86. Springer, Heidelberg (2012)
26. Doersch, C., Singh, S., Gupta, A., Sivic, J., Efros, A.: What makes paris look like paris? ACM Transactions on Graphics 31(4), 101 (2012)
27. Grauman, K., Darrell, T.: Unsupervised learning of categories from sets of partially matching image features. In: CVPR (2006)
28. Wang, F., Huang, Q., Guibas, L.: Image co-segmentation via consistent functional maps. In: ICCV (2013)
29. Wang, F., Huang, Q., Ovsjanikov, M., Guibas, L.: Unsupervised multi-class joint image segmentation. In: CVPR (2014)
30. Wilson, K., Snavely, N.: Network principles for SfM: disambiguating repeated structures with local context. In: ICCV (2013)
31. Zach, C., Klopschitz, M., Pollefeys, M.: Disambiguating visual relations using loop constraints. In: CVPR (2010)
32. Huang, Q.X., Guibas, L.: Consistent shape maps via semidefinite programming. In: SGP (2013)
33. Zhou, T., Lee, Y.J., Yu, S.X., Efros, A.A.: FlowWeb: joint image set alignment by weaving consistent, pixel-wise correspondences. In: CVPR (2015)
34. Zhang, S., Yang, M., Cour, T., Yu, K., Metaxas, D.N.: Query specific fusion for image retrieval. In: Fitzgibbon, A., Lazebnik, S., Perona, P., Sato, Y., Schmid, C. (eds.) ECCV 2012, Part II. LNCS, vol. 7573, pp. 660–673. Springer, Heidelberg (2012)
35. Dekel, T., Oron, S., Rubinstein, M., Avidan, S., Freeman, W.T.: Best-buddies similarity for robust template matching. In: CVPR (2015)
36. Wei, Y., Wen, F., Zhu, W., Sun, J.: Geodesic saliency using background priors. In: Fitzgibbon, A., Lazebnik, S., Perona, P., Sato, Y., Schmid, C. (eds.) ECCV 2012, Part III. LNCS, vol. 7574, pp. 29–42. Springer, Heidelberg (2012)
37. Krähenbühl, P., Koltun, V.: Geodesic object proposals. In: Fleet, D., Pajdla, T., Schiele, B., Tuytelaars, T. (eds.) ECCV 2014, Part V. LNCS, vol. 8693, pp. 725–739. Springer, Heidelberg (2014)
38. Wang, W., Shen, J., Porikli, F.: Saliency-aware geodesic video object segmentation. In: CVPR (2015)
39. Floyd, R.W.: Algorithm 97: shortest path. Commun. ACM 5(6), 345 (1962)
40. Deng, J., Dong, W., Socher, R., Li, L.J., Li, K., Fei-Fei, L.: ImageNet: A large-scale hierarchical image database. In: CVPR (2009)
41. Sánchez, J., Perronnin, F., Mensink, T., Verbeek, J.: Image classification with the fisher vector: theory and practice. IJCV 105(3), 222–245 (2013)
42. Jia, Y., Shelhamer, E., Donahue, J., Karayev, S., Long, J., Girshick, R., Guadarrama, S., Darrell, T.: Caffe: convolutional architecture for fast feature embedding. In: ACM MM (2014)
43. Everingham, M., Van Gool, L., Williams, C.K., Winn, J., Zisserman, A.: The PASCAL visual object classes (VOC) challenge. IJCV 88(2), 303–338 (2010)
44. Krizhevsky, A., Hinton, G.: Learning multiple layers of features from tiny images. Master's thesis, Computer Science Department, University of Toronto (2009)
45. Wah, C., Branson, S., Welinder, P., Perona, P., Belongie, S.: The Caltech-UCSD birds-200-2011 dataset. Technical report, California Institute of Technology (2011)

46. Quattoni, A., Torralba, A.: Recognizing indoor scenes. In: CVPR (2009)
47. Krähenbühl, P., Doersch, C., Donahue, J., Darrell, T.: Data-dependent initializations of convolutional neural networks. In: ICLR (2016)
48. Rasmus, A., Berglund, M., Honkala, M., Valpola, H., Raiko, T.: Semi-supervised learning with ladder networks. In: NIPS (2015)

Seed, Expand and Constrain: Three Principles for Weakly-Supervised Image Segmentation

Alexander Kolesnikov$^{(\boxtimes)}$ and Christoph H. Lampert

IST Austria, Klosterneuburg, Austria
{akolesnikov,chl}@ist.ac.at

Abstract. We introduce a new loss function for the weakly-supervised training of semantic image segmentation models based on three guiding principles: to *seed* with weak localization cues, to *expand* objects based on the information about which classes can occur in an image, and to *constrain* the segmentations to coincide with object boundaries. We show experimentally that training a deep convolutional neural network using the proposed loss function leads to substantially better segmentations than previous state-of-the-art methods on the challenging PASCAL VOC 2012 dataset. We furthermore give insight into the working mechanism of our method by a detailed experimental study that illustrates how the segmentation quality is affected by each term of the proposed loss function as well as their combinations.

Keywords: Weakly-supervised image segmentation · Deep learning

1 Introduction

Computer vision research has recently made tremendous progress. Many challenging vision tasks can now be solved with high accuracy, assuming that sufficiently much annotated data is available for training. Unfortunately, collecting large labeled datasets is time consuming and typically requires substantial financial investments. Therefore, the creation of training data has become a bottleneck for the further development of computer vision methods. Unlabeled visual data, however, can be collected in large amounts in a relatively fast and cheap manner. Therefore, a promising direction in the computer vision research is to develop methods that can learn from unlabeled or partially labeled data.

In this paper we focus on the task of semantic image segmentation. Image segmentation is a prominent example of an important vision task, for which creating annotations is especially costly: as reported in [4,29], manually producing segmentation masks requires several worker-minutes per image. Therefore, a large body of previous research studies how to train segmentation models from weaker forms of annotation.

Electronic supplementary material The online version of this chapter (doi:10. 1007/978-3-319-46493-0_42) contains supplementary material, which is available to authorized users.

© Springer International Publishing AG 2016
B. Leibe et al. (Eds.): ECCV 2016, Part IV, LNCS 9908, pp. 695–711, 2016.
DOI: 10.1007/978-3-319-46493-0_42

A particularly appealing setting is to learn image segmentation models using training sets with only per-image labels, as this form of weak supervision can be collected very efficiently. However, there is currently still a large performance gap between models trained from per-image labels and models trained from full segmentations masks. In this paper we demonstrate that this gap can be substantially reduced compared to the previous state-of-the-art techniques.

We propose a new composite loss function for training convolutional neural networks for the task of weakly-supervised image segmentation. Our approach relies on the following three insights:

- Image classification neural networks, such as AlexNet [19] or VGG [33], can be used to generate reliable object localization cues (**seeds**), but fail to predict the exact spatial extent of the objects. We incorporate this aspect by using a **seeding loss** that encourages a segmentation network to match localization cues but that is agnostic about the rest of the image.
- To train a segmentation network from per-image annotation, a global pooling layer can be used that aggregates segmentation masks into image-level label scores. The choice of this layer has large impact on the quality of segmentations. For example, max-pooling tends to underestimate the size of objects while average-pooling tends to overestimate it [26]. We propose a **global weighted rank pooling** that is leveraged by **expansion loss** to expand the object seeds to regions of a reasonable size. It generalizes max-pooling and average pooling and outperforms them in our empirical study.
- Networks trained from image-level labels rarely capture the precise boundaries of objects in an image. Postprocessing by fully-connected conditional random fields (CRF) at test time is often insufficient to overcome this effect, because once the networks have been trained they tend to be confident even about misclassified regions. We propose a new **constrain-to-boundary loss** that alleviates the problem of imprecise boundaries already at training time. It strives to **constrain** predicted segmentation masks to respect low-level image information, in particular object boundaries.

We name our approach **SEC**, as it is based on three principles: **S**eed, **E**xpand and **C**onstrain. We formally define and discuss the individual components of the SEC loss function in Sect. 3. In Sect. 4 we experimentally evaluate it on the PAS-CAL VOC 2012 image segmentation benchmark, showing that it substantially outperforms the previous state-of-the-art techniques under the same experimental settings. We also provide further insight by discussing and evaluating the effect of each of our contributions separately through additional experiments.

2 Related Work

Semantic image segmentation, i.e. assigning a semantic class label to each pixel of an image, is a topic of relatively recent interest in computer vision research, as it required the availability of modern machine learning techniques, such as discriminative classifiers [5,31] or probabilistic graphical models [21,28]. As the creation of fully annotated training data poses a major bottleneck to the further improvement of these systems, weakly supervised training methods were soon proposed in order to save annotation effort. In particular, competitive methods were developed that only require partial segmentations [11,37] or object bounding boxes [8,20,52] as training data.

A remaining challenge is, however, to learn segmentation models from just image-level labels [35,36]. Existing approaches fall into three broad categories. *Graph-based models* infer labels for segments or superpixels based on their similarity within or between images [27,43,46–48]. Variants of *multiple instance learning* [1] train with a per-image loss function, while internally maintaining a spatial representation of the image that can be used to produce segmentation masks [38–40]. Methods in the tradition of *self-training* [30] train a fully-supervised model but create the necessary pixel-level annotation using the model itself in an EM-like procedure [44,45,49]. Our SEC approach contains aspects of the latter two approaches, as it makes use of a per-image loss as well as per-pixel loss terms.

In terms of segmentation quality, currently only methods based on deep convolutional networks [19,33] are strong enough to tackle segmentation datasets of difficulty similar to what fully-supervised methods can handle, such as the PASCAL VOC 2012 [9], which we make use of in this work. In particular, *MIL-FCN* [25], *MIL-ILP* [26] and the approaches of [4,18] leverage deep networks in a multiple instance learning setting, differing mainly in their pooling strategies, i.e. how they convert their internal spatial representation to per-image labels. *EM-Adapt* [23] and *CCNN* [24] rely on the self-training framework and differ in how they enforce the consistency between the per-image annotation and the predicted segmentation masks. *SN_B* [41] adds additional steps for creating and combining multiple object proposals. As far as possible, we provide an experimental comparison to these methods in Sect. 4.

3   Weakly Supervised Segmentation from Image-Level Labels

In this section we present a technical description of our approach. We denote the space of images by $\mathcal{X}$. For any image $X \in \mathcal{X}$, a segmentation mask Y is a collection, $(y_1, \ldots, y_n)$, of semantic labels at n spatial locations. The semantic labels belong to a set $\mathcal{C} = \mathcal{C}' \cup \{c^{\mathrm{bg}}\}$ of size k, where $\mathcal{C}'$ is a set of all foreground labels and c^{bg} is a background label. We assume that the training data, $\mathcal{D} = \{(X_i, T_i)\}_{i=1}^{N}$, consists of N images, $X_i \in \mathcal{X}$, where each image is weakly annotated by a set, $T_i \subset \mathcal{C}'$, of foreground labels that occur in the image. Our goal is to train a deep convolutional neural network $f(X; \theta)$, parameterized by θ, that models the conditional probability of observing any label $c \in \mathcal{C}$ at any location $u \in \{1, 2, \ldots, n\}$, i.e. $f_{u,c}(X; \theta) = p(y_u = c | X)$. For brevity we will often omit the parameters θ in our notation and write $f(X; \theta)$ simply as $f(X)$.

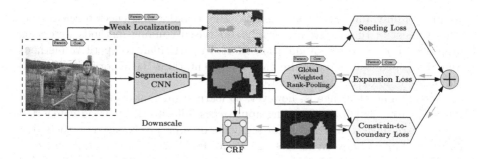

Fig. 1. A schematic illustration of SEC that is based on minimizing a composite loss function consisting of three terms: *seeding loss, expansion loss* and *constrain-to-boundary loss*. See Sect. 3 for details.

3.1 The SEC Loss for Weakly Supervised Image Segmentation

Our approach for learning the parameters, θ, of the segmentation neural network relies on minimizing a loss function that has three terms. The first term, L_{seed}, provides localization hints to the network, the second term, L_{expand}, penalizes the network for predicting segmentation masks with too small or wrong objects, and the third term, $L_{\text{constrain}}$, encourages segmentations that respect the spatial and color structure of the images. Overall, we propose to solve the following optimization problem for parameter learning:

$$\min_{\theta} \sum_{(X,T)\in\mathcal{D}} \left[L_{\text{seed}}(f(X;\theta),T) + L_{\text{expand}}(f(X;\theta),T) + L_{\text{constrain}}(X,f(X;\theta)) \right]. \quad (1)$$

In the rest of this section we explain each loss term in detail. A schematic overview of the setup can be found in Fig. 1.

Seeding Loss with Localization Cues. Image-level labels do not explicitly provide any information about the position of semantic objects in an image. Nevertheless, as was noted in many recent research papers [3,22,32,50], deep image classification networks that were trained just from image-level labels, may be successfully employed to retrieve cues on object localization. We call this procedure *weak localization* and illustrate it in Fig. 2.

Unfortunately, localization cues typically are not precise enough to be used as full and accurate segmentation masks. However, these cues can be very useful to guide the weakly-supervised segmentation network. We propose to use a *seeding loss* to encourage predictions of the neural network to match only "landmarks" given by the weak localization procedure while ignoring the rest of the image. Suppose that S_c is a set of locations that are labeled with class c by the weak localization procedure. Then, the *seeding loss* L_{seed} has the following form:

$$L_{\text{seed}}(f(X),T,S_c) = -\frac{1}{\sum_{c\in T}|S_c|} \sum_{c\in T} \sum_{u\in S_c} \log f_{u,c}(X). \quad (2)$$

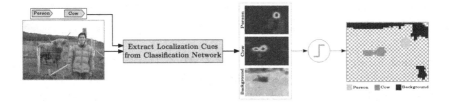

Fig. 2. The schematic illustration of the weak localization procedure.

Note that for computing L_{seed} one needs the weak localization sets, S_c, so that many existing techniques from the literature can be used, essentially, as *black boxes*. In this work, we rely on [50] for weakly localizing foreground classes. However, this method does not provide a direct way to select confident background regions, therefore we use the gradient-based saliency detection method from [32] for this purpose. We provide more details on the weak localization procedure in Sect. 4.

Expansion Loss with Global Weighted Rank Pooling. To measure if a segmentation mask is consistent with the image-level labels one can aggregate segmentation scores into classification scores and apply the standard loss function for multi-label image classification. In the context of weakly-supervised segmentation/detection various techniques were used by researches to aggregate score maps into a classification scores. The most prominent ones are *global max-poling* (GMP) [22] that assigns any class c in any image X a score of $\max\limits_{u \in \{1,...,n\}} f_{u,c}(X)$ and *global average-pooling* [50] that assigns it a score of $\frac{1}{n}\sum\limits_{u=1}^{n} f_{u,c}(X)$.

Both ways of aggregation have been successfully used in practice. However, they have their own drawbacks. For classes which are present in an image GMP only encourages the response for a single location to be high, while GAP encourages all responses to be high. Therefore, GMP results in a segmentation network that often underestimates the sizes of objects, while network trained using GAP, in contrast, often overestimates them. Our experiments in Sect. 4 support this claim empirically.

In order to overcome these drawbacks we propose a *global weighted rank-pooling (GWRP)*, a new aggregation technique, which can be seen as a generalization of GMP and GAP. GWRP computes a weighted average score for each class, where weights are higher for more promising locations. This way it encourages objects to occupy a certain fraction of an image, but, unlike GAP, is less prone to overestimating object sizes.

Formally, let an index set $I^c = \{i_1, \ldots, i_n\}$ define the descending order of prediction scores for any class $c \in C$, i.e. $f_{i_1,c}(x) \geq f_{i_2,c}(x) \geq \cdots \geq f_{i_n,c}(x)$ and let $0 < d_c <= 1$ be a decay parameter for class c. Then we define the GWRP classification scores, $G_c(f(X), d_c)$, for an image X, as following:

$$G_c(f(X); d_c) = \frac{1}{Z(d_c)} \sum_{j=1}^{n} (d_c)^{j-1} f_{i_j,c}(X), \text{ where } Z(d_c) = \sum_{j=1}^{n} (d_c)^{j-1}. \quad (3)$$

Note, that for $d_c = 0$ GWRP turns into GMP (adopting the convention that $0^0 = 1$), and for $d_c = 1$ it is identical to GAP. Therefore, GWRP generalizes both approaches and the decay parameter can be used to interpolate between the behavior of both extremes.

In principle, the decay parameter could be set individually for each class and each image. However, this would need prior knowledge about how large objects of each class typically are, which is not available in the weakly supervised setting. Therefore, we only distinguish between three groups: for object classes that occur in an image we use a decay parameter d_+, for object classes that do not occur we use d_-, and for background we use d_{bg}. We will discuss how to choose their values in Sect. 4.

In summary, the *expansion loss* term is

$$L_{\mathrm{expand}}(f(X), T) = -\frac{1}{|T|} \sum_{c \in T} \log G_c(f(X); d_+) \quad (4)$$

$$-\frac{1}{|\mathcal{C}' \backslash T|} \sum_{c \in \mathcal{C}' \backslash T} \log(1 - G_c(f(X); d_-)) - \log G_{c^{\mathrm{bg}}}(f(X); d_{\mathrm{bg}}).$$

Constrain-to-boundary Loss. The high level idea of the *constrain-to-boundary loss* is to penalize the neural network for producing segmentations that are discontinuous with respect to spatial and color information in the input image. Thereby, it encourages the network to learn to produce segmentation masks that match up with object boundaries.

Specifically, we construct a fully-connected CRF, $Q(X, f(X))$, as in [17], with unary potentials given by the logarithm of the probability scores predicted by the segmentation network, and pairwise potentials of fixed parametric form that depend only on the image pixels. We downscale the image X, so that it matches the resolution of the segmentation mask, produced by the network. More details about the choice of the CRF parameters are given in Sect. 4. We then define the *constrain-to-boundary loss* as the mean KL-divergence between the outputs of the network and the outputs of the CRF, i.e.:

$$L_{\mathrm{constrain}}(X, f(X)) = \frac{1}{n} \sum_{u=1}^{n} \sum_{c \in \mathcal{C}} Q_{u,c}(X, f(X)) \log \frac{Q_{u,c}(X, f(X))}{f_{u,c}(X)}. \quad (5)$$

This construction achieves the desired effect, since it encourages the network output to coincide with the CRF output, which itself is known to produce segmentation that respect image boundaries. An illustration of this effect can be seen in Fig. 1.

3.2 Training

The proposed network can be trained in an end-to-end way using back-propagation, provided that the individual gradients of all layers are available. For computing gradients of the fully-connected CRF we employ the procedure from [34], which was successfully used in the context of semantic image segmentation. Figure 1 illustrates the flow of gradients for the backpropagation procedure with gray arrows.

4 Experiments

In this section we validate our proposed loss function experimentally, including a detailed study of the effects of its different terms.

4.1 Experimental Setup

Dataset and Evaluation Metric. We evaluate our method on the PASCAL VOC 2012 image segmentation benchmark, which has 21 semantic classes, including background [9]. The dataset images are split into three parts: training (*train*, 1464 images), validation (*val*, 1449 images) and testing (*test*, 1456 images). Following the common practice we augment the training part by additional images from [10]. The resulting *trainaug* set has 10,582 weakly annotated images that we use to train our models. We compare our approach with other approaches on both *val* and *test* parts. For the *val* part, ground truth segmentation masks are available, so we can evaluate results of different experiments. We therefore use this data also to provide a detailed study of the influence of the different components in our approach. The ground truth segmentation masks for the *test* part are not publicly available, so we use the official PASCAL VOC evaluation server to obtain quantitative results. As evaluation measure we use the standard PASCAL VOC 2012 segmentation metric: mean intersection-over-union (mIoU).

Segmentation Network. As a particular choice for the segmentation architecture, in this paper we use *DeepLab-CRF-LargeFOV* from [6], which is a slightly modified version of the 16-layer VGG network [33]. The network has inputs of size 321×321 and produces segmentation masks of size 41×41, see [6] for more details on the architecture. We initialize the weights for the last (prediction) layer randomly from a normal distribution with mean 0 and variance 0.01. All other convolutional layers are initialized from the publicly available VGG model [33]. Note, that in principle, our loss function can be combined with any deep convolutional neural network.

Localization Networks. The localization networks for the foreground classes and the background class are also derived from the standard VGG architecture. In order to improve the localization performance, we finetune these networks for solving a multilabel classification problem on the *trainaug* data. Due to space

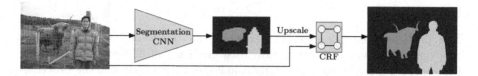

Fig. 3. The schematic illustration of our approach at test time.

limitations we provide exact details on these networks and optimization para-meters in the technical report [16].

Note, that in order to reduce the computational effort and memory con-sumption required for training SEC it is possible to precompute the localization cues. If precomputed cues are available SEC imposes no additional overhead for evaluating and storing the localization networks at training time.

Optimization. For training the network we use the batched stochastic gradient descent (SGD) with parameters used successfully in [6]. We run SGD for 8000 iterations, the batch size is 15 (reduced from 30 to allow simultaneous training of two networks), the dropout rate is 0.5 and the weight decay parameter is 0.0005. The initial learning rate is 0.001 and it is decreased by a factor of 10 every 2000 iterations. Overall, training on a `GeForce TITAN-X` GPU takes 7–8 h, which is comparable to training times of other models, reported, e.g., in [23,24].

Decay Parameters. The GWRP aggregation requires specifying the decay parameters, d_-, d_+ and d_{bg}, that control the weights for aggregating the scores produced by the network. Inspired by the previous research [23,24] we do so using the following rules-of-thumb that express prior beliefs about natural images:

- for semantic classes that are not present in the image we want to predict as few pixels as possible. Therefore, we set $d_- = 0$, which corresponds to GMP.
- for semantic classes that are present in the image we suggest that the top 10 % scores represent 50 % of the overall aggregated score. For our 41×41 masks this roughly corresponds to $d_+ = 0.996$.
- for the background we suggest that the top 30 % scores represent 50 % of the overall aggregated score, resulting in $d_{\text{bg}} = 0.999$.

Fully-connected CRF at Training Time. In order to enforce the segmen-tation network to respect the boundaries of objects already at training time we use a fully-connected CRF [17]. As parameters for the pairwise interactions, we use the default values from the authors' public implementation, except that we multiply all spatial distance terms by 12 to reflect the fact that we downscaled the original image in order to match the size of the predicted segmentation mask.

Inference at Test Time. Our segmentation neural network is trained to pro-duce probability scores for all classes and locations, but the spatial resolution of a predicted segmentation mask is lower than the original image. Thus, we upscale the predicted segmentation mask to match the size of the input image, and then apply a fully-connected CRF [17] to refine the segmentation. This is a common practice, which was previously employed, e.g., in [6,23,24]. Figure 3 shows a schematic illustration of our inference procedure at test time.

Reproducibility. In our experiments we rely on the *caffe* deep learning framework [13] in combination with a *python* implementation of the SEC loss. The code and pretrained models are publicly available[1].

4.2 Results

Numeric Results. Table 1 compares the performance of our weakly supervised approach with previous approaches that are trained in the same setup, i.e. using only images from PASCAL VOC 2012 and only image-level labels. It shows that SEC substantially outperforms the previous techniques. On the *test* data, where the evaluation is performed by an independent third party, the PASCAL VOC evaluation server, it achieves 13.5 % higher mean intersection-over-union score than the state-of-the-art approaches with new best scores on 20 out of 21 semantic classes. On the validation data, for which researchers can compute scores themselves, SEC improves over the state-of-the-art by 14.1 %, and achieves new best scores on 19 out of the 21 classes.

Results of other weakly-supervised methods on PASCAL VOC and the fully-supervised variant of DeepLab are summarized in Table 2. We provide these results for reference but emphasize that they should not simply be compared to Table 1, because the underlying methods were trained on different (and larger) training sets or were given additional forms of weak supervision, e.g. user clicks. Some entries need further explanation in this regard: [23] reports results for the EM-Adapt model when trained with weak annotation for multiple image crops. The same model was reimplemented and trained with only per-image supervision in [24], so these are the values we report in Table 1. The results reported for SN_B [41] and the *seg* variant of the MIL+ILP+SP [26] are incomparable to others because they were obtained with help of *MCG* region proposals [2] that were trained in a fully supervised way on PASCAL VOC data. Similarly, MIL+ILP+SP-*bb* makes use of bounding box proposals generated by the BING method [7] that was trained using PASCAL VOC bounding box annotation.

Note that we do include the *sppxl* variant of MIL+ILP+SP in Table 1. While it is trained on roughly 760.000 images of the ImageNet dataset, we do not consider this an unfair advantage compared to our and other methods, because those implicitly benefit from ImageNet images as well when using pretrained classification networks for initialization.

Qualitative Results. Figure 4 illustrates typical successful segmentations. It shows that our method can produce accurate segmentations even for non-trivial images and recover fine details of the boundary. Figure 5 illustrates some failure cases. As is typical for weakly-supervised systems, SEC has problems segmenting objects that occur almost always in front of the same background, e.g. boats

---

[1] https://github.com/kolesman/SEC.

Table 1. Results on PASCAL VOC 2012 (mIoU in %) for weakly-supervised semantic segmentation with only per-image labels

PASCAL VOC 2012 *val* set	[4] (Img+Obj)	[14] (stage1)	EM-Adapt (re-impl. of [24])	CCNN [24]	MIL+ILP +SP-sppxl[b] [26]	SEC (proposed)	PASCAL VOC 2012 *test* set	MIL-FCN [25]	CCNN [24]	MIL+ILP +SP-sppxl[b] [26]	Region score pooling [18]	SEC (proposed)
Background		71.7[a]	67.2	68.5	77.2	**82.4**	Background	≈ 71[c]	74.7	≈ 74[c]		**83.5**
Aeroplane		30.7[a]	29.2	25.5	37.3	**62.9**	Aeroplane		24.2	38.8	33.1		**56.4**
Bike		**30.5**[a]	17.6	18.0	18.4	26.4	Bike		19.9	19.8	21.7		**28.5**
Bird		26.3[a]	28.6	25.4	25.4	**61.6**	Bird		26.3	27.5	27.7		**64.1**
Boat		20.0[a]	22.2	20.2	**28.2**	27.6	Boat		18.6	21.7	17.7		**23.6**
Bottle		24.2[a]	29.6	36.3	31.9	**38.1**	Bottle		38.1	32.8	38.4		**46.5**
Bus		39.2[a]	47.0	46.8	41.6	**66.6**	Bus		51.7	40.0	55.8		**70.6**
Car		33.7[a]	44.0	47.1	48.1	**62.7**	Car		42.9	50.1	38.3		**58.5**
Cat		50.2[a]	44.2	48.0	50.7	**75.2**	Cat		48.2	47.1	57.9		**71.3**
Chair		17.1[a]	14.6	15.8	12.7	**22.1**	Chair		15.6	7.2	13.6		**23.2**
Cow		29.7[a]	35.1	37.9	45.7	**53.5**	Cow		37.2	44.8	37.4		**54.0**
Diningtable		22.5[a]	24.9	21.0	14.6	**28.3**	Diningtable		18.3	15.8		**29.2**	28.0
Dog		41.3[a]	41.0	44.5	50.9	**65.8**	Dog		43.0	49.4	43.9		**68.1**
Horse		35.7[a]	34.8	34.5	44.1	**57.8**	Horse		38.2	47.3	39.1		**62.1**
Motorbike		43.0[a]	41.6	46.2	39.2	**62.3**	Motorbike		52.2	36.6	52.4		**70.0**
Person		36.0[a]	32.1	40.7	37.9	**52.5**	Person		40.0	36.4	44.4		**55.0**
Plant		29.0[a]	24.8	30.4	28.3	**32.5**	Plant		33.8	24.3	30.2		**38.4**
Sheep		34.9[a]	37.4	36.3	44.0	**62.6**	Sheep		36.0	44.5	48.7		**58.0**
Sofa		23.1[a]	24.0	22.2	19.6	**32.1**	Sofa		21.6	21.0	26.4		**39.9**
Train		33.2[a]	38.1	38.8	37.6	**45.4**	Train		33.4	31.5	31.8		**38.4**
TV/monitor		33.2[a]	31.6	36.9	35.0	**45.3**	TV/monitor		38.3	41.3	36.3		**48.3**
Average	32.2	33.6[a]	33.8	35.3	36.6	**50.7**	Average	25.7	35.6	35.8	38.0	**51.7**

([a]results from unpublished/not peer-reviewed manuscripts, [b]trained on ImageNet, [c]value inferred from average)

Table 2. Summary results (mIoU %) for other methods on PASCAL VOC 2012. Note: the values in this table are not directly comparable to Table 1, as they were obtained under different experimental conditions

Method	val	test	Comments
DeepLab [6]	67.6	70.3	Fully supervised training
STC [42]	49.8[a]	51.2[a]	Trained on Flickr
TransferNet [12]	52.1	51.2	Trained on MS COCO; additional supervision: from segmentation mask of other classes
[4] (1Point)	42.7	–	Additional supervision: 1 click per class
[4] (AllPoints-weighted)	43.4	–	Additional supervision: 1 click per instance
[4] (squiggle)	49.1	–	Additional supervision: 1 squiggle per class
EM-Adapt [23]	38.2	39.6	Uses weak labels of multiple image crops
SN_B [41]	41.9	43.2	Uses MCG region proposals (see text)
MIP+ILP+SP-seg [26]	42.0	40.6	Trained on ImageNet, MCG proposals (see text)
MIL+ILP+SP-bb [26]	37.8	37.0	Trained on ImageNet, BING proposals (see text)

([a]results from manuscripts that are currently unpublished/not peer-reviewed)

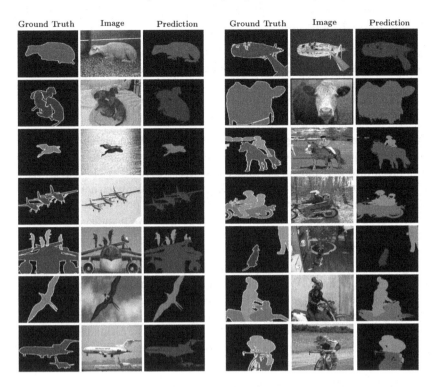

Fig. 4. Examples of predicted segmentations (*val* set, successfull cases).

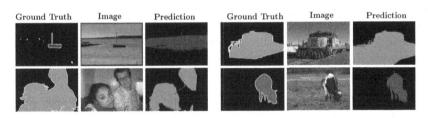

Fig. 5. Examples of predicted segmentations (*val* set, failure cases).

on water, or trains on tracks. We addressed this problem recently in follow-up work [15]. A second failure mode is that object regions can be segmented correctly, but assigned wrong class labels. This is actually quite rare for SEC, which we attribute to the fact that the DeepLab network has a large field-of-view and therefore can make use of the full image when assigning labels. Finally, it can also happen that segmentations cover only parts of objects. This is likely due to imperfections of the weak localization cues that tend to reliably detect only the most discriminative parts of an object, e.g. the face of a person. This might not be sufficient to segment the complete object, however, especially when objects overlap each other or consist of multiple components of very different appearance.

4.3 Detailed Discussion

To provide additional insight into the working mechanisms of the SEC loss function, we performed two further sets of experiments on the *val* data. First, we analyze different global pooling strategies, and second, we perform an ablation study that illustrates the effect of each of the three terms in the proposed loss function visually as well as numerically.

Effect of Global Pooling Strategies. As discussed before, the quality of segmentations depends on which global pooling strategy is used to convert segmentation mask into per-image classification scores. To quantify this effect, we train three segmentation networks from weak supervision, using either GMP, GAP or GWRP as aggregation methods for classes that are present in the image. For classes that are not present we always use GMP, i.e. we penalize any occurrence of these classes. In Fig. 6 we demonstrate visual results for every pooling strategy and report two quantities: the fraction of pixels that are predicted to belong to a foreground (fg) class, and the segmentation performance as measured by mean IoU. We observe that GWRP outperforms the other method in terms of segmentation quality and the fractions of predicted foreground pixels supports our earlier hypothesis: the model trained with GMP tends to underestimate object sizes, while the model trained with GAP on average overestimates them. In contrast, the model trained with GWRP, produces segmentations in which objects are, on average, close to the correct size[2].

Effect of the different loss terms. To investigate the contribution of each term in our composite loss function we train segmentation networks with loss functions in which different terms of the SEC loss were omitted. Figure 7 provides numerical results and illustrates typical segmentation mistakes that occur when certain loss terms are omitted. Best results are achieved when all three loss terms are present. However, the experiments also allow us to draw two interesting additional conclusions about the interaction between the loss terms.

Semi-supervised Loss and Large Field-of-View. First, we observe that having L_{seed} in the loss function is crucial to achieve competitive performance. Without this loss term our segmentation network fails to reflect the localization of objects in its predictions, even though the network does match the global label statistics rather well. See the third column of Fig. 7 for the illustration of this effect.

We believe that this effect can be explained by the large (378×378) field-of-view (FOV) of the segmentation network[3]: if an object is present in an image, then the majority of the predicted scores may be influenced by this object, no matter where object is located. This helps in predicting the right class labels, but can negatively affect the localization ability. Other researchers addressed

---

[2] Note that these experiments were done after the network architecture and parameters were fixed. In particular, we did not tune the decay parameters for this effect.

[3] We report the theoretical fields-of-view inferred from the network architecture. The empirical field-of-view that is actually used by the network can be smaller [51].

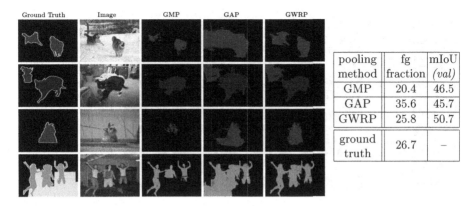

pooling method	fg fraction	mIoU (val)
GMP	20.4	46.5
GAP	35.6	45.7
GWRP	25.8	50.7
ground truth	26.7	–

Fig. 6. Results on the *val* set and examples of segmentation masks for models trained with different pooling strategies.

this problem by explicitly changing the architecture of the network in order to reduce its field-of-view [23]. However, networks with a small field-of-view are less powerful and often fail to recognize which semantic labels are present on an image. We conduct an additional experiment (see the technical report [16] for details) that confirm that SEC with a small (211×211) field-of-view network performs clearly worse than with the large (378×378) field-of-view network, see Fig. 8 for numeric results and visual examples. Thus, we conclude that the seeding loss provides the necessary localization guidance that enables the large field-of-view network to still reliably localize objects.

Effects of the Expansion and Constrain-to-Boundary Losses. By construction, the constrain-to-boundary loss encourages nearby regions of similar color to have the same label. However, this is often not enough to turn the weak localization cues into segmentation masks that cover a whole object, especially if the object consists of visually dissimilar parts, such as people wearing clothes of different colors. See the sixth column of Fig. 7 for an illustration of this effect.

The expansion loss, based on GWRP, suppresses the prediction of classes that are not meant to be in the image, and it encourages classes that are in the image to have reasonable sizes. When combined with the seeding loss, the expansion loss actually results in a drop in performance. The fifth column of Fig. 7 shows an explanation of this: objects sizes are generally increased, but the additionally predicted regions do not match the image boundaries.

In combination, the seeding loss provides reliable seed locations, the expansion loss acts as a force to enlarge the segmentation masks to a reasonable size, and the constrain-to-boundary loss constrains the segmentation mask to line up with image boundaries, thus integrating low-level image information. The result are substantially improved segmentation masks as illustrated in the last column of Fig. 7.

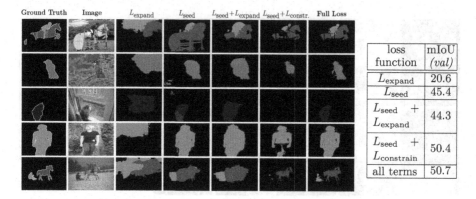

loss function	mIoU (val)
L_{expand}	20.6
L_{seed}	45.4
$L_{seed} + L_{expand}$	44.3
$L_{seed} + L_{constrain}$	50.4
all terms	50.7

Fig. 7. Results on the *val* set and examples of segmentation masks for models trained with different loss functions.

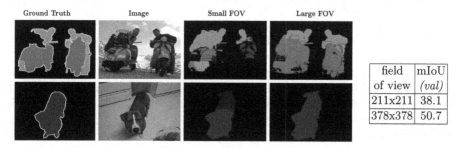

field of view	mIoU (val)
211x211	38.1
378x378	50.7

Fig. 8. Results on the *val* set and examples of segmentation masks for models with small or large field-of-views.

5   Conclusion

We propose a new loss function for training deep segmentation networks when only image-level labels are available. We demonstrate that our approach outperforms previous state-of-the-art methods by a large margin when used under the same experimental conditions and provide a detailed ablation study.

We also identify potential directions that may help to further improve weakly-supervised segmentation performance. Our experiments show that knowledge about object sizes can dramatically improve the segmentation performance. SEC readily allows incorporating size information through decay parameters, but a procedure for estimating object sizes automatically would be desirable. A second way to improve the performance would be stronger segmentation priors, for example about shape or materials. This could offer a way to avoid mistakes that are currently typical for weakly-supervised segmentation networks, including ours, for example that boats are confused with the water in their background.

Acknowledgments. This work was funded by the European Research Council under the European Unions Seventh Framework Programme (FP7/2007-2013)/ERC grant agreement no 308036. We gratefully acknowledge the support of NVIDIA Corporation with the donation of the GPUs used for this research. We also thank Vittorio Ferrari for helpful feedback.

References

1. Andrews, S., Tsochantaridis, I., Hofmann, T.: Support vector machines for multiple-instance learning. In: NIPS (2002)
2. Arbeláez, P., Pont-Tuset, J., Barron, J., Marques, F., Malik, J.: Multiscale combinatorial grouping. In: CVPR (2014)
3. Bazzani, L., Bergamo, A., Anguelov, D., Torresani, L.: Self-taught object localization with deep networks. In: WACV (2016)
4. Bearman, A., Russakovsky, O., Ferrari, V., Fei-Fei, L.: What's the point: Semantic segmentation with point supervision. In: ECCV (2016)
5. Carreira, J., Sminchisescu, C.: CPMC: Automatic object segmentation using constrained parametric min-cuts. IEEE T-PAMI 34(7), 312–1328 (2012)
6. Chen, L.C., Papandreou, G., Kokkinos, I., Murphy, K., Yuille, A.L.: Semantic image segmentation with deep convolutional nets and fully connected CRFs. In: ICLR (2015)
7. Cheng, M.M., Zhang, Z., Lin, W.Y., Torr, P.H.S.: BING: Binarized normed gradients for objectness estimation at 300fps. In: CVPR (2014)
8. Dai, J., He, K., Sun, J.: BoxSup: Exploiting bounding boxes to supervise convolutional networks for semantic segmentation. In: ICCV (2015)
9. Everingham, M., Van Gool, L., Williams, C.K., Winn, J., Zisserman, A.: The PASCAL visual object classes (VOC) challenge. IJCV 88(2), 303–338 (2010)
10. Hariharan, B., Arbelaez, P., Bourdev, L., Maji, S., Malik, J.: Semantic contours from inverse detectors. In: ICCV (2011)
11. He, X., Zemel, R.S.: Learning hybrid models for image annotation with partially labeled data. In: NIPS (2009)
12. Hong, S., Oh, J., Lee, H., Han, B.: Learning transferrable knowledge for semantic segmentation with deep convolutional neural network. In: CVPR (2016)
13. Jia, Y., Shelhamer, E., Donahue, J., Karayev, S., Long, J., Girshick, R., Guadarrama, S., Darrell, T.: Caffe: Convolutional architecture for fast feature embedding. arXiv preprint arXiv:1408.5093v1 (2014)
14. Kim, H., Hwang, S.: Scale-invariant feature learning using deconvolutional neural networks for weakly-supervised semantic segmentation. arXiv preprint arXiv:1602.04984v2 (2016). http://arxiv.org/abs/1602.04984v2
15. Kolesnikov, A., Lampert, C.H.: Improving weakly-supervised object localization by micro-annotation. In: BMVC (2016)
16. Kolesnikov, A., Lampert, C.H.: Seed, expand and constrain: Three principles for weakly-supervised image segmentation. arXiv preprint arXiv:1603.06098 (2016). http://arxiv.org/abs/1603.06098
17. Krähenbühl, P., Koltun, V.: Efficient inference in fully connected CRFs with gaussian edge potentials. In: NIPS (2011)
18. Krapac, J., Šegvic, S.: Weakly-supervised semantic segmentation by redistributing region scores to pixels. In: GCPR (2016)
19. Krizhevsky, A., Sutskever, I., Hinton, G.E.: ImageNet classification with deep convolutional neural networks. In: NIPS (2012)
20. Liu, S., Yan, S., Zhang, T., Xu, C., Liu, J., Lu, H.: Weakly supervised graph propagation towards collective image parsing. IEEE T-MM 14(2), 361–373 (2012)

21. Nowozin, S., Gehler, P.V., Lampert, C.H.: On parameter learning in CRF-based approaches to object class image segmentation. In: Daniilidis, K., Maragos, P., Paragios, N. (eds.) ECCV 2010, Part VI. LNCS, vol. 6316, pp. 98–111. Springer, Heidelberg (2010)
22. Oquab, M., Bottou, L., Laptev, I., Sivic, J.: Is object localization for free? - weakly-supervised learning with convolutional neural networks. In: CVPR, pp. 685–694 (2015)
23. Papandreou, G., Chen, L.C., Murphy, K.P., Yuille, A.L.: Weakly- and semi-supervised learning of a deep convolutional network for semantic image segmentation. In: ICCV (2015)
24. Pathak, D., Krähenbühl, P., Darrell, T.: Constrained convolutional neural networks for weakly supervised segmentation. In: ICCV (2015)
25. Pathak, D., Shelhamer, E., Long, J., Darrell, T.: Fully convolutional multi-class multiple instance learning. In: ICLR (2015)
26. Pinheiro, P.O., Collobert, R.: From image-level to pixel-level labeling with convolutional networks. In: CVPR (2015)
27. Pourian, N., Karthikeyan, S., Manjunath, B.: Weakly supervised graph based semantic segmentation by learning communities of image-parts. In: CVPR (2015)
28. Rabinovich, A., Vedaldi, A., Galleguillos, C., Wiewiora, E., Belongie, S.: Objects in context. In: ICCV (2007)
29. Russakovsky, O., Deng, J., Su, H., Krause, J., Satheesh, S., Ma, S., Huang, Z., Karpathy, A., Khosla, A., Bernstein, M., Berg, A.C., Fei-Fei, L.: ImageNet large scale visual recognition challenge. IJCV 115(3), 211–252 (2015)
30. Scudder, H.J.: Probability of error of some adaptive pattern-recognition machines. IEEE T-IT 11(3), 363–371 (1965)
31. Shotton, J., Winn, J., Rother, C., Criminisi, A.: Textonboost: Joint appearance, shape and context modeling for multi-class object recognition and segmentation. In: ECCV (2006)
32. Simonyan, K., Vedaldi, A., Zisserman, A.: Deep inside convolutional networks: visualising image classification models and saliency maps. In: ICLR (2014)
33. Simonyan, K., Zisserman, A.: Very deep convolutional networks for large-scale image recognition. In: ICLR (2015)
34. Toyoda, T., Hasegawa, O.: Random field model for integration of local information and global information. IEEE T-PAMI 30(8), 1483–1489 (2008)
35. Vasconcelos, M., Vasconcelos, N., Carneiro, G.: Weakly supervised top-down image segmentation. In: CVPR (2006)
36. Verbeek, J., Triggs, B.: Region classification with Markov field aspect models. In: CVPR (2007)
37. Verbeek, J., Triggs, W.: Scene segmentation with CRFs learned from partially labeled images. In: NIPS (2008)
38. Vezhnevets, A., Buhmann, J.M.: Towards weakly supervised semantic segmentation by means of multiple instance and multitask learning. In: CVPR (2010)
39. Vezhnevets, A., Ferrari, V., Buhmann, J.M.: Weakly supervised semantic segmentation with a multi-image model. In: ICCV (2011)
40. Vezhnevets, A., Ferrari, V., Buhmann, J.M.: Weakly supervised structured output learning for semantic segmentation. In: CVPR (2012)
41. Wei, Y., Liang, X., Chen, Y., Jie, Z., Xiao, Y., Zhao, Y., Yan, S.: Learning to segment with image-level annotations. Pattern Recognition (2016)
42. Wei, Y., Liang, X., Chen, Y., Shen, X., Cheng, M., Zhao, Y., Yan, S.: STC: a simple to complex framework for weakly-supervised semantic segmentation. arXiv preprint arXiv:1509.03150v1 (2015). http://arxiv.org/abs/1509.03150

43. Xie, W., Peng, Y., Xiao, J.: Weakly-supervised image parsing via constructing semantic graphs and hypergraphs. In: Multimedia (2014)
44. Xu, J., Schwing, A.G., Urtasun, R.: Tell me what you see and I will show you where it is. In: CVPR (2014)
45. Xu, J., Schwing, A.G., Urtasun, R.: Learning to segment under various forms of weak supervision. In: CVPR (2015)
46. Zhang, L., Gao, Y., Xia, Y., Lu, K., Shen, J., Ji, R.: Representative discovery of structure cues for weakly-supervised image segmentation. IEEE T-MM **16**(2), 470–479 (2014)
47. Zhang, L., Song, M., Liu, Z., Liu, X., Bu, J., Chen, C.: Probabilistic graphlet cut: Exploiting spatial structure cue for weakly supervised image segmentation. In: CVPR (2013)
48. Zhang, L., Yang, Y., Gao, Y., Yu, Y., Wang, C., Li, X.: A probabilistic associative model for segmenting weakly supervised images. IEEE T-IP **23**(9), 4150–4159 (2014)
49. Zhang, W., Zeng, S., Wang, D., Xue, X.: Weakly supervised semantic segmentation for social images. In: CVPR (2015)
50. Zhou, B., Khosla, A., A., L., Oliva, A., Torralba, A.: Learning deep features for discriminative localization. In: CVPR (2016)
51. Zhou, B., Khosla, A., Lapedriza, A., Oliva, A., Torralba, A.: Object detectors emerge in deep scene CNNs. In: ICLR (2015)
52. Zhu, J., Mao, J., Yuille, A.L.: Learning from weakly supervised data by the expectation loss SVM (e-SVM) algorithm. In: NIPS (2014)

Patch-Based Low-Rank Matrix Completion for Learning of Shape and Motion Models from Few Training Samples

Jan Ehrhardt$^{(\boxtimes)}$, Matthias Wilms, and Heinz Handels

Institute of Medical Informatics, University of Lübeck, Lübeck, Germany
ehrhardt@imi.uni-luebeck.de

Abstract. Statistical models have opened up new possibilities for the automated analysis of images. However, the limited availability of representative training data, e.g. segmented images, leads to a bottleneck for the application of statistical models in practice. In this paper, we propose a novel patch-based technique that enables to learn representative statistical models of shape, appearance, or motion with a high grade of detail from a small number of observed training samples using low-rank matrix completion methods. Our method relies on the assumption that local variations have limited effects in distant areas. We evaluate our approach on three exemplary applications: (1) 2D shape modeling of faces, (2) 3D modeling of human lung shapes, and (3) population-based modeling of respiratory organ deformation. A comparison with the classical PCA-based modeling approach and FEM-PCA shows an improved generalization ability for small training sets indicating the improved flexibility of the model.

Keywords: Statistical modeling · High-dimension-low-sample-size problem · Low-rank matrix completion · Virtual samples

1 Introduction

Statistical models play an important role in several tasks in computer vision and image analysis, such as image segmentation and object classification. These models aim to represent properties like shape or intensity of a class of objects based on a population of observed instances. However, collecting an adequately large and representative training population is often laborious and challenging, particularly if dimensionality and complexity of the observed objects increase. Therefore, many applications suffer from the high-dimension-low-sample-size (HDLSS) problem. In the application of statistical shape models (SSMs) [7] or eigenfaces (eigenimages) [27] for segmentation or recognition tasks, a small sample size results in a limited flexibility of the model and details can not be represented adequately (see Fig. 1).

This paper proposes a method for statistical shape, appearance, and motion modeling with increased ability to adapt to local details, thus, increasing the

© Springer International Publishing AG 2016
B. Leibe et al. (Eds.): ECCV 2016, Part IV, LNCS 9908, pp. 712–727, 2016.
DOI: 10.1007/978-3-319-46493-0_43

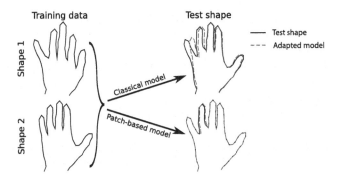

Fig. 1. Example application of the patch-based modeling approach using only two training shapes: classical models only learn the global transition between the two shapes. The patch-based model combines local shape details, and can adapt to test shapes showing local properties of both shapes.

flexibility of models generated from few training samples. The method is based on the assumption of locality, i.e. we assume that local variations in shape, intensity, or motion have limited effects in distant areas. This allows the model to combine local variations observed in different training samples while preserving overall object properties, i.e. generating valid instances. During the learning phase, the objects are partitioned into patches and distant patches of different samples are fused into virtual samples. By doing so, a very large number of virtual samples can be generated from few training instances. To avoid the problem of discontinuities at patch borders, a sparse sampling is performed and the model generation is formulated as a low-rank matrix completion problem. Thus, its left to the model to "fill in" fitting information between patches of different training instances. We validate the proposed approach using three exemplary applications in the fields of computer vision and medical image analysis: (1) 2D shape modeling of faces, (2) 3D modeling of human lung shapes, and (3) population-based modeling of respiratory organ deformation. Evaluations show that our model features an increased generalization ability for problems of different complexity while generated instances are still valid.

1.1 Related Work

Statistical Shape Models. Since their introduction in the early 1990s [7], statistical shape models have proven to be effectively addressing a large number of image segmentation problems. The most generic method to generate a SSM is to build a *point distribution model* (*PDM*) by applying a principal component analysis (PCA) to the sample matrix $\mathbf{X} = (\boldsymbol{x}_1, \dots, \boldsymbol{x}_n)$ containing a given set of n training shapes. Each training shape $\boldsymbol{x}_i$ is represented as a m-dimensional vector composed by landmark points or pseudo-landmarks $\boldsymbol{x}_i = (x_1, y_1, z_1, \dots, x_{\frac{m}{3}}, y_{\frac{m}{3}}, z_{\frac{m}{3}})^T$. There is a variety of other shape representations (see [13] for an overview), but landmark-based systems are the most popular ones.

Eigenimages and Population-Based Deformation Models. Eigenfaces (or eigen-images) [27] is the application of PCA-based methods for intensity modeling, where each training image is represented in a sample vector x_i by concatenating the pixel values. Similar to eigenfaces, PCA-based methods can be applied to a population of deformation fields. This approach has many applications in medical image analysis, e.g. to model respiratory or cardiac organ deformations [10], for morphometric studies in computational anatomy or as priors for atlas-patient matching [24,25]. The typical dimensionality of those models is between several ten thousands and several millions, and the HDLSS problem is intensified by the limited availability of medical image data and the laborious generation of application-specific training sets.

The HDLSS Problem in Statistical Modeling. Generally, two different ways exist to tackle the HDLSS problem in statistical modeling: (1) Only observed training samples are used but changes are made to the modeling process to allow for higher flexibility. (2) The modeling approach remains (largely) unchanged but additional virtual training samples are generated. Common patch-based and hierarchical techniques applied in shape modeling, object classification, or recognition tasks [5,8,16,19,29–31] belong to the first category. In patch-based approaches for object classification [16,31], the samples are subdivided to model features of small regions independently. These approaches are, however, limited to classification tasks as they do not learn a consistent generative model as needed for, e.g., segmentation tasks. The patch-based shape modeling approach for medical image segmentation proposed in [30] follows the same idea and independently models different parts of an object. This approach also does not generate a consistent model and thus the consistency needs to be enforced during model application. Hierarchical approaches used in shape modeling [5,8] subdivide the (generative) model into several parts for increased flexibility. Common approaches belonging to the second category generate virtual samples by applying (random/heuristic) transformations to individual training instances or simulate different noise levels, location errors or lightning effects [6,15,29].

Conceptually, our approach belongs to the second category. However, our work differs from previous works and contributes to the state-of-the art in two major aspects: (1) We use sparse virtual samples combining information of *different* observed samples and (2) elegantly unify virtual sample completion and learning of a generative model. The second aspect guarantees the reconstruction of valid (but perpetuated) instances, and although our method is motivated by the HDLSS problem occurring in medical applications, it could be of interest for other applications, e.g. for data augmentation in the context of deep learning.

2   Methods

We begin by briefly describing the generation of classical point distribution models and its relation to matrix factorization. As introduced in the last section, our training samples are given by m-dimensional vectors x_i that are assembled in the data matrix $\mathbf{X} = (\boldsymbol{x}_1, \ldots, \boldsymbol{x}_n)$. The central step to build a PDM is a principal component analysis of the data matrix $\mathbf{X}$ and a dimensionality reduction by selecting only the principal components corresponding to the k largest eigenvalues [7]. The problem can be formulated as the low-rank approximation

$$\hat{\mathbf{M}} = \arg \min_{\mathbf{M}} \|\tilde{\mathbf{X}} - \mathbf{M}\|_F^2 \quad \text{s.t.} \; rank(\mathbf{M}) = k, \tag{1}$$

where $\tilde{\mathbf{X}}$ is the centered data matrix. A singular value decomposition (SVD) $\tilde{\mathbf{X}} = \tilde{\mathbf{U}}\tilde{\mathbf{\Sigma}}\tilde{\mathbf{V}}^T$ can be applied to solve Eq. (1), followed by selecting the right and left singular vectors associated with the k largest singular values $\sigma_1 \geq \sigma_2 \geq \ldots \sigma_k$. $\hat{\mathbf{M}}$ is then given by the truncated matrices $\hat{\mathbf{M}} = \tilde{\mathbf{U}}_k \tilde{\mathbf{\Sigma}}_k \tilde{\mathbf{V}}_k^T$. The number of basis vectors k is usually controlled by setting a threshold as follows

$$\sum_{i=1}^{k} \sigma_i^2 \Big/ \sum_{i=1}^{n} \sigma_i^2 \geq \tau, \tag{2}$$

where common values for τ are $0.9 - 0.98$. The truncated matrix $\tilde{\mathbf{U}} \in \mathbb{R}^{m \times k}$ defines an orthonormal basis and together with a distribution of the shape parameters (the weights associated with each basis vector) they define the *classical statistical model*.

Now, let us assume that data is missing in the observed samples and let Ω be the subset of $[m] \times [n]$ of the available entries in the data matrix $\mathbf{X} \in \mathbb{R}^{m \times n}$. A statistical model can be generated by solving the following low-rank matrix completion problem:

$$\hat{\mathbf{M}} = \arg \min_{\mathbf{M}} \|\mathcal{P}_\Omega(\mathbf{X}) - \mathcal{P}_\Omega(\mathbf{M})\|_F^2 \quad \text{s.t.} \; rank(\mathbf{M}) = k, \tag{3}$$

with $\mathcal{P}_\Omega$ being the projection operator

$$(\mathcal{P}_\Omega(\mathbf{X}))_{ij} = \begin{cases} \mathbf{X}_{ij} & (i,j) \in \Omega \\ 0 & \text{else} \end{cases}. \tag{4}$$

If a solution of Eq. (3) is found, basis and variances of the model are given by the SVD $\hat{\mathbf{M}} = \mathbf{U}\mathbf{\Sigma}\mathbf{V}^T$.

The theoretical properties of low-rank matrix completion (MC) and conditions for a successful matrix recovery are well studied, see e.g. [4]. Available methods to solve Eq. (3) can be roughly divided into methods based on nuclear norm minimization (e.g., singular value thresholding (SVT) [3] and the projected proximal point algorithm (ProPPA) [17]) and algorithms based on minimization on the Grassmann manifold (e.g., OptSPACE, GROUSE and GRASTA [12]). A disadvantage of the Grassmannian-based approaches is that an upper-bound guess of the desired rank is needed, on the other hand, some of these algorithms, like GROUSE and GRASTA, allow online matrix completion and therefore the application in large scale problems.

In our applications, difficulties arise from the ill-conditioned nature of the data matrix $\mathbf{X}$ resulting in large reconstruction errors and slow convergence for many MC algorithms [21]. However, recently, several algorithms were proposed to improve the performance for those matrices [14,21,22]. Among these, polar incremental matrix completion (PIMC) is based on the GROUSE algorithm and can be applied to streaming data [14].

2.1   Low-Rank Matrix Completion of Ill-Conditioned matrices

This section briefly introduces the polar incremental matrix completion (PIMC) algorithm used to solve Eq. (3) in our applications. For a more detailed derivation and description we refer the reader to [14].

To enable an online update of the model, the incremental update of basis $\mathbf{U}$ and singular values $\boldsymbol{\Sigma}$ is needed. Let $\mathbf{M}_t = \mathbf{U}_t \mathbf{R}_t^T$ be the estimated rank k-factorization of the (sparse) data matrix $\mathbf{X}_t \in \mathbb{R}^{m \times t}$ for t observed samples. Given a new sample $\boldsymbol{x}_{\Omega_t}$ with observed entries $\Omega_t \subset \{1, \ldots, m\}$, we can compute weights $\boldsymbol{w}_t = \arg\min_w \|\mathbf{U}_{\Omega_t} \boldsymbol{w} - \boldsymbol{x}_{\Omega_t}\|_2^2$ to interpolate values at unobserved entries

$$\tilde{\boldsymbol{x}}_t = \begin{cases} \boldsymbol{x}_{\Omega_t} & \text{on } \Omega_t \\ \mathbf{U}_t \boldsymbol{w}_t & \text{otherwise} \end{cases}, \tag{5}$$

where $\mathbf{U}_{\Omega_t}$ contains only the rows Ω_t of $\mathbf{U}$. To update $\mathbf{M}_t$ according to the new sample, we have to solve for

$$\min_{\mathbf{M}} \|[\mathbf{U}_t \mathbf{R}_t^T \; \tilde{\boldsymbol{x}}_t] - \mathbf{M}\|_F^2 \quad \text{s.t. } rank(\mathbf{M}) = k. \tag{6}$$

Given that $\mathbf{R}_t = \mathbf{V}_t \boldsymbol{\Sigma}_t$ for an orthogonal matrix $\mathbf{V}_t$, iterative SVD [2] can be used to efficiently solve Eq. (6) using

$$[\mathbf{U}_t \mathbf{R}_t^T \; \tilde{\boldsymbol{x}}_t] = \begin{bmatrix} \mathbf{U}_t & \dfrac{\boldsymbol{r}_t}{\|\boldsymbol{r}_t\|} \end{bmatrix} \begin{bmatrix} \boldsymbol{\Sigma}_t & \boldsymbol{w}_t \\ 0 & \|\boldsymbol{r}_t\| \end{bmatrix} \begin{bmatrix} \mathbf{V}_t^T & 0 \\ 0 & 1 \end{bmatrix} \tag{7}$$

and performing an SVD on the central $(k+1) \times (k+1)$ matrix $\begin{bmatrix} \boldsymbol{\Sigma}_t & \boldsymbol{w}_t \\ 0 & \|\boldsymbol{r}_t\| \end{bmatrix} = \hat{\mathbf{U}}\hat{\boldsymbol{\Sigma}}\hat{\mathbf{V}}^T$ followed by the update

$$\mathbf{U}_{t+1} = \begin{bmatrix} \mathbf{U}_t & \dfrac{\boldsymbol{r}_t}{\|\boldsymbol{r}_t\|} \end{bmatrix} \hat{\mathbf{U}}, \mathbf{V}_{t+1} = \begin{bmatrix} \mathbf{V}_t^T & 0 \\ 0 & 1 \end{bmatrix} \hat{\mathbf{V}}$$

$$\boldsymbol{\Sigma}_{t+1} = \hat{\boldsymbol{\Sigma}}, \text{ or } \mathbf{R}_{t+1} = \mathbf{V}_{t+1}\hat{\boldsymbol{\Sigma}} \tag{8}$$

and dropping the smallest singular value and corresponding singular vector to obtain a rank k factorization.

As shown in [2,14], this algorithm is equivalent to GROUSE for a specific step size, if setting $\boldsymbol{\Sigma}_t = \mathbf{I}$ and $\mathbf{V}_t = \mathbf{R}_t$ in Eq. (7) and using the updates in Eq. (8). This reveals the sensitivity of GROUSE to ill-conditioned matrices, because constant singular values are assumed.

To overcome this restriction, the authors of [14] propose to use the following approach to update the model in each step: Let $\mathbf{R}_t = \tilde{\mathbf{V}}_t \tilde{\mathbf{S}}_t$ be the polar decomposition of $\mathbf{R}_t$ into the matrix $\tilde{\mathbf{V}}_t \in \mathbb{R}^{m \times k}$ with orthonormal columns, and a positive semidefinite matrix $\tilde{\mathbf{S}}_t \in \mathbb{R}^{k \times k}$. Although $\tilde{\mathbf{S}}_t$ is not diagonal it presents an estimate of the singular values in the current subspace. Let further $\gamma_t = \dfrac{\kappa_0 \sum_t \|\boldsymbol{x}_{\Omega_t}\|_2}{\|\tilde{\mathbf{S}}_t\|_F}$ be a scaling value, then Eq. (7) can be rewritten as

$$[\mathbf{U}_t \mathbf{R}_t^T \; \tilde{\boldsymbol{x}}_t] = \begin{bmatrix} \mathbf{U}_t & \dfrac{\boldsymbol{r}_t}{\|\boldsymbol{r}_t\|} \end{bmatrix} \begin{bmatrix} \gamma_t \tilde{\mathbf{S}}_t & \boldsymbol{w}_t \\ 0 & \|\boldsymbol{r}_t\| \end{bmatrix} \begin{bmatrix} \dfrac{1}{\gamma_t}\tilde{\mathbf{V}}_t^T & 0 \\ 0 & 1 \end{bmatrix}, \tag{9}$$

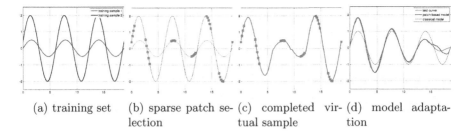

(a) training set   (b) sparse patch se- (c) completed vir- (d) model adapta-
                    lection   tual sample   tion

Fig. 2. Demonstrative example describing the patch-based modeling method using two sinusoidal training shapes (see text for details).

and Eq. (8) are used to update the model. In contrast to iterative SVD, the re-computation of $\tilde{\mathbf{S}}_t$ using the polar decomposition is required, because wrong estimates of the singular values may appear due to the missing data. Further, the interpolated data vectors $\tilde{\boldsymbol{x}}_t$ are used in the update, i.e. the singular values will increase according to the interpolated data and not according to the observed data $\boldsymbol{x}_{\Omega_t}$. Therefore, a rescaling to the norm of the actual observed data is performed using the parameter γ_t, with $\kappa_0 \ll 1$ preventing abrupt changes.

2.2 Patch-Based Model Generation

We now come back to the HDLSS problem in statistical modeling (cf. Sect. 1). To overcome this problem, several approaches for SSM generation propose to learn local models by dividing the shape into parts. A difficulty arises in recombining these local models to a global shape.

The main idea of the presented method is to combine local information of different training shapes in artificially generated virtual samples. Instead of learning individual local models or recombining these local variations into complete new training samples, we provide only partial information to learn the model. Thus, we exploit the low-rank structure of the subspace to find a model that fits the generated samples. In previous work probabilistic PCA was used to learn shape models from partial information [20]. Our approach for model generation is illustrated using the simple one-dimensional example in Fig. 2. The training samples are given by two scaled and shifted sine functions. A large number of sparse virtual samples is generated by selecting small patches randomly from both training samples (Fig. 2(b)). The virtual samples are agglomerated in the sparse data matrix $\mathbf{X}$ and the low-rank matrix completion problem given in Eq. (3) is solved to compute the completed matrix $\mathbf{M} = \mathbf{U}\mathbf{R}^T$ of given rank k. Figure 2(c) shows the reconstructed virtual samples. The computed basis $\mathbf{U}$ can now be applied to approximate a new sample $\boldsymbol{y}$ by

$$\hat{\boldsymbol{y}} = \mathbf{U}\hat{\boldsymbol{w}} \quad \text{with} \quad \hat{\boldsymbol{w}} = \arg\min_{\boldsymbol{w}} \|\mathbf{U}\boldsymbol{w} - \boldsymbol{y}\|_2^2, \tag{10}$$

as illustrated in Fig. 2(d). Here, a damped sine function is used to show the approximation quality. Although the function resembles the second training sample near zero and approaches the first sample near 5π, classical global models can not achieve a good fitting result. In contrast, the patch-based method can combine *local* properties of both training samples and allows for a good approximation of the damped sine function. Interestingly, the approximation quality decreases in the interval $[5\pi, 6\pi]$ and the approximated curve is forced to be periodic. This behavior results from the fact that we learned the periodicity of the training functions by applying periodic boundary condition during the patch-selection (see Fig. 2(c)).

We can summarize the patch-based model generation algorithm as follows:

Algorithm 1. Patch-based model generation (batch)

Require: N training samples $x_i \in \mathbb{R}^m, i = 1, \ldots, N$, estimated rank k, sparsity $p \in (0, 1)$, number of virtual samples $n \gg N$

  Generate sparse virtual samples:
    for each $x_{\Omega_j}, j = 1, \ldots, n$ **do**
      Apply a *patch selection strategy* to select random patches from different training
      samples until at least $p \cdot m$ entries of x_{Ω_j} are filled
      Agglomerate x_{Ω_j} in sparse matrix $\mathbf{X} \in \mathbb{R}^{m \times n}$
    end for
  Solve low-rank matrix completion:
    Compute $\mathbf{M} = \mathbf{U}\mathbf{R}^T$ of rank k by solving Eq. (3)
      using the algorithm described in Sect. 2.1
  Estimate a distribution of the shape parameters from matrix $\mathbf{R}$ or from estimated
  singular values $\hat{\boldsymbol{\Sigma}}$ (Eq. (8))

Output: Model defined by orthonormal basis $\mathbf{U}$ and associated distribution of the shape parameters, e.g. $w \sim \mathcal{N}(\boldsymbol{\mu}, diag(\sigma_1, \ldots, \sigma_k))$

To select suitable parameters for Algorithm 1, the dependency $p \cdot mn \geq \zeta(m + n - k)k$ can be used, where ζ is the *oversampling ratio* [21]. Most algorithms for matrix completion yield robust results with $\zeta \approx 6$. In our applications we selected a sparsity of $p = 0.3$, lower values increase the training size and higher values complicate the selection of suitable patches. The estimated rank k is application dependent and will be discussed in Sect. 3. To estimate a distribution of the model parameters, one possibility is to assume a normal distribution $\mathcal{N}(\hat{\boldsymbol{\mu}}, \hat{\sigma}_1, \ldots, \hat{\sigma}_k)$ and compute standard deviations and mean from the matrix $\mathbf{R}$.

2.3 Patch Selection and Domain Partitioning

The remaining component of the algorithm is the generation of virtual samples, i.e. the selection of patches to fill the entries of x_{Ω_j}. This step affects the properties of the generated model and at the same time interacts with the matrix factorization algorithm. In general, the applied patch selection strategy depends on the regarded application. Here, we purposely apply simple sampling strategies to show the strength of the presented approach in different applications without elaborate fine tuning.

The guiding assumption is that local variations have limited influence in distant areas. Consequently, global variations in pose and orientation have to be removed from the training set before model generation. Furthermore, prior knowledge about the minimum distance between independent areas is needed to partition the domain of interest (surface mesh or image space), and each partition should be able to reflect local domain properties, e.g. orientation or curvature. For each virtual sample to generate, partitions are randomly assigned to different training samples. The number of training samples used to generate each virtual sample influences the globality of the model and the needed rank – a small number (two or three) was sufficient in our tests.

Sampling large partitions would lead to block-like structures in the data matrix, which impedes the convergence of the matrix completion algorithm [14]. Therefore, many smaller patches drawn from each partition are used to fill the (incomplete) data matrix. Patches sampled from different training shapes should be *detached* to avoid the learning of discontinuities at patch stitches.

A partitioning of the domain is obvious if multiple objects are modeled together, e.g. the facial structures in Fig. 3. For applications like eigenfaces or deformation models the partitioning is simple because the rectangular image space can easily be divided. For surface models existing mesh partitioning methods [26] can be used. In our experiments, we apply a generic mesh partitioning approach, which randomly partitions a triangulated genus-0 surface into equally sized parts. First, the triangulated surface is mapped onto a unit sphere using an unconstrained energy-based method [11] and subsequently the unit sphere is partitioned into regions of equal area [18].

3   Experiments and Applications

To demonstrate the practicability of our approach, we evaluate the patch-based model for three different types of models: 2D contour data, 3D surface meshes, and 2D deformation fields. The proposed algorithm is compared with the classical modeling approach (see Sect. 2) and systematically evaluated using different training sizes. For 2D contour data, our approach is further compared with the FEM-PCA model of Cootes and Taylor [6] combining the standard PCA and finite element method (FEM). This approach also addresses the HDLSS problem and has shown to perform among the best in [15]. FEM-PCA manipulates the data covariance matrix and can therefore only be applied for data of moderate size.

Generalization error and *specificity error* introduced by Davies et al. [9] are used as quantitative performance measures for the statistical models. The generalization error describes the ability to model unseen shapes, and is measured by the distance of the closest model instance to the samples in a test set. The specificity error indicates the validity of the shapes produced by the model. For specificity estimation, a high number of random model instances are generated and the minimal distance to one of the samples in the database is computed. Note that small values indicate better models for both measures.

Fig. 3. 50 example contours of the IMM face database [23] (left), and randomly generated contours from $N = 4$ training samples using the classical model (middle) and the patch-based model (right). The patch-based model shows a higher variability while the overall shape is preserved.

3.1 2D Contour Data of the IMM Face Database

In our first experiment, we apply our algorithm to facial annotations contained in the IMM face database [23]. This database provides 58 facial landmarks of 40 subjects with 6 different expressions (240 in total). Three of the expressions in the database contain rotations of the head, which contradicts our assumption of locality. Therefore, these expressions are excluded and 120 samples (40 subjects, 3 expressions) were used in total. Figure 3 shows 50 example contours of the provided faces after alignment with similarity transformations.

Experiment Design: To evaluate the performance of the patch-based approach, models are generated for varying numbers N of available training samples. For each model generalization ability and specificity are computed and compared to the classical model using identical training and test sets. The N training samples are chosen randomly from the 120 available samples together with a disjunct test set of 30 samples. For each size N the experiments are repeated 60 times and the resulting measures are averaged. After model computation each sample in the test set is approximated using Eq. (10) and average landmark distances are computed to determine the generalization ability. To measure the specificity, 1000 random samples are generated using the computed model basis $\mathbf{U}$ and normally distributed weights $\boldsymbol{w} \sim \mathcal{N}(\hat{\boldsymbol{\mu}}, \hat{\boldsymbol{\Sigma}} = \mathrm{diag}(\hat{\sigma}_1^2, \ldots, \hat{\sigma}_k^2))$, with standard deviations and mean computed from the estimated matrix $\mathbf{R}$.

Virtual Sample Generation: Each facial landmark in the IMM database is labeled with the associated facial structure (eyebrows, eyes, nose, mouth and jaw) so that a partitioning is already given. The different parts are not connected whereby the patch selection strategy is further simplified. The following strategy is applied to generate one virtual sample $\boldsymbol{x}_{\Omega_j}$: Two training samples $\boldsymbol{x}_A$ and $\boldsymbol{x}_B$ are selected randomly (possibly $A = B$) and each partition is randomly assigned to one of the drawn samples $\boldsymbol{x}_A$ or $\boldsymbol{x}_B$. Then, patches of size 1 (landmarks) are drawn randomly and depending on the associated facial structure the coordinates (values) are taken from $\boldsymbol{x}_A$ or $\boldsymbol{x}_B$. The last step is repeated until $p \cdot m$ of the entries of $\boldsymbol{x}_{\Omega_j}$ are known.

Determining the Model Parameters: We computed a rank of 13 for the complete set of 120 samples using Eq. 2 with a threshold of $\tau = 0.95$ for the ratio of the total variance. Therefore, for the classical PDM the rank $k = 13$ if $N > 13$ and $k = N$ otherwise is used. The proposed patch-based modeling method is designed to learn additional variations beside the inter-sample variance, this is taken into account by using a higher rank of $k = 13 + \delta$, where δ is set arbitrary to 10 in this experiment. To show the ability to generate a reasonable and feasible model independent of the number of training samples the rank is left constant for all training sizes. The other parameters are chosen as $p = 0.3$ and $n = 400$. The FEM-PCA model uses the same rank as the patch-based approach and the control parameter is set to $\alpha = \alpha_1/N$ as suggested in [6] with $\alpha_1 = 20$.

3.2   3D Lung Surfaces of the LIDC Database

In the second experiment, 3D shape models of the right lung are generated. This experiment is based on image data from the publicly available LIDC-IDRI database [1] that provides > 1000 thoracic 3D CT images of patients with lung nodules. Here, we use a subset of $N = 160$ randomly selected images and extract the lungs via thresholding. Based on these segmentations, an average lung shape is computed as described in [10], which is subsequently triangulated and decimated to obtain 2000 pseudo-landmarks. After registering the atlas to all images by applying an open-source registration method [28], the resulting deformation fields are used to propagate the landmarks to all 160 lungs to define correspondences for the shape modeling process.

For virtual sample generation, the lungs are partitioned into 10 randomly placed areas of equal size generated by the approach described in Sect. 2.3. Using these partitions, the same strategy as used for the face data in the first experiment is applied. The rank estimation leads to a rank of 21 ($\tau = 0.95$) for the complete set of 160 shapes. The experiments are repeated 25 times, and the parameters of our approach are set to $\delta = 20, p = 0.3$, and $n = 1000$.

3.3   Respiratory Lung Motion

At last, we use the proposed method to generate population-based models for respiratory lung motion. We use 2D sagittal slices of lung CT images of $N = 38$ patients and a size of 160×200 pixels acquired at two breathing phases: end inspiration and end expiration. An open-source image registration toolbox [28] is applied to estimate a dense deformation field to describe the respiration-related organ deformations. Following the approach in [10], all images and the associated deformation fields are transformed into a common atlas space to establish anatomical correspondence between the patients. Figure 4 shows example images and computed motion fields for two patients.

Let $\mathbf{\Phi}_1, \dots, \mathbf{\Phi}_N$ be the (aligned) deformation fields with each pixel $\mathbf{\Phi}(x, y) = (u, v)$ describing the displacement from inspiration to expiration. By concatenating the u and v components of all pixels, each image can be represented by a sample vector of dimension $m = 64000$. Virtual sample generation starts by

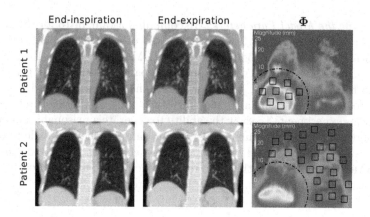

Fig. 4. CT images of two patients for different breathing phases and magnitudes of associated motion fields describing the respiratory lung deformation. The dotted line indicates the partitioning of the image domain, and the squares show the patch selection for one sparse virtual sample.

random selection of two training samples $\mathbf{\Phi}_A$ and $\mathbf{\Phi}_B$ and a seed pixel (s_x, s_y). Then, random patch centers (p_x, p_y) are determined and all displacements inside a patch of size 9×9 are used for the virtual sample. If the distance between (s_x, s_y) and (p_x, p_y) is below ϵ the values are sampled from $\mathbf{\Phi}_A$ and from $\mathbf{\Phi}_B$ otherwise. The distances between patch centers are required to be larger than $\kappa > 9\sqrt{2}$. Patches are selected until $p \cdot m$ entries are filled. The generation of one virtual samples is sketched in Fig. 4(right).

The estimated rank for all available training samples is $k = 27$ ($\tau = 0.95$) and the parameters are set to $\delta = 10, p = 0.3, n = 800, \epsilon = \frac{\sqrt{(160^2 + 200^2)}}{3}$ and $\kappa = 15$. The experiments are repeated 25 times for each size of the training set.

4   Results

The condition numbers of the complete data matrices were computed for all experiments using the largest and lowest singular values by $\frac{\sigma_1}{\sigma_k}$ where k is the rank at $\tau = 0.95$. The computed condition numbers are 423 for the IMM faces, 783 for the 3D lung surfaces and 95 for the deformation fields, showing that all problems are highly ill-conditioned, particularly the surface modeling. To validate the suitability of PIMC for our applications, random matrices of size 6000×1000 with condition number 1000 and rank 20 were generated as described in [14]. Figure 5 shows the average residual error and the required computation time for GROUSE, PIMC and ProPPA [17] and illustrates the suitability of the PIMC algorithm for that type of problems.

ROC-Like Analysis: $N = 10$ training samples of the IMM face database are used to compute a classical PCA model, a FEM-PCA model, and a patch-based model. Generalization and specificity of these shape models can be controlled by

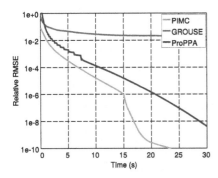
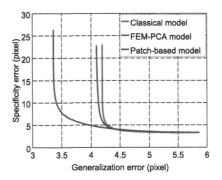

Fig. 5. Performance of three different matrix–completion algorithms for an ill–conditioned matrix (see text for details).

Fig. 6. ROC-like analysis: generalization and specificity for the IMM faces ($N = 10$) and varying variances of shape parameters (see text for details).

restricting the variances of the shape parameters. Figure 6 shows generalization and specificity for varying variances characterizing the dependencies between the two measures for the three different shape modeling approaches (average of 30 repeated experiments). The graph shows that for each given level of specificity our model clearly outperforms PCA and FEM-PCA models in terms of generalization, except for very low specificity errors where our model performs equal to the PCA model. For all remaining experiments we use the same model parameter restrictions for all shape models.

2D Contour Data of the IMM Face Database: Figure 7 (left) compares the generalization ability and specificity of the patch-based, the classical model, and FEM-PCA for varying numbers of available training samples. For small training sets ($N \leq 13$) the proposed method improves the generalization error by $\approx 22\%$, for larger training sets the improvement is less prominent ($\approx 13\%$). FEM-PCA shows no substantial improvement compared to the classical model for training sizes $N \leq 20$. As expected, the improvements in terms of generalization ability come along with higher landmark errors in the specificity tests. Both results reveal the desired increased variability of the model. However, model generated instances still represent valid face contours as indicated by an average specificity value of ≈ 10 pixels and as shown in Fig. 3.

3D Lung Surfaces: Figure 8 shows the mean surface and associated deformation modes generated from the patch-based model ($N = 10$ training shapes). Although only local information is provided to the model, it learns global deformations in the most important modes. Figure 7 (middle row) presents generalization ability and specificity depending on the number of training samples. The generalization ability is improved for small training sizes but approaches the classical model for $N \geq 20$. For this data, the localization error of the pseudo-landmarks is ≥ 2 mm due to a voxel spacing of 1.5 mm^3 of the underlying image data and an average registration error of ≈ 1.2 mm (see [28]). Therefore, by

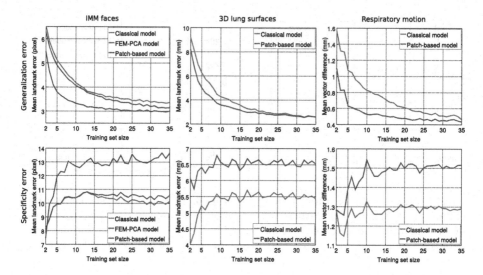

Fig. 7. Generalization and specificity errors for three experiments comparing the patch-based model (blue), the classical model (red), and the FEM-PCA model [6] (green, IMM faces only) given a varying numbers of training samples. Smaller values indicate better models. (Color figure online)

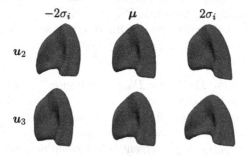

Fig. 8. Mean surface and two associated deformation modes of the 3D lung model generated by the proposed patch-based approach.

using the estimated rank of $k = 21$ a separation of noise and content in the data is obtained, and hence no further improvements in terms of adaption accuracy can be achieved without directly learning the noise.

Respiratory Lung Motion: In this application, the model obtains the most evident improvements compared with the classical model, particularly for small training sizes; e.g. an improvement of 41 % was achieved for $N = 5$, and 36 % for $N = 10$. The L-shape of the curve indicates that even small training sizes produce models with low approximation errors. The specificity measures for lung surfaces and lung motion in Fig. 7 reflects that the dependency of the generated model on the randomly selected training samples is more prominent for small training sizes.

5 Discussion and Conclusion

The contribution of this paper is a patch-based approach for learning of representative statistical shape, appearance, and motion models from few training samples. Our approach is based on the assumption that local variations have limited effects in distant areas and the model generation is formulated as a low-rank matrix completion problem that can be efficiently solved using recent algorithms capable of handling ill-conditioned matrices. In contrast to other patch-based algorithms used to tackle the HDLSS problem, our approach learns a consistent generative model and contrary to hierarchical techniques, our approach does not rely on the explicit and non-trivial definition a hierarchy.

Our experiments show that the proposed method can be applied for a variety of problems and leads to an increased flexibility and generalization ability while the validity of generated model instances is preserved. We have furthermore shown that the chosen PIMC algorithm is well suited for our intended applications. Its ability to solve the MC problem online is a key advantage for large scale problems as arising in deformation modeling where the data needed oftentimes exceeds the available memory. A disadvantage of this approach is the need to provide an estimated rank, however, in our experience an accurate choice is not crucial. It has to be noted that the presented patch-based modeling approach is not restricted to a specific MC algorithm, and any method that can handle ill-conditioned matrices can be used, e.g. ProPPA [17] (see Fig. 5). An important part of our approach is the patch selection strategy because it affects the generated model directly. But, even simple strategies lead to improved performance compared to other modeling approaches as shown in our experiments. Furthermore, application-specific prior-knowledge such as a left-right symmetry or other non-local relations could easily be incorporated.

An investigation of the computed variation modes revealed that although only local information was provided to our algorithm, the proposed method was able to learn the global shape variability as well (see Fig. 8). In this way, our approach combines local flexibility with well-known properties of classical models. In future work, we will further analyze the effects of the patch selection on the generated model. By using varying partitions (e.g., from large to small) during the virtual sample generation it should be possible to directly enforce the learning of a consistent hierarchical model with different levels of locality.

Acknowledgement. This work was supported by the German Research Foundation (DFG EH 224/6-1).

References

1. Armato, S.G., et al.: The lung image database consortium (LIDC) and image database resource initiative (IDRI): a completed reference database of lung nodules on CT scans. Med. Phys. **38**(2), 915–931 (2011)
2. Balzano, L., Wright, S.J.: On GROUSE and incremental SVD. In: Computational Advances in Multi-sensor Adaptive Processing (CAMSAP), pp. 1–4 (2013)

3. Cai, J.F., Candès, E.J., Shen, Z.: A singular value thresholding algorithm for matrix completion. SIAM J. Optim. **20**(4), 1956–1982 (2010)
4. Candès, E.J., Recht, B.: Exact matrix completion via convex optimization. Found. Comput. Math. **9**(6), 717–772 (2009)
5. Cerrolaza, J.J., Reyes, M., Summers, R.M., Ballester, M.A.G., Linguraru, M.G.: Automatic multi-resolution shape modeling of multi-organ structures. Med. Image Anal. **25**(1), 11–21 (2015)
6. Cootes, T.F., Taylor, C.J.: Combining point distribution models with shape models based on finite element analysis. Image Vis. Comput. **13**(5), 403–409 (1995)
7. Cootes, T.F., Taylor, C.J., Cooper, D.H., Graham, J.: Active shape models-their training and application. Comput. Vis. Image Underst. **61**(1), 38–59 (1995)
8. Davatzikos, C., Tao, X., Shen, D.: Hierarchical active shape models, using the wavelet transform. IEEE Trans. Med. Imaging **22**(3), 414–423 (2003)
9. Davies, R.H., Twining, C.J., Cootes, T.F., Waterton, J.C., Taylor, C.J.: A minimum description length approach to statistical shape modeling. IEEE Trans. Med. Imaging **21**(5), 525–537 (2002)
10. Ehrhardt, J., Werner, R., Schmidt-Richberg, A., Handels, H.: Statistical modeling of 4D respiratory lung motion using diffeomorphic image registration. IEEE Trans. Med. Imaging **30**(2), 251–265 (2011)
11. Friedel, I., Schröder, P., Desbrun, M.: Unconstrained spherical parameterization. J. Graph. GPU Game Tools **12**(1), 17–26 (2007)
12. He, J., Balzano, L., Szlam, A.: Incremental gradient on the grassmannian for online foreground and background separation in subsampled video. CVPR **2012**, 1568–1575 (2012)
13. Heimann, T., Meinzer, H.P.: Statistical shape models for 3D medical image segmentation: a review. Med. Image Anal. **13**(4), 543–563 (2009)
14. Kennedy, R., Taylor, C.J., Balzano, L.: Online completion of ill-conditioned low-rank matrices. In: IEEE Global Conference on Signal and Information Processing (GlobalSIP), pp. 507–511 (2014)
15. Koikkalainen, J., Tolli, T., Lauerma, K., Antila, K., Mattila, E., Lilja, M., Lotjonen, J.: Methods of artificial enlargement of the training set for statistical shape models. IEEE Trans. Med. Imaging **27**(11), 1643–1654 (2008)
16. Kumar, R., Banerjee, A., Vemuri, B.C., Pfister, H.: Maximizing all margins: pushing face recognition with kernel plurality. ICCV **2011**, 2375–2382 (2011)
17. Lai, R.Y., Yuen, P.C.: ProPPA: a fast algorithm for ℓ_1 minimization and low-rank matrix completion, May 2012. arXiv preprint arXiv:1205.0088
18. Leopardi, P.: A partition of the unit sphere into regions of equal area and small diameter. Electr. Trans. Numer. Anal. **25**(12), 309–327 (2006)
19. Lu, J., Tan, Y.P., Wang, G.: Discriminative multi-manifold analysis for face recognition from a single training sample per person. ICCV **2011**, 1943–1950 (2011)
20. Lüthi, M., Albrecht, T., Vetter, T.: Building shape models from lousy data. In: Yang, G.-Z., Hawkes, D., Rueckert, D., Noble, A., Taylor, C. (eds.) MICCAI 2009, Part II. LNCS, vol. 5762, pp. 1–8. Springer, Heidelberg (2009)
21. Mishra, B.: A Riemannian approach to large-scale constrained least-squares with symmetries. Ph.D. thesis, Université de Namur (2014)
22. Ngo, T., Saad, Y.: Scaled gradients on grassmann manifolds for matrix completion. NIPS **2012**, 1412–1420 (2012)
23. Nordstrøm, M.M., Larsen, M., Sierakowski, J., Stegmann, M.B.: The IMM face database-an annotated dataset of 240 face images. Technical report, Technical University of Denmark, DTU Informatics (2004)

24. Onofrey, J., Papademetris, X., Staib, L.: Low-dimensional non-rigid image registration using statistical deformation models from semi-supervised training data. IEEE Trans. Med. Imaging **34**(7), 1522–1532 (2015)

25. Rueckert, D., Frangi, A.F., Schnabel, J.A.: Automatic construction of 3D statistical deformation models using non-rigid registration. In: Niessen, W.J., Viergever, M.A. (eds.) MICCAI 2001. LNCS, vol. 2208, pp. 77–84. Springer, Heidelberg (2001)

26. Shamir, A.: A survey on mesh segmentation techniques. Comput. Graph. Forum **27**(6), 1539–1556 (2008)

27. Turk, M.A., Pentland, A.P.: Face recognition using eigenfaces. In: CVPR 1991, pp. 586–591. IEEE (1991)

28. Werner, R., Schmidt-Richberg, A., Handels, H., Ehrhardt, J.: Estimation of lung motion fields in 4D CT data by variational non-linear intensity-based registration: a comparison and evaluation study. Phys. Med. Biol. **59**, 4247–4260 (2014)

29. Zhang, D., Chen, S., Zhou, Z.H.: A new face recognition method based on SVD perturbation for single example image per person. Appl. Math. Comput. **163**(2), 895–907 (2005)

30. Zhao, Z., Aylward, S.R., Teoh, E.-K.: A novel 3D partitioned active shape model for segmentation of brain MR images. In: Duncan, J.S., Gerig, G. (eds.) MICCAI 2005. LNCS, vol. 3749, pp. 221–228. Springer, Heidelberg (2005)

31. Zhu, P., Zhang, L., Hu, Q., Shiu, S.C.K.: Multi-scale patch based collaborative representation for face recognition with margin distribution optimization. In: Fitzgibbon, A., Lazebnik, S., Perona, P., Sato, Y., Schmid, C. (eds.) ECCV 2012, Part I. LNCS, vol. 7572, pp. 822–835. Springer, Heidelberg (2012)

Chained Predictions Using Convolutional Neural Networks

Georgia Gkioxari[1]([✉]), Alexander Toshev[2], and Navdeep Jaitly[2]

[1] University of California, Berkeley, USA
gkioxari@eecs.berkeley.edu
[2] Google Inc., Mountain View, USA
toshev@google.com, ndjaitly@google.com

Abstract. In this work, we present an adaptation of the sequence-to-sequence model for structured vision tasks. In this model, the output variables for a given input are predicted sequentially using neural networks. The prediction for each output variable depends not only on the input but also on the previously predicted output variables. The model is applied to spatial localization tasks and uses convolutional neural networks (CNNs) for processing input images and a multi-scale deconvolutional architecture for making spatial predictions at each step. We explore the impact of weight sharing with a recurrent connection matrix between consecutive predictions, and compare it to a formulation where these weights are not tied. Untied weights are particularly suited for problems with a fixed sized structure, where different classes of output are predicted at different steps. We show that chain models achieve top performing results on human pose estimation from images and videos.

Keywords: Structured tasks · Chain model · Human pose estimation

1 Introduction

Structured prediction methods have long been used for various vision tasks, such as segmentation, object detection and human pose estimation, to deal with complicated constraints and relationships between the different output variables predicted from an input image. For example, in human pose estimation the location of one body part is constrained by the locations of most of the other body parts. Conditional Random Fields, Latent Structural Support Vector Machines and related methods are popular examples of structured output prediction models that model dependencies among output variables.

A major drawback of such models is the need to hand-design the structure of the model in order to capture important problem-specific dependencies amongst the different output variables and at the same time allow for tractable inference. For the sake of efficiency, a specific form of conditional independence amongst output variables is often assumed. For example, in human pose estimation, a predefined kinematic body model is often used to assume that each body part is independent of all the others except for the ones it is attached to.

© Springer International Publishing AG 2016
B. Leibe et al. (Eds.): ECCV 2016, Part IV, LNCS 9908, pp. 728–743, 2016.
DOI: 10.1007/978-3-319-46493-0_44

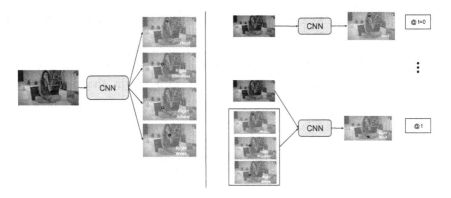

Fig. 1. A description of our model for the task of body pose estimation compared to pure feed forward nets. **Left**: Feed forward networks make independent predictions for all body parts simultaneously and fail to capture contextual cues for accurate predictions. **Right**: Body parts are predicted sequentially, given an image and all previously predicted parts. Here, we show the chain model for the prediction of *Right Wrist*, where predictions of all other joints in the sequence are used along with the image.

To alleviate some of the above modeling simplifications, structured prediction problems have been solved with sequential decision making, where all earlier predictions influence later predictions. The SEARN algorithm [1] introduced a very general formulation for this approach, and demonstrated its application to various natural language processing tasks using losses from binary classifiers. A related model recently introduced, the sequence-to-sequence model, has been applied to various sequence mapping tasks, such as machine translation, speech recognition and image caption generation [2–4]. In all these models the output is a sentence - where the words of the sentence are predicted in a first to last order. This model maximizes the log probability for output sequence conditioned on the input, by decomposing the probability of an output sequence with the multiplicative chain rule of probability; at each index of the output, the next prediction is made conditioned on all previous outputs and the input. A recurrent neural network is used at every step of the output and this allows parameter sharing across all the output steps.

In this paper we borrow ideas from the above sequence-to-sequence model and propose to extend it to more general structured outputs encountered in computer vision – human pose estimation from a single image and video. The contributions of this work are as follows:

- A *chain model for structured outputs*, such as human pose estimation. The body part locations are predicted sequentially, where the prediction of each body part is dependent on *all previously predicted* body parts (See Fig. 1). The model is formulated using a neural network in which the feature extraction and prediction models are learned end-to-end. Since we apply the model to spatial labelling tasks we use convolutional neural networks in both the inputs and outputs. The output convolutional neural networks is a multi-scale

deconvolution that we call *deception* because of its relationship to deconvolution [5,6] and inception models [7].

- We demonstrate *two formulations of the chain model* - one without weight
sharing between different predictors (poses in images) to allow semantic-
specific flow of information and the other with weight sharing to enforce
recurrence in time (poses in videos). The latter model is a RNN similar to
the sequence-to-sequence model.

The above model achieves top performing results on the MPII human pose
dataset – 86.1 % PCKh. We achieve state-of-the art performance for pose estimation on the PennAction video dataset – 91.8 % PCK.

2   Related Work

Structured output prediction as sequence prediction. The use of sequential models
for structured predictions is not new. The SEARN algorithm [1] laid down a
broad framework for such models in which a sequence of actions is generated by
conditioning the next action on previous actions and the data. The optimization
method proposed in SEARN is based on iterative improvement over policies
using reinforcement learning.

A similar class of models are the more recent sequence-to-sequence models [2,8] that map an input sequence to an output sequence of fixed vocabulary.
The models produce output variables, one at a time, conditioned on inputs and
previous output variables. A next-step loss function is computed at each step,
using a recurrent neural network. Sequence-to-sequence models have been shown
to be very effective at a variety of language tasks including machine translation [2], speech recognition [3], image captioning [4] and parsing [9]. In this
paper we use the same idea of chaining predictions for structured prediction on
two vision problems - human pose estimation in individual frames and in video
sequences. However, as exemplified in the pose estimation case, since we have a
fixed output structure we are not limited to using recurrent models.

In the pose prediction problem, we used a fixed ordering of joints, that is
motivated by the kinematics of the human body. Prior work in sequential modelling has explored the idea of choosing the best ordering for a task [10–12]. For
example, Vinyals et al. [10] explored this question and found that for some problems, such as geometric problems, choosing an intuitive ordering of the outputs
results in slightly better performance. However for simpler problems most order-
ings were able to perform equally well. For our problem, the number of joints
being predicted is small, and tree based ordering of joints from head to torso to
the extremities seems to be the intuitively correct ordering.

Human pose estimation. Human pose estimation has been one of the major
playgrounds for structured prediction models in computer vision. Historically,
most of the research has focused on graphical models, starting with tree-based
decompositions [13–16] motivated by kinematic models of the human body.

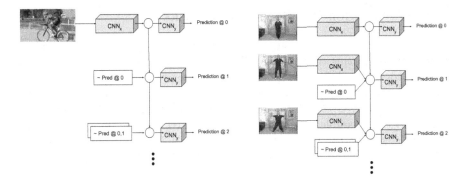

Fig. 2. A visualization of our chain model. **Left:** single image case. **Right:** video case. In both cases, an image is encoded with a CNN (CNN$_x$). At each step, the previous output variables are combined with the hidden state, through the sequential modules. A CNN decoder (CNN$_y$) makes predictions each step, t. There are two differences between the two cases: (i) for video CNN$_x$ receives at each step a frame as an input, while for single image there is no such input; (ii) for video CNN$_y$ share parameters across steps, while for single image the parameters are untied.

Many of these models assume conditional independence of a body part from all other parts except the parent part as defined by the kinematic body model (see pictorial structure model [13]). This simplification comes at a performance cost and has been addressed in various ways: mixture model of parts [17]; mixtures of full body models [18]; higher-order spatial relationships [19]; image dependent pictorial structures [20–23]. Like these above approaches, we assume an order among the body parts. However, this ordering is used only to decompose the joint probability of the output joints into a particular ordering of variables in the chain rule of probability, and not to make assumptions about the structure of the probability distribution. Because no simplifying assumptions are made about the joint distribution of the output variables it leads to a more expressive model, as exemplified in the experimental section. The model is only constrained by the ability of neural networks to model the conditional probability distributions that arise from the particular ordering of the variables chosen. In addition, the correlations among parts are learned through a set of non-linear operations instead of imposing binary term constraints on hand-designed image features (e.g. RGB values, location) as done in CRFs.

It is worth noting that there have been models for pose estimation where parts are sequentially refined [24–27]. In these models an initial prediction is made of all the parts; in subsequent steps, all part predictions are refined based on the image and earlier part predictions. However, note that the predictions are initially independent of each other.

3   Chain Models for Structured Tasks

Chain models exploit the structure of the tasks they are designed to tackle by sequentially predicting their outputs. To capture this structure each output prediction is conditioned on all outputs predicted already. This philosophy has been exploited in language processing where sentences, expressed as word sequences, need to be predicted [2,8] from inputs. In recent automatic image captioning work [4,28], for example, a sentence Y is generated from an image X by maximizing the likelihood $P(Y \mid X)$. The chain rule is applied, consecutively to model each output Y_t (here a word) given the image X and all the previous outputs $Y_{<t}$ in the output sequence.

In computer vision, recognition problems, such as segmentation, detection and pose estimation, demonstrate rich structure with complex dependencies. In this work, we model this structure with a simple and efficient recognition machine that makes little to no assumptions about the structure, other than the ability of a neural network to model complex, incremental conditional distributions.

Mathematically, let $Y = \{Y_t\}_{t=0}^{T-1}$ be the T objects to be detected. For example, for the pose prediction problem, Y_t is the location of the t-th body part. In video prediction problems, Y_t is the location of an object in the t-th frame of a video. Using the chain rule we decompose $P(Y = y \mid X)$ as follows:

$$P(Y = y \mid X) = P(Y_0 = y_0 \mid X) \prod_{t=1}^{T-1} P(Y_t = y_t \mid X, y_0, ..., y_{t-1}) \qquad (1)$$

From the above equation, we see that the likelihood of assigning value y_t to the t-th variable is given by $P(Y_t = y_t \mid X, y_0, ..., y_{t-1})$, and depends on both the input X as well as the assignment of previous variables. In this work, we model the likelihood $P(Y_t = y_t \mid X, y_0, ..., y_{t-1})$ with a convolutional neural network (CNN). The direct dependence of the current prediction on the ground truth values of previous variables allows for the model to capture all necessary relationships without making any assumption about the joint distributions of all the variables, other than assuming that each successive conditional distribution, $P(Y_t = y_t \mid X, y_0, ..., y_{t-1})$, can be computed with a neural network.

3.1   Chain Models for Single Images

In the case of single images, the input X is the image while the t-th variable Y_t can be, for example, the location of the t-th object in image X (see Fig. 2).

The probability of each step in the decomposition of Eq. (1) is defined through a hidden state h_t at step t, which carries information about the input as well as states at previous steps. In addition it incorporates the values $y_{<t}$ from previous steps. The final probability for variable Y_t is computed from the hidden state:

$$h_t = \sigma(w_t^h * h_{t-1} + \sum_{i=0}^{t-1} w_{i,t}^y * e(y_i)) \qquad (2)$$

$$P(Y_t = y_t \mid X, y_0, ..., y_{t-1}) = \text{Softmax}(m_t(h_t)) \qquad (3)$$

In the above equation, the previous variables are first transformed through a full neural net $e(\cdot)$. Parameters w_t^h and $w_{i,t}^y$ then linearly transform the previous hidden state and a function of previous output variables, $e(\cdot)$, and a non-linearity σ is then applied to each dimension of this output. The nonlinearity σ of choice is a Rectified Linear Unit. Finally, $*$ denotes multiplication. In image applications, however, the hidden state h can be a feature map and the prediction y a location in the image. In such cases, $*$ denotes convolution and e is a CNN. Note that, as long as we feed in just the last variable y_{t-1} in this equation, the recurrent equation insures that we condition on the entire history of joints. However feeding in more of the previous joints makes it easier for the model to learn the conditional distributions directly. In the computation of the conditional probability of y_t from h_t we use another neural net m_t, which produces scores for potential object location. By applying a softmax function over these scores we convert them to a probability distribution over locations.

The initial state h_0 is computed based solely on the input X: $h_0 = \mathrm{CNN}(X)$.

This formulation is reminiscent of recurrent networks (RNNs), the equations define how to transform a state from one step to the next. We differ, however, from RNNs in one important aspect, the parameters in Eqs. (2–3) are not necessarily tied. Indeed, parameters w_t^h and $w_{i,t}^y$ are indexed by the step. This design choice is appropriate for tasks such as human pose estimation where the number of outputs T is fixed and where each step is different from the rest. In other applications, e.g. video, we tie these parameters: $w_t^h = w_0^h$ and $w_{i,t}^y = w_{i,0}^y$, $\forall i, t$.

3.2   Chain Models for Videos

For videos, the input is a sequence of images $X = \{X_t\}_{t=0}^{T-1}$ (Fig. 2). Predictions are made at each step, as the images are fed in. At each step t, we make predictions for the image X_t at that step, using the past images, and the past output variables. Thus, we modify the equation for the hidden state as follows:

$$h_t = \sigma(w_t^h * h_{t-1} + \mathrm{CNN}(X_t) + \sum_{i=t-T_H}^{t-1} w_{t-i,t}^y * e(y_i)) \qquad (4)$$

where we add features extracted from image X_t using a CNN. The final probability is computed as in Eq. (3).

In videos we often need to predict the same type of information at each step, e.g. location of all body joints of the person in the current frame. As such, the predictors can have the same weights. Thus, we tie the parameters w_t^h, $w_{i,t}^y$, and m_t together, which results in a convolutional RNN.

As before, the connections from hidden state at the previous step guarantees that the prediction at each time step uses output variables from all previous steps, as long as the previous output variable Y_{t-1} is fed in at time t. However, feeding in a larger time horizon T_H leads to an easier learning problem.

3.3 Improved Learning with Scheduled Sampling

So far, we have described the method as using the input and only ground truth values of the previous output variables when making a prediction for the next output variable. However, it has previously been observed that for sequence-to-sequence models overfitting can be mitigated by probabilistically substituting ground truth values of previous output variables with samples from the probability distribution predicted by the model [29]. One challenge that arises in this is that, at the start of the training, the predicted probability distributions are wildly inaccurate and thus, feeding in samples from the distribution is counter-productive. The authors of [29] propose a method, called *scheduled sampling*, that uses an annealing schedule that feeds in only the ground truth outputs at the start of the training and increases the rate of sampling from the predictions of the model towards the end of the training. We use the idea of scheduled sampling in our paper and find that it leads to improved results.

4 Experimental Evaluation

To evaluate the proposed model, we apply it on human pose estimation, which is challenging and of great interest due to the complex relationship among body parts. In the single image case, we use the chain model to capture the structure of pose in space, i.e. how the location of a part influences others. For the videos, our model captures the constraints and dynamics of the body pose in time.

Tasks and Datasets. For our single image experiments we use the MPII Human Pose dataset [30], which consists of about 40 K instances of people performing various actions. All frames come with a maximum of 16 annotated joints (e.g. *Top Head, Right Ankle, Left Knee*, etc.). For the task of pose estimation in video we use the Penn Action dataset [31], which consists of 2326 video sequences of people performing various sports. All frames come with a maximum of 13 annotated joints. During evaluation, if a joint prediction lies within a predefined distance, proportional to the size of the person, from the ground truth location it is counted as a correct detection. This metric is called PCK [30,32].

Our model is illustrated in Fig. 2. We experiment with two choices for CNN_x, the network which encodes the input image. First, a shallow CNN which consists of six layers each followed by a rectified linear unit [33] and Batch Normalization [34]. The first four layers include max pooling with stride 2, leading to an effective stride of 16. This network is described in Fig. 3. Second, we experiment with a deeper network of identical architecture to inception-v3 [35]. We discard the last convolutional layer of inception-v3 and connect the output to CNN_y.

The CNN_y network decodes the hidden state to a heatmap over possible locations of a single body part. This heatmap is converted to a probability distribution over locations using a softmax. The network consists of two towers of deconvolutional layers each of which increases the width and height of the feature maps by a factor of 2. Note that the deconvolutional towers are multi-scale - in one layer, different filter sizes are used and combined together. This is similar to the inception model [7], with the difference that here it is applied with the deconvolution operation, and hence we call it *deception*.

4.1 Pose Estimation from a Single Image

In this application case, we use the chain model to predict the joints sequentially. The sequence with which the joints are processed is fixed and is motivated by the marginal distributions of the joints. In particular, we sort the joints in descending order according to the detection rates of an unchained feed forward net. This allows for the easy cases to be processed first (e.g. *Torso, Head*) while the harder cases (e.g. *Wrist, Ankle*) are processed last, and as a result use the contextual information from the joints predicted before them.

Inference. At test time, we use beam search to infer the optimal location of the joints. Note that exact inference is infeasible, due to the size of the search space (a total of $(HW)^T$ possible solutions, where $H \times W$ is the size of the prediction heatmap and T are the number of joints). At each step t, the best B predictions are stored, where each prediction is the sequence of the first t joints. The quality of a full body pose prediction is measured by its log-probability, which is the sum of the log-probabilities corresponding to the individual joint predictions.

An exact implementation of chain rule conditions on predictions made at every step. Alternatively, one could skip the non-differentiable sampling operation and use the probability distributions directly. Even though this is not an

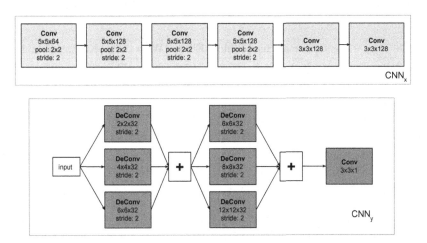

Fig. 3. Description of the components of our network, CNN_x and CNN_y. Each box represents a convolutional or deconvolutional layer, where $w \times h \times f$ denotes the width w, the height h of the filters and f denotes the number of filters. In each layer the filter is applied with stride 1 if not noted otherwise. Finally, in each layer after the filtering operation a ReLU and batch normalization are applied.

exact application of the chain rule, it allows for the gradients to flow back to the output of each task. We found that this approximation led to very similar performance - it slowed down training time by a factor of 3 and sped up inference by a factor of B.

Learning Details. We use an SGD solver with momentum to learn the model parameters by optimizing the loss. The loss for one image X is defined as the sum of losses for individual joints. The loss for the k-th joint is the cross entropy between the predicted probability P_k over locations of the joint and the ground-truth probability P_k^{gt}. The former is defined based on the heatmap h_k output by CNN$_y$ for the k-th joint: $P_k(x,y) = \frac{e^{h_k(x,y)}}{\sum_{(x',y')} e^{h_k(x',y')}}$. The latter is defined based on a distance r – all locations within radius r of the ground-truth joint location are assigned same nonzero probability $P_k^{\text{gt}}(x,y) = 1/N$, all other locations are assigned probability 0. N is a normalizer guaranteeing P_k^{gt} is a probability.

Table 1. PCKh performance on the MPII validation set. Rows 1 and 2 show results for 9-layered CNN models, with multi-scale (deception) and single scale deconvolutions. Row 3 show results for a 24-layer model with deception, but without chained outputs. Row 4 shows results for our chain model with comparable depth and number of parameters as the 24-layer model, but with chained predictions. We observe clear improvement over the baselines. The performance is further improved using multiple crops of the input at test time, at row 5. Row 6 shows the performance of the oracle, where the correct values of previous output is fed into the network at each step. Row 7 and 8 show the performance for a base and chain model when inception-v3, pre trained on ImageNet, is used as the encoder network. Using a deeper architecture leads to substantially improved results across all joints.

PCKh (%)	Torso	Head	Shldr	Elbow	Wrist	Hip	Knee	Ankle	Mean
Base Network	86.8	91.9	85.8	74.5	69.0	71.1	61.4	50.6	73.9
Base Net. w/single deconv.	86.0	91.7	85.1	72.9	68.0	69.4	59.7	48.5	72.6
Very Deep Base Network	88.1	92.0	86.1	74.1	67.7	73.7	64.7	58.0	75.6
Chain Model	86.8	93.2	88.3	79.4	74.6	77.8	71.4	65.2	79.6
Chain Model w/multi-crop	88.7	94.4	90.0	82.6	78.6	80.2	74.8	68.4	82.2
Oracle Chain Model	87.2	95.9	93.4	83.3	82.3	95.2	77.6	72.3	85.9
Inception Base Network	91.1	95.0	90.2	81.0	77.4	77.2	73.7	64.6	81.3
Inception Chain Model	91.7	95.7	92.2	85.3	82.2	82.9	80.0	72.4	85.3

The final loss for X reads as follows:

$$L(\{h_k\}_{k=0}^{T-1}) = \sum_{k=0}^{T-1} \sum_{(x,y)} P_k^{\text{gt}}(x,y) \log P_k(x,y) \tag{5}$$

We use batch size of 16; initial learning rate of 0.003 that was decayed every 100 K steps (50 K for the inception model); radius of $r = 0.01 \times (W+H)/2$. The model was trained for 120 K iterations (55 K for the inception model). Our images are rescaled to 224×224 (299×299 for the inception model). The weights of the network are initialized by sampling from a normal distribution of zero mean and 0.01 standard deviation. For the inception model, we initialize the weights of CNN_x with weights from an ImageNet model.

Results. Table 1 shows the PCKh performance on the MPII validation set of our chain model and our baseline variants.

Rows 1, 2 & 3 show the performance of pure feed forward networks for the task in question. The 1st row shows the performance of a 9-layer network, shallow $\text{CNN}_x + \text{CNN}_y$, which we call base network. The 2nd row is a similar network, where each deconvolutional tower, which we call *deception*, in CNN_y is replaced by a single deconvolution. The difference in performance shows that multi-scale deconvolutions lead to a better and very competitive baseline. Finally, the 3rd row shows the performance of a very deep network consisting of 24 layers. This network has the same number of parameters and the same depth as our chain model and serves as the baseline which we improve upon using the chain model.

Row 4 shows the performance of our chain model. This model improves significantly over all the baselines. The biggest gains are observed for *Wrists* and *Ankles*, which is a clear indication that conditioning on the predictions of previous joints provides cues for better localization.

Row 5 shows the performance of the chain model with multi-crop evaluation, where at test time we average the predictions from flipping and jittering of the input image.

Row 6 shows the performance of an *oracle* chain model. For this model, at each step t we use the oracle (ground truth) locations of all previous joints. This model is an estimate of the upper bound performance of our chain model, as it predicts the location of a joint given perfect knowledge of the location of all other joints which precede it in the sequence.

Row 7 shows the performance of the inception base network, $\text{CNN}_x + \text{CNN}_y$, where CNN_x is the inception-v3 [35]. We observe significant gains when using the inception-v3 architecture compared to a shallower 6-layer network for the encoder network, at the expense of more computations.

Row 8 shows the performance of the inception chain model. For both the inception base and chain model we use multi-crop evaluation. In both cases, the inception-v3 parameters were initialized with weights from an ImageNet model. The inception chain model leads to significant gains compared to its base network (row 7). The improvements are more evident for the joints of *Wrist, Knee, Ankle*.

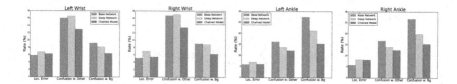

Fig. 4. Error analysis of the predictions made by the base network (blue), the very deep model (red) and our chain model (green), for *Wrist* and *Ankle*. Each figure shows the error rates, categorized in three classes, localization error, confusion with other joints and confusion with the background. (Color figure online)

Error Analysis. Digging deeper into the models, we perform an error analysis for the base network $CNN_x + CNN_y$, the very deep network and our chain model. For this analysis, the 6-layer encoder network CNN_x is used for all models. Similar to [36], we categorize the erroneous predictions into the three distinct classes: (a) localization error, i.e. the prediction is within $[\alpha, \beta] \times HeadSize$ of the true location, (b) confusion with other joints, i.e. the prediction is within $\alpha \times HeadSize$ of a different joint, and (c) confusion with the background, i.e. the prediction lies somewhere else in the image. According to PCKh, a prediction is correct if it falls within $0.3 \times HeadSize$. We set $\beta = 0.5$.

Figure 4 shows the error analysis for the hardest joints, namely *Wrist* and *Ankle*. Each plot consists of three sets of bars, the rates for error localization, confusion with other joints and confusion with background. According to the plots, the chain model reduces the misses due to confusion with other joints and the background. For *Wrists*, the confusion with other joints is the dominating error mode, and further analysis shows that the main source of confusion comes mainly from the opposite wrist and then the nearby joints. For *Ankles*, the biggest error mode comes from confusion with the background, which is not surprising since lower legs are usually heavily occluded and lack strong appearance cues.

Figure 5 shows some examples of our predictions on the MPII dataset.

Fig. 5. Examples of predictions by our chain model on the MPII dataset.

Table 2. Performance on the MPII test set. A comparison of our chain model, with a shallow 6 layer and an inception-v3 encoder, with leading approaches in the field.

Method	Head	Shoulder	Elbow	Wrist	Hip	Knee	Ankle	Total
Carreira et al. [26]	95.7	91.7	81.7	72.4	82.8	73.2	66.4	81.3
Tompson et al. [38]	96.1	91.9	83.9	77.8	80.9	72.3	64.8	82.0
Hu and Ramanan [39]	95.0	91.6	83.0	76.6	81.9	74.5	69.5	82.4
Pishchulin et al. [40]	94.1	90.2	83.4	77.3	82.6	75.7	68.6	82.4
Lifshitz et al. [41]	97.8	93.3	85.7	80.4	85.3	76.6	70.2	85.0
Wei et al. [27]	97.8	95.0	88.7	84.0	88.4	82.8	79.4	88.5
Newell et al. [37]	97.6	95.4	90.0	85.2	88.7	85.0	80.6	89.4
Chain model	93.8	91.8	84.2	79.4	84.4	77.9	70.7	84.1
Inception Chain Model	97.9	93.2	86.7	82.1	85.2	81.5	74.0	86.1

Comparison to Other Approaches. We evaluate our approach on the MPII test set and compare to other methods on the task of pose estimation from a single image. Table 2 shows the results of our approach and other leading methods in the field. We show the performance of both versions of our chain model, using a shallow 6-layer encoder as well as the inception-v3 architecture. For the shallow chain model, we ensemble two chain models trained at different input scales. For the inception chain model, no ensembling was performed.

The leading approaches by Wei *et al.* [27] and Newell *et al.* [37] rely on iteratively refining predictions. In particular, predictions are made initially for all joints independently. These predictions, which are quite poor (see [27]), are fed subsequently into a network for further refinement. Our approach produces only one set of predictions via a single chain model and does not refine them further. One could combine the two ideas, the one of chained predictions and the one of iterative refinement, to achieve better results.

4.2 Pose Estimation from Videos

Our chain models in time are described in Eq. 4 and illustrated in Fig. 2. Here, the task is to localize body parts in time across video frames. The output variables from the joints of the previous frames are used as inputs to make a prediction for the joints in the current frame. We apply the chaining in two different ways - first, only in time, where each joint is predicted independently of the other joints (as in our baseline models), but chaining is done in time, and second, with chaining both in time and in joints.

Pose Estimation in Time. As shown in Fig. 2, the chain model sequentially processes the video frames. The predictions at the previous time steps are used through a recurrent module in order to make a prediction at the current time step. Again, we use a heatmap to encode the location of a part in the frame.

Table 3. PCK performance on the Penn Action test set. We show the performance of our chain model for two choices of the time horizon T_H and compare against the per-frame model, with and without temporal smoothing, and a baseline convolutional RNN model. The chain model with $T_H = 3$ improves the localization accuracy across all joints. The method by Nie *et al.* [42] is shown for comparison.

PCK (%)	Head	Shldr	Elbow	Wrist	Hip	Knee	Ankle	Mean
Nie *et al.* [42]	64.2	55.4	33.8	24.4	56.4	54.1	48.0	48.0
Base Network	94.1	90.3	84.2	83.5	88.7	87.2	87.7	87.5
Base Network w/smoothing	93.1	91.8	85.7	78.8	90.2	91.9	91.1	88.6
RNN	95.3	92.5	87.9	87.5	91.1	89.8	90.1	90.1
Chain Model, $T_H = 1$	95.8	93.2	88.9	89.6	91.3	89.8	91.2	91.0
Chain Model, $T_H = 3$	95.8	94.1	90.0	90.2	91.3	90.6	91.8	91.7
Chain Model in time & joints, $T_H = 3$	95.6	93.8	90.4	90.7	91.8	90.8	91.5	91.8

The details of our learning procedure are identical to the ones described for the single image case. The only difference is that each training example is now a sequence of images $X = \{X_t\}_{t=0}^{T-1}$ each of which has a ground-truth pose. Thus, the loss for X is the sum over the losses for each frame. Each frame loss is defined as in the case of single image (see Eq. (5)).

We train our model for 120 K iterations using SGD with momentum of 0.9, a batch size of 6 and a learning rate of 0.003 with step decay 100 K. Images are rescaled to 256 × 256. A relative radius of $r = 0.03$ is used for the loss. The weights are initialized randomly from a normal distribution with zero mean and standard deviation of 0.01.

Table 3 shows the performance on the Penn Action test set. For consistency with previous work on the dataset [42], a prediction is considered correct if it lies within $0.2 \times \max(s_h, s_w)$, where s_h, s_w is the height and width, respectively, of the instance in question. We refer to this metric as PCK. (Note that this is a weaker criterion than the one used on the MPII dataset). We show the per frame performance, as produced by a base network $\text{CNN}_x + \text{CNN}_y$ trained to predict the location of the joints at each frame. We also provide results after applying temporal smoothing to the predictions via the Viterbi algorithm where the transition function is the Euclidean distance of the same joints in two neighboring frames. Additionally, we show the performance of a convolutional RNN with $w_{i,t}^y = 0, \forall i, t$ in Eq. 4. This model corresponds to a standard convolutional RNN where the output variables of the previous time steps are not connected to the hidden state. All networks have roughly the same numbers of parameters, to ensure a fair comparison. For our chain model in time, we show results for two choices of time horizon T_H. Namely, $T_H = 1$, where predictions of only the previous time step are being considered and $T_H = 3$, where predictions of the

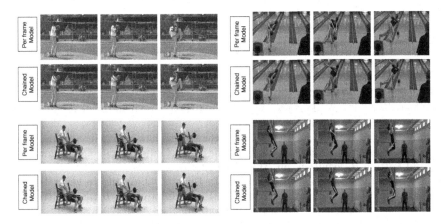

Fig. 6. Examples of predictions on the Penn Action dataset. Predictions by the per frame model (top) and by the chain model (bottom) are shown in each example block.

past 3 frames are considered at each time step. Finally, we show the performance of a chain model in time and in joints, with a time horizon of $T_H = 3$.

We compare to previous work on the Penn Action dataset [42]. This model uses action specific pose models, with shallow hand-crafted features, and improves upon Yang and Ramanan [32].

We observe a gain in performance compared to the per frame CNN as well as the RNN across all joints. Interestingly, chain models show bigger improvement for arms compared to legs. This is due to the fact that the people in the videos play sports which involve big arm movements, while the legs are mostly unoccluded and less kinematic. In addition, we see that $T_H = 3$ leads to better performance, which is not surprising since the model makes a decision about the location of the joints at the current time step based on observation from 3 past frames. We did not observe additional gains for $T_H > 3$. Chaining in time and in joints does not improve performance even further, possibly due to the already high accuracy achieved by the chain model in time.

Figure 6 shows examples of predictions by our chain model on the Penn Action dataset. We also show the predictions made by the per frame detector. We see that the chain model is able to disambiguate right-left confusions which occur often due to the constant motion of the person while performing actions, while the per frame detector switches very often between erroneous detections.

5   Conclusions

In this paper, motivated by sequence-to-sequence models, we show how chained predictions can lead to a powerful tool for structured vision tasks. Chain models allow us to sidestep any assumptions about the joint distribution of the output variables, other than the capacity of a neural network to model conditional distributions. We prove this point experimentally by showing top performing results on the task of pose estimation from images and videos.

References

1. Daumé Iii, H., Langford, J., Marcu, D.: Search-based structured prediction. Mach. Learn. **75**(3), 297–325 (2009)
2. Sutskever, I., Vinyals, O., Le, Q.V.: Sequence to sequence learning with neural networks. In: NIPS (2014)
3. Chan, W., Jaitly, N., Le, Q.V., Vinyals, O.: Listen, attend and spell. arXiv preprint arXiv:1508.01211 (2015)
4. Vinyals, O., Toshev, A., Bengio, S., Erhan, D.: Show and tell: a neural image caption generator. In: Proceedings of the IEEE Conference on Computer Vision and Pattern Recognition, pp. 3156–3164 (2015)
5. Dosovitskiy, A., Tobias Springenberg, J., Brox, T.: Learning to generate chairs with convolutional neural networks. In: Proceedings of the IEEE Conference on Computer Vision and Pattern Recognition, pp. 1538–1546 (2015)
6. Long, J., Shelhamer, E., Darrell, T.: Fully convolutional networks for semantic segmentation. In: Proceedings of the IEEE Conference on Computer Vision and Pattern Recognition, pp. 3431–3440 (2015)
7. Szegedy, C., Liu, W., Jia, Y., Sermanet, P., Reed, S., Anguelov, D., Erhan, D., Vanhoucke, V., Rabinovich, A.: Going deeper with convolutions. In: CVPR (2015)
8. Bahdanau, D., Cho, K., Bengio, Y.: Neural machine translation by jointly learning to align and translate. CoRR abs/1409.0473 (2014)
9. Vinyals, O., Kaiser, L., Koo, T., Petrov, S., Sutskever, I., Hinton, G.: Grammar as a foreign language. In: Advances in Neural Information Processing Systems, pp. 2755–2763 (2015)
10. Vinyals, O., Bengio, S., Kudlur, M.: Order Matters: sequence to sequence for sets. ArXiv e-prints, November 2015
11. Goldberg, Y., Elhadad, M.:An efficient algorithm for easy-first non-directional dependency parsing. In: Human Language Technologies: The 2010 Annual Conference of the North American Chapter of the Association for Computational Linguistics, Association for Computational Linguistics, pp. 742–750 (2010)
12. Ross, S., Gordon, G.J., Bagnell, J.A.: A reduction of imitation learning and structured prediction to no-regret online learning. ArXiv e-prints, November 2010
13. Felzenszwalb, P.F., Huttenlocher, D.P.: Pictorial structures for object recognition. Int. J. Comput. Vis. **61**(1), 55–79 (2005)
14. Ramanan, D.: Learning to parse images of articulated bodies. In: NIPS (2006)
15. Andriluka, M., Roth, S., Schiele, B.: Pictorial structures revisited: people detection and articulated pose estimation. In: CVPR (2009)
16. Eichner, M., Ferrari, V.: Better appearance models for pictorial structures (2009)
17. Yang, Y., Ramanan, D.: Articulated pose estimation with flexible mixtures-of-parts. In: CVPR (2011)
18. Johnson, S., Everingham, M.: Learning effective human pose estimation from inaccurate annotation. In: CVPR (2011)
19. Tian, Y., Zitnick, C.L., Narasimhan, S.G.: Exploring the spatial hierarchy of mixture models for human pose estimation. In: Fitzgibbon, A., Lazebnik, S., Perona, P., Sato, Y., Schmid, C. (eds.) ECCV 2012, Part V. LNCS, vol. 7576, pp. 256–269. Springer, Heidelberg (2012). doi:10.1007/978-3-642-33715-4_19
20. Wang, F., Li, Y.: Beyond physical connections: tree models in human pose estimation. In: CVPR (2013)
21. Sapp, B., Taskar, B.: Modec: multimodal decomposable models for human pose estimation. In: CVPR (2013)

22. Pishchulin, L., Andriluka, M., Gehler, P., Schiele, B.: Poselet conditioned pictorial structures. In: CVPR (2013)
23. Karlinsky, L., Dinerstein, M., Harari, D., Ullman, S.: The chains model for detecting parts by their context. In: CVPR (2010)
24. Toshev, A., Szegedy, C.: Deeppose: human pose estimation via deep neural networks. In: CVPR (2014)
25. Ramakrishna, V., Munoz, D., Hebert, M., Andrew Bagnell, J., Sheikh, Y.: Pose machines: articulated pose estimation via inference machines. In: Fleet, D., Pajdla, T., Schiele, B., Tuytelaars, T. (eds.) ECCV 2014, Part II. LNCS, vol. 8690, pp. 33–47. Springer, Heidelberg (2014). doi:10.1007/978-3-319-10605-2_3
26. Carreira, J., Agrawal, P., Fragkiadaki, K., Malik, J.: Human pose estimation with iterative error feedback (2015)
27. Wei, S.E., Ramakrishna, V., Kanade, T., Sheikh, Y.: Convolutional pose machines. In: CVPR (2016)
28. Xu, K., Ba, J., Kiros, R., Cho, K., Courville, A.C., Salakhutdinov, R., Zemel, R.S., Bengio, Y.: Show, attend and tell: neural image caption generation with visual attention. CoRR abs/1502.03044 (2015)
29. Bengio, S., Vinyals, O., Jaitly, N., Shazeer, N.: Scheduled sampling for sequence prediction with recurrent neural networks. In: NIPS (2015)
30. Andriluka, M., Pishchulin, L., Gehler, P., Schiele, B.: 2D human pose estimation: new benchmark and state of the art analysis. In: CVPR (2014)
31. Zhang, W., Zhu, M., Derpanis, K.: From actemes to action: a strongly-supervised representation for detailed action understanding. In: ICCV (2013)
32. Yang, Y., Ramanan, D.: Articulated human detection with flexible mixtures-of-parts. PAMI (2012)
33. Nair, V., Hinton, G.E.: Rectified linear units improve restricted boltzmann machines. In: Proceedings of the 27th International Conference on Machine Learning (ICML-10), pp. 807–814 (2010)
34. Ioffe, S., Szegedy, C.: Batch normalization: accelerating deep network training by reducing internal covariate shift. arXiv preprint arXiv:1502.03167 (2015)
35. Szegedy, C., Vanhoucke, V., Ioffe, S., Shlens, J., Wojna, Z.: Rethinking the inception architecture for computer vision. CoRR abs/1512.00567 (2015)
36. Hoiem, D., Chodpathumwan, Y., Dai, Q.: Diagnosing error in object detectors. In: Fitzgibbon, A., Lazebnik, S., Perona, P., Sato, Y., Schmid, C. (eds.) ECCV 2012, Part III. LNCS, vol. 7574, pp. 340–353. Springer, Heidelberg (2012). doi:10.1007/978-3-642-33712-3_25
37. Newell, A., Yang, K., Deng, J.: Stacked hourglass networks for human pose estimation. CoRR abs/1603.06937 (2016)
38. Tompson, J., Goroshin, R., Jain, A., LeCun, Y., Bregler, C.: Efficient object localization using convolutional networks. In: CVPR (2015)
39. Hu, P., Ramanan, D.: Bottom-up and top-down reasoning with hierarchical rectified gaussians. CVPR (2016)
40. Pishchulin, L., Insafutdinov, E., Tang, S., Andres, B., Andriluka, M., Gehler, P., Schiele, B.: Deepcut: joint subset partition and labeling for multi person pose estimation. CVPR (2016)
41. Lifshitz, I., Fetaya, E., Ullman, S.: Human pose estimation using deep consensusvoting. CoRR abs/1603.08212 (2016)
42. Xiaohan Nie, B., Xiong, C., Zhu, S.C.: Joint action recognition and pose estimation from video. In: The IEEE Conference on Computer Vision and Pattern Recognition (CVPR), June 2015

Multi-region Two-Stream R-CNN
for Action Detection

Xiaojiang Peng$^{(\boxtimes)}$ and Cordelia Schmid

Thoth team, Laboratoire Jean Kuntzmann, Inria, Grenoble, France
{xiaojiang.peng,cordelia.schmid}@inria.fr

Abstract. We propose a multi-region two-stream R-CNN model for
action detection in realistic videos. We start from frame-level action
detection based on faster R-CNN, and make three contributions: (1) we
show that a motion region proposal network generates high-quality proposals, which are complementary to those of an appearance region proposal network; (2) we show that stacking optical flow over several frames
significantly improves frame-level action detection; and (3) we embed
a multi-region scheme in the faster R-CNN model, which adds complementary information on body parts. We then link frame-level detections
with the Viterbi algorithm, and temporally localize an action with the
maximum subarray method. Experimental results on the UCF-Sports,
J-HMDB and UCF101 action detection datasets show that our approach
outperforms the state of the art with a significant margin in both frame-
mAP and video-mAP.

Keywords: Action detection · Faster R-CNN · Multi-region CNNs ·
Two stream R-CNN

1 Introduction

Action recognition in videos has many realistic applications such as surveillance,
human computer interaction, and content-based retrieval. Most research efforts
have concentrated on action classification [1–4], where a class label is assigned to
an entire video. However, given a video stream, actions occur at precise spatio-
temporal extents. Action detection aims at determining these location, which
has attracted increasing attention recently [5–8]. It is a challenging problem due
to large intra-class variations, background clutter and in particular the large
spatio-temporal search space.

Several previous works address only temporal localization [9–11], i.e. they
only provide the start and end time of an action. State-of-the-art results are
obtained with a temporal sliding window and dense trajectory features [10].
For spatio-temporal detection, several recent works extend 2D object detection
models to 3D ones. For example, Tian *et al.* [5] extend the 2D deformable part
model [12] to a 3D deformable part model and Wang *et al.* [6] extend poselets [13]
to a dynamic poselet model. More recent works first detect actions at a frame

B. Leibe et al. (Eds.): ECCV 2016, Part IV, LNCS 9908, pp. 744–759, 2016.
DOI: 10.1007/978-3-319-46493-0_45

level by using Convolutional Neural Networks (CNNs) features and then either link them or track some selected detections to obtain video action detections [7, 8]. Thanks to the excellent performance of CNNs for object detection, these frame-level based approaches achieve state-of-the-art performance. This suggests that the quality of the frame-level action detections impacts directly the quality of action detection in videos.

Thus, a crucial point is how to improve the frame-level action detection. Weinzaepfel *et al.* [8] improve frame-level action detection by using a better proposal algorithm, i.e. EdgeBoxes [14]. Gkioxari *et al.* [15] boost R-CNN based action detection in still images by adding contextual features. Indeed, these two approaches indicate two important issues for frame-level detection: (1) high-quality proposals help CNNs to extract action representations precisely; and (2) the action representation is vital for detection.

In this paper we focus on the frame-level based action detection method, and aim to advance the state-of-the-art with respect to these two key aspects: frame-level action proposal and action representation.

Frame-level action proposal. One of the bottleneck for object detection based on region proposals is the accurate localization of these proposals [16–18]. To address this issue for action detection, we first evaluate three proposal methods for frame-level action localization on RGB data: selective search (SS) [19], EdgeBoxes (EB) [14], and region proposal network (RPN) [17]. We show that the RPN approach on appearance information achieves consistently better results than the others with higher inter-section-over-union (IoU) score. Furthermore, we extend the appearance RPN to motion RPN trained on optical flow data. We observe that motion RPN obtains high quality proposals, which are shown to be complementary to appearance RPN.

Action representation. Action representation is crucial for good performance, see for example [20,21]. Here, we propose an improved action representation inspired by the two-stream CNNs for action classification [22] and multi-region CNNs [18]. First, we stack multiple frame optical flows for the faster R-CNN model which significantly improves the motion R-CNN. Second, we select multiple body regions (i.e., upper body, lower body and border region) for both appearance and motion R-CNN, which boosts the performance of frame-based action detection.

In summary, this paper introduces a multi-region two-stream R-CNN model for action detection with state-of-the-art results on UCF-Sports, J-HMDB and UCF101 datasets. Our contributions are as follows: (1) we introduce a motion RPN which generates high-quality proposals and is complementary to the appearance RPN. (2) We show that stacking optical flows significantly improves frame-level detections. (3) We embed a multi-region scheme in the faster R-CNN model which is shown to improve the results.

The remained of this paper is organized as follows. In Sect. 2, we review related work on action recognition and region CNNs. We introduce the two-stream R-CNN with the motion RPN and stacked optical flows in Sect. 3. Our multi-region embedded R-CNN is described in Sect. 4 and the temporal linking and localization in Sect. 5. We present experimental results in Sect. 6.

2 Related Work

Action recognition and Convolutional Neural Networks (CNNs) have been extensively studied in recent years [23,24]. This section only covers the approaches directly related to our method.

Action classification and detection. For action classification, most methods focus on how to represent the entire video [1–4]. Popular video representations are bag-of-visual-words (BoW) [25] and its variants which aggregate local video features [1], CNN representations [22,26], and slow feature representations [27]. Wang *et al.* [1] use Fisher Vectors [28] and dense trajectories with motion compensation. Peng *et al.* [3] combine this approach with stacked Fisher Vectors. Simonyan *et al.* [22] design the two-stream CNNs based on RGB data and optical flow. Karpathy *et al.* [26] explore several approaches for fusing information over time based on appearance CNN. Wang *et al.* [4] extract two-stream CNNs along dense trajectories.

For action detection, [9,10,29,30] use local features to represent actions and rely on a sliding window scheme for either temporal or spatio-temporal localization. Rodriguez *et al.* [31] and Derpanis *et al.* [32] conduct global template matching. Tran *et al.* [33] use a BoW representation and implement the optimal spatio-temporal path for action detection. Tian *et al.* [5] extend the 2D deformable part model [12] to 3D space-time volumes for action localization. Wang *et al.* [6] apply dynamic poselets and a sequential skeleton model to jointly detect actions and poses.

Region CNN for detection. Region CNN (R-CNN) [16] has achieved a significant improvement for object detection in static image. This approach first extracts region proposals using selective search [19] and rescales them to a fixed size, and then uses a standard CNN network [34] to train and extract features. The features are subsequently fed into a SVM classifier with hard negative mining and a bounding box regressor. SPP-net improved it by removing the limitation of a fixed input size with a spatial pyramid pooling strategy [35]. Fast R-CNN speeds up the R-CNN by introducing a RoI pooling scheme and training classifier and bounding box regressor simultaneously [36]. Faster R-CNN further accelerates the fast R-CNN by replacing the selective search proposal method with a region proposal network [17]. Spyros *et al.* [18] added multi-region and segmentation-aware CNN features to make the R-CNN representation more discriminative. Inspired by R-CNN, Gkioxari and Malik [7] extract proposals by using the selective search method on RGB frames and then applied the original R-CNN on per frame RGB and optical flow data for frame-level action detection, and finally link detections by the Viterbi algorithm [37] to generate action tubes. Weinzaepfel *et al.* [8] replaced the selective search method by EdgeBoxes [14] for proposal extraction, and performed tracking on selected frame-level detections.

Our work differs from the above mentioned approaches in four ways: (1) we generate rich proposals from both RGB and optical flow data by using region proposal networks; (2) we use stacked optical flows to enhance the discriminative

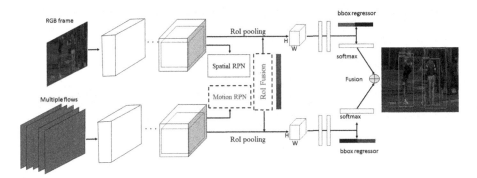

Fig. 1. Overview of our two-stream faster R-CNN. (Color figure online)

capacity of motion R-CNN; (3) we further improve the performance by embedding a multi-region scheme in faster R-CNN; and (4) we build an end-to-end multi-region two-stream CNN model for frame-level action detection.

3   End-to-end Two-Stream Faster R-CNN

Figure 1 gives an overview of our two-stream faster R-CNN (TS R-CNN) approach. Stacking optical flow has shown to be effective for CNN based action classification [22]. We believe this can also be the case for R-CNN based action detection. Our TS R-CNN takes as input an RGB frame f_t and *several optical flow maps* extracted for frame f_t and its neighboring frames (we take half of the frames before time t and half of them after). The network then processes them with several convolutional and max pooling layers, independently in the appearance and the motion stream. For each stream, the last convolutional layer is fed into an appearance or motion region proposal network and a region of interest (RoI) pooling layer. Here we introduce a RoI fusion layer, which merges the proposals from both the appearance RPN and the motion RPN. Both the appearance and the motion RoI pooling layer take all the RoIs and perform max-pooling for each of them with a $H \times W$ grid. For each stream, these fixed-length feature vectors are then fed into a sequence of fully connected layers that finally branch into a softmax layer and a bounding box regressor. The final detection results from both streams can be combined by several methods which will be evaluated in Sect. 6.3. Best performance is obtained by simply combining the softmax scores.

Training and testing. We train each of the two-stream faster R-CNNs separately. For both streams, we fine-tune the VGG-16 model [38] pre-trained on the ImageNet dataset [39]. One frame optical flow data is transformed to a 3 channel image by stacking the x-component, the y-component and the magnitude of the flow as in [8]. In case of multiple optical flow maps, where the input channel number is different from that of VGG-16 net, we just duplicate the VGG-16 filters of the first layer multiple times. We use the ground-truth bounding boxes of

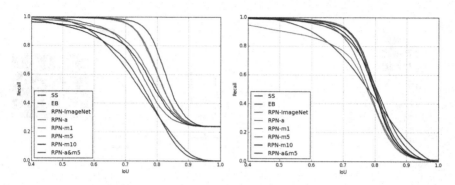

Fig. 2. Comparision of frame-level proposals on UCF-Sports and J-HMDB split 1: selective search proposals (SS), EdgeBoxes proposals (EB), RPN-ImageNet, RPN-a, RPN-m and the fusion of RPN-a and RPN-m proposals. RPN-mk indicates k frame optical flows. Left: UCF-Sports. Right: J-HMDB split 1.

the middle frame for training. For testing, we first combine the learned appearance and motion R-CNN models into one model by adding a RoI fusion layer, see Fig. 1. We then put frame-flow pairs to the end-to-end model and average the softmax scores from both streams as the final action region detection scores. The bounding box regressor is applied to corresponding RoIs of each stream (see the red and blue solid bars in Fig. 1). The concatenation of these boxes is the final detection result.

Evaluation of our action proposals. To show the quality of our motion RPN (RPN-m), we compare it to several other proposal methods. Figure 2 compares the recall over intersection-over-union (IoU) for different proposal methods described in the following. Selective search (SS) [19] generates regions by using a bottom-up grouping scheme with features from color, texture and box sizes. We keep the default setting and obtain 2 k proposals. EdgeBoxes (EB) [14] are obtained based on the observation that the number of contours entirely contained in a bounding box is indicative of the objectness. Again we use the default setting and obtain 256 proposals. The RPN method first generates several anchor boxes for each pixel with multiple scales and ratios, and then scores and regresses them with the learned features. For training RPN, positive objectness labels are obtained for those anchors that have high IoU overlap with ground-truth boxes. For the comparison, we keep RPN 300 proposals and use one scale with a fixed minimum side of 600 pixels. We also extend the RPN method to optical flow and report results for single flow and stacked flows.

Figure 2 shows that RPN-a method consistently outperforms SS and EB, i.e. it obtains best results when using RGB frames. Interestingly, on UCF-Sports it obtains perfect detections (IoU = 1) 25 % of the time (i.e., recall = 0.25 for IoU = 1). For fair comparison with SS and EB (both are non-tuned methods for action datasets), we show the results of RPN pre-trained on ImageNet as RPN-ImageNet in Fig. 2. It also consistently outperforms SS and EB on both datasets. Moreover, the motion RPN with a single frame optical flow also provides very

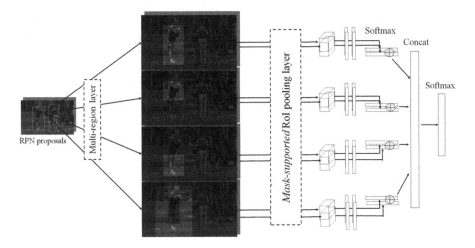

Fig. 3. Overview of the multi-region two-stream faster R-CNN architecture.

good action proposals. They are better than RPN-a on UCF-Sports, but worse on J-HMDB. This can be explained by more significant motion occurring on UCF-Sports compared to J-HMDB, which contains a number of daily activities without significant motion, such as "brush_hair", "pour" and "wave". The recall increases with 5 stacked flows (RPN-m5) and decreases with 10 stacked flows (RPN-m10). A possible explanation is that stacking optical flows makes the representation more discriminative, but that there is a saturation for a higher number of frames due to the non-aligned temporal boxes. Combining the proposals from both appearance and motion RPN achieves the best performance and outperforms SS and EB by a significant margin.

4   Multi-region Two-Stream Faster R-CNN

The multi-region two-stream faster R-CNN (MR-TS R-CNN) architecture is illustrated in Fig. 3. It is built on the two-stream faster R-CNN by embedding a multi-region generation layer between the RPNs and the RoI pooling layer. Given proposals from both appearance RPN and motion RPN, the multi-region layer generates 4 RoIs for each RPN proposal. We describe the 4 types of regions relevant for action representation in the following.

Original regions are the original RPN proposals. A network along this channel is guided to capture the whole action region. The network is exactly the same as the TS R-CNN. The bounding box regressor is only applied on this channel.

"*Upper half*" and "*bottom half*" regions are the upper and bottom halfs of the RPN proposals, see second and third rows in the multi-region layer in Fig. 3. Instead of left/right/upper/bottom half regions used for objects in [18], we only use the upper/bottom half regions due to the mostly symmetric vertical structure of bodies in action videos. Networks based on these parts are not only robust w.r.t occlusions but also more discriminative for action categories for which body part features are dominant. For example, "golf" and "swing_baseball" are easier to recognize by only the upper half region, while "climb_stairs" and "kick_ball" by only the bottom half region.

"*Border*" regions are rectangular rings around the original proposals. Given a RPN proposal, we generate the inner box of a border region by scaling the proposal by a factor of 0.8 and the outer box by a factor of 1.5. For the appearance stream, a network along this channel is expected to jointly capture the appearance border of human and nearby objects which may be helpful for action recognition. For motion stream, this channel has high probability to focus on the motion boundary region which was demonstrated to be very useful for hand-crafted features [1].

Training. The two-stream network for original regions is copied from the one presented in the previous section. For training the two-stream networks of the other regions, we fine-tune the network of the original regions separately for each region. In particular, we only tune the fully connected layers, and fix all the *convolutional* layers as well as the RPN to ensure that all the region networks share the same proposals. Regarding the "Border" region two-stream network, we introduce a mask-supported RoI pooling layer which sets the activations inside the inner box to zero similar to [18,40]. After training the region networks, we combine them by further training another softmax layer based on the softmax layers of multi-region two-stream networks, see Fig. 3. Note that the multi-region R-CNNs share all the *conv* layers and hence the computation cost during testing increases only by a factor of 1.8.

5   Linking and Temporal Localization

Based on the above described method, we obtain frame-level action detections. In order to achieve video-level detection, we apply linking similar to [7] and temporal localization based on the maximum subarray algorithm [41].

Given two regions R_t and R_{t+1} from consecutive frames t and $t+1$, we define the linking score for an action class c by

$$s_c(R_t, R_{t+1}) = \{s_c(R_t) + s_c(R_{t+1}) + \beta\ ov(R_t, R_{t+1})\} \bullet \psi(ov), \qquad (1)$$

where $s_c(R_i)$ is the class score of region R_i, ov is the intersection-over-union overlap of the two regions and β is a scalar. $\psi(ov)$ is a threshold function defined by $\psi(ov) = 1$ if ov is larger than τ, $\psi(ov) = 0$ otherwise. We experimentally observe that our linking score is better than the one in [7] and more robust due to the additional overlap constraint. After computing all the linking scores of an action, we obtain video-level action detections by determining the optimal path iteratively with the Viterbi algorithm. We finally score a video-level action detection $\Re = [R_1, R_2, ..., R_T]$ by $\overline{s_c(\Re)} = \frac{1}{T}\sum_{i=1}^{T} s_c(R_i)$.

In order to determine the temporal extent of an action detection within a video track, one can apply a sliding window approach with multiple temporal scales and strides as [8]. Here we rely on an efficient maximum subarray method. Given a video-level detection $\mathfrak{R}$, we aim to find a detection from frame s to frame e which satisfies the following objective,

$$s_c(\mathfrak{R}^{\star}_{(s,e)}) = \underset{(s,e)}{\mathrm{argmax}}\{\frac{1}{L_{(s,e)}} \sum_{i=s}^{e} s_c(R_i) - \lambda \frac{|L_{(s,e)} - L_c|}{L_c}\}, \qquad (2)$$

where $L_{(s,e)}$ is the track length and L_c is the average duration of class c on the training set. We propose to approximately solve this objective by three steps: (1) subtract from all the frame-level action scores the video-length action score $\overline{s_c(\mathfrak{R})}$, (2) find the maximum subarray of the subtracted array by using Kadane's algorithm [41], (3) extend or shorten the optimal range to L_c. Our solution searches the track only once. For each video-length action detection, we only keep the best extent as spatio-temporal detection. Note that the threes-step heuristic is an approximation to Eq. (2), and step (3) sets the length of the optimal tube from step (2) to the average length to avoid degenerate solutions.

6   Experiments

In this section, we first present the details of datasets and the evaluation metrics and describe the implementation details. We then evaluate our method comprehensively and compare to the state of the art.

6.1   Datasets and Evaluation Metrics

In our experiments, we evaluate action detection on three datasets: UCF-Sports, J-HMDB and UCF-101. We briefly review them in the following and present the metrics used for evaluation.

UCF-Sports [31] contains 150 short videos of 10 different sport classes. Videos are truncated to the action and bounding boxes annotations are provided for all frames. We use the standard training and test split defined in [31].

J-HMDB [20] consists of 928 videos for 21 different actions such as brush hair, swing baseball or jump. Video clips are restricted to the duration of the action. Each clip contains between 15 and 40 frames. Human silhouettes are annotated for all frames. The ground-truth bounding boxes are inferred from the silhouettes. There are 3 train/test splits and evaluation averages the results over the three splits.

UCF-101 [42] is dedicated to action classification with more than 13000 videos and 101 classes. For a subset of 24 labels and 3207 videos, the spatio-temporal extents of the actions are annotated. All experiments are performed on the first split only. In contrast to UCF-Sports and J-HMDB where the videos are truncated to the action, UCF-101 videos are longer and the localization is both spatial and temporal.

Evaluation metrics. We use three metrics in our experiments: (i) *frame-AP*, the average precision of detection at the frame level as in [7]; (ii) *video-AP*, the

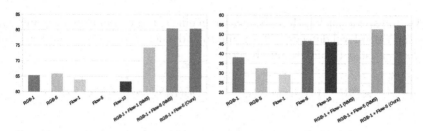

Fig. 4. Evaluation of different frames types (RGB and flow), number of frames (x = 1, 5, 10) used for detection and combination strategies (NMS or score combination–ours). Left: UCF-Sports. Right: J-HMDB split 1.

average precision at the video level as in [7,8]. We fix the IoU threshold to [0.2, 0.5] for frame-AP and video-AP measurement on the UCF-Sports and J-HMDB, and [0.05, 0.1, 0.2, 0.3] on UCF101.

6.2   Implementation Details

We implement our method based on the Caffe open source toolbox[1]. Optical flow is estimated using the online code from Brox *et al.* [43]. For both appearance and motion R-CNN, we use the same setting except that motion R-CNN uses $128, 128, 128$ as the mean data values. Similar to [36], we use a single sample, i.e. either a single image or a stacked optical flow map annotated with ground-truth boxes at every training iteration. When fine-tuning the VGG-16 model, we only update layers from $conv3\_1$ and up as observed to be efficient in [36]. For action region proposal network training, we set the regions with IoU larger than 0.7 as positive regions, and the regions with IoU less than 0.3 as negative regions. For the classification part of faster R-CNN, we use 256 proposals with a quarter of them as positive bounding boxes from the RPN, where the IoU of a positive box is larger than 0.5 and of a negative between 0.1 and 0.5. When training the two-stream R-CNN on UCF-Sports and J-HMDB, we initialize the learning rate to 10^{-3}, decrease it to 10^{-4} after 50 K iterations, and stop training after 70 K iterations. When training the *multi-region* two-stream R-CNN, we only fine-tune the fully-connected layers of the TS R-CNN model and set the learning rate to 10^{-4}, change it to 10^{-5} after 7 K iterations, and stop after 10 k iterations. We double the mentioned iterations on the UCF101 dataset empirically since it is a much larger dataset. The grid of RoI pooling layer is fixed to 7×7. The dropout rates of fully connected layers are set to 0.5 in all cases. The threshold τ of function $\psi(ov)$ is fixed to 0.2 empirically.

6.3   Evaluation of Multi-region Two-Stream Faster R-CNN

In this section, we first evaluate our method for frame-level detection with respect to four aspects: RGB/flow stacking, stream combination, multi-scale training and

---

[1] https://github.com/rbgirshick/py-faster-rcnn.

Table 1. Evaluation of different training and testing scales. All detections from different scales are combined by the NMS, and RGB-1 and Flow-5 streams are combined by score averaging. We report results for UCF-Sports and J-HMDB, split 1.

Test scales	Train scales	RGB-1		Flow-5		RGB-1 + Flow-5	
		UCF-Sports	J-HMDB	UCF-Sports	J-HMDB	UCF-Sports	J-HMDB
{600}	{600}	65.30	38.05	74.24	46.71	-	-
	{480, 600, 800}	68.07	38.71	73.62	47.74	-	-
{480, 600, 800}	{600}	68.47	39.90	**76.77**	47.05	-	-
	{480, 600, 800}	**69.29**	**40.02**	75.81	**48.60**	**82.30**	**56.60**

testing and multi-region scheme. We then present the spatio-temporal detection at the video level and the action classification results based on detection.

RGB and optical flow faster R-CNN with several frames. We compare appearance and motion faster R-CNN with one or multiple frames for frame-level detection (mean AP), see Fig. 4. For this evaluation, the training/testing scale is fixed to 600 which corresponds to the shorter side of an *input image*. We can observe that appearance R-CNN extracted for one frame (RGB-1) outperforms motion R-CNN extracted for one frame (Flow-1) on both UCF-Sport and J-HMDB. Increasing the number of frames for the appearance model (RGB-5) does not improve the performance. However, using 5 frames for flow significantly improves the performance for motion R-CNN, i.e. we gain 10.27 % on UCF-Sports and 17.39 % on J-HMDB split 1. This is mainly due to the fact that motion information from one frame is not discriminative enough, see a similar observation for action classification in [22]. Stacking more flows (Flow-10) decreases the result significantly on UCF-Sports, and slightly on J-HMDB partly due to the degraded proposals as mentioned in Sect. 3. We observe that the decrease in performance is more important on the strongly moving actions such as "Diving", "Swinging at the high bar", "Kicking", and "Jump". This can be explained by the fact the stacking does not align the actors and hence the detected bounding boxes are more imprecise. In summary, Flow-5 performs best and is complementary to RGB-1. We discuss different combination schemes next.

Two streams combination. We explore two schemes for combining the appearance and motion R-CNN: box-level non maximum suppression (NMS) and score fusion with a RoI fusion layer (our end-to-end pipeline, see Fig. 1). The NMS method perform detection for appearance and motion R-CNN separately, and then fuses all the detected bounding boxes from both streams with NMS. As shown in Fig. 4, for the fusion of RGB-1 and Flow-5 streams, the score fusion (indicated by "Ours") obtains 2.02 % improvement over the NMS fusion on J-HMDB and performs on par on UCF-Sports. Compared to the NMS fusion, the score fusion uses both appearance and motion information for bounding box scoring which is more discriminative. In the remained of this paper, we use score fusion for the combination of appearance and motion R-CNNs, and use "RGB-1 + Flow-5" for two-stream R-CNN by default.

Multi-scale training and testing. An action can occur on arbitrary scales. Here we explore robustness to scale changes by using multi-scale training and

Table 2. Per-class frame-AP of individual regions and multi-region two-stream faster R-CNN on UCF-Sports.

Region	Diving	Golf	Kicking	Lifting	Riding	Run	SkateBoarding	Swing1	Swing2	Walk	mAP
Org	94.68	66.34	72.06	98.53	97.54	**84.04**	**59.67**	79	98.20	72.87	82.30
Upper half	95.84	**80.44**	33.61	99.10	97.51	81.45	17.08	60.78	98.08	69.87	73.38
Bottom half	88.34	48.12	67.62	96.86	**97.61**	79.75	57.98	**84.16**	98.12	72.91	79.15
Border	95.91	69.54	66.74	**99.95**	97.02	80.53	50.53	52.14	98.15	**76.52**	78.67
Multi-region	**96.12**	**80.47**	**73.78**	99.17	97.56	82.37	57.43	83.64	**98.54**	75.99	**84.51**
Gkioxari *et al.* [7]	75.8	69.3	54.6	99.1	89.6	54.9	29.8	88.7	74.5	44.7	68.1
Weinzaepfel *et al.* [8]	60.71	77.55	65.26	100.00	99.53	52.60	47.14	88.88	62.86	64.44	71.9

Table 3. Per-class frame-AP of individual regions and multi-region two-stream faster R-CNN on J-HMDB (average on 3 splits).

Region	brushHair	catch	clap	climbStairs	golf	jump	kickBall	pick	pour	pullup	push	run	shootBall	shootBow	shootGun	sit	stand	swingBaseball	throw	walk	wave	mAP
Org	70.5	**39**	60.1	60.2	99.3	11.2	**35.9**	**59.1**	97	97.4	78	32.4	**52.9**	90.1	52.4	29.2	**49.3**	53.9	**27.8**	**60.5**	**38.1**	56.9
Upper half	**77.9**	33.1	60.8	48.6	94.7	5.40	20	44	89.6	93.9	62.9	24.5	46.4	83.5	57.9	**36.7**	38.2	**62.6**	20.5	49.4	29.3	51.4
Bottom half	36.4	29.4	32.3	**68.1**	97.3	6.90	32.9	26.5	87	93.7	67.1	31.9	33	72.6	21.7	20.8	41.3	44.3	18	38.1	24.9	44.0
Border	64.9	34.6	58.9	52.6	99.5	11.4	35	49.6	94.6	95.2	71.3	32.4	46.5	83.8	50.9	25.1	46.9	45.6	22.9	56.1	32.3	52.9
Multi-region	75.8	38.4	**62.2**	62.4	**99.6**	12.7	35.1	57.8	96.8	97.3	**79.6**	**38.1**	52.8	**90.8**	**62.7**	33.6	48.9	62.2	25.6	59.7	37.1	**58.5**
[7]	65.2	18.3	38.1	39.0	79.4	7.3	9.4	25.2	80.2	82.8	33.6	11.6	5.6	66.8	27.0	32.1	34.2	33.6	15.5	34.0	21.9	36.2
[8]	73.3	34.0	40.8	56.8	93.9	5.9	13.8	38.5	88.1	89.4	60.5	21.1	23.9	85.6	37.8	34.9	49.2	36.7	16.8	40.5	20.5	45.8

testing. We fix the scale to 600 for single scale training/testing, and to {480, 600, 800} for the multi-scale case. The results are shown in Table 1. The results of multi-scale training is on par of single-scale training when testing on one scale only. However, multi-scale training with multi-scale testing achieves consistent better results than the other settings. In particular, it improves the single-scale training and testing by 4 % for the RGB-1 R-CNN model on UCF-Sports. Our two-stream R-CNN with multi-scale setting obtains 82.3 % and 56.6 % on UCF-Sports and J-HMDB, respectively. In the remained of the paper, we fix the setting to multi-scale training and testing.

Multi-region R-CNN. For the multi-region evaluation, we use the two-stream model RGB-1 + Flow-5 and the multi-scale setting for all part R-CNN models. We report the per-class results of our region R-CNN models in Table 2 for UCF-Sports and in Table 3 for J-HMDB. Among all the R-CNN models on both datasets, the *Org* R-CNN achieves the best performance in mean AP, which indicates the whole body is essential for an action. On UCF-Sports, the *Bottom half* and *Border* models get similar results as the *Org* model, while the *Upper half* model is worse than the *Org* model by a margin of 9 %. In contrast, on J-HMDB the *Bottom half* model gets the worst result and the other region models obtain similar results with the *Org* model. This reflects the different type of actions in the two datasets, i.e., J-HMDB is dominated by upper body actions (everyday actions), while for UCF-Sports the bottom part of the action is most characteristic (sport actions). The multi-region two-stream R-CNN (MR-TS R-CNN) model improves the *Org* R-CNN model by 2.21 % and 1.6 % on UCF-Sports and J-HMDB datasets, respectively. It also outperforms the state-of-the-art methods [7,8] with a large margins on both datasets.

Furthermore, we observe that individual part R-CNN models perform better than the *Org* model for some actions. For example, the *Upper half* model gains 14.1 % for "Golf" on UCF-Sports and 8.7 % for "swingBaseball" on J-HMDB over the *Org* model. Also, the *Bottom half* model gains 5.16 % for "Swing 1" on

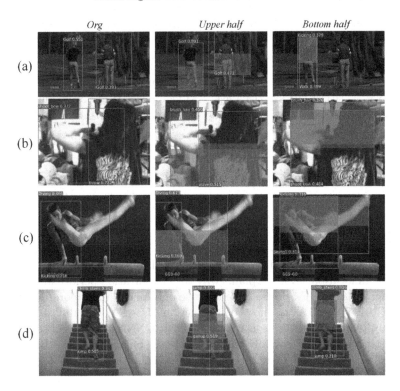

Fig. 5. Examples of action detection with different region R-CNN models. We only show the top two detections after performing NMS. Overlayed yellow regions indicate the regions invisible for the part R-CNN models. (Color figure online)

UCF-Sports and 7.9 % for "climbStairs" on J-HMDB. Figure 5 illustrates this with a few examples. Actions in row (a) and (b) are better detected by *Upper half* R-CNN model, while row (c) and (d) by *Bottom half* R-CNN model. We can observe that the detected boxes and their scores vary significantly between the different models. By focusing on the bottom part, the example of "climb_stairs" (row d, column 3) gets a high confidence detection due to the discriminative cue of stairs and legs.

Linking and temporal localization. We evaluate our linking and temporal localization methods for both the two stream R-CNN model and its multi-region version. Table 4 shows the video mAP results with IoU threshold of δ on UCF-Sports, J-HMDB, and UCF101 datasets. Both of our approaches obtain excellent video-level performance on these datasets which is mainly due to the high-quality frame-level detections. We obtain 94.82 % and 70.88 % on UCF-Sports and J-HMDB (split 1) with our linking method, respectively. The corresponding numbers are 94.81 % and 68.97 with the linking method in [7]. Results improve on J-HMDB, but are the similar for UCF-Sports, where detections are near perfect. Multi-region TS R-CNN consistently outperforms the original TS R-CNN model on J-HMDB and UCF101, and performs similarly on UCF-Sports. The lack in

Table 4. Video mAP on UCF-Sports, J-HMDB and UCF101 (split 1) with variant IoU thresholds.

	UCF-Sports		J-HMDB		UCF101 (with temporal loc)				UCF101 (w/o)
δ	0.2	0.5	0.2	0.5	0.05	0.1	0.2	0.3	0.2
TS R-CNN	94.82	**94.82**	71.1	70.6	54.13	49.51	41.17	31.13	40.67
MR-TS R-CNN	**94.83**	94.67	**74.3**	**73.09**	**54.46**	**50.39**	**42.27**	**32.70**	40.95

Table 5. Classification results on UCF-Sports and J-HMDB by detection.

	FAT [7]	IDT+FV [1]	P-CNN (w/o GT) [21]	TS R-CNN	MR-TS R-CNN
UCF-Sports	-	88.0	-	91.49	**95.74**
J-HMDB	62.5	65.9	61.1	70.52	**71.08**

improvement on UCF-Sports might be explained by the mistakes in the spatio-temporal annotation, which explains why the classification performance actually does improve for UCF-Sports. Note that we only perform temporal localization on UCF101. Nevertheless, most of the action classes cover almost the entire video. By temporal localization with MR-TS R-CNN model, we observe a gain of 1.3 % in video-mAP for IoU threshold of 0.2, but on actions "Basketball", "BasketballDunk", and "CricketBowling", we gain 19.6 %, 16.2 %, and 9.6 % respectively.

Classification by detection. Similar to [7], our approach can be also extended to action classification of the videos. We leverage the best action track (i.e., the track with maximum action score) in a video to predict the action label. Table 5 reports the average class accuracy on UCF-Sports and J-HMDB. Both of our models achieve outstanding performance, with the multi-region version improving the results in both cases. In particular, our MR-TS R-CNN model obtains 95.74 % and 71.08 % on UCF-Sports and J-HMDB, respectively. The results are significantly better than those of the IDT method [1] and the pose-based CNN method [21] which perform only classification. This suggests that classification can be improved by *precise localization* and *detection-aware* features.

6.4   Comparison to the State of the Art

We conclude the experimental evaluation with a comparison to the state of the art in Table 6. In both frame-level and video-level mAP, our TS R-CNN already outperforms the state-of-the-art results on both UCF-Sports and J-HMDB, and is on par with [8] on UCF101. In particular, our MR-TS R-CNN approach outperforms the state of the art by 12.6 %, 12.7 % and 4.79 % in frame-mAP, 4.3 %, 12.4 % and 0.2 % on UCF-Sports, J-HMDB and UCF101, respectively. Both [7,8] also make use of frame-level action detection with R-CNN. Weinzaephel *et al.* [8] select the top two frame-level detections for each class from the entire video and then track with them based on class-level and instance-level scores.

Table 6. Comparison to the state of the art on three datasets. The IoU threshold δ for frame-mAP is fixed to 0.5.

		UCF-Sports		J-HMDB		UCF101 (split 1)			
	δ	0.2	0.5	0.2	0.5	0.05	0.1	0.2	0.3
Video-mAP	Gkioxari *et al.* [7]	-	75.8	-	53.3	-	-	-	-
	Weinzaepfel *et al.* [8]	-	90.5	63.1	60.7	54.3	51.7	46.8	37.8
	Yu *et al.* [44]	-	-	-	-	49.9	42.8	26.5	14.6
	Our TS R-CNN	94.8	**94.8**	71.1	70.6	54.1	49.5	41.2	31.1
	Our MR-TS R-CNN	**94.8**	94.7	**74.3**	**73.1**	**54.5**	50.4	42.3	32.7
Frame-mAP	Gkioxari *et al.* [7]	68.1		36.2		-			
	Weinzaepfel *et al.* [8]	71.9		45.8		35.84			
	Our TS R-CNN	82.3		56.9		**39.94**			
	Our MR-TS R-CNN	**84.5**		**58.5**		39.63			

This allows them to increase the video-mAP relative to their frame mAP, in particular for difficult datasets such as UCF101. Yet, such an additional tracking step is complementary to our approach. Compared to [7,8], our method benefits from two key points: (1) the high-quality proposals from both appearance and motion RPN and (2) the discriminative frame-level action representation based on stacked optical flows and multiple parts.

7   Conclusion

This paper introduces a multi-region two-stream R-CNN action detection approach, which takes full advantage of three recent methods, namely faster R-CNN, two-stream CNNs with optical flow stacking and multi-region CNNs. We propose a novel framework for action detection which builds on these methods. It significantly outperforms the state of the art [7,8]. In our experiments on UCF101, we observed that a limitation lies in handling low-quality videos and small bounding boxes, which will be addressed in future work.

Acknowledgments. This work was supported in part by the ERC advanced grant ALLEGRO, the MSR-Inria joint project, a Google research award, a Facebook gift, the Natural Science Foundation of China (No. 61502152) and the Open Projects Program of National Laboratory of Pattern Recognition. We gratefully acknowledge the support of NVIDIA with the donation of GPUs used for this research.

References

1. Wang, H., Schmid, C.: Action recognition with improved trajectories. In: ICCV, pp. 3551–3558 (2013)
2. Jain, A., Gupta, A., Rodriguez, M., Davis, L.: Representing videos using mid-level discriminative patches. In: CVPR, pp. 2571–2578 (2013)

3. Peng, X., Zou, C., Qiao, Y., Peng, Q.: Action recognition with stacked fisher vectors. In: Fleet, D., Pajdla, T., Schiele, B., Tuytelaars, T. (eds.) ECCV 2014, Part V. LNCS, vol. 8693, pp. 581–595. Springer, Heidelberg (2014)
4. Wang, L., Qiao, Y., Tang, X.: Action recognition with trajectory-pooled deep-convolutional descriptors. In: CVPR, pp. 4305–4314 (2015)
5. Tian, Y., Sukthankar, R., Shah, M.: Spatiotemporal deformable part models for action detection. In: CVPR, pp. 2642–2649 (2013)
6. Wang, L., Qiao, Y., Tang, X.: Video action detection with relational dynamic-poselets. In: Fleet, D., Pajdla, T., Schiele, B., Tuytelaars, T. (eds.) ECCV 2014, Part V. LNCS, vol. 8693, pp. 565–580. Springer, Heidelberg (2014)
7. Gkioxari, G., Malik, J.: Finding action tubes. In: CVPR, pp. 759–768 (2015)
8. Weinzaepfel, P., Harchaoui, Z., Schmid, C.: Learning to track for spatio-temporal action localization. In: ICCV, pp. 3164–3172 (2015)
9. Gaidon, A., Harchaoui, Z., Schmid, C.: Temporal localization of actions with actoms. PAMI 35(11), 2782–2795 (2013)
10. Oneata, D., Verbeek, J., Schmid, C.: Efficient action localization with approximately normalized Fisher vectors. In: CVPR, pp. 2545–2552 (2014)
11. Escalera, S., et al.: ChaLearn looking at people challenge 2014: dataset and results. In: Agapito, L., Bronstein, M.M., Rother, C. (eds.) ECCV 2014. LNCS, vol. 8925, pp. 459–473. Springer, Heidelberg (2015). doi:10.1007/978-3-319-16178-5_32
12. Felzenszwalb, P., McAllester, D., Ramanan, D.: A discriminatively trained, multi-scale, deformable part model. In: CVPR, pp. 1–8 (2008)
13. Bourdev, L., Malik, J.: Poselets: body part detectors trained using 3D human pose annotations. In: ICCV, pp. 1365–1372 (2009)
14. Zitnick, C.L., Dollár, P.: Edge boxes: locating object proposals from edges. In: Fleet, D., Pajdla, T., Schiele, B., Tuytelaars, T. (eds.) ECCV 2014, Part V. LNCS, vol. 8693, pp. 391–405. Springer, Heidelberg (2014)
15. Gkioxari, G., Girshick, R., Malik, J.: Contextual action recognition with R*CNN. In: ICCV, pp. 1080–1088 (2015)
16. Girshick, R., Donahue, J., Darrell, T., Malik, J.: Rich feature hierarchies for accurate object detection and semantic segmentation. In: CVPR, pp. 580–587 (2014)
17. Ren, S., He, K., Girshick, R., Sun, J.: Faster R-CNN: towards real-time object detection with region proposal networks. In: NIPS, pp. 91–99 (2015)
18. Gidaris, S., Komodakis, N.: Object detection via a multi-region and semantic segmentation-aware CNN model. In: ICCV, pp. 1134–1142 (2015)
19. Uijlings, J.R., van de Sande, K.E., Gevers, T., Smeulders, A.W.: Selective search for object recognition. IJCV 104(2), 154–171 (2013)
20. Jhuang, H., Gall, J., Zuffi, S., Schmid, C., Black, M.: Towards understanding action recognition. In: ICCV, pp. 3192–3199 (2013)
21. Chéron, G., Laptev, I., Schmid, C.: P-CNN: pose-based CNN features for action recognition. In: ICCV, pp. 3218–3226 (2015)
22. Simonyan, K., Zisserman, A.: Two-stream convolutional networks for action recognition in videos. In: NIPS, pp. 568–576 (2014)
23. Aggarwal, J.K., Ryoo, M.S.: Human activity analysis: a review. ACM Comput. Surv. (CSUR) 43(3), 16 (2011)
24. LeCun, Y., Bengio, Y., Hinton, G.: Deep learning. Nature 521(7553), 436–444 (2015)
25. Sivic, J., Zisserman, A.: Video Google: a text retrieval approach to object matching in videos. In: ICCV, pp. 1470–1477 (2003)

26. Karpathy, A., Toderici, G., Shetty, S., Leung, T., Sukthankar, R., Fei-Fei, L.: Large-scale video classification with convolutional neural networks. In: CVPR, pp. 1725–1732 (2014)
27. Sun, L., Jia, K., Chan, T.H., Fang, Y., Wang, G., Yan, S.: DL-SFA: deeply-learned slow feature analysis for action recognition. In: CVPR, pp. 2625–2632 (2014)
28. Perronnin, F., Sánchez, J., Mensink, T.: Improving the fisher kernel for large-scale image classification. In: Daniilidis, K., Maragos, P., Paragios, N. (eds.) ECCV 2010, Part IV. LNCS, vol. 6314, pp. 143–156. Springer, Heidelberg (2010)
29. Laptev, I., Pérez, P.: Retrieving actions in movies. In: ICCV 2007, pp. 1–8 (2007)
30. Yuan, J., Liu, Z., Wu, Y.: Discriminative subvolume search for efficient action detection. In: CVPR, pp. 2442–2449 (2009)
31. Rodriguez, M.D., Ahmed, J., Shah, M.: Action MACH a spatio-temporal maximum average correlation height filter for action recognition. In: CVPR, pp. 1–8 (2008)
32. Derpanis, K.G., Sizintsev, M., Cannons, K., Wildes, R.P.: Efficient action spotting based on a spacetime oriented structure representation. In: CVPR, pp. 1990–1997 (2010)
33. Tran, D., Yuan, J., Forsyth, D.: Video event detection: from subvolume localization to spatiotemporal path search. PAMI **36**(2), 404–416 (2014)
34. Krizhevsky, A., Sutskever, I., Hinton, G.E.: ImageNet classification with deep convolutional neural networks. In: NIPS, pp. 1097–1105 (2012)
35. He, K., Zhang, X., Ren, S., Sun, J.: Spatial pyramid pooling in deep convolutional networks for visual recognition. PAMI **37**(9), 1904–1916 (2015)
36. Girshick, R.: Fast R-CNN. In: ICCV, pp. 1440–1448 (2015)
37. Viterbi, A.J.: Error bounds for convolutional codes and an asymptotically optimum decoding algorithm. Inf. Theory **13**(2), 260–269 (1967)
38. Simonyan, K., Zisserman, A.: Very deep convolutional networks for large-scale image recognition. arXiv:1409.1556 (2014)
39. Russakovsky, O., Deng, J., Su, H., Krause, J., Satheesh, S., Ma, S., Huang, Z., Karpathy, A., Khosla, A., Bernstein, M., et al.: ImageNet large scale visual recognition challenge. IJCV **115**(3), 211–252 (2015)
40. Dai, J., He, K., Sun, J.: Convolutional feature masking for joint object and stuff segmentation. In: CVPR, pp. 3992–4000 (2015)
41. Bentley, J.: Programming pearls: algorithm design techniques. Commun. ACM **27**(9), 865–873 (1984)
42. Soomro, K., Zamir, A.R., Shah, M.: UCF101: a dataset of 101 human actions classes from videos in the wild. arXiv:1212.0402 (2012)
43. Brox, T., Bruhn, A., Papenberg, N., Weickert, J.: High accuracy optical flow estimation based on a theory for warping. In: Pajdla, T., Matas, J.G. (eds.) ECCV 2004. LNCS, vol. 3024, pp. 25–36. Springer, Heidelberg (2004)
44. Yu, G., Yuan, J.: Fast action proposals for human action detection and search. In: CVPR, pp. 1302–1311 (2015)

Semantic Co-segmentation in Videos

Yi-Hsuan Tsai[1]($\boxtimes$), Guangyu Zhong[1,2], and Ming-Hsuan Yang[1]

[1] UC Merced, Merced, USA
{ytsai2,gzhong,mhyang}@ucmerced.edu
[2] Dalian University of Technology, Dalian, China

Abstract. Discovering and segmenting objects in videos is a challenging task due to large variations of objects in appearances, deformed shapes and cluttered backgrounds. In this paper, we propose to segment objects and understand their visual semantics from a collection of videos that link to each other, which we refer to as *semantic co-segmentation*. Without any prior knowledge on videos, we first extract semantic objects and utilize a tracking-based approach to generate multiple object-like tracklets across the video. Each tracklet maintains temporally connected segments and is associated with a predicted category. To exploit rich information from other videos, we collect tracklets that are assigned to the same category from all videos, and co-select tracklets that belong to true objects by solving a submodular function. This function accounts for object properties such as appearances, shapes and motions, and hence facilitates the co-segmentation process. Experiments on three video object segmentation datasets show that the proposed algorithm performs favorably against the other state-of-the-art methods.

1 Introduction

Objects may appear at any location in various shapes and appearances with different visual semantics across videos. Given a set of videos, localizing and segmenting all the objects is a challenging task, especially when the visual categories are unknown. In this work, we propose an algorithm to segment objects and understand visual semantics from a video collection, which we refer to as *semantic co-segmentation*. Within the proposed co-segmentation framework, we aim to find the common representation for each semantic category and exploit relations between objects. For instance, dogs from different videos may share more commonalities and have stronger relations between each other than objects with other semantics (see Fig. 1).

Numerous algorithms have been proposed for video object co-segmentation [3,6,26,34]. However, most existing methods [3,6,26] assume that at least one common object appears all the time in two or more videos, which limits the

---

Y.-H. Tsai and G. Zhong—These authors contribute equally to this work.

Electronic supplementary material The online version of this chapter (doi:10.1007/978-3-319-46493-0_46) contains supplementary material, which is available to authorized users.

B. Leibe et al. (Eds.): ECCV 2016, Part IV, LNCS 9908, pp. 760–775, 2016.
DOI: 10.1007/978-3-319-46493-0_46

applicability in real world scenarios. In this work, we propose an algorithm to segment semantic objects from a collection of videos containing various categories despite large variations in appearances, shapes, poses and sizes.

We exploit semantic information to facilitate co-segmentation to associate objects of the same category from different videos. Visual semantics has been used as prior information for object segmentation in weakly labeled videos [28,31,35]. In semantic video object segmentation, an object detector or a segmentation algorithm is first applied to localize objects according to the video label. However, for videos without any semantic label, an object detector may find noisy segments that do not belong to any semantic object (i.e., due to the trade-off between recall and precision). In this work, we propose an algorithm to associate semantic representations between objects in different videos and help the object co-segmentation process, where non-object detections can be removed.

Toward this end, we first extract semantic objects in each video. Compared with methods that use region proposals [34,35] to localize objects, we develop a proposal-free tracking-based approach that generates multiple tracklets of regions (segments) across the video. Each tracklet maintains temporal connections and contains a predicted category that is initialized by an image-based semantic segmentation algorithm. After collecting tracklets from all videos, we link the relations between tracklets for each object category by formulating a submodular optimization problem, which maximizes the similarities between object regions (segments). With this formulation, prominent objects in each video can be discovered and segmented based on similarities of regions.

We first conduct experiments on the Youtube-Objects dataset [22] in a weakly-supervised manner. Then we evaluate the proposed method in a more generalized setting without knowing any semantic information as a prior. Both results show that our algorithm performs favorably against the state-of-the-art methods. In addition, we compare our method to the other video object co-segmentation approaches on the MOViCS [3] and Safari [34] datasets. Experimental results on three datasets show that the proposed algorithm performs favorably in terms of visual quality and accuracy.

The contributions of this work are summarized as follows. First, we propose a semantic co-segmentation method that considers relations between objects from a collection of videos, where object categories can be unknown. Second, a proposal-free tracking-based method is developed to segment object-like tracklets while maintaining temporal consistency in videos. Third, a submodular function is formulated to carry out semantic co-segmentation from tracklets in all videos.

2   Related Work

Video Object Segmentation/Co-segmentation. Object segmentation from one single video has been studied extensively in the literature [10,14,15,21,29,33]. In general, these approaches are developed to use spatial-temporal graphical models based on object proposals [14,33], segments [15], motion cues [21] or propagating foreground regions [10,19,29]. Recently, co-segmentation methods are developed to segment common objects in images [11,25,30] and videos [3,6, 8,26,34]. Most co-segmentation schemes assume that all the input videos contain at least one common target object [3,6,8,26], which is rarely true in real world scenarios. With a less strict assumption in [34], objects with unknown number of categories can be segmented from a collection of videos by tracking and matching object proposals. However, another assumption underlying the above-mentioned methods is that usually common objects have almost identical appearances. In contrast, the proposed algorithm is not constrained by these factors and is able to segment objects with large variations in appearances without any assumption, e.g., number of object instances and number of object categories.

Object Segmentation in Weakly-Supervised Videos. Weakly-supervised methods have attracted attention due to their effectiveness for facilitating the segmentation process with known video-level object categories. Several learning-based approaches are proposed to collect semantic samples for training segment classifiers [9,28] or performing label transfer [16], and then identify the target object in videos. However, these methods rely on training instances and may generate inaccurate segmentation results. Zhang et al. [35] propose to segment semantic objects via detection without the need of training process. In this method, object detections and proposals are integrated within an optimization framework to refine the final tracklets for segmentation. In contrast, the proposed algorithm does not require object proposals or video-level annotations. More importantly, we link objects between different videos and construct a graph for submodular optimization, and hence help recognize each semantic object.

Object Discovery and Co-localization. Object discovery and co-localization methods are developed in a way similar to object co-segmentation, and these methods assume that input images or videos contain object instances from the same category. Recent image-based approaches [2,4,24,27] are proposed to overcome the problem of large amounts of intra-class variations and inter-class diversity. Several video-based methods are extended to account for temporal information. In [31], superpixel-level labels are propagated across frames via a boosting algorithm. However, this approach requires supervision from a few frame-level annotations. Kwak et al. [12] propose a video object discovery method by matching correspondences across videos and tracking object regions across frames. Different from the above-mentioned schemes, this work focuses on video object co-segmentation without any assumption on objects appearing in videos, in a way that we incorporate semantic information and analyze relations between object-like tracklets.

3   Proposed Algorithm

3.1   Overview

Given a set of videos with unknown object categories, our goal is to discover and segment prominent objects, as well as assign each object a semantic label. To achieve this, we first utilize a fully convolutional network (FCN) [17] trained

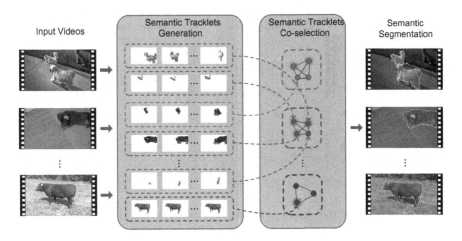

Fig. 1. Overview of the proposed algorithm. Given a collection of videos without providing category labels, we aim to segment semantic objects. First, a set of tracklets is generated for each video, and each tracklet is associated with a predicted category illustrated in different colors (e.g., blue represents the dog and red represents the cow). Then a graph that connects tracklets as nodes from all videos is constructed for each object category. We formulate it as the submodular optimization problem to co-select tracklets that belong to true objects (depicted as glowing nodes), and produce final semantic segmentation results. (Color figure online)

on the PASCAL VOC 2011 dataset [5] to segment objects in each frame, where each segment has a predicted category. To reduce noisy segments in each video, we cluster segments and eliminate clusters containing noisy segments through the video. Among the selected clusters with object segments, we randomly choose a few of them as initializations and apply a spatial-temporal graph-based tracking algorithm to generate tracklets. Each tracklet maintains coherent appearances of an object region (segment) in the spatial and temporal domains.

However, tracklets may still contain only object parts or noisy background clutters, and the available visual information is limited within each video. We construct a graph that connects tracklets within the same category from all videos as nodes, and utilize a submodular function to define the corresponding relations based on their appearances, shapes and motions. After maximizing this submodular function, tracklets are ranked according to their mutual similarities, and hence prominent objects can be discovered in each video. Figure 1 shows the overview of the proposed algorithm.

3.2 Semantic Tracklet Generation

Video object segmentation methods usually utilize object proposals in each frame to detect where instances may appear [6,14,15,34]. One challenge is to associate thousands of proposals from different objects while maintaining temporal connections for each of them across all sequences. Here, we propose to utilize a semantic segmentation algorithm (e.g., FCN) to generate object segments as

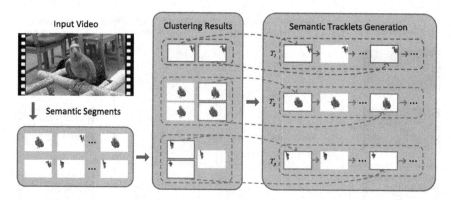

Fig. 2. Illustration of the proposed method for semantic tracklet generation. Given an input video, we first utilize the FCN algorithm to produce semantic segments in each frame. We then cluster all segments within each object category into different groups, where each color denotes one category (e.g., two green groups for birds and one blue group for dogs). Within each group, we randomly select a few segments as multiple initializations (depicted as rectangular boxes with solid color lines) and utilize a tracking-based approach to generate semantic tracklets T_i. Note that we only show the forward tracklets in this figure (similar process when generating backward tracklets). (Color figure online)

initializations, and then construct a spatial-temporal graphical model to track each object segment and form tracklets. The procedure to generate tracklets is illustrated in Fig. 2.

Selecting Objects Segments via Clustering. We first apply the FCN algorithm to extract object segments in each frame of one video. To reduce noisy segments that are not likely to be any object, a simple yet effective clustering method is utilized to select object-like segments through each video. Since the number of object instances is unknown, we apply the mean shift clustering method on all the segments within each object category based on color histograms in the RGB space. Then we select the N largest clusters (i.e., top 80 % of the largest ones) while removing the others.

The object segments in selected clusters are considered as initializations for tracking. We randomly choose a few segments from each cluster, while ensuring the selected segments are within a certain time frame (e.g., at least 20 frames apart between two selected segments) to increase the diversity. However, these initializations may not contain the entire object region or include background clutters. To refine each initialized segment, we learn an online SVM model based on color histograms (as used in the clustering stage), and re-estimate the foreground region using an iterative scheme (e.g., one iteration is sufficient in this work) as in the GrabCut method [23].

Tracking Object Segments. Based on multiple initializations from the previous step, we aim to track segments and generate consistent tracklets (as illus-

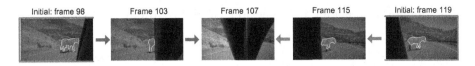

Fig. 3. An example to track the object under heavy occlusions based on the proposed bi-directional approach with multiple initializations, where initialized segments are denoted as colored rectangular boxes.

trated in Fig. 2). The tracking scheme can better localize objects that may be missed by detection algorithms in a single frame, while maintaining temporal connections between object segments. Since selected segments within the same cluster share similar appearances, we track multiple segments in both forward and backward directions, and group them into two tracklets. Hence, we obtain $2N$ tracklets for each cluster. We note that the bi-directional approach facilitates tracking segments under heavy occlusions (see Fig. 3 for an example). Further note that each initialized segment only tracks a small number of frames until reaching the next initialization, as most tracking methods perform well within a number of frames.

Considering the case of forward tracking from frame $t-1$ to t, the goal is to assign each pixel $x_i^t \in X$ with a foreground or background label $\in \{0, 1\}$. We define an energy function in a Conditional Random Field (CRF):

$$E(X) = U_t(X) + \gamma^s \sum_{(i,j,t) \in \mathcal{N}_t} V_t(x_i^t, x_j^t) + \gamma^t \sum_{(i,j,t) \in \mathcal{N}_t} W_t(x_i^{t-1}, x_j^t), \qquad (1)$$

where U_t is the unary potential to be foreground or background, and V_t and W_t are pairwise potentials for spatial and temporal smoothnesses with weights γ^s and γ^t, respectively. The pairwise terms are defined in a way similar to those in [21]. To reduce the computational load and the effect of background noise, we only segment the object within an estimated object location R_t, obtained as in [29]. Note that we also define $\mathcal{N}_t$ as the neighboring set within this region. For the unary term in (1), we compute appearance and location energies defined by:

$$U_t(X) = \alpha \sum_{(i,t) \in R_t} \Phi_a(x_i^t) + \beta \sum_{(i,t) \in R_t} \Phi_l(x_i^t), \qquad (2)$$

where Φ_a is the appearance term, and Φ_l is the location term. For the appearance term, we learn a SVM model based on color histograms (as used in the clustering stage) from the first frame, and an online SVM model with CNN features [18] updated every frame. The weight α consists of α^{col} and α^{cnn} for the color and CNN features, respectively. By minimizing (1) using the graph cut method [1], we obtain labels and thus the object mask within R_t, and continue to track segments in the next frame.

3.3   Semantic Tracklet Co-selection via Submodular Function

For each video, we generate a set of tracklets where each one is assigned to an object category from the FCN method. However, these tracklets are usually noisy (false negatives) and may not belong to any true object (false positives). In addition, objects within the same category usually share more similarities. To better select object-like tracklets, we collect all those within the same category from all videos to help each other. That is achieved by constructing a graph where the tracklets are nodes, and formulating it as a submodular optimization problem which aims to find a subset that shares more similarities. Once tracklets are selected in each video, we rank different semantic objects based on the submodular energies and find prominent objects.

Graph Construction on Tracklets. We first collect tracklets from all videos where each one is associated with an object category from a set of M categories $\mathcal{L} = \{1, 2, \cdots, M\}$. For each category $l \in \mathcal{L}$, we can find a tracklet set $\mathcal{O}$, and construct a graph $G = (\mathcal{V}, \mathcal{E})$ containing tracklets from all videos (with the same category l), where each node $v \in \mathcal{V}$ is a tracklet and the edges $e \in \mathcal{E}$ model the pairwise relations. For each G, we aim to discover an object-like tracklet set $\mathcal{A}$ of $\mathcal{O}$ by iteratively selecting elements of $\mathcal{O}$ into $\mathcal{A}$.

Submodular Function. Our submodular objective function is designed to find tracklets that meet two criteria: (1) sharing more similarities, (2) maintaining high quality object-like segments. To achieve this, we model the submodular function with a facility location term [13,36] to compute similarities, and a unary term that measures how likely the tracklet belongs to the true object. We first introduce the facility location term defined as:

$$\mathcal{F}(\mathcal{A}) = \sum_{i \in \mathcal{A}} \sum_{j \in \mathcal{V}} w_{ij} - \sum_{i \in \mathcal{A}} \phi_i, \tag{3}$$

where w_{ij} is the pairwise relation between a potential facility v_i and a node v_j, and ϕ_i is the cost to open a facility fixed to a constant ϵ. In (3), we define w_{ij} as the similarity $S(v_i, v_j)$ to encourage the model to find a similar facility v_i to v_j such that the final selected tracklets share more similarities.

To compute the similarity between two tracklets, we represent each tracklet by a feature vector F_i, and compute their inner product, $S(v_i, v_j) = \langle F_i, F_j \rangle$, as the similarity. For each tracklet, we extract CNN features (same as mentioned in (2)) in each frame and utilize an average pooling method to compute a feature vector that represents each object. Then F_i is computed by averaging feature vectors from all the frames to represent each tracklet. Note that F_i represents appearance of the tracklet in semantics that is learned from CNN, and hence tracklets within the same category are likely to have higher mutual similarities.

However, with only the facility location term, it is not effective in removing all the noisy tracklets in the selected subset $\mathcal{A}$. Hence we propose to include a unary term in the submodular function that can measure the quality of tracklets while preserving the submodularity. The proposed unary term is defined as:

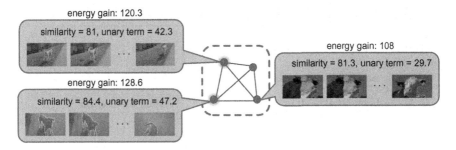

Fig. 4. Illustration of the proposed submodular function for tracklet co-selection. We show three tracklets within the dog category, where the left two tracklets are selected as true objects (denoted as glowing nodes). For each tracklet, we show energy gain, unary term and summed pairwise energy (similarity) in the facility location term. While all three tracklets have high similarity scores, the right tracklet (false positive) has lower energy gain due to low unary term resulting from inconsistent motions and shapes, and hence it is not selected as the object.

$$\mathcal{U}(\mathcal{A}) = \lambda_o \sum_{i \in \mathcal{A}} \Phi_o(i) + \lambda_m \sum_{i \in \mathcal{A}} \Phi_m(i) + \lambda_s \sum_{i \in \mathcal{A}} \Phi_s(i), \tag{4}$$

where $\Phi_o(i)$ measures how likely v_i belongs to the true object (objectness score), and $\Phi_m(i)$ and $\Phi_s(i)$ evaluate the quality of v_i based on the consistency of motions and shapes.

First, we compute $\Phi_o(i) = p_o(i)$ by utilizing probabilities from the FCN output layer according to its category, where $p_o(i)$ is the average probability on all the pixels in v_i. For motion consistency, we use a method similar to [33] and compute motion scores around segment boundaries based on the average gradient magnitude of optical flow estimations [32]. Then we compute $\Phi_m(i)$ by averaging all the motion scores obtained for every two frames. The shape consistency is also considered by computing the intersection-over-union (overlap) ratio between two object segments in adjacent frames. We then compute the variance $\nu_s(i)$ of these overlap ratios, and define $\Phi_s(i) = 1 - \nu_s(i)$, which reflects that larger variance has lower consistency.

Optimization for Tracklet Co-selection. We aim to formulate a submodular function such that tracklets in the selected set $\mathcal{A}$ share more similarities and maintain object-like as well as consistent segments. We combine the facility location term (3) and the unary term (4) with a weight δ into an objective function, and the submodularity is preserved by linearly combining two non-negative terms:

$$\max_{\mathcal{A}} \mathcal{C}(\mathcal{A}) = \max_{\mathcal{A}} \mathcal{F}(\mathcal{A}) + \delta \mathcal{U}(\mathcal{A}),$$
$$\text{s.t. } \mathcal{A} \subseteq \mathcal{O} \subseteq \mathcal{V}, \ \mathcal{N}_{\mathcal{A}} \leq \mathcal{N},$$
$$\mathcal{H}(\mathcal{A}^i) \geq 0,$$
$$\mathcal{H}(\mathcal{A}^i) \geq \rho \cdot \mathcal{H}(\mathcal{A}^{i-1}), \tag{5}$$

Algorithm 1. Tracklet Co-selection for Each Category

Input: $G = (\mathcal{V}, \mathcal{E}), \mathcal{N}, \rho$

Initialization: $\mathcal{A}^0 \leftarrow \emptyset, \mathcal{O}^0 \leftarrow \mathcal{V}, i \leftarrow 1$

loop

    $a^* = \arg \max_{\{\mathcal{A}^i \in \mathcal{V}\}} \mathcal{H}(\mathcal{A}^i)$, where $\mathcal{A}^i = \mathcal{A}^{i-1} \cup a$

    if $\mathcal{N}_{\mathcal{A}} > \mathcal{N}$ or $\mathcal{H}(\mathcal{A}^i) < 0$ or $\mathcal{H}(\mathcal{A}^i) < \rho \cdot \mathcal{H}(\mathcal{A}^{i-1})$ when $i \geq 2$ **then**

        break

    end if

    $\mathcal{A}^i \leftarrow \mathcal{A}^{i-1} \cup a^*, \mathcal{O}^i \leftarrow \mathcal{O}^{i-1} - a^*, i = i + 1$

end loop

Output: $\mathcal{A} \leftarrow \mathcal{A}^i, \mathcal{O} \leftarrow \mathcal{O}^i$

---

where $\mathcal{N}_{\mathcal{A}}$ is the number of open facilities, and $\mathcal{H}(\mathcal{A}^i)$ is the energy gain at iterations i during iterative optimization, which is defined as: $\mathcal{C}(\mathcal{A}^i) - \mathcal{C}(\mathcal{A}^{i-1})$. We adopt a greedy algorithm to optimize (5) in a way similar to [36]. We start from an empty set of $\mathcal{A}$ and iteratively add an element $a \in \mathcal{V} \backslash \mathcal{A}$ to $\mathcal{A}$ that provides the largest energy gain. The iterative process stops when one of the following conditions is satisfied. First, the number of selected nodes is reached, i.e., $\mathcal{N}_{\mathcal{A}} > \mathcal{N}$. Second, the energy gain is negative, i.e., $\mathcal{H}(\mathcal{A}^i) < 0$. Third, the ratio of increased energy gain is below a threshold, i.e., $\mathcal{H}(\mathcal{A}^i) < \rho \cdot \mathcal{H}(\mathcal{A}^{i-1})$, when $i \geq 2$. We show the main steps of the tracklet co-selection algorithm for each category l in Algorithm 1 and Fig. 4 illustrates the effectiveness of the proposed submodular function.

After optimizing (5) for each graph G within one category, we select a set of tracklets $\mathcal{T}_l$ for each category l. Considering each video, we can obtain a few tracklets from different sets of $\mathcal{T}_l$, where l can be any category among $\mathcal{L}$. In each video, we then compute the normalized energy gain for each obtained tracklet and re-rank all of them. This is, a normalized gain for a tracklet with category l added at iteration i during optimization is computed as $\mathcal{G}_l^i = \frac{\mathcal{H}(\mathcal{A}^i)}{\mathcal{C}(\mathcal{A}^1)}$, where $\mathcal{C}(\mathcal{A}^1)$ is the energy as the normalization term after adding the first tracklet. Based on the re-ranked results, a threshold (i.e., 0.85 in this work) is applied to all $\mathcal{G}_l^i$ for selecting a set of semantic tracklets that represent prominent objects. To obtain final semantic segmentation results, since object segments from different tracklets may overlap to each other, we choose the one with larger $\mathcal{G}_l^i$ in overlapped regions.

4   Experimental Results

We evaluate the proposed co-segmentation algorithm against the state-of-the-art methods on numerous benchmark datasets. The MATLAB code will be made available at https://sites.google.com/site/yihsuantsai/.

4.1   Experimental Settings

For tracklet generation, we learn an online SVM model with CNN features combining the first three convolutional layers [17] (i.e., 448 dimensional vectors).

For parameters in the graphical model (1) and (2), we use $\alpha^{col} = 1, \alpha^{cnn} = 1, \beta = 0.5, \gamma^s = 3.5$ and $\gamma^t = 1$. In the submodular function, we set ϵ as 3 in the facility location term of (3), and use $\lambda_o = \lambda_m = \lambda_s = 1$ in the unary term of (4). During submodular optimization, we use $\delta = 20$ in (5), and set $\mathcal{N} = 10$ and $\rho = 0.8$ to determine stopping conditions. All these parameters are fixed in the experiments for fair evaluations.

4.2 Youtube-Objects Dataset

The Youtube-Objects dataset [22] contains 10 object categories, and the length of each sequence is up to 400 frames. We evaluate the proposed algorithm in a subset of 126 videos with more than 20000 frames, where the pixel-wise annotations in every 10 frames are provided by [10]. Note that, different from previous video co-segmentation datasets [3,34], appearances and shapes of objects from the same category in this dataset are significantly different.

We first conduct experiments in a weakly supervised manner, where a semantic label is given for each video. Next, we evaluate our algorithm in a way that object categories are unknown in videos. Table 1 shows segmentation results of the proposed method and other state-of-the-art approaches. We use the intersection-over-union (overlap) ratio to evaluate all the methods.

Weakly Labeled Videos. For the video labeled with a semantic category, we use FCN segments belonging to its video-level category as initializations, such that tracklets generated in each video (as described in Sect. 3.2) are all associated with the same category. We compare our approach with other supervised tracking-based [7,20] or weakly supervised [35][1] methods. Table 1 shows that the proposed method with weak supervision performs favorably in terms of overlap ratio, especially in 7 out of 10 categories.

In general, our method performs well on non-rigid objects (*bird, cat, dog, horse*) and fast moving objects (*car, train*). As the appearances and shapes of these objects vary significantly, it is challenging to segment these objects from all videos accurately. Although the recent method [35] utilizes object detectors and generates proposals to localize objects in each frame, it is less effective for videos with large appearance and shape variations as the generated proposals are usually noisy and less consistent across videos. In contrast, the proposed tracking-based algorithm is able to capture detailed appearance and shape changes, and hence generate tracklets consistently for segmentation.

Semantic Co-segmentation. In addition to weakly supervised settings, the proposed algorithm can segment objects and discover the corresponding object categories without any supervision. Table 1 shows our segmentation results compared with the state-of-the-art unsupervised method [21]. The proposed algorithm generates more accurate segmentation results in most categories with significant improvement (e.g., more than 10 % gain in *boat, cat* and *train*).

---

[1] [35] evaluates the method on their annotated images, and we obtain their results on the same annotation set [10] directly from the authors.

Table 1. Segmentation results on the Youtube-Objects dataset with the overlap ratio.

Category	[7]	[35]	Ours	[20]	[21]	Baseline (FCN)	Ours
Supervised?	Y	weakly	weakly	N	N	N	N
Aeroplane	**73.6**	72.4	69.3	13.7	**70.9**	60.8	69.3
Bird	56.1	66.6	**76.1**	12.2	70.6	69.7	**76.0**
Boat	**57.8**	43.0	57.2	10.8	42.5	44.7	**53.5**
Car	33.9	58.9	**70.4**	23.7	65.2	60.3	**70.4**
Cat	30.5	36.4	**67.7**	18.6	52.1	53.9	**66.8**
Cow	41.8	58.2	**59.7**	16.3	44.5	**52.8**	49.0
Dog	36.8	48.7	**64.2**	18.0	**65.3**	52.8	47.5
Horse	44.3	49.6	**57.1**	11.5	53.5	42.4	**55.7**
Motorbike	**48.9**	41.4	44.1	10.6	44.2	**47.3**	39.5
Train	39.2	49.3	**57.9**	19.6	29.6	**54.7**	53.4
Mean	46.3	52.4	**62.3**	15.5	53.8	53.9	**58.1**

It demonstrates the effectiveness of our co-segmentation scheme that links relations between semantic objects from all videos, which is not addressed in [21].

To evaluate the effectiveness of the proposed tracking-based algorithm for tracklet generation, we establish a baseline method which directly groups FCN segments from every frame into a tracklet for each category (i.e., without using tracking). We then use the same submodular function for tracklet co-selection (Sect. 3.3). Compared to this baseline method, the proposed algorithm performs well on most categories, especially for deformable objects such as *bird*, *cat* and *horse*, as consistent tracklets can be extracted. However, the proposed algorithm does not perform well in some videos (*cow*, *motorbike*) as some segments are not initialized well, which causes inaccurate tracking results in these videos.

Compared to the proposed algorithm with weakly supervised setting, the results on categories such as *aeroplane*, *bird* and *car* have identical and high overlap ratios. It shows that without providing video-level labels, our co-segmentation approach can reduce noisy segments that are generated from other false categories, and hence retain high accuracies as with weakly supervised setting. Moreover, it is worth noticing that the proposed algorithm without supervision, already performs favorably against the state-of-the-art method that requires weak supervision [35].

Different from other methods [21,35], the proposed algorithm can segment objects as well as discover object categories (labels). We evaluate the classification accuracy for predicting object categories based on ranked tracklets, and the average precision (AP) is 85.3 on average over all categories. The results show that with the proposed submodular function and re-ranking in each video, false positives can be reduced, and hence prominent objects are discovered. We show qualitative results in Fig. 5, and more results are presented in the supplementary material.

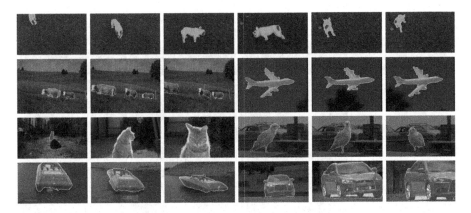

Fig. 5. Example results for semantic co-segmentation on the Youtube-Objects dataset (without knowing object categories). The colors overlapping on the objects indicate different semantic labels. The results show that our method is able to track and segment (multiple) objects under challenges such as occlusions, fast movements, deformed shapes, scale changes and cluttered backgrounds. Best viewed in color with enlarged images. (Color figure online)

4.3 MOViCS Dataset

The MOViCS dataset [3], which contains 4 sets with 11 sequences, is used for evaluation on multi-class video co-segmentation. For each set, at least one common object appears in all videos, while the number of object categories is unknown. The proposed algorithm is evaluated against three state-of-the-art methods including image co-segmentation (ICS) [11], video co-segmentation (VCS) [3] and RMWC [34]. We use the unsupervised method [21] as a baseline and produce segments in each frame as initializations for tracklet generation (Sect. 3.2). In addition, since categories are not known for different segments at this stage, one graph including tracklets from all videos is constructed for co-selecting tracklets in each video.

Based on the evaluation metric in [3], Table 2 shows that the proposed algorithm performs well in all the video sets, especially in the *tiger* set. As the variations of objects in some videos are large, other approaches are less effective in segmenting objects in these videos. In contrast, our method works for objects with various appearances in different videos by utilizing the submodular optimization that accounts for appearances, shapes and motions together to co-select tracklets containing common objects. We show qualitative comparisons to other methods in Fig. 6.

4.4 Safari Dataset

In addition to co-segmentation in videos where each set contains at least one common object, our method is able to segment objects given a collection of sequences without any prior knowledge. The Safari dataset [34] contains 9 videos with 5

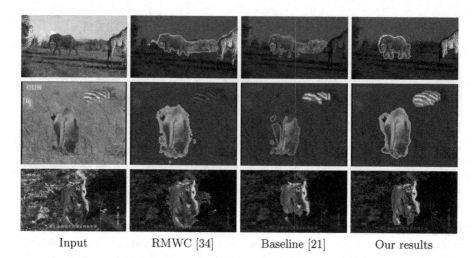

Input   RMWC [34]   Baseline [21]   Our results

Fig. 6. Example results for object co-segmentation on the MOViCS dataset. Segmentation outputs are indicated as colored contours, where each color represents an instance. Compared to the state-of-the-art approach [34] and the baseline method [21] that often produce noisy segments or missing objects, our method obtains better segmentation results. Best viewed in color. (Color figure online)

Table 2. Segmentation results on the MOViCS dataset with the overlap ratio.

Video Set	ICS [11]	RMWC [34]	VCS [3]	Baseline [21]	Ours
Chicken & Turtle	8.0	86.0	65.0	73.6	**87.7**
Zebra & Lion	23.0	58.8	48.0	45.9	**71.3**
Giraffe & Elephant	7.0	52.8	52.0	36.5	**59.0**
Tiger	30.0	33.6	30.0	44.1	**70.9**
Mean	17.0	57.8	48.8	50.0	**72.2**

object categories, where each video may contain one or two object categories. To evaluate the proposed algorithm, we input these 9 videos together and segment common objects. Note that, we use [21] as the baseline method for single video object segmentation. Then we initialize these segments to generate tracklets and construct a graph for tracklet co-selection.

Table 3 shows the results by the proposed algorithm and two state-of-the-art methods. In 4 out of 5 categories, our method achieves better results over the other methods. The VCS [3] method is not effective for the general setting when videos contain unknown types of object categories, and hence generates less accurate results. The RMWC method [34] relies on object proposals and does not generate consistent tracklets across videos when more than one object category is involved. In our proposed algorithm, we utilize tracking-based method to generate consistent tracklets, and segment objects via submodular optimization

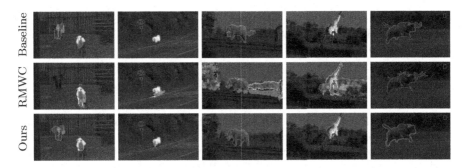

Fig. 7. Example results for object co-segmentation on the Safari dataset. Segmentation outputs are indicated as colored contours, where each color represents an instance. Compared to the state-of-the-art approach [34] (second row) and the baseline method [21] (first row) that often produce noisy segments, false positives or missing objects, our method obtains better segmentation results. Best viewed in color.

Table 3. Segmentation results on the Safari dataset with the overlap ratio.

Object	RMWC [34]	VCS [3]	Baseline [21]	Ours
Buffalo	86.9	68.6	90.0	**91.3**
Elephant	35.3	26.6	73.8	**74.9**
Giraffe	2.4	2.4	9.8	**15.8**
Lion	**31.7**	30.2	19.0	21.9
Sheep	36.3	4.8	32.3	**65.8**
Mean	38.5	26.5	45.0	**54.0**

in multiple videos without any assumption on the commonality of objects in the videos. We show some example results in Fig. 7.

5   Concluding Remarks

In this paper, we present a novel algorithm to segment objects and understand their visual semantics from a collection of videos. To exploit semantic information, we first assign a category for each discovered segment in videos via the FCN method. A tracking-based approach is presented to generate consistent tracklets across videos. We then link the relations between videos by constructing graphs which contain tracklets from different videos. Without any assumption of objects appearing in videos, we formulate a submodular optimization problem and co-select tracklets, which accounts for their appearances, shapes and motions. This step considers other sequences and reduces noisy tracklets that can not be filtered out within a single video. As a result, prominent objects are discovered and segmented in videos. Extensive experimental results on the Youtube-Objects, MOViCS and Safari datasets show that our method performs favorably against the state-of-the-art approaches in terms of visual quality and accuracy.

Acknowledgments. This work is supported in part by the NSF CAREER grant #1149783, NSF IIS grant #1152576, and gifts from Adobe and Nvidia. G. Zhong is sponsored by China Scholarship Council.

References

1. Boykov, Y., Kolmogorov, V.: An experimental comparison of min-cut/max-flow algorithms for energy minimization in vision. PAMI **26**(9), 1124–1137 (2004)
2. Chen, X., Shrivastava, A., Gupta, A.: Enriching visual knowledge bases via object discovery and segmentation. In: CVPR (2014)
3. Chiu, W.C., Fritz, M.: Multi-class video co-segmentation with a generative multi-video model. In: CVPR (2013)
4. Cho, M., Kwak, S., Schmid, C., Ponce, J.: Unsupervised object discovery and localization in the wild: Part-based matching with bottom-up region proposals. In: CVPR (2015)
5. Everingham, M., Gool, L.J.V., Williams, C.K.I., Winn, J.M., Zisserman, A.: The pascal visual object classes (VOC) challenge. IJCV **88**(2), 303–338 (2010)
6. Fu, H., Xu, D., Zhang, B., Lin, S.: Object-based multiple foreground video co-segmentation. In: CVPR (2014)
7. Godec, M., Roth, P.M., Bischof, H.: Hough-based tracking of non-rigid objects. In: ICCV (2011)
8. Guo, J., Cheong, L.-F., Tan, R.T., Zhou, S.Z.: Consistent foreground co-segmentation. In: Cremers, D., Reid, I., Saito, H., Yang, M.-H. (eds.) ACCV 2014. LNCS, vol. 9006, pp. 241–257. Springer, Heidelberg (2015)
9. Hartmann, G., Grundmann, M., Hoffman, J., Tsai, D., Kwatra, V., Madani, O., Vijayanarasimhan, S., Essa, I., Rehg, J., Sukthankar, R.: Weakly supervised learning of object segmentations from web-scale video. In: ECCV Workshop (2012)
10. Jain, S.D., Grauman, K.: Supervoxel-consistent foreground propagation in video. In: Fleet, D., Pajdla, T., Schiele, B., Tuytelaars, T. (eds.) ECCV 2014, Part IV. LNCS, vol. 8692, pp. 656–671. Springer, Heidelberg (2014)
11. Joulin, A., Bach, F., Ponce, J.: Multi-class cosegmentation. In: CVPR (2012)
12. Kwak, S., Cho, M., Laptev, I., Ponce, J., Schmid, C.: Unsupervised object discovery and tracking in video collections. In: ICCV (2015)
13. Lazic, N., Givoni, I., Frey, B., Aarabi, P.: Floss: Facility location for subspace segmentation. In: ICCV (2009)
14. Lee, Y.J., Kim, J., Grauman, K.: Key-segments for video object segmentation. In: ICCV (2011)
15. Li, F., Kim, T., Humayun, A., Tsai, D., Rehg, J.M.: Video segmentation by tracking many figure-ground segments. In: ICCV (2013)
16. Liu, X., Tao, D., Song, M., Ruan, Y., Chen, C., Bu, J.: Weakly supervised multi-class video segmentation. In: CVPR (2014)
17. Long, J., Shelhamer, E., Darrell, T.: Fully convolutional networks for semantic segmentation. In: CVPR (2015)
18. Ma, C., Huang, J.B., Yang, X., Yang, M.H.: Hierarchical convolutional features for visual tracking. In: ICCV (2015)
19. Nagaraja, N.S., Schmidt, F., Brox, T.: Video segmentation with just a few strokes. In: ICCV (2015)
20. Ochs, P., Malik, J., Brox, T.: Segmentation of moving objects by long term video analysis. PAMI **36**(6), 1187–1200 (2014)

21. Papazoglou, A., Ferrari, V.: Fast object segmentation in unconstrained video. In: ICCV (2013)
22. Prest, A., Leistner, C., Civera, J., Schmid, C., Ferrari, V.: Learning object class detectors from weakly annotated video. In: CVPR (2012)
23. Rother, C., Kolmogorov, V., Blake, A.: Grabcut: Interactive foreground extraction using iterated graph cuts. In: SIGGRAPH (2004)
24. Rubinstein, M., Joulin, A., Kopf, J., Liu, C.: Unsupervised joint object discovery and segmentation in internet images. In: CVPR (2013)
25. Rubio, J.C., Serrat, J., Antonio, L., Paragios, N.: Unsupervised co-segmentation through region matching. In: CVPR (2012)
26. Rubio, J.C., Serrat, J., López, A.: Video co-segmentation. In: Lee, K.M., Matsushita, Y., Rehg, J.M., Hu, Z. (eds.) ACCV 2012, Part II. LNCS, vol. 7725, pp. 13–24. Springer, Heidelberg (2013)
27. Tang, K., Joulin, A., Li, L.J., Fei-Fei, L.: Co-localization in real-world images. In: CVPR (2014)
28. Tang, K., Sukthankar, R., Yagnik, J., Fei-Fei, L.: Discriminative segment annotation in weakly labeled video. In: CVPR (2013)
29. Tsai, Y.H., Yang, M.H., Black, M.J.: Video segmentation via object flow. In: CVPR (2016)
30. Vicente, S., Rother, C., Kolmogorov, V.: Object cosegmentation. In: CVPR (2011)
31. Wang, L., Hua, G., Sukthankar, R., Xue, J., Zheng, N.: Video object discovery and co-segmentation with extremely weak supervision. In: Fleet, D., Pajdla, T., Schiele, B., Tuytelaars, T. (eds.) ECCV 2014, Part IV. LNCS, vol. 8692, pp. 640–655. Springer, Heidelberg (2014)
32. Wulff, J., Black, M.J.: Efficient sparse-to-dense optical flow estimation using a learned basis and layers. In: CVPR (2015)
33. Zhang, D., Javed, O., Shah, M.: Video object segmentation through spatially accurate and temporally dense extraction of primary object regions. In: CVPR (2013)
34. Zhang, D., Javed, O., Shah, M.: Video object co-segmentation by regulated maximum weight cliques. In: Fleet, D., Pajdla, T., Schiele, B., Tuytelaars, T. (eds.) ECCV 2014, Part VII. LNCS, vol. 8695, pp. 551–566. Springer, Heidelberg (2014)
35. Zhang, Y., Chen, X., Li, J., Wang, C., Xia, C.: Semantic object segmentation via detection in weakly labeled video. In: CVPR (2015)
36. Zhu, F., Jiang, Z., Shao, L.: Submodular object recognition. In: CVPR (2014)

Attribute2Image: Conditional Image Generation from Visual Attributes

Xinchen Yan[1(✉)], Jimei Yang[2], Kihyuk Sohn[3], and Honglak Lee[1]

[1] Computer Science and Engineering,
University of Michigan, Ann Arbor, USA
{xcyan,honglak}@umich.edu
[2] Adobe Research, San Francisco, USA
jimyang@adobe.com
[3] NEC Labs, Cupertino, USA
ksohn@nec-labs.com

Abstract. This paper investigates a novel problem of generating images from visual attributes. We model the image as a composite of foreground and background and develop a layered generative model with disentangled latent variables that can be learned end-to-end using a variational auto-encoder. We experiment with natural images of faces and birds and demonstrate that the proposed models are capable of generating realistic and diverse samples with disentangled latent representations. We use a general energy minimization algorithm for posterior inference of latent variables given novel images. Therefore, the learned generative models show excellent quantitative and visual results in the tasks of attribute-conditioned image reconstruction and completion.

1 Introduction

Generative image modeling is of fundamental interest in computer vision and machine learning. Early works [20, 21, 26, 30, 32, 36] studied statistical and physical principles of building generative models, but due to the lack of effective feature representations, their results are limited to textures or particular patterns such as well-aligned faces. Recent advances on representation learning using deep neural networks [16, 29] nourish a series of deep generative models that enjoy joint generative modeling and representation learning through Bayesian inference [1, 9, 14, 15, 28, 34] or adversarial training [3, 8]. Those works show promising results of generating natural images, but the generated samples are still in low resolution and far from being perfect because of the fundamental challenges of learning unconditioned generative models of images.

In this paper, we are interested in generating object images from high-level description. For example, we would like to generate portrait images that all match the description "a young girl with brown hair is smiling" (Fig. 1). This

Electronic supplementary material The online version of this chapter (doi:10.1007/978-3-319-46493-0_47) contains supplementary material, which is available to authorized users.

B. Leibe et al. (Eds.): ECCV 2016, Part IV, LNCS 9908, pp. 776–791, 2016.
DOI: 10.1007/978-3-319-46493-0_47

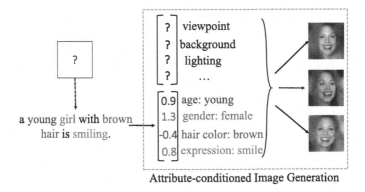

Attribute-conditioned Image Generation

Fig. 1. An example that demonstrates the problem of conditioned image generation from visual attributes. We assume a vector of visual attributes is extracted from a natural language description, and then this attribute vector is combined with learned latent factors to generate diverse image samples. (Color figure online)

conditioned treatment reduces sampling uncertainties and helps generating more realistic images, and thus has potential real-world applications such as forensic art and semantic photo editing [12,19,40]. The high-level descriptions are usually natural languages, but what underlies its corresponding images are essentially a group of facts or visual attributes that are extracted from the sentence. In the example above, the attributes are (hair color: brown), (gender: female), (age: young) and (expression: smile). Based on this assumption, we propose to learn an attribute-conditioned generative model.

Indeed, image generation is a complex process that involves many factors. Other than enlisted attributes, there are many unknown or latent factors. It has been shown that those latent factors are supposed to be interpretable according to their semantic or physical meanings [4,17,27]. Inspired by layered image models [23,38], we disentangle the latent factors into two groups: one related to uncertain properties of foreground object and the other related to the background, and model the generation process as layered composition. In particular, the foreground is overlaid on the background so that the background visibility depends on the foreground shape and position. Therefore, we propose a novel layered image generative model with disentangled foreground and background latent variables. The entire background is first generated from background variables, then the foreground variables are combined with given attributes to generate object layer and its shape map determining the visibility of background and finally the image is composed by the summation of object layer and the background layer gated by its visibility map. We learn this layered generative model in an end-to-end deep neural network using a variational auto-encoder [15] (Sect. 3). Our variational auto-encoder includes two encoders or recognition models for approximating the posterior distributions of foreground and background latent variables respectively, and two decoders for generating a foreground image and a full image by composition. Assuming the latent variables are Gaussian, the whole network can be trained end-to-end by back-propagation using the reparametrization trick.

Generating realistic samples is certainly an important goal of deep generative models. Moreover, generative models can be also used to perform Bayesian inference on novel images. Since the true posterior distribution of latent variables is unknown, we propose a general optimization-based approach for posterior inference using image generation models and latent priors (Sect. 4).

We evaluate the proposed model on two datasets, the Labeled Faces in the Wild (LFW) dataset [10] and the Caltech-UCSD Birds-200-2011 (CUB) dataset [37]. In the LFW dataset, the attributes are 73-dimensional vectors describing age, gender, expressions, hair and many others [18]. In the CUB dataset, the 312-dimensional binary attribute vectors are converted from descriptions about bird parts and colors. We organize our experiments in the following two tasks. First, we demonstrate the quality of attribute-conditioned image generation with comparisons to nearest-neighbor search, and analyze the disentangling performance of latent space and corresponding foreground-background layers. Second, we perform image reconstruction and completion on a set of novel test images by posterior inference with quantitative evaluation. Results from those experiments show the superior performance of the proposed model over previous art. The contributions of this paper are summarized as follows:

- We propose a novel problem of conditioned image generation from visual attributes.
- We tackle this problem by learning conditional variational auto-encoders and propose a novel layered foreground-background generative model that significantly improves the generation quality of complex images.
- We propose a general optimization-based method for posterior inference on novel images and use it to evaluate generative models in the context of image reconstruction and completion.

2   Related Work

Image Generation. In terms of generating realistic and novel images, there are several recent work [3,4,8,9,17,25] that are relevant to ours. Dosovitskiy et al. [4] proposed to generate 3D chairs given graphics code using deep convolutional neural networks, and Kulkarni et al. [17] used variational auto-encoders [15] to model the rendering process of 3D objects. Both of these models [4,17] assume the existence of a graphics engine during training, from which they have (1) virtually infinite amount of training data and/or (2) pairs of rendered images that differ only in one factor of variation. Therefore, they are not directly applicable to natural image generation. While both work [4,17] studied generation of rendered images from complete description (e.g., object identity, view-point, color) trained from synthetic images (via graphics engine), generation of images from an incomplete description (e.g., class labels, visual attributes) is still under-explored. In fact, image generation from incomplete description is a more challenging task and the one-to-one mapping formulation of [4] is inherently limited. Gregor et al. [9]

developed recurrent variational auto-encoders with spatial attention mechanism that allows iterative image generation by patches. This elegant algorithm mimics the process of human drawing but at the same time faces challenges when scaling up to large complex images. Recently, generative adversarial networks (GANs) [3,7,8,25] have been developed for image generation. In the GAN, two models are trained to against each other: a generative model aims to capture the data distribution, while a discriminative model attempts to distinguish between generated samples and training data. The GAN training is based on a min-max objective, which is known to be challenging to optimize.

Layered Modeling of Images. Layered models or 2.1D representations of images have been studied in the context of moving or still object segmentation [11,23,38,39,41]. The layered structure is introduced into generative image modeling [20,35]. Tang et al. [35] modeled the occluded images with gated restricted Boltzmann machines and achieved good inpainting and denoising results on well cropped face images. Le Roux et al. [20] explicitly modeled the occlusion layer in a masked restricted Boltzmann machine for separating foreground and background and demonstrated promising results on small patches. Though similar to our proposed gating in the form, these models face challenges when applied to model large natural images due to its difficulty in learning hierarchical representation based on restricted Boltzmann machine.

Multimodal Learning. Generative models of image and text have been studied in multimodal learning to model joint distribution of multiple data modalities [22,31,33]. For example, Srivastava and Salakhutdinov [33] developed a multimodal deep Boltzmann machine that models joint distribution of image and text (e.g., image tag). Sohn et al. [31] proposed improved shared representation learning of multimodal data through bi-directional conditional prediction by deriving a conditional prediction model of one data modality given the other and vice versa. Both of these works focused more on shared representation learning using hand-crafted low-level image features and therefore have limited applications such as conditional image or text retrieval than actual generation of images.

3   Attribute-Conditioned Generative Modeling of Images

In this section, we describe our proposed method for attribute-conditioned generative modeling of images. We first describe a conditional variational auto-encoder, followed by the formulation of layered generative model and its variational learning.

3.1   Base Model: Conditional Variational Auto-Encoder (CVAE)

Given the attribute $y \in \mathbb{R}^{N_y}$ and latent variable $z \in \mathbb{R}^{N_z}$, our goal is to build a model $p_\theta(x|y, z)$ that generates realistic image $x \in \mathbb{R}^{N_x}$ conditioned on y and z. Here, we refer p_θ a generator (or generation model), parametrized by θ. Conditioned image generation is simply a two-step process in the following:

1. Randomly sample latent variable z from prior distribution $p(z)$;
2. Given y and z as conditioning variable, generate image x from $p_\theta(x|y,z)$.

Here, the purpose of learning is to find the best parameter θ that maximizes the log-likelihood $\log p_\theta(x|y)$. As proposed in [15,28], variational auto-encoders try to maximize the variational lower bound of the log-likelihood $\log p_\theta(x|y)$. Specifically, an auxiliary distribution $q_\phi(z|x,y)$ is introduced to approximate the true posterior $p_\theta(z|x,y)$. We refer the base model a conditional variational auto-encoder (CVAE) with the conditional log-likelihood

$$\log p_\theta(x|y) = KL(q_\phi(z|x,y)||p_\theta(z|x,y)) + \mathcal{L}_{\mathrm{CVAE}}(x,y;\theta,\phi),$$

where the variational lower bound

$$\mathcal{L}_{\mathrm{CVAE}}(x,y;\theta,\phi) = -KL(q_\phi(z|x,y)||p_\theta(z)) + \mathbb{E}_{q_\phi(z|x,y)}\left[\log p_\theta(x|y,z)\right] \quad (1)$$

is maximized for learning the model parameters.

Here, the prior $p_\theta(z)$ is assumed to follow isotropic multivariate Gaussian distribution, while two conditional distributions $p_\theta(x|y,z)$ and $q_\phi(z|x,y)$ are multivariate Gaussian distributions whose mean and covariance are parametrized by $\mathcal{N}\left(\mu_\theta(z,y), diag(\sigma_\theta^2(z,y))\right)$ and $\mathcal{N}\left(\mu_\phi(x,y), diag(\sigma_\phi^2(x,y))\right)$, respectively. We refer the auxiliary proposal distribution $q_\phi(z|x,y)$ a recognition model and the conditional data distribution $p_\theta(x|y,z)$ a generation model.

The first term $KL(q_\phi(z|x,y)||p_\theta(z))$ is a regularization term that reduces the gap between the prior $p(z)$ and the proposal distribution $q_\phi(z|x,y)$, while the second term $\log p_\theta(x|y,z)$ is the log likelihood of samples. In practice, we usually take as a deterministic generation function the mean $x = \mu_\theta(z,y)$ of conditional distribution $p_\theta(x|z,y)$ given z and y, so it is convenient to assume the standard deviation function $\sigma_\theta(z,y)$ is a constant shared by all the pixels as the latent factors capture all the data variations. We will keep this assumption for the rest of the paper if not particularly mentioned. Thus, we can rewrite the second term in the variational lower bound as reconstruction loss $L(\cdot,\cdot)$ (e.g., ℓ_2 loss):

$$\mathcal{L}_{\mathrm{CVAE}} = -KL(q_\phi(z|x,y)||p_\theta(z)) - \mathbb{E}_{q_\phi(z|x,y)}L(\mu_\theta(y,z),x) \quad (2)$$

Note that the discriminator of GANs [8] can be used as the loss function $L(\cdot,\cdot)$ as well, especially when ℓ_2 (or ℓ_1) reconstruction loss may not capture the true image similarities. We leave it for future study.

3.2 Disentangling CVAE with a Layered Representation

An image x can be interpreted as a composite of a foreground layer (or a foreground image x_F) and a background layer (or a background image x_B) via a matting equation [24]:

$$x = x_F \odot (1 - g) + x_B \odot g, \quad (3)$$

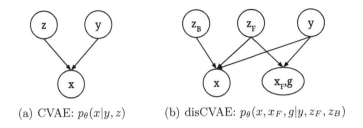

(a) CVAE: $p_\theta(x|y,z)$ (b) disCVAE: $p_\theta(x, x_F, g|y, z_F, z_B)$

Fig. 2. Graphical model representations of attribute-conditioned image generation models (a) without (CVAE) and (b) with (disCVAE) disentangled latent space.

where $\odot$ denotes the element-wise product. $g \in [0,1]^{N_x}$ is an occlusion layer or a gating function that determines the visibility of background pixels while $1 - g$ defines the visibility of foreground pixels. However, the model based on Eq. (3) may suffer from the incorrectly estimated mask as it gates the foreground region with imperfect mask estimation. Instead, we approximate the following formulation that is more robust to estimation error on mask:

$$x = x_F + x_B \odot g. \tag{4}$$

When lighting condition is stable and background is at a distance, we can safely assume foreground and background pixels are generated from independent latent factors. To this end, we propose a disentangled representation $z = [z_F, z_B]$ in the latent space, where z_F together with attribute y captures the foreground factors while z_B the background factors. As a result, the foreground layer x_F is generated from $\mu_{\theta_F}(y, z_F)$ and the background layer x_B from $\mu_{\theta_B}(z_B)$. The foreground shape and position determine the background occlusion so the gating layer g is generated from $s_{\theta_g}(y, z_F)$ where the last layer of $s(\cdot)$ is sigmoid function. In summary, we approximate the layered generation process as follows:

1. Sample foreground and background latent variables $z_F \sim p(z_F)$, $z_B \sim p(z_B)$;
2. Given y and z_F, generate foreground layer $x_F \sim \mathcal{N}\left(\mu_{\theta_F}(y, z_F), \sigma_0^2 I_{N_x}\right)$ and gating layer $g \sim Bernoulli\left(s_{\theta_g}(y, z_F)\right)$; here, σ_0 is a constant. The background layer (which correspond to x_B) is implicitly computed as $\mu_{\theta_B}(z_B)$.
3. Synthesize an image $x \sim \mathcal{N}\left(\mu_\theta(y, z_F, z_B), \sigma_0^2 I_{N_x}\right)$ where $\mu_\theta(y, z_F, z_B) = \mu_{\theta_F}(y, z_F) + s_{\theta_g}(y, z_F) \odot \mu_{\theta_B}(z_B)$.

Learning. It is very challenging to learn our layered generative model in a fully-unsupervised manner since we need to infer about x_F, x_B, and g from the image x only. In this paper, we further assume the foreground layer x_F (as well as gating variable g) is observable during the training and we train the model to maximize the joint log-likelihood $\log p_\theta(x, x_F, g|y)$ instead of $\log p_\theta(x|y)$. With disentangled latent variables z_F and z_B, we refer our layered model a disentangling conditional variational auto-encoder (disCVAE). We compare the graphical models of disCVAE with vanilla CVAE in Fig. 2. Based on the layered generation process, we write the generation model by

$$p_\theta(x_F, g, x, z_F, z_B | y) = p_\theta(x|z_F, z_B, y)p_\theta(x_F, g|z_F, y)p_\theta(z_F)p_\theta(z_B), \quad (5)$$

the recognition model by

$$q_\phi(z_F, z_B | x_F, g, x, y) = q_\phi(z_B | z_F, x_F, g, x, y)q_\phi(z_F | x_F, g, y) \quad (6)$$

and the variational lower bound $\mathcal{L}_{\text{disCVAE}}(x_F, g, x, y; \theta, \phi)$ is given by

$$
\begin{aligned}
\mathcal{L}_{\text{disCVAE}}&(x_F, g, x, y; \theta, \phi) = \\
&- KL(q_\phi(z_F|x_F, g, y)\|p_\theta(z_F)) - \mathbb{E}_{q_\phi(z_F|x_F, g, y)}\big[KL(q_\phi(z_B|z_F, x_F, g, x, y)\|p_\theta(z_B))\big] \\
&- \mathbb{E}_{q_\phi(z_F|x_F, g, y)}\big[L(\mu_{\theta_F}(y, z_F), x_F) + \lambda_g L(s_{\theta_g}(y, z_F), g)\big] \\
&- \mathbb{E}_{q_\phi(z_F, z_B|x_F, g, x, y)}L(\mu_\theta(y, z_F, z_B), x)
\end{aligned} \quad (7)
$$

where $\mu_\theta(y, z_F, z_B) = \mu_{\theta_F}(y, z_F) + s_{\theta_g}(y, z_F) \odot \mu_{\theta_B}(z_B)$ as in Eq. (4). We further assume that $\log p_\theta(x_F, g|z_F, y) = \log p_\theta(x_F|z_F, y) + \lambda_g \log p_\theta(g|z_F, y)$, where we introduce λ_g as additional hyperparameter when decomposing the probablity $p_\theta(x_F, g|z_F, y)$. For the loss function $L(\cdot, \cdot)$, we used reconstruction error for predicting x or x_F and cross entropy for predicting the binary mask g. See the supplementary material for details of the derivation. All the generation and recognition models are parameterized by convolutional neural networks and trained end-to-end in a single architecture with back-propagation. We will introduce the exact network architecture in the experiment section.

4   Posterior Inference via Optimization

Once the attribute-conditioned generative model is trained, the inference or generation of image x given attribute y and latent variable z is straight-forward. However, the inference of latent variable z given an image x and its corresponding attribute y is unknown. In fact, the latent variable inference is quite useful as it enables model evaluation on novel images. For simplicity, we introduce our inference algorithm based on the vanilla CVAE and the same algorithm can be directly applied to the proposed disCVAE and the other generative models such as GANs [3,7]. Firstly we notice that the recognition model $q_\phi(z|y, x)$ may not be directly used to infer z. On one hand, as an approximate, we don't know how far it is from the true posterior $p_\theta(z|x, y)$ because the KL divergence between them is thrown away in the variational learning objective; on the other hand, this approximation does not even exist in the models such as GANs. We propose a general approach for posterior inference via optimization in the latent space. Using Bayes' rule, we can formulate the posterior inference by

$$
\begin{aligned}
\max_z \log p_\theta(z|x, y) &= \max_z \big[\log p_\theta(x|z, y) + \log p_\theta(z|y)\big] \\
&= \max_z \big[\log p_\theta(x|z, y) + \log p_\theta(z)\big]
\end{aligned} \quad (8)
$$

Note that the generation models or likelihood terms $p_\theta(x|z, y)$ could be non-Gaussian or even a deterministic function (e.g. in GANs) with no proper probabilistic definition.

Thus, to make our algorithm general enough, we reformulate the inference in (8) as an energy minimization problem,

$$\min_z E(z, x, y) = \min_z \left[L(\mu(z, y), x) + \lambda R(z) \right] \tag{9}$$

where $L(\cdot, \cdot)$ is the image reconstruction loss and $R(\cdot)$ is a prior regularization term. Taking the simple Gaussian model as an example, the posterior inference can be rewritten as,

$$\min_z E(z, x, y) = \min_z \left[\|\mu(z, y) - x\|^2 + \lambda \|z\|^2) \right] \tag{10}$$

Note that we abuse the mean function $\mu(z, y)$ as a general image generation function. Since $\mu(z, y)$ is a complex neural network, optimizing (9) is essentially error back-propagation from the energy function to the variable z, which we solve by the ADAM method [13]. Our algorithm actually shares a similar spirit with recently proposed neural network visualization [42] and texture synthesis algorithms [6]. The difference is that we use generation models for recognition while their algorithms use recognition models for generation. Compared to the conventional way of inferring z from recognition model $q_\phi(z|x, y)$, the proposed optimization contributed to an empirically more accurate latent variable z and hence was useful for reconstruction, completion, and editing.

5   Experiments

Datasets. We evaluated our model on two datasets: Labeled Faces in the Wild (LFW) [10] and Caltech-UCSD Birds-200-2011 (CUB) [37]. For experiments on LFW, we aligned the face images using five landmarks [43] and rescaled the center region to 64×64. We used 73 dimensional attribute score vector provided by [18] that describes different aspects of facial appearance such as age, gender, or facial expression. We trained our model using 70% of the data (9,000 out of 13,000 face images) following the training-testing split (View 1) [10], where the face identities are distinct between train and test sets. For experiments on CUB, we cropped the bird region using the tight bounding box computed from the foreground mask and rescaled to 64×64. We used 312 dimensional binary attribute vector that describes bird parts and colors. We trained our model using 50% of the data (6,000 out of 12,000 bird images) following the training-testing split [37]. For model training, we held-out 10% of training data for validation.

Data Preprocessing and Augmentation. To make the learning easier, we pre-processed the data by normalizing the pixel values to the range $[-1, 1]$. We augmented the training data with the following image transformations [5, 16]: (1) flipping images horizontally with probability 0.5, (2) multiplying pixel values of each color channel with a random value $c \in [0.97, 1.03]$, and (3) augmenting the image with its residual with a random tradeoff parameter $s \in [0, 1.5]$. Specifically, for CUB experiments, we performed two extra transformations: (4) rotating images around the centering point by a random angle $\theta_r \in [-0.08, 0.08]$, (5) rescaling images to the scale of 72×72 and performing random cropping of 64×64 regions. Note that these methods are designed to be invariant to the attribute description.

Architecture Design. For disCVAE, we build four convolutional neural networks (one for foreground and the other for background for both recognition and generation networks) for auto-encoding style training. The foreground encoder network consists of 5 convolution layers, followed by 2 fully-connected layers (convolution layers have 64, 128, 256, 256 and 1024 channels with filter size of 5×5, 5×5, 3×3, 3×3 and 4×4, respectively; the two fully-connected layers have 1024 and 192 neurons). The attribute stream is merged with image stream at the end of the recognition network. The foreground decoder network consists of 2 fully-connected layers, followed by 5 convolution layers with 2-by-2 upsampling (fully-connected layers have 256 and $8 \times 8 \times 256$ neurons; the convolution layers have 256, 256, 128, 64 and 3 channels with filter size of 3×3, 5×5, 5×5, 5×5 and 5×5. The foreground prediction stream and gating prediction stream are separated at the last convolution layer. We adopt the same encoder/decoder architecture for background networks but with fewer number of channels. See the supplementary material for more details.

For all the models, we fixed the latent dimension to be 256 and found this configuration is sufficient to generate 64×64 images in our setting. We adopt slightly different architectures for different datasets: we use 192 dimensions to foreground latent space and 64 dimensions to background latent space for experiments on LFW dataset; we use 128 dimensions for both foreground and background latent spaces on CUB dataset. Compared to vanilla CVAE, the proposed disCVAE has more parameters because of the additional convolutions introduced by the two-stream architecture. However, we found that adding more parameters to vanilla CVAE does not lead to much improvement in terms of image quality. Although both [4] and the proposed method use segmentation masks as supervision, naive mask prediction was not comparable to the proposed model in our setting based on the preliminary results. In fact, the proposed disCVAE architecture assigns foreground/background generation to individual networks and composite with gated interaction, which we found very effective in practice.

Implementation Details. We used ADAM [13] for stochastic optimization in all experiments. For training, we used mini-batch of size 32 and the learning rate 0.0003. We also added dropout layer of ratio 0.5 for the image stream of the encoder network before merging with attribute stream. For posterior inference, we used the learning rate 0.3 with 1000 iterations. The models are implemented using deep learning toolbox Torch7 [2].

Baselines. For the vanilla CVAE model, we used the same convolution architecture from foreground encoder network and foreground decoder network. To demonstrate the significance of attribute-conditioned modeling, we trained an unconditional variational auto-encoders (VAE) with almost the same convolutional architecture as our CVAE.

5.1   Attribute-Conditioned Image Generation

To examine whether the model has the capacity to generate diverse and realistic images from given attribute description, we performed the task of attribute-conditioned image generation. For each attribute description from testing set, we generated 5 samples by the proposed generation process: $x \sim p_\theta(x|y, z)$, where z is sampled from isotropic Gaussian distribution. For vanilla CVAE, x is the only output of the generation.

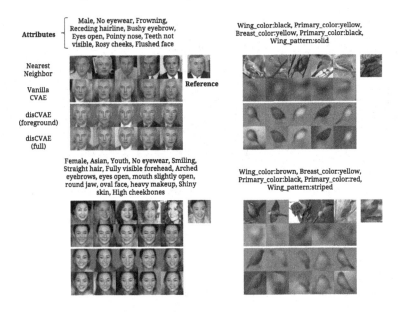

Fig. 3. Attribute-conditioned image generation.

In comparison, for disCVAE, the foreground image x_F can be considered a by-product of the layered generation process. For evaluation, we visualized the samples generated from the model in Fig. 3 and compared them with the corresponding image in the testing set, which we name as "reference" image. To demonstrate that model did not exploit the trivial solution of attribute-conditioned generation by memorizing the training data, we added a simple baseline as experimental comparison. Basically, for each given attribute description in the testing set, we conducted the nearest neighbor search in the training set. We used the mean squared error as the distance metric for the nearest neighbor search (in the attribute space). For more visual results and code, please see the supplementary material and the project website: https://sites.google.com/site/attribute2image/.

Attribute-conditioned Face Image Generation. As we can see in Fig. 3, face images generated by the proposed models look realistic and non-trivially different from each other, especially for view-point and background color. Moreover, it is clear that images generated by disCVAE have clear boundaries against the background. In comparison, the boundary regions between the hair area and background are quite blurry for samples generated by vanilla CVAE. This observation suggests the limitation of vanilla CVAE in modeling hair pattern for face images. This also justifies the significance of layered modeling and latent space disentangling in our attribute-conditioned generation process. Compared to the nearest neighbors in the training set, the generated samples can better reflect the input attribute description.

Attribute-conditioned Bird Image Generation. Compared to the experiments on LFW database, the bird image modeling is more challenging because the bird images

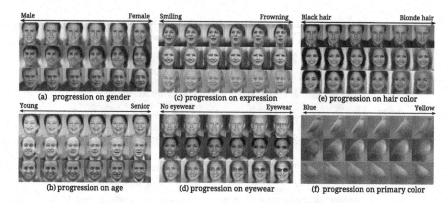

Fig. 4. Attribute-conditioned image progression. The visualization is organized into six attribute groups (e.g., "gender", "age", "facial expression", "eyewear", "hair color" and "primary color (blue vs. yellow)"). Within each group, the images are generated from $p_\theta(x|y,z)$ with $z \sim \mathcal{N}(0,I)$ and $y = [y_\alpha, y_{rest}]$, where $y_\alpha = (1-\alpha)\cdot y_{min} + \alpha\cdot y_{max}$. Here, y_{min} and y_{max} stands for the minimum and maximum attribute value respectively in the dataset along the corresponding dimension. (Color figure online)

have more diverse shapes and color patterns and the binary-valued attributes are more sparse and higher dimensional. As we can see in Fig. 3, there is a big difference between two versions of the proposed CVAE model. Basically, the samples generated by vanilla CVAE are blurry and sometimes blended with the background area. However, samples generated by disCVAE have clear bird shapes and reflect the input attribute description well. This confirms the strengths of the proposed layered modeling of images.

Attribute-conditioned Image Progression. To better analyze the proposed model, we generate images with interpolated attributes by gradually increasing or decreasing the values along each attribute dimension. We regard this process as *attribute-conditioned image progression*. Specifically, for each attribute vector, we modify the value of one attribute dimension by interpolating between the minimum and maximum attribute value. Then, we generate images by interpolating the value of y between the two attribute vectors while keeping latent variable z fixed. For visualization, we use the attribute vector from testing set.

As we can see in Fig. 4, samples generated by progression are visually consistent with attribute description. For face images, by changing attributes like "gender" and "age", the identity-related visual appearance is changed accordingly but the viewpoint, background color, and facial expression are well preserved; on the other hand, by changing attributes like "facial expression", "eyewear" and "hair color", the global appearance is well preserved but the difference appears in the local region. For bird images, by changing the primary color from one to the other, the global shape and background color are well preserved. These observations demonstrated that the generation process of our model is well controlled by the input attributes.

Analysis: Latent Space Disentangling. To better analyze the disCVAE, we performed the following experiments on the latent space. In this model, the image generation

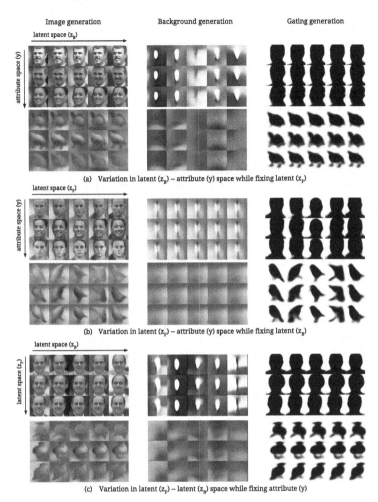

Image generation   Background generation   Gating generation

latent space (z_B)

attribute space (y)

(a) Variation in latent (z_B) – attribute (y) space while fixing latent (z_F)

latent space (z_F)

attribute space (y)

(b) Variation in latent (z_F) – attribute (y) space while fixing latent (z_B)

latent space (z_B)

latent space (z_F)

(c) Variation in latent (z_F) – latent (z_B) space while fixing attribute (y)

Fig. 5. Analysis: latent space disentangling.

process is driven by three factors: attribute y, foreground latent variable z_F and background latent variable z_B. By changing one variable while fixing the other two, we can analyze how each variable contributes to the final generation results. We visualize the samples x, the generated background x_B and the gating variables g in Fig. 5. We summarized the observations as follows: (1) The background of the generated samples look different but with identical foreground region when we change background latent variable z_B only; (2) the foreground region of the generated samples look diverse in terms of viewpoints but still look similar in terms of appearance and the samples have uniform background pattern when we change foreground latent variable z_F only. Interestingly, for face images, one can identify a "hole" in the background generation. This can be considered as the location prior of the face images, since the images are relatively aligned. Meanwhile, the generated background for birds are relatively uniform, which demonstrates our model learned to recover missing background in the training set and also suggests that foreground and background have been disentangled in the latent space.

5.2 Attribute-Conditioned Image Reconstruction and Completion

Image Reconstruction. Given a test image x and its attribute vector y, we find z that maximizes the posterior $p_\theta(z|x, y)$ following Eq. (9).

Image Completion. Given a test image with synthetic occlusion, we evaluate whether the model has the capacity to fill in the occluded region by recognizing the observed region. We denote the occluded (unobserved) region and observed region as x_u and x_o, respectively. For completion, we first find z that maximizes the posterior $p_\theta(z|x_o, y)$ by optimization (9). Then, we fill in the unobserved region x_u by generation using $p_\theta(x_u|z, y)$. For each face image, we consider four types of occlusions: occlusion on the eye region, occlusion on the mouth region, occlusion on the face region and occlusion on right half of the image. For occluded regions, we set the pixel value to 0. For each bird image, we consider blocks of occlusion of size 8×8 and 16×16 at random locations.

In Fig. 6, we visualize the results of image reconstruction (a, b) and image completion (c–h). As we can see, for face images, our proposed CVAE models are in general good at reconstructing and predicting the occluded region in unseen images (from testing set). However, for bird images, vanilla CVAE model had significant failures in general. This agreed with the previous results in attribute-conditioned image generation.

In addition, to demonstrate the significance of attribute-conditioned modeling, we compared our vanilla CVAE and disCVAE with unconditional VAE (attribute is not given) for image reconstruction and completion. It can be seen in Fig. 6(c) and (d), the generated images using attributes actually perform better in terms of expression and eyewear ("smiling" and "sunglasses").

For quantitative comparisons, we measured the pixel-level mean squared error on the entire image and occluded region for reconstruction and completion, respectively. We summarized the results in Table 1 (mean squared error and standard error).

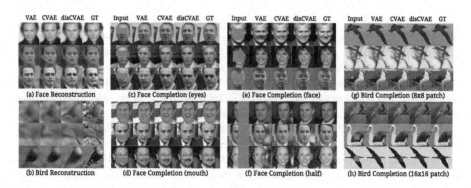

Fig. 6. Attribute-conditioned image reconstruction and completion.

Table 1. Quantitative comparisons on face reconstruction and completion tasks.

Face	Recon: full	Recon: fg	Comp: eye	Comp: mouth	Comp: face	Comp: half
VAE	11.8 ± 0.1	9.4 ± 0.1	13.0 ± 0.1	12.1 ± 0.1	13.1 ± 0.1	21.3 ± 0.2
CVAE	11.8 ± 0.1	9.3 ± 0.1	12.0 ± 0.1	12.0 ± 0.1	12.3 ± 0.1	20.3 ± 0.2
disCVAE	10.0 ± 0.1	7.9 ± 0.1	10.3 ± 0.1	10.3 ± 0.1	10.9 ± 0.1	18.8 ± 0.2
Bird	Recon: full	Recon: fg	Comp: 8×8	Comp: 16×16		
VAE	14.5 ± 0.1	11.7 ± 0.1	1.8 ± 0.1	4.6 ± 0.1		
CVAE	14.3 ± 0.1	11.5 ± 0.1	1.8 ± 0.1	4.4 ± 0.1		
disCVAE	12.9 ± 0.1	10.2 ± 0.1	1.8 ± 0.1	4.4 ± 0.1		

The quantitative analysis highlighted the benefits of attribute-conditioned modeling and the importance of layered modeling.

6   Conclusion

To conclude, this paper studied a novel problem of attribute-conditioned image generation and proposed a solution with CVAEs. Considering the compositional structure of images, we proposed a novel disentangling CVAE (disCVAE) with a layered representation. Results on faces and birds demonstrate that our models can generate realistic samples with diverse appearance and especially disCVAE significantly improved the generation quality on bird images. To evaluate the learned generation models on the novel images, we also developed an optimization-based approach to posterior inference and applied it to the tasks of image reconstruction and completion with quantitative evaluation.

Acknowledgement. This work was supported in part by NSF CAREER IIS-1453651, ONR N00014-13-1-0762, Sloan Research Fellowship, and a gift from Adobe. We acknowledge NVIDIA for the donation of GPUs. We also thank Yuting Zhang, Scott Reed, Junhyuk Oh, Ruben Villegas, Seunghoon Hong, Wenling Shang, Ye Liu, Kibok Lee, Lajanugen Logeswaran, Rui Zhang, Changhan Wang and Yi Zhang for helpful comments and discussions.

References

1. Bengio, Y., Thibodeau-Laufer, E., Alain, G., Yosinski, J.: Deep generative stochastic networks trainable by backprop. arXiv preprint arXiv:1306.1091 (2013)
2. Collobert, R., Kavukcuoglu, K., Farabet, C.: Torch7: a matlab-like environment for machine learning. In: BigLearn, NIPS Workshop (2011)
3. Denton, E., Chintala, S., Szlam, A., Fergus, R.: Deep generative image models using a Laplacian pyramid of adversarial networks. In: NIPS (2015)
4. Dosovitskiy, A., Springenberg, J.T., Brox, T.: Learning to generate chairs with convolutional neural networks. In: CVPR (2015)
5. Eigen, D., Puhrsch, C., Fergus, R.: Depth map prediction from a single image using a multi-scale deep network. In: NIPS (2014)

6. Gatys, L.A., Ecker, A.S., Bethge, M.: Texture synthesis using convolutional neural networks. In: NIPS (2015)
7. Gauthier, J.: Conditional generative adversarial nets for convolutional face generation. Technical report (2015)
8. Goodfellow, I., Pouget-Abadie, J., Mirza, M., Xu, B., Warde-Farley, D., Ozair, S., Courville, A., Bengio, Y.: Generative adversarial nets. In: NIPS, pp. 2672–2680 (2014)
9. Gregor, K., Danihelka, I., Graves, A., Wierstra, D.: DRAW: a recurrent neural network for image generation. In: ICML (2015)
10. Huang, G.B., Ramesh, M., Berg, T.: Labeled faces in the wild: a database for studying, 07–49 (2007)
11. Isola, P., Liu, C.: Scene collaging: analysis and synthesis of natural images with semantic layers. In: ICCV (2013)
12. Kemelmacher-Shlizerman, I., Suwajanakorn, S., Seitz, S.M.: Illumination-aware age progression. In: CVPR (2014)
13. Kingma, D., Ba, J.: ADAM: a method for stochastic optimization. In: ICLR (2015)
14. Kingma, D.P., Mohamed, S., Rezende, D.J., Welling, M.: Semi-supervised learning with deep generative models. In: NIPS (2014)
15. Kingma, D.P., Welling, M.: Auto-encoding variational Bayes. In: ICLR (2014)
16. Krizhevsky, A., Sutskever, I., Hinton, G.E.: Imagenet classification with deep convolutional neural networks. In: NIPS (2012)
17. Kulkarni, T.D., Whitney, W., Kohli, P., Tenenbaum, J.B.: Deep convolutional inverse graphics network. In: NIPS (2015)
18. Kumar, N., Berg, A.C., Belhumeur, P.N., Nayar, S.K.: Attribute and simile classifiers for face verification. In: ICCV (2009)
19. Laput, G.P., Dontcheva, M., Wilensky, G., Chang, W., Agarwala, A., Linder, J., Adar, E.: Pixeltone: a multimodal interface for image editing. In: Proceedings of the SIGCHI Conference on Human Factors in Computing Systems (2013)
20. Le Roux, N., Heess, N., Shotton, J., Winn, J.: Learning a generative model of images by factoring appearance and shape. Neural Comput. **23**(3), 593–650 (2011)
21. Lee, H., Grosse, R., Ranganath, R., Ng, A.Y.: Convolutional deep belief networks for scalable unsupervised learning of hierarchical representations. In: ICML (2009)
22. Ngiam, J., Khosla, A., Kim, M., Nam, J., Lee, H., Ng, A.Y.: Multimodal deep learning. In: ICML (2011)
23. Nitzberg, M., Mumford, D.: The 2.1-d sketch. In: ICCV (1990)
24. Porter, T., Duff, T.: Compositing digital images. In: ACM Siggraph Computer Graphics, vol. 18, pp. 253–259. ACM (1984)
25. Radford, A., Metz, L., Chintala, S.: Unsupervised representation learning with deep convolutional generative adversarial networks. arXiv preprint arXiv:1511.06434 (2015)
26. Ranzato, M., Mnih, V., Hinton, G.E.: Generating more realistic images using gated MRFS. In: NIPS (2010)
27. Reed, S., Sohn, K., Zhang, Y., Lee, H.: Learning to disentangle factors of variation with manifold interaction. In: ICML (2014)
28. Rezende, D.J., Mohamed, S., Wierstra, D.: Stochastic backpropagation and approximate inference in deep generative models. In: ICML (2014)
29. Simonyan, K., Zisserman, A.: Very deep convolutional networks for large-scale image recognition. arXiv preprint arXiv:1409.1556 (2014)
30. Smolensky, P.: Information processing in dynamical systems: foundations of harmony theory. In: Rumelhart, D.E., McClelland, J.L. (eds.) Parallel Distributed Processing, vol. 1 (1986)

31. Sohn, K., Shang, W., Lee, H.: Improved multimodal deep learning with variation of information. In: NIPS (2014)

32. Srivastava, A., Lee, A.B., Simoncelli, E.P., Zhu, S.C.: On advances in statistical modeling of natural images. J. Math. Imaging Vis. **18**(1), 17–33 (2003)

33. Srivastava, N., Salakhutdinov, R.R.: Multimodal learning with deep Boltzmann machines. In: NIPS (2012)

34. Tang, Y., Salakhutdinov, R.: Learning stochastic feedforward neural networks. In: NIPS (2013)

35. Tang, Y., Salakhutdinov, R., Hinton, G.: Robust boltzmann machines for recognition and denoising. In: CVPR (2012)

36. Tu, Z.: Learning generative models via discriminative approaches. In: CVPR (2007)

37. Wah, C., Branson, S., Welinder, P., Perona, P., Belongie, S.: The Caltech-UCSD birds-200-2011 dataset (2011)

38. Wang, J.Y., Adelson, E.H.: Representing moving images with layers. IEEE Trans. Image Process. **3**(5), 625–638 (1994)

39. Williams, C.K., Titsias, M.K.: Greedy learning of multiple objects in images using robust statistics and factorial learning. Neural Comput. **16**(5), 1039–1062 (2004)

40. Yang, F., Wang, J., Shechtman, E., Bourdev, L., Metaxas, D.: Expression flow for 3D-aware face component transfer. In: SIGGRAPH (2011)

41. Yang, Y., Hallman, S., Ramanan, D., Fowlkes, C.C.: Layered object models for image segmentation. PAMI **34**(9), 1731–1743 (2012)

42. Yosinski, J., Clune, J., Nguyen, A., Fuchs, T., Lipson, H.: Understanding neural networks through deep visualization. arXiv preprint arXiv:1506.06579 (2015)

43. Zhu, S., Li, C., Loy, C.C., Tang, X.: Transferring landmark annotations for cross-dataset face alignment. arXiv preprint arXiv:1409.0602 (2014)

Modeling Context Between Objects for Referring Expression Understanding

Varun K. Nagaraja$^{(\boxtimes)}$, Vlad I. Morariu, and Larry S. Davis

University of Maryland, College Park, MD, USA
{varun,morariu,lsd}@umiacs.umd.edu

Abstract. Referring expressions usually describe an object using properties of the object and relationships of the object with other objects. We propose a technique that integrates context between objects to understand referring expressions. Our approach uses an LSTM to learn the probability of a referring expression, with input features from a region and a context region. The context regions are discovered using multiple-instance learning (MIL) since annotations for context objects are generally not available for training. We utilize max-margin based MIL objective functions for training the LSTM. Experiments on the Google RefExp and UNC RefExp datasets show that modeling context between objects provides better performance than modeling only object properties. We also qualitatively show that our technique can ground a referring expression to its referred region along with the supporting context region.

1 Introduction

In image retrieval and human-robot interaction, objects are usually queried by their category, attributes, pose, action and their context in the scene [1]. Natural language queries can encode rich information like relationships that distinguish object instances from each other. In a retrieval task that focuses on a particular object in an image, the query is called a *referring expression* [2,3]. When there is only one instance of an object type in an image, a referring expression provides additional information such as attributes to improve retrieval/localization performance. More importantly, when multiple instances of an object type are present in an image, a referring expression distinguishes the referred object from other instances, thereby helping to localize the correct instance. The task of localizing a region in an image given a referring expression is called the *comprehension task* [4] and its inverse process is the *generation task*. In this work we focus on the comprehension task.

Referring expressions usually mention relationships of an object with other regions along with the properties of the object [5,6] (See Fig. 1). Hence, it is important to model relationships between regions for understanding referring expressions. However, the supervision during training typically consists of annotations of only the referred object. While this might be sufficient for modeling attributes of an object mentioned in a referring expression, it is difficult to model relationships between objects with such limited supervision. Previous work on

© Springer International Publishing AG 2016
B. Leibe et al. (Eds.): ECCV 2016, Part IV, LNCS 9908, pp. 792–807, 2016.
DOI: 10.1007/978-3-319-46493-0_48

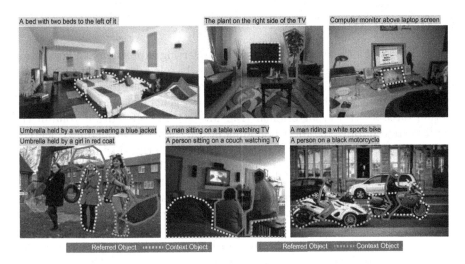

Fig. 1. Context between objects is specified using spatial relationships between regions such as "above", "to the right", "to the left" etc. It is also represented using interactions between objects such as "riding", "holding" etc. When there are multiple instances of the same type of object, context helps in referring to the appropriate instance.

referring expressions [2,4,7] generally ignores modeling relationships between regions. In contrast, we learn to map a referring expression to a region and its supporting context region. Since the bounding box annotations of context objects are not available for training, we learn the relationships in a weakly supervised framework.

We follow the approach of Mao et al. [4] to perform the comprehension task. The probability of a referring expression is measured for different region proposals and the top scoring region is selected as the referred region. The input features in our model are obtained from a {*region, context_region*} pair where the image itself is considered as one of the context regions. The probability of a referring expression for a region can then be pooled over multiple pairs using the max function or the noisy-or function. We use an LSTM [8] for learning probabilities of a referring expression similar to Mao et al. [4]. Since the bounding boxes for context objects are not known during training, we train using a Multiple-Instance Learning (MIL) objective function. The max-margin based LSTM training of Mao et al. [4] is extended to max-margin MIL training for LSTMs. The first formulation is similar to MI-SVM [9] which has only negative bag margin and the second formulation is similar to mi-SVM [9] which has both positive and negative bag margins. Experiments are performed on the Google RefExp dataset [4] and UNC RefExp dataset [10]. Our results show that modeling objects in context for the comprehension task provides better performance than modeling only object properties. We also qualitatively show that our technique can ground the correct context regions for those referring expressions which mention object relationships.

2   Related Work

The two tasks of localizing an object given a referring expression and generating a referring expression given an object are closely related. Some image caption generation techniques [11,12] first learn to ground sentence fragments to image regions and then use the learned association to generate sentences. Since the caption datasets (Flickr30k-original [13], MS-COCO [14]) do not contain the mapping from phrases to object bounding boxes, the visual grounding is learned in a weakly supervised manner. Fang et al. [15] use multiple-instance learning to learn the probability of a region corresponding to different words. However, the associations are learned for individual words and not in context with other words. Karpathy et al. [16] learn a common embedding space for image and sentence with an MIL objective such that a sentence fragment has a high similarity with a single image region. Instead of associating each word to its best region, they use an MRF to encourage neighboring words to associate to common regions.

Attention based models implicitly learn to select or weigh different regions in an image based on the words generated in a caption. Xu et al. [17] propose two types of attention models for caption generation. In their stochastic hard attention model, the attention locations vary for each word and in the deterministic soft attention model, a soft weight is learned for different regions. Neither of these models are well suited for localizing a single region for a referring expression. Rohrbach et al. [18] learn to ground phrases in sentences using a two stage model. In the first stage, an attention model selects an image region and in the second stage, the selected region is trained to predict the original phrase. They evaluate their technique on the Flickr 30k Entities dataset [12] which contains mappings for noun phrases in a sentence to bounding boxes in the corresponding image. The descriptions in this dataset do not always mention a salient object in the image. Many times the descriptions mention groups of objects and the scene at a higher level and hence it becomes challenging to learn object relationships.

Kong et al. [19] learn visual grounding for nouns in descriptions of indoor scenes in a supervised manner. They use an MRF which jointly models scene classification, object detection and grounding to 3D cuboids. Johnson et al. [20] propose an end-to-end neural network that can localize regions in an image and generate descriptions for those regions. Their model is trained with full supervision with region descriptions present in the Visual Genome dataset [21].

Most of the works on referring expressions learn to ground a single region by modeling object properties and image level context. Rule based approaches to generating referring expressions [22,23] are restricted in the types of properties that can be modeled. Kazemzadeh et al. [2] designed an energy optimization model for generating referring expressions in the form of object attributes. Hu et al. [7] propose an approach with three LSTMs which take in different feature inputs such as region features, image features and word embedding. Mao et al. [4] propose an LSTM based technique that can perform both tasks of referring expression generation and referring expression comprehension. They use a max-margin based training method for the LSTM wherein the probability of a referring expression is high only for the referred region and low for every other region. This type of training significantly improves performance. We extend their max-margin approach to multiple-instance learning based training objectives for the LSTM. Unlike previous work, we model context between objects for comprehending referring expressions.

3   Modeling Context Between Objects

Given a referring expression S and an image I, the goal of the comprehension task is to predict the (bounding box of the) region R^* that is being referred to. We adopt the method of Mao et al. [4] and start with a set of region proposals ($\mathcal{C}$) from the image. We learn a model that measures the probability of a region given a referring expression. The maximum scoring region $R^* = \arg\max_{R \in \mathcal{C}} p(R|S, I)$ is then selected as the referred region. Mao et al. [4] rewrite the scoring function as $R^* = \arg\max_{R \in \mathcal{C}} p(S|R, I)$ by applying Bayes' rule and assuming a uniform prior for $p(R|I)$. This implies that comprehension can be accomplished using a model trained to generate sentences for an image region.

Many image and video captioning techniques [11, 24, 25], learn the probability of a sentence given an image or video frame using an LSTM. The input features to the LSTM consist of a word embedding vector and CNN features extracted from the image. The LSTM is trained to maximize the likelihood of observing the words of the caption corresponding to the image or the region. This model is used by Mao et al. [4] as the baseline for referring expression comprehension. Along with the word embedding and region features, they also input CNN features of the entire image and bounding box features to act as context. They further propose a max-margin training method for the LSTM to enforce the probability of a referring expression to be high for the referred region and low for all other regions. For a referring expression S, let $R_n \in \mathcal{C}$ be the true region and $R_i \in \mathcal{C} \setminus R_n$ be a negative region; then the training loss function with a max-margin component is written as

$$J(\theta) = - \sum_{R_i \in \mathcal{C} \setminus R_n} \left\{ \begin{array}{l} \log p(S|R_n, I, \theta) \\ -\lambda \max(0, M - \log p(S|R_n, I, \theta) + \log p(S|R_i, I, \theta)) \end{array} \right\} \quad (1)$$

where θ are the parameters of the model, λ is the weight for the margin loss component and M is the margin. The max-margin model has the same architecture as the baseline model but is trained with a different loss function.

In the above model, the probability of a referring expression is influenced by the region and only the image as context. However, many referring expressions mention an object in relation to some other object (e.g., "The person next to the table") and hence it is important to incorporate context information from other regions as well. One of the challenges for learning relationships between regions through referring expressions is that the annotations for the context regions are generally not available for training. However, we can treat combinations of regions in an image as bags and use Multiple Instance Learning (MIL) to learn the probability of referring expressions. MIL has been used by image captioning

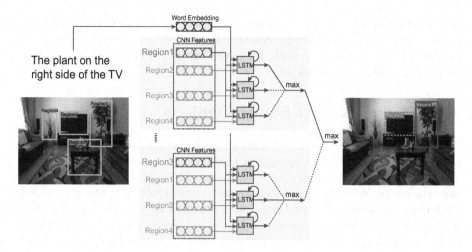

Fig. 2. We identify the referred region along with its supporting context region. We start with a set of region proposals in an image and consider pairs of the form {*region, context_region*}. The entire image is also considered as a potential context region. The probability is evaluated using an LSTM which takes as input region CNN features, context region CNN features, bounding box features and an embedding vector for words in the referring expression. All the LSTMs share the same weights. The probability of a referring expression for an individual region is obtained by finding the maximum over its pairs with context regions. The noisy-or function can be used instead of the max function. After pooling over context regions, the top scoring region (along with its context region) is selected as the referred region

techniques [15,16,26] to associate phrases to image regions when the ground-truth mapping is not available.

We learn to map a referring expression to a region and its supporting context region. We start with a set of region proposals in an image and consider pairs of the form {*region, context_region*}. The image is included as one of the context regions. The probability of a referring expression is learned for pairs of regions where the input features include visual features and bounding box features for both regions. The probability of an individual region is then obtained by pooling from probabilities of the region's combinations with its potential context regions. After pooling, the top scoring region (along with its context region) is selected as the referred region. Figure 2 shows an overview of our system.

Let $\mathcal{C} = \{I, R_1, R_2, \ldots, R_n\}$ be the set of candidate context regions which includes the entire image, I, and other regions generated by the object proposal algorithm. The minimum size of the context region set is one since it always includes I and the model in that case would be equivalent to Mao et al. [4]. We now define the probability of a sentence S given a region R as

$$p(S|R) = \max_{R_i \in \mathcal{C} \setminus R} p(S|R, R_i) \tag{2}$$

This implies that the probability of a sentence given a region is defined as the maximum probability obtained by any of the region's combination with a context region. The referred region can now be selected as the top scoring region from the max-pooled probabilities.

$$R^* = \arg\max_{R \in \mathcal{C} \setminus I} \left\{ \max_{R_i \in \mathcal{C} \setminus R} p(S|R, R_i) \right\} \tag{3}$$

The noisy-or function can be used instead of the max function in Eq. 2. Then the referred region is selected as

$$R^* = \arg\max_{R \in \mathcal{C} \setminus I} \left\{ 1 - \prod_{R_i \in \mathcal{C} \setminus R} (1 - p(S|R, R_i)) \right\} \tag{4}$$

The noisy-or function can integrate context information from more than one pair of regions and it is more robust to noise than the max function.

We learn the probability function $p(S|R_i, R_j)$ using multiple-instance learning. In our MIL framework, a positive bag for a referring expression consists of pairs of regions of the form (R_t, R_i). The first element in the pair is the region R_t referred to in the expression and the second element is a context region $R_i \in \mathcal{C} \setminus R_t$. A negative bag consists of pairs of regions of the form (R_i, R_j) where $R_i \in \mathcal{C} \setminus R_t$ and $R_j \in \mathcal{C}$. Figure 3 shows an example of bags constructed for a sample referring expression.

An LSTM is used to learn the probability of referring expressions and we define multiple-instance learning objective functions for training. Similar to the max-margin training objective defined in Eq. 1, we apply the max-margin approach of MI-SVM and mi-SVM [9] here to train the LSTM. In MI-SVM, the margin constraint is enforced on all the samples from the negative bag but only on the positive instances from the positive bag. The training loss function with a margin for the negative bag is given by

$$J'(\theta) = - \sum_{\substack{R_i \in \mathcal{C} \setminus R_t, \\ R_j \in \mathcal{C}}} \left\{ \begin{array}{l} \log p(S|R_t, \theta) \\ -\lambda_N \max(0, M - \log p(S|R_t, \theta) + \log p(S|R_i, R_j, \theta)) \end{array} \right\} \tag{5}$$

The difference between the max-margin Eqs. 1 and 5 is that the probability of the referred region is now obtained from Eq. 2 and the negative samples are not just pairs of regions with the entire image.

The loss function in Eq. 5 ignores potential negative instances in the positive bag. We can attempt to identify the negative instances and apply a margin to those pairs as well. In mi-SVM, the labels for instances in positive bags are assumed to be latent variables. The goal is to maximize the margin between all positive and negative instances jointly over the latent labels and the discriminant hyperplane. In many referring expressions, there is usually one other object mentioned in context. We assume that there is only one positive pair in the positive bag and assign a positive label for the instance with the maximum

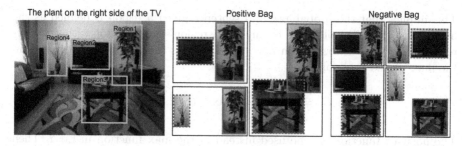

Fig. 3. Given a set of region proposals in an image, we construct positive and negative bags containing pairs of regions. In this example, the plant in *Region*1 is the referred object. Hence the positive bag consists of pairs of the form (*Region*1,R_i) where R_i is one of the remaining regions. The negative bag consists of pairs of the form (R_i, R_j) where the first region R_i can be any region except *Region*1 and the second region R_j can be any region including *Region*1

probability. The remaining pairs in the positive bag are assigned a negative label. Without loss of generality, let (R_t, R_c) be the positive instance from the positive bag. The training loss function with margins for both positive and negative bags is given by,

$$
J''(\theta) = - \sum_{\substack{R_i \in \mathcal{C} \backslash R_t, \\ R_j \in \mathcal{C}}} \left\{ \begin{aligned} &\log p(S|R_t, R_c, \theta) \\ &-\lambda_N \max(0, M - \log p(S|R_t, R_c, \theta) + \log p(S|R_i, R_j, \theta)) \end{aligned} \right\}
$$
$$
- \sum_{R_k \in \mathcal{C} \backslash R_c} \left\{ \begin{aligned} &\log p(S|R_t, R_c, \theta) \\ &-\lambda_P \max(0, M - \log p(S|R_t, R_c, \theta) + \log p(S|R_t, R_k, \theta)) \end{aligned} \right\}
$$
$$(6)$$

In the training algorithm proposed by Andrews et al. [9] for mi-SVM, the latent labels for instances in a positive bag are obtained in an iterative manner. The mi-SVM algorithm iterates over two steps: use the current hyperplane to determine the latent labels, then use the labels to train a new hyperplane. Since neural networks are trained over multiple epochs of the data, the training process is similar to the iterative algorithm used to train mi-SVM. During an epoch, the positive instance (R_t, R_c) in the positive bag is determined as

$$
R_c = \arg\max_{R_i \in \mathcal{C} \backslash R_t} p(S|R_t, R_i) \tag{7}
$$

The parameter θ is updated by applying the loss function in Eq. 6 with R_c substituted into it. In the following epoch, R_c is updated using the model with updated parameter θ.

The assumption that there is one positive instance in the positive bag holds true when a referring expression uniquely identifies an object and its context object. Such referring expressions are present in the Google RefExp dataset (e.g., "A white truck in front of a yellow truck"). The UNC RefExp dataset contains referring expressions which do not always uniquely refer to an object with its context object (e.g., "Elephant towards the back"). Hence the two different formulations (Eqs. 5 and 6) harness different characteristics of referring expressions between the two datasets.

4 Experiments

4.1 Datasets

We perform experiments on the Google RefExp dataset [4] and the UNC RefExp dataset [10]. Both datasets contain referring expressions for images in the Microsoft COCO dataset [14].

The dataset partition accompanying the current release of Google RefExp dataset was created by randomly selecting 5000 objects for validation and 5000 objects for testing. This type of partitioning results in overlapping images between training, validation and test sets. To avoid any overlap between the partitions, we create our own partition for the training and validation sets. Our training partition contains 23199 images with 67996 objects. Some objects have multiple referring expressions and hence the total number of referring expressions is 85,408. The validation partition contains 2600 images with 7623 objects and 9602 referring expressions. The results of the baseline and max-margin techniques did not differ much between our partition and the Mao et al. [4] partition. However, we perform experiments with our partition since we model context from many regions in an image and that information should not leak into the test stage. We will make our partition publicly available. The test set of this dataset has not been released yet. Hence, we use 4800 referring expressions from the training set for validation.

The UNC RefExp dataset was collected by applying the ReferIt game [2] on MS-COCO images. The training partition contains 16994 images, 42404 objects and 120624 referring expressions. The validation partition contains 1500 images, 3811 objects and 10834 referring expressions. The testing partition contains two splits. TestA partition contains 750 images, 1975 objects and 5657 person-centric referring expressions. TestB partition contains 750 images, 1810 objects and 5095 object-centric referring expressions. While Mao et al. [4] create their own test partition of the UNC RefExp data from a random subset of objects, we work with the partitioning provided by Yu et al. [10].

The evaluation is performed by measuring the Intersection over Union (IoU) ratio between a groundtruth box and the top predicted box for a referring expression. If the IoU >0.5, the prediction is considered a true positive and this is the Precision@1 score. The scores are then averaged over all referring expressions.

4.2 Implementation Details

Our neural network architecture is the same as Mao et al. [4]. We use an LSTM to learn probabilities of referring expressions. The size of the hidden state vector is 1024. We extract CNN features for a region and its context region using the 16 layer VGGNet [27] pre-trained on the ImageNet dataset. We use the 1000 dimensional features from the last layer (fc8) of VGGNet and fine tune only the last layer while keeping everything else fixed. The CNN features for each region are concatenated with bounding box features of the form $[\frac{x_{min}}{W}, \frac{y_{min}}{H}, \frac{x_{max}}{W}, \frac{y_{max}}{H}, \frac{Area_{bbox}}{Area_{image}}]$ where (W, H) are the width and height of the image. The resulting feature length for both the region and the context region is 2010. We scale the features to lie between -0.5 and 0.5 before feeding them into the LSTM. The scaling factors were obtained from the training set. We use a vector embedding of size 1024 for the words in a referring expression. The size of the vocabulary is 3489 and 2020 for the Google RefExp and UNC RefExp datasets respectively. The vocabularies are constructed by choosing words that occur at least five times in the training sets. We also filter out special characters of length 1.

We implement our system using the Caffe framework [28] with LSTM layer provided by Donahue et al. [24]. We train our network using stochastic gradient descent with a learning rate of 0.01 which is halved every 50,000 iterations. We use a batch size of 16. The word embedding and LSTM layer outputs are regularized using dropout with a ratio of 0.5.

While Mao et al. [4] used proposals from the Multibox [29] technique, we use proposals from the MCG [30] technique. We obtain top 100 proposals for an image using MCG and evaluate scores for the 80 categories in the MS-COCO [14] dataset. We then discard boxes with low values. The category scores are obtained using the 16 layers VGGNet [27] CNN fine-tuned using Fast RCNN [31]. The category scores of proposals are not used during the testing stage by the referring expression model.

4.3   Comparison of Different Techniques

We compare our MIL based techniques with the baseline and max-margin models of Mao et al. [4]. The model architecture is the same for all the different variants of training objective functions.

Our implementation of the max-margin technique provided better results than those reported in Mao et al. [4]. We use a margin $M = 0.1$ and margin weight $\lambda = 1$ in the max-margin loss function. The margin is applied on word probabilities in the implementation. For each referring expression and its referred region, we sample 5 "hard MCG negatives" for training, similar to their "hard Multibox negatives". The "hard MCG negatives" are MCG proposals that have the same predicted object category as the referred region. The object category of a proposal is obtained during the proposal filtering process. For our MIL based loss functions, we randomly sample 5 ground-truth proposals as context regions for training. We also sample 5 hard MCG negatives. We use a margin $M = 0.1$ and margin weights $\lambda_N = 1, \lambda_P = 1$ in the MIL based loss functions. During testing, we combine the scores from different context regions using the noisy-or function (Eq. 4). We sample a maximum of 10 regions for context during the testing stage.

Table 1. Precision@1 score of different techniques. The results are obtained using the noisy-or function for pooling context information from multiple pairs. We experiment with both ground-truth (GT) and MCG proposals

Proposals	GT	MCG	Proposals	GT	MCG
Google RefExp - Val			UNC RefExp - TestA		
Max Likelihood [4]	57.5	42.4	Max Likelihood [4]	65.9	53.2
Max-Margin [4]	65.7	47.8	Max-Margin [4]	74.9	58.4
Ours, Neg.Bag Margin	**68.4**	49.5	Ours, Neg. Bag Margin	**75.6**	58.6
Ours, Pos. & Neg. Bag Mgn.	**68.4**	**50.0**	Ours, Pos. & Neg. Bag Mgn.	75.0	**58.7**
UNC RefExp - Val			UNC RefExp -TestB		
Max Likelihood [4]	67.5	51.8	Max Likelihood [4]	70.6	50.0
Max-Margin [4]	74.4	56.1	Max-Margin [4]	76.3	55.1
Ours, Neg. Bag Margin	**76.9**	57.3	Ours, Neg. Bag Margin	**78.0**	**56.4**
Ours, Pos. & Neg. Bag Mgn.	76.1	**57.4**	Ours, Pos. & Neg. Bag Mgn.	76.1	56.3

Table 1 shows the Precision@1 scores for the different partitions of both datasets. We show results using ground-truth proposals and MCG proposals to observe the behavior of our framework with and without proposal false positives. The results show that our MIL loss functions perform significantly better than the max-margin technique of Mao et al. [4] on the validation partitions of both datasets and the TestB partition of UNC RefExp dataset. The results on the TestA partition show only a small improvement over the max-margin technique and we investigate this further in the ablation experiments.

We observe on the Google RefExp dataset that the MIL loss function with both positive and negative bag margin performs better than the one with negative bag margin only. In this dataset, referring expressions which mention context between objects usually identify an object and its context object uniquely. Hence there is only one positive instance in the positive bag of region and context region pairs. This property of the referring expressions satisfies the assumption for using the loss function with both positive and negative bag margin.

On the UNC RefExp dataset, we observe that the MIL loss function with negative bag margin performs better or similar to the loss function with both positive and negative bag margin. Unlike the Google RefExp dataset, the referring expressions in the dataset do not always uniquely identify a context object. Many times the context object is not explicitly mentioned in a referring expression e.g., in Fig. 6b, the elephant in the front is implied to be context but not explicitly mentioned. The assumption of one positive instance in the positive bag does not always hold. Hence, the performance is better using the loss function with negative bag margin only.

4.4   Ablation Experiments

In Table 1, the results for the MIL based methods use the noisy-or function for measuring the probability of a referring expression for a region. The noisy-or

Table 2. Pooling context in different ways during testing. We compare the performance of pooling context using noisy-or function, max function and also restricting to image as context. The bold values indicate the best performance obtained for the corresponding dataset among all settings

MIL with Negative Bag Margin			MIL with Pos. & Neg. Bag Margin		
Proposals	GT	MCG	Proposals	GT	MCG
Google RefExp - Val			Google RefExp - Val		
Noisy-Or	**68.4**	49.5	Noisy-Or	**68.4**	**50.0**
Max	66.5	48.6	Max	67.2	49.3
Image context only	65.9	48.1	Image context only	67.9	49.3
UNC RefExp - Val			UNC RefExp - Val		
Noisy-Or	**76.9**	57.3	Noisy-Or	76.1	**57.4**
Max	75.5	56.5	Max	75.3	56.5
Image context only	76.4	56.7	Image context only	76.1	56.6
UNC RefExp - TestA			UNC RefExp - TestA		
Noisy-Or	75.6	58.6	Noisy-Or	75.0	58.7
Max	74.1	57.9	Max	73.4	58.2
Image context only	**76.2**	58.8	Image context only	75.5	**58.9**
UNC RefExp - TestB			UNC RefExp - TestB		
Noisy-Or	**78.0**	**56.4**	Noisy-Or	77.5	56.3
Max	76.8	55.3	Max	76.1	55.3
Image context only	77.0	55.0	Image context only	76.1	55.0

function integrates context information from multiple pairs of a regions. We can also use the max function to determine the probability of a referring expression for a region. In this case, the probability for a region is defined as the maximum probability obtained by any of its pairings with other regions. We also experiment with restricting the context region set to include only the image during testing.

The results in Table 2 show that noisy-or pooling provides the best performance on all partitions except the UNC RefExp TestA partition. It is also more robust when compared to max pooling, which does not exhibit consistent performance. Our models with just image context perform better than the max-margin model of Mao et al. [4] which also used only image as context. The reason for this improvement is that our MIL based loss functions mine negative samples for context during training. In the max-margin model of Mao et al. [4], the model was trained on negative samples for only the referred region and it was not possible to sample negatives for context.

Figures 4 and 5 show a few sample results from the Google RefExp dataset. We observe that our model can localize the referred region and its supporting context region. When there is only one instance of an object in an image, the presence of a supporting context region helps in localizing the instance more accurately when compared to using just the image as context. When there are multiple instances of an object type, the supporting context region resolves ambiguity and helps in localizing the correct instance.

Fig. 4. Google RefExp results. We show results from the model trained with positive and negative bag margin. We compare the grounding between using image context only and pooling the context from all regions using noisy-or. A box with dashed line indicates the context region. We first identify the referred region using noisy-or function. The context region is then selected as the one which produces maximum probability with the referred region. The last row shows images with misplaced context regions

Fig. 5. Google RefExp failure cases. We observe errors when there is wrong grounding of attributes or when there is incorrect localization of context region

The sample results in Fig. 6 from the TestB partition of the UNC RefExp dataset shows that our method can identify the referred region even when the context object is not explicitly mentioned. Since our method considers pairs of regions, it can evaluate the likelihood of a region relative to another region. For example, when there are two instance of the same object on the left, our method can evaluate which of those two instances is more to the left than the other. On the TestA partition of UNC RefExp dataset, we observe that adding context did not improve performance. Samples from this partition are shown in Fig. 7.

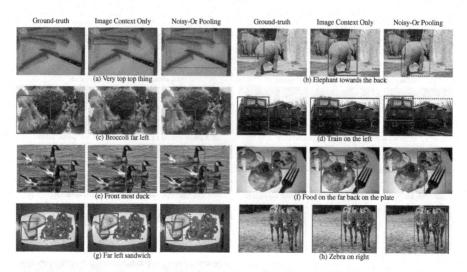

Fig. 6. UNC RefExp results from TestB partition. We show results from the model trained with negative bag margin. We observe that our method can identify the referred region even when the context object is not explicitly mentioned

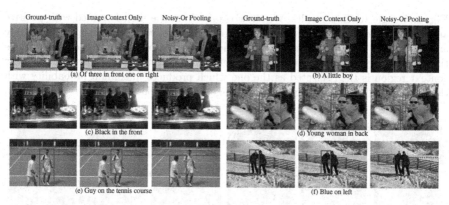

Fig. 7. UNC RefExp failure cases from TestA partition. We show results from the model trained with negative bag margin. This partition contains terse referring expressions. Most of the time, the referring expressions do not uniquely identify the people

The referring expressions in this partition deal with people only and are usually terse. They do not always refer to a unique region in the image. We also observe that many referring expressions do not mention that they are referring to a person.

To observe the effect of spatial relationships between objects, we move the referred region to different locations in the image and evaluate the likelihood of the referred region at different locations. Figure 8 shows sample heat-maps of the likelihood of a referred object. We first select the entire image as context and observe that the likelihood map is not indicative of the location of the referred

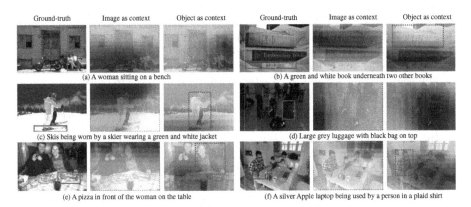

Fig. 8. Spatial likelihood of referred region given a context region. We fix the context region and evaluate the likelihood of the referred object being present in various locations of the image. When the entire image is used as context, the high likelihood regions do not necessarily overlap with the location of the referred region. However when the context region is fixed, the high likelihood regions overlap with the referred region

object. However, when the relevant context object is selected, the regions of high likelihood overlap with the location of referred object.

5   Conclusions

We have proposed a technique that models the probability of a referring expression as a function of a region and a context region using an LSTM. We demonstrated that multiple-instance learning based objective functions can be used for training LSTMs to handle the lack of annotations for context objects. Our two formulations of the training objective functions are conceptually similar to MISVM and mi-SVM [9]. The results on Google RefExp and UNC RefExp dataset show that our technique performs better than the max-margin model of Mao et al. [4]. The qualitative results show that our models can identify a referred region along with its supporting context region.

Acknowledgement. This research was supported by contract N00014-13-C-0164 from the Office of Naval Research through a subcontract from the United Technologies Research Center. The GPUs used in this research were donated by the NVIDIA Corporation. We thank Junhua Mao, Licheng Yu and Tamara Berg for helping with the datasets. We also thank Bharat Singh for helpful discussions.

References

1. Johnson, J., Krishna, R., Stark, M., Li, L.J., Shamma, D., Bernstein, M., Fei-Fei, L.: Image retrieval using scene graphs. In: CVPR (2015)
2. Kazemzadeh, S., Ordonez, V., Matten, M., Berg, T.: Referitgame: referring to objects in photographs of natural scenes. In: EMNLP (2014)

3. Krahmer, E., van Deemter, K.: Computational generation of referring expressions: a survey. Comput. Linguist. **38**(1), 173–218 (2012)
4. Mao, J., Huang, J., Toshev, A., Camburu, O., Yuille, A.L., Murphy, K.: Generation and comprehension of unambiguous object descriptions. In: CVPR (2016)
5. Mitchell, M., van Deemter, K., Reiter, E.: Natural reference to objects in a visual domain. In: INLG (2010)
6. Viethen, J., Dale, R.: The use of spatial relations in referring expression generation. In: INLG (2008)
7. Hu, R., Xu, H., Rohrbach, M., Feng, J., Saenko, K., Darrell, T.: Natural language object retrieval. In: CVPR (2016)
8. Hochreiter, S., Schmidhuber, J.: Long short-term memory. Neural Comput. **9**, 1735–1780 (1997)
9. Andrews, S., Tsochantaridis, I., Hofmann, T.: Support vector machines for multiple-instance learning. In: NIPS (2003)
10. Yu, L., Poirson, P., Yang, S., Berg, A.C., Berg, T.L.: Modeling context in referring expressions. In: ECCV (2016)
11. Vinyals, O., Toshev, A., Bengio, S., Erhan, D.: Show and tell: a neural image caption generator. In: CVPR (2015)
12. Plummer, B.A., Wang, L., Cervantes, C.M., Caicedo, J.C., Hockenmaier, J., Lazebnik, S.: Flickr30k entities: collecting region-to-phrase correspondences for richer image-to-sentence models. In: ICCV (2015)
13. Young, P., Lai, A., Hodosh, M., Hockenmaier, J.: From image descriptions to visual denotations: New similarity metrics for semantic inference over event descriptions. TACL **2**, 67–78 (2014)
14. Lin, T.-Y., Maire, M., Belongie, S., Hays, J., Perona, P., Ramanan, D., Dollár, P., Zitnick, C.L.: Microsoft COCO: common objects in context. In: Fleet, D., Pajdla, T., Schiele, B., Tuytelaars, T. (eds.) ECCV 2014, Part V. LNCS, vol. 8693, pp. 740–755. Springer, Heidelberg (2014)
15. Fang, H., Gupta, S., Iandola, F., Srivastava, R.K., Deng, L., Dollár, P., Gao, J., He, X., Mitchell, M., Platt, J.C., et al.: From captions to visual concepts and back. In: CVPR (2015)
16. Karpathy, A., Fei-Fei, L.: Deep visual-semantic alignments for generating image descriptions. In: CVPR (2015)
17. Xu, K., Ba, J., Kiros, R., Cho, K., Courville, A.C., Salakhutdinov, R., Zemel, R.S., Bengio, Y.: Show, attend and tell: neural image caption generation with visual attention. In: ICML (2015)
18. Rohrbach, A., Rohrbach, M., Hu, R., Darrell, T., Schiele, B.: Grounding of textual phrases in images by reconstruction. In: ECCV (2016)
19. Kong, C., Lin, D., Bansal, M., Urtasun, R., Fidler, S.: What are you talking about? text-to-image coreference. In: CVPR (2014)
20. Johnson, J., Karpathy, A., Li, F.: Densecap: fully convolutional localization networks for dense captioning. In: CVPR (2016)
21. Krishna, R., Zhu, Y., Groth, O., Johnson, J., Hata, K., Kravitz, J., Chen, S., Kalantidis, Y., Li, L.J., Shamma, D.A., Bernstein, M.S., Li, F.F.: Visual genome: connecting language and vision using crowdsourced dense image annotations. In: IJCV (2016)
22. Mitchell, M., Van Deemter, K., Reiter, E.: Two approaches for generating size modifiers. In: European Workshop on Natural Language Generation (2011)
23. FitzGerald, N., Artzi, Y., Zettlemoyer, L.S.: Learning distributions over logical forms for referring expression generation. In: EMNLP (2013)

24. Donahue, J., Anne Hendricks, L., Guadarrama, S., Rohrbach, M., Venugopalan, S., Saenko, K., Darrell, T.: Long-term recurrent convolutional networks for visual recognition and description. In: CVPR(2015)
25. Venugopalan, S., Rohrbach, M., Donahue, J., Mooney, R., Darrell, T., Saenko, K.: Sequence to sequence-video to text. In: ICCV (2015)
26. Karpathy, A., Joulin, A., Li, F.F.: Deep fragment embeddings for bidirectional image sentence mapping. In: NIPS (2014)
27. Simonyan, K., Zisserman, A.: Very deep convolutional networks for large-scale image recognition. In: ICLR (2015)
28. Jia, Y., Shelhamer, E., Donahue, J., Karayev, S., Long, J., Girshick, R., Guadarrama, S., Darrell, T.: Caffe: convolutional architecture for fast feature embedding. arXiv preprint (2014). arXiv:1408.5093
29. Erhan, D., Szegedy, C., Toshev, A., Anguelov, D.: Scalable object detection using deep neural networks. In: CVPR (2014)
30. Arbeláez, P., Pont-Tuset, J., Barron, J., Marques, F., Malik, J.: Multiscale combinatorial grouping. In: CVPR (2014)
31. Girshick, R.: Fast R-CNN. In: ICCV (2015)

Friction from Reflectance: Deep Reflectance Codes for Predicting Physical Surface Properties from One-Shot In-Field Reflectance

Hang Zhang[1]([⊠]), Kristin Dana[1], and Ko Nishino[2]

[1] Department of Electrical and Computer Engineering,
Rutgers University, New Brunswick, USA
`zhang.hang@rutgers.edu`, `kdana@ece.rutgers.edu`
[2] Department of Computer Science, Drexel University, Philadelphia, USA
`kon@drexel.edu`

Abstract. Images are the standard input for vision algorithms, but one-shot in-field reflectance measurements are creating new opportunities for recognition and scene understanding. In this work, we address the question of what reflectance can reveal about materials in an efficient manner. We go beyond the question of recognition and labeling and ask the question: What intrinsic physical properties of the surface can be estimated using reflectance? We introduce a framework that enables prediction of actual friction values for surfaces using one-shot reflectance measurements. This work is a first of its kind vision-based friction estimation. We develop a novel representation for reflectance disks that capture partial BRDF measurements instantaneously. Our method of *deep reflectance codes* combines CNN features and fisher vector pooling with optimal binary embedding to create codes that have sufficient discriminatory power and have important properties of illumination and spatial invariance. The experimental results demonstrate that reflectance can play a new role in deciphering the underlying physical properties of real-world scenes.

Keywords: Surface friction · Reflectance · Material recognition · Binary embedding

1 Introduction

Reflectance describes the characteristics of light interaction with a surface, which is uniquely determined by how the surface is made up at a microscopic (e.g., pigments in the surface medium) and mesoscopic scale (e.g., geometric 3D texture). Naturally, reflectance provides an invaluable clue about the surface, including what it is made of (i.e., material), and how it is shaped (i.e., surface roughness). Reflectance has recently been used to classify surfaces based on the underlying materials [26,47]. and to recover fine-grained geometry [12,44]. Reflectance, however, encodes richer information about the surface than just the material category and surface geometry.

© Springer International Publishing AG 2016
B. Leibe et al. (Eds.): ECCV 2016, Part IV, LNCS 9908, pp. 808–824, 2016.
DOI: 10.1007/978-3-319-46493-0_49

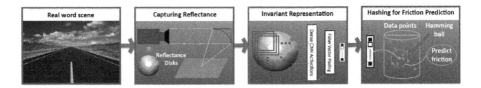

Fig. 1. Deep reflectance codes for *friction-from-reflectance*. Reflectance is captured using one-shot in-field measurements. The binary embedding of Fisher Vector CNN preserves physical properties and provides invariant representation. The resulting hash codes is used in prediction of surface friction.

In this paper, we show that reflectance can be used to estimate tactile properties of the surface: determine the touch from appearance. We, in particular, build the first approach for *friction-from-reflectance*. An image-based friction estimation method has important implications in many applications. For example, robotics can plan how to grasp an object easily with an estimated friction coefficient. A mobile robot or autonomous automobile can use friction information to select an optimized driving mode. For this, we introduce a novel representation of reflectance patterns using a state-of-the-art texture representation that builds on key aspects of deep learning and binary embedding. We demonstrate the power of our approach called *deep reflectance codes*, first in conventional material recognition and then on predicting friction from one-shot measurements.

Reflectance measurements encode rich information that raw images do not. Recognizing materials using ordinary internet-mined photographs has shown great promise [2,7,37,39]. Reflectance information provides a different, complementary approach [47] based on the measurement of the material characteristics, instead of phenomenological appearance. As introduced by Zhang et al. [47], reflectance disks provide a sampling of a surface BRDF without requiring a lab based dome-like measurement system. The disk images are acquired using a concave parabolic mirror positioned over a surface. Due to the mirror geometry, each pixel corresponds to the reflected surface light from a different viewing direction. One of the key innovations, that we introduced in [47] is the use of *angular gradients* in representing surface appearance for recognition and other algorithms. While spatial filtering such as orientation gradients have been commonly used in recognizing texture and materials, angular gradients in the BRDF have been relatively unexplored and our prior work was the first to show that angular filtering is critical for material recognition. Spatial filtering the images comprising reflectance disks corresponds to angular filtering of the surface reflectance. The representation is learned in a multilayer deep learning approach.

These computational models of reflectance disks need to be sufficiently descriptive and yet have invariance to illumination and surface tilt. The measured appearance of a surface changes under multiple illumination angles. The illumination direction affects the position of the specular peak within the reflectance disk, necessitating translation invariance within the representation. The distribution of patterns in the reflectance disk also necessitates a shift-invariant representation similar to desired properties of texture representations. Prior work in representing reflectance disks [47] used hashing to create a binary code for fast recognition and retrieval in high dimensional spaces. Classic methods of texton histograms and texton maps have been replaced in recent years with deep representations for texture such as deep filter banks [8]. We introduce a novel material representation, which we refer to as *deep reflectance codes (DRC)*, that builds on these two concepts. Deep reflectance codes achieve necessary descriptive power and invariance by applying binary embedding to fisher vector convolutional neural nets (FV-CNN) [8]. To demonstrate the general discriminatory power of this new material representation, we test it in both image-based and reflectance disk-based material recognition and show that their performance surpasses past representations on several existing material datasets. Figure 1 shows an overview of our approach.

Deep reflectance codes provide a compact binary representation of the intrinsic phyiscal characteristics of the underlying material. We demonstrate this by showing, for the first time, that reflectance can be used to estimate the friction coefficient of a surface. For this, we collect a first-of-its-kind database of friction coefficients and reflectance disks measured for 137 surfaces that can be grouped into 21 classes (shown in Fig. 2). For exploratory analysis of how reflectance disks encode surface friction, we find a manifold showing the proximal layout of deep reflectance codes using t-SNE [27] as well as a corresponding friction map in t-SNE space. The experimental results show that the reflectance disks and their deep codes encode sufficient information to accurately predict the friction of a surface from its one-shot in-field reflectance measurements. The practical implications of this novel vision-based friction estimation is significant. Current friction sensors are tactile such as tire sensors that measure slip [14,20,28]. Appearance modeling in a fine-grained precise manner allows non-contact friction estimation (e.g. before the tire hits the road patch), which would be useful for various applications such as road surface ice detection, robot locomotion control, and the integration of haptics and graphics.

In summary, there are three main novel contributions: 1) deep reflectance codes for material representation, 2) friction estimation from reflectance, 3) and a database of friction coefficients and reflectance disks.

2   Related Work

Friction from reflectance is an entirely new area. Prior work in friction measurement requires surface contact. These contact friction sensors have been used for real-world friction estimates in applications such as haptics for textiles [3,33], automobile tire sensors [14,20,28], and sheet metal rolling in manufacturing [29]. The ability to estimate friction with vision-based methods will have significant impact on these application areas and many others. Non-contact enables higher speeds and larger distances. Furthermore, material characterization based on friction does not depend on a semantic label and may have greater utility in applications that interact with surfaces.

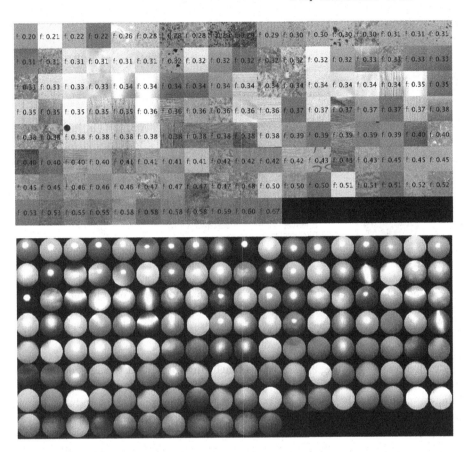

Fig. 2. (Top) Images of the 137 material surfaces for the friction-material database ordered by friction coefficient. (Bottom) Example reflectance disks for corresponding material surfaces. The names for all material classes and the number of instances captured per class are shown in Table 1. As examples of material class names, the list of names for the first surface in each row are as follows: Smooth Ceramic Tile, Automotive Paint, Marble, Composite Flooring, Asphalt, Nylon, Linen, Leather and Sand Paper. As expected, samples such as Smooth Ceramic Tile have lower coefficients of friction (0.2) than samples such as Sand Paper (0.53).

In prior work [47], reflectance disks have been used for material recognition. Their work combines material descriptor of textons distribution with similarity preserving binary embedding methods such as circulant binary embedding (CBE) [46], bilinear embedding [16], iterative quantization (ITQ) [18], angular quantization-based binary codes (AQBC) [17], spectral hashing (SH) [45], locality-sensitive binary codes from shift-invariant kernels (SKLSH) [32], and locality sensitive hash (LSH) [5]. Traditional methods of texton histograms [9,10,25,41] have a weakness in their discriminatory power.

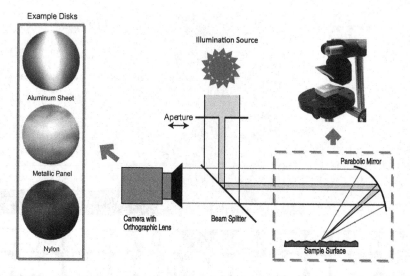

Fig. 3. Schematic of the mirror-based camera. Reflectance disks are obtained by viewing a single point under multiple viewing directions using a concave parabolic mirror viewed by a telecentric lens. The off-axis concave parabolic mirror is shown in the upper right.

Fisher Vector pooling as part of deep learning frameworks has been shown to have excellent performance in texture recognition problems [8]. Binary embedding combined with Fisher Vector pooling [30] has been explored for image retrieval. Deep learning is known for discovering discriminant and robust feature representations. The combination of deep learning and binary compact hash codes is an interesting path that combines the efficiency of binary codes (hamming distance is fast) with the robust performance of deep learning. Semantic hashing [36,40] builds a deep binary model by quantizing a pre-trained and fine-tuned stack of Restricted Boltzmann Machines (RBMs). Deep hashing [15] develops a neural network to learn multiple hierarchical non-linear transformations mapping raw images to compact binary hash codes. However, these hashing techniques rely on hand-crafted visual features as input.

Recent work shows that deep convolutional neural networks trained on a sufficiently large dataset such as ImageNet [35] can be transferred to other computer vision tasks [8,13,19,34]. Lower convolutional layers remain similar on different datasets [49]. CNN activations are still sensitive to translation, rotation and scale [19]. Recognizing reflectance disks from unknown illumination and surface tilts is very similar to texture recognition. It is the distribution of features and visual structures, not their particular spatial location, that is most important. Therefore, dense pooling methods are essential. Multi-scale orderless pooling [19] and deep filter banks [8] using VLAD pooling [21] and Fisher Vector pooling of CNN activations achieve state-of-the-art results on texture, material and scene recognition tasks. We leverage Fisher vector pooling of CNN activations for exploring compact hash codes as binary representations of data.

3 One-Shot In-Field Reflectance Disks

We follow Zhang et al. [47] and use a mirror-based camera [11,12] to measure reflectance of surface points. The camera components are an off-axis parabolic mirror, a CCD camera, a movable aperture and a beam splitter (as shown in Fig. 3). The parabolic mirror is fixed so that its focus is at the surface point to be measured. The illumination source is a collimated beam of light parallel to the global plane of the surface passing through a movable aperture. The angle of the incident ray at the surface is determined by the intersection point with the mirror. Therefore, the illumination direction can be controlled by planar translations of the aperture. Similarly, light reflected from the surface point is reflected by the mirror to a set of parallel rays directed through a beam splitter to the camera. Each pixel of this camera image corresponds to a viewing direction of the surface point. Therefore, the recorded image, referred to as a *reflectance disk*, is an observation of a single point on the surface but from a dense sampling of viewing directions.

4 Deep Reflectance Codes

Reflectance naturally encodes the intrinsic physical properties of the surface, but its measurement is sensitive to illumination changes. For reflectance disks, the illumination changes correspond to translational shifts of image features; e.g. the specularity position shifts. We explore translation invariant representation to extract the physical information. Pre-trained CNN features have been applied to a number of computer vision tasks with great success [22–24], but CNN features are fairly sensitive to translation and rotation. Dense pooling of CNN activations removes the globally spatial information and therefore is robust to pattern translation and rotation. VLAD-CNN and FV-CNN achieved the state-of-the-art results in scene understanding and material recognition [8,19]. We leverage the shift-invariance representation of dense pooling CNN for exploring compact hash codes. The resulting hash codes potentially preserve the similarities of surface physical characteristics, which we refer to as *deep reflectance codes*. A key difference from Cimpoi *et al.* [8] is that we introduce a unsupervised hashing approach rather than a material descriptor for supervised SVM material classification.

Visualizing the effect of the FV-CNN representation can be done with t-SNE [27]. Figure 4 shows reflectance disk representations using (a) raw reflectance disk data and (b) texton maps. The representation of FV-CNN in Fig. 4 (c) shows significantly better class discrimination. This figure depicts many material instances under multiple illumination directions and we can see that our reflectance descriptor provides sufficient invariance and allows grouping of similar materials.

The challenge of using FV-CNN for retrieval is the high dimensionality of the Fisher vector representation ($64K$ dimensions for our implementation described in Sect. 6.1). To achieve a more compact representation, we integrate a binary embedding strategy which preserves the similarity of the Fisher vectors.

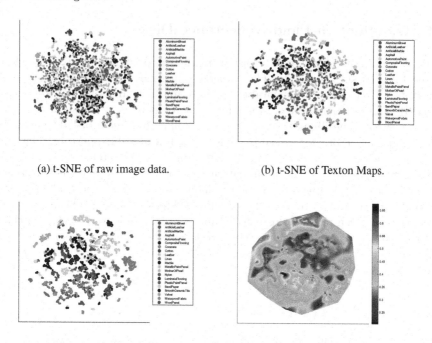

(a) t-SNE of raw image data.   (b) t-SNE of Texton Maps.

(c) Material Manifold of t-SNE FV-CNN.   (d) Friction Manifold in t-SNE space.

Fig. 4. (a) and (b) shows t-SNE of raw image data and traditional texton representation. (c) t-SNE embedding of deep reflectance codes representation. Classes are color-coded (21 classes). There are 5–10 instances per class (137 material surfaces). For some classes there is significant intra-class reflectance variation, but most group well within the t-SNE manifold. (d) Friction map generated in the t-SNE space. Each instance can have a different friction value, as shown in Table 1.

The resulting hash codes are suitable for both material recognition and friction estimation. In this work, the recognition experiments are used to evaluate the quality of the representation in order to use it for friction estimation.

DRC. For binary embedding, projection to a lower dimensional subspace that preserves the similarity is a key component. The Johnson-Lindenstrauss (J-L) Lemma implies that with high probability, the relative distances between all pair of points are approximately preserved under random projection [1]. Therefore, by randomly projecting the high-dimensional data into lower dimension, we can still achieve a comparative results with a linear classifier. Additionally, learning a kernel classifier using Fisher kernel is equivalent to learning a linear classifier on the Fisher vector [31]. By quantizing the randomly projected Fisher vector to binary hash codes, we are able to approximate the behavior of linear classifier using Fisher Vectors, approximating a kernel classifier using Fisher Kernel. The dot product has been shown as a good measurement of similarity for Fisher vectors and we can use Local Sensitivity Hashing (LSH) [5] to binarize the Fisher Vector as in [30] quantizing the randomly projected data using the hyper-planes

Table 1. The measured friction coefficients of the material dataset; the friction sensor is shown at the right bottom corner. The collection of 137 material surfaces are grouped into classes. Each class has multiple distinct instances numbered from 1 to 10.

Friction	AVG.	STD.	1	2	3	4	5	6	7	8	9	10
AluminumSheet	**0.354**	**0.018**	0.354	0.344	0.364	0.384	0.344	0.335				
ArtificialLeather	**0.463**	**0.099**	0.325	0.510	0.577	0.404	0.499					
ArtificialMarble	**0.296**	**0.013**	0.287	0.306	0.306	0.306	0.296	0.296	0.315	0.296	0.277	0.277
Asphalt	**0.398**	**0.043**	0.384	0.404	0.414	0.335	0.466	0.384				
AutomotivePaint	**0.342**	**0.019**	0.344	0.306	0.335	0.344	0.335	0.354	0.344	0.374		
CompositeFlooring	**0.371**	**0.016**	0.384	0.374	0.384	0.354	0.344	0.384	0.384	0.354	0.384	0.364
Concrete	**0.453**	**0.060**	0.424	0.364	0.435	0.456	0.521	0.521				
Cotton	**0.449**	**0.006**	0.445	0.445	0.456	0.445	0.456					
Leather	**0.494**	**0.108**	0.466	0.477	0.466	0.675	0.384					
Linen	**0.467**	**0.031**	0.499	0.510	0.466	0.435	0.445	0.445				
Marble	**0.320**	**0.028**	0.344	0.306	0.335	0.325	0.277	0.287	0.296	0.344	0.364	0.325
MetallicPaintPanel	**0.331**	**0.018**	0.344	0.335	0.335	0.315	0.306	0.354				
MotherOfPearl	**0.333**	**0.023**	0.306	0.306	0.344	0.344	0.335	0.364				
Nylon	**0.412**	**0.015**	0.435	0.424	0.424	0.394	0.404	0.404	0.414	0.394		
LaminateFlooring	**0.394**	**0.018**	0.394	0.384	0.374	0.384	0.404	0.424				
PlasticPaintPanel	**0.343**	**0.042**	0.325	0.325	0.414	0.315	0.374	0.306				
SandPaper	**0.547**	**0.039**	0.510	0.532	0.499	0.577	0.577	0.589				
SmoothCeramicTile	**0.224**	**0.021**	0.259	0.203	0.222	0.213	0.222					
Velvet	**0.564**	**0.026**	0.601	0.532	0.554	0.577	0.554					
WaterproofFabric	**0.394**	**0.014**	0.404	0.414	0.394	0.394	0.384	0.374				
WoodPanel	**0.346**	**0.031**	0.364	0.354	0.354	0.344	0.374	0.287				

across the origin. The cosine similarities of all pairs of data are preserved under random projection [38]. Therefore the hamming distance of generated hash codes preserves the similarity of Fisher vectors. We use quantized random projection of Fisher representation in one variation of our approach, and we refer to this method as *DRC - deep reflectance codes.*

DRC-opt. LSH directly quantizes the randomly projected data into hash codes. Let $v \in \mathbb{R}^d$ represent a projected data point and the hash function $\text{sgn}(v)$ maps the data to the vertex of the hyper-cube $\{-1, 1\}^d$. The quantization error can be written as $\|\text{sgn}(v) - v\|^2$. Following the iterative quantization method [18], in order to preserve the local similarity of the data, a better hash code can be learned by rotating the data to minimize the quantization error:

$$\sum_{i=1}^{N} \|b_i - v_i R\|_2^2, \tag{1}$$

where N is the number of training data, the binary code is given by $b_i = \text{sgn}(v_i R)$, $R \in \mathbb{R}^{d \times d}$ is a rotation matrix. We use this combination of fisher vector CNN with this optimized binary embedding and we refer to it as *DRC-opt optimized deep reflectance codes.*

5   Friction from Reflectance

Deep reflectance codes give us a compact representation that encodes the reflectance disks which we expect to encode rich information about the physical properties of the material itself. We are particularly interested in probing tactile properties of a surface from its reflectance appearance. For this, we focus on estimating friction from reflectance disks. In this section, we introduce the first-of-its-kind friction-reflectance database and then apply deep reflectance codes to estimate friction from one-shot in-field reflectance disks.

5.1   Friction-Reflectance Database

We collect 137 different materials (shown in Fig. 2) and group them into 21 categories: aluminum sheet, artificial leather, artificial marble, asphalt, automotive paint, composite flooring, concrete, cotton, leather, linen, marble, metallic paint panel, mother of pearl, nylon, painted wood flooring, plastic paint panel, sand paper, smooth ceramic tile, velvet, waterproof fabric, wood panel. Our database includes 5–10 different material samples (instances) per category, and we measure 2 different surface spots per sample with 7 illumination directions $(-20°, -10°, 0, 10°, 20°)$ along axis and $(-10°, 10°)$ off axis, where $0°$ is frontal illumination aligned with the surface normal. Additionally, images with 3 exposure settings are collected for high dynamic range imaging. The total number of reflectance disks are 5754.

Friction of a surface is an intrinsic physical property of a surface that can readily be measured non-visually with a contact device. The coefficient of kinetic friction multiplied by the force normal (due to gravity) is the force of friction which act to hold an object in place on a surface. We adopt a simple approach for measuring kinetic friction coefficient by using an inclined plane. In the experiments, we hold the object just above the surface of the inclined plane and release it. At low angles, the object should does not move. As the angle increases, the object begins to slide down at a constant velocity. The angle θ is recorded, and the kinetic friction coefficient is calculated as $\mu = \tan\theta$. For a thin material such as cloth, we attach it to a solid object for the friction measurement. The measured kinetic friction coefficients for all 137 surfaces and the inclined plane friction measurement device are shown in the Table 1. The measured kinetic friction coefficients are shown in Table 1.

5.2   Hashing for Friction Prediction

Deep reflectance codes encode rich information of physical properties of material surface from reflectance disks. The similarities of material physical properties are preserved in Hamming distance by compact hash codes. Figure 4 (c, d) visualizes the correspondence between the friction distribution and the representation using t-SNE, and we are able to see the material surfaces with similar friction coefficients are likely to have small distance. Therefore, our approach of deep reflectance codes can be used for friction estimation. We build a binary hash

Table 2. Comparison of encodings and hashing methods (using 1024-bit hash codes) on different material datasets. The recognition precision over 10 runs, large standard deviation of reflectance and KTH dataset due to randomly selecting one sample surface from each class as test set in each iteration (described in Sect. 6.1).

dataset	FV-SIFT-Hash	CNN-ITQ	VLAD-CNN-KBE	FV-CNN-KBE	DRC	DRC-opt
reflectance	$64.5_{\pm5.8}$	$51.9_{\pm7.0}$	$60.1_{\pm6.7}$	$58.8_{\pm7.1}$	$59.9_{\pm4.8}$	$60.2_{\pm5.1}$
FMD	$48.3_{\pm4.5}$	$65.0_{\pm1.7}$	$59.4_{\pm2.8}$	$57.7_{\pm2.7}$	$64.8_{\pm2.8}$	$65.5_{\pm3.0}$
DTD	$43.6_{\pm1.4}$	$52.6_{\pm1.3}$	$52.3_{\pm1.4}$	$53.1_{\pm0.9}$	$55.4_{\pm1.2}$	$55.8_{\pm1.4}$
KTH	$72.0_{\pm4.3}$	$73.7_{\pm3.4}$	$75.6_{\pm6.2}$	$74.4_{\pm5.2}$	$76.6_{\pm5.2}$	$77.2_{\pm6.4}$

table with the DRC as the key and the corresponding surface friction coefficient as the hash value. The binary representations are compact and amenable for fast nearest neighbor retrieval. The predicted friction coefficient of a sample is given by the average of friction coefficients of retrieved samples.

6   Experimental Results

To evaluate the proposed approach of deep reflectance codes in spatial invariance representation and friction prediction, we conduct two groups of experiments. We first apply deep reflectance codes on retrieval for material recognition as a litmus test of the representation and then evaluate the performance of friction prediction from one-shot measurements.

6.1   Hashing for Material Recognition

Material and texture are typically modeled by orderless pooling of visual patterns, *i.e.* texton distributions, as the shape and spatial information are not important. We apply deep reflectance codes on image retrieval for material recognition to demonstrate the discriminative power and the spatial invariance of our representation.

Additional Datasets. We also consider three other material datasets to evaluate our DRC approach for general material recognition. The first one is Flickr Material Dataset (FMD) [37], which contains 10 material classes. The second one is the Describable Texture Datasets (DTD) [7], containing texture images labeled with 47 describable attributes. The third texture dataset is KTH-TIPS-2b (KTH) [4], which contains 11 material categories with 4 samples per category and a number of example images for each sample. For this unsupervised hashing for material recognition experiments, the training set means the retrieval set for nearest neighbor search. For the DTD and FMD, the test set are given by randomly selected 20 % images, and the rest are for training. The test set of reflectance database and KTH-TIPS are given by randomly selecting one sample of each material category, and the remaining samples are used for training. The experimental results are averaged in 10 runs.

Baseline Methods. For general evaluation of our DRC in material recognition, we compare it with the following methods and settings: FV-SIFT-Hash [30], CNN-ITQ [18], VLAD-CNN-KBE [48], FV-CNN-KBE. FV-SIFT-Hash is binarized fisher vector pooling of SIFT feature as in [30]. CNN-ITQ is iterative quantization binary hashing [18] on 4096-dimensional CNN activations, which is typically compared as a baseline for deep hashing algorithm. KBE represents a latest work Kronecker Binary Embedding [48] (randomized orthogonal version with order 2 is used in this experiment, which is good for high-dimension data). We define ground truth as the given class label of material, and use the mode of labels from 10 retrieved nearest neighbors of hash codes in Hamming Distance as the predicted label. The mean recognition precision is computed over all inquiries from test set averaged over 10 runs.

In our experiments, a pre-trained VGG-M model [6] is used for computing CNN activations. CNN activations for VLAD are taken by the output on the first fully connected layer (full6) with a 4096 dimension. We extract activations for 128×128 paches sampled with a stride of 32 pixels, and use PCA to reduce them to 512 dimensions [19]. We use 64 k-means centers for computing VLAD pooling, the vector is given by assigning each patch to its nearest clustering center and aggregating the residuals of patches minus the center. Hence, the dimension of VLAD pooling CNN is 32 K. The CNN activations for FV pooling are taken from the output of the first convolutional layer with 512 dimensions (conv5 of VGG-M). We use 64 Gaussian components for the FV representation, resulting in $65K$ dimensions FV-CNN descriptors. The implementations are based on MatConvNet [43] and VLFeat [42].

Table 2 shows material recognition results comparing different encodings and hashing methods. We can see the randomized and optimized version of DRC hashing outperform the other methods in FTD, DTD and KTH datasets. Note that our compact unsupervised binary hashing methods can achieve comparable results with training SVM on FV-CNN as reported in [7]. FV pooling provides domain transfer of CNN activations and we have found it make the use of the property that FV pooling essentially discarding the influence the CNN activations corresponding to frequent background structures that are often domain specific. DRC-opt (60.2 %) is much better than directly using CNN activations (CNN-ITQ 51.9 %) for the reflectance dataset. The methods using CNN features are slightly worse than hashing with FV pooling SIFT feature, since the reflectance disks dataset is very different from the CNN pre-trained dataset, ImageNet, which consists real world images. Reflectance Hashing with textons [47] has an overall recognition precision of 56.69 % on this reflectance dataset. We test this method on the reflectance dataset only since it is specifically developed for reflectance disks. Our evaluation indicates the utility of this binary code representation both for general material recognition and specifically for reflectance disk representation.

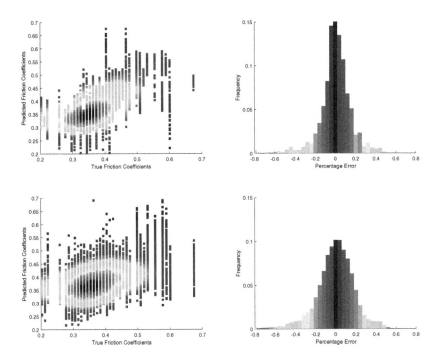

Fig. 5. (Top-left) Friction prediction scatter plot, colored by density. (Top-right) Percentage error distribution, the average percentage error is 11.15 %. (Bottom row) The friction prediction with neural net regression has the average percentage error of 14.74 %.

6.2   Friction Prediction

For friction prediction experiments, we use 1024-bit deep reflectance codes to estimate the surface friction from one-shot in-field reflectance disks. For reflectance-friction dataset, each surface instance (from same or different material class) can have a different friction coefficient, as shown in Table 1. We use leave-one-out cross-validation as training test splits. Each time the disks of one surface is selected as test set and the disks of the rest 136 surfaces are used for training (retrieval). The predicted friction coefficient is given by calculating the average of retrieved 10 neighbors.

Baseline Method. To evaluate our hash codes on friction prediction, we use a regression network as a baseline method. The feedforward network takes the material reflectance representation to directly predict the friction coefficients by fitting a parameterized functional form using FV-CNN representation as input (projected into 1024 dimension). Each neuron in the network nonlinearly transforms the weighted received inputs into outputs. Our regression net has two hidden layers with 16 and 8 neurons respectively and apply a sigmoid function as activation function. The optimal values for parameters are learned by minimizing the sum of the square errors between measured friction coefficients and those predicted by the network.

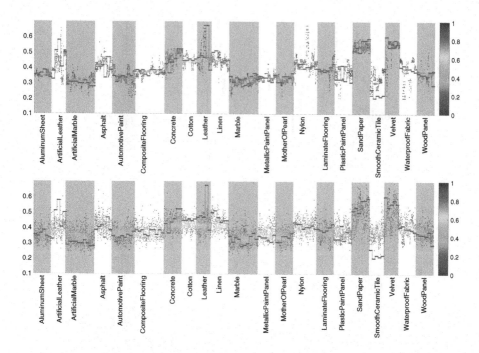

Fig. 6. (Top) Per-class friction prediction results, colored by local density. The red line is the ground truth of friction coefficients. The mean percentage error is 11.15 %. The predicted coefficients match the overall friction variation with material class. Friction-from-reflectance has never been attempted to our knowledge and these results show great promise for this challenging task. (Bottom) The friction prediction with neural net regression has the average percentage error of 14.74 %. (Colour figure online)

Figure 5 shows the prediction results of DRC and the baseline method. The scatter plot (top-left) is color coded and the colors represent the local density around each point. The plot shows the largest density of points have low prediction error. The top-right figure shows a histogram of the error percentage. The predicted data mainly fall into small error bins and the overall mean percentage error is 11.15 %. The results of baseline method are shown at the bottom and the overall mean percentage error is 14.74 %.

Figure 6 provides a more detailed view of the friction-from-reflectance prediction by showing the per-class recognition performance. The red line is the ground truth of friction coefficients, and the points are predicted values colored by the local density of points. Our DRC approach outperforms the baseline method. However, the DRC as a hashing approach has the limitation for predicting the surface with extremely high or low friction due to absence of certain data from retrieval set.

7 Conclusions

We have presented the first-of-its kind friction-from-reflectance framework. Using a unique method for capturing one-shot reflectance, we obtain a simple snapshot of local reflectance. We implement a representation of reflectance with the goal of using this representation for physical property inference. As an evaluation of the quality of the representation, we consider its use in retrieval of reflectance disks and also in general image retrieval; a representation that is sufficiently descriptive for recognition is a good candidate for input to our novel image-based friction prediction. Friction-from-prediction will have good practical value in applications including automated assessment of road conditions prior to vehicular contact, planning robotic grasping of unknown objects, attribute tagging in scene analysis. The paradigm of inferring physical surface properties from image data is the major contribution of the work. The database of reflectance disks, surface images, and corresponding friction measurements will be made publicly available for future research.

Acknowledgment. This work was supported by National Science Foundation award IIS-1421134 to KD and KN and Office of Naval Research grant N00014-16-1-2158 (N00014-14-1-0316) to KN.

References

1. Arriaga, R., Vempala, S., et al.: An algorithmic theory of learning: robust concepts and random projection. In: 40th Annual Symposium on Foundations of Computer Science, pp. 616–623. IEEE (1999)
2. Bell, S., Upchurch, P., Snavely, N., Bala, K.: Material recognition in the wild with the materials in context database. In: Computer Vision and Pattern Recognition (CVPR) (2015)
3. Bertaux, E., Lewandowski, M., Derler, S.: Relationship between friction and tactile properties for woven and knitted fabrics. Text. Res. J. **77**(6), 387–396 (2007)
4. Caputo, B., Hayman, E., Mallikarjuna, P.: Class-specific material categorisation. In: Tenth IEEE International Conference on Computer Vision, ICCV 2005, vol. 2, pp. 1597–1604. IEEE (2005)
5. Charikar, M.S.: Similarity estimation techniques from rounding algorithms. In: Proceedings of the Thiry-Fourth Annual ACM Symposium on Theory of Computing, pp. 380–388. ACM (2002)
6. Chatfield, K., Simonyan, K., Vedaldi, A., Zisserman, A.: Return of the devil in the details: delving deep into convolutional nets. In: British Machine Vision Conference (2014)
7. Cimpoi, M., Maji, S., Kokkinos, I., Mohamed, S., Vedaldi, A.: Describing textures in the wild. In: 2014 IEEE Conference on Computer Vision and Pattern Recognition (CVPR), pp. 3606–3613. IEEE (2014)
8. Cimpoi, M., Maji, S., Vedaldi, A.: Deep filter banks for texture recognition and segmentation. In: Proceedings of the IEEE Conference on Computer Vision and Pattern Recognition, pp. 3828–3836 (2015)

9. Cula, O.G., Dana, K.J.: Compact representation of bidirectional texture functions. In: IEEE Conference on Computer Vision and Pattern Recognition, vol. 1, pp. 1041–1067 (2001)

10. Cula, O.G., Dana, K.J.: Recognition methods for 3d textured surfaces. In: Proceedings of SPIE Conference on Human Vision and Electronic Imaging VI, vol. 4299, pp. 209–220 (2001)

11. Dana, K.J.: BRDF/BTF measurement device. In: International Conference on Computer Vision, vol. 2, pp. 460–466 (2001)

12. Dana, K., Wang, J.: Device for convenient measurement of spatially varying bidirectional reflectance. J. Opt. Soc. Am. A **21**, 1–12 (2004)

13. Donahue, J., Jia, Y., Vinyals, O., Hoffman, J., Zhang, N., Tzeng, E., Darrell, T.: DeCAF: a deep convolutional activation feature for generic visual recognition. In: Proceedings of the 31st International Conference on Machine Learning, pp. 647–655 (2014)

14. Erdogan, G., Alexander, L., Rajamani, R.: A novel wireless piezoelectric tire sensor for the estimation of slip angle. Meas. Sci. Technol. **21**(1), 015201 (2010)

15. Erin Liong, V., Lu, J., Wang, G., Moulin, P., Zhou, J.: Deep hashing for compact binary codes learning. In: Proceedings of the IEEE Conference on Computer Vision and Pattern Recognition, pp. 2475–2483 (2015)

16. Gong, Y., Kumar, S., Rowley, H.A., Lazebnik, S.: Learning binary codes for high-dimensional data using bilinear projections. In: IEEE Conference on Computer Vision and Pattern Recognition, pp. 484–491 (2013)

17. Gong, Y., Kumar, S., Verma, V., Lazebnik, S.: Angular quantization-based binary codes for fast similarity search. In: Advances in Neural Information Processing Systems, pp. 1196–1204 (2012)

18. Gong, Y., Lazebnik, S., Gordo, A., Perronnin, F.: Iterative quantization: a procrustean approach to learning binary codes for large-scale image retrieval. IEEE Trans. Pattern Anal. Mach. Intell. **35**(12), 2916–2929 (2013)

19. Gong, Y., Wang, L., Guo, R., Lazebnik, S.: Multi-scale orderless pooling of deep convolutional activation features. In: Fleet, D., Pajdla, T., Schiele, B., Tuytelaars, T. (eds.) ECCV 2014, Part VII. LNCS, vol. 8695, pp. 392–407. Springer, Heidelberg (2014)

20. Gustafsson, F.: Slip-based tire-road friction estimation. Automatica **33**(6), 1087–1099 (1997)

21. Jégou, H., Douze, M., Schmid, C., Pérez, P.: Aggregating local descriptors into a compact image representation. In: 2010 IEEE Conference on Computer Vision and Pattern Recognition (CVPR), pp. 3304–3311. IEEE (2010)

22. Jia, Y., Shelhamer, E., Donahue, J., Karayev, S., Long, J., Girshick, R., Guadarrama, S., Darrell, T.: Caffe: convolutional architecture for fast feature embedding. In: Proceedings of the ACM International Conference on Multimedia, pp. 675–678. ACM (2014)

23. Krizhevsky, A., Sutskever, I., Hinton, G.E.: Imagenet classification with deep convolutional neural networks. In: Advances in Neural Information Processing Systems, pp. 1097–1105 (2012)

24. LeCun, Y., Bengio, Y., Hinton, G.: Deep learning. Nature **521**, 436–444 (2015)

25. Leung, T., Malik, J.: Representing and recognizing the visual appearance of materials using three-dimensional textons. Int. J. Comput. Vis. **43**(1), 29–44 (2001)

26. Liu, C., Yang, G., Gu, J.: Learning discriminative illumination and filters for raw material classification with optimal projections of bidirectional texture functions. In: The IEEE Conference on Computer Vision and Pattern Recognition (CVPR), June 2013

27. Van der Maaten, L., Hinton, G.: Visualizing data using t-SNE. J. Mach. Learn. Res. **9**(2579–2605), 85 (2008)

28. Matsuzaki, R., Todoroki, A.: Wireless strain monitoring of tires using electrical capacitance changes with an oscillating circuit. Sens. Actuators A: Phys. **119**(2), 323–331 (2005)

29. Nyahumwa, C., Jeswiet, J.: A friction sensor for sheet-metal rolling. CIRP Ann. Manufact. Technol. **40**(1), 231–233 (1991)

30. Perronnin, F., Liu, Y., Sánchez, J., Poirier, H.: Large-scale image retrieval with compressed fisher vectors. In: 2010 IEEE Conference on Computer Vision and Pattern Recognition (CVPR), pp. 3384–3391. IEEE (2010)

31. Perronnin, F., Sánchez, J., Mensink, T.: Improving the fisher kernel for large-scale image classification. In: Daniilidis, K., Maragos, P., Paragios, N. (eds.) ECCV 2010, Part IV. LNCS, vol. 6314, pp. 143–156. Springer, Heidelberg (2010)

32. Raginsky, M., Lazebnik, S.: Locality-sensitive binary codes from shift-invariant kernels. In: Advances in Neural Information Processing Systems, pp. 1509–1517 (2009)

33. Ramkumar, S., Wood, D., Fox, K., Harlock, S.: Developing a polymeric human finger sensor to study the frictional properties of textiles part I: artificial finger development. Text. Res. J. **73**(6), 469–473 (2003)

34. Razavian, A.S., Azizpour, H., Sullivan, J., Carlsson, S.: CNN features off-the-shelf: an astounding baseline for recognition. In: 2014 IEEE Conference on Computer Vision and Pattern Recognition Workshops (CVPRW), pp. 512–519. IEEE (2014)

35. Russakovsky, O., Deng, J., Su, H., Krause, J., Satheesh, S., Ma, S., Huang, Z., Karpathy, A., Khosla, A., Bernstein, M., Berg, A.C., Fei-Fei, L.: Imagenet large scale visual recognition challenge. Int. J. Comput. Vis. (IJCV) **115**, 1–42 (2015)

36. Salakhutdinov, R., Hinton, G.: Semantic hashing. Int. J. Approx. Reason. **50**(7), 969–978 (2009)

37. Sharan, L., Liu, C., Rosenholtz, R., Adelson, E.H.: Recognizing materials using perceptually inspired features. Int. J. Comput. Vis. **103**(3), 348–371 (2013)

38. Shi, Q., Shen, C., Hill, R., Hengel, A.: Is margin preserved after random projection? In: Proceedings of the 29th International Conference on Machine Learning (ICML 2012), pp. 591–598 (2012)

39. Su, S., Heide, F., Swanson, R., Klein, J., Callenberg, C., Hullin, M., Heidrich, W.: Material classification using raw time-of-flight measurements. In: Proceedings of the IEEE Conference on Computer Vision and Pattern Recognition, pp. 3503–3511 (2016)

40. Torralba, A., Fergus, R., Weiss, Y.: Small codes and large image databases for recognition. In: IEEE Conference on Computer Vision and Pattern Recognition, CVPR 2008, pp. 1–8. IEEE (2008)

41. Varma, M., Zisserman, A.: Classifying images of materials: achieving viewpoint and illumination independence. In: Heyden, A., Sparr, G., Nielsen, M., Johansen, P. (eds.) ECCV 2002, Part III. LNCS, vol. 2352, pp. 255–271. Springer, Heidelberg (2002)

42. Vedaldi, A., Fulkerson, B.: VLFeat: an open and portable library of computer vision algorithms (2008). http://www.vlfeat.org/

43. Vedaldi, A., Lenc, K.: Matconvnet-convolutional neural networks for matlab (2015)

44. Wang, J., Dana, K.J.: Relief texture from specularities. IEEE Trans. Pattern Anal. Mach. Intell. **28**(3), 446–457 (2006)

45. Weiss, Y., Torralba, A., Fergus, R.: Spectral hashing. In: Koller, D., Schuurmans, D., Bengio, Y., Bottou, L. (eds.) Advances in Neural Information Processing Systems, vol. 21, pp. 1753–1760. Curran Associates, Inc. (2009). http://papers.nips.cc/paper/3383-spectral-hashing.pdf

46. Yu, F.X., Kumar, S., Gong, Y., Chang, S.F.: Circulant binary embedding. In: International Conference on Machine Learning (2014)

47. Zhang, H., Dana, K., Nishino, K.: Reflectance hashing for material recognition. In: IEEE Conference on Computer Vision and Pattern Recognition (CVPR), pp. 3071–3080 (2015)

48. Zhang, X., Yu, F.X., Guo, R., Kumar, S., Wang, S., Chang, S.F.: Fast orthogonal projection based on kronecker product. In: International Conference on Computer Vision (2015)

49. Zhou, B., Lapedriza, A., Xiao, J., Torralba, A., Oliva, A.: Learning deep features for scene recognition using places database. In: Advances in Neural Information Processing Systems, pp. 487–495 (2014)

Saliency Detection with Recurrent Fully Convolutional Networks

Linzhao Wang[1], Lijun Wang[1], Huchuan Lu[1(✉)], Pingping Zhang[1],
and Xiang Ruan[2]

[1] School of Information and Communication Engineering,
Dalian University of Technology, Dalian, China
{linzertling,wlj,jssxzhpp}@mail.dlut.edu.cn, lhchuan@dlut.edu.cn
[2] TIWAKI Corporation, Iwaki, Japan
ruanxiang@gmail.com

Abstract. Deep networks have been proved to encode high level semantic features and delivered superior performance in saliency detection. In this paper, we go one step further by developing a new saliency model using recurrent fully convolutional networks (RFCNs). Compared with existing deep network based methods, the proposed network is able to incorporate saliency prior knowledge for more accurate inference. In addition, the recurrent architecture enables our method to automatically learn to refine the saliency map by correcting its previous errors. To train such a network with numerous parameters, we propose a pre-training strategy using semantic segmentation data, which simultaneously leverages the strong supervision of segmentation tasks for better training and enables the network to capture generic representations of objects for saliency detection. Through extensive experimental evaluations, we demonstrate that the proposed method compares favorably against state-of-the-art approaches, and that the proposed recurrent deep model as well as the pre-training method can significantly improve performance.

Keywords: Saliency detection · Recurrent fully convolutional network

1 Introduction

Saliency detection can be generally divided into two subcategories: salient object segmentation [12,16,38] and eye-fixation detection [7,26]. This paper mainly focus on salient object segmentation, which aims to highlight the most conspicuous and eye-attracting object regions in images. It has been used as a pre-processing step to facilitate a wide range of vision applications and received increasingly more interest from the community. Although much progress has been made, it is still a very challenging task to develop effective algorithms capable of handling real world adverse scenarios.

Electronic supplementary material The online version of this chapter (doi:10.1007/978-3-319-46493-0_50) contains supplementary material, which is available to authorized users.

B. Leibe et al. (Eds.): ECCV 2016, Part IV, LNCS 9908, pp. 825–841, 2016.
DOI: 10.1007/978-3-319-46493-0_50

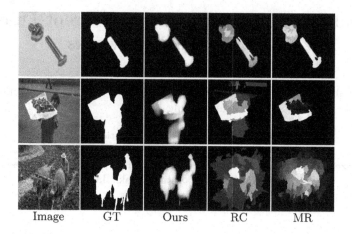

Image   GT   Ours   RC   MR

Fig. 1. Saliency detection results by different methods. From left to right: original image, groundtruth mask, our proposed RFCN, RC [2], MR [36]

Most existing methods address saliency detection with hand-crafted models and heuristic saliency priors. For instance, *contrast prior* formulates saliency detection as center-surrounding contrast analysis and captures salient regions either characterized by global rarity or locally standing out from their neighbors. In addition, *boundary prior* regards boundary regions as background and detects foreground objects by propagating background information to the rest image areas. Although these saliency priors have been proved to be effective in some cases (Fig. 1 first row), they are not robust enough to discover salient objects in complex scenes (Fig. 1 second row). Furthermore, saliency prior based methods mainly rely on low-level hand-crafted features which are incapable to capture the semantic concept of objects. As demonstrated in the third row of Fig. 1, high-level semantic information, in some cases, plays a central role in distinguishing foreground objects from background with similar appearance.

Recently, deep convolutional neural networks (CNNs) have delivered record breaking performance in many vision tasks, *e.g.* image classification [15,28], object detection [5,27], object tracking [32,33], semantic segmentation [21,22], *etc.* Existing methods suggest that deep CNNs can also benefit salinecy detection and are very effective to handle complex scenes by accurately identifying semantically salient objects (Fig. 1 third row). Though better performance has been achieved, there are still three major issues of prior CNN based saliency detection methods. Firstly, saliency priors, which are shown to be effective in previous work, are completely discarded by most CNN based methods. Secondly, CNNs predict the saliency label of a pixel only considering a limited size of local image patch. They mostly fail to enforce spatial consistency and may inevitably make incorrect predictions. However, with feed-forward architectures, CNNs can hardly refine the output predictions. Lastly, saliency detection are mainly formulated as binary classification problems, *i.e.*, either foreground or background. Compared with image classification tasks with thousands of categories, the supervision of binary labels is relatively weak to effectively train a deep CNN with a huge number of parameters.

To mitigate the above issues, we investigate recurrent fully convolutional networks (RFCNs) for saliency detection. In each time step, we feed forward both the input RGB image and a saliency prior map through the RFCN to obtain the predicted saliency map which in turn serves as the saliency prior map in the next time step. The prior map in the first time step is initialized by incorporating saliency priors indicative of potential salient regions. Our RFCN architecture has two advantages over existing CNN based methods: a) saliency priors are exploited to make training deep models more easier and yield more accurate prediction; b) in contrast to feed-forward networks, the output of our RFCN network is provided as the feedback signal, such that the RFCN is capable to refine the saliency prediction by correcting its previous mistakes until producing the final prediction in the last time step. To train the RFCN for saliency detection, a new pre-training strategy is developed, which leverage rich attribute information of semantic segmentation data for supervision. Figure 2 demonstrates the architecture overview of the proposed RFCN model.

In summary, the contributions of this work are three folds. Firstly, we propose a saliency detection method using recurrent fully convolutional network which is able to refine the previous predictions. Secondly, saliency priors are incorporated into the network to facilitate training and inference. Thirdly, we design a RFCN pre-training method for saliency detection using semantic segmentation data to both leverage strong supervison from multiple object categories and capture the intrinsic representation of generic objects. The proposed saliency detection method yields more accurate saliency maps and outperforms state-of-the-art approaches with a considerable margin on four benchmark data sets.

2   Related Work

Existing saliency detection methods can be mainly classified into two categories, *i.e.*, either hand-crafted models or learning based approaches. Most hand-crafted methods ca be traced back to the feature-integration theory [30], where important visual features are selected and combined to model visual attention. Later on, Itti *et al.* [8] propose to measure saliency by center-surround contrast of color, intensity and orientation features. Xie *et al.* [34] formulate saliency detection in a Bayesian framework and estimate visual saliency by a likelihood probability. In [3], a soft image abstraction is developed by considering both appearance similarity and spatial distribution of image pixels for saliency measurement. Meanwhile, background prior is also commonly used by many hand-crafted models [6,10,36,38], where the fundamental hypothesis is that image boundary regions are more likely to be background. Salient regions can then be recognized by label propagation using boundary regions as background seeds.

Hand-crafted saliency methods are efficient and effective, however they are not robust in handling complex scenarios. Recently, learning based methods have

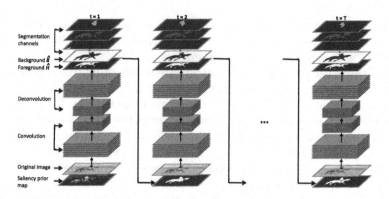

Fig. 2. Architecture overview of our RFCN model.

received more attention from the community. These methods can automatically learn to detect saliency by training detectors (*e.g.*, random forests [12,19], deep networks [17,31,37] *etc.*) on image data with annotations. Among others, deep networks based saliency models have shown very competitive performance. For instance, Wang *et al.* [31] propose to detect salient region by training a DNN-L and a DNN-G network for local estimation and global search, respectively. In [16], a fully connected network is trained to regress the saliency degree of each superpixel by taking multi-scale CNN features of the surrounding region. Both methods conduct patch-by-patch scanning in order to obtain the saliency map of the input image, which is very computational expensive. In addition, they directly train deep models on saliency detection data sets and ignore the problem of weak supervision from binary labels. To address the above issues, Li *et al.* [17] propose to detect saliency using a fully convolutional network (FCN) trained under a multi-task learning framework. Though bears a similar spirit, our method significantly differs from [17] in three aspects. Firstly, saliency priors are leveraged for network training and inference, which are ignored in [17]. Secondly, instead of using the feed-forward architecture in [17], we design a recurrent architecture capable of refining the generated predictions. Thirdly, our pre-training method for deep network allows to learn both class specific features and generic object representations using segmentation data. In contrast, [17] trains the network on segmentation data only for the task of distinguishing objects of different categories, which is essentially different from the task of salient object detection.

Recurrent neural networks (RNNs) have been applied to many vision tasks [20,25]. The recurrent architecture in our method mainly serves as a refinement mechanism to correct previous errors. Compared to existing RNNs that strongly rely on hidden units from last step, RFCN takes only the final output of last step as prior. Hence, it takes fewer steps to converge and is more easier to train.

3   Saliency Prediction by Recurrent Networks

A conventional CNN used for image classification consists of convolutional layers followed by fully connected layers, which takes an image of fixed spatial size as input and produces a label vector indicating the category of the input image. For tasks requiring spatial labels, like segmentation, depth prediction *etc.*, some methods apply CNNs for dense predictions in a patch-by-patch scanning manner. However, the overlap between patches leads to redundant computations and thus significantly increases computational overhead. Unlike existing methods, we consider the fully convolutional network (FCN) architecture [22] for our recurrent model, which generates predictions with the same size of the input image. In Sect. 3.1, we formally introduce FCN network for saliency detection. Section 3.2 presents our saliency methods based on RFCN network. Finally, we show how to train the RFCN network for saliency detection in Sect. 3.3.

3.1   Fully Convolutional Networks for Saliency Detection

Convolutional layers as building blocks of CNNs are defined on a translation invariance basis and have shared weights across different spatial locations. Both the input and the output of convolutional layers are 3D tensors called feature maps, where output feature map is obtained by convolving convolution kernels on the input feature map as

$$f_s(\boldsymbol{X}; \boldsymbol{W}, \boldsymbol{b}) = \boldsymbol{W} *_s \boldsymbol{X} + \boldsymbol{b}, \tag{1}$$

where $\boldsymbol{X}$ is the input feature map; $\boldsymbol{W}$ and $\boldsymbol{b}$ denote kernel and bias, respectively; $*_s$ represents convolution operation with stride s. As a result, the resolution of the output feature map $f_s(\boldsymbol{X}; \boldsymbol{W}, \boldsymbol{b})$ is downsampled by a factor of s. Typically, convolutional layers are interleaved with max pooling layers and non-linear units (*e.g.*, ReLUs) to further improve translation invariance and representation capability. The output feature map of the last convolutional layer can then be fed into a stack of fully connected layers which discard the spatial coordinates of the input and generates a global label for the input image (See Fig. 3 (a)).

For efficient dense inference, [22] converts CNNs to fully convolutional networks (FCNs) (Fig. 3(b)) by casting fully connected layers into convolutional layers with kernels that cover their entire input regions. This allows the network to take input images of arbitrary sizes and generate spatial output by one forward pass. However, due to the stride of convolutional and pooling layers, the final output feature maps are still coarse and downsampled from the input image by a factor of the total stride of the network. To map the coarse feature map into a pixelwise prediction of the input image, FCN upsamples the coarse map via a stack of deconvolution layers (Fig. 3(c))

$$\hat{\boldsymbol{Y}} = U_S\left(F_S(\boldsymbol{I}; \boldsymbol{\theta}); \boldsymbol{\psi}\right), \tag{2}$$

where $\boldsymbol{I}$ is the input image; $F_S(\cdot; \boldsymbol{\theta})$ denotes the output feature map generated by the convolutional layers of FCN with total stride of S and parameterized

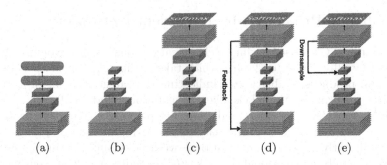

Fig. 3. Comparison of different deep models. (a) Convolution network. (b) Fully convolution network. (c) Fully convolution network with deconvolution layers. (d)(e) Recurrent fully convolution networks with different recurrent architectures.

by $\boldsymbol{\theta}$; $U_S(\cdot; \boldsymbol{\psi})$ denotes the deconvolution layers of FCN networks parameterized by $\boldsymbol{\psi}$ that upsamples the input by a factor of S to ensure the same spatial size of the output prediction $\hat{\boldsymbol{Y}}$ and the input image $\boldsymbol{I}$. Different from simple bilinear interpolation, the parameters $\boldsymbol{\psi}$ of deconvolution layers are jointly learned. To explore the fine-scaled local appearance of the input image, the skip architecture [22] can also be employed to combine output feature maps of both lower convolutional layers and the final convolutional layer for more accurate inference.

In the context of saliency detection, we are interested in measuring the saliency degree of each pixel in an image. To this end, the FCN takes the RGB image $\boldsymbol{I}$ of size $h \times w \times 3$ as input and generates the output feature map $\hat{\boldsymbol{Y}} = U_S\left(F_S(\boldsymbol{I}; \boldsymbol{\theta}); \boldsymbol{\psi}\right)$ of size $h \times w \times 2$. We denote the two output channels of $\hat{\boldsymbol{Y}}$ as background map $\hat{\boldsymbol{B}}$ and salient foreground map $\hat{\boldsymbol{H}}$, indicating the scores of all the pixels being background and foreground, respectively. By applying softmax function, these two scores are transformed into foreground probability as

$$p(l_{i,j} = fg|\boldsymbol{\theta}, \boldsymbol{\psi}) = \frac{\exp(\hat{\boldsymbol{H}}_{i,j})}{\exp(\hat{\boldsymbol{H}}_{i,j}) + \exp(\hat{\boldsymbol{B}}_{i,j})}, \tag{3}$$

where $l_{i,j} \in \{fg, bg\}$ indicates the foreground/background label of the pixel indexed by (i, j). The background probability $p(l_{i,j} = bg|\boldsymbol{\theta}, \boldsymbol{\psi})$ can be computed in a similar way. Given the training set $\{\boldsymbol{Z} = (\boldsymbol{I}, \boldsymbol{C})\}_1^N$ containing both training image $\boldsymbol{I}$ and its pixelwise saliency annotation $\boldsymbol{C}$, the FCN network can be trained end-to-end for saliency detection by minimizing the following loss

$$\arg\min_{\boldsymbol{\theta}, \boldsymbol{\psi}} - \sum_{\boldsymbol{Z}} \sum_{i,j} \mathbf{1}(C_{i,j} = fg) \ln p(l_{i,j} = fg|\boldsymbol{\theta}, \boldsymbol{\psi})$$

$$+ \mathbf{1}(C_{i,j} = bg) \ln p(l_{i,j} = bg|\boldsymbol{\theta}, \boldsymbol{\psi}), \tag{4}$$

where $\mathbf{1}(\cdot)$ is the indicator function. The network parameters $\boldsymbol{\theta}$ and $\boldsymbol{\psi}$ can then be iteratively updated using stochastic gradient descent (SGD) algorithm.

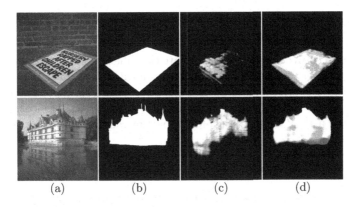

Fig. 4. Saliency maps generated by our model. (a) Original images. (b) Ground truth. (c)(d) Saliency maps without and with prior maps, respectively.

3.2 Recurrent Network for Saliency Detection

The above FCN network is trained to approximate the direct nonlinear mapping from raw pixels to saliency values and ignores the saliency priors which are widely used in existing methods. Although, heuristic saliency priors have their limitations, they are easy to compute and shown to be very effective under a variety of cases. Thus, we believe that leveraging saliency prior information can facilitate faster training and more accurate inference. This has been verified by our experiments. We also note that the output prediction by FCN may be very noisy and lack of label consistency. However, the feed forward architecture of FCN fails to consider feedback information, which makes it impossible to correct prediction errors. Based on these observations, we make two improvements over the FCN network and design the RFCN by: (i) incorporating saliency prior into both training and inference; and (ii) recurrently refining the output prediction (Fig. 4).

Saliency Prior Maps. We encode prior knowledge into a saliency prior map which serves as the input to the network. We first oversegment the input image into M superpixels, $\{s_i\}_1^M$. The color contrast prior for s_i is calculated by

$$\mathcal{G}(s_i) = \frac{1}{\Gamma_i} \sum_{j=1}^{M} \|\mu_{s_i} - \mu_{s_j}\|^2 \exp(-\frac{\|p_{s_i} - p_{s_j}\|^2}{2\delta^2}), \tag{5}$$

where μ and p denote the mean RGB value and the center position of a superpixel, respectively; Γ_i is the normalization factor; and δ is a scale parameter (fixed to 0.5). The intensity contrast $\mathcal{I}(s_i)$ and orientation feature contrast $\mathcal{O}(s_i)$ can be computed in a similar way by replacing the color values in (5) with corresponding feature values. The saliency prior map $\boldsymbol{P}$ is obtained by

$$\boldsymbol{P}(s_i) = \mathcal{U}(s_i) \times (\mathcal{G}(s_i) + \mathcal{I}(s_i) + \mathcal{O}(s_i)), \tag{6}$$

where $P(s_i)$ denotes the saliency prior value of superpixel s_i; and the central prior [11] $\mathcal{U}(s_i)$ penalizes0 the distance from superpixel s_i to the image center.

Recurrent Architecture. To incorporate the saliency prior maps into our approach, we consider two recurrent architectures for RFCN network. As in Sect. 3.1, we divide the network into two parts, *i.e.*, convolution part $F(\cdot, \boldsymbol{\theta})$ and deconvolution part $U(\cdot, \boldsymbol{\psi})$. Our first recurrent architecture (Fig. 3 (d)) incorporates the saliency prior map $\boldsymbol{P}$ into the convolution part by modifying the first convolution layer as

$$f(\boldsymbol{I}) = \boldsymbol{W_I} * \boldsymbol{I} + \boldsymbol{W_P} * \boldsymbol{P} + \boldsymbol{b}, \tag{7}$$

where $\boldsymbol{I}$ and $\boldsymbol{P}$ denote input image and saliency prior, respectively; $\boldsymbol{W_I}$ and $\boldsymbol{W_P}$ represent corresponding convolution kernels; $\boldsymbol{b}$ is bias parameter. In the first time step, the RFCN network takes the input image and saliency prior map as input and produces the final feature map $\hat{\boldsymbol{Y}}^1 = U\left(F(\boldsymbol{I}, \boldsymbol{P}; \boldsymbol{\theta}); \boldsymbol{\psi}\right)$ comprising both foreground map $\hat{\boldsymbol{H}}^1$ and background map $\hat{\boldsymbol{B}}^1$. In the following each time step, the foreground map $\hat{\boldsymbol{H}}^{t-1}$ generated in the last time step is fed back as saliency prior map to the input. The RFCN then refine the saliency prediction by considering both the input image and the last prediction as

$$\hat{\boldsymbol{Y}}^t = U\left(F(\boldsymbol{I}, \hat{\boldsymbol{H}}^{t-1}; \boldsymbol{\theta}); \boldsymbol{\psi}\right). \tag{8}$$

For the above recurrent architecture, forward propagation of the whole network is conducted in every time step, which is very expensive in terms of both computation and memory. An alternative recurrent architecture is to incorporate the saliency prior maps into the deconvolution part ((Figure 3 (e))). Specifically, in the first time step, we feed the input image $\boldsymbol{I}$ into the convolution part to obtain the convolution feature map $F(\boldsymbol{I}; \boldsymbol{\theta})$. The deconvolution part then takes the convolution feature map as well as saliency prior map $\boldsymbol{P}$ as input to infer the saliency prediction $\hat{\boldsymbol{Y}}^1 = U\left(F(\boldsymbol{I}; \boldsymbol{\theta}), \boldsymbol{P}; \boldsymbol{\psi}\right)$. In the t-th time step, the predicted foreground map $\hat{\boldsymbol{H}}^{t-1}$ in the last time step serves as saliency prior map. The deconvolution part takes the convolution feature map $F(\boldsymbol{I}; \boldsymbol{\theta})$ as well as the foreground map $\hat{\boldsymbol{H}}^{t-1}$ to refine the saliency prediction $\hat{\boldsymbol{Y}}^t$:

$$\hat{\boldsymbol{Y}}^t = U\left(F(\boldsymbol{I}; \boldsymbol{\theta}), \hat{\boldsymbol{H}}^{t-1}; \boldsymbol{\psi}\right). \tag{9}$$

Note that, for each input image, forward propagation of deconvolution part is repeatedly conducted in each time step, whereas the convolution part is only required to be fed forward once in the first time step. Since the deconvolution part has approximately 10 times fewer parameters than the convolution part, this recurrent architecture can effectively reduce computational complexity and save memory. However, we find in our preliminary experiments that the second recurrent architecture can only achieve similar performance compared to the FCN based approach (*i.e.*, without recurrent). This may be attributed to the fact

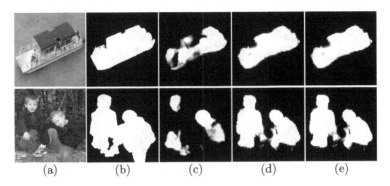

Fig. 5. Saliency maps predicted by the proposed RFCN in different time steps. (a) Original images. (b) Ground truth. (c)–(e) Saliency maps predicted by RFCN in the 1st–3rd time step, respectively.

that the prior saliency map is severely downsampled to the same spatial size of the last convolution feature map $F(I; \theta)$ (downsampled by a factor of $1/32$ from the input). With less prior information, the downsampled prior saliency map can hardly facilitate network inference. Therefore, we adopt the first recurrent architecture in this work. In our experiments, we observe that the accuracy of the saliency maps almost converges after the second time step (Compare Fig. 5(a) and (e)). Therefore, we set the total time step of the RFCN to $T = 2$.

3.3   Training RFCN for Saliency Detection

Our RFCN training approach consists of two stages: pre-training and fine-tuning. Pre-training is conducted on the PASCAL VOC 2010 semantic segmentation data set. Saliency detection and semantic segmentation are highly correlated but essentially different in that saliency detection aims at separating generic salient objects from background, whereas semantic segmentation focuses on distinguishing objects of different categories. Our pre-training approach enjoys strong supervision from segmentation data and also enables the network to learn general representation of foreground objects. Specifically, for each training pair $Z = (I, S)$ containing image I and pixelwise semantic annotation S, we generate an object map G to label each pixel as either foreground (fg) or background (bg) as follow

$$G_{i,j} = \begin{cases} bg & \text{if } S_{i,j} = 0 \\ fg & \text{otherwise} \end{cases}, \tag{10}$$

where $S_{i,j} \in \{0, 1, \dots, C\}$ denotes the semantic class label of pixel (i, j), and $S_{i,j} = 0$ indicates the pixel belonging to background. In the pre-training stage, the final feature map $\hat{Y}^t$ (Sect. 3.1) generated by the RFCN consists of $C + 3$ channels, where the first $C+1$ channels correspond to the class scores for semantic segmentation and the last 2 channels, $i.e.$, $\hat{H}^t$ and $\hat{B}^t$ (Sect. 3.1), denotes

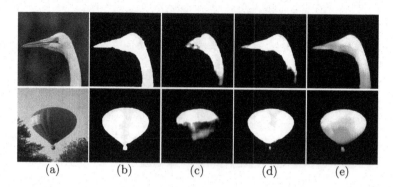

(a)   (b)   (c)   (d)   (e)

Fig. 6. Saliency detection results on different stages. (a) Original images. (b) ground truth. (c) results of pre-trained RFCN. (d) results of fine-tuned RFCN. (e) result after post-processing.

the foreground/background scores. By applying softmax function, we obtain the conditional probability $p(c_{i,j}|I, \hat{H}^{t-1}, \theta, \psi)$ and $p(l_{i,j}|I, \hat{H}^{t-1}, \theta, \psi)$ predicted by the RFCN for segmentation and foreground detection, respectively. The loss function for pre-training across all time steps is defined as

$$L(\theta, \psi) = -\sum_{t=1}^{T}\sum_{Z}\sum_{i,j} \ln p(c_{i,j} = S_{i,j}|I, \hat{H}^{t-1}, \theta, \psi)$$

$$+ \ln p(l_{i,j} = G_{i,j}|I, \hat{H}^{t-1}, \theta, \psi), \quad (11)$$

where T is the total time step and $\hat{H}^0$ is initialized by the saliency prior map P (Sect. 3.2). Pre-training is conducted via back propagation through time.

After pre-training, we modify the RFCN network architecture by removing the first $C + 1$ channels of the last feature map and only maintaining the last two channels, *i.e.*, the predicted foreground and background maps. Finally, we fine-tune the RFCN network on the saliency detection data set as described in Sect. 3.2. As demonstrated in Fig. 6(c), the pre-trained model, supervised by semantic labels of multiple object categories, captures generic object features and can already discriminate foreground objects (of unseen categories in pre-training) from background. Fine-tuning on the saliency data set can further improve the performance of the RFCN network (Fig. 6(d)).

3.4   Post-processing

The trained RFCN network is able to accurately identify salient objects. To more precisely delineate the compact and boundary-preserving object regions, we adopt an efficient post-processing approach. Given the final saliency score map $\hat{H}^T$ predicted by the RFCN, we first segment the image into foreground and background regions by thresholding $\hat{H}^T$ with its mean saliency score. A spatial confidence $SC_{i,j}$ and a color confidence $CC_{i,j}$ are computed for each pixel (i,j). The spatial confidence is defined considering the spatial distance of the pixel to the center of the foreground region

$$SC_{i,j} = \exp(-\frac{\|loc_{i,j} - loc_s\|_2}{\sigma}), \tag{12}$$

where $loc_{i,j}$ and loc_s denote the coordinates the pixel (i,j) and the center of foreground, respectively; σ is a scale parameter. The color confidence is defined to measure the similarity of the pixel to foreground region in RGB color space

$$CC_{i,j} = \frac{N_{i,j}}{N_s}, \tag{13}$$

where $N_{i,j}$ is the number of foreground pixels that have the same color feature with pixel (i,j) and N_s is the total number of foreground pixels.

We then weight the predicted saliency scores by spatial and color confidences to dilate the foreground region

$$\tilde{H}_{i,j} = SC_{i,j} \times CC_{i,j} \times \hat{H}^T. \tag{14}$$

After an edge-aware erosion procedure [4] on the dilated saliency score map $\tilde{H}$, we obtain the final saliency map. As demonstrated in Fig. 6 (e), the post-processing step can improve the detection precision to a certain degree.

4 Experiments

4.1 Experimental Setup

Detailed architecture of the proposed RFCN can be found in the supplementary materials[1]. We pre-train the RFCN on the PASCAL VOC 2010 semantic segmentation data set with 10103 training images belonging to 20 object classes. The pre-training is converged after 200k iterations of SGD. We then fine-tune the pre-trained model for saliency detection on the THUS10K [2] data set for 100k iterations. In the test stage, we apply the trained RFCN in three different scales and fuse all the results into the final saliency maps [12]. Our method is implemented in MATLAB with the Caffe [9] wrapper and runs at 4.6 s per image on a PC with a 3.4 GHz CPU and a TITANX GPU. The source code will be released (see footnote 1).

We evaluate the proposed algorithm (RFCN) on five benchmark data sets: SOD [24], ECSSD [35], PASCAL-S [19], SED1 [1], and SED2 [1]. The evaluation result on SED2 and additional analysis on the impact of recurrent time step are included in the supplementary materials. Three metrics are utilized to measure the performance, including precision-recall (PR) curves, F-measure and area under ROC curve (AUC). The precision and recall are computed by thresholding

---

[1] http://ice.dlut.edu.cn/lu/index.html.

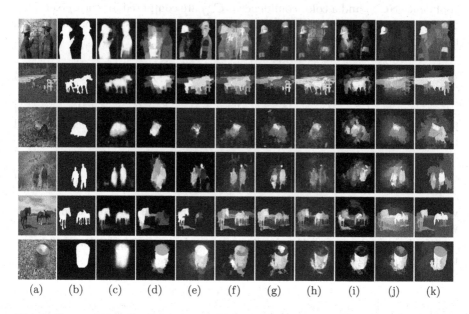

Fig. 7. Comparisons of saliency maps. Top, middle and bottom two rows are images from the SOD, ECSSD, PASCAL-S and SED1 data sets, respectively.(a) Original images, (b) ground truth, (c) our RFCN method, (d) LEGS, (e) MDF, (f) DRFI, (g) wCtr, (h) HDCT, (i) DSR, (j) MR, (k) HS.

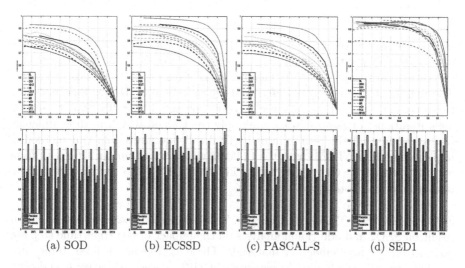

Fig. 8. Performance of the proposed algorithm compared with other state-of-the-art methods on the SOD, ECSSD, PASCAL-S and SED1 databases, respectively.

Table 1. F-measure and AUC (Area Under ROC Curve) on the SOD, ECSSD, PASCAL-S and SED1 data sets. The best two results are shown in italic and bold fonts respectively. The proposed methods rank first and second on the four data sets.

*	SOD		ECSSD		PASCAL-S		SED1	
	F-measure	AUC	F-measure	AUC	F-measure	AUC	F-measure	AUC
RFCN	0.7426	0.9053	0.8340	0.9714	0.7468	0.9453	0.8502	0.9640
MTDS	0.6978	0.9233	0.7589	0.9009	0.7310	0.9287	-	-
LEGS	0.6492	0.8117	0.7887	0.9230	0.6951	0.8857	0.8414	0.9328
MDF	0.6966	0.8532	0.7557	0.9180	0.6562	0.8806	0.8194	0.9710
BL	0.5723	0.8503	0.6825	0.9147	0.5668	0.8633	0.7675	0.9528
DRFI	0.6031	0.8464	0.7337	0.9391	0.6159	0.8913	0.8024	0.9528
wCtr	0.5978	0.8014	0.6774	0.8779	0.5972	0.8433	0.7889	0.9159
DSR	0.5968	0.8210	0.6636	0.8604	0.5513	0.8079	0.7877	0.9086
MR	0.5697	0.7899	0.6932	0.8820	0.5881	0.8205	0.8255	0.9223
HS	0.5210	0.8145	0.6363	0.8821	0.5278	0.8330	0.7426	0.9161
PCA	0.5370	0.8212	0.5796	0.8737	0.5298	0.8371	0.6256	0.9030
UFO	0.5480	0.7840	0.6442	0.8587	0.5502	0.8088	-	-

the saliency map, and comparing the binary map with the ground truth. The PR curves demonstrate the mean precision and recall of saliency maps at different thresholds. The F-measure can be calculated by $F_\beta = \frac{(1+\beta^2)Precision \times Recall}{\beta^2 \times Precision + Recall}$, where *Precision* and *Recall* are obtained using twice the mean saliency value of saliency maps as the threshold, and set $\beta^2 = 0.3$.

4.2   Performance Comparison with State-of-the-art

We compare the proposed algorithm (RFCN) with twelve state-of-the-art methods, including MTDS [17], LEGS [31], MDF [16], BL [29], DRFI [12], UFO [13], PCA [23], HS [35], wCtr [38], MR [36], DSR [18] and HDCT [14]. We use either the implementations or the saliency maps provided by the authors for fair comparison. Note that MTDS, LEGS and MDF are deep learning based methods. Among others, MTDS exploits fully convolution network for saliency detection and leverages segmentation data for multi-task training. As demonstrated in Fig. 8 and Table 1, the proposed RFCN method can consistently outperform existing methods across almost all the data sets with a considerable margin in terms of PR curves, F-measure as well as AUC scores. Compared with other deep learning based methods, the three contributions of our method (*i.e.*, integration of saliency priors, recurrent architecture and pre-training approach) ensures more accurate saliency detection. Figure 7 shows that our saliency maps can reliably highlight the salient objects in various challenging scenarios.

Table 2. Different settings of variants of the proposed RFCN method. "Pre-train" denotes that the network is pre-trained on segmentation data only for semantic segmentation task. "Pre-train$_+$" indicates the proposed pre-training method using segmentation data for both semantic segmentation and foreground background separation.

Settings	FCN	FCN$_p$	RFCN-A	RFCN-B	RFCN
Prior map		√	√	√	√
Feed-forward	√	√			
Recurrent			√	√	√
Pre-train	√	√	√		
Pre-train$_+$				√	√
Post-processing					√

Table 3. Comparison of the proposed approach. The best results are shown in bold fonts.

*	SOD		ECSSD		PASCAL-S		SED1	
	F-measure	AUC	F-measure	AUC	F-measure	AUC	F-measure	AUC
FCN	0.6985	0.7810	0.8116	0.8864	0.7179	0.8387	0.7924	0.8452
FCN$_p$	0.7248	0.8210	0.8252	0.9145	0.7315	0.8733	0.8335	0.8823
RFCN-A	0.7276	0.8213	0.8312	0.9119	0.7372	0.8784	0.8500	0.8967
RFCN-B	**0.7487**	0.8331	**0.8534**	0.9310	**0.7734**	0.9028	**0.8527**	0.9006
RFCN	0.7426	**0.9053**	0.8340	**0.9714**	0.7468	**0.9453**	0.8502	**0.9640**

4.3   Ablation Studies

To analyze the relative contributions of different components of our methods, we evaluate four variants of the proposed RFCN method with different settings as demonstrated in Table 2. The performance in terms of F-measure and AUC are reported in Table 3. The comparison between FCN and FCN$_p$ suggests that saliency priors ignored by existing deep learning based methods can indeed benefit network training and inference. The comparison between FCN$_p$ and RFCN-A indicates that the proposed recurrent architecture is capable of correcting previous errors and refining the output saliency maps. In addition, the RFCN-B method with the proposed pre-training strategy can significantly outperform the RFCN-A method simply pre-trained for segmentation, which verifies that our pre-training method can effectively leverage the strong supervision of segmentation and simultaneously enable the network to caputre generic feature representation of foreground objects. After the proposed post-processing step, our RFCN method achieves considerable improvements over RFCN-B in terms of AUC scores with a slight performance degrade in terms of F-measure.

5   Conclusions

In this paper, we propose a recurrent fully convolutional network based saliency detection methods. Heuristic saliency priors are incorporated into the network to facilitate training and inference. The recurrent architecture enables our method to refine saliency maps based on previous output and yield more accurate predictions. A pre-training strategy is also developed to exploit the strong supervision of segmentation data sets and explicitly enforce the network to learn generic feature representation for saliency detection. Extensive evaluations verify that the above three contributions can significantly improve performance of saliency detection. State-of-the-art performance has been achieved by the proposed method in five widely adopted data sets.

Acknowledgement. The work is supported by the National Natural Science Foundation of China under Grant 61528101 and Grant 61472060.

References

1. Alpert, S., Galun, M., Brandt, A., Basri, R.: Image segmentation by probabilistic bottom-up aggregation and cue integration. PAMI **34**(2), 315–327 (2012)
2. Cheng, M., Mitra, N.J., Huang, X., Torr, P.H., Hu, S.: Global contrast based salient region detection. PAMI **37**(3), 569–582 (2015)
3. Cheng, M.M., Warrell, J., Lin, W.Y., Zheng, S., Vineet, V., Crook, N.: Efficient salient region detection with soft image abstraction. In: ICCV, pp. 1529–1536 (2013)
4. Gastal, E.S., Oliveira, M.M.: Domain transform for edge-aware image and video processing. ACM Trans. Graph. (TOG) **30**, 69 (2011)
5. Girshick, R., Donahue, J., Darrell, T., Malik, J.: Rich feature hierarchies for accurate object detection and semantic segmentation. In: CVPR, pp. 580–587 (2014)
6. Han, J., Zhang, D., Hu, X., Guo, L., Ren, J., Wu, F.: Background prior-based salient object detection via deep reconstruction residual. CSVT **25**(8), 1309–1321 (2015)
7. Huang, X., Shen, C., Boix, X., Zhao, Q.: Salicon: reducing the semantic gap in saliency prediction by adapting deep neural networks. In: ICCV (2015)
8. Itti, L., Koch, C., Niebur, E.: A model of saliency-based visual attention for rapid scene analysis. PAMI **11**, 1254–1259 (1998)
9. Jia, Y., Shelhamer, E., Donahue, J., Karayev, S., Long, J., Girshick, R., Guadarrama, S., Darrell, T.: Caffe: convolutional architecture for fast feature embedding. In: Proceedings of the ACM International Conference on Multimedia, pp. 675–678 (2014)
10. Jiang, B., Zhang, L., Lu, H., Yang, C., Yang, M.H.: Saliency detection via absorbing markov chain. In: CVPR, pp. 1665–1672 (2013)
11. Jiang, H., Wang, J., Yuan, Z., Liu, T., Zheng, N., Li, S.: Automatic salient object segmentation based on context and shape prior. In: BMVC, vol. 6, p. 9 (2011)
12. Jiang, H., Wang, J., Yuan, Z., Wu, Y., Zheng, N., Li, S.: Salient object detection: a discriminative regional feature integration approach. In: CVPR, pp. 2083–2090 (2013)

13. Jiang, P., Ling, H., Yu, J., Peng, J.: Salient region detection by ufo: uniqueness, focusness and objectness. In: ICCV, pp. 1976–1983 (2013)

14. Kim, J., Han, D., Tai, Y.W., Kim, J.: Salient region detection via high-dimensional color transform. In: CVPR, pp. 883–890 (2014)

15. Krizhevsky, A., Sutskever, I., Hinton, G.E.: Imagenet classification with deep convolutional neural networks. In: NIPS, pp. 1097–1105 (2012)

16. Li, G., Yu, Y.: Visual saliency based on multiscale deep features. In: CVPR, pp. 5455–5463 (2015)

17. Li, X., Zhao, L., Wei, L., Yang, M., Wu, F., Zhuang, Y., Ling, H., Wang, J.: Deepsaliency: multi-task deep neural network model for salient object detection. arXiv preprint arXiv:1510.05484 (2015)

18. Li, X., Lu, H., Zhang, L., Ruan, X., Yang, M.H.: Saliency detection via dense and sparse reconstruction. In: ICCV, pp. 2976–2983 (2013)

19. Li, Y., Hou, X., Koch, C., Rehg, J., Yuille, A.: The secrets of salient object segmentation. In: CVPR, pp. 280–287 (2014)

20. Liang, M., Hu, X.: Recurrent convolutional neural network for object recognition. In: Computer Vision and Pattern Recognition, pp. 3367–3375 (2015)

21. Liang-Chieh, C., Papandreou, G., Kokkinos, I., Murphy, K., Yuille, A.: Semantic image segmentation with deep convolutional nets and fully connected crfs. In: ICLR (2015)

22. Long, J., Shelhamer, E., Darrell, T.: Fully convolutional networks for semantic segmentation. In: CVPR, pp. 3431–3440 (2015)

23. Margolin, R., Tal, A., Zelnik-Manor, L.: What makes a patch distinct? In: CVPR, pp. 1139–1146 (2013)

24. Movahedi, V., Elder, J.H.: Design and perceptual validation of performance measures for salient object segmentation. In: CVPR, pp. 49–56 (2010)

25. Pinheiro, P.H., Collobert, R.: Recurrent convolutional neural networks for scene labeling. In: ICML, pp. 82–90 (2014)

26. Ramanathan, S., Katti, H., Sebe, N., Kankanhalli, M., Chua, T.-S.: An eye fixation database for saliency detection in images. In: Daniilidis, K., Maragos, P., Paragios, N. (eds.) ECCV 2010, Part IV. LNCS, vol. 6314, pp. 30–43. Springer, Heidelberg (2010)

27. Ren, S., He, K., Girshick, R., Sun, J.: Faster R-CNN: towards real-time object detection with region proposal networks. In: NIPS, pp. 91–99 (2015)

28. Simonyan, K., Zisserman, A.: Very deep convolutional networks for large-scale image recognition. arXiv preprint arXiv:1409.1556 (2014)

29. Tong, N., Lu, H., Ruan, X., Yang, M.H.: Salient object detection via bootstrap learning. In: CVPR, pp. 1884–1892 (2015)

30. Treisman, A.M., Gelade, G.: A feature-integration theory of attention. Cogn. Psychol. 12(1), 97–136 (1980)

31. Wang, L., Lu, H., Ruan, X., Yang, M.H.: Deep networks for saliency detection via local estimation and global search. In: CVPR, pp. 3183–3192 (2015)

32. Wang, L., Ouyang, W., Wang, X., Lu, H.: Visual tracking with fully convolutional networks. In: ICCV, pp. 3119–3127 (2015)

33. Wang, L., Ouyang, W., Wang, X., Lu, H.: Stct: sequentially training convolutional networks for visual tracking. In: CVPR (2016)

34. Xie, Y., Lu, H.: Visual saliency detection based on bayesian model. In: ICIP, pp. 645–648 (2011)

35. Yan, Q., Xu, L., Shi, J., Jia, J.: Hierarchical saliency detection. In: CVPR, pp. 1155–1162 (2013)

36. Yang, C., Zhang, L., Lu, H., Ruan, X., Yang, M.H.: Saliency detection via graph-based manifold ranking. In: CVPR, pp. 3166–3173 (2013)
37. Zhao, R., Ouyang, W., Li, H., Wang, X.: Saliency detection by multi-context deep learning. In: CVPR, pp. 1265–1274 (2015)
38. Zhu, W., Liang, S., Wei, Y., Sun, J.: Saliency optimization from robust background detection. In: CVPR, pp. 2814–2821 (2014)

Deep3D: Fully Automatic 2D-to-3D Video Conversion with Deep Convolutional Neural Networks

Junyuan Xie[1]([✉]), Ross Girshick[1], and Ali Farhadi[1,2]

[1] University of Washington, Seattle, USA
{jxie,rbg,ali}@cs.washington.edu
[2] Allen Institute for Artificial Intelligence, Seattle, USA

Abstract. As 3D movie viewing becomes mainstream and the Virtual Reality (VR) market emerges, the demand for 3D contents is growing rapidly. Producing 3D videos, however, remains challenging. In this paper we propose to use deep neural networks to automatically convert 2D videos and images to a stereoscopic 3D format. In contrast to previous automatic 2D-to-3D conversion algorithms, which have separate stages and need ground truth depth map as supervision, our approach is trained end-to-end directly on stereo pairs extracted from existing 3D movies. This novel training scheme makes it possible to exploit orders of magnitude more data and significantly increases performance. Indeed, Deep3D outperforms baselines in both quantitative and human subject evaluations.

Keywords: Monocular stereo reconstruction · Deep convolutional neural networks

1 Introduction

3D movies are popular and comprise a large segment of the movie theater market, ranging between 14 % and 21 % of all box office sales between 2010 and 2014 in the U.S. and Canada [1]. Moreover, the emerging market of Virtual Reality (VR) head-mounted displays will likely drive an increased demand for 3D content (Fig. 1).

3D videos and images are usually stored in stereoscopic format. For each frame, the format includes two projections of the same scene, one of which is exposed to the viewer's left eye and the other to the viewer's right eye, thus giving the viewer the experience of seeing the scene in three dimensions.

There are two approaches to making 3D movies: shooting natively in 3D or converting to 3D after shooting in 2D. Shooting in 3D requires costly special-purpose stereo camera rigs. Aside from equipment costs, there are cinemagraphic

Electronic supplementary material The online version of this chapter (doi:10.1007/978-3-319-46493-0_51) contains supplementary material, which is available to authorized users.

B. Leibe et al. (Eds.): ECCV 2016, Part IV, LNCS 9908, pp. 842–857, 2016.
DOI: 10.1007/978-3-319-46493-0_51

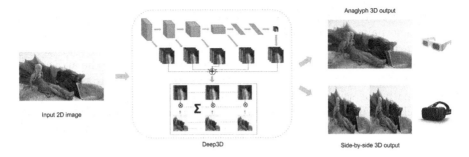

Fig. 1. We propose Deep3D, a fully automatic 2D-to-3D conversion algorithm that takes 2D images or video frames as input and outputs stereo 3D image pairs. The stereo images can be viewed with 3D glasses or head-mounted VR displays. Deep3D is trained directly on stereo pairs from a dataset of 3D movies to minimize the pixel-wise reconstruction error of the right view when given the left view. Internally, the Deep3D network estimates a probabilistic disparity map that is used by a differentiable depth image-based rendering layer to produce the right view. Thus Deep3D does not require collecting depth sensor data for supervision.

issues that may preclude the use of stereo camera rigs. For example, some inexpensive optical special effects, such as forced perspective[1], are not compatible with multi-view capturing devices. 2D-to-3D conversion offers an alternative to filming in 3D. Professional conversion processes typically rely on "depth artists" who manually create a depth map for each frame. Standard Depth Image-Based Rendering (DIBR) algorithms can then be used to combine the original frame with the depth map in order to arrive at a stereo image pair [2]. However, this process is still expensive as it requires intensive human effort.

Each year about 20 new 3D movies are produced. High production cost is the main hurdle in the way of scaling up the 3D movie industry. Automated 2D-to-3D conversion would eliminate this obstacle.

In this paper, we propose a fully automated, data-driven approach to the problem of 2D-to-3D video conversion. Solving this problem entails reasoning about depth from a single image and synthesizing a novel view for the other eye. Inferring depth (or disparity) from a single image, however, is a highly under-constrained problem. In addition to depth ambiguities, some pixels in the novel view correspond to geometry that's not visible in the available view, which causes missing data that must be hallucinated with an in-painting algorithm.

In spite of these difficulties, our intuition is that given the vast number of stereo-frame pairs that exist in already-produced 3D movies it should be possible to train a machine learning model to predict the novel view from the given view. To that end, we design a deep neural network that takes as input the left eye's view, internally estimates a soft (probabilistic) disparity map, and then renders

---

[1] Forced perspective is an optical illusion technique that makes objects appear larger or smaller than they really are. It breaks down when viewed from another angle, which prevents stereo filming.

a novel image for the right eye. We train our model end-to-end on ground-truth stereo-frame pairs with the objective of directly predicting one view from the other. The internal disparity-like map produced by the network is computed only in service of creating a good right eye view and is not intended to be an accurate map of depth or disparity. We show that this approach is easier to train for than the alternative of using a stereo algorithm to derive a disparity map, training the model to predict disparity explicitly, and then using the predicted disparity to render the new image. Our model also performs in-painting implicitly without the need for post-processing.

Evaluating the quality of the 3D scene generated from the left view is non-trivial. For quantitative evaluations, we use a dataset of 3D movies and report pixel-wise metrics comparing the reconstructed right view and the ground-truth right view. We also conduct human subject experiments to show the effectiveness of our solution. We compare our method with the ground-truth and baselines that use state-of-the-art single view depth estimation techniques. Our quantitative and qualitative analyses demonstrate the benefits of our solution.

2   Related Work

Most existing automatic 2D-to-3D conversion pipelines can be roughly divided into two stages. First, a depth map is estimated from an image of the input view, then a DIBR algorithm combines the depth map with the input view to generate the missing view of a stereo pair. Early attempts to estimate depth from a single image utilize various hand engineered features and cues including defocus, scattering, and texture gradients [3,4]. These methods only rely on one cue. As a result, they perform best in restricted situations where the particular cue is present. In contrast, humans perceive depth by seamlessly combining information from multiple sources.

More recent research has moved to learning-based methods [5–9]. These approaches take single-view 2D images and their depth maps as supervision and try to learn a mapping from 2D image to depth map. Learning-based methods combine multiple cues and have better generalization, such as recent works that use deep convolutional neural networks (DCNNs) to advance the state-of-the-art for this problem [10,11]. However, collecting high quality image-depth pairs is difficult, expensive, and subject to sensor-dependent constraints. As a result, existing depth data set mainly consists of a small number of static indoor and, less commonly, outdoor scenes [12,13]. The lack of volume and variations in these datasets limits the generality of learning-based methods. Moreover, the depth maps produced by these methods are only an intermediate representation and a separate DIBR step is still needed to generate the final result.

Monocular depth prediction is challenging and we conjecture that performing that task accurately is unnecessary. Motivated by the recent trend towards training end-to-end differentiable systems [14,15], we propose a method that requires stereo pairs for training and learns to directly predict the right view from the left view. In our approach, DIBR is implemented using an internal probabilistic disparity representation, and while it learns something akin to a disparity map the system is allowed to use that internal representation as it likes in service of predicting the novel view. This flexibility allows the algorithm to naturally handle in-painting. Unlike 2D image/depth map pairs, there is a vast amount of training data available to our approach since roughly 10 to 20 3D movies have been produced each year since 2008 and each has hundreds of thousands frames.

Our model is inspired by Flynn et al.'s DeepStereo approach [16], in which they propose to use a probabilistic selection layer to model the rendering process in a differentiable way so that it can be trained together with a DCNN. Specifically we use the same probabilistic selection layer, but improve upon their approach in two significant ways. First, their formulation requires two or more calibrated views in order to synthesize a novel view—a restriction that makes it impossible to train from existing 3D movies. We remove this limitation by restructuring the network input and layout. Second, their method works on small patches (28 × 28 pixels) which limits the network's receptive field to local structures. Our approach processes the entire image, allowing large receptive fields that are necessary to take advantage of high-level abstractions and regularities, such as the fact that large people tend to appear close to the camera while small people tend to be far away.

3   Method

Previous work on 2D-to-3D conversion usually consists of two steps: estimating an accurate depth map from the left view and rendering the right view with a Depth Image-Based Rendering (DIBR) algorithm. Instead, we propose to directly regress on the right view with a pixel-wise loss. Naively following this approach, however, leads to poor results because it does not capture the structure of the task (see Sect. 5.4). Inspired by previous work, we utilize a DIBR process to capture the fact that most output pixels are shifted copies of input pixels. However, unlike previous work we don't constrain the system to produce an accurate depth map, nor do we require depth maps as supervision for training. Instead, we propose a model that predicts a probabilistic disparity-like map as an intermediate output and combines it with the input view using a differentiable selection layer that models the DIBR process. During training, the disparity-like map produced by the model is never directly compared to a true disparity map and it ends up serving the dual purposes of representing horizontal disparity and performing in-painting. Our model can be trained end-to-end thanks to the differentiable selection layer [16].

3.1   Model Architecture

Recent research has shown that incorporating lower level features benefits pixel wise prediction tasks including semantic segmentation, depth estimation, and optical flow estimation [10,17]. Given the similarity between our task and depth estimation, it is natural to incorporate this idea. Our network, as shown in Fig. 2,

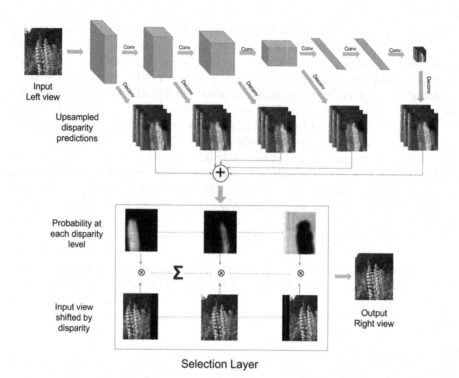

Fig. 2. Deep3D model architecture. Our model combines information from multiple levels and is trained end-to-end to directly generate the right view from the left view. The base network predicts a probabilistic disparity-like map which is then used by the selection layer to model Depth Image-Based Rendering (DIBR) in a differentiable way. This also allows implicit in-painting. (Color figure online)

has a branch after each pooling layer that upsamples the incoming feature maps using so-called "deconvolution" layers (i.e., a learned upsampling filter). The upsampled feature maps from each level are summed together to give a feature representation that has the same size as the input image. We perform one more convolution on the summed feature representation and apply a softmax transform across channels at each spatial location. The output of this softmax layer is interpreted as a probabilistic disparity-like map. We then feed this disparity-like map and the left view to the selection layer, which outputs the right view.

Bilinear Interpolation by Deconvolution. Similar to [17] we use "deconvolutional" layers to upsample lower layer features maps before feeding them to the final representation. Deconvolutional layers are implemented by reversing the forward and backward computations of a convolution layer.

We found that initializing the deconvolutional layers to be equivalent to bilinear interpolation can facilitate training. Specifically, for upsampling by factor S, we use a deconvolutional layer with $2S$ by $2S$ kernel, S by S stride, and $S/2$ by

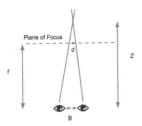
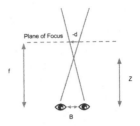

Object further than imaginary screen plane   Object nearer than imaginary screen plane

Fig. 3. Depth to disparity conversion. Given the distance between the eyes B and the distance between the eyes and the plane of focus f, we can compute disparity from depth with Eq. 3. Disparity is negative if object is closer than the plane of focus and positive if it is further away.

$S/2$ padding. The kernel weight w is then initialized with:

$$C = \frac{2S - 1 - (S \bmod 2)}{2S} \tag{1}$$

$$w_{ij} = \left(1 - |\frac{i}{S - C}|\right)\left(1 - |\frac{j}{S - C}|\right) \tag{2}$$

3.2 Reconstruction with Selection Layer

The selection layer models the DIBR step in traditional 2D-to-3D conversion. In traditional 2D-to-3D conversion, given the left view I and a depth map Z, a disparity map D is first computed with

$$D = \frac{B(Z - f)}{Z} \tag{3}$$

where the baseline B is the distance between the two cameras, Z is the input depth and f is the distance from cameras to the plane of focus. See Fig. 3 for illustration. The right view O is then generated with:

$$O_{i,j+D_{ij}} = I_{i,j}. \tag{4}$$

However this is not differentiable with respect to D so we cannot train it together with a deep neural network. Instead, our network predicts a probability distribution across possible disparity values d at each pixel location $D_{i,j}^d$, where $\sum_d D_{i,j}^d = 1$ for all i, j. We define a shifted stack of the left view as $I_{i,j}^d = I_{i,j-d}$, then the selection layer reconstructs the right view with:

$$O_{i,j} = \sum_d I_{i,j}^d D_{i,j}^d \tag{5}$$

This is now differentiable with respect to $D_{i,j}^d$ so we can compute an L1 loss between the output and ground-truth right view Y as the training objective:

$$L = |O - Y| \tag{6}$$

We use L1 loss because recent research has shown that it outperforms L2 loss for pixel-wise prediction tasks [18].

We note that D is only an intermediate result optimized for producing low error reconstructions while not intended to be an accurate disparity prediction. In fact, we observe that in practice D serves the dual purpose of depth estimation and in-painting. Low texture regions also tend to be ignored as they do not significantly contribute to reconstruction error.

3.3 Scaling up to Full Resolution

Modern movies are usually distributed in at least 1080p resolution, which has 1920 pixel by 800 pixel frames. In our experiments, We reduce input frames to 432 by 180 to preserve aspect ratio and save computation time. As a result, the generated right view frames will only have a resolution of 432 by 180, which is unacceptably low for movie viewing.

To address this issue, we first observe that the disparity map usually has much less high-frequency content than the original color image. Therefore we can scale up the predicted disparity map and couple it with the original high resolution left view to render a full resolution right view. The right view rendered this way has better image quality compared to the naively 4x-upsampled prediction.

4   Dataset

Since Deep3D can be trained directly on stereo pairs without ground-truth depth maps as supervision, we can take advantage of the large volume of existing stereo videos instead of using traditional scene depth datasets like KITTI [13] and NYU Depth [12]. We collected 27 non-animation 3D movies produced in recent years and randomly partitioned them to 18 for training and 9 for testing. Our dataset contains around 5 million frames while KITTI and NYU Depth only provide several hundred frames. During training, each input left frame is resized to 432 by 180 pixels and a crop of size 384 by 160 pixels is randomly selected from the frame. The target right frame undergoes the same transformations. We do not use horizontal flipping.

5   Experiments

In our main experiments we use a single frame at a time as input without exploiting temporal information. This choice ensures a more fair comparison to single-frame baseline algorithms and also allows applying trained models to static photos in addition to videos. However, it is natural to hypothesize that motion provides important cues for depth, thus we also conducted additional experiments that use consecutive RGB frames and computed optical flow as input, following [19]. These results are discussed in Sect. 5.4.

5.1 Implementation Details

For quantitative evaluation we use the non-upsampled output size of 384 by 160 pixels. For qualitative and human subject evaluation we upsample the output by a factor of 4 using the method described in Sect. 3.3. Our network is based on VGG16, which is a large convolutional network trained on ImageNet [20]. We initialize the main branch convolutional layers (colored green in Fig. 2) with VGG16 weight and initialize all other weights with normal distribution with a standard deviation of 0.01.

To integrate information from lower level features, we create a side branch after each pooling layer by applying batch normalization [21] followed by a 3×3 convolution layer. This is then followed by a deconvolution layer initialized to be equivalent to bilinear upsampling. The output dimensions of the deconvolution layers match the final prediction dimensions. We use batch normalization to connect pretrained VGG16 layers to randomly initialized layers because it solves the numerical instability problem caused by VGG16's large and non-uniform activation magnitude.

We also connect the top VGG16 convolution layer feature to two randomly initialized fully connected layers (colored blue in Fig. 2) with 4096 hidden units followed by a linear layer. We then reshape the output of the linear layer to 33 channels of 12 by 5 feature maps which is then fed to a deconvolution layer. We then sum across all up sampled feature maps and do a convolution to get the final feature representation. The representation is then fed to the selection layer. The selection layer interprets this representation as the probability over empty or disparity -15 to 16 (a total of 33 channels).

In all experiments Deep3D is trained with a mini-batch size of 64 for $100,000$ iterations in total. The initial learning rate is set to 0.002 and reduce it by a factor of 10 after every $20,000$ iterations. No weight decay is used and dropout with rate 0.5 is only applied after the fully connected layers. Training takes two days on one NVidia GTX Titan X GPU. Once trained, Deep3D can reconstruct novel right views at more than 100 frames per second. Our implementation is based on MXNet [22] and available for download at https://github.com/piiswrong/deep3d.

5.2 Comparison Algorithms

We used three baseline algorithms for comparison:

1. Global Disparity: the right view is computed by shifting the left view with a global disparity δ that is determined by minimizing Mean Absolution Error (MAE) on the validation set.
2. The DNN-based monocular depth estimation algorithm of Eigen et al. [10] plus a standard DIBR method as described in Sect. 3.2.
3. DNN-based Monocular depth estimation trained to predict disparity estimation from stereo block matching algorithms, plus standard DIBR method.
4. Ground-truth stereo pairs. We only show the ground-truth in human subject studies since in quantitative evaluations it always gives zero error.

To the best of our knowledge, Deep3D is the first 2D-to-3D conversion algorithm that can be trained directly on stereo pairs, while all previous methods requires ground-truth depth map for training. As one baseline, we take the model released by Eigen et al. [10], which is trained on NYU Depth [12], and evaluate it on our test set. However, it is a stretch to hope that a model trained on NYU Depth will generalize well to 3D movies. Therefore, for a more fair comparison, we also a retrain monocular depth estimation network with estimated depth from stereo block matching algorithms on the same 3D movie dataset. Since Eigen et al. did not release training code, we instead use the same VGG-based network architecture proposed in this paper. This also has the added benefit of being directly comparable to Deep3D.

Because [10] predicts depth rather then disparity, we need to convert depth to disparity with Eq. 3 for rendering with DIBR. However, [10] does not predict the distance to the plane of focus f, a quantity that is unknown and varies across shots due to zooming. The interpupillary distance B is also unknown, but it is fixed across shots. The value of B and f can be determined in two ways:

1. Optimize for MAE on the validation set and use fixed values for B and f across the whole test set. This approach corresponds to the lower bound of [10]'s performance.
2. Fix B across the test set, but pick the f that gives the lowest MAE for each *test* frame. This corresponds to having access to oracle plane of focus distance and thus the upper bound on [10]'s performance.

We do both and report them as two separate baselines, [10] and [10] + Oracle. For fair comparisons, we also do this optimization for Deep3D's predictions and report the performance of Deep3D and Deep3D + Oracle.

5.3   Results

Quantitative Evaluation. For quantitative evaluation, we compute Mean Absolute Error (MAE) as:

$$MAE = \frac{1}{HW}|y - g(x)|, \tag{7}$$

where x is the left view, y is the right view, $g(\cdot)$ is the model, and H and W are height and width of the image respectively. The results are shown in Table 1. We observe that Deep3D outperforms baselines with and without oracle distance of focus plane.

Qualitative Evaluation. To better understand the proposed method, we show qualitative results in Fig. 5. Each entry starts with a stereo pair predicted by Deep3D shown in anaglyph, followed by 12 channels of internal soft disparity assignment, ordered from near (-3) to far ($+8$). We observe that Deep3D is able to infer depth from multiple cues including size, occlusion, and geometric structure.

Table 1. Deep3D evaluation. We compare pixel-wise reconstruction error for each method using Mean Absolute Error (MAE) as metric.

Method	MAE
Global disparity	7.75
[10]	7.75
DNN trained on estimated depth	7.29
Deep3D (ours)	**6.87**
[10] + Oracle	6.31
Deep3D + Oracle	**5.47**

Table 2. Human subject evaluation. In each entry, the first number represents the frequency of the row method being preferred to the column method by human subjects, while the second number represents their certainty (i.e. the percentage of people who gave an answer instead of "not sure"). Note that 66 % of times subjects prefer Deep3D to [10] and 24 % of the times Deep3D is preferred over the ground truth.

	Global disparity	[10] + Oracle	Deep3D (ours)	Ground truth
Trivial	N/A	27.21 %/56 %	25.28 %/74 %	7.80 %/77 %
Eigen et al.	72.79 %/56 %	N/A	33.53 %/71 %	10.19 %/77 %
Ours	74.72 %/74 %	66.47 %/71 %	N/A	24.43 %/81 %
Ground truth	92.20 %/77 %	89.81 %/77 %	75.57 %/81 %	N/A

Fig. 4. Human subject study setup. Each subject is shown 50 pairs of 3D anaglyph images. Each pair consists of the same scene generated by 2 randomly selected methods. The subjects are instructed to wear red-blue 3D glasses and pick the one with better 3D effects or "not sure" if they cannot tell. The study result is shown in Table 2. (Color figure online)

Fig. 5. Qualitative results. Column one shows an anaglyph of the predicted 3D image (best viewed in color with red-blue 3D glasses). Each anaglyph is followed by 12 heat maps of disparity channels −3 to 8 (closer to far). In the first example, the man is closer and appears in the first 3 channels while the woman is further away and appears in 4th-5th channels; the background appears in the last 4 channels. In the second example, the person seen from behind is closer than the other 4 people fighting him. In the third example, the window frame appears in the first 3 channels while the distant outside scene gradually appears in the following channels. (Color figure online)

Fig. 6. Comparison between [10] and Deep3D. The first column shows the input image. The second column shows the prediction of [10] and the third column shows Deep3D's prediction. This figure shows that Deep3D is better at delineating people and figuring out their distance from the camera.

We also compare Deep3D's internal disparity maps (column 3) to [10]'s depth predictions (column 2) in Fig. 6. This figure demonstrates that Deep3D is better at delineating people and figuring out their distance from the camera.

Note that the disparity maps generated by Deep3D tend to be noisy at image regions with low horizontal gradient, however this does not affect the quality of the final reconstruction because if a row of pixels have the same value, any disparity assignment would give the same reconstruction. Disparity prediction only needs to be accurate around vertical edges and we indeed observe that Deep3D tends to focus on such regions.

Human Subject Evaluation We also conducted a human subject study to evaluate the visual quality of the predictions of different algorithms. We used four algorithms for this experiment: Global Disparity, [10] + Oracle, Deep3D without Oracle, and the ground-truth.[2]

For the human subject study, we randomly selected 500 frames from the test set. Each annotator is shown a sequence of trials. In each trial, the annotator sees two anaglyph 3D images, which are reconstructed from the same 2D frame by two algorithms, and is instructed to wear red-blue 3D glasses and pick the one with better 3D effects or select "not sure" if they are similar. The interface for this study is shown in Fig. 4. Each annotator is given 50 such pairs and we collected decisions on all $C_4^2 500$ pairs from 60 annotators.

Table 2 shows that Deep3D outperforms the naive Global Disparity baseline by a 49 % margin and outperforms [10] + Oracle by a 32 % margin. When facing

---

[2] [10] without Oracle and Deep3D + Oracle are left out due to annotator budget Note that a change in average scene depth only pushes a scene further away or pull it closer and usually doesn't affect the perception of depth variation in the scene.

against the ground truth, Deep3D's prediction is preferred 24.48 % of the time while [10] + Oracle is only preferred 10.27 % of the time and Global Disparity baseline is preferred 7.88 % of the time.

5.4   Algorithm Analysis

Ablation Study. To understand the contribution of each component of the proposed algorithm, we show the performance of Deep3D with parts removed in Table 3. In Deep3D w/o lower level feature we show the performance of Deep3D without branching off from lower convolution layers. The resulting network only has one feed-forward path that consists of 5 convolution and pooling module and 2 fully connected layers. We observe that the performance significantly decreases compared to the full method.

In Deep3D w/o direct training on stereo pairs we show the performance of training on disparity maps generated from stereo pairs by block matching algorithm [23] instead of directly training on stereo pairs. The predicted disparity maps are then fed to DIBR method to render the right view. This approach results in decreased performance and demonstrates the effectiveness of Deep3D's end-to-end training scheme.

We also show the result from directly regressing on the novel view without internal disparity representation and selection layer. Empirically this also leads to decreased performance, demonstrating the effectiveness of modeling the DIBR process.

Temporal Information. In our main experiment and evaluation we only used one still frame of RGB image as input. We made this choice for fair comparisons and more general application domains. Incorporating temporal information into Deep3D can be handled in two ways: use multiple consecutive RGB frames as input to the network, or provide temporal information through optical flow frames similar to [19].

We briefly explored both directions and found moderate performance improvements in terms of pixel-wise metrics. We believe more effort along this direction, such as model structure adjustment, hyper-parameter tuning, and

Table 3. Ablation studies. We evaluate different components of Deep3D by removing them from the model to further understand the contribution of each component. Note that removing lower level features and selection layer both result in performance drop.

Method	MAE
Deep3D w/o lower level feature	8.24
Deep3D w/o direct training on stereo pairs	7.29
Deep3D w/o selection layer	7.01
Deep3D	6.87

Table 4. Temporal information. We incorporate temporal information by extending the input to include multiple consecutive RGB frames or optical flow frames. We observe that additional temporal information leads to performance gains.

Method	MAE
Deep3D with 5 RGB frames	6.81
Deep3D with 1 RGB frames and 5 optical flow frames	6.86
Deep3D	6.87

explicit modeling of time will lead to larger performance gains at the cost of restricting application domain to videos only (Table 4).

6 Conclusions

In this paper we proposed a fully automatic 2D-to-3D conversion algorithm based on deep convolutional neural networks. Our method is trained end-to-end on stereo image pairs directly, thus able to exploit orders of magnitude more data than traditional learning based 2D-to-3D conversion methods. Quantitatively, our method outperforms baseline algorithms. In human subject study stereo images generated by our method are consistently preferred by subjects over results from baseline algorithms. When facing against the ground truth, our results have a higher chance of confusing subjects than baseline results.

In our experiment and evaluations we only used still images as input while ignoring temporal information from video. The benefit of this design is that the trained model can be applied to not only videos but also photos. However, in the context of video conversion, it is likely that taking advantage of temporal information can improve performance. We briefly experimented with this idea but found little quantitative performance gain. We conjecture this may be due to the complexity of effectively incorporating temporal information. We believe this is an interesting direction for future research.

Acknowledgements. This work is in part supported by ONR N00014-13-1-0720, NSF IIS-1338054, Allen Distinguished Investigator Award and contracts from the Allen Institute for Artificial Intelligence.

References

1. Motion Picture Association of America: Theatrical market statistics (2014)
2. Fehn, C.: Depth-image-based rendering (DIBR), compression, and transmission for a new approach on 3D-tv. In: Electronic Imaging 2004, International Society for Optics and Photonics, pp. 93–104 (2004)
3. Zhuo, S., Sim, T.: On the recovery of depth from a single defocused image. In: Jiang, X., Petkov, N. (eds.) CAIP 2009. LNCS, vol. 5702, pp. 889–897. Springer, Heidelberg (2009)

4. Cozman, F., Krotkov, E.: Depth from scattering. In: IEEE Computer Society Conference on Computer Vision and Pattern Recognition, Proceedings, pp. 801–806. IEEE (1997)

5. Zhang, L., Vázquez, C., Knorr, S.: 3D-tv content creation: automatic 2D-to-3D video conversion. IEEE Trans. Broadcast. **57**(2), 372–383 (2011)

6. Konrad, J., Wang, M., Ishwar, P., Wu, C., Mukherjee, D.: Learning-based, automatic 2D-to-3D image and video conversion. IEEE Trans. Image Process. **22**(9), 3485–3496 (2013)

7. Appia, V., Batur, U.: Fully automatic 2D to 3D conversion with aid of high-level image features. In: IS&T/SPIE Electronic Imaging, International Society for Optics and Photonics, p. 90110W (2014)

8. Saxena, A., Sun, M., Ng, A.Y.: Make3D: learning 3D scene structure from a single still image. IEEE Trans. Pattern Anal. Mach. Intell. **31**(5), 824–840 (2009)

9. Baig, M.H., Jagadeesh, V., Piramuthu, R., Bhardwaj, A., Di, W., Sundaresan, N.: Im2depth: scalable exemplar based depth transfer. In: 2014 IEEE Winter Conference on Applications of Computer Vision (WACV), pp. 145–152. IEEE (2014)

10. Eigen, D., Fergus, R.: Predicting depth, surface normals and semantic labels with a common multi-scale convolutional architecture. In: Proceedings of the IEEE International Conference on Computer Vision, pp. 2650–2658 (2015)

11. Liu, F., Shen, C., Lin, G.: Deep convolutional neural fields for depth estimation from a single image. In: Proceedings of the IEEE Conference on Computer Vision and Pattern Recognition, pp. 5162–5170 (2015)

12. Silberman, N., Hoiem, D., Kohli, P., Fergus, R.: Indoor segmentation and support inference from RGBD images. In: Fitzgibbon, A., Lazebnik, S., Perona, P., Sato, Y., Schmid, C. (eds.) ECCV 2012, Part V. LNCS, vol. 7576, pp. 746–760. Springer, Heidelberg (2012)

13. Geiger, A., Lenz, P., Stiller, C., Urtasun, R.: Vision meets robotics: the kitti dataset. Int. J. Rob. Res. (IJRR) **32**, 1231–1237 (2013)

14. Zheng, S., Jayasumana, S., Romera-Paredes, B., Vineet, V., Su, Z., Du, D., Huang, C., Torr, P.H.: Conditional random fields as recurrent neural networks. In: Proceedings of the IEEE International Conference on Computer Vision, pp. 1529–1537 (2015)

15. Levine, S., Finn, C., Darrell, T., Abbeel, P.: End-to-end training of deep visuomotor policies. arXiv preprint arXiv:1504.00702 (2015)

16. Flynn, J., Neulander, I., Philbin, J., Snavely, N.: Deepstereo: learning to predict new views from the world's imagery. arXiv preprint arXiv:1506.06825 (2015)

17. Fischer, P., Dosovitskiy, A., Ilg, E., Häusser, P., Hazırbaş, C., Golkov, V., van der Smagt, P., Cremers, D., Brox, T.: Flownet: learning optical flow with convolutional networks. arXiv preprint arXiv:1504.06852 (2015)

18. Mathieu, M., Couprie, C., LeCun, Y.: Deep multi-scale video prediction beyond mean square error. arXiv preprint arXiv:1511.05440 (2015)

19. Wang, L., Xiong, Y., Wang, Z., Qiao, Y.: Towards good practices for very deep two-stream convnets. arXiv preprint arXiv:1507.02159 (2015)

20. Simonyan, K., Zisserman, A.: Very deep convolutional networks for large-scale image recognition. arXiv preprint arXiv:1409.1556 (2014)

21. Ioffe, S., Szegedy, C.: Batch normalization: accelerating deep network training by reducing internal covariate shift. arXiv preprint arXiv:1502.03167 (2015)

22. Chen, T., Li, M., Li, Y., Lin, M., Wang, N., Wang, M., Xiao, T., Xu, B., Zhang, C., Zhang, Z.: Mxnet: a flexible and efficient machine learning library for heterogeneous distributed systems. arXiv preprint arXiv:1512.01274 (2015)
23. Hirschmüller, H.: Stereo processing by semiglobal matching and mutual information. IEEE Trans. Pattern Anal. Mach. Intell. **30**(2), 328–341 (2008)

Temporal Model Adaptation for Person Re-identification

Niki Martinel[1,3]([✉]), Abir Das[2], Christian Micheloni[1],
and Amit K. Roy-Chowdhury[3]

[1] University of Udine, 33100 Udine, Italy
`niki.martinel@uniud.it`
[2] University of Massatchussets Lowell, Lowell, MA 01852, USA
[3] University of California Riverside, Riverside, CA 92507, USA

Abstract. Person re-identification is an open and challenging problem in computer vision. Majority of the efforts have been spent either to design the best feature representation or to learn the optimal matching metric. Most approaches have neglected the problem of adapting the selected features or the learned model over time. To address such a problem, we propose a temporal model adaptation scheme with human in the loop. We first introduce a similarity-dissimilarity learning method which can be trained in an incremental fashion by means of a stochastic alternating directions methods of multipliers optimization procedure. Then, to achieve temporal adaptation with limited human effort, we exploit a graph-based approach to present the user only the most informative probe-gallery matches that should be used to update the model. Results on three datasets have shown that our approach performs on par or even better than state-of-the-art approaches while reducing the manual pairwise labeling effort by about 80 %.

Keywords: Person re-identificaion · Metric learning · Active learning

1 Introduction

Person re-identification is the problem of matching a person acquired by disjoint cameras at different time instants. The problem has recently gained increasing attention (see [1] for a recent survey) due to its open challenges like changes in viewing angle, background clutter, and occlusions. To address these issues, existing approaches seek either the best feature representations (e.g., [2–4]) or propose to learn optimal matching metrics (e.g., [5–7]). While they have obtained reasonable performance on commonly used datasets (e.g., [8–10]), we believe that these approaches have not yet considered a fundamental related problem: how to learn from the data being continuously collected in an installed system and

Electronic supplementary material The online version of this chapter (doi:10.1007/978-3-319-46493-0_52) contains supplementary material, which is available to authorized users.

B. Leibe et al. (Eds.): ECCV 2016, Part IV, LNCS 9908, pp. 858–877, 2016.
DOI: 10.1007/978-3-319-46493-0_52

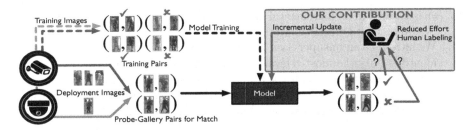

Fig. 1. Illustration of the re-identification pipeline highlighting our contribution. Dashed lines indicate the training stage, solid lines the deployment stage. Existing methods do not consider the information provided by a matched probe-gallery pair to update the model. We propose to use such information to improve the model performance by adapting it to the dynamic environmental variations.

adapt existing models to this new data. This is an important problem to address if re-identification methods have to work on long time-scales.

To illustrate such a problem, let us consider a simplified scenario in which at every time instant a conspicuous amount of visual data is being generated from two cameras. From each camera we obtain a large set of *probe* and *gallery* persons that have to be matched. Since this is a task that evolves over time, it is unlikely that the *a-priori* selected features or the learned model return the correct gallery match for every probe at any instant. In addition, after each of such matches is computed, the information provided by the considered images is discarded. This results in a loss of valuable information which could have been used to update the model, thus ideally yielding better performance over time.

The above problem could be overcome if the data could be exploited in a continuous learning process in which the model can be updated with every single *probe-gallery* match. Since we do not know whether a match is correct or not, the model might be updated with the wrong information. To tackle this issue, manual labeling of each match can be performed, but, doing so with a large corpus of data is clearly impossible. However, if the human labor is kept to a minimum, the model can ideally be adapted over time without compromising performance. Thus, *the main idea of the paper is a person re-identification solution based on an incremental adaptation of the learned model with human in the loop.*

Contributions: As shown in Fig. 1, this work brings in two main contributions: (i) an incremental learning algorithm that allows the model to be adapted over time, and (ii) a method to reduce the human labeling effort required to properly update the model. These objectives are achieved as follows.

(i) We propose a low-rank sparse similarity-dissimilarity metric learning method (Sect. 3.2) which
  (a) learns two low-rank projections onto discriminant manifolds providing optimal embeddings for a similarity and a dissimilarity measure;
  (b) introduces sparsity inducing regularizers that allow identification and exploitation of the most discriminative dimensions for matching; and

    (c) is trained in an incremental fashion through a stochastic derivation of the Alternating Directions Methods of Multipliers (ADMM) [11].

 (ii) We introduce an unsupervised graph-based approach which, for every probe, identifies only the most relevant gallery persons among a large set of available ones (Sect. 3.3). Such a set, obtained by exploiting dominant sets clustering [12], contains the most informative gallery persons which are first provided to the human labeler, then exploited to update the model.

To substantiate our contributions we have conducted the experiments on three benchmark datasets for person re-identification. Results demonstrate that (i) the proposed approach for identifying the most informative gallery persons yields better re-identification performance than using completely labeled data; (ii) the proposed low-rank sparse similarity-dissimilarity approach trained in an incremental fashion with such informative gallery persons, hence with significantly less manual labor, performs on par or even better than state-of-the-art methods trained on 100 % labeled data. In fact, with only 15 % labeled data we improve the previous best rank 1 results by more than 8 % on the PRID450S dataset. These experiments show how re-identification models can be continuously adapted over time with limited human effort and without sacrifice in performance.

2   Relation to Existing Work

The person re-identification problem has been studied from different perspectives, ranging from partially seen persons [13] to low resolution images [14] – also considered in camera networks [15], which can eventually be synthesized in the open-world re-identification idea [16]. In the following, we focus on metric and active learning methods relevant to our work.

    Metric Learning approaches focus on learning discriminant metrics which aim to yield an optimal matching score/distance between a gallery and a probe image.

    Since the early work of [17], many different solutions have been introduced [18]. In the re-identification field, metric learning approaches have been proposed by relaxing [19] or enforcing [20] positive semi-definite (PSD) conditions as well as by considering equivalence constraints [21–23]. While most of the existing methods capture the global structure of the dissimilarity space, local solutions [24–27] have been proposed too. Following the success of both approaches, methods combining them in ensembles [5,7,28] have been introduced.

    Different solutions yielding similarity measures have also been investigated by proposing to learn listwise [29] and pairwise [30] similarities as well as mixture of polynomial kernel-based models [9]. Related to these similarity learning models are the deep architectures which have been exploited to tackle the task [31–33].

    With respect to all such methods, the closest ones to our approach are [6,20]. Specifically, in [6], authors jointly exploit the metric in [21] and learn a low-rank projection onto a subspace with discriminative Euclidean distance. The solution is obtained through generalized eigenvalue decomposition. In [20], a soft-margin PSD constrained metric with low-rank projections is learned via a proximal gradient method. Both works exploit a batch optimization approach.

Though sharing the idea of finding discriminative low-rank projections, there are significant differences with our method. Specifically, we introduce (i) an incremental learning procedure along with a stochastic ADMM solver which can handle noisy observations of the true data; (ii) a low-rank similarity-dissimilarity metric learning which brings significant performance gain with respect to each of its components; (iii) additional sparsity regularizers on the low-rank projections that allow self-discovery of the relevant components of the underlying manifold.

Active Learning: In an effort to bypass tedious labeling of training data there has been recent interest in "active learning" [34] to intelligently select unlabeled examples for the experts to label in an interactive manner.

This can be achieved by choosing one sample at a time by maximizing the value of information [35], reducing the expected error [36], or minimizing the resultant entropy of the system [37]. More recently, works selecting batches of unlabeled data by exploiting classifier feedback to maximize informativeness and sample diversity [38,39] were proposed. Specific application areas in computer vision include, but are not limited to, tracking [40], scene classification [35,41], semantic segmentation [42], video annotation [43] and activity recognition [44].

Active learning has been a relatively unexplored area in person re-identification. Including the human in the loop has been investigated in [8,45,46]. These methods focused on post-ranking solutions and exploit human labor to refine the initial results by relying on full [8] or partial [45] image selection. In [46], authors introduce an active learning strategy that exploits mid level attributes to train a set of attribute predictors aiding active selection of images.

Different from such approaches, in our proposed method human labor is not required to improve the post-rank visual search, but to reliably update the learned model over time. We do not rely on additional attribute predictors which require a proper training that calls for a large number of annotated attributes. Thus bypassing the need for attribute annotation, we reduce both the computational complexity as well as the additional manual effort. We introduce a graph-based solution that exploits the information provided by a single probe-gallery match as well as the information shared between all the persons in the entire gallery. With this, a small set of highly informative probe-gallery pairs is delivered to the human, whose effort is thus limited.

3 Temporal Model Adaptation for Re-identification

An overview of the proposed solution is illustrated in Fig. 2. Specifically, to achieve model adaptation over time, we first introduce a similarity-dissimilarity metric learning approach which can be trained in an incremental fashion (Sect. 3.2). Then, to limit the human labeling effort required to properly update the model, we propose an unsupervised graph-based approach that identifies only the most informative probe-gallery samples (Sect. 3.3).

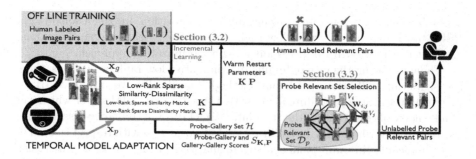

Fig. 2. Proposed temporal model adaptation scheme. An off-line procedure exploits labeled image pairs to train the initial similarity-dissimilarity model. As new unlabeled pairs are obtained, a score for each of those is obtained using the learned model. These are later used to identify a relevant set of gallery persons for each probe. Such a set, containing the most informative samples, is exploited to construct the relevant pairs which are first provided to the human annotator, then considered to update the model.

3.1 Preliminaries

Let $\mathcal{P} = \{\mathbf{I}_p\}_{p=1}^{|\mathcal{P}|}$ and $\mathcal{G} = \{\mathbf{I}_g\}_{g=1}^{|\mathcal{G}|}$ be the set of probe and gallery images acquired by two disjoint cameras. Let $\mathbf{x}_p \in \mathbb{R}^d$ and $\mathbf{x}_g \in \mathbb{R}^d$ be the feature representations of $\mathbf{I}_p$ and $\mathbf{I}_g$ of two persons p and g. Let $\mathcal{X} = \{(\mathbf{x}_p, \mathbf{x}_g; y_{p,g})^{(i)}\}_{i=1}^n$ denote the training set of $n = |\mathcal{P}| \times |\mathcal{G}|$ probe-gallery pairs where $y_{p,g} \in \{-1, +1\}$ indicates whether p and g are the same person $(+1)$ or not (-1). Finally, let an *iteration* be a parameter update computed by visiting a single sample and let an *epoch* denote a complete cycle on the training set.

3.2 Low-Rank Sparse Similarity-Dissimilarity Learning

Objective: The image feature representations $\mathbf{x}$ might be very high-dimensional and contain non-discriminative components. Hence, learning a metric in such a feature space might yield to non-optimal generalization performance. To overcome such a problem we propose to learn a low-rank metric which self-determines the discriminative dimensions of the underlying manifold.

Towards such an objective, inspired by the success of similarity learning on image retrieval tasks [47–49], we propose to learn a similarity function

$$\sigma_{\mathbf{K}}(\mathbf{x}_p, \mathbf{x}_g) = \mathbf{x}_p^T \mathbf{K}^T \mathbf{K} \mathbf{x}_g \qquad (1)$$

parameterized by the low-rank projection matrix $\mathbf{K} \in \mathbb{R}^{r \times d}$, with $r \ll d$. This provides an embedding in which the dot product between the projected feature vectors is "large" if p and g are the same person, "small" otherwise. The similarity function is then coupled with the output of a metric learning solution that aims to find a matrix $\mathbf{P} \in \mathbb{R}^{r \times d}$ that projects the high-dimensional vectors to a low-dimensional manifold with a discriminative Euclidean dissimilarity

$$\delta_{\mathbf{P}}(\mathbf{x}_p, \mathbf{x}_g) = \|\mathbf{P}\mathbf{x}_p - \mathbf{P}\mathbf{x}_g\|_2^2 = (\mathbf{x}_p - \mathbf{x}_g)^T \mathbf{P}^T \mathbf{P}(\mathbf{x}_p - \mathbf{x}_g) \qquad (2)$$

which is "small" if p and g are the same person, "larger" otherwise. This results in the score function

$$S_{\mathbf{K},\mathbf{P}}(p,g) = y_{p,g}(\underbrace{\sigma_{\mathbf{K}}(\mathbf{x}_p, \mathbf{x}_g)}_{\uparrow \text{for } p=g, \downarrow \text{for } p \neq g} - \underbrace{(1/2)\delta_{\mathbf{P}}(\mathbf{x}_p, \mathbf{x}_g))}_{\downarrow \text{for } p=g, \uparrow \text{for } p \neq g} \tag{3}$$

which included in a margin hinge loss yields

$$\ell_{\mathbf{K},\mathbf{P}}(p,g) = \max(0, 1 - S_{\mathbf{K},\mathbf{P}}(p,g)). \tag{4}$$

Notice that zero loss is achieved if $S_{\mathbf{K},\mathbf{P}}(p,g) \geq 1$, i.e., when the difference between $\sigma_{\mathbf{K}}$ and $\frac{1}{2}\delta_{\mathbf{P}}$ is either greater than or equal to 1 for positive pairs or less than or equal to -1 for negative ones. In other cases a linear penalty is paid.

Obtaining the low-rank projections through Eq. (4) with fixed r implies that such a value should be carefully selected before the learning process begins. To overcome such a problem, we impose additional constraints on the low-rank projection matrices. In particular, the $\ell_{2,1}$ norm has shown to perform robust feature selection through the induced group sparsity [50–53]. Motivated by such findings, we can set $r = d$, then leverage on an $\ell_{2,1}$ norm regularizer to drive the rows of $\mathbf{P}$ and $\mathbf{K}$ to decay to zero. This corresponds to rejecting non discriminative dimensions of the underlying manifold.

Let $\Omega_{\mathbf{K},\mathbf{P}} = \alpha\|\mathbf{K}\|_{2,1} + \beta\|\mathbf{P}\|_{2,1}$ be the cost associated with the low-rank projection matrix regularizers where α and β are the corresponding trade-off parameters controlling the regularization strength. Then, considering that we want to optimize the empirical risk over $\mathcal{X}$, we can write our objective as

$$\arg\min_{\mathbf{K},\mathbf{P}} \mathcal{J}_{\mathbf{K},\mathbf{P}} + \Omega_{\mathbf{K},\mathbf{P}} \qquad \text{where} \qquad \mathcal{J}_{\mathbf{K},\mathbf{P}} = \frac{1}{n}\sum_{i=1}^{n} \ell_{\mathbf{K},\mathbf{P}}\left(p^{(i)}, g^{(i)}\right) \tag{5}$$

and $p^{(i)}$ and $g^{(i)}$ denote the identities of persons p and g in the i-th pair of $\mathcal{X}$.

Incremental Learning: The objective function in Eq. (5) is a sum of two functions which are both convex but non-smooth. A solution to such kind of a problem that allows us to perform incremental updates can be obtained using the ADMM optimization algorithm [11].

ADMM solves optimization problems defined by means of the corresponding augmented Lagrangian. By introducing two additional constraints $\mathbf{K} - \mathbf{U} = \mathbf{0}$ and $\mathbf{P} - \mathbf{V} = \mathbf{0}$ we can define the augmented Lagrangian for Eq. (5) as

$$L_{\mathbf{K},\mathbf{P},\mathbf{U},\mathbf{V},\mathbf{\Lambda},\mathbf{\Psi}} = \mathcal{J}_{\mathbf{K},\mathbf{P}} + \Omega_{\mathbf{U},\mathbf{V}} + \langle\mathbf{\Lambda}, \mathbf{K} - \mathbf{U}\rangle + \langle\mathbf{\Psi}, \mathbf{P} - \mathbf{V}\rangle$$
$$+ \frac{\rho}{2}\left(\|\mathbf{K} - \mathbf{U}\|_F^2 + \|\mathbf{P} - \mathbf{V}\|_F^2\right) \tag{6}$$

where $\mathbf{\Lambda} \in \mathbb{R}^{r \times d}$ and $\mathbf{\Psi} \in \mathbb{R}^{r \times d}$ are two Lagrangian multipliers, $\langle\cdot,\cdot\rangle$ denote the inner product, $\|\cdot\|_F$ is the Frobenius norm and, $\rho > 0$ is a penalty parameter.

To solve the optimization problem, at each epoch s, ADMM alternatively minimizes L with respect to a single parameter, $\mathbf{K}$, $\mathbf{P}$, $\mathbf{U}$, $\mathbf{V}$, $\mathbf{\Lambda}$ or $\mathbf{\Psi}$, keeping others fixed. The result of each minimization gives the updated parameter.

Standard deterministic ADMM implicitly assumes true data values are available, hence overlooking the existence of noise [54]. Noticing that only $\mathbf{K}$ and $\mathbf{P}$ depend on the data samples, we define the corresponding update rules using the scalable stochastic ADMM approach [55,56] which can handle such an issue.

Update K and P: Let $\frac{\partial}{\partial \mathbf{K}}\mathcal{J}_{\mathbf{K},\mathbf{P}} = \frac{1}{n}\sum_{i=1}^{n}\frac{\partial}{\partial \mathbf{K}}\ell_{\mathbf{K},\mathbf{P}}(p^{(i)}, g^{(i)})$ and $\frac{\partial}{\partial \mathbf{P}}\mathcal{J}_{\mathbf{K},\mathbf{P}} = \frac{1}{n}\sum_{i=1}^{n}\frac{\partial}{\partial \mathbf{P}}\ell_{\mathbf{K},\mathbf{P}}(p^{(i)}, g^{(i)})$ denote the subgradients components of Eq. (4) computed for all samples with respect $\mathbf{K}$ and $\mathbf{P}$, respectively. Then, at each iteration t, i.e., for the t-th random sample, we compute

$$\tilde{\mathbf{K}}^{(t+1)} = \tilde{\mathbf{K}}^{(t)} - \eta\left(\frac{\partial}{\partial \tilde{\mathbf{K}}^{(t)}}\ell_{\tilde{\mathbf{K}}^{(t)},\tilde{\mathbf{P}}^{(t)}}(p^{(t)}, g^{(t)}) - \frac{\partial}{\partial \mathbf{K}^{(s)}}\ell_{\mathbf{K}^{(s)},\mathbf{P}^{(s)}}(p^{(t)}, g^{(t)})\right.$$
$$\left. + \frac{\partial}{\partial \mathbf{K}^{(s)}}\mathcal{J}_{\mathbf{K}^{(s)},\mathbf{P}^{(s)}} + \rho\left(\tilde{\mathbf{K}}^{(t)} - \mathbf{U}^{(s)} + \mathbf{\Lambda}^{(s)}/\rho\right)\right) \tag{7}$$

$$\tilde{\mathbf{P}}^{(t+1)} = \tilde{\mathbf{P}}^{(t)} - \eta\left(\frac{\partial}{\partial \tilde{\mathbf{P}}^{(t)}}\ell_{\tilde{\mathbf{K}}^{(t+1)},\tilde{\mathbf{P}}^{(t)}}(p^{(t)}, g^{(t)}) - \frac{\partial}{\partial \mathbf{P}^{(s)}}\ell_{\mathbf{K}^{(s)},\mathbf{P}^{(s)}}(p^{(t)}, g^{(t)})\right.$$
$$\left. + \frac{\partial}{\partial \mathbf{P}^{(s)}}\mathcal{J}_{\mathbf{K}^{(s)},\mathbf{P}^{(s)}} + \rho\left(\tilde{\mathbf{P}}^{(t)} - \mathbf{V}^{(s)} + \mathbf{\Psi}^{(s)}/\rho\right)\right) \tag{8}$$

where η is the step size and $\tilde{\mathbf{K}}^{(t)}$ and $\tilde{\mathbf{P}}^{(t)}$ denote the parameters for a specific iteration t, while $\mathbf{K}^{(s)}$ and $\mathbf{P}^{(s)}$ represent the parameters obtained for epoch s. Once T iterations are completed, the two low-rank matrices are updated as

$$\mathbf{K}^{(s+1)} = \frac{1}{T}\sum_{t=1}^{T}\tilde{\mathbf{K}}^{(t)} \qquad \mathbf{P}^{(s+1)} = \frac{1}{T}\sum_{t=1}^{T}\tilde{\mathbf{P}}^{(t)} \tag{9}$$

Update U and V: To derive the updates for the two regularizers, we first compute the partial derivatives of Eq. (6) with respect to $\mathbf{U}$ and $\mathbf{V}$ while keeping other parameters fixed. Then, solving for a stationary point yields

$$\mathbf{U}^{(s+1)} = \left(\mathbf{K}_{i,:}^{(s+1)} + \mathbf{\Lambda}_{i,:}^{(s)}/\rho\right)\max\left(0, 1 - \alpha/\left(\rho\left\|\mathbf{K}_{i,:}^{(s+1)} + \mathbf{\Lambda}_{i,:}^{(s)}/\rho\right\|_{2}\right)\right) \tag{10}$$

$$\mathbf{V}^{(s+1)} = \left(\mathbf{P}_{i,:}^{(s+1)} + \mathbf{\Psi}_{i,:}^{(s)}/\rho\right)\max\left(0, 1 - \beta/\left(\rho\left\|\mathbf{P}_{i,:}^{(s+1)} + \mathbf{\Psi}_{i,:}^{(s)}/\rho\right\|_{2}\right)\right) \tag{11}$$

whose closed form solutions have been obtained using the group soft-thresholding technique [51] and $i = 1, \cdots, r$ denotes the i-th row of a parameter matrix.

Update $\mathbf{\Lambda}$ and $\mathbf{\Psi}$: Results from Eq. (9) and Eqs. (10–11) can be finally used to update the duals for the Lagrangian multipliers as

$$\mathbf{\Lambda}^{(s+1)} = \mathbf{\Lambda}^{(s)} + \rho(\mathbf{K}^{(s+1)} - \mathbf{U}^{(s+1)}) \tag{12}$$

$$\mathbf{\Psi}^{(s+1)} = \mathbf{\Psi}^{(s)} + \rho(\mathbf{P}^{(s+1)} - \mathbf{V}^{(s+1)}) \tag{13}$$

To conclude, after S epochs have been performed, the optimal estimates for the two low-rank projection matrices are given by $\mathbf{K}^{(S)}$ and $\mathbf{P}^{(S)}$.

3.3   Model Adaptation with Reduced Human Effort

In the previous section we have presented a similarity-dissimilarity learning model which can be trained in an incremental fashion. To achieve model adaptation over time, we propose to perform incremental steps to minimize Eq. (6) with new image pairs that are progressively acquired as time passes. This requires human labeling of such pairs. To limit such a manual effort and improve model generalization, we aim to select only a small set of informative gallery persons to update the model. These are persons for which the positive/negative association with the probe is very uncertain. Given a probe, such gallery persons form its *probe relevant set*.

Probe Relevant Set Selection: Let $\mathcal{H} = \{\mathbf{x}_p, \mathbf{x}_g \mid g = 1, \ldots, |\mathcal{G}|\}$ denote the probe-gallery set for probe p. We represent such a set as an undirected graph with no loops. More precisely, let $G = (V, E, \mathbf{W})$ denote a graph where $V = \{p, g | g = 1, \ldots, |\mathcal{G}|\}$ is the set of vertices, $E \subseteq V \times V$ is the set of edges and $\mathbf{W} \in \mathbb{R}_+^{|V| \times |V|}$ denotes the adjacency symmetric matrix of positive edge weights such that, for any two vertices i and j, $\mathbf{W}_{i,j} = f(S_{\mathbf{K},\mathbf{P}}(i,j))$ if $i \neq j$, $\mathbf{W}_{i,j} = 0$, otherwise. $f(\cdot)$ is the Platt function [57] used to ensure a positive edge weight.

To obtain the probe relevant set, we aim to cluster G in such a way that (i) a cluster contains the probe and gallery persons which are similar to each other, and (ii) all persons outside a cluster should be dissimilar to the ones inside. To achieve such an objective, we exploit the dominant sets clustering technique [12].

Dominant set clustering partitions a graph into dominant sets on the basis of the coherency between vertices as measured by the edge weights. A dominant set is a subset of the graph nodes having high internal and low external coherency.

To obtain such partitions, the dominant sets approach is based on the participation vector $\mathbf{h}$. It expresses the probability of participation of the corresponding person in the cluster. More precisely, the objective is

$$\hat{\mathbf{h}} = \arg\max_{\mathbf{h}} \mathbf{h}^T \mathbf{W} \mathbf{h} \qquad \text{s.t.} \quad \mathbf{h} \in \mathcal{S} \qquad (14)$$

where $\mathcal{S}$ is the standard simplex of $\mathbb{R}^{|V|}$.

Let the participation vector be initialized to a uniform distribution, i.e., $h_i = 1/|V|$, for $i = 1, \ldots, |V|$[1]. Then, as shown in [12], a solution to the optimization problem can be obtained by an iterative procedure that, at each iteration k, updates the participation vector as

$$h_i^{(k+1)} = h_i^{(k)} \frac{(\mathbf{W} \mathbf{h}^{(k)})_i}{(\mathbf{h}^{(k)})^T \mathbf{W} \mathbf{h}^{(k)}} \qquad \text{for } i = 1, \ldots, |V| \qquad (15)$$

The iterative updates are applied until the objective function difference between two consecutive iterations is higher than a predefined threshold ϵ. When such a condition is not satisfied a local optima is obtained and the non-zero

---

[1] Effect of this initialization is checked by adding random noise to each element of $\mathbf{h}$. Results show that in 96 % of the cases the output cluster is the same.

Algorithm 1. Temporal Model Adaptation for Person Re-Identification

Off-Line Training

Input: $\mathcal{X}, \eta > 0, \rho > 0, T > 0, S > 0$

Output: Discriminative low rank projection matrices $\mathbf{K}$ and $\mathbf{P}$

Initialize: $\mathbf{K}^{(1)}$ and $\mathbf{P}^{(1)}$ to random, $\mathbf{\Lambda}^{(1)}$ and $\mathbf{\Psi}^{(1)}$ to $\mathbf{0}$

Set: $\mathbf{U}^{(1)} = \mathbf{K}^{(1)}, \mathbf{V}^{(1)} = \mathbf{P}^{(1)}$

Iterate *for* $s = 1, \ldots, S$

   1. Consider all the n training samples to pre-compute the average hinge loss subgradients with respect to $\mathbf{K}^{(s)}$ and $\mathbf{P}^{(s)}$

   2. Set $\tilde{\mathbf{K}}^{(t)} = \mathbf{K}^{(s)}, \tilde{\mathbf{P}}^{(t)} = \mathbf{P}^{(s)}$, then run T iterations and update $\tilde{\mathbf{K}}^{(t)}$ and $\tilde{\mathbf{P}}^{(t)}$ as in Eqs. (7) and (8)

   3. Average over the T updates as in Eq. (9) to obtain $\mathbf{K}^{(s+1)}$ and $\mathbf{P}^{(s+1)}$

   4. Update the constraints $\mathbf{U}^{(s)}$ and $\mathbf{V}^{(s)}$ using Eqs. (10) and (11)

   5. Compute the dual updates for the Lagrangian multipliers as in Eqs. (12) and (13)

6. Obtain the optimal estimates $\mathbf{K} = \mathbf{K}^{(S)}$ and $\mathbf{P} = \mathbf{P}^{(S)}$

Temporal Model Adaptation

Input: $\mathbf{K}, \mathbf{P}, \mathcal{H}, \eta > 0, \rho > 0, \hat{T} > 0, \hat{S} > 0, \epsilon > 0$

Output: Updated discriminative low rank projection matrices $\mathbf{K}$ and $\mathbf{P}$

1. Compute the scores for each possible probe-gallery pair via $S_{\mathbf{K},\mathbf{P}}$ to obtain $\mathbf{W}$

2. Solve the problem in Eqs. (14) – using Eq. (15)– to obtain the probe relevant set $\mathcal{D}_p$

3. Form the set of probe relevant pairs

4. Update $\mathbf{K}$ and $\mathbf{P}$ by performing *off-line training* steps **1–6** with the probe relevant pairs, $S = \hat{S}$ and $T = \hat{T}$

entries in the participation vector $\hat{\mathbf{h}}$ specify the relevant nodes included in the dominant set. Notice that the dominant sets clustering can be easily extended to cluster a graph in multiple dominant sets. This is obtained by removing the person identities included in the current dominant set from $\mathcal{H}$, creating the new graph structure and then repeating the process. In our approach such a procedure is applied until the dominant set containing the probe person p is found. This is the probe relevant set for person p and is denoted as $\mathcal{D}_p = \{i \mid i \neq p \wedge h_i > 0\}$.

Incremental Model Update: Armed with the probe relevant set, we can now achieve temporal model adaptation by performing the incremental learning steps described in Sect. 3.2. Towards this objective, we first ask the human annotator to label only the probe relevant pairs in $\{(\mathbf{I}_p, \mathbf{I}_g) \mid g \in \mathcal{D}_p\}$. Then, using the current parameters $\mathbf{K}$ and $\mathbf{P}$ as a "warm-restart", we exploit the newly labeled samples to run $\hat{S}$ epochs, each providing $\hat{T}$ incremental iterations. When such a process is completed the updated model parameters $\mathbf{K}$ and $\mathbf{P}$ are obtained.

3.4 Discussion

Through the preceding sections we have introduced two main contributions that allow us to obtain model adaptation over time. Specifically, the goal has been achieved (i) by proposing a stochastic similarity-dissimilarity metric learning procedure that can be incrementally updated and (ii) by introducing a graph-based approach that allows to identify the most informative pairs that should be labeled by the human. All the steps are summarized in Algorithm 1.

MLAPG [20] and XQDA [6], which learn a discriminant subspace as well as a distance function in the learned subspace, are close to the proposed approach.

(a)   (b)   (c)

Fig. 3. 15 image pairs from the (a) VIPeR, (b) PRID450S and (c) Market1501 datasets. Columns correspond to different persons, rows to different cameras.

However, both of them do not update the model over time. In addition, our solution differs in the stochastic ADMM optimization, the combination of both a similarity and a dissimilarity measure, as well as the sparsity regularization.

4   Experimental Results

Datasets: We evaluated our approach on three publicly available benchmark datasets[2], namely VIPeR [58], PRID450S [59], and Market1501 [60] (see Fig. 3 for few sample images). Following the literature, we run 10 trials on the VIPeR and PRID450S dataset, while we use the available partitions for Market 1501. We report on the average performance using the Cumulative Matching Characteristic (CMC). We refer to our method as Temporal Model Adaptation (TMA).

VIPeR [58] is considered one of the most challenging datasets. It contains 1,264 images of 632 persons viewed by two cameras. Most image pairs have viewpoint changes larger than 90°. Following the general protocol, we split the dataset into a training and a test set each including 316 persons.

PRID450S [59] is a more recent dataset containing 450 persons viewed by two disjoint cameras with viewpoint changes, background interference and partial occlusion. As performed in literature [61,62], we partitioned the dataset into a training and a test set each containing 225 individuals.

Market1501 [60] is the largest currently available person re-identification dataset. It contains 32,668 images of 1,501 persons taken from 6 disjoint cameras. Multiple images of a same person have been obtained by means of a state-of-the-art detector, thus providing a realistic setup. To run the experiments, we used the available code[3] to get the same BoW feature representation as well as the same train/test partitions containing 750 and 751 person identities each.

Implementation: To model person appearance we adopted the Local Maximal Occurrence (LOMO) representation [6]. We selected $\alpha = 0.001$, $\beta = 0.001$, $\eta = 1$, and $\rho = 1$ by performing 5-fold cross validation on $\{1, 0.5, 0.1, 0.05, 0.01, 0.001\}$. The temporal model adaptation followed the common batch framework used in

---

[2] See supplementary for additional results on the 3DPeS and CUHK03 datasets.

[3] http://www.liangzheng.com.cn.

Table 1. Comparison with state-of-the-art methods on the VIPeR dataset. Best results for each rank are in boldface font.

Rank →	1	10	20	50	Labeled [%]	Reference
TMA_4+LADF	**48.19**	**87.65**	93.54	98.41	20.32+100	Proposed + [24]
TMA_0	43.83	83.86	91.45	97.47	100	Proposed
LMF+LADF	43.29	85.13	**94.12**	–	100	CVPR 2014 [63]+[24]
TMA_4	41.46	82.65	92.46	**99.65**	20.32	Proposed
MLAPG	40.73	82.34	92.37	–	100	ICCV 2015 [20]
XQDA	40.00	80.51	91.08	–	100	CVPR 2015 [6]
TMA_3	37.97	75.00	87.66	96.52	12.56	Proposed
SCNCDFinal	37.80	81.20	90.40	97.0	100	ECCV 2014 [61]
PKFM	36.8	83.7	91.7	97.8	100	CVPR 2015 [9]
TMA_2	36.08	71.84	81.96	94.62	6.78	Proposed
TMA_1	35.13	69.94	81.01	93.35	4.91	Proposed
QALF	30.17	62.44	73.81	–	100	CVPR 2015 [60]
ISR	27.43	61.06	72.92	86.69	100	TPAMI 2015 [3]
WFS	25.81	69.56	83.67	95.12	100	TPAMI 2015 [64]
KISSME	19.60	62.20	77.00	91.80	100	CVPR 2012 [21]

active learning [34]. It partitioned each training set into 4 disjoint *batches*. Due to the adopted randomization procedure, each batch contains approximately $z = (|\mathcal{P}|/4) \times (|\mathcal{G}|/4)$ pairs[4]. We have used the first batch to train the initial model with $T = 2z$, $S = 200$, and no further stopping criteria. The remaining ones have been used for the batch-incremental updates with $\hat{T} = 2z$ and $\hat{S} = 150$ (in the following, the subscript of TMA indicates the number of model updates that are achieved for every probe in each batch). Finally, to select the relevant gallery images in each batch we have set $\epsilon = 0.1$ (see Table 5).

4.1   State-of-the-art Comparisons

In the following we compare the results of our approach with existing methods. In addition to the incremental performance, we also provide our results when no model adaptation is exploited and all the training data is included in one single batch (TMA_0).

VIPeR: Results in Table 1 show that our approach has better performance than recent solutions even in the case only about 5 % of the data is used. This result indicates that, partially due to the feature representation (see results of KISSME in Table 4), our approach produces a robust solution to viewpoint variations. Incremental updates bring TMA_4 to be the second best. In such a case, only

---

[4] The percentage of labeled pairs is computed with respect to n.

Table 2. Comparison with state-of-the-art methods on the PRID 450S dataset. Best results for each rank are in boldface font.

Rank →	1	5	10	20	50	Labeled [%]	Reference
TMA_0	**54.22**	73.78	83.11	90.22	97.33	100	Proposed
TMA_4	52.89	**76.00**	**85.78**	**93.33**	**97.78**	14.25	Proposed
TMA_3	50.22	75.56	85.33	92.89	97.64	10.18	Proposed
TMA_2	48.89	75.33	84.01	91.1	97.33	8.64	Proposed
TMA_1	45.33	72.00	83.11	89.78	96.02	6.42	Proposed
CSL	44.4	71.6	82.2	89.8	96.0	100	ICCV2015 [62]
SCNCDFinal	41.6	48.9	79.4	87.8	95.4	100	ECCV2014 [61]
SCNCD	41.5	66.6	75.9	84.4	92.4	100	ECCV2014 [61]
KISSME	33	–	71	79	90	100	CVPR2012 [21]

LMF+LADF performs better. However, such an approach is a combination of two methods, which, as shown in [5], generally improves the performance. Indeed, a rank 1 recognition rate of 48.19 % is achieved by summing TMA_0 and LADF scores. If the same batches as TMA_{1-4} are considered to train LADF, the fused rank 1 performances are of 35.6 %, 37.9 %, 40.8 % and 43.4 %, respectively – which represent an average improvement of 11 % over standalone LADF.

Finally, results obtained with TMA_0 show that the best rank 1 is achieved, but performance on higher ranks is slightly worse than the one obtained using incremental updates (TMA_4). Hence, using all the available data requires additional manual labor and might also drive to decreasing performance. This strengthens our contribution showing that, by identifying the most informative samples to train with, better results can be achieved with reduced human effort.

PRID450S: In Table 2 we report on the performance comparisons between existing method and our approach on the PRID450S dataset. Results show that our solution outperforms the methods used for comparisons regardless of the amount of data used for training. In particular, using only 14.25 % of the data an 8 % improvement with respect to the best existing approach is obtained at rank 1. By training only with the initially available data (i.e., TMA_1), our solution outperforms SCNCDFinal [61], which, on the VIPeR dataset, had better performance (until the 3rd batch update). This may suggest that our approach is robust to background clutter and occlusions which PRID450S suffer from.

Market1501: Comparisons of our approach with existing methods on the Market 1501 dataset are shown in Table 3. The obtained performance are consistent with the ones achieved on the VIPeR and PRID450S datasets. Our approach has significantly better performance than methods used for comparisons even by using 5.23 % of labeled data. Incremental updates bring in relevant improvements and with TMA_4 we achieve the best rank 1 recognition rate, i.e., 44.74 %. Using the LOMO feature representation instead of the BoW one provided by [60], about a 3 % rank 1 performance gain is obtained. Results on such dataset

Table 3. Rank 1 and mAP performance comparison with existing methods on the Market 1501 dataset. Best result is in boldface font.

Method	BoW [60]	LMNN BoW [60]	ITML BoW [60]	KISSME BoW [60]	TMA$_1$ BoW	TMA$_2$ BoW	TMA$_3$ BoW	TMA$_4$ BoW	TMA$_4$ LOMO
Rank 1	42.64	38.91	27.08	43.03	28.77	34.68	39.81	44.74	**47.92**
mAP	19.47	17.34	8.13	19.98	8.69	14.56	17.89	20.92	**22.31**
Labeled [%]	100	100	100	100	5.23	8.71	12.09	14.36	13.58

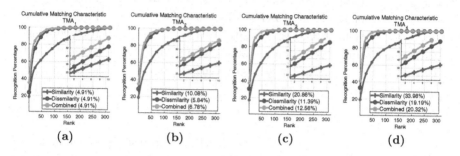

Fig. 4. Comparison of the similarity-dissimilarity learning components. (a)–(d) show the results on the VIPeR dataset computed using incremental batch updates. For each curve, the percentage of manually labeled samples is indicated in parenthesis. The inside picture show the results for rank range 1–10.

demonstrate that our approach can scale to a real scenario and achieve competitive performance with significantly less manual labor. The reason for the improved performance with much less training data is because our method identifies the most discriminating examples to train with, and does not waste labeling effort on those that will add little or no value to the re-identification accuracy.

4.2 Influence of the Temporal Model Adaptation Components

To better understand the achieved performance, we have run additional experiments by separately considering the similarity-dissimilarity metric learning approach and the probe relevant set selection method.

Similarity-Dissimilarity Metric: In the following, we first analyze the contribution of the similarity and the dissimilarity components. Then, we compare our performance with existing methods using the same LOMO representation.

Contribution of the components: In Fig. 4, we report on the results obtained using either the learned similarity, the learned dissimilarity or both. Results show that most of the performance contribution is provided by the dissimilarity. The similarity has significantly lower performance and calls for more labeled pairs. This is due to the fact that the majority of the edges of the corresponding graph have weak weights, thus causing the maximization procedure to select more samples before the stop condition. Enforcing agreement on a specific pair by jointly optimizing the similarity and the dissimilarity measure results in the best

Table 4. Comparison with metric learning approaches on the VIPeR dataset. Results obtained using truncated projections (100 dimensions) are given for three representative ranks. Last row shows the percentage of manually labeled samples. Best results for each rank are in bold. Most of the results are from [20].

Rank ↓	MLAPG	XQDA	KISSME	LMNN	LADF	ITML	LDML	PRDC	TMA_1	TMA_2	TMA_3	TMA_4
1	39.21	38.23	33.54	28.42	27.63	19.02	13.99	12.15	32.28	34.81	36.07	**39.88**
10	**81.42**	81.14	79.30	72.31	75.47	52.31	38.64	35.82	69.62	73.10	76.27	81.33
20	**92.50**	92.18	90.47	85.32	88.29	67.34	48.73	48.26	81.33	58.79	90.19	91.46
Labeled [%]	100	100	100	100	100	100	100	100	4.91	6.91	11.48	15.77

performances. With respect to the dissimilarity approach, this yields negligible increase of manual labor and improved results (7 % at rank 1).

Comparison with existing methods: In Table 4, we report on the comparison of our similarity-dissimilarity approach with general state-of-the-art metric learning approaches, namely ITML [65], LMNN [66], LDML [67], and re-identification tied ones namely, PRDC [30], KISSME [21], LADF [24], XQDA [6], and MLAPG [20]. To provide a fair comparison, we used the same settings in [20]. Precisely, the 100 principal components found by PCA have been exploited to train LMNN, ITML, KISSME, and LADF. Since other methods, i.e., XQDA, PRDC, LDML, MLAPG and TMA, are able to discover the discriminative features, we used all the principal components. For a fair comparison, projection learned by XQDA, MLAPG and TMA were truncated to 100 dimensions.

Results in Table 4 show that our approach, trained with only 4.91 % of the available data, has the 4th best rank 1 result. As shown in Fig. 4, such a successful result is due to the competition between the similarity and the dissimilarity approaches. Performing incremental updates yields significant improvements and, after the 4th update is completed, the best rank 1 recognition rate is achieved. At higher ranks, TMA performs on par with other methods but with substantially less labeled pairs (i.e., 15.77 % of all possible annotations).

Discussion: Results have demonstrated that, while the dissimilarity metric has more impact on the performance, by enforcing competition with the similarity measure better results can be obtained. Additional evaluations showed that by removing the $\ell_{2,1}$ norms the degradation is of 3 %. Comparisons with existing approaches have shown that, under the same conditions, our approach achieves good results using only 1/6 of the data. Incremental updates produce considerable improvements with a significantly reduced human effort. This substantiates the benefits of the proposed similarity-dissimilarity learning approach and demonstrate the feasibility of temporal model adaptation for the task.

Probe Relevant Set Selection: In the following, we provide an analysis of the graph-based solution to identify the most informative gallery persons. We report on the effects of the ϵ parameter, then we compare with three approaches.

Influence of ϵ: To verify the influence of the ϵ parameter, we have computed the results in Table 5. These show that, large values of ϵ produce coarse under-segmented sets, hence identify a large number of relevant pairs to label.

872   N. Martinel et al.

Table 5. Analysis of the ϵ parameter used to obtain the probe relevant set. Each entry in the table shows the rank 1 performance as well as the percentage of labeled data (in brackets). Best results for each rank are in bold.

$\epsilon \rightarrow$	0.5	0.3	0.1	0.05	0.01
TMA_1	35.13 (4.91)	35.13 (4.91)	35.13 (4.91)	35.13 (4.91)	35.13 (4.91)
TMA_2	**36.08** (7.87)	35.76 (7.26)	**36.08** (6.78)	34.49 (6.62)	34.49 (6.20)
TMA_3	37.03 (11.36)	36.23 (10.59)	**37.97** (12.56)	36.71 (8.97)	34.81 (7.95)
TMA_4	38.61 (14.74)	38.92 (13.50)	**41.46** (20.32)	39.87 (11.49)	37.97 (9.81)

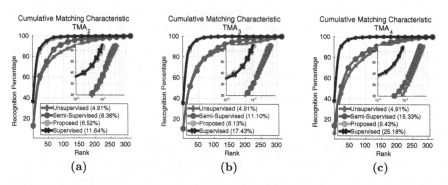

Fig. 5. Re-Identification performance on the VIPeR dataset computed using four different probe relevant set selection criteria. (a)–(c) show the performances achieved using the 2nd-4th batch incremental updates. The percentage of manually labeled samples is given within parenthesis. The inside picture show the results on a log-scale reduced rank range, i.e., 1–50.

Small values of ϵ, e.g., 0.01, produce over segmented-graphs, hence small dominant sets. Indeed, after the 4th update, less than 10 % of all the available pairs has been used for training. This results in achieving similar performance improvements, but with a different manual effort. The reason behind this is that, in the former case, the probe relevant sets contain additional persons which are not "similar" to the probe and any other gallery person. This causes the model to be updated with uninformative pairs which weaken its discriminative power. In the latter, too few informative pairs are found and the model overfits such samples.

Selection Criteria Comparison: In Fig. 5, we compare our probe relevant set selection approach with three different criteria. Before exploiting such criteria, we applied Platt scaling [57] to the obtained scores to get the probability of each probe-gallery pair being positive.

(i) *Unsupervised*: Each pair having probability less than 0.5 has been assigned the negative label, remaining ones have been assigned the positive label.

(ii) *Semi-Supervised*: Top and bottom 20 ranked pairs have been labeled as positive or the negative, respectively. Remaining pairs have been human labeled.

(iii) *Supervised*: Every pair has been human labeled.

Results show that using the unsupervised or the semi-supervised criteria, the performance obtained with incremental updates tends to decrease. This behavior is due to the fact that, right after the first update, the produced scores induce very small or very large probabilities. This yields zero manual labor, but, as a consequence, the model is updated with a large portion of mislabeled samples. Using our solution, performance reaches the ones obtained using a fully-supervised approach. In particular, with the 4th batch update our approach yields the highest rank 1 recognition rate (41.46 % vs 39.87 %) with 5 % less manual labor. Additional experiments considering the human mislabeling error $C \in \{5, \ldots, 95\}\%$ show that the model update is effective when $C \leq 15\%$.

Discussion: In this section, we have shown that our approach is moderately sensible to the selection of ϵ, which to some extent, controls the human effort. In addition, it performs better than a fully supervised approach in which all the samples are manually labeled. This demonstrates that the proposed approach identifies the most informative pairs that should be used to update the model.

4.3   Computational Complexity

In Table 6, we compare the computational performance of deterministic ADMM and our stochastic solution. While achieving similar rank 1 performance, deterministic ADMM brings in more complexity, hence the training time is considerably higher. In particular, while d might be arbitrarily large, n and K are usually small (those depend on the number of samples which are manually labeled), thus our solution is more desirable in a continuous learning scenario.

Finally, notice that, while the initial training is more expensive than existing approaches, e.g., KISSME [21], the proposed incremental learning solution is more effective in the long term since it does not require re-training like others.

Table 6. Comparison between deterministic ADMM and our stochastic solution. VIPeR result computed by running MATLAB code on an Intel Xeon 2.6 GHz. Complexity is computed for the parameters updates which differs from the two solutions

Method ↓	TMA$_1$ - Rank 1	Per-Epoch complexity	Training time [s]
Deterministic ADMM	34.84	$\mathcal{O}\left(2(n2d^2 + d^3)\right)$	12051.19
Stochastic ADMM	35.15	$\mathcal{O}\left(2(n3d^2 + K3d^2)\right)$	2948.38

5   Conclusion

In this paper we have proposed a person re-identification approach based on a temporal adaptation of the learned model with human in the loop. First, to allow temporal adaptation, we have proposed a similarity-dissimilarity metric learning approach which can be trained in an incremental fashion by means of a stochastic version of the ADMM optimization method. Then, to update the model with the proper information, we have included the human in the loop and proposed a graph-based approach to select the most informative pairs that should be manually labeled. Informative pairs selection has been obtained through the dominant sets graph partition technique. Results conducted on three datasets have shown that similar or better performances than existing methods can be achieved with significantly less manual labor.

Acknowledgment. The work was partially supported by US NSF grant IIS-1316934.

References

1. Vezzani, R., Baltieri, D., Cucchiara, R.: People reidentification in surveillance and forensics. ACM Comput. Surv. **46**(2), 1–37 (2013)
2. Wu, Z., Li, Y., Radke, R.J.: Viewpoint invariant human re-identification in camera networks using pose priors and subject-discriminative features. IEEE Trans. Pattern Anal. Mach. Intell. **37**(5), 1095–1108 (2015)
3. Lisanti, G., Masi, I., Bagdanov, A.D., Bimbo, A.D.: Person re-identification by iterative re-weighted sparse ranking. IEEE Trans. Pattern Anal. Mach. Intell. **37**(8), 1629–1642 (2015)
4. Martinel, N., Micheloni, C.: Sparse matching of random patches for person re-identification. In: International Conference on Distributed Smart Cameras, pp. 1–6 (2014)
5. Xiong, F., Gou, M., Camps, O., Sznaier, M.: Using kernel-based metric learning methods. In: European Conference Computer Vision, pp. 1–16 (2014)
6. Liao, S., Hu, Y., Zhu, X., Li, S.Z.: Person re-identification by local maximal occurrence representation and metric learning. In: International Conference on Computer Vision and Pattern Recognition (2015)
7. Paisitkriangkrai, S., Shen, C., Hengel, A.V.D.: Learning to rank in person re-identification with metric ensembles. In: International Conference on Computer Vision and Pattern Recognition (2015)
8. Liu, C., Loy, C.C., Gong, S., Wang, G.: POP: person re-identification post-rank optimisation. In: International Conference on Computer Vision (2013)
9. Chen, D., Yuan, Z., Hua, G., Zheng, N., Wang, J.: Similarity learning on an explicit polynomial kernel feature map for person re-identification. In: International Conference on Computer Vision and Pattern Recognition (2015)
10. Garcia, J., Martinel, N., Micheloni, C., Gardel, A.: Person re-identification ranking optimisation by discriminant context information analysis. In: International Conference on Computer Vision (2015)
11. Boyd, S., Parikh, N., E Chu, B.P., Eckstein, J.: Distributed optimization and statistical learning via the alternating direction method of multipliers. Found. Trends Mach. Learn. **3**(1), 1–122 (2010)
12. Pavan, M., Pelillo, M.: Dominant sets and pairwise clustering. IEEE Trans. Pattern Anal. Mach. Intell. **29**(1), 167–172 (2007)
13. Zheng, W.S., Li, X., Xiang, T., Liao, S., Lai, J., Gong, S.: Partial person re-identification. In: International Conference on Computer Vision, pp. 4678–4686 (2015)

14. Li, X., Zheng, W.S., Wang, X., Xiang, T., Gong, S.: Multi-scale learning for low-resolution person re-identification. In: International Conference on Computer Vision, pp. 3765–3773 (2015)
15. Martinel, N., Foresti, G.L., Micheloni, C.: Person reidentification in a distributed camera network framework. IEEE Trans. Cybern. 1–12 (in press, 2016)
16. Zheng, W.S., Gong, S., Xiang, T.: Towards open-world person re-identification by one-shot group-based verification. IEEE Trans. Pattern Anal. Mach. Intell. **8828**(2), 1–1 (2015)
17. Xing, E.P., Ng, A.Y., Jordan, M.I., Russell, S.: Distance metric learning, with application to clustering with side-information. Adv. Neural Inf. Process. Syst. **15**, 505–512 (2002)
18. Bellet, A., Habrard, A., Sebban, M.: A Survey on Metric Learning for Feature Vectors and Structured Data. ArXiv e-prints, June 2013
19. Hirzer, M., Roth, P.M., Köstinger, M., Bischof, H.: Relaxed pairwise learned metric for person re-identification. In: Fitzgibbon, A., Lazebnik, S., Perona, P., Sato, Y., Schmid, C. (eds.) ECCV 2012, Part VI. LNCS, vol. 7577, pp. 780–793. Springer, Heidelberg (2012). doi:10.1007/978-3-642-33783-3_56
20. Liao, S., Li, S.Z.: Efficient PSD constrained asymmetric metric learning for person re-identification. In: International Conference on Computer Vision, pp. 3685–3693 (2015)
21. Kostinger, M., Hirzer, M., Wohlhart, P., Roth, P.M., Bischof, H.: Large scale metric learning from equivalence constraints. In: International Conference on Computer Vision and Pattern Recognition, pp. 2288–2295 (2012)
22. Tao, D., Jin, L., Wang, Y., Yuan, Y., Li, X.: Person re-identification by regularized smoothing KISS metric learning. IEEE Trans. Circ. Syst. Video Technol. **23**(10), 1675–1685 (2013)
23. Tao, D., Jin, L., Wang, Y., Li, X.: Person reidentification by minimum classification error-based KISS metric learning. IEEE Trans. Cyber. **45**(2), 1–11 (2014)
24. Li, Z., Chang, S., Liang, F., Huang, T.S., Cao, L., Smith, J.R.: Learning locally-adaptive decision functions for person verification. In: International Conference on Computer Vision and Pattern Recognition, pp. 3610–3617. IEEE, June 2013
25. Pedagadi, S., Orwell, J., Velastin, S.: Local fisher discriminant analysis for pedestrian re-identification. In: International Conference on Computer Vision and Pattern Recognition, pp. 3318–3325 (2013)
26. Martinel, N., Micheloni, C.: Classification of local eigen-dissimilarities for person re-identification. ieee sig. process. lett. **22**(4), 455–459 (2015)
27. García, J., Martinel, N., Gardel, A., Bravo, I., Foresti, G.L., Micheloni, C.: Modeling feature distances by orientation driven classifiers for person re-identification. J. Vis. Commun. Image Representation **38**, 115–129 (2016)
28. Martinel, N., Micheloni, C., Foresti, G.L.: Kernelized saliency-based person re-identification through multiple metric learning. IEEE Trans. Image Process. **24**(12), 5645–5658 (2015)
29. Chen, J., Zhang, Z., Wang, Y.: Relevance metric learning for person re-identification by exploiting listwise similarities. IEEE Trans. Image Process. **7149**(c), 1–1 (2015)
30. Zheng, W.S., Gong, S., Xiang, T.: Re-identification by relative distance comparison. IEEE Trans. Pattern Anal. Mach. Intell. **35**(3), 653–668 (2013)
31. Li, W., Zhao, R., Xiao, T., Wang, X.: DeepReID: deep filter pairing neural network for person re-identification. In: Conference on Computer Vision and Pattern Recognition, pp. 152–159, June 2014

32. Ahmed, E., Jones, M., Marks, T.K.: An improved deep learning architecture for person re-identification. In: IEEE International Conference on Computer Vision and Pattern Recognition (2015)

33. Zhang, R., Lin, L., Zhang, R., Zuo, W., Zhang, L.: Bit-Scalable deep hashing with regularized similarity learning for image retrieval and person re-identification. IEEE Trans. Image Process. **24**(12), 4766–4779 (2015)

34. Settles, B.: Active learning. Synth. Lect. Artif. Intell. Mach. Learn. **6**(1), 1–114 (2012)

35. Joshi, A.J., Porikli, F., Papanikolopoulos, N.P.: Scalable active learning for multi-class image classification. IEEE Trans. Pattern Anal. Mach. Intell. **34**(11), 2259–2273 (2012)

36. Aodha, O.M., Campbell, N.D.F., Kautz, J., Brostow, G.J.: Hierarchical subquery evaluation for active learning on a graph. In: IEEE Conference on Computer Vision and Pattern Recognition (2014)

37. Biswas, A., Parikh, D.: Simultaneous active learning of classifiers & attributes via relative feedback. In: IEEE Conference on Computer Vision and Pattern Recognition (2013)

38. Chakraborty, S., Balasubramanian, V.N., Panchanathan, S.: Optimal batch selection for active learning in multi-label classification. In: ACM International Conference on Multimedia, pp. 1413–1416 (2011)

39. Elhamifar, E., Sapiro, G., Yang, A., Sasrty, S.S.: A convex optimization framework for active learning. In: IEEE International Conference on Computer Vision, pp. 209–216 (2013)

40. Vondrick, C., Ramanan, D.: Video annotation and tracking with active learning. In: Advances in Neural Information Processing Systems (2011)

41. Vijayanarasimhan, S., Grauman, K.: Large-scale live active learning: training object detectors with crawled data and crowds. In: IEEE Conference on Computer Vision and Pattern Recognition (2011)

42. Vezhnevets, A., Buhmann, J.M., Ferrari, V.: Active learning for semantic segmentation with expected change. In: IEEE Conference on Computer Vision and Pattern Recognition, pp. 3162–3169 (2012)

43. Karasev, V., Ravichandran, A., Soatto, S.: Active frame, location, and detector selection for automated and manual video annotation. In: IEEE Conference on Computer Vision and Pattern Recognition (2014)

44. Hasan, M., Roy-Chowdhury, A.K.: Context aware active learning of activity recognition models. In: IEEE International Conference on Computer Vision (2015)

45. Wang, Z., Hu, R., Liang, C., Leng, Q., Sun, K.: Region-based interactive ranking optimization for person re-identification. In: Ooi, W.T., Snoek, C.G.M., Tan, H.K., Ho, C.-K., Huet, B., Ngo, C.-W. (eds.) PCM 2014. LNCS, vol. 8879, pp. 1–10. Springer, Heidelberg (2014). doi:10.1007/978-3-319-13168-9_1

46. Das, A., Panda, R., Roy-Chowdhury, A.: Active image pair selection for continuous person re-identification. In: International Conference on Image Processing (2015)

47. Chechik, G., Sharma, V., Shalit, U., Bengio, S.: Large scale online learning of image similarity through ranking. J. Mach. Learn. Res. **11**, 1109–1135 (2010)

48. Guo, Z.C., Ying, Y.: Guaranteed classification via regularized similarity learning. Neural Comput. **26**(3), 497–522 (2013)

49. Xia, H., Hoi, S.C.H., Jin, R., Zhao, P.: Online multiple kernel similarity learning for visual search. IEEE Trans. Pattern Anal. Mach. Intell. **36**(3), 536–549 (2014)

50. Nie, F., Huang, H., Cai, X., Ding, C.H.: Efficient and robust feature selection via joint L2, 1-norms minimization. In: Advances in Neural Information Processing Systems, pp. 1813–1821 (2010)

51. Bach, F., Jenatton, R., Mairal, J., Obozinski, G.: Convex optimization with sparsity-inducing norms. In: Sra, S., Nowozin, S., Wright, S.J. (eds.) Optimization for Machine Learning, pp. 1–35. The MIT Press (2011)

52. Cao, X., Zhang, H., Guo, X., Liu, S., Chen, X.: Image retrieval and ranking via consistently reconstructing multi-attribute queries. In: European Conference on Computer Vision, pp. 569–583 (2014)

53. Zhang, C., Fu, H., Liu, S., Liu, G., Cao, X.: Low-Rank tensor constrained multiview subspace clustering. In: International Conference on Computer Vision, pp. 1582–1590 (2015)

54. Ouyang, H., He, N., Tran, L., Gray, A.: Stochastic alternating direction method of multipliers. In: International Conference on Machine Learning, pp. 80–88 (2013)

55. Zhao, S.Y., Li, W.J., Zhou, Z.H.: Scalable stochastic alternating direction method of multipliers. arXiv preprint arXiv:1502.03529 (2015)

56. Johnson, R., Zhang, T.: Accelerating stochastic gradient descent using predictive variance reduction. Adv. Neural Inf. Process. Syst. **1**(3), 1–9 (2013)

57. Platt, J.: Probabilistic outputs for support vector machines and comparisons to regularized likelihood methods. In: Smola, A.J., Bartlett, P., Schölkopf, B., Schuurmans, D. (eds.) Advances in large margin classifiers, pp. 61–74. The MIT Press (1999)

58. Gray, D., Brennan, S., Tao, H.: Evaluating appearance models for recongnition, reacquisition and tracking. In: IEEE International Workshop on Performance Evaluation of Tracking and Surveillance (PETS), Rio De Janeiro, Brazil, October 2007

59. Roth, P.M., Hirzer, M., Koestinger, M., Beleznai, C., Bischof, H.: Mahalanobis distance learning for person re-identification. In: Gong, S., Cristani, M., Yan, S., Loy, C.C. (eds.) Person Re-Identification, pp. 247–267 (2014)

60. Zheng, L., Shen, L., Tian, L., Wang, S., Wang, J., Tian, Q.: Scalable person re-identification: a benchmark. In: International Conference on Computer Vision (2015)

61. Yang, Y., Jimei, Y., Junjie, Y., Liao, S.: Salient color names for person re-identification. In: European Conference on Computer Vision (2014)

62. Shen, Y., Lin, W., Yan, J., Xu, M., Wu, J., Wang, J.: Person re-identification with correspondence structure learning. In: International Conference on Computer Vision, pp. 3200–3208 (2015)

63. Zhao, R., Ouyang, W., Wang, X.: Learning mid-level filters for person re-identification. In: International Conference on Computer Vision and Pattern Recognition, pp. 144–151. IEEE, June 2014

64. Martinel, N., Das, A., Micheloni, C., Roy-Chowdhury, A.K.: Re-identification in the function space of feature warps. IEEE Trans. Pattern Anal. Mach. Intell. **37**(8), 1656–1669 (2015)

65. Davis, J.V., Kulis, B., Jain, P., Sra, S., Dhillon, I.S.: Information-theoretic metric learning. In: International Conference on Machine Learning, pp. 209–216. ACM Press, New York (2007)

66. Weinberger, K.Q., Saul, L.K.: Distance metric learning for large margin nearest neighbor classification. J. Mach. Learn. Res. **10**, 207–244 (2009)

67. Guillaumin, M., Verbeek, J., Schmid, C.: Is that you? metric learning approaches for face identification. In: International Conference on Computer Vision, pp. 498–505. IEEE, September 2009

Author Index

Printed in the United States
By Bookmasters